D0460706

Praise for *The Complete Guide to Windows Server 2008*

"John Savill's *The Complete Guide to Windows Server 2008* is comprehensive without being overwhelming. At over 1500 pages, the book is not light reading, but Savill does a superb job of explaining the features and functions of Windows Server 2008 in a way that the reader can understand and apply. Rather than investing in a library of books, an administrator can just keep this book handy as a reference resource for all their Windows Server 2008 questions and needs."

—**Tony Bradley**, CISSP, Microsoft MVP, Director of Security, Evangelyze Communications

"John Savill's book is the kind of technology bible you don't mind reading cover to cover. Often I find books with this much information just too deadly dull to actually read, but this is an exception. If you are an old hat, you might end up skipping the starts of chapters, as John makes few assumptions about what you already know—a very good thing overall."

—**Patrick Hynds**, CTO, CriticalSites Microsoft Regional Director

"Of all the recent books on Windows Server 2008 I've read, this one provides the most complete coverage in an easy to digest manner. An aptly titled publication that I recommend for anyone working with Windows Server 2008."

—**Alan Le Marquand**, Content Architect, Technical Audience Global Marketing Team

"With the number of changes being introduced in Windows Server 2008, a book like *The Complete Guide to Windows Server 2008* is essential in any IT professional's library. John Savill does an excellent job of introducing these changes. He also gives clear instructions on how to implement them. I would highly recommend to anyone who's planning on making Microsoft's latest server operating system part of their infrastructure to buy and read this book from cover to cover."

—**Ed Roberts**, Lethos Incorporated

"This book is an invaluable one-stop reference for deploying, configuring, and managing Windows Server 2008. It's filled with John's unique and hard-earned nuggets of advice, helpful scripts, and shortcuts that will save you time and money."

—**Mark Russinovich**, Technical Fellow, Platform and Services Division, Microsoft

"*The Complete Guide to Windows Server 2008* by John Savill is, indeed, just that. It begins with one of the most clear, concise, and understandable explanations of the evolution of Windows from its earliest days that I have ever read. I expected to learn about Windows Server 2008, but along the way learned a great deal about Windows in general and Vista in particular. If you are looking for a guide to help you navigate the rapids on the way to implementing, running, and troubleshooting Windows Server 2008, this is an excellent choice."

—**Jerry Tibor**, Microsoft MVP, Windows Server

"If you've got questions about Windows Server 2008, John Savill has the answers. Written by one of the industry's true heavyweights, *The Complete Guide to Windows Server 2008* is just that, your complete guide to planning, deploying, configuring, and administering a computing environment based on the latest and greatest version of Windows Server. Highly recommended!"

—**Paul Thurrott**, Windows IT Pro Magazine and SuperSite for Windows

THE COMPLETE GUIDE TO WINDOWS SERVER 2008

The Complete Guide to Windows Server 2008

John Savill

Addison-Wesley

Upper Saddle River, NJ • Boston • Indianapolis • San Francisco
New York • Toronto • Montreal • London • Munich • Paris • Madrid
Cape Town • Sydney • Tokyo • Singapore • Mexico City

The publisher offers excellent discounts on this book when ordered in quantity for bulk purchases or special sales, which may include electronic versions and/or custom covers and content particular to your business, training goals, marketing focus, and branding interests. For more information, please contact:

U.S. Corporate and Government Sales
(800) 382-3419
corpsales@pearsontechgroup.com

For sales outside the United States please contact:

International Sales
international@pearsoned.com

Visit us on the Web: www.informit.com/aw

Library of Congress Cataloging-in-Publication Data:

Savill, John, 1975-
The complete guide to Windows server 2008 / John Savill.
p. cm.
ISBN 0-321-50272-8 (pbk. : alk. paper) 1. Microsoft Windows server. 2. Operating systems (Computers) I. Title.

QA76.76.O63S35654 2008
005.4'476—dc22

2008025996

ISBN-13: 978-0-321-50272-8
ISBN-10: 0-321-50272-8
Text printed in the United States on recycled paper at Edwards Brothers in Ann Arbor, Michigan.
First printing September 2008

Dedicated to Julie,
for showing me love and support that I never knew existed

Contents at a Glance

Contents

Acknowledgments

Many people helped in the creation of this book. I want to start by thanking Joan Murray, acquisitions editor at Addison-Wesley, who I worked with on this book. She had the faith to support this project.

Those who know me know that I think and talk very fast; I quickly jump from one subject to the next. That does not translate well for a book, so I am extremely lucky that Addison-Wesley gave me an amazing development editor team to make my manuscript readable—a huge thanks you to Sheri Cain and Susan Brown Zahn.

When the development edit was complete, the technical editors verified that my content was technically accurate and digestible by the reading public, so I thank my technical editors Khaki Cohen and John Ruley.

There are many other people at Addison-Wesley who I'll probably never communicate with—such as copy editors, designers, proofreaders, and the publisher—so here's a big thank you to all of them.

Microsoft provided a great deal of input into this book, which was facilitated by Emily Ohlsen and Melissa Dingle who handled my interaction with the Microsoft program managers. There are too many people at Microsoft to thank individually—so I want to make this a big thank-you to everyone at Microsoft who helped me with my many questions and for providing their insight.

Writing this book has taken up a huge amount of my life over the last 24 months. I would like to thank my colleagues at EMC for their support throughout this process.

I feel I should also thank my two best friends, Brad Bartholow and David Covich, who are always there with life advice, keep me focused on what is important, and put up with me insulting them 24/7.

I want to thank my parents for making me the person I am—which some people will curse them for. Along with Arnold Schwarzenegger, my father has always been my hero and the person I want to be.

Throughout everything, Julie, my fiancée, has always been there with unconditional love, understanding, and full support for this project. My son, Kevin, has always been there to make me smile, highlight what's most important in the world, and put everything into perspective.

About the Author

John Savill, B.S., MCSE, M.S. ITP Server Administrator, M.S. ITP Enterprise Administrator, Clustering MVP, is the Central U.S. manager for EMC's Microsoft technical infrastructure practice and chief Microsoft architect. John has worked in infrastructure solutions for 15 years in different industries. At the age of 19, John started a frequently asked questions site for Windows NT that evolved into the www.ntfaq.com site, which became the most used NT FAQ on the Internet. John is a frequent writer for *Windows IT Pro* magazine and other major publications such as *TechNet Magazine*, and this work is John's fourth solo book project. John is a speaker at many major technology shows, including Tech Ed 2006, 2007, and 2008.

Outside of technology, John enjoys fitness activities, such as cycling, running, and weightlifting in addition to practicing martial arts, which he has done since the age of 7. John has lived in the United States since 2004 and received his green card (finally) at the beginning of 2008.

PREFACE

Everyone knows the saying, "Be careful what you wish for." It had long been my goal to write a complete guide to Windows Server, but I never felt I had sufficient time to do justice to the subject. In the middle of 2006, I convinced myself that I could organize my time to allow the undertaking of writing a book on the largest Microsoft server release ever—from scratch. I started writing the book a few months later and finished the final copy editing in June 2008, basically two years from start to finish. Fortunately, Microsoft delayed the release of Windows Server 2008 enough that this book will hit bookshelves while Windows Server 2008 is still new to the market.

With this book, I tried to create a resource that explains the major features of Windows Server 2008, when to use them, how to design the best implementation, and how to manage the deployed environment.

Windows Server 2008 has so many features that I had to leave some out. Those features not discussed are ones I felt would not be interesting to most readers; however, I point out what is not covered and suggest some resources. Windows 2008 is trying to put books out of business; however, although the online help is great, it is task focused. Therefore, I encourage you to follow the online help tool. I concentrate on items that require more design, decision, or are just cool.

Windows Server 2008 is very customer-focused and focuses on a key number of areas such as virtualization, the Web, and security. Usability is also a major area for Windows 2008. A customer does not point to a server and say "that's my windows server"; a customer says "that's my domain controller" or "that's my file server." Windows Server 2008 is designed around how the server is used. Only the basic functions are installed; additional components are installed as roles, and features are added to the server and their management tools accessed through a single server manager interface.

Design of Microsoft-based systems will change in the future. I predict that the process we perform today to design the best practice implementation for our environment will be automated entirely within ten years—

and I'll need a new day job. Think of the process today: We look at the environment and how to use it and then create a design following experience and best practices. We have a number of tools today to help with this: Best Practice Analyzers that check that an installation follows guidelines; System Center Capacity Planner that allows a designer to input information about locations, users, servers, and bandwidth and then creates a server design that services needs; and Microsoft Solution Accelerators that help create solutions with Microsoft technologies. The next step is bringing these together. System Center Configuration Manager and System Center Operations Manager can ascertain the information needed about an environment. This information can then be automatically fed into Capacity Planner-type solutions to produce a best practice design and periodically verify that the design still meets requirements. With the move to virtualization, the design tools will partner with deployment technologies to automatically build new virtual machines for services, as needed, without administrator intervention. Microsoft already has a direction to this type of environment with the Dynamic Systems Initiative. Our involvement will likely be telling these tools about new initiatives and services needed to know what infrastructure to put in place. New versions of software such as Exchange can be downloaded and applied automatically, assuming organizations still have local servers and software. It's entirely possible everything will be a service offered by a "cloud" on the Internet which companies subscribe to.

So with all of that, why is there snow on the cover? Snow makes anything look calm and beautiful. I hope the cover is calming. If ever you start panicking about content in this book, just stop and look at the cover. Like they said in the book *The Hitchhiker's Guide to the Galaxy*, "Don't panic."

Audience for This Book

I've written this book with the IT administrator and architect in mind. Although a background from Windows and networking in general is advantageous, I introduce the basics of each subject, explain how the technologies work, and then build on that transferred understanding until we get to advanced concepts and best practices.

This is not a Microsoft Certified IT Professional study guide, although I did take the exams for both the MS ITP Server Administrator and Enterprise Administrator without studying. I used what I knew from writing this book and easily passed all the exams with high marks. So if you understand and can apply the information in this book, I would expect you to do well on the Microsoft exams.

This Book's Organization

It would be great if you could sit and read this book from start to finish. Although you may not be able to learn all the features, you may remember items that are possible in day-to-day work and then re-read details of specific features. In the same manner that a chef expects you to eat all courses of a meal instead of picking at each one, I expect this book to be "digested" more like a buffet. You might want to consume the parts relevant to you. I urge you, however, to read a chapter at a time, and not just part of a chapter because each one builds on a subject. In addition, I typically start each chapter with details for you to thoroughly understand the concepts so that we can cover other concepts more quickly.

I want to teach you to drive, not to understand the internal parts of the engine. I'm not big on giving detail on components that don't do you any good from a design or management perspective, but I do give internal details when it aids in learning a technology.

Structure of This Book

This book is made up of 24 chapters:

- **Chapter 1, "Windows 101: Its Origins, Present, and the Services It Provides,"** introduces the major new features of Windows Server 2008. It highlights the key differentiators between the editions of Windows Server 2008 from Web edition through Datacenter.
- **Chapter 2, "Windows Server 2008 Fundamentals: Navigating and Getting Started,"** walks you through the key interface and management components of Windows Vista and Windows Server 2008. The log-on experience for Windows in both workgroup and domain environments is detailed along with the changes to how the built-in Administrator account is handled in Vista and 2008. The chapter discusses User Access Control and how it impacts how to use Windows. Also, key Windows elements, including the Start menu, task bar, and the system tray, are examined along with the available customizations.

Most of your time with Windows Server 2008 is spent in Task Manager, Explorer, and the Microsoft Management Console, so Chapter 2 looks at the major elements of these powerful tools and finishes off with a quick look at the Control Panel.

- **Chapter 3, "Installing and Upgrading Windows Server 2008,"** walks you through the basic system requirements of Windows Server 2008 in terms of memory, processor, and disk space. Windows Server 2008 has a number of activation options, and this chapter looks at both Multiple Activation Keys and Key Management Service.

  The next section walks through performing an upgrade from Windows Server 2003 SP1 to Windows Server 2008, and the various options and limitations associated with an in-place upgrade. The chapter ends with automating local installations using XML answer files.
- **Chapter 4, "Securing Your Windows Server 2008 Deployment,"** discusses security. It looks at authentication and authorization methods, along with the importance of the physical environment that houses your servers. It also discusses BitLocker and how to use it most efficiently.

  This chapter also looks at the built-in certification service in Windows Server 2008, Active Directory Certificate Services (ADCS), and how it is used in (and out) of an organization.

  Finally, Chapter 4 discusses the Security Configuration Wizard and the Security Configuration and Analysis tool that can increase the security of an environment. Increasing network security is handled via the Windows Firewall and IPsec, which this chapter details, along with more information on the User Access Control.
- **Chapter 5, "File System and Print Management Features,"** looks at the facilities that the Windows Server 2008 platform provides for the critical storing of an organization's data. After discussing the new capabilities of NTFS, this chapter looks at creating and managing volumes for data storage. The file permission and ownership capabilities are explained and the concept of shares are introduced and walked through. Then, more advanced subjects are covered, including using quotas to control how much data users can store, file screening technologies to control how the storage is used, and reporting capabilities.

  The second section of Chapter 5 deals with print management, which has taken some big steps in Windows Server 2008. For the deployment of printers to users, Group Policy can now be used to assign printers to users based on their physical location so that as a user moves, he can be assigned printers that are physically close to him. The chapter closes with a detailed look at printer configuration options.

- **Chapter 6, "TCP/IP,"** starts from the ground up with Internet Protocol (IP). Network Address Translation (NAT) is explored as a means for sharing public IP addresses between multiple computers on a private network. Then, this chapter looks at Transmission Control Protocol (TCP) and User Datagram Protocol (UDP) as methods to provide levels of reliability and extra service to IP communication.

  Chapter 6 rounds off with a look at troubleshooting IP communication through various utilities. It also looks at tracing network traffic, which is invaluable for resolving issues and understanding more complex protocols.
- **Chapter 7, "Advanced Networking Services,"** looks at two main capabilities that make the Internet Protocol more usable and manageable in an environment: Dynamic Host Configuration Protocol (DHCP) and Domain Name System (DNS). The chapter ends with a brief look at WINS and how its capabilities are hopefully no longer required.
- **Chapter 8, "Remote Access and Securing and Optimizing the Network,"** looks at extending the visibility of our enterprises resources to external users in a controlled manner via a virtual private network (VPN). It also looks at the different types of VPN that are available and the pros and cons of each. NAT is explained and its impact on VPNs explored.

  Finally, Chapter 8 looks at one of the major features in Windows Server 2008: Network Access Protection (NAP). It walks through the various types of NAP available, how to use NAP, and how best to configure it. It looks at implementation options for NAP to ensure the most secure environment while minimizing potential impact to the organizations users, thus, avoiding business impact.
- **Chapter 9, "Terminal Services,"** kicks off with an overview of Terminal Services (TS) before walking through the basic steps to enable Remote Desktop and then use Remote Desktop. New security features related to Remote Desktop are examined. Licensing is key with TS, and licensing options are documented and advice given

on which of the licensing modes work in different types of organizations.

The next section looks at installing the full TS role in Windows Server 2008 and its role services, which include TS Gateway for access over SSL and Remote Applications to enable seamless application execution on a terminal server without having a full desktop on the remote server visible. Tied in with Remote Applications, the chapter looks at TS Web, which gives a Web-based portal to launch remote applications.

As TS becomes more important in an organization, it will be necessary to ensure that users can get sessions and good responses, so that multiple terminal servers are pooled together into a farm. Chapter 9 looks at the technologies to facilitate terminal server farms.

- **Chapter 10, "Active Directory Domain Services Introduction,"** looks at the history of domains in Windows and the basic building blocks of Active Directory Domain Services (ADDS). It looks at trust relationships and how they are a core part of Active Directory (AD) hierarchical structure. The chapter then expands on the structure of ADDS by looking at features such as Organization Units, Global Catalog servers, and the special Flexible Single Master of Operations (FSMO) roles.

  Replication is key to ADDS, and this chapter looks at the site components that document to ADDS the physical structure of the environment, the subnets for each location, and the links between each location. Chapter 10 ends with a look at the various domain and forest modes that enable additional features.
- More advanced AD concepts are explored in **Chapter 11, "Designing and Installing Active Directory."** This chapter begins by adding a replica domain controller to an existing domain to give the domain high availability and support for more users and distributed environments.

  For Windows Server Core installations and automated AD deployments, an unattended approach is required. The unattended answer format is explored along with an easy way to create the answer file that is new in Windows Server 2008.

  Management functions related to the FSMO domain controllers are explored, including normal movement of FSMO actions and exception FMO movement options. The last setting the chapter looks at is Global Catalog creation.

The next section deals with creating a new domain, but more importantly, the reasons of when and why a new domain is created. Steps related to verifying a new domain controller are described. The chapter then looks at demoting a domain controller to a normal member server.

One of the major new features in Windows Server 2008 is the Read-Only Domain Controller (RODC); the chapter looks in detail at the capabilities of RODC, its usage considerations, and the restrictions.

Chapter 11 closes with a detailed look at the various types of trust relationships and how to create them.

- **Chapter 12, "Managing Active Directory and Advanced Concepts,"** looks at managing AD, backing up and restoring the AD, and other more advanced features. It looks at AD management tools, both graphical and command line-based.

  This chapter also looks at how backing up the AD has changed in Windows Server 2008, using new AD snapshots and restoring deleted objects.

  Chapter 12 closes with a look at changing the replication technology from FRS to DFS-R when you are running a pure Windows Server 2008 domain controller environment.
- **Chapter 13, "Active Directory Federated Services, Lightweight Directory Services, and Rights Management,"** deals with the other role services that complement ADDS, namely Active Directory Lightweight Directory Services (AD LDS), Active Directory Rights Management Services (AD RMS), and Active Directory Federated Services (AD FS).
- **Chapter 14, "Server Core,"** starts with an overview of server core followed by how to perform a Windows Server 2008 installation for a server core instance. When the installation is complete, the hard part is configuring and managing because you don't have the same local graphic tools available that are normally present in a full Windows Server 2008 instance.

  The various command line utilities are explored to perform configuration in addition to walking through configurations that can be done with limited graphical tools such as the Registry editor. Along with this configuration, the chapter explores how to keep a server core patched and what applications can be installed on a server core installation. Finally this chapter looks at managing a server core installation.

- **Chapter 15, "Distributed File System,"** discusses one of the greatest challenges in a distributed environment: managing data and making the data available to all users in a timely fashion. The Distributed File System (DFS) consists of two components: Distributed File System Namespace (DFSN) and Distributed File System Replication (DFSR).

  Chapter 15 closes with a look at best practices to design a DFSR topology and how to troubleshoot and monitor the overall health of replication.
- **Chapter 16, "Deploying Windows,"** starts with a brief history of deployment and then introduces the technologies required to deploy modern operating systems (OSs).

  Installing and configuring WDS is covered, along with the considerations of running WDS and DHCP together and separately. After WDS installation is explained, the process of importing images is introduced and the process discussed. Automated installations are key in large environments, and the process of creating an unattended answer file using the Windows System Image Builder is explained.

  Chapter 16 also looks at creating custom images from reference installations and then maintaining the images by installing fixes, additional drivers, and even language packs. Finally, multicast deployments are explored.
- **Chapter 17, "Managing and Maintaining Windows Server 2008,"** looks at the major tasks and utilities that relate to managing and maintaining Windows Server 2008. The majority of the chapter is spent exploring Server Manager: how to manage the roles and features of Windows Server 2008 using Server Manager and, more than just management actions, how Server Manager gives consolidated insight into each role and is a go-to point to troubleshoot.

  Chapter 17 then looks at Windows Server Backup, the major changes in Windows Server 2008, and details on the Volume Shadow Copy Service (VSS).

  Patch Updates are critical to keeping your environment healthy and secure. The chapter looks at the options for patching systems, their advantages and disadvantages, and finally, the Registry.
- **Chapter 18, "Highly Available Windows Server 2008,"** looks at the two high availability features of Windows Server 2008: Network Load Balancing (NLB) and Failover Cluster. Validating hardware for Windows Server 2008 clustering is shown, as well as the process

to create and manage a Failover Cluster. Chapter 18 finishes with the migration options from a Windows 2003-based failover cluster.

- **Chapter 19, "Virtualization and Resource Management,"** focuses on two main virtualization technologies: machine virtualization and the new hypervisor-based virtualization solution in Windows 2008, Hyper-V, including how to install Hyper-V, and best practices of configuring and managing. We then complete the section with a look at high availability solutions for Hyper-V through failover-clustering.

  Chapter 19 closes with Windows Server Resource Management. It is not a virtualization technology but allows multiple applications/services to be run on a single OS instance while allocating a specific amount of memory and processor to processor. This allocation of resources allows performance guarantees to be made when consolidating multiple OSs running an application, down to a single OS instance running multiple applications.
- **Chapter 20, "Troubleshooting Windows Server 2008 and Vista Environments,"** starts with the basic building blocks of the OS in terms of processes, threads, jobs, and handles—these are key items that are manipulated when troubleshooting. The chapter looks at the boot options for Windows and then delves into the Windows Recovery Environment (RE) that fixes problem systems from outside of Windows.

  The Reliability and Performance Monitoring interface gives access to performance attributes of an OS instance in addition to a historical view of issues on the system for a general "health" view.

  The Event Viewer is covered extensively because it is the main portal to see what is going on in the Windows installation. When there are problems, an event log is typically written to see the system events, pertinent event logs, and how to receive specific event logs from other systems in our environment.

  Chapter 20 closes with a look at System Center, which has solutions that help monitor an environment and preemptively troubleshoot and resolve issues before users are impacted. It's better to fix something before it's a problem.
- **Chapter 21, "Group Policy,"** starts with an overview of Group Policy, its architecture, and basic usage, before going into detail about the Group Policy Management Console (GPMC), the tool of choice for group policy management. Using the GPMC, advanced

concepts are covered, such as using no override, block inheritance, and filtering capabilities. Resultant Set of Policy features are explored that help ascertain how policy is applied for a user/computer and how policy is applied in different circumstances, for example, if the user was moved to another Organizational Unit.

Chapter 21 then looks at features that are new to Windows Server 2008, including the new Starter GPO functionality and Group Policy Preferences capability to set initial configurations for a computer that the user can override.

- **Chapter 22, "The Command Prompt and PowerShell,"** kicks off with a look at the old style command prompt (cmd.exe) environment with information on customization and how to access and set environment variables, before moving onto more advanced concepts such as chaining commands and redirecting output.

  The Windows Scripting Host is explored as a way to create more complicated sequences of logic with some VBScript examples.

  PowerShell is explored with focus on its structure and capabilities for forming complex action sequences. PowerShell can interact with the environment including system processes, the Registry, and file systems. Scripting with PowerShell is explored and some scripts are showcased to further explain capabilities and error handling features.
- **Chapter 23, "Connecting Windows Server 2008 to Other Environments,"** discusses integration with UNIX and NetWare, an important capability in mixed environments. Windows Server has capabilities to integrate and migrate with both UNIX and NetWare environments
- **Chapter 24, "Internet Information Services,"** looks at the Internet Information Services role in Windows Server 2008. The chapter starts with the new architecture that is a radical change from in previous versions, giving administrators and developers greater power to customize IIS processing.

  The configuration of IIS is explained, as well as the various levels of configuration made possible by the new configuration architecture of IIS 7. The process of IIS role service installation is shown along with the steps required to create and access new web sites.

  The chapter looks at new capabilities in IIS 7 including URL authorization that allows specific users to access a site and new management delegation capabilities. IIS is one of the roles supported by

Windows Server Core, and the restrictions associated with this IIS support are communicated. Chapter 24 concludes with the Windows Web Server 2008 SKU.

Code and Command Entry

Some code statements presented in this book are too long to appear on a single line. In these cases, a code continuation character (➥) indicates that the following line is a continuation of the current statement. Scripts can be found at www.savilltech.com/completeguidetowindows2008.

CHAPTER 1

Windows 101: Its Origins, Present, and the Services It Provides

I believe in learning by understanding, rather than remembering pieces of information, and seeing how and why a technology evolved facilitates that. This chapter first looks at how the Windows OS and Windows Server 2008 got to where it is with an overview tour of the major Windows Server 2008 components. You then learn how to choose the right version of Windows Server 2008; the chapter ends with a quick look at licensing.

Windows powers around 97 percent of desktops and over half of all servers, making it the dominant OS today. No matter where you are, Windows surrounds you. How did Microsoft achieve this incredible feat?

Origin of the Windows Operating System

Microsoft provided Microsoft Disk Operating System (MS-DOS), which it purchased from another company and provided it to hardware companies to bundle with their computers. IBM renamed MS-DOS to PC-DOS for use on IBM computers. Other hardware manufacturers, such as Compaq and Tandy, also bundled a relabeled MS-DOS. The first MS-DOS, version 1.25, shipped May 1982. New versions released with features such as

- Support for subdirectories and hard drives (2.0)
- Support for hard disk partitions up to 32MB (3.0)
- Microsoft networking (3.1)
- Support for 3.5 inch, 720KB floppy disk drivers (3.2)

The first version of DOS I used was 5.0 when my dad brought home a PC from his company. Version 5.0 was the first version to include the QBasic programming language and was my introduction to PC programming.

Windows Hits the Big Time

Windows 3.0, which ran on top of the MS-DOS, released around the same time. The first two versions of Windows were unsuccessful, but Windows 3.0 achieved broad commercial success. It introduced the Program Manager and File Manager that were prevalent until WNT 4.0. Windows for Workgroups 3.11 introduced peer-to-peer networking along with networking support for domains (which was vital to fully utilize WNT Server 3.1). It was widely used in corporate, mobile, and home environments.

DOS continued to evolve and became the base operating system (OS) to run the home line of Windows OSs. Windows 95 ran on MS-DOS 7.0, Windows 95B and Windows 98 ran on MS-DOS 7.1, and Windows Me ran on top of MS-DOS 8.0.

In 1984, Microsoft worked closely with IBM on OS/2 to create a new multitasking OS using the new Intel 80286 processor. However, Microsoft wanted to concentrate on the in-development 80386 processor, feeling it was superior. Microsoft worked on new versions of OS/2 with IBM until version 3.0, when joint development of OS/2 stopped and Microsoft went its own direction. Microsoft renamed the in-development new version of OS/2 (3.0) to Windows New Technology (NT), a 32-bit, hardware-independent OS. The Windows line was doing well for Microsoft, which was another reason for Microsoft to part ways from IBM. Microsoft built WNT from the ground up, and for the first time Windows was not based on DOS. IBM continued development on the OS/2 line, but it never caught on.

IBM was not the only company with which Microsoft created OSs. Microsoft also worked closely with 3Com to create the LAN Manager Network Operating System (NOS). LAN Manager used the NetBEUI protocol, which until recently still shipped with the latest versions of Windows: Even Windows XP included NetBEUI in the Valueadd folder. But given the nonroutable nature of LAN Manager in nearly all environments, TCP/IP is the superior choice. LAN Manager's development stopped with version 2.2 when Microsoft released Windows NT Server. Windows Server contains hints of LAN Manager; for example, it uses the old password hash used by LAN Manager.

Combining the knowledge of creating OSs and with new design help from great experts such as David Cutler, who Microsoft recruited from

Digital Equipment Corporation as the designer of the DEC VMS OS, Microsoft released Windows NT. It's a fallacy that Windows NT (WNT) got its name just to be one letter up on VMS (aka HAL, the computer from *2001: A Space Odyssey* and IBM). Released on July 27, 1993, WNT 3.1 was a milestone for Microsoft. At the time of its release, Bill Gates said, "Windows NT represents nothing less than a fundamental change in the way that companies can address their business computing requirements." He was spot on.

Introduction of Windows NT

Why was the first version of WNT version 3.1? Microsoft states that the version number was to keep WNT in line with its 16-bit OSs—the current version at the time was Windows 3.1. But unlike the 16-bit Windows 3.1, WNT 3.1 was 32-bit all the way.

Both workstation and server editions were released with WNT 3.1 (at the time, the workstation version was not named Workstation, simply WNT 3.1). The workstation version was popular for high-end application users and developers with its Win32 application programming interface (API). Features included built-in networking, domain security, subsystems for OS/2, POSIX support, and as per one of its original goals, support for multiple hardware platforms. The Hardware Abstraction Layer (HAL), which sits between the computer's hardware and the OS kernel, device drivers, and the rest of the Windows executive components, facilitated support for multiple hardware platforms. This allowed a single kernel and OS code base to use nonhardware-specific functions, which translate to hardware-specific instructions via the HAL.

Also new in WNT 3.1 was the New Technology File System (NTFS), a much needed file system improvement over the File Allocation Table (FAT) file system. FAT had severe limitations for a serious file system, including a lack of security, a limitation on partition size (2GB in most cases), no journaling, a limited number of files (65,000), and the 8.3 file-naming restriction. However, support for FAT continued along with support for the OS/2 High Performance File System (HPFS) file system. NTFS had 2TB maximum volume sizes, a practically unlimited number of files, a maximum file size limited only by the size of the partition, and file-names up to 255 characters. NTFS also included a Unicode character set that made it internationally usable, per-object permissions, compression, and streaming capabilities. Each NTFS volume had a mirrored master file table (MFT) to aid recovery in the case of MFT corruption.

The WNT 3.1 Advanced Server, the official name of the server flavor of NT 3.1, included software RAID 0, 1, and 5, which are the RAID levels supported in today's latest server products. Redundant Array of Independent Disks (RAID) levels are detailed in Chapter 5, "File System and Print Management Features." RAID 0 is disk striping in which data is written over multiple disks, making the data more susceptible to loss because if one disk in the set is lost, all the data is lost. Because more disk heads are in use, however, RAID 0 is faster than a single-disk volume. RAID 1 mirrors the content of one volume to another volume on another disk, providing higher availability and some performance improvements. RAID 5 also spreads data over multiple disks, but this time check data is also written. If a single disk is lost, the check data and data on the remaining disks recalculate the missing content.

WNT 3.1 provided capabilities for not only Microsoft networks but also for Novell NetWare and Banyan VINES, which was vital in aiding people to migrate to the Microsoft Server platform from other server technologies. NT Advanced Server strengthened as the host OS for other Microsoft technologies, such as its SQL Server platform, mail solutions, and communication server products such as Microsoft SNA Server. For native networking, the Windows domain model provided a centralized security database and, therefore, single-logon capability to access all resources in the enterprise.

Windows NT 3.5

A little more than a year later, Microsoft released WNT Server and Workstation version 3.5, which was a performance-enhanced release that ran significantly faster. The server version enhanced support for the NetWare and UNIX environments, including tools to aid in support NetWare interoperability. NT 3.5 also had improved remote support via its upgraded Remote Access Service (RAS).

Windows NT 3.51 (released in 1995) added support for the PowerPC processor and was the last version to use the Windows 3.1 Program Manager–type interface. Windows 95 also released in 1995 and replaced the previous separate products of Windows 3.1, Windows for Workgroups, and MS-DOS as the single mass-market desktop OS. Windows 95 was a 32-bit OS, had built-in TCP/IP support, and included new plug-and-play technologies. Plug-and-play greatly improved the usability of Windows for end users to install new hardware and software, and cemented Windows as the OS of choice. Windows 95 introduced support for long filenames on the FAT file system via the Virtual File Allocation Table (VFAT) file system, which used a file system workaround to enable filenames beyond the 8.3 limitation. Windows 95 also had a new interface based around the Start button and Windows Explorer, which made the old Program Manager interface extinct. This new interface was available for WNT 3.51 as the "Shell Update Release" download.

Windows NT 4.0

A new version of NT in 1996, Windows NT 4.0, used the Windows 95–style Start menu interface and Windows Explorer in addition to the Windows 95 introduced "My" items, such as My Documents and so forth. For the first time, different versions of the server were available. The basic WNT 4.0 Workstation product released along with WNT 4.0 Server. The following year, a WNT 4.0 Enterprise Edition released for higher-volume and business-critical services. It introduced clustering capabilities with the Microsoft Cluster Server (MSCS), which allowed two servers to be joined via a shared small computer serial interface (SCSI)–connected storage hard drive, providing permanently available state-aware services for failover between the two servers. The Enterprise edition included the Windows NT Load Balancing Service (WLBS), which allowed up to 32 servers to load balance incoming requests across all the members. This was useful for nonstate-aware services, such as web sites.

In 1998, Microsoft released Windows NT 4.0 Terminal Server edition. It allowed users running terminals and terminal emulators to remotely connect to the server and run 32-bit applications and a full desktop environment via the Remote Desktop Protocol (RDP).

Windows 98 (And the Other One)

In 1998, Microsoft released Windows 98, the first consumer-oriented OS. It had superior Internet access (Internet Explorer 4.0 was part of Windows 98), and better hardware support, including accelerated graphics port (AGP) graphics card support, Universal Serial Bus (USB) support, DVD support, the FAT32 file system, which offered support for much larger drives, and true long filename support. FAT32 was added to Windows 95 OSR2, an update made available to system builders.

Windows 98 had a second edition in 1999. It included Internet Explorer 5.0, media improvements, and network connectivity solutions such as Internet Connection Sharing (ICS) because more homes had more than one computer. In 2000, Windows Millennium Edition (Me) released. Windows Me had numerous problems and instabilities and was the last OS release based on Windows 95/DOS. The year 2000 also introduced Windows NT 5.0. It was four years after the last version of WNT, but WNT

5.0 was not to be its name. The WNT OSs continued to use many components, and its increment reflects the degree of change made to the OS core.

Windows 2000 and a True Directory Service

Windows 2000 was a long time in the making. Windows 2000 Professional (instead of Workstation) replaced all previous versions of Windows in a business environment, desktop or laptop. Windows 2000 Professional had plug-and-play support, an improved network for both wired and wireless networks, and full USB and infrared support, which was important for laptop users. Windows 2000 also included Internet Explorer 5.01.

The server versions introduced Active Directory, which was Microsoft's first true directory service offering. Until Windows 2000, centralized accounts and management were based around the domain concept, using the Security Accounts Manager (SAM), which was a flat structure consisting of users, computers, and groups, with relationships to other domains via manually maintained, nontransitive trusts. (You learn about transitive versus nontransitive in Chapter 10, "Active Directory Domain Services Introduction.") Active Directory was a true directory service that enabled Microsoft-centric networks to offer far more sophisticated solutions with a more granular management structure. Windows 2000 also included a replacement for NT LAN Manager (NTLM) authentication: Kerberos, which provided a far more scalable authentication.

Windows 2000 provided a new administrative environment: the Microsoft Management Console (MMC). The MMC was a GUI shell that could load one or more snap-ins that provided administrative tool–type functionality (such as a Computer Management snap-in that allowed management of computer functions, such as services, disks, and so on). Windows 2000 also introduced NTFS5, which had quotas and encryption. A recovery console came as a separate environment that the operator could boot to when a problem could not be resolved inside the OS.

Each version of the now familiar Windows 2000 Server line contained the same core OS but had different features and supported different amounts of processor and memory. As of Windows 2000, support for MIPS, Alpha, and PowerPC dropped from the retail channel but could be obtained from embedded system vendors. The three versions were Windows 2000 Server (the base version), Windows 2000 Advanced Server (support for addition processors and memory and supported clusters), and Windows 2000 Datacenter Server (support for large amounts of memory and CPUs).

Because of Active Directory and its different management structure, adoption of Windows 2000 was slow. It took time for people to understand Active Directory and its huge advantages over its predecessor. Coupled with changes made to Exchange 2000, which had to run on Windows 2000 and Active Directory, migration was mainly a case of "when" and not "if."

Windows XP

At the end of 2001, Microsoft released Windows XP, which did away with separate business and consumer product lines (Windows 2000 and Windows Me/9x). Windows XP built on the Windows 2000 code base. Its name came from "eXPerience" to reflect its comprehensive built-in support for all types of media. Windows XP had an updated user interface, a new green Start button, and enhanced dialogs. The default theme in XP is Luna; however, themes were available with various color options and other choices, as shown in Figures 1-1 and 1-2.

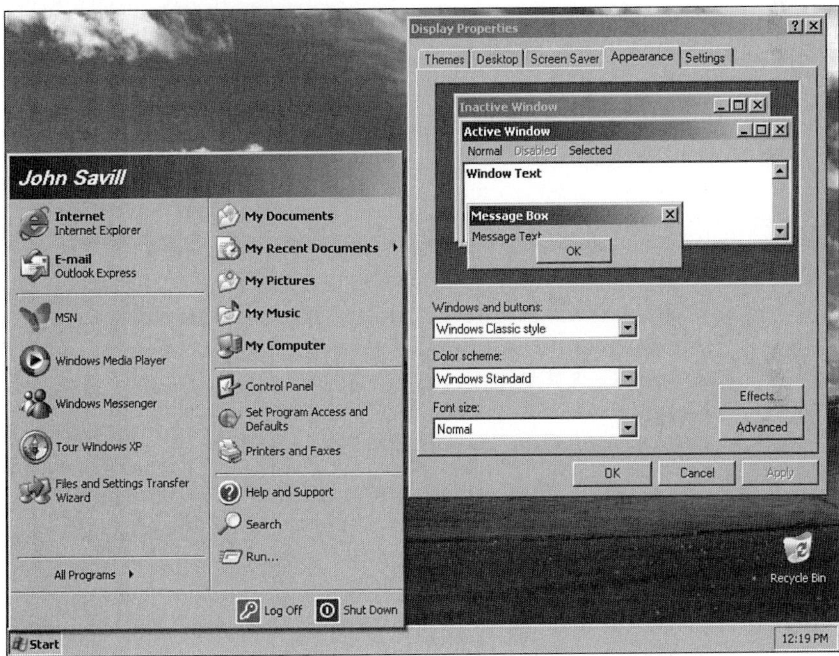

FIGURE 1-1 The older, classic style with the new Start menu structure.

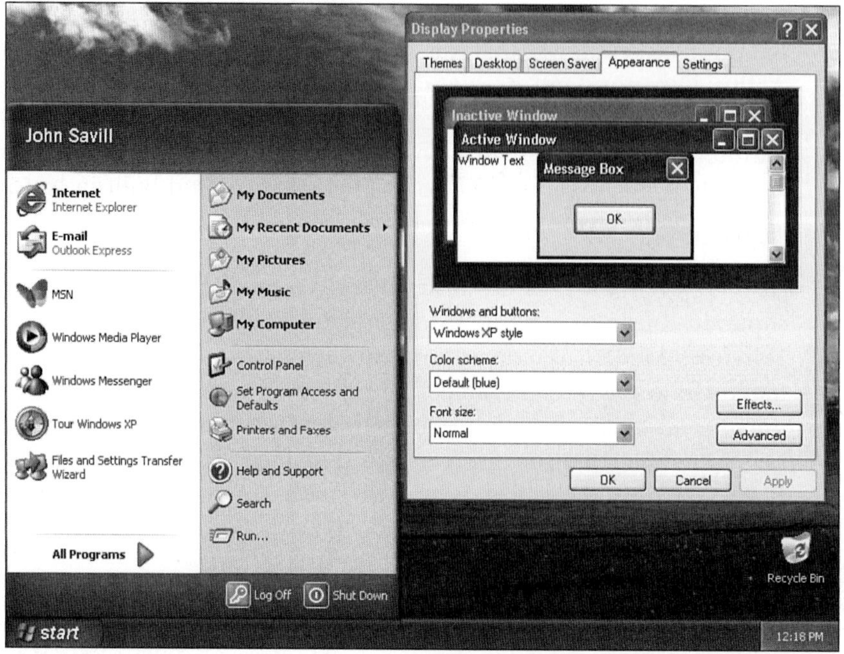

FIGURE 1-2 The new XP style gives a more modern look and feel, removing the earlier gray, flat scheme.

Two versions of Windows XP were released:

- **Windows XP Home Edition**. Targeted toward the home user not in a domain environment
- **Windows XP Professional**. Targeted toward power and business users

Home Edition could use only one processor, whereas XP Professional could use two processors. Also, the Encrypting File System (EFS) was available in XP Professional but not in the Home Edition. A 64-bit edition of Windows XP was released for the Intel Itanium processor, which was a landmark as the first 64-bit client OS from Microsoft. (A 64-bit edition of Windows 2000 had been released named Windows 2000 Advanced Server Limited Edition.) The Internal NT version number for XP was 5.1 (Windows 2000 was 5.0), showing this was not a major kernel upgrade.

Microsoft built on the Windows XP base in 2002 to create media-based products. Windows XP Media Center Edition was available only with computers targeted as in-home media centers. It featured a full-screen Media Center application designed for operation by remote control and gave full access to all visual content known to your computer. The Tablet PC edition was for the new laptop that featured a rotating screen for use in a tablet fashion. This version of XP was available only with the purchase of a Tablet PC. Windows XP for Tablet PC included built-in handwriting recognition and pen support.

Windows Server 2003

In 2003, Microsoft released Windows 2003 (WNT 5.2). This was the first server-only release, and there was no Windows 2003 Professional. Microsoft made up for that with a new server version, releasing four Windows Server 2003 products. Table 1-1 summarizes these products, which are also available in 64-bit versions for the x64 processor in 2005.

Table 1-1 Windows 2003 Product Edition Feature Comparison Table

Feature	Web Server Edition	Standard Server Edition	Enterprise Server Edition	Datacenter Server Edition
Maximum number of processors	2	4	8	32 (64 in the 64-bit edition)
Maximum amount of RAM	2 GB	4GB (32GB in the 64-bit edition)	64GB (1TB in the SP1 64-bit edition)	128GB (2TB in the SP2 64-bit edition, 1TB in the SP1 64-bit edition)
Active Directory	No, can only be member of a domain	Yes	Yes	Yes
Network load balancing	Yes	Yes	Yes	Yes
Clustering	No	No	8 nodes (up from 2 in 2000)	8 nodes (up from 4 in 2000)
Terminal Server capabilities	Only for remote management	Yes	Yes	Yes
Virtualized OS rights	None	None	4 (R2 edition)	Unlimited

The new Web edition was a much-scaled-back version of the Windows Server product and aimed at combating the trend of using free Linux-based services for hosting web sites.

You might run Windows 2000 servers today, so the following list covers the new features of Windows 2003. These features carried into Windows Server 2008, so they are still reasons to migrate to the latest server OS.

- The Microsoft .NET Framework became a core part of the OS.
- New Active Directory features provided prune and graft functionality, allowing you to move and rename domains within an Active Directory forest.
- Domain controllers were added via a system state backup of another domain controller, instead of copying all domain information over the network.
- Internet Information Services (IIS) 6.0 offered improved security with its default state of lockdown and new management features. IIS 6.0 also featured improved reliability and allowed consolidation where appropriate.
- Updated Terminal Services allowed access to and control of the server console via the `/console` switch of the mstsc application.
- Virtual Disk Service (VDS) provided single interface for disk management.
- Volume Shadow Copy Service (VSS) allowed point-in-time copies of information known as shadow copies and provided client side-access to previous "versions" of a share, enabling clients to restore deleted information without administrators performing time-consuming tape restorations.
- Windows Server 2003 included the visual style of Windows XP but disabled it by default. It is accessible if the Themes service is enabled and the Windows XP theme is selected for the display properties.

An important term to mention here is service pack. Feature packs deliver new features to the OS; however, as with every piece of software, errors creep into the released product. These errors require fixing and Microsoft often releases repairs as hot fixes. After some interval, Microsoft combines the fixes into a service pack, which might also contain customer-requested updates. Microsoft makes each service pack available from its web site at no charge. The user installs the service pack onto an installed OS (or directly onto installation media in later versions of Windows). This brings the OS up-to-date with the latest set of fixes and sometimes adds new functionality, although not features or changes that cause compatibility issues. In Service Pack 1 for Windows 2003, Microsoft added the Security Configuration Wizard, which was a core part of helping to lock down server installations. Service packs are cumulative, so Service Pack 2 contains everything in Service Pack 1. If you install a new computer, only install the latest service pack—you don't need to install all the previous service packs. In the past, if you added new OS components to an installed OS (for example, enabling domain name service [DNS] on a server), you had to reapply the service packs. This is no longer required because the content of the service pack is stored locally on the server to ensure that the newest code is always used.

Microsoft continued to add new features to Windows 2003 via downloadable feature packs. Major new features were not made available in service packs due to past complications, so feature packs were a great compromise. Users who didn't want to wait for the next major release could get features as Microsoft released them. Other users were free from installing features they did not want and that could introduce complexity or potential security considerations. Feature packs available for download include the following:

- **Active Directory Application Mode (ADAM)**. Active Directory "lite," enabling multiple directories to exist on a single Windows 2003 or XP machine without the full infrastructure of DNS and other components normally required for a domain. ADAM stores data related to an application that does not require the availability associated with data stored in an AD-based domain.
- **Group Policy Management Console (GPMC)**. Enables policy backup and restoration of policies, task scripting, better management, and HTML reports.
- **Identity Integration Feature Pack (IIFP)**. Allows replication among AD, ADAM, and Exchange directory service (2000 and 2003). This is useful in multiforest situations to sync the Global Address List (GAL). IIFP is MS Identity Integration Server (MIIS) lite!
- **ISCSI support**. Enables IP-based storage area network (SAN) connectivity via the Internet Small Computer System Interface (iSCSI).
- **Windows Software Update Services (SUS)**. Deploys critical updates throughout a company in a manager manner.
- **Windows Rights Management Services (RMS)**. Provides rights management protection with RMS-enabled applications to

safeguard digital info when online or offline. Controls, for example, what a person can do when received (cut/paste, forward, and so on).

- **Windows Services for NetWare/UNIX**. Offers greater integration and migration capabilities than previous versions.
- **Windows SharePoint Services (WSS) update**. Improved SharePoint capabilities and security.
- **Windows Automated Installation Kit**. Contains tools and information for the deployment of Windows Vista from a Windows 2003–based infrastructure including Windows Deployment Services (WDS), which replaces Remote Installation Service (RIS) and forms a core part of Windows Server 2008.

R2 on Disk 2, R2D2

At the end of 2005, Microsoft started a new tradition, releasing Windows 2003 R2 (short for Release 2). There are two important factors for this R2 release:

- Windows 2003 R2 is Windows 2003 with Service Pack 1 built in.
- It has no new kernel changes or modifications to the core OS. The R2 relates to a second supplied CD that contains new features originally slated for and built in to the Windows Server 2008 OS.

R2 releases will be seen in other products in the Microsoft line. Windows 2003 R2 comprises two CDs: the first CD contains Windows 2003 with SP1, and the second contains the new content. After installation of the first disc, the installer prompts the user to insert the second CD. If a server is already running Windows 2003 SP1, only the second CD has to be inserted.

The only actual change made to the core OS is that a new version of the MMC (3.0) is installed before the second CD is executed and new features are added. The new version of the MMC allows for new functionality provided by the updated management console, which some of the R2 component snap-ins require. Add/Remove Programs is updated to allow for the installation of the new R2 components, and the Manage/Configure Your Server Wizard introduces a new SharePoint role and updates the File and Printer Server roles. View the R2 as a collection of useful feature packs, but installing them does not affect the core OS. There are no separate service packs for Windows 2003 and Windows 2003 R2 because they are the same core OS. You don't need to retest your software and recertify applications any more than if you installed a feature pack on a server.

The only testing to perform is to ensure that any MMC snap-ins run with MMC 3.0.

You run a mixture of Windows 2003 and Windows 2003 R2 systems in your environment. Upgrade to R2 only those servers that require some of the new features R2 contains—don't upgrade every server. For an existing Windows 2003 Service Pack 1 system, only use the second CD of R2, which "upgrades" it to R2. (It updates the MMC and modifies Add/Remove Programs to let you add the new R2 features.)

R2 contains a mixture of brand new features and features previously available as feature pack downloads (for example, ADAM and SharePoint services). The new features are summarized as follows:

- The new Distributed File System Replication (DFSR) engine facilitates simplified branch office management by performing delta replication of files between locations. Delta replication means that only the changes to a file replicate instead of replicating the whole file. This saves bandwidth between locations. DFSR is also more self-fixing and tolerant than FRS, making it far less likely to "break" and require administrative effort to restart replication. Although the engine's name is DFSR, use it separately from Distributed File System (DFS) name spaces to replication information in many different scenarios. A new Print Management Console allows a centralized view and management of printers in distributed environments, allowing centralized driver upgrades, printer discovery on remote subnets, form configuration, and notification options if a printer becomes unavailable, which includes executing a script or sending an e-mail.
- Active Directory Federated Services (AD FS) extends the visibility of a trusted organization's directory service to allow its users access to Web-based applications in another organization. For detailed information, see www.windowsitpro.com/Windows/Article/ArticleID/48252/48252.html.
- WSS SP2 is .NET 2.0–compatible and certified to run on 64-bit. (It is 32-bit code but is certified to run in Windows on the Windows subsystem that 64-bit OSs use to run 32-bit code.) SharePoint Services SP2 supports Kerberos authentication and fully integrates with Windows (now shows as a Server role and in Add/Remove Windows Components).

  Add all R2 components as entries in the Windows Components dialog.

- Improved UNIX integration and management capabilities, including password synchronization between UNIX and Windows. Mixed mode support enables a mixture of Windows and Interix libraries.
- .NET 2.0 is included as well as the Common Log File System (CLFS), a callable driver that provides a robust sequential logging environment for use by applications as required.
- Improved hardware management. A Simple SAN MMC snap-in enables full life-cycle control of most small-to-medium SAN environments via the Virtual Disk Service (VDS), which includes creation and assigning of logical unit numbers (LUNs), configuring connections, creating partitions, and so on. A WS-Management (Web Services) implementation is included—for supported hardware that means remote access to servers, even in a crash or preboot scenario. Interaction with the Baseboard Management Controller (BMC) allows Windows-based reading and writing of hardware configuration, reading of the hardware's equivalent of the event log (System Event Log [SEL]) via the Windows Event Viewer, and triggering actions using standard Windows mechanisms, if required.
- A new Quota Management component comprising three technologies. One component is a new quota system based on the physical space (rather than logical size) used on a disk. If users compress files, they store more data, which was not the case in a logical size quota. The quotas can be set on a folder or disk level, so you can configure a specific folder not to exceed 500MB. A file-screening component allows for real-time file type checking. If a type of file tries to write to a folder that has a rule stopping that type, an I/O error generates and the file write stops. One useful scenario for this technology is for blocking video/audio files to company file shares. For both quotas and file screening, comprehensive actions occur when a user attempts to breach policy. Actions could include e-mailing the offender, e-mailing an administrator/manager, and performing an action. Storage reports are the third technology, providing detailed reports of file system status in a variety of formats.

Why put out an R2 release? Microsoft already set a precedent with feature packs that added functionality to the Windows 2003 product as free downloads from the Microsoft site, so why not just have the R2 features provided as downloads as separate feature packs? There are two trains of thought on this issue. It's important to realize that Windows 2003 R2 is a separate product; there is no upgrade version or free update. You have to purchase Windows 2003 R2, even if you already own Windows 2003. However, after release, Windows 2003 R2 replaced Windows 2003 in the retail channel. So, if you purchased Windows 2003 on or after December 6, 2005, you automatically got Windows 2003 R2.

The first and probably official reason for the R2 version is that the functionality added by the R2 release is too significant to give away as a free download, requires more support, and warrants a new "version." The second reason is slightly more sinister, but understandable. Before you look at it, however, let's review how Microsoft sells software.

Purchasing Windows

The most basic way to purchase server products is as needed. When a new version releases, you can go to the store or a web site and purchase a new or upgrade version. This gives you control over the upgrade purchase; however, you must buy each update. If many new versions come out, this method of buying upgrades gets expensive and hard to budget for.

To alleviate this complicated method of purchasing, Microsoft has two other methods for licensing procurement:

- Software Assurance is a part of the Volume Licensing program for which a company signs an agreement of *x* years and pays a fee. Software Assurance gives the company the right to any upgrades to software covered under the agreement without purchasing per product upgrades for each version. It is available for most products, including the Windows line and Office. Additionally, Software Assurance customers get free training, at-home rights for employees, additional phone support, access to the Windows Pre-Installation Environment (now part of the Windows Automated Installation Kit—a free download), and access to Windows Vista Enterprise Edition, which is available *only* to Software Assurance clients. By default, Software Assurance is a three-year contract with one-year or three-year renewals.
- Like Software Assurance, Microsoft offers Enterprise Agreement for organizations with more than 250 desktop PCs. It bundles software products and client access licenses over a three-year term, including Software Assurance benefits based mainly around Office and Windows desktops and the core client access license.

The transition to selling subscriptions of services from selling boxes of software is important for any software company. When you consider just how good the existing versions are, why pay a lot of money for a new version?

Software Assurance has a cost, so it's a benefit only if new versions release during the term of the agreement. Likewise, one great benefit of an Enterprise Agreement is the Software Assurance feature. To help sell these three-year, contract-based products, clients need to know that a new version is going to release within the three years of their coverage!

This is where the R2 versions help. Previously, a new version of the OS might or might not release within three years. With R2 releases, Microsoft is committing to a set release cycle, which Figure 1-3 illustrates.

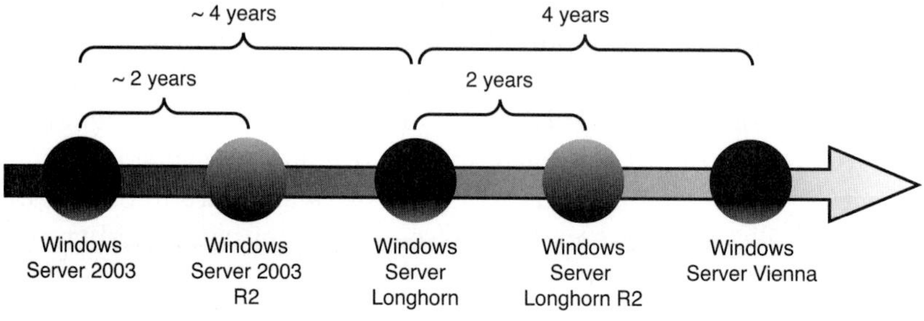

FIGURE 1-3 Microsoft now promises a new OS every two years.

This new OS release schedule promises, every four years, a major version that contains a new kernel and, therefore, supports additional types of hardware and technology. A major release might change fundamental concepts (such as security and application compatibility) and the behavior of core services such as Active Directory. Major versions require significant testing to ensure that the new major version coexist cleanly with existing OSs and applications and that hardware still correctly functions. Two years after release of the major version, a minor or update version will release, the R2, which consists of the last major version with the latest service pack integrated, any relevant feature packs available for download, and new features that do not conflict with existing core functionality. Because the update release is just the last major release with extra features, there are no compatibility problems, and it integrates easily into the existing infrastructure.

Note, however, that it is already believed Microsoft will skip the R2 for Windows Server 2008 and release a major version sometime in 2009/2010 (Windows 7), with the next version arriving sometime in 2011 or later.

Why does this matter? Customers now have a defined schedule of when new products will be available. If you sign up for a three-year agreement, at least one new OS will release in that time. This fact makes it easier to justify purchasing the agreement, which makes it easier for Microsoft to sell it. However, this is good news for customers, too. From planning, manpower, and budget perspectives, it's useful to know when new OSs will be available.

Windows Vista

Microsoft released Windows Vista at the end of 2006. The next chapter covers Vista but, in brief, it introduced many new features, new editions, and another new interface style. The new interface, Aero, features translucent borders of Windows and cool sharpshooting of running applications, which you see in Chapter 2, "Windows Server 2008 Fundamentals: Navigating and Getting Started." For organizations, one of Vista's biggest draws is file system and Registry redirection, which improves application compatibility for applications that write to otherwise protected areas of the file system or Registry. With redirection, the application thinks it's writing to the area but is redirected to a lower privilege area. Other draws include user access control (lowers privileges of users by default), better support for low rights users (thanks to the redirection technologies), and new BitLocker technology (encrypts entire drives). Protected mode in Internet Explorer 7 restricts ActiveX control execution, and a new granular USB Group Policy setting suite helps control the use of USB devices.

Deployment of Vista radically changed. Gone is the structure of many files installed and registered during setup in favor of a new imaging format that is a SYSPREPd image of a deployed installation. This image format leads to a much faster installation time with only a mini-setup wizard executing during setup. Thanks to the image format, a separate image for each HAL type is no longer necessary. You can choose the HAL during the final installation phases because the image contains all HALs. boot.ini, which has existed since the start of Windows, was removed in favor of boot configuration data (BCD) and its management tool.

Windows Server 2008

At the end of 2007, Microsoft released Windows Server 2008. Some of the major new features include but are not limited to the following:

- **Network Access Protection (NAP)**. This feature is also part of Windows Vista and available as an update for Windows XP SP2. It requests a statement of health (SoH) from each connecting machine, and checks the SoH against health policies for the network. If the connecting machine does not meet the network health level, Windows Server quarantines it and, optionally, sends updates to bring it up to required health levels.

- **Internet Information Services (IIS) 7**. IIS fully integrates with Windows Communication Foundation (WCF), Windows SharePoint Services, and Web Services. IIS is highly componentized, allowing the installation of specific modules, and is managed via an IIS Manager interface.
- **Initial Configuration Tasks (ICT)**. ICT shortens the time between installation and enterprise use by giving administrators a more intuitive interface for the initial configuration of items. ICT absorbs the Post-Setup Security Updates (PSSU) stage that Windows 2003 SP1 introduced. ICT locks down a server until the latest fixes are applied and the firewall is configured, as shown in Figure 1-4.

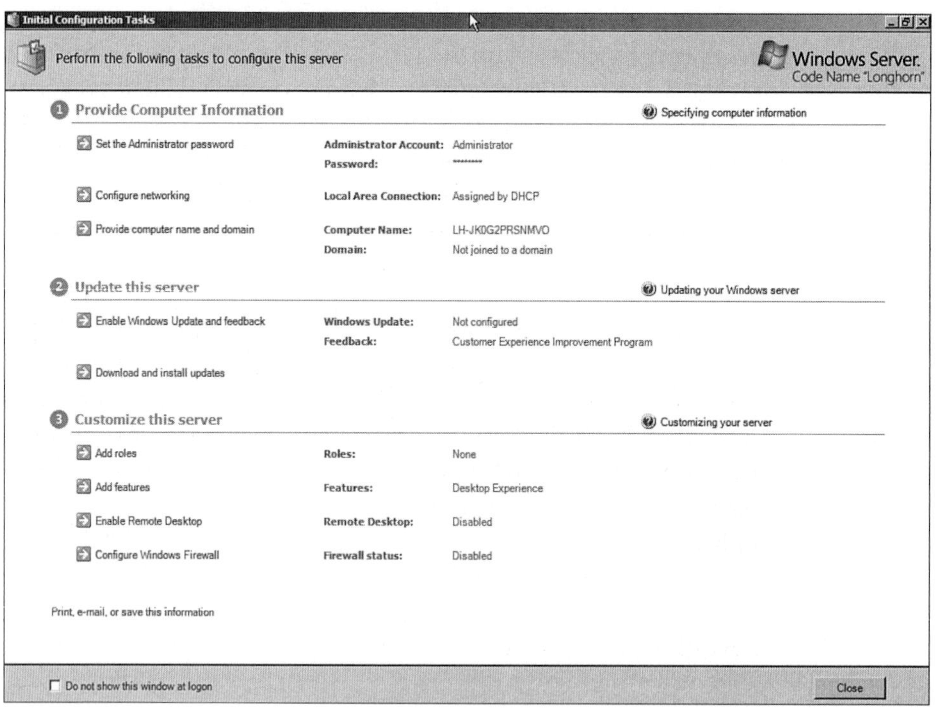

FIGURE 1-4 ICT provides a single interface to perform all initial server configurations instead of trawling through multiple dialogs and locations.

- **Server Manager MMC snap-in**. This snap-in gives a single portal to view and administers nearly all information relating to a server's production health and functionality status.
- **Windows PowerShell**. This command-line shell and scripting technology will be the standard foundation for most future Microsoft service technologies. Use PowerShell for any task you do via a GUI. Exchange 2007 and System Center are just two of the back office products built on PowerShell.
- **Server Core**. As Microsoft adds functionality to Windows, the overhead gets higher and more maintenance is necessary. Server Core is an install mode for a Windows Server 2008 that at installation time allows a server to be nominated as a server core installation. As a result, only the services and components needed for the supported server functions are installed. Any services or components not needed for any of the eight supported roles are not installed, including the Windows GUI—the command prompt is the default interface for a server core's management. Because of the scaled-down installation, the server requires fewer updates and less maintenance. Because there are fewer components, security risks and attack vectors are minimized. A server core installation requires only about 1GB of disk space for the OS components.
- **Read-Only Domain Controller (RODC)**. Before Active Directory, a single primary domain controller held a fully writeable copy of the SAM database. One or more backup domain controllers held a read-only copy of the SAM database for fault-tolerance and load-balancing purposes. With Active Directory, all domain controllers have fully writeable copies of the database that are kept synchronized through multimaster replication. With Windows Server 2008, you can designate a domain controller as read-only. This is useful for remote locations that lack the physical security to place a traditional domain controller but whose performance benefits from having a local authentication source. In addition, configures a read-only domain controller to store security information of only particular accounts and not to store certain sensitive attributes.
- **Terminal Services (TS)**. Third-party terminal server technologies have the capability to stream remote applications instead of entire sessions. For example, assume that Word is running on a terminal server. Instead of a user having a complete session to run Word, he uses an application window on the terminal server running Word. To the user, Word appears to be running locally but is running on the remote terminal server in a seamless window fashion. Windows

Server 2008 now has this capability, with users able to run applications on remote terminal servers (known as "Terminal Services Remote Programs") side-by-side with applications running locally. This works with Windows XP SP2 and Vista clients.
TS availability increased by adding Terminal Services (TS) Gateway functionality, which allows Remote Desktop Protocol (RDP) traffic to be sent over encrypted HTTP. This reduces the firewall holes required for terminal server access from the Internet. For those familiar with Exchange 2003, this works in a similar fashion to RPC over HTTP.

Other advancements provided as part of TS in Windows Server 2008 include Web-based access to TS and single sign on, which allows connection to a terminal server using the credentials of the current locally logged-on session.

- **Windows Deployment Services**. Although available as an update for Windows Server 2003 as part of the Windows Automated Installation Kit, WDS allows the network-based deployment of Windows Vista and Windows Server 2008 images.
- **NTFS**. NTFS now self-heals in the event of volume corruptions, instead of requiring chkdsk.exe execution. Transactional support added to NTFS allows transacted file system operations and ensures that operations in a transaction are atomic.
- **Internet Protocol, Version 6 (IPv6)**. Windows Server 2008, like Windows Vista, has full support for IPv6.
- **Failover clustering**. Windows Server 2008 has a completely rewritten failover clustering feature that is easy to configure and maintain, with a wizard-driven process to validate that the hardware configuration is cluster-supported.

Windows Server 2008 runs Windows Vista clients with a number of features exposed. The "utopian" combination is discussed throughout the book, but a few included features are worth mentioning here. Some additions are client-side rendering of print jobs before sending them to the print server; improved client-side caching of server data, ensuring higher availability of information; and the new Server Message Block (SMB) 2.0, which gives a better performing and more secure communication path between clients and servers.

As with Windows Server 2003, the different versions of Windows Server 2008 have different capabilities and resource constraints, as shown in Table 1-2. In addition to the four main versions of Windows Server 2008 (namely Web, Standard, Enterprise, and Datacenter), there is an Itanium edition for use in specific roles. Note that the amount of memory supported for the 64-bit editions is more than for the 32-bit editions.

Table 1-2 Different Capabilities and Resource Constraints of Different Editions of Windows Server 2008

Feature	Web	Standard	Enterprise	Datacenter	Itanium
Processors	4	4	8	32 (x86) 64 (x64)	64
RAM (x86/x64)	4GB/32GB	4GB/32GB	64GB/2TB	64GB/2TB	2TB
Failover clustering	No	No	16 nodes	16 nodes	8 nodes
Virtual image use rights	0	1	4	Unlimited	Unlimited
Hot add memory	No	No	Yes	Yes and replace	Yes and replace
Hot add processors	No	No	No	Yes and replace	Yes and replace
Cross-file replication (DFS-R)	No	No	Yes	Yes	Yes
TS Gateway	No	250	Unlimited	Unlimited	No
Routing and Remote Access Services (RRAS) connections	No	250	Unlimited	Unlimited	2
Internet Authentication Service (IAS) connections	No	50	Unlimited	Unlimited	No

Features of the Windows Server 2008 Product Line

This chapter has touched on some of the new features of 2008. But why do you need what you have available? What benefit does a server or other back office service bring to an organization?

A number of core changes were made to Windows Server 2008. Many were part of Windows Vista kernel changes (Windows Server 2008 and Vista have essentially the same kernel), but some are Windows Server

2008–specific. Not all kernel features in Vista are present in Windows Server 2008. Many of the more multimedia and lower-end performance improvements are not available in Windows Server 2008.

If you want some good background on the kernel changes in Vista and Windows Server 2008, look at *TechNet* magazine from February, March, and April 2007. Those issues have a great series from Mark Russinovich, and you can download them at no cost. Highlighted here are some of the main Windows Server 2008–only changes, but this is not definitive—there are entire books written about the kernel. Other updates to the core are discussed throughout the book, but here are some other items not discussed heavily elsewhere:

- One version of the kernel exists for 64-bit Windows Server 2008 (in both checked and nonchecked versions). 32-bit Windows also has a Physical Address Extension (PAE) version. There are no single-core versus multicore versions of the kernel anymore because most systems now have multiple cores. The extra work to lock multicore systems is such a small overhead on today's systems that it is of negligible benefit to remove for single-core systems.
- Windows Hardware Error Architecture (WHEA) provides a simplified experience and crash-handling process for sending crash information to Microsoft. If the cause is known, information about a cause or resolution is communicated to the system administrator.
- Internal changes were made to how threads are allocated CPU cycles, so threads now get a fairer share of the processor. Other changes were made in how I/O completion is handled. The kernel is now kinder and gives better performance.
- Kernel Transaction Manager allows file and Registry changes to be placed in a transaction and atomically committed or rolled back as one unit. These transactions cross processes and even systems. System protection and Windows Update use this to safely apply updates. If the system crashes in the middle of an update, the transaction is not applied until the update is complete, so no changes have taken place.
- Dynamic addition/removal and changing of processors and memory—known as dynamic partitioning. Error-correcting code (ECC) memory notifies of pending failure and Windows Server 2008 moves information off the failing memory so that it can be replaced. Hot processor addition is great; however, by default, applications have to request to be able to "see" additional processors. This is to protect the application because some applications perform certain preparation at startup based on the number of processors. If another core

was suddenly visible and the application did not set up structures for it, the application crashes.

- Self-healing NTFS, facilitated by an NTFS worker thread that runs in the background performing chkdsk-type corrections when it detects a corrupt file or folder in NTFS. The administrator gets balloon tooltip notification that the system is performing a repair and when the repair finishes. This avoids many manual chkdsk executions.
- SMB 2.0 offers huge performance increases over the old SMB.

Let's take a high-level look at the activities performed by a client and examine how Windows Server 2008 addresses them. The rest of the book goes into detail about the features.

Data Storage and Printing

The most basic function users perform is file manipulation—be it editing a Word document, viewing a spreadsheet, checking a text file for a product key, or using OneNote to manage notes from a meeting. All these actions depend on physical files for persistent information storage. Even though files can be stored locally on end-user workstations, this approach has many problems, including the lack of centralized backup for local data. If a hard disk becomes corrupted or a laptop misplaced, the data is lost unless the user performs backups to a memory key or someone hands in the laptop to the lost and found.

Data sharing is also an issue for locally stored data. Copying local data to a floppy disk or memory key or burning to a CD/DVD is inconvenient, time-consuming, and impractical for sharing between multiple parties. A far better approach is for the data to be stored centrally, which alleviates all the problems of local storage and offers an improved end-user experience. Windows Server 2008 implemented this simple file service as a share, and it provides many highly useful features. A folder or volume can be shared with the share name accessed by users as \\name. For example, a share named data, on server fileserver, is \\fileserver\data. Permissions can be assigned at the root of the share. Permissions control who can access, read from, and write to the share. Share permissions are not normally used; taking its place is the superior underlying NTFS security. Figure 1-5 demonstrates how users interact with a file server to read and write documents and other data types.

At the heart of Windows Server is NTFS, which is the optimal file system to use with Windows to ensure that the full functionality of the OS is available. Although legacy file systems such as FAT and FAT32 are supported, many features are unavailable when files are stored on FAT/FAT32 volumes, and legacy file systems do not have the storage capabilities of NTFS.

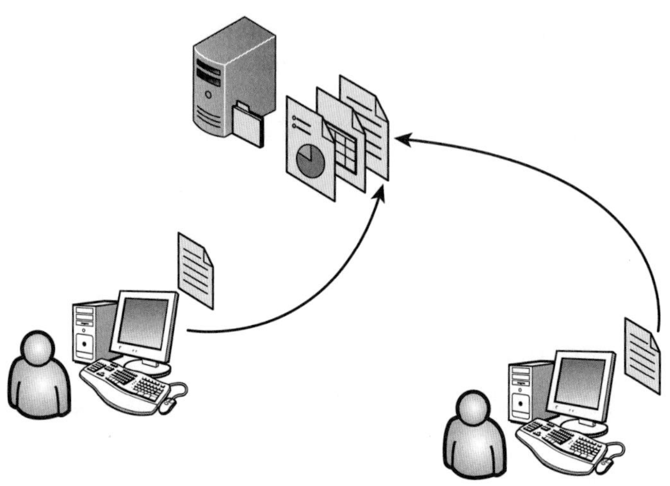

Figure 1-5 With file services, the Windows Server 2008 environment provides a common storage point for users of the network to safely and securely save and access data.

NTFS supports storage of terabytes of data, but as storage devices become cheaper, data management becomes the biggest driving factor and challenge for file server storage. A 500GB disk might take minutes to install but hours every night to back up or restore. Windows Server 2008 has a highly flexible backup and recovery component to ensure that data is backed up regularly. That is in addition to the Volume Shadow Copy service, which allows point-in-time copies of directly attached or SAN-based storage to provide backups with high integrity and maximize uptime of business applications during the backup. Other solutions exist, such as the Data Protection Manager, which is used in place of tape backups and to pull data back from branch offices into a central hub location.

Although any amount of data can be backed up, to avoid the backup of unnecessary data, a quality file server platform helps ensure that only the right data is being stored on the file server. Windows 2000 introduced disk quotas on physical size used, on a per-volume and per-user basis. This meant that, for each user, a quota could be configured on each volume to limit the amount of logical space that could be used. This quota system carried into Windows 2003. Windows 2003 R2 and Windows Server 2008 introduce a new quota system as part of the File Server Resource Management (FSRM) subsystem. The new quota system allows quotas to be set at a volume or folder level based on the physical size used, which means the amount of space used on the disk. So, if the users compress data, they use less of the quota and have more storage.

Obviously, quotas are great for restricting how much data is written to file servers. But you're just controlling how much data is written, not *what* can be written, which is far more useful. A user might fill a 500MB quota with 10MB of work-related Microsoft Word documents and the other 490MB with an MP3 collection. If you block storage of media type files on the file server, only 10MB of the quota is used. Windows Server 2008 has this capability, known as file screening. A real-time engine checks the extensions of files being written or modified on the file server and rejects blocked file types (if an active file screen is configured, as opposed to a passive screen that allows the write). It also performs a set of defined actions, such as e-mailing the user to explain why the file write failed.

If this quota and file-screening does not satisfy your needs, Windows Server has a comprehensive reporting capability to show how a volume or folder is being used in terms of types of files, biggest, most used, least used, by which users, and so forth.

The next facility, in addition to just having a network viewable location to store and retrieve data, is to ensure that data on shared areas is accessible to only the people who should have access. Obviously, data security is a big component and is where the NTFS file system is used. Whereas file systems such as FAT and FAT32 have no security to speak of, NTFS has a granular, inheritable access control structure that allows each folder and file to have an Access Control List (ACL). Each ACL has one or more Access Control Entry (ACE) that states which objects have permissions to the file or folder and what permissions they have. These permissions are normally based around domain accounts. For file security to work, you have to assume that the domain security is solid (which you just trust for now but demonstrate later).

Using technologies such as the EFS locally on workstations and on the file servers gives an additional layer of security. Improvements over initial implementations allow EFS access to additional users and encrypted file access for offline files.

Offline files? The whole point of having the file servers was so that data is not stored on workstations, correct? Absolutely. You want data to be stored on file servers to ensure that it's backed up and available for sharing, but there are times when that file server is not available. If you take your laptop away from the office, you want data to be available even when you are not connected to the corporate network. Offline files use a cache, known as the client-side cache (CSC), on the user's workstation for files and folders from the network. The CSC synchronizes when connected, giving access to network resources even when network connectivity is not available. As far as the end user is concerned, the files are on the network even when he is not connected; no special action or data copying data is required on the end-user side. Imagine that a user is editing a file in offline mode and then connects to the network. The data synchronizes and the file handle automatically switches to the file on the file server instead of the local cached version. Combine this with the ability to redirect users' My Documents to a network location, so users save their data to their documents area, which automatically writes to the network for secure storage and caches it locally for availability offline

Distributed Storage

High availability for data via clustering is discussed later, but file server clusters are fully supported, allowing data to be stored on external storage including a SAN with multiple servers servicing the storage. With multiple servers serving the storage, a single server outage does not interrupt access to data. However, that is just one method of making data highly available. Clusters do not assist in distributed environments where users travel between offices that might have copies of the same data. Ideally, as a user travels, he accesses the nearest copy of data. Additionally, the number of file servers is increasing in many environments, so knowing which server to go to for a share or which mapped drive to use is problematic for the user.

DFS uses a namespace that is stored as part of the domain consisting of links that are logical names having one or more link targets that point to a share on a file server. This allows the user to see a single share, which is the actual DFS namespace. When the user navigates through the various links of the DFS, which appear simply as folders, the user is redirected to the closest file server that contains the data without even knowing it, as shown in Figure 1-6. In the example, the user is accessing the Sales "folder" of the DFS and is redirected to the share Sales on the Fileserver2 server. If the user accessed Documents, he could be redirected to either of the copies or, if spread geographically, to the closest version.

In addition to the namespace, a sophisticated delta-based replication engine keeps multiple copies of the same share synchronized. This is a big improvement over the FRS present in Windows 2000 and Windows 2003. In our example, the replication keeps the two copies of the Documents share synchronized.

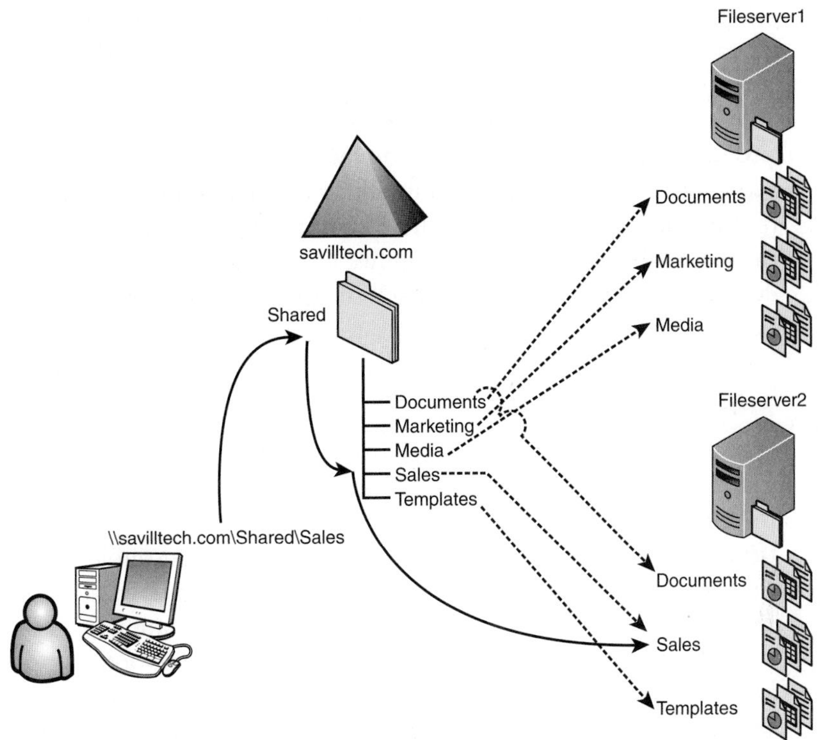

FIGURE 1-6 Although DFS can have link targets to shares on hundreds of servers, in this example, the domain-based DFS named Shared in the savilltech.com domain has links to just two file servers with different shared folder names, but each holds a copy of Documents and the DFS namespace points to both.

In addition to safe and easy data storage and access, users want their data restored when they lose it. Windows uses the VSS for backups and to provide Shadow Copy Restore (also known as Previous Versions), which allows a user to right-click a file or folder and see previous versions of the data at points in the past. This functionality allows users to restore their own data, cutting the need for administrator intervention. In Windows Vista, this is also available on the clients' local disks!

Users also want an easy way to find their data. Windows Server has a content indexer component that indexes the information on the file server and gives easy access to query the index via the users' local Search option from the Start menu.

File storage is great but sometimes a greater collaboration environment is required, for example, the ability to check out files for editing and then check them back in, and combine the data with calendaring, contacts, list data, and the other components required for full collaboration and project success. Microsoft provides Windows SharePoint Services (WSS) to supply a Web-based environment to facilitate end user collaboration.

Windows Server 2008 delivers everything needed for your Windows infrastructure, and for interoperation with other environments such as NetWare and UNIX via both platform-specific solutions and network standards such as the Network File System (NFS).

Printing

Despite drives to a paperless environment and more online collaboration, the requirement to print data still exists. Although it is possible to connect printers to each user's workstation, it is not efficient. Even though many printers connect directly to the network, it is not desirable for each client to connect directly to a network printer. The Windows Server platform provides printer-sharing capabilities and print job queuing (a print job is simply a set of data to print), which allows prioritization of printing and limits maximum print job size at certain times of the day. Additionally, to simplify driver management when a client connects to a printer via a Windows print server, the server sends the locally needed driver to the client machine for installation, minimizing the actions needed to set up the client to be able to print. With Windows Vista and Windows Server 2008, clients can fully render print jobs before sending them to the print server to cut down on the workload of the print server, which increases the availability of the print server.

There have always been discussions regarding the best placement of a print server in distributed environments. Obviously the physical printer has to exist in the remote location so that the users can pick up the print job. Placing a print server locally increases management tasks, such as updating drivers. But *not* placing a local print server means a job has to be sent over the WAN to the print server and then back over the WAN to the actual printer. With Windows Server 2008, the Print Management Console gives a central control point and allows printer driver deployment and updates to multiple print servers. It includes automatic printer discovery on the server, which is useful because it enables a subnet to be specified and any printers in the subnet to be found and configured with a print queue on the print server.

Networking Services of Windows Server 2008

Today almost all communication takes place over Transmission Control Protocol/Internet Protocol (TCP/IP) version 4, in which each computer has a 32-bit address that is commonly viewed as four numbers separated by decimals. For example, 10.10.10.5 is an IP address for a machine. Although it is possible to manually configure each machine with an IP address (known as static IP configuration because it doesn't change), doing so is cumbersome in large environments and is hard to track if machines are reinstalled or replaced. The Windows Server platform provides the DHCP service, which allows clients, at startup, to send a request over the network for an IP address (a DHCP lease request). A DHCP server that has a database of IP addresses that can be given out, and leases that can be offered, services the request. The duration of this IP address lease is configurable, but is 8 days by default. At the midpoint of the lease duration, the client attempts to contact the DHCP server and renew the lease so that it can keep the IP address. If you have computers that connect and then are reinstalled or replaced at the end of the lease duration, the IP address is marked as available again—no IP addresses are "lost" and no manual effort is needed to track them. In addition to an IP address, the DHCP server sends additional information, such as DNS servers, domain information, and time services.

Each machine, be it a server or workstation, now has an IP address. Humans, however, don't do well with 32-bit addresses. I'm far more likely to remember juliespc than 10.132.43.175. Every machine has a "friendly" name, it's known as the machine's hostname, but you can't just talk to juliespc. (That's not quite true: On a local network, machines have the capability to ask, "Is juliespc out there?" but it's not ideal to flood a network with this broadcast traffic.) Therefore, you need a lookup list so that you can check which IP address belongs to a specific hostname.

A legacy solution still used today is Windows Internet Name Service (WINS), which maps a 15-character NetBIOS name to an IP address. However, this is being retired as quickly as possible. WINS allows machines, on startup, to tell the WINS server its name and IP address, and other computers could then ask WINS for the IP address for a specific PC. But WINS is limited and designed for NetBIOS, which is neither a future direction for networks nor an Internet standard.

The domain name system (DNS) is used every day. www.microsoft.com is a hostname that has to be resolved to an IP address. DNS has traditionally been a manually managed database: The DNS administrators added records for hosts and their IP addresses, which were based around zones. For example, one or more DNS servers host a DNS zone for Microsoft.com. In that zone is a manually created record named www that resolves to an IP address (possibly more than one IP address in the case of a big web site).

However, the role of DNS grew significantly with the introduction of Active Directory, which uses DNS as the locator service. This meant many new records and types of records in DNS for every domain controller, and managing them manually became too troublesome and prone to errors. Therefore dynamic DNS (DDNS) was introduced. DDNS is an Internet standard and allows each machine to register its hostname-to-IP-address mappings and additional records that are vital to many services. This also works well for clients that get IP addresses from DHCP and register their hostname-to-IP addresses.

Figure 1-7 shows two workstations connected to a network. The DHCP server has a database of IP addresses it uses to give IP addresses to workstations. In this example, you see the following:

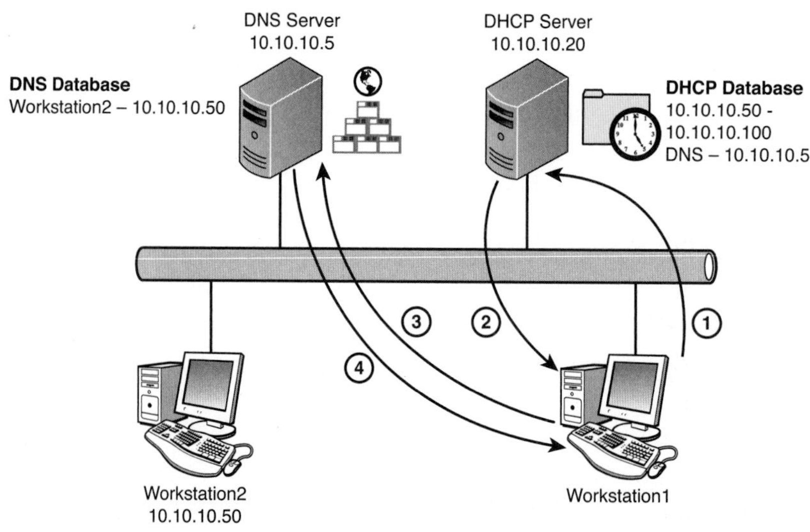

FIGURE 1-7 An overview of some of the steps a dynamically configured client goes through for its IP-based communication.

1. Workstation1 turns on and sends out a DHCP lease request over the network. Note that it is not sending to a DHCP server if it's newly connected to the network; it just sends out a broadcast for an IP address over its local network.

2. The DHCP server responds with an IP address for it to use (for example, 10.10.10.51).
3. Workstation1 now wants to talk to Workstation2; however, it does not know the IP address for Workstation2. So, Workstation1 makes a request to the DNS server to find the IP address for the known hostname.
4. The DNS server responds with the IP address of Workstation2, allowing communication between Workstation1 and Workstation2.

TCP/IP version 4, the 32-bit address, was discussed earlier. A while back, people panicked because everything was becoming Internet-aware and had an address. The concern was that the world would run out of addresses. (Thirty-two bits gives just over four thousand million addresses.) Technologies such as Network Address Translation (NAT) have widely circumvented the problem. NAT allows a company to use an IP addressing scheme internally, and Internet requests to pass through gateway computers that have "real" Internet addresses and communicate to the Internet on the client's behalf. Some features of TCP/IP were not optimal, including a lot of wasted space due to the fixed format of the TCP header, lack of security, and the autoconfiguration nature of addresses. IPv6 was created to solve those problems and is supported in Windows Vista and Windows Server 2008. IPv6 addresses are 128 bits in length, so no one remembers an address, making the DHCP and dynamic DNS services even more important.

Security

Beyond the basic connectivity services of one machine talking to another, network security is paramount. Traffic is just packets of data sent over a network cable, and depending on the traffic, it might be "clear text," meaning that someone can put a scanner on the network or run a piece of software on his computer that captures all the traffic being sent—traffic that might contain sensitive data. Although applications encrypt their data, this does not apply to all traffic. IP security (IPsec) sets policies to encrypt all data to and from specific computers or even the entire network. IPsec allows the encryption of all traffic, and if a client does not support the encryption or is not listed as an allowed communication partner, traffic is blocked.

Users love working from home. This normally entails access to corporate resources, which is accomplished via a connection from a home computer into the corporate network. In the past, this might have been a modem dial-up connection into a bank of modems at a company. However, nearly every home now has Internet access via DSL or cable and doesn't possess a modem, so access to the organization's infrastructure from the Internet is required. One obvious answer is to connect a company to the Internet (which most companies do). But given some of the unscrupulous types on the Internet, this connection is not left open. A system known as a firewall is placed between an organization and the Internet to block all but a configured type of communication.

Because a user might access many system types over many types of protocol from many locations, opening holes in the firewall for all the types of communication is not practical. Instead, a pipe opens between the remote user and the company infrastructure. This pipe is a virtual private network (VPN) and is only a single "hole" in the firewall that allows all types of communication to flow over. Security is used on these VPN connections, with authentication performed before the pipe opens for traffic because after the VPN connection is made, the remote client can perform functions as if it were sitting inside the network. Checks are performed on VPN connections to ensure that clients have certain levels of patch and antivirus updates before connections are allowed.

A welcomed feature in Windows Server 2008 allows health checking of machines that connect to the local network, not via a VPN. A new component for Windows Vista and Windows XP is available from Microsoft. This component allows an SoH to be made by the clients, which is checked against a required level for network access. If the machine lacks certain aspects of the required health level, it is placed in a quarantine network where it is sent the patches and antivirus updates necessary before full network access is granted. Only certain clients are supported by this health validation process, which is discussed in full detail in Chapter 8, "Remote Access and Securing and Optimizing the Network."

Authorization and Authentication

The words authorization and authentication are often used interchangeably, but that is not correct. Authentication is proving you are who you say you are. Commonly this is accomplished by something you know (such as a password), something you have (such as a USB token), or something you are (biometric tests such as fingerprints). You might hear of two-factor authentication that requires two types of authentication: for example, a USB token that also requires a pass code to be entered.

Authorization indicates what an authenticated person can do, which includes accessing certain data from a file server, printing to a certain printer, or manipulating objects in a directory service.

Windows facilitates both authorization and authentication via Active Directory, which is used as the central account repository (and much more). Information is stored in a highly secure form and authentication from a client to the directory is encrypted along with authorization handled by Kerberos. You explore this topic fully in Chapter 10.

The actual Active Directory is stored on one or more domain controllers. (In reality this is two or more for fault tolerance purposes.) Through a process called multimaster replication, changes are made at any domain controller from a client. These changes propagate in the most bandwidth efficient manner to all domain controllers, even those in different physical locations. There have always been concerns over the physical security of domain controllers. Obviously they hold the database for every account and password that although encrypted can be deciphered given enough time. So, the general rule is that a location can have a local domain controller only if physical security can be guaranteed.

Why is a local domain controller even desired? Consider a location that has a number of local file servers—application servers. For a user sitting next to the server to access any resources, he must authenticate and receive authorization to access them, a process requiring communication with a domain controller. The domain controller can sit in a remote location, and the authentication and authorization requests can be sent over a WAN link, which might use bandwidth and take a little time, but that's no big problem. But imagine that a WAN link is unavailable. The client has no way to get the tickets needed to talk to the servers, and even though he can see the server, he can't get to the data. With a local domain controller, WAN link failures do not affect the access to local resources. You don't want to jeopardize a company's security, so with Windows Server 2008, a new RODC has been introduced that stores certain aspects of Active Directory but can be configured with what level of data to store, even down to storing passwords for some users but not others to avoid risking the security of the entire organization.

Deployment

Another big drive for the Windows platform is the actual deployment of the OS itself. Previously, different technologies were used for server deployment and client deployment. Windows 2003 Enterprise edition included the Automated Deployment Services (ADS) imaging technology, which was designed for server deployments and included many features needed for server hardware deployment.

An example of server-specific functionality provided by ADS is the capability to capture floppy disk content to an image and then remotely send it to a server—this is useful for performing initial BIOS updates and hardware RAID configurations that are vital for server configurations. For clients, Remote Installation Services (RIS) has long been the Microsoft solution that could send the installation files from the media to a machine over the network and perform an installation. Although ADS was a good solution for servers, RIS had a poor reputation due to its slow installation speed and the fact it used installation files. With Windows Vista and Windows Server 2008, the installation media contains an image of the OS. The i386 folder is gone, so new deployment solutions are needed to work with this new format.

This Windows Imaging (WIM) format was first used as part of the OS deployment feature pack for Systems Management Server (SMS). But it was based on a .9 version of the image format and not initially compatible with Vista (although an update was released at the launch of Vista to make operating system deployment [OSD] Vista WIM-format compatible), but Windows Vista brought the format into the mainstream. In essence, Windows Vista contains a prebuilt copy of a Vista machine that it lays down on your hard drive, performs some hardware-specific detection, and the machine is ready to be used.

Windows Server 2008 contains WDS, which deploys the WIM file of the OS over the network along with other components used to tailor the contents of the image format and prepare XML files to answer questions normally asked during installation and for more advanced granular configuration. The basic process of an OS deployment via Windows Deployment Services consists of the following:

1. The client boots over the network using PXE Boot.
2. The WDS server responds and sends a Windows PE environment that contains the WDS client, which allows the downloading and application of WIM files along with performing any tasks outlined in the XML configuration files.
3. After the WIM file extracts to disk, further actions are performed from within the Windows PE.
4. The client computer reboots into the deployed OS and performs machine-specific hardware detection and configuration along with other customizations.
5. The computer boots normally and applies any Group Policy settings applicable to the computer account and, on user logon, any user-specific Group Policy options.

Although you just learned about using WDS to deploy the Windows Vista client, server deployments use the same technology. You finally have a common deployment methodology and infrastructure to control deployment of the entire organization. Although the deployment is Windows Server 2008 and Vista out of the box, you can create images of older OSs such as 2003 and XP to give one unified deployment infrastructure. Other technologies, such as System Center Configuration Manager 2007, build on WDS to offer additional features such as application and patch deployment during the OS deployment, but are not required.

Licensing

Microsoft has a number of licensing models available to customers. The client side of licensing is generally far more costly than server licensing, so let's look at the client option. You can go to your retail channel and purchase Windows off the shelf. You can purchase a number of different versions of Windows Vista: Windows Vista Home Basic, Windows Vista Home Premium, Windows Vista Business, and Windows Vista Ultimate. This is probably the most expensive option for most businesses, even small ones. There is a relationship with a reseller and/or Microsoft to purchase in bulk via Volume Licensing, which gives cheaper prices and better support levels from Microsoft. For Volume Licensing customers that also have Software Assurance (a program where automatic rights to new versions within a defined period are made available), an additional version of Vista is available: Windows Vista Enterprise. Like its big brother Vista Ultimate, Enterprise edition includes BitLocker technology that allows the encryption of the entire hard drive using hardware-based data encryption, better compatibility with UNIX applications via the Subsystem for UNIX-based Applications (SUA) that allows UNIX applications to run on Vista with no changes, and multilingual capabilities. Additionally, Enterprise edition (not Ultimate) allows users of the free Virtual PC application the right to run four additional copies of the OS (or a down-level OS such as XP). An overview of the upgrade flow improving features is shown in Figure 1-8. Both the home and business lines have a basic and advanced version with Ultimate being the Ultimate version!

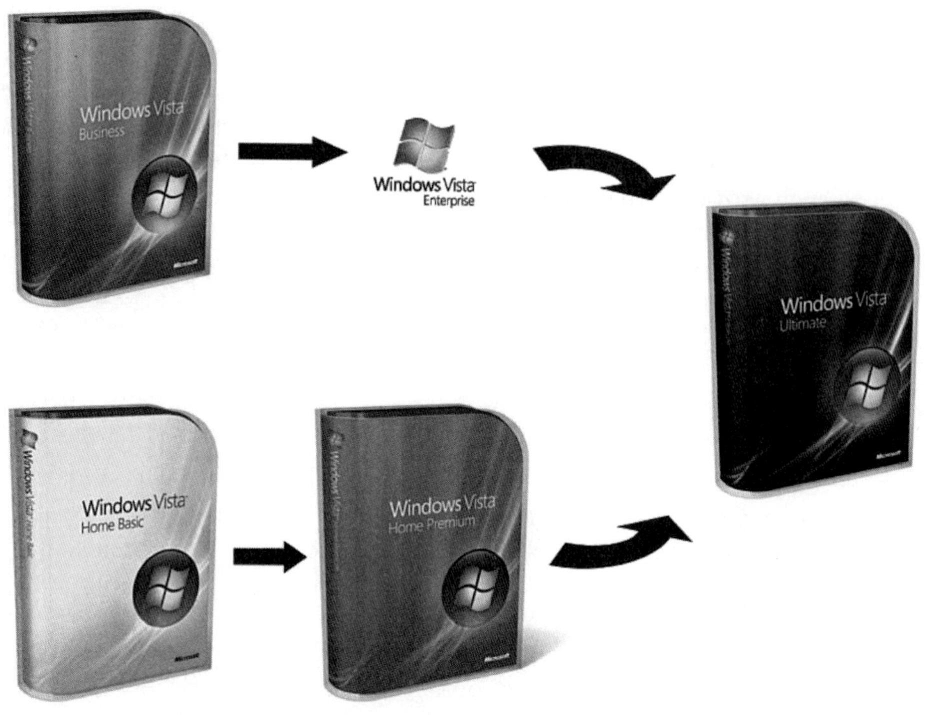

FIGURE 1-8 The two threads of Windows Vista OS, business and home, and how the Ultimate edition includes the best of both.

Something of interest to customers who qualify for Windows Vista Enterprise edition: They are eligible for the Microsoft Desktop Optimization Pack, which comprises five solutions at the time of writing. All five solutions were previously separate third-party products that were purchased by Microsoft and updated to meet Microsoft coding standards and practices to form an attractive suite:

- **Microsoft SoftGrid (formerly Softricity SoftGrid)**. Instead of installing software onto computers through writes to the file system, placement of DLLs, and changes to the Registry, applications are captured to a data stream. When users need to run the application, the data is streamed and cached to the computer in the order that the data is needed as the application starts, minimizing start times. The application runs entirely in this sandboxed environment. No Registry or file system changes are made on the computer receiving the application, minimizing compatibility and regression testing issues. This data stream is also cached locally for execution when not connected to the network.

- **Microsoft Asset Inventory Service (formerly AssetMetrix)**. For users of SMS, the ability to gather applications installed on a PC by interrogating Add/Remove Programs is common. But what about software that does not register itself in Add/Remove Programs? The Microsoft Asset Inventory Service scans the computer, collects data, and compares it to its database of more than 430,000 titles to identify, in a friendly format, the actual applications installed. Users of SMS will be pleased to know this information hooks into SMS for one central view of all inventory information.
- **Microsoft Advanced Group Policy Management (formerly Desktop Standard GPOVault)**. This provides a change management structure for Group Policy plus the ability to rollback Group Policy changes. More granular control of GPO management is possible via a role-based administration and delegation model with change request approval built-in.
- **Microsoft Diagnostics and Recovery Toolset (formerly Winternals IT Admin Pak)**. For users of Winternals ERD Commander, this will be familiar. (It is simply the tool repackaged.) Microsoft Diagnostics and Recovery Toolset is an amazing environment that allows access to unbootable or corrupted systems to extract data and repair the environment. Repair occurs via automated utilities that check the system for common causes of an unbootable system, and via utilities to manually manipulate the file system, Registry, and nearly every aspect of the OS. Beyond data access and resolution of system problems, the toolset includes components that allow a system to be set back to a system restore point; a crash analyzer that uses a point-and-click GUI; LockSmith, which allows the password to be reset on any local user account; and File Restore capabilities for hard deleted files (that is, not in the Recycle Bin). Another tool enables you to see interactions between a client and the Active Directory. The software includes a utility to wipe a disk to Department of Defense security levels, a partition management utility, and an offline hotfix removal tool.
- **Microsoft System Center Desktop Error Monitoring**. This tool enables monitoring, at an enterprise level, of all errors that occur on desktop computers, giving a view into the entire error status of your organization and providing control over the errors reported to Microsoft.

This amazing set of tools has a per-desktop price of around $7 to $10, depending on the number of desktops, and so on. You just have to have Software Assurance, which is the driver behind the Desktop Optimization Pack (DOP). It's a huge value-add for SA customers, but it's a nonperpetual license; use the Desktop Optimization Pack only while you pay its annual fee, which is possible only while Software Assurance is in effect. What Microsoft has done with DOP is give a compelling reason for customers to keep SA or to get it if they don't have it. Even small organizations are normally eligible for some kind of SA deal with Microsoft.

You learned about the server versions earlier in the chapter, and the hardware you run the OS on and the features you need available will lead your purchasing decision. If you need failover clustering, purchase the Enterprise version of Windows Server 2008.

Virtualization

The final area of discussion is virtualization. Previously each type of service or application had one or more server of its own. You had batch processing servers, application servers for each application, file servers, and so on, and for good reason. Each system had a vital job and placing multiple applications/services on a single OS introduces undesirable risks and problems, for example:

- **Resource conflict**. One application might use a large portion of the processor or memory, leaving the other contending applications bottlenecked and performing poorly. This even happens with disk space. Applications use up the entire disk, leaving the others unable to write data and hang or crash.
- **Uptime**. A failure on an application might require the ultimate fix: reboot. That's fine if an application is on its own server, but when multiple applications share a server, the reboot knocks the neighbors out as well, which causes a bigger problem than the one the reboot was fixing. Obviously a reboot is the nice scenario; an application that causes an OS to crash brings down other systems in an uncontrolled state that could lead to corruption.
- **OS requirements**. Different applications/services might have varying OS requirements, such as different service pack levels, different versions of .NET, ActiveX Data Objects (ADO), or even the entire OS. If an application runs only on NT 4.0, you have to keep a whole NT 4.0 server.

- **Compatibility**. Running more services/applications on a single box increases the amount of testing anytime something changes in any one of the applications because of the possibility it might affect the OS in some manner that affects the other applications.

Physical servers are expensive in terms of a hardware perspective, rack space perspective, maintenance costs, management costs (for example patching, updating, backing up), and licensing. Ideally, you run everything on a single box. That's not practical, but there is a middle ground.

Windows Server 2008 (like Windows Server 2003) has Windows Server Resource Management (WSRM) that allows each application/service to be allocated limits on memory and processor usage with different amounts configurable for different times of the day. This calendaring flexibility is useful in the instance of a single server running applications that operate at different times of the day. For example, an application server has to have priority over the processor usage during the day but at night is not used because all the clients are tucked up in bed. So, a batch-processing service is given 80 percent of the CPU between the hours of 8 p.m. and 4 a.m. In the event the batch took longer, it could continue running, but after 4 a.m. is limited to only 10 percent of the processor to ensure that the application server gets the resources it needs during the day.

WSRM gathers accounting type data to track how much resource an application or service uses, which is useful in the scenario where the IT department bills business units based on usage. WSRM is a great solution from a number of angles. It minimizes the number of servers; you run only one copy of the OS (although WSRM is only on Enterprise and Datacenter editions, so one copy of a quite expensive OS, but still good); and you have one OS to patch and maintain. WSRM manages resource contention nicely, but it fails in other areas. For example, if an application needs a reboot, so do all the others. The applications are also still all on one OS, meaning compatibility issues. Because they are all on one OS, they have to accept the same OS, patch levels, .NET version, and so on. So, although WSRM solves some problems, it does not solve everything.

An alternative to using WSRM is virtualization, and you see a *lot* of detail on this topic in Chapter 19, "Virtualization and Resource Management." A service runs on the server that emulates multiple virtual computers, each with its own allocations of processor and memory, with virtual disks that map to large files on the host server's file system. Each of these virtual computers run any OS such as Windows NT 4, Windows 2000, XP, Windows 2003, Vista, and Windows Server 2008. Different solutions exist for virtualization, such as from VMWare; however, this book concentrates on the Microsoft solutions of Virtual PC and Virtual Server, which accomplish a similar goal in slightly different implementations.

With several virtual environments on a single physical server, you can run multiple virtual server instances totally separate from the others, with their own OS version, service packs, and other components. Also each of these virtual machines restarts entirely separate from the others (with the exception of the host server; if the host server shuts down, obviously all the "guest" OSs also shut down). Consider also that if each virtual machine runs one application or service, compatibility testing is minimized because each service/application is in its own environment and does not share any resources with other services and applications. If one virtual machine crashes, the other virtual machines are not affected, so virtualization solves compatibility, OS requirements, uptime, and resource conflict. It's perfect, right? Yes and no. Yes, the virtual servers solve the problem areas of consolidation, but remember the reasons for consolidation in the first place:

- **Physical servers are expensive both from a hardware perspective**. You consolidated, so this issue is solved.
- **Rack space perspective**. Yes, you consolidated the number of servers.
- **Maintenance costs**. Yes, again, you consolidated the number of servers, so hardware maintenance is minimized.
- **Management costs (for example patching, updating, backing up)**. You still have separate OSs in each virtual, so each virtual has to be patched, monitored, backed up, and so on. But you have Microsoft Operations Manager (MOM) for monitoring and it has management packs for Virtual Server. You have a good patch management strategy in place, so that's not a big deal; it's a pain, but not a deal breaker.
- **Licensing**. You have to buy a server license for every virtual you run? That's expensive. You were so close—no wonder Microsoft gives away free virtualization software.

Microsoft jumped on the virtualization bandwagon, so in addition to giving away its virtualization products, it relaxed the licensing requirements. As mentioned, Windows Vista Enterprise Edition allows four guest client OSs to run under the one license—well, Vista Enterprise is not alone.

With the release of Windows 2003 R2, Microsoft introduced the concept of license-cost free virtual instances. Whereas licenses used to be based on number of installations of the software, they were now based on the number of instances that are run on a server at any one time; for example, you could have 10 installations of Windows Server as virtuals but run only 4 at a time. These license-free virtuals are available on Windows 2003 R2 Enterprise and Datacenter editions. Windows 2003 R2 Enterprise edition, like Vista Enterprise, may run four concurrent virtuals running Windows Server 2003 R2 Enterprise or Standard edition (or previous versions; for example, Windows 2000). If you need more than four concurrent virtuals, purchase a license for them or consider upgrading to Datacenter. With the Datacenter edition, an unlimited number of virtualization instances run Datacenter, Enterprise, or Standard edition, and it again includes previous versions.

With Windows Server 2008, these rights are one virtual instance right for Standard edition, four for Enterprise, and unlimited for Datacenter and Itanium editions.

Summary

Organizations obviously expect features such as overall security, stability, and easy maintenance, and they all improved with Windows Server 2008, including new interfaces and recovery processes. Higher availability (via clustered groups of servers) and rich experiences (via terminal servers and remote applications) are important in most environments. In addition, far more powerful clustering technologies overall make Windows Server 2008 compelling not only for use on its own, but also other technologies such as Exchange Server 2007 take advantage of new OS features to offer better services to its users.

You now move on to examining each aspect of the Windows Server 2008 platform in the detail needed to understand the technology and utilize best practices in your day-to-day environment. Let's start by looking at the GUI and finding out what Aero Glass is.

CHAPTER 2

WINDOWS SERVER 2008 FUNDAMENTALS: NAVIGATING AND GETTING STARTED

Before you embark on an expedition, you need to know how to read a map. This chapter looks at the Windows environment from a navigational standpoint: How do you use Windows? What facilities does Windows offer to help you do your job? In many situations, you won't manage your servers from the servers themselves; instead, you'll manage them remotely via the various management tools and interfaces. Therefore, this chapter looks at the client experience and the differences between the environment of Windows Vista/Server 2008 and previous operating systems.

With earlier versions of Windows, the installation process was very interactive. Installing Windows Server 2008 is much simpler, as discussed in Chapter 3, "Installing and Upgrading Windows Server 2008." This chapter looks at how to interact with the operating system in various situations.

Chapter 1, "Windows 101: Its Origins, Present, and the Services It Provides," discusses the various versions of Windows Server 2008. This chapter looks at the various versions of Vista that are available and their features. It then examines the main features that apply to both Windows Vista and Windows Server 2008.

With Windows 2000, the server and client operating systems shared a common code base, and service packs and updates were made available for clients and servers concurrently. With Windows Server 2003, there was pressure to release the client early, so the Windows XP client was split from the Windows Server 2003 code base, and there were separate kernels for the operating system, as well as separate service packs and updates. This system was difficult to manage, and with Windows Server 2008, the goal was to get back to a common code base for the client and server.

However, Vista was released early, creating a separation between client and server. At the same time that the Windows Server 2008 operating system (OS) was released, changes made to the OS were replicated into Windows Vista Service Pack 1. The Release To Manufacture (RTM) of Windows Server 2008 is the Service Pack 1 build. The first released service pack for Windows Server 2008 will be Service Pack 2, and it will be a shared pack for both Vista and Server 2008. Thanks to the servicing stack in the OS, this shared service pack and update strategy is fine because only updates to components installed will be downloaded and applied. (So, for example, a domain name system [DNS] server update will be not downloaded to a Windows Vista client.) All this talk of code bases and service packs matters because it has to do with a common core for Windows Vista and Windows Server 2008.

NOTE This chapter doesn't look at the Starter edition of Vista, which was designed for emerging markets with basic computers and limits the number of concurrent applications and the types of network connectivity. It also doesn't look at the "N" editions for the European market that do not include the integrated media player or media-related components.

Windows Vista at 30,000 Feet

Table 2-1 shows the features available in the various versions of Windows Vista. All the editions of Vista shown in the table—Home Basic, Home Premium, Business, Enterprise, and Ultimate—come in both 32- and 64-bit editions.

Table 2-1 Feature Comparison of the Windows Vista Versions

Feature	Home Basic	Home Premium	Business	Enterprise	Ultimate
Domain membership and group policy	N	N	Y	Y	Y
Encrypted file system	N	Y	Y	Y	Y
Windows Aero	N	Y	Y	Y	Y

Feature	Home Basic	Home Premium	Business	Enterprise	Ultimate
Remote Desktop	N	N	Y	Y	Y
Media Center	N	Y	N	N	Y
Offline folders	N	N	Y	Y	Y
BitLocker drive encryption	N	N	N	Y	Y
Subsystem for UNIX applications	N	N	N	Y	Y
Multilanguage user interface (MUI)	N	N	N	Y	Y
Tablet PC support	N	Y	Y	Y	Y
Single-session virtual PC	N	N	N	Y	Y
Volume shadow copy	N	N	Y	Y	Y
Number of physical processors	1	1	2	2	2
Maximum amount of memory	8GB	16GB	Machine maximum	Machine maximum	Machine maximum

In a corporate environment, you run the Windows Vista Business edition (unless you have Software Assurance, which gives you access to Windows Vista Enterprise edition). At a minimum, in such an environment, you have a domain to centralize security and account management, which necessitates a business flavor of Vista.

The additional cost of the Ultimate edition and its nonbusiness features make it unlikely to be used in a corporation, except perhaps on a few specific-purpose machines, such as a media center box in a conference room.

Because corporations don't use the home editions, all their machines are domain member-capable and group policy-aware. If some users use their personal machines to access corporate resources, they could run one of the home editions; however, those computers would not be actual members of the corporate domain, so these home machines do not need to run corporate policies (nor would it be desirable for them to do so).

If you work for an enterprise that has Software Assurance and are trying to decide whether to buy the Business or Enterprise edition, check to see if any specific features you want are in Enterprise edition only (for example, the BitLocker drive encryption that can help protect laptop content).

The Logon Experience

The first component of the operating system you normally interact with is the logon environment. As in Windows XP, the logon in Windows Server 2008 has different options, depending on whether you are a member of a domain or workgroup.

Windows XP Logon

Under Windows XP, the Welcome screen is available for a machine that is a member of a workgroup. An example of the XP Welcome screen is shown in Figure 2-1.

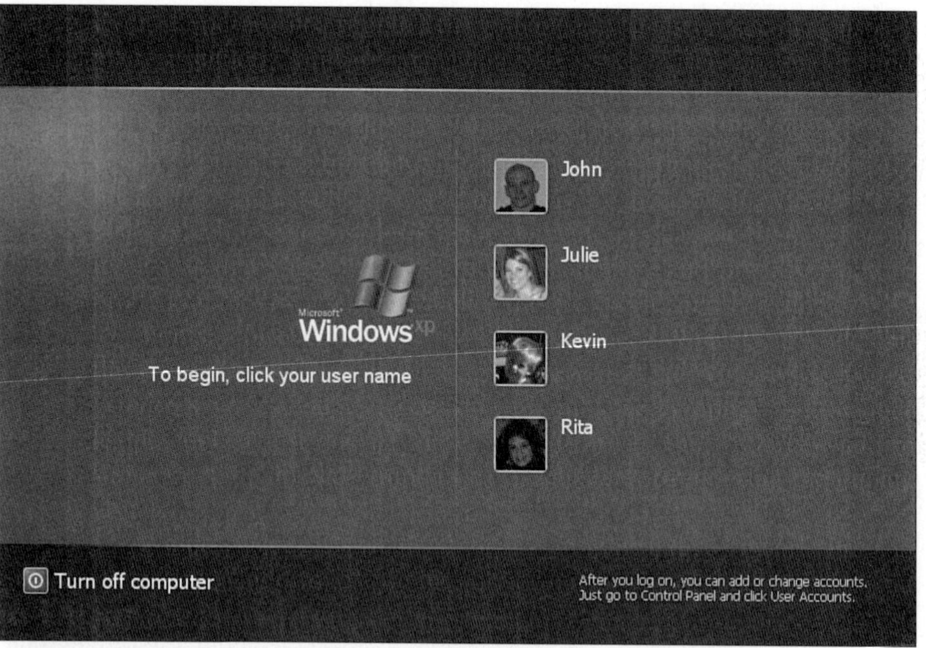

FIGURE 2-1 The Windows XP logon screen for computers in a workgroup environment shows the local accounts.

By default, the administrator account does not appear on the Welcome screen, but you can access it by pressing Ctrl+Alt+Del twice. When you do this, a standard logon dialog appears, allowing you to type a username instead of selecting from the Welcome screen. Enable the administrator account to appear on the Welcome screen by making the following Registry change:

1. Start the Registry editor (regedit.exe).
2. Navigate to HKEY_LOCAL_MACHINE\SOFTWARE\Microsoft\Windows NT\CurrentVersion\Winlogon\SpecialAccounts\UserList.
3. From the Edit menu, select New, DWORD Value.
4. Enter a name for the administrator account and press Enter.
5. Double-click the new value and set it to 1. Click OK. The administrator account now appears on the Welcome screen.

Windows Vista Logon

By default, Windows Vista uses the Welcome screen for a machine that belongs to a workgroup. Like Windows XP, it does not show the administrator account, as shown in Figure 2-2.

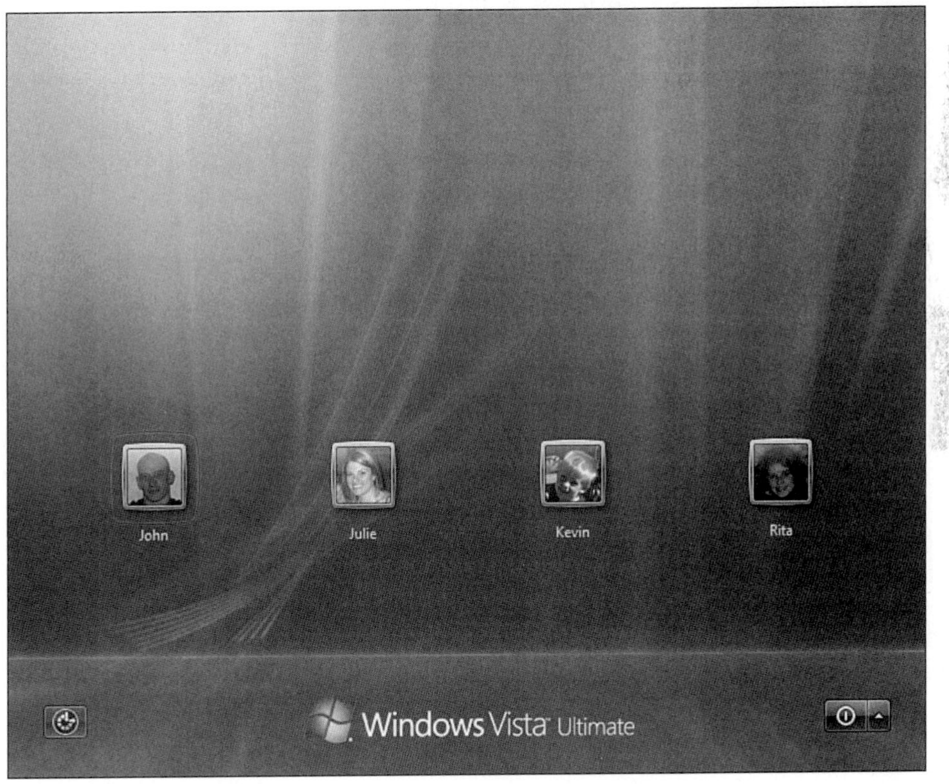

FIGURE 2-2 The Windows Vista logon screen for computers in a workgroup environment shows the local accounts and the version of Vista.

The fact that the administrator account does not appear on the Welcome screen with Windows Vista is part of a focus change regarding protecting users from themselves that is known as user account control (UAC) discussed later in this chapter. In the past, the administrator account was created by default with a blank password during the out-of-box experience. That was not great security, so with Windows Vista, the administrator account is disabled by default. When you upgrade from Windows XP, the administrator account is disabled on a workgroup-joined machine unless there are no other local administrator accounts active; for a domain-joined machine, the administrator account is always disabled. Because the logon screen shows only active accounts that can be logged into, the administrator account does not show. To be listed on the logon screen, the administrator account needs to be enabled and also have a password configured. You can accomplish this with the Computer Management Microsoft Management Console (MMC) console, where you enable administrator via Local Users and Groups.

Windows Server 2008 Logon

On a fresh installation of Windows Server 2008, the administrator account is enabled but has a blank password. After the installation is complete, first change the administrator password; until the password change is complete, you cannot do anything else. Figure 2-3 shows the Windows Server 2008 Welcome screen for a workgroup machine.

With both Windows Vista and Windows Server 2008, if a machine is a member of a domain, local accounts are not displayed for selection. Instead, by default, the user most recently logged on is displayed, allowing easy access. (If required for security reasons, you can disable this feature.) If you want to use another account for logon, click the Switch User button, select Other User, and enter the username and password (see Figure 2-4).

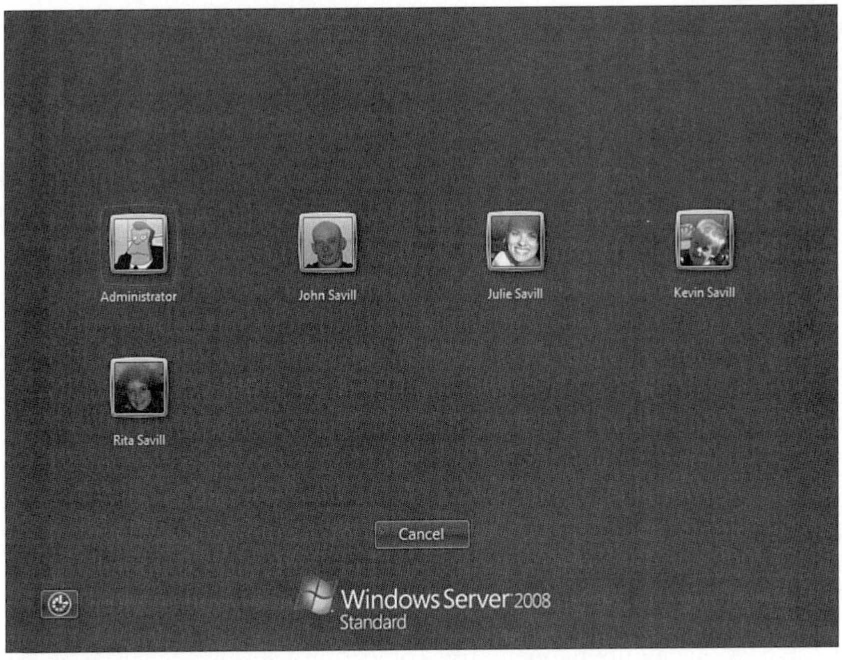

FIGURE 2-3 The logon process in a workgroup-joined Windows Server 2008 machine.

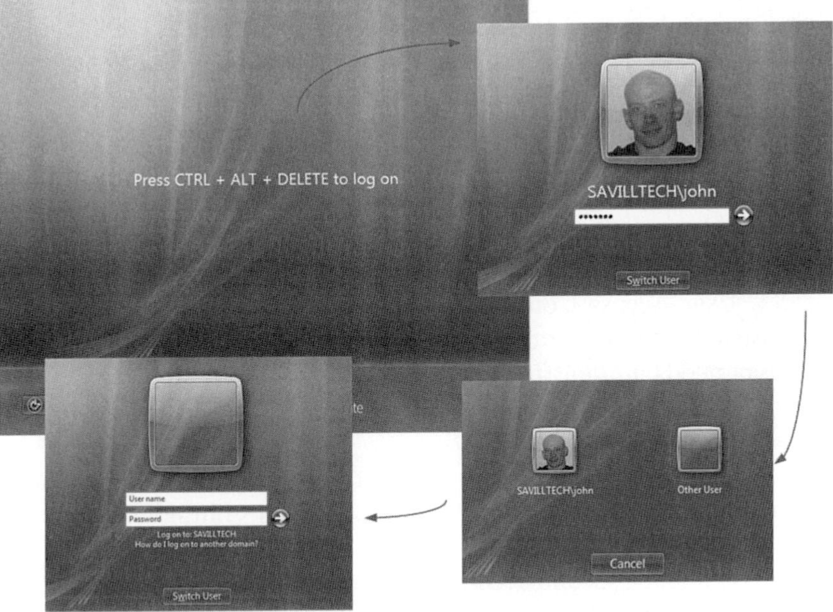

FIGURE 2-4 In the Windows Vista and Windows Server 2008 logon process for a domain-joined machine, you have a Switch User option.

User Access Control

What is the UAC and why do we have it? There have long been a few best practices for administrators. The most important one is that you should never share the administrator account because when multiple users use the administrator account, there is no accountability. If a problem occurs, auditing will show only that administrator did something, not which of the 30 people who know the administrator password performed the action. In general, don't share accounts. Instead of letting multiple people use the administrator account, make each user who requires administrator-type powers a member of the local administrators group in a workgroup environment or a member of the Domain Admins group. Or give these users some lower-level set of permissions that are still powerful compared to a normal user account. For several reasons, you don't want users performing normal day-to-day actions such as surfing the Web or playing *Lego Star Wars* (with your son, of course) when logged on with administrator credentials:

- Accidents happen. You could run a script or click something that might just cause inconvenience if running with normal user credentials but could wipe out an entire company's files or delete entire groups of users when running with administrator credentials.
- Malware exists. As with accidents, while a piece of malware executed by a normal user causes a certain level of havoc or exposure, that same piece of malware run by a user with administrator credentials can be a serious problem.
- An organization will see a much lower total cost of ownership (TCO) when running with managed systems, which is possible only when users are not all running with administrator permissions.

User Access Control allows users to run with standard user rights instead of administrator credentials which mitigates these risks. When a user needs administrative credentials, he can elevate his permissions to those of an administrator as described in the "Elevation of Privilege" section.

When do you use an administrator account? Administrators need administrative credentials for certain functions but not others, so the solution is to have two accounts for each administrative person: a normal user account and a second account that has Administrator privileges. For example, if my normal user account is jsavill, my administrator account might be jsavill-a. Some organizations name each administrator account something totally different from the user's name (for example, characters from *The Simpsons*) so the administrator accounts are not easily guessed. When an action requires administrator credentials, I could use my jsavill-a or Homer account. However, logging out of the normal user account and logging in as the administrator user is an inconvenience, so instead you can use the Run As functionality, which allows a user to execute a command or program in the context of another user (in this case, using administrator account credentials).

To enable simpler operation, administrators sometimes create shortcuts that include their administrator credentials as part of the program initialization. However, it does not happen often, and administrators run with their administrator credentials all the time, and even normal users are often made local administrators of their machines to enable basic functions such as installing printers and software installation. What's the solution? The first part is to minimize when administrator credentials are needed. To reduce the number of people who need local administrator permissions, several changes were made in Windows Vista:

- Users are redirected from the file system and Registry. In previous versions of Windows, during installation, applications would try to write to the Program Files folder or the HKEY_LOCAL_MACHINE\Software Registry branches, and unless the user had administrator permissions, the action would fail. Windows Vista has built in redirection that intercepts any attempt to write to areas that the user does not have permission for and redirects to an area of their profile and subsequently also redirects any attempt to read the data back. This redirection is shown in Figure 2-5. Note that this virtualization of key file system and Registry locations is not supported in native 64-bit applications.
  It's important to note, however, that software that is certified for Windows Vista works without this redirection and virtualization of protected areas, so longer-term redirection should not be required.
- Users can view the system clock and calendar.
- Users can now change the time zone of their computer (but cannot change the actual time or date).
- Users can change power management settings.
- Users can create and manage virtual private network connections.
- Users can modify wireless network security settings.
- Users can download and install critical Windows updates.

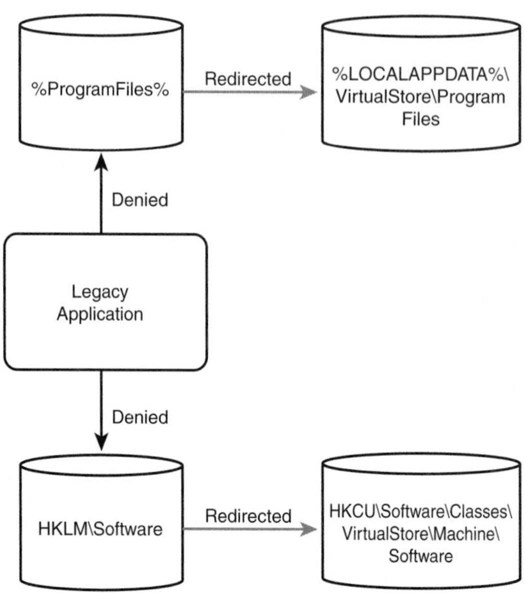

FIGURE 2-5 When legacy applications try to write to protected areas of the Registry and file system, they are redirected.

- Users can install ActiveX controls (subject to the group policy that specifies from which web sites users can install ActiveX controls via the ActiveX Installer Service).
- Users can install hardware that has locally available installed drivers in the Vista Driver Store. The Driver Store can be populated with any trusted drivers you may need in the organization. The type of hardware that users can install is governed by group policy settings that specify the class ID of the types of devices users may install (for example, printers).

In addition to all these new capabilities for a standard user, if group policy is used to deploy software, users can install software from the Add/Remove Programs Control Panel applet, which runs with elevated rights requiring no special user permission. More details on UAC can be found in Chapter 4, "Securing Your Windows Server 2008 Deployment."

Elevation of Privilege

There are fewer instances when you need administrator permissions in Vista, but what about when you do? How can a user tell if he can perform a function? Windows Vista has a shield icon that shows when a certain program or task requires administrator privileges (see Figure 2-6). It protects us from ourselves and from software doing evil things. Such a program or task has XML embedded into its code that sets the requestedExecutionLevel to the value requireAdministrator. When the code is executed, the UAC reads the program's manifest is read, sees requireAdministrator, and presents the consent dialog.

NOTE The shield icon is not automatically added to software based on the program's manifest, but the software should display it as part of Microsoft's design guidelines.

Figure 2-6 The shield icon on the Change Date and Time button shows that administrator credentials are needed to perform the action.

A normal user who clicks a button that contains a shield icon is prompted to enter a set of administrator-level credentials to allow the functionality. This is useful in several situations. For example, when an administrator logs on with a normal user account for most actions, when she needs to run an administrative function, she can just enter the administrator credentials when needed. Or when an administrator is visiting a user desktop, rather than making the user log out, she can run the administrator parts with her administrator account. This type of rights elevation is known as Over the Shoulder (OTS) elevation because in most cases, an IT administrator types in her administrator credentials over the user's shoulder when helping to resolve a problem. If a client is part of a workgroup, the administrator accounts are displayed, and you simply choose the appropriate account and enter its password (see Figure 2-7). If a client is part of a domain, manually enter an administrator account, as shown in Figure 2-8.

FIGURE 2-7 In a workgroup environment, the administrator accounts are displayed.

FIGURE 2-8 In a domain environment, no list of administrators is shown. Instead, the user must enter an administrative account username and password.

Even with all the safeguards of UAC, Microsoft decided that administrators could not be trusted to use a separate, normal user account during the 99% of the time when they don't need elevated permissions. Therefore, Microsoft implemented a token system. With Windows Vista and Windows Server 2008, during the logon process, your account permissions and rights are evaluated, and if you have administrator privileges, you get a token that details these attributes. You also get a standard user token, which has the administration type privileges filtered out. The standard user token is the default token that is used for the logon session. This process is shown in Figure 2-9, along with an example of where the two different tokens are used.

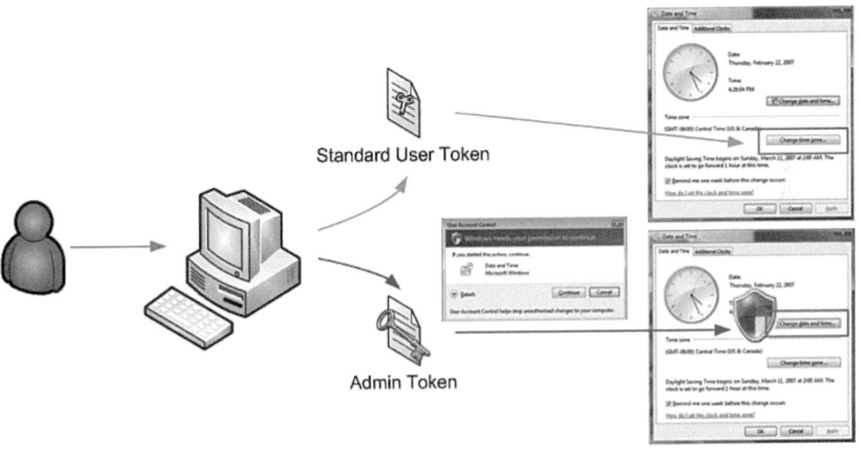

Figure 2-9 This administrator gets two tokens at logon. Only when an operation requires administrative permissions is the Admin Approval Mode (AAM) consent displayed and the unfiltered token used.

As with OTS rights elevation, when an administrator tries to perform an action that requires administrative credentials, a consent dialog is displayed, which by default just requires confirmation that the administrative token can be used (although this behavior can be changed, as seen in Chapter 4). This elevation is known as Admin Approval Mode (AAM) because no second set of credentials is used, and the administrator is just invoking his elevated powers. If an application is not marked as requiring administrative credentials but you want to run it with the admin token, right-click on it and select Run as Administrator, as shown in Figure 2-10.

This is useful, for example, for launching an elevated-privileges command prompt session.

When you launch a command prompt session with your elevated privileges, the OS is kind enough to add Administrator: to the title of the command prompt window so you know you are running with privileges. If you run the `whoami /all` command in both elevated and nonelevated command prompt sessions, you see that the nonelevated account has far fewer privileges. If you examined the integrity flags of the processes, you see that the nonelevated session has a Mandatory Label\Medium Mandatory level, while the elevated session has a High integrity level. You can view the integrity flags through applications such as Process Explorer from System Internals via the Security tab of the process properties.

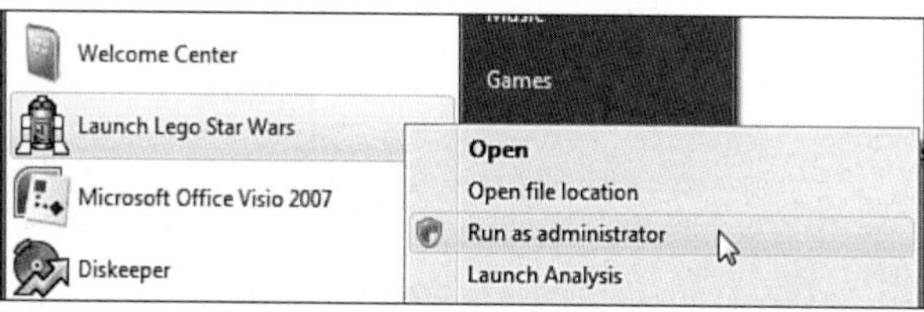

FIGURE 2-10 You can launch anything with administrative credentials, although what those credentials do for you in a video game is unknown.

NOTE UAC was one of the most talked-about and controversial features of the Windows Vista product. Many people complained that it is intrusive, but this negative press was based on beta versions, where the functionality was not yet tuned. UAC involves changes in how you perform your job, including consent prompts and elevation requirements, but is a powerful feature that, when used correctly, is beneficial to organizations.

Windows Elements

After you have logged in, what is the next thing you see? The basic and most-used interface is the Start menu, Taskbar, and notification area (also known as the system tray). Figure 2-11 shows these three core elements, which allow you to control and access nearly every part of the operating system. Notice on the right side of the figure is an area that contains various gadgets. You can configure this area, known as the Windows Sidebar, to show various elements, and you can import new gadgets to perform different actions and show configurable information, such as the weather and news feeds. The Sidebar is a feature of Windows Vista and is not part of Windows Server 2008.

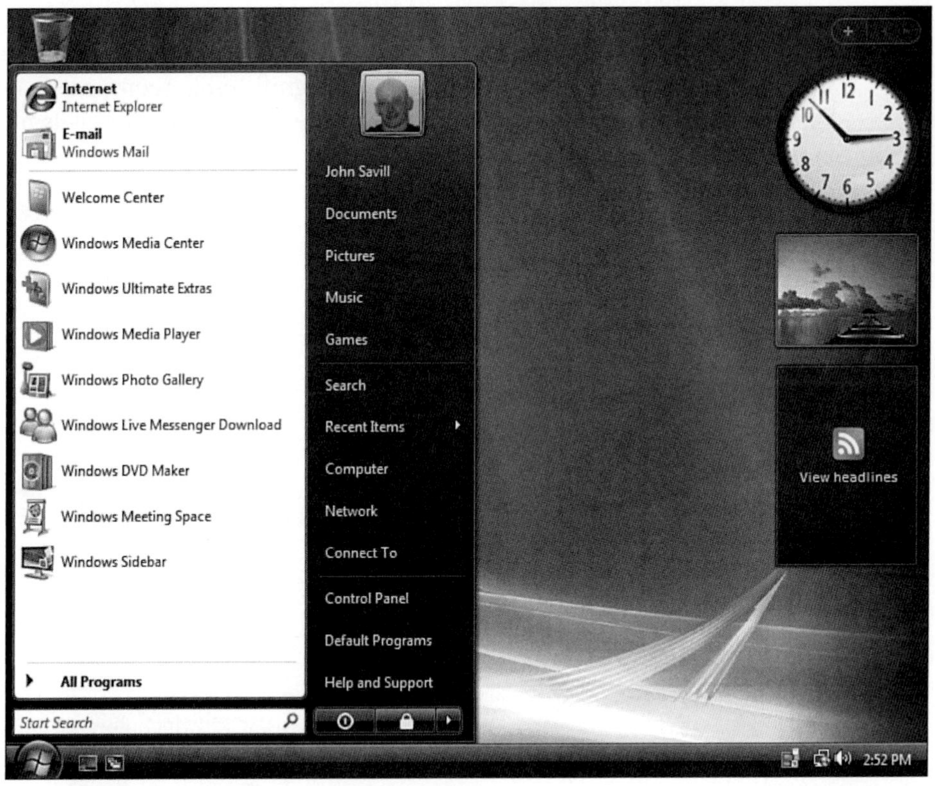

FIGURE 2-11 The three main components of the Windows experience are the Start menu, Taskbar, and notification area.

The Start Menu

The Start menu is where you access most of the installed components and applications on a machine, including Administrative Tools and the Control Panel, which you use to perform most configuration and management functions. When you right-click the Start button and select Properties, you can choose one of two modes:

- The default Start menu is adaptive and displays shortcuts to applications that are most used.
- The "classic" Start menu (as used in Windows 2000) has a static menu structure.

In Windows XP, each submenu of the Start menu opened up to the side of the existing menu, which took up significant screen space. With Windows Vista and Windows Server 2008, the Start menu display is much more compact and easy to navigate, as shown in Figure 2-12.

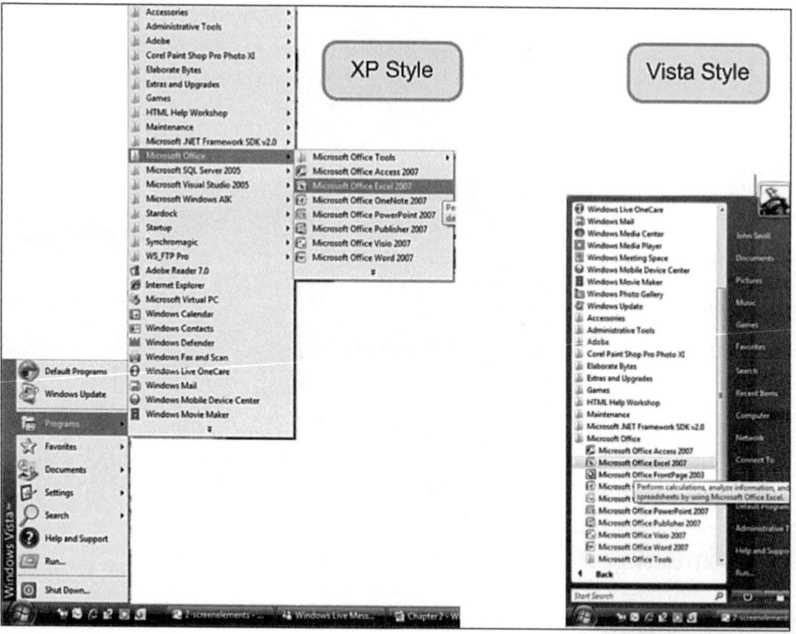

FIGURE 2-12 The XP-style menu on the left takes up far more screen real estate to access the required submenu and shortcut than the Windows Vista and Windows Server 2008 version.

In addition to configuring the type of Start menu to display, you can configure what elements to display in the Start menu (for example, Administrative Tools, Favorites).

A new feature of the Start menu in Vista and Server 2008 is the instant search text entry box, which has the default focus when the Start menu is selected or you click the Windows key. You can quickly search by simply clicking the Windows key and then typing the name of the file you want to find or the application you want to run, as shown in Figure 2-13. As you type in the search box, Windows dynamically displays close matches, and you can simply press Enter to select the correct choice when it appears. If the choice you're looking for doesn't appear, you can manually enter your whole search string and press Enter. All data on the machine, including documents and their contents, e-mail messages, and programs, is indexed and accessible via the instant search.

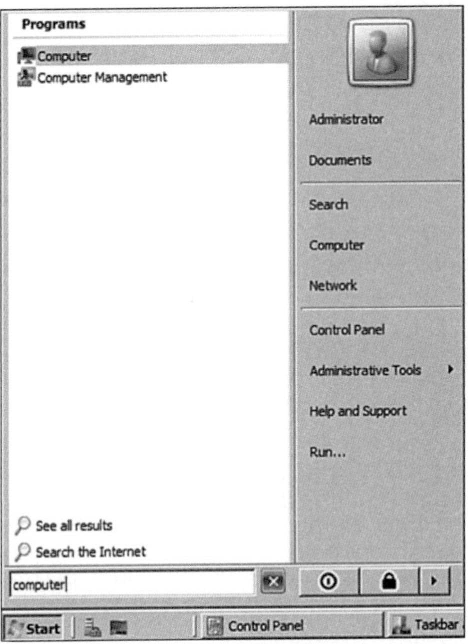

FIGURE 2-13 The new Start menu provides access to many applications in a little bit of screen real estate, and the instant search provides fast access to applications and other types of data.

You also access basic features such as logging off and restarting the computer via the Start menu.

NOTE In Windows Server 2008 and Vista, the Ctrl+Alt+Del key combination performs the same function as in previous versions: When you press it, the Windows Security screen appears, giving you options to change your password, lock the computer (which can also be accomplished by clicking the Start menu or Windows key and then pressing L), log off, switch user, and start the Task Manager. Notice the addition of the Switch User option, which was previously reserved for Windows XP workgroup machines but has been expanded to all configurations under Windows Vista and Windows Server 2008. The other visual change from previous operating systems is that Windows Security is no longer a dialog box. It's now an entire screen in the same visual style as the logon screen, but the options are the same as in earlier versions.

The Taskbar

The Taskbar displays a list of all the applications that are currently running on the system. In the standard graphical mode, if you hover your mouse over an application listed on the Taskbar, a pop-up displays the full title of the application, as shown in Figure 2-14. When the Taskbar is full, it stacks together multiple copies of the same application that are running so that they take up only one slot on the Taskbar. Instead of clicking an application on the Taskbar, you can select it by clicking the Windows key and typing the number that corresponds to the application's position on the Taskbar.

FIGURE 2-14 The Taskbar allows easy access to running applications.

The Taskbar can host several additional toolbars. When you right-click the Taskbar, from the context menu that appears, select the additional toolbars you want to be displayed on the Taskbar. For example, the quick launch toolbar is useful for displaying icon-only shortcuts to the applications you use the most.

NOTE A *context menu* is the menu that appears when you right-click an object. It is called a *context* menu because the content of the menu is generated based on the object selected and so it is context aware.

In addition to using the Taskbar to switch between running applications, you can also press the Alt and Tab keys at the same time to bring up a minidialog that shows the icon for each running application (see Figure 2-15). While holding down Alt, press Tab to toggle through the applications shown. If you hold down the Shift+Alt while pressing Tab, you move backward through the list.

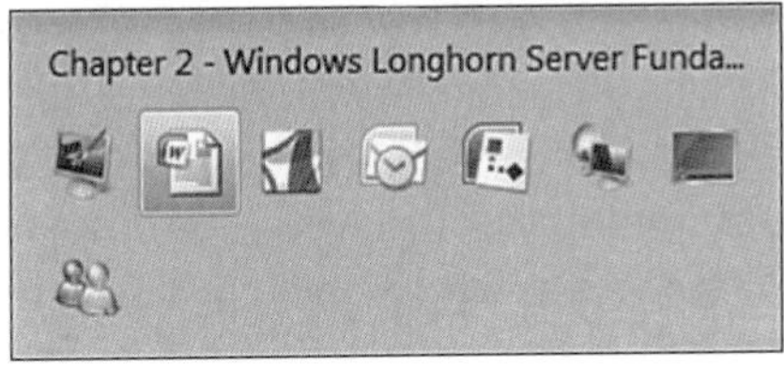

FIGURE 2-15 The standard Alt+Tab list displays the shortcut icon for each running application, allowing for keyboard-based switching between applications.

The System Tray

Windows uses the system tray (aka the notification area) to communicate information about services and applications. For example, the Networking and Sharing center, which is the central location for managing all network connectivity faculties of the operating system, displays the connectivity state in its system tray entry. For example, if network connectivity exists, but there's no Internet connection, the system tray displays an icon showing just two computers; if Internet connection exists, then a globe appears over the two computers icon; and if no network connectivity exists, a red X overlays the two computers (see Figure 2-16).

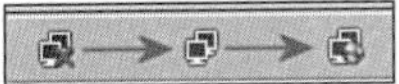

FIGURE 2-16 The system tray shows icons that indicate the status of various services and applications.

The Windows Sidebar

A useful addition to Windows Vista is the Sidebar, which by default on a fresh installation displays a clock, an image slideshow, and a news component. At

the top of the sidebar (which is shown on the right side of the screen) is a control that allows you to add new Sidebar gadgets. The main purpose of the Windows Sidebar is to help you quickly perform common tasks and control information flow, and its gadgets are designed to perform tasks or consolidate and summarize information.

If you add to the Sidebar more gadgets than can be displayed in a single view, the right and left arrows become enabled so you can scroll through the various views. In addition, if you select the spanner icon when you hover the mouse over a gadget, you can access the options for a gadget. Or alternatively if you right-click a gadget, its context menu is displayed, allowing you to remove the gadget and in some instances change configuration options.

FIGURE 2-17 This Sidebar has default gadgets selected, including the calendar, picture gallery, clock, and CPU/memory meter. In the Sidebar shown here, a Remote Desktop gadget allows fast connections to remote servers.

When the Sidebar is closed, right-click its Taskbar icon (shown in a red box at the bottom of Figure 2-17), and select Open. If you right-click the Sidebar and select Properties, the main properties are displayed, and you can select where to display the Sidebar, whether the Sidebar should start at Windows startup, and other settings. You can also access the Sidebar properties by selecting Windows Sidebar Properties from the Appearance and Personalization Control Panel area.

If you drag gadgets onto the main desktop from the Sidebar, they stay running even if the Sidebar is minimized, but they close if you exit the Sidebar. When you drag some gadgets off the Sidebar, they display additional information and have a new appearance.

Additional gadgets for the Windows Vista Sidebar are available at http://vista.gallery.microsoft.com/vista/SideBar.aspx. When you download a .gadget file, and execute it, you are prompted to install it. After it is installed, it is available in the Add Gadget dialog. To uninstall a gadget, simply right-click it in the Add Gadget dialog and select Uninstall. From an administrative perspective, one of the most useful gadgets is the Terminal Services gadget, which allows you to quickly connect to remote systems.

Although the Sidebar is not available in Windows Server 2008 at press time, it may be added in the future. It is possible to use the Windows Sidebar provided in Vista on Windows Server 2008 with a few tweaks outlined here:

1. Copy the Windows Sidebar folder from a Windows Vista SP1 installations Program Files folder that is the same architecture as the Windows Server 2008 box you intend to enable Windows Sidebar on. If you are running Windows Server 2008 64-bit, copy from a 64-bit Windows Vista SP1 installation.
2. Copy the Windows Sidebar copy into the Program Files folder of the Windows Server 2008 installation. (If 64 Windows Server 2008, copy to the Program Files folder and not the Program Files [x86] folder.)
3. Run the following commands from a prompt with administrative credentials:

```
regsvr32 atl.dll
regsvr32 "C:\Program Files\Windows
  Sidebar\sbdrop.dll"
regsvr32 "C:\Program Files\Windows
  Sidebar\wlsrvc.dll"
"C:\Program Files\Windows Sidebar\sidebar.exe"
  /RegServer
```

4. Copy the content of the Sidebar Registry area from your Vista box to the 2008 box (HKEY_LOCAL_MACHINE\SOFTWARE\Microsoft\Windows\CurrentVersion\Sidebar). The Registry content is the same for 32 bit and 64 bit, so you can just type the following into sidebar.reg and execute (by double-clicking) to save any copying between machines:

```
Windows Registry Editor Version 5.00
[HKEY_LOCAL_MACHINE\SOFTWARE\Microsoft\Windows\
CurrentVersion\Sidebar]
[HKEY_LOCAL_MACHINE\SOFTWARE\Microsoft\Windows\
CurrentVersion\Sidebar\Compatibility]
[HKEY_LOCAL_MACHINE\SOFTWARE\Microsoft\Windows\
CurrentVersion\Sidebar\Settings]
"SidebarDockedPartsOrder"="0x1,0x2,0x3,0x4
```

5. You can now launch Sidebar with the C:\Program Files\Windows Sidebar\sidebar.exe command.
6. Now access the Properties of Sidebar (right-click on a blank area of that Sidebar and select Properties) and check the State Sidebar when Windows starts option.

If you are managing a server from a Vista client, you can take advantage of many gadgets that make server administration easier, such as Remote Desktop gadgets, server status gadgets, and gadgets that report status from monitoring solutions such as System Center Operations Manager.

The Desktop Windows Manager (DWM)

One of the hot topics related to Windows Vista is the new graphical improvements. Many of these improvements are also part of Windows Server 2008. By default, the enhanced visuals discussed here are not enabled in Windows Server 2008, but if you install the Desktop Experience feature and enable the Themes service, and if the server has the correct hardware and graphics drivers, the enhanced visuals are usable. Even if you are not running the enhanced visuals on server consoles, in many instances, you are managing servers via Vista. So, understanding what it can do enhances the overall management experience.

Windows XP introduced a new visual style, the Windows XP theme, which featured 3D buttons with shaded color schemes and a more colorful Taskbar. By default, the XP theme was not available in Windows Server 2003, which instead used the flat, gray Windows Classic theme. The argument was that you don't need to waste memory and processor power on pretty graphics on a server, which is there to perform processing or to service clients. However, if you wanted the enhanced visuals, you could enable the Windows XP theme in the Themes service. Like Windows Server 2003, Windows Server 2008 can operate with enhanced graphics, but by default, it does not; it just doesn't make sense to waste the resources, and most servers don't ship with graphics cards capable of rendering the enhanced visuals.

Windows Vista has changed the way graphical drivers work. Previously, the entire Windows XP graphics driver ran as part of the kernel (the internals of the operating system), and if a problem occurred, it could crash the entire OS; Microsoft investigations show that 20% of blue screens of death (BSODs) in XP are caused by display drivers. With Windows Vista, the graphics driver is split into two: a streamlined kernel mode driver (KMD) and a user-mode driver that performs most of the intensive graphical functions and is, therefore, more likely to experience problems. This split makes a crash of the entire OS far less likely because the kernel mode piece does far less, and problems are limited to a single application rather than the entire OS. This new device driver model is known as the Windows Device Driver Model (WDDM), and graphics hardware requires a WDDM driver to qualify for the Aero experience (discussed later in this chapter).

NOTE The BSOD—a blue background screen with white text that gives an error code and some basic information about the crash—appears when Windows crashes. Depending on the OS version, a dump of the memory is also written to file to help you troubleshoot at a later time. BSODs are officially known as Stop errors. If you see a BSOD, it may ruin your day, especially if it happens on a server. If you want to scare another administrator, download a screen saver that emulates the BSOD (see www.microsoft.com/technet/sysinternals/Miscellaneous/BlueScreen.mspx). It's not very kind and may bring bad karma, but it might provide a laugh.

In Vista, more than the driver model was changed; the whole approach to graphics was changed. Instead of each application drawing directly to the screen itself, a new technology, the Desktop Windows Manager (DWM), controls the display and updating of windows on the desktop. In previous Windows versions, applications painted their visible display area directly to the buffer that was displayed by the video card. This old approach meant that if you moved a window, the window might leave a trail or just blank area (see Figure 2-18) because the application that was behind the moving window had to be woken up and asked to repaint its display region via the `WM_PAINT` command.

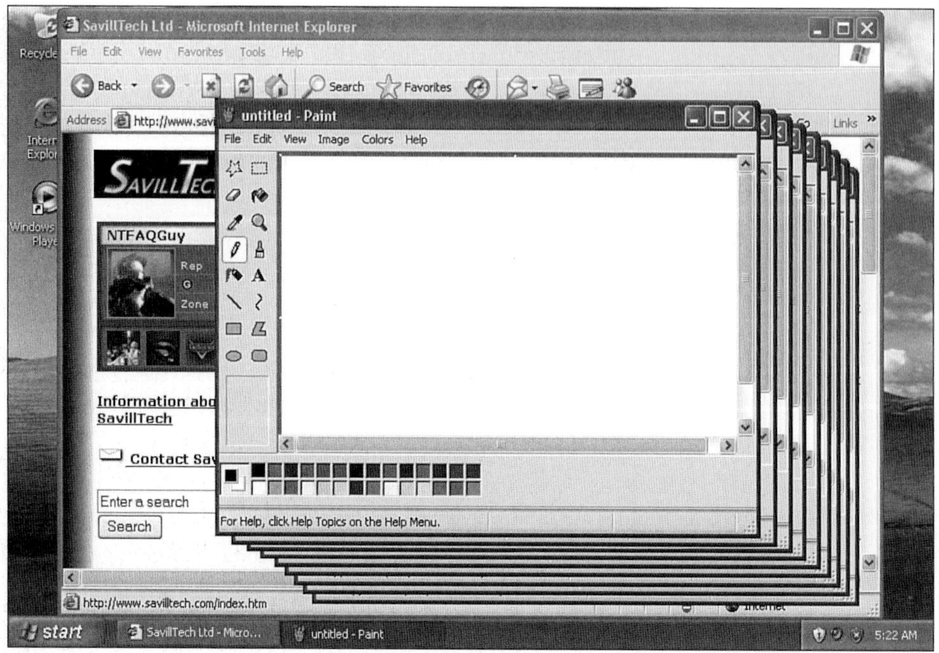

FIGURE 2-18 In pre-Windows Vista, if the computer was busy or an application was under stress and could not redraw its screen buffer fast enough, a trail was left behind any moving windows.

DWM uses an offscreen buffer to composite the various applications' individual offscreen graphical display buffers together and then draws the composite image to the onscreen buffer. The DWM has the graphical content of each application, and for each screen refresh, it does not need the application to redraw its content; instead, it has a snapshot of the last display update it received from each application and uses that to composite the latest buffer onscreen, and it uses that snapshot rather than leaving a trail or a blank spot. In Figure 2-19, you can see that each application draws to its own offscreen buffer. The DWM then composites each of these application-specific buffers together, based on their location on the screen, and then writes the completed composite offscreen buffer to the onscreen buffer to ensure a smooth display experience, no matter how busy an application is. Although the DWM process is always running, it is essentially idle except when you run in Windows Aero graphical mode. If you run in any other graphical mode, including Vista Basic, the DWM is not heavily used, and the trailing behavior still occurs because the display is not composited, and the features covered next are not available. The DWM process still runs even in non-Windows Aero because it handles Windows ghosting, in which a nonresponsive window takes on a frosted appearance and says "(Not Responding)" to the end of the windows title.

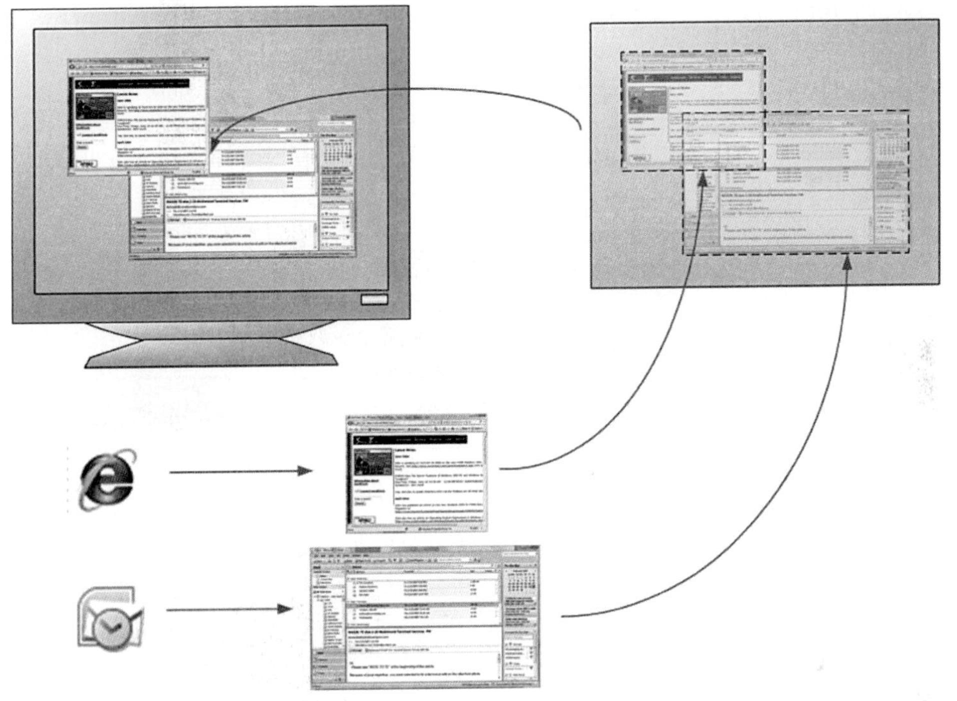

FIGURE 2-19 A high-level overview of how DWM works via the virtual graphical buffers.

Windows Aero Effects

The fact that Vista has separate graphical buffers for each application allows for several facilities that create a far richer graphical environment. The standard interface, as discussed previously, allows you to press Alt+Tab to cycle through the various running applications, but only minimal information is shown about each application. For Windows Vista machines that run Windows Aero, the Alt+Tab task switcher looks different. Instead of the application's icon being displayed in the list, a thumbnail of the actual applications screen buffer is shown (see Figure 2-20). This is possible because the DWM has each application's screen buffer stored and can use it for purposes other than just drawing to screen. In addition, as the screen output from the application changes, so does its thumbnail, so if you were watching a video, the thumbnail on the task switcher would also be playing in real-time. This new task switcher is known as Windows Flip. Without switching to the application, you can get a quick idea of what the application is doing. If you press Ctrl+Alt+Tab, the task switcher stays onscreen, and you can scroll through applications with the arrow keys.

FIGURE 2-20 With Windows Aero, the actual content of each application is displayed in the task switcher instead of just a static icon.

This new graphical feature doesn't greatly affect your processor, but a good graphics card is recommended for Windows Vista to support Windows Aero and its associated features, such as Flip. Most of the processing to render these new graphical features is passed to the graphical processing unit (GPU) on the graphics card instead of the main computer processor, which prevents too much additional overhead.

The main feature that is immediately visible in Windows Aero is the new translucent edges to applications (hence the previous name, Aero Glass), which are possible because the DWM has the content of each application in a separate buffer and can calculate what is required to be displayed, including adding light effects and shadows. Figure 2-21 shows Aero (A) and non-Aero (Vista Basic) (B) versions of the same screen. The application window edges are translucent in the Aero version, allowing you to see information behind the window. Notice also that a button glows when selected. The non-Aero screen displays none of the "glass" characteristics and does not look as polished.

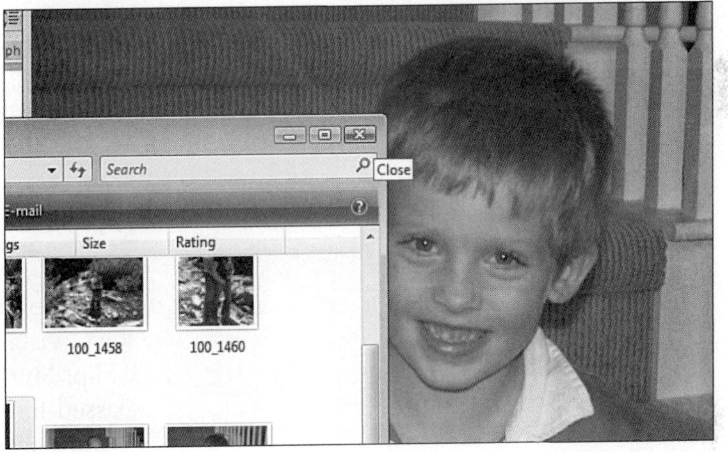

FIGURE 2-21 The screen section on the top is from a machine running Windows Aero; the one on the bottom is the Vista Basic theme.

The DWM and Windows Aero mode provide two more fun features. When the mouse hovers over an application on the Taskbar, you now see a thumbnail of the application, as shown in Figure 2-22.

The final major visual enhancement is Flip 3D, which performs exactly the same function as the normal Windows Flip task switcher but instead presents each window in a 3D stacked fashion (see Figure 2-23). You accessed Flip 3D by clicking the Windows button (now called Start key) and Tab (or click Ctrl to avoid having to hold down the Windows key).

FIGURE 2-22 The live Taskbar thumbnails show a miniature version of the application's entire display buffer in real-time.

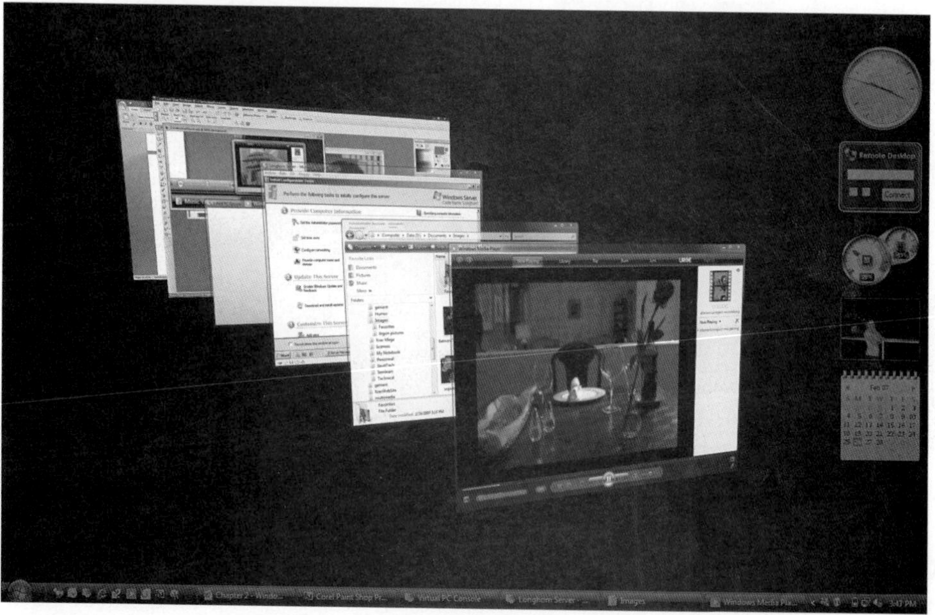

FIGURE 2-23 With Flip 3D, a larger thumbnail of every application is shown in real-time.

Now that you know about the graphical and layout elements of the Windows Server 2008 and Vista interfaces, let's dive deeper into the other components and structures you use when interfacing with Windows Server.

Task Manager

What is the Task Manager, and why do we need to use it? The Task Manager has been around since the earliest versions of Windows NT and is a useful tool for ascertaining certain information about the state of the operating system. You can launch the Task Manager via the Windows Security dialog, by pressing Ctrl+Shift+Esc, or by right-clicking the Taskbar and selecting Task Manager. You can also execute taskmgr.exe as you would any other program.

By default, the Task Manager is always displayed on top, even when another window is selected. You can change this setting via the Options menu of Task Manager, but generally you want the Task Manager to stay on top because if other windows cover the Task Manager, it is difficult to use Task Manager to get the information you need. In addition, when you right-click the system tray icon that shows a CPU meter for the system (see Figure 2-24), the Task Manager is always on top.

FIGURE 2-24 The Task Manager icon that appears in the system tray gives a quick indication of CPU usage on the system.

The Applications Tab

The first tab of the Task Manager is the Applications tab, which lists all the applications running on the system along with their status (see Figure 2-25). When an application's status is Running, the application is behaving normally. The status Not Responding indicates that an application is not responding in a timely fashion, perhaps because the application is hanging or busy; don't try to take action on an application immediately if its status is Not Responding. If you try to close an application and the normal method of clicking the close button (the X button at the top right of the application's window) for the application does not work, select the application from the Task Manager's application list and click the End Task button. This asks the application to close nicely before forcing the process to terminate if it doesn't do as it's told. You can also give an application the focus (which means it's the selected application) by selecting the application from the list and clicking the Switch To button, and you can start a new task by clicking the New Task button and entering the name of an image (executable) associated with the task or clicking the Browse button and navigating the file system.

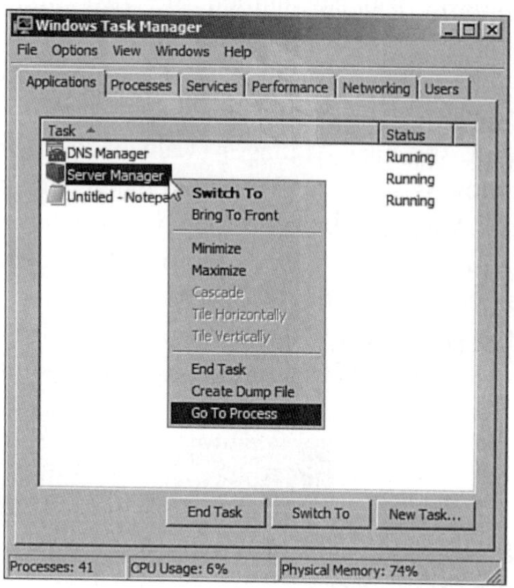

FIGURE 2-25 The Applications tab shows all running applications. Select an application and stop it by clicking End Task, give it the focus by clicking Switch To, or right-click for additional options.

If you right-click an application on the Applications tab, you have additional options. For example, you can maximize and minimize the application's window and even go to its process.

The Applications tab works from a list of all the running processes on the system. It ascertains which of them have visible windows, and lists only those that do. In fact, there are many more processes running on the system, but they simply don't have visible user windows. If you see an application on your desktop, it shows on the Applications tab, and if you can't see it, then it won't.

The Processes Tab

The Processes tab of the Task Manager (see Figure 2-26), lists all processes running on the system and provides selectable information about each process, including by default the image name (the executable), the username under which the process is running, the percentage of CPU it is using, the amount of memory it is using, and a description. At the bottom of the dialog is the option Show Processes from All Users, which you can check to see all processes for the system, including those of other users who may also be logged on to the server as part of a remote session or fast user switching. You need administrator credentials to show the processes from other users. For example, Figure 2-26 shows processes for the users Administrator (the current user), John (who is also logged on but switched out currently), and Brad (who is connected via Remote Desktop).

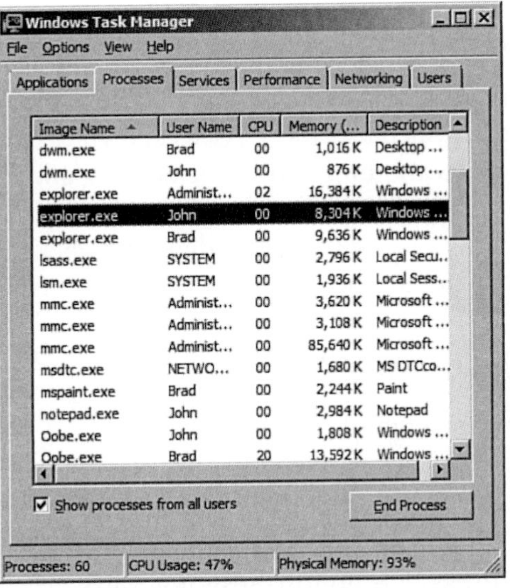

FIGURE 2-26 The Processes tab shows all the processes running on the system, and you can sort the list by any of the columns. For example, if the system is running at high CPU use, sort the display by CPU, so you can more easily spot the high CPU users.

Selecting View, Select Columns opens up a large variety of selectable process information attributes, such as the CPU time used by a process, the number of threads, the path to the image, and the command line. If you right-click a process, you get a context menu that allows you to stop the process or its entire process tree, which also stops any processes started by the selected process. For example, if you start a cmd.exe instance (a command window) and in that command window start notepad.exe, you can then select the cmd.exe process in Task Manager and choose to end the process tree to end both the command window and the Notepad instance. The context menu for a process also allows you to configure processor affinity (that is, in a multiprocessor system, you can specify which processors a process can use), whether virtualization is enabled (which for user processes redirects file system and Registry activity from protected areas to a safe area that is part of the user's workspace), and change the priority of a process. Finally, if a process is part of a service, select the option Go to Service(s) to switch to the Services tab and show the service for the process. The Processes tab is one of the most useful places you can go to troubleshoot performance issues and to quickly see who is using what.

The Services Tab

New to Windows Vista and Windows Server 2008 is the Services tab of the Task Manager, which lists the services known to the system and the process IDs (which you can jump to by right-clicking and selecting Go to Process), status, and service group of each one. You can use this tab to start and stop services. If you need more control than this, click the Services button at the bottom of the tab to start the Services MMC snap-in.

The Performance Tab

The Performance tab of the Task Manager (see Figure 2-27) gives a high-level view of the system, including processor usage (for example, the ability to show kernel process usage via the View menu's Show Kernel Times option), memory usage, and overall system numbers (such as the number of threads, processes, and handles; the page file use; and the amount of time the system has been running).

Clicking the Resource Monitor button launches the new Resource Monitor snap-in, which gives more detail about the system in a more easily digestible format than the standard Performance Monitor tool. If the system does not seem to be behaving as expected, one of the first places to go is the Performance tab of the Task Manager to quickly look for processor or memory bottlenecks; if you find bottlenecks, you can then jump to the Processes tab to identify the offending process.

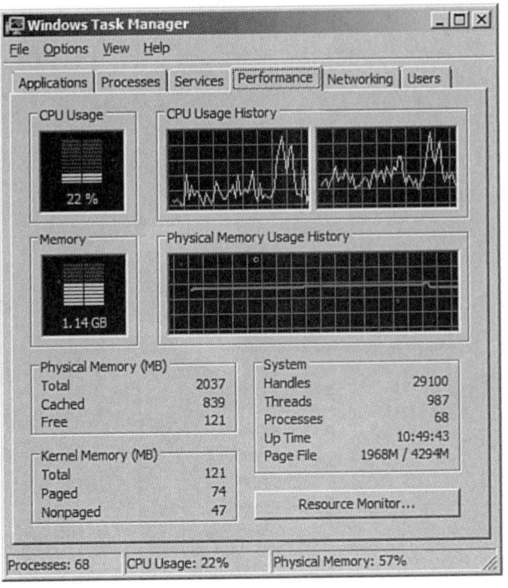

FIGURE 2-27 Overall CPU usage, per-processor usage, and overall system states are available via the Performance tab, which gives a high-level view of the system.

The Networking Tab

The Networking tab of the Task Manager (see Figure 2-28) allows you to view the network utilization of any connected network. This tab shows a graph of network history usage on a variable vertical scale, depending on the bandwidth usage. The bottom of the dialog provides more specific information about the networks, and you can choose View, Select Columns and enable the information you want to see displayed. For example, this tab shows whether the data is unicast. (Unicast network traffic is data sent to a specific IP address. Nonunicast, for example multicast, data is sent out once by a server to multiple addresses or the entire network as a broadcast.) The View menu also provides an option to display separate lines on the graph for bytes in and bytes out in addition to the default line that shows the total number of bytes. Figure 2-28 is from a Vista laptop and demonstrates how multiple networks are displayed. Notice that the vertical axis of the graph (y) scales is based on the network usage rather than being set in stone between 0 and 100, which makes it difficult to look for differences because in the local area connection, the network usage never goes above 1%.

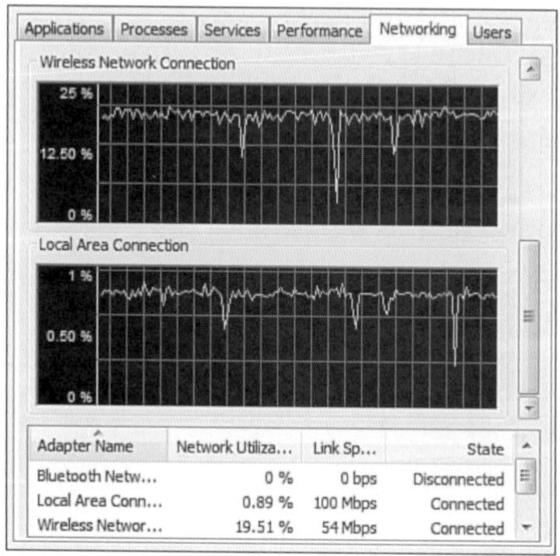

FIGURE 2-28 The Networking tab of the Task Manager lists all networks known to the machine.

The Users Tab

In Windows XP, the Users tab of the Task Manager was shown only if the machine was in a workgroup and had Fast User Switching enabled. In Vista and Windows Server 2008, the Users tab (see Figure 2-29) is always available because switching users is now available under all circumstances.

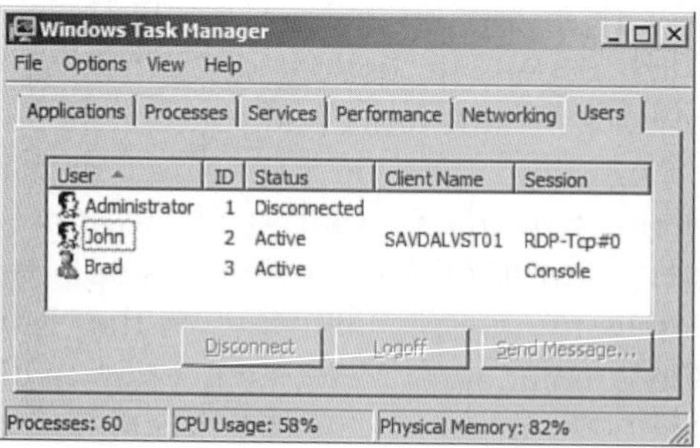

FIGURE 2-29 All user sessions—including a local logged-on sessions that have been switched out or Remote Desktop sessions—are equal and can be interchanged on the Users tab.

If you have administrator privileges and right-click a user session, you can conduct basic functions such as sending the user a message or logging the user off. You can also connect to another session and effectively take it over if you can enter the password for the user, and you can also remotely Control a session to help a user in the event of a problem. The only configuration option on this tab, which you access via the Options menu, is to display the user's full name (which would include the user's domain or, if a local account, the name of the computer).

Fast User Switching

As mentioned earlier in this chapter, switching users in XP was possible only with workgroup-joined machines. Windows Server 2008 and Vista support the ability to switch users without having to log out the current session in all scenarios. In addition, disconnected Remote Desktop/Terminal Services-style sessions are treated the same way as switched-out users: They are fully interchangeable. For example, say that I log on to a server as John and then switch users to Administrator. I can then go home, use Remote Desktop to access the server, log on as John, and take over the switched-out user session, with all open applications available. After I disconnect from the remote session and physically switch back to John on the server the next morning, my session state is maintained from my remote session.

The technology used for user switching and remote sessions is built on Terminal Services technology. It consists of running multiple desktop environments, one for each user session, which at a minimum consists of a user-specific explorer.exe instance (with an accompanying dwm.exe process). When a user logs in either remotely or locally, the Session Manager Subsystem (SMSS) checks to see if an existing session exists for the user logging on, and if it does, the existing session is used; if no session exists, a new one is created. When the user wants to finish working, he can log out, which ends the session and any associated processes. With a remote desktop session, the user can disconnect (and keep the session from terminating), and with a local session, the user can click Switch User. Figure 2-30 shows the process of sharing local and remote sessions. In previous versions of Windows, a session 0 was reserved for the local physical console session; however, with Windows Server 2008, session 0 is reserved for services only, and the first session is 1, the next is 2, and so on. Chapter 9, "Terminal Services," provides more detail on this.

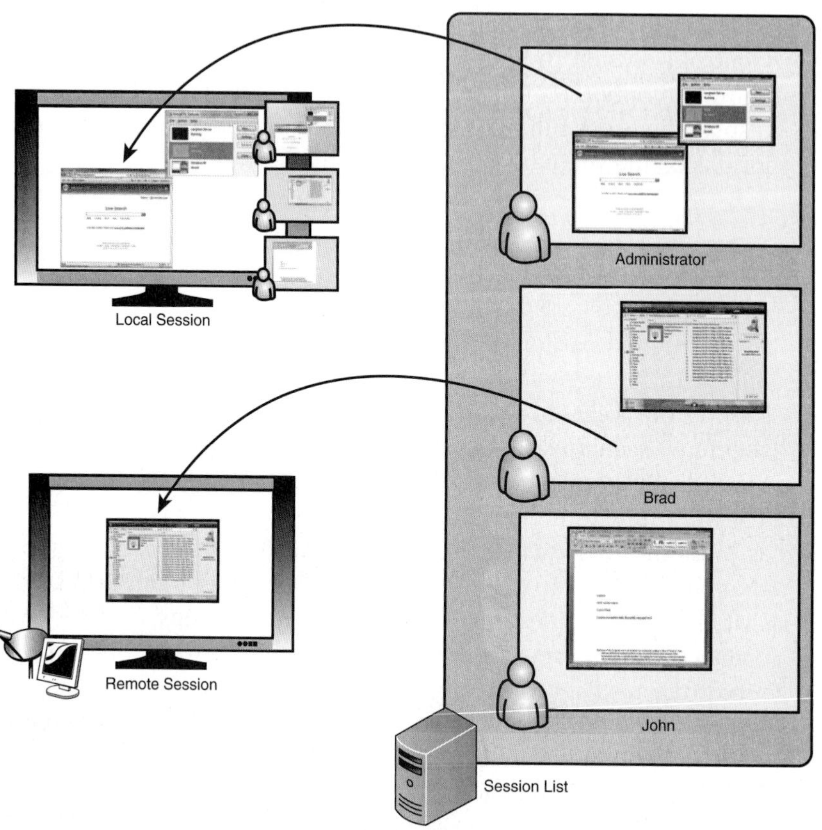

FIGURE 2-30 The multiuser kernel of Windows Server stores each session as an individual session, and every session is accessible via the physical server console or remotely, regardless of the manner in which it was initiated.

Windows Explorer

Windows Explorer was first introduced into the Windows NT product line with version 4.0 after initially debuting in Windows 95. With Windows Vista and Windows Server 2008, its features have been expanded from previous versions. Windows Explorers, which now provide better integration with searching capabilities, is now consistent among nearly all Windows components, giving a single feel to the OS and making it more intuitive.

NOTE The term *Explorers* is used instead of just *Explorer* because the old My Documents, My Pictures, and so on have been replaced with different Explorers (for example, Documents Explorer, Music Explorer, Pictures Explorer, Search Explorer).

The Explorer Interface

Windows Vista and Windows Server 2008 share the same Explorer interface (which is logical because both OSs are built on the same core OS). Thanks to Vista's goal of providing a richer environment for media and a simpler way to locate information, the Explorer interface has several new features (see Figure 2-31).

The old Explorer-style menus that were present pre-Vista are no longer present by default, but you can view them by simply pressing Alt. However, most of the functionality and settings exposed by the static menus are now made available in a more intuitive form via the various elements of Explorer:

- **Address bar**. The address bar still displays the current location, but it now has drop-down menus for every component of the current navigation path, allowing easy backtracking of the path to other locations or even forward to an alternative to the current folder, as shown in Figure 2-32. At the far left of the address bar is a drop-down that shows all the available areas of the computer, such as drives, shared folder areas, and the Control Panel. Right-click the address bar for the option Copy Address and then paste the object in the navigation bar. For example, after you copy an address, paste it onto another folder to copy the folder and its contents. Another option is Copy Address as Text, which places a textual representation of the address in the Clipboard (for example, D:\documents\books\Complete Windows Longhorn). Finally, use Edit Address if you don't want to navigate to a folder and would prefer to just type in the name. As with Internet Explorer, Windows Explorer now provides Back and Forward buttons to make it easier to navigate back from folders you have visited recently. Figure 2-32 shows the various address bar options.

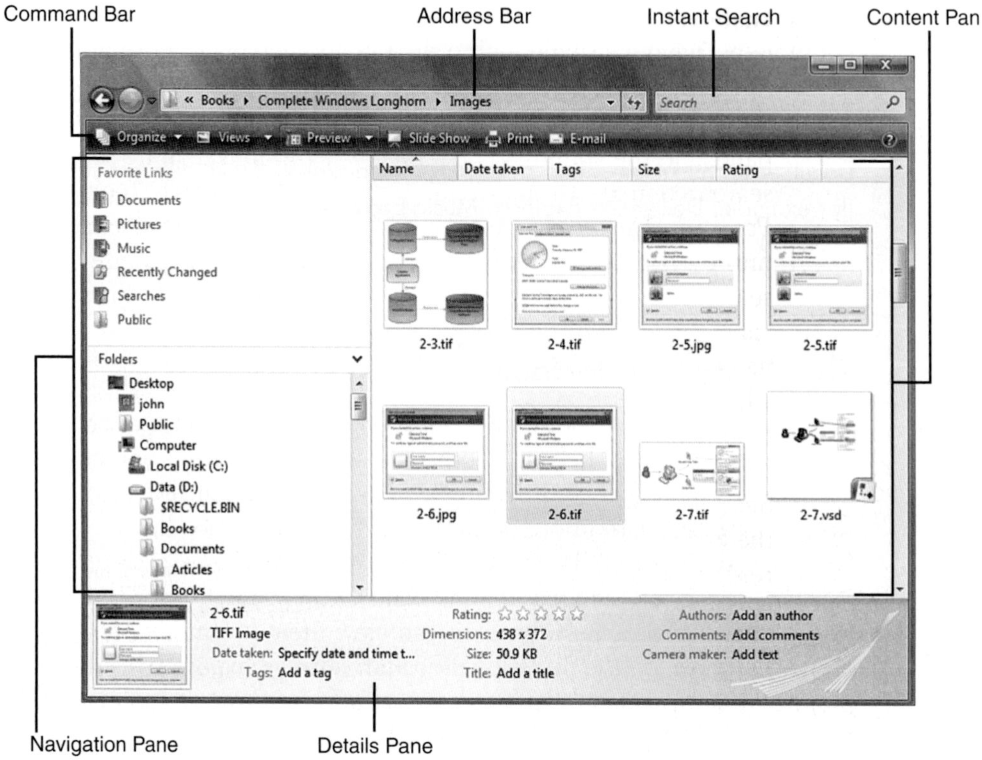

FIGURE 2-31 Explorer is now a rich environment that performs far more than just presenting the raw information of the file system. Dynamic additional views such as stacking and grouping, combined with powerful search capabilities, make Explorer a highly usable interface.

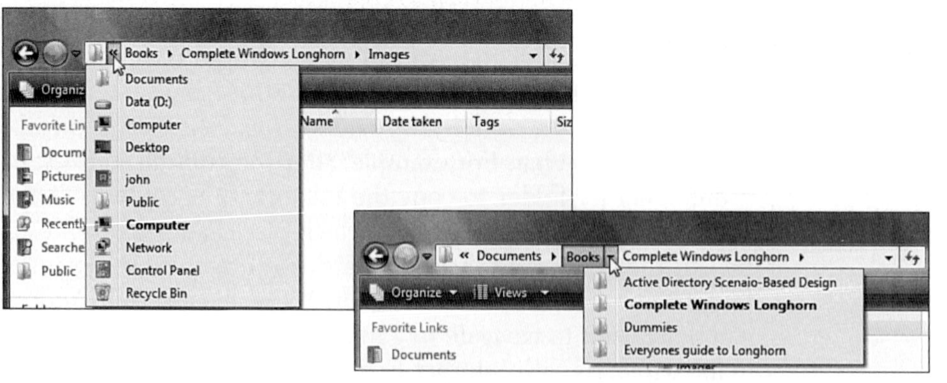

FIGURE 2-32 The address bar is now a powerful navigation aid that you can use in conjunction with the standard Navigation pane.

- **Instant search**. Like the Start menu search option, the Explorer search option is focused on finding results in the current folder and, by default, any search folders. (Although you can change this behavior.) When you perform a search, the results appear in the Content pane, and the command bar changes to options that are sensitive to search content. To fine-tune a search, select Search Tools, Search Pane to change what to display (for example, just documents or music). You can also select Advanced Search to enter more granular search criteria, as shown in Figure 2-33. You can also tune a search via the instant search box. For example, if you want to search for the name of a file that contains *Longhorn*, instead of typing *longhorn*, which returns results with *longhorn* in the data of the document, type *name:longhorn*. If you have a search that you might want to reuse, click Save Search in the command bar to save it to your user Searches folder with the file extension search-ms. Then navigate to the Searches folder to see all searches and select one to quickly get results. These search capabilities rely on the Windows Search service, which allows you to use the Indexing Options Control Panel applet to configure what is indexed and the type of files to index.

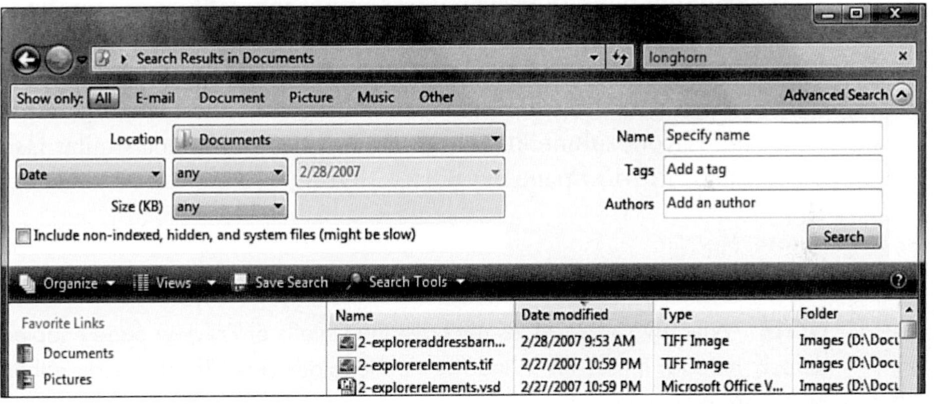

FIGURE 2-33 Advanced search opens increase your ability to fine-tune a search to find exactly what is needed.

- **Command bar**. This new Explorer component lists actions that are related to the object that currently has the focus. You can still access the old style menu by pressing Alt.

- **Navigation pane**. By default, the Navigation pane consists of two components: the standard Folders view and Favorites, which shows the most popular areas you can navigate to and can be modified to include a user's favorite locations.
- **Content pane**. The Content pane features scalable live icons that show thumbnails of the file content. These thumbnails give a good indication of what is contained in a file; for example, a PowerPoint file icon might show the first slide of the presentation.
- **Details pane**. When a file is selected, the Details pane (see Figure 2-34) shows elements of the files metadata, such as comments in the file and its author. From this preview pane, you can edit the metadata of the file.

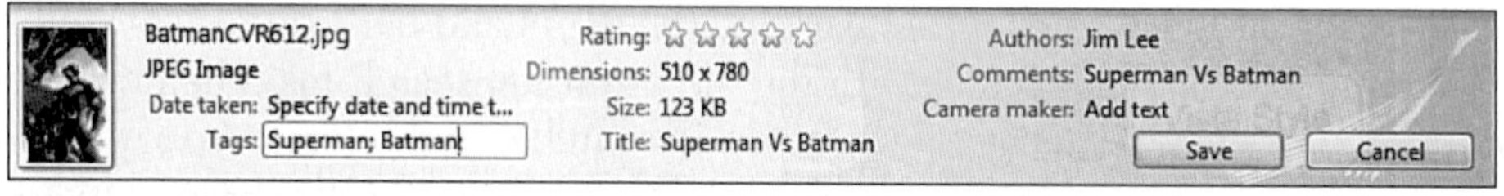

FIGURE 2-34 The Preview pane provides easy access to a file's content and its metadata.

- **Preview pane**. For even more insight into a file's content than you get with the Details pane, you can enable the Preview pane by selecting Organize, Layout, Preview Pane from the command bar. (You can also turn on and off the Navigation and Details panes from the Layout submenu.) The Preview pane works in a similar fashion to the Preview pane in Outlook, letting you see the actual data of a file.

NOTE Windows Server does not have the Details or Preview pane enabled by default. Instead, it uses the Windows classic folder view. This is because those panes are very much for rich viewing of data, which is not normally required on a server as it is on a client machine. To enable the Details and Preview panes, select Tools, Folder Options in Explorer (press Alt to view the menus), and in the General tab change the Tasks option to Show Preview and Filters. Then you can enable the Details and Preview panes via the Layout menu.

Explorer Capabilities

Beyond just the layout of the Explorer interface, some new capabilities have been introduced to better allow viewing of file-based data. Previously in Explorer, you could sort by the various Details view columns, such as filename, file size, or type of file. Windows Server 2008 introduces three new concepts: filtering, grouping, and stacking.

Filtering

With filtering, you can have a view show only objects that meet the criteria of the filter. For example, if you select the Type column of the results, a drop-down lists all the different types of files in the folder, and you can check and uncheck the various file types to affect what is displayed (see Figure 2-35). You can do the same thing on any of the other columns. Remember that you can right-click the column bar to select which column headings are displayed and govern the filter criteria you can use. The filtering options are specific to each attribute type, so, for example, if selecting size yields various sizing categories, such as 0–10KB, 10KB–100KB, and 100KB–1 MB.

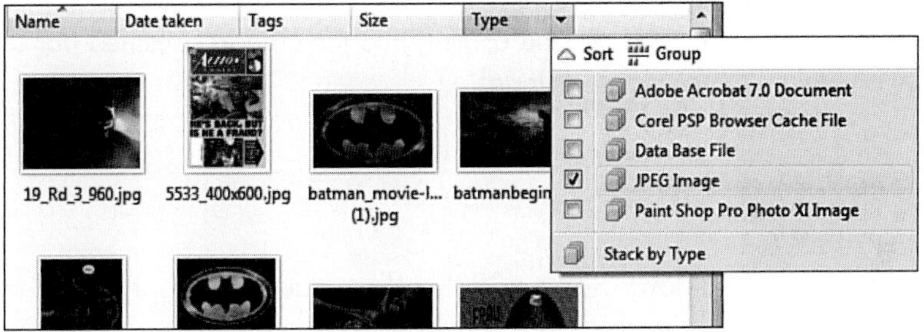

FIGURE 2-35 The columns of the Content pane are usable areas, and clicking on the column enables you to filter based on several criteria.

Grouping

Grouping works in a similar way to filtering, except that the items are separated into sections on the screen. Enable grouping by right-clicking the Content pane and selecting the relevant grouping criteria from the context menu, as shown in Figure 2-36. As with filtering, with grouping, any attribute that can be selected as a column is available for use as the group criterion.

FIGURE 2-36 Grouping breaks down the content into the criteria specified (for example, type, name, or any other selectable criteria).

Stacking

Vista and Windows Server 2008 offer a new concept called stacking. A *stack* is collection of related files that have some common criteria, such as author, file type, or size range. In the same manner as grouping, right-click the Content pane and select criteria by which to stack. (Or select Stack when you select a column heading by which to stack.) However, stacking also places the content from subfolders into the relevant stacks instead of just stacking the currently displayed data. This allows you to view data by the criteria you specify, no matter where it physically resides. If you open a stack, Windows fetches the matching results from all the locations that were used for the stack calculation (see Figure 2-37).

FIGURE 2-37 Stacking enables you to handle data no matter where it sits. Combined with the new search capabilities, stacking makes physical location of data far less important than it was in previous versions of Windows.

Advanced Explorer Features

You can configure advanced Explorer features by pressing Alt+T and selecting Folder Options. The View tab of the Folder Options dialog is useful for configuring what is displayed in Explorer. For example, select Show Hidden Files and Folders and do not select Hide Protected Operating System Files (see Figure 2-38). These options prevent system-type folders from being visible, which is normally a good thing; however, it's beneficial to your productivity not to have information hidden.

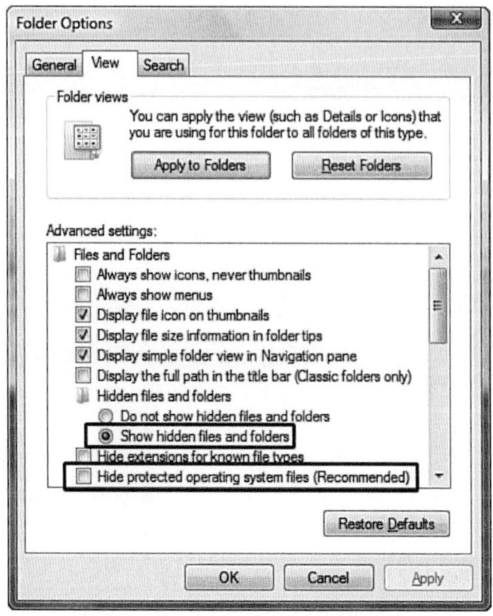

FIGURE 2-38 You can easily configure advanced options via the View tab of the Folder Options dialog.

The Microsoft Management Console

The Microsoft Management Console (MMC) was introduced in Windows 2000 to solve the age-old problem of every management tool being a separate application with its own control structure and layout. In the days before the MMC, it was difficult to learn management and impossible to create a single dashboard-type environment to manage and configure different facets of the environment. The MMC is a container into which you can import one or more snap-ins. The snap-ins provide their own functionality, but each one behaves in a consistent manner, so MMC snap-ins are intuitive to use. The MMC provides a single "go to" place for the management of the entire infrastructure, and most add-on services, such as Exchange, provide snap-ins.

Details of the MMC snap-ins are covered throughout this book, but this chapter looks at the basics of the MMC so you understand the structure. Initiate the MMC by using the mmc.exe image, which has three parameter options in addition to the passing of a saved snap-in console configuration (an .MSC file, for Microsoft Saved Console):

- **/a**. Use this parameter to open the MMC in author mode, which allows you to make changes to an MMC snap-in console. Normally an .MSC file is opened in a read-only mode (known as the user mode), which means changes are not saved and no additional snap-ins can be added.
- **/64**. On a 64-bit OS, this parameter opens the 64-bit version (mmc64) of the MMC and is used to run 64-bit snap-ins.
- **/32**. On a 64-bit OS, this parameter opens the 32-bit version (mmc32) of the MMC and is used to run 32-bit snap-ins.

If you look at the Administrative Tools link in the Program menu group of the Start menu, you see that all the links are shortcuts to .MSC files. (If the Administrative Tools link doesn't appear in the Start menu, select Customize and ensure that administrative tools are displayed.) By default, .MSC files are associated with the MMC image, which you can see by using the `assoc` and `ftype` commands. Use these commands to manage the file type of extensions and the file type action to perform, respectively:

```
C:\Windows\System32>assoc .msc
.msc=MSCFile

C:\Windows\System32>ftype mscfile
mscfile=%SystemRoot%\system32\mmc.exe "%1" %*
```

As this output shows, when an .MSC file is called, it simply is passed to the MMC image, along with any additional parameters that may be specified in the shortcut for the .MSC files. These .MSC files are stored in the `%SystemRoot%\system32` folder by default, although other applications may place them in other folders. Because the MSC is associated with the MMC, it's possible to call an .MSC file by just typing its name; for example, you could type compmgm.msc in the Run dialog or from a command line to start the Computer Management MMC snap-in console.

NOTE %<*name*>%<$I%<name>% environment variable><$Ienvironment variables;%<name>%> is an environment variable that is translated to system- or user-specific values when used. For example, %SystemRoot% normally translates to C:\Windows if Windows was installed into the Windows folder on the C:\ drive. To see a list of all environment variables, type the `set` command at the command prompt or use the Environment Variables button on the Advanced tab of the System Control Panel applet.

Figure 2-39 shows the main components of the MMC, with the Computer Management snap-in loaded.

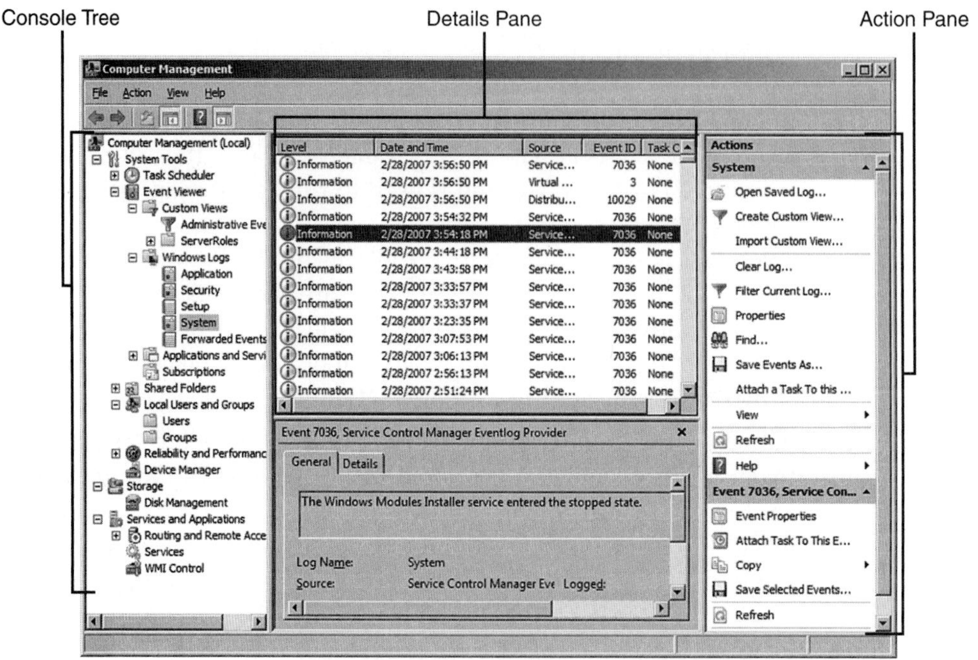

FIGURE 2-39 In addition to the standard application menu (including File, Action, View, and Help options), a context-sensitive toolbar sits below the menu bar.

The MMC includes the standard menu that is present in most applications. The File and Help menu items include static content (with the File menu having different options available, depending on the mode of the MMC session, such as author or user), while the Action and View menu items' content is dynamically populated based on the focus object of the MMC. In author mode, the File menu contains options to add and remove snap-ins from the console. Under the menu is a toolbar whose options also change depending on the object selected. The toolbar contains buttons to control visibility of the console tree and the Actions pane in addition to standard Explorer-style navigation controls to move back and forward through areas in the MMC previously visited (see Figure 2-40). The Export list outputs the content of the selected item to a tabbed-delimited text file.

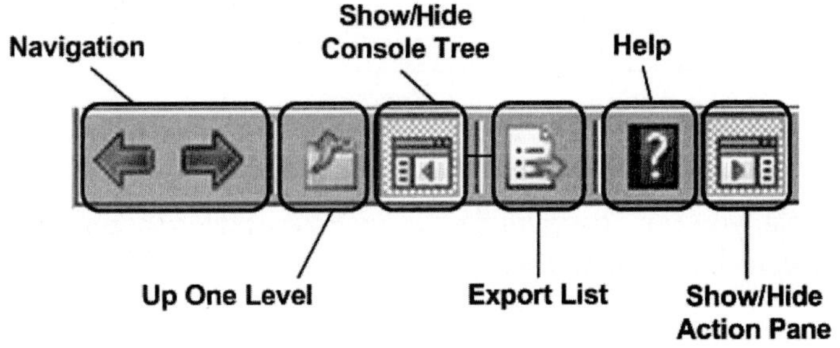

FIGURE 2-40 While other elements may be shown on the toolbar, these buttons are the core toolbar controls.

The Console Tree

Use the console tree to navigate the high-level options around the snap-ins. If you run only a single snap-in that does not have subnavigation items, you can turn off the console tree to save screen real estate, but generally you leave this pane enabled, especially if you load multiple snap-ins to a single console, because it provides the means to move between the snap-ins.

Some items in the console tree have context menus that expose functionality. For example, right-click on the Users leaf of the Local Users and Groups branch under Computer Management and select to create a new user.

The actual computer you are connected to displays at the root of each snap-in (if it supports remote management). By default, most snap-ins connect to the local computer and therefore show (Local) next to the name of the snap-in or, for domain-based snap-ins, show the name of the domain. In most cases where the target is variable, right-click the snap-in root and select to connect to a different computer or domain or whatever the snap-in manipulates, as shown in Figure 2-41.

It's also common to specify as a parameter to the MSC a nonlocal object to be the target. For example, with the Computer Management snap-in, you could use the `/computer=<computername>` to automatically change focus to another machine, as in this example:

```
compmgmt.msc /computer=johnpc
```

FIGURE 2-41 One useful feature of the MMC framework is its capability to manage both local and remote resources or select different targets based on the functionality of the snap-in. For example, you can configure the Group Policy Editor snap-in to select which Group Policy Object it should be editing.

The Details Pane

The Details pane is where you perform the bulk of your management work. The node selected from the console tree drives the Details pane content. Information in the Details pane can be graphical or textual. For example, the Resource Monitor node has full graphs that show system activity. In most cases, to perform actions on an object displayed in the Details pane, right-click on the object and select the action via the displayed context menu or to modify attributes of the object select the Properties option. Or select an option and then select actions from the Action menu.

The Actions Pane

The Actions pane sits on the right side of the screen and displays the actions that apply to the currently selected object in the MMC. The actions listed normally equate to the items that would be listed as actions for the context menu of an item. However, this does not have to be the case; the Actions pane can be coded to display anything the developer desires. The Actions pane provides an easier way to quickly see what actions apply to the selected object than the standard context menu.

Creating a Customized Console

To create a customized console configuration, start the MMC on its own by running the MMC image in an empty console. When the console is open, add snap-ins by selecting File, Add or Remove Snap-ins or pressing Ctrl+M to open the new MMC 3.0 Add or Remove Snap-ins dialog, as shown in Figure 2-42. This dialog is a big improvement over the 2.0 interface. The available snap-ins are displayed on the left side of the dialog, and you can select them and load them into the console by clicking the Add button. Depending on the snap-in you add, an additional dialog may appear, asking you to specify additional options. For example, if the Computer Management snap-in is loaded, a dialog asks if the local computer has the focus, whether a remote computer should have the focus, and if the target computer can be modified via command-line execution of the saved console.

After you add a snap-in, edit the extensions that are available for the snap-in by clicking the Edit Extensions button. While snap-ins are self-contained units of functionality, a snap-in extension, as the name implies, extends the functionality of a snap-in; it is essentially a snap-in for a snap-in. Clicking the Advanced button allows you to specify the parent of each loaded snap-in. By default, each snap-in is a child of the root of the console tree. However, by enabling the ability to change the parent of a snap-in, you can specify a snap-in's position by specifying an alternate parent.

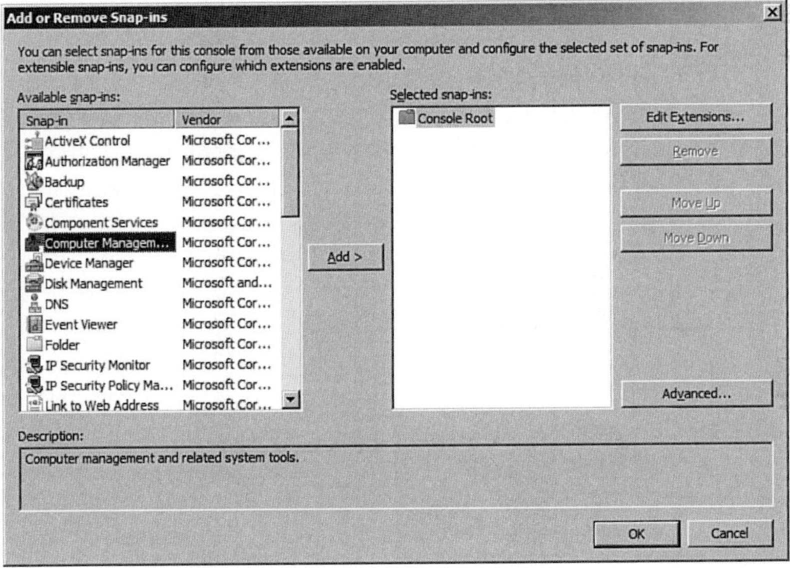

FIGURE 2-42 The new Add or Remove Snap-ins dialog is far simpler to use than the old option and allows multiple snap-ins to be added with a small number of mouse clicks.

After your console is created, configure multiple windows within the console by selecting Window, New Window or pressing Ctrl+W to open a complete copy of the main window. You can also right-click an item in the console tree and select New Window from Here to create a new window with only the options from the selected point, which allows you to move windows around in the console and view multiple areas simultaneously. For example, right-click Reliability and Performance within the Computer Management snap-in and select a new window from that location. On that new window, you could turn off the console tree and the Actions pane options to just have a window showing performance graphs as part of the console.

When you have finished designing your console, save it to an .MSC file by selecting File, Save. By default, your custom .MSC files are saved to the Administrative Tools programs folder that is part of your user profile and are available as shortcuts in the Administrative Tools menu for your logon. If you look at the Options menu, you see the console mode, which by default is the author mode because the console was just created; however, you can select from the following modes:

- **Author mode**. Grants users full access to all MMC functionality, including the ability to add or remove snap-ins, create new windows, manage extensions, and view all portions of the console tree.
- **User mode—full access**. Grants users full access to all window management commands and to the console tree. Prevents users from adding or removing snap-ins or changing console properties.
- **User mode—limited access, multiple window**. Grants users access only to the areas of the console tree that were visible when the console was saved. Users can create new windows but cannot close existing windows.
- **User mode—limited access, single window**. Grants users access only to the areas of the console tree that were visible when the console was saved. Prevents users from opening new windows.

Being able to select a mode is especially important if you intend to share your console with other users.

If you change mode and subsequently need to open an .MSC file in author mode, start the .MSC file with the /a switch or right-click the .MSC file and select Author from the context menu. By default, the full path for your custom MSC files is C:\Users\<*username*>\AppData\Roaming\Microsoft\Windows\Start Menu\Programs\Administrative Tools.

The Control Panel

The Control Panel consists of several applets that allow specific areas of the OS to be configured and are .CPL files, the majority of which are stored in the system32 folder. The Control Panel applets are discussed in more detail in future chapters, as they apply to functionality. This chapter briefly looks at the overall Control Panel options. The Control Panel, which you access via the Start menu, has two view options:

- **Control Panel home**. This default view breaks all the components of the Control Panel into ten major categories of configuration that you can select to see all available applets. In addition, the most popular categories are available as subitems on the Control Panel home screen (see Figure 2-43).
- **Classic view**. Classic view simply lists all available Control Panel applets in alphabetical order, not grouped by functionality area.

There may be times when you access Control Panel applets from outside the Control Panel interface. For example, if you right-click the desktop and select Personalize from the context menu, the Personalize Control Panel applet launches. Likewise, selecting Networking and Sharing Center from the context menu of the network notification tray icon launches this Control Panel applet.

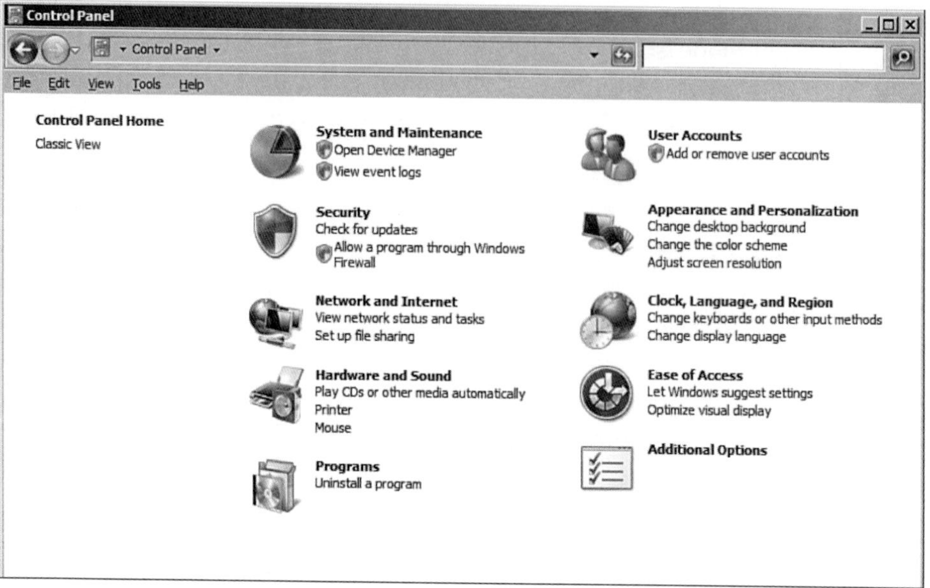

FIGURE 2-43 Select one of the ten major areas of functionality by clicking the title to view the Control Panel applets that relate to that area.

Searching the Control Panel

In both Control Panel views, the Search box is available in the top right of the window, enabling you to quickly limit the applets displayed to those that match your search criteria. However, depending on the view, you get different results for the same search.

In classic view, you can only perform a search based on the names of Control Panel applets, so in classic view typing *monitor* brings up no results because no Control Panel applets have the word *monitor* in them. However, in the Control Panel home view, a search checks the functionality of each applet; so in this case, a search on *monitor* brings up a list of matching tasks related to the term, as shown in Figure 2-44. This is useful when you are not sure which Control Panel applet you need to use for a particular configuration area.

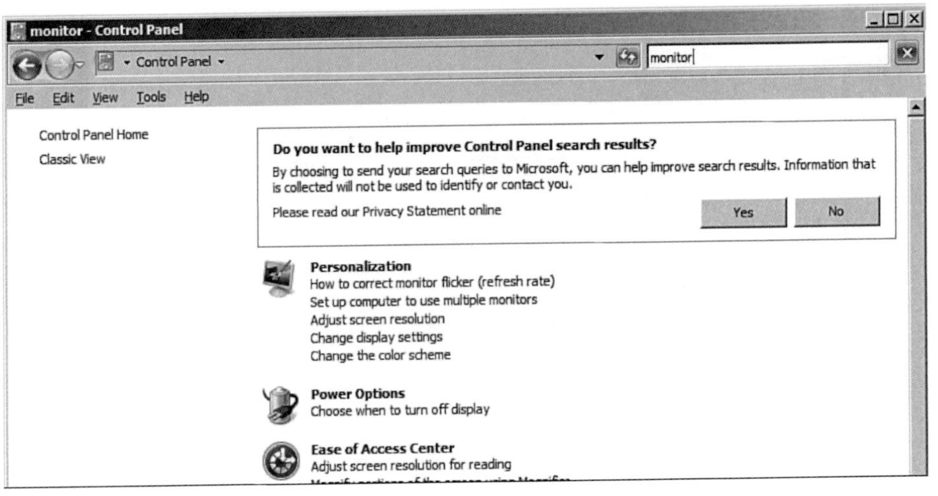

FIGURE 2-44 A list of tasks related to the searched keyword(s) (in this example, *monitor*) are displayed in order of relevance.

Control Panel Programs and Features

One of the Control Panel applets that has undergone a major overhaul is the old Add or Remove Programs applet. There used to be separate areas for changing/removing existing installed applications, adding a new application, and adding/removing Windows components. The new Programs Explorer, called Program and Features, replaces the old-style interface. The default Tasks view still lists installed applications and allows you to modify or remove them, but it also offers the option View Installed Updates, which lists updates not only to the OS but also to applications. To modify components of the OS, use Turn Windows Features On or Off, which for Windows Server launches Server Manager. The Server Manager breaks functionality into features, including items such as Desktop Experience and MSMQ; you access items such as DNS and DHCP via the Roles area. In Windows Vista, a separate Windows Features application that lists all the available components (see Figure 2-45) controls OS component installation.

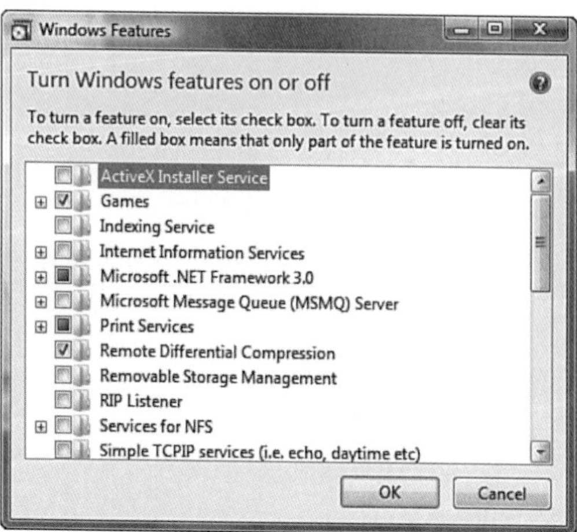

FIGURE 2-45 The interface for feature configuration with Windows Vista.

NOTE You cannot turn Windows Features on or off using the Control Panel in Windows Server 2008. Instead, you must use Service Manager to add or remove roles and features.

Navigating and launching all the Control Panel applets is worth your time because they expose a great deal of functionality and flexibility in the OS, and if there is something you dislike about the usability of the system, it may be configurable via the Control Panel.

Summary

This chapter examines the overall interface elements of Windows Vista and Windows Server 2008, including visual elements such as Windows Flip and Flip 3D. The main Start menu, the Taskbar, and the system tray have undergone many changes over the years but are still great tools for quickly getting information about your system. Thanks to the new functionality of Explorer, the Control Panel, and the Start menu, you no longer need to remember where programs, configuration parameters, and data reside. Search capabilities are embedded in all parts of the OS, allowing you to search more easily.

This chapter provides a glimpse into the major interface structures in Windows Server 2008 and some that are Vista-specific. Some of the major areas, such as UAC, certainly require some adjustment, but they definitely provide a safer environment. The rest of the book expands on these concepts and looks at more aspects of the interface, including utilities such as the Registry editor, which allows direct access to the operating system's internal configuration database; numerous support tools; and command-line and scripting interfaces. In addition, this book covers other critical information areas, such as the event logs.

CHAPTER 3

INSTALLING AND UPGRADING WINDOWS SERVER 2008

This book looks at the features and usage of a Windows Server 2008 environment. However, before you can enjoy Windows Server 2008, you need to install it.

Chapter 16, "Deploying Windows," discusses deploying operating systems (OSs), which also applies to installing Windows Server 2008; therefore, network-based installation is not covered in this chapter. This chapter focuses on the local installation of the OS and the initial configuration of a new installation, which applies to both a local and network-based installation. With a network-based installation, you commonly automate a majority of the initial configuration via an unattended answer file. This chapter shows how to achieve that with a local installation.

Installing Windows Server 2008

Let's start with a basic installation of Windows Server 2008.

NOTE One item not covered in this section is installing Windows Server 2008 to a virtual environment; the process, however, is essentially the same. The only additional option is to create a library of template OS installations that have been prepared for duplication. Creating this library prevents you from installing the OS for each new virtual instance. When you need a new virtual instance, copy the virtual hard disk (VHD) file to the new virtual instance and then boot. Doing so runs a quick setup, making the installation unique and allowing the computer name to be configured (see Chapter 19, "Virtualization and Resource Management").

Installation Requirements

Before installing Windows Server 2008, make sure the hardware meets the minimum requirements of the OS and the tasks and applications you intend to use:

- **Memory**. Windows Server 2008 does not run without at least 512MB RAM. (Ideally, you need at least 2GB.) For 32-bit, the maximum amount of memory is 4GB for Standard and 64GB for Enterprise and Datacenter. For 64-bit, 32GB of memory is the maximum for Standard edition or 2TB for Enterprise and Datacenter.
- **Disk**. 10GB of space is a functional minimum, but there's no breathing room. Shoot for 40GB minimum. If you run more than 16GB of memory, you need more disk space because of the paging and dump files. If you enable hibernation, consider that the hibernation file is the size of the memory amount.
- **Processor**. The minimum is 1GHz for x86 processors, 1.4GHz for x64 processors, and Itanium 2 for Itanium-based installations.

Have a plan for your drive space. If you plan to use this system in a production environment, you must implement some kind of Redundant Array of Independent Disks (RAID). (Chapter 5, "File System and Print Management Features," provides more information about RAID.) In most cases, the RAID will be hardware-implemented, and typically, you'll use RAID 1 for the system disk. Before you install the OS, configure RAID on the server and update the basic input/output system (BIOS).

Decide how to logically divide the disk. If the server stores large amounts of data, do not store it on the boot volume where the OS resides. In the event of volume corruption, there are more controllable data subsets to locate and restore. (For example, restore only the OS volume but not the 300GB of data partitioned on its own volume.) Some products have their own disk best practices. For example, Exchange best practice requires placing transaction logs on different physical disks from the databases to limit the chance of failure affecting the logs and the database. If you have any direct attached storage (DAS), a storage area network (SAN), or access to network attached storage (NAS), the data may reside on these solutions. Only the OS and binaries for services will be locally installed, so the OS can take up most of the local disk space. It is also common to place the paging file on a separate physical disk to minimize disk head movement on the OS/application drives related to page file activity.

If you intend to use BitLocker drive encryption, ensure that at least 1.5GB remains available as unpartitioned space. The storage is required as a special BitLocker system volume that contains the files needed to start the Windows OS load after the BIOS boots. (Note that, if needed, you can shrink existing partitions to claim this space.)

Fresh Installation of Windows Server 2008

To begin installation, you need Windows Server 2008 media and, ideally, the product key. The key is not needed for installation, but it activates Windows Server after installation is complete.

There are two ways to install Windows Server 2008 outside of a network: You can boot from the Windows Server 2008 media, or you can initiate the installation from another OS. When you initiate the installation from within another OS, you might receive an option to upgrade (depending on the existing OS), but the next chapter covers that. In this section, you use the custom installation option and install the 2008 OS to an empty partition. This provides a dual boot scenario, which leaves the existing OS intact and installs Server 2008 on another volume, allowing you to choose the OS at boot time. In a production situation, this is rarely used and is considered a waste of resources because you have two OSs on one box, and both require patching, licensing, and so forth.

Installing from Media

The first question you might have is what media to use: "I have only one Windows Server 2008 DVD, but I want to install Web Edition, Enterprise," and so on. Like Windows Vista, all editions of Windows Server 2008 are contained on a single version of the media, in a single instance store WIM file. Chapter 16 goes into detail on WIM, but if you have one 2008 media DVD, you have every edition. The version that gets installed is based on the product key you enter, or you can skip entering a product key and just select the version you want to install. You have to promise that you have a key for that version and will activate it soon:

1. Insert the 2008 DVD and boot the server from the DVD drive. The DVD boots the server to the Windows PE 2.0 environment contained in the boot.wim file on the Windows Server 2008 DVD. Windows PE is used as the installation environment for Windows Server 2008, which gives a rich installation environment that's more intuitive than previous installation environments with Windows.
2. The first installation choices are to select the language for the installation, the time and currency format, and the keyboard

layout. By default, English media contains only the English language. However, you could create a custom installation media containing multiple languages by injecting additional language packs into the boot.wim file. This is common to Windows Server 2008 and Windows Vista, which is why you have a language-neutral core operating system. You just add language packs, which you can do at any stage in an operating system's life. Download these language packs from www.microsoft.com; just search for Windows Server 2008 Multilingual User Interface Language Packs.

3. After you make the choices, as shown in Figure 3-1, the main part of the installation can commence.

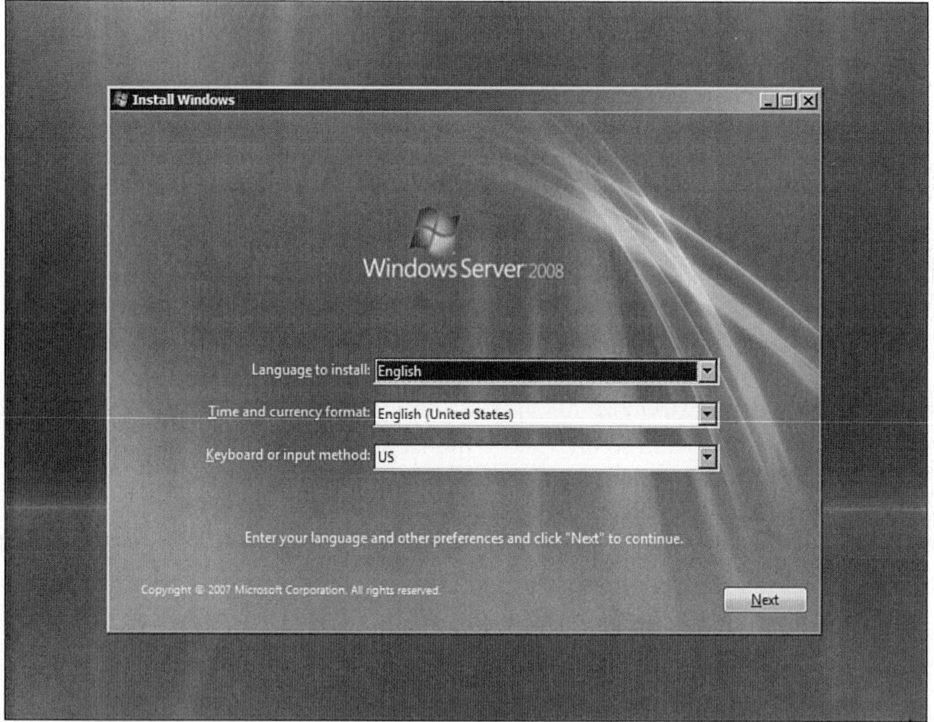

FIGURE 3-1 The initial configuration controls all display and input during the setup process.

4. The next screen gives you the option to Install Now; however, notice the option to repair the computer, which is covered in Chapter 20, "Troubleshooting Windows Server 2008 and Vista Environments." Click the Install Now link to start installing Windows Server 2008, as shown in Figure 3-2.

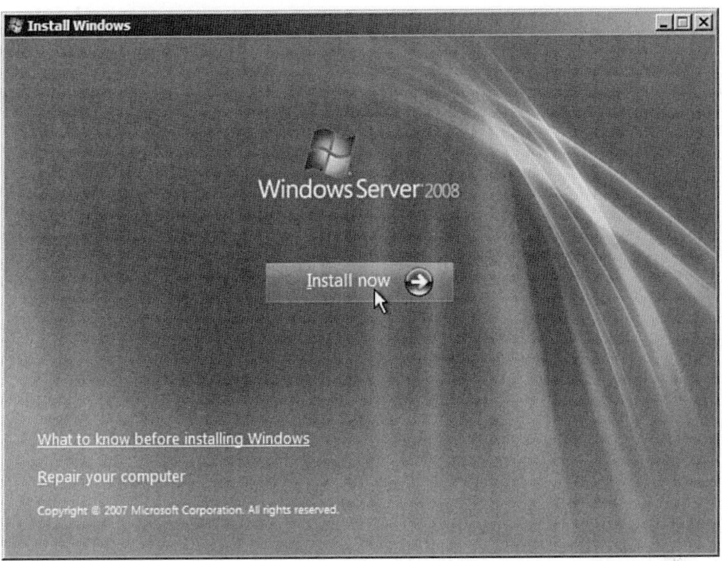

FIGURE 3-2 Not much to configure here, but that link for repair at the bottom is powerful.

5. The actual installation process now initiates in two phases. Rather than ask questions throughout the entire install process, the install process asks all needed information upfront in the first phase. It then proceeds with phase 2, which is the actual installation without any user interaction. So, have a nice cup of tea during the installation.

   The first part of the collection information phase is requesting the product key. This action tells the installation process which version of 2008 to install and gives the option to tell Windows Server to automatically activate when it's next online. You can omit entering a product key and just click Next, as shown in Figure 3-3. A dialog confirms that you should enter a product key because, if you don't, you might install the wrong version of Windows, one that you have no key for and then have to reinstall. If you want to continue without entering a product key, click No to avoid typing the 25-character key. (You can just cut and paste it during the activation process after installation. Also, if you're using a Microsoft Developer Network [MSDN] key, you'll have to re-enter the key anyway.)

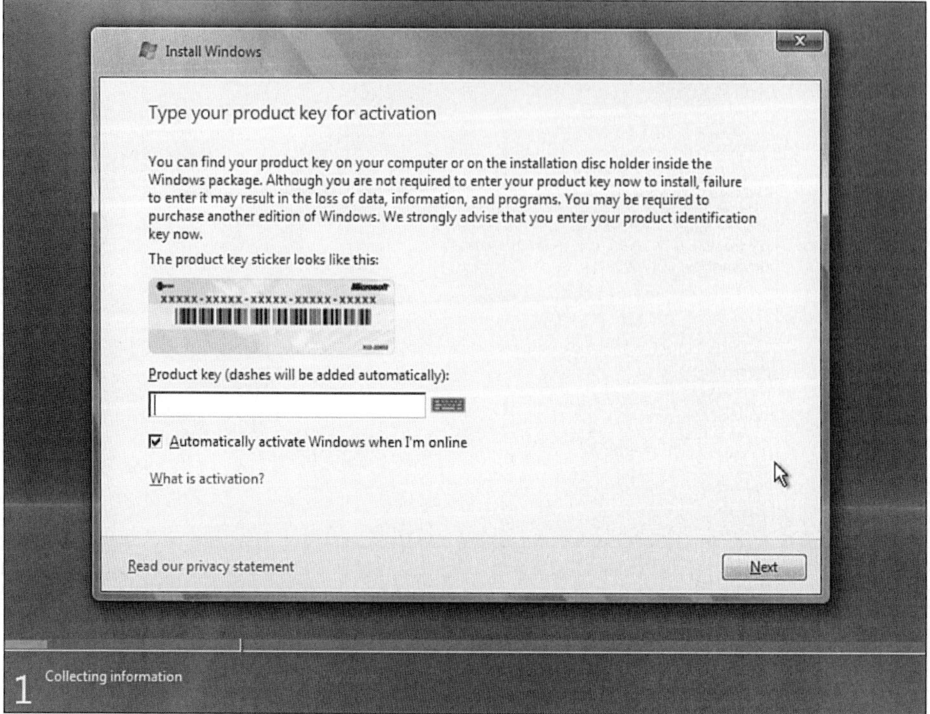

FIGURE 3-3 Enter the product key for the Server 2008 version you want to install.

6. If you entered a product key, you are prompted about which version of Windows Server to install (unless you are installing Web Edition, which has only one type). The two installation type choices are Full Install and Server Core Install.
   If you did not enter a product key, you have six types of installation available: Standard, Enterprise, and Datacenter, and whether each type of install is full or server core, as shown in Figure 3-4. Notice if you did not enter a product key, you also have to check the box confirming you have selected the Windows version for which you purchased a product key. If you install Enterprise edition and only have a standard key, you won't be able to activate the server installation, so it goes into the nag mode, reminding you to activate constantly. Although it is the organization's fault for installing the wrong version, there would be grumbling aimed at Microsoft for letting you install the wrong version, so it's all about double-checking. Until you check I Have Selected the Edition of Windows That I Purchased, you cannot continue the installation.

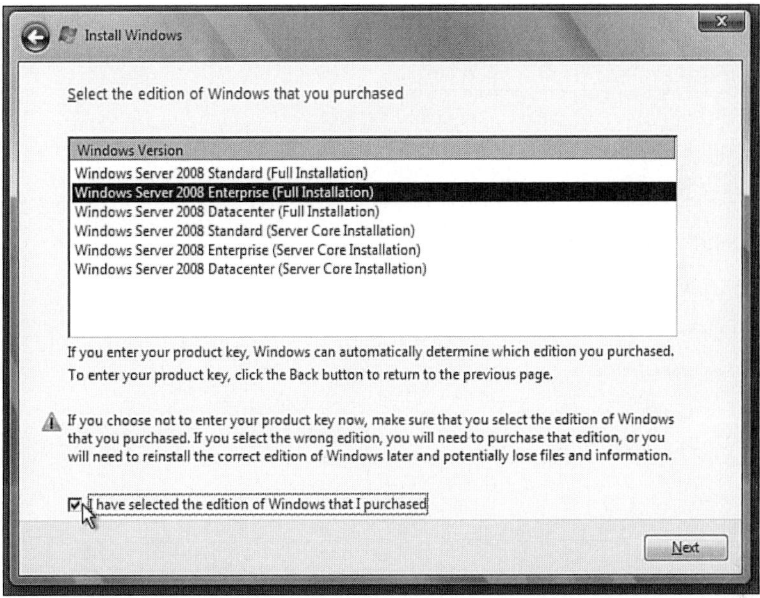

FIGURE 3-4 This is another confirmation that the 2008 media contains all versions.

7. The Windows Server 2008 license agreement appears. Check the I Accept the License Terms box after reading it in detail (as we all do). Click Next. Again, you cannot continue the installation until you accept the license agreement.
8. The install type is now selectable, which because you booted from media is only a custom installation as opposed to an upgrade, as shown in Figure 3-5. To perform an in-place upgrade, you have to start the install from within the Windows installation being upgraded. If you have an existing Windows installation on the server, you must install Windows Server 2008 on a new volume; otherwise, the existing installation will be deleted.
9. The last part of the information-gathering process is installing the actual volume. As shown in Figure 3-6, a list of volumes displays. Our example is a new machine with no existing volumes. By default, you can just select a volume or unpartitioned space to install to and, if it's currently unallocated, a New Technology File System (NTFS) volume is automatically created on it.

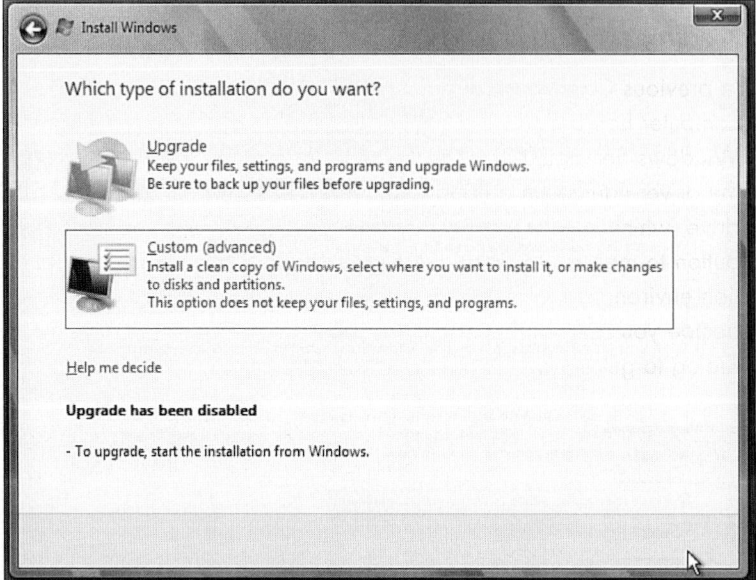

Figure 3-5 A fresh installation is a Custom installation type.

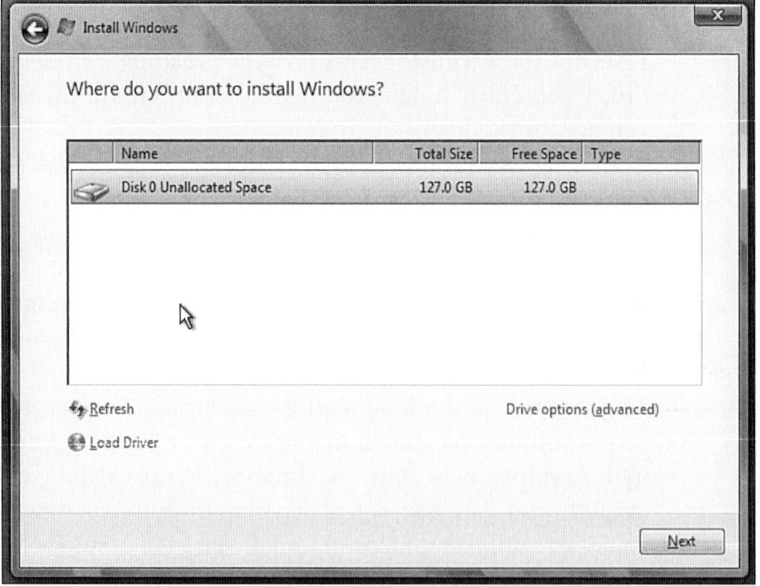

Figure 3-6 In this case, no partitions exist.

Adding Drivers

In previous OSs, you could press F6 to install additional storage drivers if the computer had a storage controller unknown to the built-in storage library. With Windows Server 2008, click the Load Driver link. If you select Load a Driver, the driver can be on a floppy, CD, DVD, or Universal Serial Bus (USB) flash drive, which is a nice capability (see Figure 3-7). You can also click the Browse button to manually select a location from any file system known to the installation environment, and a list of drivers that you can select is displayed. If you decide you don't want to add a driver, click the back arrow at the top left of the dialog to get back to the dialog that allows you to select installation.

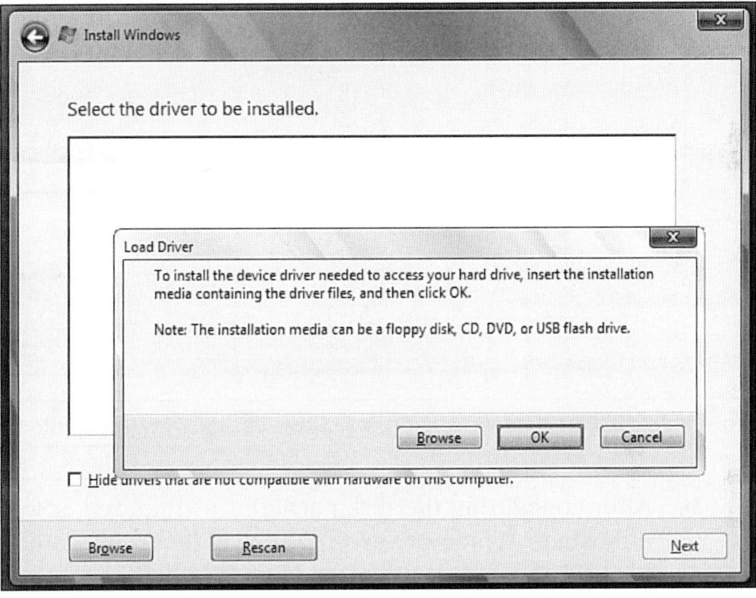

FIGURE 3-7 Option to install additional drivers from multiple sources.

If you don't want to install Windows into an entire unallocated space but rather a smaller portion of the space, click the Drive Options (Advanced) link, which adds additional buttons to delete volumes, create new volumes, extend a volume into unallocated space, and perform a format. To create a new partition, click the New button and select a size for the new partition up to the maximum of the unallocated space, as shown in Figure 3-8. After

creating the partition, select it, and you have the option to format the partition as NTFS.
To extend a partition, select the partition you want to extend and the amount of unallocated space to have available after creating the selected partition.

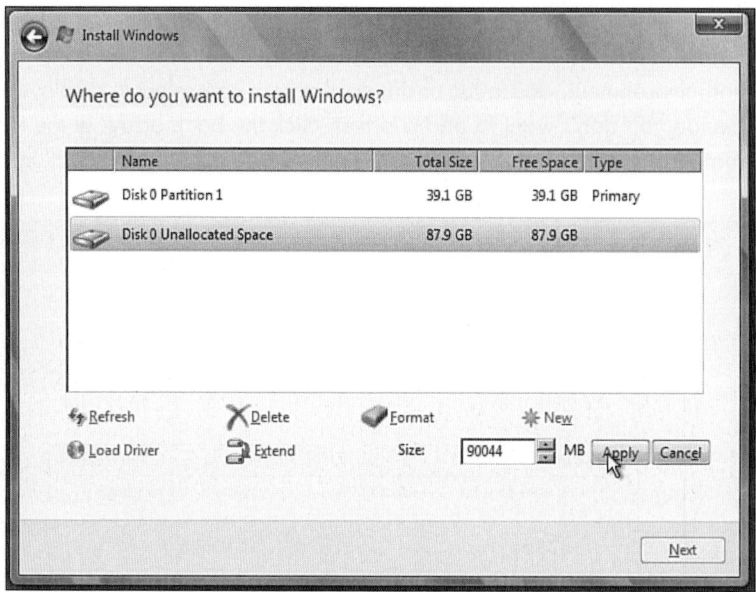

FIGURE 3-8 You have created a new partition and have clicked New to create another one.

10. After configuring the disk partitions as required, select the partition where Windows Server 2008 will be installed and click Next. Phase 1 is now complete and the installation continues with no user interaction, as shown in Figure 3-9. The installation progress installation displays in the dialog. During the second phase, the server reboots into the Windows Server 2008 environment.

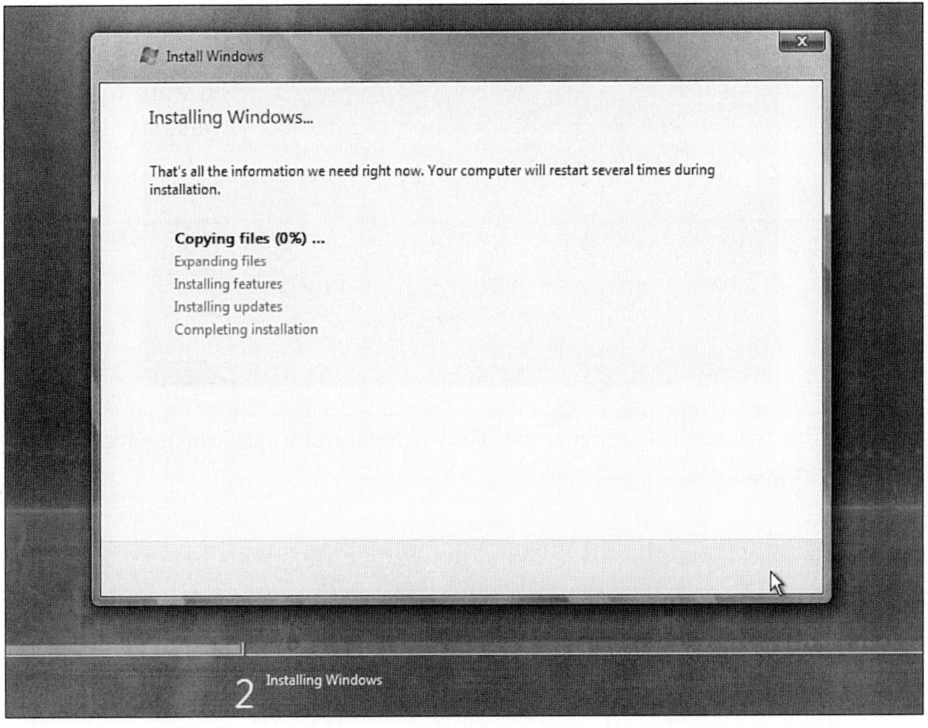

FIGURE 3-9 The remaining installation stages are automated.

Performing Initial Configuration of a Server

When the installation is complete, you have a fully installed Windows Server 2008 environment. However, because you gave no information during the installation process, its configuration is currently highly generic with a Dynamic Host Configuration Protocol (DHCP)–assigned Internet Protocol (IP) address, automatically generated hostname, and so on. Notice also that during installation you never set a password for the Administrator account. So, instead of seeing a logon screen, you are prompted to change the user's password before logging on the first time, as shown in Figure 3-10. Click OK, enter the new Administrator password twice, and click the proceed arrow. The screen displays a message that the password is changing and confirmation that the change is finished. Click OK to continue. Then you can log on as Administrator.

FIGURE 3-10 The first item is modifying the blank Administrator password, which is probably not a good idea.

For those that used Windows Server 2003 with Service Pack 1 integrated (which included Windows 2003 R2) after a fresh installation, the first activity was to complete the Post Setup Security Update (PSSU) process to get any important updates from Windows Update and then configure the server for automatic updates. It made sure administrators got the server up-to-date and kept it that way. With Windows Server 2008, you have the PSSU on steroids with the Initial Configuration Tasks (ICT) interface.

The ICT interface is not a Microsoft Management Console (MMC) snap-in but is, in fact, the Windows Server 2008 Out-of-Box-Experience (OOBE) (see Figure 3-11). It is the oobe.exe executable, which you can run or perform the configuration at any time; however, you have better options. The ICT just brings together initial configuration items. Although the ICT is a way to graphically configure the server, the configuration can also be done from the command line (covered in Chapter 14, "Server Core").

The ICT is broken into three sections. The first part is the configuration previously performed during the OS installation: configuring the time zone, network, and computer name and domain. Each ICT item is a link to the OS component normally used for the configuration item. The actual ICT is just a page of links to give the administrator a series of steps to follow to make sure all vital configuration areas are finished. You don't have to use the ICT. For example, clicking the Set Time Zone link opens the Date and Time Control Panel applet, which allows you to set the time zone by clicking the Change Time Zone button, as shown in Figure 3-12.

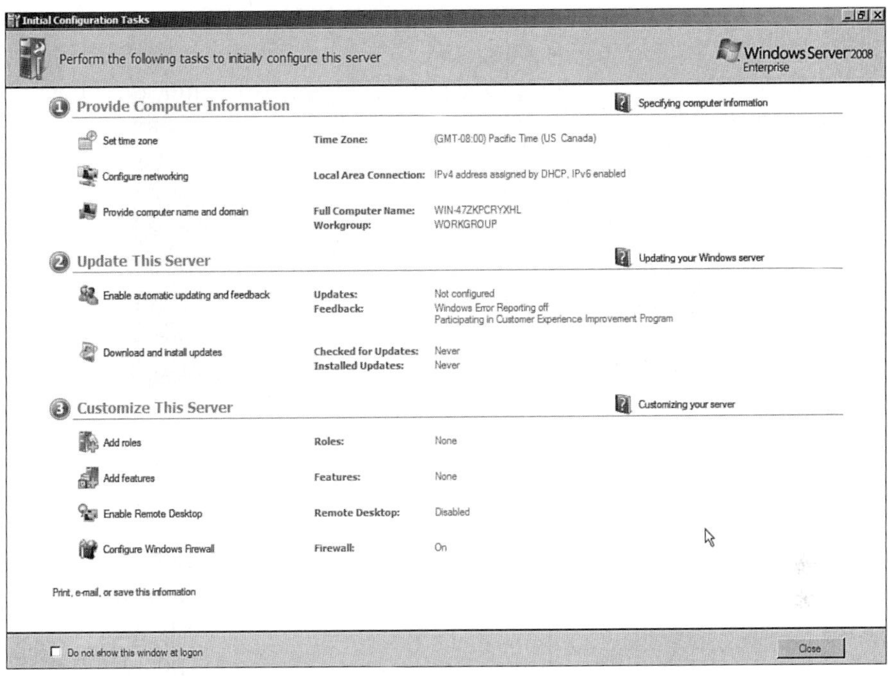

FIGURE 3-11 The ICT interface helps complete server installation and perform the configuration previously done during installation.

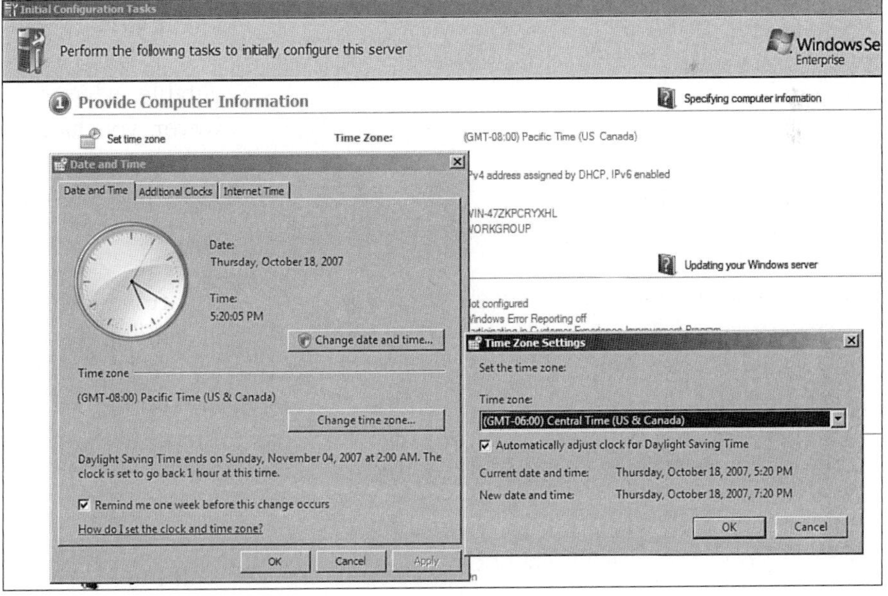

FIGURE 3-12 Setting the time zone is important for an environment.

After configuring the time zone, click the Configure Networking link to open the Network Connections Control Panel applet. This applet displays the network connections on the server. By default, the network connections have DHCP-configured IP addresses; however, in most cases, your servers want a static IP address. Therefore, each adapter for the server displays. You can configure each one by selecting the adapter properties and configuring Internet Protocol Version 4 (TCP/IPv4) with static address information. You can also configure the Version 6 properties; however, you most likely utilize DHCP even for servers with IPv6.

The final part of the computer information section is to click the Provide Computer Name and Domain link, which opens the System Control Panel applet on the Computer Name tab. Click the Change button, as shown in Figure 3-13, to modify the computer name. You can modify the domain/workgroup from this screen. If you change the domain, you get a prompt for an account with permission to join to the domain. After changing the computer name and/or domain, you receive a prompt to reboot the server. Why do you still need to reboot? So many services rely on the computer name and domain membership that it's cleaner to reboot the server. If you intend to make the server a domain controller, leave the server in a workgroup. Then when you run the domain controller promotion process, the server is automatically placed into the domain.

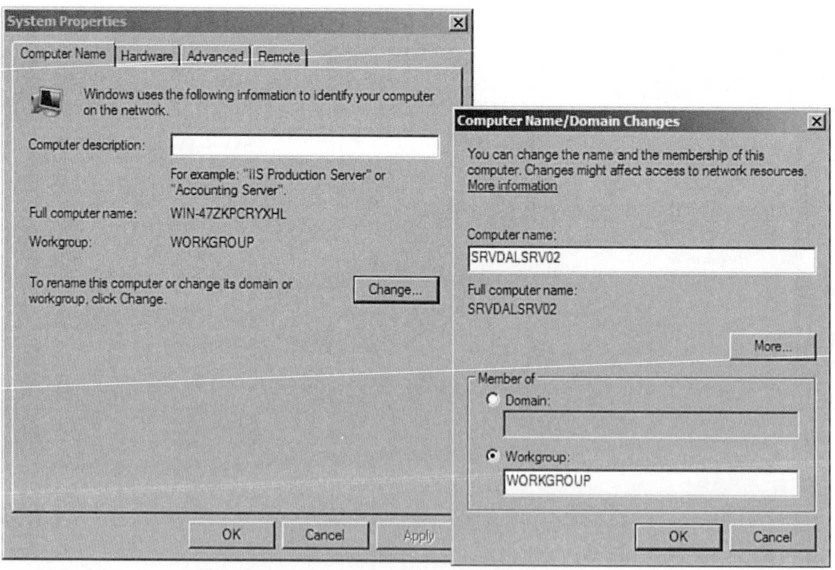

FIGURE 3-13 The computer name is important to configure because the automatically generated name is less than ideal.

After the reboot, the ICT opens and phase 2 begins, which consists of configuring server updates. The first configuration item is to configure the automatic updating of the server by clicking the Enable Automatic Updating and Feedback link. This opens a dialog that has an easy button to enable automatic updating, or you can choose to manually configure the settings, which (as Figure 3-14 shows) allows you to choose from among the individual elements of automatic update, error reporting, and the customer experience improvement program. The manual configuration allows you to granularly configure whether updates are downloaded and applied automatically or just downloaded and manually installed. If they install automatically, you can configure at what time and what days. (By default, the updates install automatically at 3:00 a.m. daily.) Also note the option to apply recommended updates and not just the critical updates. If you have an internal patch deployment solution to deploy fixes, such as Windows Update Services or System Center Configuration Manager, leave the automatic updating disabled. Your organization probably does testing on updates prior to enabling them for deployment, so servers should not directly pull down updates that might not have passed internal certification from Microsoft.

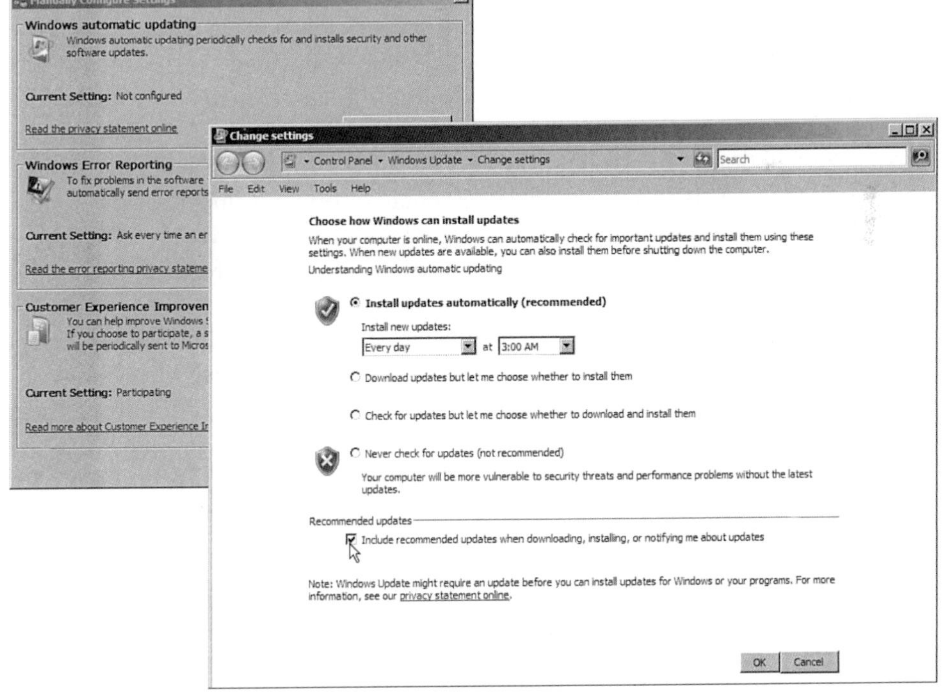

FIGURE 3-14 The manual configuration options for the update application.

After configuring the server for automatic updating, click the Download and Install Updates link. This launches the Windows Update Control Panel applet, which attempts to find any missing fixes and drivers by connecting to Microsoft. If you don't enable automatic updates, ensure that you regularly run the Windows Update Control Panel applet to look for changes. A large percentage of system outages result from problems and attacks for which fixes exist but were not applied. Again, if you have an internal solution for updating servers, skip this step.

NOTE Notice you have not enabled the firewall. This is because Windows Server 2008 enables the Windows Firewall by default, giving you protection as soon as you install the OS.

The final step of configuration guided by the ICT is server customization. You have an installed 2008 server, but it does nothing; it offers no services. Therefore, you need to add roles and features to the server. This is not a new concept. In Windows Server 2003, you had the ability to add server roles; however, most people simply used the Add/Remove Programs Control Panel applet and added Windows components. However, this is no longer an option.

Roles and features, and how to add each via a different interface, has been covered. Why the two types? A role is a primary purpose of a server, such as a DNS server, DHCP server, or domain controller. A feature helps a server in its duty (for example, Failover Clustering, BitLocker Drive Encryption). On its own, the Failover Clustering feature is not useful, but if you apply it to a file server or Exchange server, it improves the functionality of that installed role. After initial configuration, roles and features are easily added and modified via the Server Manager interface.

For now, make this server a domain controller; therefore, Active Directory Domain Service (ADDS) is needed. Click the Add Roles link to start the wizard to let you select roles. Notice that several roles are available, and their great capability is you don't have to worry about which services are necessary for the role to function. For example, just select Windows SharePoint Services and do not worry about Web Server, .NET, or any other components that SharePoint needs. Any required services are automatically installed as part of the role. Check the roles you want. You can normally select multiple roles. However, ADDS has to be installed on its own first, so if you want to create a domain controller, select only ADDS, as shown in Figure 3-15. Don't worry: If you wanted DNS as well, it gives you the option to install the DNS server in the additional domain controller options section later in the domain controller creation process.

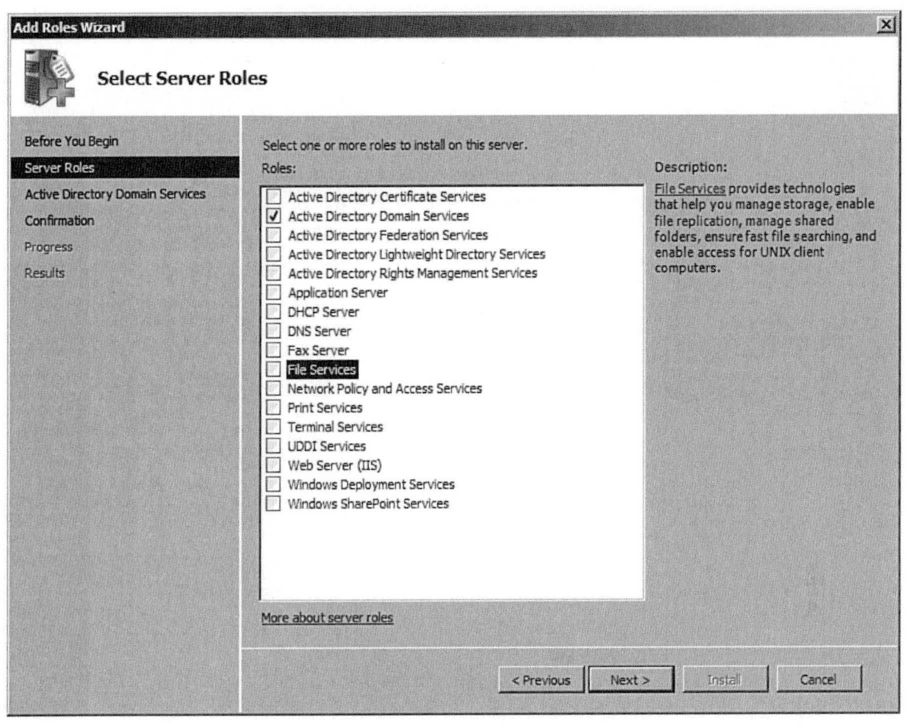

FIGURE 3-15 Installing roles for a server.

Depending on the roles selected, you are asked for different levels of information. In the case of ADDS, adding the role simply adds the binaries needed to create a domain controller. You still have to run DCPROMO after adding the binaries to promote the server to a domain controller, so you are not asked anything. Other roles that have subfeatures prompt you for which elements you want to install and basic configuration items necessary for installation. (This book looks at those options as they relate to the topic of the chapter, but the Role Installation Wizard does a great job of explaining the options available.)

After you install roles, you can add features, which depend on the roles installed and the extra features needed. Click the Add Features link and select the features desired, as shown in Figure 3-16. Some features, such as roles, have dependencies on other features. For example, if you add Windows Server Backup Features, you also need the Windows Recovery Disc feature, which is automatically enabled by the wizard. Typically, features do not require configuration when installed because a role uses them.

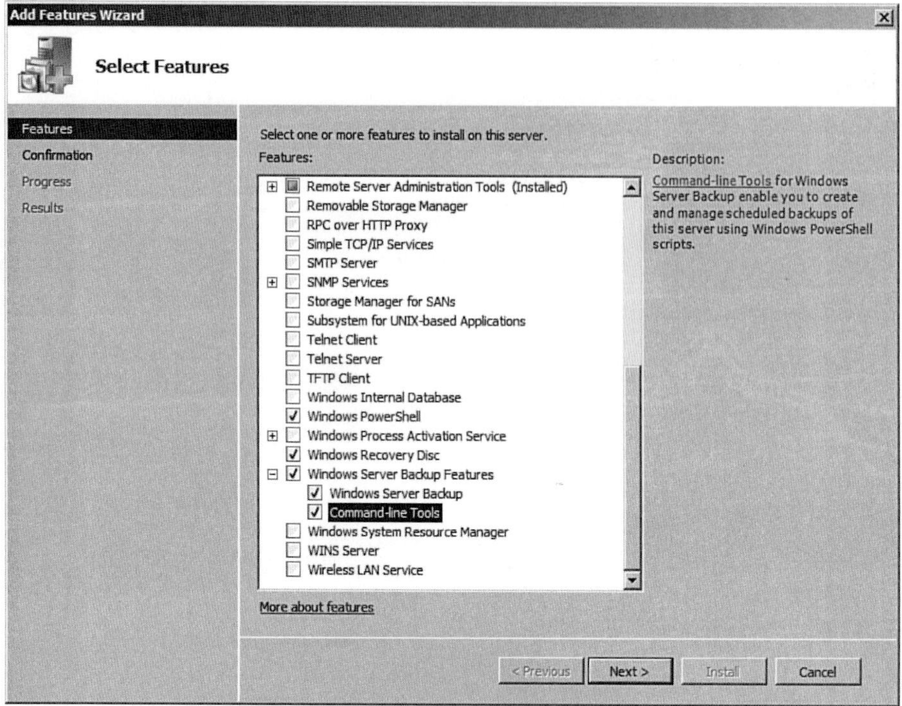

FIGURE 3-16 Many features are available that complement the core server roles.

After installing the features and roles, the last two configuration items via the ICT are to enable Remote Desktop and configure the Windows Firewall. Click the Enable Remote Desktop link to open the System Control Panel applet on the Remote tab. By default, Remote Desktop is disabled; however, it can be enabled from any version of the Remote Desktop client or only versions that support network level authentication (NLA) (see Figure 3-17). The only Remote Desktop version that supports NLA natively is the version that ships with Windows Vista and 2008. However, an updated client is available for Windows XP and Server 2003 that adds NLA. When you enable Remote Desktop, an exception is automatically enabled in Windows Firewall. You can also select users who can connect via Remote Desktop by clicking the Select Users button. By default, this allows any member of the Administrators group to connect, but anyone can be given permission.

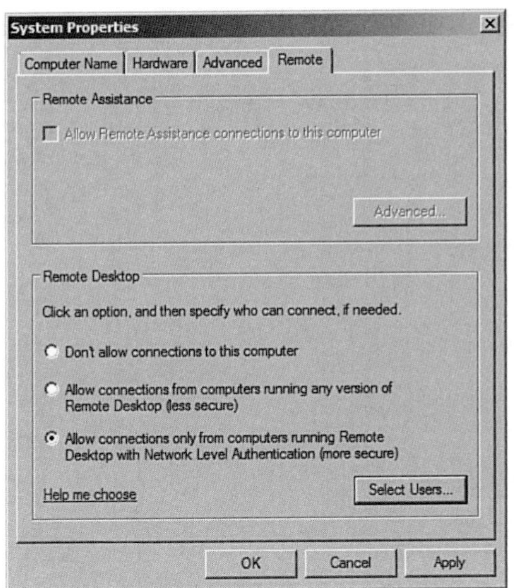

FIGURE 3-17 Selecting the Remote Desktop.

The final configuration item via the ICT is to configure Windows Firewall. By default, as you add roles and features, you create exceptions in Windows Firewall, which is enabled by default. However, additional configuration is possible via the Windows Firewall Control Panel applet (covered in Chapter 4, "Securing Your Windows Server 2008 Deployment").

You are now finished with the ICT, so you can check the Do Not Show This Window at Logon check box so that it does not launch at system start-up (as shown in Figure 3-18) and click Close. The Server Manager then launches. (Server Manager is covered in Chapter 12, "Managing Active Directory and Advanced Concepts.") You have now completed the basic configuration items.

Activating the Installation

You can now activate your installation. You are prompted via the system tray, but you can also activate via the System Control Panel applet. Access this applet via the Control Panel or by right-clicking Start, Computer, and selecting Properties. As shown in Figure 3-19, you can click the Activate Windows Now link, which runs the Windows Activation dialog that can activate via the Internet. If you have not entered a key, you are prompted for one. If you are using an MSDN key, click the Change Product Key link and enter the MSDN key that activates the installation.

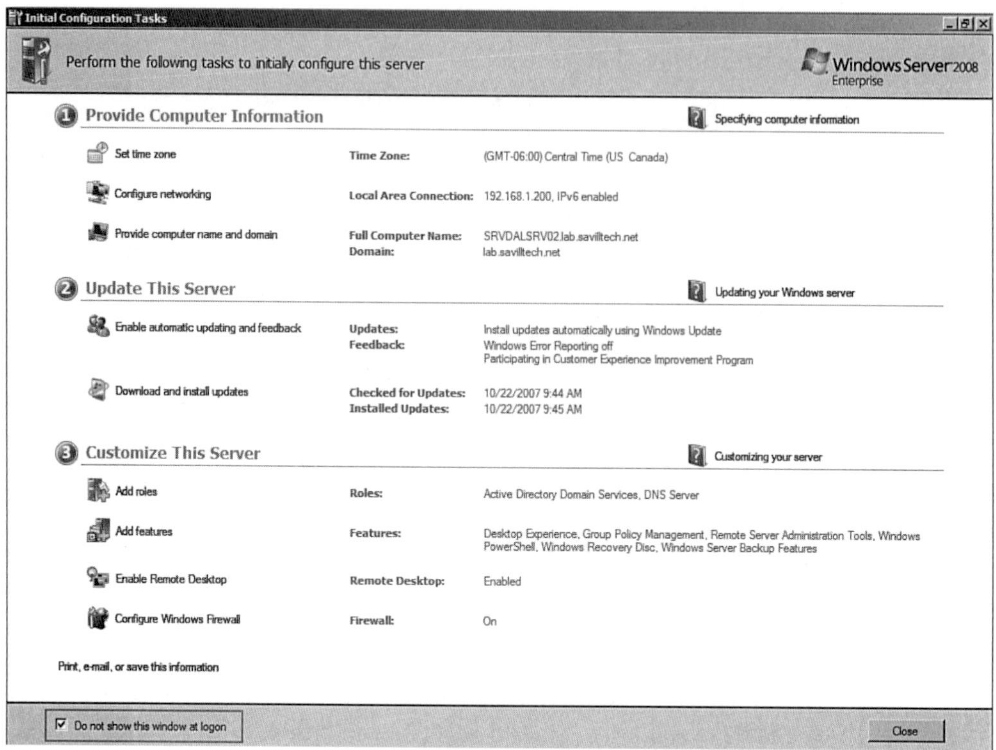

FIGURE 3-18 Next to each step, you can see the configuration made, showing that the actions were taken.

In Windows Vista before Service Pack 1, if you did not activate Vista, it went into a reduced functionality mode. This was removed in Windows Vista SP1 and Windows Server 2008. Instead, you have notification, also known as nag mode, which gives you a black background with a tattoo in the bottom-right corner of the screen telling you that the installation is not genuine, and you get a balloon pop-up once an hour telling you to activate. The logon screen also tells you to activate.

Here, assume that you are activating your installation using a Multiple Activation Key (MAK). There is another option if your organization has a local Key Management Server (KMS), in which case you don't need to enter any key. It happens automatically for you, assuming that KMS is correctly configured in the organization.

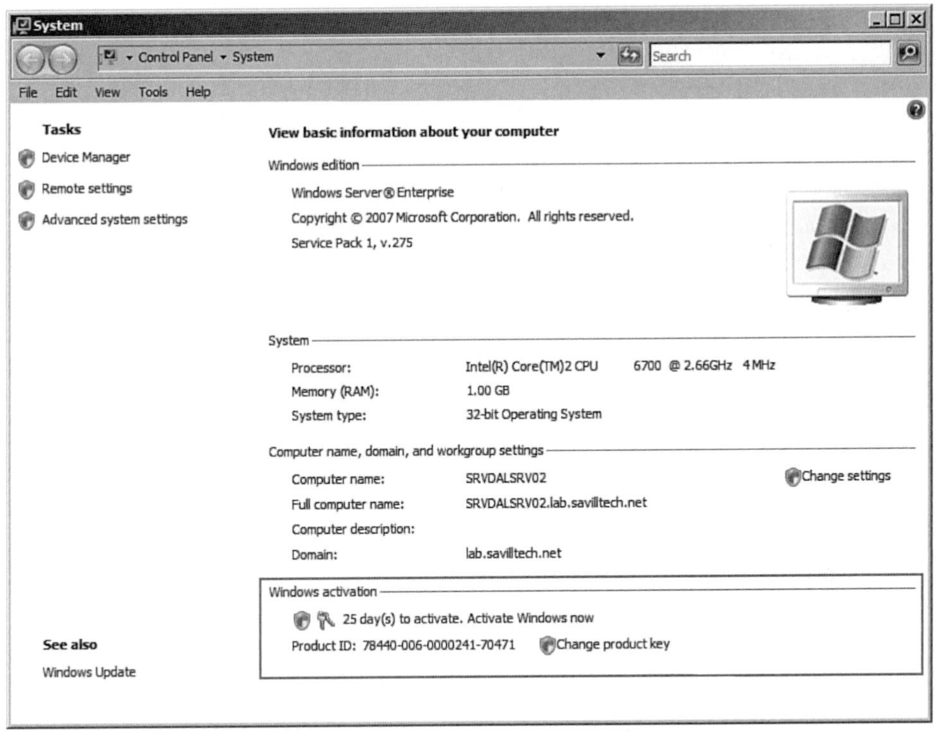

FIGURE 3-19 You get 30 days before activation is required and the server goes into notification or nag mode.

Activation Options

With Windows Vista and Windows Server 2008, you have two different activation schemes, as previously mentioned: MAK and KMS. Of course, there are also single-use retail keys, but if you're reading this book, you are using a MAK or KMS.

One important thing to remember: KMS and MAK are not for license enforcement. Microsoft is clear on that matter. If you are using MAK and have run out of activations, a phone call to Microsoft doubles those activations without a question asked. The activation is to ensure that you are running genuine Windows, which protects both you and Microsoft.

Multiple Activation Keys (MAKs)

MAKs work the same as the keys with Windows Server 2003 and XP volume license keys: You get a key that is entered on each computer. However, the difference is that a computer using a MAK still must be activated, unlike with XP/2003 volume license keys (VLKs). Each server contacts Microsoft and receives an activation code. If you have a lot of machines using MAK, you can install the Volume Activation Management Tool (VAMT), which acts as a proxy for communication with the Microsoft activation servers and activates machines in batches via a single connection or phone call to Microsoft. The VAMT is useful for enabling an administrator to monitor the activations within the environment via the MAK key and can be downloaded from Microsoft—search for VAMT.

When activated with a MAK, the client/server stays activated forever (or at least until a major hardware change, which requires reactivation).

Key Management Service (KMS)

With KMS, you enable a computer, known as the KMS host, within your organization (or multiple KMS servers for load balancing) via a KMS key you receive from Microsoft, which comes in four flavors. The KMS host activates itself to Microsoft, and from that point on, the KMS host activates machines within the environment. No data goes to Microsoft; it's an honor system.

Before the KMS host can activate any computers, you need the following:

- **To activate a Windows Server 2008 box**. At least five *physical* machines running Vista or Server 2008
- **To activate a Windows Vista box**. At least 25 *physical* machines running Vista or Server 2008

Virtual machines do not count. This stops people using a KMS to bypass activation in small environments. Your KMS server must maintain these numbers of clients or it stops being able to activate computers. If you originally have only 20 computers, the activation requests queue on the KMS server until it hits 25 before it activates Vista machines. (Of course, with 20 it happily activates your 2008 boxes.)

Clients find the KMS host through auto-configuration via DNS service records (`_vlmcs._tcp.<domain>`) or the clients can be manually configured with the KMS server name and port (1688, by default) using the slmgr.vbs script with the `/skms` switch, for example:

```
Cscript c:\windows\system32\slmgr.vbs /skms <KMS FQDN or
➥IPv4 or IPv6 or NetBIOS name>:<port>
```

By default, KMS hosts auto-register the DNS service records, so there is little configuration to perform.

The KMS host is part of Vista and Windows Server 2008; you don't have to install any software. The only configuration is from an elevated command prompt. Run the following commands to specify the KMS key, and then activate over the Internet:

```
Cscript c:\windows\system32\slmgr.vbs /ipk <KMS Key>
Cscript c:\windows\system32\slmgr.vbs /ato
```

NOTE A Windows Vista KMS host can activate only Windows Vista computers, not servers. A Windows Server 2008 KMS host can activate Vista and Windows Server 2008. You can also run KMS on Windows Server 2003 that can activate Vista and Server 2008, but first download the Key Management Service 1.1 update from Microsoft. You cannot run KMS host on a Windows server core installation.

The default activation method for Windows Vista for Windows Server 2008 uses KMS. However, you can change this by setting a MAK as the product key. If you want to revert to KMS for a computer, enter the KMS client setup key, which is listed at technet.microsoft.com. (Search for KMS_Client_Setup.) Note that these are useless without an activated KMS host in your environment. All these keys do is tell your computer to use KMS for activation.

A computer that activates via KMS must reactivate every 180 days and by default attempts to reactivate every 7 days. You, therefore, need to ensure that computers using KMS connect into a network KMS at least once every 180 days. Otherwise the computer goes into grace mode again, and after the grace period has expired, the computer goes into nag (notification) mode until KMS is contacted.

As mentioned earlier, there are four flavors of the KMS key. The flavors specify which machines a KMS host can activate:

- **Client**. Windows Vista
- **Server Group A**. Windows Server 2008 Web
- **Server Group B**. Windows Server 2008 Standard and Enterprise
- **Server Group C**. Windows Server 2008 Datacenter and Itanium

Only one key is on your KMS because a KMS key can activate its class of OS and any below it. For example, a Server Group A key can activate

Windows 2008 Web and Windows Vista; a Server Group B key can activate Windows Server 2008 Web, Standard, and Enterprise and Windows Vista; and a Server Group C key can activate any version of Windows Server 2008 and Windows Vista.

Which Activation Method to Use

The best option is to use KMS if you can—using KMS is the way Microsoft prefers. It requires less work on the client side and is especially important if you are using virtualization because of how activation works on a virtual machine.

Remember that if a machine has a large hardware change, it must reactivate. A virtual machine moving to another virtual server counts as a large hardware change, so you must reactivate it. If you have an environment in which you move virtual machines around frequently, or have technologies such as System Center Virtual Machine Manager, which dynamically moves virtual machines for best performance, you might be reactivating constantly. KMS solves this with an easy automatic activation that stops you worrying about activation counts associated with a MAK. This also applies to a virtual machine running on a cluster of virtual servers. If the virtual machine moved to another node in the cluster, you have to reactivate it.

There are still times when a MAK is required. If you have machines that disconnect from the network for long periods, such as on an oil rig, use MAK on them. You don't have to pick only one. For corporate machines that have frequent connectivity, use KMS; for machines that don't, use MAK.

You don't need high availability with KMS. If the KMS server dies, just fire up a new one and activate it with Microsoft. Its past activation history isn't needed. However, if you are interested, make sure you are backing up the Key Management Service log under Application and Services logs in Event Viewer. It contains all the activation events (12290 event ID).

In terms of how many KMS servers are needed in your organization, probably one. Each activation is a tiny payload—around 500 bytes. Microsoft has 400,000 KMS clients and just two KMS servers. You don't need to put a KMS server at each location.

Other Important Items

Although the OS core configuration and getting the OS updated and the firewall configured are important, many other items still require attention. Ensure that you apply corporate standards to the server. You can apply some of these configurations via items, such as Group Policy. However, you also need to get antivirus solutions installed and configured to ensure that the server receives updated virus definition files. Depending on the role of the server, install backup agents to ensure routine content and state backups. If you are using Data Protection Manager (DPM), you must deploy the DPM agent.

You might have to install other agents, such as System Center Operations Manager and System Center Configuration Manager, to ensure that the server is monitored and maintained.

You can now install additional roles and features on the server (if required) or install additional services such as Exchange, System Center, or anything else for the role of the server.

If this new install is a replacement for an existing Windows server, you might need to migrate resources, such as file storage and printer queues. There are normally tools available to help with resource migration. For example, the Print Management Console can migrate printers between servers.

When installing additional applications, it is not the best practice to install any application data or user data on the critical system volumes. This keeps the critical volumes small, enabling better system recovery and state protection. Also, in case of disk failure, the system is isolated from data so that if the data volume fails, the OS is available for data volume recovery. If the OS volume fails, a System Recovery Only operation is performed without repartitioning disks to get the server up and running without data loss or information roll back.

Installing from an Existing OS

Installing Windows Server 2008 from an existing OS and not performing an upgrade is the same as installing from media. Instead of the first phase of the installation occurring from within the media's Windows PE 2.0 environment, it occurs within the current OS. There is one side effect, however. The partition on which you want to install Windows Server 2008 must exist because you cannot manipulate partitions from within the setup routine (as you could when booted from the 2008 media in the Windows PE 2.0 environment). Create the partition prior to running 2008 setup from the Disk Management snap-in, which is available via the Storage section of the Computer Management MMC snap-in:

1. When performing the installation, the first screen is the Install Windows dialog, as shown in Figure 3-20, which is the dialog after you selected the language from the Windows media boot.

However, the language selection and keyboard layout information isn't necessary because the existing OS is interrogated for them. Also, notice that you don't have the option to repair the computer because you are not booted from the Windows PE environment. Therefore, you can't launch the recovery environment or other recovery tools.

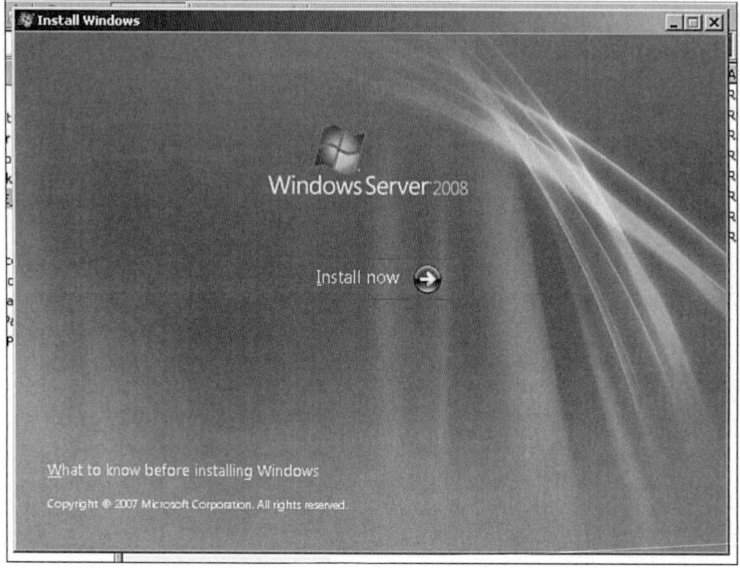

FIGURE 3-20 Install Windows screen.

2. After clicking Install Now, the installation process is the same as installing from media except that you get one additional installation option. Because you are running the first phase of installation from an existing OS with network connectivity, the setup routine gives you the option to go online and check for any updates, as shown in Figure 3-21. If updates exist, they are installed along with the Windows Server 2008 OS. These downloads are restricted to core updates, such as security updates and hardware drivers, plus the latest version of the Malicious Software Removal Tool. If you select to go online to check updates, an updates search occurs and installation then continues as normal.
3. When asked for the product key, select the OS version and accept the license agreement.

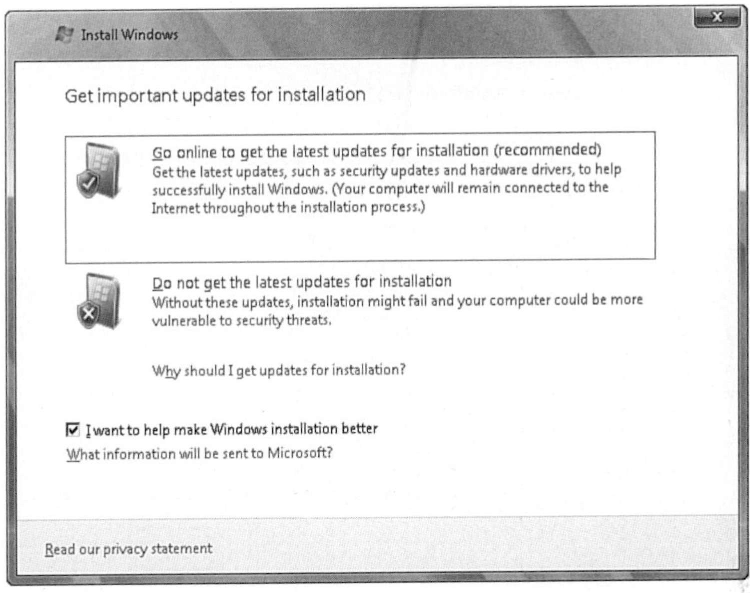

FIGURE 3-21 The option to go online and download updates and drivers is useful and might save you setup headaches.

4. You are prompted for the installation type. If you are running Windows Server 2003 SP1 or above with at least 512MB of memory, the prompt might include an option to upgrade. For now, select the Custom (Advanced) option because you want a new installation of 2008, the same as when you booted from the distribution media.
5. The partitions list displays, but there is a difference now. When you are running installation from within an OS, you cannot make any modifications to the partitions as discussed earlier; you can only use an existing partition. If you forgot, don't worry—start the Computer Management MMC snap-in while Setup is still running and create the partition via the Disk Management component and format it as NTFS. Then switch back to the setup routine and click the Refresh link. This forces the setup routine to recheck the disks available. It sees your new partition and allows you to select it as an install target, as shown in Figure 3-22.

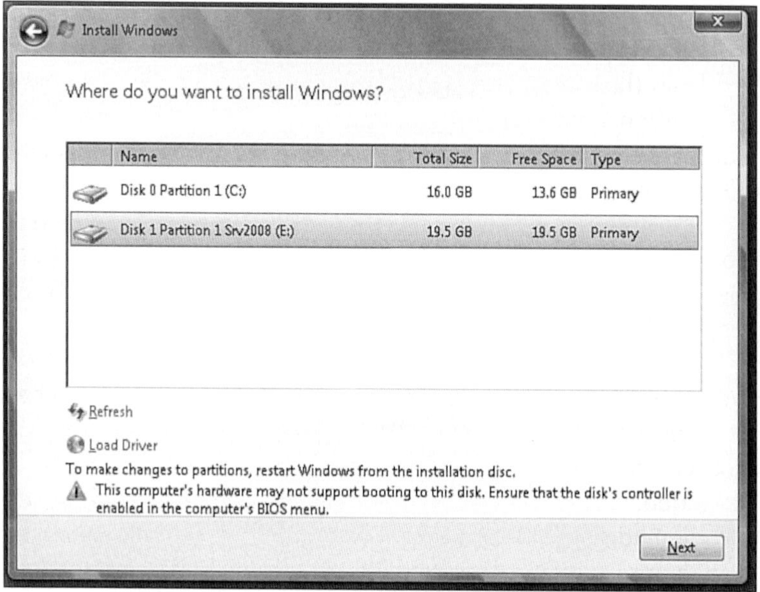

FIGURE 3-22 Selecting the target partition for Windows Server 2008 installation.

The setup routine lets you select the partition that contains the existing OS. Remember you did not choose to perform an upgrade; you are performing a clean install. If you select a partition that has an existing Windows installation, any conflicting folders such as Windows and Program Files move to a Windows.old folder, and the old OS becomes unusable. If the existing folder does not conflict, it does not move. For example, if Windows was previously installed to the WINNT folder, that folder is not moved.

6. The setup routine continues the same as for a normal install from media and reboots after the PE environment has been expanded on the file system and the install.wim from the media is copied to the local disk drive. The rest of the installation is the same as installing from media, including the execution of the Initial Configuration Tasks after the Administrator password is set.

Upgrading to Windows Server 2008

Generally, an in-place upgrade is not a good idea when a possible major OS upgrade accompanies a server hardware refresh such that Windows

Server 2008 is installed on the new server hardware. After the new OS installation on the new hardware is complete, the services can be migrated from the old server to the new. The best practice and industry recommendation is a fresh installation. In the case of an existing server, this includes a wipe and load: Wipe away the existing OS and then load the new OS. An upgrade is messy; however, it is possible in certain scenarios.

An upgrade is supported from Windows Server 2003 SP1 and above for the same architecture. For example, you can go from 32-bit Windows Server 2003 SP1 to 32-bit Windows Server 2008 but not to 64-bit Windows Server 2008.

The upgrade process for Windows Server 2008 is much the same as for Windows Vista: the OS components first and then everything else. The OS is replaced with Windows Server 2008, any additional features from the source are identified, the Windows Server 2008 equivalent role or feature is added, and all configuration migrates. The "everything else" can be problematic and limits the systems that can be upgraded in place. Few server applications and services support an in-place upgrade. For example, if you have a 64-bit Windows Server 2003 box running Exchange 2007, an in-place upgrade to 64-bit Windows Server 2008 is not supported. That is not to say it won't work, but Microsoft will not support it. Check any software installed on a server to ensure that an upgrade is supported.

As with any normal installation, check compatibility with all the software running on the server. For example, is the antivirus software compatible with Server 2008? The backup agent? And so on for all your software.

NOTE There is one other consideration when upgrading: If the server is a domain controller, you cannot upgrade the domain controller to Windows Server 2008 until the domain and forest have been prepared with the Windows Server 2008 adprep process. (Chapters 10, 11, and 12 cover this topic.)

On the plus side, when you run the Windows Server 2008 installation from within a 2003 SP1 OS, if an in-place upgrade is not possible, the Upgrade Wizard displays the reason. For example, it notifies you that the domain has not been updated to support 2008 domain controllers if you try to upgrade a domain controller and the upgrade process runs a compatibility check. Let's walk through an upgrade.

An upgrade has to initiate from within the OS being upgraded. This allows the install process to better capture user and machine state data and perform checks on the OS suitability for an upgrade.

After the installation process has been initiated and the normal stages of entering a product key, accepting the End User License Agreement, and checking for updates online have all been completed, the type of installation is requested. So far in this chapter you have always selected Custom (Advanced), not an upgrade. This time, select Upgrade, which launches a compatibility check of the installation process. The check looks for items that flat-out stop the system from functioning if it upgrades and, therefore, stop the install process, as shown in Figure 3-23. It also identifies items that might have issues after upgrade and require attention, as shown in Figure 3-24. If you receive a critical problem that stops installation, perform the advisory steps in the compatibility report and rerun installation. (For example, uninstall a troublesome piece of software.)

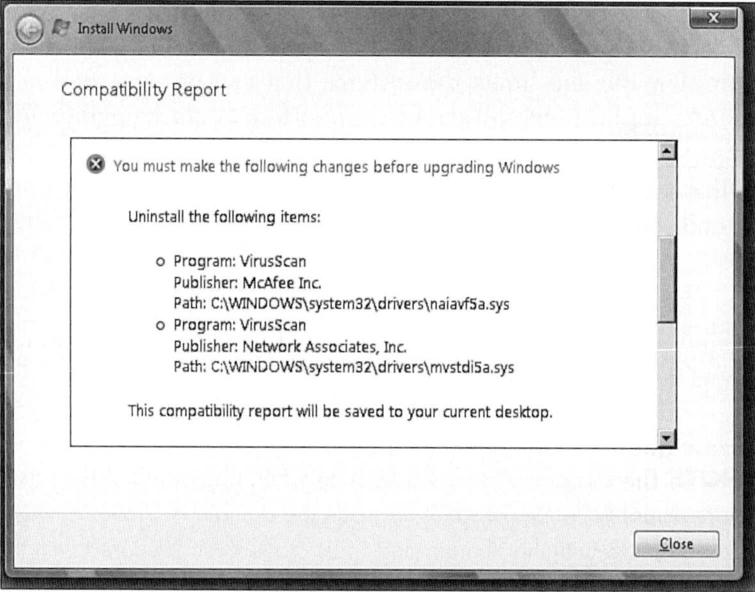

FIGURE 3-23 In this case, the antivirus software installed on the Windows Server 2003 installation stops Windows Server 2008 from functioning, so you cannot upgrade.

A full compatibility report is saved to the desktop for viewing outside of the Installation Wizard. You can share this report with others in the organization, use it as an action plan, or just file it away for reference. If performing an upgrade, keep the compatibility report for your records and check it again after the upgrade completes to verify that all actions occurred. Printing the report is ideal.

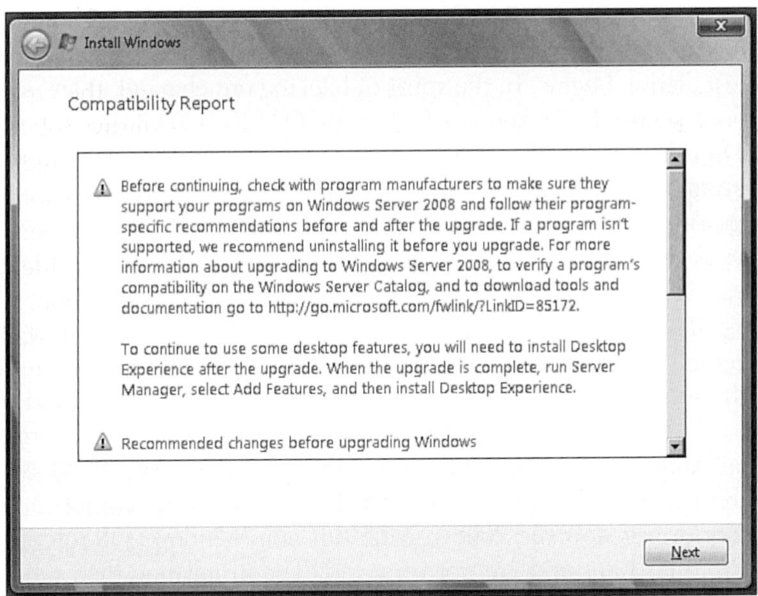

Figure 3-24 This is a nicer compatibility report. You have some recommendations, which are generic, and you can continue with the upgrade.

Assuming that the compatibility check passes and installation can continue, the install process begins its detail analysis of the current OS and puts in numerous safeguards so that, even in the worse case, you won't end up with a dead server. Because you are upgrading, you are not asked the same questions as a normal installation.

In the down-level phase of installation, which happens in the existing (previous) OS, the installation process creates four new folders:

- **$UPGRADE.~OS**. Contains information required from the OS being upgraded around drivers and stores of migration information
- **$WINDOWS.~BT**. Contains the content of the boot.wim from the 2008 media, which is the Windows PE 2.0 environment used to reboot the server
- **$WINDOWS.~LS**. Contains the install.wim from the 2008 media, which contains the Windows Server 2008 OS and any updates that were downloaded from the Internet during the initial part of the upgrade process
- **Boot**. Contains the new boot configuration environment used by Vista and Windows Server 2008

The system then reboots from the $WINDOWS.~BT folder via a modified boot sector, and the Windows Preinstall Environment (PE) phase of installation begins. In the spirit of backing out changes at any stage, the old boot sector is backed up to the BOOTSECT.BAK file for safekeeping. There are also other files created at the root of the file system, including `$DRVLTR$`, which contains the drive letter for the system in addition to empty files that help identify the partitions such as the boot drive (`$bootdrive$`), migration drive (`$drvmig$`), `$dwnlvldrive$`, `$lsdrive$`, and `$installdrive$`.

The bulk of the upgrade work happens during this boot. This is the actual laying down of the Windows Server 2008 environment, but first the entire Windows Server 2003 environment is backed up to the $WINDOWS.~Q folder. The Windows Server 2008 environment is then laid down on the disk. At the end of the PE phase, the Windows folder and the Program Files folder contain the 2008 versions; for example, Internet Explorer is now the 2008 version but non-Windows OS folders are still in Program Files and are not removed. The installation then reboots into the 2008 environment, the upgrade completes, and any additional roles and features are installed and configured.

Advanced Installation

Although it would be great if all installations went smoothly, in reality, you will hit hiccups during installations. With Windows PE facilitating one cool feature of the installation, it's possible to bring up a command prompt that runs with full system privileges at any stage during the installation (when in the Windows PE phases). This feature allows you to inspect the environment as the installation is taking place to help troubleshoot and potentially resolve problems.

To open the command prompt, press Shift and F10 simultaneously. While the command prompt is open, the installation does not reboot the computer, giving you as much time as necessary to troubleshoot.

As shown in Figure 3-25, the command prompt runs and has full interaction with the environment. In this example, I used DISKPART to create a 20GB partition and then refreshed the Install Windows Wizard, which could then see this new partition as available for Windows installation. By default, you start on the X drive. What is the X drive? The Windows PE environment that expanded from the boot.wim on the 2008 media is loaded into a RAM drive at boot time. It receives the X drive letter to avoid conflicting with any local drive letters.

From within this command prompt, you can run any commands normally associated with PE such as disk partitioning and WDSCapture, which captures an installed environment. Chapter 20 looks at many of these utilities. Remember to close the command prompt when you are finished, or the installation will not continue because the install cannot reboot.

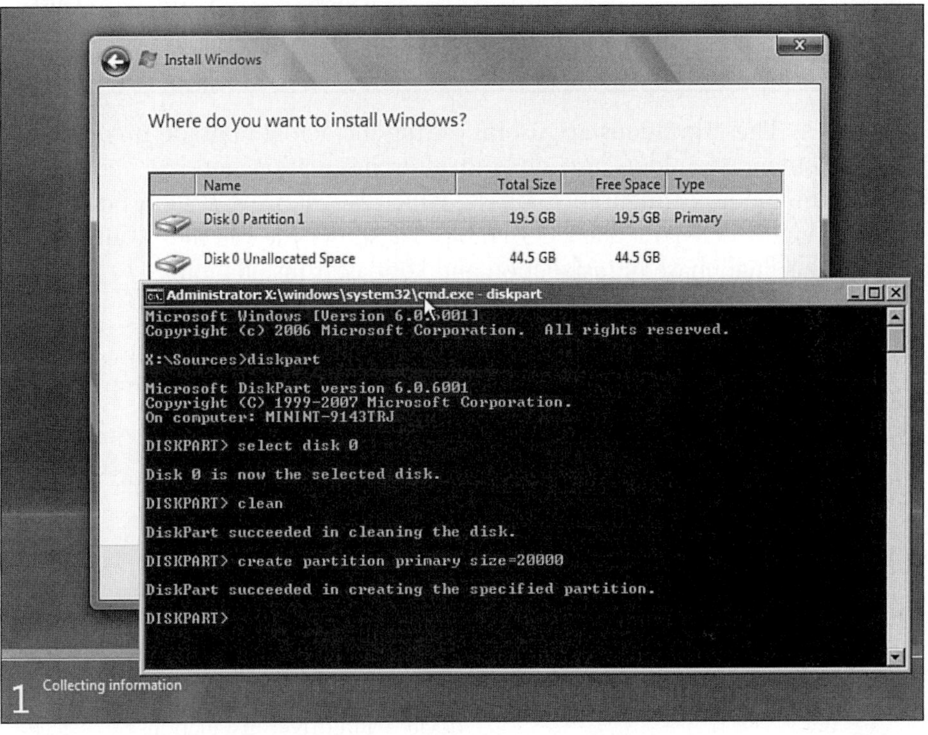

Figure 3-25 Notice that the default drive letter is X.

Viewing Installation Log Files

What do you do when there are installation problems? One useful item is to look at the log files generated by setup. There are *lots* of them, and they vary based on the stage of the installation.

If you are performing an in-place upgrade, the down-level phase of the installation generates the log files, as shown in Table 3-1. If you are performing a clean installation, the same log files are created; however, they may be created on the Windows PE RAM drive (X) instead of the C: drive.

Table 3-1 Log Files

C:\$WINDOWS.~BT\Sources\Panther\setupact.log	Contains information about setup actions during the installation.
C:\$WINDOWS.~BT\Sources\Panther\setuperr.log	Contains information about setup errors during the installation.
C:\$WINDOWS.~BT\Sources\Panther\miglog.xml	Contains information about the user directory structure. This information includes security identifiers (SIDs).

These locations are useful during the actual upgrade process, but the temporary folders are deleted after installation and are moved during the online configuration phase, which is when the system boots into the Windows Server 2008 OS. Table 3-2 shows the log files available during this final phase of installation and kept after installation.

Table 3-2 Log files Available During Final Installation Phase

C:\WINDOWS\PANTHER\setupact.log	Contains information about setup actions during the installation.
C:\WINDOWS\PANTHER\setuperr.log	Contains information about setup errors during the installation. Hopefully, this file is empty.
C:\WINDOWS\PANTHER\miglog.xml	Contains information about the user directory structure. This information includes SIDs. If a fresh installation is performed, this file will not exist.
C:\WINDOWS\INF\setupapi.dev.log	Contains information about plug and play devices and driver installation.
C:\WINDOWS\INF\setupapi.app.log	Contains information about application installation which includes components of the OS and configuration.

The setupact.log file contains information about the setup and the phases. If the installation is new, the log file starts from phase 2, which is the PE portion of the installation. A sample section follows, presenting the initial information and the source of your installation. In the event of problems or if your installation does not complete as expected, check the logs for any errors or warnings.

```
2007-10-24 10:18:57, Info                  IBS
InstallWindows:Successfully loaded resource language [en-US]
2007-10-24 10:18:57, Info       [0x0601c1] IBS
InstallWindows:Install Path = X:\Sources
2007-10-24 10:18:57, Info       [0x0601c2] IBS
InstallWindows:Setup Phase = 2
2007-10-24 10:18:57, Info       [0x0601e9] IBS
CheckWinPEVersion:Compatible WinPE Version 6.0.6001 sp 1.0
2007-10-24 10:18:57, Info       [0x0601c9] IBS
InstallWindows:Starting a new install from WinPE
2007-10-24 10:18:57, Info                  IBS
InstallWindows: Setup working directory = X:\windows\panther
2007-10-24 10:18:57, Info       [0x0601ce] IBS
Setup has started phase 2 at 2007-10-24 10:18:57
2007-10-24 10:18:57, Info       [0x0601cf] IBS
Install source is X:\Sources
```

Automating Installation

You can also automate locally, although the best automation is via the Windows Deployment Services (WDS) environment, which can stream the 2008 OS over the network and pass the information required for automation via an answer file. Chapter 16 covers this topic in detail.

The simplest way to initiate installation from another OS or PE is to pass an unattended install answer file to the `setup` command. For example, insert the 2008 media and, from the command prompt, run this command:

```
Setup /unattend:<path to unattend file>\unattend.xml
```

Use the Windows Automated Installation Kit (version 1.1 and above has 2008 support) to create an answer file for automating Windows Server 2008 installation. See Chapter 16 for more information.

An alternative is to create the answer file and pass that to a media-based installation by naming the answer file autounattend.xml and placing it on a floppy disk or USB drive that you insert as the 2008 install process starts. This answer file is read and automates the installation. Like a deployment from WDS, there are minimum requirements to automate the installation. These include setting the language and keyboard layout options, partitioning the disk, selecting the install partition target, and the actual selection of the OS. Figure 3-26 is a sample file that performs an automated installation of Windows Server 2008, Enterprise edition. You can save this as autounattend.xml to a floppy or USB. Update the product key.

The important part of this autounattend.xml file that differs from Windows Vista is the OS selection. With Windows Vista, the product key defines the version to install. But with Windows Server 2008, for any version, there are two flavors: the full install and the core install. Specify which version to install by using the InstallFrom section of the ImageInstall - OSImage part of the Windows Setup component in the answer file, as shown in Figure 3-26.

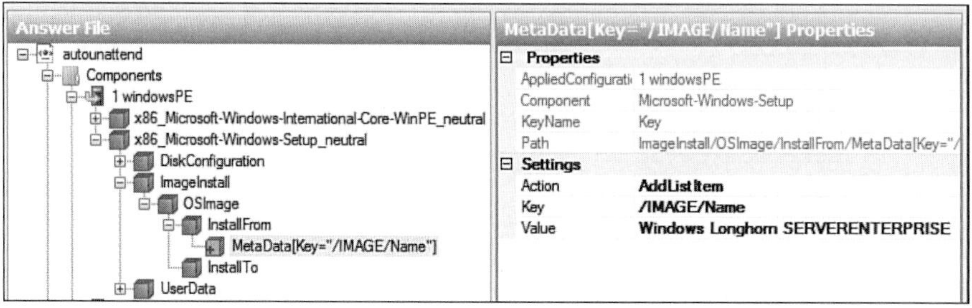

FIGURE 3-26 This autounattend.xml file installs the full version of Windows Server 2008 Enterprise.

The key to use is /IMAGE/Name, the value is the name of the OS (which is "Windows Longhorn SERVER"), and the SKU (for example, for Enterprise, "Windows Longhorn SERVERENTERPRISE"). If you wanted the core version, for example, add this to the end: "Windows Longhorn SERVERENTERPRISECORE". (This data comes directly from the WIM file header.) Instead of /IMAGE/Name, you could also use the index of the WIM image or the description:

```
  <?xml version="1.0" encoding="utf-8" ?>
- <unattend xmlns="urn:schemas-microsoft-com:unattend">
- <settings pass="windowsPE">
- <component name="Microsoft-Windows-International-Core-WinPE"
processorArchitecture="x86" publicKeyToken="31bf3856ad364e35"
language="neutral" versionScope="nonSxS"
xmlns:wcm="http://schemas.microsoft.com/WMIConfig/2002/State"
xmlns:xsi="http://www.w3.org/2001/XMLSchema-instance">
- <SetupUILanguage>
  <UILanguage>en-US</UILanguage>
  </SetupUILanguage>
  <UILanguage>en-US</UILanguage>
```

```
  <InputLocale>0409:00000409</InputLocale>
  <SystemLocale>en-US</SystemLocale>
  <UserLocale>en-US</UserLocale>
  <UILanguageFallback>en-US</UILanguageFallback>
  </component>
- <component name="Microsoft-Windows-Setup"
processorArchitecture="x86" publicKeyToken="31bf3856ad364e35"
language="neutral" versionScope="nonSxS"
xmlns:wcm="http://schemas.microsoft.com/WMIConfig/2002/State"
xmlns:xsi="http://www.w3.org/2001/XMLSchema-instance">
- <UserData>
- <ProductKey>
  <Key>XXXXX-XXXXX-XXXXX-XXXXX-XXXXX</Key>
  <WillShowUI>OnError</WillShowUI>
  </ProductKey>
  <AcceptEula>true</AcceptEula>
  </UserData>
- <ImageInstall>
- <OSImage>
- <InstallTo>
  <DiskID>0</DiskID>
  <PartitionID>1</PartitionID>
  </InstallTo>
  <InstallFrom>
- <MetaData wcm:action="add">
  <Key>/IMAGE/Name</Key>
  <Value>Windows Longhorn SERVERENTERPRISE</Value>
  </MetaData>
  </InstallFrom>
  </OSImage>
  </ImageInstall>
- <DiskConfiguration>
- <Disk wcm:action="add">
- <CreatePartitions>
- <CreatePartition wcm:action="add">
  <Order>1</Order>
  <Size>40000</Size>
  <Type>Primary</Type>
  </CreatePartition>
  </CreatePartitions>
- <ModifyPartitions>
- <ModifyPartition wcm:action="add">
  <PartitionID>1</PartitionID>
  <Order>1</Order>
  <Letter>C</Letter>
```

```
  <Format>NTFS</Format>
  <Extend>false</Extend>
  </ModifyPartition>
  </ModifyPartitions>
  <DiskID>0</DiskID>
  <WillWipeDisk>true</WillWipeDisk>
  </Disk>
  </DiskConfiguration>
  </component>
  </settings>
- <settings pass="oobeSystem">
- <component name="Microsoft-Windows-International-Core"
processorArchitecture="x86" publicKeyToken="31bf3856ad364e35"
language="neutral" versionScope="nonSxS"
xmlns:wcm="http://schemas.microsoft.com/WMIConfig/2002/State"
xmlns:xsi="http://www.w3.org/2001/XMLSchema-instance">
  <UserLocale>en-US</UserLocale>
  <UILanguage>en-US</UILanguage>
  <SystemLocale>en-US</SystemLocale>
  <InputLocale>en-US</InputLocale>
  </component>
- <component name="Microsoft-Windows-Shell-Setup"
processorArchitecture="x86" publicKeyToken="31bf3856ad364e35"
language="neutral" versionScope="nonSxS"
xmlns:wcm="http://schemas.microsoft.com/WMIConfig/2002/State"
xmlns:xsi="http://www.w3.org/2001/XMLSchema-instance">
- <OOBE>
  <HideEULAPage>true</HideEULAPage>
  </OOBE>
- <UserAccounts>
- <AdministratorPassword>

<Value>UABhADUANQB3AG8AcgBkAEEAZABtAGkAbgBpAHMAdAByAGEAdABvAHIA
UABhAHMAcwB3AG8AcgBkAA==</Value>
  <PlainText>false</PlainText>
  </AdministratorPassword>
  </UserAccounts>
  </component>
  </settings>
- <settings pass="specialize">
- <component name="Microsoft-Windows-Shell-Setup"
processorArchitecture="x86" publicKeyToken="31bf3856ad364e35"
```

```
language="neutral" versionScope="nonSxS"
xmlns:wcm="http://schemas.microsoft.com/WMIConfig/2002/State"
xmlns:xsi="http://www.w3.org/2001/XMLSchema-instance">
  <ProductKey>XXXXX-XXXXX-XXXXX-XXXXX-XXXXX</ProductKey>
  <RegisteredOrganization>SavillTech</RegisteredOrganization>
  <RegisteredOwner>SavillTech</RegisteredOwner>
  <ComputerName>*</ComputerName>
  </component>
  </settings>
  <cpi:offlineImage
cpi:source="wim:d:/os%20images/install.wim#Windows Longhorn
SERVERENTERPRISE" xmlns:cpi="urn:schemas-microsoft-com:cpi" />
  </unattend>
```

The unattend file is saved in the Windows\Panther folder, so it's easy to go back and check on any unattended options that were configured during an installation. The answer file has any sensitive data, such as product key, domain passwords, and local administrator passwords removed.

Another option using a similar method is (when syspreping an installation for automated installation) placing an answer file in the image so that the Welcome Wizard portion, the OOBE, is automated. This is useful if you want to create your own images that can be deployed and self-configure without connecting to any network location or require administrator action. To do this, create the answer file and save as unattend.xml in the sysprep folder, which is `c:\windows\system32\sysprep`.

When executing the sysprep, ensure that you add the `/unattend:unattend.xml` switch. The full command looks like the following:

```
C:\windows\system32\sysprep\sysprep.exe /generalize /oobe
➥/shutdown /unattend:unattend.xml
```

When SYSPREP executes, the machine shuts down, as shown in Figure 3-27. The closed machine is imaged via WDS, the WDSCapture utility, or imagex. On restart, it configures automatically.

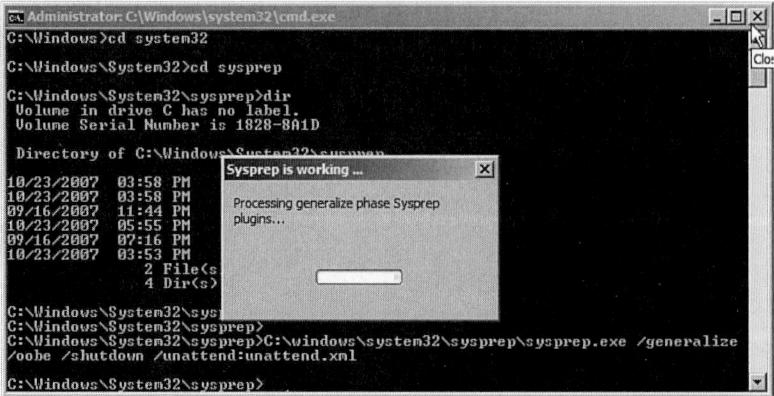

FIGURE 3-27 The SYSPREP process executing after being given an unattend answer file to use for the OOBE phase.

The following code is a bare minimum unattend.xml file that avoids the console being asked any questions. It sets the local Administrator password. In reality, you want this answer file to do more (for example, join a domain or set a time zone). The Windows Automated Installation Kit document details all the various values that can be in an unattended answer file.

```
  <?xml version="1.0" encoding="utf-8" ?>
- <unattend xmlns="urn:schemas-microsoft-com:unattend">
- <settings pass="oobeSystem">
- <component name="Microsoft-Windows-International-Core"
processorArchitecture="x86" publicKeyToken="31bf3856ad364e35"
language="neutral" versionScope="nonSxS"
xmlns:wcm="http://schemas.microsoft.com/WMIConfig/2002/State"
xmlns:xsi="http://www.w3.org/2001/XMLSchema-instance">
  <UserLocale>en-US</UserLocale>
  <UILanguage>en-US</UILanguage>
  <SystemLocale>en-US</SystemLocale>
  <InputLocale>en-US</InputLocale>
  </component>
- <component name="Microsoft-Windows-Shell-Setup"
processorArchitecture="x86" publicKeyToken="31bf3856ad364e35"
language="neutral" versionScope="nonSxS"
xmlns:wcm="http://schemas.microsoft.com/WMIConfig/2002/State"
xmlns:xsi="http://www.w3.org/2001/XMLSchema-instance">
- <OOBE>
  <HideEULAPage>true</HideEULAPage>
```

```
  </OOBE>
- <UserAccounts>
- <AdministratorPassword>

<Value>UABhADUANQB3AG8AcgBkAEEAZABtAGkAbgBpAHMAdAByAGEAdABvAHIA
UABhAHMAcwB3AG8AcgBkAA==</Value>
  <PlainText>false</PlainText>
  </AdministratorPassword>
  </UserAccounts>
  </component>
  </settings>
- <settings pass="specialize">
- <component name="Microsoft-Windows-Shell-Setup"
processorArchitecture="x86" publicKeyToken="31bf3856ad364e35"
language="neutral" versionScope="nonSxS"
xmlns:wcm="http://schemas.microsoft.com/WMIConfig/2002/State"
xmlns:xsi="http://www.w3.org/2001/XMLSchema-instance">
  <ProductKey>PUTYO-URKEY-INFIE-LDNO-TMINE</ProductKey>
  <RegisteredOrganization>SavillTech</RegisteredOrganization>
  <RegisteredOwner>SavillTech</RegisteredOwner>
  <ComputerName>*</ComputerName>
  </component>
  </settings>
  <cpi:offlineImage
cpi:source="wim:d:/os%20images/install.wim#Windows Longhorn
SERVERENTERPRISE" xmlns:cpi="urn:schemas-microsoft-com:cpi" />
  </unattend>
```

Summary

In this chapter, you learned how to perform a manual installation of Windows Server 2008. You also examined associated best practices, such as a fresh installation versus an upgrade, activation options, and where to install applications. Although you can manually configure Windows Server 2008, you saw how an unattended answer file can automate the process. This gives you a more consistent environment that is easier to maintain. If you have multiple servers to deploy, consider using WDS, which can also use unattended installation files, to enable installation over the network.

CHAPTER 4

Securing Your Windows Server 2008 Deployment

This chapter looks at the security aspects of Windows Server 2008, including making Windows Server 2008 a secure platform and the features that are available to secure the entire infrastructure.

One aspect of security that's often overlooked is the physical aspect. All the technological security in the world is worthless if servers are left in the middle of an office floor, where anyone can physically access them and perhaps even obtain passwords that are left on sticky notes on monitors. I thought that was a joke until an old company of mine was having an audit. On the last day of the audit, the auditor was leaving; all had gone well. He asked to use a phone to call a taxi to take him to the airport. He used a phone at one technology guy's desks. Thirty seconds later, he laughs and hands me a post-it note with two words: Password Ach1lle5. It didn't matter that it was a password for a lab virtual computer; the perception was we had poor process regarding security. Fortunately, the auditor had a sense of humor and after firing the IT guy and assuring the auditor that the IT admin and his family would be homeless within the week, he agreed to not write it up in his report. (Just a joke!)

Throughout this book, many key items are touched on that are considered big security gains in Windows Server 2008. (For example, Active Directory Rights Management Services [AD RMS], Active Directory Federated Services [AD FS], the new read-only domain controller functionality, improved control over device installation via group policy, Network Access Protection [NAP].) This chapter concentrates on items that are purely security-focused and do not fall into other technology areas.

TIP Keep your servers and desktops patched. Many attacks occur because a server has not been patched with an already available fix. Implementing a good patch deployment mechanism and process will help protect your infrastructure.

Authentication and Authorization

Before we look at the environmental factors affecting security, let's talk about authentication and authorization. What is the difference between the two?

Authentication

Authentication is proving you are who you say you are. There are three ways to do this. To authenticate a user, you can use any of the following:

- Something you know, such as a password
- Something you have, such as a passcard or secure ID token
- Something you are, such as a fingerprint or retina scan

The most common of these is a password. When you log on to your computer or access Amazon to buy the latest season of *The Simpsons*, you enter your e-mail address and password. This is generally considered sufficient for many situations. At my company, if my laptop is connected to the wired network, I need to enter only my username and password to get onto the domain. This is because, to get on the wired network, I have already entered through a secure physical door that requires a passcard (something I have). To gain access via the wired network, I have used two forms of authentication: something I need to get into the area and something I know to access resources. This is known as *two-factor authentication*. With two-factor authentication, two different forms of authentication are required. In my company, for example, to access resources from the Internet, I have to use my passcode (something I know) along with a token generated on my secureID keyfob (something I have). This would be considered a better form of two-factor authentication than the earlier example.

The appropriate authentication method depends on the environment and the sensitivity of the resources being accessed. In movies, you often see a card being slid across a scanner (something someone has) and then a retina scan, a thumbprint scan, a voice analyzer, or a breath analysis.

Numerous protocols are used to perform authentication on the secret information provided. (This subject is discussed later in this chapter, in the section "Authentication Protocols.")

Authorization

Authorization is the process of an authenticated person being authorized to access certain resources, such as permissions on a New Technology File System (NTFS) file. Authorization is commonly performed on resources where discretionary Access Control Lists (ACLs) are set to detail security principals that have rights and what those rights are. Commonly, these security principals would be users or groups. If the permission is set on a group to which a user belongs, when the user logs on, a token is generated that lists the individual's group memberships and is used when accessing resources.

There are various best practices in the industry; however, in the security world, even best practices are questioned. For example, one best practice is to rename the built-in administrator account so it's not such an obvious attack point; however, counterarguments say that this won't fool an experienced hacker, and the fact that the administrator accounts always have the same relative ID still creates an easy target. In general, renaming built-in accounts is still a good option and does give some increased protection; just don't consider it hacker proof.

Another best practice is to avoid using the built-in administrator account. Allowing multiple people to use such generic accounts makes it impossible to track who performed a change. Each user and administrator should have his own accounts that he uses to perform his job. The best practice used to be that each domain administrator had a normal user account and he would use Run As to use his domain admin account only when needed. With User Access Control, as you see later in this chapter, that happens automatically now.

The Physical Environment

In many ways, your computer security is only as good as the physical security protecting the physical servers. For example, you can lock down your domain controller with the best set of server-hardening and group policies, but if you place it in the lobby of a building, physical access is easy and increases the ability of a hacker to compromise the data by pulling out hard drives and attaching to other servers to gain access to data, such as file and directory databases that contain passwords.

You can take advantage of a number of advancements that help protect servers when you can't guarantee their physical security. Windows Server 2008 provides the new BitLocker technology, first released with Windows Vista, which allows you to encrypt the entire operating system (OS) partition. This is something you could not do before with the encrypted file system. You also have the new Read-Only Domain Controller (RODC) capability, which allows you to store passwords for only a limited set of users that reside in the location of the domain controller, based on group membership. When you use both RODC and BitLocker, you have a secure server that, even if it's physically compromised, contains limited information. This is especially useful for branch office environments that typically don't have a real server room and the associated physical security.

Pay close attention to the networking "doors" into your infrastructure, such as your connection to the Internet via an Internet service provider. You should have firewall protection and, for servers that need to offer services to the Internet, consider using a demilitarized zone (DMZ), where computers can exist and communicate with the Internet, and the DMZ is separated from the internal network by another firewall server.

NOTE This chapter doesn't discuss the full range of safety measures, including fire protections for servers and adequate air-conditioning, but those are vital elements when you plan a data center environment.

Your backups contain vital information for your enterprise; ensure that you have backups stored offsite in case of a building disaster. Also ensure that the service you use for offsite backups can return backups to you in a timely manner in case a restoration is needed. Depending on your business, implement disaster recovery plans to activate in the event of a building-level disaster. To create a disaster recovery site, plan for alternate office space, with servers that are ready to restore your backups and therefore need to match your hardware; this is a large expense. Several services provide disaster recovery capabilities, with a range of server types that are available to companies for a monthly fee. Of course, the more servers you virtualize, the easier it is to restore backups to other hardware because a virtual server is abstracted from the underlying hardware, and it can run on any type of physical server.

Discard your retired hardware—both servers and desktop machines—with care. There are numerous programs that perform multiple cycle writes to hard drives, removing their contents and stopping software that can restore data, even data that's overwritten by other data. Numerous tools can perform this secure disk wiping; for example, Microsoft provides the Cipher tool, which has the capability to securely obscure previous data on a disk by writing all 0s, then all 1s, and then a random sequence of numbers. For maximum security, run the Cipher tool multiple times. To use it, you format the disk first and then run Cipher with the drive letter, as in the following example:

```
Format <drive>: /fs:ntfs /v:wipeme /x
Cipher /w:<drive>:\
```

What about security for laptops? You have likely heard a story about a top-secret laptop that was left in the front seat of a car and was stolen. You can't control the facts that laptops will get stolen, and laptops will be left at security points at airports. But you can protect the content of your laptop, using the same technology as for protecting servers: BitLocker.

BitLocker

Windows Vista Enterprise and Ultimate editions and Windows Server 2008 (including Server Core installations) provide BitLocker drive encryption, which is used to encrypt the entire system boot volume. For Windows Server 2008 (and Vista with SP1 installed), data volumes can also be encrypted for offline protection. For Windows Vista, the technology is targeted at laptops; because the entire drive is encrypted and can be accessed only with the passkey, nothing on the drive will be accessible to a thief. For Windows Server 2008, use BitLocker on any server that you cannot physically secure. When a machine is running, however, BitLocker does not offer protection, so online protection technologies such as Encrypted File System and Rights Management should be employed.

When BitLocker is enabled, at machine boot time, a secret key is requested before the encrypted drive can be accessed. This secret key can be stored on a Universal Serial Bus (USB) key and/or in the form of a PIN. The drive is encrypted with a Full-Volume Encryption Key (FVEK), and without the key, nothing on the drive can be accessed. Therefore, protecting the FVEK is vital, and this is why a Trusted Platform Module (TPM) chip on the motherboard can be used to provide security services. On most computers, go into the BIOS to enable TPM. The FVEK can be unlocked in and of four ways:

- TPM only, with no user input required
- USB only, which means the USB device must be connected for boot to succeed and useful for computers without TPM support
- TPM with a 4- to 20-digit PIN
- TPM with a USB key

NOTE Why would you bother with the TPM-only mode with no user input or USB key required? What protection does that offer? The disks do not work unless they are in the server! If someone wants to steal data at a physical level, taking the disks out of the server is an easy way to bypass OS security; the thief can then install them as an additional drive in another computer, giving the most portability. Because disks are much smaller than a server, someone will notice you walking out of a building with a server under your shirt. If the disk doesn't have access to the TPM in the server, the disk is encrypted, and the data is unavailable, so the TPM-only option protects the disk from being removed from the server. This can work the other way, too: If you have a motherboard failure and you replace the motherboard, you have lost the TPM, and you need to use the recovery key.

With Bitlocker Drive Encryption, because the entire volume is encrypted, a second partition is needed to store the system information. This second partition contains the boot files needed for BitLocker to function and the FVEK in protected form. It's always the S: drive, and it must be marked as active and should be at least 1.5GB. For Windows Vista Ultimate and Enterprise, a utility is available to automatically set up the drive configuration (see http://support.microsoft.com/kb/930063). For Windows Server 2008, you currently need to configure the environment manually.

BitLocker works on only simple disks and NTFS partitions. The active partition also needs to contain the boot configuration database and the boot files and not the main bulk of the OS. This is why when you install Windows Server, it is a good idea to create a 1.5GB partition at the start of the disk and make it active. Then you can create additional partitions to install the actual bulk of the OS, as shown in Figure 4-1. This sets you up to easily add BitLocker in the future in addition to a locally installed Windows Recovery Environment (Windows RE) instance.

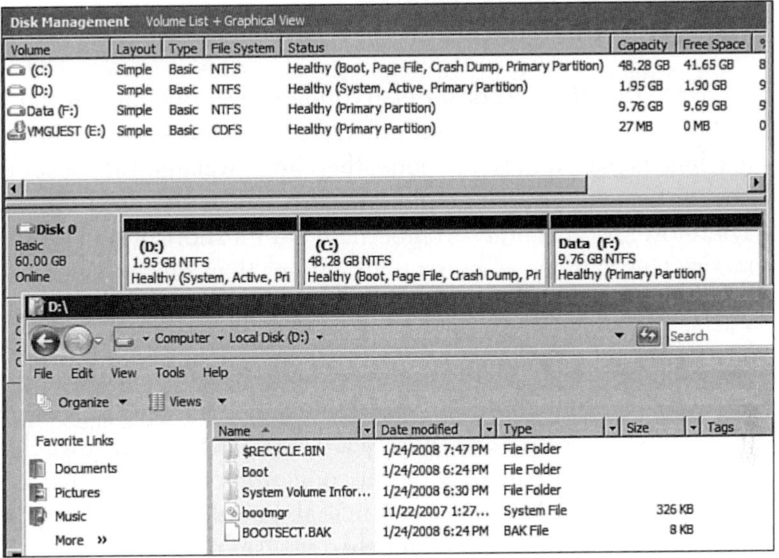

FIGURE 4-1 A typical disk configuration for BitLocker implementation.

The easiest way to create this disk configuration is during the Windows Server 2008 installation process. Before you perform the disk configuration via the graphical user interface (GUI), press Shift+F10 to open a command prompt window. From there, you can use `diskpart` to create partitions. The following commands clean disk 0 of all content, create an active S: partition of 1.5GB, create a C: partition using the remaining disk space, and format both partitions as NTFS. If you did not want C to use all space on the disk, add a `size=` option in the same manner as for the S: drive.

```
C:\>diskpart
Select disk 0
Clean
Create partition primary size=1500
Assign letter=S
Active
```

```
Create partition primary
Assign letter=C
Exit
C:\>format c: /y /q :fs:NTFS
C:\>format s: /y /q :fs:NTFS
C:\>exit
```

Note that the BitLocker encryption takes effect only if the machine is shut down (that is, powered off, either via shutdown or hibernate). If a machine is placed in sleep mode, then upon waking, BitLocker checking is not performed. (For example, no USB key is required for disk access.) Therefore, set machines to hibernate after a short period of time in sleep mode. This is more of an issue for laptops than for servers, but it is a consideration.

The configuration to enable the TPM needs to be done in the BIOS of the computer. The TPM Windows Management Instrumentation (WMI) interface provides some capability to enable elements of TPM, which are exposed with the `manage-bde.wsf` script via the `-tpm` switch. However, there is normally still BIOS-level configuration needed that is facilitated via a reboot. A TPM MMC snap-in is also available for aspects of the TPM management, and it can be launched via tsm.msc.

It is possible to configure BitLocker without a TPM. Doing so requires the use of a USB key for each computer boot, but this is an option for non-TPM-capable hardware. You can modify the computer's policy to enable non-TPM BitLocker, which you can do by editing the local computer policy or by setting a Group Policy Object (GPO) that is applied to the applicable servers. The setting is in the Computer Configuration, Administrative Templates, Windows Components, BitLocker Drive Encryption area, and you need to enable Control Panel Setup: Enable Advanced Startup Options and set the Allow BitLocker Without a Compatible TPM option, as shown in Figure 4-2.

BitLocker drive encryption is a feature in Windows Server 2008 that is not installed by default; add it via the Add Features Wizard, which you access via Server Manager. After you install it, restart the server. To install on the server core, use the `ocsetup` command, as in the following example:

```
Start /w ocsetup BitLocker
```

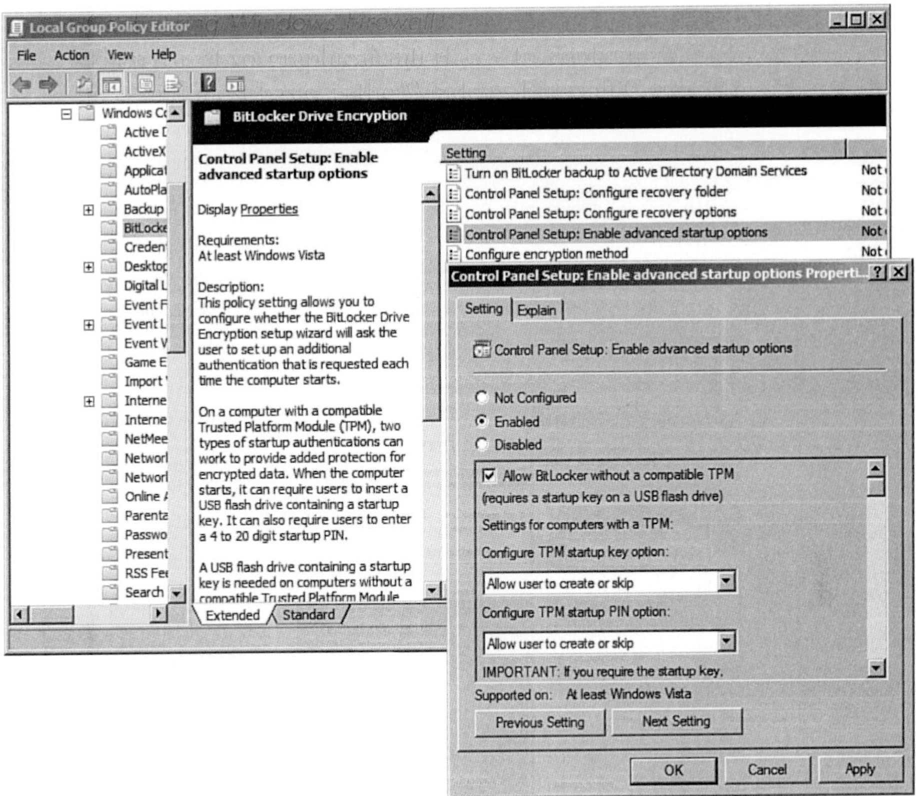

FIGURE 4-2 Enabling BitLocker without a TPM.

You can configure BitLocker in two ways: via the BitLocker Drive Encryption Control Panel applet, which is installed as part of the BitLocker feature installation, or via the manage-bde.wsf script that is also provided. To use the method, start the BitLocker Drive Encryption Control Panel applet, which shows that BitLocker is currently disabled for each drive. Then click the Turn on BitLocker link for the Windows volume, and when the confirmation dialog appears, click Continue with BitLocker Drive Encryption, as shown in Figure 4-3.

The list of options that can be used for BitLocker is then displayed (for example, Use BitLocker Without Additional Keys, Require PIN at Every Startup, and Require a USB Key at Every Startup, which is the only option if you don't have a TPM enabled in the server). If you are using a TPM that is not initialized, you are prompted to initialize the TPM security hardware via a wizard that requires a reboot of the server. If you selected a PIN, you are prompted for the PIN, and if you selected a USB key, you are prompted for a USB memory device, where the startup key will be saved.

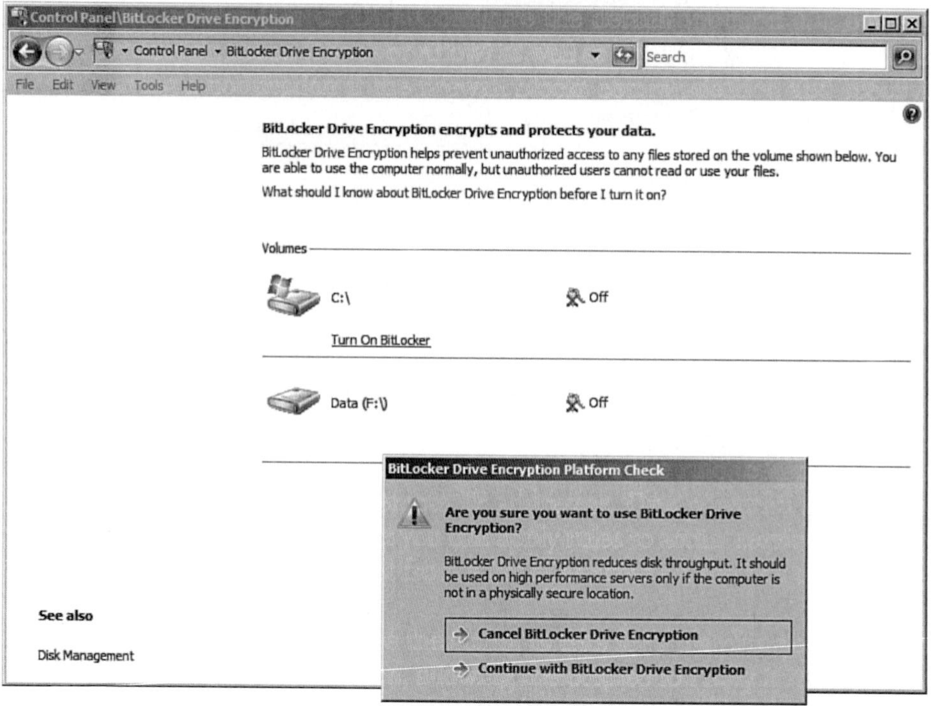

FIGURE 4-3 Performing the initial BitLocker configuration.

The next step involves how to store the recovery key, as shown in Figure 4-4. You can save the password to a USB key, save the password to a file, or just print the password and store it securely. After you save or print the password, the Next button is enabled, and you can configure encryption of the volume and a BitLocker system check, which will result in a reboot of the server and then encryption being in use (see Figure 4-5). To turn on BitLocker for other drives, select the option for the drive, and you are prompted for which recovery key storage to use. The startup key is the same as for the first drive encrypted, so there are no questions about whether a USB key or PIN is used, and a reboot is not required; the actual encryption process is shown onscreen and happens immediately.

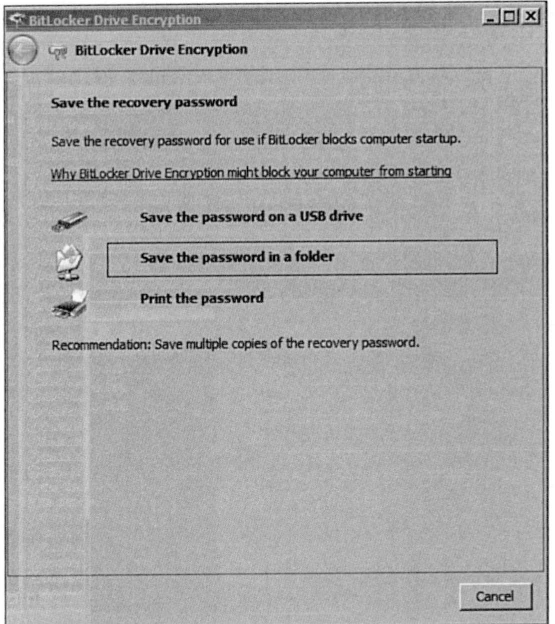

FIGURE 4-4 Selecting the location for the recovery password.

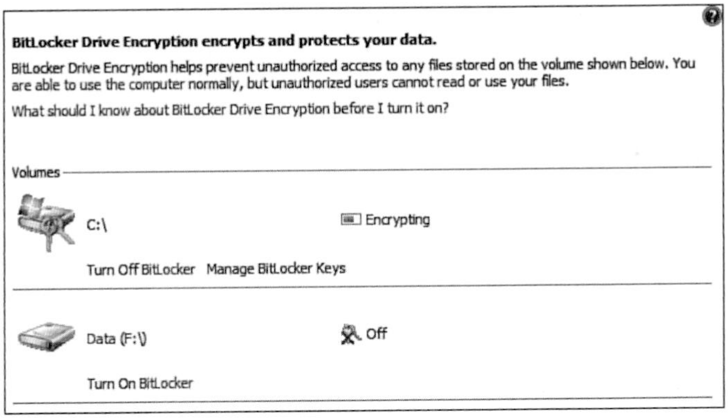

BitLocker Drive Encryption encrypts and protects your data.

BitLocker Drive Encryption helps prevent unauthorized access to any files stored on the volume shown below. You are able to use the computer normally, but unauthorized users cannot read or use your files.

What should I know about BitLocker Drive Encryption before I turn it on?

Volumes

C:\ Encrypting

Turn Off BitLocker Manage BitLocker Keys

Data (F:\) Off

Turn On BitLocker

FIGURE 4-5 The BitLocker state after reboot.

Instead of using the GUI, enable BitLocker from the command line. The manage-bde.wsf script has full BDE management capabilities, including enabling you to view the status of BitLocker on the system and view which drives can be encrypted with BitLocker.

```
C:\Users\Administrator>cscript
➥c:\windows\system32\manage-bde.wsf -status
Microsoft (R) Windows Script Host Version 5.7
Copyright (C) Microsoft Corporation. All rights reserved.

Disk volumes that can be protected with
BitLocker Drive Encryption:
Volume C: []
[OS Volume]

    Size:                 48.28 GB
    Conversion Status:    Fully Decrypted
    Percentage Encrypted: 0%
    Encryption Method:    None
    Protection Status:    Protection Off
    Lock Status:          Unlocked
    Key Protectors:       None Found

Volume F: [Data]
[Data Volume]

    Size:                 9.76 GB
    Conversion Status:    Fully Decrypted
    Percentage Encrypted: 0%
    Encryption Method:    None
    Protection Status:    Protection Off
    Lock Status:          Unlocked
    Automatic Unlock:     Disabled
    Key Protectors:       None Found
```

To perform the encryption, use the `-on` switch with the drive letter. You can then use various other options, such as `-rp`, which says to use a numeric recovery key that you print or save, and `-sk` to target a specific external device to contain the key (which needs to therefore be inserted at each reboot). Note that if you use the command line, you can use a floppy drive as a location for the BitLocker key, which is useful for virtual testing.

```
C:\>cscript c:\windows\system32\manage-bde.wsf -on C: -rp -sk f:
Microsoft (R) Windows Script Host Version 5.7
Copyright (C) Microsoft Corporation. All rights reserved.
```

```
Volume C:
[OS Volume]
Key Protectors Added:

    Recovery Key:
      ID: {25665FC0-A95E-4332-B341-F0E5B348E782}
      External Key File Name:
        25665FC0-A95E-4332-B341-F0E5B348E782.BEK

    Saved to directory f:

    Numerical Password:
      ID: {2867192F-70A3-4FFC-A7D3-7732FBA1A707}
      Password:
        576411-392634-161348-117491-324764-672672-286902-114169

ACTIONS REQUIRED:
    1. Save this numerical recovery password in a secure loca-
tion away from your computer:
    576411-392634-161348-117491-324764-672672-286902-114169
    To prevent data loss, save this password immediately. This
password helps ensure that you can unlock the encrypted volume.
    2. Insert a USB flash drive with an external key file into
the computer.
    3. Restart the computer to run a hardware test.
   (Type "shutdown /?" for command line instructions.)
    4. Type "manage-bde -status" to check if the hardware test
succeeded.
NOTE: Encryption will begin after the hardware test succeeds.
```

When the reboot is complete, the encryption starts, as with the GUI configuration.

One cool feature with the command-line interface is that you can pause the encryption if it's having a system performance (but this is uncommon on modern hardware) via the `-pause` switch with manage-bde.wsf, as in the following example:

```
c:\windows\system32\manage-bde.wsf -pause C:
```

To resume encryption, use the following:

```
c:\windows\system32\manage-bde.wsf -resume c:
```

BitLocker does have an integrity concern if you use a PIN or USB key to unlock the FVEK: If you lose the USB key or forget the PIN, because you won't be able to unlock the drive, the data you were trying to secure is now so secure you can't access it. Therefore, when you enable BitLocker, you can configure a recovery password as an emergency access control, and this recovery password should be kept in a secure location so it's not lost but also can't be easily accessed. As an alternative, you can store the recovery password in Active Directory (AD). (This process is documented on TechNet. Search http://technet.microsoft.com for "BitLocker drive encryption Active Directory back up.")

If you ever need to use the restoration password—for example, if you can't remember the PIN or if you lose the USB device—you are prompted to enter the recovery password automatically.

To decrypt a BitLocker-enabled drive, use the `-off` switch with the volume name. You have some options here. There are times when you need to disable the normal BitLocker process (for example, during a major upgrade, such as an in-place upgrade but not a normal service pack or hotfix application). Other situations, such as BIOS updates and TPM firmware and other component changes, might modify the boot environment and also require BitLocker to be disabled. Notice this is *disable* and not *decrypt*. When you decrypt, the entire drive is decrypted and is stored in clear form. When you *disable* BitLocker, the drive is left encrypted, but the BitLocker volume master key is encrypted with a clear key that is stored on the local drive in an unencrypted form, meaning access to the BitLocker encrypted drive is possible without any USB, PIN, or TPM help. This saves the time of decrypting and then encrypting again (which could take hours) after the changes but still relies on booting from the S: drive initially, which does not work for system upgrades, hence the need for certain scenarios requiring a decryption first.

To decrypt/disable, access the BitLocker Drive Encryption Control Panel applet and click the Turn Off BitLocker link. A dialog appears, giving you the option to disable or decrypt, as shown in Figure 4-6. If you disable and then want to enable again, just go back to the BitLocker Drive Encryption Control Panel applet and select the Turn On BitLocker link.

One snippet of information you may have heard about BitLocker is that its "unbreakable encryption" is vulnerable to a cold boot attack. A cold boot attack is nothing new; its use against BitLocker is just a new twist on an old technique, facilitated by the fact that when you turn off a computer, the volatile RAM keeps the information stored for between 2.5 and

30 seconds under normal circumstances and even minutes if you cool the RAM chips. This is mainly a problem for DRAM memory, which uses a capacitor for each bit. With a cold boot attack, a hacker powers off a computer and then boots it to a special program that copies the content of the memory to a USB key. Then the hacker can scan the dump of the memory for the old information and extract keys that are used for the disk encryption. There are some algorithms available that make finding the encryption keys among all the memory dumped quite easy.

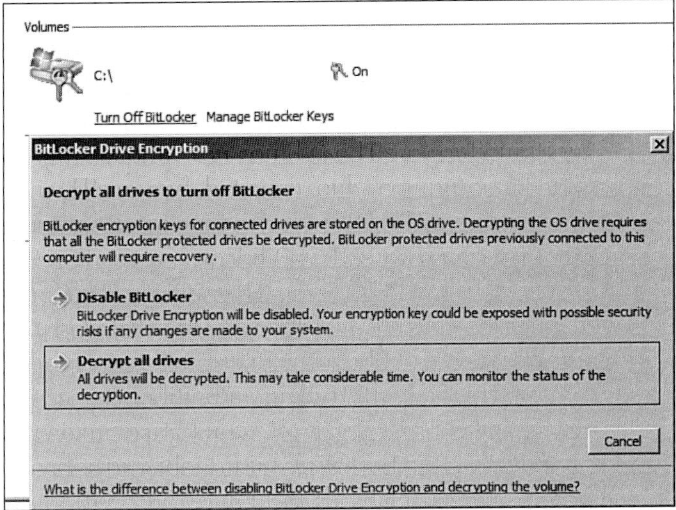

FIGURE 4-6 To turn off BitLocker, use Disable to avoid decrypting the entire drive.

To protect against cold boot attacks, exercise good physical security on your servers and disable booting from USB devices. These measures cannot stop an attack, but they make an attack harder to accomplish. If an attacker has the physical box, she can power it down, take out the RAM, and put it in another box (unless you solder the RAM to the motherboard). To protect against these attacks on laptops, power them off and do not leave them in sleep mode in public. The use of a TPM does not help because the TPM stores the key initially and then puts it in memory to do decryption.

You can see a video of cold boot attacks in action at www.hackaday.com/2008/02/21/breaking-disk-encryption-with-ram-dumps/, and you can find a full paper on these attacks at http://citp.princeton.edu/pub/coldboot.pdf.

Active Directory Certificate Services (ADCS)

Multiple places in this book speak of certificates, particularly regarding Secure Sockets Layer (SSL) and the encryption of data. You have seen a number of options, including self-signed certificates, which require extra steps on clients to use the certificates. At the other end of the scale, you can purchase certificates from Internet trusted certificate authorities (CAs), such as VeriSign and RapidSSL, which are trusted by all Internet clients but cost money. In the middle are domain certificates, which are issued by a CA that exists within your infrastructure. A domain certificate is a great solution for services that are used internally in an organization or only by clients who are part of the domain and so will trust the domain's CA.

When you make a server a CA, you cannot change its name or domain membership. You can't even promote or demote its domain controller status, so make sure your server is as needed from a configuration perspective before you install ADCS on it.

ADCS is a vast and complex topic. This section skims over the main concepts and walks through a few usage examples, but if you need to use ADCS within your organization, go to the Microsoft web site for great information and walkthroughs on public key infrastructure. ADCS help in Windows Server 2008 is also thorough.

Types of CAs

A CA is a core piece of ADCS that provides a number of services, including verifying the identity of a party requesting a certificate, issuing certificates to a verified requestor, and managing the revocation of certificates, where needed.

There are a number of different types of CA available:

- A root CA is the topmost CA in the CA hierarchy and is also the most important because the entire rest of the CA hierarchy is based around certificates issued by the root CA. A root CA certificate is self-issued, and there is always a root CA in the hierarchy. The root CA issues certificates to other CAs in the enterprise and optionally to users, computers, services, and so on, depending on the CA hierarchy. It is common for the root CA to be an offline CA, which means it is disconnected from the network and locked away somewhere safe after it has given certificates to subordinate CAs in the enterprise, and it is brought out only when its direct subordinate CAs need their certificates renewed.

- An intermediate CA is a CA that is subordinate to another CA—for example, subordinate to the root CA or even subordinate to a CA that is subordinate to the root CA. The structure of the CAs will depend on the size and needs of an organization. A special type of intermediate CA is known as a policy CA, and its only job is to issue certificates to other CAs.
- An issuing CA is a CA that issues certificates to users, computers, services, and network devices.

These three types of CA typically create a hierarchy of CA services, as shown in Figure 4-7. However, it would also be possible for an issuing CA to be subordinate to the root CA, but this is just not common if there are intermediate CAs.

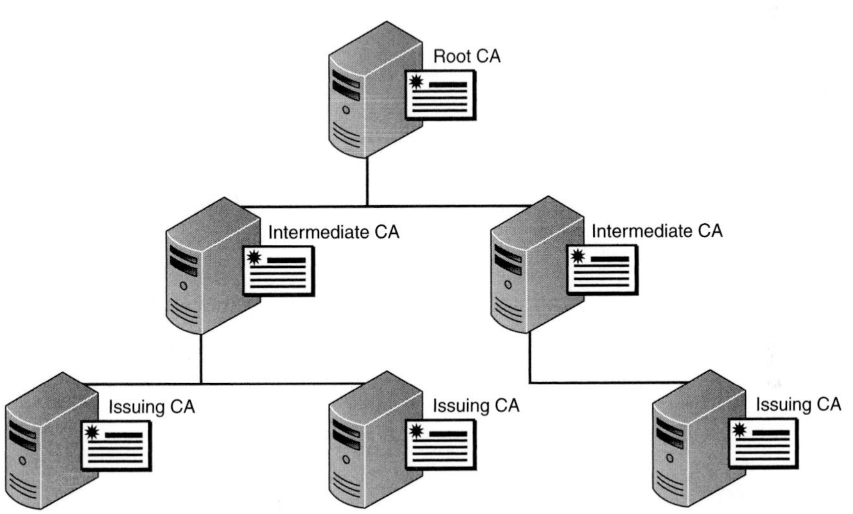

Figure 4-7 Typical CA hierarchy.

The reasons for having more than one CA of any type vary and can include geography of the infrastructure (for example, you may want local CAs at certain locations), load balancing, fault tolerance, and the usage type of certificates. (For example, you may want a CA to give out only certain types of certificate.)

In addition to the placement of a CA in the hierarchy, the Windows Server 2008 ADCS supports two types of CAs: enterprise and stand-alone CAs.

An enterprise CA must be part of a domain, and it uses group policy to distribute its certificate to the Trusted Root Certification Authorities certificate store for all users and computers in the domain; all users and computers in the domain will trust certificates issued by the enterprise CA. An enterprise CA also publishes user certificates and the Certificate Revocation List (CRL) to AD and can even publish to other domains, provided that the CA is a member of the other domains' Certificate Publishers group. Certificate templates can be used to facilitate the automatic issuing of certain types of certificate, which is useful in a domain environment.

A stand-alone CA does not use AD, and it requires more manual work (such as manual configuration of clients to trust the stand-alone CA because certificate templates cannot be used) and manual certificate request approval.

Consider your certificate needs and plan your CA hierarchy and the roles of each CA. It is common to make the root CA an offline stand-alone root so that after it issues certificates to the intermediate/issuing CAs, the root CA is removed from the network. Make the root CA stand-alone because you plan to remove it from the network, and if it were part of the domain, its computer account would expire when it was removed from the network, and that would cause problems. The intermediate and issuing CAs are enterprise CAs and take advantage of AD. In contrast, in a small environment with a few hundred users, you could have a single enterprise root CA that issues certificates to users and computers without any separate intermediate or issuing CAs.

Installing ADCS

Like everything else in Windows Server 2008, install ADCS via the Server Manager. And because ADCS is a primary function of a server, it is a role and not a feature. After you select the ADCS role, perform a number of configuration steps via the Add Roles Wizard.

ADCS includes a number of services. The core service is the CA, which is selected by default. There is also a CA Web enrollment page, which provides a handy way to requests certificates via a Web browser.

The Online Responder component of ADCS is an alternative to a CRL, and it contains a list of all revoked certificates. Online Responder performs a similar function to a CRL, but instead of publishing a list, it allows a client to query the status of a specific certificate, and then it responds with the status of the queried certificate. This has the advantage of requiring less data to be sent over the network; in addition, the company does not share all of its revoked or suspended certificates.

The Network Device Enrollment Service allows devices that do not have network accounts to request certificates.

Let's look at an example of enabling the CA and CA Web enrollment. The first configuration required is the type of CA to install, as described in the "Types of CAs" section. Say that you have a small organization that requires a single CA integrated into AD, which will be the root CA and issue certificates. You therefore need to select an enterprise CA instead of stand-alone. On the next screen, because this is the first CA server in the environment, select that this is a root CA.

The next screen asks if a new private key should be generated or if an existing one can be used. You can accept the default for ADCS to create a new private key. Next, you specify the cryptography to use for the new private key, as shown in Figure 4-8. The default options are fine for most environments. The strong private key feature sounds nice but requires a password to be entered each time the private key is used, which is anytime a cryptographic operation is performed, so unless this CA is going to be a nonissuing root CA that is effectively offline most of the time, you don't want to enable that option.

By default, the name for the CA is `<`*`domain name`*`>-<`*`server name`*`>-CA` (if it is part of a domain). This name is placed in all issued certificates. Modify it to something else if you want (for example, savilltech-CA) and leave the distinguished name suffix unmodified because that will be your domain name. You are prompted for the certificate validity, which is five years by default, and you may need to shorten this time based on the usage for the CA and the security in place to protect it. The shorter the time, the more secure it can be considered, but there may then be additional work during certificate renewal.

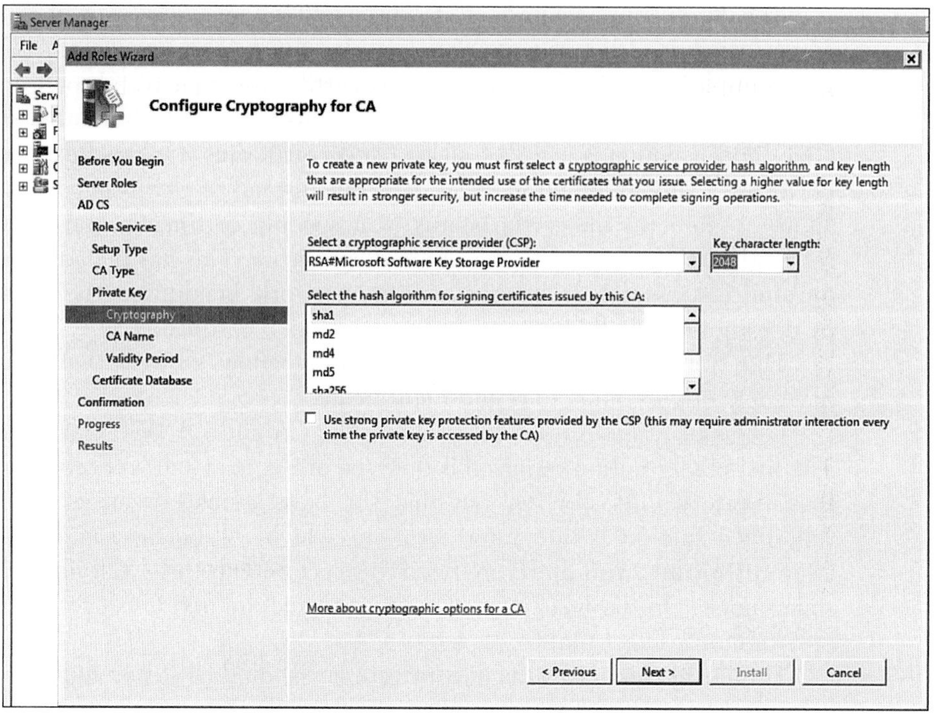

FIGURE 4-8 Configuring cryptography for the new private key.

Finally, the location for the certificate database and log files is requested; by default, it is %windir%\system32\CertLog. The best practice is to place the database files on one set of disks and the log files on a separate set of disks for high-availability purposes and to minimize any data loss due to disk failure. After you make all settings, click Install to perform the actual installation and enable ADCS in your domain.

Trusting Your New CA

After you install your new enterprise CA, the next step is to make all domain clients trust the new CA to avoid issues with the CA not being a trusted root. When you created the new CA, the certificate should have been published into AD, and an event should have been written by the CA into the Application event log (event ID 103), informing you of the steps to perform to verify and remediate if not present, as shown in the following example.

```
Log Name:      Application
Source:        Microsoft-Windows-CertificationAuthority
Date:          1/16/2008 4:15:20 PM
Event ID:      103
Task Category: None
Level:         Warning
Keywords:      Classic
User:          SYSTEM
Computer:      savdaldc01.savilltech.net
Description:
Active Directory Certificate Services added the root certificate
of certificate chain 0 to the downloaded Trusted Root Certifica-
tion Authorities Enterprise store on the CA computer. This
store will be updated from the Certification Authorities con-
tainer in Active Directory the next time Group Policy is
applied. To verify that the CA certificate is published cor-
rectly in Active Directory, run the following command:
certutil -viewstore "ldap:///CN=savilltech-CA,
CN=CertificationAuthorities,CN=Public KeyServices,CN=Services,
CN=Configuration,DC=savilltech,
DC=net?cACertificate?base?objectClass=certificationAuthority"
(You must include the quotation marks when you run this com-
mand). If the root CA certificate is not present, use the Cer-
tificates console on the root CA computer to export the
certificate to a file, and then run the following command to pub-
lish it to Active Directory: Certutil -dspublish %certificate-
filename% Root.
```

You see your root certificate now (see Figure 4-9). The actual certificate is pushed to members of the domain as part of group policy refresh.

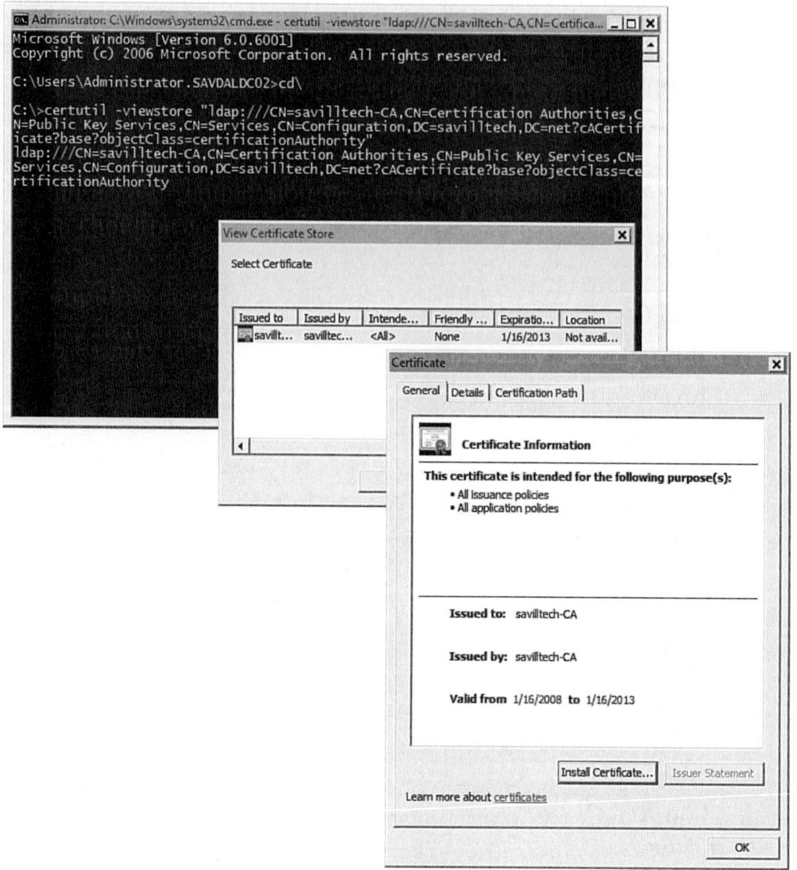

FIGURE 4-9 Verifying certificate publishing state in AD.

Managing ADCS

The ADCS area in Server Manager links to three snap-ins. The first, Enterprise PKI (PKIView), is a tool that was part of the Windows Server 2003 resource kit and is used to analyze the health of a CA, as shown in Figure 4-10. It is a good place to go to for an overview of the Enterprise PKI hierarchy and health.

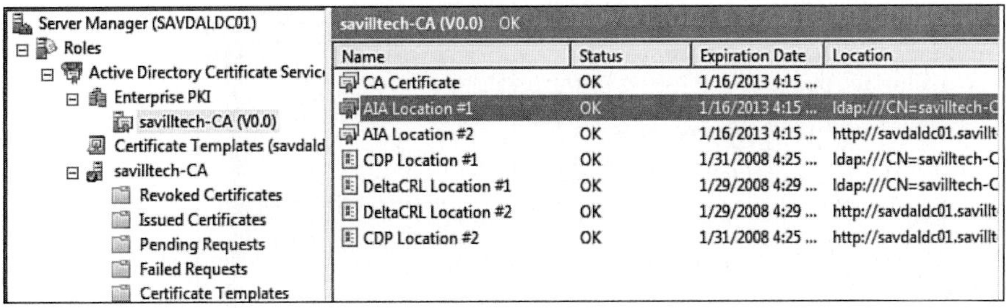

Server Manager (SAVDALDC01)
Roles
Active Directory Certificate Servic
Enterprise PKI
savilltech-CA (V0.0)
Certificate Templates (savdald
savilltech-CA
Revoked Certificates
Issued Certificates
Pending Requests
Failed Requests
Certificate Templates

savilltech-CA (V0.0) OK

Name	Status	Expiration Date	Location
CA Certificate	OK	1/16/2013 4:15 ...	
AIA Location #1	OK	1/16/2013 4:15 ...	ldap:///CN=savilltech-C
AIA Location #2	OK	1/16/2013 4:15 ...	http://savdaldc01.savillt
CDP Location #1	OK	1/31/2008 4:25 ...	ldap:///CN=savilltech-C
DeltaCRL Location #1	OK	1/29/2008 4:29 ...	ldap:///CN=savilltech-C
DeltaCRL Location #2	OK	1/29/2008 4:29 ...	http://savdaldc01.savillt
CDP Location #2	OK	1/31/2008 4:25 ...	http://savdaldc01.savillt

FIGURE 4-10 Viewing CA health with Enterprise PKI.

The second snap-in, Certificate Templates, displays all certificate templates configured on the selected server, which by default is the local server. The key item here is that these templates all perform certain functions and are configured around the format and content of a certificate. There are three versions of certificate templates:

- **Version 1**. Version 1 templates, created by default on a new CA, support many different types of certificate use and are supported by Windows 2000 and above.
- **Version 2**. Introduced with Windows Server 2003, Version 2 templates add features such as autoenrollment capabilities and allow customization of most settings in the template. They are supported on XP/2003 and above.
- **Version 3**. Introduced with Windows Server 2008, Version 3 templates allow the use of Suite B cryptographic settings, which offer advanced options for encryption, digital signatures, key exchange, and hashing. These templates are supported only on Windows Server 2008 and Windows Vista.

Convert preconfigured certificate templates to Version 2 or Version 3 templates by selecting the certificate template and selecting the Duplicate Template action, as shown in Figure 4-11. Selecting Windows 2003 Server creates a Version 2 certificate template and selecting 2008 creates a Version 3 certificate template.

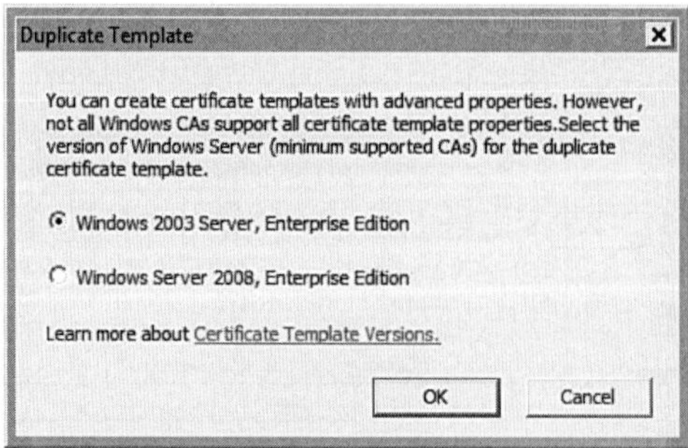

FIGURE 4-11 Turning a Version 1 certificate template into a Version 2 or Version 3 template.

Autoenrollment

Let's use a certificate template by configuring the Exchange Signature Only certificate template as autoenrolled so all users in the domain receive an Exchange Signature-style certificate:

1. Right-click the Exchange Signature Only template and select Duplicate Template from the context menu.
2. Enter a name for the new template on the General tab (for example, Exchange Signature Only Custom). As shown in Figure 4-12, do not enable publishing in AD for digital signatures; it is not needed for signatures because the certificate is enabled in the payload of the message sent. If you were creating a certificate for mail encryption, such as Exchange User, enable publishing to AD. This would result in the public certificate being placed in the user's `userCertificate` attribute. This public certificate for the user is queried via the global catalog by the sending party and will be visible under the Published Certificates tab for the user in the AD Users and Computer's MMC snap-in. Under Request Handling, set the Purpose to Encryption.
3. On the Request Handling tab, set the purpose to Signature. Select Enroll Subject Without Requiring Any User Input and check the Allow Private Key to Be Exported box. Optionally (if the option is not grayed out because it is applicable to the type of certificate you are duplicating), check Archive Subject's Encryption Private Key if you have archiving enabled. (If you don't have this configured on the CA and you check this option, it causes autoenrollment to fail. It is advisable to enable the key archived in case a private key is lost.)

4. On the Subject Name tab, set Build from This Active Directory Information, set Subject Name Format to Fully Distinguished Name, and check Include E-Mail Name in Subject Name.
5. On the Security tab, ensure that Read, Enroll, and Autoenroll are enabled for the users who will autoenroll (for example, Domain Users). Use any global or universal group here (not a domain local), as shown in Figure 4-13. Some companies have a process whereby users are added to a group if they require certain certificate autoenrollments, which then are processed on their next login or group policy refresh.
6. Click OK to create the new template.
7. Under Certificate Templates within the Certification Authority MMC snap-in, right-click and select New, Certificate Template to Issue. This important step tells the CA which type of certificate templates it can use to issue certificates to requestors.
8. Select a certificate you want to issue (for example, the new Exchange Signature Only Custom template, as shown in Figure 4-14) and click OK. (Certificates that are already being issued are not shown in the dialog box.) Ensure that you choose the copied template that you created and not the original. The base template supplied does not have autoenroll permitted; you have to use your customized copy.

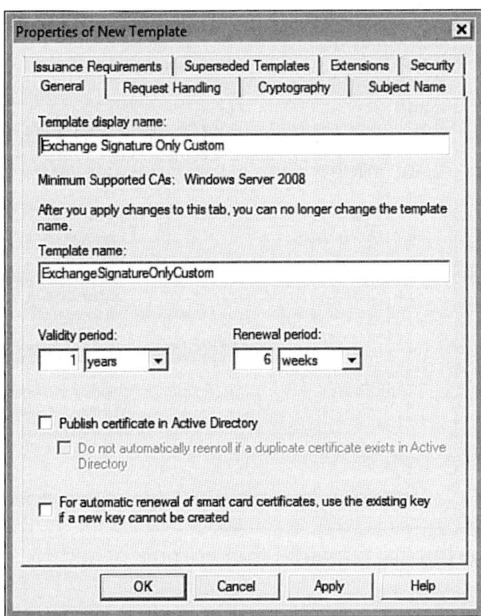

FIGURE 4-12 Configuring the General properties of the new certificate template.

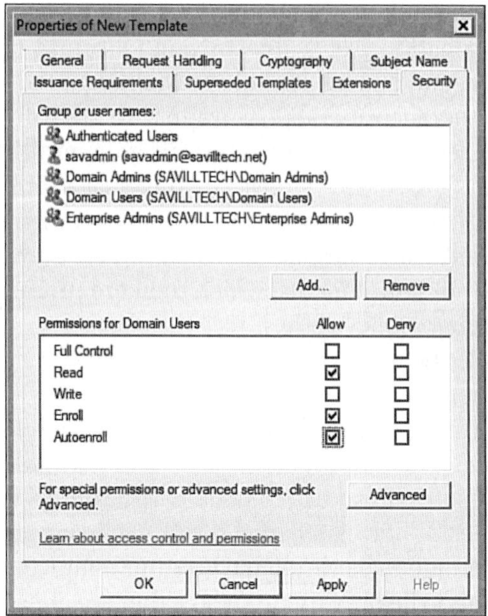

FIGURE 4-13 Configuring the Security properties of the new certificate template.

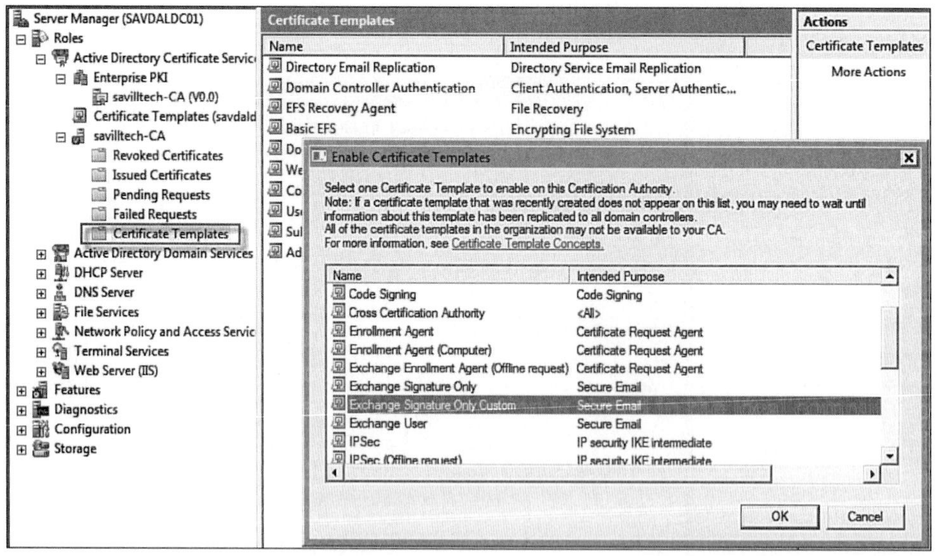

FIGURE 4-14 Adding a certificate template that can be issued by a server.

The new certificate template can now be issued by the CA, and with the security you configured, autoenrollment is permitted. The last step is to use group policy to configure autoenrollment. Open a GPO that is linked to the domain, site, or organizational unit (OU) that contains the users/computers that should participate in autoenrollment. Then navigate to Computer Configuration, Policies, Windows Settings, Security Settings, Public Key Policies and double-click Certificate Services Client, Autoenrollment. Set the policy to Enabled and also enable the boxes to automatically renew certificates and update certificates as well as to notify when a certificate reaches a certain percentage of its lifetime. Repeat this configuration on the user configuration, as shown in Figure 4-15.

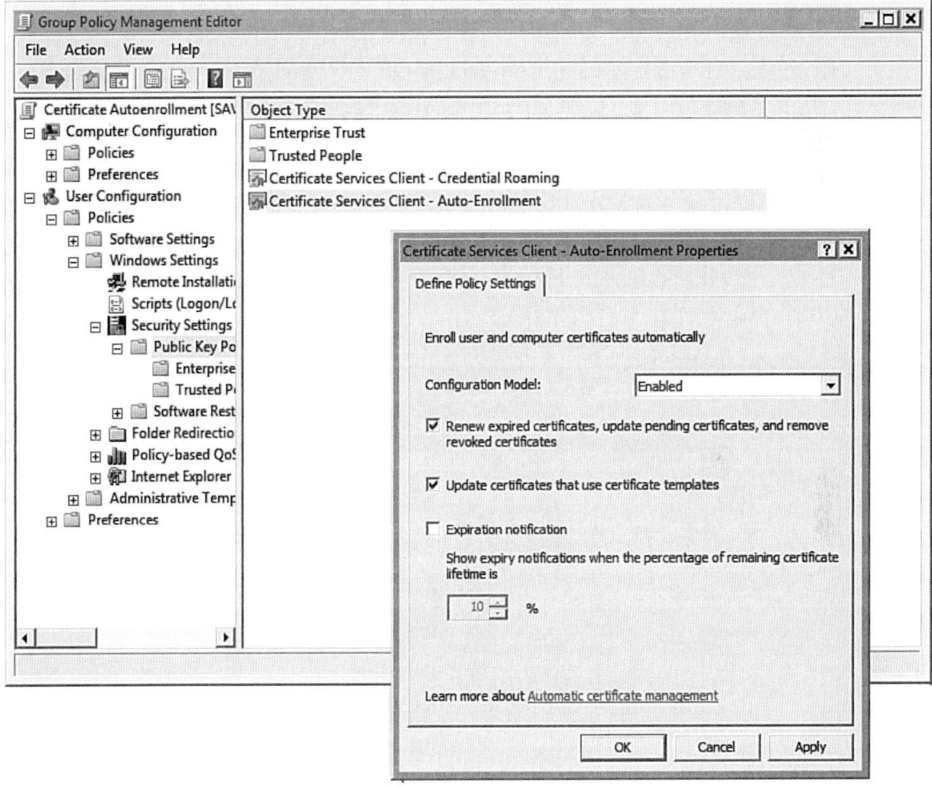

FIGURE 4-15 Enabling autoenrollment for users.

When the user or computer refreshes group policy via a logon/startup or via `gpupdate`, the new autoenrollment setting is read, and the user/computer checks for templates for which it can autoenroll. A log is written to the Application event log of ID 19, showing the autoenrollment event and failures write an event ID 13. The process of receiving a certificate may take up to 90 seconds.

You can view certificates via the Certificates MMC snap-in. If you are looking for a user-issued certificate, ensure that you select the user's certificate store when adding the snap-in to your MMC instance.

Manual Certificate Requests

More commonly than receiving certificates via autoenrollment, you receive them via manual requests, which can be done using the Certificates MMC snap-in or, if Web enrollment was installed on the CA, via the CA's Web page.

To use the Certificates MMC snap-in, select Request New Certificate from the All Tasks action item to launch the Certificate Enrollment screen. Click Next, and a list of the supported templates for the CA is displayed, as shown in Figure 4-16. Check the types of certificates you want to receive and click the Enroll button. The request is sent to the CA, and after a few seconds, you see a dialog that lists the certificate request as Succeeded. This hands-off approach is possible thanks to the integration with AD. If the certificate shows as Enrollment Pending, it must be manually approved on the CA.

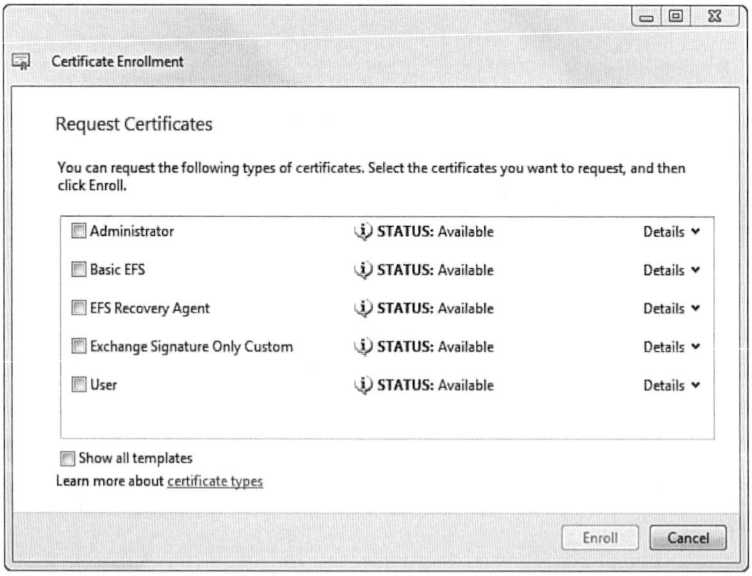

FIGURE 4-16 Requesting a new certificate.

You can also perform a more complex certificate request via All Tasks, Advanced Operations, Create Custom Request. This allows a similar set of functionality, but the request can be saved to a file for offline processing, which means it can be serviced by any CA and not just the enterprise CA.

Viewing Certificates on the CA

You can see the certificates that a CA has issued and revoked in addition to viewing the pending and failed requests via the main Certificates snap-in. The Failed Request node shows the reason for a certificate issuance failure (for example, insufficient information in the request to complete the certificate enrollment).

By default, an enterprise CA automatically issues certificates. However, you can modify this behavior via the Policy Module tab of the Properties dialog, as shown in Figure 4-17. You can configure all pending requests to be manually approved. This is not the best practice; you should instead configure manual authorization as part of the certificate template configuration under Issuance Requirements by enabling the CA Certificate Manager Approval option under the Issuance Requirements tab of the certificate template properties.

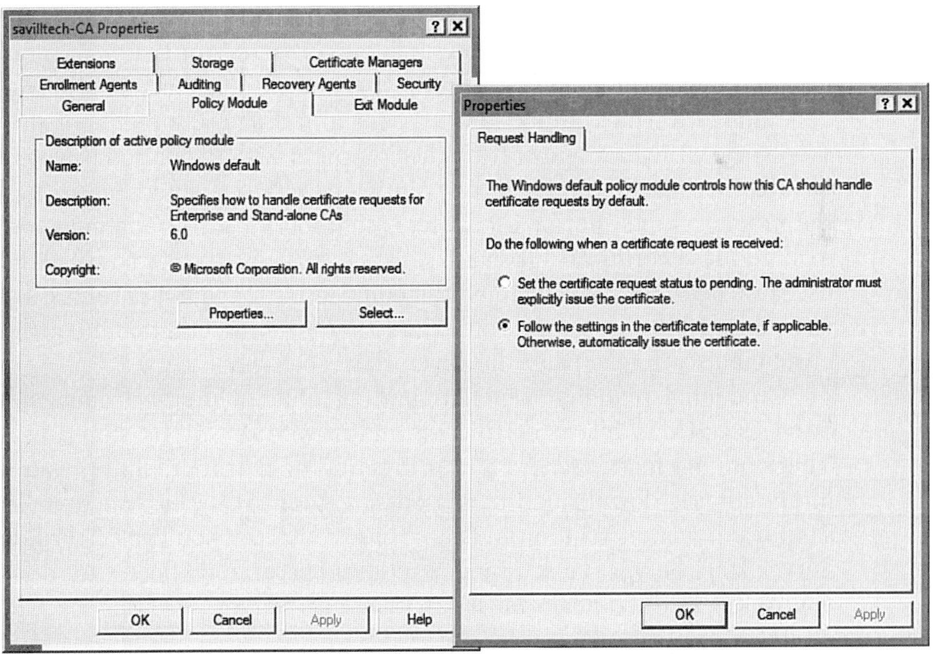

FIGURE 4-17 Configuring the automatic approval.

If there are requests in the Pending Requests node, you can issue or deny (as part of the All Tasks action) them, and you might want to examine whether these requests are ones you want to manually authorize if you are getting a lot of them; in that case, remove the CA Certificate Manager Approval option on the certificate template, or perhaps the server is configured to not allow automatic approval as per the setting mentioned previously.

The Certificate Templates node shows all the certificate templates the CA can issue. Remember to use New, Certificate Template to Issue to enable the CA to issue a new certificate template type.

Credential Roaming

Take care when using autoenrollment for the Exchange User certificate, which encrypts messages if users log on to more than one machine to access mail.

Encrypted messages are encrypted using a generated symmetric key (meaning it both encrypts and decrypts the message), and the symmetric key is transmitted with the message encrypted with the recipient's public key. This means that only the recipient's private key can decrypt the symmetric key and thus decrypt the message.

If autoenrollment is used and a user logs on to multiple machines, a new set of private and public keys will be generated for that user on each machine (because a separate profile is used on each machine), and so depending on which public key encrypts a message, the recipient will be able to open the message only on the computer with the paired private key. On all other machines, the corresponding private key would be missing, so the message would not be readable. A solution for this problem would be to store these certificates (private keys) on smart cards that travel with the user instead of on the machines. You could also use roaming profiles, so the user always has the same profile, and therefore, no additional certificate enrollments will take place; however, this is cumbersome.

Credential roaming, which is part of Digital Identity Management Services (DIMS), allows certificates and private keys to be stored in AD. Therefore, no matter where a user logs on, the certificate and private key information is downloaded to her session from AD. This functionality is supported only on Windows Vista, Windows XP Service Pack 2, Windows Server 2003 Service Pack 1, and Windows Server 2008 boxes. All domain controllers in the domain must run Windows Server 2003 Service Pack 1 or above.

To enable credential roaming, use group policy: Select User Configuration, Policies, Windows Settings, Security Settings, Public Key Policies and double-click the Certificate Services Client – Credential Roaming policy. Set the policy to Enabled, and the default options work for most environments but can be modified if required, as shown in Figure 4-18.

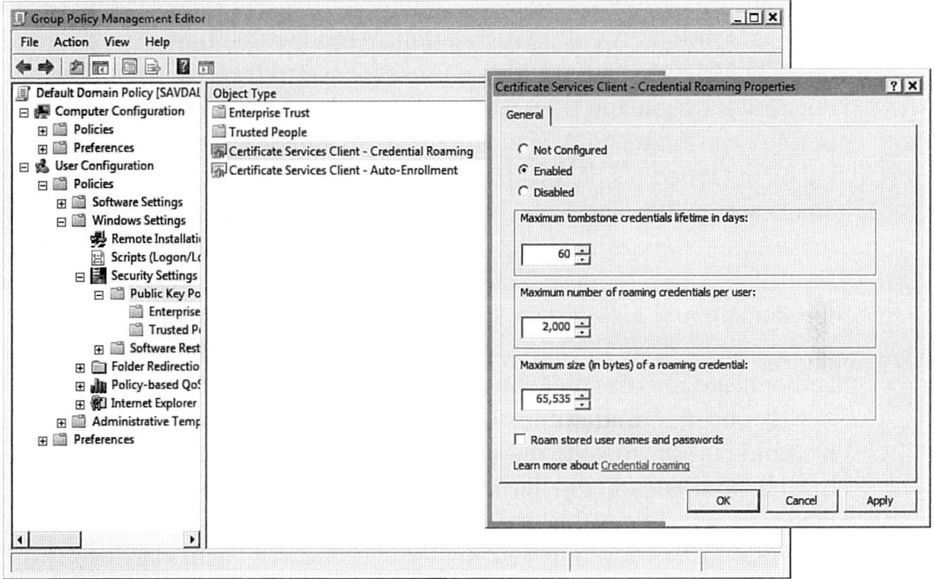

FIGURE 4-18 Enabling credential roaming.

The first time a user logs on and sees that credential roaming has been enabled, all the certificates in the user's store are copied to AD, and from that point on, any new certificates are synchronized between AD and any computer the user logs on to.

Authentication Protocols

As mentioned earlier, security involves both authentication and authorization. The topic of authorization—in particular, accurate authorization—is critical because everything done regarding security is based on ensuring that users are who they say they are, so the protocols used need to be foolproof. Two such protocols are NTLM and Kerberos.

NTLM and LAN Manager

Prior to Windows Server 2000 and AD, NTLM Authentication was the recommended challenge/response authentication system. It was developed for use with the Windows Server NT line and its enterprise client versions, such as Windows NT 4.0 Workstation, Windows 2000 Professional, and so on. NTLM worked by running a user's password through a complex mathematical function and then storing the result, known as the *password hash*, in the Security Account Manager (SAM) database. When a user wanted to log on, he typed his password, which was then run through the same mathematical function, and if the hash matched that stored in the SAM, the user must have entered the correct password and was considered authenticated for that resource request. Those requests included logging on to a client in the domain and accessing a server resource, and every time, the resource being accessed would have to communicate with a domain controller to authenticate the user, which was a burden on the server.

However, if all that the client sent was the hash of the password, then it would be easy to sniff the value on the network and fake requests from the client. Instead, the hash is used as part of the NTLM challenge/response, which goes like this:

1. The user wants access to a resource on a server she has not communicated with as part of the logon session, and so the user sends the server her username in plain text.
2. The server makes up a random 16-byte number and sends it to the client. This is the challenge.
3. The client encrypts the challenge with the hash of the user's password and sends it to the server.
4. The server sends to a domain controller the username, the challenge sent to the client, and the response received from the client.
5. The domain controller looks up the password hash based on the username and uses the hash to run the encryption on the challenge that was sent to the client. If the result matches that generated by the user, she had the right password, and she is authenticated.

With this process, the user's raw hash is not sent over the network.

Prior to NTLM, there was just LAN Manager authentication, which is weak by today's standards because, among other reasons, the hash generated is easier to break than the NTLM hash. With LAN Manager, the password is stored as all uppercase characters, reducing the number of combinations possible, and the password is broken into two seven-character chunks, making it easier to break. With Windows Vista and Windows Server 2008, the LAN Manager hash is not stored. There are two versions of NTLM:

- **NTLM Version 1**. A more secure challenge/response authentication than LAN Manager, using 56-bit encryption for protocol security and passwords stored as NT hashes. It is used by clients running Windows NT 4.0 Service Pack 3 and below.
- **NTLM Version 2**. The current version of NTLM, which uses 128-bit encryption and is used for machines running Windows NT 4.0 Service Pack 4 and above. This is the most secure challenge/response authentication available.

Kerberos

NTLM is an old protocol, and although it still works and is effective, it has some limitations:

- It's not a fast protocol and has a high overhead.
- Each client access requires the server to contact a domain controller for verification, putting a load on the server.
- It is a proprietary protocol, which reduces its supportability.
- It provides no support for delegation of authentication.
- It does not allow servers to authenticate with other servers.

For AD, Microsoft chose Kerberos as the default protocol. (Although NTLM Versions 1 and 2 are still supported for backward-compatibility.) Kerberos is an industry standard defined in RFC 1510, and it is named for the three-headed dog that guards the gates of Hades because Kerberos involves three parts: the client, the server the client wants to talk to, and the Key Distribution Center (KDC) enabling the secure communication (see Figure 4-19). Users contact the KDC for access to a server, and services on servers also contact the KDC to enable access to other servers; this communication is a key part of the AD-based secure infrastructure.

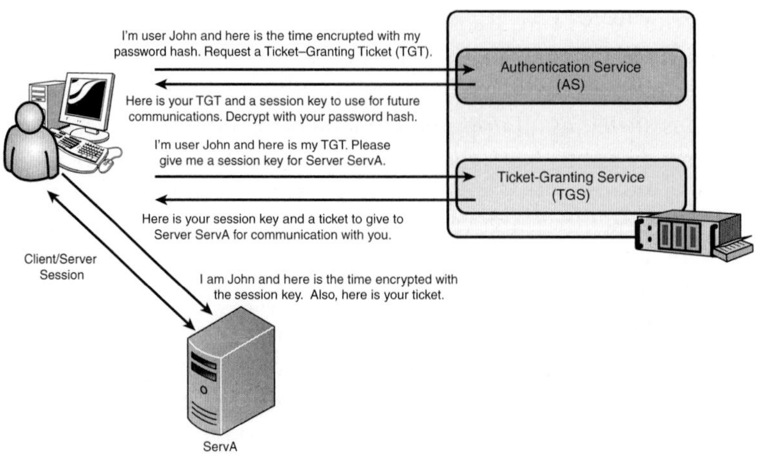
I'm user John and here is the time encrupted with my password hash. Request a Ticket–Granting Ticket (TGT).
Authentication Service (AS)
Here is your TGT and a session key to use for future communications. Decrypt with your password hash.
I'm user John and here is my TGT. Please give me a session key for Server ServA.
Ticket-Granting Service (TGS)
Here is your session key and a ticket to give to Server ServA for communication with you.
Client/Server Session
I am John and here is the time encrypted with the session key. Also, here is your ticket.
ServA

FIGURE 4-19 The basic steps for Kerberos-based client/server communication.

The idea is if two people know a secret, they can communicate, and they also know the other person is who they say they are. You can't just send a secret over the network as just text because anyone with a network sniffer could find it. The Kerberos protocol solves this problem by using secret key cryptography. Rather than sharing a password, communication partners share a cryptographic key. This key is symmetric in nature, which means a single key can both encrypt and decrypt. The process starts when the user first logs on to the domain and continues as follows:

1. The user enters his username and password at the logon screen. The local Kerberos client converts the password to an encryption key by creating a one-way hash value.
2. The local client time is encrypted with the generated encryption key, and a KRB_AS_REQ (Kerberos authentication service request) is generated, containing the user's name, the request for a ticket-granting ticket, and the encrypted time. This is sent to the Authentication Service component of the KDC.
3. The KDC (which is a domain controller and therefore has access to AD) looks up the user's information, including the password hash, and uses it to decrypt the time. If it is within five minutes (this five-minute limit can be changed) of the server's time, it knows it is not a replay. When the user is confirmed, the KDC creates a session key that is used for future communication between the user and the KDC. This generated session key is encrypted

with the user's encryption key (the hash of the password) and also encrypted with the KDC's own long-term key, which is known as the ticket-granting ticket. This is sent back as a KRB_AS_REP (Kerberos authentication service reply).

4. The client now wants to talk to a server. It sends a request to the ticket-granting service component of the KDC that contains the ticket-granting ticket and the server it wants to talk to in a KRB_TGS_REQ (Kerberos ticket-granting service request).
5. The KDC decrypts the KRB_TGS_REQ, using the ticket-granting ticket (which it decrypts with its own secret key), and it passes authenticator testing; the KDC generates a session key to use for communication between the user and the desired server. This session key is encrypted with the user's encryption key and also with the server's long-term key, in the form of a ticket. These are then sent to the user in a KRB_TGS_REP (Kerberos ticket-granting service reply).
6. Now the client can initiate communication with the server by sending a KRB_AP_REQ (Kerberos application request), which contains the user's name and the time encrypted with the session key, to be used between the user and the server along with the server's ticket (which is the session key encrypted with the server's long-time key).
7. The server decrypts the ticket using its long-term key and extracts the session's key. It can then decrypt the encrypted time, and if it passes, the server can trust that the client is who it says it is. If the client asked for mutual authentication, the server then encrypts the time, using the session key it shares with the user, and sends back a KRB_AP_REP (Kerberos application reply).
8. The client at the user's workstation then decrypts the KRB_AP_REP if requested. If the authenticator passes, then the client knows the server could decrypt and use the ticket, proving it is who it said it is. The client and the server now have a mutual session key, which they can use to encrypt any required communication.

Notice that at no time do any of the servers have to remember anything about the client. The client always sends the server a ticket generated by the KDC for its use with all client communication. The server never has to contact the KDC directly during client/server session initialization.

For each server the user needs to communicate with, a separate ticket is created, and the KRB_TGS_REQ, KRB_TGS_REP, KRB_AP_REQ, KRB_AQ_REP process is performed. These tickets last only a certain amount of time, and the KDC does not keep track or notify clients of their expiration, but in the case of an expired ticket or even an expired ticket-granting ticket, a new one will be requested using the same steps. The user's password hash is normally cached, but if for some reason it is no longer cached, the user may be prompted for his credentials again.

You notice that in nearly all steps, the time is encrypted with the session key to prove it's not just a replay. The fact that time is part of the encryption technology is why machines using Kerberos need to be time synchronized with a Simple Network Time Protocol (SNTP) service.

There are more steps involved if the server and the user are in different domains. The user's domain gives her a referral ticket, which is just another ticket-granting ticket to give to a domain controller in the other domain where the resource exists, assuming that the user's domain is directly trusted by the domain with the resource. If there are multiple domains between the user and the resource—for example, in a forest where the user is in Europe.savilltech.net and the resource is in America.savilltech.net. Without manual trust creation, there is no trust between Europe and America directly; instead, both domains have trusts with savilltech.net, and so a chain of referrals is performed. Europe refers the user to savilltech.net, which then gives the user a referral ticket to America, where a domain controller could give the user a ticket to talk to the server hosting the resource.

Setting Authentication Methods for a Domain

By default, a Windows AD domain supports all authentication methods (LAN Manager, NTLM Versions 1 and 2, and Kerberos), but the most secure shared authentication is always attempted. For example, a Windows NT 4.0 Service Pack 6 box uses NTLM Version 2 when talking to an AD domain controller because although AD understands Kerberos, the client can only support NTLM Version 2 at best.

To restrict the protocols that are supported by domain controllers and clients, modify the Network Security LAN Manager Authentication Level policy to set which authentication protocols is used:

1. Open the GPO you want to modify. For example, you could create a policy that applies to the entire domain by linking the GPO at a domain level, or a policy that affects only domain controllers by setting the Domain Controllers OU. The default domain controllers GPO already has this setting defined, so you could open the existing default domain controllers GPO to target just domain controllers.
2. Navigate to the Computer Configuration, Policies, Windows Settings, Security Settings, Local Policies, Security Options portion of the group policy.
3. Double-click the Network Security: LAN Manager Authentication Level policy.
4. Check the Define this policy setting option, and select the required level from the drop-down, as shown in Figure 4-20. Click OK.
6. Close the GPO. When the policy is refreshed, the level of LAN Manager/NTLM support is modified for the clients and servers to which the policy is applied.

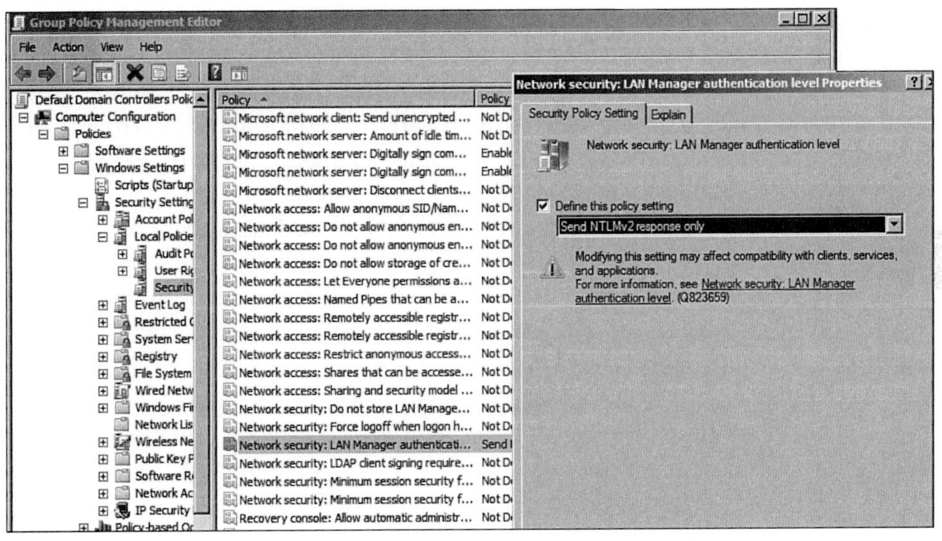

Figure 4-20 The default setting for a Windows Server 2008 domain.

The various policy options have different effects, and the policy options affect the clients and domain controllers differently:

- **Send LM & NTLM responses**. Clients send only LAN Manager and NTLM v1 (not NTLM v2), although domain controllers support NTLM v2. This ensures that clients can always authenticate with servers even pre-Windows NT 4.0 with Service Pack 4.
- **Send LM & NTLM - use NTLMv2 session security if negotiated**. Clients and servers can use LAN Manager, NTLM Version 1, and NTLM Version 2. Where possible, NTLM Version 2 is used.
- **Send NTLM response only**. Clients use only NTLM Version 1 and NTLM Version 2 (not LAN Manager), although domain controllers still accept LAN Manager. This stops clients authenticating with Windows 95, Windows 98, and Windows Me because Windows 9x clients cannot speak NTLM.
- **Send NTLMv2 response only**. Clients use only NTLM Version 2 (not LAN Manager or NTLM Version 1) authentication, although domain controllers still accept all forms of authentication (LAN Manager, NTLM Version 1, and NTLM Version 2). This stops clients communicating with any box pre-Windows NT 4.0 Service Pack 4.
- **Send NTLMv2 response only\refuse LM**. Clients only use NTLM Version 2 authentication, and domain controllers refuse LAN Manager authentication. (Domain controllers still accept NTLM Version 1 and NTLM Version 2.)
- **Send NTLMv2 response only\refuse LM & NTLM**. Clients use only NTLM Version 2, and domain controllers accept only NTLM Version 2 authentication. This means any pre-Windows NT 4.0 Service Pack 4 box is unable to authenticate to clients or domain controllers.

If you have an environment of all Windows 2000 and above, configure the last option, which allows only NTLM Version 2. (Although Kerberos will still be the preferred authentication method.)

While looking at the group policy and settings, you can also see the disabling of the LAN Manager hash storage on Windows Server 2008 via the setting Network Security: Do Not Store LAN Manager Hash Value on Next Password Change. If you open the local computer policy of any Vista or Windows Server 2008 box, you see this set to Enabled, which is why

LAN Manager hash values are no longer stored on Vista and Windows Server 2008 platforms by default. (However, if you set the aforementioned policy to Disabled, the LAN Manager hash is stored at the next password change if a particular application needed the LAN Manager hash that you had to use, but you don't want to store LAN Manager hash if possible.)

Securing Windows Server 2008

The Security section of the Windows Server 2008 management environment concentrates on four items: configuring the server to receive updates, the firewall, the Internet Explorer Enhanced Security Configuration mode, and the Security Configuration Wizard. Chapter 3, "Installing and Upgrading Windows Server 2008," discusses configuring the server to receive updates. This section looks at the other three areas and then expands into some other vital concepts not covered elsewhere in the book.

NOTE Windows Server 2008 is much more locked down out of the box than previous OSs. The firewall is locked down, and exceptions are opened only as components that require connectivity are enabled. However, there are still services and configurations that may be unnecessary and thus increase vulnerabilities.

The Security Configuration Wizard (SCW)

The group policy options are vast; you can use them to configure many different aspects of a server and the interaction with the client population. (For example, which authentication protocols are used depends on the types of clients on the network.) To help select the right options and to get the network as locked down as possible as quickly as possible, Microsoft created the Security Configuration Wizard (SCW), which walks you through a number of questions and performs various detections to ascertain the optimal configuration for the server and create a policy that can be applied to other servers. You can later edit the policies you create with the SCW, and if you apply a policy to a server and the policy is found to cause problems, you can roll back the policy application to reset the server back to its configuration prior to the policy application.

You can also use the SCW for audit purposes by allowing a server to be compared to the settings in a security policy. This is an easy way to quickly spot any settings that do not comply with policy.

Because the SCW creates policies to lock down a server based in a large part on the configuration of the server it is being run against, it is a good idea to run the SCW against multiple servers that run different roles to create a number of role-based SCW configuration files. You can then apply these SCW role-based configuration files to servers performing the same role and that have the right configuration, including firewall exceptions. Running a security policy created for a domain controller on a SQL Server machine, for example, would not allow the correct communication or other settings, so this is not a one-size-fits-all process.

You can access the SCW via the Server Manager main page, through a link under Administrative Tools, or by running its executable, SCW.EXE, directly. The first page of the wizard advises you to make sure the server is running any applications or services that it runs as part of its normal duties. This is because the SCW performs an inbound port detection that it uses later as part of the server lockdown configuration.

The Configuration Action page allows you to create a new security policy (the default action), edit an existing policy, apply an already existing policy, or roll back the last policy that was applied. In this example, you want to create a new policy, so accept the default to create a new policy.

Because the SCW is based on detections, select a base server that is used for the detection portions of the SCW functionality, which by default is the local server. You can select a remote server, but you must have administrative permissions on any server you select.

The SCW performs a scan on the selected server, which generates a security configuration database that contains information on the server roles, client features, services, firewall configuration, and various other installed components. You can view this security configuration database information by clicking the View Configuration Database button, which loads the information into the SCW Viewer. You are then prompted to allow an ActiveX component, which you should do. If you view the database, you see information on the configuration, with a list of dependence and security implications. For example, the database shows all the roles that are available as well as whether that role is installed and whether it has the services needed for the role to run and the firewall exceptions for it to communicate with other servers and clients.

The next stage is role-based service configuration, where you answer questions to help the SCW decide which services should be running. Make sure you answer correctly, or services needed may be disabled. The first page shows installed roles on the selected server, including required services and required roles (see Figure 4-21). You can check/uncheck roles if you don't want the roles to be considered as part of the generated security policy or if you want a role that is not installed to be included in the policy. The next page shows installed features, and you can enable/disable features for consideration in the policy.

NOTE As you complete this information, you do not enable/disable roles and features on the server. You just tell the SCW to consider them when it decides what services should be running and what other server configurations, such as firewall exceptions, are needed. However, after the security policy is created, if you applied it to a server, it could possibly break roles/features that were not included in the policy.

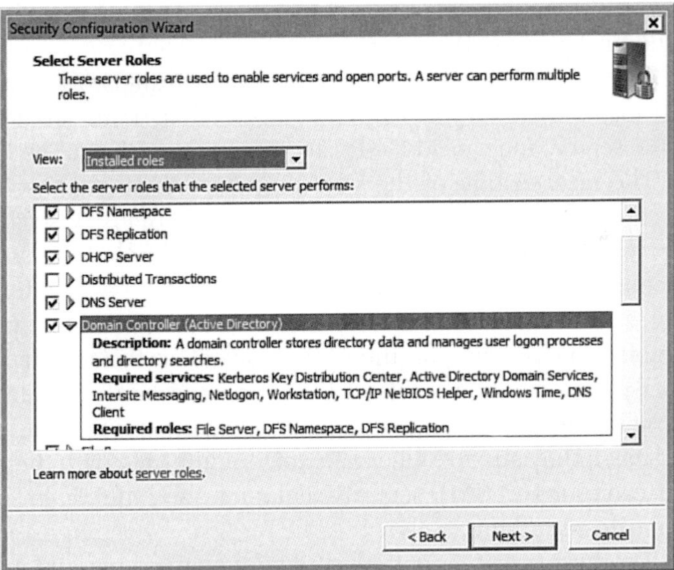

FIGURE 4-21 Viewing installed roles.

The next section allows configuration of other options and administration, such as error reporting, and once again, you can make changes. The next screen shows additional services on the machine such as third-party installed services (for example, Virtual Server, SQL Server).

The next screen is important; it asks what to do with services that are not specified with the policy (for example, a service that did not exist on the server on which the policy was created). The default is to not change the configuration of any unspecified services, which is a safe option. However, if you have 50 servers that should all be the same, and you run the SCW on 1 of those servers, then if 1 of the other 49 servers has another service, it is out of configuration with the others. You might, therefore, want to choose the Disable the Service option to ensure that all servers have the same service configuration.

The SCW then does some calculations and shows any services that will have their startup mode changed. It shows each service's current startup mode and the startup mode after the policy is applied, along with the services that typically use the service. It is common for the policy to set lots of services to Disabled. Look through these services and ensure that none of them were needed. (For example, perhaps something was just not running at the time you ran the service.)

The next section of the wizard deals with network security. The first page displays the firewall rules that are needed, based on the installed roles on the server. You can add, edit, and remove rules from the list, if required.

The next section of the wizard deals with Registry settings and asks questions about the environment to modify Registry settings that affect how features of the OS are used. For example, the first screen asks if all computers are Windows NT 4.0 Service Pack 6a or later, as shown in Figure 4-22, in addition to asking whether the server has spare processing capability. Depending on the options selected, the Server Message Block (SMB) signing option is set, which improves security of data sent via SMB. If you say all computers meet the requirements and you have computers that don't, they are no longer able to communicate with the server because they can't support SMB security signatures, and the server would not communicate with them.

The next screen asks if all directory-enabled computers are Windows 2000 Service Pack 3 or later, which allows Lightweight Directory Access Protocol (LDAP) signing to be a requirement for communication, once again improving security.

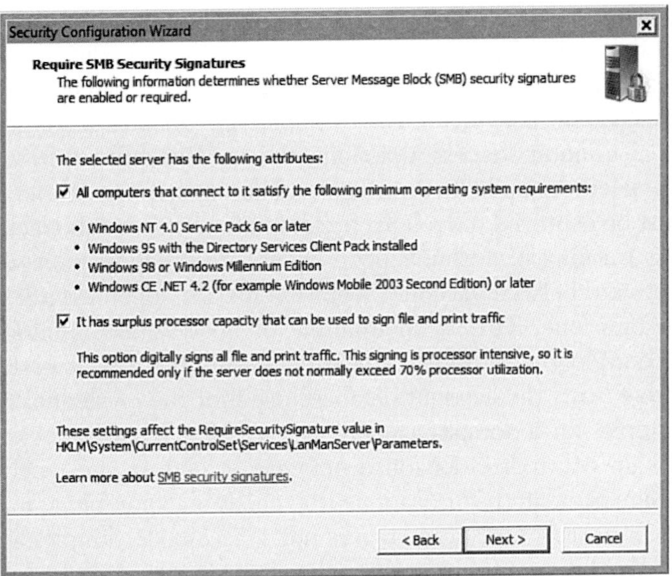

FIGURE 4-22 Setting the SMB signing configuration.

The next screen asks what types of accounts are used for outbound access to resources, which by default include only domain accounts. However, local accounts on remote computers and file sharing passwords for connection to Windows 95, Windows 98, and Windows Me are also available as options and ascertain the LAN Manager authentication level that should be used.

If domain accounts were selected, you are prompted for information about the client computers. You are presented with two options for outgoing authentication: whether the computer OSs the server will communicate with are all Windows NT 4.0 Service Pack 6a or later and whether the times on computers are synchronized with each other. The next stage deals with incoming authentication methods, and you are prompted for the types of computers that are supported to connect (for example, computers that are not configured to use NTLM Version 2, computers that need LAN Manager authentication, and RAS/VPN servers that are not Windows Server 2003 Service Pack 1 or above). After you answer these questions, the list of new Registry settings is displayed. It includes lmcompatibilitylevel, lmhash storage, ldap signing, and SMB security signatures.

The next stage deals with audit configuration. It allows you to select whether auditing will be performed and what to audit. (For example, track successful actions, so you can see how changes occurred or to also track unsuccessful activities.) This is not as universal as it sounds. Even if you select to audit successful actions, the SCW is still security conscious and will select to audit certain types of failures; for example, logon failures must be captured to look for break-in attempts, so this tracking is enabled, as is tracking of account logon events. You may wonder what the differences are between account logon events and logon events, and you're not the only one. This is an example of not-so-good naming at Microsoft. Account logon events are credential events and are generated on the server that hosts the account database used for the credential validation. (For example, for a domain account, the account logon event is logged on the domain controller.) Logon events are logged on the machine where the session is created (for example, the client machine being logged on to or a server hosting a resource that is being accessed). Simple, huh?

Finally, save the security policy to an XML file, which by default is in the C:\Windows\security\msscw\Policies\ folder. When this is saved, you are prompted about whether to apply the policy. If there are a lot of changes, test the policy on a test or nonimportant server rather than just executing on a live, in-use server, just in case things break.

To modify a policy, run the SCW again and select to edit an existing policy. Then select the XML file, and the SCW runs through the whole wizard again, with the answers from the XML file selected by default. You can make any changes needed to modify these settings.

To use the generated security policy, copy the XML file to each server and then use the SCW to apply it. However, that is cumbersome for multiple servers; instead you can use the scwcmd.exe tool to convert the XML security policy file into a GPO, which you can then easily link to an OU/domain/site that contains the target servers. Remember don't just apply a GPO generated from a security template to servers of different roles, or it will break them. Be diligent about creating security templates that are based on the role of the server, testing the security policy, and then converting to a GPO and linking to an OU that contains only that type of server (which may mean you need to restructure the AD so servers are in different OUs, based on their role).

The actual conversion of a security policy XML file to a GPO is simple: Just use the `transform` function of `scwcmd` and pass the name of the XML file and the name of the GPO you want to create, as in the following example.

```
C:\>scwcmd transform /p:
➥C:\Windows\security\msscw\Policies\domaincontroller.xml
➥/g:"DC Sec Policy"
Command completed successfully.
```

A new GPO is then available in the domain of the server that ran the scwcmd command and can be linked as needed. Figure 4-23 shows the generated GPO and some of the settings that were configured.

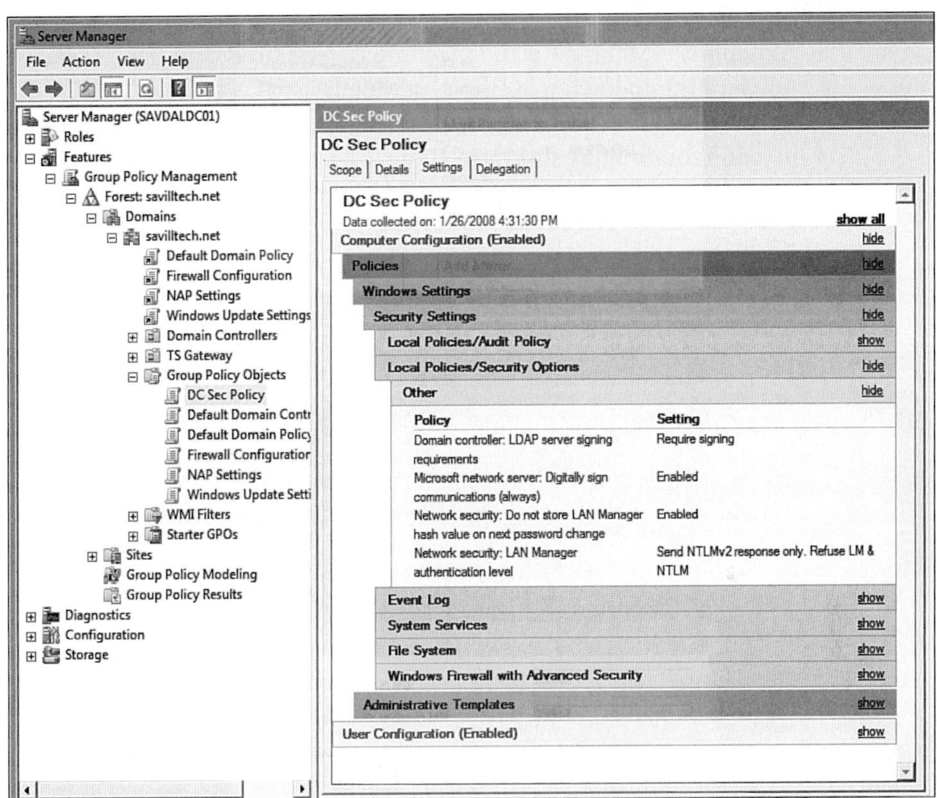

FIGURE 4-23 A GPO generated by the `scwcmd` transform command.

Use scwcmd.exe to apply a security policy XML file via the `configure` switch (that is, `scwcmd configure /p:domaincontroller.xml`) in addition to rolling back a policy.

The neat `analyze` capability can compare a server's current configuration to that of a security policy and report back any differences, as shown in the following example. Run `analyze` against a remote machine by using the `/m:`<*server name*> switch and configure a specific folder for the output to be written to with the `/o:`<*folder path*> switch.

```
C:\>scwcmd analyze /p:C:\Windows\security\
➥msscw\Policies\domaincontroller.xml
   *    1/1 100%
Command completed successfully.
Result file: C:\SAVDALDC01.xml
```

When the XML file for the machine is generated, run the `view` option, as shown in the following example. scwanalysis.xsl is part of the SCW. This analysis loads in the SCW Viewer, which allows easy viewing of differences in the configuration, as shown in Figure 4-24.

```
C:\>scwcmd view /x:savdaldc01.xml
➥/s:c:\windows\security\msscw\transformfiles\scwanalysis.xsl
Command completed successfully.
```


Audit Event Type	Policy Value	System Value
System Events	Success, failure	Success
Logon Events	Success, failure	Success
Object Access	Success	Not audited
Process Tracking	Success	Not audited
Account Logon Events	Success, failure	Success

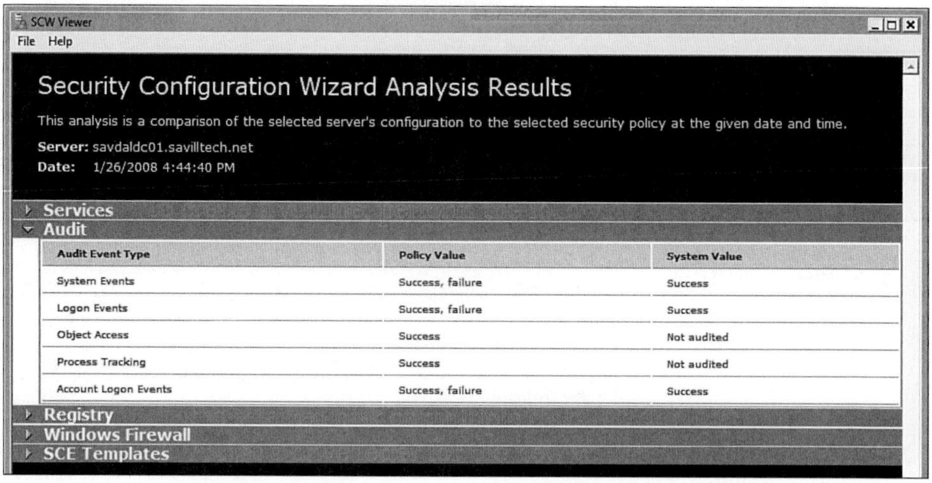

FIGURE 4-24 Viewing differences between a server and the security policy.

The SCW is a great tool to help create a policy to lock down your server, and with the rollback tool, it's easy to undo any problems that a policy may cause. Still, don't rush to push out policies to live servers without testing.

Security Configuration and Analysis

The SCW performs elements of security configuration and analysis based on the questions it asks and the discovery it performs. The Security Configuration and Analysis snap-in gives you a more granular ability to analyze a machine and apply security configuration. The Security Configuration and Analysis snap-in comprises a number of elements, but the whole solution is based on security template files that allow configuration of all the main elements of the security settings found in the Computer configuration of a GPO: Account Policies, Local Policies, Event Log, Restricted Groups, System Services, Registry, and File System.

By using these templates, you can configure certain settings for various types of servers within your environment and then manually apply the settings to a server or just use the template to compare the settings in the template to those configured on the server and find any that do not match. For example, you could create a security template for a secure domain controller. In that template, define certain local policy configuration, system services settings, and account policies. Then run that secure domain controller template file against a domain controller you have in an analysis mode and quickly see any discrepancies between settings in the template and those configured on the server. Then apply the template to the domain controller so that the domain controller's security settings match those in the template.

Many security solutions provide additional templates to help you configure servers easily, without having to step through manually configuring hundreds of settings. For example, the Windows Server 2008 security guide provides a number of security templates for enterprise client and specialized security environments. There are three tools you can use for security configuration and analysis snap-in:

- **Security Templates**. Use this MMC snap-in to view security templates, create new security templates, and modify existing templates.
- **Security Configuration and Analysis**. Use this MMC snap-in to evaluate a system's security configuration compared to a selected template and then apply the template configuration, if desired.
- **secedit.exe**. Use this command-line tool for command-line evaluation and application of security templates.

In addition, use the Group Policy Editor to import a security template to quickly apply settings from the security template to a GPO for easy deployment to multiple computers. There are no shortcuts to either of the MMC snap-ins; create a custom console by running mmc.exe and then adding the Security Templates snap-in and the Security Configuration and Analysis snap-in, as shown in Figure 4-25.

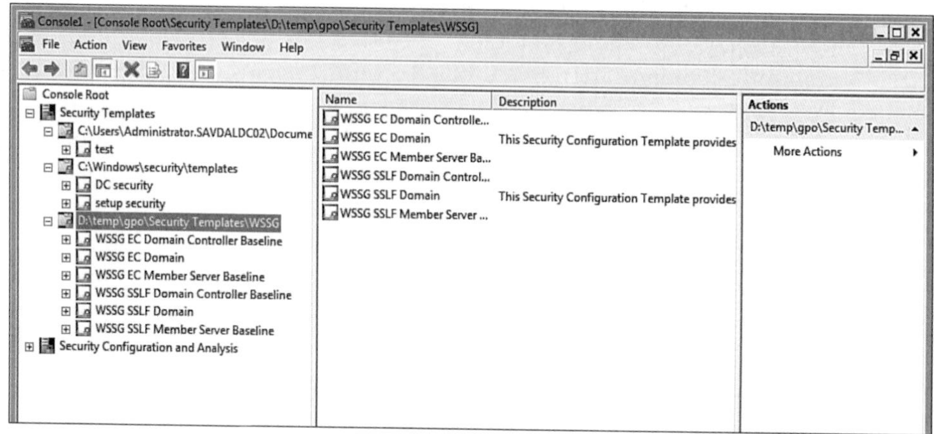

FIGURE 4-25 A custom MMC console with two MMC snap-ins loaded for security configuration and analysis.

Let's look at the main components of security configuration and analysis.

Security Templates

The security templates are the key to security configuration and analysis. A template provides the settings you want to configure via the template. When you first open the Security Templates snap-in, it has a single location—the Documents folder for the logged-on user, which doesn't yet contain any templates but is the location where you can create your own templates.

Windows Server 2008 supplies a number of templates, found in the %windir%\security\templates folder. At the time of this writing, two templates are provided that help define initial security for servers and a separate configuration for domain controllers; however, in previous OSs, additional templates were provided that should also be available for Windows Server 2008:

- **SecureWS**. For workstations and servers that have security settings that are suitable for a secure environment, such as increased security for account policy and auditing.
- **SecureDC**. For domain controllers with settings suitable for a secure environments.
- **HiSecWS**. For workstations and servers that require a highly secure configuration that specifies the use of digital signatures and encryption for network communication.
- **HiSecDC**. For domain controllers in a highly secure environment.

Select the New Template Search Path action when Security Templates is selected to add additional paths to look for security templates (for example, c:\windows\security\templates to view the supplied templates). In addition, if you have installed solution accelerators such as the Windows Server 2008 security guide that include additional security templates, you can add those locations.

You can open security templates and view the settings that are configured, and if you want to modify settings, it is best to not modify templates that are provided by the OS but instead use the Save As action for the template you want to modify and save to a new filename in your documents location. Figure 4-26 shows the domain password policy settings that the Windows Server 2008 security guide template for an enterprise client domain specifies, and it's important to note that you don't have to define all settings. Define only settings that you want to be part of the template; all other settings are left as Not Defined. Create a new template by using the New Template action and specifying a name and description for the template.

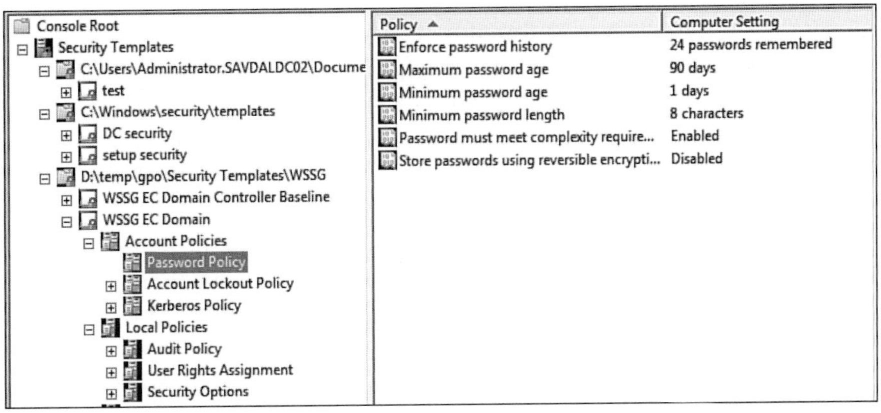

FIGURE 4-26 Viewing settings defined in a template.

After you define the settings you want to include in a template, you can use the template.

Security Configuration and Analysis

The first step in using the Security Configuration and Analysis snap-in is to open a security database that is used to store configuration setting information and select the security template to be used. If this is your first use, you do not have a security database, so for this example, create a new one. This security database is used to load the security templates settings to allow comparisons between the template settings and the computer settings. The Security Configuration and Analysis snap-in works from the security database only, and the only time the security templates are used is to import settings from the template into the security database.

Select the Open Database action at the root of the Security Configuration and Analysis snap-in and type in the name of the new security database. For example, you may use the server's name as the database name, which generates a new security database (.sdb) file. You are then asked for the security template to use for analysis and application.

You can now use the template to configure your server with the settings contained in the template via the Configure Computer Now action. Or to analyze your configuration against the settings in the template, you use the Analyze Computer Now action. For both actions, you are prompted for a log file.

For this example, start with the analysis, and after a scan of the computer is performed, you can read its configuration. You can go through all the settings in the seven main sections of the security template to see the database settings, which are the settings defined in the security template and then the computer's setting. If the computer's setting matches the setting in the template, a green tick is shown on the setting, and if the computer's setting does not match, the setting has a red cross displayed, as shown in Figure 4-27. If a setting is not defined in the template, the policy does not have a tick or cross, and the database setting is set as Not Defined.

If you have reviewed all the settings and want to apply the template, then run the Configure Computer Now action. But before you run that action, keep in mind that unlike with the SCW, there is no rollback option from the Security Configuration and Analysis MMC snap-in. The command-line tool secedit.exe enables you to create rollback information, so it's a good idea to create a rollback file in case the application of a template causes problems.

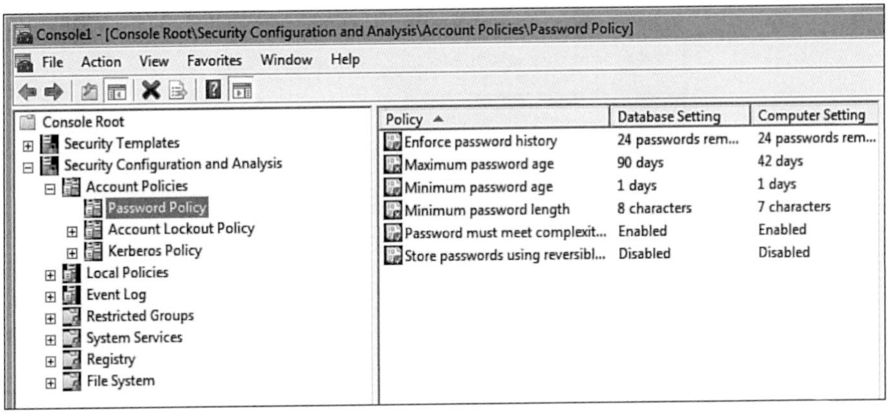

FIGURE 4-27 Viewing settings on the server compared to those defined in the template.

If you want to load another security template into the security database, select the Import Template option, which allows a new template to be opened. Notice on the Import Template dialog the option Clear This Database Before Importing. If you don't select this option, the policy settings from the previous security template are left in the database, so the previous settings are left in the database. This means the settings from the new template are added to the security database, which effectively merges the settings from the previously loaded template and this new template.

When the template is loaded, run the Analyze Computer Now action again to run checks against the computer compared to the new template and then use the template to configure the server as normal.

If you want to use a different setting, modify the settings stored in the security database by double-clicking the policy setting to open a dialog that shows the computer's current setting. You can configure whether the setting should be defined in the security database and, if so, what the value should be, as shown in Figure 4-28. Remember that you are modifying the value in the security database; you are not modifying the computer until you configure the computer with the information in the security database.

If you make a number of changes to the security database by either changing settings or loading multiple templates, save the content of the security database to a security template via the Export Template action.

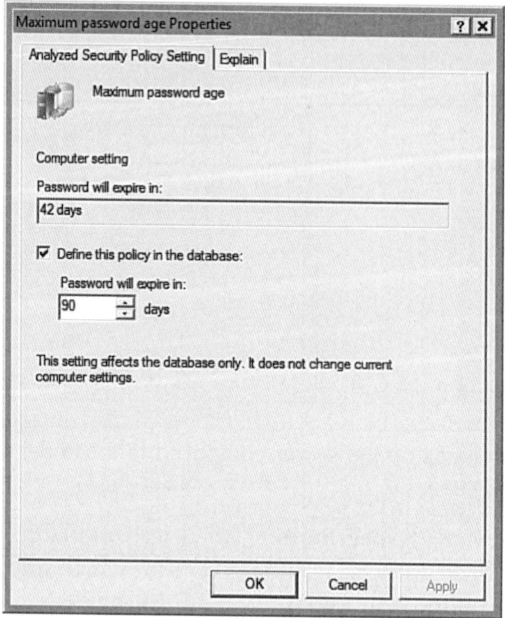

FIGURE 4-28 Modifying a setting in the security database.

Figure 4-29 provides a quick recap about how core the security database is. Note that the security database is maintained in the file you specified, so if you close the Security Configuration and Analysis snap-in, you can open an existing security database (.sdb file) to once again see all the settings configured in the database in addition to the data gathered from the server that was analyzed.

Integration with Group Policy

Group policy fully supports security templates, and if you have a security template that contains policies you want to deploy via group policy, you can create or edit a GPO and navigate to Computer Configuration, Policies, Windows Settings, Security Settings. Then right-click Security Settings and select Import Policy from the context menu, as shown in Figure 4-30, and you are prompted for the .inf file to import, which then loads all the settings defined into the GPO.

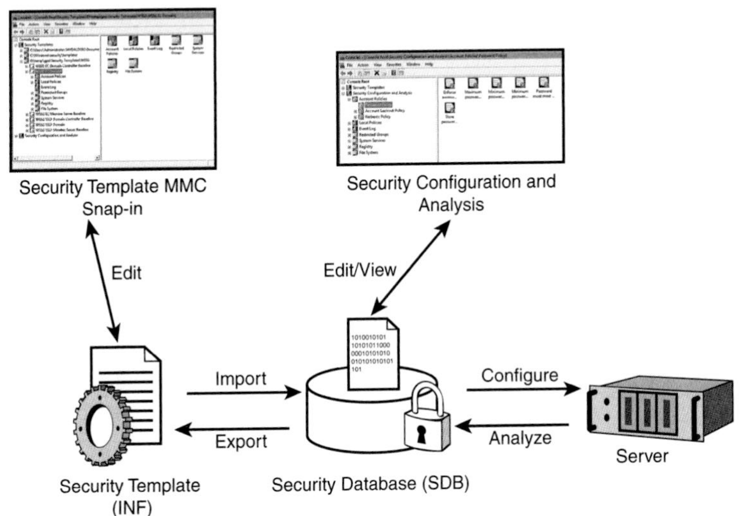

Figure 4-29 The security configuration and analysis process.

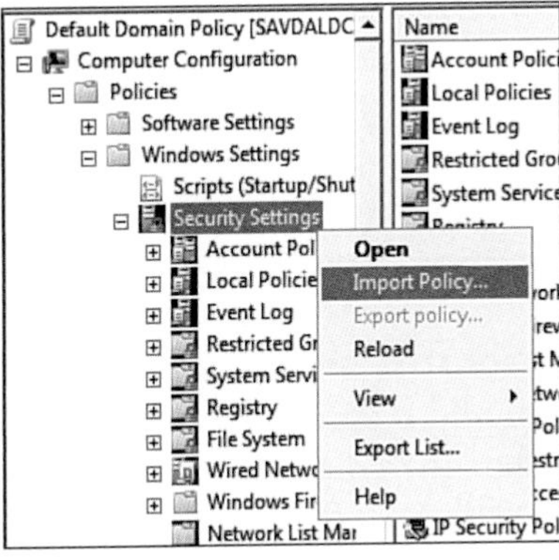

Figure 4-30 Applying a security template into a GPO.

secedit.exe

The secedit.exe command-line utility allows you to configure and analyze security from the command line, including performing analysis of a server compared to a template and applying the settings in a security template. The command-line tool can also do something you can't do with the Security Configuration and Analysis MMC snap-in: It can create a rollback file of all the settings that is replaced when a security template is applied, and it implements this rollback file as another security template file.

To perform an analysis from the command line, specify a database name and the template file you want to use for the configuration, along with optional log file location. By default, logs are written to %windir%\security\logs. For example, to perform the analysis on a server, use the following.

```
C:\sectemp>secedit /analyze /db savsand.sdb /cfg
➥"WSSG EC Member Server Baseline.inf"
```

```
The task has completed successfully.
See log %windir%\security\logs\scesrv.log for detail info.
```

To apply a security template, use the `/configure` switch instead of `/analyze`, and also add the `/overwrite` switch to ensure that the database is blank before applying any configuration so that the only settings are those stored within the security template specified on the command line.

You can also use the `/import` and `/export` switches, which provide the same functionality that is available via the MMC snap-in for template importing and exporting. However, one area of additional functionality is possible. Unlike the snap-in, the command-line tool allows you to define the specific parts of a template to import or export via the `/areas` switch, and use the following area options of content to import/export:

- **SECURITYPOLICY**. Includes account policies, audit policies, event log settings, and security options
- **GROUP_MGMT**. Includes restricted group settings
- **USER_RIGHTS**. Includes user rights assignment
- **REGKEYS**. Includes Registry permissions
- **FILESTORE**. Includes file system permissions
- **SERVICES**. Includes system service settings

To use the rollback functionality, use the `/generaterollback` switch, which requires you to specify the security template that is applied via the `/cfg` switch and then the name of the security template to create to store the settings to be saved for rollback via the `/rbk` switch, as in the following example:

```
C:\sectemp>secedit /generaterollback /cfg
➥"WSSG EC Member Server Baseline.inf"
➥/rbk rollbacksand.inf
Rollback is not supported for File Security and
Registry Security.
Do you want to continue this operation ? [y/n] y
Rollback template being generated...

The task has completed successfully.
See log %windir%\security\logs\scesrv.log for detail info.
```

A rollback does not document the current file system and Registry security settings, so any changes made by a policy to file system security or Registry security cannot be undone with a rollback file, but all other settings can be rolled back. Pass the security template you are going to apply so the rollback knows which current settings to back up because only the settings that are replaced by the specified template are backed up to the rollback template—not every possible setting. It is, therefore, important to specify the correct template that you are planning to apply in the `generaterollback` command. The template created by the rollback has the same settings defined as the template to be applied, just with the values current on the machine.

If you have created a custom template and you want to verify its integrity, you can use the `/validate` switch, which verifies that the format of the template file is correct.

Windows Firewall with Advanced Security

A firewall is a service that controls the traffic flowing through it, allowing only authorized traffic to traverse and keeping out the bad people. Why the addition of *Advanced Security* to the title? With Windows Vista and Windows Server 2008, you not only configure the firewall via the Windows Firewall with Advanced Security MMC snap-in, you also use Internet Protocol Security (IPsec), although the older Policy and Monitor snap-ins are still included to manage older client computers, such as Windows 2000, Windows XP, and Windows Server 2003. The firewall is enabled by default on a new installation, providing protection from the point of OS installation in a locked-down state. For upgraded OSs, the firewall state is maintained from the previous OS, so if the firewall was disabled in Windows Server 2003, the firewall is still disabled after an upgrade to Windows Server 2008.

Windows Firewall

Windows Firewall is discussed throughout the book because all the roles and features in Windows Server 2008 understand the firewall and automatically add and enable exceptions to ensure that the firewall doesn't cause a break in functionality by blocking a port that is required for the role or feature to function. However, you can also perform configuration directly via the MMC interface or by using the `netsh` command-line tool to perform custom exceptions and configuration.

Windows Firewall performs both inbound and outbound checking of all Internet Protocol version 4 (IPv4) and Internet Protocol version 6 (IPv6) traffic and is a state-based firewall, so inbound data is allowed only in if it's in response to a previous outbound request, unless there is a specific firewall exception for that type of traffic. (For example, a DNS server has an exception to allow inbound TCP/UDP port 53 traffic, which is the port over which DNS requests are sent.) Custom exceptions can be based on ports, services, or application names, giving granular levels of control. An exception is a rule that allows in a certain type of traffic. The firewall also monitors outgoing traffic for certain services to ensure that communication is as expected. Or perhaps an administrator wants to block sensitive outgoing content. However, in general, all outgoing traffic is allowed unless it matches a specific outgoing rule.

You can configure different firewall behavior, depending on the network to which the computer is connected. This is of more use to laptop machines that may connect to multiple networks than it is to servers. For servers, configure all the various connectivity profiles the same. There are three different network location types, and each can have a different firewall exception behavior:

- **Domain**. A situation in which a member server is connected to a network that allows communication with a domain controller for the member server's domain.
- **Private**. A network that the user has selected as a trusted network and is typically more restrictive than the domain profile because most of the services and applications a computer uses are most likely not available outside the domain network.
- **Public**. The default network type for any new network a computer is placed on and is the most restrictive.

The default configuration of all three profiles is on the main page of WFAS.

Configuring Windows Firewall

There are two graphical interfaces to configure Windows Firewall. The first, and most basic, is the Windows Firewall Control Panel applet, which allows you to configure basic exceptions and to add new exceptions based on a port (see Figure 4-31). If you configure an exception based on a port, you can configure the port number and whether the protocol is TCP or UDP.

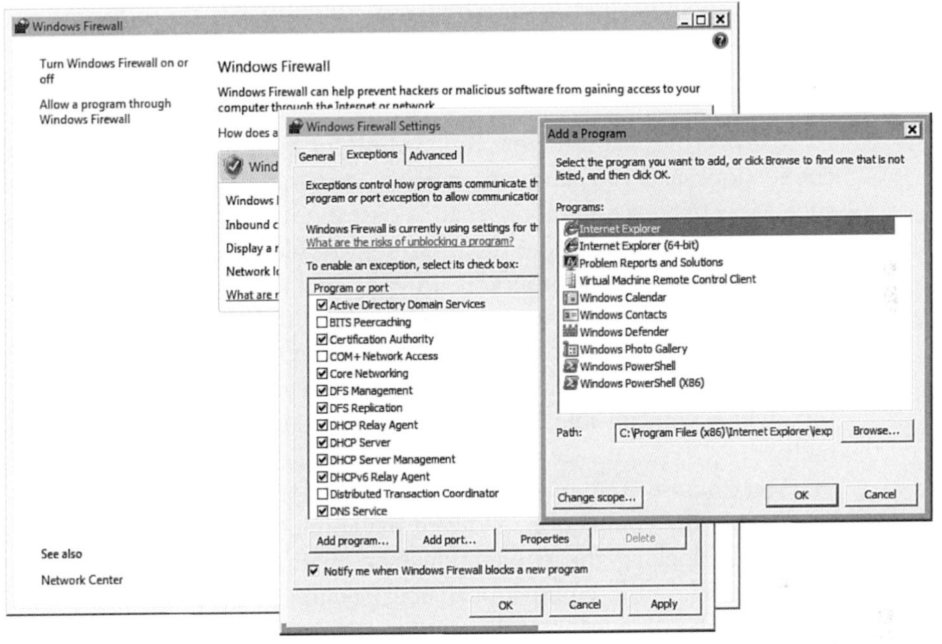

FIGURE 4-31 Configuration available via the Windows Firewall Control Panel applet.

The General tab allows configuration of the state of the firewall (On or Off) and provides an option to block all incoming connections and ignore any exceptions that may have been configured; use this when connecting to less secure networks. The Advanced tab allows configuration of which networks the firewall will protect, plus the ability to reset the configuration back to the defaults that are set on installation.

For more advanced configuration, use the Windows Firewall with Advanced Security (WFAS) MMC snap-in, which breaks the configuration into inbound and outbound rules in addition to connection security rules, which are used for IPsec configuration (discussed later in this chapter).

All the rules are displayed in the Inbound Rules and Outbound Rules sections, along with the profiles to which they apply. If you select the root node in the console tree, Windows Firewall with Advanced Configuration, and select Properties, you can configure the firewall state for each of the three profiles (On or Off). Configure the default inbound and outbound connection action (Block or Allow) as well as advanced options, such as displaying a notification if the firewall blocks communication and specifying whether unicast responses are allowed to multicast broadcasts. You can also set logging options, which by default write to C:\Windows\system32\LogFiles\Firewall\pfirewall.log, which does not log anything; however, you can configure logging of dropped packets and successful connections.

Create rules via the New Rule action for both inbound and outbound connections, and you can base a rule on a program or port; predefine a rule such as a DNS exception; or create a custom rule (see Figure 4-32). If you create a custom rule, select the program to which the rule applies or allow the rule to apply to all programs, the protocol and ports to which the rule applies, and the IP address scope that allows the rule to apply to specific local IP addresses and remote IP addresses. One powerful feature when using a custom rule is that you can apply rules to actual services on the system, which you can select from a list of services on the box or enter manually.

You can also configure the action to take for a matching scenario, such as allowing the connection, allowing the connection only if it's secured via IPsec, or blocking the connection (see Figure 4-33). If you select the option to allow the connection if it is secure, you are also prompted to select whether you want to allow connections only from specified computers and users.

Finally, select the profile that the rule applies to—which can be domain, private, and public—along with a name for the new rule. When a rule is complete, right-click it and select Properties to configure all the settings via the tabs in the Properties dialog box. Enable and disable rules via the Disable/Enable Rule action.

Outbound rules behave the same way as inbound rules and allow you to specify actions for certain programs, services, and ports. For example, you could choose to block all outbound communication and then create rules to allow only certain programs and services to communicate outbound from the server.

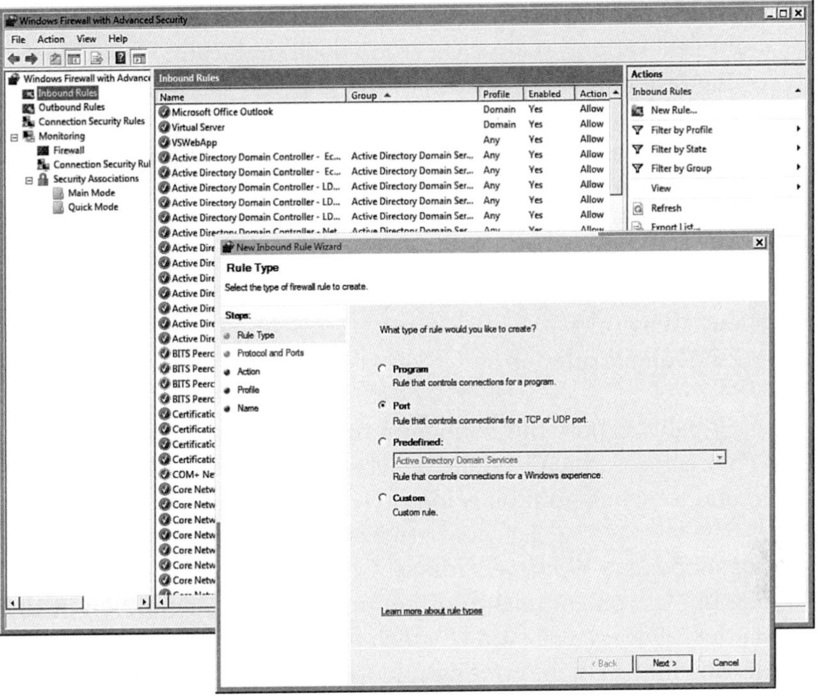

FIGURE 4-32 Creating a new rule.

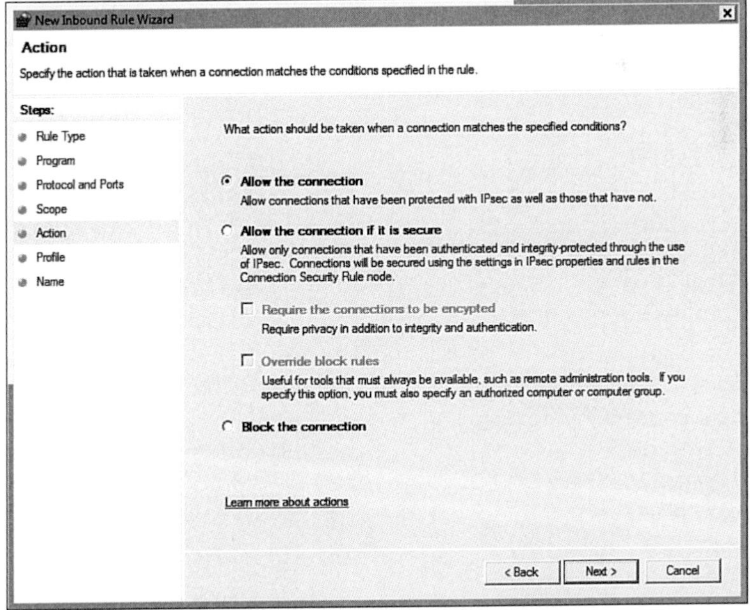

FIGURE 4-33 An action for a new rule.

Numerous types of rules are available, and the rules can be applied in multiple locations, such as via group policy or locally. Apply rules in the following order, allowing control of the final rule set that a firewall uses:

- Service restrictions, which have the highest priority because services typically are a target for hackers due to their power
- Connection security rules
- Authenticated bypass rules
- Block rules
- Allow rules
- Default rules

Finally, export the configuration of a server to a file via the Export Policy action, which is available when the root console tree item is selected and the configuration is imported via the Import Policy action.

Command-Line Windows Firewall Configuration

Use the `netsh` command for command-line configuration of the firewall via the `advfirewall` switch, which exposes a lot of functionality, including viewing information. For example, you can view the configuration of a profile (for example, the domain profile) by using the following command.

```
C:\>netsh advfirewall show domainprofile

Domain Profile Settings:
----------------------------------------------------------------
State                                 ON
Firewall Policy                       BlockInbound,AllowOutbound
LocalFirewallRules                    N/A (GPO-store only)
LocalConSecRules                      N/A (GPO-store only)
InboundUserNotification               Disable
RemoteManagement                      Disable
UnicastResponseToMulticast            Enable

Logging:
LogAllowedConnections                 Disable
LogDroppedConnections                 Enable
FileName                              C:\Windows\system32\LogFiles\
Firewall\pfirewall.log
MaxFileSize                               4096

Ok.
```

Export and import configuration via the `netsh advfirewall export <filename>` and `netsh advfirewall import <filename>` commands.

To create rules, use the `netsh advfirewall firewall add rule` command along with a number of options, such as the rule name, protocol, port, direction, and action. Examples of the various commands are available in the command-line help, which is thorough.

You can quickly turn off Windows Firewall for all profiles by using `netsh advfirewall set allprofiles state off`, and you can use `netsh advfirewall set allprofiles state on` to enable it.

Monitoring

The monitoring section allows monitoring of the enabled firewall rules on the server via the Firewall section, and the Connection Security Rules section shows information on enabled connection security rules.

The Security Associations area displays information about security associations between machines using IPsec, including information on the IP addresses, authentication, and encryption used.

Group Policy Options

The Group Policy area for Windows Firewall with Advanced Configuration is detailed and allows rules to be defined in group policy, configuration of whether local rules should be used, and IPsec configuration.

Under Computer Configuration, Policies, Windows Settings, Security Settings, Windows Firewall with Advanced Security, Windows Firewall with Advanced Security (yes, twice), you can perform full configuration, such as configuration of the various states for the domain, private and public profiles, and rules. As shown in Figure 4-34, the dialogs you use are the same as those used via the Windows Firewall with Advanced Configuration MMC snap-in, even the rule creation wizards. The only real difference is that with the GPO editor, you don't get an Actions pane.

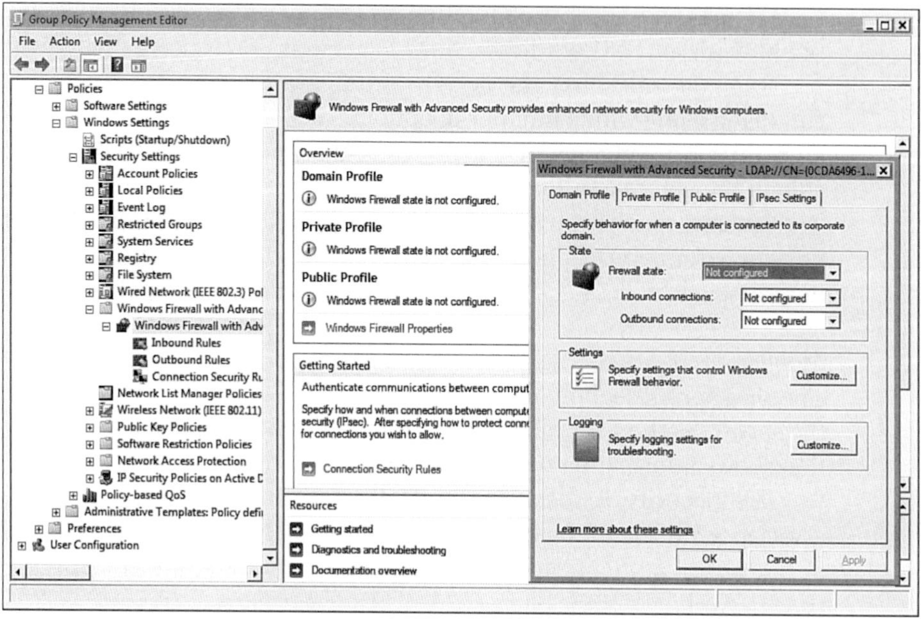

FIGURE 4-34 Configuration via GPO of firewall configuration.

There are some settings you can apply only via group policy. For example, the application of local firewall and connection security rules can be enabled/disabled via the Customize button for the settings of a profile within a GPO, which allows you to set whether locally configured rules on a server/desktop are ignored. Everything else is the same as using the GPO Editor for firewall configuration, and sometimes configuring multiple servers/computers by using the GPO Editor makes the most sense, especially when we consider IPsec.

IPsec

IPsec enables you to encrypt IP information sent between two servers to protect the information being transmitted. Because IPsec operates at Layer 3 in the protocol stack, there are no changes to any applications or services that use IP; the encryption takes place without the knowledge of any user of IP. IPsec provides end-to-end security between two machines, and it is useful if there are IP services or applications that inherently are not secure and perhaps send password information unencrypted (for example, Telnet,

File Transfer Protocol [FTP]). If IPsec is enabled between the client and the FTP server, then all the information is encrypted.

IPsec configuration is commonly performed to configure a server to allow communication only if it is encrypted with IPsec, which helps secure all access and is the base of a type of Network Access Protection (NAP). IPsec as a requirement means communication is possible only with computers that are part of a trusted infrastructure; this is commonly known as domain isolation and means that only members of the domain are allowed to participate in the IPsec communication. You can also be more granular and use IPsec configuration to provide server isolation by configuring specific servers to allow only communication from domain members, specific computers, or hosts in a specific AD security group. Imagine that you had a sensitive SQL Server database server that contained human resources (HR) information. You could use IPsec configuration to allow communication via IPsec and between only computers that were part of the AD domain and were a members of the HR computers AD group.

IPsec has two capabilities: It can provide an authentication guarantee via the Authentication Header (AH), which provides integrity assurance for IP packets by creating a hash value based on the content of the packet and the routing information in addition to sequence information. If the packet were modified in any way, the hash in the AH does not match, and the receiving party knows the packet had been compromised. Whereas the AH header provides an integrity and authenticity guarantee, it does nothing to protect the content of the data from being snooped on. The other capability is the Encapsulating Security Payload (ESP) protocol which encrypts the payload content and also provides integrity and authenticity via its own ESP header and trailer, which surround the original packet. You don't have to use AH if you are using ESP (but you can).

There are two IPsec modes: transport and tunnel. Transport mode is designed to be used between two hosts, and only the payload, which is the data being transferred, is encrypted/authenticated; the IP header is not modified. If you use IPsec authentication, which uses a hash value to ensure that the packet has not been modified, you cannot translate the IP address, for example, if going over a network that uses network address translation (NAT) because the IPsec AH uses the IP address as part of the hash value algorithm, and if the IP address changed, the hash calculation would be invalid.

Tunnel mode solves the NAT issue by encrypting/authenticating the entire IP packet (headers and the payload) and then encapsulating the encryption packet into another IP packet for routing purposes. Because the original IP packet was encrypted/authenticated and an additional IP header is used for the actual data transmission, the communication between hosts can be through NAT networks and also typically creates tunnels between networks.

With Windows Vista and Windows Server 2008, the encryption and key exchange cryptographic algorithms were enhanced to support new compliance requirements, and you now can use the following:

- **Encryption**. Encryption protocols include Data Encryption Standard (DES), which uses a 56-bit key and is not recommended; Triple DES (3DES), which uses three 56-bit keys; and Advanced Encryption Standard, which has a 128-bit key size (AES-128), AES-192 (192-bit key size), and AES-256 (256-bit key size). You can use AES only on Windows Vista and Windows Server 2008.
- **Key exchange**. Key exchange protocols include Diffie-Hellman Group 1, 2, and 14; Elliptic Curve Diffie-Hellman P256 (ECDH P-256); and ECDH P-384. You can use ECDH P-256/384 only when all systems involved in the communication are running either Windows Vista or Windows Server 2008.

Server Configuration

Configure IPsec via connection security rules and the IPsec settings as part of the computer's properties, as shown in Figure 4-35. The IPsec settings are broken out in the key exchange, data protection, and authentication settings. Notice the terms Main Mode and Quick Mode in this dialog. You also see them when you look at the security associations under monitoring. What are these modes?

Security associations (SAs) contain the information needed to determine how traffic is to be secured between systems participating in IPsec as well as details of the security services, protection mechanisms, and the cryptographic keys that will be used. For communication, there are two types of SA: Internet Security Association and Key Management Protocol (ISAKMP) and IPsec. The ISAKMP SA is known as the main mode SA and is used for the initial IPsec security negotiation. The initial negotiation is used to agree on the suite of cipher settings (known as the ciphersuite) and keys that will be used for the main communication between the two computers, in addition to authentication of the computers. The use of the

ISAKMP SA ensures that all communication related to IPsec is encrypted, even the traffic that is used to agree on what configuration to use.

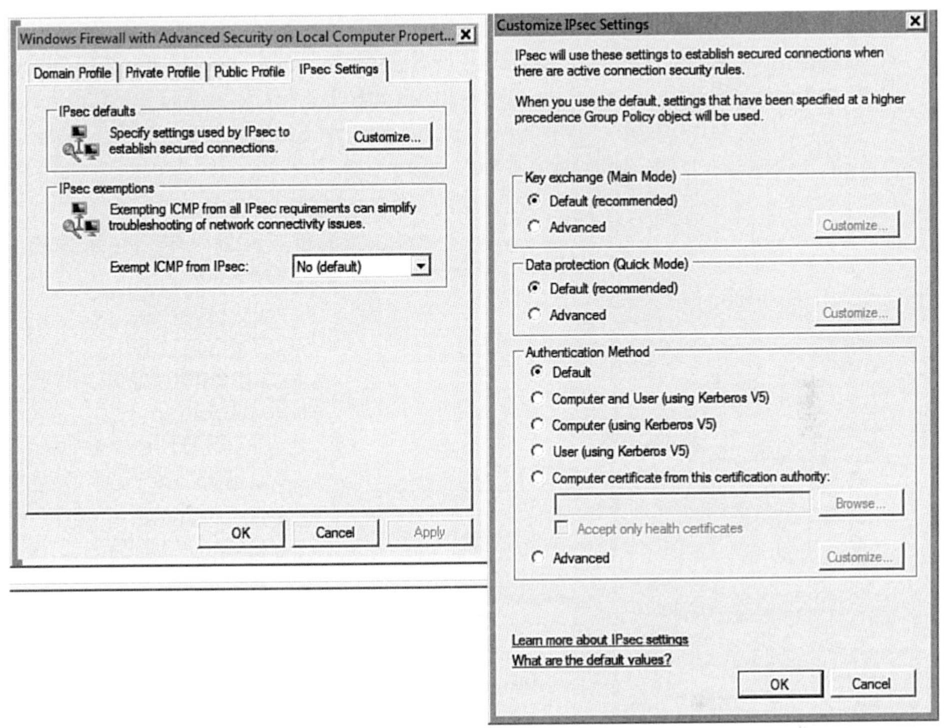

FIGURE 4-35 IPsec server-level options.

When the ISAKMP SA is complete, the IPsec SA is used. This is known as the quick mode SA, and it protects the traffic sent between the IPsec computers. There are always two IPsec SAs, one inbound and one outbound (from the perspective of one of the servers). The inbound IPsec SA for Server A would be the outbound IPsec SA for Server B.

Now that you understand the two modes, main and quick, let's look at specific options. For both cases, leaving the default settings is recommended. However, you can set advanced options, and for the main mode (key exchange), this allows you to specify a specific key exchange algorithm and security method, which by default includes 3DES and AES-128. However, you can add more security methods via the Add button, as shown in Figure 4-36. Remember that for two hosts to communicate with IPsec, there has to be a common security method, so don't remove security methods that may be the only configured methods on nodes a server may need to talk to. The default key exchange of Diffie-Hellman Group 2 provides good key exchange functionality and security and is supported by all versions of Windows, so it is a good default. If you selected a ECDHP key exchange algorithm, you have stronger protection, but only Vista and Windows Server 2008 would be supported.

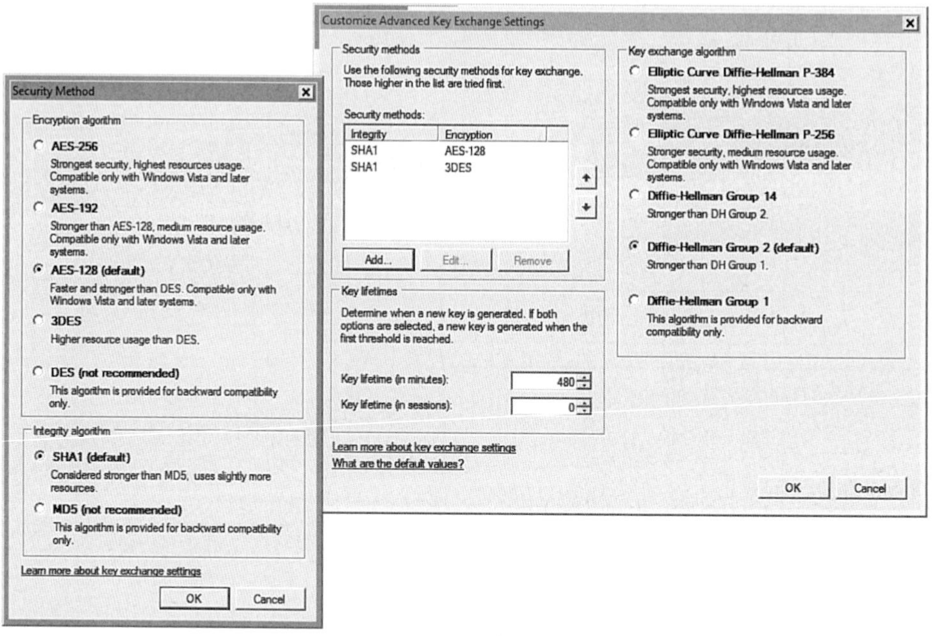

FIGURE 4-36 Configuring specific advanced settings for key exchange.

The same configuration is also available for the data protection area (quick mode) and allows you to define the various data integrity and encryption algorithm combinations that are used between IPsec hosts. The two nodes involved go through their list of algorithms from top to bottom, and the first common algorithm is used, so the ordering is important. You can add additional data integrity algorithms, which just allow you to specify whether ESP or AH is used (ESP is preferred because it supports NAT) and the algorithm (SHA1 versus MD5) plus the key lifetime, in minutes, and KB.

For data integrity with encryption, you have exactly the same options, but this time you can also choose the algorithm to use for the actual encryption, as shown in Figure 4-37.

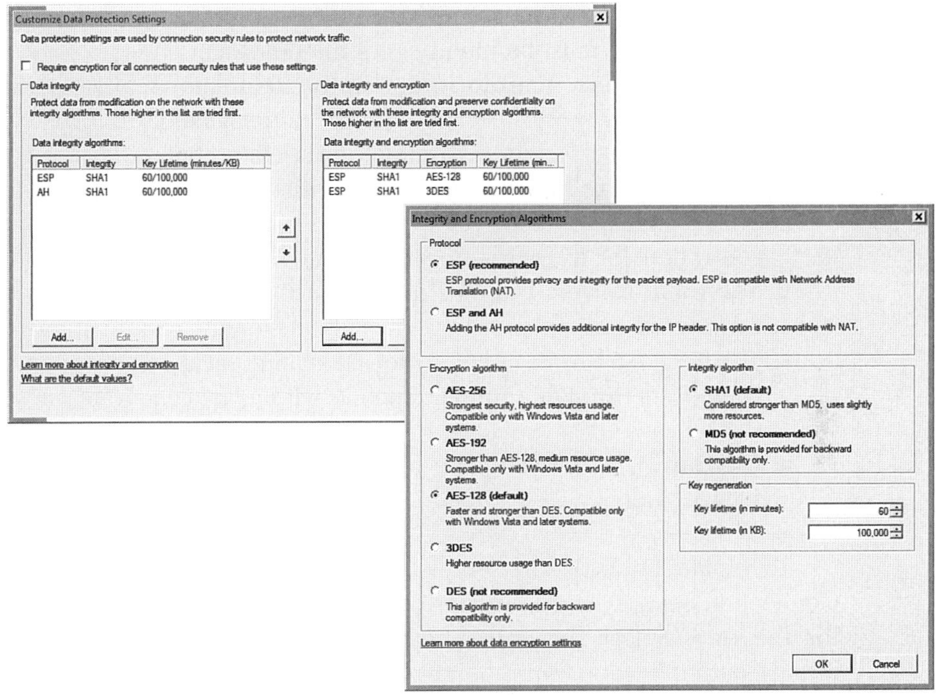

FIGURE 4-37 The IPsec data protection advanced options.

The final server-level setting is the authentication method, which by default is computer Kerberos Version 5 authentication. However, you can change this to combinations of computer and user in addition to using a computer certificate from an organization's CA that leverages PKI or even configure the use of NTLM Version 2 or a preshared key, which is not recommended because this key would be stored in plaintext.

Connection Security Rules

Use connection security rules to control IPsec-based connection security. A number of template connection security rules are available via the wizard, and you can also create custom rules. The actual connection security rules are all in the same format, but the templates configure different settings to achieve different results. The templates are as follows:

- **Isolation**. Use this template to isolate a server by specifying criteria that must be met for computers wanting to communicate (for example, that they must be members of the domain).
- **Authentication Exemption**. Use this template to allow specific computers, groups of computer, or IP address ranges to be excluded from being required to authenticate themselves. This is commonly used to allow communication with computers before the type of authentication configured is possible (for example, with domain controllers for Kerberos).
- **Server-to-server**. Use this template to authenticate between two computers, groups of computers, subnets, or any combination.
- **Tunnel**. Use this template to secure communications between two computers through a tunnels such as with a virtual private network (VPN).
- **Custom**. Use this template to tailor all aspects of the connection security rule.

To create an Isolation template rule, select New Rule from the Connection Security Rules Actions pane and then select the Isolation type for the rule. Select the authentication requirement, which can be to request authentication for inbound and outbound connections, but it is not required. Select to require authentication for inbound connections and request it for outbound connections, which says anyone wanting to communicate with the server must use authentication and is a common setting to use. Finally, configure authentication to be required for inbound and outbound connections.

When the authentication requirements are selected, select the authentication method, which by default uses the method configured in the server settings. Alternatively, you can select a specific authentication method. Finally, select the profile where the connection security rule should be applied (domain, private, or public), and although a server should never move, ensure that the rule is set for all profiles.

Set a name and description for the new connection security rule, and it is displayed when viewing the connection security rules via the MMC snap-in. You can edit these rules via their properties, which gives you control over the computers/IP addresses the rule applies to, the authentication to use, and advanced settings such as the interfaces the rule applies to and IPsec tunneling behavior.

Based on the connection security rule, communication is encrypted with IPsec, provided that both servers trying to communicate have a connection security rule defined. Therefore, using Group Policy to configure the IPsec configuration makes the most sense. If you have a server that requires inbound authentication but you have machines that have no connection security rules configured, they are unable to communicate. An acceptable combination is to configure specific servers to require inbound authentication and then the rest of the computers configured to request inbound and outbound authentication. This configuration allows negotiation to take place and IPsec to be enabled.

When you have connections, you can see the detailed connections under the Monitoring, Security Associations, Main/Quick Mode, as shown in Figure 4-38. This example shows two connections that are being authenticated and encrypted via ESP.

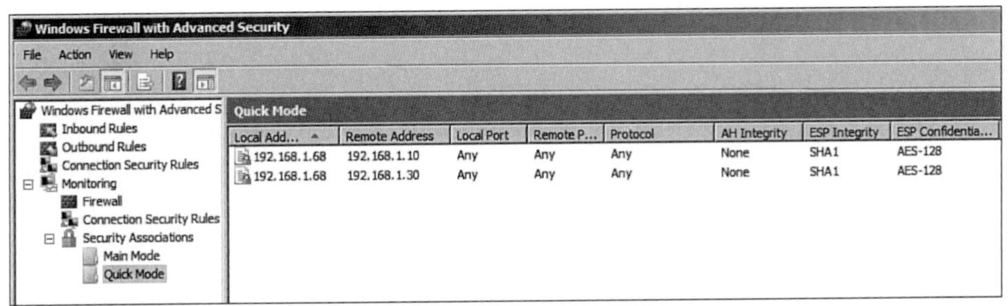

FIGURE 4-38 Viewing IPsec security associations.

Windows Defender

Windows Server 2008 includes Windows Defender, which is enabled if the Desktop Experience feature is installed. It requires no configuration, and it monitors for spyware on the server and attempts to stop any spyware installation. Windows Defender can be configured to use Microsoft SpyNet, an online network that can be used to look up behavior that is currently not classified within the Windows Defender spyware definition file to see how other users in the community have treated the software.

Manual scans can be triggered to search the system for spyware in addition to periodically scanning the Tools menu. Any suspect items are placed in the Quarantined Items bin, which allows the administrator to restore the program to an operational state or remove it if it's not desired.

To bulk configure machines, use the group policy Windows Defender settings, which are found under Computer Configuration, Policies, Administrative Templates, Windows Components, Windows Defender.

Internet Explorer Enhanced Security Configuration

The Internet Explorer Enhanced Security Configuration (IE ESC) is designed to reduce the risks related to Web browsing performed on a server; it is enabled by default. Ideally, you should not be surfing the Web on a server, but sometimes it is convenient to jump onto the Web to look for something, and there is always a risk you will be redirected to a site with malware that on a desktop is a pain but on a server could be devastating.

For this protection, IE ESC restricts the content that web sites can display and utilize. For example, for Internet web sites, Microsoft ActiveX controls, Microsoft VM for HTML content, and file downloads are all disabled, and this is based on the Internet Explorer Security zones. Internet sites are set to a High security level, whereas for sites on the local intranet, the security level is set to Medium-low. The automatic detection of intranet sites is disabled by default, which means your credentials are not passed through automatically, so you are prompted for credentials until you manually add an intranet site to the Local intranet zone.

Other settings, including the following, are made when IE ESC is enabled:

- The enhanced security configuration dialog is displayed when a site tries to use blocked content, such as scripting or ActiveX controls.
- Browser extensions are disabled.
- On-demand installation of Internet Explorer components is disabled.
- Playing of media content in the Internet Explorer media bar is disabled.
- Music, sounds, animations, and videos are disabled in Web pages.
- Revocation of certificates used by web sites is enabled.
- Signatures are checked for downloaded programs.
- Encrypted pages cannot be saved to the temporary Internet files folder.

- A warning is issued when you move from a secure to nonsecure site.
- The Web files cache is emptied when Internet Explorer is closed.
- Windows Updates is added to the Trusted Sites zone, allowing updates to be applied seamlessly, as is the Windows error reporting site, which allows problems to be reported.

When you first start Internet Explorer with no URL selected, Internet Explorer informs you of its mode; by default, it informs you that IE ESC is enabled. This status display is facilitated by configuring a default home page.

If you select Tools, Internet Options and select the Security tab, if you are an administrator, you can modify the security level for each of the site zones. Normal users and administrators can add sites to zones, as shown in Figure 4-39. (For example, add a Web page to the Trusted Sites zone to enable additional functionality, such as ActiveX.)

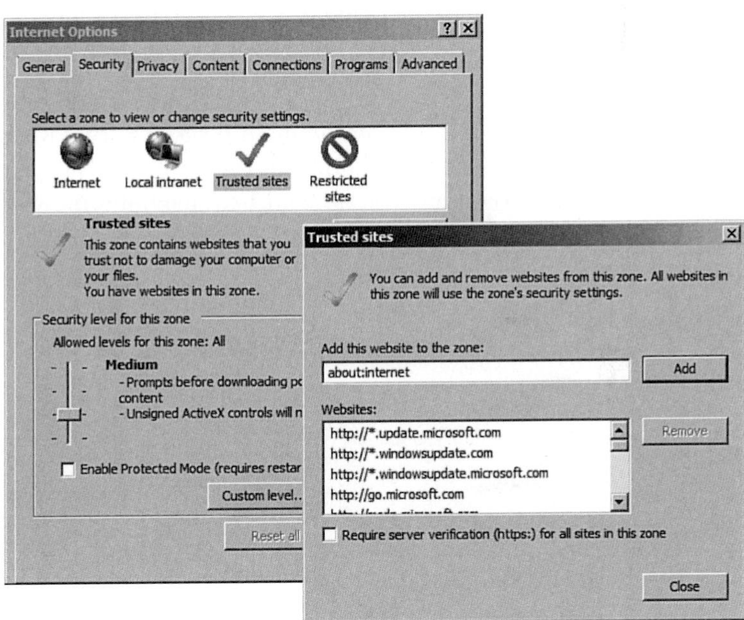

FIGURE 4-39 When configuring sites in zones, notice the default members of the Trusted Sites zone when in IE ESC mode.

If you access a nontrusted site that tries to run content that is blocked by IE ESC, you see the enhanced security content dialog, shown in Figure 4-40, which allows you to add the site to the Trusted Sites zone to enable full functionality or just click Close to continue to load the page but with the blocked content unavailable.

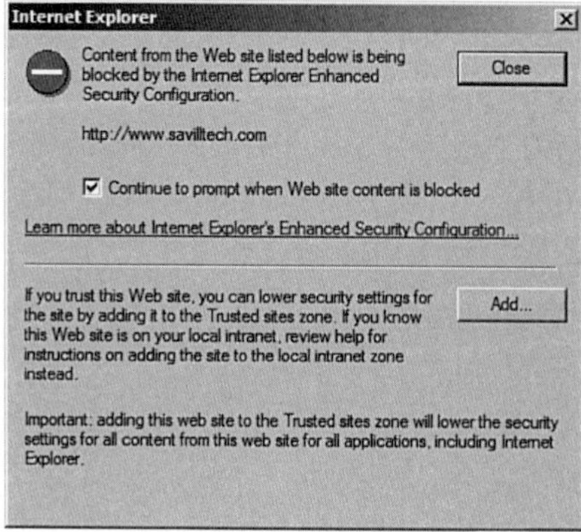

FIGURE 4-40 The IE ESC message for a site trying to run content that is blocked by IE ESC.

You can turn IE ESC on and off at the administrator and user levels via the Configure IE ESC link on the main page of Server Manager in the Security Information section, as shown in Figure 4-41. The best practice is to leave this turned on; however, on your test machines on which you may do multiple functions, you may want to turn it off so you more easily research items.

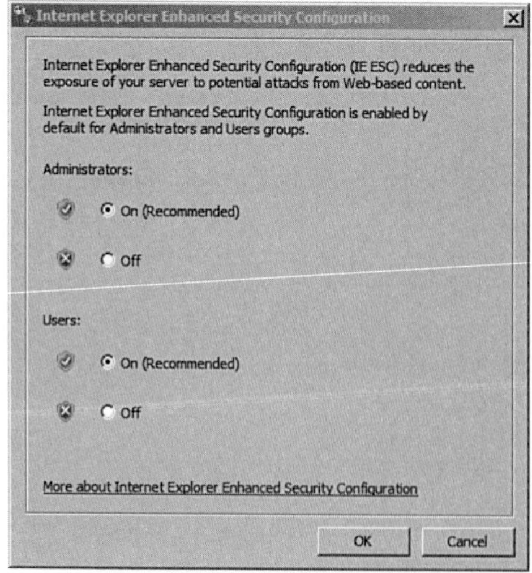

FIGURE 4-41 IE ESC configuration.

User Access Control (UAC)

Chapter 2, "Windows Server 2008 Fundamentals: Navigating and Getting Started," looked at User Access Control (UAC) as a way to protect administrator sessions from issues caused by the privileges associated with administrator accounts. UAC has solved this problem by creating two tokens for an administrator, one with the administrator privileges, and one with just normal credentials. The administrator session runs with the normal-user-privileges token by default, and only when higher credentials are needed is the administrator prompted for consent (known as prompt for consent) to authorize the use of the elevated powers to perform administrative functions. This also works for nonadministrators, who, when trying to perform a function that requires higher privileges, are prompted for an administrator account username and password, allowing an administrator to provide Over the Shoulder (OTS) assistance without having to log out the user (known as prompt for credentials). You can also configure administrators to be prompted for credentials to elevate privileges in highly secure environments, but your administrators won't like it! With this functionality, you can use numerous configurations to control how UAC functions in the environment.

By default, the built-in administrator account has Admin Approval Mode (AAM) disabled, so the administrator never sees prompts to grant administrator permissions, but UAC is still a part of Windows Server 2008. For example, a domain administrator (not the built-in domain administrator) trying to modify the time on a server might receive the UAC consent dialog, as shown in Figure 4-42. Notice that the rest of the screen has been grayed out. This is a security feature of the UAC dialogs, designed to stop malware from trying to interfere with the UAC prompts in case you're entering administrator credentials and to prevent malware from taking over a prompt to OK the use of your administrator credential token. Your interface normally is the interactive or user desktop, where your applications interface with you and any process can perform input/output. A second desktop, known as the secure desktop, is used by UAC dialogs, and only Windows processes can write to it. When Windows wants to display a UAC dialog, it flips to the secure desktop, and the user desktop is displayed behind the secure desktop, with the user desktop content grayed out to show that it's not in focus. It would be possible for a malware application to fake a UAC prompt by graying out the rest of the screen, but this would be useful only if it prompted for administrator credentials to harvest the password because a fake AAM dialog would just get you to click Continue and would not give any privileges due to the fact that the real elevation process would not have been activated. Vista has other controls in place to stop malware from trying to harvest passwords using a fake UAC prompt.

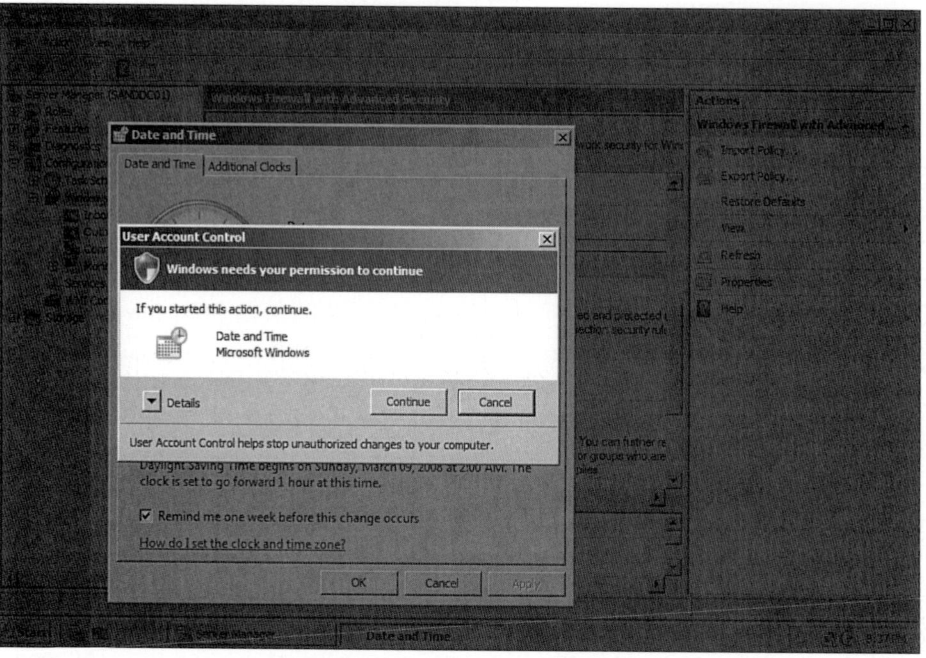

FIGURE 4-42 The UAC consent dialog.

You can manually configure the UAC via a number of methods, and you can use group policy settings for granular control. These settings are available at Computer Configuration, Policies, Windows Settings, Security Settings, Local Policies, Security Options. They are also available as local settings in the local computer policy for a server (and, indeed, a Vista client). In fact, the UAC configuration is stored in the local computer policy by default, but group policy can be used to override those settings. The settings available for Windows Server 2008 and Windows Vista are shown here, and the defaults are consistent for both OSs:

- **User Account Control: Admin Approval Mode for the Built-in Administrator account. [Default – Disabled].** Controls whether the AAM is used for the built-in administrator account. By default, AAM is disabled for the built-in administrator account, but you can enable it by setting this policy to Enabled.

- **User Account Control: Allow UIAccess applications to prompt for elevation without using the secure desktop [Default – Disabled]**. Applies to User Interface Accessibility (UIA) programs, particularly Remote Assistance and how elevation prompts are displayed. By default, during a Remote Assistance session, any elevation prompts are displayed on the interactive user's session, and the Remote Assistance user gets a grayed-out screen. If the Remote Assistance user needs to be answering the elevation prompts remotely, the elevation prompts cannot be displayed on the secure desktop and instead need to be displayed on the interactive desktop so that they are shown to the Remote Assistance session. Setting this setting to Enabled configures elevation prompts during UIA sessions to be displayed in the user desktop. It should be noted that with Remote Assistance, the user can allow the Remote Assistance expert to respond to the UAC prompts, but doing so requires a UAC prompt itself, which kind of defeats the purpose and hence why we have this option.
- **User Account Control: Behavior of the elevation prompt for administrators in Admin Approval Mode [Default – Prompt for consent]**. If administrators are configured to run in the AAM, this option controls whether they are prompted for consent (the default), whether the administrator has to enter her credentials (Prompt for Credentials), or whether the administrator is not prompted and is elevated automatically (Elevate without Prompting). The last option should not be used because although UAC is in effect so you run as a normal user token, any time more privileges are needed, the elevation occurs automatically, defeating the purpose.
- **User Account Control: Behavior of the elevation prompt for standard users [Default – Prompt for credentials].** Controls how UAC works for nonadministrators. By default, the user is prompted for an administrator set of credentials (an account and a password in a domain or an administrator account and a password in a workgroup). As an alternative, this can be set to Automatically Deny Elevation Requests, which means the user will not be prompted, and any action or process that requires elevation will fail.

- **User Account Control: Detect application installations and prompt for elevation [Default – Enabled**. Allows Vista to detect whether an application installer that requires elevation is running, and if so, the elevation prompt will be displayed. Setting this to Disabled turns off this check and suppresses the elevation dialog and would be used in environments where technologies such as group policy or System Center Configuration Manager (SCCM) are used to deploy software that uses delegated installation to avoid permission issues. By default, this option is set to Disabled for Windows Vista Enterprise edition.
- **User Account Control: Only elevate executables that are signed and validated [Default – Disabled]**. Allows only executables that are signed by a trusted certificate chain to request elevation. Because of the implications of the enterprise configuration needed to ensure that all the correct chains are trusted, this option is disabled by default, but in a locked-down environment, this setting can be useful to further protect systems from malware-type applications
- **User Account Control: Only elevate UIAccess applications that are installed in secure locations [Default – Enabled]**. Applies to the UIA applications and ensures that only applications in the "normal" program areas, such as under %systemroot%\Program Files [(x86) for 64-bit also] and %windir%, can be treated as UIAccess applications per their manifest requests. The manifest is a header for each program that makes statements about what the program does and things it needs. Turning it off would allow applications installed anywhere to use the UIAccess UAC prompt options, which could be dangerous.
- **User Account Control: Run all administrators in Admin Approval Mode [Default – Enabled]**. By default, all administrators except the built-in administrator account run in AAM and so are prompted for elevation consent/credentials (depending on the AAM setting for administrators). By default, Enabled is the optimal setting, and it should not be disabled as that would turn off UAC for all administrator accounts, and those are the users who need it the most.
- **User Account Control: Switch to the secure desktop when prompting for elevation [Default – Enabled]**. Controls whether UAC elevation requests are displayed on the secure desktop (with

the user desktop grayed out in the background), which is the default, and it offers protection against malware UAC hijacking and emulations. If it is disabled, UAC elevation prompts will display on the normal user desktop.

- **User Account Control: Virtualize file and Registry write failures to per-user locations [Default – Enabled].** With this feature, as discussed in Chapter 2, if a process tries to write to an area of the Registry or file system that is considered secure, such as %program files% or %windir%, then instead of failing the write request, it is redirected to an area under the user's profile that allows the application to function. This option is enabled by default, and if it is disabled, applications simply fail, as they would have done pre-Vista. This is an important setting when you consider that the switch to Vista will see many normal users lose their local administrative rights.

All these settings are in the Registry under HKEY_LOCAL_MACHINE\SOFTWARE\Microsoft\Windows\CurrentVersion\Policies\System. For example, to disable UAC, set EnableLUA to 0 and reboot. Set the elevation prompt for administrators via ConsentPromptBehaviorAdmin, where 2 prompts for consent and 1 prompts for credentials, while 0 does not prompt at all. It's not a good idea to modify the Registry directly. If you need to change settings for one machine, use gpedit.msc to edit the local computer policy, and if you need to change settings for multiple machines, use a GPO to link to a domain or an OU (or even a site) that contains the computers that should use the new UAC configuration.

Also at a local machine level, you can control whether UAC is enabled or disabled via the User Accounts Control Panel applet and use the Turn User Account Control On or Off link, which allows you to disable or enable UAC at a computer level, as shown in Figure 4-43. Again, this is not recommended. There is also a tool in MSCONFIG that you can use to disable and enable UAC, but the command that gets run just modifies the EnableLUA Registry value discussed earlier, so it's no different from using policy or the User Accounts Control Panel applet.

Remember that you can run any application with the administrative token by typing the application name in the Start menu search area and then right-clicking and selecting Run as Administrator.

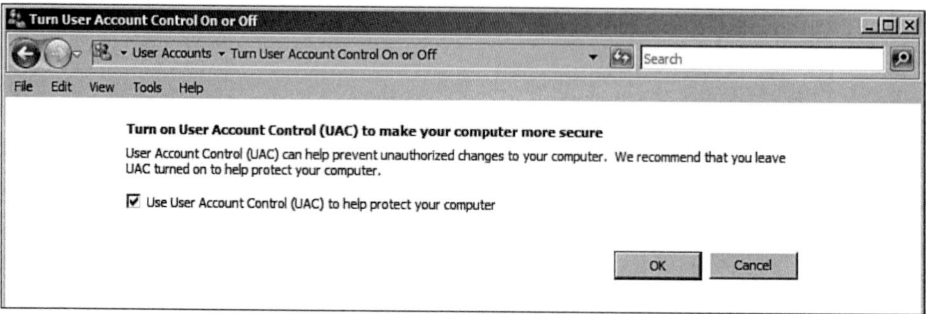

FIGURE 4-43 Manual UAC control.

In short, UAC is a great technology, and sometimes there is a temptation to just turn it off at the first sign of inconvenience. But if you look at the longer-term protection it offers, you see that it's a good idea to use UAC, particularly on your servers, where damage impact could be huge.

SysKey

SysKey is a utility designed to increase the security of the accounts database by encrypting its content. SysKey is enabled by default and cannot be disabled. However, by default the key required to decrypt is stored locally on the server. If you click the Update button, configure a password to be entered or store the startup key on a floppy disk that would need to be entered at each system startup, as shown in Figure 4-44. In general, do not tamper with the configuration.

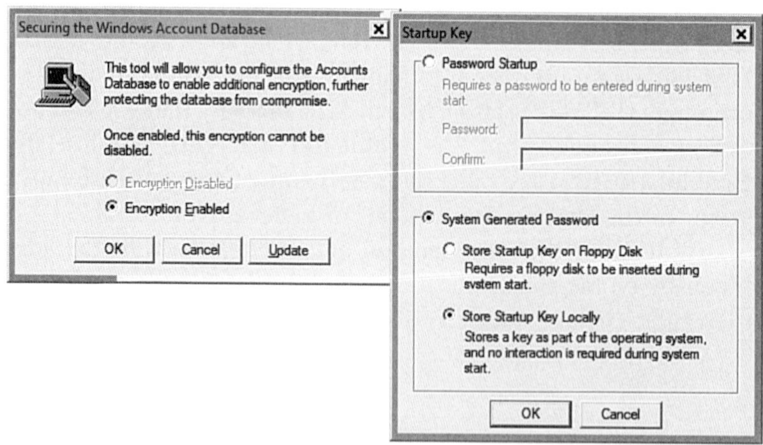

FIGURE 4-44 Configuring SysKey.

Account Policies

Account Policies are a critical area of configuration that is often overlooked and misconfigured. As seen in this chapter and as throughout the rest of this book, Microsoft offers huge amounts of security technology, and in most environments, the key to the door is via your username and password, so you need to make sure your passwords are sufficiently complex that they won't be easily guessed or hacked.

To enforce a certain password standard, use account policies, which are defined in the Default Domain Policy and are broken into three areas: Password Policy, Account Lockout Policy, and Kerberos Policy. These policies apply to all domain accounts, so any user in the domain will be forced to use these settings.

Password Policy allows the configuration of six key aspects of a password:

- **Enforce password history**. Keeps track of the last 0 to 24 passwords, depending on the configuration. By default, on a domain controller, this is set to the maximum of 24. A user cannot change his password to any password stored in the password history.
- **Maximum password age**. The maximum age a password can be before it must be changed. A user is prompted when his password is about to expire, and when a password has expired, the user must change the password before logging on. By default, this is 42 days.
- **Minimum password age**. The amount of time a password must be set before it can be changed. Why might you need this? With password history enabled and no minimum password age, a user could just change his password 25 times and get back to the original password because the password history would have deleted the oldest password, which was the original. When you force a password to be used for a period of time, such as a day, users can't just change their passwords repeatedly and work around the password history.
- **Minimum password length**. The minimum number of characters the password must be. Seven is the default, and it originates the way the LAN Manager hash of a password was stored as two seven-character chunks; it was more secure to have a seven-character password than an eight-character password because the last character could easily be broken and might hint at the rest of the password.

- **Password must meet complexity requirements**. When this setting is enabled, passwords must meet the following criteria:
  - Not contain the user's account name or parts of the user's full name that exceed two consecutive characters
  - Be at least six characters in length
  - Contain characters from three of the following four categories:

    English uppercase characters (A through Z)

    English lowercase characters (a through z)

    Base 10 digits (0 through 9)

    Nonalphabetic characters (for example, !, $, #, %)
  - Meet complexity requirements when they are changed or created
- **Store passwords using reversible encryption**. Disabled by default but is required if Challenge-Handshake Authentication Protocol (CHAP) is used for remote access or digest authentication with Internet Information Services (IIS). Enabling this option is not recommended.

By default, on a newly created domain, the settings implemented are strong; check your environment to ensure that you have similar settings. In many companies, password complexity is turned off, which is a disaster, and although it may be politically challenging to convince executives that they need a complex password, it is for the good of the company. Remember that account policies can be configured only at the domain level. If you create a GPO and configure account settings and then link at an OU or site level, those account settings will have no effect for domain accounts and will instead affect only local accounts on the computers within the OU or site. Prior to Windows Server 2008, you could have only one account policy per domain, and this is still the case in Windows Server 2008, except with a Windows Server 2008 mode domain, you have fine-grained password policy capabilities that allow you to specify addition password policies based on a user's group membership (see Chapter 12, "Managing Active Directory and Advanced Concepts.")

Account Lockout Policy defines what you do if a password for an account is incorrect. It is designed to lock out an account and make it unusable after a specified number of incorrect password attempts in a certain amount of time. By default, this is not enabled, but it should be. The following are the three areas of configuration:

- **Account lockout duration**. The amount of time an account is locked out, in minutes. A setting of 0 means the account stays locked out until it is manually enabled. A common value is 30 minutes, which is a good balance. We don't want a value of 0 because an attacker who just wants to disrupt your company from working would just have to target each account with a wrong password five times (if five were the number of incorrect password attempts before lockout), and the account would be locked out until it was manually enabled. If the attacker hit every account in the domain, every account would be locked out forever, and you would have no way to log in to enable it. This is why 30 minutes is a good amount of time. A hacker trying to hack the password would get five tries and then have to wait 30 minutes, then try another five, and so on. They are not likely to crack a password with only ten tries per hour.
- **Account lockout threshold**. The number of incorrect password attempts before lockout. 0 means the account is never locked out. 5 is a common value to use.
- **Reset account lockout counter after**. Configures the counter of incorrect passwords to be reset after a configured number of minutes. Again, 30 minutes is typically used.

The Kerberos Policy area should not be modified and is part of the internal workings of Kerberos.

If you want to view account logon failures on a domain controller, view the Security log and look for `Audit Failure` keyword event logs with the events ID 4771. You can filter the security log view to show only failure audits by setting the current filter to have `Audit Failure` for the keywords. The following is an example of a logon failure event log:

```
Log Name:       Security
Source:         Microsoft-Windows-Security-Auditing
Date:           1/27/2008 9:15:49 PM
Event ID:       4771
Task Category: Kerberos Authentication Service
Level:          Information
Keywords:       Audit Failure
```

```
User:           N/A
Computer:       savdaldc01.savilltech.net
Description:
Kerberos pre-authentication failed.

Account Information:
      Security ID:              SAVILLTECH\dutch
      Account Name:             dutch

Service Information:
      Service Name:             krbtgt/SAVILLTECH

Network Information:
      Client Address:           ::ffff:192.168.1.80
      Client Port:              54361

Additional Information:
      Ticket Options:           0x40810010
      Failure Code:             0x12
      Pre-Authentication Type:     0

Certificate Information:
      Certificate Issuer Name:
      Certificate Serial Number:
      Certificate Thumbprint:

Certificate information is only provided if a certificate was
used for pre-authentication.

Pre-authentication types, ticket options and failure codes are
defined in RFC 4120.

If the ticket was malformed or damaged during transit and could
not be decrypted, then many fields in this event might not be
present.
```

You might need to make a change to see these failure event logs. Configure this on the local computer policy of your domain controller or on all domain controllers via group policy, and set the Audit Account Logon Events setting under Computer Configuration, Windows Settings, Security Settings, Local Policies, Audit Policy to Success, Failure.

If an account is locked out, the option Unlock Account is available via the user's Account tab, as shown in Figure 4-45.

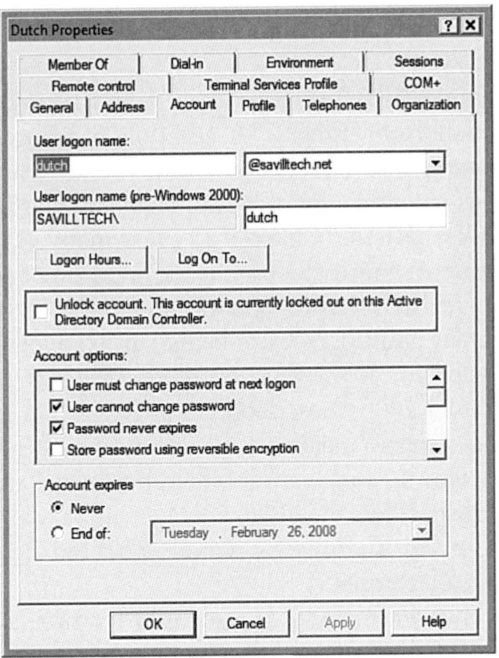

FIGURE 4-45 Unlocking a locked-out account.

By default, the information related to lockout information and good and bad logons is stored on each domain controller and not easily viewable across all domain controllers. However, for Windows Server 2003, an additional account information DLL, acctinfo.dll, was available as part of the resource kit and when it was registered with command `regsvr32 acctinfo.dll`, a new tab for user objects displayed the following:

- The last time the password was set
- The domain password policies
- When the password will expire
- The lockout status
- The last good and bad logons

Windows Server 2008 mode domains provide a much better way to track good and bad logons, as discussed in Chapter 12.

Summary

Windows Server 2008 has had a great deal of attention paid to its security and protection from attacks. In addition to improvements to Windows Firewall, components enabled only when needed, and the other items discussed in this chapter, a lot of kernel-level changes have made it more difficult to hack a system. (Chapter 2 covers many of these.) One key bit of protection that is security focused is the addition of address space load randomization (ASLR). Before Windows Server 2008, the kernel, HAL, and key executables and DLLs were loaded at fixed locations in memory. This made it easier for a process to try to attack these memory areas. In Windows Server 2008, these modules are placed in 1 of 256 random points in the address space, making it far more difficult to attack. A service can auto restart only 10 times, after which the server must reboot before the service can restart; this means an attacker can't try all 256 because the server will reboot. So if you see a server rebooted because of service retry, check for hack attempts.

In this chapter, many of the security features are discussed at a high level, which is an unfortunate limitation when trying to cover such a huge topic. As mentioned at the beginning of this chapter, many security-related technologies are discussed throughout the entire book; this chapter focuses on technologies that are purely security. This chapter helps you see what is available and how to use the various features. Security is often discussed but not emphasized enough in organizations. Taking some time to understand the features that are available to you and spending some time now securing your environment will save you a lot of time later, when you're not hacked.

If you want to lock down your environment, download the *Microsoft Windows Server 2008 Security Guide*. It has 200 pages of lockdown information, and it even includes some group policy templates and updates for the Security Configuration and Analysis snap-in.

CHAPTER 5

FILE SYSTEM AND PRINT MANAGEMENT FEATURES

One of the greatest and most used features of an operating system is the file system. At its most basic level, the file system allows you to store and read data in a persistent manner. In this chapter, you look at the facilities for server-based file storage offered by Windows Server 2008. Server-based file storage is vital in any organization because client-side storage cannot be relied upon from a resiliency perspective, and client-side data is not available to the organization.

You start off with a basic view of the file systems and their features you use in Windows Server 2008, including basic management of file systems, volume creation, maintenance, and more advanced concepts.

After you have data, you sometimes need to print it. So, the second half of the chapter deals with print server capabilities with Windows Server 2008, including managing the properties of an individual print server, print queues, and multiple print servers from a central management location.

File System Types and Management

Windows Server offers a number of file systems that can be used on media connected to the server. Although you use only one of the file systems for fixed media, you look at all the options.

File Allocation Table (FAT)

File Allocation Table (FAT) is a remnant from the MS-DOS days and was limited to 8.3 filename restrictions until Long File Name (LFN) support was added. Although FAT has been largely replaced by more sophisticated file systems, many media, such as memory cards, still use FAT because of its support across nearly all operating systems.

LFNs worked behind the scenes. The LFN for a file was stored using a series of linked directory entries. An LFN uses one directory entry for its alias (an automatically generated 8.3 name) and a hidden secondary directory entry for every 13 characters in its name. If you had a 200-character filename, it would use 17 entries.

The alias is generated using the first six characters of the LFN, then a ~, and then a number for the first four versions of a files with the same first six characters. For example, for the file john savills file.txt, the names generated would be johnsa~1.txt, johnsa~2.txt, and so on. After the first four versions of a file, only the first two characters of the filename are used, and the last six are generated, as in jo0E38~1.txt.

FAT is a basic file system. It has no capability to set security on files or audit access. Files on FAT volumes become fragmented because no map is kept of free space on the volume, and FAT has no built-in corruption recovery.

FAT32

Introduced with Windows 95 OSR2, FAT32 is designed to address some of the size limitations of FAT as hard drives increase in size. As with FAT, the same 8.3 filenames exist, although LFN's 255-character filenames are available.

New Technology File System (NTFS)

New Technology File System (NTFS) was introduced with the first version of Windows NT (3.1) and was a completely rewritten file system instead of an upgrade for FAT. NTFS introduced metadata for objects on the file system, allowing many more file system capabilities, such as security configuration and auditing information. A subset of the metadata for each file is stored in the master file table (MTF), which is used to quickly see free space on a volume, determine where to place new files, and cut down on fragmentation. Fragmentation occurs when a file is written to disk but not to a contiguous block of space. The file is scattered over separate areas of the disk. Why is this a problem? This fragmentation means that when the data is read, instead of one disk seek (a slow operation), many disk seeks are needed to read the data.

Numerous versions of NTFS exist. Windows XP, 2003, Vista, and Windows Server 2008 all run version 3.1. The version of an NTFS volume (seen in the third line of the following output) can be checked with the `fsutil` command:

```
C:\>fsutil fsinfo ntfsinfo c:\
NTFS Volume Serial Number :       0x886a8ca26a8c8f1e
Version :                         3.1
Number Sectors :                  0x0000000009c3ffff
Total Clusters :                  0x0000000001387fff
Free Clusters  :                  0x000000000104b337
Total Reserved :                  0x0000000000000040
Bytes Per Sector  :               512
Bytes Per Cluster :               4096
Bytes Per FileRecord Segment    : 1024
Clusters Per FileRecord Segment : 0
Mft Valid Data Length :           0x0000000003cb0000
Mft Start Lcn  :                  0x00000000000c0000
Mft2 Start Lcn :                  0x00000000009c3fff
Mft Zone Start :                  0x00000000000c3ca0
Mft Zone End   :                  0x00000000000cc820
RM Identifier:        827C9D5C-FCD5-11DB-9486-E19769CE1781
```

The output shows version 3.1; the number of sectors, clusters, and so forth; the location of the start of the MFT; and the location of MFT2. The MFT2 is a mirror of the first 16 records of the MFT, which describe the metadata files themselves and are, therefore, the most vital. The MFT2 is stored at the end of the partition as a spare copy of the MFT in case of corruption. The MFT2 can be used to make your NTFS volume usable again. (Search the Microsoft Knowledge Base for details on how.) These files are stored at the root of the C: drive as super hidden files $MFT and $MFTMirr. There is no way to view them within Windows itself. More of these super hidden files exist, such as the following:

- **$AttrDef**. A description of the metadata that can be used as attributes of data stored on the volume
- **$BadClus**. List of all clusters on the disk that are marked as bad
- **$Bitmap**. Map of the clusters on the volume, including which are currently free
- **$Boot**. Copy of the boot sector
- **$LogFile**. Transaction log file for the volume
- **$Quota**. Quota entries on the volume for NTFS 5.0 volumes
- **$UpCase**. Table to convert filenames to Unicode
- **$Volume**. Key information about the volume, such as the NTFS version, creation time, and volume name

The core features of NTFS are discussed later, but let's start off with some new NTFS features introduced with Windows Server 2008.

New NTFS Features in Windows Server 2008

Windows Server 2008 introduced significant changes to NTFS, namely transaction NTFS, self-healing NTFS, and enhanced symbolic linking.

Transaction NTFS

A major part of any multiaction operation is that if one part fails, all the actions must roll back. These actions are grouped into a transaction. A transaction often has to pass the atomic, consistent, isolated, and durable (ACID) test. This means the transaction should completely apply at one time and not affect other elements outside the transaction.

Windows Server 2008 introduces support for transactions via the NTFS file system. Changes to NTFS can now be made part of a larger transaction, which could include other changes to the system, SQL updates, and anything else that supports transactions. This feature is intended for developers who write code that requires transactions. Transactions can be monitored and managed using the `fsutil transaction` command. This supports viewing current transactions and committing and rolling back a transaction.

Self-Healing NTFS

Even with the latest version of NTFS, errors in the file system can occur. Many factors can cause errors, including physical drive corruption. When this corruption occurs, traditionally you use the `chkdsk` utility to locate errors and report, or try to recover data from bad sectors, and repair the disk.

The new self-healing NTFS reduces the need to run `chkdsk` by automatically attempting to recover and repair problems on the disk without requiring manual intervention. If the automatic process discovers a problem beyond the scope of self-healing, it alerts the console user to perform remedial steps. The self-healing is enabled by default and automatically detects and recovers/repairs/removes corruptions on the NTFS volume, boot sector, or contained files. A NTFS source event is logged in the system event log (130 and 55 event IDs) when any repairs are performed.

Symbolic Linking

A symbolic link is a file system object that points to another file system object (the destination object). Symbolic links appear as regular folders and files to users and are a standard part of the operating system. This allows a single interface point on the file system to access data in multiple locations on local and remote computers without the user needing to know.

Windows 2000 and XP had the capability to create junction points to folders and volumes on the local computer. These were hard to manage natively and have been replaced with the new symbolic linking feature.

Windows Vista and Windows Server 2008 provide the `mklink` utility, which creates both file and directory symbolic links. The command has three optional parameters:

- **/D**. Creates a directory symbolic link instead of the default file symbolic link
- **/H**. Creates a hard link instead of a symbolic link
- **/J**. Creates a directory junction

Let's say you have calc.exe in the windows\system32 folder. However, you want to run it as addup.exe. To do this, use the following command:

```
C:\Windows\System32>mklink addup.exe calc.exe
symbolic link created for addup.exe <<===>> calc.exe

C:\Windows\System32>dir addup.exe
 Volume in drive C has no label.
 Volume Serial Number is E0BA-564B

 Directory of C:\Windows\System32

05/17/2007  11:08 AM    <SYMLINK>      addup.exe [calc.exe]
               1 File(s)              0 bytes
               0 Dir(s)  235,354,234,880 bytes free
```

The directory entry shows that it's a symbolic link with the real filename in square brackets.

If you use `/H` instead and create a hard link, this makes the entry appear as if it's the file instead of a shortcut. This is what you get by default. For example, in the following output, you see a standard symbolic link and then a hard link:

```
D:\temp>mklink /H addup2.exe calc.exe
Hardlink created for addup2.exe <<===>> calc.exe

D:\temp>dir
05/17/2007  11:10 AM    <SYMLINK>      addup.exe [calc.exe]
```

```
11/02/2006  10:00 AM            188,416 addup2.exe
11/02/2006  10:00 AM            188,416 calc.exe
```

To delete the links, use the `del` command from the command line or via Explorer. Deleting a link does not delete the file to which it links.

For folders, you have the same symbolic link and hard link (known as a junction point) options. These are created with the `/D` and `/J` switches, respectively. With either type of link you can navigate to the folders. Any added or deleted content updates the target folder because this is a link to the data.

```
D:\temp>mklink /d testlnk test1
symbolic link created for testlnk <<===>> test1

D:\temp>mklink /j testlnkhd test1
Junction created for testlnkhd <<===>> test1

D:\temp>dir
05/17/2007  11:20 AM    <DIR>          test1
05/17/2007  11:21 AM    <SYMLINKD>     testlnk [test1]
05/17/2007  11:21 AM    <JUNCTION>     testlnkhd
[D:\temp\test1]
```

File System Review

Table 5-1 shows a summary of the various file system attributes and limitations, concentrating on the main file systems available for your data storage needs.

Table 5-1 System Attributes/Limitations of File Systems

File System Feature	FAT16	FAT32	NTFS
Maximum File Size	2GB	4GB	16TB (theoretical is 16EB)
Maximum Volume Size	2GB	8TB; format support is limited to 32GB during setup in Windows 2000 and above	256TB (theoretical is much higher)
Maximum Number of Files	65,517	268,435,437	
Maximum Filename Size	8.3 or 255 with LFN	255	

Formatting and Managing File Systems

A new computer has one or more physical drives that might be combined into a single visible drive in a highly available configuration (for example, Redundant Array of Inexpensive Disks [RAID] 1 mirror drives or individual drives). Before these disk areas can be used, partitions must be created on the disk space. This can be done during the operating system installation, covered in Chapter 3, "Installing and Upgrading Windows Server 2008," or within the installed operating system using the Disk Management Microsoft Management Console (MMC) snap-in. Both graphical and command-line interfaces exist for managing disk partitions.

Disk Management Microsoft Management Console Snap-In

The Disk Management MMC snap-in is part of the Computer Management console. It is available in the Administrative Tools program group within the Storage section of the navigation pane (see Figure 5-1).

The physical drives are shown in the bottom part of the details pane. Within each physical disk space volume, the various partitions and any available unallocated disk space are shown. At the top of the details window is a list of the actual partitions with their type, layout, file system, and status.

The layout refers to the type of the volume. For example, a volume comprising of space on a single disk is known as a simple volume. Just as hardware disk configuration such as mirroring and striping with parity (RAID 5) is possible, software versions of these disk configurations are part of the Windows operating system. The complete list of disk configurations is as follows:

- **Simple**. A single block of contiguous space on a single physical disk
- **Spanned**. Multiple blocks of contiguous space on single or multiple physical disks
- **Striped (RAID 0)**. Multiple blocks of contiguous space on multiple physical disks
- **Mirrored (RAID 1)**. Two blocks of equal contiguous space on two separate physical disks with the same information
- **RAID 5**. Multiple blocks of contiguous space on at least three physical disks with parity information stored across the disks

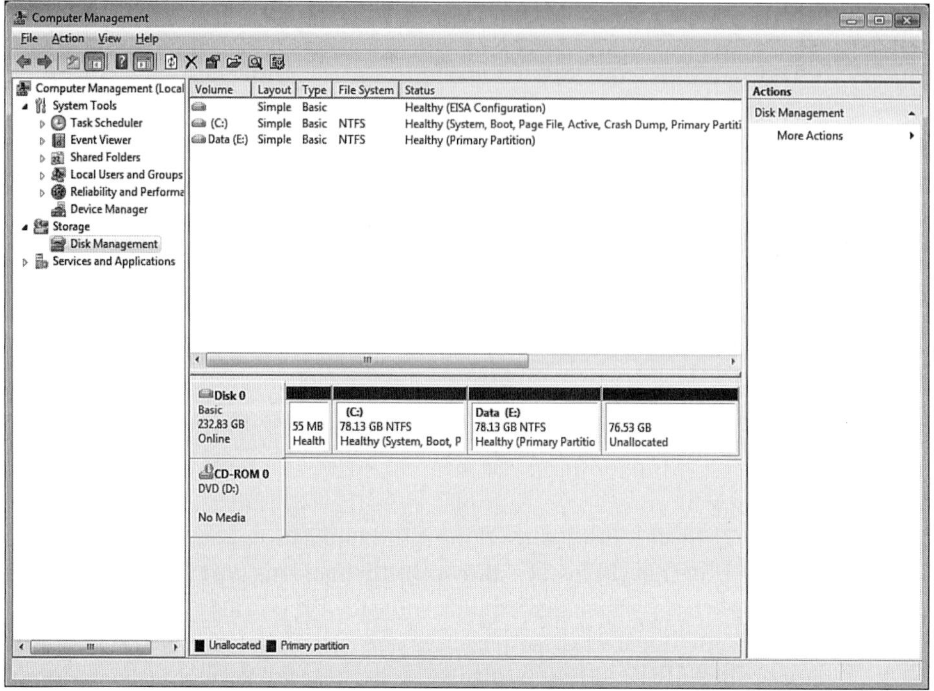

Figure 5-1 The Disk Management snap-in shows the physical space visible to the operating system and how it is portioned.

Only mirroring and RAID 5 increase availability because data is spread over multiple physical drives with data redundancy. If one disk is unavailable, its content is either duplicated on another disk in the set or can be calculated by parity information spread over the other members of the set.

The type of disk refers to whether the disk is a basic disk, dynamic disk, or GUID Partition Table (GPT) disk. A basic disk is the traditional disk type of storage, similar to that used by MS-DOS, and is based on partition tables that can contain basic volume types such as primary, extended, and logical drives. The only type of volume you can have on a basic disk is a simple volume. Dynamic disks contain dynamic volume types, such as spanned, striped, mirrored, and RAID 5. Dynamic disks are not understood by pre–Windows 2000 operating systems. A basic disk can be upgraded to a dynamic disk by right-clicking on the disk and selecting Convert to Dynamic Disk from the context menu. After you convert a disk to dynamic, the only way to convert it back to basic is to delete all volumes on the disk. The third type of available disk is the GPT disk. GPT was created as part of the Extensible Firmware Interface (EFI) initiative and is designed to give a far more flexible approach to volume management. GPT disks support 128 primary partitions, a lot compared to the four supported by traditional MBR type disks, and volumes greater than 2TB (the MBR limit).

Windows Vista and Windows Server 2008 introduced the capability via the Disk Management snap-in to shrink and extend volumes via the context menu of a partition, as shown in Figure 5-2.

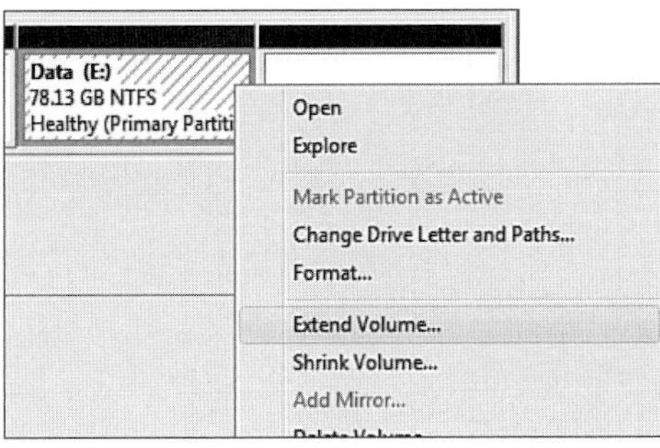

FIGURE 5-2 The Extend Volume and Shrink Volume options give easy access to modifying the size of existing volumes.

If you select the Shrink Volume option, the disk management interface ascertains the amount of space at the end of the disk that can be shrunk. This can be modified as required, as shown in Figure 5-3. After the amount of space is selected, click Shrink to resize the partition.

Shrink E:
Total size before shrink in MB: 80000
Size of available shrink space in MB: 39947
Enter the amount of space to shrink in MB: 39947
Total size after shrink in MB: 40053
Size of available shrink space can be restricted if snapshots or pagefiles are enabled on the volume.
Shrink Cancel

FIGURE 5-3 The Shrink dialog shows the amount of space that can be shrunk. The amount of space to shrink and the size after shrinking are configurable.

The Extend Volume option selects free space next to the partition to increase the partition size and keeps it as a simple volume, or selects disk space from another area on the disk or another disk entirely to create a spanned volume (see Figure 5-4).

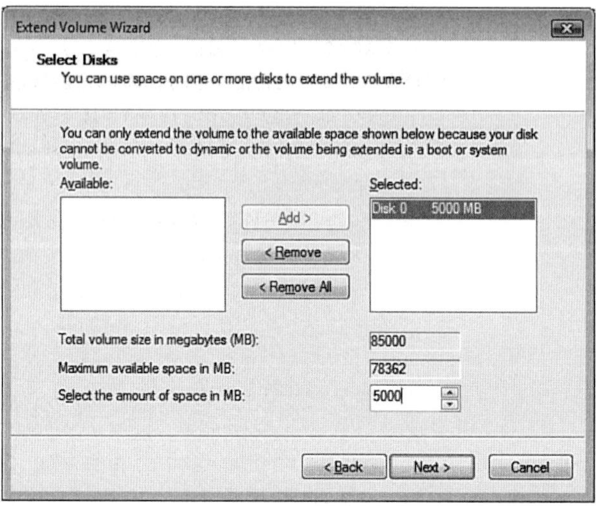

FIGURE 5-4 The Extend Volume Wizard allows disk space to be added to a volume either from the same disk or from a disk on another disk.

To create a volume, perform the following steps:

1. Right-click on an area of unallocated disk space and select a new type of volume (simple, mirrored, and so forth).
2. Click Next to the New Volume Wizard introduction screen.
3. Depending on the type of volume selected, select disk space from the selected disk or multiple disks. Click Next.
4. Assign a drive letter for the new volume or mount the partition as a folder on an existing volume as a junction point. If you want to assign letters or paths later, select the option to not assign a letter or folder (see Figure 5-5). Click Next.
5. The final dialog formats the new volume (see Figure 5-6). After options are selected, click Next. The Quick Format option does not perform the normal bad sector check. If you are formatting a disk that you have used for a while and that you know is good, you could perform a quick format. The Enable File and Folder Compression option means that all data on the new volume should be compressed. The allocation unit defines how big the smallest unit of allocation is on a volume. The larger the allocation unit, the

fewer number of units are required for each file, resulting in more efficient and faster disk access. However, you also risk wasting space. If you have many 1KB files and the allocation unit is 64KB, each file has 63KB of wasted space. If you know you are storing large files, set a large allocation unit size; if you are storing lots of small files, set a low allocation unit size. Normally the default works fine. Click Next.

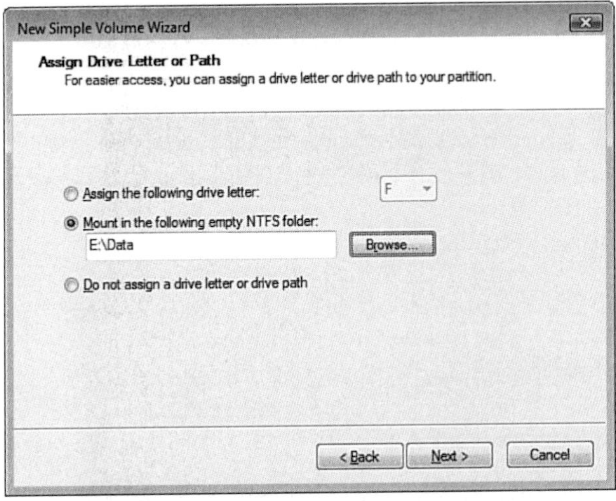

FIGURE 5-5 In this example, the new volume is available as a subfolder of the existing E: drive.

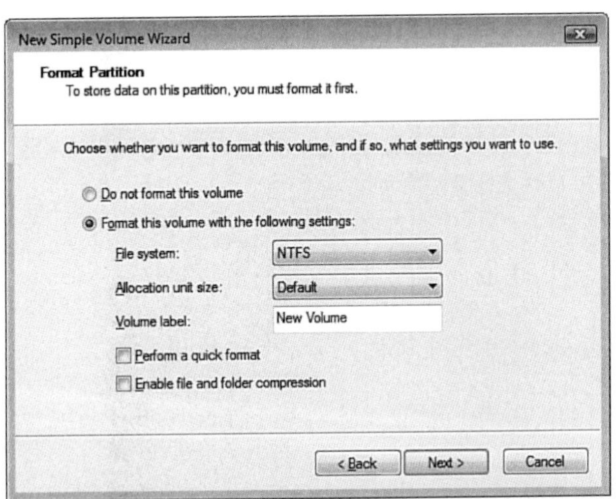

FIGURE 5-6 File system, volume, quick format, and compression options are available for new volumes.

6. A summary of the new volume creation is displayed. After confirming options, click Finish.

A partition format can be performed by right-clicking on the partition and selecting Format from the context menu. This can also be performed via Explorer by right-clicking on the volume and selecting Format.

Command-Line Management

As with the graphical interfaces, all the same options can be performed from the command line, which is mostly facilitated via the `diskpart` command-line utility.

The basic read type operations are available with `diskpart`, such as listing all the disks and viewing partitions on a disk, as shown here:

```
DISKPART> list disk

  Disk ###  Status      Size     Free     Dyn  Gpt
  --------  ----------  -------  -------  ---  ---
  Disk 0    Online        16 GB   280 MB   *
  Disk 1    Online        31 GB  4399 MB   *    *
  Disk 2    Online        16 GB    15 GB   *    *

DISKPART> select disk 0

Disk 0 is now the selected disk.

DISKPART> list part

  Partition ###  Type              Size     Offset
  -------------  ----------------  -------  -------
  Partition 2    Dynamic Data       993 KB    32 KB
  Partition 1    Dynamic Data        15 GB  1024 KB
  Partition 3    Dynamic Data      1382 MB    15 GB

DISKPART> select part 3

Partition 3 is now the selected partition.

DISKPART> detail partition

Partition 3
Type  : 42
```

```
Hidden: Yes
Active: No

  Volume ###  Ltr Label  Fs    Type     Size     Status     Info
  ----------  --- ------ ----  -------  -------  --------   -----
* Volume 3    F   RAID1  NTFS  Mirror   500 MB   Healthy
```

To create volumes, use the Create Volume context menu action on dynamic disks or Create Partition on basic disks.

The power of `diskpart` is useful for scripting. For example, the following commands to create and format partitions can be saved as a text file and then passed to the `diskpart` command:

```
select disk 0
clean
create partition primary
select partition 1
assign letter=c:
active
format
exit
```

To pass the text to `diskpart`, use the `/s` switch:

```
diskpart /s partcleanandcreate.txt
```

To create more complex disk sets, such as a RAID 5, you need to pass the disks you want to use as part of the set; for example:

```
DISKPART> create volume raid size=6000 disk=1,2,3
DiskPart successfully created the volume.
```

Here, the `disk=` are the disks to use and the `size=` is the space to take from each disk. To see a list of all commands, run `help` from within `diskpart`.

Converting File Systems

If a FAT or FAT32 partition were created, it can be converted to NTFS and maintain its content. Any other type of conversion requires the data to be backed up and the partition to be re-formed. The `convert` command can be used to perform the file system conversion. The following example shows a conversion from FAT32 to NTFS. Notice you have to enter the volume label for the volume.

```
C:\Users\Administrator>convert i: /fs:ntfs
The type of the file system is FAT32.
Enter current volume label for drive I: TEST2
Volume TEST2 created 5/17/2007 3:52 PM
Volume Serial Number is D435-A9D2
Windows is verifying files and folders...
File and folder verification is complete.
Windows has checked the file system and found no problems.

  242,606,336 bytes total disk space.
      104,096 bytes in 2 hidden files.
  142,600,192 bytes available on disk.

        2,048 bytes in each allocation unit.
       69,632 total allocation units on disk.
       69,629 allocation units available on disk.

Determining disk space required for file system conversion...
Total disk space:                 243360 KB
Free space on volume:             139258 KB
Space required for conversion:      2394 KB
Converting file system
Conversion complete
```

Disk Defragmentation

One of the advantages of NTFS is that it has a map of free space on the volume. This enables new files to be written contiguously where possible, avoiding fragmentation. However, defragmentation is still necessary, and Microsoft made Disk Defragmenter part of its Windows 2000 product line.

Available from Accessories, System Tools, Disk Defragmenter, it gives a view of the volumes on the computer. When executed, a check is initially performed on the file system (see Figure 5-7). Also, advice is given on the state of the file system and what action should be performed.

If you choose to perform a defragmentation, the list of volumes is shown. Select the volumes to be defragmented, as shown in Figure 5-8. Additionally, you can select to Run on a Schedule (Recommended) by checking the box (refer to Figure 5-7). Decide when, how often, and on which volumes to perform the defragmentation.

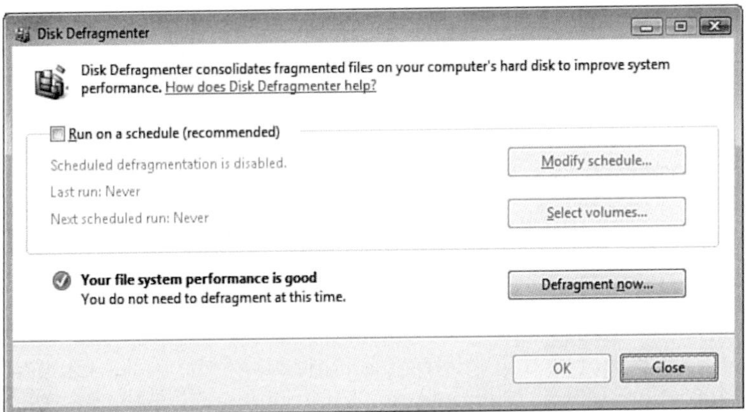

Figure 5-7 The Windows Server 2008 disk defragmenter runs an analysis when first executed and defragments if required.

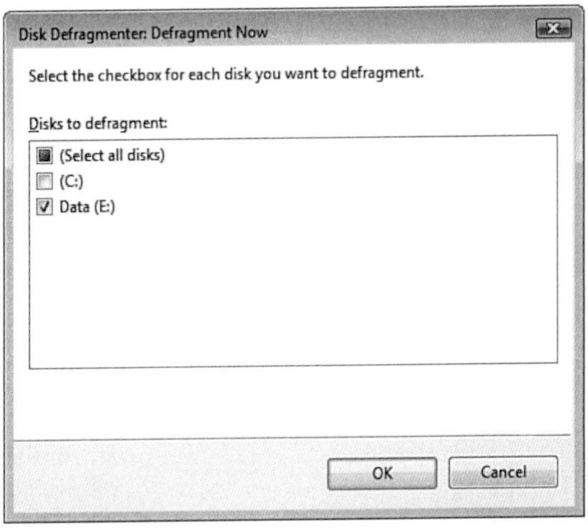

Figure 5-8 The volumes to be defragmented must be selected.

A command-line interface for defrag.exe is available. This is useful for scripting execution of the disk defragmentation and more customized scheduling of the execution. The -a switch performs analysis only and gives details of the fragmentation state, as shown here:

```
C:\Windows\system32>defrag c: -a
Windows Disk Defragmenter
Copyright (c) 2006 Microsoft Corp.
```

```
Analysis report for volume C:

    Volume size                              = 78.12 GB
    Free space                               = 65.16 GB
    Largest free space extent                = 39.06 GB
    Percent file fragmentation              = 2 %

    Note: On NTFS volumes, file fragments larger than 64MB are
not included in the fragmentation statistics.
    You do not need to defragment this volume.
```

-w performs a full defragmentation, and the -r switch performs a fast defragmentation (only defragmenting files smaller than 64MB). Full help can be seen with the -? switch. The paging file is not defragmented with the free utility. Purchase a third-party defragmentation utility if you want to defragment the paging file. However, the paging file usually doesn't fragment too much if you reboot regularly because the page file is shrunk to its original size at each reboot.

File Management

Data management is vital in any environment, and Windows is no exception. In a number of environments, storing data is worse than not storing data because data is often sensitive, and you need to ensure only the right people can get to it. In addition, as you store more data, tracking who is using data, where, and for what; ownership; the type of information; and reporting become more important.

File Ownership

The rest of this chapter discusses NTFS, which stores data more reliably and allows other facilities because of its metadata-based approach.

One of the attributes of a file or folder is its owner. This is derived from the creator of the file or folder and can be viewed by right-clicking the file or folder, selecting Properties, selecting the Security tab, clicking the Advanced button, and then selecting the Owner tab. The owner information can be seen in Figure 5-9.

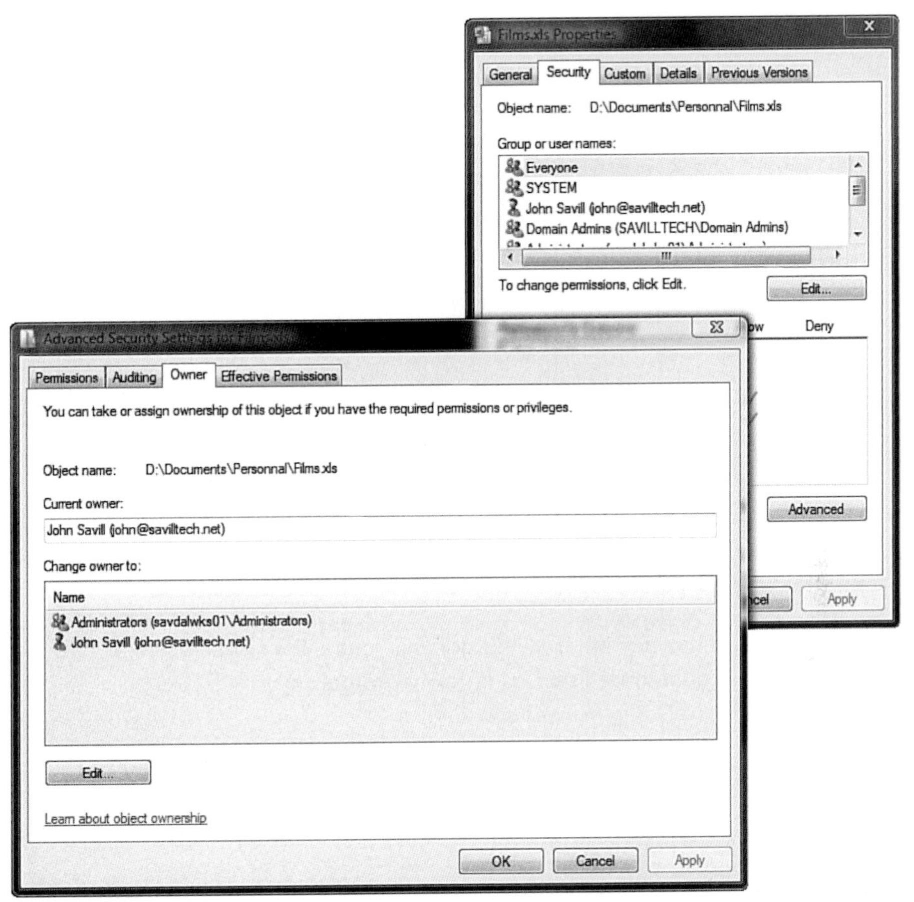

FIGURE 5-9 In this example, the file owner is shown as John Savill.

If you have the correct permissions, you can change the owner to yourself or to the Administrators group using the same dialog box. If you click the Edit button, you can search the local computer's account database or an Active Directory (AD) and select any user by clicking the Other Users or Groups button, as shown in Figure 5-10. After being selected, any user can be given the ownership.

The process is identical for folders except that if ownership is modified for a folder, an additional Replace Owner on Subcontainers and Objects check box is available. If enabled, it changes the owner on subfolders and files.

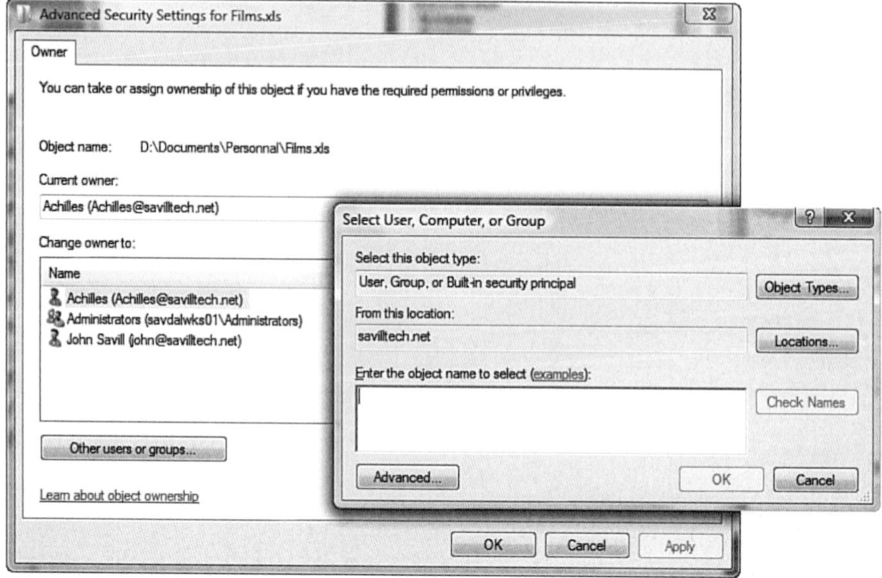

FIGURE 5-10 Beyond the current user and administrators, the Other Users or Groups button allows any account to be listed as an owner target.

Windows Vista retains the `takeown` command that allows the ownership of a file to be taken from the command line. A number of switches specify a remote system (`/s`), username (`/u`), and password (`/p`). To see all switches, use `takeown /?`.

Here is a basic example of taking ownership of a specific file:

```
D:\Documents>takeown /f music.xls

SUCCESS: The file (or folder): "D:\Documents\music.xls" now
owned by user "SAVILLTECH\john".
```

To take ownership of a folder and all its content, add the `/r` switch for recursive execution:

```
D:\Documents\takeown /f . /r

SUCCESS: The file (or folder): "D:\Documents" now owned by user
"SAVILLTECH\john".

SUCCESS: The file (or folder): " D:\Documents\music.xls " now
owned by user "SAVILLTECH\john".
```

You can also use the /a switch to make the ownership go to the Administrators group instead of the current user:

```
D:\Documents>takeown /f music.xls /a

SUCCESS: The file (or folder): "D:\Documents\music.xls" now
owned by the administrators group.
```

File Permissions

The owner of a file is simply who owns the file, but without permissions, the owner is fairly meaningless other than for quota purposes. Who gains access to a file is determined by the security on files and folders, not ownership.

Security on files and folders is viewed and managed via the Security tab of the file Properties. This is most easily accessed via Explorer. The Security tab displays a dialog listing any users or groups with explicit permissions both allowing and denying access, as shown in Figure 5-11.

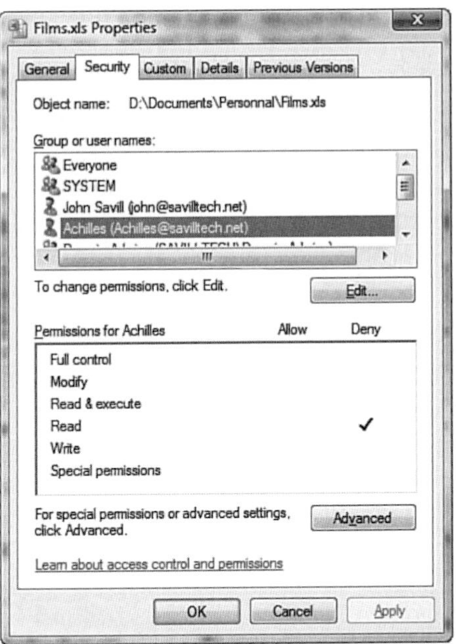

FIGURE 5-11 The Security tab displays the users who have permissions on a file. In this case, Achilles has explicit deny read access, which takes precedence over any allow permissions.

A number of basic permissions are available for each user or group:

- **Full control**: Users can modify, add, move, and delete files and their associated properties and directories. In addition, users can change permission settings for all files and subdirectories, including ownership.
- **Modify**: Users can view and modify files and file properties, including deleting and adding files to a directory or file properties to a file.
- **Read and execute**: Users can run executable files, including scripts.
- **Read**: Users can view files and file properties.
- **Write**: Users can write to a file.

Folders have an additional List Folder Contents permission that allows the objects' names in the folder to be traversed.

One important item to remember is that a deny always takes precedence over an allow. If a user is a member of a group that has permissions to read a file but is also a member of a group that has deny read permission, the user is able to read the file. Apart from denies, permissions are cumulative. If a user is a member of a group that has read permissions and of another group that has modify permissions, the user has both read and modify access.

Special permissions allow more complex combinations of access and control inherited permissions. Inheritance means that permissions on a folder are automatically applied to any new object (file or folder) created within. Additional permissions beyond those inherited can be set on an object. This brings an exception to the "a deny always takes precedence over an allow" rule. Inherited permissions have a different order of precedence. Permissions are checked in the following order and when a match for the user is found, the user is either granted or denied access:

1. An explicit deny
2. An explicit allow
3. An inherited deny
4. An inherited allow

This order means that an explicit allow on a file would override a deny that was inherited. For example, if a folder had deny set for a group and a file within the folder had explicit allow for the group, the members of that group would have access to the file.

To access special permissions, click the Advanced button on the Security tab and then select the Effective Permissions tab of the Advanced Security Settings dialog. Each permission on the object is displayed, along with whether the permission is explicitly defined on the object or inherited from the parent (see Figure 5-12).

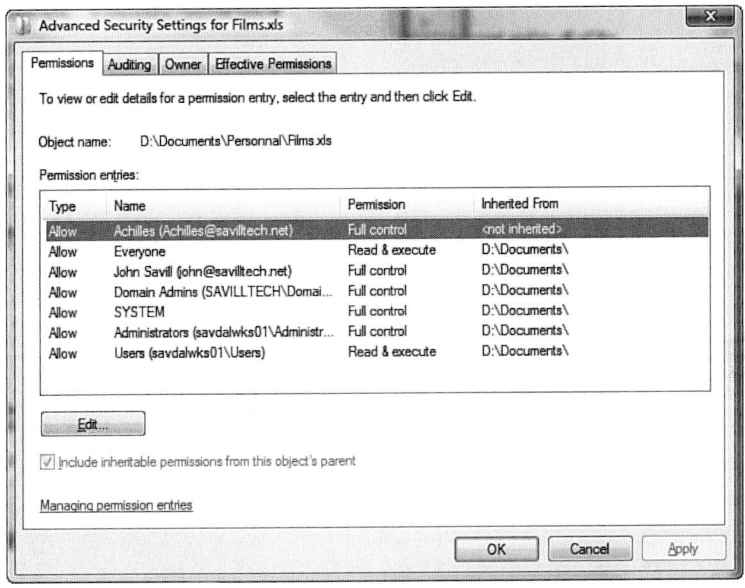

FIGURE 5-12 The advanced view shows the permissions and where they originated.

If the Edit button in the Advanced Security Settings dialog is selected, new permissions can be added and existing permissions can be modified and removed. A larger number of options are available if you change permissions via this advanced view. The advanced permission screen is shown in Figure 5-13. The additional advanced permissions are the following:

- **Traverse folder/execute file**. Users can navigate through folders to reach other files or folders, even if they have no permissions for the traversed files or folders. By default this is not required because the Bypass Traverse Checking user right is assigned via group policy to everyone.

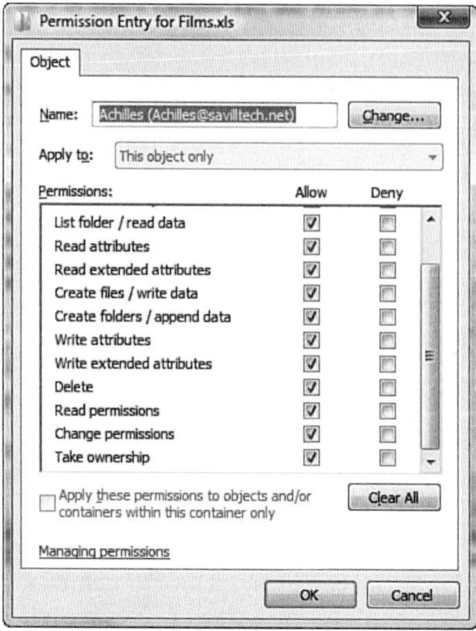

FIGURE 5-13 The advanced permissions are far more granular than standard permissions.

- **List folder/read data**. Users can view a list of a folder's contents and data files.
- **Read attributes**. Users can view the attributes, such as read-only and hidden, of a file or folder.
- **Read extended attributes**. Users can view the extended attributes of a file or folder.
- **Create files/write data**. The Create Files permission applies to folders and allows users to create files within the folder. The Write Data permission applies to files and allows users to make changes to the specified file and overwrite existing content.
- **Create folders/append data**. The Create Folders permission allows users to create folders within a folder. The Append Data permission applies to files only and allows users to make changes to the end of the file, but it does not grant change, delete, or overwrite permissions for the existing data.
- **Write attributes**. Users can change the attributes, such as read-only or hidden, of a file or folder.
- **Write extended attributes**. Users can change the extended attributes of a file or folder.
- **Delete**. Users can delete the file or folder.

- **Read permissions**. Users have read permissions on the file or folder.
- **Change permissions**. Users have change permissions on the file or folder.
- **Take ownership**. Users can take ownership of the file or folder. The owner of a file or folder can always change permissions on it, regardless of any existing permissions that protect the file or folder.

Along with the various security options on an object, you can stop permissions inheritance from an object's parent by unselecting the Include Inheritable Permissions from this Object's Parent check box. If this is unchecked, a dialog box is displayed that gives the option to copy or remove the permissions that have been inherited or to cancel the operation altogether.

The final issue with basic permissions is how they work when copying or moving data. If you move a file, its explicit permissions remain. Any inherited permissions are replaced with those of the new parent folder. If you move a folder between volumes, this is a copy-and-delete operation. Any explicit permissions are lost, and the permissions are those inherited from the new parent folder.

If you want to copy a file and maintain its permissions and ownership information, use the `XCOPY` command with the `/o` switch.

Numerous commands query permissions from the command line. To list all files that a user has permissions defined on, use the `icacls` command. The `icacls` command has the capability to back up and restore Access Control Lists (ACLs) on entire directory structures to a file. It can also swap security identifiers (SIDs) in ACLs or just find all entries that contain a certain SID. For example, to find all files with savilltech/john in the ACL, use the following:

```
D:\Documents\Personnal>icacls *.* /findsid savilltech\john
SID Found: American Express TRS Membership Awards.doc.
SID Found: cissp.
Successfully processed 24 files; Failed processing 0 files
```

Full information on using the utility can be found by running `icacls /?`. This command also gives examples for using the various functions of the `icacls` command.

Shares

Shares provide remote access to information stored on a server. By default, a number of shares exist on a server, which can easily be seen by running the `net share` command:

```
C:\Users\john> net share

Share name   Resource                        Remark

-------------------------------------------------------------------
C$           C:\                             Default share
E$           E:\                             Default share
IPC$                                         Remote IPC
ADMIN$       C:\Windows                      Remote Admin
The command completed successfully.
```

The `IPC$` share is used for interprocess communication between local and remote processes. The other default shares are mapped to certain file system folders. The `ADMIN$` folder points to the Windows folder. The other volumes have a share for its volume, allowing access to the root of the folder. Why does the share have a dollar sign? The dollar sign hides the share from normal network browsing.

Shares can be created from the Explorer interface by right-clicking a folder, selecting Properties, and viewing the Sharing tab, as shown in Figure 5-14.

Clicking the Share button opens up a simple dialog that allows groups and users to be added to the share access list. Then one of three levels of access is granted (see Figure 5-15). The three levels of access that can be granted are the following:

- **Reader**. This is read-only access to the content, so no modifications or additions to existing content can be made
- **Contributor**. Allows full read-and-write access to the content
- **Co-owner**. Full control of the content, including changing permissions on the share

After access has been granted, click the Share button to complete the share-creation process. A confirmation dialog and a link to the new share are displayed, making it easy to share the new location with users (see Figure 5-15). The Advanced Share permission works in a similar fashion but exposes the raw full control, change, and read rights and enables the option to deny the levels of access. The advanced interface also allows comments and a maximum number of simultaneous users to be configured for the share.

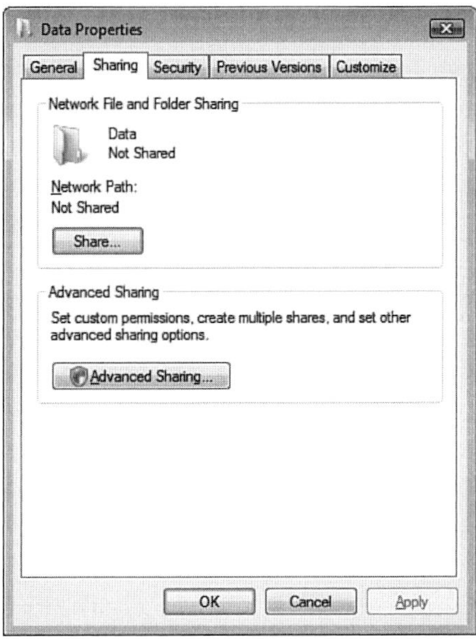

FIGURE 5-14 The basic Share option and the Advanced Sharing option.

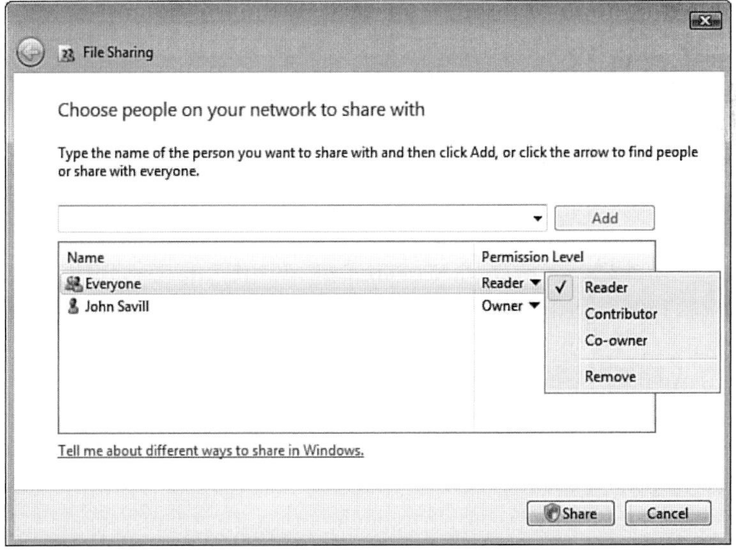

FIGURE 5-15 The File Sharing dialog is an easy interface to control access to shares.

NOTE The whole issue of share permissions is interesting. In many environments, shares are not used to govern access because the files and folders already have NTFS permissions. I prefer to set shares so that domain users have full control and then use NTFS permissions to restrict actual levels of access to the data.

To create a share from the command line, use the following format:

```
net share <share name>=<drive>:<dir> /remark="<description>"
net share john=c:\data\johndrv /remark="Johns drive"
```

NTFS Quotas

Since Windows 2000, disk quotas have been available through the NTFS file system. This simplistic quota capability allowed only an amount of logical disk space for individual users for an entire disk. The NTFS quota facility has no capability for a shared quota for groups of users nor does it base the quota on a subfolder of the disk. In most instances, the file server resource management's quota component should be used, which is explored later in the "File Server Resource Manager" section. Let's now look at the basic quota component of NTFS.

To enable quotas on a disk, right-click the disk and select its Quota tab. By default, quotas are disabled. Click the Enable Quota Management option and the Apply button to gain access to the other quota configurable options, as shown in Figure 5-16.

A default quota amount and a warning level can be specified for all users of the disk. If the Deny Disk Space to Users Exceeding Quota Limit is selected, the user cannot write any more data after the quota is reached. As shown in Figure 5-16, options are available to log events when users reach the quota limit or warning levels. These default values apply to all users of the disk. However, if you select the Quota Entries button, specific quotas for individual users can be set.

Any user that owns files on the disk is displayed, along with the amount of disk space he is using and how much of his total quota the used space equates to. If you right-click on a user and select Properties, the individual quota settings can be configured, as shown in Figure 5-17. You can also create quota entries for people who are not yet using space on the drive by selecting New Quota Entry from the Quota menu, selecting their AD account, and setting quota limits for them.

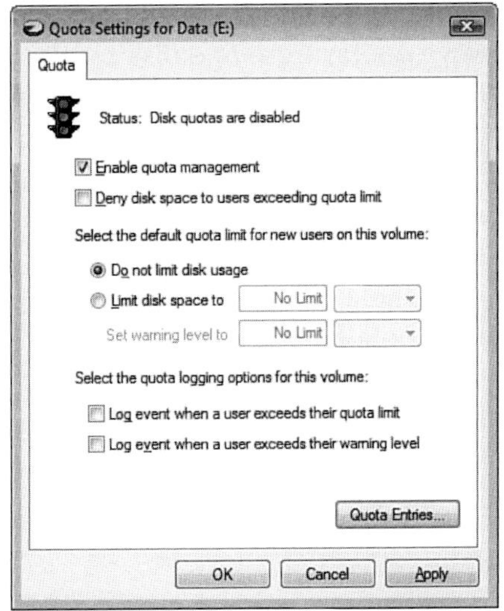

FIGURE 5-16 The quota allows disk space usage to be limited to a certain predefined amount.

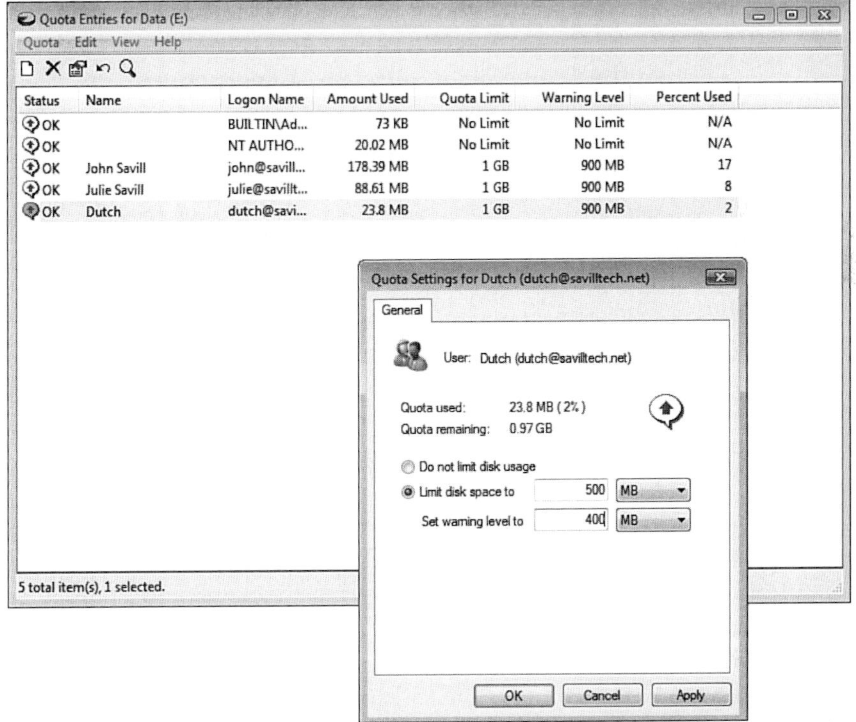

FIGURE 5-17 This shows how individual quota entries beyond the generic setting can be set.

You might have invested a lot of time setting up specific quotas for each user. To move quotas from one disk to another, export them and then import them. To export quotas from a volume, perform the following:

1. Start Explorer.
2. Right-click on the volume that has the quotas you want to copy and select Properties.
3. Select the Quota tab.
4. Click the Quota Entries button.
5. From the Quota menu, select the Export option.
6. Enter a filename for the export file and click Save.
7. Close the Quota dialog.

To import the freshly exported quota information, perform the same tasks, substituting export with import:

1. Start Explorer.
2. Right-click on the volume that will import the quotas and select Properties.
3. Select the Quota tab.
4. Click the Quota Entries button.
5. From the Quota menu, select the Import option.
6. Select the exported file and click Open.
7. For any quotas that already exist, you are asked if you want to replace them and if this action should be performed on all clashes. Click OK.
8. Close the Quota dialog.

Again, while this type of quota system does exist, the File Server Resource Manager (FSRM) version is far superior and allows granular quotas with a wide range of actions to be performed if a quota is reached.

Encrypted File System (EFS)

NTFS is a secure file system. However, an increasing number of people are using portables and utilities such as NTFSDos that bypasses NTFS security. Another layer of protection is needed for these more mobile environments. The Encrypted File System (EFS) was new for Windows 2000 and the NTFS 5-0 file system. EFS uses public and private key encryption and the CryptoAPI architecture. EFS can use any symmetric encryption algorithm to encrypt data and includes support for Microsoft Enhanced and Strong cryptographic service providers.

No preparation is needed to encrypt files. The first time a user encrypts a file, an encryption certificate for the user and a private key are automatically created.

Encrypted files stay encrypted when they are moved. New files in an encrypted folder are automatically encrypted. There is no need to decrypt a file before use; the operating system automatically handles this for you in a secure manner. If a user's private key is lost (either by reinstallation or new user creation), the EFS recovery agent can decrypt the files. In a domain environment, the recovery agent should be configured as part of the secure certificate services environment to ensure that the recovery agent is a domain-based account instead of a domain administrator account (for domain-joined machines). This is achieved by defining a Recovery Agent Policy.

An enhancement with the Windows 2003 and XP implementation of EFS was the capability to encrypt a file for multiple Data Recovery Agents (DRAs), which allowed multiple users to be given access to encrypted data. To encrypt a file, perform the following:

1. Right-click on the file and select Properties from the context menu.
2. Under the General tab, click the Advanced button.
3. Check the Encrypt Contents to Secure Data and click OK.
4. Click OK to perform the encryption and close the Properties dialog for the file.
5. You might be prompted to encrypt just the file or also its parent folder, as shown in Figure 5-18. This is to offer protection in case software that accesses the file creates temporary versions of the file in its folder. These are unencrypted unless the folder is configured to be encrypted. Then any content is automatically encrypted.

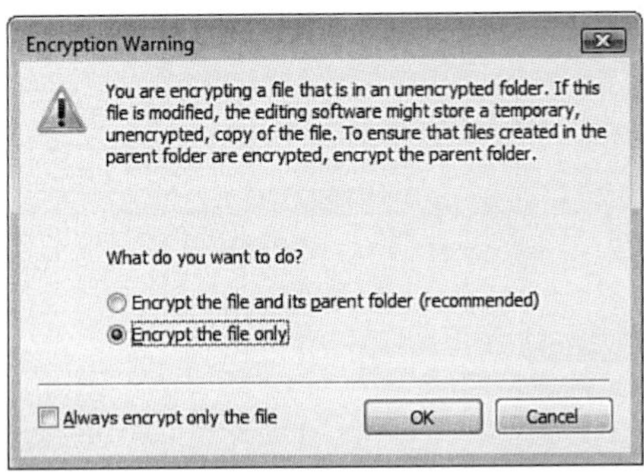

FIGURE 5-18 For added security. the EFS process offers confirmation if the folder's parent should also be encrypted.

After the file is encrypted, additional users can be granted access:

1. Right-click on the file and select Properties from the context menu.
2. Under the General tab, click the Advanced button.
3. Click the Details button in the Advanced Attributes dialog, as shown in Figure 5-19.

FIGURE 5-19 The Details button allows configuration of additional users for the encrypted data.

4. A list of users who have access to the file is shown. Click the Add button to give additional users access. (The users must have a valid EFS certificate in the AD.) Users who are trusted on the machine are displayed, as shown in Figure 5-20, and can be selected. Or click Find User to enable other users in the forest. After the users are added, click OK.

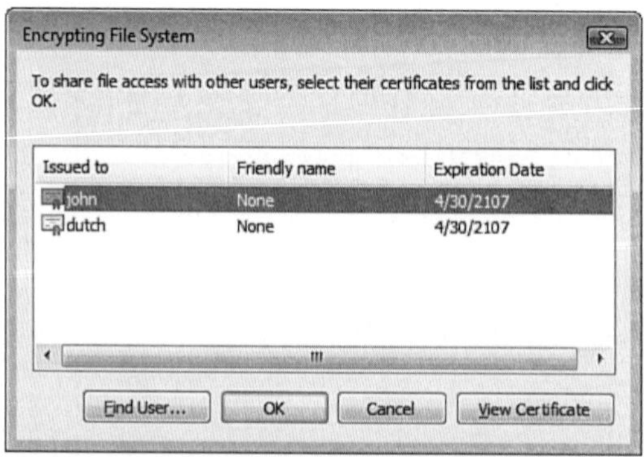

FIGURE 5-20 The list of trusted users on the computer is displayed.

5. The new users who have been granted access are listed (see Figure 5-21). Click OK to all dialogs to close.

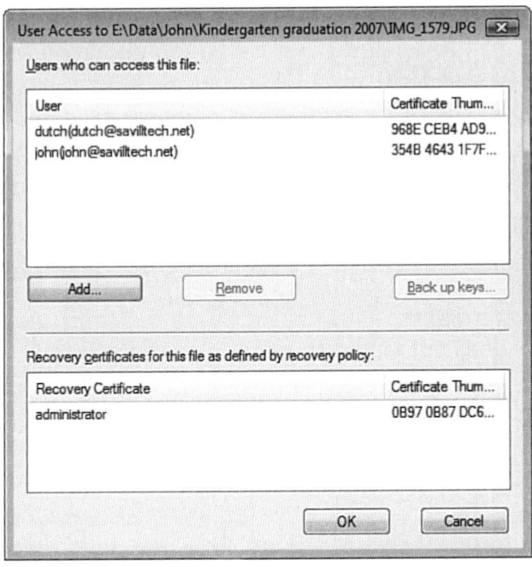

FIGURE 5-21 This file now has access by users John and Dutch with recovery access from the administrator.

The EFS is a useful feature for individual or groups of files. However, the Windows Vista BitLocker functionality allows encryption of the entire drive and might be a better solution than EFS. When you copy a file that is encrypted with EFS to another NTFS volume, the file stays encrypted. If you copy to a FAT/FAT32 volume, the file is unencrypted.

Shadow Copy Feature

One common administrator burden is restoring data from backups. Windows Server 2003 and Windows Server 2008 have a wonderful Volume Shadow Copy Service (VSS). This creates shadow copies, or previous versions. Shadow copies enable users to select the Previous Versions tab of the Properties dialog of a share, see point-in-time copies of the share, and perform self-restoration of data stored on NTFS volumes.

At configurable intervals/times of the day, VSS takes a snapshot of the state of the content of selected volumes (that's right, the entire volume, not just share content). Even at the file level, only the changes are stored. If there is a small change to a 1GB file, only the small change is stored. Up to 64 versions of a share can be made available. This limit is imposed by the previous version client and the amount of disk space available. When the 65th snapshot is taken, the oldest one is deleted. Likewise, if the amount of disk space allocated for shadow copies has run out, the eldest snapshots is deleted to make space for the newest snapshot.

Some clients need a new software component installed that adds a tab to the share's Properties dialog. This tab allows them to select a point-in-time view of the share and access its content. Newer operating systems, such as Vista, have VSS built-in. This is great for users and administrators. If a user deletes a file, she doesn't need to trouble an Administrator. The user can view the share as it was at a point in the past and copy over the file. Likewise, if a file has been corrupted, the user can view the share as it was in the past and copy over the uncorrupted version.

NOTE VSS does not replace performing backups because only the changes are stored. If your file system was lost, the shadow copy information on its own would be of no use. Microsoft has also stated that in times of exceptionally high I/O, shadow copies might be lost.

The amount of disk space used for the shadow copies is not based on the size of the volume, but rather the size and frequency of changes. This is driven by the applications used. For example, if an application only writes changes to the file when data is changed, this uses far less shadow copy space than an application that rewrites the entire file.

When accessing previous states of a share, the ACLs on files and folders still apply. If you did not have access to the file before, you won't have access when viewing it via the Previous Versions client.

The shadow copy file or folder information is stored in the System Volume Information of the volume selected to hold the information and cannot be accessed outside of the shadow copy client.

Finally, although the whole content of the volume is protected by VSS, you can only view previous states via share properties. If you need to recover a file that is not within a current share, create a new share that contains the file and then connect to the share. Notice that if you create a new share, you see a full history of all previous versions equivalent to existing shares. This happens because VSS logs the entire file system, not just existing shares.

You can enable VSS for a drive or volume with the following steps. If you want to create from the command line, use the `vssadmin` command with the `create shadow /for=<volume>:` parameters.

1. Right-click the drive and select Configure Shadow Copies from the context menu.

2. Select the volume for which you want to enable shadow copies from the Select a Volume area.
3. Click the Settings button to change the default. The default configuration creates a shadow copy at 7:00 and 12:00 each week day, storing the data on the selected drive.
4. In the dialog, you can choose which drive the shadow copy files are saved to (drive only, you cannot select folders) and the maximum amount of space that can be used (you need at least 100MB). Make your choices and click the Schedule button.
5. The Schedule dialog has a drop-down at the top that shows the current scheduled executions of the shadow copy. You can select one (click the drop-down arrow) and then use the options to change how often it runs. The Weekly option allows a time to be selected and on which days to run. You can also click New to create a new schedule. For example, you might want a schedule that runs just once on Saturday and Sunday at 7:00. Click OK when all options are made.
6. Click OK to the main Settings dialog.
7. The shadow copy is now enabled. (You don't need to click the Enable button.) You can optionally click the Create Now button to create a starting snapshot. The Create Now button can be used at any time to force creation of a shadow copy.

Windows Vista clients (Business and Ultimate editions) have a Restore Previous Versions context menu item for shares. This can be used to view the contents of the shadow copies and restore or copy data from them. Windows XP SP2 also has VSS built-in. For other operating system support, check out www.microsoft.com/technet/downloads/winsrvr/shadowcopyclient.mspx.

File Server Resource Manager

Windows Server 2008 includes the File Server Resource Manager (FSRM) component that is part of the File Server role. Data storage is getting cheaper and disk sizes are increasing, leading to the "just buy more disk space" mindset. However, the physical disk space is not the most expensive component of storing data. For many companies, data is the most important company asset and must be securely stored and recoverable. Managing data can cost three times as much as the physical storage devices, so although the disks might be cheap, the effort to maintain the data is not. As more data is created, the cost of management increases accordingly. This increase in total cost of ownership (TCO) leads to a number of customer requirements for the next release of Windows:

- Better reporting capabilities to identify how storage is being used
- Allow more granular controls on how storage can be used
- Define quotas on folders and volumes that consider actual disk space usage
- Easy-to-use tools to implement the new functionality

Three core components make up the FSRM, each building upon the last. Before we discuss components, let's install it.

Installation

The FSRM component is one of the optional services of the File Services role. To install it, perform the following:

1. Launch Server Manager (Administrative Tools, Server Manager).
2. Navigate to Roles in the navigation pane and select File Services.
3. Click Add Role Services, as shown in Figure 5-22.

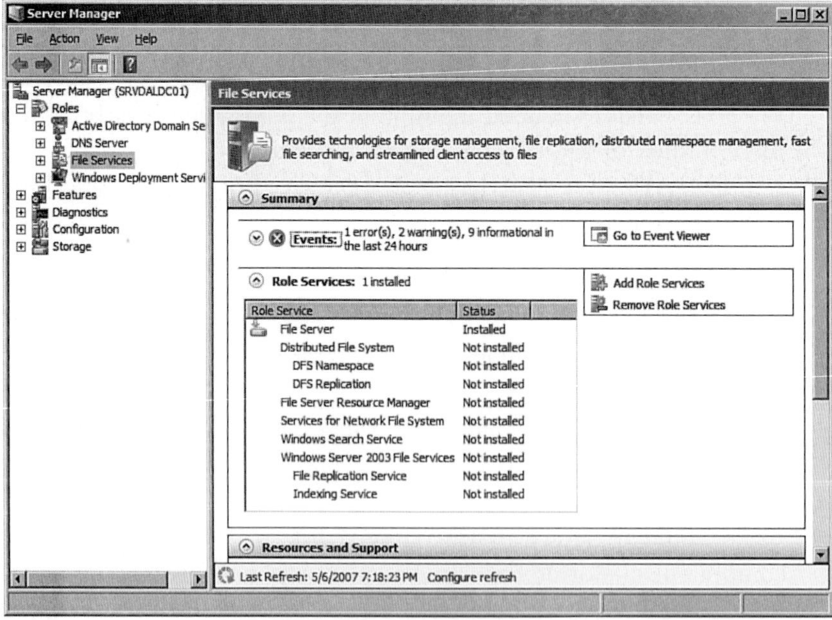

FIGURE 5-22 The File Server Resource Manager service is one of many available as part of the File Services role.

4. Select File Server Resource Manager, as shown in Figure 5-23.

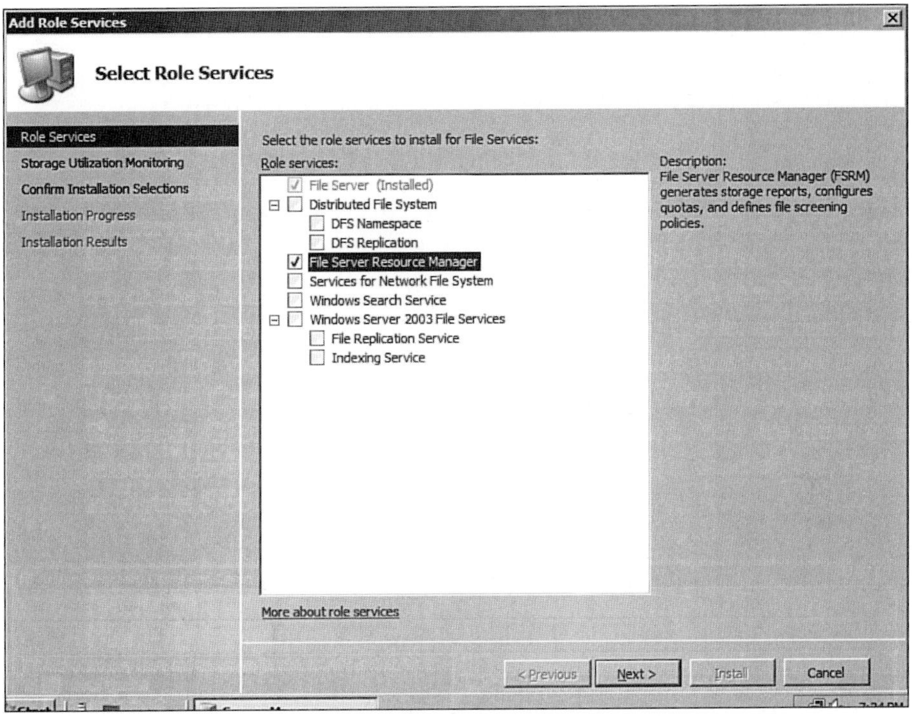

FIGURE 5-23 Selecting the File Server Resource Manager service.

5. FSRM allows you to choose to monitor the overall disk usage of volumes local to the server. FSRM can notify relevant parties, such as the administrators, that a disk is nearly full, as shown in Figure 5-24. By default, both Files by Owner and Files by File Type reports are triggered when a partition reaches 85% of capacity. Report triggers can be changed by clicking the Edit button.
6. If volumes were selected for usage monitoring, the notification options must be selected. These options include a folder to write the reports to, an e-mail address to send the reports to, and an SMTP server to transmit the mail messages (see Figure 5-25).

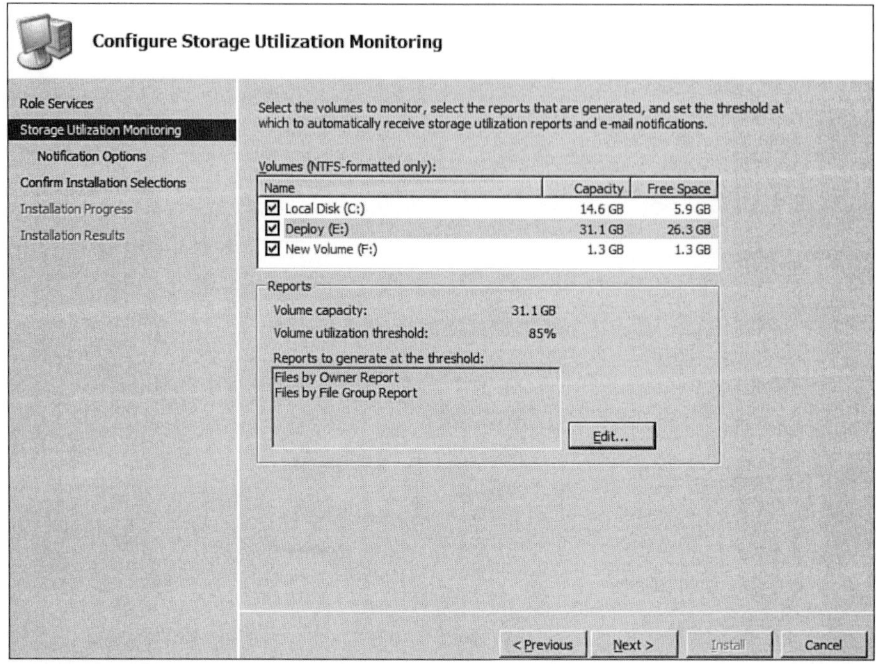

FIGURE 5-24 Using the FSRM capabilities to monitor overall disk usage on a system makes sense and avoids the problem of finding out a disk is out of space when the users tell you.

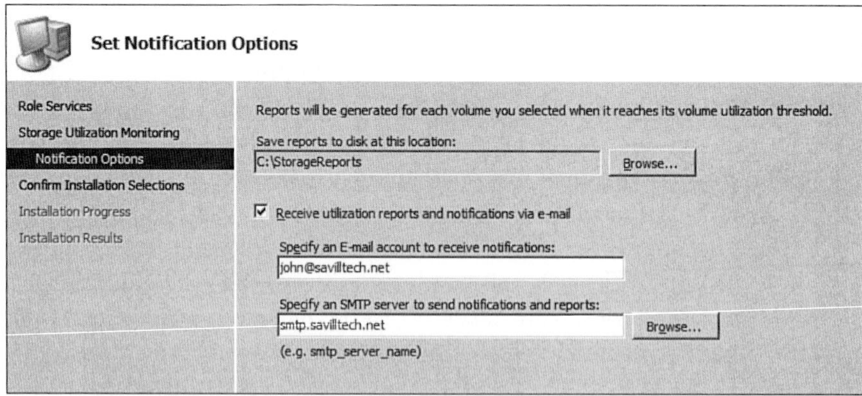

FIGURE 5-25 The notification options are useful for automatic notification of overall system usage.

7. A summary of the options selected is displayed. Confirm your choices by clicking Install, which starts installing the FSRM

component. The install progress is shown on screen. After it is complete, click the Close button.

NOTE For those who used FSRM under Windows 2003 R2, you no longer have to reboot to ensure the drivers are correctly placed in the I/O stack.

During installation, two application services and two mini-filter file system drivers are installed:

- **DataScrn (datascren.sys)**. A kernel-mode mini-filter file system driver that implements file screening checks in real time on configured volumes and folders.
- **Quota (quota.sys)**. A kernel-mode mini-filter file system driver that implements quota checks in real time on configured volumes and folders.
- **SrmSvc (srmsvc.dll)**. An application-type service running as a stand-alone process. It is seen as File Server Resource Manager and starts automatically on system startup.
- **SrmReports (srmhost.exe)**. An application-type service running as a stand-alone process. It is seen as File Server Storage Reports Manager and is configured to be manually started when scheduled reports are configured.

FSRM configuration is stored in the System Volume Information\SRM folder for each volume in metadata files. This configuration is read and processed by the drivers at startup in conjunction with information from the main SrmSvc service after it has started. The configuration is then cached in memory. In the event of a change in the quota or file screen entries, the SrmSvc service notifies the mini-filter of the new entry set. Likewise, if the quota mini-filter file system driver detects that a folder is created or deleted, it notifies SrmSvc to update any quota entries that might be affected. You never need to access this system volume information. All configuration is via the MMC snap-in and the command-line tools. The three tools are dirquota.exe for quotas, filescrn.exe to manage file screening, and storrept.exe for storage reporting needs. Configuration is backed up by NTBACKUP as part of system state and other backup utilities that take advantage of the FSRM VSS writer.

After FSRM is installed, it is administered via the File Server Resource Manager MMC snap-in, placed in the Administrative Tools folder. The navigation pane of the MMC shows the three functionality areas of FSRM:

Quota Management, File Screening Management, and Storage Reports Management.

If the root FSRM item is selected in the navigation pane, one of the actions in the actions pane is Configure Options, as shown in Figure 5-26. You can also access Configure Options via the Action menu of the MMC. Also notice that you can connect to another FSRM server for easy remote management via the actions pane or the Actions menu by selecting Connect to Another Computer.

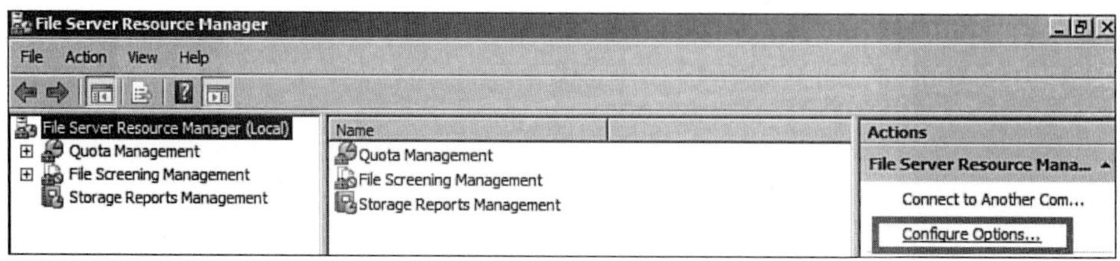

FIGURE 5-26 The MMC 3.0 layout action pane makes the administration experience far more intuitive by making available options more prevalent.

File Server Resource Manager Options

The options for FSRM are broken into five areas: e-mail notifications, notification limits, storage reports, report locations, and file screen audits.

E-Mail Notifications

The E-mail Notifications tab configures which SMTP server sends notifications via e-mail. If you configured storage utilization monitoring during installation of FSRM and entered mail server information, the installation information is already entered in the tab. The e-mail address that the e-mails originate from can be configured (replace with a valid address for your environment).

A Default Administrator Recipients field is set to [Admin E-mail] by default but should be changed to a group containing administrators for the environment. This is used as the recipient for any e-mail where the [Admin E-mail] variable is used as the target, such as for an e-mail about reports or quota/file screening violations.

After you have made your configurations, click the Send Test E-mail button. FSRM sends a test message to confirm the settings are correct, as shown in Figure 5-27.

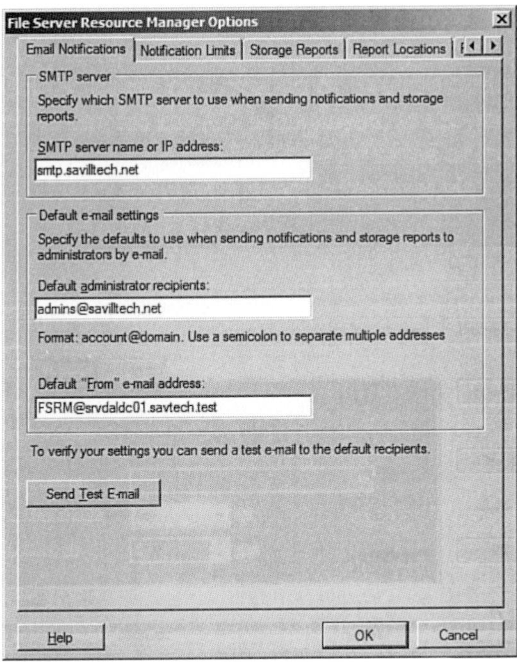

FIGURE 5-27 E-mail notifications are one of the greatest features of the FSRM, so ensure that you get the mail configuration correct.

Notification Limits

The Quota and File Screening components allow various actions to be performed when a violation occurs, such as going over quota or writing an illegal file type. To avoid flooding the user with e-mails or writing excessive event logs in a short amount of time, only one notification of each type per hour for one issue is raised by default. The Notification Limits tab allows you to change these defaults for each of the action types (e-mail, event log, command, and report), as shown in Figure 5-28. For most scenarios, the default of 60 minutes works well.

There can be a temptation to set the time to 0 so every instance of an issue is raised. However, consider trying to write a blocked file type, such as an MP3 file. Windows tries to copy a file once. If it fails, it tries again. If that fails, it tries once more before giving up and throwing an error. This means if you set the notification to 0, all those internal attempts to copy the file generate three exceptions via e-mail, event log, and so on. This is not an attractive situation.

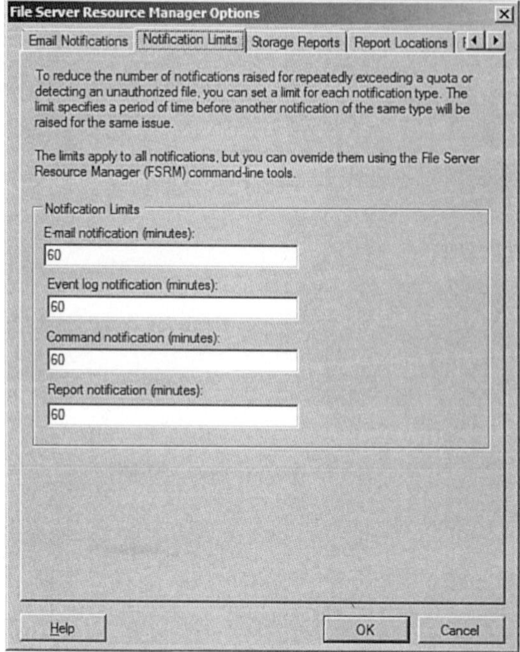

FIGURE 5-28 The default of 60 minutes works best in most environments to avoid flooding both users and internal system resources.

Storage Reports

The Storage Reports tab configures the default parameters for each report type to avoid having to define them each time a report is used. These parameters should be configured to best meet your environment, but they can be changed for specific report executions. This is discussed in the "Reporting" section. For now, remember you can change the defaults for the server.

Report Locations

FSRM has three types of reports:

- **Incident reports**. A report generated as a result of a violation, such as a quota threshold or unauthorized file type
- **Scheduled reports**. A report created based on a scheduled report execution

- **On-demand reports**. A manually triggered report; also known as an interactive report

Each report type has its own save location, which by default is a subfolder of the %systemdrive%\StorageReports folder. The Report Locations tab allows the storage location to be modified, as shown in Figure 5-29.

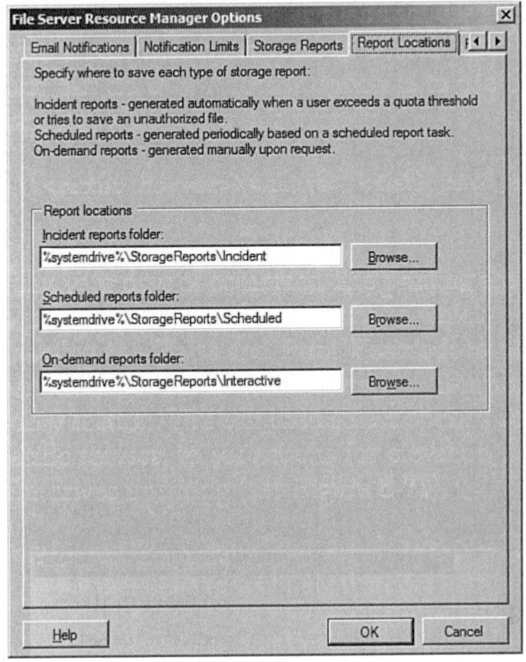

FIGURE 5-29 Each report by default saves to a subdirectory of StorageReports. However, any local location can be configured.

File Screen Audit

The File Screen Audit tab has just one check box, Record File Screening Activity in Auditing Database (see Figure 5-30). One of the reports in the next section runs a report of all file screening exceptions. This report is not generated by searching for event logs but by an internal database of file screen activity. By default, writing to the internal file screen database is not enabled. If you want to run the File Screen Auditing Report, enable this option, so any file screen exceptions are written to the database for parsing by the report.

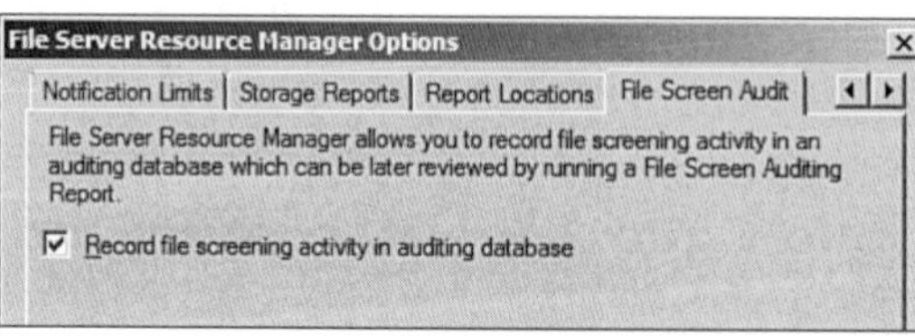

FIGURE 5-30 This is a critical check box if you want to run reports about file screening exceptions.

Reporting

The first component you examine for FSRM is the Storage Report system. It addresses the everyday question, "Where did all my space go?" Current mechanisms to ascertain usage of disk space are manual at best. There is no solution to quickly find out how much space is wasted due to duplicate files, how the disk space is used by file type, and what are the least and most used files, and then present this information in a readable manner.

The Storage Report system addresses this need by defining a number of key scenario reports that can be customized through a number of user-definable parameters and run on an as-needed basis or on a defined schedule. The built-in reports are defined via the Extensible Style sheet Language (XSL) format. Modifying them is not recommended. The included reports are the following:

- **Duplicate files**. Files that share a common size and last modified date. This information can be used to reclaim wasted disk space.
- **File screening audit**. This scans the screening audit events to find violations of screening policies.
- **Files by file group**. Finds disk usage by the type of file and can be configured to report on all files or only files of certain types, such as audio and video or e-mail.
- **Files by owner**. Finds usage by the file owner for all users or selected users. It can be fine-tuned to report only on certain filename patterns, such as *.mp3.
- **Large files**. List all files above a certain definable size and, optionally, based on a certain filename pattern.
- **Least recently accessed files**. List all files that have not been accessed for a definable number of days and, optionally, matching a certain filename pattern.

- **Most recently accessed files**. List all files that have been accessed within a definable number of days and, optionally, matching a certain filename pattern.
- **Quota usage**. List all quotas and their current usage that meet a certain percent of quota used.

The reports can be outputted in a variety of formats, such as HTML, dynamic HTML (allows re-sorting of data within the Web browser), comma-separated values (CSV), text, and XML. After the reports are created, they are saved to a defined location (C:\StorageReports by default) and optionally delivered to a mailbox or distribution list to target multiple users.

Select the Storage Reports Management leaf in the navigation pane. The main details pane shows any existing scheduled reports (if any) and the actions pane gives three options: Schedule a New Report Task allows a new scheduled report to be configured, Add or Remove Reports for a Report Task allows modifications to an existing scheduled report, and Generate Reports Now to initiate a report interactively.

Scheduling a New Report

One of the best ways to use the FSRM reports is to schedule the reports to run periodically at quiet times (for example 2:00 AM) and then post the output to a SharePoint site or by e-mail to managers responsible for a data area. To accomplish this, select the Schedule a New Report Task from the Actions menu or actions pane. You now have three tabs for configuration.

The Settings tab allows you to select which areas are included as part of the report. Volumes, folders, and multiple areas can be selected for each report by clicking the Add button in the Scope section of the tab, as shown in Figure 5-31.

After you select the scope of the report, select which reports to be run. By default, all reports are selected, but you probably want to unselect most of them and run only a specific report. For each report, the Edit Parameters button can be selected. Depending on the report, it allows additional configuration to be performed. For example, for the File Screening Audit report, you can set a minimum number of days since the file screen events occurred and whether the report should be for all users or specific users, as shown in Figure 5-32.

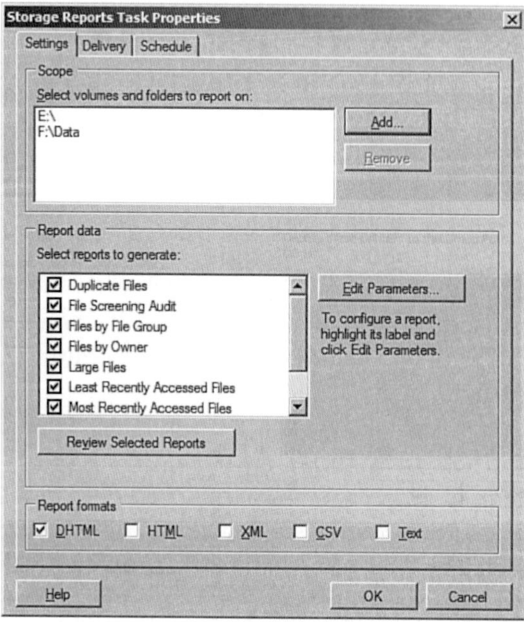

FIGURE 5-31 The Settings tab configures the report.

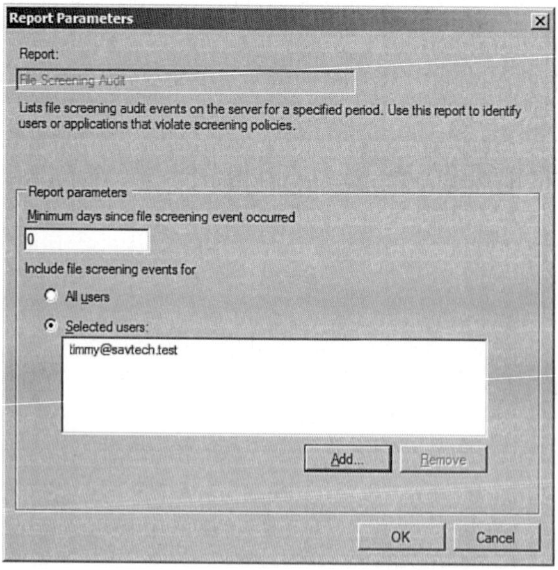

FIGURE 5-32 For this report, only Timmy is reported on.

The final configuration on the Settings tab is the output format, which can be dynamic HTML (DHTML), regular HTML, XML, CSV, and plain text. Choose HTML or DHTML for interactive viewing. The difference between DHTML and HTML is that DHTML tables of information can be sorted dynamically by clicking the various column headings. The XML format is most useful for importing the report into another system, such as a data warehouse where you can then run more complex reporting.

The Delivery tab specifies to which e-mail addresses the reports are mailed if the Send Reports to the Following Administrators option is selected. By default, this is not enabled. The Delivery tab also confirms where the report is saved to. You can change this using the Configure options, but it cannot be set on a per-report basis.

The Schedule tab configures when to run the report. Click the Create Schedule button to open the Schedule dialog, as shown in Figure 5-33.

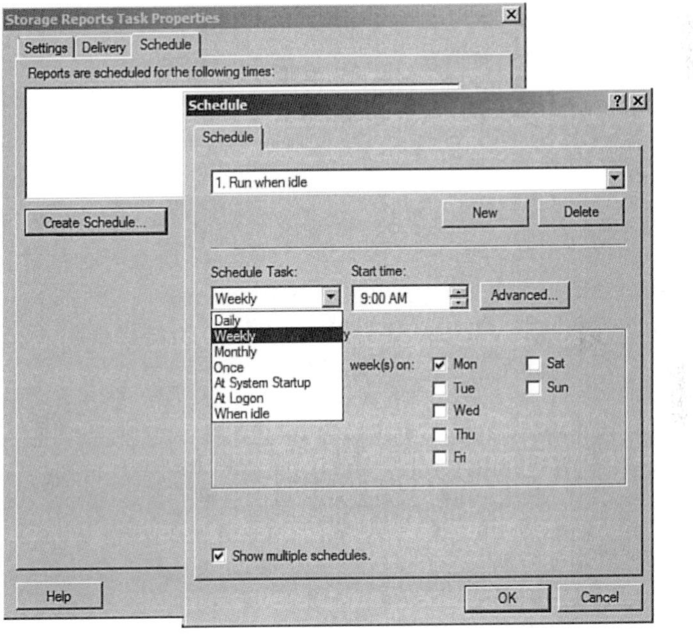

Figure 5-33 A large number of options are configurable.

Click the New button and options for the configuration are displayed. Options include frequency of execution, which could be daily, weekly (with the option to select which days to run on), monthly, at system startup, when the system has been idle for a configurable number of minutes, and once (runs the report once at a configured time and date). You can click New multiple times to create combinations of report executions. You are not limited to just one schedule—you can easily run the report daily and at system startup. The Show Multiple Schedules option at the bottom of the Schedule dialog needs to be selected to run multiple schedules. Click OK after all options are configured. The Storage report is now listed in the details pane, as shown in Figure 5-34.

Schedules reports can be modified by right-clicking the report and selecting Properties or by clicking the Add or Remove Reports for a Report Task. This lists the scheduled reports.

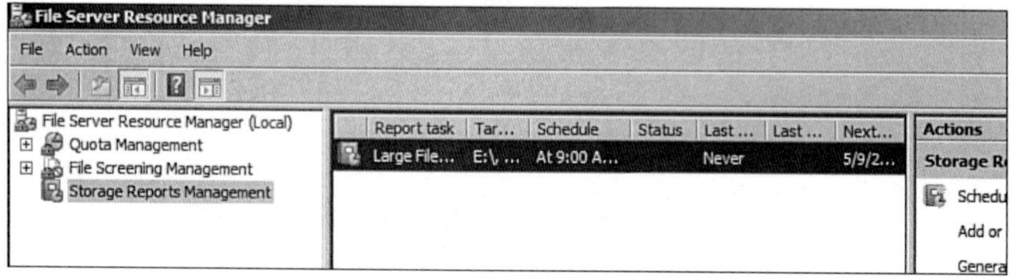

FIGURE 5-34 Over time your list of scheduled reports grows. You likely have many scheduled reports for various data areas that are sent to different mail distribution groups.

If you need a report immediately, you can right-click on a scheduled report and select Run Report Task Now from its context menu. You might create scheduled reports just to have an easy and quick way to run them interactively. If you want to run a report you don't have defined, click the Generate Reports Now link in the actions pane. This gives you exactly the same options as a scheduled report.

If you opt to run reports manually, you have two options. The report can run and then automatically show you the results. The report can run in the background, and you can view it manually later by looking at the reports area (interactive) on disk. Depending on the configuration, the report can be mailed to you. This dialog is shown in Figure 5-35.

Now navigate to the StorageReports\Interactive folder. You see a number of files. (The number depends on the reports selected and the output format.) Let's take the most interesting, the dynamic HTML file. (It still has a HTML extension.) When you open the file, you get an Internet Explorer warning, as shown in Figure 5-36. This is because a script loads to render the dynamic HTML. Right-click the warning and select Allow Blocked Content. Then click Yes on the confirmation dialog.

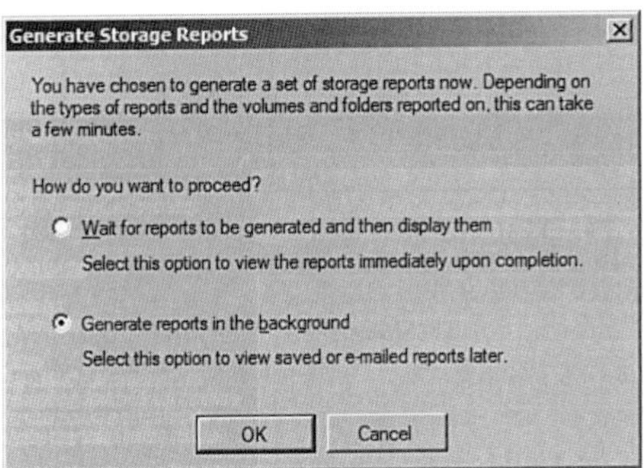
Generate Storage Reports
You have chosen to generate a set of storage reports now. Depending on the types of reports and the volumes and folders reported on, this can take a few minutes.
How do you want to proceed?
Wait for reports to be generated and then display them
Select this option to view the reports immediately upon completion.
Generate reports in the background
Select this option to view saved or e-mailed reports later.
OK
Cancel

FIGURE 5-35 Depending on the amount of data, waiting for the report to complete might be impractical.

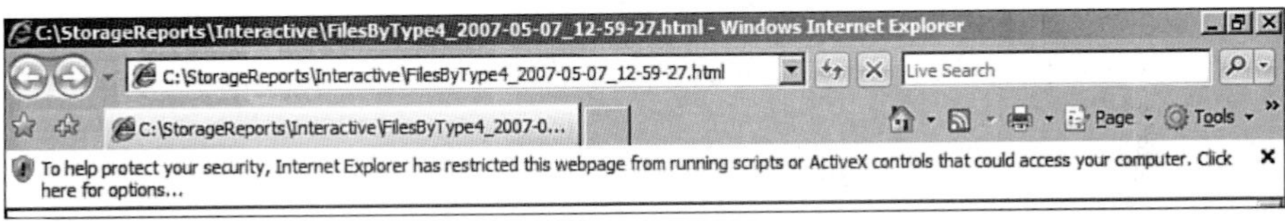
C:\StorageReports\Interactive\FilesByType4_2007-05-07_12-59-27.html - Windows Internet Explorer
C:\StorageReports\Interactive\FilesByType4_2007-05-07_12-59-27.html
Live Search
C:\StorageReports\Interactive\FilesByType4_2007-0...
Page
Tools
To help protect your security, Internet Explorer has restricted this webpage from running scripts or ActiveX controls that could access your computer. Click here for options...

FIGURE 5-36 It's protecting us, just remember that.

The DHTML file can now be viewed. Clicking the various table column headings sorts the data (see Figure 5-37). This allows one report to be usable for nearly any purpose. (For example, one person might want to see the data listed in order of owner, by biggest file, and by smallest files.)

Take some time running reports, and you see the real benefit to the organization. If your company charges business areas for its disk space usage, now you can automatically run a report each night that gets mailed to the areas, showing them why they are using so much disk space. From an operational standpoint, reports that find duplicate files identify wasted disk space. Reports showing file space usage by file type prove that most of your space is used by MP3 files.

Scheduling storage reports is controlled via the Task Scheduler component of Windows Server. Reports are executed by the storrept.exe image. It passes a task identifier so `storrept` knows which scheduled report to execute. An example of this format is as follows:

```
C:\WINDOWS\system32\storrept.exe reports generate /scheduled
➥ /Task:"FSRM_Report_Task{8900e594-08ce-49f7-82d3-
➥531d0ce6ac6a}"
```

View the scheduled task using the Task Scheduler system tool (accessed by clicking Start, Programs, Accessories, System Tools). Select the root Task Scheduler Library leaf of the navigation pane, and the report task is listed in the details pane. Each entry can be selected to see the detail of its execution, as shown in Figure 5-38.

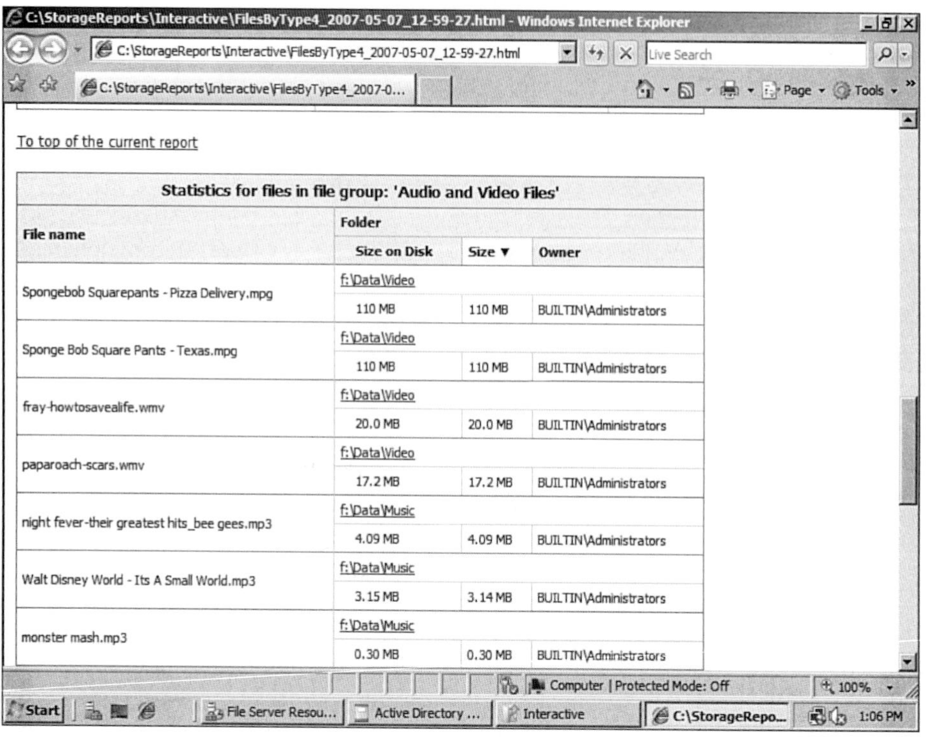

FIGURE 5-37 A strange collection of data.

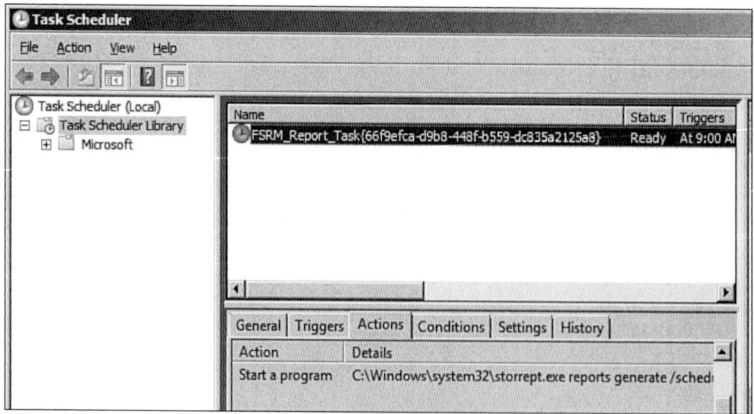

FIGURE 5-38 Task Scheduler is a great interface to see what is running on your system.

Cluster installations are fully supported. Practically, this means that if a scheduled report is defined on one node in the cluster, it is accessible from the other nodes that might share disks. This is possible because the entire FSRM configuration is stored on the actual volume.

Quotas

Windows 2000 introduced disk quotas, which allowed a maximum amount of logical disk space to be defined on a per-volume and per-user basis. When the quota was exceeded, either the user couldn't write additional information in the case of a hard limit, or an event log was written if a soft limit was reached.

This quota system had limitations; each user had her own entry, and quotas did not work for shared areas. Also, the quota was for an entire disk. File server users might have access to many different shares and areas on a single volume, and different quota limits should be possible at that level of granularity. For shared areas, a quota on the total folder size should be shared between anyone who has write permissions.

The quota management subsystem of FSRM provides exactly this level of granularity, based on physical disk usage rather than logical usage. The Windows 2000–type quotas based the disk usage on the logical size of the data, which is not the space used on the actual physical disk. If you compress a 10MB (logical size) Word document, it might only use 350KB (physical size) on disk. Under the legacy quota, this compressed file would use 10MB of the user's quota. Under the FSRM quota solution, the physical size (350KB) is used. That drives users to be more diligent in compressing their information because it directly affects the amount of data they can store.

Quota management (like file screening) offers a flexible set of rich notifications that can be defined in the event of a quota breach or when a certain percentage of the quota is reached. This feature is only available on NTFS, nonremovable volumes.

A big change here is that quotas are defined on a per-volume or per-folder basis; no user or group is specified. NTFS permissions should be used to restrict who can write to a folder. Quotas are not a security mechanism. They control how much can be written, and NTFS controls who can write it. After a quota is applied to a folder or volume, anyone with write permissions is encompassed by the total quota limit.

FSRM quotas are highly flexible. First, the quota can be configured as a hard or soft quota. A hard quota enforces the quota limit and cancels an I/O request if it would result in the quota being exceeded. A soft quota is not enforced and allows continued I/O beyond the quota size. So why bother having a soft quota? When a quota is reached, or at a defined percentage of the quota, one or more actions can be triggered:

- **E-mail message**. Sends a message to a defined administrator and/or the user performing the I/O with configurable message content that can contain a number of variables. For example, variables for the quota used in MB, the percentage used, the server, and so on, exist. The user simply receives an access denied message when a hard quota is exceeded and he might not understand. The e-mail message is sent to him within seconds, and you could use it to recommunicate what quotas are in force and the policies behind their use.
- **Event log**. A warning event can be written to the application event log, which can contain configurable content based on a number of variables.
- **Command**. Run a script or command with a defined set of arguments. It can be run as the local service, network service, or local system context.
- **Report**. A storage report, as described in the previous section, can be called. When a quota is exceeded, a storage report is run and then e-mailed to the user who exceeded the quota. This helps the user understand what data has caused her to exceed her quota and take action to free space. Use caution with this, based on the resources required to run the reports. Running large storage reports in the middle of the day can cause a considerable performance hit. There are situations where running in the day would be okay—for example, a common use might be to run a report on a user's home folder, which is small and would, therefore, run a report quickly.

These options are powerful. When sets of actions are used, such as warning a user when he reaches 85% of his quota and performing a more definitive action at 100%, a lot of configuration is needed. Do not repeat it on the various different folders and volumes on which quotas are required. Thankfully, templates are supported, which allow a set of actions to be defined at various percentage states of a defined quota and can then be quickly applied to various volumes and folders.

Microsoft has a number of templates that can be customized to your exact requirements, as shown in Figure 5-39. These are accessed via the Quota Templates leaf under Quota Management in the navigation pane. You can modify a template by right-clicking it and selecting Edit Template Properties.

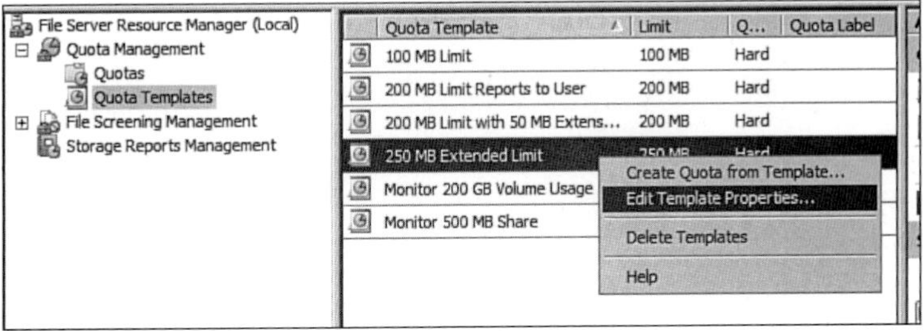

FIGURE 5-39 These six templates form the basis of anything you need to do and show what can be done.

Quota Properties

The properties of a quota template show the type of the quota (hard or soft) and the quota limit in terabytes, gigabytes, megabytes, and kilobytes. The four types of actions available can be configured at different threshold points in any combination (for example, at 85% of a quota, 95% of a quota, and then 100%). A good template to look at is the 200MB Limit with 50MB Extension template. Look at the properties of that template, which should look like Figure 5-40. This template has a 200MB limit, and when the limit is reached, the quota is extended by an additional 50MB. This gives a total quota of 250MB.

Select the Warning (100%) threshold notification and click Edit so you can see all the options available. These options are broken into four tabs relating to the four types of actions.

E-Mail Message

The E-mail Message tab allows an e-mail account or distribution group to be selected as the target for an e-mail message. You can opt to send an e-mail to the actual user who exceeds the threshold, as shown in Figure 5-41.

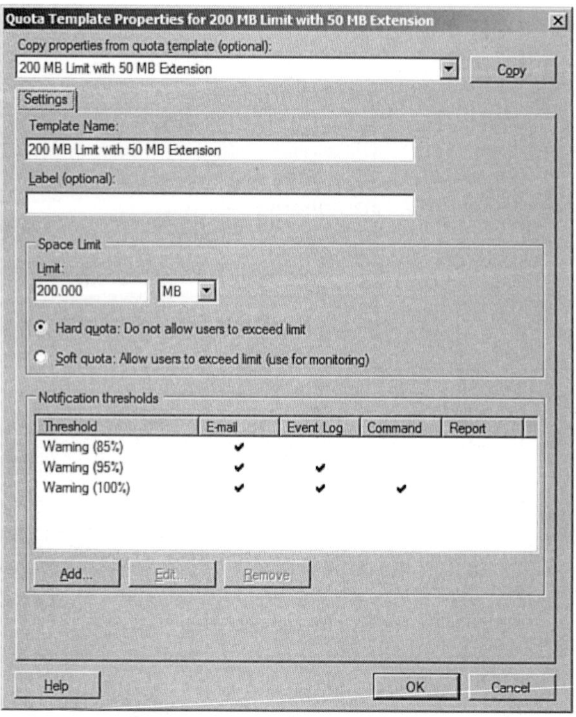

FIGURE 5-40 This template uses different actions based on the closer you get to the actual quota limit.

A subject and body for the e-mail can be configured. Notice that a number of FSRM variables can be inserted into the header and body to make the message content specific to the notification. The example shows using the Source I/O Owner variable to insert the user who made the I/O request that exceeded the threshold. Quota Path shows the actual location where the quota is set. If you select the variable drop-down box, all the available variables are displayed.

If you want to configure options such as who the message is from, a reply-to, CC, and BCC, click the Additional E-mail Headers button, which allows this extra information to be input.

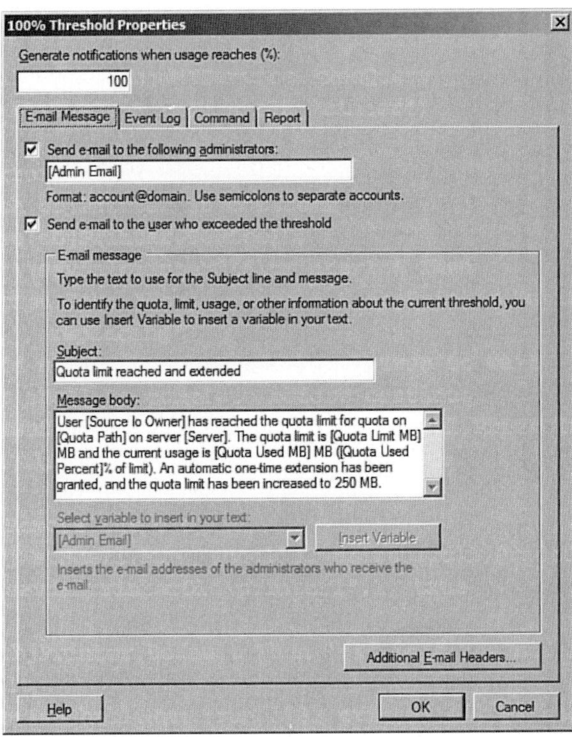

FIGURE 5-41 The e-mail notification is one of the most used actions because it gives a direct way to notify the quota-exceeding user of what has happened.

Event Log

The Event Log tab works in a similar fashion to the E-mail Message tab, except this time you can just configure the body of text with variables written to the Application Event Log, as shown in Figure 5-42.

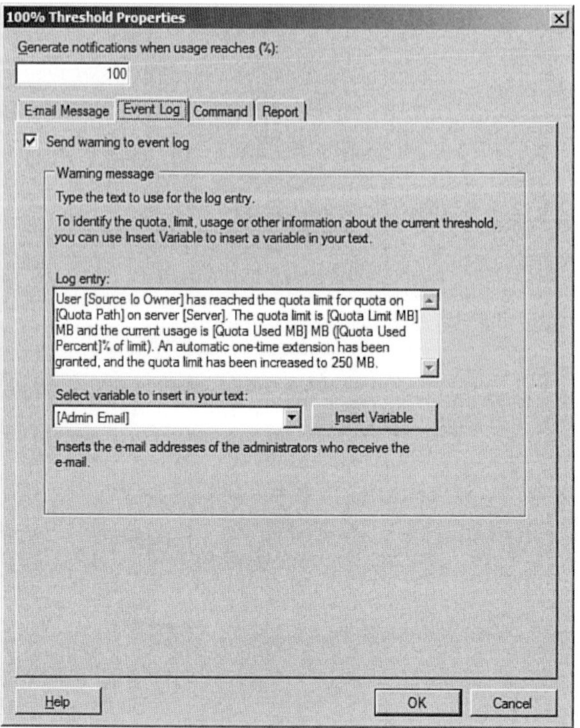

FIGURE 5-42 The event log text for this quota.

Command

The Command tab enables you to run any command that can be called from a command line. Arguments to the command can be configured along with a working directory. The use of this is shown with the 200MB Limit with a 50MB Extension quota, as shown in Figure 5-43.

At 100% of the quota, the command runs the quota command-line interface tool, `dirquota`, to extend the quota by 50MB. It does this by replacing the 200MB limit template with a 250MB limit template. As a side point, this reinforces that everything that can be done through the GUI can also be configured using the command-line tools and that some sophisticated combinations are possible.

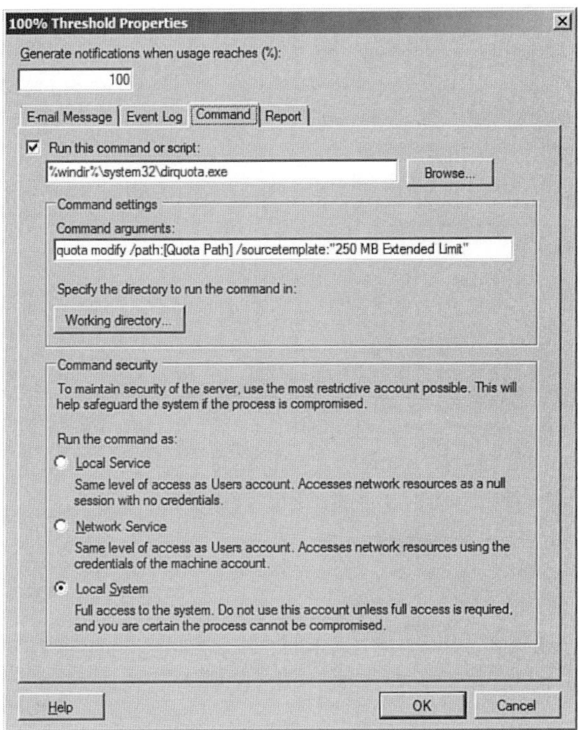

FIGURE 5-43 Extending a quota by 50MB

Select the account in which to run the command from the local service, network service, or local system (the default).

Report

The Report tab is used to run any of the reports you have seen before (although without customizable options). A report can be sent to a defined administrator and to the user who exceeded the threshold, as shown in Figure 5-44.

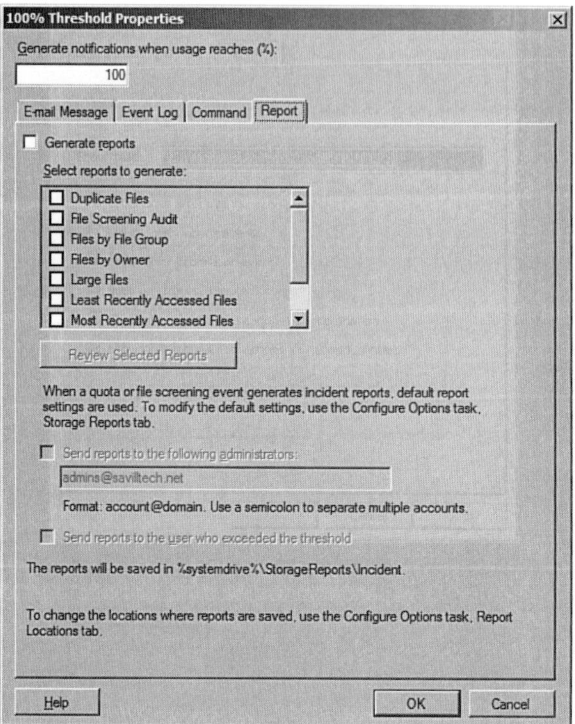

FIGURE 5-44 Running reports might not be the best option from a resource-usage perspective.

Assigning Quotas

After the templates are defined, a new quota entry is easily created by selecting Create Quota from the actions pane within the Quotas leaf of Quota Management. If you selected to use FSRM for usage monitoring when installing FSRM, there is already one soft quota entry for each volume that was selected.

The Create Quota dialog, as shown in Figure 5-45, allows the selection of a template or a custom set of criteria. The recommended way is to use a quota template rather than manually defining criteria (hence the whole point of quotas). After all options are selected, click the Create button.

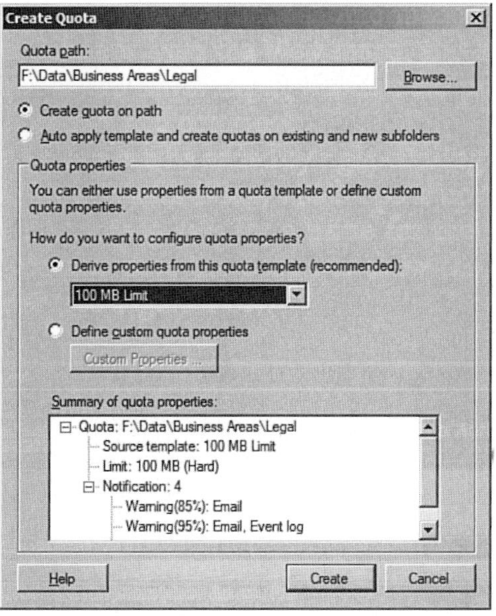

FIGURE 5-45 It is possible to create a custom quota, but this should be the exception. Use templates in most situations.

Notice at the top of Figure 5-45 that a Create Quota on Path or an Auto Apply Template and Create Quotas on Existing and New Subfolders option is available. The normal option is to select Create Quota on Path, which applies the template or custom properties onto the selected quota path. The second option is useful on folders that might contain dynamically created subfolders that each need their own quota, such as a folder that houses user home folders. Each user's folder should have its own quota applied. When Auto Apply is selected, all existing subfolders have the quota selected applied individually. As new folders are created, they automatically have their own copy of the selected quota applied to them. This is shown in Figure 5-46.

Note that only the first quota, D:\Data\Users*, was manually created. All the others were automatically created because the quota type was set as Auto Apply. Another useful feature is that if the template is modified, you can opt to apply this change to all template instances. If you change the limit from 200MB to 500MB in the template and select the appropriate option to propagate to derived template uses, all the entries in Figure 5.46 would change to a 500MB limit.

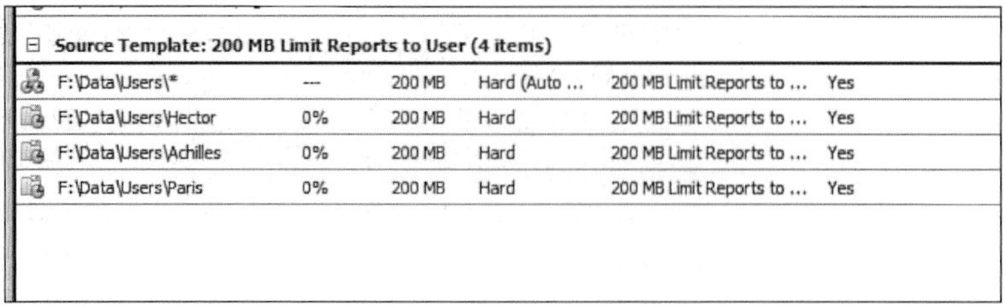

⊟ Source Template: 200 MB Limit Reports to User (4 items)					
F:\Data\Users*	---	200 MB	Hard (Auto ...	200 MB Limit Reports to ...	Yes
F:\Data\Users\Hector	0%	200 MB	Hard	200 MB Limit Reports to ...	Yes
F:\Data\Users\Achilles	0%	200 MB	Hard	200 MB Limit Reports to ...	Yes
F:\Data\Users\Paris	0%	200 MB	Hard	200 MB Limit Reports to ...	Yes

FIGURE 5-46 Although four quotas are shown, only one was manually added.

If you navigate a volume with quotas locally, the free space changes based on the prevalent quota, as shown in the following code. Notice that the free space changes as you move through the volume.

```
F:\Data\Users>dir
 Volume in drive F is New Volume
 Volume Serial Number is 50E8-E6EE

 Directory of F:\Data\Users

05/07/2007  02:18 PM    <DIR>          .
05/07/2007  02:18 PM    <DIR>          ..
05/07/2007  02:18 PM    <DIR>          Achilles
05/07/2007  02:18 PM    <DIR>          Hector
05/07/2007  02:18 PM    <DIR>          Paris
               0 File(s)              0 bytes
               5 Dir(s)   1,131,294,720 bytes free

F:\Data\Users>cd hector

F:\Data\Users\Hector>dir
 Volume in drive F is New Volume
 Volume Serial Number is 50E8-E6EE

 Directory of F:\Data\Users\Hector

05/07/2007  02:18 PM    <DIR>          .
05/07/2007  02:18 PM    <DIR>          ..
               0 File(s)              0 bytes
               2 Dir(s)     209,711,104 bytes free
```

With Server Message Block (SMB) 1.0 (used prior to Windows Vista and Windows Server 2008), a remote location's free space stayed the same as the free space of the point of connection, such as the root share. With SMB 2.0, the free space changes for remote paths. The following code shows a remote connection from a Vista client. Notice the space change is the same as the local.

```
C:\Users\john>net use * \\192.168.1.180\f$
Drive Z: is now connected to \\192.168.1.180\f$.

The command completed successfully.

C:\Users\john>z:

Z:\>cd data

Z:\Data>cd users

Z:\Data\Users>dir
 Volume in drive Z is New Volume
 Volume Serial Number is 50E8-E6EE

 Directory of Z:\Data\Users

05/07/2007  02:18 PM    <DIR>          .
05/07/2007  02:18 PM    <DIR>          ..
05/07/2007  02:18 PM    <DIR>          Achilles
05/07/2007  02:18 PM    <DIR>          Hector
05/07/2007  02:18 PM    <DIR>          Paris
               0 File(s)              0 bytes
               5 Dir(s)   1,131,294,720 bytes free

Z:\Data\Users>cd paris

Z:\Data\Users\Paris>dir
 Volume in drive Z is New Volume
 Volume Serial Number is 50E8-E6EE

 Directory of Z:\Data\Users\Paris

05/07/2007  02:18 PM    <DIR>          .
05/07/2007  02:18 PM    <DIR>          ..
               0 File(s)              0 bytes
               2 Dir(s)     209,711,104 bytes free
```

Templates can be exported and imported using the command-line tools but not via the MMC snap-in. Currently, exporting and importing is the only way to perform template management over multiple machines. You look at the syntax of exporting and importing in the file screening section—the syntax is the same for both quota and file screens.

SMB 2.0 Windows Vista and Windows Server 2008 support SMB 2.0, a major improvement over SMB 1.0. The real power of SMB 2.0 is performance. The original SMB was optimized around 60KB data packages, which are uncommon in today's networks that handle files that are megabytes, if not gigabytes, in size. Whereas SMB 1.0 used a fixed window size where packets had to arrive in sequence, SMB 2.0 uses a variable window size. Packets can be sent without an acknowledgment from the preceding packets, allowing data to be sent 30 to 40 times faster under SMB 2.0. SMB 2.0 also supports symbolic links. SMB 2.0 can only be used if both ends of a link support SMB 2.0. If XP is talking to a Windows Server 2008 box, SMB 1.0 is used.

File Screening

Quotas are a great feature, but they have one major flaw: They work on the assumption that the administrator's intention for the disk space matches the end user's intention for the disk space. Conflict can quickly escalate when administrators fail to appreciate that users' most important data is their MP3 collection, which must be highly available and recoverable at all times. A quota does not govern how users fill their 500MB folder with their Britney Spears' collection. It is vital that administrators understand how the users do their job.

Although storage reports tell you how data is used and quotas define how much data can be stored, file screens define what data can be stored. Like quotas, this is performed in real time. Any attempt to write an illegal file type results in an "Access is denied" error message on the client.

Everything you discussed with quotas applies to file screening. File screen templates define what type of file groups should be blocked, such as audio, video, or image files.

Microsoft provides several file groups that contain all the popular file extensions for the group type. The content of these file groups can be modified and new file groups defined as needed. To view the file groups, select the File Groups leaf of the File Screening Management component, as shown in Figure 5-47.

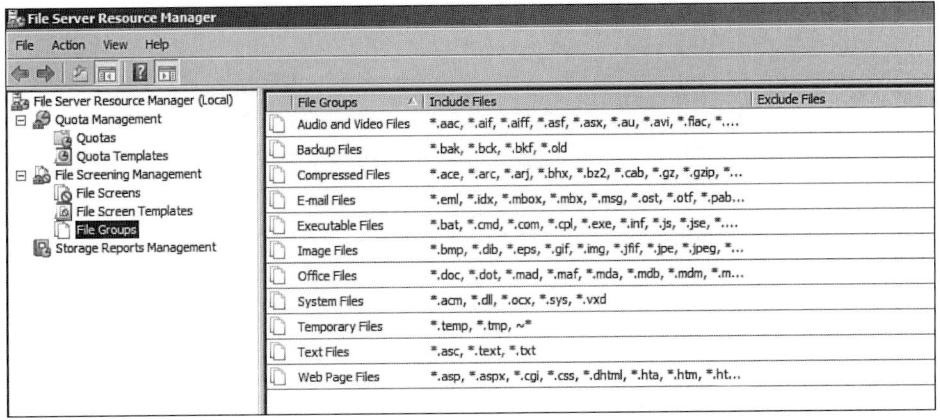

FIGURE 5-47 Default and custom file groups are useful.

Templates are used for file screening the same as quotas, and any combination of the four actions (e-mail, event log, command execution, or storage report) can be configured. File screens have no configurable thresholds. You can't have 95% of an MP3 file being written, so instead, simply select which file groups to block. If you want a custom file type, click Create, as shown in Figure 5-48.

Like quotas, file screening has an active or passive mode. Active mode stops an illegal file type from being written to the volume or folder. Passive mode allows the file to be created and runs the defined set of actions, such as paging the large security guard to escort the user off the company premises.

After the templates are created, you can apply a screen. Let's say you have a media folder and no media types should be written to the root of the folder. Apply a screen at the root using these steps:

1. Select the File Screens node of File Screening Management.
2. Select Create File Screen from the actions pane.
3. Select the path for the file screen by clicking the Browse button. Select the template to use, as shown in Figure 5-49.
4. Click Create.

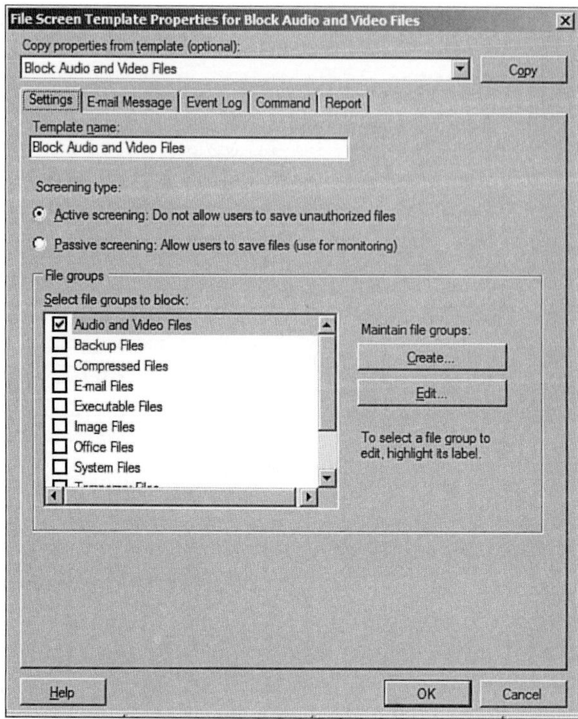

FIGURE 5-48 The only different configuration area between file screens and quotas.

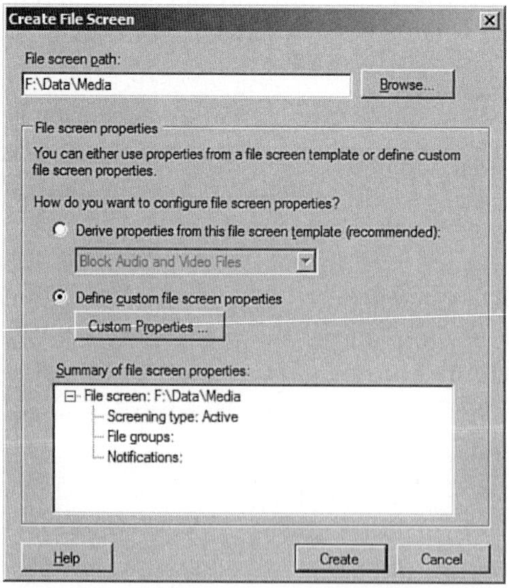

FIGURE 5-49 Creating a file screen from a template is simple.

Now you can go back and edit a screen. Let's say you selected Audio and Video originally, but now you want to add images. To do this, right-click the file screen and select its properties. Now select other file groups to block, such as image files. When you now view the file screen instance, the column showing if it matches the template now reads "No" because you've changed the groups, as shown in Figure 5-50.

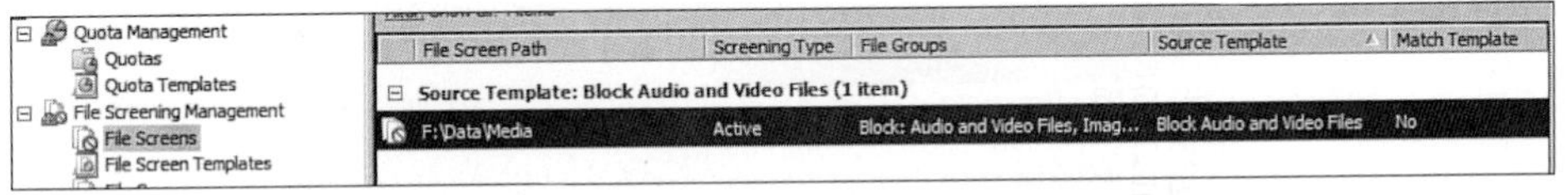

FIGURE 5-50 The slightly customized file screen.

At this point, attempting to copy or create a file type that matches the audio, video, or image file groups results in an access denied message. Any files that are already in the location of the blocked type can still be accessed and read/executed. They cannot be edited or renamed because the file screen looks for write and modify operations. Because you get a basic access denied message, sending e-mail notification to the user explaining why he was denied access is crucial. Otherwise, he simply raises help desk tickets, saying something is wrong in the environment.

Additionally, exceptions can be defined to allow certain file groups. Let's go back to the folder where you blocked all audio, video, and image files. You can create an Images subfolder onto which you create an exception to explicitly allow image files. This would stop users writing image files to anywhere in the folder structure except in the Images subfolder. This lends itself to a organized file storage environment.

Exceptions are created the same way as normal file screens, except you select Create File Screen Exception in the actions pane. As Figure 5-51 shows, you select the file groups to be excluded. With this exception in place, images can be written to the Images subfolder but not to the parent media.

When combined with a comprehensive communications policy to ensure that users are aware of the company rules, file screening and e-mail notification are great features. The notifications should be just that—a reminder. It should not be the first time the users are informed to not store this type of media on company resources.

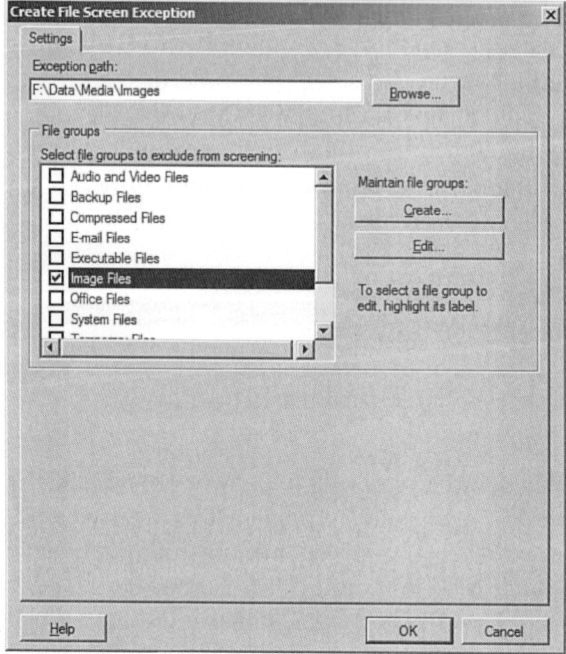

FIGURE 5-51 A file screen exception allows file groups on a path.

Finally, file screening works on file extensions. It is not designed to stop the determined user from renaming all his MP3 files to another extension. The screening is designed to prevent unintentional file placement. Future versions of file screening might use content/signature screening instead of the file extension.

Exporting and Importing File Screens and Quotas

Configuring multiple servers is not easy. You have three options—the first is to configure everything via the command-line utilities, which are the following:

- **`dirquota.exe`**. Used to define, configure, and manage quotas on directories, quota templates, and global options
- **`filescrn.exe`**. Used to define, configure, and manage file screens, file screen exceptions, file screen templates, and global options on directories
- **`storrept.exe`**. Used to define, configure, and manage reports

Manually performing all the configuration via the command-line utilities and then running the commands on all the servers is one option, but it means you need to be an expert in the command line.

The second option is using the same command-line tools to export configuration from one server and then import it into all the other servers. Each tool has good help, but to export a file screen, you just need to give a filename to export to and the name of the template. For example, let's say you have a custom block MP3 template. To export it, use the following:

```
C:\ >filescrn template export /file:f:\data\fsrm\filescreenmp3.xml
➥/template:"Block MP3"

Templates exported successfully.
```

You also created a custom file group, so you need to export it using the same format:

```
C:\ >filescrn filegroup export /file:f:\data\fsrm\mp3filegroup.xml
➥/filegroup:"MP3 Files"

File groups exported successfully.
```

After a template is exported, you can open up the XML and change the settings if required. To import, use the same commands, but with `import` instead of `export`. For example:

```
filescrn template import /file:f:\data\fsrm\filescreenmp3.xml
➥/template:"Block MP3"
```

To add a file screen, use the `filescrn screen add` command with the parameters shown in the help. For example, to apply the custom block MP3 template, use the following:

```
C:\>filescrn screen add /path:f:\data\media\music\wma
➥/sourcetemplate:"Block MP3"

File screen successfully created for "f:\data\media\music\wma".
```

The third option is to script all the actions, discussed in the following section.

Scripting

With Windows Server 2008, a public application programming interface (API) is now available for FSRM as a document on the Microsoft MSDN web site. Although the API can be used in many ways, one easy way is via a VBScript. The following example applies a 100MB quota to the `e:\data` folder:

```
Dim quotaManager
Set quotaManager = CreateObject("Fsrm.FsrmQuotaManager")


Dim quota
Set quota = quotaManager.CreateQuota("e:\data")

quota.ApplyTemplate("100 MB Limit")

quota.Commit()
```

Notice that you create an object of type Fsrm.QuotaManager and then use the object to create a quota instance.

Print Management

In any corporate environment, you rarely see each computer hooked up to its own USB printer. Instead, shared printers are used that offer superior features. Although each desktop could directly connect to the shared printer via an IP connection, each client would have to maintain the configuration of the connection and manually install the printer driver. Central management of printer use or a repository of printers available would not be possible.

The Windows Server 2008 platform offers a great deal of functionality for print services, including features that benefit users and administrators. Today, organizations have many branch locations, each with local print servers. Windows Server 2008 helps meet the challenge by managing multiple print servers as one.

Windows Vista and Windows Server 2008 saw the integration of the XML Paper Specification (XPS), which was previously made available as part of the XPS Essentials Pack for XP and Windows Server 2003. The XPS capability enabled the XPS print path, which spooled documents in the XPS format. This gave greater fidelity, performance, and security to the printing process. This requires an XPSDrv printer driver.

This XPS spooling also applies for server-side spooling, assuming that client-side rendering is enabled (which is the default). The client renders to XML and sends to the printer's spool file. Newer printers are XPS-enabled, maintaining the XPS data from the client to the server to the printer with no conversions. These printers are known as direct-consumption printers. Non-XPS printers have to provide a filter that converts the XPS spool file to the native Page Description Language (PDL) of the printer. The old Graphics Device Interface (GDI) print path is still provided for non-XPSDrv printer drivers and results in the old style Enhanced Metafile (EMF) spool file storage and subsequent rendering. If you have an older Win32 application that uses GDI graphics that is sent to an XPSDrv printer, a GDI-to-XPS conversion is performed so you still get the XPS spooling and other XPS advantages previously discussed. The opposite applies as well. If you print from a Windows Presentation Foundation application that natively outputs to XPS and you are using an non-XPSDrv, an XPS-to-GDI conversion takes place. XPS-based client-server printing is one of those "better together" Vista/Windows Server 2008 winners. If you want to know the ins and outs of XPS-based printing, Microsoft has a whitepaper on the entire XPS printing pipe at www.microsoft.com/whdc/device/print/XPSDrv_FilterPipe.mspx.

Now let's manage some printing.

Installing the Windows Server 2008 Print Management Components

Like all the 2008 components, you install the Print Services Role via the Server Manager interface. After it is selected, three subservices are associated with the Print Services role:

- **Print Server**. Includes the Print Management MMC snap-in that manages print servers and their prints, plus the capability to migrate printers between print servers. This is the same MMC that is part of Windows Vista Business, Enterprise, and Ultimate editions. Vista can manage your Windows Server 2008 printer environment in small environments (up to 10 concurrent network connections).
- **LPD Service**. An implementation of the Line Printer Daemon designed to provide print support to UNIX-based clients. Implementations of Line Printer Remote (LPR) are available for other platforms, including Windows Vista.
- **Internet Printing**. Has two features: The first enables Web-based print server management, and the second provides support for the

Internet Printing Protocol, which allows printing to the print server from the Web. Because the Internet Printing feature operates via a web site, the print server must also have the Web Server role installed. This role is automatically selected and enabled during the selection of the Internet Printing subrole.

The LPD Service requires no special configuration. During installation, the local server firewall is updated to allow inbound connection on port 515, over which LPR operates.

Print Management MMC

The Print Management MMC functionality is focused around three main activity areas. As shown in Figure 5-52, the navigation pane displays a Custom Filters node, a Print Servers node, and a Deployed Printers node.

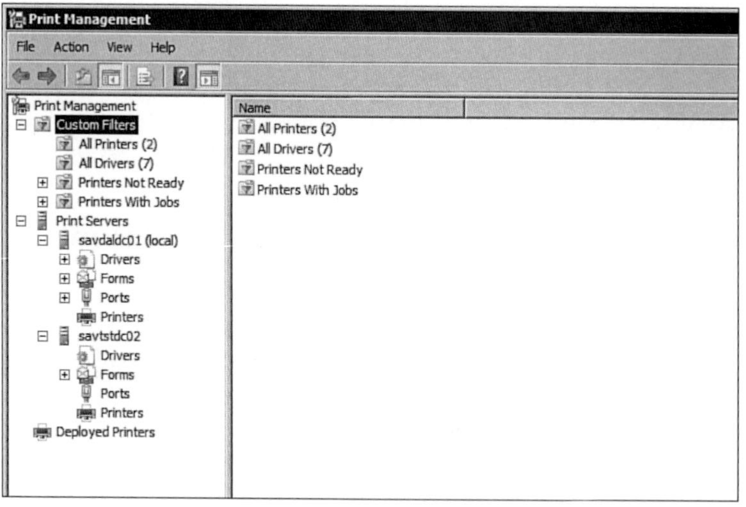

FIGURE 5-52 In this example, two print servers are known to the Print Management console.

By default, four custom filters exist, which list all known printers, all known drivers, any printers that are not in a ready state (indicating a problem), and all printers with print jobs. Additional filters can be created to allow quick access to groups of printers. Think of these filters as ways to view all information known to the Print Management console in groups that might make your job easier, such as all laser printers in Building Four. You'll create some custom filters later.

The next major navigation node shows the print servers that are known to the Print Management MMC. By default, the local printer server is listed. For each print server, four areas of information are available: the drivers currently installed on the print server; the forms available for printing; ports used for printing local, terminal server, and IP; and the printers to which the server has connections.

The Deployed Printers node enables an easy view of the printers that are being deployed via group policy. This was a new capability in Windows 2003 R2 that used a combination of group policy and a client-side PushPrinterConnections.exe executable to check the group policy for printers and then add them. This client-side tool is not needed with Windows Vista/2008 clients.

Adding Printer Servers

The Print Management console is not just for managing Windows Server 2008 print servers. Print servers run Windows Server 2000, 2003, XP, and Vista.

To add an additional print server, right-click on the Print Servers navigation node item and select Add/Remove Servers from the node's context menu. You can browse for new printers or enter in the name of the print server directly to add a server. If the local server is not currently displayed in the printer servers list, click the Add the Local Server button, as shown in Figure 5-53.

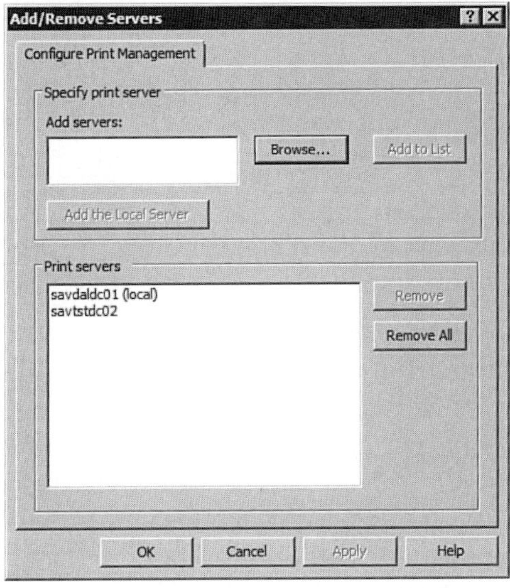

FIGURE 5-53 The Add/Remove Servers dialog allows new servers to be added or existing servers to be removed.

Adding a New Printer

One of the goals of the Print Management console is to make management of print server environments simpler, especially for the branch office with no local administrator to help set up the printers.

You can statically add a printer by right-clicking the Printers navigation node item for a specific print server and selecting Add Printer from the context menu. This launches the Network Printer Installation Wizard, as shown in Figure 5-54. Other options include adding a printer on a server's existing port, such as LPT, COM devices, a file device, ports associated with terminal services printers, and the XPSPort used for XPS printing to files. You might have additional or less ports on your server depending on your hardware. Nearly all modern printers are network-based, so our discussion focuses on that for now.

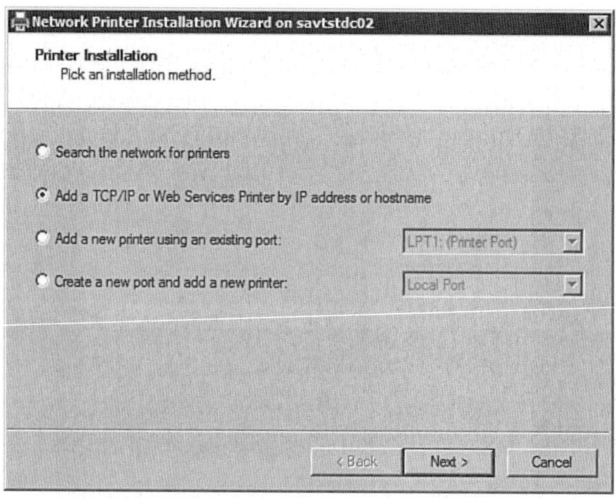

FIGURE 5-54 There are four ways to add a printer via the Print Management console.

Nearly every printer purchased today has a network capability that automatically grabs an IP address via DHCP but allows static configuration via a simple menu. Many home printers even have wireless capabilities. After the printer has an IP address and that IP address is known to the administrator, the printer can be added via the Add a TCP/IP or Web Services Printer by IP Address or Hostname option. This opens up a new dialog asking for the name or IP of the printer, as shown in Figure 5-55. By default, the Network Printer Installation Wizard auto-detects the type of printer, but it can be manually configured as a TCP/IP or Web Services printer. Also notice that by default, the Network Printer Installation Wizard attempts to detect the correct driver to use.

WEB SERVICES FOR PRINTING The concept of Web Services printers might be new to some. Web Services are considered the next wave of the Internet evolution. It is an architecture to allow applications and services to talk to each other. The goal of Web Services printing is to emulate the plug-and-play experience seen when a printer is plugged into a PC via USB; the printer is seen and installed automatically. With Web Services printing, you also get better communication between the printer and the print client. You can now receive real end-of-job completion notifications from the printer instead of just being notified when the job had been sent to the spooler. The security of the print communication is assured and that's just the beginning.

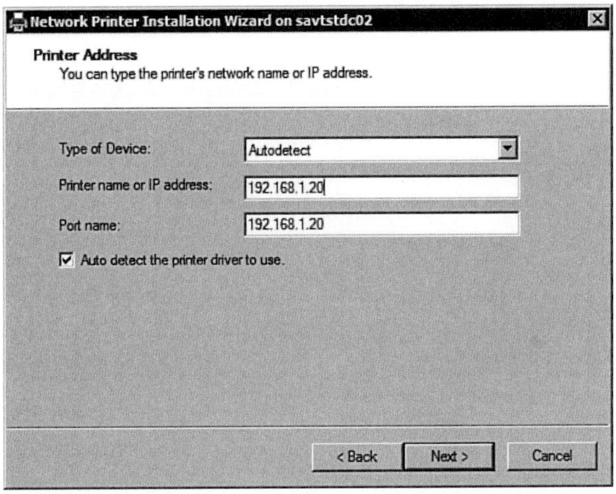

FIGURE 5-55 The port name can be set to any value, but by default it matches the IP address.

After entering the IP address of the printer, the Network Printer Installation Wizard contacts the printer to ascertain information about it, such as make and model, to calculate the drivers it should use.

If the printer has a driver that is part of the operating system, it is selected automatically. However, if it's a newer printer that is not known to the OS, you need to install a new driver or use the Microsoft XPS Document Writer or the Terminal Services Easy Print. (The Easy Printer driver is covered in Chapter 9, "Terminal Services.") The Microsoft XPS Document writer is a print-to-file driver that acts like a normal printer target but the output is a file in the XPS format. You would never want to use this driver for a real printer, but it is good for printing to an XPS file.

If you are installing a new printer driver, select the Install a New Driver option. This opens a dialog with a list of all the drivers known to the OS. You can select a driver to work with the printer or select the Have Disk button to install a new driver from media or the network. A list of all printers that are serviced by the driver file selected are displayed. Select the relevant driver.

The final dialog specifies a name for the printer. If you have a large or small environment, give the printer a meaningful name that might describe its type, location, and capabilities (such as color, dual-sided, and so on), as shown in Figure 5-56. The same dialog allows a share to be created for the printer. The share has separate location and comment fields, which allows greater detail to be given.

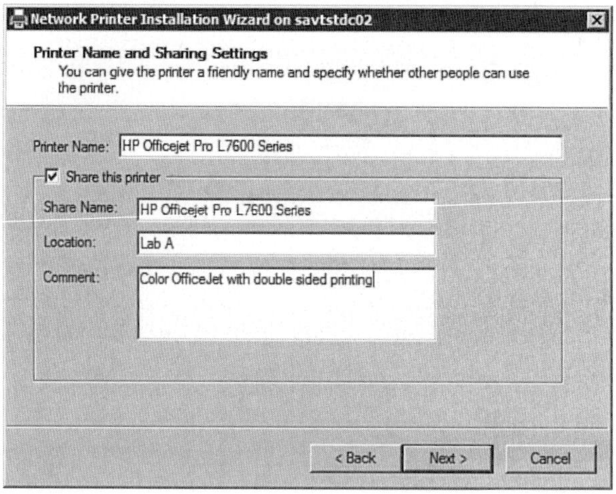

FIGURE 5-56 Creating a new printer share during the Network Printer Installation Wizard.

A confirmation screen for the settings is displayed. Click Next to install any additional drivers that are required and to complete the installation of the printer to the print server. The completion dialog displays the status of the driver and printer installation, an option to print a test page, and an option to keep the wizard running and add another printer. Select any options and click Finish.

After the printer is added to a print server, its properties can be examined. However, if you are looking at a printer on a remote print server, you might get warnings that the driver for the remote printer is not loaded on the local computer. Not all of the printer properties might be available, and you are given the option of installing the driver for the printer to remedy the situation.

The context menu of a printer gives a number of options, including opening the print queue, pausing/resuming printing on the queue (useful for planned maintenance on a device), canceling all pending jobs, printing a test page, managing sharing (which is just a shortcut to the Sharing tab of the printer properties), and viewing the properties of the printer. Depending on the printer's current list status in the AD, you can select the List in Directory or Remove from Directory option.

If you open the queue of a printer, you can see all the pending print jobs. The administrator or the person delegated for printer permissions can delete individual jobs or change the properties of a print job, such as its priority and when it can print (see Figure 5-57). Changing the priorities of a print item is useful if you need it to print ahead of other items in the queue. The other tabs available vary based on the type of target printer and the local availability of the driver for the printer. All printers have an Advanced tab with a standard interface to printing options. Figure 5-57 shows three additional tabs because this computer runs the Print Management console and has the driver for the HP printer installed, so all the enhanced properties provided by the printer driver are displayed.

If you want an easy, fast view of a printer's queue, enable the Extended View via the Printers navigation node item's context menu. This option adds a pane in the console that has two tabs. The first tab shows the jobs for the printer, and the second tab loads the Web page from the printer if it has one. This avoids the need to launch a separate process to manage some aspects of the device that might not be possible via the console or to expose information that is otherwise not available (see Figure 5-58). The printer's Web page might also be useful for troubleshooting.

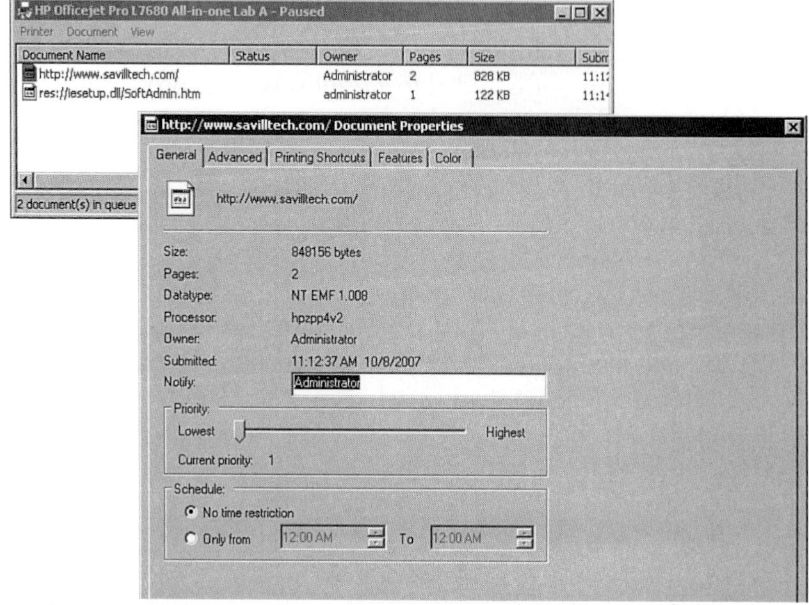

FIGURE 5-57 Granular control on a print item is possible.

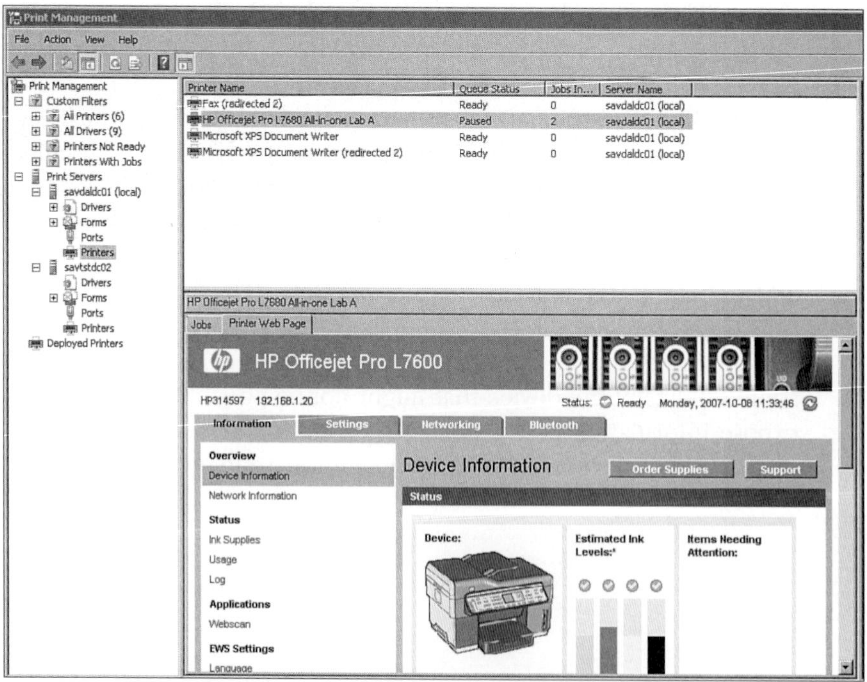

FIGURE 5-58 Most IP printers have a Web page to help manage the printer, and it is now seamlessly available via the Print Management console.

Printer Properties

Printers in Windows Server 2008 have many configuration options that help control how the printers can be used and their accessibility. The options are accessible through tabs in the Properties dialog.

General Tab

The General tab gives access to the name of the printer, location, and comment that you configured when you first added the printer. Information about the printer features is displayed, including print speed, maximum resolution, and if the printer is color capable, double-sided, and can staple documents. A list of the paper types in the printer is also shown.

A test print can be sent from the General tab. You can also set the default print job properties, such as printing quality, the paper to use, one- or two-sided, and so on.

Sharing Tab

The Sharing tab has the basic option to share the printer along with the name of the share. Two additional options are also available. The first is to render the print jobs locally on the client computers prior to sending them to the print server. This is the default option and tells the client computer to create the print ready format. The second option is to list the printer in the AD.

One of the great advantages to using a printer server is driver management. The Sharing tab gives access to adding additional drivers via the Additional Drivers button. By default, when you add a printer, only the driver for the architecture of Windows Server 2008 is loaded. For example, if it's a 32-bit server, only x86-based drivers are installed. The dialog allows additional drivers to be selected, and the options vary based on the type of printer (see Figure 5-59). If you have a 64-bit server, add the drivers for the 32-bit platform by enabling the x86 processor, so 32-bit clients can use the printer. You are prompted for the location of the additional drivers being added. In some cases, your printer drivers are available on media supplied with the printer or as a download from the manufacturer's web site, which requires extracting the driver files. If the downloaded driver file does not support extraction and requires installation, install the driver download onto a client computer. Then run the Print Management console on the client computer to import the driver to the print server.

When you load a driver for another architecture, the server operating system needs information about the other architecture, so you are also prompted for the ntprint.inf file for the architecture of the driver you are importing. This is not as easy to get as you might think because operating systems are now stored in an image file, so inserting the media for another architecture does nothing. Instead, you need to have an instance of the other architecture installed on the network somewhere. Navigate to the folder C:\Windows\System32\DriverStore\FileRepository\ntprint.inf_xxxxxxxx on the other architecture machine (the xxxxxxxx is a unique hexadecimal string for each machine) for the ntprint.inf file, and then the driver can be installed. This will hopefully be resolved in a future release.

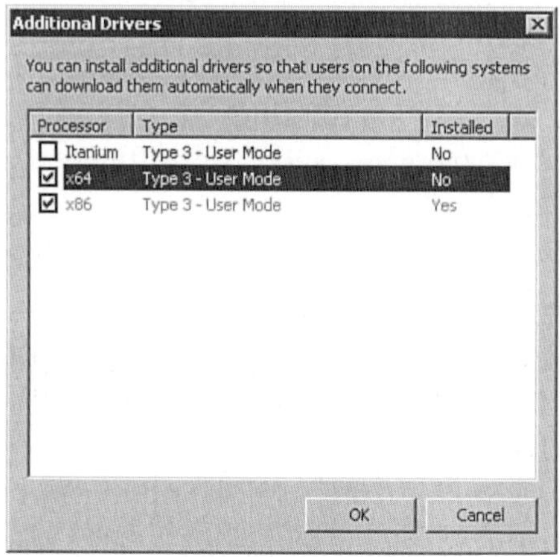

FIGURE 5-59 Enabling the driver for the 64-bit platform.

Ports Tab

The Ports tab allows ports that the printer operates over to be added, removed, and configured. For example, you could change the IP address that a printer resides on by modifying its port and switching protocols between RAW and LPR.

You also have the option to Simple Network Management Protocol (SNMP)-enable the port. This allows management and monitoring via SNMP, along with the option to specify a specific SNMP community name.

You can also enable bidirectional support, which is used for printers directly connected via parallel cables and to enable printer pooling. Printer pooling allows multiple devices to be selected for a single printer instance. This means that all the printers have to be the same type and use the same driver. It allows a single printer share to be connected to multiple printer devices, and any print jobs are distributed to all the selected ports. Printer pooling supports a mixture of local and network print devices. If you do not select Enable Printer Pooling, only one port may be selected.

Advanced Tab

The Advanced tab shown in Figure 5-60 allows configuration of the more "down and dirty" settings. By default, a printer is available at all hours, but it is possible to configure a printer to only be available during certain hours. A loud printer could be prevented from printing during the day, and any jobs would queue until printing was allowed during night hours. You could also set two print queues to one device. One print queue could be for large documents that would print at night and not interfere with normal documents printed during the day. You might have experienced the misery of trying to print an urgent one-page document and adding paper to the printer for the kind soul who prints a 50-page document and does not keep an eye on it.

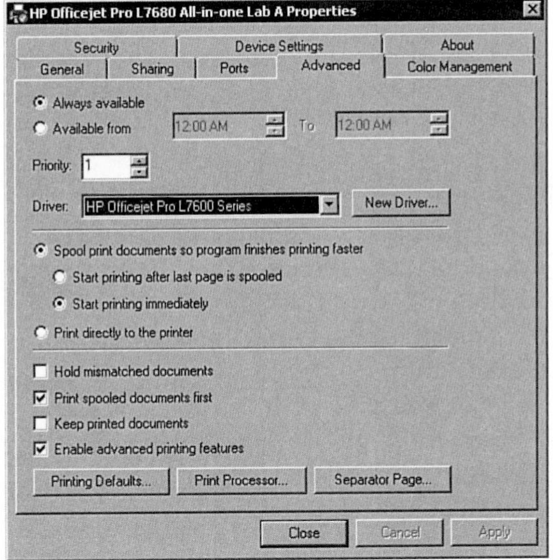

FIGURE 5-60 The Advanced tab gives you access to less used features.

The priority sets the default priority for print jobs and higher priority print jobs print before lower priority jobs. This is only useful if you create multiple print queues pointing to the same physical printer. An example use would be to give executives access to the high priority printer queue so their documents would print before everyone else's low priority jobs. For this to work, the multiple printer queues must be hosted on the same Windows print server.

You could certainly combine the availability and priority options to have two printer queues to one device, setting nighttime printing to a lower priority than the daytime print queue, just in case someone is working late.

The driver used for the device can be updated by selecting the new driver from the drop-down, or by clicking the New Driver button, which opens up the Add Printer Driver Wizard. Select the new driver from the wizard. Then it is uploaded to the print server and automatically deployed to the client users of the printer the next time they attempt to print.

Because the generation of a printable job format takes less time than the actual printing, by default, documents are spooled to the print server and then sent to the printer. The actual printing is started as soon as the document starts to spool. You have the option to not start the actual printing until the entire document is spooled to the print server, which might be useful in the event a document takes longer to render than to print or a large document is canceled from the application during the printing. (Then nothing is sent to the printer). You can also configure the printing to go directly to the printer and not spool at all. This is not commonly used because it bypasses many of the advantages of a print server.

Additionally, spooling options are available:

- **Hold mismatched documents**. This is not selected by default but if enabled, the spooler holds print jobs that don't match the setup for the printer. A good use would be for a printer that has selectable print trays or forms. With this option enabled, print jobs that are for a configuration other than the one currently selected would hold until the printer configuration matches the print job.
- **Print spooled documents first**. Enabled by default and allows jobs that have completed spooling to print before jobs in the process of spooling, no matter what the document priorities are.
- **Keep printed documents**. By default, print jobs are deleted after printing. With this option, print jobs are kept after printing.
- **Enable advanced printing features**. A print job can be sent in a raw format that is suitable for the printer or in an enhanced metafile (EMF) format. EMF saves some print job processing done by the spooler, which means the application printing prints faster but generates a larger spool file. Enabling advanced printing features turns on the EMF mode of printing. If you have problems with some types of printing, a common fix is to turn off the advanced printing features, which disables EMF and makes the application generate the output ready for the destination print device.

A button to set printing defaults for the printer might be displayed if extra drivers are installed on the computer running the Print Management snap-in plus. There is also a button to select the print processor. The Separator button allows a SEP extension file to be printed at the start of each print job. The separator file has a specific format, and example separator files are found in the system32 folder for both PCL mode and postscript mode. PCL is the Printer Control Language originally created by Hewlett-Packard as a printer language without all the bells and whistles of postscript, which was one of the first languages designed to describe page layout and content for printers.

Security Tab

The Security tab is the last core tab of a printer and allows you to control who can print to the device, who can manage the properties of the printer, and who can manage print jobs on the printer queue. As shown in Figure 5-61, server operators and print operators have permission to manage the printer and documents on the printer. These are both local groups on the computer, so an easy way to give a person permission to manage a printer and the documents is to add her to the Print Operators group. However, this gives her permission to manage any printer on the server.

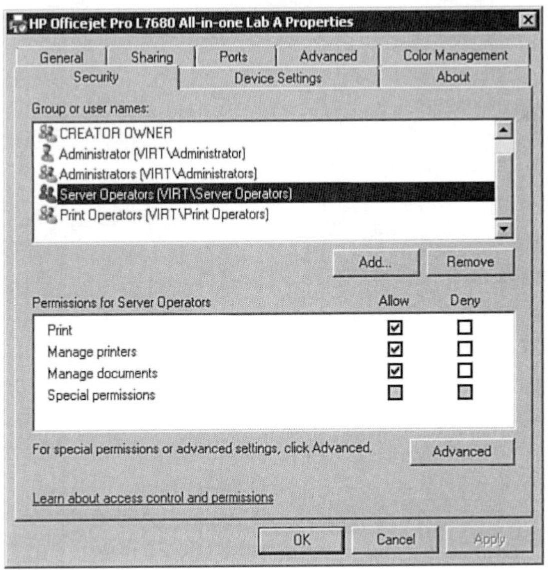

FIGURE 5-61 Server operators have permission to manage printers and documents.

At a more granular level, you can give users and groups permissions to manage printers and/or documents by adding them to the Security list and granting them allow permissions for the Manage Printers and/or Manage Documents permissions.

By default, the Everyone group has permission to print, which means everyone can print to the device. If you want to restrict who can print, you can either delete the Everyone group entry or leave the Everyone group entry and add specific users/groups to the dialog and set the Print permission to deny, which would stop only them from printing. The best option depends on your goal. If you are creating a print queue for just executives, the easiest option would be to remove the Everyone entry, add the Executive group, and grant it to allow permission for Print. If you're trying to stop Joe McTroublesome from using the printer, leave everyone intact, add Joe's user account, and set the Print permission to deny.

NOTE Don't deny the Everyone group Print permissions. A deny always take precedence over an allow, and that would stop anyone from ever printing.

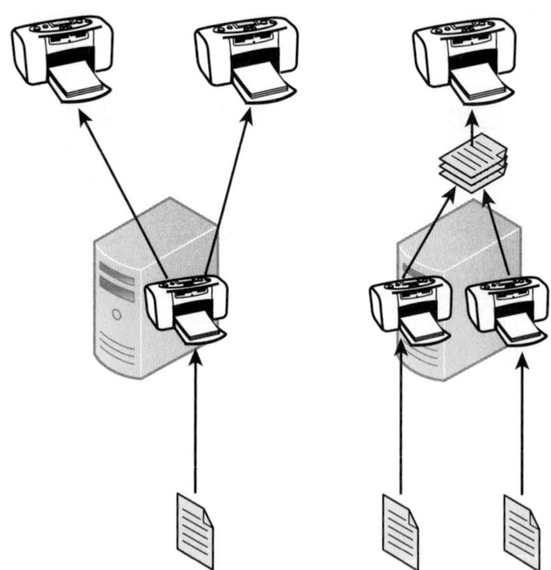

FIGURE 5-62 Print pooling shown on the left and multiple print queues for one printer on the right.

In Figure 5-62, on the left, you see printer pooling, where one print queue points to multiple printers. On the right you see multiple printer queues that point to the same printer. The right scenario allows one queue for certain users/documents to be given a different priority than the other, allowing one queue to be printed before documents from the other queue. As can be seen on the right side, documents from both queues go to a shared spool, which merges the print jobs and their prioritization to the printer.

Just as an item of interest, notice the entry for CREATOR OWNER, which has permissions to manage documents. This allows users to manage their own submissions to the print queue. They can delete their own jobs from the print queue.

If you click the Advanced button, you get access to additional areas, two of which are useful: Auditing and Effective permissions, which are common to nearly all object types. The Effective permissions allow a user or group to be specified and their permissions on the printer are displayed. This helps in troubleshooting permission problems, as shown in Figure 5-63.

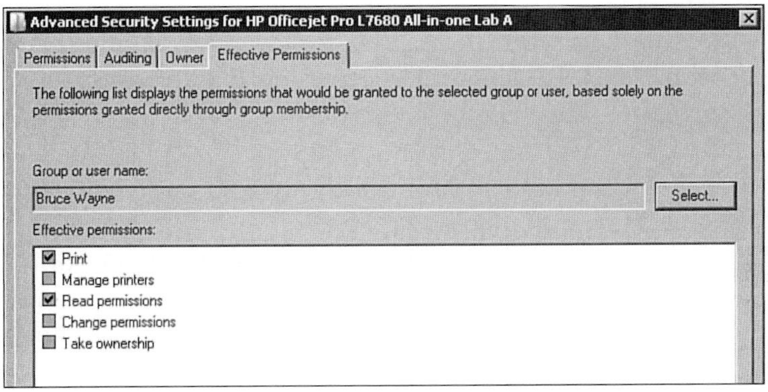

FIGURE 5-63 Bruce, in this case, can just print and view the print queue.

The Auditing tab allows auditing to be enabled on a printer for a selected user or group, which includes selecting the Everyone group if the auditing should apply to all users. After the group or user is selected, you can audit successful or failed actions based on six areas (see Figure 5-64). A successful audit log means the action was a successful attempt; a failed audit log means the attempt was not successful.

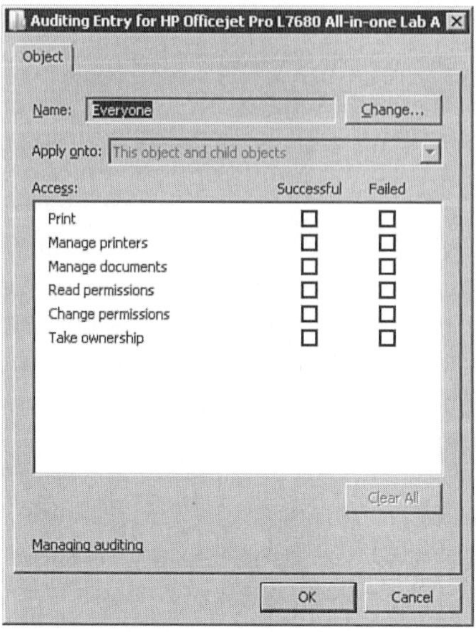

FIGURE 5-64 Success and/or failures can be audited for print actions.

Obviously, printers print often. Be careful of auditing successful printing requests as this fills up the event log. The types of audit are the following:

- **Print**. Audit the printing of documents and modifying of document printing preferences
- **Manage printers**. Audit changing of document printing defaults, printer share or property changes, and deleting a printer
- **Manage documents**. Audit the changes to a document job properties, any modification to the printing/deleting of a document, and changing document printing defaults
- **Read permissions**. Audit when the permissions of a printer are read
- **Change permissions**. Audit any change to the permissions of a printer
- **Take ownership**. Audit where a change in ownership occurs

Other Tabs

You might see other tabs that are based on the printer driver. These might offer access to other print items, such as color configuration and format options.

Listing a Printer in the Active Directory

Share printer options have not been discussed yet. You can list shared printers in the AD by selecting the List in Directory context menu option for the printer. You can also enable the printer to be listed via the Sharing tab of the printer's properties and checking the List in the Directory box.

The printer object is created by default under the server that hosts the printer. To view the directory-listed printers, use the Active Directory Users and Computers MMC snap-in. From the View menu, select Users, Contacts, Groups, and Computers as Containers. You are now able to select a server, and the printer object is shown as a child object, as shown in Figure 5-65.

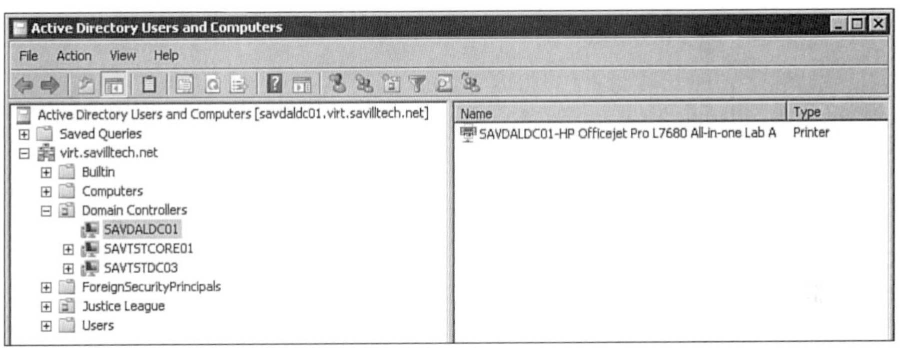

FIGURE 5-65 The printer that is listed in the Active Directory shows under the server with the Viewing Objects as Containers view turned on.

You can right-click this printer object and move it, open its print queue, and view some basic properties. You can manually create these entries in the AD by right-clicking a domain or organization unit and selecting New, Printer from the context menu. Enter the URL of the shared printer, such as \\server\printer share, and the printer object is created for you in that location.

The following script searches the AD and lists all printers that are published:

```
Const ADS_SCOPE_SUBTREE = 2

' Check all arguments required have been passed
If Wscript.Arguments.Count < 1 Then
    Wscript.Echo "Arguments <root DN> required. For example:" &
vbCrLf & "cscript searchprinters.vbs dc=savilltech,dc=com"
    Wscript.Quit(0)
End If

strRootSearch = Wscript.Arguments(0)

Set objConnection = CreateObject("ADODB.Connection")
Set objCommand = CreateObject("ADODB.Command")
objConnection.Provider = "ADsDSOObject"
objConnection.Open "Active Directory Provider"
Set objCommand.ActiveConnection = objConnection
objCommand.CommandText = "Select printerName, serverName from "
➥& " 'LDAP://" & strRootSearch & "' where objectClass=
'printQueue'"
objCommand.Properties("Page Size") = 1000
objCommand.Properties("Timeout") = 30
objCommand.Properties("Searchscope") = ADS_SCOPE_SUBTREE
objCommand.Properties("Cache Results") = False
Set objRecordSet = objCommand.Execute
objRecordSet.MoveFirst
Do Until objRecordSet.EOF
    Wscript.Echo "Printer Name: " & objRecordSet.Fields
("printerName").Value
    Wscript.Echo "Server Name: " & objRecordSet.Fields
("serverName").Value
    objRecordSet.MoveNext
Loop
```

To use the script, just execute via the `cscript` interpreter and paste the distinguished name that you want to search from. For example, if you want to search the entire virt.savilltech.net domain, the DN would be `dc=virt,dc=savilltech,dc=net`. If you just wanted to search within the Justice League organizational unit (OU), use `ou=justice league,dc=virt,dc=savilltech,dc=net`. For example:

```
C:\Tools>cscript searchprinters.vbs
➥dc=virt,dc=savilltech,dc=net
Microsoft (R) Windows Script Host Version 5.7
Copyright (C) Microsoft Corporation. All rights reserved.

Printer Name: HP Officejet Pro L7680 All-in-one Lab A
Server Name: savdaldc01.virt.savilltech.net
Printer Name: HP Photosmart C5100 series
Server Name: savdaldc01.virt.savilltech.net
```

Why publish printers in the AD? It makes it easier for administrators to find printers for management purposes, but most importantly, it helps users find them.

Connecting Users to Network Printers

All these printer options are fantastic, but right now no one is using them. What are the options for getting the clients connected?

If the user knows the server that the printer is hosted on, he can just type the server name in the Run box or browse the network, and all shared printers are listed, as shown in Figure 5-66.

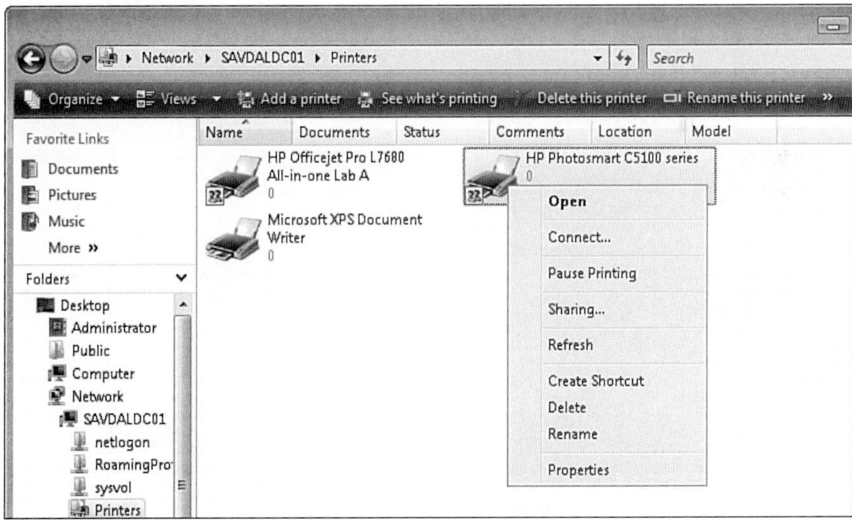

FIGURE 5-66 This is an easy way to install if you know on which server the printer is hosted.

The user can then right-click a printer and select Connect, which connects the computer to the printer. If the driver is not local to the client, he is prompted to click the Install Driver button and voilà, the printer is mapped and ready to print.

This method is great, and the user can browse through servers to find the printer he wants, but now imagine you have 1,000 servers, 20 of which are print servers. Even assuming you have a good naming scheme, that is still a lot of browsing. This is why you list printers in the directory.

For an end-user to add a printer, go to the Printers control panel applet on the client computer and select Add Printer, which launches the Add Printer Wizard. Two options are displayed in Windows Vista: adding a local printer or adding a network, wireless, or Bluetooth printer. Select the latter option for a network printer and click Next.

By default, the Add Printer Wizard searches the local subnet of the client for network printers and any shared printers that are available, which is a big improvement over the XP experience. However, if the printer desired is not there, the user can click The Printer That I Want Isn't Listed button, which takes him to a dialog that allows more detail to be entered (see Figure 5-67).

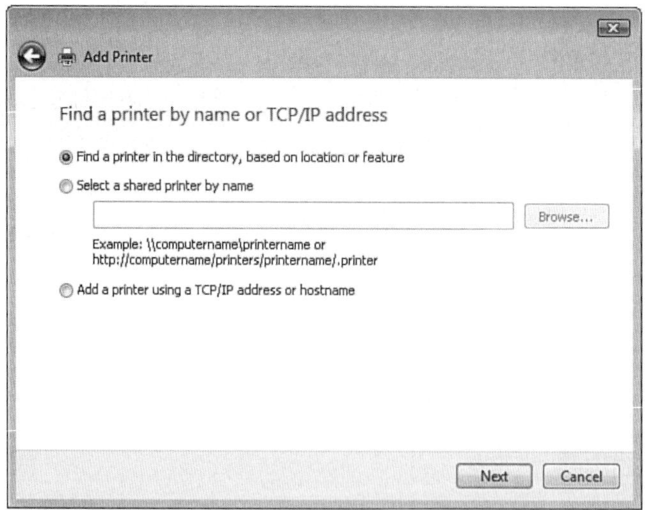

FIGURE 5-67 You have options to search the directory for a printer, manually enter the server and printer share, or add via network printer TCP/IP or hostname.

Users enter the share name of a printer in the format of `\\<server>\<share>`. To search the AD, they can select the Find a Printer in the Directory, Based on Location or Feature option and click Next.

A search dialog for the AD is displayed, as shown in Figure 5-68. Using this dialog, they enter parts of the printer name or location via the Printers tab or search for printers with specific features via the Features tab.

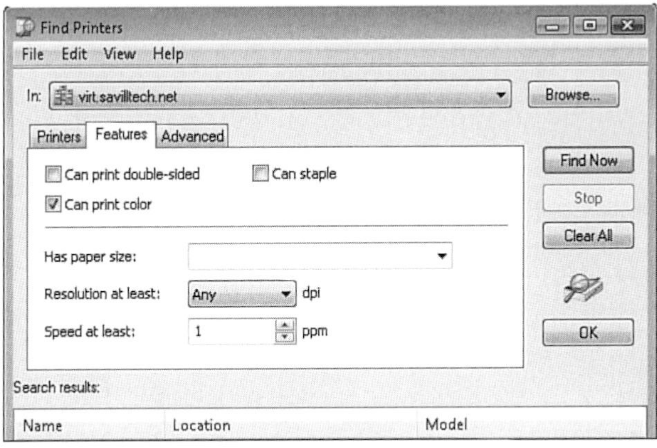

FIGURE 5-68 Searching for specific printer attributes.

After the printer is found, the printer can be connected to the client and used.

The process is similar with Windows XP clients. The user launches the Printers and Faxes interface from the Start menu and runs the Add a Printer task, which launches the Add Printer Wizard. The user is prompted for a local or network printer. Select the A Network Printer, or a Printer Attached to Another Computer option (see Figure 5-69).

The user is then prompted to find a printer in the directory and enter the name of the printer in the `\\<share name>\<printer>` format. If she is using Internet Printing, enter the URL, as shown in Figure 5-70. The rest of the process is the same as Windows Vista; the printer is selected and added automatically.

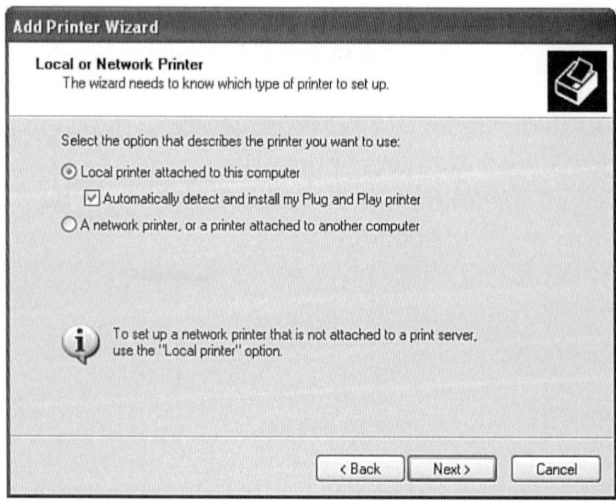

FIGURE 5-69 Selection of the XP printer. For a printer on a print server, select the second option.

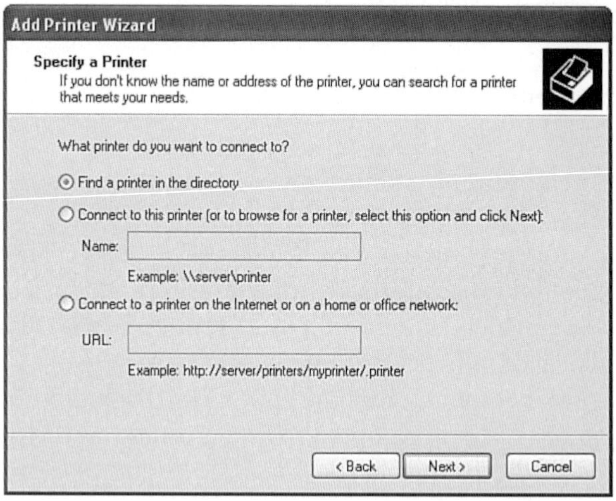

FIGURE 5-70 The three options with Windows XP are the same as with Windows Vista.

If you want to access a printer from the command line, you can map an LPT port to the network printer. For example, in the following command, you map LPT2 to a network printer:

```
C:\>net use lpt2 "\\savtstdc01\HP Officejet Pro L7680 - LabA"
The command completed successfully.
```

Notice that the printer share is in double quotes because the name has spaces. You can then copy files to LPT2: and it prints to the network printer. You can add `/persistent:yes` at the end of the command to map the printer at each logon. To delete a mapped printer, use the `net use lptn /del` command.

If you are a nonadministrator, you must map an LPT port that is not physically mapped on the hardware. For instance, LPT1 is normally mapped to the parallel port, and so a normal user does not have permission to remap a port that is assigned to a local parallel port. However, an administrator can do this. Another option is to use the `print` command without mapping, which uses this format:

```
Print /D:\\<print server>\<share> <full path and name of file
to print>
```

Hopefully, your days of command-line printing are in the past, however.

Group policy can be used to restrict to which print server users can print by enabling the Point and Print Restrictions policy, which is found under User Configuration, Administrative Templates, Control Panel, Printers Policy section. You can then select options so that users can print only to specific servers, to set actions for elevation during driver installations and for driver updating (see Figure 5-71).

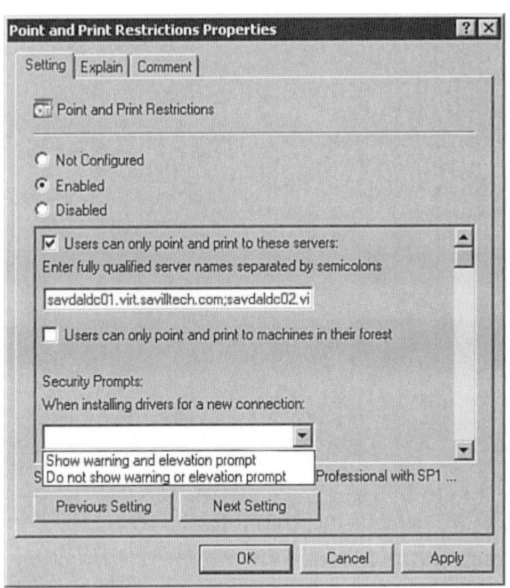

FIGURE 5-71 Some of these settings apply to XP and Vista, and some to Vista only. This is shown in the help for each setting.

After the group policy object is configured, make sure it is linked to a domain, site, or OU that matches the users that should be restricted.

Deploying Printers Using Group Policy

Deploying printers to clients was a messy process. Many times printers would be manually added by administrators, mapped as part of logon scripts, or installed by users from the AD. However, issues associated with permissions needed to install printer drivers often came up.

With Windows Server 2008 and Windows Vista clients, printers can be deployed using group policy with no other actions. A printer can be deployed in the same way desktop settings can be configured. This is the best way to deploy printers.

Because group policy can be assigned to a domain, OU, and a site, you have the option to deploy printers to a site, which allows users to get different printers deployed to them depending on their location. This is especially useful for mobile users who might visit different offices.

The Print Management console makes it easy to deploy a printer via group policy. Right-click on the printer and select Deploy with Group Policy from its context menu, which opens the Deploy with Group Policy dialog. Click the Browse button to select or create the Group Policy Object (GPO) that deploys the printer, as shown in Figure 5-72.

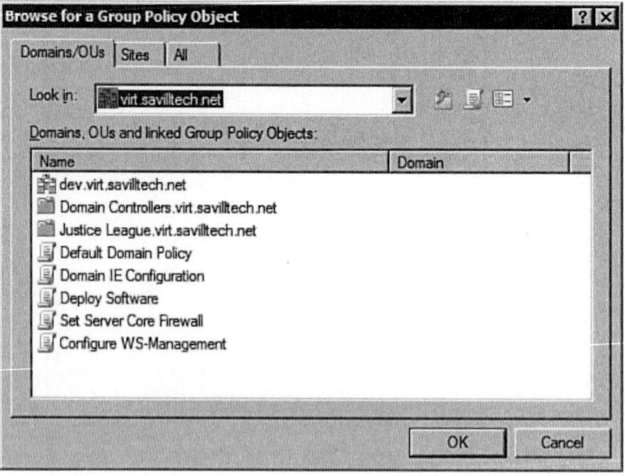

FIGURE 5-72 All the GPOs that are in the domain are selected. The New button (on the right side of the domain name) allows you to create a new GPO.

After a GPO has been selected, select if the printers are deployed to users and/or computers. If the printer is deployed to the computer, any user of the Windows XP or above computer can access the printer. A printer deployed to users can only be used by the users receiving the policy.

The last and most important step is to add the printer that you selected and want to deploy by clicking the Add button. This adds the printer to the list of deployed printers in the list with the GPO. Notice that after the printer is added, you can select additional GPOs via which you want to deploy the printer. It is added to the list, as shown in Figure 5-73. After all GPOs you want to deploy the printer via have been added, click Apply. A dialog is displayed confirming that the deployment or removal operation succeeded. Click OK.

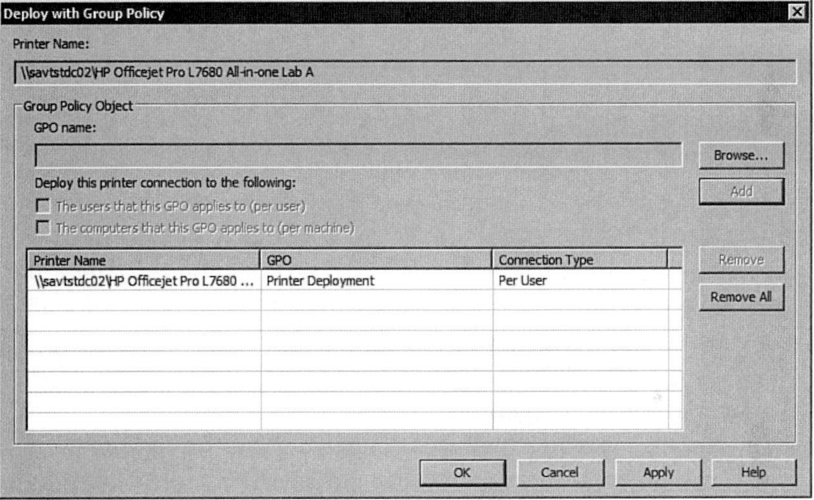

FIGURE 5-73 This dialog is printer-centric. When you click Add, you are adding GPOs that publish the specific printer.

If you created a new GPO for the printer deployment via the Deploy with Group Policy dialog, you can use the Group Policy Management Console to link the GPO to other targets, such as an OU or site. (By default, the GPO is linked at the domain level, which might not be desired.) If you edit the GPO, per-computer printers are found under the Computer Configuration, Windows Settings, Deployed Printers; per-user printers are found under User Configuration, Windows Settings, Deployed Printers.

You can also deploy printers from the Group Policy Management Console. Instead of the process being printer-centric, the process is GPO-centric, with the capability to add additional shared printers by entering the printer share name and clicking Add (see Figure 5-74).

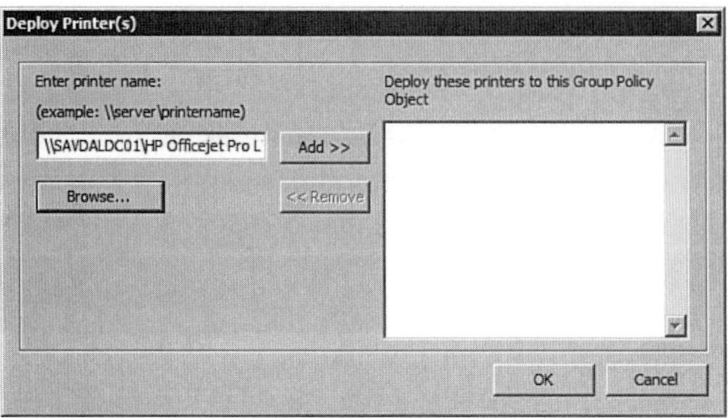

FIGURE 5-74 You can quickly add multiple printers to be deployed via a GPO using the Group Policy Management Console. Printers can be browsed for if the server and print share are not known.

The next time the group policy is refreshed on the client, the printers are automatically added and made available. Computers don't need to be logged off or restarted.

To remove a printer deployed with group policy, select Deploy with Group Policy from the printer's context menu and select the GPO from the list that the printer should no longer deploy through. Click Remove or Remove All to stop the printer from being deployed via any group policies. After the client refreshes the policy, the printer is removed. Once again, no logoff or shutdown is required.

Notice your pre–Windows Vista clients ignore these printer deployments. The Deployed Printer Connections group policy client-side extension does not present pre–Windows Vista, and so the Client Side Extensions (CSEs) have no knowledge of deployed printers and cannot process them. Fortunately, the PushPrinterConnections.exe utility can be used on pre–Windows Vista operating systems to process the deployed printers via group policy. The behavior differs for printers deployed via PushPrinterConnections.exe. Per-user printers are added at logon time and per-computer printers are added at computer startup. To enable the

PushPrinterConnections for computers to process group policy defined printers, perform the following:

1. Open the GPO that was used for the printer deployment in the Group Policy Object editor.
2. If the printer is deployed to users, navigate to User Configuration, Windows Settings, Scripts (Logon/Logoff). If printers were deployed to computers, navigate to Computer Configuration, Windows Settings, Scripts (Startup/Shutdown).
3. Right-click Startup or Logon, and then click Properties.
4. In the Logon Properties or Startup Properties dialog, click Show Files. The location is shown in the Address field.
5. Copy the PushPrinterConnections.exe file from the c:\windows\system32 folder to this location by copy and pasting. Close the window.
6. In the Logon Properties or Startup Properties dialog, click Add.
7. Type **`PushPrinterConnections.exe`** in the Script Name box. If you want to enable logging, type **`-log`** in the Script Parameters box. Log files are written to %windir%\Temp\PpcMachine.log for per-computer connections and to %temp%\PpcUser.log for per-user connections on the computer on which the policy is applied.
8. Click OK.

Allowing Nonadministrators/Power Users to Install Printers

To add a local printer to a computer in pre–Windows Vista world, the user had to be a member of the local Administrators group or be a member of the Power Users group and have the user right to load/unload device drivers. Loading drivers is the issue. Unless the driver is part of the OS, the normal user does not have permission to install the drivers needed. This is one reason normal users were made members of the local Administrators group.

With Windows Vista, the user no longer needs to be a local administrator. In Vista, a normal user can add a printer if the driver is in-box (part of the operating system) and the user is physically at the Vista machine. The in-box drivers are those contained in the trusted driver store that is part of the new Vista functionality. Any driver in the driver store is trusted and therefore available to a user.

The best practice is for administrators to add the drivers used by printers within the environment to the driver store of the desktop machines using the pnputil.exe driver store utility. Thus, all the drivers needed for the environment are available. If it's not possible to keep the driver store maintained to always include all needed drivers, users can be delegated permission to install printer drivers via group policy settings.

This policy allows digitally signed and trusted drivers to be installed by a standard user. Drivers should be digitally signed by Microsoft, a commercially acquired certificate, or an internally trusted certificate. The GUID of the device class that is being given permission to be added by a user is selected by the policy. A full list of the device classes can be found at http://msdn2.microsoft.com/en-us/library/ms791130.aspx and http://msdn2.microsoft.com/en-us/library/ms791134.aspx. Here are some common ones:

- **Printers**. {4d36e979-e325-11ce-bfc1-08002be10318}
- **Network clients**. {4d36e973-e325-11ce-bfc1-08002be10318}
- **SCSI/I394 printers**. {4658ee7e-f050-11d1-b6bd-00c04fa372a7}

To allow users to install drivers, enable the policy setting found in Computer Configuration, Administrative Templates, System. In the driver installation part of a GPO, enable the Allow Non-administrators to Install Drivers for These Device Setup Classes policy. After it is enabled, click the Show button, which sets the GUIDs that relate to device classes, as shown in Figure 5-75. Only normal printer drivers that can be installed by users who receive the policy are enabled in Figure 5-75. Only administrators can install nonsigned drivers, so it's important that devices come with signed drivers.

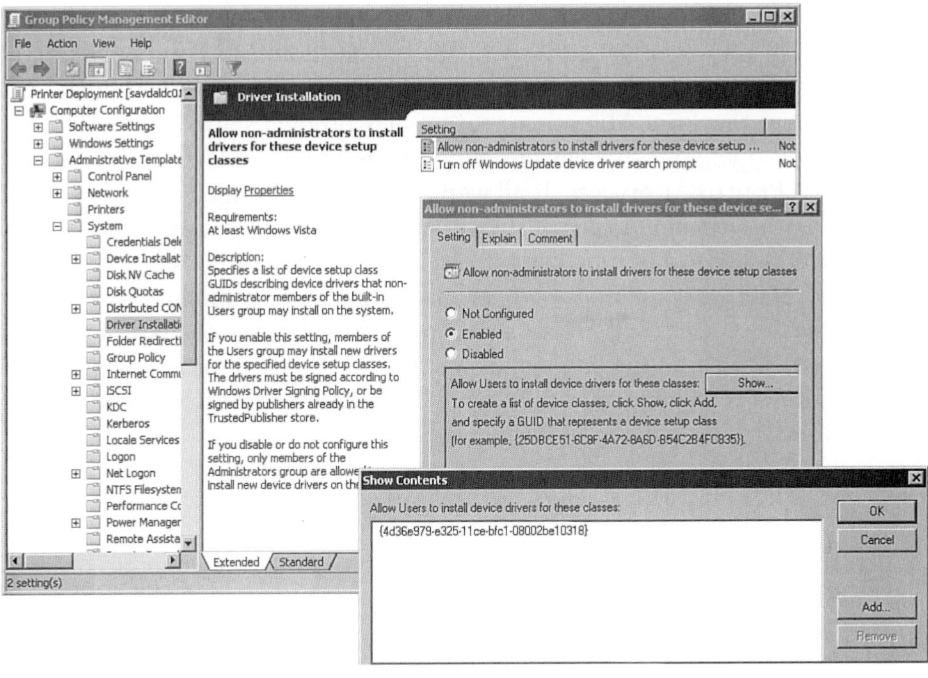

FIGURE 5-75 Allows users who receive this policy to install printer device class drivers.

Migrating a Printer

The Print Management console is not just for managing printers on multiple print servers. It's also useful for moving printers between print servers. Printers can be migrated between all the types of print server supported by the Print Management console: Windows 2000, XP, 2003,Vista, and 2008.

Moving a printer between print servers used to be accomplished via the downloaded Print Migrator tool. It allowed printer details to be exported to a cabinet file that contained all details, shares, and drivers for the printer, and then it was imported onto the target print server. This process is essentially the same but instead of needing to download and use a separate tool, the functionality is part of the Print Management console.

To start the migration process, right-click the print server from which you want to migrate a printer and select Export Printers to a File from the context menu. The Print Migration Wizard launches with all printers selected. A summary of the actions to be performed is displayed and clicking Next requests a location and file to where the export is saved.

The dialog shows the progress of the export. Upon completion, the status of the export is displayed with information about any errors encountered. If any errors are listed, click the Open Event Viewer button. This is where the Print Migration process logs problems and details. The Event log is opened with a custom filter enabled to list only events generated by the PrintBRM process. If all went well with the migration, you should see four information logs that show that the printer object, the printer queues, the printer driver, and the printer forms were all exported.

The export can also be performed from the command line. However, the command used, `printbrm`, is not in a folder that is part of the default search path, so the command can only be executed by first passing the full path of the command or changing the current folder to that containing the executable, as in the following code:

```
E:\PrintDrives\Exports>cd /d %windir%\system32\spool\tools
```

The `/d` is added to the change directory (`cd`) command to change the drive just in case you are not currently on the boot volume. You then run `printbrm` by passing the source server, the backup switch (`-b`), and the file to save the configuration of the print server to.

```
C:\Windows\System32\spool\tools>printbrm -s \\savtstdc02 -b -f
E:\PrintDrives\Exports\savtstdc02exportcmd.printerExport
Operation mode: backup
Target server: \\savtstdc02
Target file path:
E:\PrintDrives\Exports\savtstdc02exportcmd.printerExport.
Queue publish mode: none
Overwrite Mode: keep existing settings

LISTING PRINT QUEUES
HP Officejet Pro L7680 All-in-one Lab A
LISTING PRINTER DRIVERS
HP Officejet Pro L7600 Series, Windows NT x86, PCL hpz3l4v6
LISTING PRINT PROCESSORS
hpzpp4v2 Windows NT x86 hpzpp4v2.dll
LISTING PRINTER PORTS
192.168.1.20, TCP

Saving Print Queues…
Saved print queue HP Officejet Pro L7680 All-in-one Lab A
Saving Print Processors…
Saved print processor hpzpp4v2, Windows NT x86, hpzpp4v2.dll
Saving Printer Drivers…
```

```
Saved printer driver HP Officejet Pro L7600 Series, Windows NT
x86, 3
Saving Printer Ports…
Saved printer port 192.168.1.20, TCP
************ 100% ************
```

This is exactly the same output as the graphical interface. The Print Management console just acts as a graphical overlay to the `printbrm` functionality. Notice that both methods export only the printers that have been added to the print server and not the built-in XPS-based printer.

After the export file is created, it can be imported onto the target print server. This can be run remotely. You have more options when importing than exporting. To initiate the import process, select Import Printers from a File from the context menu of the target print server. You are prompted to select the export file. Click Next to continue the import process. A summary of the file content is displayed, listing the print queues, drivers, ports, and processors that will be imported into the target print server.

As shown in Figure 5-76, you have some additional options when importing the printers. By default, if a printer being imported already exists on the target server, the printer is not imported, and the existing printer is kept. You can select to overwrite existing printers to replace any duplicate printers on the target server.

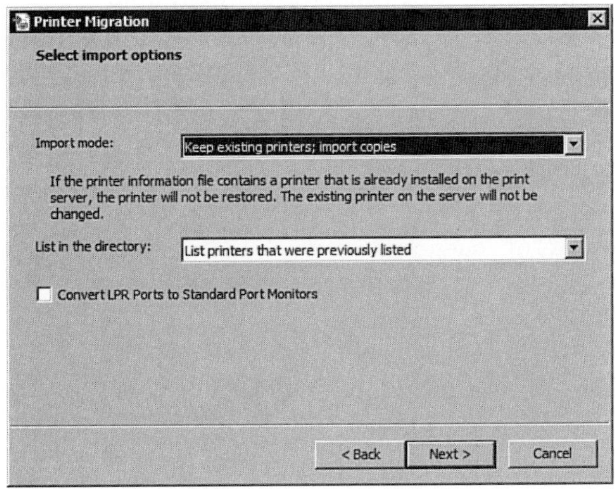

FIGURE 5-76 The import screen of the Printer Migration import wizard gives you options for the printers being imported.

You also have options around listing printers in the AD (covered earlier), including options to list the printer in the directory if it was listed in the directory on the source print server, to list all the printers, or to not list any of the printers.

An option to convert LPR ports to standard port monitors is available. If you are importing LPR printers, this option is advantageous. Standard port monitors give a better performance than LPRs.

As with the export, the final dialog displays the completion status with a summary of any errors encountered. A link to open the event viewer with a filter to just the `printbrm`-generated event logs is available.

To import from the command line, use the `printbrm` command. Instead of the `-b` switch, use the `-r` switch. The rest of the syntax is the same. However, you do have additional switches that can be used to match the options available in the graphical interface import options. You can configure duplicate printer handling, list the printer in the AD, and convert LPR ports to standard ports. The options are as follows:

- **`-o force`**. This option replaces any existing objects. If the printer already exists on the target server, it is overwritten.
- **`-p add|orig`**. This option controls the publishing of the printers to the AD. Using the `add` option adds any imported printer to the AD-published printers. The `orig` switch publishes only in the AD if the source print server had the printer published in the AD.
- **`-lpr2tcp`**. This option converts the LPR ports to standard TCP/IP printer ports.

If you don't overwrite duplicate printers and there is a clash on execution from the command line, the following text is displayed:

```
Skipped print queue HP Officejet Pro L7680 All-in-one Lab A
because a queue with the same name (or same share name)
already exists
```

Here is an example import of the export file you created earlier. Notice the `-o force` parameter, which sets the overwrite mode to force new settings.

```
C:\Windows\System32\spool\tools>printbrm -s \\savtstdc01 -r -o
➥force -f
➥E:\PrintDrives\Exports\savtstdc02exportcmd.printerExport
Operation mode: restore
```

```
Target server: \\savtstdc01
Target file path:
E:\PrintDrives\Exports\savtstdc02exportcmd.printerExport.
Queue publish mode: none
Overwrite Mode: force new settings

LISTING PRINT QUEUES
HP Officejet Pro L7680 All-in-one Lab A
LISTING PRINTER DRIVERS
HP Officejet Pro L7600 Series, Windows NT x86, None
LISTING PRINTER PORTS
192.168.1.20, TCP
LISTING PRINT PROCESSORS
hpzpp4v2 Windows NT x86 hpzpp4v2.dll

Restoring Printer Drivers...
Restored printer driver HP Officejet Pro L7600 Series, Windows
NT x86, 3
Restoring Printer Ports...
Restored printer port 192.168.1.20, TCP
Restoring Print Processors...
Restored print processor Windows NT x86, hpzpp4v2.dll,
hpzpp4v2
Restoring Print Queues...
Restored print queue HP Officejet Pro L7680 All-in-one Lab A
************ 100% ************

Successfully finished operation.
```


One final use of the `printbrm` command is to query the printer information of a server and an export file. This is useful if you have a printerExport file but are unsure of its content. The content is displayed with the `-q` switch. If you want to see information about a server instead of a printer export file, use the `-s` switch with the server name instead of the `-f` filename switch.

```
C:\Windows\System32\spool\tools>printbrm -q -f
➥E:\PrintDrives\Exports\savtstdc02exportcmd.printerExport
Operation mode: query
Target server: local machine
Target file path:
E:\PrintDrives\Exports\savtstdc02exportcmd.printerExport.
Queue publish mode: none
```

```
Overwrite Mode: keep existing settings

LISTING PRINT QUEUES
HP Officejet Pro L7680 All-in-one Lab A
LISTING PRINTER DRIVERS
HP Officejet Pro L7600 Series, Windows NT x86, None
LISTING PRINTER PORTS
192.168.1.20, TCP
LISTING PRINT PROCESSORS
hpzpp4v2 Windows NT x86 hpzpp4v2.dll

Displaying print hierarchy.
HP Officejet Pro L7680 All-in-one Lab A
        HP Officejet Pro L7600 Series (Windows NT x86) #1
        192.168.1.20 #1
Unassociated:
```

Notice in this process that the printer is not removed from the source print server. This is to aid a smooth migration because you still need to move clients from pointing to the old print server to the new print server. If you just removed the print queue from the old server before the clients were moved, you would have an unhappy client base. After all the users are migrated to the new printer server, remove the printers from the old print server.

In terms of updating the clients to use the new print server, ideally you are using group policy to deploy the printers to the user base and so the process is fairly simple. Deploy the printer on the new print server to the same group used on the old print server. Delete the deployment of the printer via the old print server. Clients then get the new printer at the same time the old one is removed in a seamless fashion.

If group policy is not an option, use a script that swaps a printer for another via a logon script. Here is a basic script that replaces one printer mapping for another:

```
Option Explicit
Dim objWMIService, objPrinter, colItems, strComputer
Dom objWshShell, strDefaultState

strComputer =″.″

Set objWshShell = WScript.CreateObject(″WScript.Shell″)

Set objWMIService = GetObject(″winmgmts:\\″ & strComputer & _
```

```
   "\root\CIMV2")

Set colItems = objWMIService.ExecQuery _
       ("SELECT * FROM Win32_Printer")

' On Error Resume Next
For Each objPrinter In colItems
If UCase(objPrinter.DeviceID) =
UCase("\\savdalprinterOld\printer1") Then
   Wscript.Echo "Found match " & objPrinter.DeviceID & _
       ", replacing"
   ' Add new printer. Need the ,1,true to wait
   'for shell to complete before continue
   objWshShell.Run "rundll32 printui.dll,PrintUIEntry /in /Gw
➥/q /n \\savdaldc01\printerNew",1, true

➥    ' Remove the old
➥    objWshShell.Run "rundll32 printui.dll,PrintUIEntry /dn /q
➥/n \\savdalprinterOld\printer1",1, true

   If objPrinter.Default Then ' if it's the default set as
➥default
     objWshShell.Run "rundll32 printui.dll,PrintUIEntry /y /n
➥\\savdaldc01\printerNew",1, true
   End If

End If
Next

WScript.Quit
```

If you use this, you'll need to replace the old and new printer in three places in the script. Reading from the script gives you ideas on how to manage printers via scripting interfaces. For example, you enumerate all the printers on the local computers by querying WMI and selecting all entries from the Win32_Printer class.

To remove and add printers, use the printui dynamic link library (dll). You also use it to set it as the default printer (if the printer you are replacing was the default).

Automatic Network Print Addition

Earlier, you added a printer by adding the printer's IP address to the print server. The driver for the printer is discovered automatically by the server, but you still had to enter the IP address of the print server. In a corporate location, that is fine. When a new network printer is added to the network, the administrator configures the printer with a static IP address and network information. In a branch office, however, a printer might be placed on the network with a DHCP address and the administrator has no clue how to get to the printer. In addition, talking a local user through the process is complex.

Thankfully, the Print Management console has the option to scan the network of the print server for any printers and automatically configure them on the print server. The scan is performed from the computer that the Print Management console is executing on, so only the local subnet of the computer running the Print Management console is scanned. If the scan is for a remote location, you need to remotely connect to the print server at the remote location and run the scan from the Print Management console on that remote computer.

Select Add Printer from the context menu of the print server. The Add Printer Wizard launches. Select the Search the Network for Printers option and click Next. Figure 5-77 shows a summary of all the printers found on the network.

Select the printer that you want to install and click Next. At this point, the printer installation is the same as for a normal printer installation with driver prompt, sharing options, and so on.

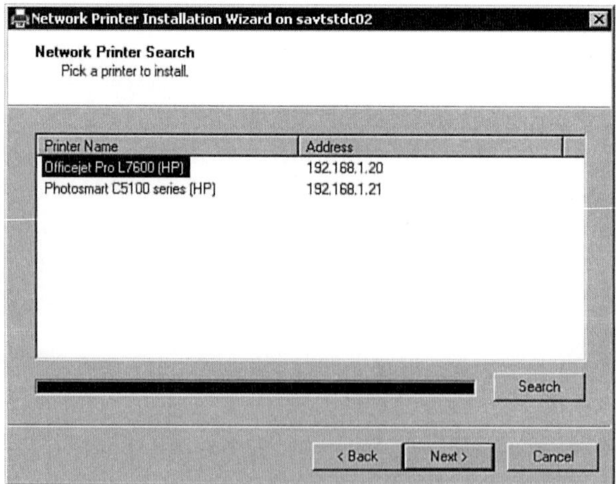

FIGURE 5-77 Results of a network search.

Print Server Configuration

The Print Management console gives easy access to the overall view of a print server. Instead of having to manage elements that relate to each printer installed on a server, you can manage the entire print server's elements in terms of drivers, forms, ports, and printers.

Let's look at the three areas of the Print Management console: driver management, forms management, and ports.

Driver Management

The Drive tab of the Print Management console for a print server shows all the drivers that are loaded and being used on the print server. From this single area, it is possible to quickly add a new printer driver or remove printer drivers. This tab has the same content as that displayed in the Drivers tab of the print server properties.

Forms Management

The Forms tab shows all the forms that are print target sizes for both the built-in and loaded drivers. From this area, forms can be deleted or new forms added of any custom size. This tab has the same content as that displayed in the Forms tab of the print server properties.

Ports

The Ports tab gives access to creating new ports on the print server or modifying existing ports. This tab has the same content as that displayed in the Ports tab of the print server properties or the printer properties.

Advanced Features

One final area of customization is available by right-clicking on the print server and selecting Properties. The Advanced tab gives you access to some additional configuration, as shown in Figure 5-78.

The spooler folder is where the print jobs are spooled prior to printing, and it can be moved if you expect large amounts of spool information. You can also change what logging is performed for the print server in terms of errors, warnings, and information events. By default, only errors and warning events are written to the Application log and the source is SpoolerSpools.

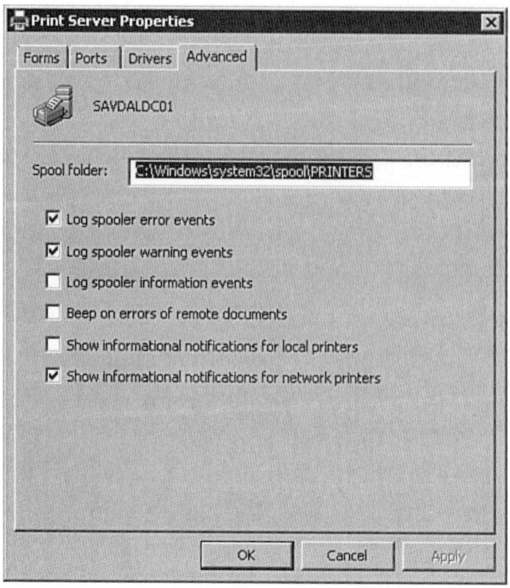

FIGURE 5-78 Extra configuration of print server options.

Customizing Views of Information

The Custom Filters node of the Print Management console gives you a great way to quickly see the status of the entire print environment. By default, four filters are provided, which list all print drivers, all printers, all printers not in a ready state, and all printers with jobs. If you have 20 print servers added to the Print Management console and you want to look for any printers not in a ready state, select the Printers Not Ready custom view. Any nonready printer is listed, with its state, number of jobs, and server, as shown in Figure 5-79.

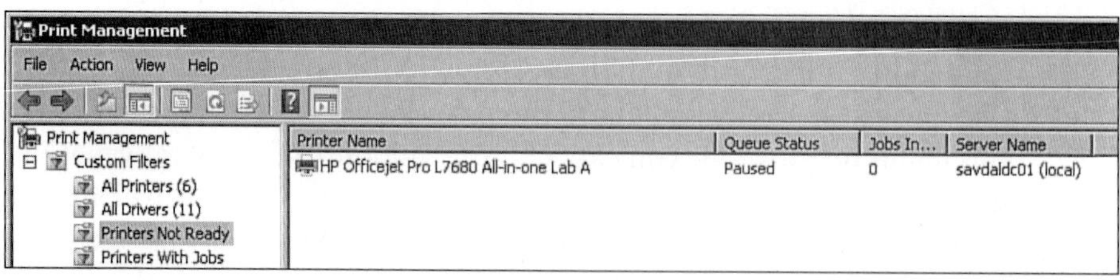

FIGURE 5-79 If you are managing a large number of printers, the custom filters prove invaluable in giving fast insight into the overall printing environment state.

If you want to view additional information for the filter, select Add/Remove Columns from the View menu, and additional columns can be added, such as the driver name, whether the printer is shared, and its share name, location, and comments.

Additional filters can be added by right-clicking on Custom Filters and selecting Add New Printer Filter, which opens up the New Printer Filter Wizard. The first screen asks for a name for the filter and a comment. Notice that you also have the option to show the number of items that match the filter (see Figure 5-80).

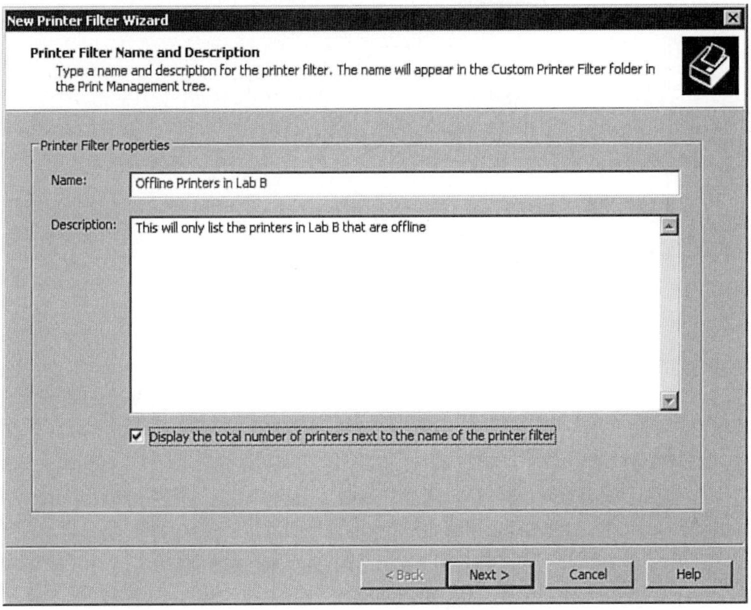

New Printer Filter Wizard

Printer Filter Name and Description
Type a name and description for the printer filter. The name will appear in the Custom Printer Filter folder in the Print Management tree.

Printer Filter Properties

Name: Offline Printers in Lab B

Description: This will only list the printers in Lab B that are offline

☑ Display the total number of printers next to the name of the printer filter

< Back | Next > | Cancel | Help

Figure 5-80 The name and description of the new filter.

The next screen is the real power of the print filter, and it allows up to six fields to be tested for possible values, as shown in Figure 5-81. The conditions vary depending on the field. As with the condition, if the field is a defined type, the values possible are constrained. In Figure 5-81, you check the Queue Status field for exactly being offline and the Location field for containing B (for your Lab B). After the conditions are selected, click Next.

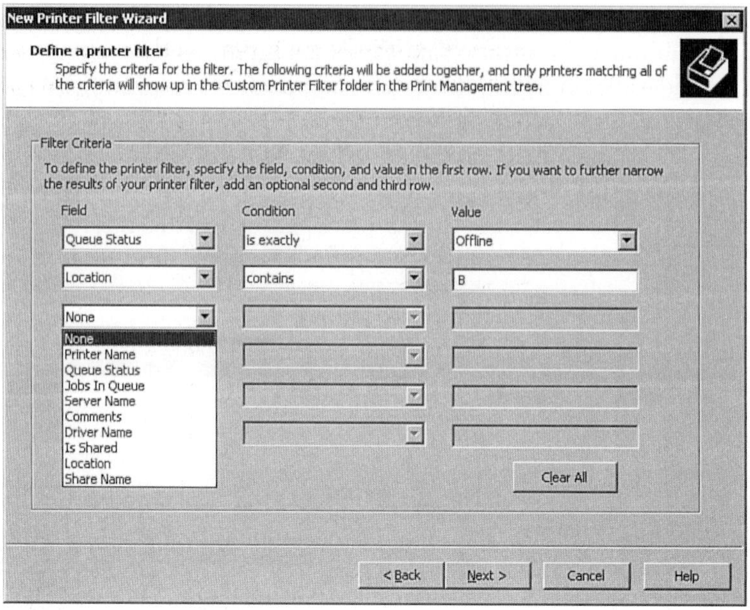

FIGURE 5-81 A range of possible attributes to examine.

The final screen allows a notification to be configured. When a printer meets the criteria in the filter, you can send an e-mail with a certain message and/or run a script. This is optional but is useful if you created a filter for errors and so forth. In the event that a printer goes into an error condition, you could be mailed an alert of the error status. Enter the e-mail address that receives the e-mail and an address from which the alert appears to come (see Figure 5-82).

Click Finish after configuring the notification options or just leave them unselected. The custom filter now lists a new entry that you've created with any offline printers in Lab B. You can always change a filter by right-clicking it and selecting Properties.

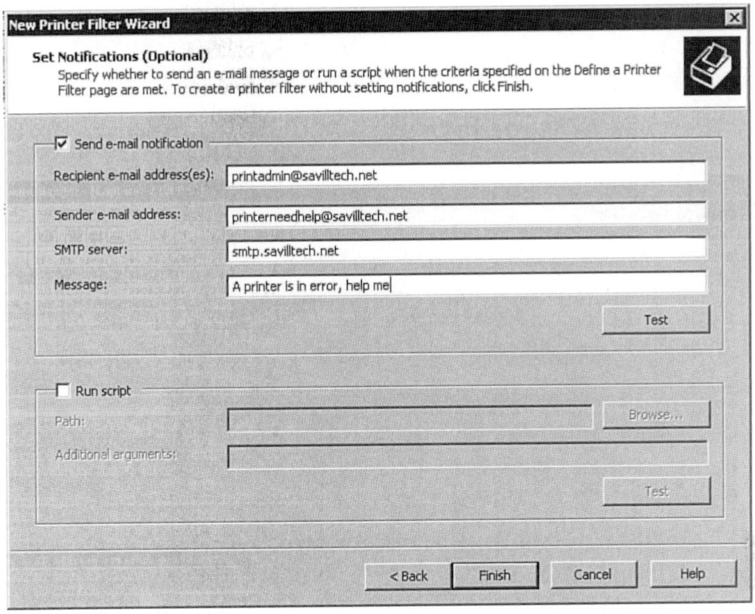

Figure 5-82 When a printer meets the filter criteria, the print administrator gets an e-mail.

Notifications

Notifications are possible when a printer meets the criteria configured in a filter. You can also add a notification for a print server. If you right-click a print server, select Set Notifications from the context menu. This allows an e-mail notification or script to be executed in the event of a print server failure with the same options as a filter notification. If a print server goes offline, restart the print spooler from a script (`net stop spooler`, then `net start spooler`).

Internet Printing

The final piece in this printing puzzle is Web-based printing. This allows users to view and install printers via an Internet Information Services–hosted Web page. The good news is that it's done automatically if you selected the Internet Printing sub-role of Print Services, which takes care of Internet Information Services installation and configuration. Go to http://<*print server*>/printers to see a Web page like that shown in Figure 5-83, listing the printers on the server.

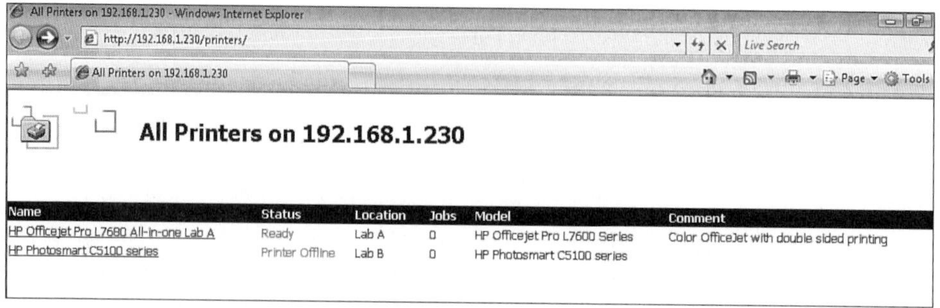

FIGURE 5-83 Web-based printing access.

A user can click a printer to see the queue of the printer and depending on the user permissions, he has options to pause, resume, and cancel documents. The Connect option is displayed as shown in Figure 5-84.

When you connect to a printer, the connection first tries via remote procedure call as normal. If this connection is not possible, the Internet Printing Protocol (IPP) is used. Communication for printing is via IPP encapsulated in HTTP packets over standard port 80, which is open in most environments. This is all done automatically.

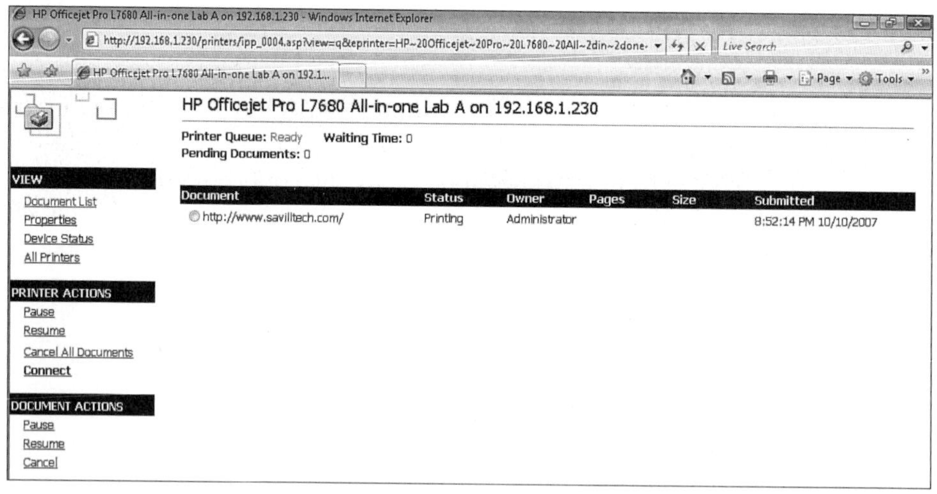

FIGURE 5-84 View of a printer from the Web interface. You get a feed of the print jobs and options for printer and job management.

Summary

This chapter contained a lot of information and for good reason. If you look at what your job involves, you'll see that a large part is reading and writing data that you need to ensure is available and secure. In nearly all environments, you use NTFS, which you examined how to manage and maintain. The file system resource management capabilities allow you to set limits on how much disk space can be used and what it's used for. This is a great and welcome feature for any file system administrator.

Printing is powerful in Windows Server 2008, and the new role-based structure makes some elements such as Internet printing automatic. The Print Management console is heavily used in any organization with more than one print server and especially those in distributed environments. With these new file server and printing features, Windows Server 2008 is a viable choice for your organization.

CHAPTER 6

TCP/IP

Windows Server 2008 has many great features, but if it could only be used sitting locally at the server console, it would probably not sell anywhere near the number of units Microsoft estimated. Even the name, a Network Operating System (NOS), stresses the importance of connectivity to the enterprise. The Internet revolution has made providing services beyond your organization a key component to most organization's futures.

In this chapter, you look at the services the operating system provides across the entire organization and beyond to enable networking communication. This chapter focuses on the core communication capabilities, which are centered on the Internet Protocol (IP) and its configuration, management, and troubleshooting.

By understanding how to troubleshoot IP, you are well suited to troubleshoot any service that uses IP and to build on your knowledge with more advanced services that are discussed in Chapter 7, "Advanced Networking Services."

The year is 2008. For previous operating systems, I would have gone over the legacy communication protocols—NetBEUI for example, the original core protocol used by Windows for Workgroups and Windows NT before TCP/IP became dominant. However, in this day and age, you use Transmission Control Protocol/Internet Protocol (TCP/IP), and I'm not going to waste time on a pure history lesson.

So what is TCP/IP? It's two separate parts. Let's look at IP first.

Internet Protocol (IP)

IP was originally used on a private network called Advanced Research Protocol Agency Network (ARPANET), which initially joined a number of institutions via the first shared packet-switching network. Other networks wanted to join, but they all used different protocols. A common protocol was required to hide the specifics of each network and thus sprang forth the IP. IP was used on the networks connected to ARPANET, which later became known as the Internet. Each host connected to the Internet had its own IP address that was statically allocated and configured.

This chapter concentrates on version 4 of IP (IPv4) because it is the primary version used on the Internet today. However, IPv6 is also discussed as one of the new features of Windows Vista and Windows Server 2008.

A computer can have various format names. A NetBIOS name (16 characters or less, for example, johns-pc) is the only item that still affects us from the NetBEUI days. It is being phased out with each new Windows release, in favor of the domain name system (DNS) (or host) name. The DNS is part of a hierarchal namespace with the left part being the name of the host (for example, johns-pc.savilltech.net). The hostname is the primary name used for computers in today's networks. Neither of these names are usable by computers to talk to each other, and later in this chapter, you see how those names are used. They have to be translated to an IPv4 address, which is a 32-bit address used to transmit data. It's normally written in dotted-quad format, meaning it is represented as four one-byte chunks (a byte being eight bits) or octets. When converted to decimal, you get the familiar xxx.xxx.xxx.xxx format, where the byte values range from 0 to 255. (For example, 192.168.1.1 is a valid IP address.)

OSI MODEL If you are going to be picky, I said IP is used for the computers to communicate. In fact, it's not. For the old timers among us, the Open Systems Interconnection Basic Reference Model (OSI model) still haunts our dreams. The various layers and where they sit are shown in Figure 6-1. IP sits three layers up from the bottom in the network layer.

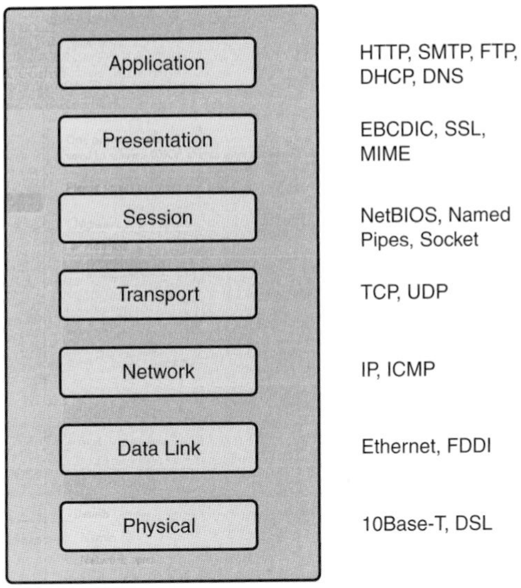

FIGURE 6-1 The seven layers of the OSI model and examples of the technologies that fall into each layer.

Data Link Layer and the MAC Address

The Data Link layer (the second layer of the OSI model) facilitates transferring data between communications. Many organizations use Ethernet, so let's look at how it works. Ethernet gives each device on the network—such as a network card—a Media Access Control (MAC) address. This address is 48 bits in length and is normally written in hexadecimal (base 16, which means it ranges from 0 to F for each digit) with six one-byte sets. Each hexadecimal character is four bits, so they're two characters per byte. To look at your MAC address, run the `ipconfig` command with the `/all` parameter. Each network device's physical address is listed, as shown here:

```
C:\Users\john>ipconfig /all

Windows IP Configuration

   Host Name . . . . . . . . . . . . : savdalm65
   Primary Dns Suffix  . . . . . . . : savilltech.net
   Node Type . . . . . . . . . . . . : Hybrid
```

```
   IP Routing Enabled. . . . . . . . : No
   WINS Proxy Enabled. . . . . . . . : No
   DNS Suffix Search List. . . . . . : savilltech.net

Wireless LAN adapter Wireless Network Connection:

   Connection-specific DNS Suffix  . : savilltech.net
   Description . . . . . . . . . . . : Intel(R) PRO/Wireless
3945ABG Network Connection
   Physical Address. . . . . . . . . : 00-19-D2-92-5C-DA
   DHCP Enabled. . . . . . . . . . . : Yes
..
..
   NetBIOS over Tcpip. . . . . . . . : Enabled

Ethernet adapter Local Area Connection:

   Connection-specific DNS Suffix  . : geniant.net
   Description . . . . . . . . . . . : Broadcom NetXtreme 57xx
Gigabit Controller
   Physical Address. . . . . . . . . : 00-19-B9-5D-42-9E
..
```

Notice that each adapter has its own MAC address. It is not created or set by the operating system, and it is hard-coded onto the actual network adapter.

Computers communicate through the MAC address, and when data packets are sent out, they list the source and destination MAC addresses and broadcast the data over the wire. Network cards ignore traffic not meant for their MAC address, and only the targeted recipient card reads and processes the data. Because it's broadcast, this traffic only works on local network segments. Traffic for computers on other physical segments that filter broadcasts is sent to the MAC of the gateway for that segment and then forwarded onward. (You get to that when you read more about IP.)

For now, remember when you want to talk to hosts, the IP address is converted to a MAC address. The sender initially sends out a broadcast asking, "Hey, which MAC address is handling this IP address? My MAC is *x*; please let me know." The sender stores the response in its Address Resolution Protocol (ARP) cache for that and future communications. (By default it's only kept for two minutes). Static entries of IP to MAC mappings that are always available can be added, but by default the entries are dynamic and added as discovered and removed after the timeout period. To look at the content of your ARP cache, use the arp command with the -a switch:

```
C:\Users\john>arp -a

Interface: 10.10.12.129 --- 0x9
  Internet Address      Physical Address      Type
  10.10.12.38           00-17-f2-40-0f-fb     dynamic
  10.10.12.134          00-0d-93-43-b2-54     dynamic
  10.10.15.1            00-c0-9f-0c-f9-9a     dynamic
  10.10.15.60           00-0d-9d-01-78-77     dynamic
  10.10.15.255          ff-ff-ff-ff-ff-ff     static
  224.0.0.22            01-00-5e-00-00-16     static
```

Subnet Masks

So back to the IP addresses. You have an IP address, 192.168.1.13, and you want to talk to 192.168.1.25. What if you want to talk to 192.168.2.5? Remember how the communication works: These IP addresses are converted to MAC addresses, and, assuming they are on the same segment, direct communication is possible. If they are not on the same segment, the traffic is sent to a gateway for onward transmission. How do you know if an IP address is on the same segment of the network—or in IP terms, the same subnet?

Numerous attributes exist for IP configuration, one of which is the subnet mask. Subnet masks identify which parts of the IP address are part of the network address and which are part of the host address. IP addresses with the same network address are, therefore, on the same network (or subnet) and can communicate directly. Think of it as a street address, 13 Baker Street.

As humans, you can see that 13 is the house number (in IP terms, the host address), and Baker Street is the road name or network address. Say you want to send a letter to 24 Baker Street. (I have no clue who lives there, maybe Watson; if this makes no sense, do an Internet search for the original address—number 13.) You see the road name is the same, so you walk down and deliver the letter yourself.

In IP terms, how do you know if 192.168.1.13 is on the same road as 192.168.1.25? Along with the IP address, you also have a subnet mask to identify which parts of the IP address are the hosts and networks. The subnet mask is 32 bits and written as the dotted-quad format (for example 255.255.255.0). Where the bit is a 1, that part of the IP address is the network; where the bit is a 0, that part is the host. So let's look at these IP address (see Figure 6-2).

192	168	1	13
1 1 0 0 0 0 0 0	1 0 1 0 1 0 0 0	0 0 0 0 0 0 0 1	0 0 0 0 1 1 0 1
255	255	255	0
1 1 1 1 1 1 1 1	1 1 1 1 1 1 1 1	1 1 1 1 1 1 1 1	0 0 0 0 0 0 0 0
Network Address			Host Address
192	168	1	13

FIGURE 6-2 How the subnet mask breaks an IP address into its network and host address component.

The network address, 192.168.1, is the first 24 bits, nearly the first three of the dotted quads (also known as octets). The last part is the host address, 13. This means any IP address starting with 192.168.1 is on the same subnet as 192.168.1.13. Sometimes the network address is written with the number of bits as the subnet after the address; for instance, 192.168.1.0/24. This shows 24 bits out of the address given make up the network address.

Apply this procedure to the target of 192.168.1.25. The first 24 bits are the same, and the same network address is 192.168.1. This is the same "road" as the sender, so you can deliver the packet directly. Various classes of IP addresses normally dictate the subnet mask and the size of the network ID:

- **Class A**. The first byte/octet denotes the network address, and the last three octets/bytes are the host portion. Any IP address whose first octet is between 1 and 126 is a class A address. Note that 0 is reserved as a part of the default address, and 127 is reserved for internal loopback testing. You can see this if you contact 127.0.01, known as the loopback address. On any computer this is you.

- **Class B**. The first two octets denote the network address, and the last two octets are the host portion. Any address whose first octet is in the range 128 to 191 is a class B address.
- **Class C**. The first three octets denote the network address, and the last octet is the host portion. The first octet range of 192 to 223 is a class C address.
- **Class D**. Used for multicast. Multicast IP addresses' first octets are in the range 224 to 239.
- **Class E**. Reserved for experimental usage and includes the range of addresses with a first octet from 240 to 255.

In reality, if your company was given a class A or B network, you would not use a subnet mask of 255.0.0.0 or 255.255.0.0. Remember that the subnet defines when a target is on a local segment. Not every machine is on one physical network, so you use subnetting to break up the address range into separate networks to enable more efficient communication and management. For example, if you had a class B of 130.20.0.0/16, you can break it up into multiple class C networks with 255.255.255.0 subnet masks, such as 130.20.1.0/24 and 130.20.2.0/24.

Subnet masks don't have to be full octets. It is any value that identifies which bits of the address are part of the network. If more than 254 hosts are on a network, you need a bigger part of the address dedicated to the host address instead of the network address. For example, 500 hosts would not fit within one normal class C network because it uses only 8 bits for the host address. One solution is to use multiple subnets and put gateways between them, but that might not work, and machines might not be physically connected that way. Instead, devote 9 bits to the host ID, giving a maximum number of 510 hosts. (2^9 is 512, but you lose two addresses—one to the network base address of 0 and the other to the broadcast, which is all bits of the host set to 1.) The subnet mask is now 23 bits, which is 255.255.254.0—notice 254 instead of 255 because the last bit of the third octet is now used for the host address and not the network. 11111110 converted to decimal is 254 (see Figure 6-3 for an example).

<table>
<tr><td colspan="8">192</td><td colspan="8">168</td><td colspan="8">2</td><td colspan="8">0</td></tr>
<tr><td>1</td><td>1</td><td>0</td><td>0</td><td>0</td><td>0</td><td>0</td><td>0</td><td>1</td><td>0</td><td>1</td><td>0</td><td>1</td><td>0</td><td>0</td><td>0</td><td>0</td><td>0</td><td>0</td><td>0</td><td>0</td><td>0</td><td>1</td><td>0</td><td>0</td><td>0</td><td>0</td><td>0</td><td>1</td><td>1</td><td>0</td><td>1</td></tr>
<tr><td colspan="8">255</td><td colspan="8">255</td><td colspan="8">254</td><td colspan="8">0</td></tr>
<tr><td>1</td><td>1</td><td>1</td><td>1</td><td>1</td><td>1</td><td>1</td><td>1</td><td>1</td><td>1</td><td>1</td><td>1</td><td>1</td><td>1</td><td>1</td><td>1</td><td>1</td><td>1</td><td>1</td><td>1</td><td>1</td><td>1</td><td>1</td><td>0</td><td>0</td><td>0</td><td>0</td><td>0</td><td>0</td><td>0</td><td>0</td><td>0</td></tr>
<tr><td>1</td><td>1</td><td>0</td><td>0</td><td>0</td><td>0</td><td>0</td><td>0</td><td>1</td><td>0</td><td>1</td><td>0</td><td>1</td><td>0</td><td>0</td><td>0</td><td>0</td><td>0</td><td>0</td><td>0</td><td>0</td><td>0</td><td>1</td><td>0</td><td>0</td><td>0</td><td>0</td><td>0</td><td>0</td><td>0</td><td>0</td><td>0</td></tr>
<tr><td colspan="23">Network address, e.g. 192.168.1.0 and 192.168.2.0</td><td colspan="9">Host address 1 through 511</td></tr>
</table>

FIGURE 6-3 Less bits in the subnet mask can create networks that span multiple traditional class networks.

What happens is a bitwise AND operation between the IP address and the subnet mask. For example:

1 AND 1=1

1 AND 0=0

0 AND 1=0

0 AND 0=0

That final number is the network address, which is the fifth row in Figure 6-3.

The example shows if 192.168.2.0/23 is the subnet address, those addresses starting with 192.168.3.0 are also considered part of the same network. 192.168.1 is not the same network as 192.168.2 because the .1 is part of the eighth bit and, therefore, considered part of the host address. (The .2 is part of the seventh bit and part of the network address.) If you want 192.168.1/23, the other network address is 192.168.0/23.

To make it easier, go to www.subnet-calculator.com, a graphical interface that lets you type in the information you want. If you are not sticking to the traditional classes or subnets, use the classless version at www.subnet-calculator.com/cidr.php (see Figure 6-4). It gives more flexibility in the options around number of bits for the mask and shows the number of addresses possible and the ranges used.

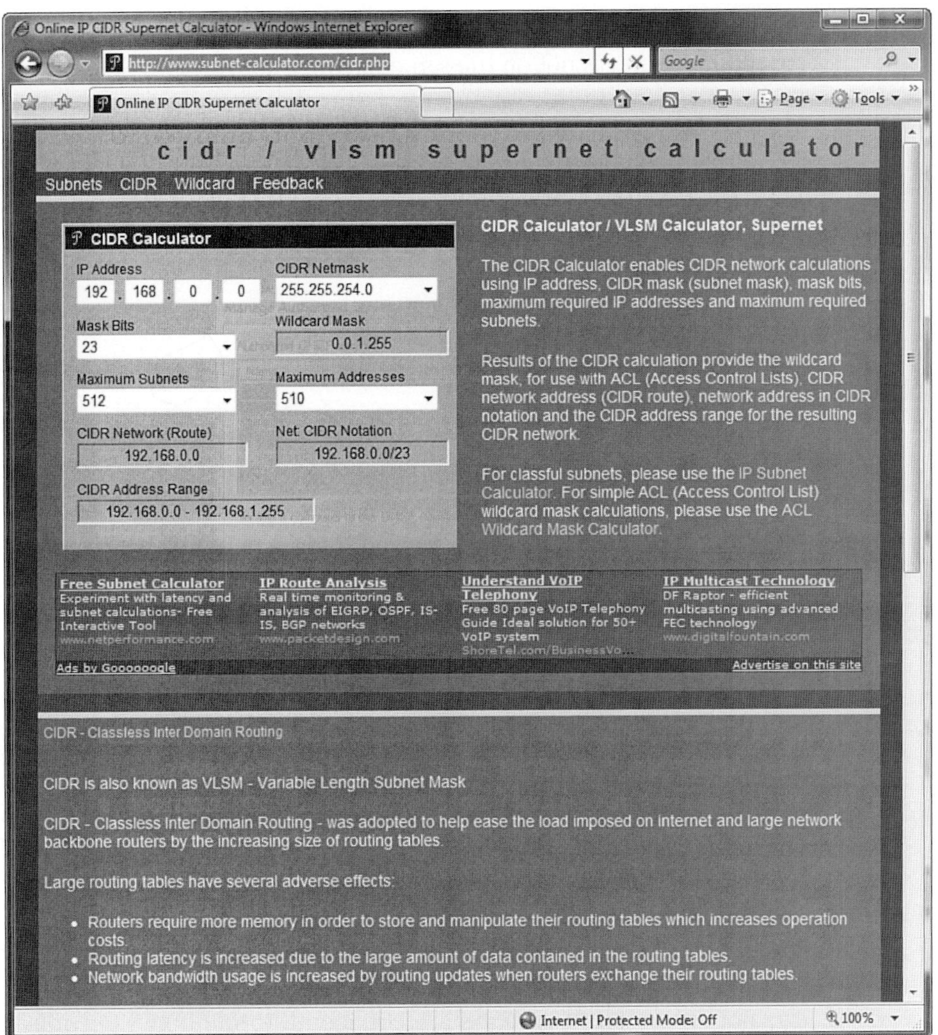

FIGURE 6-4 The calculator allows the number of bits used to be selected along with the IP address and displays the address ranges you would use with full notation options.

Routing Between Subnets

What if a computer is not on the same network address and data cannot be sent directly to it? Let's continue the letter delivery analogy. If the street was the same, you could delivery it yourself. If it were on a different street, you would pop it in the mailbox at the street corner and let the postal office deliver it to its destination because the mailbox is connected to both streets. Figure 6-5 shows the letter going from 13 Baker Street to 2 Grocer Street.

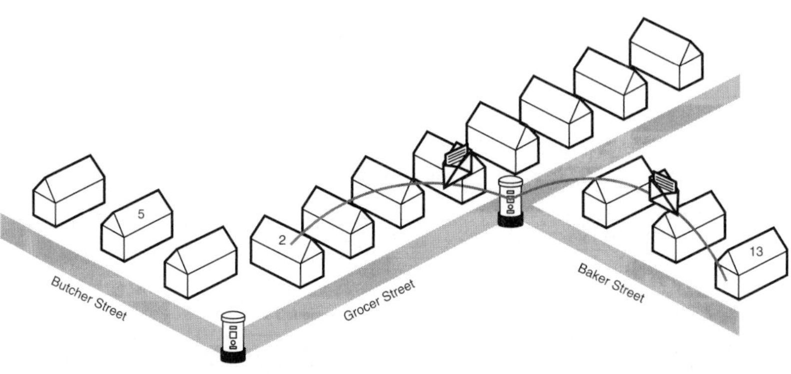

FIGURE 6-5 How letters are delivered between streets.

This concept is the same for IP traffic. So far you have seen that a computer has an IP address and a subnet mask. It also has a gateway configured, and this gateway tells it where to send traffic that is not part of its local subnet; this is the equivalent of the mailbox. The gateway then works out where to send the traffic, either the destination if the gateway is connected to the target network subnet or the next gateway to send the traffic if it is not connected. Gateways are connected to multiple networks with IP addresses on each one it is connected to. If your letter was addressed to 5 Butcher Street, the route looks like Figure 6-6.

These hops are common between gateways. The more correct name for gateway is router because it is routing traffic between different parts of the network. The router is the "gateway" for the computers because it opens up communication to other networks. If a router has traffic for a network address it does not have a connection to, it checks its routing table to see where it should send the data to ensure that it reaches its correct destination.

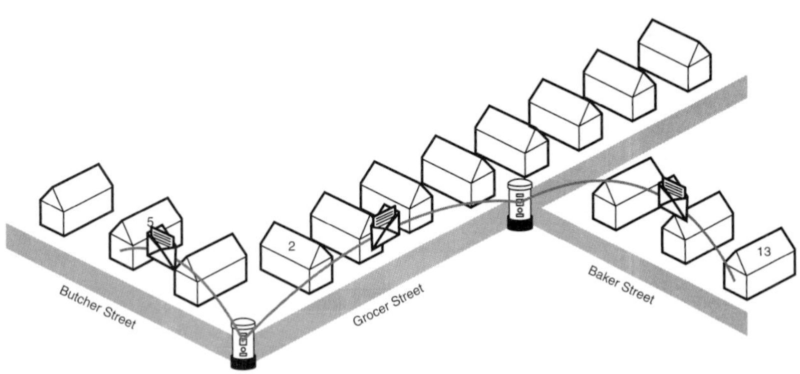

FIGURE 6-6 The destination is not attached to the gateway, so it's sent to another gateway for final delivery.

WIRELESS COMMUNICATION You might wonder how wireless devices work, and the good news is, exactly the same. Remember the OSI model? The only difference between a wired and wireless connection is the physical layer, which does not affect the use of MAC address for the routing. The wireless hub forwards on traffic to its connected wireless clients in the same way a switch works.

Setting an IP Address

To set the IP address for a computer or to view its properties, perform the following:

1. Right-click the Network Status system tray icon and select Network and Sharing Center (or select it from the Control Panel). See Figure 6-7.

FIGURE 6-7 The Network Status system tray icon.

2. In the Network and Sharing Center, click the Manage Network Connections task (see Figure 6-8).

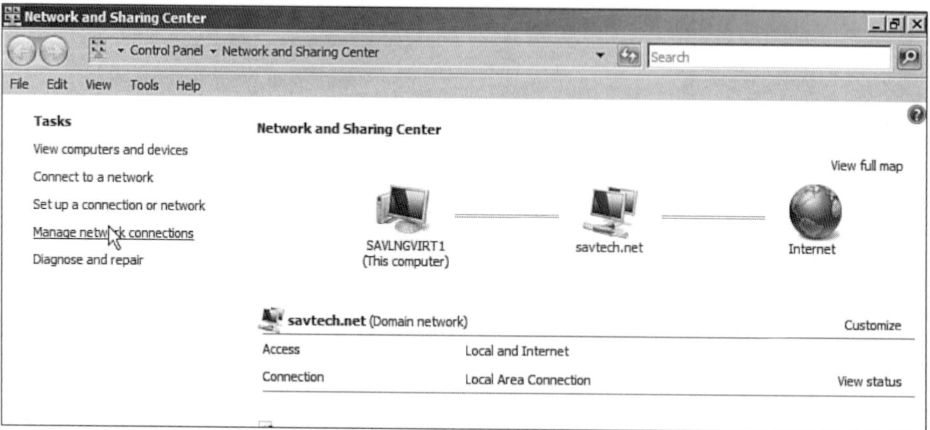

FIGURE 6-8 Overview screen of Network and Sharing Center.

3. A list of network connections appears. Right-click the connection you want to inspect and select Properties.
4. Select Internet Protocol Version 4 (TCP/IPv4) and click Properties (see Figure 6-9).

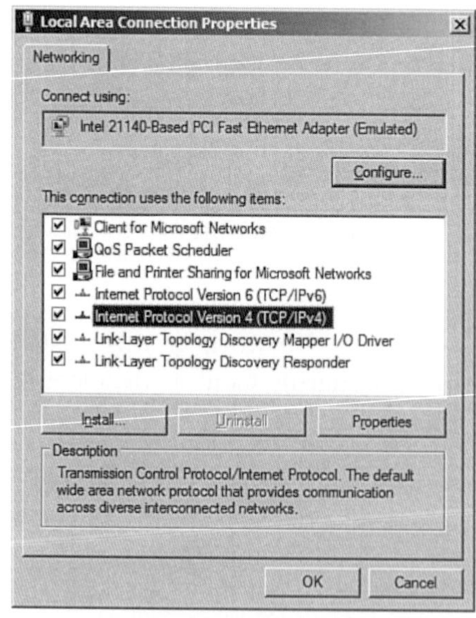

FIGURE 6-9 The various services associated with the network connection. Notice you have IP version 4 and 6, but for now you care only about version 4.

5. The basic properties for the connection appear, which you can change as required (see Figure 6-10).

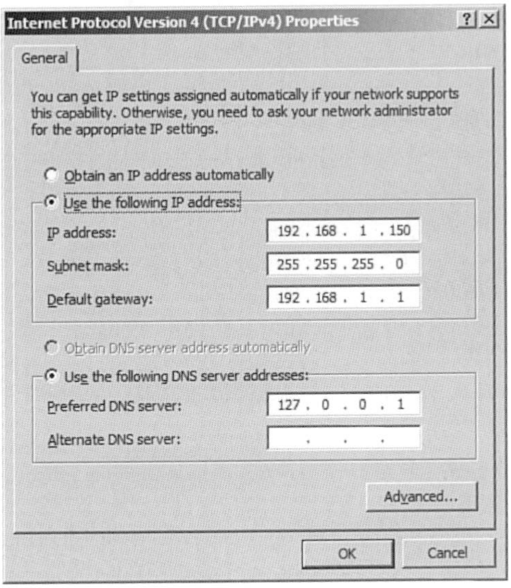

FIGURE 6-10 Basic TCP/IPv4 configuration screen.

In Figure 6-10, you had the option to automatically assign IP addresses, which is covered in detail in Chapter 7. For now stick with statically defining the IP address.

You can also see your IP information using the `ifcongif` command with no parameters. (Add the `/all` parameter for more information, including DNS and WINS, which are covered in Chapter 7.)

```
C:\Users\john.SAVILLTECH>ipconfig

Windows IP Configuration


Ethernet adapter Local Area Connection:

   Connection-specific DNS Suffix  . :
   Link-local IPv6 Address . . . . . : fe80::40b:144b:956:f7de%7
   IPv4 Address. . . . . . . . . . . : 192.168.1.190
   Subnet Mask . . . . . . . . . . . : 255.255.255.0
   Default Gateway . . . . . . . . . : 192.168.1.1
```

This ifcongif shows the IP address, subnet mask, and the default gateway. The computer uses this gateway information in the same way a router works. Each machine has a routing table of where to send packets, depending on the destination. To see the routing table, run the route print command:

```
C:\Users\john.SAVILLTECH>route print
===========================================================================
Interface List
  7 ...00 13 d4 7e d4 11 ...... NVIDIA nForce Networking Controller
  1 ........................... Software Loopback Interface 1
  9 ...02 00 54 55 4e 01 ...... Teredo Tunneling Pseudo-Interface
 17 ...00 00 00 00 00 00 00 e0  isatap.{E474F6C1-08C7-4E8D-B744-
                                1B97936E733F}
===========================================================================

IPv4 Route Table
===========================================================================
Active Routes:
Network Destination        Netmask          Gateway       Interface  Metric
          0.0.0.0          0.0.0.0      192.168.1.1    192.168.1.190    266
        127.0.0.0        255.0.0.0         On-link         127.0.0.1    306
        127.0.0.1  255.255.255.255         On-link         127.0.0.1    306
  127.255.255.255  255.255.255.255         On-link         127.0.0.1    306
      192.168.1.0    255.255.255.0         On-link     192.168.1.190    266
    192.168.1.190  255.255.255.255         On-link     192.168.1.190    266
    192.168.1.255  255.255.255.255         On-link     192.168.1.190    266
        224.0.0.0        240.0.0.0         On-link         127.0.0.1    306
        224.0.0.0        240.0.0.0         On-link     192.168.1.190    266
  255.255.255.255  255.255.255.255         On-link         127.0.0.1    306
  255.255.255.255  255.255.255.255         On-link     192.168.1.190    266
===========================================================================
Persistent Routes:
  Network Address          Netmask  Gateway Address  Metric
          0.0.0.0          0.0.0.0      192.168.1.1  Default
===========================================================================
```

The destination shows the network destination of the route along with the netmask (another term for subnet mask) to specify the scope of addresses it represents. 0.0.0.0 for the network destination and the netmask show this is the default route. This is also written as 0.0.0.0/0 or 0/0. If you have multiple Network Interface Cards (NICs), only define default gateways on one of them. Only one default route is used, so if multiple default gateways are defined, the one with the fastest speed is chosen. If the speeds match, the interface with the highest binding order to TCP/IP is selected. You can have a subnet mask of 255.255.255.255, which is a host-specific route and enables a path to be taken to reach specific machines.

Gateway Configuration

The gateway represents where to send traffic that matches the network and netmask, the interface shows which address in the computer the route represents (127.0.0.1 is the loopback), and the metric shows the route's priority (the lower the metric the higher its priority). The most specific route is chosen first, and so the default is only used if no other route can be found. In the old days of Windows 2003 and earlier, the metric was based on a basic list of network speeds (see Table 6-1).

Table 6-1 Link Speed Metrics

Link Speed	Metric
Greater than 200Mb	10
Greater than 20Mb and less than or equal to 200Mb (Windows XP SP2 introduced a separate metric of 25 for 20–80Mb, with 80–200Mb being 20)	20
Greater than 4Mb and less than or equal to 20Mb	30
Greater than 500Kb and less than or equal to 4Mb	40
Less than or equal to 500Kb	50

With Windows Vista and Windows Server 2008, the metric is not as neat and uses a far more complex algorithm to define the metric, but it is still based on network speed.

To set the metric manually, click the Advanced button on the TCP/IP properties of the adapter. On the IP Settings tab, click Edit for the gateway and unselect Automatic Metric. Configure your own value, as shown in Figure 6-11.

NOTE Although you can change the metrics, ensure sensible values are selected. Wrong metrics change how traffic is routed, potentially causing undesirable results. You might change a metric if you want a particular route to be used or not used, and the modified metric would depend on the metric of other routes that exist on the system.

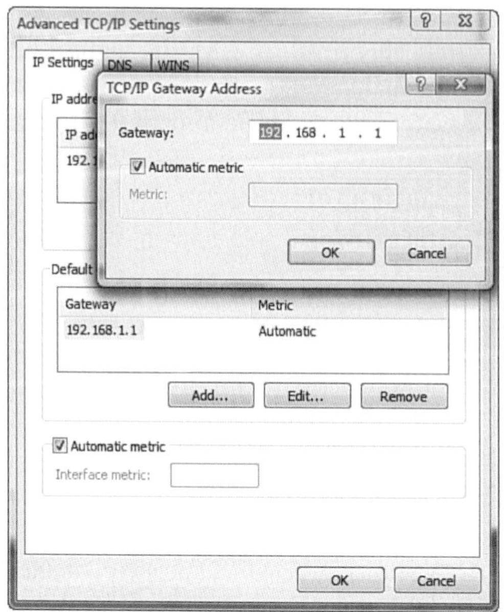

FIGURE 6-11 Changing the default metric location.

You can statically add routes if required. If a computer has multiple network cards, and you want to define if a certain NIC can be used to reach a certain network, add a route. Adding routes is accomplished with the `route` command, and help is available by typing `route` without any parameters:

```
route ADD 192.168.5.0 MASK 255.255.255.0  192.168.1.100 METRIC
5 IF 7
```

This says to get to network 192.168.5/24 and go via gateway 192.168.1.100 on interface (IF) 7. (The list of interfaces is listed at the top of the `route print` command.)

Static IP and IPv4 Limitations

Every computer and any device that wants to communicate via IP in an environment needs an IP address. So if a company has 1,000 users, it needs at least four class C networks (possibly more based on the number of servers, printers, photocopies, and fish webcams on the network). Class C networks range from 192 to 223, giving you 32 networks each with around

65,000 class Cs. That means just over two million class C networks are available for companies to buy. Now do you see the problem with IPv4? There aren't enough addresses, and the routing tables on the Internet would be impossibly large. IPv4 was intended for a specific purpose and scope of machine, and not for something the size of today's Internet.

IPv6 was created to address this by giving us 128-bit addresses, meaning everything can have an IP address (including the cat), and you would never run out. IPv6 is radically different, though, and has had little chance of being adopted quickly. Around the same time, two other technologies were widely implemented: Dynamic Host Control Protocol (DHCP) and Network Address Translation (NAT). DHCP is a service that gives clients IP addresses dynamically. NAT allows a single Internet address to be shared by all the computers in an organization.

Automatic Private IP Addressing

You might have seen an address starting with 169.254. What is this? With Windows 2000, Microsoft tried to make it as easy as possible to set up TCP/IP on a small network, and by default machines were set up to use DHCP. A very small network might not have a DHCP server or cable modem to give out addresses. Rather than failing to initialize TCP/IP, Microsoft added code so that the machines use an address not in use on the local network in the class B address range: 169.254.x.x. This IP address range is reserved for internal use only and so should not clash with any "real" IP addresses on your network.

Automatic address allocation uses conflict detection via a NetBIOS naming broadcast, so each machine gets an IP address from the 169.254.x.x range that is not in use. The actual address initially chosen is random.

If any of your machines have a 169.254.x.x address, it just means they could not contact a DHCP server, so check your network connectivity. This automatic IP addressing is known as Automatic Private IP Addressing (APIPA) and is commonly referred to as a private IP addressing.

Private Network IP Address Allocations

In your home networks, you probably see your router gets an IP address in the network 192.168.1. Why that address? If the "real" owner of that address is on the Internet, and you try to access it, it would fail, right? Fear not—batches of IP addresses are reserved for internal use only and do not exist on the Internet. They are not routed by routers that are part of the Internet. These addresses are defined in RFC 1918:

- **10.0.0.0–10.255.255.255**. A single class A network
- **172.16.0.0–172.31.255.255**. A group of 16 contiguous class B networks
- **192.168.0.0–192.168.255.255**. A contiguous group of 256 class C networks

Nearly all companies have IP addresses in this range and a few Internet registered addresses given by your ISP that connect your company to the actual Internet. Like the APIPA addresses, these addresses only work on the internal network and so are also private IP addresses.

WHAT IS AN RFC? The Internet is guided by the Internet Engineering Task Force (IETF) that consists of many network designers, researchers, and other organizations. When a change or new standard for the Internet is proposed, a Request for Comment (RFC) document is created and posted. These can be viewed at www.ietf.org/rfc.html. All of the major protocols for the Internet are defined in RFC documents.

Network Address Translation

Network Address Translation (NAT) is the process in which the gateway router at a company that connects to the Internet has a "real" Internet IP address, and then all other computers that send requests to the Internet do so via the firewall or router. The gateway device rewrites the source and/or destination address's content in the data packet with that of the firewall/router and then sends/receives to the Internet. NAT translates private IP addresses to public IP addresses.

This means companies no longer buy a class C network from one of the central Internet registries (like InterNIC). Instead they use Classless Inter-Domain Routing (CIDR) and buy one or two public IP addresses from their Internet Service Provider (ISP). The ISP purchases blocks of addresses from the Internet Registry. You can see this if you run a router in your house. You plug in your DSL or cable modem into the router and then hang off your three home servers, workstation, and wireless network, which all normally get a 192.168.1-something address given to it by the router. Our router status shows the address the router was given by the

ISP; in my case it has an address of 75.9.40.x. Now 75 is a class A network, so does my ISP have a whole class A network, one of only 126? No, these networks have been allocated and broken up into smaller chunks to providers of Internet services. If you look at IANA.ORG you can see the IP address allocations: http://www.iana.org/assignments/ipv4-address-space shows the IP address allocations.

Three main types of NAT start simply and grow in complexity:

- **Static NAT**. The NAT router maintains a table and for each internal IP address has a corresponding external, legitimate IP address used for communication with the Internet. This does not save on registering Internet addresses but can be useful where devices need to be accessible from the Internet. Static is not widely used.
- **Dynamic NAT**. The NAT router has a list of registered legitimate IP addresses, and each time an internal client tries to access the Internet, it is mapped to one of the currently unused registered Internet IP addresses. This means you need only legitimate IP addresses for the number of concurrent Internet users.
- **Single Address NAT/Overloading/Masquerading/Network Address Port Translation (NAPT)**. The NAT router has only one registered Internet IP address, and each internal user that needs to communicate with the Internet is mapped to a different port. This is written in the form x.x.x.x:y. 10.0.0.1:100 is IP address 100.0.0.1, port 100. When the NAT gateway receives responses from the Internet, the originating port is included, which it maps to the originating IP address on the local intranet. This is the most popular form of NAT.

In Figure 6-12, the NAT device has a mapping table of the IP addresses internally and the ports it uses for the external configuration. The NAT device can inspect incoming traffic for the source port, so it can forward the traffic to the internal computer (see Table 6-2). Windows Server 2008 provides this NAT functionality, which is covered in Chapter 8, "Remote Access and Securing and Optimizing the Network."

Table 6-2 Mapping of Original to Externally Addressable IP Addresses

Original IP Address	Address Used for External Communication
192.168.1.51	74.9.40.53:58250
192.168.1.52	74.9.40.53:58251
192.168.1.53	74.9.40.53:58252

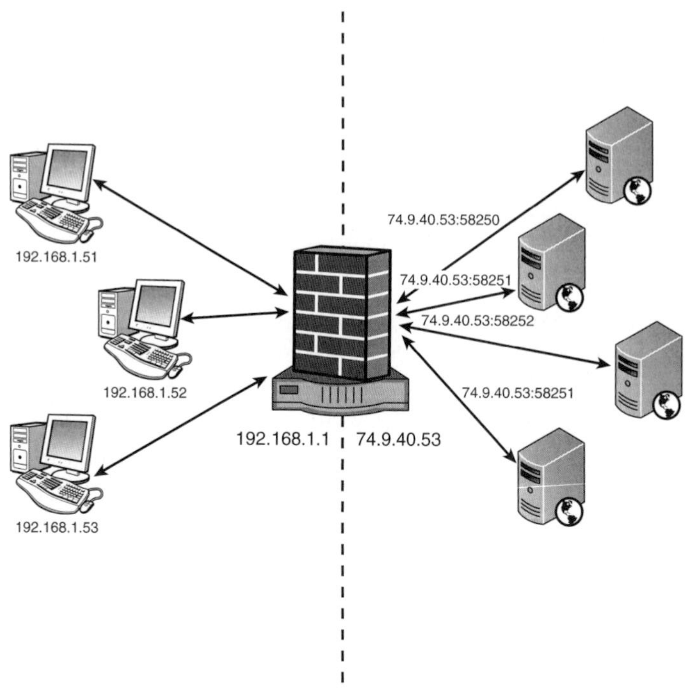

FIGURE 6-12 A Single Address NAT in progress. The NAT device maintains a table of ports for its single external address of 74.9.40.53 that maps to the computers on the internal network.

IP facilitates communication, but it's a best-effort service with no guarantee of delivery. It's like tying a letter you want to deliver around your cat's neck, telling him the address, and then setting the cat about his way. (You're assuming it's an intelligent cat.) You have no way of knowing if the letter got there. That's IP—the packet goes out onto the network, but you get no verification of delivery. IP packets can be corrupted, lost, arrive at the destination out of order, or get delivered multiple times. The transmission of an IP packet and its routing is enabled via its header, which is simple (see Figure 6-13).

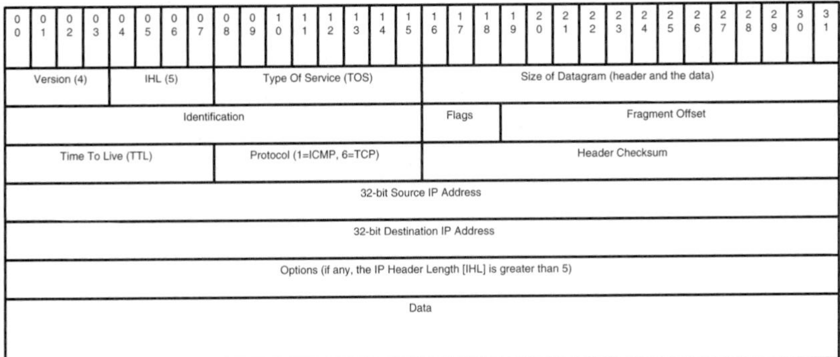

0 0
0 1
0 2
0 3
0 4
0 5
0 6
0 7
0 8
0 9
1 0
1 1
1 2
1 3
1 4
1 5
1 6
1 7
1 8
1 9
2 0
2 1
2 2
2 3
2 4
2 5
2 6
2 7
2 8
2 9
3 0
3 1
Version (4)
IHL (5)
Type Of Service (TOS)
Size of Datagram (header and the data)
Identification
Flags
Fragment Offset
Time To Live (TTL)
Protocol (1=ICMP, 6=TCP)
Header Checksum
32-bit Source IP Address
32-bit Destination IP Address
Options (if any, the IP Header Length [IHL] is greater than 5)
Data

FIGURE 6-13 IP header format.

As you can see, not much is in here. You can tell it the type of protocol, the size of the packet, where it is from, and where it's going. The Time to Live (TTL) says how many hops between routers the packet can survive. Each hop at a router decreases the TTL by 1, and when it reaches 0, it stops being routed. This is designed to stop packets from being routed in a circle indefinitely.

Although IP allows communication and actual data transfer, other protocols that sit above it in the Transport layer of the OSI model are needed.

Transmission Control Protocol (TCP)

Transmission Control Protocol (TCP) sits on top of IP in the OSI stack and adds reliability to IP's communication capabilities. TCP creates a connection between the hosts communicating and provides guaranteed data delivery by resending data packets if they don't arrive. TCP also ensures the data is presented in the correct order and follows a sequence of creating the connection, having a data transfer session, and then terminating the connection after the transfer is complete. Each of these connections uses a TCP port, which can be between 1 and 65535. Some of these ports are reserved for specific applications types that listen on a port for requests. For example:

- **Port 21**. File Transfer Protocol (FTP).
- **Port 23**. Telnet for character-based communication to a remote computer.

- **Port 25**. Simple Mail Transfer Protocol (SMTP).
- **Port 80**. Hypertext Transfer Protocol (HTTP)—the most used because it powers all those Web browser sessions. When you tell your Web browser to go to http://www.msn.com, you are telling it to use protocol http to talk to server www.msn.com. The Web browser opens a request to port 80 on server www.msn.com.

TCP is great because it adds reliability to your services, but it adds overhead in terms of data size sent over the network, and the time it takes to initiate the connection before "useful" data transfer can start.

Figure 6-14 shows the TCP header. Notice it does not have details about the source or destination address. This is because the TCP header just sits inside the IP data, which already contains the source and destination information. Notice you have port information now along with sequence space.

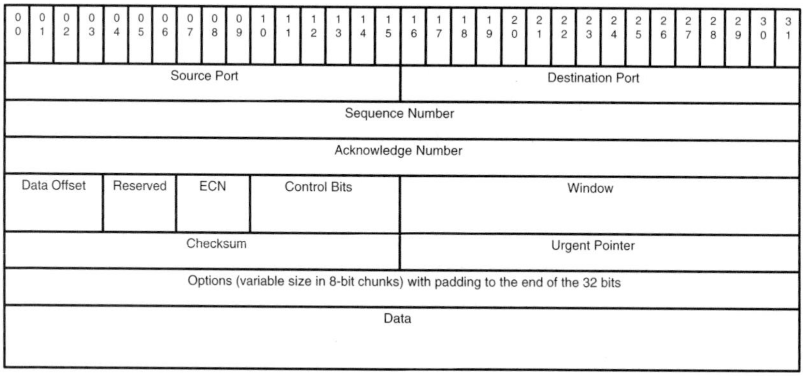

00 01 02 03 04 05 06 07 08 09 10 11 12 13 14 15 16 17 18 19 20 21 22 23 24 25 26 27 28 29 30 31

Source Port | Destination Port

Sequence Number

Acknowledge Number

Data Offset | Reserved | ECN | Control Bits | Window

Checksum | Urgent Pointer

Options (variable size in 8-bit chunks) with padding to the end of the 32 bits

Data

FIGURE 6-14 TCP header.

User Datagram Protocol (UDP)

User Datagram Protocol (UDP) is the skinny sister of TCP. Although it still uses ports to enable structured communication, UDP does not provide the reliability or ordering of TCP. This is a good thing for shorter types of communication because it does not have the session creation prerequisites of TCP. This makes UDP faster than TCP. UDP is typically used for broadcast-type communication where data packets are sent to multiple computers, such as broadcasts and multicast transmissions. (Multicast is traffic broadcast to multiple recipients, and unicast is traffic targeted for a single destination.) Remember the TCP header shown in Figure 6-14? The UDP header is much simpler (see Figure 6-15).

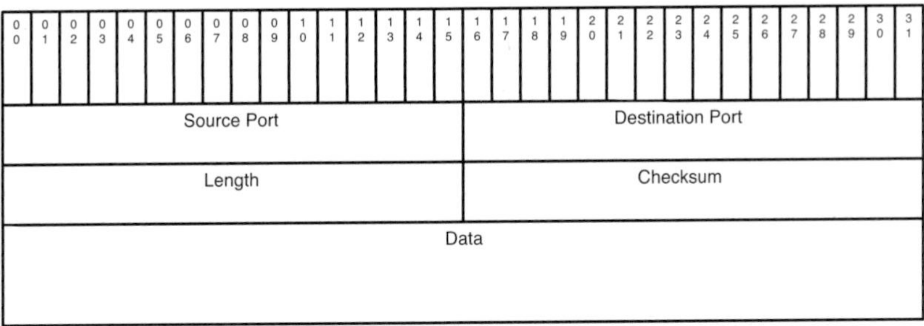

FIGURE 6-15 UDP header.

Because UDP offers so few extra services, its users have to take care of its nonacknowledge or guaranteed delivery. The service that uses UDP checks for responses and is responsible for resending or requesting data that is it not confirmed as being received.

Network Monitoring

It's great talking about the various headers and how traffic is sent, but it helps to see it. IP with TCP or UDP does nothing more than send data. The actual workload, such as a DNS request or sending an e-mail, sits on top of these protocols. Different types of traffic and different services use the most relevant protocol.

Numerous troubleshooting techniques and investigations for TCP/IP exist, but let's take a quick look at network monitoring so that you can see the headers and data you have been reading about. Being able to see the traffic flowing over the network can be an invaluable tool in diagnosing problems.

Microsoft Network Monitor

Windows Vista and Windows Server 2008 have a new version of Microsoft Network Monitor that you can download from www.microsoft.com/downloads/details.aspx?familyid=18b1d59d-f4d8-4213-8d17-2f6dde7d7aac&displaylang=en. It comes in both 32-bit and 64-bit versions. The good news is that this improved network monitor also runs on Windows Server 2003 and XP. The new version has an advantage over the old version—it can operate in promiscuous and nonpromiscuous mode.

PROMISCUOUS? Promiscuous mode means the Network Monitor monitors all network traffic from everywhere. Nonpromiscuous mode means the Network Monitor monitors only network traffic from and to itself.

Figure 6-16 shows the interface of Network Monitor 3. To get started, select Create a New Capture Tab. At the bottom of the screen are the network connections you want to monitor. If you enable the P-mode (promiscuous), you can see all traffic on the network and not just traffic to/from the monitoring machine.

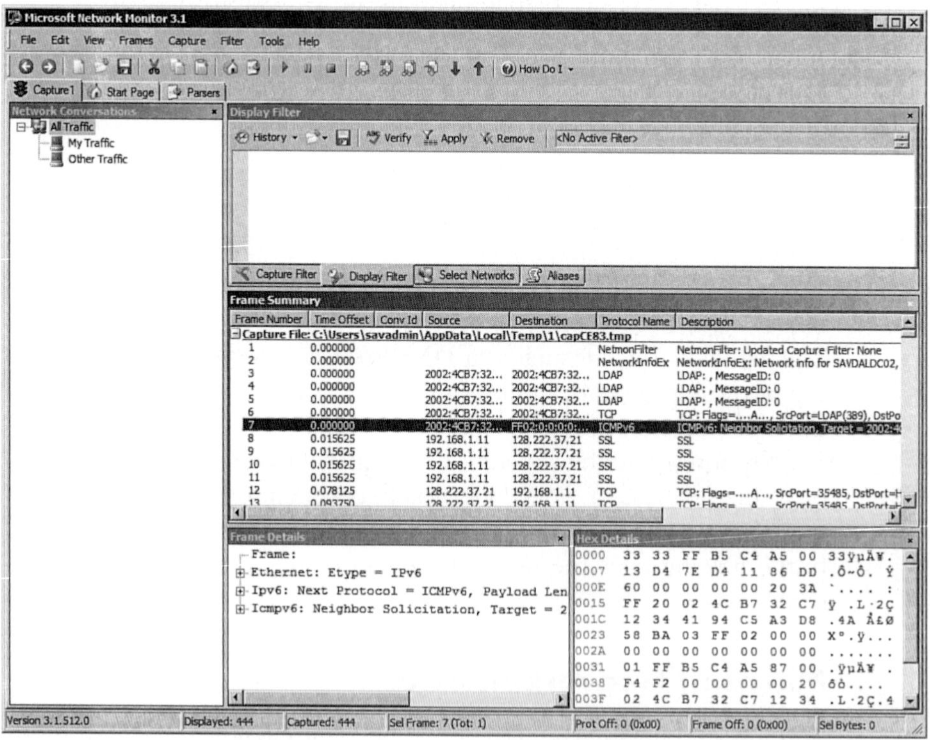

FIGURE 6-16 Overview of monitoring via Network Monitor.

Capture tabs, capture filters, and capture displays are now part of the application. Templates are provided for you. It's more intuitive than previous versions. For example, to see only DNS traffic, type `DNS` in the display filter and click the Apply Filter button (the note icon with the red pin through it).

Network Monitor has a programming-like syntax for its filters that understands the attributes of various classes of objects that can be filtered. For example, if you type `protocol` in the filter editor, a drop-down shows all the known protocols that you can select (see Figure 6-17).

Multiple lines can be added to a filter joined via AND and OR conditions. Group multiple conditions by surrounding them in brackets (). If you want to exclude types of data or protocol, use `NOT` or `!` in front of the expression. For example, to stop all RDP traffic showing, type `NOT protocol.RDP` or `!protocol.RDP`.

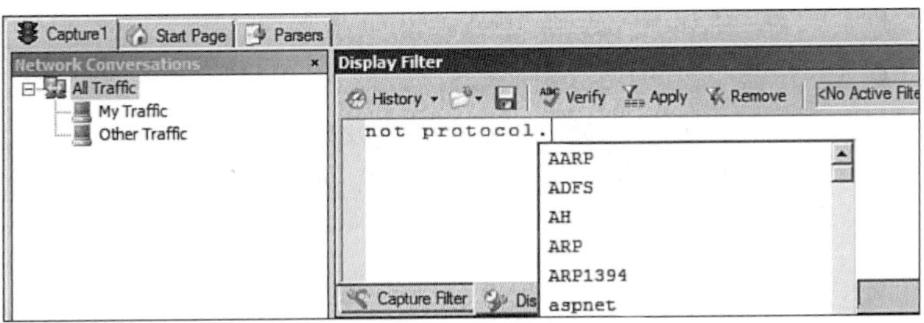

FIGURE 6-17 Attribute-aware filter screen.

After changing filters, click the Verify button to check that the syntax is correct and click Apply to apply the filter to the capture. You can apply filters to the capture to only capture specific frames or apply filters to what is displayed. The best practice is to use a broader filter to capture too much traffic and then hone in on the traffic you want to see in the display filter.

The content of packets can be searched using the Contains action. For example, to search the ascii payload (binary cannot be searched) of a TCP packets payload, use

```
property.TCPPayload.contains("secretstuff")
```

You can apply these filters at both the capture level, which means packets are only captured that meet the criteria, and at the display level, which searches the packets captured for those matching the filter. You could use a capture filter to trim down what is captured and then a display

6. TCP/IP

filter to show only specific information. Let's say you run the following command so you can look at captured data. Although DNS is covered in Chapter 7, for now understand that DNS acts like a phonebook, converting a machine's name to an IP address. In this example you are trying to find the IP address for the name www.savilltech.net.

```
C:\Users\john.SAVILLTECH>nslookup www.savilltech.net
Server:  savdaldc01.savilltech.net
Address:  192.168.1.10:53

Name:    savdaldc01.savilltech.net
Address:  192.168.1.10
Aliases:  www.savilltech.net
```

Network Monitor has a series of eight packets (see Figure 6-18).

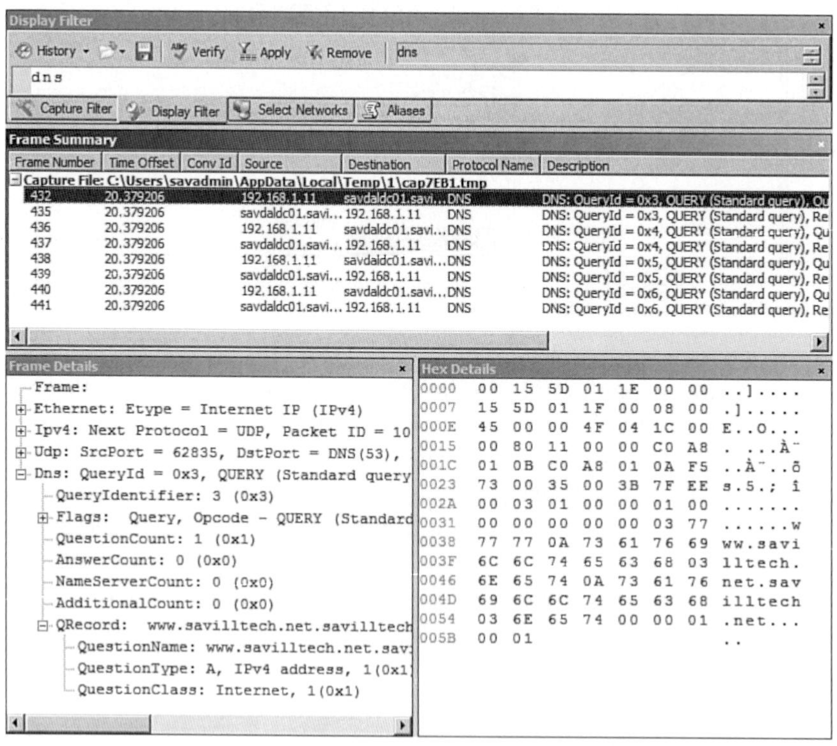

FIGURE 6-18 The DNS detail in the packet.

In Figure 6-18, the bottom-left pane shows the various layers of the data. Frame is first; then the Ethernet information that has the MAC address information; then the IP protocol that has the full IP header, including the source and destination; then the UDP header; and then the DNS information. Notice you use UDP because it's a fast, short request, and the actual DNS requester simply re-asks for the answer if it gets no response.

DNS Communication Explained

Why are multiple packets sent? If you look at the Network Monitor output, the first item is the IP address of the DNS server and its name. The client does not know the name of the DNS server, only its IP address. So the first two packets are the client asking the DNS server the name of the host with IP address 192.168.1.10 (which is the DNS server configured on the client). This is a reverse lookup that tells you the name from an IP address. The next query looks up www.savillltech.net.savilltech.net. Why savilltech.net twice? A default DNS domain is configured on your computer, and the `nslookup` client is assuming you are lazy and did not type the fully qualified domain name (FQDN), such as typing www instead of `www.savilltech.net`. You can prove this:

```
C:\Users\john.SAVILLTECH>nslookup www
Server:  savdaldc01.savilltech.net
Address:  192.168.1.10:53

Name:    savdaldc01.savilltech.net
Address:  192.168.1.10
Aliases:  www.savilltech.net
```

See, it still worked. The fourth packet in the trace returns an error code, Name Does Not Exist. At this point, the `nslookup` client re-queries but without adding the default DNS domain for the computer. This time, the DNS server has a response and sends back the results (see Figure 6-19). You get even more packets because you have IPv6, and both A and AAAA records are checked for across both IPv4 and IPv6.

Two DNS resource records were returned. This is because www is an alias for a real host `savdaldc01`, and so the alias record and the actual host record are returned. What is important is to see how the layers of communication exist and add value to the communication.

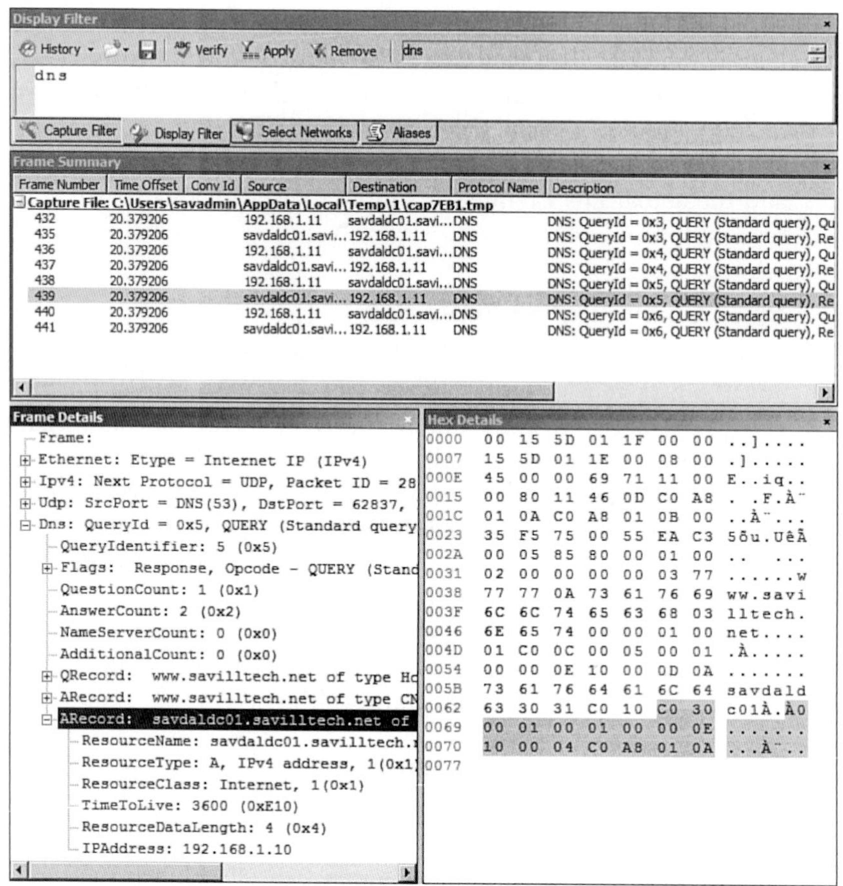

FIGURE 6-19 The data returned for a DNS request.

IPv6

IPv6 will eventually replace IPv4. This change will take a long time, given how ingrained IPv4 is. You might see IPv4 and IPv6 side-by-side forever.

Remember how IPv4 with its 32-bit addresses would eventually run out and, although NAT seemingly solves it, there would still be problems? IPv4 also has other limitations that IPv6 fixes. The following are the main IPv6 advantages over IPv4:

- Greater flexibility to provide additional functionality for next generation–type communication.
- Reduce size of routing tables on backbone routers on the Internet (which currently have about 85,000 entries).
- Easier configuration without the need for DHCP or static configuration that is prevalent today through an auto-configuration scheme. In reality, there will likely still be some IPv6 configuration through DHCP in organizations.
- Improved Quality of Service (QOS) enabling real-time delivery.
- Security at the IP level that is built-in unlike the add-on IPsec for IPv4.

NOTE Windows Vista and Windows Server 2008 have a brand new, next generation TCP/IP stack in which IPv4 and IPv6 are integrated together, sharing common transport and framing layers. Security, reliability, and scalability are radically improved.

IPv6 is a core part of the operating system and enabled by default in Windows Vista and Windows Longhorn Server. For Windows Server 2003 and XP, it is very much a separate component. There is no IPv6 for Windows 2000 or 98, and such.

What is IPv6? Also known as IP the Next Generation (IPng), IPv6's appeal is the size of the addresses. At 128 bits and four times the size of IPv4, IPv6 expands the number of possible addresses from about 4 billion to 3.4×10^{38} (or 340,282,366,920,938,463,463,374,607,431,768,211,456).

This larger address space is designed to allow multiple levels of subnetting for better traffic routing from the Internet backbone to subnets within companies and remove the need for address translation techniques, such as NAT.

The header format is simpler than that of IPv4 because IPv6 is designed to have extension headers as needed, depending on the type of traffic. These extension headers, and IPv6 in general, are defined in RFC 2460, found at www.faqs.org/rfcs/rfc2460.html. Even though it's a simpler header (see Figure 6-20), IPv6 is still twice the size because the addresses it has to store are four times the size.

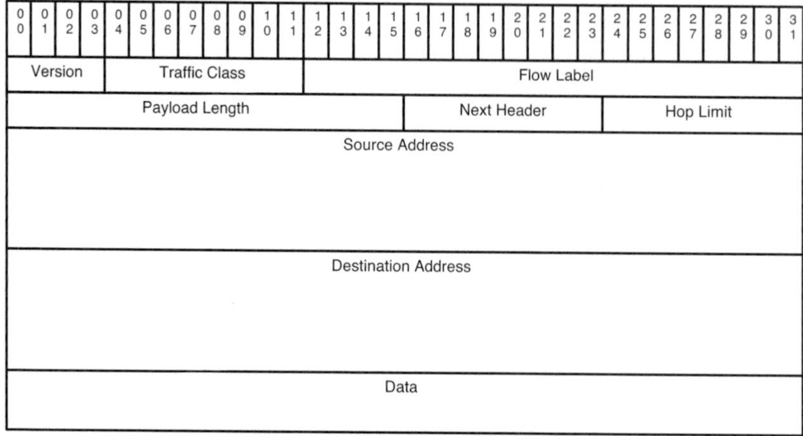

FIGURE 6-20 IPv6 header.

Don't write an address the same as IPv4. IPv6 addresses are expressed as

XXXX:XXXX:XXXX:XXXX:XXXX:XXXX:XXXX:XXXX

Each X is a hexadecimal integer (16 bits). Each digit is 4 bits and so can be between 0 and F. (F is 15 in hexadecimal.) Examples of valid addresses are

2001: BA98:4136:e378:2845:ef02:b4f6:d71b

1080:0:0:0:8:800:200C:417A

In the second address, you can leave off any leading 0s, but you must have at least one numeral in each part. For example, :0800: can be written as :800:. You might have a large sequence of 0s in the address, and it is possible to have a single gap by writing ::. This fills the gap with 0s. For example:

1080:0:0:0:8:800:200C:417A

can be written as

1080::8:800:200C:417A

You can only use :: once in an address for blocks of 0s. If you used it more than once, there would be no way of knowing how many blocks of 0s should be in each instance and, therefore, no way of reading the actual address. 0:0:0:0:0:0:0:1 is the loopback address (the same as 127.0.0.1 in IPv4) and can be written as ::1.

A third format is available when dealing with a mixed environment of IPv4 and IPv6 nodes:

xxxx:xxxx:xxxx:xxxx:xxxx:xxxx:ddd.ddd.ddd.ddd

The x's are the hexadecimal values of the six high-order 16-bit pieces of the address, and the d's are the decimal values of the four low-order 8-bit pieces of the address (standard IPv4 representation). Examples include

0:0:0:0:0:0:13.1.68.3

0:0:0:0:0:FFFF:129.144.52.38

or in compressed form:

::13.1.68.3

::FFFF:129.144.52.38

The subnet mask is now replaced by a number appended to the network address specifying the number of bits making up the network part (CIDR notation), in the form of ipv6.address/prefix-length:

12AB:0000:0000:CD30:0000:0000:0000:0000/60

12AB:0000:0000:CD30::/60

/60 means the first 60 bits make up the network part of the address.

When writing a node address and a node address prefix (the node's subnet prefix), the two can combined as follows:

The node address 11AC:0:0:CA20:123:4567:89AB:CDEF.

Its subnet number 11AC:0:0:CA20::/60.

This can be abbreviated as
11AC:0:0:CA20:123:4567:89AB:CDEF/60.

Let's look at `ipconfig` again:

```
C:\Users\Administrator>ipconfig

Windows IP Configuration


Ethernet adapter Local Area Connection:

   Connection-specific DNS Suffix  . :
   Link-local IPv6 Address . . . . . : fe80::bd36:fdf4:b60c:
e29a%9
   IPv4 Address. . . . . . . . . . . : 192.168.1.150
   Subnet Mask . . . . . . . . . . . : 255.255.255.0
   Default Gateway . . . . . . . . . : 192.168.1.1
```

The address looks slightly different—you have a `%9` at the end because no IPv6 addresses are manually configured or a process set up to allocate addresses in the environment. This means Link-Local Addresses are used (explained a little further on). For all addresses, the first 64 bits make up the network ID, and the last 64 bits are the interface ID. Here are the types of addresses that can exist:

- **Global unicast addresses**. These are like the public IPv4 addresses routable across the entire IPv6 Internet and allocated by the Internet Assigned Numbers Authority (IANA at www.iana.org). Global unicast addresses are formatted as follows:
  - **3 bits**. Set to 001 (known as the format prefix).
  - **45 bits**. Identify the Global Routing Prefix that is specific for an organization. These 45 bits are split in a 13-bit Top Level Aggregation Identifier (TLA ID) that are granted to local Internet registries by IANA; then 8 bits are reserved, and 24 bits are for a Next Level Aggregation Identifier (NLA ID) to identify customer sites from the TLA.
  - **16 bits**. The subnet within an organization.
  - **64 bits**. The interface of the computer within the subnet.
    This address separation allows layers of routing, meaning the central Internet routing tables potentially contain 8,192 TLA IDs, and those would then link to the NLA.
- **Link-local addresses**. This is the equivalent of the Automatic Private IP Addressing (APIPA) for IPv4, which uses the 169.254.0.0/16 network and is given to hosts that don't have an IP address and cannot contact a stateful configuration server (such as a DHCP server that provides configuration about IP). This can only be used to communicate with nodes on the same network. These

addresses all start with fe80, and the rest of the subnet is zeroed out with the last 64 bits making up the interface ID. A zone ID is added to the end of the address after the percent (%) sign, which is an integer. You can list these with the `netsh interface ipv6 show interface` command.

The auto-generated address is automatically generated with Windows Vista and Windows Server 2008, unlike previous versions that used the MAC address of the network card in part. You can enable the older style behavior using the following command:

```
netsh interface ipv6 set global randomizeidentifiers
➥=disabled
```

If the `ipconfig` is checked, the MAC address is now part of the IPv6 address:

```
   Physical Address. . . . . . . . . : 00-13-D4-7E-D4-11
   Link-local IPv6 Address . . . . . :
fe80::213:d4ff:fe7e:d411%7(Preferred)
```

- **Site-local addresses**. This is for internal organizations, similar to the IPv4 local address space (10.0.0.0/8, 172.16.0.0/12, and 192.168.0.0/16). These addresses all start with fec0, and once again the last 64 bits of the address are the interface ID. The lower 16 bits of the network ID make up a subnet mask that allows subnets to be created in the IPv6 address range. The rest of the network ID is zeroed out. This was depreciated in favor of the unique local address because the site-local address caused confusion.

- **Unique local address**. The replacement for the site-local address and is designed to be used within an organization. The first eight bits are always 11111101, meaning all unique local addresses start with fd. The next 40 bits make up the global ID used to identify buildings or a location within an organization. The network ID's last 16 bits is the subnet ID, allowing multiple subnets within a location. Generate the global ID portion randomly and do not just start with 1. You might need to combine networks with another network in the future, as might happen in a company merger, and if both companies randomly generated the global ID, the chance of them both using the same address is unlikely. Also an allocation starting with fc is managed by a body for allocation not currently in existence.

It is unlikely you will ever want to configure static IPv6 addresses given their size. You are more likely to use an IPv6 DHCP service (see Figure 6-21). However, you can configure a static address via the Internet Protocol Version 6 (TCP/IPv6) properties of the network connection. You can also configure a manual address using the `netsh` command, for example:

```
netsh interface ipv6 set address
➥"Local Area Connection" fec0::0:0:1
```

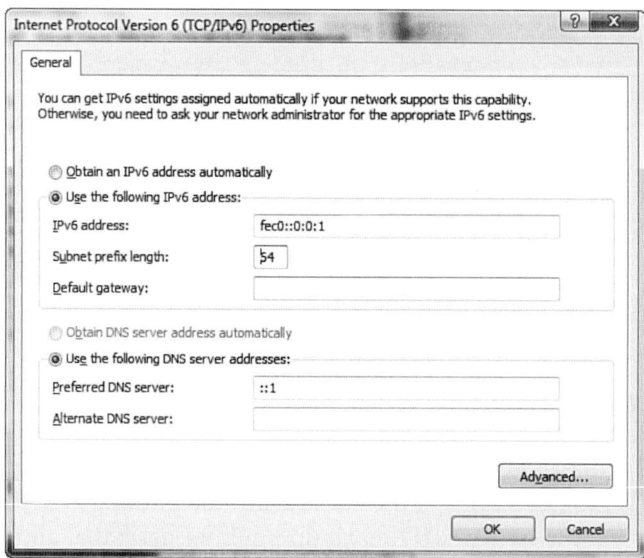

FIGURE 6-21 Option to statically define IPv6 address properties.

Communication Testing

This chapter has concentrated on local IP address configuration, but its purpose is to communicate with other hosts on the same network. You have already seen the `ipconfig` command, which gives you information about the IP configuration, and you can add `/all` to get extended information.

Ping is the first communication testing tool to use. It performs a basic IP communication test by sending an IP address an echo request packet. This tells the receiving computer to send the data back to the source computer. If the computer receives the data back, it knows the IP address is active and responsive.

The first test for communication verification is to ping the loopback address of 127.0.0.1. This should always work, and if it does not, it implies something is corrupt in the TCP driver or that the network adapter is not enabled or is not functioning:

```
Ping 127.0.0.1
```

If you want to see if IPv6 is functioning properly, ping the IPv6 loopback address:

```
Ping ::1
```

The next communication test is to ping your local IP address. If this fails, you might have the incorrect IP address, or the network adapter driver might not be functioning correctly:

```
Ping 192.168.1.190
```

Ping consists of ICMP Type 8 (echo requests). Internet Control Message Protocol (ICMP) exists at the same level as IP (OSI layer three). Although ICMP is part of the same network layer, it still exists inside an IP packet (as you can see from the following trace). Now ping a host on your same local subnet. For example, 192.168.1.10, a domain controller:

```
C:\Users\john.SAVILLTECH>ping 192.168.1.10

Pinging 192.168.1.10 with 32 bytes of data:

Reply from 192.168.1.10: bytes=32 time=1ms TTL=128
Reply from 192.168.1.10: bytes=32 time<1ms TTL=128
Reply from 192.168.1.10: bytes=32 time<1ms TTL=128
Reply from 192.168.1.10: bytes=32 time<1ms TTL=128

Ping statistics for 192.168.1.10:
    Packets: Sent = 4, Received = 4, Lost = 0 (0% loss),
Approximate round trip times in milli-seconds:
    Minimum = 0ms, Maximum = 1ms, Average = 0ms
```

The output of the ping shows the number of bytes each ping request sent, the amount of time taken, and the time to live of each packet. After the ping is complete, an overview of the test is shown, including minimum, maximum, and average times (see Figure 6-22).

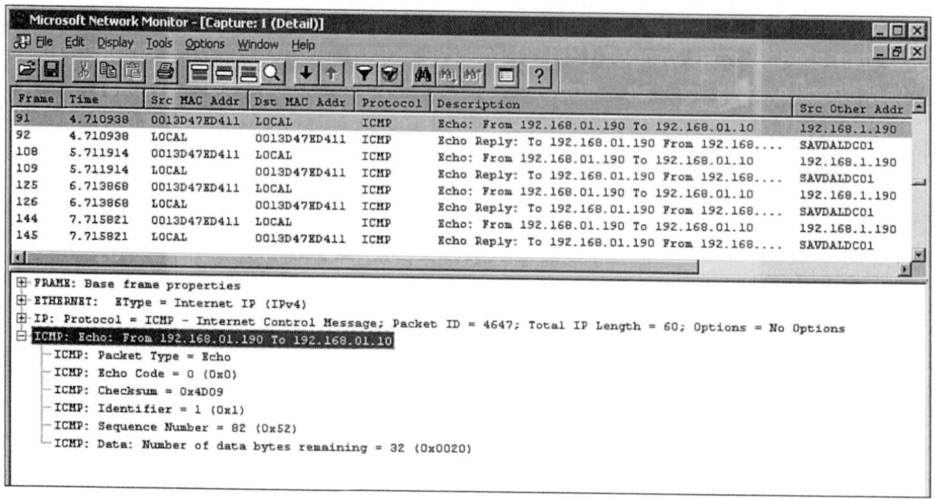

FIGURE 6-22 You have a series of four sets of send and receive packets at one second intervals, matching how the `ping` command sent the requests.

If the ping to a remote host on the local network fails, it could mean communication is not functioning between the nodes, or firewall software might be enabled on the remote server. If you are using the Windows Firewall, you can confirm by accessing the Windows Firewall Control Panel applet and selecting the Advanced tab. Click the Settings button in the ICMP section and ensure Allow Incoming Echo Request is enabled (see Figure 6-23).

NOTE Enabling the incoming echo request aids in troubleshooting configuration. Be careful of enabling this on Internet-facing servers because doing so exposes the server to possible attack. The ping of death attack overloads a server with constant ping requests.

If you can ping a local host, next try pinging the gateway that is your route to computers outside your local subnet:

```
Ping 192.168.1.1
```

After you can contact the gateway, you can ping to a remote computer. If it fails, confirm ICMP echo is enabled. Further tests include pinging by the hostname, but this is discussed with DNS.

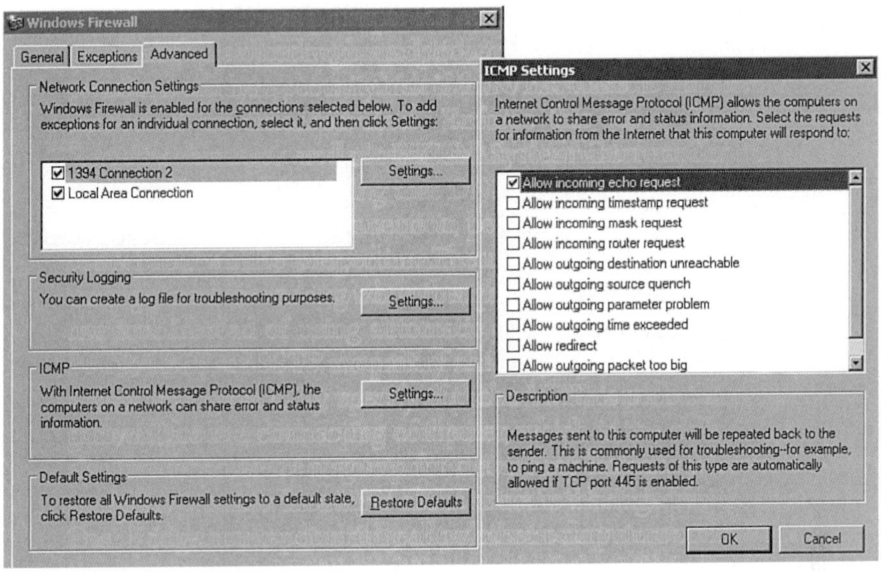

FIGURE 6-23 Enabling incoming echo requests in the firewall.

Again, these tests all work with IPv6, for example:

```
C:\Users\Administrator>ping fe80::bd36:fdf4:b60c:e29a%9

Pinging fe80::bd36:fdf4:b60c:e29a%9 from fe80::bd36:fdf4:b60c:
e29a%9 with 32 bytes of data:
Reply from fe80::bd36:fdf4:b60c:e29a%9: time=87ms
Reply from fe80::bd36:fdf4:b60c:e29a%9: time<1ms
Reply from fe80::bd36:fdf4:b60c:e29a%9: time<1ms
Reply from fe80::bd36:fdf4:b60c:e29a%9: time=1ms

Ping statistics for fe80::bd36:fdf4:b60c:e29a%9:
    Packets: Sent = 4, Received = 4, Lost = 0 (0% loss),
Approximate round trip times in milli-seconds:
    Minimum = 0ms, Maximum = 87ms, Average = 22ms
```

To test the route of a certain destination, use the `tracert` command, which shows all the hops between servers between the sender and recipient system. For example, to get to a DNS server at SBC Global (my ISP) from my local network host of 192.168.1.190, I see the following:

```
C:\Users\john.SAVILLTECH>tracert 68.94.156.1

Tracing route to dnsr1.sbcglobal.net [68.94.156.1]
over a maximum of 30 hops:

  1     3 ms     3 ms     2 ms  192.168.1.1
  2     3 ms     3 ms     3 ms  192.168.0.1
  3    13 ms    13 ms    15 ms  bras23-10.rcsntx.sbcglobal.net
[151.164.182.7]
  4    11 ms    11 ms    11 ms  dist1-vlan130.rcsntx.sbcglobal.
net [151.164.162.
130]
  5    12 ms    11 ms    11 ms  151.164.93.188
  6    12 ms    11 ms    12 ms  srvr1-vlan20.rcsntx.sbcglobal.
net [151.164.1.138
]
  7    11 ms    12 ms    11 ms  dnsr1.sbcglobal.net
[68.94.156.1]

Trace complete.
```

This output shows the hops, the IP version of the mailboxes between streets. Notice the traffic first goes to my gateway on the 192.168.1 network (192.168.1.1). It is next sent to the gateway on the router's network (192.168.1.0) and then between various routers on the SBC network before reaching the destination for a total of seven hops. That is quite close. If the trace route fails, use the `route print` command to view the gateways used for the target IP address specified.

If a `tracert` demonstrates a full route to a host, the next tool you can use is `pathping`, which combines `tracert` with `ping` and sends ping requests to each hop on the route. Failures might be because the router has ICMP echo response disabled.

The same test is run to the DNS server with `pathping`. The time taken depends on the number of hops.

```
C:\Users\john.SAVILLTECH>pathping 68.94.156.1

Tracing route to dnsr1.sbcglobal.net [68.94.156.1]
over a maximum of 30 hops:
  0  savdalwks01.savilltech.net [192.168.1.190]
  1  192.168.1.1
  2  192.168.0.1
  3  bras23-10.rcsntx.sbcglobal.net [151.164.182.7]
  4  dist1-vlan130.rcsntx.sbcglobal.net [151.164.162.130]
```

```
  5  151.164.93.188
  6  srvr1-vlan20.rcsntx.sbcglobal.net [151.164.1.138]
  7  dnsr1.sbcglobal.net [68.94.156.1]

Computing statistics for 175 seconds...
            Source to Here   This Node/Link
Hop  RTT    Lost/Sent = Pct  Lost/Sent = Pct  Address
  0
savdalwks01.savilltech.net [192.16
8.1.190]
                                0/ 100 =  0%   |
  1    2ms     0/ 100 =  0%     0/ 100 =  0%  192.168.1.1
                                0/ 100 =  0%   |
  2    2ms     0/ 100 =  0%     0/ 100 =  0%  192.168.0.1
                                0/ 100 =  0i%   |
  3   13ms     0/ 100 =  0%     0/ 100 =  0%  bras23-
10.rcsntx.sbcglobal.net [15
1.164.182.7]
                                0/ 100 =  0%   |
  4  ---     100/ 100 =100%   100/ 100 =100%  dist1-
vlan130.rcsntx.sbcglobal.net
 [151.164.162.130]
                                0/ 100 =  0%   |
  5  ---     100/ 100 =100%   100/ 100 =100%  151.164.93.188
                                0/ 100 =  0%   |
  6   11ms    52/ 100 = 52%    52/ 100 = 52%  srvr1-
vlan20.rcsntx.sbcglobal.net
[151.164.1.138]
                                0/ 100 =  0%   |
  7   11ms     0/ 100 =  0%     0/ 100 =  0%  dnsr1.
sbcglobal.net [68.94.156.1]


Trace complete.
```

In this trace, you can see that several of the routers (hops 4 and 5) had ICMP echo disabled because no pings were responded to.

At a graphical level, the Windows Help and Support (Start, Help and Support) gives you step-by-step guides to many network issues. A useful new feature of Windows Server 2008 (and Vista) is the Network and Sharing Center, which is available via the Control Panel or by right-clicking the system tray icon (see Figure 6-24). Right-clicking the system tray icon also gives instant access to Diagnose and Repair, which starts an instant check and remediation of the network.

The Network and Sharing Center shows the connectivity of the network and if Internet is available. More detailed information about the connections is available by clicking the View Status link, which shows the state of both IPv4 and IPv6, the duration of the link, and the link speed. Expand the basic network map by clicking View Full Map. By default this is disabled on domain networks because the new Link Layer Topology Discovery (LLTD) protocol responsible for discovering information about a network is disabled when a Vista machine is part of a domain. It is only enabled when the network is designated as Home and not Work or Public. If you try to select the View Full Map from the Network and Sharing Center, a message says, "Network mapping is disabled by default on domain networks. Your network administrator can use Group Policy to enable mapping."

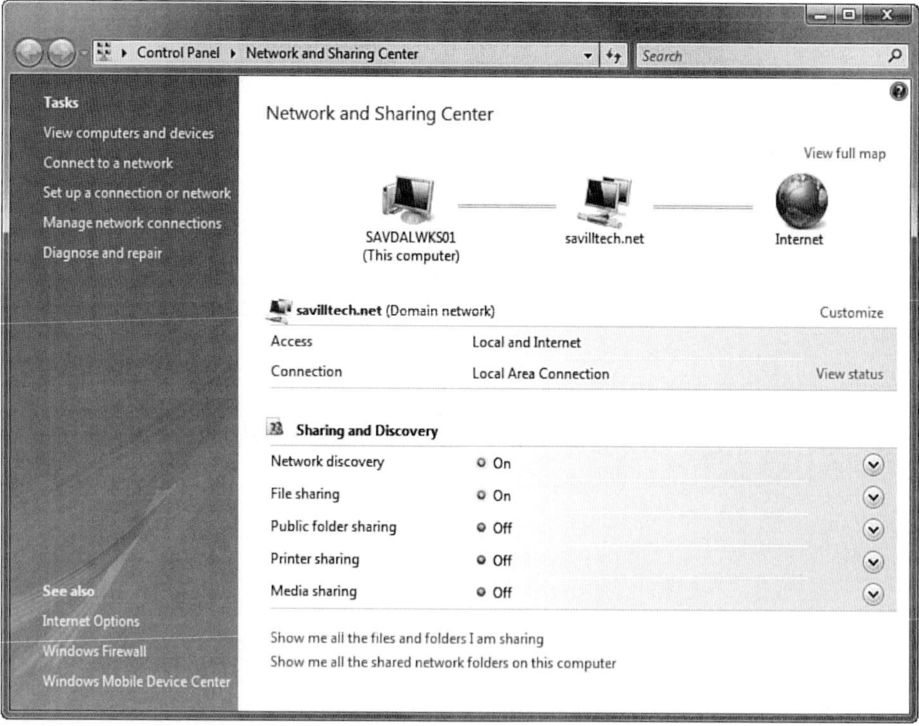

FIGURE 6-24 The Network and Sharing Center gives a single interface to manage and view nearly all aspects that relate to the network.

To enable network mapping locally on a machine, start `gpedit.msc` as an administrator and navigate to the Local Computer Policy or domain-based Group Policy Object by clicking Computer Configuration, Administrative Templates, Network, Link-Layer Topology Discovery branch. Double-click Turn on Mapper I/O (LLTDIO) Driver and set it to Enabled with the Allow Operation While in Domain check box (and optionally in a public network). Click Apply, OK, and close the Group Policy editor.

The other option, Turn on Responder (RSPNDR) Driver, enables the machine to participate and return information to LLTP requests from other machines and again can be enabled for domain environments (see Figure 6-25).

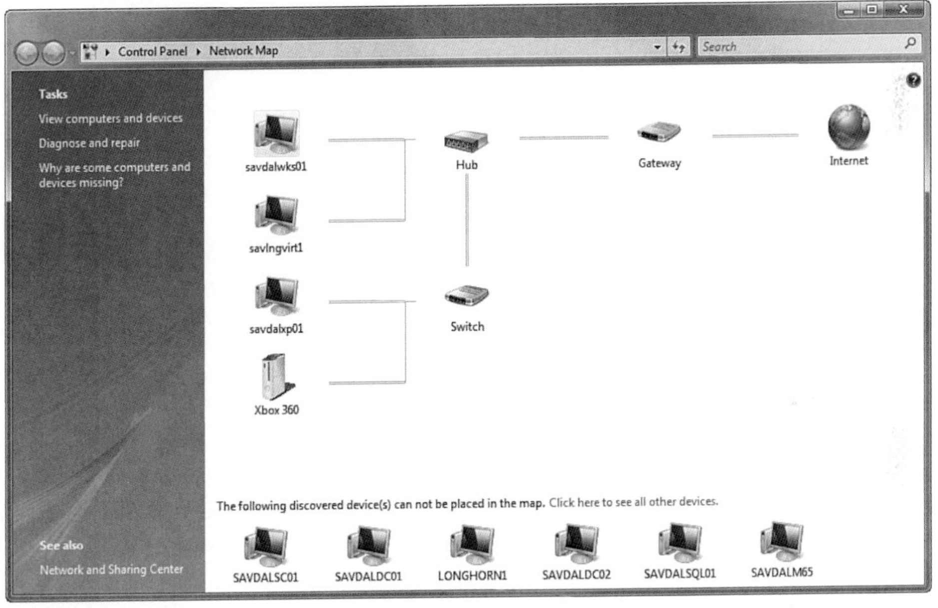

FIGURE 6-25 An example network map generated by Vista.

NOTE There is not currently an LLTP responder for any other operating systems, such as Windows 2003, which is why many computers cannot be placed in Figure 6-25.

Back to the main Network and Sharing Center interface. On the left side of the screen are common tasks, such as viewing all computers, connecting to a network, setting up a new connection or network, managing network connections (grants access to the old-style network adapter properties), and diagnosing and repairing the connection. Under the list of tasks are links to Internet Options and Windows Firewall for fast configuration.

Many of the new fault detection and resolution features are thanks to the new TCP/IP stack, which has the Network Diagnostics Framework architecture fully integrated. This includes

- Incorrect IP address
- Default gateway (router) is not available
- Incorrect default gateway
- NetBIOS over TCP/IP (NetBT) name resolution failure
- Incorrect DNS settings
- Local port is already being used
- The DHCP Client service is not running
- There is no remote listener
- The media is disconnected
- The local port is blocked
- Low on memory
- TCP extended statistics (ESTATS) support

Summary

It might seem like an entire section on IP is excessive, but as you have seen, a lot is going on. IP is behind everything you do on the network. By understanding how that underlying communication works and knowing how to check communication, you might find that application or service problems might just be a simple IP communications issue.

In the next chapter, you look at specific services that work with TCP/IP and give real power to the network. Remember the fundamentals you have covered and the troubleshooting you use with IP. They are often the first actions to troubleshoot any service problem.

CHAPTER 7

ADVANCED NETWORKING SERVICES

In Chapter 6, "TCP/IP," you looked at TCP/IP, which handles the communication of data across the network. You probably have no desire to manually configure every computer in the network with IP addresses, and having to communicate with systems by IP address doesn't work well. Fortunately, services for IP can simplify your life.

DHCP

You saw in the previous chapter that static IP addresses could be set for a network adapter along with subnet masks and gateway and domain name system (DNS) servers. Many more options can be configured for IP. In any environment with more than a couple of machines, a way to automatically configure IP properties is necessary.

The Dynamic Host Configuration Protocol (DHCP) is responsible for allocating IP addresses to machines on the network. Not every machine should have a dynamically allocated IP address, however. Any server that is accessed consistently by clients and that would be hampered if its IP address changed should have a static IP address. Some examples include

- Domain controllers
- DNS servers
- WINS servers
- DHCP servers
- SQL servers
- File/print servers
- Web servers

After DHCP is running on a network, configure clients to obtain IP addresses via DHCP and they automatically request an IP address upon startup. The address is assigned from a group of IP addresses known as a scope. Chapter 6 shows how to enable static IP addresses.

So how does this work; do we tell the client a DHCP server to ask for an address? This would not be very portable if computers move between networks and would still require manual configuration. The way DHCP works is when the client starts it sends out a broadcast on the network requesting an IP address from "someone," this is the same as the old BOOTP protocol that was used in "the old days" but is expanded in size to allow properties beyond just IP address; for example, DNS server and domain name can be configured using DHCP.

In most environments, when a client computer requests an IP address, routers do not forward these broadcasts beyond the local subnet. Thus, the router requires configuration to forward the DHCP requests to specified servers, or place DHCP servers on each subnets or use DHCP relay agents that communicate with central DHCP servers on behalf of the clients located on other subnets. Four packets are used in a DHCP communication. Figure 7-1 shows the process.

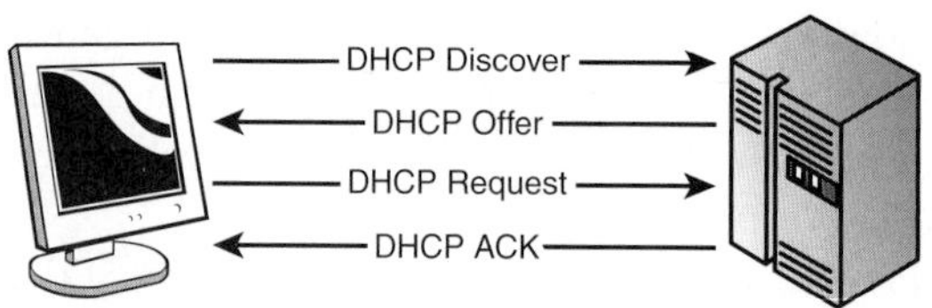

FIGURE 7-1 The four-packet structure of the DHCP process.

It is important to note that the communication is not between the two computers shown but rather broadcast over the entire subnet. If you look at a trace, you see the source address is 0.0.0.0 and the destination is 255.255.255.255, as shown in Figure 7-2.

The IP address given to the clients is not permanent and is for a specified period of time, thus the term *lease*. The actual amount of time can be configured, but do not make the lease term too short or continual lease renewal will increase network traffic. If the lease is too long, clients might be removed from the system but their IP addresses are not freed up and the DHCP server might run out of available addresses. During configuration, you are asked if the addresses are for a wired or wireless lease and the lease time is adjusted accordingly (six days for wired, eight hours for wireless). You can override this. DHCP clients attempt to renew their lease at 50% of the lease duration. If this is successful, a client could keep the same

IP address for its entire lifetime. The renewal process is a basic DHCP request from the client directly to the DHCP server that leased the address originally and then an acknowledgement (ACK) from the DHCP server that confirms the options that relate to the address.

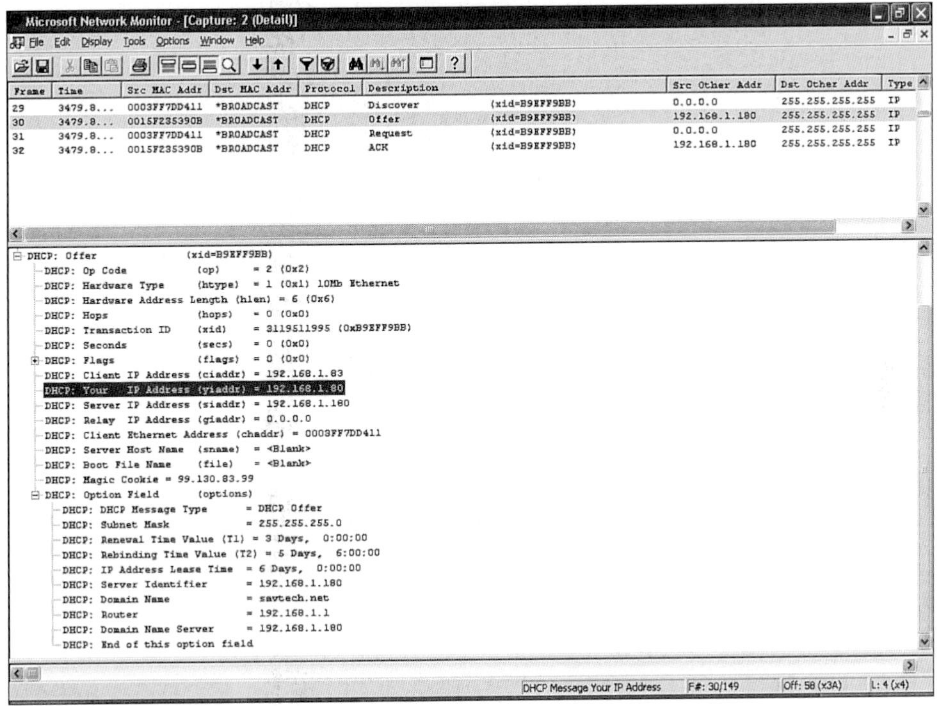

FIGURE 7-2 The second packet is the offer from the DHCP server and shows the IP address being offered along with the additional options, such as lease time, DNS servers, router, and so forth.

This process demonstrates that DHCP helps keep IP address management simple and that lease time is important. Clients receive updates to the environment when they renew their leases. If you are planning to make essential changes to the environment, reduce the lease time of the addresses perhaps a week before the change is planned. This gives clients a chance to pick up the new lease time and therefore start checking in more often. The other options are to force a renewal or simply ensure all machines are rebooted, which causes them to renew their IP address.

Renew a lease using the ipconfig command:

```
C:\>ipconfig /renew

Windows IP Configuration


Ethernet adapter Local Area Connection:

   Connection-specific DNS Suffix  . . : savtech.net
   Link-local IPv6 Address . . . . . :
fe80::a4f5:1e4d:547a:e313%8
   IPv4 Address. . . . . . . . . . . : 192.168.1.80
   Subnet Mask . . . . . . . . . . . : 255.255.255.0
   Default Gateway . . . . . . . . . : 192.168.1.1

Tunnel adapter Local Area Connection* 6:

   Media State . . . . . . . . . . . : Media disconnected
   Connection-specific DNS Suffix  . . :

Tunnel adapter Local Area Connection* 7:

   Connection-specific DNS Suffix  . . : savtech.net
   Link-local IPv6 Address . . . . . :
fe80::5efe:192.168.1.80%10
   Default Gateway . . . . . . . . . :
```

After the renewal is complete, you are shown the parameters for the connection. If you currently have a DHCP lease and want to release it, use the /release parameter to tell the client to send the DHCP server a DHCP Release message.

If a client is configured for DHCP but it is ignored and not given an IP address, it uses Automatic Private IP Addressing (APIPA) to assign itself an address in the 169.254.0.0 scope. Instead of using an address from the APIPA scope, configure an alternate configuration for when a DHCP server cannot be found. Use the Alternate Configuration tab of the IPv4 Properties dialog, as shown in Figure 7-3. This is useful in environments where you use static IP at home but use DHCP at work. You can configure the alternate configuration to match IP at your home.

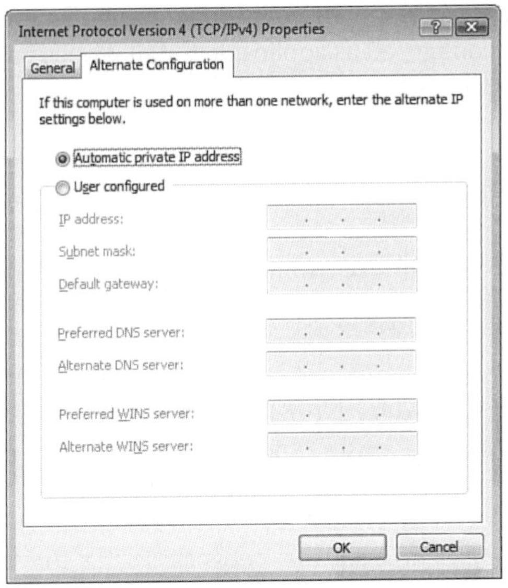

FIGURE 7-3 The alternate configuration provides a method to configure IP properties when a DHCP server cannot be found, which might better suit your environment.

However, you probably do run DHCP at home. Cable/DSL modems or Linksys routers act as DHCP servers. Cable modems normally give out addresses in the 192.168.0.0/24 subnet and Linksys uses the 192.168.1.0/24 range. If you implement DHCP via Windows Server, disable the DHCP on the Linksys (or whatever brand router you use) to keep it from clashing.

Installing and Performing DHCP Initial Configuration

The DHCP service is a role within Windows 2008 and can be installed via the Initial Configuration Tasks (ICT), which is part of the Out of Box Experience (Oobe.exe) or via the Server Manager MMC snap-in. Like nearly all of the Windows 2008 roles, basic configuration is done during the roles' installation to make it functional straight away. So before you install the DHCP role, let's quickly cover the core configurations to perform.

The IP addresses given to clients and the additional options such as DNS servers are defined as part of a scope. Each DHCP server has one or more scopes assigned, which are a range of IP addresses, a subnet mask, and the gateway (option 003). More options allow other IP-related parameters to be configured as applicable for all scopes on the server or on a per-scope basis. Some common options are

- **DNS servers (option 006)**. This is the list of DNS servers. These are normally per enterprise in most small and medium companies, so it can be set at the per-server level.
- **DNS domain name (option 015)**. The domain name used for the resolution of hostnames.
- **WINS/NBNS servers (option 044)**. A list of the Windows Internet Name Service (WINS) servers on the network in order of priority used for NetBIOS name resolution.
- **WINS/NBT node type (option 046)**. The node type for NetBIOS resolution. NetBIOS names can be resolved in two ways. They can be looked up via a WINS server to find an IP address or a broadcast can be sent over the network asking for the NetBIOS name to respond with its IP address. The node type controls how the NetBIOS resolution works as follows:
    - **B-node.** (Broadcast 0x1.) Broadcasts are used for name registration and name resolution. Depending on the gateway configuration, these packets might not be sent beyond the local subnet. B-node is not suitable for large networks. Microsoft modified the standard b-node type by performing LMHOST cache checking before broadcasting, and then checking the actual LMHOSTS file if the broadcast failed.
    - **P-node**. (Point to point 0x2.) Broadcast is never used and the machines register their names with the configured WINS server on startup. When a resolution is required, the request is sent to the WINS server. This method works well provided the WINS server is up and running. If the WINS server fails, resolution is not possible.
    - **M-node**. (Mixed 0x4.) This mode uses b-node first and if that fails to resolve, p-node is used. This is not the best solution as it still uses broadcasts, initially wasting time and network resources.
    - **H-node**. (Hybrid 0x8.) This mode uses p-node first and if that fails to resolve, b-node is used. Therefore broadcast is tried only if the WINS lookup failed (which is not likely). This is normally the best method to use. This is the default mode.

Now that you understand the basic configuration options, let's get DHCP installed and a scope created.

1. Select the Add Roles link within the Roles section of the tool (either ICT or Server Manager), as shown in Figure 7-4.

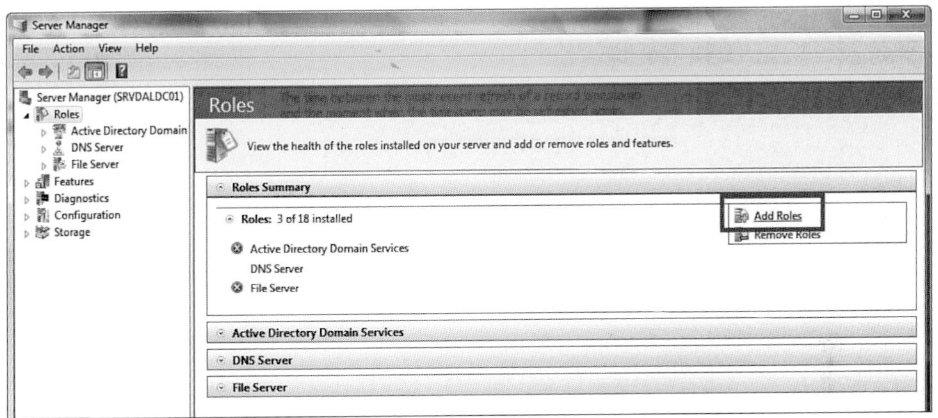

FIGURE 7-4 The Add Roles option is also available via the ICT environment.

2. The Add Roles wizard is displayed and gives warnings that you should ensure the Administrator has a strong password, a static IP address, and the latest updates. Click Next
3. A list of all roles is displayed. Select DHCP Server and click Next (see Figure 7-5).
4. The wizard now guides you through the basic configuration of DHCP with seven steps. Click Next.

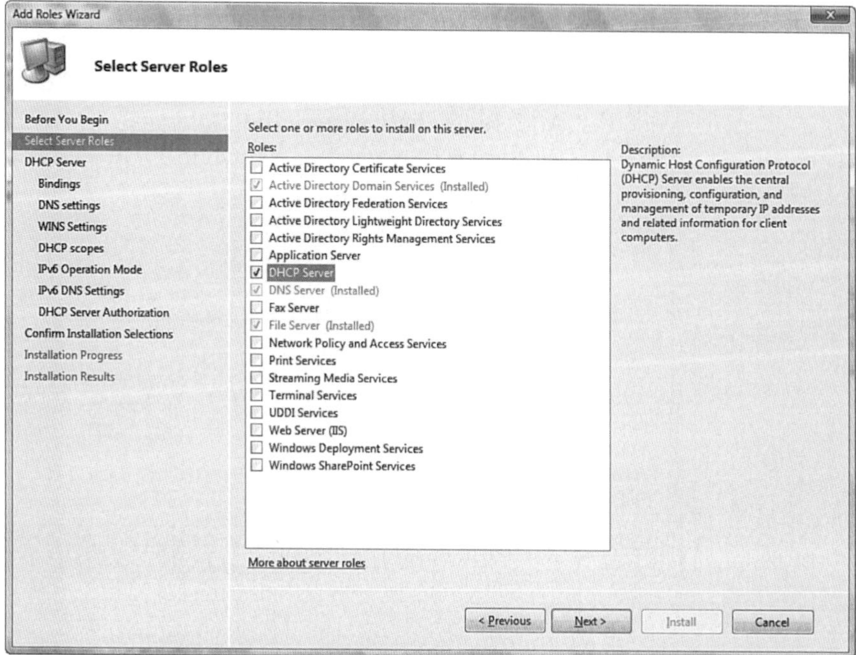

FIGURE 7-5 The role-based method is far more attractive than the old style Add/Remove Windows Components in previous versions.

5. The first step is determining which network connections are bound for the DHCP server. All connections with a static IP address are listed. Confirm that the bindings are correct and click Next (see Figure 7-6).
6. The DNS information that is given to clients, including the DNS domain of the client parent, the primary DNS server, and the secondary DNS server (if available), is configured. Click Next (see Figure 7-7). This configuration is set at the global level and so applies to all scopes created on the DHCP server.

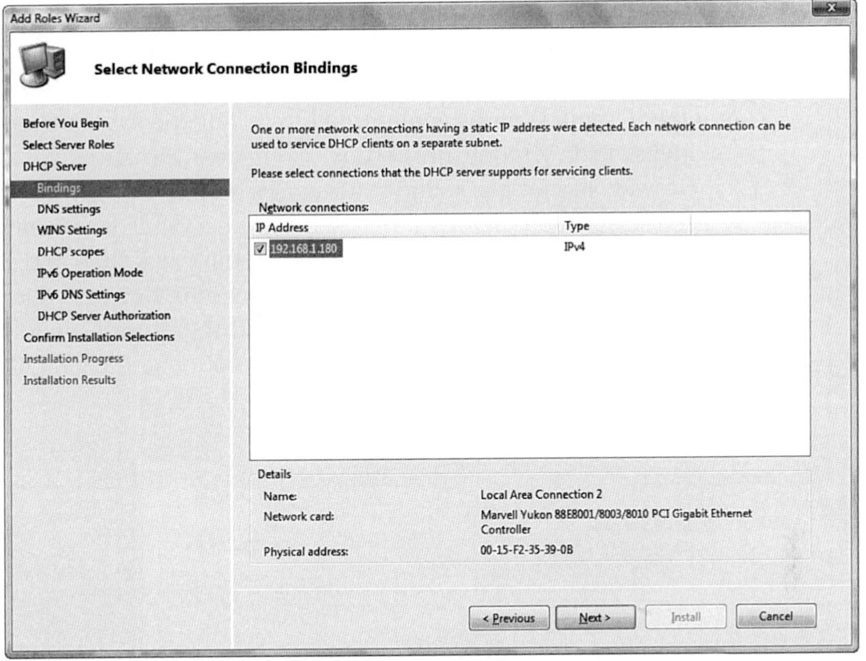

Figure 7-6 Selecting the network connections with which the DHCP server provides service.

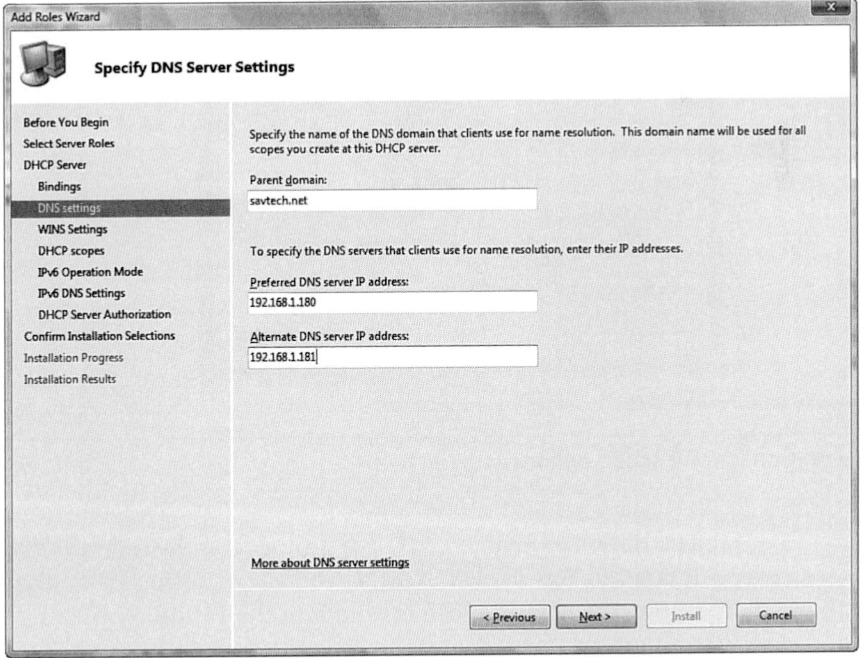

Figure 7-7 Configuring the DNS domain and servers for the DHCP server.

7. The next screen configures WINS (if required). If any of your applications still use NetBIOS names, configure the WINS servers. Click Next.
8. DHCP scopes can be configured by clicking the Add button, which opens up the scope properties. Configure the name, its default gateway, subnet mask, and starting and ending IP address. You can also select the type of subnet (see Figure 7-8). If it's wireless, this generally assumes devices are connected for less time and so have a lease of only eight hours. Wired devices are normally more permanent fixtures in the environment and therefore have a lease of six days. Check the Activate the Scope option and click OK. Click Next after scopes have been defined.

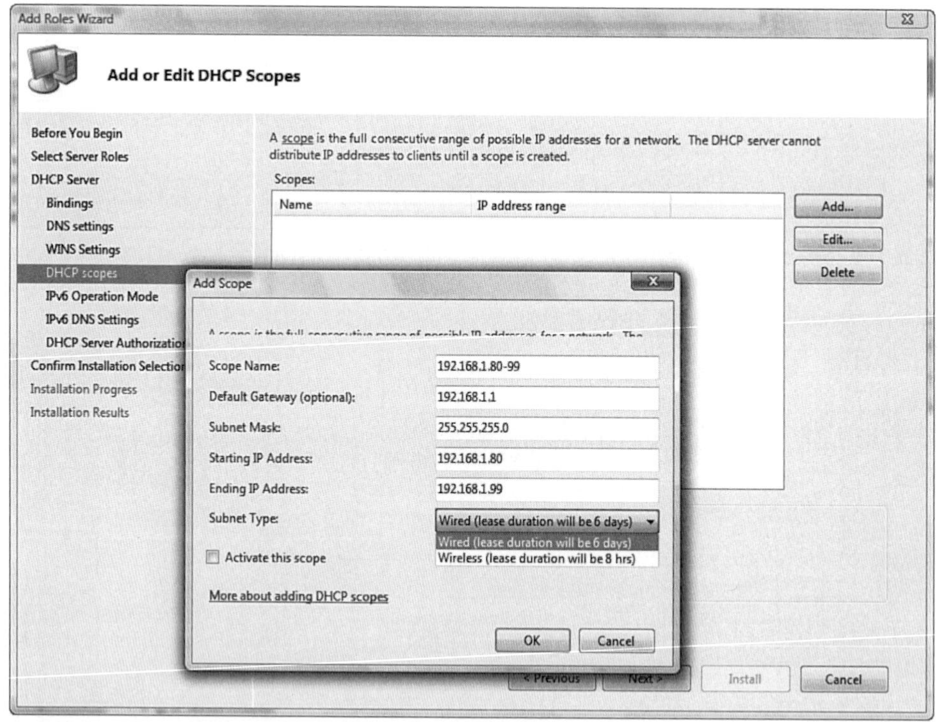

FIGURE 7-8 Configuring scope options.

9. The option to enable DHCPv6 protocol on the server is displayed. It is set to Yes, so click Next. If you are not using IPv6, disable this setting for now. You can enable it in the future.

10. The DNS settings for IPv6 DNS must be configured if you selected to enable DHCPv6. After the configuration is done, click Next.
11. Finally, the DHCP server must be authorized with the current credentials or an alternate set of credentials. You can also decide to skip the authorization. Make a choice and click Next (see Figure 7-9).

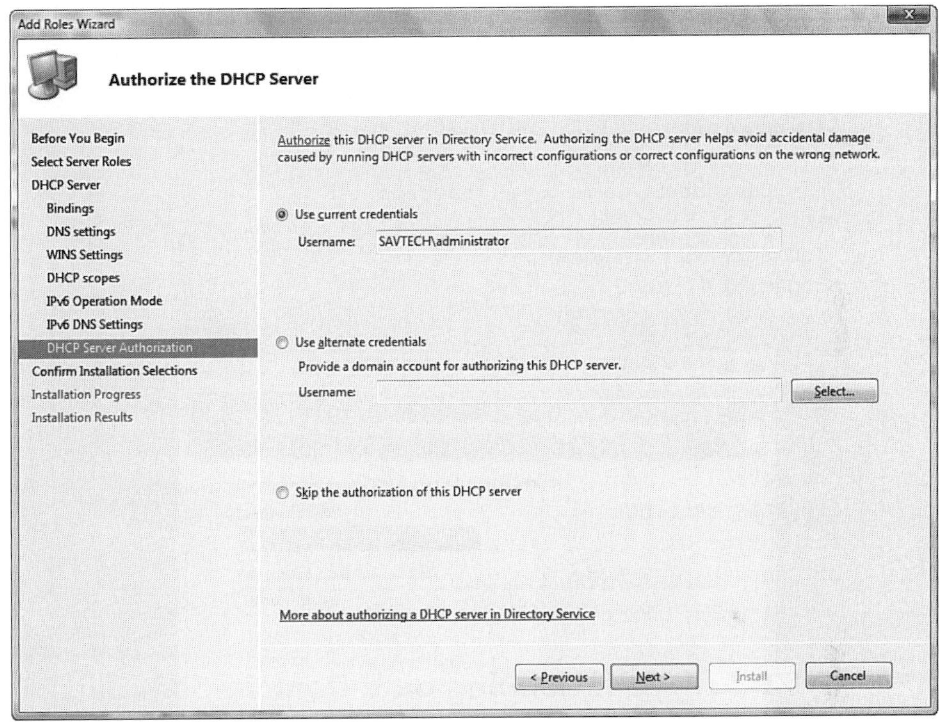

FIGURE 7-9 Selecting credentials for authorizing a DHCP server.

12. A summary of the configuration is displayed, which can be output to an HTML file and opened in Internet Explorer (see Figure 7-10). Click Install to start the DHCP installation. After the install is complete, a summary is displayed. Click Close.

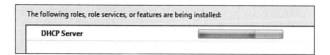

The following roles, role services, or features are being installed:

DHCP Server

FIGURE 7-10 DHCP server role installation progress display.

The following is an example of the output given in the summary section when creating a new scope:

```
DHCP Server
NIC bindings     192.168.1.180 (IPv4)
IPv4 DNS settings
     Dns parent domain     savtech.net
DNS servers     192.168.1.180, 192.168.1.181
WINS Servers     None
Scopes
Name     192.168.1.80-99
Default gateway     192.168.1.1
Subnet mask     255.255.255.0
IP address range     192.168.1.80 - 192.168.1.99
Subnet type     Wired (lease duration will be 6 days)
Activated     Yes
IPv6 DNS settings
Dns parent domain     savtech.net
DNS servers     None
```

DHCP Actions If Running on a Domain Controller

If DHCP is enabled on a domain controller, credentials from the DHCP service should be configured for Dynamic DNS registrations using the `netsh dhcp server set dnscredentials` command. Why? The DHCP service runs under the local system account, which is the computer account of the server. If the DHCP server is a domain controller, the computer account has full control over all objects in the Active Directory (AD), including the DNS objects. This means an early DHCP client might use the domain controller's account to overwrite DNS entries that it should not. By configuring the `dnscredentials`, an alternate account with fewer privileges can be configured to handle the DNS entries. The account specified should be a normal user account with no expiry or restrictions.

To set the user account that the DHCP Server service uses for DNS registrations, use the following command:

```
netsh dhcp server set dnscredentials
➥ <user name> <domain name> <password>
```

Use an asterisk (*) in place of the password variable, which prompts the user to type a password; for example:

```
C:\ >netsh dhcp server set dnscredentials !dnscredacct savtech *

Enter the password:

Command completed successfully.
```

After configuring the `dnscredentials`, restart the DHCP Server service for these changes to take effect. Right-click on the server within the DHCP MMC snap-in and select Restart from the All Tasks menu. Or, from the command prompt:

```
C:\Users\Administrator>net stop dhcpserver
The DHCP Server service is stopping.
The DHCP Server service was stopped successfully.


C:\Users\Administrator>net start dhcpserver
The DHCP Server service is starting...
The DHCP Server service was started successfully.
```

To delete the user account that the DHCP Server service uses for DNS registrations, use the following command (restart DHCP after this change):

```
netsh dhcp server delete dnscredentials dhcpfullforce
```

To check the account that is being used, use the `show` option, for example:

```
C:\ >netsh dhcp server show dnscredentials

The credentials used for DNS Dynamic registrations:
        User Name  : !dnscredacct
        Domain     : savtech
```

If the account you have specified has the password that expires (which is best practice for security purposes), remember to update the password in the DHCP service for the `dnscredentials` by rerunning the `netsh set dnscredentials` command. You can also set these credentials via the IPv4 Properties, Advanced tab, and Credentials button (see Figure 7-11).

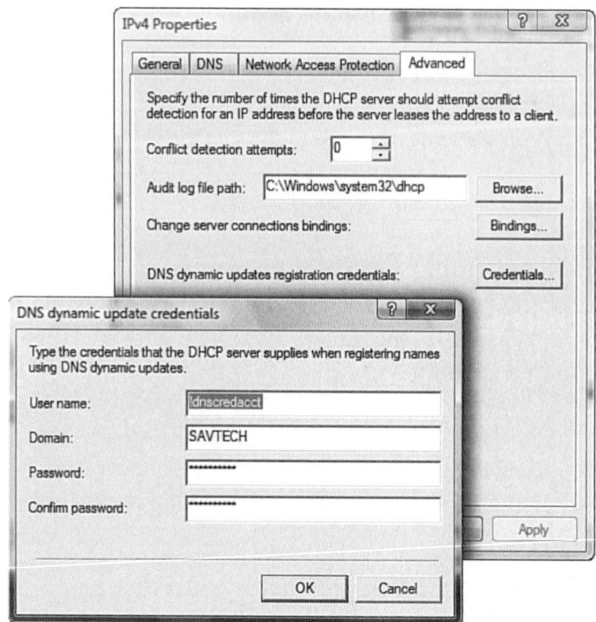

FIGURE 7-11 This gives the same access as the command line to the DNS credential account.

DHCP Server Activation

To secure your network and stop potential rogue servers from giving out IP addresses, a Windows 2000, 2003, and 2008 server must be authorized in the AD before it can lease IP addresses. Only domain controllers or member servers can be authorized. If you have DHCP servers that are not part of the domain, they can be used only on subnets where no AD-authorized DHCP servers exist. If a stand-alone DHCP server detects an AD-authorized DHCP server on its subnet, it stops its DHCP service. This only applies to Microsoft-based DHCP servers. A Linux-based DHCP server probably doesn't care what a Microsoft server tells it to do.

DHCP servers are authorized via the DHCP MMC snap-in's root context menu. Select Manage Authorized Servers, as shown in Figure 7-12.

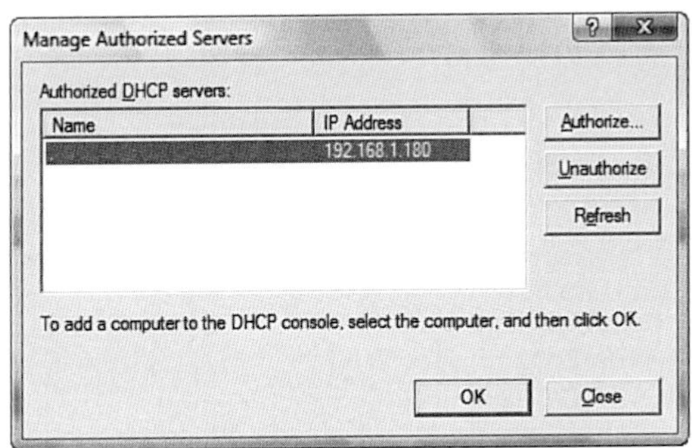

FIGURE 7-12 From this simple dialog, you can quickly authorize or unauthorize other servers.

DHCP Administration

Let's jump back a step. DHCP is managed via the DHCP MMC snap-in that has a shortcut in the Administrative Tools. When opened, the local server is loaded in the console. Other servers can be added by right-clicking on the DHCP root and selecting Add Server. By creating a console with all your DHCP servers, you can quickly get an overview and manage your entire environment from a central location without having to visit each DHCP server separately.

Setting Scope Options

Under each server is an IPv4 and IPv6 leaf that corresponds to the two DHCP protocols supported. If you created an IPv4/IPv6 scope during installation, it is listed under the IPv4/IPv6 branch. You also see a Server Options leaf. Although options can be configured for the scope, some are common for the entire enterprise. It makes no sense to keep defining these options for each scope you create. Instead, they can be set for any scope given from the server under the Server Options. For example, items like DNS Servers and Domain Name are most likely common to all scopes from the server and so you'll define them under the Server Options. Follow these steps:

1. Right-click Server Options and select Configure Options (see Figure 7-13).

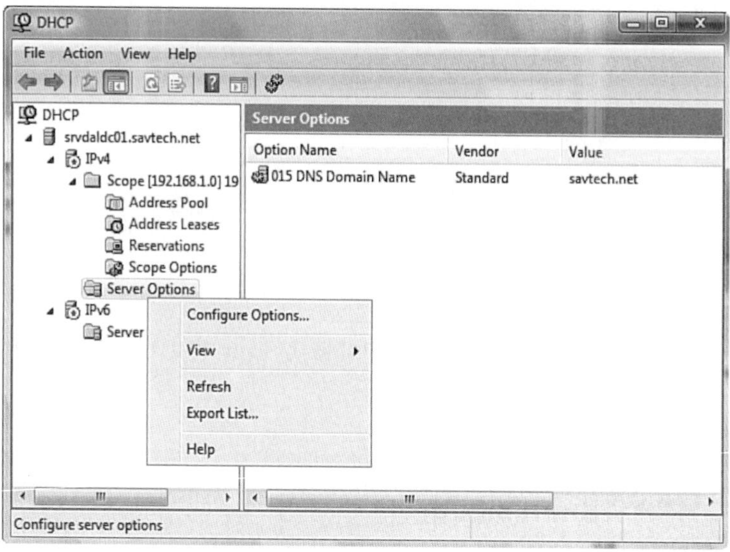

Figure 7-13 Notice the options at a scope level. Domain Name is already configured at the server level.

2. A list of options is displayed (for example, 006 for the DNS Server). Check the box to enable and enter the IP addresses of the DNS servers or type in the fully qualified domain name of the server. Click Resolve, and then click Add (see Figure 7-14).

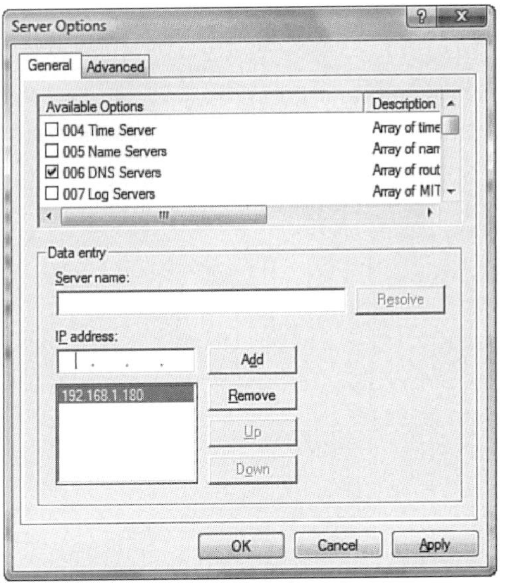

FIGURE 7-14 Setting DHCP server options.

3. The Advanced tab allows you to view specific classes of options, standard DHCP options, and Microsoft-specific ones. After all options are configured, click OK.

After the server options are configured, remove them from a scope-specific option. If a setting is defined at both the scope and server level, the more specific scope option takes precedence and the server option is ignored (they are not combined). If you forget to remove the scope option and change the server option, your new server options are ignored. In Figure 7-15, notice that both scope options and server options are displayed. This is done to help you avoid thinking a setting is not defined and duplicating a setting at the scope level.

To delete an option, just select Delete from its context menu and click OK.

Managing Scopes

Let's look at the rest of the capabilities and management tasks. If you right-click the main scope and select Display Statistics, you get a quick display of the usage of the scope, including the total number of addresses, the number in use, and the number available (see Figure 7-16).

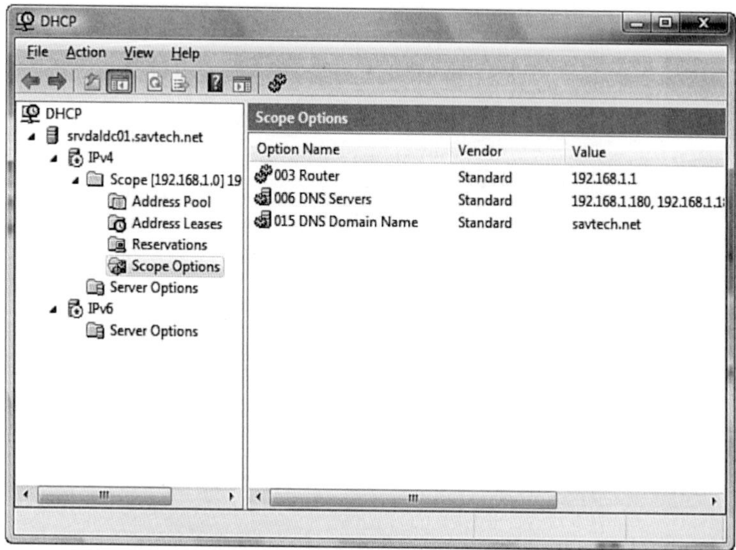

FIGURE 7-15 The options you defined for the server option have a picture with a server in the icon (006 and 015). The scope-specific router option has two cogs (003).

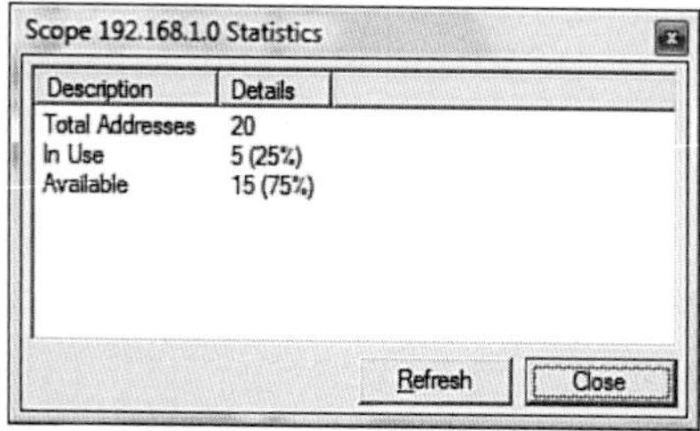

FIGURE 7-16 This gives a useful quick view of the state of the DHCP and lets you know if you need to add more addresses if you are getting near the limit.

A reconcile option is used to check for inconsistencies between the detailed IP and the quick summary information stored in the DHCP database. Clicking Reconcile compares these two sets of data and any differences are fixed.

The Properties context menu option brings up the main configuration of the scope with four tabs (see Figure 7-17).

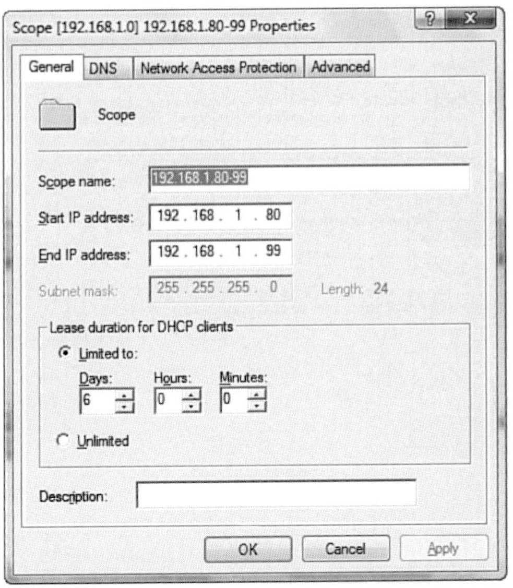

FIGURE 7-17 The main General tab allows you to change the start and end of the DHCP lease and the lease duration.

The General tab allows configuration of IP addresses given to clients and the lease time. The DNS tab controls dynamic update for DHCP clients (see Figure 7-18). Dynamic DNS allows clients to register their hostname to IP address mappings. By default, the DHCP server registers the pointer (PTR) record on behalf of the computer. The PTR record is of the IP address pointing to the hostname (used by a reverse lookup). The host (A) record (used by the normal lookup record) is dynamically updated to the client. This is the default only because this is what the client computers ask the DHCP server to do; for example, Windows 2000 or later computers request the DHCP server to register the PTR record on their behalf.

This behavior can be changed so that the DHCP server also registers the host records or only registers them for clients that don't understand dynamic update, such as Windows NT 4.0 clients. How does the DHCP server know if the client understands dynamic update? Dynamic DNS–aware DHCP clients send option 81 to the DHCP server as part of the DHCP request. This tells the DHCP server how it wants record registering handled. A trace of the DNS update request is shown in Figure 7-19.

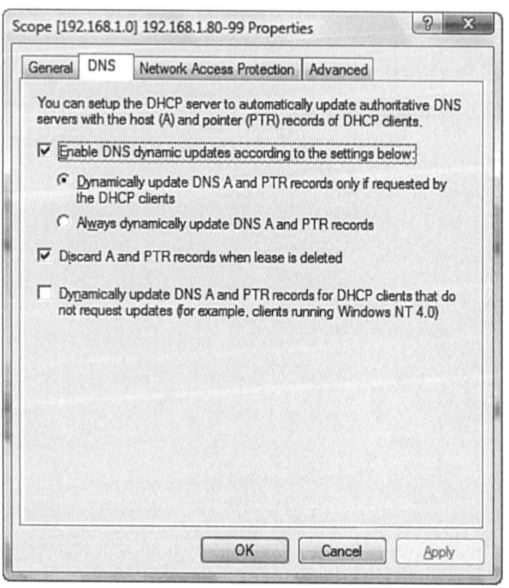

FIGURE 7-18 The default is to enable DNS Dynamic Update but only to register A (host) and PTR records if requested by the clients. Windows 2000 and above clients opt to let the DHCP server register the PTR and the client registers the host record.

```
DHCP: Server IP Address (siaddr) = 0.0.0.0
DHCP: Relay  IP Address (giaddr) = 0.0.0.0
DHCP: Client Ethernet Address (chaddr) = 0003FF7DD411
DHCP: Server Host Name  (sname)  = <Blank>
DHCP: Boot File Name    (file)   = <Blank>
DHCP: Magic Cookie = 99.130.83.99
DHCP: Option Field       (options)
  DHCP: DHCP Message Type       = DHCP Request
  DHCP: Client-identifier       = (Type: 1) 00 03 ff 7d d4 11
  DHCP: Host Name               = John-PC
  DHCP: Dynamic DNS updates     = (Length: 22) 00 00 00 4a 6f 68 6e 2d 50 43 2e 73 61 76 74 65 ...
  DHCP: Client Class information = (Length: 8) 4d 53 46 54 20 35 2e 30
  DHCP: Parameter Request List = (Length: 12) 01 0f 03 06 2c 2e 2f 1f 21 79 f9 2b
  DHCP: End of this option field
```

FIGURE 7-19 The packet responsible for DNS updates.

The third tab is the Network Access Protection tab, covered in Chapter 8, "Remote Access and Securing and Optimizing the Network." Just remember that it's here and that it is used to define a profile needed to get an address.

The Advanced tab configures which clients are supported by the DHCP server beyond the default DHCP protocol, such as using Bootstrap Protocol (BOOTP) (see Figure 7-20). If you enable BOOTP support, you can configure separate lease duration.

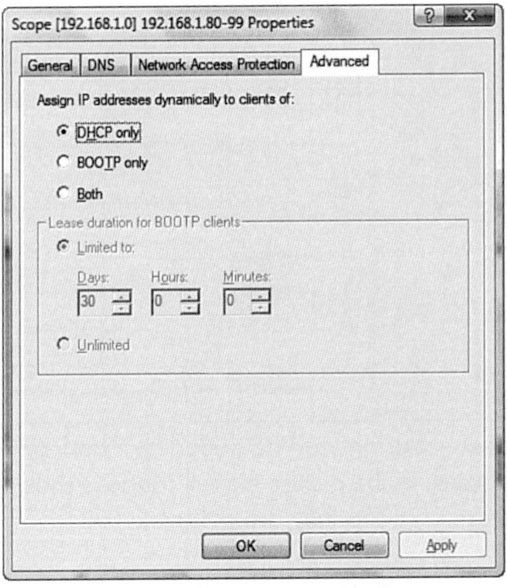

FIGURE 7-20 Advanced scope options.

The scope has four child items: Address Pool, Address Leases, Reservations, and Scope Options (scope-specific versions of the Server Options).

The Address Pool leaf shows the addresses that are part of the lease. Add an Exclusion Range (right-click on Address Pool and select New Exclusions Range). Exclusions are addresses that fall within the IP address range of the scope but that you don't want to give out to clients, such as a server's IP address (see Figure 7-21).

The Address Leases leaf shows the leases that have been given, their status, and when the lease expires (see Figure 7-22). If you know a computer no longer requires the lease, right-click on a particular lease and select Delete from its context menu. A computer icon means it's an active lease, an icon with an I in a circle means it's an expired lease, and an icon with a pen over it means it has a DNS dynamic update pending. This update is whatever updates for which the DHCP server is responsible. By default, a DHCP server is just responsible for the PTR records. If you have the pen icon, your DNS server might not have a reverse lookup zone defined for the subnet so the DHCP server cannot write the entries.

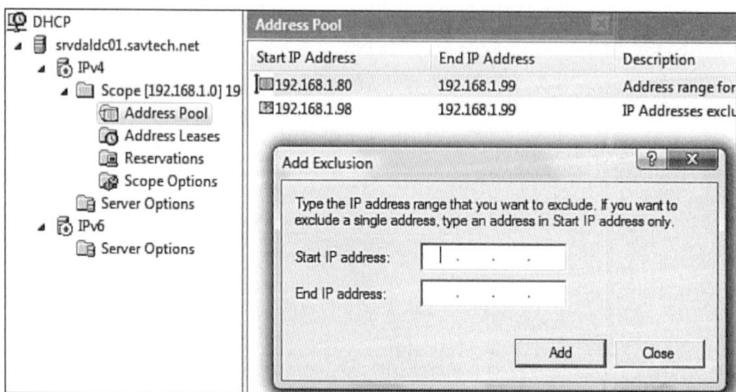

FIGURE 7-21 Single address exclusions can be added by entering the same address for both the start and end. Notice in the picture the full range is shown first and then the exclusions have a red cross, showing they are not available.

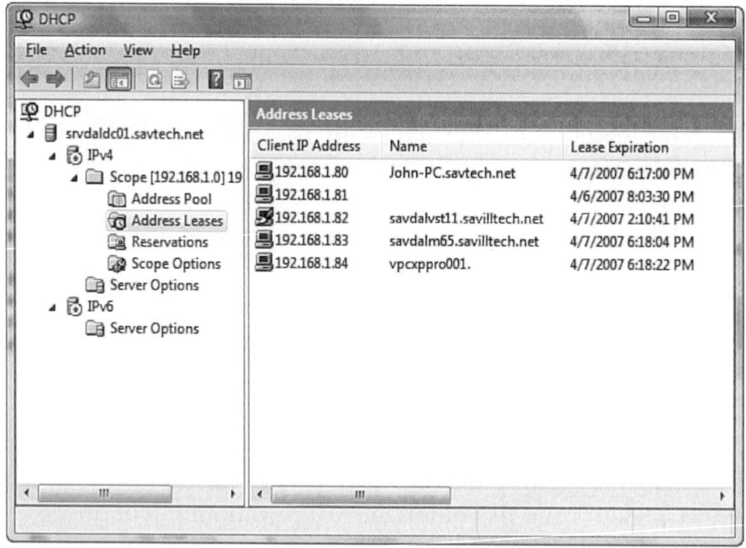

FIGURE 7-22 An easy view of the current leases.

The Reservations leaf is where you configure an IP address from the scope to be given to a particular machine (see Figure 7-23). To associate the IP address with a machine, give the MAC address of the client who receives the IP address. This chapter talked earlier about certain servers needing a static IP address. It might be possible to reserve IP addresses for certain machines so they also receive the same IP address, such as your SQL servers. You just need to ensure the services support receiving IP configuration via DHCP.

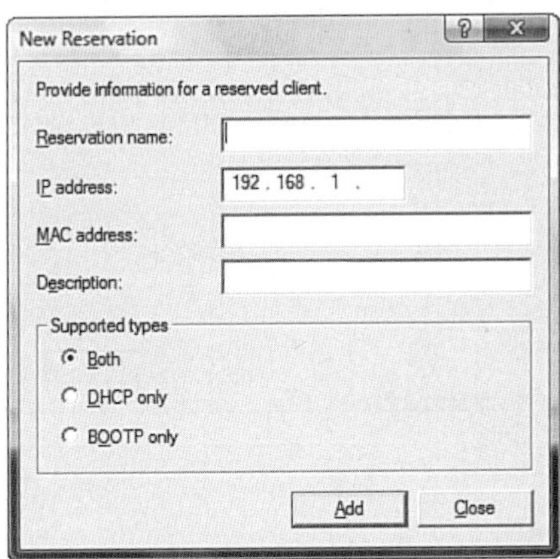

Figure 7-23 Configure an IP address to a client with a specific MAC address. This means you know the IP address the client can be contacted with, but you still get the advantages of IP configuration from the DHCP server, such as changing the DNS and WINS configuration.

Creating a New Scope

To create new scopes on a server, right-click on IPv4, select New Scope from the displayed context menu, and follow the prompts, which are the same as the ones during the installation of the DHCP server:

1. Click Next at the New Scope wizard screen.
2. Enter a name for the scope and a description.
3. Enter the starting address and the ending address for the scope along with the subnet mask (see Figure 7-24).
4. An Exclusions screen is displayed to add any exclusions.
5. The duration of the lease is requested, which can be configured in a combination of days, hours, or minutes (see Figure 7-25).

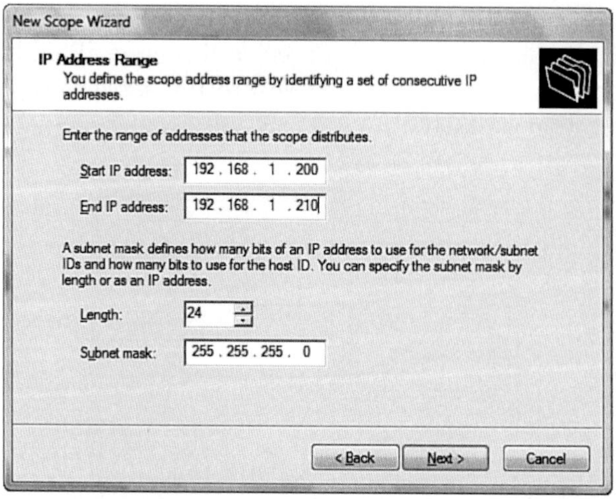

FIGURE 7-24 Creating a new scope.

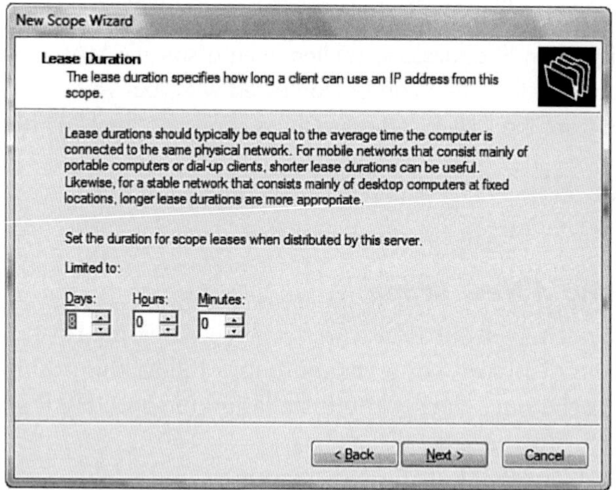

FIGURE 7-25 Setting lease duration.

6. Configure scope options and if selected, the gateway, DNS, and WINS options.
7. Select to enable or disable the scope.
8. Click Finish to create.

If you want to stop leasing addresses from a scope but do not want to delete it, right-click on the scope and select Deactivate. It now displays with a red down arrow. If you want to enable it, right-click it again and select Activate.

Backing Up a Scope

Back up the state of the DHCP service by right-clicking on the server and selecting Backup, which stores information about all scopes, leases, settings, and so forth. By default, a backup is made every 60 minutes to the %systemroot%\system32\dhcp\backup folder. The Restore option is a good way to migrate a DHCP scope if you plan to move to a new DHCP server. You cannot just add a new DHCP server, turn off the scope on the old server, and re-create it on the new server because active leases would clash with those given out by the new server (unless you turned on the conflict detection). A better approach is to back up the scope on the original server, stop the DHCP service, copy the backup to the new server, and restore the backup to the new server.

Also back up from the command line via `netsh.exe` using the export and import commands. For example:

```
C:\temp>netsh
netsh>dhcp server v4
netsh dhcp server v4>export c:\temp\tempdb all

Command completed successfully.
netsh dhcp server v4>dhcp server v6
netsh dhcp server v6>export c:\temp\tempdbv6 all

Command completed successfully.
```

If you only wanted to export specific scopes, add the name of the scope to the export command instead of the `all` parameter; for example, `export <file> <scope>`. The import format is the same: `import <file> all` or `import <file> <scope>`.

DHCPv6

New to Windows Server 2008 is the IPv6 node item under the DHCP server in the navigation pane, which allows for IPv6 DHCPv6 functionality. The original purpose for DHCP was to give out IP addresses, but IPv6 takes care of this automatically. DHCPv6 might still be useful for configuring options such as DNS servers and setting an address range to use, which allows subnet-specific, routable IPv6 address space usage.

There are two modes for DHCPv6, stateless and stateful. In stateless mode, the host uses DHCP just to find configuration options and the IPv6 address used is assigned elsewhere. In stateful mode, the host uses DHCP for both configuration and address assignment. The mode of the host is based on a router advertisement the host receives in response to a router solicitation and two flags in the returned advertisement, namely flags M and O. If both flags are set to 1, the host uses stateful mode; if only O (options) is set, stateless mode is used although options such as DNS are configured via the DHCP.

DHCPv6 does not work like DHCPv4. Instead of a broadcast, the DHCPv6 client sends a multicast Solicit message to locate a DHCPv6 server. DHCPv6 servers respond with an advertisement of a lease, the client picks one and makes a request, the server sends a reply, and the lease is complete. UDP port 547 is used by DHCPv6 servers.

Just like with a new IPv4 scope, right-click on IPv6, select New Scope, and enter a name and description. Instead of a start and end range, you are asked for a 64-bit prefix and a preference (see Figure 7-26). The preference is between 0 and 255. If a client receives multiple DHCP offers, the offer from the higher preference server is used (255 is the highest).

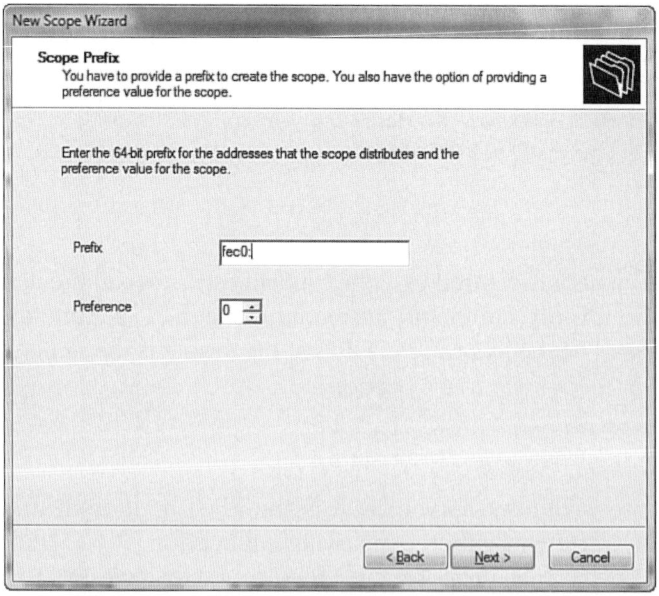

FIGURE 7-26 Enter the prefix for the 64-bit scope and a preference value.

Like an IPv4 scope, exclusions can be configured by specifying the address ranges to exclude (see Figure 7-27). You must enter all bytes for the interface ID, for example 0:0:0:10 and not just 10. Next, the lease time must be configured for both Identity Association for Non-Temporary Addresses (IANA) and Identity Association for Temporary Addresses (IATA), which are settings on the client informing the server of the type of lease it requires. As usual, you can activate the scope immediately.

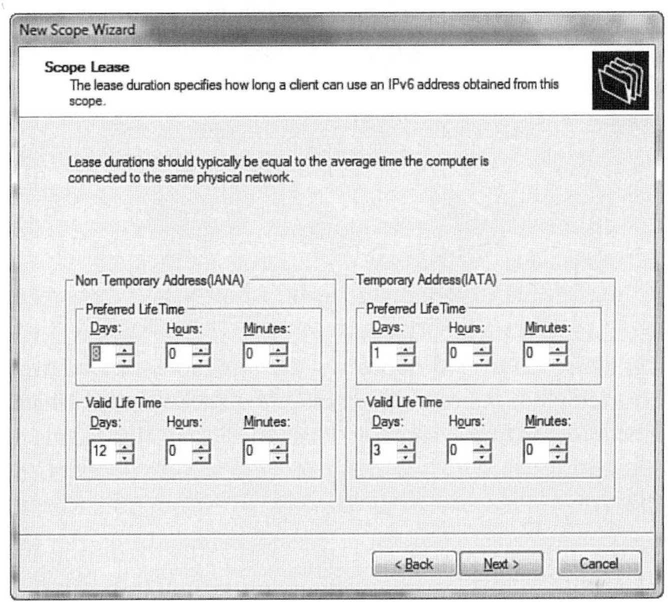

FIGURE 7-27 Configuring lease times for the IPv6 scope.

There are leases, exclusions, reservations, scope options, and server-specific options. DHCPv6 configuration and management is the same as for IPv4—you just have bigger addresses and a slightly more complicated lease time configuration.

DHCP High Availability

So far, so good. However, there is a catch. For fault tolerance reasons it is common to have multiple DHCP servers with scopes broken up using the 80/20 rule. This means that two DHCP servers are configured to assign addresses for the same subnet. This leads to an obvious problem: If you have two DHCP servers on the same subnet, they might both lease the same IP address to different machines, causing a conflict on the network. To avoid this, separate exclusions are set on each of the DHCP scopes with one of the servers leasing 80% of the available addresses, the other leasing the remaining 20%. You get to exclusions in a second. Figure 7-28 shows an example of this configuration.

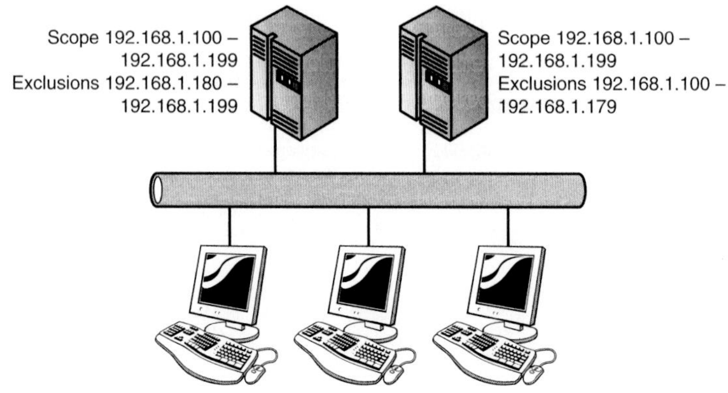

FIGURE 7-28 Out of the scope of 100 addresses, the first server has 80 available to lease and the other server only has the other 20 (look at the exclusions; anything not in the exclusion is available for the DHCP server to lease to clients). This means no overlap and no conflict.

If the primary server (the one with 80%) is not available, the other server is able to service some clients until the other server can be brought back into the environment. How do you prevent clients from automatically leasing from the second server? Place the primary DHCP server on the subnet with the clients it is leasing to and the spare DHCP server on a separate server. The router between the subnets should be configured to forward BOOTP/DHCP requests. This means when a client requests an address, the DHCP server on the local subnet would service it first. To ensure the local DHCP server always responds first, set a delay on the router that is acting as a DHCP relay agent to a value that ensures the local DHCP server always responds first. The second DHCP server has 80% of the addresses for its local subnet and the primary has 20% of its subnet addresses (thus each server giving the other redundancy).

Remember, DHCP gives out a lease to a client for a set amount of time. If the DHCP server stops working, clients are not immediately affected. They still have their lease that they can continue to use. They need to contact the DHCP server only when the lease is due for renewal (beginning at 50% of the lease length), when the machine restarts, or when a renewal is manually forced (`ipconfig /renew`). The DHCP client attempts to directly contact the DHCP server that leased it the address, but if it is not available, the client broadcasts to the network.

Other options exist for DHCP redundancy. If you right-click the IPv4 leaf of the DHCP snap-in and access its Properties, you get options that apply to all IPv4 scopes, including options of when to update stats, DHCP audit logging options, and DNS settings. The Advanced tab has a Conflict Detection Attempts option, set to 0 (see Figure 7-29). This number can be between 0 and 6 and is how many times a DHCP server performs a `ping` to the address before leasing to a client.

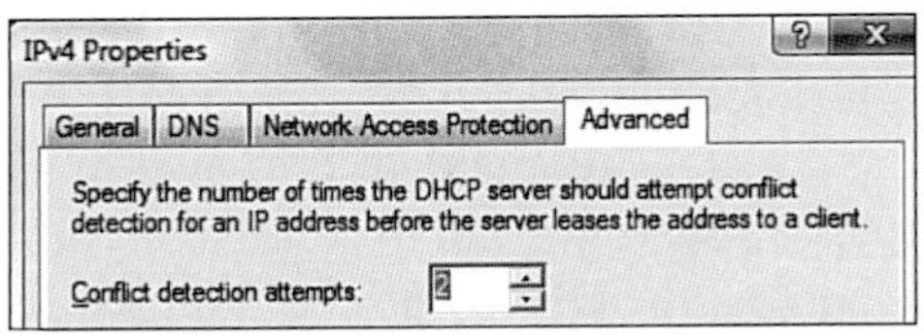

FIGURE 7-29 Each attempt is a ping and, therefore, a one second increase in time before the IP address is given. Two is the maximum recommended setting to avoid long delays to the client.

If you enable conflict detection, you could define the entire scope of DHCP to another server in addition to the primary (forgetting about the 80/20 split) but leave it disabled. In the event the primary DHCP server becomes unavailable, simply enable the scope on the second server, and it checks if the address is in use before giving it to the client. This approach does introduce a slight delay to clients getting addresses, but it ensures a DHCP server failure is detected so you can bring up the new server.

DHCP Secure DNS Update

The option of secure update dynamic entries (which is covered in detail in the "Domain Name System" section) can pose a problem. With secure update, the computer that registers a new resource record becomes its owner and only the owner can update it. The DHCP server registers records on behalf of the clients, so the DHCP server is the owner of the records. Thus, when the second DHCP server tries to update a client resource record, it fails because it is not the owner of the record.

To resolve this problem, a group exists called the DnsUpdateProxy Security group. Any resource record created by a member of this group does not have any security or owner applied to it. This means if you place your DHCP servers in this group, the records created by them can be updated by other DHCP servers. The first time a computer modifies a record that is not a member of the DnsUpdateProxy, it becomes the owner. This becomes important when upgrading your legacy computers to the latest client, allowing the client to start registering its own DNS records.

As with everything else so far, the DnsUpdateProxy group introduces a problem if you are running DHCP on your domain controllers. If a domain controller is in the DnsUpdateProxy group (which is required if it was one of a number of DHCP servers), all the records it creates are open, including all of its service records registered by the NETLOGON service. They could potentially be modified by a hostile on the network.

It is therefore recommended to not run DHCP on a domain controller when dynamic updates are enabled. However, many small- and medium-sized companies do not have the necessary physical infrastructure to warrant separate servers for DHCP. So the minimal risk is accepted or, more commonly, DHCP scopes are not split over multiple DHCP servers. The security of domain controllers should be priority number one.

Domain Name System

Just as remembering a name is easier than remembering a Social Security number, server names are easier to remember than IP addresses, especially when naming conventions are used. A naming convention is simply a standard you apply when you name servers and workstations. An example of a convention might be

- Three characters refer to the name of the company.
- Three characters are for the location.
- Two characters are for the type of server.
- Three characters identify the unique instance of the server.

For example, a domain controller in Dallas for SavillTech would be SAVDALDC01. The first three characters are SAV for the company, the next three characters are DAL for the location, the next two characters are

DC for the type of server, for example, DC for Domain Controller, and EX for Exchange server (although I recommend XC instead to avoid childish giggling in case the 3 letter location ends in S), FS for File Server, etc., then 01 for the unique instance. There are arguments both ways about using company names in the naming standard. I prefer to use part of the company name to eliminate duplicate naming in case of a merger. You might change this naming scheme however you like; it's just important to have one.

The problem is that computers identify each other by IP address and so you need a phonebook-type system that can give you the address based on a name. This is exactly what DNS does—it takes the name of a computer and returns the requested computer's IP address. It also offers the reverse, getting a hostname by a machine's IP address.

DNS is prevalent today. The days of WINS are basically gone (it's covered briefly at the end of this chapter), and it is only needed for legacy applications. Use DNS for everything network-related you do.

How DNS Works

DNS is hierarchal. Each part of the name separated by a dot (.) is a level in the DNS space, with the right-most being the highest level. Take www.savilltech.com as an example. The .com part of the name is the top-level domain that is serviced by a number of Internet DNS services. The savilltech component is a second-level domain registered to a company that is hosted by DNS servers within the company or by an ISP. The www is the host part of the name and is the record looked up on the savilltech.com DNS server. This resolves to one or more IP addresses, as Figure 7-30 shows. Going left to right you see the top of that hierarchy has the root (.) with some of the top-level domains, such as com, org, and co (a country-specific top-level domain with countries as child domains, such as uk for the United Kingdom and de for Germany). The second-level domains include domains such as msn, savilltech, and county codes. Under those domains are further levels for domains or host records, such as www.

How does a local DNS server get an IP address that might be mapped on one of millions of DNS servers available from the Internet? The process starts at the top of the DNS tree, which knows the DNS servers for the top-level domains. Those top-level domains know the second-level DNS servers for zones that are part of their namespace, and so on.

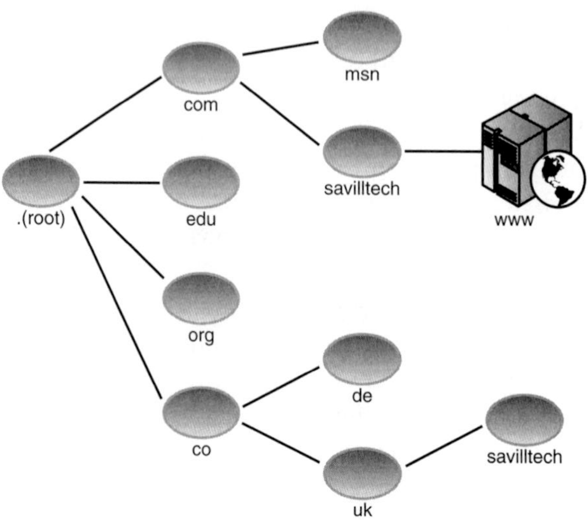

FIGURE 7-30 An example of the DNS hierarchy.

Let's perform a simple lookup using Name Server Lookup (`nslookup`).

```
C:\Users\john.SAVILLTECH>nslookup www.weddings.com
Server:  savdaldc01.savilltech.net
Address:  192.168.1.10:53

Name:    weddings.com
Address:  170.224.69.43
Aliases:  www.weddings.com
```

Figure 7-31 shows this process and the following list contains details.

1. The client checks its DNS cache and if no entry for www.weddings.com is found (or it's expired), the client sends a recursive query request to its local DNS server. A recursive query is one in which the requester is asking the server to assume all responsibility for returning a full answer to the query.
2. The local DNS server checks its cache and if www.weddings.com is not found, it looks in its database. After seeing it does not hold the weddings.com zone, it checks its list of root DNS servers and picks one to ask. It then sends an iterative query to the chosen server asking for a resolution for www.weddings.com. The iterative query means the DNS server should just return its best answer and is not responsible for providing the correct answer.

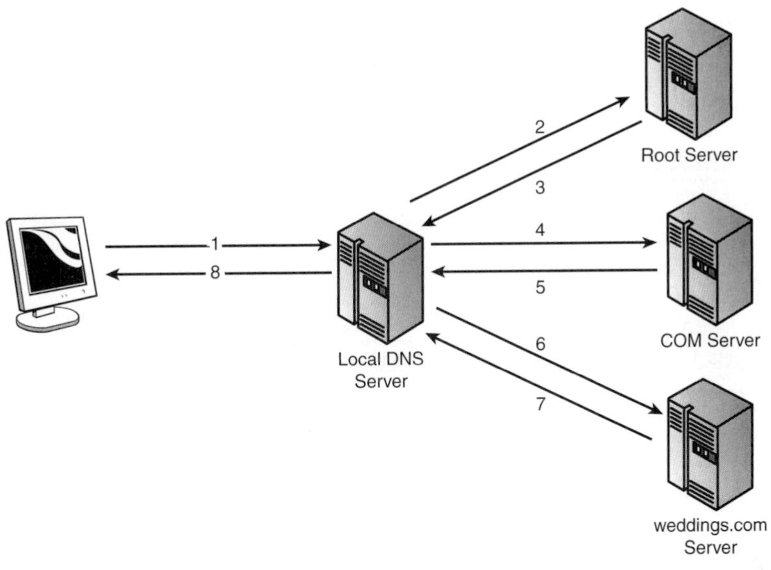

FIGURE 7-31 How the DNS lookup works—there's lots of communication just to look up a web site!

3. The root DNS server receives the request for www.weddings.com but cannot resolve it. Instead, it gives the address of all the DNS servers that know about .com, and this is its best answer.
4. The local DNS server now sends an iterative query request for www.weddings.com to one of the DNS servers who knows about .com.
5. Again this server does not know but knows the DNS server that holds the weddings.com zone.
6. The request for www.weddings.com is now sent to the DNS server who is responsible for savilltech.com.
7. The record is found and the IP address for www in the weddings.com zone is returned.
8. The local DNS server returns the IP address of www.weddings.com to the requesting client.

Figure 7-32 shows this entire transfer. The top-level name server (192.36.148.17) is contacted; (192.36.148.17) did not have an answer for www.weddings.com in frame 129. The name server passed back a list of DNS servers for .COM for the server to contact to try and get an answer.

One of these servers is contacted and again was referred to another name server (the one for wedding.com) which it then asked and got an answer which it passed back to the client.

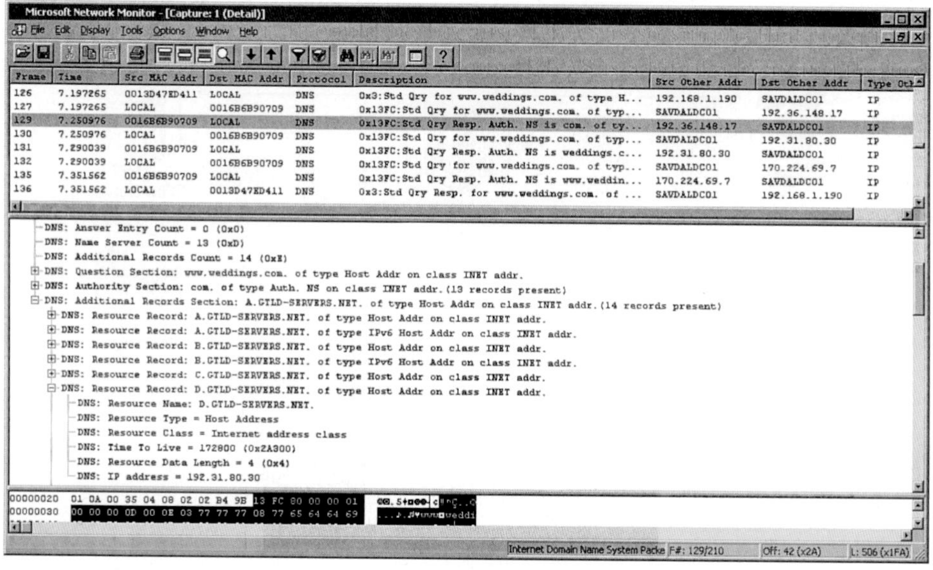

FIGURE 7-32 An example of the DNS response information.

The authoritative DNS server is the server that holds a full copy of the zones data locally, can answer queries about the zone without needing to query other servers, and can be trusted as the final word when trying to resolve a record. If the authoritative DNS server for a zone says it cannot find the requested address, the process stops.

Why does the DNS server do all this resolution for you instead of the client? Primarily it's because the DNS server has a cache of records it has looked up in the past, so next time someone asks for the same record, it does not have to go through the whole process again. It just gives the result from the last time it checked. Obviously, records change, so each record has a Time To Live (TTL), a length of time records are allowed to be cached on other DNS servers. When the TTL has expired, the record is deleted from the DNS server's cache. Another reason is that you don't want all your clients directly talking to different servers on the Internet. It's better to control all access through specific servers that can be locked down for security.

Each DNS server has a list of the root DNS servers that it pings at random when performing initial queries to find domain name servers for top-level domains, which it then caches (see Figure 7-33). Notice the names end with a period (.), which is the correct notation, even though no one ever adds it. This information is accessed by right-clicking on a server in the DNS MMC snap-in and selecting Properties. The Root Hints tab shows the root servers it knows about.

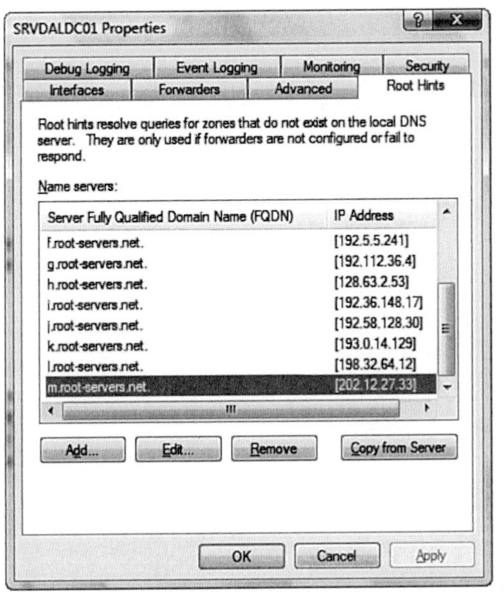

FIGURE 7-33 The default Root Hint servers.

Installing DNS

Installing DNS is done the same as installing DHCP via Server Manager or Initial Configuration Tasks and choosing the DNS Server role (see Figure 7-34).

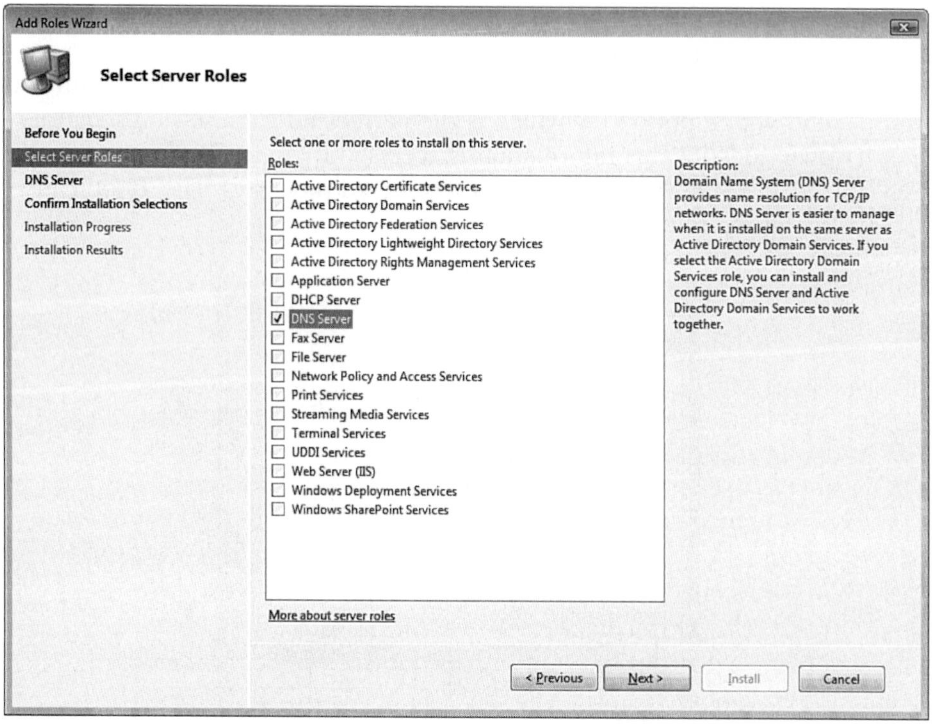

FIGURE 7-34 Adding the DNS role.

Unlike DHCP, no questions are asked during DNS installation (in part because in many instance DNS is automatically installed when you create a server as a domain controller). All that is displayed is an overview screen (see Figure 7-35). Click Next and continue the normal role installation.

Managing DNS

After DNS server is installed, you administer the server via the DNS MMC snap-in. If the DNS server is also a domain controller, you notice certain zones already exist under Forward Lookup Zones, which are the normal zones for finding IP addresses from hostnames.

As a quick aside, if you ever want to confirm the hostname of your machine, run the `hostname` command:

```
C:\Users\john.SAVILLTECH>hostname
savdalwks01
```

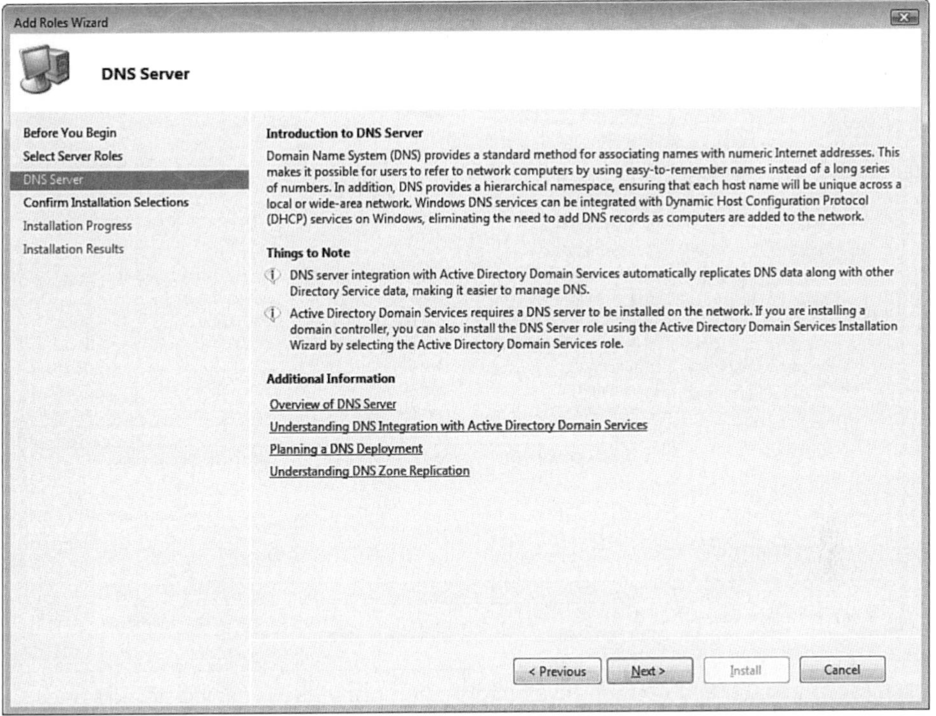

FIGURE 7-35 Links to useful information on DNS, which mostly center on its cohabitation with AD.

Before you start creating records, let's first discuss how the DNS server responds to DNS clients and how DNS information can be structured.

Record Response Behavior

What do you see in the zones of a domain controller (see Figure 7-36)? You see some host records that give the IP addresses for the host names. Many types of records exist, but the most common are host (A) records that provide a map from the name to IP addresses. You also see alias (CNAME) records that are "also known as" names for existing host records. It is common to create a www alias record that points to one or more servers that serve a Web page. You also see Mail Exchange (MX) records that tell systems which servers process mail for a given domain. Right-click on a zone and select Other New Records to see the whole list of possible record types and a description for each (see Figure 7-37).

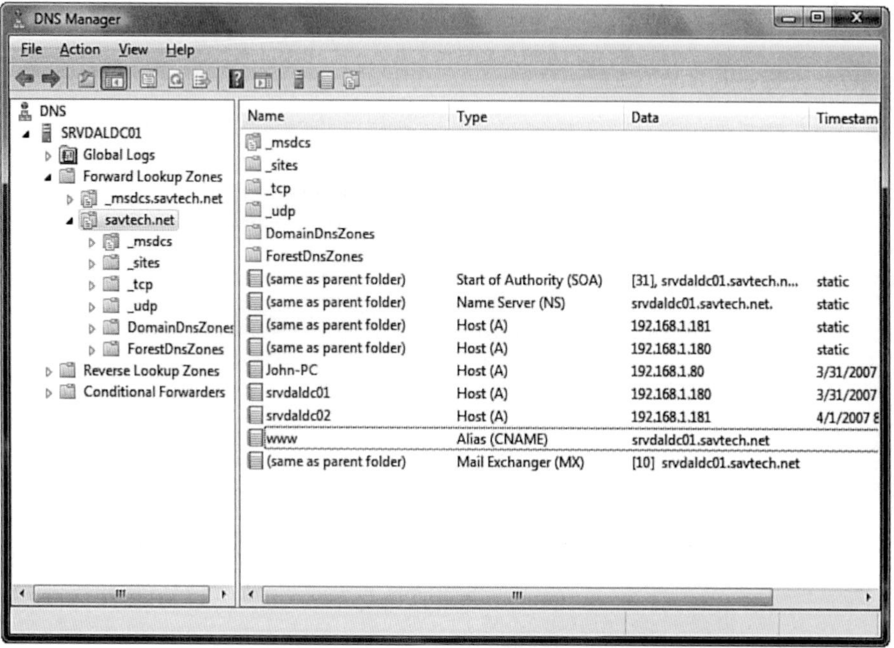

FIGURE 7-36 The main DNS screen gives information about the top-level stored zones.

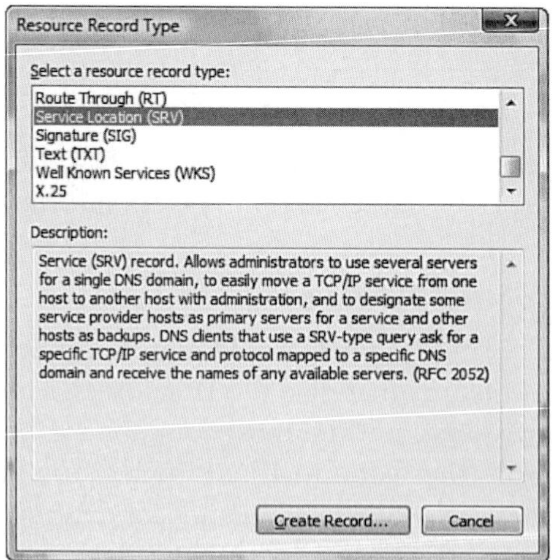

FIGURE 7-37 A lot of DNS record types exist; here, you see the service record type along with its description.

If multiple records for a single name exist, which ones does the DNS server return? Let's take a CRM application that has an address of crm.savtech.net, but might be hosted on multiple servers. The DNS server might have three address records for one host name:

crm.savilltech.net.IN A192.168.1.150

crm.savilltech.net.IN A192.168.1.151

crm.savilltech.net.IN A192.168.1.152

When a DNS server is queried for a host, it returns multiple matching records. To keep all clients going to the first record every time, it uses a round robin algorithm (this is described in the Request for Comment document 1794). This means the record's order is rotated each time to get an even distribution of host usage. For example, the first time the DNS server is queried, it returns in order:

192.168.1.150 192.168.1.151 192.168.1.152

The second time it returns
192.168.1.151 192.168.1.152 192.168.1.150

The third time it returns
192.168.1.152 192.168.1.150 192.168.1.151

This cycle repeats. This would be fine except in some instances the client making the request might be directly connected to a subnet one of the returned addresses exists in, so it makes more sense from a network use point of view for the client to communicate with the address on a local subnet. This is known as subnet prioritization and is a feature of the client DNS resolver. Results are sorted into order of direct subnet connectivity.

The local DNS resolver subnet prioritization cancels out the DNS server round robin if one of the results is on a local subnet. This reduces network traffic but does not load balance the server load.

The subnet prioritization can also be set via the DNS Management Console (Start, Programs, Administrative Tools, DNS Management Console). Right-click on the server and select Properties, select the Advanced tab, and clear/set the Enable Netmask Ordering (see Figure 7-37).

The round robin functionality is also set via the Advanced tab Enable Round Robin option. Table 7-1 shows the expected functionality depending on the values set.

Table 7-1 Record Return Order

Subnet Prioritization Round Robin	Disabled	Enabled
Disabled	Records returned in order added to database	Records returned in local net priority order
Enabled	Records returned in rotated order based on order added to database	Records returned rotated based on local net priority order

Creating New Domains

You can also create other domains under an existing domain, creating a deeper hierarchy. For example, right-click on savtech.net and select New Domain (DNS Domain, not Active Directory Domain) and enter a name. Then create records in that zone (see Figure 7-38).

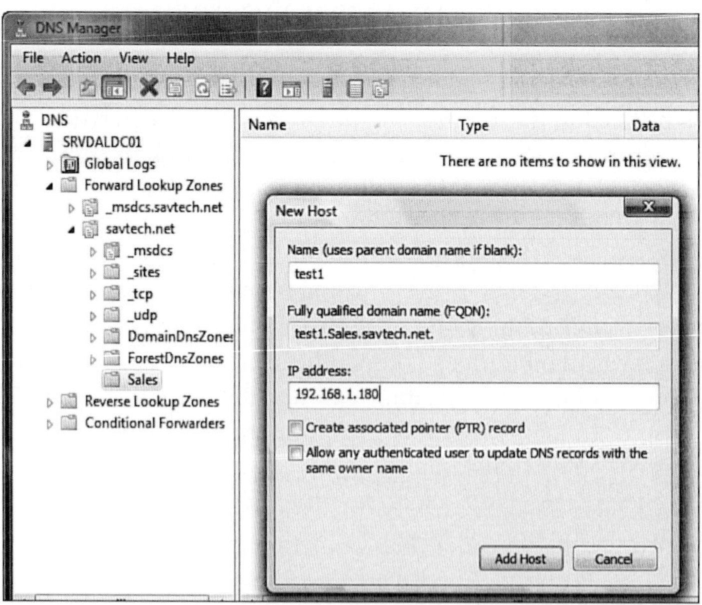

FIGURE 7-38 When a new domain is created, it shows in the DNS hierarchy and is treated in the same way as any other. It can have records or child domains of its own.

The entries in your new domain are available by their fully qualified domain name:

```
C:\Users\Administrator>nslookup test1.sales.savtech.net
Server:   srvdaldc01.savtech.net
Address:  192.168.1.180

Name:     test1.sales.savtech.net
Address:  192.168.1.180
```

Creating DNS Zones

Zones are boundaries of storage for DNS information. Right-click on the DNS server and select New Zone to start the New Zone wizard (see Figure 7-39). Click Next to begin.

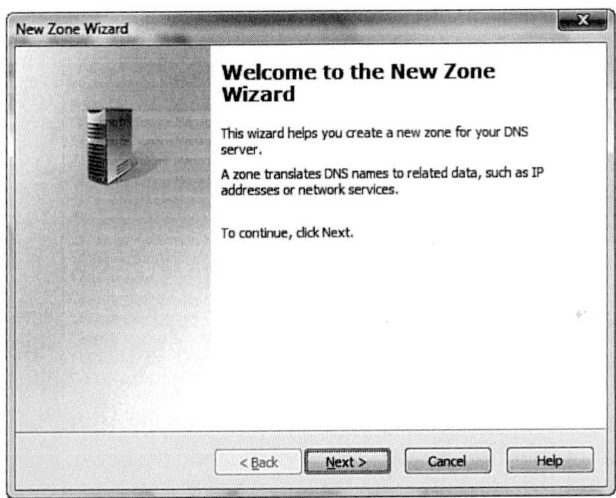

FIGURE 7-39 Creating a new zone.

The first question asks for the type of zone (see Figure 7-40). It also asks if it's primary or a stub zone, and if you want to store in the AD (which is useful if you want to enable secure updating of records). You cannot store a secondary zone in AD.

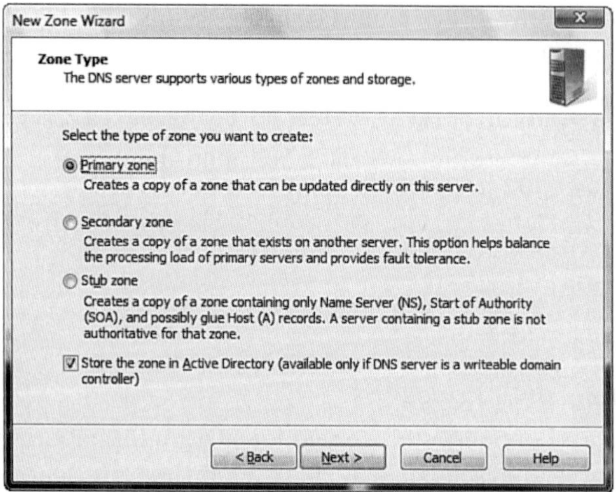

FIGURE 7-40 Three types of zone.

With pre–Windows 2000 incarnations of DNS, there was a single option for storing the DNS database. For each zone, a zone file was created that held the content of the zone. These files were named *<name of zone>*.dns and were stored in the %systemroot%\system32\dns folder.

The first DNS server onto which a zone was created was the primary DNS server, and it held a writeable copy of this zone file. Having a single copy of the database was not practical for load balancing and fault tolerance purposes, however.

To resolve this shortcoming, secondary copies of the DNS zone could be hosted by other DNS servers. These secondary copies contained a read-only copy of the zone, which was periodically updated by the secondary servers pulling the changes from the primary server. Originally this update consisted of the entire zone being re-copied on every update and was a full transfer (or AXFR request). With Windows 2000, an incremental transfer (or IXFR request) was introduced in accordance with Request for Comment (RFC) 1995 that allows the secondary server to only pull down the changes.

An update specified in RFC 1996 allowed the primary DNS server to notify its secondary servers when updates were available rather than them waiting for the refresh interval to expire. This was implemented in the Windows implementation of DNS.

With this method, there was still only one writeable copy of the database to which all changes had to be directed. This was mainly due to the problems of trying to synchronize the database if multiple write-enabled versions of the file existed.

AD solved this and allowed full multi-master replication. DNS piggybacks on this and providing that DNS is running on a domain controller, it is possible to configure a zone to be stored in the AD. When the zone is stored in the AD, every domain controller in the domain that has DNS installed can service the zone in a primary mode, meaning it can write to the zone.

You can still have secondary zone servers on non–domain controllers, which host a read-only version of the zone. This pulls changes from the primary AD-integrated copies of the zone.

One important thing to point out is that the zones stored in the AD do not have to match the name of the domain that the domain controller services. For example, domain controllers in domain.com can store zones of any zone name. Multiple different zones can all be stored in the AD. Because the configuration of the storage of the zone is on a per-zone basis, it's possible to have some zones stored in the AD, some zones as standard primary in a file, and some zones as secondary copies stored in a file.

You should also not have the zone AD integrated on domain controllers and then nominate another DNS server that is not AD integrated to store the zone as primary (whether a domain controller or not). Having a file-based primary DNS zone in addition to the AD-integrated zone results in a separate version of the zone with no consistency between them.

When stored in the AD DNS zone, information is written in the domain partition. Remember that the domain partition is only replicated between domain controllers in the same domain. Now imagine you have multiple domains and you would like to AD integrate the zone on domain controllers in all the domains.

The zone is replicated within the domain partition, creating a separate version of the zone in every domain, leading to inconsistent content. You are therefore constrained in that the zone can only be replicated between domain controllers in the same domain.

You should also consider that when the zone is stored in the AD, the zone is replicated to all domain controllers in the domain, not just the DNS servers in the domain controllers. This might generate excess traffic that wastes bandwidth, especially when you might have domain controllers connected over slow WAN links.

Because you selected New Zone from the server's context menu, you are prompted to indicate if the zone is a forward or reverse lookup zone. If you selected New Zone from the Forward Lookup Zones leaf on the navigation pane, you are not prompted for this. Select Forward lookup zone for now (see Figure 7-41).

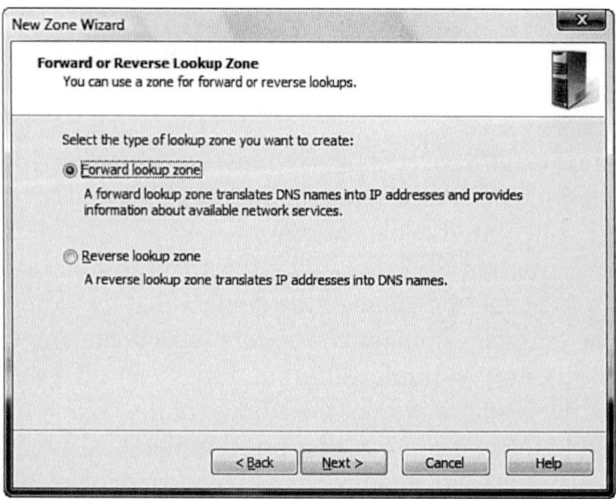

FIGURE 7-41 Forward lookup zones and reverse lookup zones behave in different ways and so the type must be specified during zone creation.

You are now prompted for the zone name (see Figure 7-42). This can be any name you want, but stick to proper naming standards and avoid single-level zones (for example, savilltech).

Now you indicate the type of dynamic update supported (see Figure 7-43). You cover dynamic update in more detail in the "DNS Security" section, but for now enabling secure dynamic update allows clients to register their own DNS updates with security set on those records so only that client can update the record. Nonsecure allows records to be written dynamically without security, and not allowing dynamic updates means no dynamic records can be written.

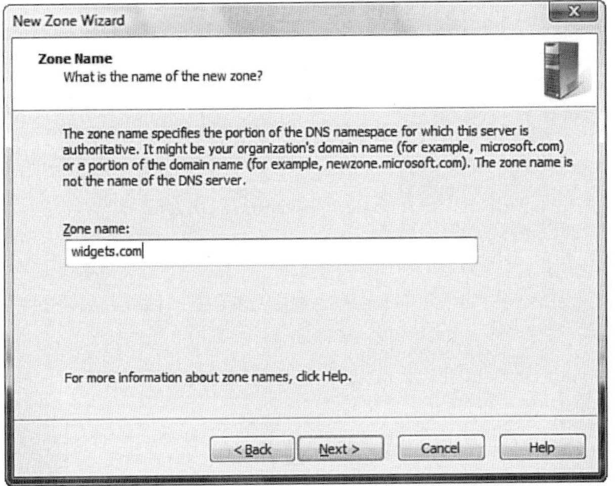

FIGURE 7-42 Setting the name of the new zone.

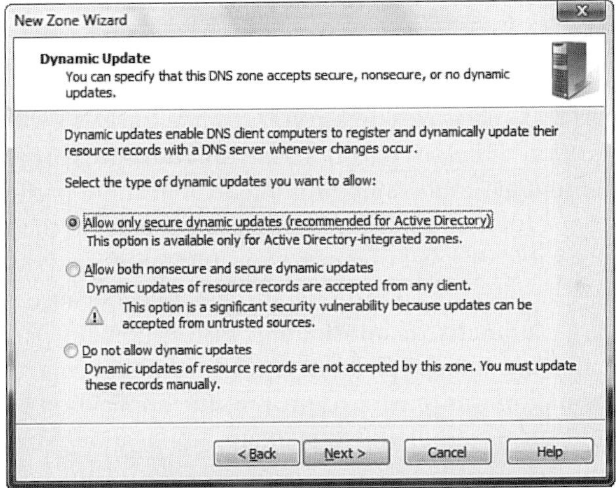

FIGURE 7-43 Disable dynamic update so all records must be manually created, or enable in a secure or nonsecure form.

A summary is displayed and the zone created (see Figure 7-44).

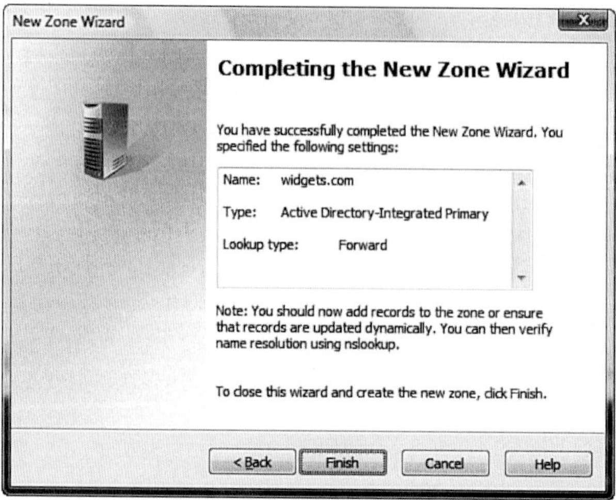

FIGURE 7-44 Confirmation of new zone configuration.

DNS Application Partitions

Windows 2003 improves on the AD storage for DNS with the introduction of application directory partitions beyond the core three types of partition: domain, schema, and configuration. Application partitions are used by applications to store information that exists outside the normal partitions. This allows a finer level of control for its replication.

These application partitions are required because many applications place large amounts of information in the domain partitions. Then that information has to be replicated to all the domain controllers, even though the information was only of use to specific applications.

Microsoft introduced two standard application partitions in Windows 2003 for use with DNS, which provided the following additional functionality:

- The capability for zone information to replicate to every domain controller in the entire forest with the DNS service installed.
- The capability for zone information to replicate only to domain controllers within a domain with the DNS service installed. Because this uses the domain as the boundary, multiple instances exist, one for each domain.

Using the first option and replicating to all DNS servers in the entire forest, a zone can be stored anywhere in the entire forest. Using the second option for only two domain controllers that are DNS servers out of the 10 domain controllers stops all the DNS data from being replicated to the other eight domain controllers.

If you upgraded from a pre–Windows 2003 server, these application partitions might not exist. Create them by right-clicking on the DNS server in the DNS MMC snap-in and selecting Create Default Application Directory Partitions. Select the option to create the per-domain or per-forest partitions. These partitions can also be created from the command line using the DNSCMD tool.

To create the domain-wide partition for the local domain, use

```
dnscmd <DNS server> /CreateBuiltinDirectoryPartitions /Domain
```

To create the domain-wide partition for all domains in the forest, use

```
dnscmd <DNS server> /CreateBuiltinDirectoryPartitions
➥/AllDomains
```

To create the forest-wide partition, use

```
dnscmd <DNS server> /CreateBuiltinDirectoryPartitions /Forest
```

To see a list of all the directory partitions on a domain controller, use the `enumdirectorypartitions` switch; for example:

```
C:\Users\Administrator>dnscmd /enumdirectorypartitions
Enumerated directory partition list:

        Directory partition count = 2

 DomainDnsZones.savtech.net                Enlisted Auto Domain
 ForestDnsZones.savtech.net                Enlisted Auto Forest

Command completed successfully.
```

This example shows that the domain controller is enlisted in both the domain (DomainDNSZones) and forest (ForestDNSZones) application partitions. Alternatively, the status could show as `Not-Enlisted Auto Domain/Forest`.

To view all the members of the replica set of a partition, use the `ntdsutil` command as shown here:

```
C:\Users\Administrator>ntdsutil
ntdsutil: activate instance ntds
Active instance set to "ntds".
ntdsutil: partition management
partition management: connection
server connections: connect to server savdaldc01
Binding to savdaldc01 ...
Connected to savdaldc01 using credentials of locally logged on
user.
server connections: quit
partition management: list
Note: Directory partition names with International/Unicode
characters will only display correctly if appropriate fonts and
language support are loaded
Found 5 Naming Context(s)
0 - CN=Configuration,DC=savilltech,DC=net
1 - CN=Schema,CN=Configuration,DC=savilltech,DC=net
2 - DC=savilltech,DC=net
3 - DC=DomainDnsZones,DC=savilltech,DC=net
4 - DC=ForestDnsZones,DC=savilltech,DC=net
partition management: list nc replica
dc=domaindnszones,dc=savilltech,dc=net
The application directory partition
dc=domaindnszones,dc=savilltech,dc=net's Replicas are:
        CN=NTDS
Settings,CN=SAVDALDC01,CN=Servers,CN=Dallas,CN=Sites,
CN=Configuration,DC=savilltech,DC=net
        CN=NTDS
Settings,CN=SAVDALDC02,CN=Servers,CN=Dallas,CN=Sites,
CN=Configuration,DC=savilltech,DC=net
partition management: quit
ntdsutil: quit
```

The code first shows starting the domain management functions of the `ntdsutil` command. You then need to connect to an actual domain controller. You tell `ntdsutil` to show you all the partitions that exist using the `list` command. Finally, you list the members of the `domaindnszones` replica set (for the savtech.net domain). If you ran this on a Windows 2003 server, use `domain management` instead of `partition management` in the code.

If you have any domain controllers listed as uninstantiated replicas, it means currently there is no replication object configured to allow the replication of the information. Force the knowledge consistency checker to run to create the replication objects as needed (use `repadmin /kcc`) and then force replication (`repadmin /syncall`).

DNS Security

Dynamic update is a useful feature. Obviously the Windows 2000/2003 implementation of DNS supports this, but if you AD-integrate the zone, you now can allow secure updates either exclusively or in combination with nonsecure updates.

With the normal nonsecure and secure mode, any computer whose domain suffix matches that of the DNS zone it is trying to update can dynamically register and modify entries in the DNS database for A and PTR resource records. For example, for the homer client to dynamically register its record in savtech.net, the computer's fully qualified domain name (FQDN) would have to be homer.savtech.net and be talking to a DNS server for the savtech.net zone.

There is some modification of the behavior when DHCP is in use. By default, the client would register its A resource record, and the DHCP server would register its PTR resource record. The problem is that with non-secure updates, it's quite easy for someone to modify another computer's resource records possibly for malicious purposes.

Fortunately, when the zone is AD integrated, the secure only mode is enabled. Resource records can only be modified by the machine that created them and only machines authenticated with the AD can register records initially. This stops someone else modifying another resource's records.

An Access Control List (ACL) is placed on the records (which are manually edited via the DNS MMC snap-in), specifying who can read, write, or delete the record. By default, only the computer account and the domain administrators have full permissions, as shown in Figure 7-45 and Figure 7-46. Everyone else only has read permission, meaning they can only resolve the record via a query but cannot modify it. Notice in the figures that the host's DNS record has full control of the host's computer account because the computer registers it. DHCP registers the PTR record and IP address for the client and so the DNS credential account has full control. For both records, the Everyone group just has read permission.

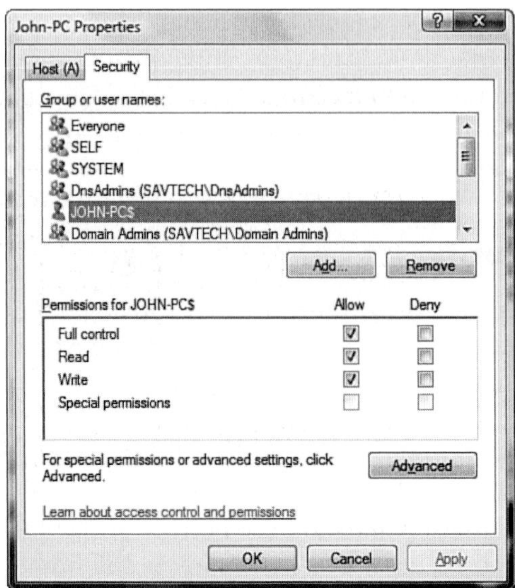

FIGURE 7-45 The computer account for the registering host has full control.

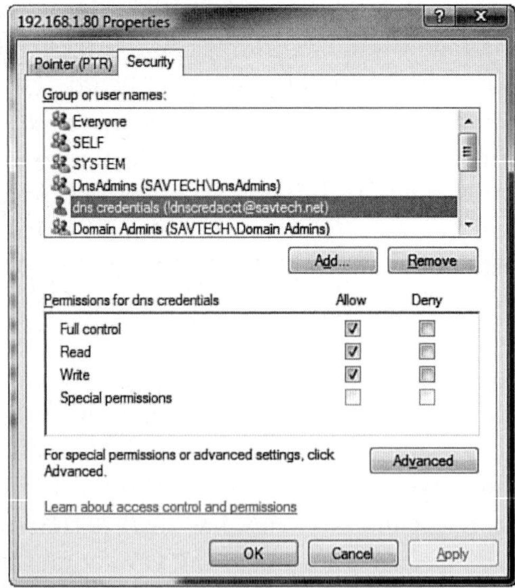

FIGURE 7-46 The DNS credentials account also has full control of the record.

By default, clients attempt an unsecured dynamic update first and if that fails, attempt a secure update.

DNS and Active Directory Domain Services

With Windows 2000 there were challenges around correctly configuring DNS to be ready for Active Directory Domain Services (ADDS). With Windows 2003 and Windows Server 2008, if DNS is not installed or configured correctly, the DNS zones that ADDS requires will be created or their configuration corrected. In Windows Server 2008, the option to install DNS is part of the domain controller promotion process. (If the installation wizard for the ADDS cannot find the correct information in DNS, it needs to create the domain.) By default it configures the DNS zone to be AD integrated and replicate to all DNS servers in the domain via the DomainDNSZones application partition. Look at this by right-clicking the zone and selecting Properties (see Figure 7-47).

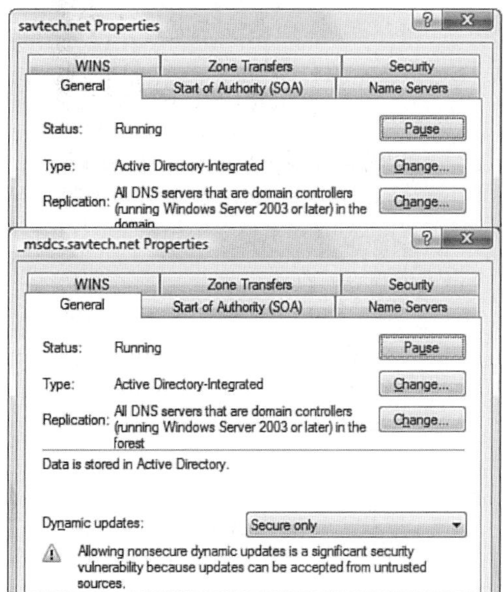

FIGURE 7-47 The difference between the storage of the normal domain zone and the forest zone.

Notice that the domain creation process creates a second zone on the DNS server for the first domain created in forest `_msdcs.<forest name>`, such as `_msdcs.savtech.net`. (This only happens if you allow the domain creation process to configure DNS.) If you examine the properties of this `_msdcs` zone, you'll notice it's configured to be stored on all DNS servers in the entire forest. Why this special treatment for this one DNS subdomain? Think of this zone as a zone for the forest and not for the domain at the top of the forest.

Every AD domain has a zone in DNS to store its resource records, which allow computers to find the services and computers they need. Since Microsoft has implemented AD using a number of industry standards, it is quite possible to have LDAP and Global Catalog services (and possibly others) offered by non-Microsoft-based services that would be advertised in DNS alongside Microsoft-offered services.

There might be times when a client needs to specifically talk to a Microsoft-based service and this is where the `_msdcs` zone comes into play. Each Microsoft-based service publishes records to the normal location in DNS. For example, a domain controller publishes its LDAP resource (among other places) as

```
_ldap._tcp.<domain>
```

For example: `_ldap._tcp.savtech.net`

It also writes an additional record under the _msdcs zone as

```
_ldap._tcp.dc._msdcs.<domain>
```

For example: `_ldap._tcp.dc._msdcs.savtech.net`

This allows a client to easily find a Microsoft LDAP server or any other Microsoft-hosted service. However, why does the forest root domain `_msdcs` zone need to be on all DNS servers in the entire forest?

The `_msdcs` zone for the forest root also includes details about the Globally Unique Identifier (GUID) for all domains in the forest and a list of all the global catalog servers in the forest. This is the key. Whenever a client in the forest needs to find a global catalog server, it has to query the `_msdcs` zone of the forest root. Therefore, by having the forest root `_msdcs` zone stored on all the DNS servers that are domain controllers in the entire forest, it is more readily available, avoiding the need for clients to have to communicate with DNS servers in the forest root domain.

Zone Properties

If you right-click on a zone and select Properties, you get access to the full properties that allow advanced configuration. You focus on the areas of interest in this section.

The General tab allows you to change where a zone is stored (AD integrated, primary, and so forth) and its replication, along with in which format dynamic updates can occur. The General tab also gives access to the Aging… options that are covered in the "DNS Scavenging" section.

The Name Servers tab (see Figure 7-48) lists all the DNS servers that are authoritative for the zone and can be modified as needed via the Add, Edit, and Remove buttons. Each name server listed also has a Name Server (NS) record at the root of the zone.

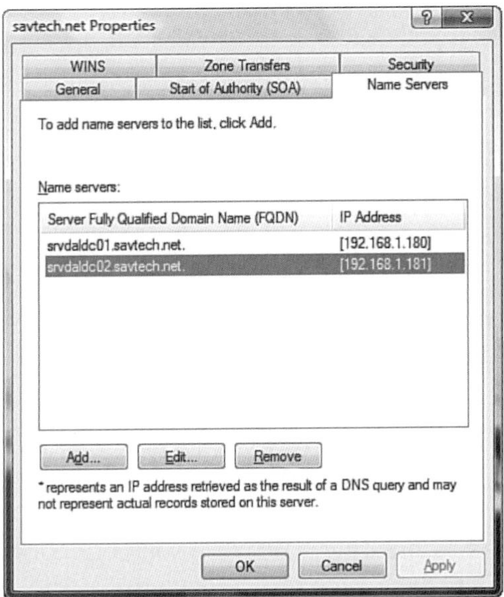

FIGURE 7-48 The Name Servers tab controls who can be authoritative for the zone.

The Start of Authority tab simply allows configuration of the authority record for the zone, the contact person for the zone, and timing settings. The Security tab is the generic security dialog, allowing control of who can perform actions on the records within the zone, such as creating new records.

The Zone Transfers tab allows control of who can perform a zone transfer from the server (see Figure 7-49). This takes every record from the server for storage and makes servicing on another server possible.

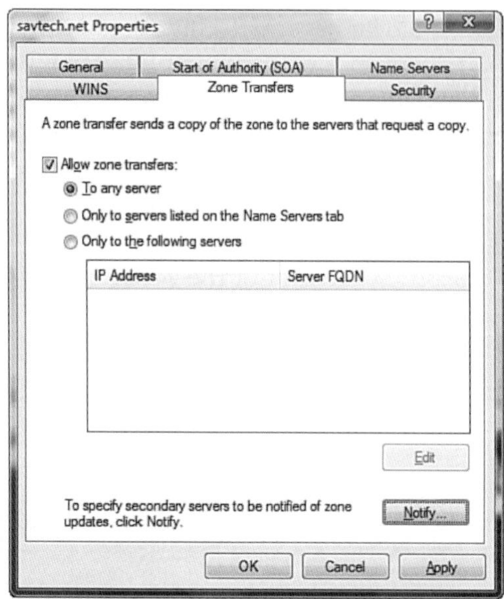

FIGURE 7-49 Three options for zone transfers exist. It is also possible to configure notification so the DNS server tells certain servers when changes have occurred.

The WINS tab allows DNS to query WINS if it cannot resolve a name itself. You configure which WINS servers to query. You can also opt to not replicate the configuration of the WINS to other DNS servers. The WINS lookup works by creating a WINS resource record at the root of the zone and a WINS-R record for reverse lookups. WINS is antiquated, however, and hopefully with Windows Server 2008 it can be retired along with NetBIOS names.

DNS Scavenging

Dynamic update allows computer and DHCP servers to register records into the DNS zone. What if machines are rebuilt with new names or retired? The DNS database becomes polluted with records for nonexistent machines.

DNS scavenging eliminates obsolete records. It can be configured on a per-zone basis via the Aging button on the General tab or for all zones by selecting Set Aging/Scavenging for All Zones from the context menu of the server. Either selection brings up the same options (see Figure 7-50).

FIGURE 7-50 Two intervals to configure: no refresh and refresh.

The two configurable options are

- **No-refresh interval**. This is used to stop unnecessary updates on an existing record, reducing replication traffic. The default is seven days. Any attempt to reregister the record within seven days is ignored and the record not updated.
- **Refresh interval**. This is the time from when the no-refresh interval has expired before the record is considered stale. So if the default of seven days is left, from the point of first registration the client would need to re-register within 14 days but not before seven days.

The actual values should be based on the DHCP lease time. The default lease time and no-refresh and refresh intervals work well together. If you reduce the lease times, you should also reduce the refresh/no-refresh times accordingly to ensure old records are not left too long. It's important that the sum of the no-refresh and refresh values are greater than the maximum refresh interval (the DHCP lease time), otherwise records could be scavenged before the DHCP lease has expired. For example, if the lease time is eight days and the no-refresh and refresh intervals are set to two days, the dynamic records are deleted after four days, even though the lease was still active and the client is likely still using it.

Additionally the actual DNS zone scavenging is not real time and occurs once a week by default. Therefore, if your refresh intervals are much smaller, configure the scavenging to also occur more regularly via the `dnscmd` command-line tool.

```
dnscmd /config /scavenginginterval <hours>
C:\ >dnscmd /config /scavenginginterval 12
Registry property scavenginginterval successfully reset.
Command completed successfully.
```

This updates Registry value `HKEY_LOCAL_MACHINE\SYSTEM\ControlSet001\Services\DNS\Parameters\scavengungunterval.`

A scavenge can be forced by right-clicking on the server in the DNS Management snap-in and selecting Scavenge Stale Resource Records. It's also possible at the server level to select scavenging for all zones rather than on a per-zone basis.

Reverse Lookup Zones

Suppose you have a phone number written on your hand from a wild night's partying. You want to phone the number but you don't know the name. You could pick up the phone book and look through each phone number and then see the name, but this would be a slow and resource-intensive process. What would be great is a reverse phone book that is organized by phone number that just gives you the name.

This is exactly what a reverse lookup zone is. You create a zone for each subnet on which you want to be able to perform reverse lookups. Now the zone names are a little strange. If the subnet was 192.168.1, you reverse the order of the subnet to 1.169.192 and add in-addr.arpa to the end. The zone is now 1.169.192.in-addr.arpa. You don't need to worry about this too much. When you create a reverse zone, the reverse zone wizard takes care of this for you.

1. Right-click the Reverse Lookup Zones leaf in the DNS navigation pane and select New Zone.
2. Click Next to the wizard welcome screen.
3. You are asked for how the zone should be stored (as per any zone creation). Click Next.
4. You are asked how the zone should be replicated if it's AD integrated. Click Next.
5. You are prompted for whether the reverse lookup is for IPv4 or IPv6. Select IPv4 (see Figure 7-51). Click Next.

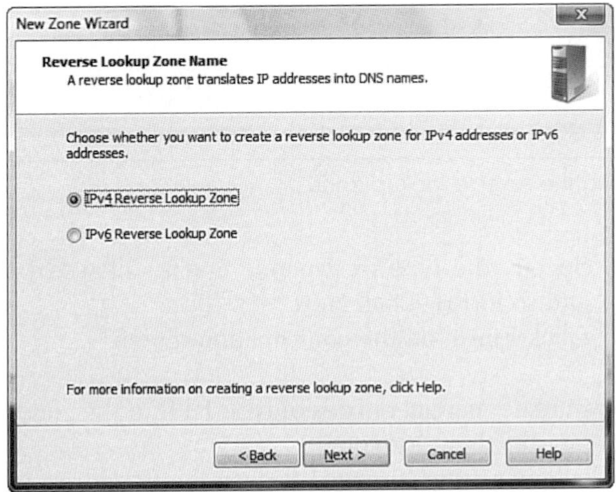

Figure 7-51 Creating a new reverse lookup zone.

6. A dialog appears prompting for the subnet for the reverse lookup. Only enter the parts that are network addresses and in the normal order; for example, 192.168.1 (see Figure 7-52). Notice you can also opt to enter the full name for the zone manually (this is not needed because the zone name is completed for you as you type). Click Next.

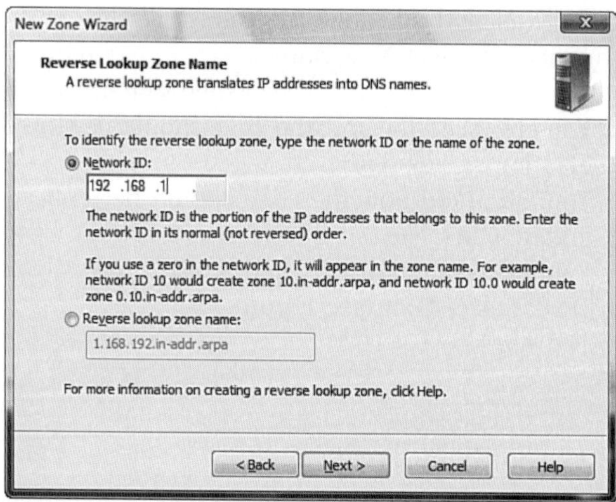

FIGURE 7-52 Naming the reverse lookup zone.

7. Specify the type of dynamic update allowed (secure, nonsecure, and so forth). Click Next.
8. Click Finish on the confirmation screen.

Now create manual entries of type PTR in the zone, or clients/DHCP servers register them for you.

To look up a reverse record, type in the IP address with the `nslookup` command:

```
C:\Users\Administrator>nslookup 192.168.1.80
Server:  srvdaldc01.savtech.net
Address:  192.168.1.180

Name:    john-pc.savtech.net
Address:  192.168.1.80
```

Reverse lookups are used by a number of services that receive a request from an IP address and want to verify the registered hostname for the IP address.

Delegation

In addition to the standard types of DNS records and creating new zones as children of existing zones, you can also decide that a portion of the namespace that belongs to a domain should be hosted separately on another DNS server. An example would be to spread the load of a large DNS hierarchy or to let child ADDS controllers host their own portion of an existing namespace. To allow another DNS server to host a subdomain of its own namespace, a DNS server delegates the child partition of the domain to another DNS server.

For example, if you wanted a new subzone, asia, that would host records about computers and services in Asia used by clients in Asia, you could delegate the asia subzone to a DNS server that was physically located in Asia. Delegation is accomplished as follows:

1. Right-click the zone for which you want to delegate part of the namespace and select New Delegation.
2. Click Next to the welcome wizard initial screen.
3. Enter the name of the domain you want to delegate (see Figure 7-53). Click Next.

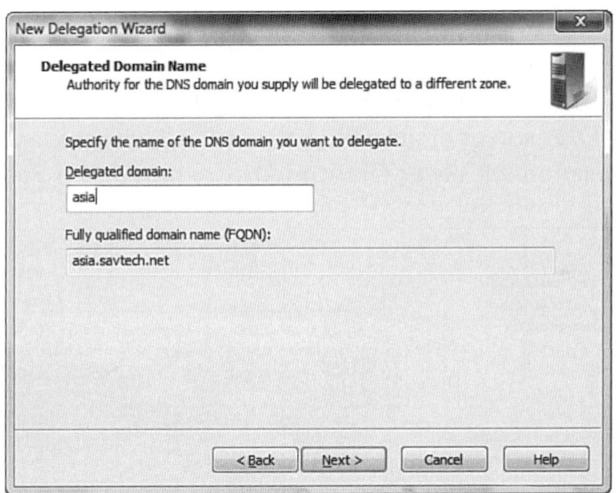

FIGURE 7-53 Delegating a domain zone.

4. Enter the list of DNS servers that will be delegated this namespace and then click Next (see Figure 7-54).

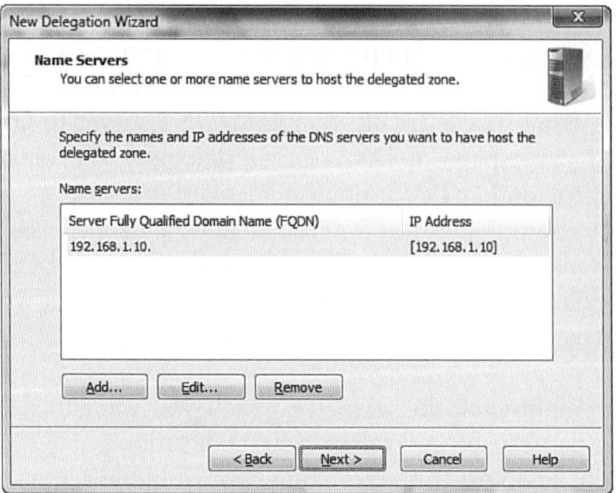

FIGURE 7-54 Specifying the name server to which to delegate a zone.

5. Click Finish.

On the delegated DNS servers, create the zone as usual. On the delegating DNS server or anywhere else, query it as usual and requests for resolution automatically are forwarded as required (see Figure 7-55).

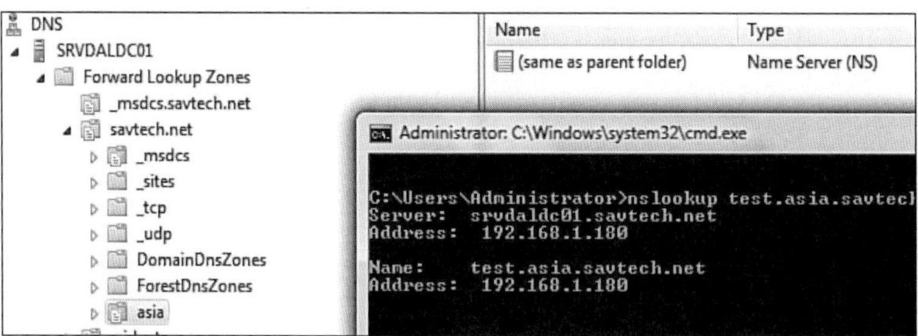

FIGURE 7-55 When you query for a record, the response is correctly returned from the delegated DNS server.

Stub Zones

Stub zones were new in Windows 2003 and allowed a DNS server to maintain some knowledge of the name servers responsible for another namespace instead of having to perform normal searches via contacting a root name server, then a COM name server, and so on. Like a normal zone, a stub zone contains records but only name server, start of authority, and special host records (known as glue records). Glue records exist only to help resolve the entries for name servers in the zone. Even though a DNS server holds a stub zone, it is not configured to be authoritative for the zone. So why create a stub zone? A stub zone keeps updated if name servers for the stub namespace change and so can query more intelligently when looking up records.

Let's create a stub zone for Savill.info. It does not have to be part of a different namespace and could be any DNS zone name.

1. Right click the Forward Lookup Zones and select New Zone.
2. Click Next to the welcome wizard initial screen.
3. Select Stub Zone for the type of zone. If you want to store in AD, check the Store the Zone in Active Directory checkbox and click Next (see Figure 7-56).

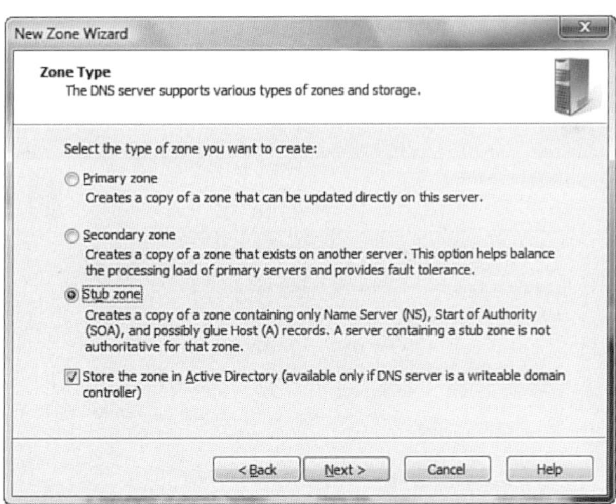

FIGURE 7-56 Creating a stub zone.

4. If you select AD integrated, specify the domain controllers that should participate in the replication. Click Next.
5. Enter a name for the stub zone and click Next (see Figure 7-57).

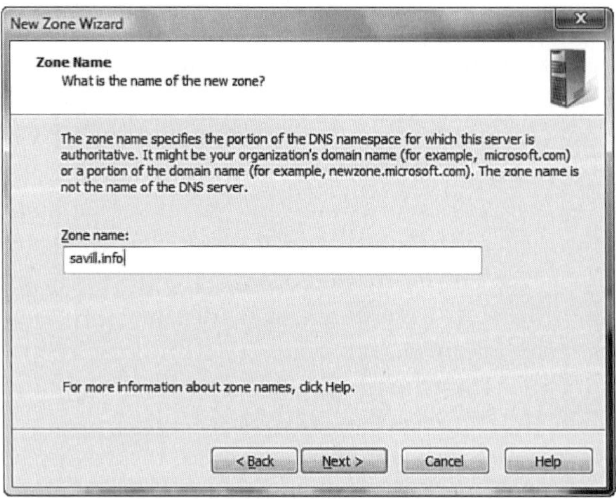

FIGURE 7-57 The name of the new stub zone.

6. Enter the FQDN of the authoritative server for the zone or its IP address (see Figure 7-58). If you enter a server that does not have the zone, you receive an error; otherwise a green tick is shown. Check the Use the Above Servers to Create a Local List of Master Servers, which causes the wizard to ask the server named for its name server records. Click Next.

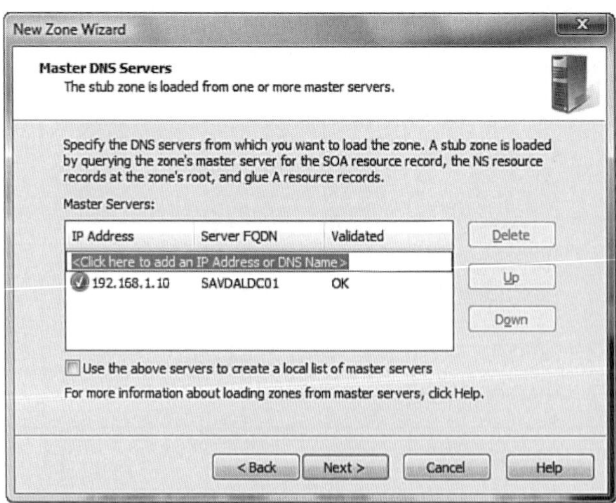

FIGURE 7-58 Specifying the master DNS zone for the stub zone.

7. Click Finish.

Now when this DNS server is asked for a record that belongs to the zone, it has a stub zone to directly ascertain a DNS server to query.

Forwarding and Conditional Forwarding

Let's say you work for a large company with lots of DNS servers for one namespace. Each DNS server can query the Internet for records it is not authoritative for and then cache the results. However, this means each DNS server is performing the same lookups that might have already been queried by another DNS server in the company. It is possible to configure forwarding on a DNS server to cause the server to send a query to the DNS server configured for resolution of queries instead of performing iterative queries to resolve itself. Therefore, each DNS server in the company could be configured to forward to one or more central DNS servers, which then query the Internet for records. The whole company can then query those servers for unknown lookups.

To create forwarders, right-click the DNS server, click Properties, and choose the Forwarders tab (see Figure 7-59). Add entries for each server to which the DNS server should forward queries. After you configure a forwarder, you can select that the DNS server uses root hints if no forwarders are available. This means the DNS server goes to the iterative root and asks root servers for a COM name server, then the name server, and so on.

Forwarders are also useful for caching, but suppose you had delegated a portion of the namespace to another DNS server, such as asia.savtech.net. Well, on the asia name servers, there are no such records to tell it to send savtech.net queries to that original server. Configure asia to forward all queries it is not authoritative for to the delegating server. Now they effectively point to each other.

Let's go back to that big company that hosts multiple namespaces on different name servers. How does each name server know which one to contact for each DNS zone? Suppose you have two namespaces, as in the following list, and then another DNS server 192.168.1.5, to which all other DNS queries should go.

- Savtech.net is hosted on 192.168.1.180 and 192.168.1.181.
- Savilltech.com is hosted on 192.168.1.10 and 192.168.1.11.

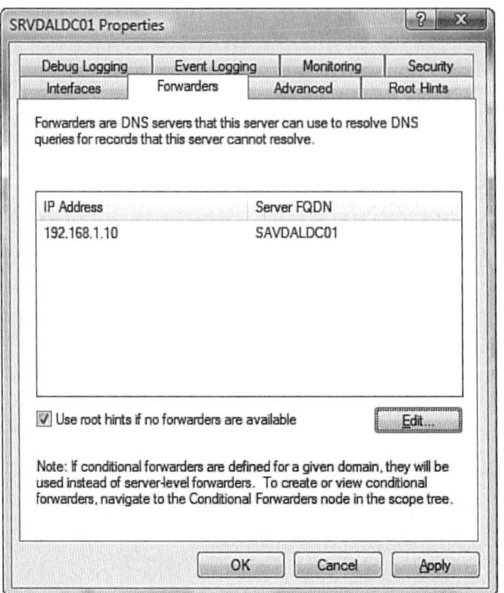

FIGURE 7-59 Multiple forwarders can be configured if required.

This would be a pain to do with normal forwarders. You forward to 192.168.1.5 and then add stub zones on 192.168.1.5 for savtech.net and savilltech.com so it would know which name servers to go to. Fortunately, you have conditional forwarders that work exactly the same as a normal forwarder but they are only for the DNS zones specified. Therefore, fix the situation as shown in Figure 7-60.

Even if a server is configured for normal forwarding, explicit conditional forwarding entries take precedence. To create the conditional forwarding rule to savilltech.com, you perform the following:

1. Right-click Conditional Forwarders under the server in the navigation pane and select New Conditional Forwarder.
2. Enter the name of the DNS domain being conditionally forwarded along with the name servers that hold the zone (see Figure 7-61).

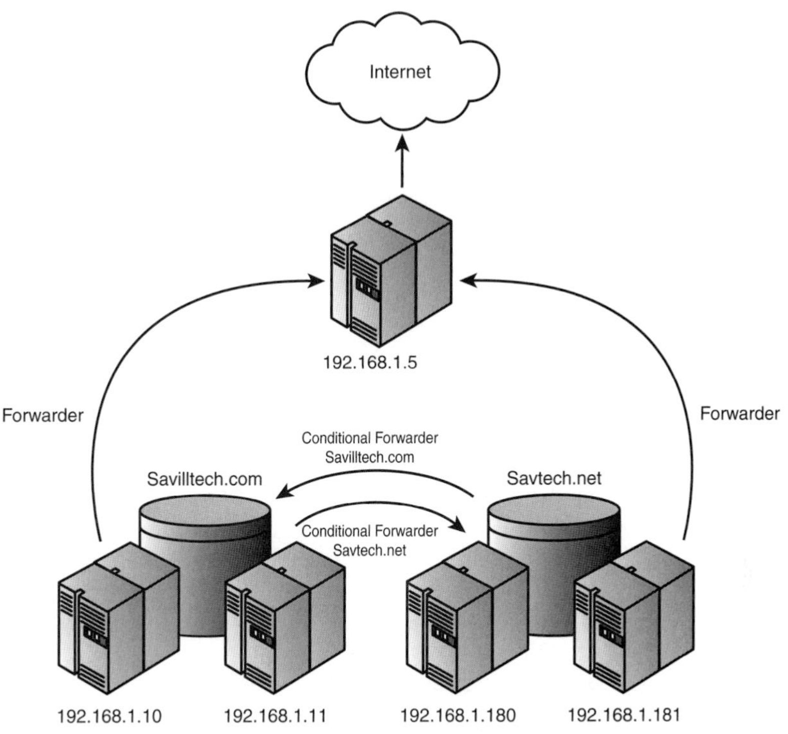

Figure 7-60 All servers at the bottom forward to the 192.168.1.5 server but are configured with a conditional forwarding rule just for the DNS zone that the other pair of DNS servers hold.

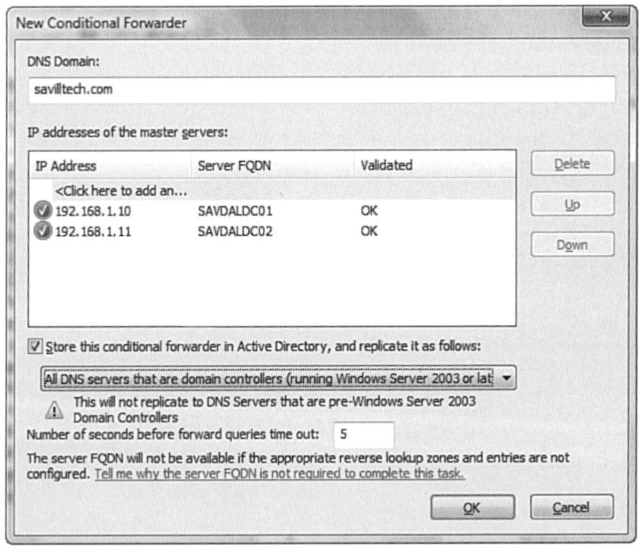

Figure 7-61 Creating a new conditional forwarder.

New to Windows Server 2008 is the option to store the conditional forwarder in the AD and configure how it is replicated.

3. Click OK.

Previously in Windows Server 2003, this could only be done via the DNSCMD utility which also works in Windows Server 2008:

```
dnscmd /ZoneAdd savilltech.com /DsForwarder 192.168.1.10
```

To configure how this is stored in AD, use the `/DP` switch in Windows Server 2008. The DNSCMD help says the following:

```
[/DP <FQDN>]        — fully qualified domain name of directory
partition where zone should be stored; or use one of:
                         /DP /domain - domain directory partition
                         /DP /forest - forest directory partition
                         /DP /legacy - legacy directory partition
```

So did it work? Let's look up a record for the savilltech.com domain.

```
C:\Users\Administrator>nslookup
Default Server:  srvdaldc01.savtech.net
Address:  192.168.1.180

> set q=srv
> _ldap._tcp.savilltech.com
Server:  srvdaldc01.savtech.com
Address:  192.168.1.180

_ldap._tcp.savilltech.com       SRV service location:
          priority       = 0
          weight         = 100
          port           = 389
          svr hostname   = savdaldc01.savilltech.com
_ldap._tcp.savilltech.com       SRV service location:
          priority       = 0
          weight         = 100
          port           = 389
          svr hostname   = savdaldc02.savilltech.net
savdaldc01.savilltech.com       internet address = 192.168.1.10
savdaldc02.savilltech.com       internet address = 192.168.1.11
> quit
```

Here, you use the `nslookup` command but tell it you want to see service type records (`set q=srv` means set query of type service) and then look up the `ldap` service records for the domain.

Caching

You previously read about DNS servers caching results, but where do they do this? If you select Advanced from the View menu, you see a new Cached Lookups branch. If selected, it shows the entire hierarchy of the DNS lookups it has performed (see Figure 7-62). Notice under the com folder, it has all the com name servers that were returned to it when it first tried to find a .com web site.

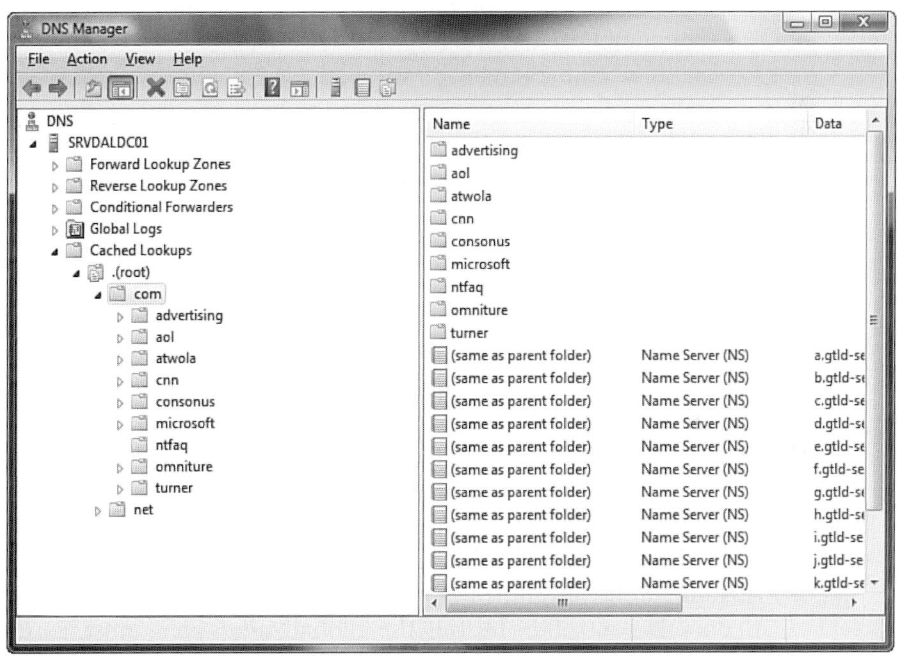

FIGURE 7-62 The content of the local cache.

To clear the cache, right-click Cached Lookups and select Clear Cache. You might want to clear the cache of a DNS server if you believe the cache has incorrect information stored. You can also perform the following from the command line:

```
C:\Users\Administrator>dnscmd /clearcache
. completed successfully.
Command completed successfully.
```

GlobalNames Zone

You spend a few pages on WINS in a minute but WINS has one neat feature—it is a single-label namespace. You don't need john-pc.savtech.net, you just query for john-pc. Now if you tried that in DNS and you had different domains you might or might not get a response depending on if john-pc.savtech.net existed and the default domain of your PC. If you were part of savilltech.com domain, it would look for john-pc.savilltech.com. How inconvenient.

The GlobalNames zone gives you this functionality back as a zone you generally replicate to all DNS servers in the entire forest. Entries in this zone would therefore resolve no matter which domain you resided in.

The obvious difference between the GlobalNames zone and WINS is that WINS is dynamic, with clients updating their own records, whereas GlobalNames is manually maintained. GlobalNames is designed for if you have a few flat names that are still needed in the environment. In general, WINS is no longer required when you combine GlobalNames and DNS suffix search names.

By default, if your single-label name is entered, the GetAddrInfo function appends the DNS domain zones configured for the client to the single-label name to attempt resolution. After the GlobalNames zone is enabled, those local zones are still checked first, and then the GlobalNames zone attempts before failing over to WINS lookups.

All domain controllers hosting the GlobalNames zone must be running Windows Server 2008. Enable global names support to enable the GlobalNames zone, and then create the actual zone in DNS.

First enable global names support on the local server via the `dnscmd` utility. Repeat this on all the DNS servers that hold a copy of the zone, such as all DNS servers in the forest if the best practice is followed and the zone is forest wide.

```
C:\>dnscmd . /config /enableglobalnamessupport 1

Registry property enableglobalnamessupport successfully reset.
Command completed successfully.
```

Now create a new zone called GlobalNames (it is not case sensitive). The best practice is to configure the zone to be stored in the AD and available to all DNS servers in the forest that store the GlobalNames zone in the ForestDNSZones application partition. The zone should be configured for no dynamic updates.

Right-click the Forward Lookup Zones node and select New Zone. Configure as described in the previous paragraph: AD integrated, forest wide, and no dynamic update. After creation, the zone's General tab should look like Figure 7-63.

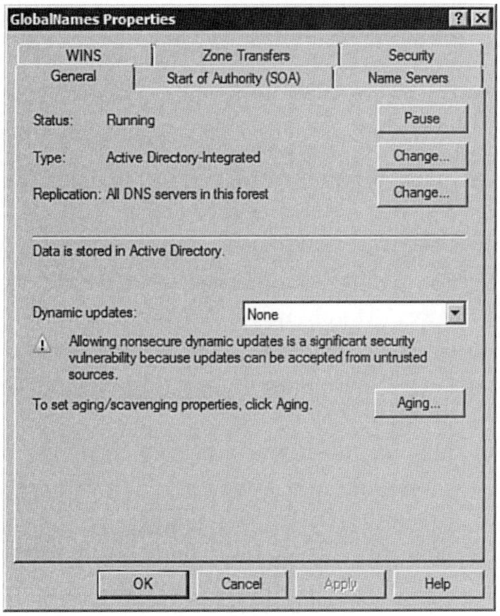

FIGURE 7-63 The correct zone information for GlobalNames zone.

Now create single label alias entries in the zone that resolve to fully qualified names. For example, in Figure 7-64, a filesrv alias is created in the GlobalNames zone. These aliases work anywhere in the forest.

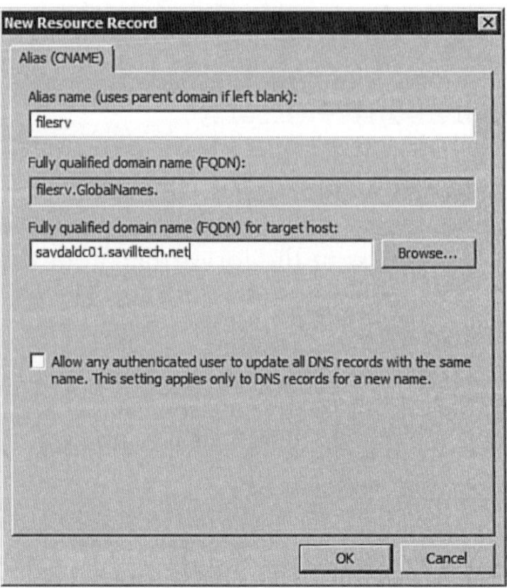

FIGURE 7-64 Creating an entry in the GlobalName.

You can also create alias entries from the command line using `dnscmd`, the command-line interface for DNS. For example:

```
C:\>dnscmd /recordadd GlobalNames filesrv2 CNAME
➥savdaldc02.savilltech.net
Add CNAME Record for filesrv2.GlobalNames at GlobalNames
Command completed successfully.
```

Microsoft has a full document on implementing the GlobalNames zone at www.microsoft.com/downloads/details.aspx?FamilyID=1C6B31CD-3DD9-4C3F-8ACD-3201A57194F1&displaylang=en. It is worth reading because it talks you through the more complex deployment considerations of multiple forests and if the GlobalNames zone is not hosted on all authoritative DNS servers. The guide discusses the use of a service resource record, `_globalnames.msdcs`, in other forests that points to a DNS server hosting global names.

IPv6 Support

DNS fully supports IPv6 both in terms of a new host record type, the AAAA record, and also a special type of reverse lookup zone via the ip6.arpa domain. All the standard interfaces and command-line tools accept both IPv4 and IPv6 formats. Functionality is equal and everything you have learned applies to IPv4 and IPv6. You just have a longer IP address with IPv6.

No special management is needed to use the AAAA IPv6 type host records. You just need to enter an IPv6 IP address for the host record to resolve to, which is why you have a separate type of host record. It needs room to store a 127-bit target instead of a 32-bit target.

WINS

WINS has been around since the days of NetBIOS and was needed for the lookup of NetBIOS names to their IP address and vice-versa. Prior to the AD, all domain names were NetBIOS names. They have a maximum length of 16 characters. NetBIOS stands for Network Basic Input/Output System and is used to separate the details of the network from an application by enabling the application to simply specify a destination for a request. NetBIOS is network independent and although it originally ran over NetBEUI, it was modified to also run over TCP/IP.

Because NetBIOS names can be up to 16 characters, the maximum length for a domain name is 15 characters. The sixteenth character is used to specify the type of resource; for example, <1C> is used to specify the resource is a domain controller. A full list of the NetBIOS suffixes is found in Knowledge Base article Q163409, which is accessed via http://support.microsoft.com.

WINS was also heavily used to help find domain controllers. NT 4 domain controllers have a NetBIOS resource entry of type 1C. There are three methods of resolving NetBIOS names and the order they are used depends on the configuration of the client and the options enabled on your network and clients:

- **WINS request**. If WINS is enabled on the network, servers and clients register their NetBIOS name to IP address mappings dynamically when they start up. When a client needs to resolve a

NetBIOS name, such as a domain name, it sends a request to the WINS server, which sends back a list of up to 25 matching entries.

- **Broadcast**. The client sends out a request to its local subnet, asking if anyone is the destination name. Due to the amount of traffic created by the broadcasts and the fact that NetBIOS broadcasts are not routable, this method is only useful for small non-routed networks.
- **LMHOSTS entry**. Each computer can have a lmhosts file that resides in the %systemroot%\system32\drivers\etc folder. (%systemroot% is an environment variable that points to the root of your Windows installation; for example, C:\Windows.) This file can have NetBIOS entries and one type can be for domain controllers. For example, the following line adds an entry for server savdaldc01 as a domain controller for savilltech at IP address 192.168.1.10.

```
192.168.1.10 savdaldc01 #PRE #DOM:savilltech #savilltech domain
controller
```

Unlike DNS, you cannot store WINS information in AD. It is stored in a file on the WINS server instead. You facilitate high availability and scalability by creating multiple WINS servers and manually configuring push/pull relationships between them to distribute the content of the WINS server's local name database.

With the AD, DNS has replaced WINS for most of the resolution requirements. However, even in a pure AD environment you might still have other applications that use NetBIOS names rather than DNS. This is rare now and hopefully with Windows Server 2008, you can finally now decommission the dreaded WINS service. When GlobalNames is combined with the new dynamic nature of DNS, hopefully you can fully remove WINS. As a word of caution: If you remove WINS and NetBIOS names are still used, there will be a lot of broadcast traffic over the network for resolution. If the machines are on different networks and broadcasts are not routed, the names won't resolve at all.

Instead of installing WINS via a role, it is tucked away as a feature (see Figure 7-65). No requested parameters appear during the installation of WINS. It behaves exactly as in the previous version, which is well documented on the Microsoft web site.

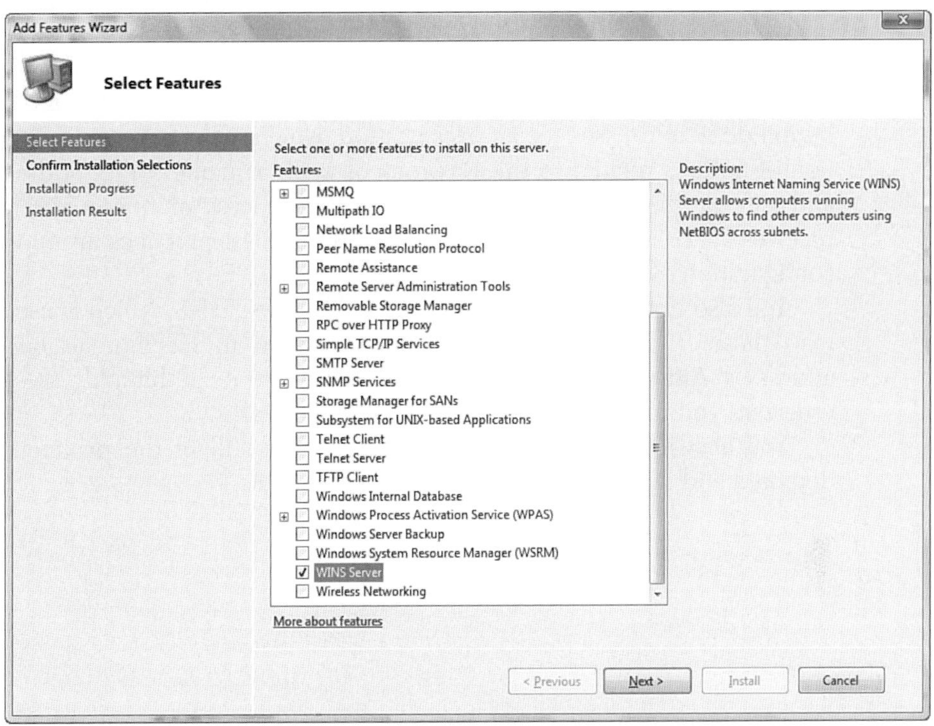

FIGURE 7-65 Installing WINS in Windows Server 2008.

You should only continue to use WINS if you maintain legacy applications that require NetBIOS names and the new GlobalNames DNS zone does not meet your requirements. No components in Windows Server 2008 or Vista require WINS, nor are there requirements in the new Microsoft services, such as Exchange 2007. Sometimes flat names are required, as in Exchange 2007 clustering that needs flat-name resolution, but this can be achieved through DNS via a suffix search list or the GlobalNames zone.

Summary

This chapter has examined ways to automate the management and distribution of IP addresses for an organization, which included the configuration of options related to the IP protocol, such as name server addresses and gateway information. You explored the process of how a machine receives an IP address automatically and some best practices around the configuration of the DHCP service.

You also examined a core service for Windows, DNS, which is used to map those friendly text names you understand to machine usable IP addresses. Although DNS was useful for IPv4 and its 32-bit addresses, it's crucial as you move to IPv6 and its 128-bit addresses.

You also found out that although WINS is still in the product, it's demoted and hopefully you won't need to touch it.

CHAPTER 8

REMOTE ACCESS AND SECURING AND OPTIMIZING THE NETWORK

In parts of this book, you look at making some great features of Windows Server 2008 available outside the internal network; for example, enabling access to Terminal Services (TS) over HyperText Transfer Protocol over Secure Sockets Layer (HTTPS) using the TS Gateway feature (see Chapter 9, "Terminal Services"). However, many types of action and access are available only on the actual internal network, the private network. This chapter focuses on two main areas: how to extend the boundary of your internal network to allow computers on the outside to access resources as if the computers were on the internal network, and how to keep your internal network as clean and secure as possible.

All the functionality discussed in this chapter is part of the Routing and Remote Access Services (RRAS) suite within Windows Server 2008. RRAS includes capabilities for virtual private networking, dial-up services, routing including network address translation (NAT), Remote Authentication Dial-in User Service (RADIUS), and even a limited firewall. A full featured solution exists in Microsoft's Internet Security and Acceleration (ISA) Server, which currently stands at version 2007. It has powerful firewall and connectivity features.

This is another area with a huge number of components. This chapter focuses on the core elements particularly needed to support Network Access Protection (NAP) plus Virtual Private Network (VPN) connectivity, which is the most frequent use of Remote Access. Fortunately, the in-box help for Remote Access is great. It includes detailed documentation and usage examples. Also in this chapter, you perform a full NAP implementation, which is a new feature of 2008.

Virtual Private Networks

As its name suggests, a Virtual Private Network (VPN) is a grouping of technologies that facilitate connections across point-to-point networks. It enables a VPN client to connect to a VPN server. After authentication and authorization, the VPN client computer can access resources on the VPN server's network as if it were locally present. Although a VPN is point-to-point from a user's perspective, after the user connects via VPN, he can connect to any resource on the connected network so that it seems like a point-to-many connection.

A tunnel is created between the client and the VPN server. All traffic between the client and the VPN server network is encapsulated in a special type of packet and sent over the tunnel in a compressed, encrypted format. This means the internal network does not need many types of exceptions in its firewall; all the traffic is sent over the port used for the VPN no matter what service is accessed on the internal network. VPNs are used widely in the industry for people to gain access to resources at the office from home, the road, or a customer site. This is a Remote Access VPN connection because it provides a single user with remote access to your internal network via VPN, as shown in Figure 8-1.

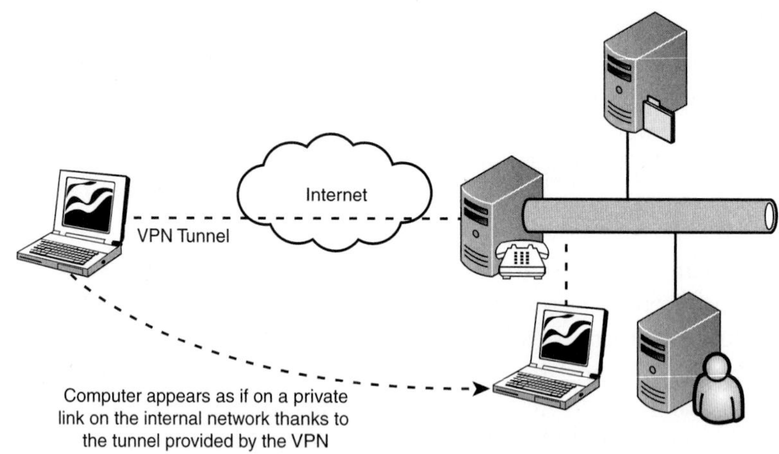

Figure 8-1 Typical Remote Access VPN.

The other type of VPN is typically used between corporate locations, and constitutes a site-to-site VPN. It is essentially the same process as a Remote Access VPN. But consider the case in which a remote office with

20 desktop computers does not have a dedicated line back to corporate. Instead, the remote office has a business-class broadband connection to the Internet via a typical Internet service provider (ISP). It would be possible for each desktop computer to VPN into the corporate environment, but doing so is a hassle for each user and a waste of connections on the VPN server. Instead, a server at the remote site can create a VPN connection to the central VPN server that acts as a router so that all the clients at the remote site can access corporate resources via this single VPN connection. In effect, a dedicated WAN link is created between the remote office and the central office via the VPN connection, as shown in Figure 8-2. All the clients at the remote site can access resources at the central office without taking any special actions.

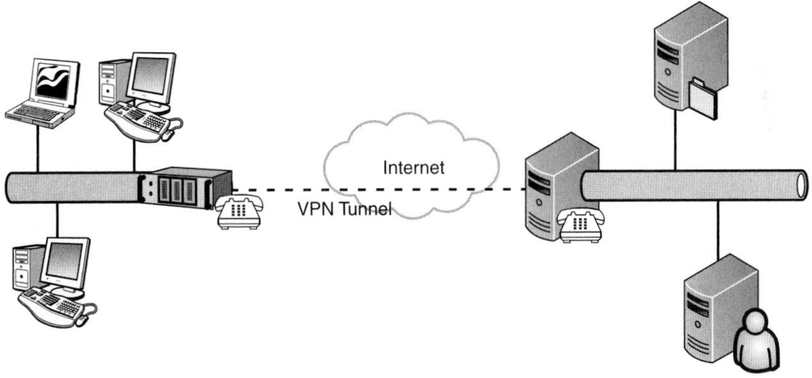

FIGURE 8-2 An example of site-to-site VPN.

The number of situations needing VPN connections has decreased as technology has evolved. Because of the many technologies supporting connectivity over typically open ports (such as HTTPS), you now have more options. For example, Outlook can now talk to its Exchange server over HTTPS (remote procedure call [RPC] over HTTPS). And, as already mentioned, TS connections can now operate over HTTPS thanks to TS Gateway. Many organizations use SharePoint for collaboration and information sharing. SharePoint operates as a web site, so it is already Internet friendly. But there are still times VPN connections are desirable. Unfortunately they are not always available because until now VPN connections operated over specific ports that corporate locations commonly block due to their potential security implications.

What are the security implications? In essence, when you connect via VPN, you connect via a private link to the network. If a vulnerability exists on that VPN network, your client machine is now open to that vulnerability. The reverse argument is also valid. When you offer a VPN service you need to ensure that your security is airtight. As soon as someone VPNs in to your network, it's as if they are sitting at a cubicle inside your building. They are virtually plugged in and can access anything that entails. Clients with a virus or vulnerability connecting via VPN can spread it over your network as if they were directly connected. That is why, as part of your VPN solution, you need to check the health of VPN clients. You need to protect your network. If many of the VPN connections are to be made from users' home computers, you could have a real problem. A home computer is far less likely to have up-to-date patches and virus definitions than your office equipment, and probably sees far more colorful web sites thanks to little Billy exposing it to more attacks.

Because of these security concerns and the importance of the data going over the VPN tunnel, three areas of functionality are offered via VPN solutions. The first is encapsulation, as discussed earlier. Encapsulation wraps any data for transmission over the VPN with information needed for its routing. The form of this encapsulation varies depending on the type of VPN tunnel you use.

The next area of functionality is authentication, and this is vital. You don't want just anyone connecting via your VPN, so you need to be certain whom you are authenticating and maintain this checking in case a VPN session is hijacked over the Internet. There are various options available for authentication. Point-to-Point Protocol (PPP) is the protocol most commonly used. It performs a user authentication at the start to confirm that a user is who he says he is, using an authentication protocol such as Password Authentication Protocol (PAP) or Extensible Authentication Protocol (EAP). Another option is mutual authentication, which is where the VPN server also confirms its identity to the client. This avoids the possibility of a server masquerading as the VPN server, harvesting credentials, and potentially giving false information. You might have heard of PPP from a dial-up perspective in which it sends data over phone lines and has largely replaced Serial Line Internet Protocol (SLIP). Other types of authentication are possible at a computer-level using Internet Key Exchange (IKE), which uses certificates or some shared key for mutual authentication. A similar approach is data origin authentication in which a cryptographic checksum based on a shared encryption key (shared between the VPN client and server) is added to the data being sent, proving the data's integrity.

The third main area is data encryption. You have many connections via the Internet with lots of possibly sensitive data moving back and forth. In addition to providing a path for this virtual private connection, you need to ensure that other parties neither read nor compromise the data. Various data encryption technologies are available to protect the data with variable length encryption keys. The longer the key, the more secure the encryption. Although tunneling does not automatically mean data is encrypted, the use of encryption is generally treated as standard and is normally included as part of the overall VPN solution.

Types of VPN Tunnel

This is an exciting area of Windows Server 2008. A new tunneling protocol addresses one of the major problems with the existing tunneling solutions, namely the need for firewall holes. Let's look at the existing solutions first so that you understand why a new tunneling protocol was introduced.

Point-to-Point Tunneling Protocol (PPTP)

PPTP is a Microsoft-authored protocol and is a standard in the industry for sending traffic using multiple protocols over an Internet Protocol (IP) network. That is also its limitation: PPTP works across IP networks only. But in today's world that is normally enough. The days of IPX support and NetBEUI are behind us.

You learned about PPP earlier, and it is still used. However, PPP needs help over IP networks, so PPTP uses a PPP frame that has a payload encrypted using Microsoft Point-to-Point Encryption (MPEE). MPEE uses MS-CHAP v2 or EAP-TLS using keys generated during the authentication process between the user and the authentication/VPN server. EAP-TLS is far stronger and the preferred choice, with MS-CHAP being only as strong as the user's password. The PPE packet then has a Generic Routing Encapsulation (GRE) header added. GRE is a Cisco-designed protocol that adds information such as a checksum, a key, a sequence number, and routing information. A standard IP header is added to the packet to enable transmission over IP networks.

PPTP uses two streams of information. At the start, Transmission Control Protocol (TCP) port 1723 initiates the PPTP connection and after initiation, 1723 is used for maintenance traffic about the PPTP connection. The tunneled data is sent over Protocol 47 (this is not UDP [User Datagram Protocol] or TCP; it is its own protocol). Many routers refer to this as VPN pass-through.

Layer Two Tunneling Protocol (L2TP)

L2TP provides all the same features as PPTP except it can work on networks other than IP such as frame relay, asynchronous transfer mode (ATM), and X.25 (although X.25 is not supported in Windows Server 2008). Also it can provide higher security by combining with IP security (IPsec). IPsec is required for any encryption or authentication services because L2TP has none natively. There is no use of MPPE for the encryption of the PPP payload with L2TP.

The encapsulation process is similar with L2TP: The PPP frame gets encapsulated with an L2TP header, a UDP header, and, optionally, an IP header if you are using L2TP over IP networks. That's just for a tunneled packet. If you want security and encryption (and you do), you have an IPsec Encapsulating Security Payload (ESP) header and trailer in addition to an IPsec authentication trailer that confirms the integrity of the message and its authenticity. Figure 8-3 shows this total L2TP packet with IPsec ESP encryption.

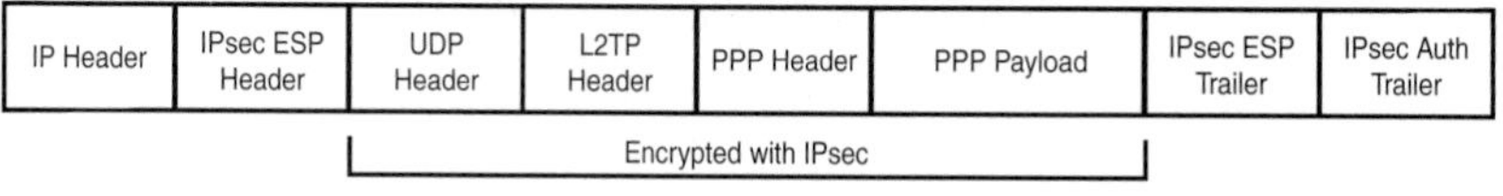

FIGURE 8-3 L2TP packet.

If you are using L2TP over IP, open UDP port 500 for IKE traffic, UDP port 4500 for IPsec NAT-T traffic, and IP Protocol 50 for the IPsec ESP traffic. Open UDP port 1701 for L2TP traffic if the VPN server is in front of a firewall so that the traffic coming through is stripped from the encrypted payload.

Secure Socket Tunneling Protocol (SSTP)

As for both PPTP and L2TP, a combination of ports and protocols must be open for your communication to work and to get your VPN up and running, which is a problem. Most clients won't open these holes in the firewall. With SSTP, Microsoft has created a new protocol that encapsulates PPP frames in HTTPS traffic, allowing communication over the Secure Sockets Layer (SSL) port 443, which is open in most environments. Because you are operating over SSL, the data is encrypted via the SSL channel.

Figure 8-4 shows the communication flow. The firewall symbols can be firewalls, Web proxy servers, NAT routers, or SSL load balancers (and network load balancing is supported). SSTP traverses them all with no issues.

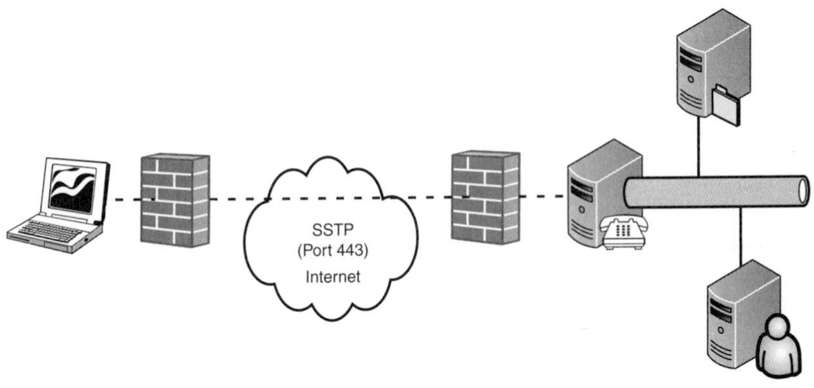

Figure 8-4 The SSTP communication flow.

From an authentication perspective, EAP-TLS is the preferred authentication method, and you can use passwords, smart cards, certificates, and even one-time password type solutions.

Only Windows Server 2008 and Windows Vista SP1 clients support SSTP, so the client base that supports SSTP is initially limited.

Which to Use?

Generally, PPTP is used the most because it works with nearly all Microsoft clients and potentially complex certificate environments are not required. However, PPTP is not as feature rich as L2TP, which has better services that can guarantee data was not modified in transit and provide proof of sender. But a smaller number of clients support L2TP, and distributing the shared key requires a certificate infrastructure or mechanism.

SSTP is the best option in terms of compatibility with firewalls and minimal port requirements, but with such a small number of supported client platforms (again, just Vista SP1 and Server 2008), it's not widely available just yet. Another great advantage of SSTP is that it doesn't care whether it's behind a Web proxy or behind a NAT router, which is typically a problem with PPTP and L2TP.

Installation

The implementation of VPN is provided as part of RRAS, a role service that is part of the Network Policy and Access Services role shown in Figure 8-5. There are no additional stages of installation for RRAS and no questions to answer. It could be because RRAS is so simple that no questions are necessary, or it could be because RRAS is a bit of a bear and the installation wizard can't contain its configuration.

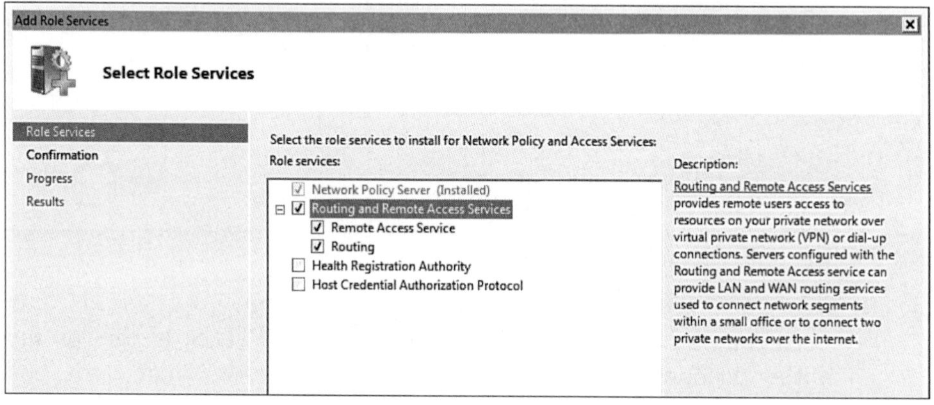

Figure 8-5 Installing the RRAS role service.

Before performing configuration, you need to make sure you have the right hardware on the RRAS server for the functionality you require. For example, if RRAS acts as a VPN server, you need at least two network interface cards (NICs): one NIC connected to a demilitarized zone (DMZ) or the Internet where incoming VPN connections originate from, and a second NIC connected to the internal, private network where the VPN clients have access. This same arrangement of network cards is necessary if the RRAS server is to act as a router between networks. It needs a network connection to each network it is routing between. This includes scenarios in which RRAS is acting as a router to the Internet for an organization to provide NAT.

After you have the NICs installed and configured with addresses, rename the network connections to something meaningful—not Local Area Connection1 and so forth. A name such as Private Network is far more useful in helping to work out which connection connects to the internal, private network. You are now ready to configure RRAS.

After installation, RRAS is disabled. First, run the Configure and Enable Routing and Remote Access action via the Routing and Remote Access snap-in for Microsoft Management Console (MMC). It walks you through a wizard to perform initial configuration and make the server useful. The initial page of the wizard is just an introduction to the process, so click Next, which displays the main configuration screen, as shown in Figure 8-6.

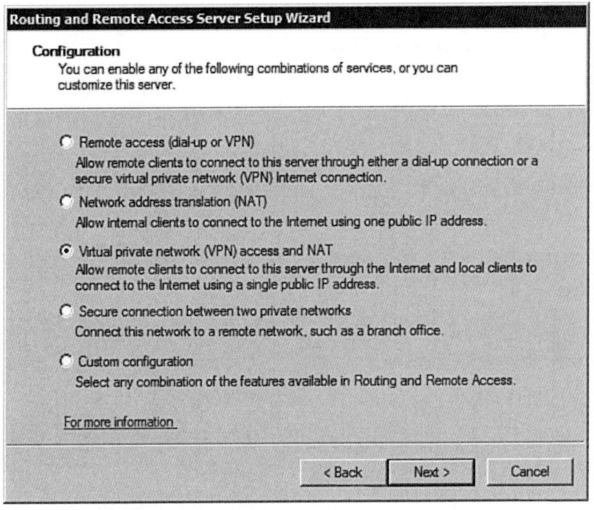

FIGURE 8-6 The initial configuration of RRAS via the wizard.

You have a number of main configuration options, including a Remote Access server that accepts connections via modem (anyone use those anymore?) and via NAT. The latter is useful if you have an internal network using a private IP range and everyone needs Internet connectivity, but you have only one valid Internet IP address (see the NAT sidebar). Those are the main types of configuration, but you might have combinations or different takes. For example, you can set things up as a VPN and NAT server, or you can connect two private networks, or use a custom configuration. Remember, this is not your only time to configure. This wizard gets you up and running quickly, but you perform full configuration outside the wizard after you enable RRAS.

Network Address Translation (NAT)

Internet Protocol version 6 (IPv6) was created because there were no more IP addresses. Although 32 bits sounds like a lot, it's only just over four billion addresses. When you consider that big chunks are lost based on how the classes of addresses are divided, there are not enough addresses for each computer to have a valid Internet IP address that enables it to directly communicate over the Internet. IPv6 solves this with a few thousand addresses for every square meter of the Earth. When change over from IPv4 occurs, NAT will not be necessary. But in the meantime, what is it?

Imagine you have a group of friends down to watch the big game on TV and you want pizza. Everyone wants their own choices, but you are the only one who has a phone. So, you communicate with the pizza man on behalf of everyone else. You take your friends' requests and relay them to the pizza man as if you were making the order, and then relay his responses/questions regarding the order back to your friends. This is the essence of what NAT is, but without cheese.

NAT enables organizations to hide their internal IP addresses and indeed to have many more computers using TCP/IP than would be possible if all the addresses had been allocated by an IP Registry. If an organization uses NAT, it can use any IP address scheme internally (although there are specific ranges set aside for internal use, as discussed in Chapter 6, "TCP/IP"). Only machines connecting directly to the Internet require legitimate addresses, but internal machines can still connect to the Internet thanks to the NAT gateways talking on their behalf and forwarding responses from the Internet to the originator on the local intranet. It's also more secure to conceal your internal IP address structure and have all communication via a NAT firewall.

For example, if a company has 20 computers and they all need Internet connectivity, they would all need legitimate IP addresses. But by using NAT, the only machines that would need legitimate Internet IP addresses would be the NAT gateway connected to the Internet. That means the company might need only one real address. All Internet communication is channeled through that single server (although in reality the company would have several NAT gateways for fault tolerance and load-balancing in larger environments).

Figure 8-7 shows this arrangement, with the NAT server performing all queries requested from the internal clients so that the Internet servers see only the IP address of the NAT server.

There are a number of different NAT types. However, in practice, only one is used today. Static and dynamic NAT do nothing more than replace the internal IP address of a computer with an Internet routable IP address and send the request on its way. However, this requires an equal number of public IP addresses for the number of concurrently connecting internal machines, which is not useful.

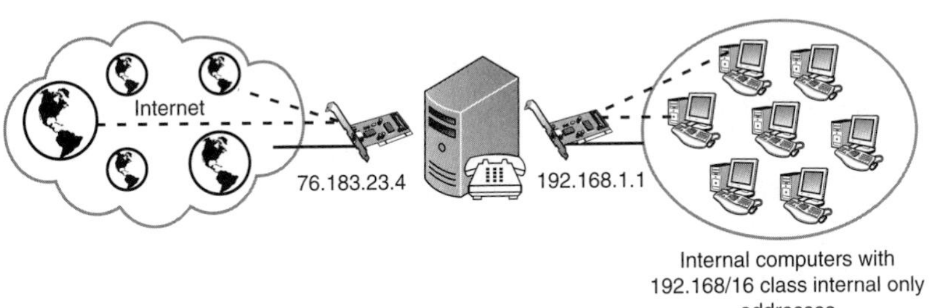

FIGURE 8-7 NAT in action.

More popular and useful is port address translation (PAT) also known as overloading, masquerading, and symmetric NAT. With this version you have only one public IP address (or possibly more, but only one is necessary). The NAT server reads internal requests to the Internet. The source IP address and port of the request are stored in a NAT mapping table on the NAT server. The source is changed to the IP of the NAT server's public IP address and a unique port number is added to the NAT mapping table. NAT uses this information to track this session. When a response comes from the Internet, the NAT server looks at the destination port in the mapping table to find out which internal machine and port to forward the response to. Figure 8-8 shows this process.

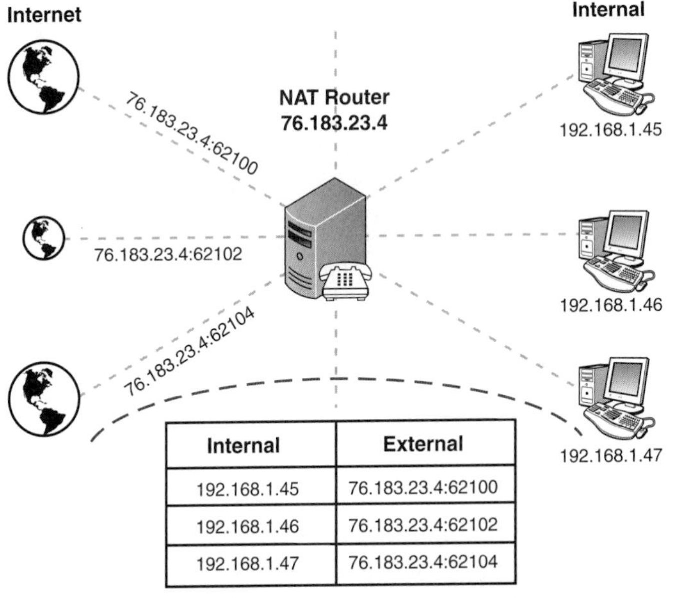

Internal	External
192.168.1.45	76.183.23.4:62100
192.168.1.46	76.183.23.4:62102
192.168.1.47	76.183.23.4:62104

FIGURE 8-8 A sample overloaded NAT in use.

Everyone uses NAT today. It has great features, although it breaks some types of service because there is no true end-to-end connection between the computer and the server on the Internet. For example, Internet phone services have issues with it, as do certain VPN technologies. However, some advancements enable a single level of NAT support.

Right now you just want to configure a VPN server. However, say you are a small shop, so this server also acts as the gateway for your internal network and provides NAT services enabling Internet communication. Pick the VPN Access and NAT option. It is obviously vital that you have a good firewall in the environment, and if your RRAS server is going to face the Internet, you must ensure that the server is as locked down and secure as possible.

The next screen requests that you indicate which connection connects to the Internet. As Figure 8-9 shows, this connection listens for VPN connections. The name of the network connection is displayed.

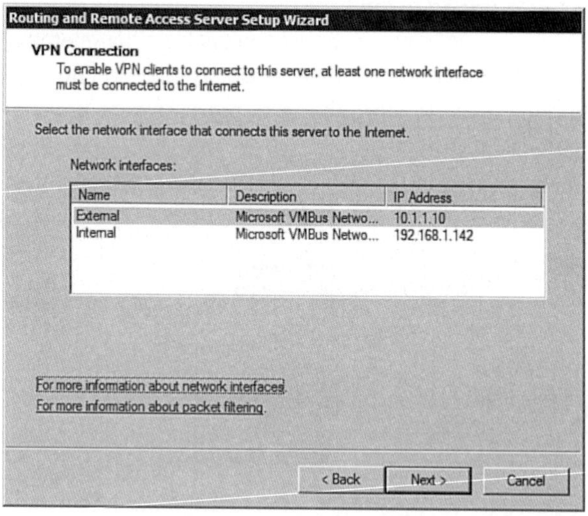

FIGURE 8-9 Selecting the external network.

The next question is how to allocate IP addresses to the VPN clients. If you consider that a tunnel is created between the VPN client and the VPN server into the internal network, the client needs an IP address by which to communicate with internal resources on the internal network. If Dynamic Host Configuration Protocol (DHCP) is already available within the network, the RRAS server can be configured to request addresses from

DHCP that can then be given to the VPN clients. Alternatively if DHCP is not available or you just want to use a different scope of addresses, a specific scope of addresses can be configured for the RRAS server to use for issuance to the VPN clients. If you configure a scope of addresses for RRAS distribution, block out that scope from DHCP so that multiple clients do not use the addresses. If you elect to use DHCP, perform some configuration after this initial setup is complete to indicate the DHCP server or servers to use.

A large part of a secure network is authenticating connection requests, which is important for VPN connections, given the scope of connectivity available after a successful connection. So, for authentication, the RRAS server uses a RADIUS server, which you learn about later in this chapter. But, for now, it uses a server that services authentication requests using a selected user store. In this Windows world, that would commonly be requests to a domain controller to authenticate against the Active Directory. RADIUS is a standard technology, and RRAS provides the Microsoft implementation of RADIUS. As shown in Figure 8-10, you are prompted to indicate whether the local RRAS server or an alternative RADIUS server is going to act as the RADIUS server. For now, use the RADIUS box as this server.

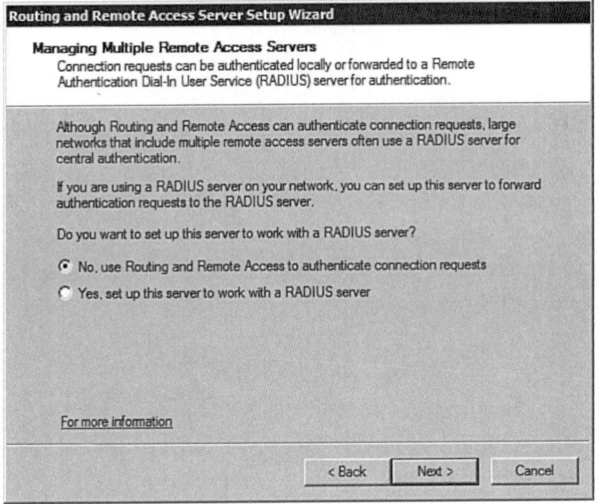

FIGURE 8-10 Using the RRAS as the RADIUS.

A summary of the choices made is displayed. Click Finish to perform the initial configurations and enable the Routing and Remote Access Service.

RRAS is now running and you can get down to the real configuration. But first things first: If you opted to use DHCP for IP address assignment, you need to configure the DHCP relay agent with the list of DHCP servers. The DHCP relay agent passes DHCP requests on behalf of clients to the specified DHCP servers; that is, it relays the requests. Do that by expanding IPv4 and editing the properties of the DHCP relay agent as shown in Figure 8-11. Just enter the IP addresses of the DHCP servers to which RRAS forwards IP address requests.

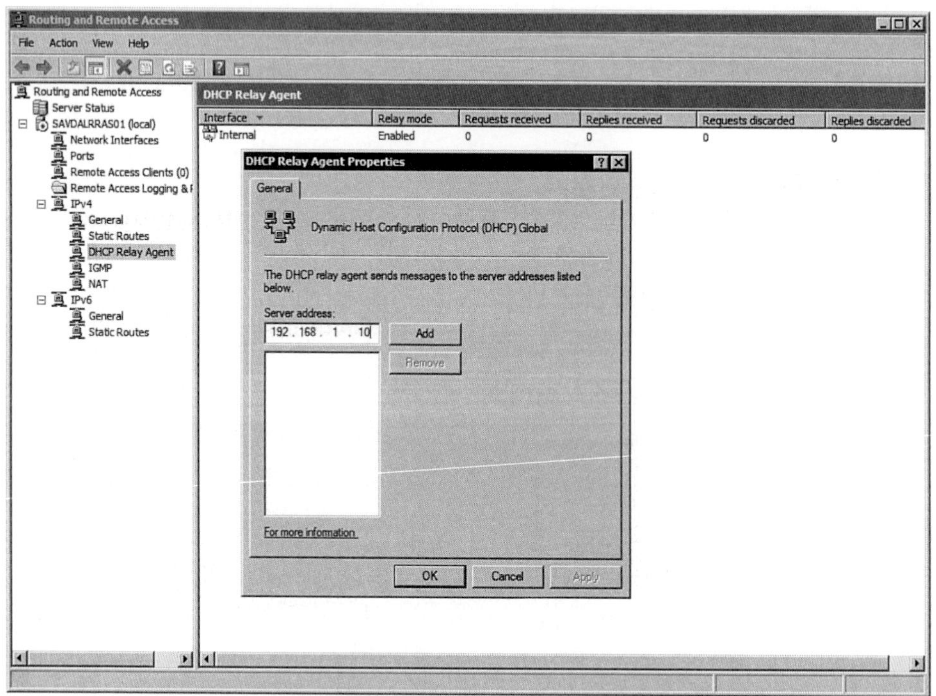

FIGURE 8-11 Initial DHCP configuration of RRAS.

At this point your server is ready to service VPN connections, and connections are ready for all three VPN types: PPTP, L2TP, and SSTP. However, this does not mean you can connect with all types of VPN because some have additional requirements.

PPTP does not require additional configuration. You defined the authentication used during the initial RRAS configuration and you specified Windows authentication, which you can verify via the Security tab of the server properties within the Routing and Remote Access MMC snap-in. If required, changes such as specifying a RADIUS server can be made. If the VPN server has not been configured to use RADIUS, and it's a member of a domain, authentication requests use Active Directory. If the VPN server is in a workgroup, authentication requests use the VPN server's own local account database.

By default Windows Server 2008 server has a firewall that blocks all communication from coming into your server. However, like most components in Windows Server 2008, the RRAS components are fully aware of the Windows Firewall. So, after the VPN capabilities are enabled for RRAS, as shown in Figure 8-12, each exception can be examined to identify the protocol used and ports opened. If you want to disable a certain type of VPN, such as PPTP, you could just disable the rule that allows the type of communication. The correct practice, however, is to remove the ports.

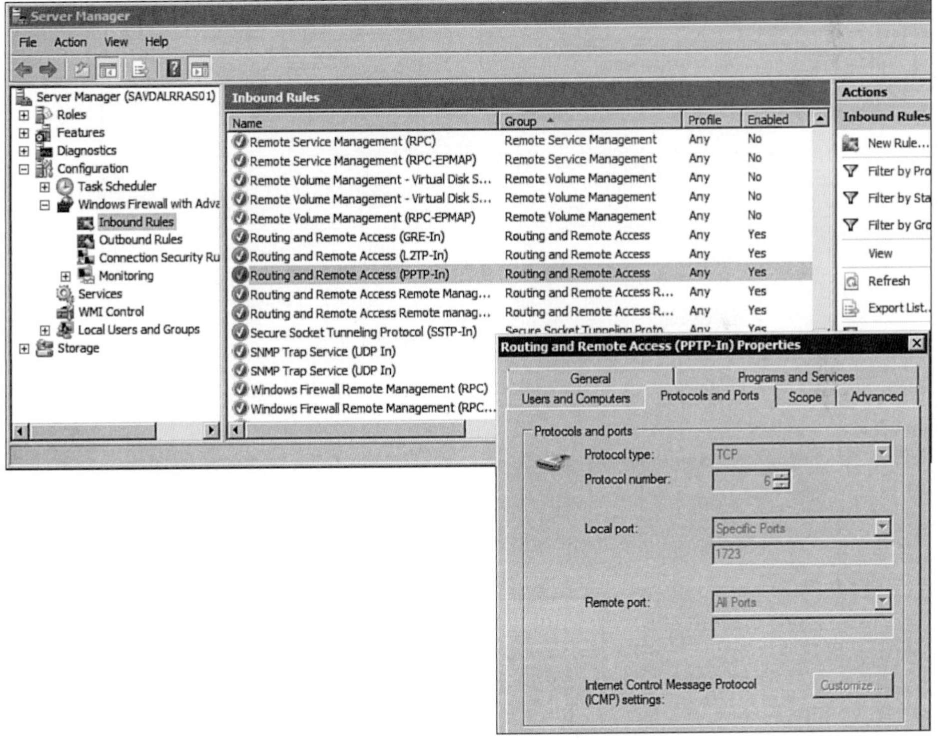

FIGURE 8-12 The firewall exceptions used by RRAS.

Try a VPN connection. If this is on the Internet, make sure you have some public domain name system (DNS) record that clients can use to resolve to your VPN server (such as pptp.savilltech.net or vpn.savilltech.net). If you are just testing, place an entry in the host's file of your client. For example, in file %windir%\system32\drivers\etc\hosts, you could place the following line:

```
10.1.1.10     vpn.savilltech.net
```

Now initiate a connection via the Set up a Connection or Network Wizard that is part of Network and Sharing Center in Windows Vista and Windows Server 2008. Because you are connecting to a VPN, you need to specify the Connect to a Workplace option. The next screen asks whether the connection is via a VPN or via a dial-up connection. Select Use My Internet Connection (VPN), as Figure 8-13 shows.

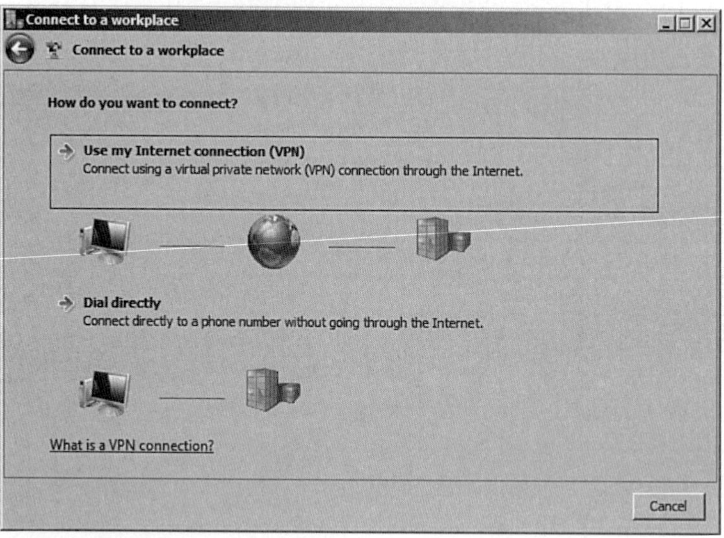

FIGURE 8-13 Choosing a VPN connection.

You then receive a prompt for an address for the VPN server and a name for the VPN connection. Use vpn.savilltech.net or an IP address with the name of VPN connection to SavillTech. Options to use a smart card for authentication and to make the connection available to other users of the computer are also available.

The next screen prompts for credentials, which include domain, username, and password with an option to remember the password. Saving the password can be a security risk if this VPN client is not secure or left unattended in an unlocked state. Enforce this via a DisableSavePassword Registry change under HKLM\System\CurrentControlSet\Services\RasMan\Parameters.

After creating the connection, perform additional configurations on the connection via the properties. The most interesting settings are available through the Networking tab and enable you to specify the type of VPN connection. Instead of using automatic detection, for example, you can force PPTP, L2TP, or SSTP. As part of the IP properties advanced configuration shown in Figure 8-14, specify that the VPN connection act as the default gateway for the connecting computer, which is the default setting. That is also the most secure scenario for a company because without this setting it would be possible for a VPN client to act as a bridge between two networks. That bridge could potentially allow other computers at the VPN client location to access the VPN server network if the VPN client has IP routing enabled. This is known as split-tunneling. With this setting enabled, a new route with a higher metric than existing connections is added on connection, so connections local to the VPN client are not available.

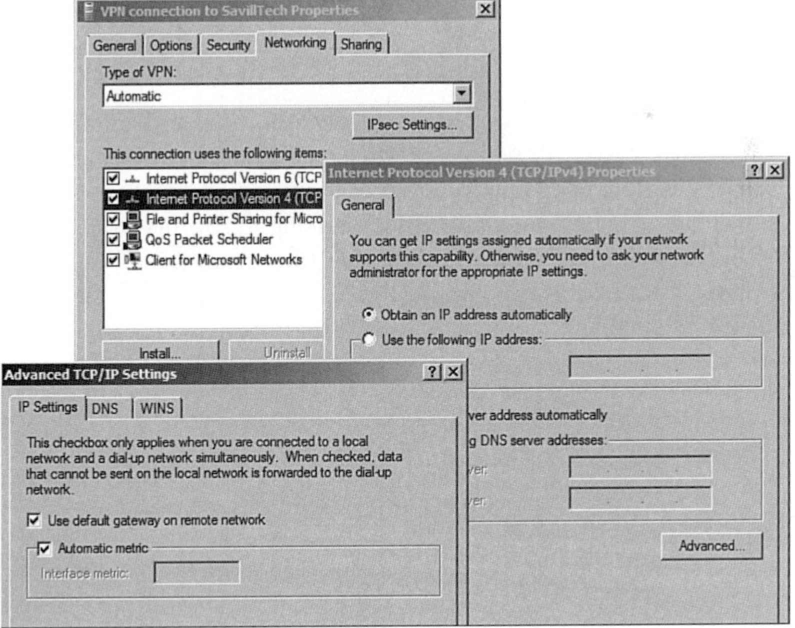

FIGURE 8-14 Advanced IP properties for a VPN connection.

After making any settings, connect to the network as shown in Figure 8-15. However, your connection fails. You are told you have an error, 812, indicating that the policy on your Remote Access Service (RAS)/VPN server does not match that of your connection attempt. Time to investigate.

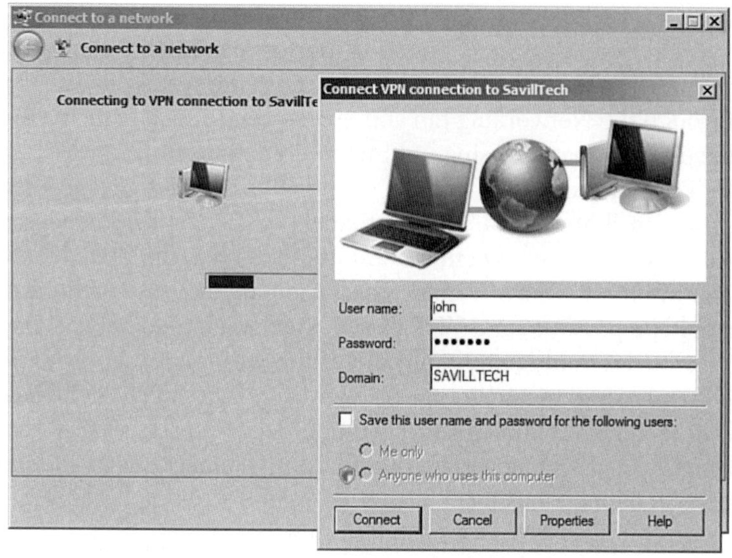

FIGURE 8-15 VPN initialization.

The first place to look is the event logs, and as with all roles in Windows Server 2008, Server Manager is the best place to start—specifically the Network Policy and Access role main page. It summarizes events over the past 24 hours, and you're looking for events from RemoteAccess. On that main page you see a number of warnings, including the following one:

```
Log Name:      System
Source:        RemoteAccess
Date:          1/15/2008 3:31:56 PM
Event ID:      20258
Task Category: None
Level:         Warning
Keywords:      Classic
User:          N/A
Computer:      savdalRRAS01.savilltech.net
Description:
```

```
CoId={CF13A840-7D95-4E63-9DE4-7B0E4B6F1E93}: The account for
user \SAVILLTECH\john connected on port VPN2-127 does not have
Remote Access privilege.  The line has been disconnected.
```

It's just a permissions issue: The user you're trying to connect with does not have rights to connect via remote means. If you examine the properties of a user using AD Users and Computers as shown in Figure 8-16, a user has a number of options related to remote connections. Although it's called Dial-in, this is just a carryover from the old days; the information applies to any form of remote access, including VPN.

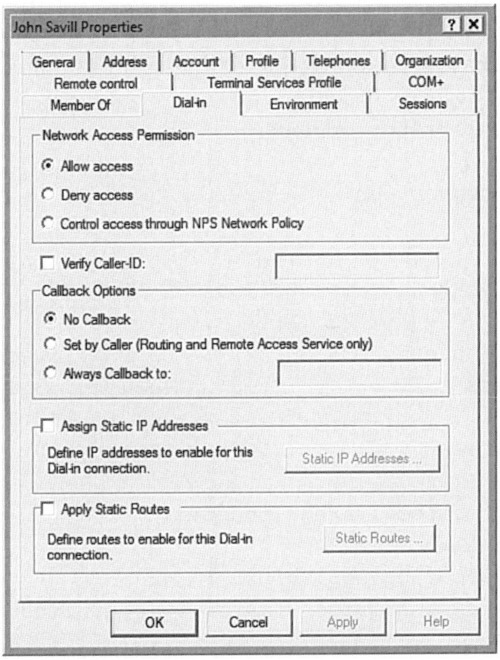

FIGURE 8-16 The user properties related to Remote Access.

The Network Access Permission is the most important. By default the permission is controlled via a Network Policy Server (NPS) network policy. However, you have not enabled this component yet, so if you want to allow this user to connect, you have to set Allow Access. This is only for interim testing, though. The best practice is to use NPS network policies.

The Verify Caller-ID and Callback options relate to dial-in (modem) connections. The options enable users to connect only if they are dialing from a specific number and either allow the NPS server to call the user back (for phone charge purposes) or to always call back, which acts as another security layer ensuring the connection is to a specific number.

The Assign Static IP Addresses option enables a specific IP address always to be given to a connection made by the user, and the Apply Static Routes area allows a number of routes to be defined for connections that are added to the routing table of the server for use by the named user.

In this case, enable your user, attempt the connection, and it works. If you look at the IP properties, you see a new connection that has an IP address from the internal network as shown in the following listing. The client has full access to the network and even out to the Internet for Web browsing via this connection, which was previously unavailable because the client was on a private network that did not allow Internet access for Web browsing. Pay attention to the PPP adapter connection configuration.

```
C:\Users\Administrator>ipconfig

Windows IP Configuration


PPP adapter VPN connection to SavillTech:

   Connection-specific DNS Suffix  . : savilltech.net
   IPv4 Address. . . . . . . . . . . : 192.168.1.63
   Subnet Mask . . . . . . . . . . . : 255.255.255.255
   Default Gateway . . . . . . . . . : 0.0.0.0

Ethernet adapter Local Area Connection 4:

   Connection-specific DNS Suffix  . :
   Link-local IPv6 Address . . . . . : fe80::c0ba:74b:75f6:afa9%13
   IPv4 Address. . . . . . . . . . . : 10.1.1.20
   Subnet Mask . . . . . . . . . . . : 255.255.255.0
   Default Gateway . . . . . . . . . : 10.1.1.10
```

You can perform additional configuration on your VPN connections, primarily through the server properties and the Ports configuration.

How do you disable a certain type of VPN connectivity? If you select the properties of the Ports console tree item, a list of the types of wide area network (WAN) miniports are displayed. The list shows the type and number of ports, which represent the maximum number of concurrent connections using that type of connection. By default, that maximum is 128. You can select each VPN connection type, and via the Configure button, modify its properties as shown in Figure 8-17. That includes the maximum number of ports, which affects the number of concurrent VPN connections. If you want to disable a type of VPN, uncheck the Remote Access Connections (Inbound Only) and Demand-Dial Routing Connections (Inbound and Outbound) check boxes.

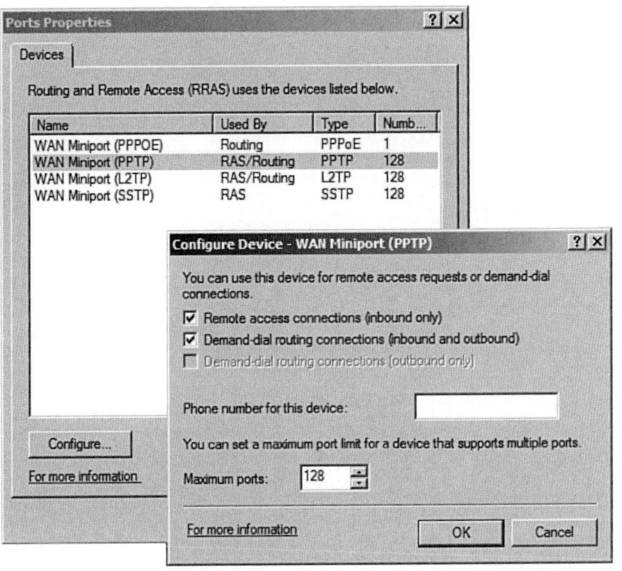

FIGURE 8-17 Configuring the PPTP properties.

The server properties provide access to general RRAS options. For example, the General tab shows whether the RRAS server acts as an IPv4 and/or IPv6 router (see the "Routing" section).

The Security tab enables specification of a RADIUS server. However, after installing NPS, you have additional functionality. On the Security tab, you can specify the IPsec policy to use with an L2TP VPN. If the NPS Role Service is installed on the server, the option to configure RADIUS authentication is not available. Instead, you must use connection request policies to configure things. However, you do get a new Authentication Methods option, as shown in Figure 8-18.

The IPv4 and IPv6 tabs allow configuration of the IP configuration of the server, including specifying whether DHCP or a static pool of addresses is used. This is the same configuration you performed during the initial activation of RRAS. In addition, you can turn off the broadcast name resolution. However, doing so is not recommended because this facilitates the resolution of names via broadcast for VPN clients. Also part of the IP dialogs is the specification of the adapter to use on the RRAS server to facilitate DHCP, DNS, and Windows Internet Name Service (WINS) requests from the clients. By default, these requests fall to the "other" adapter in the server—the one not used for the servicing of VPN requests. As shown in Figure 8-19, in my environment the internal adapter is used for these services.

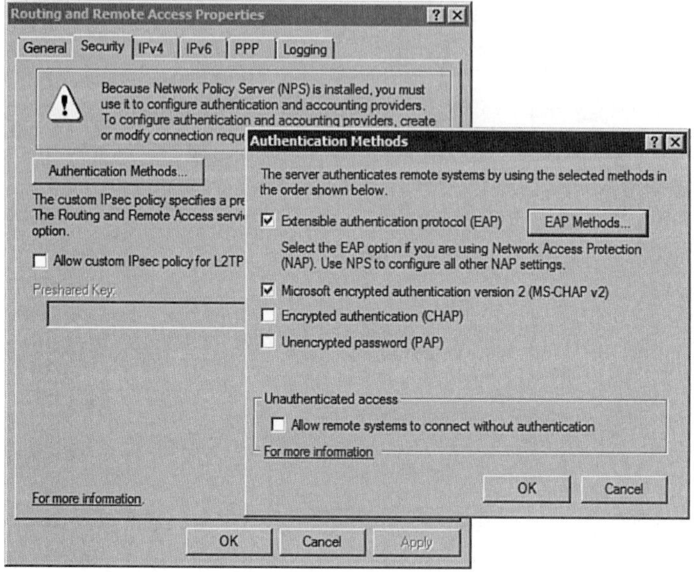

FIGURE 8-18 The Security dialog with NPS installed.

The PPP tab enables configuration of PPP-specific properties such as whether multilink connections are supported. That setting enables multiple separate connections to join into a single logical connection and is typically useful in a dial-up environment rather than VPN. Additionally, Link Control Protocol (LCP) can be disabled, which stops facilities such as time remaining, identification data regarding sessions, and whether software compression is used.

The Logging tab for a server enables configuration of the logs generated for a server (by default, errors and warnings). You can also enable advanced logging, which is useful for debugging situations in which you are trying to troubleshoot connectivity problems. Such logs write to the %windir%\tracing folder in the PPP.log file. Normally, log information is written to the event log and is summarized as part of the main role screen you saw earlier. But it can be viewed the old fashioned way in the System event log.

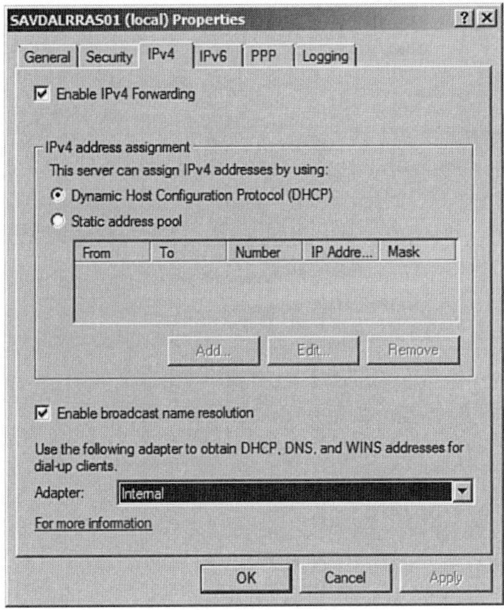

FIGURE 8-19 IPv4 properties for a server.

If you view the Ports area of RRAS, you see active connections that you can select to view details. The details include the address of the client via VPN, the amount of data sent over the connection, and the connection time. Click the headings of the display to sort by the column, so to quickly see the active connections, click the Status column and all the active ports display first. The same type of information is available on a per-user level via the Remote Access Clients area, as shown in Figure 8-20, which displays all the ports used for each user.

So, you got PPTP up and running. Let's look at SSTP now because it's a new protocol and you won't find much on its configuration. Not a huge amount of extra configuration is required except for the certificate requirement that you need to get SSL connectivity.

For SSTP you need a server/machine or all-purpose certificate and a certificate authority configured in your environment or you could request certificates from a third party. This is the same type of key you use for normal SSL connectivity to a server. You don't have to distribute this certificate to clients in advance. It is sent to the client during the SSL initiation phase. However, the clients do need to trust the certificate authority that generates the certificate for SSTP to work (in addition to the next requirement regarding the Certificate Revocation List [CRL] discussed later in this chapter). If you are using a third-party certificate, just request it as usual, making sure the common name matches the full name VPN clients use to connect, and then install it.

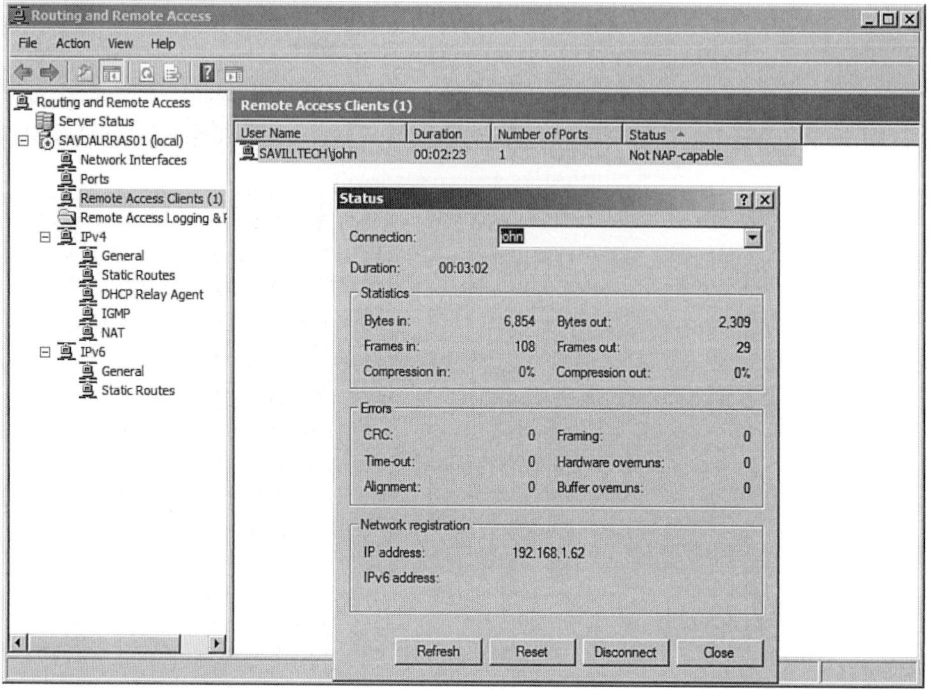

FIGURE 8-20 Viewing the connected users via RRAS.

You walked through installing the Active Directory Certificate Services in Chapter 4, "Securing Your Windows Server 2008 Deployment." However, remember that because a VPN is used outside your network, if you use an Internet certificate authority (CA) you need to ensure that the CRL Distribution Point (CDP) is available for checking certification revocation during the SSL initiation phase. Whatever approach you take, get a certificate onto the server for SSL. Then the SSTP listener binds to the installed server authentication certificate, and the SSTP VPN becomes available.

You can view the binding of the certificate to the SSL service with the `netsh http show ssl` command, which shows the binding for both IPv4 and IPv6. If you install IIS on the same server as your RRAS server, you need to be careful around the binding of a certificate to port 443 for a web site because this overrides the binding performed by SSTP. That is fine, assuming that the same certificate is used. If you remove the binding of the certificate from port 443 or if you add the certificate after installing RRAS, you can force Remote Access to check for a certificate to use by removing the certificate hash from the Registry and restarting the services. First delete any binding still in place for both IPv4 and IPv6. If you want to change the certificate, perform the same steps but first remove the old certificate from the Personal store for the computer account and load the new certificate to use into the Personal store. These steps force use of the new certificate.

```
C:\>netsh http delete ssl 0.0.0.0:443
SSL Certificate successfully deleted

C:\>netsh http delete ssl [::]:443
```

Next, delete the existing certificate hash from the Registry for the SSTP service with the following command (or you can just use RegEdit to remove the SHA256CertificateHash value):

```
C:\>reg delete
➥HKLM\SYSTEM\CurrentControlSet\Services\SstpSvc\Parameters
➥ /v SHA256CertificateHash /f
The operation completed successfully.
```

Then stop the SSTP service and then start Remote Access, which forces the SSTP to check for a certificate and rebind SSL.

```
C:\>net stop sstpsvc /y
The following services are dependent on the Secure Socket
Tunneling Protocol Service service.
Stopping the Secure Socket Tunneling Protocol Service service
will also stop these services.

   Routing and Remote Access
   Remote Access Connection Manager

The Routing and Remote Access service is stopping...
The Routing and Remote Access service was stopped
successfully.

The Remote Access Connection Manager service is stopping.
The Remote Access Connection Manager service was stopped
successfully.

The Secure Socket Tunneling Protocol Service service is
stopping.
```

```
The Secure Socket Tunneling Protocol Service service was
stopped successfully.

C:\>net start remoteaccess
The Routing and Remote Access service is starting.
The Routing and Remote Access service was started
successfully.
```

We can now run the binding check again and all should look happy.

```
C:\>netsh http show ssl

SSL Certificate bindings:
-------------------------

    IP:port                      : 0.0.0.0:443
    Certificate Hash            :
b6dadf4cbe5c08261c84f111128306199d0c0d76
    Application ID              : {ba195980-cd49-458b-9e23-
c84ee0adcd75}
    Certificate Store Name   : MY
    Verify Client Certificate Revocation     : Enabled
    Verify Revocation Using Cached Client Certificate Only     :
Disabled
    Usage Check     : Enabled
    Revocation Freshness Time : 0
    URL Retrieval Timeout    : 0
    Ctl Identifier              :
    Ctl Store Name              :
    DS Mapper Usage     : Disabled
    Negotiate Client Certificate     : Disabled

    IP:port                      : [::]:443
    Certificate Hash            :
b6dadf4cbe5c08261c84f111128306199d0c0d76
    Application ID              : {ba195980-cd49-458b-9e23-
c84ee0adcd75}
    Certificate Store Name   : MY
    Verify Client Certificate Revocation     : Enabled
    Verify Revocation Using Cached Client Certificate Only     :
Disabled
```

```
Usage Check     : Enabled
Revocation Freshness Time : 0
URL Retrieval Timeout    : 0
Ctl Identifier          :
Ctl Store Name           :
DS Mapper Usage     : Disabled
Negotiate Client Certificate    : Disabled
```

If you have multiple server authentication certificates installed on a server and need to specify which one is bound after running the Registry delete command and before stopping the SSTP service, use NETSH to force the SSLCERT mapping for IPv4 and IPv6, specifying the certificate thumbprint. It is found in the properties of the certificate, in the Field-Value section of the Details tab. The commands to run are as follows:

```
netsh http add sslcert ipport=0.0.0.0:443
➥certhash=<Certificate Thumbprint> appid={ba195980-cd49-458b-
9e23-c84ee0adcd75} certstorename=MY
netsh http add sslcert ipport=[::]:443
➥certhash=<Certificate Thumbprint> appid={ba195980-cd49-458b-
9e23-c84ee0adcd75} certstorename=MY
```

If you have connection problems, such as error 809, which is no response from the RRAS server, ensure that all firewalls between the client and the server are allowing port 443 traffic and that the client has connectivity to the server. Verify the RRAS server is listening on port 443 with NETSTAT:

```
C:\>netstat -aon | findstr 443
  TCP    0.0.0.0:443            0.0.0.0:0              LISTENING
4
  TCP    [::]:443               [::]:0                 LISTENING
4
```

NOTE Microsoft has a great blog page at http://blogs.technet.com/RRASblog/archive/2007/09/26/how-to-debug-sstp-specific-connection-failures.aspx, which talks through some common problems and things to do to fix them.

RADIUS and Policy Services

You need NPS for Windows Server 2008 to provide full RADIUS-style functionality. NPS requires no configuration when its role service is installed—that all comes after installation.

RADIUS Configuration

By default, when you install NPS it becomes a RADIUS server and can perform authentication and authorization requests for clients based on the network policies you create. NPS can use an NT 4.0 domain, Active Directory, or a local accounts database to perform the authentication requests.

You can add to the RADIUS configuration specific RADIUS clients that are devices on the network, expand the network in some way, or give access to other areas of the network. A few such devices are wireless access points and other network access servers such as VPN servers. When a RADIUS client is added via the RADIUS Clients console tree item and a friendly name for the client is given along with its IP address or DNS name, the vendor of the RADIUS client can be selected along with the shared secret used between the RADIUS server and client. You can also specify whether the RADIUS client must contain the Message-Authenticator attribute. It is like a signature and gives extra security for the authentication. Finally, you can also specify whether the device supports NAP.

You can perform configuration using the command line via the `netsh nps add client` command with various options such as name, address, shared secret, and NAP compatibility. The command-line help for `netsh` gives the required information.

It is clear here that RADIUS clients are not the everyday computers that connect via VPN and receive authentication—those are access clients. RADIUS clients are machines that authenticate clients using the RADIUS service.

Remote RADIUS server groups are used to define groups of other RADIUS servers that NPS can forward requests to if the server is configured as a RADIUS proxy. This means it receives requests for authentication and authorization and forwards them to another RADIUS server. When you configure a connection request policy, if you want to forward requests for authentication, you select a RADIUS server group and not a specific server. When you have connection request policies that forward to other RADIUS servers, you are acting as a RADIUS proxy.

Using NPS as a RADIUS proxy is great when you consider that you might have many different access clients requesting access that might need authentication by different RADIUS servers based on attributes of the client. Using NPS, you can define RADIUS server groups for the various RADIUS servers available and then use connection request policies to forward the various types of authentication and authorization requests to the relevant RADIUS server. This would apply equally well if you have clients from various domains and use NPS as the RADIUS proxy to forward the requests to the correct server in the right domain.

Policies

Earlier in this chapter, you modified a user account to enable dial-up access instead of using network policies. Network policies enable a set of conditions to be specified, and depending on the results, settings can be applied that control remote access. So an NPS enabled with network polices and used as a RADIUS server performs both authorization, which confirms someone is who they say they are, and authentication, which confirms the permissions/access someone has. This is not a new feature. Windows Server 2003 referred to network policies as remote access policies. They have just been rebranded into the network nomenclature.

By default the NPS server uses the Active Directory of the domain it is a member of as its account repository. However, if you wanted to use the local Security Accounts Manager (SAM) database, you can set that via a Registry change. Open RegEdit and navigate to HKEY_LOCAL_MACHINE\SYSTEM\CurrentControlSet\Services\RasMan\PPP\ControlProtocols\BuiltIn. Create a new String value named DefaultDomain (if it does not exist) and set it to the local NPS server name instead of a domain name.

There are three different types of policies with Network Policy Server:

- **Connection request policies**. These policies determine which RADIUS server responds to incoming requests.
- **Network policies**. These are your main interest and designate users and groups that can connect to the network.
- **Health policies**. NAP uses these policies to determine health levels for clients requesting connectivity.

Health policies are in the NAP section, so let's concentrate on network policies for now because they give the most functionality. With a network policy you can base access on many criteria such as group membership for the user, the type of connection, the access server used, and even the time of the day. You can then authorize different aspects of connection, which can include how long a session can be idle before timeout, the maximum duration of a session, and various connectivity enforcements such as encryption.

A wizard creates network policies. Select the Network Policies node under Policies in the console tree and run the New action. The first page of the dialog, as shown in Figure 8-21, enables you to specify a name for the policy and the type of access it controls. You create a VPN connection policy to control rights concerned with VPN connectivity.

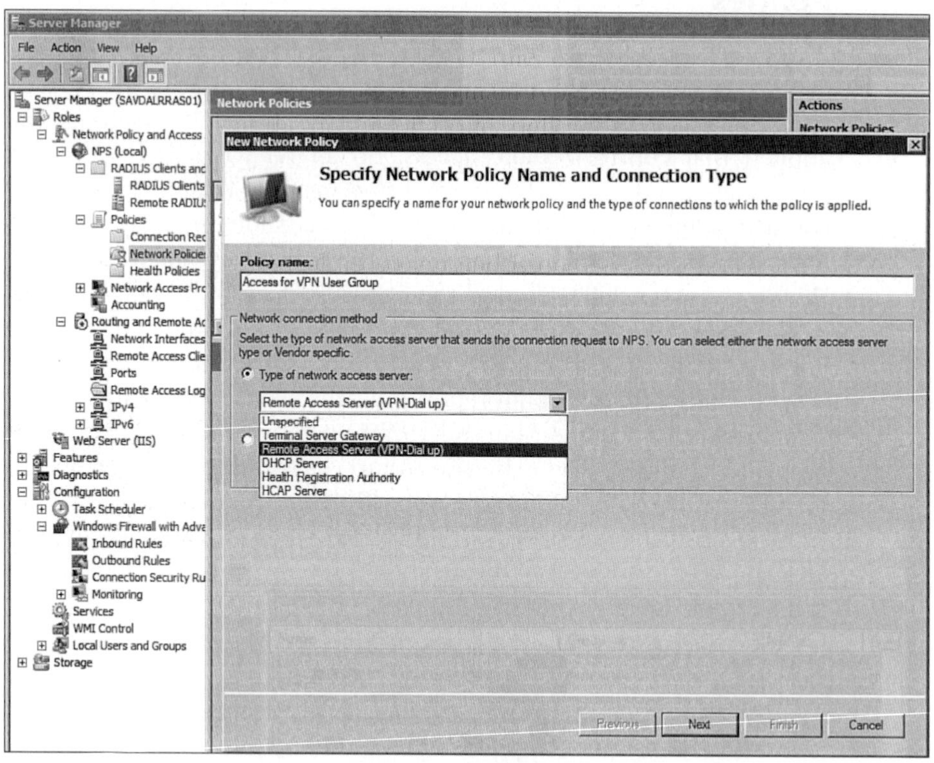

FIGURE 8-21 Selecting the type of connection the policy controls.

The next stage enables multiple conditions to be set for the network policy, which you can select from the conditions available for a network policy as shown in Figure 8-22. There is a broad range of conditions from basic level group membership checks, communication with Host

Credential Authorization Protocol (HCAP) servers, date, time down to hourly granularity for all the days of the week, and operating system information such as version, service pack, health information, connection details, and gateway. A full description of the conditions is in the Windows Server 2008 NPS help file, Network Policy Conditions Properties.

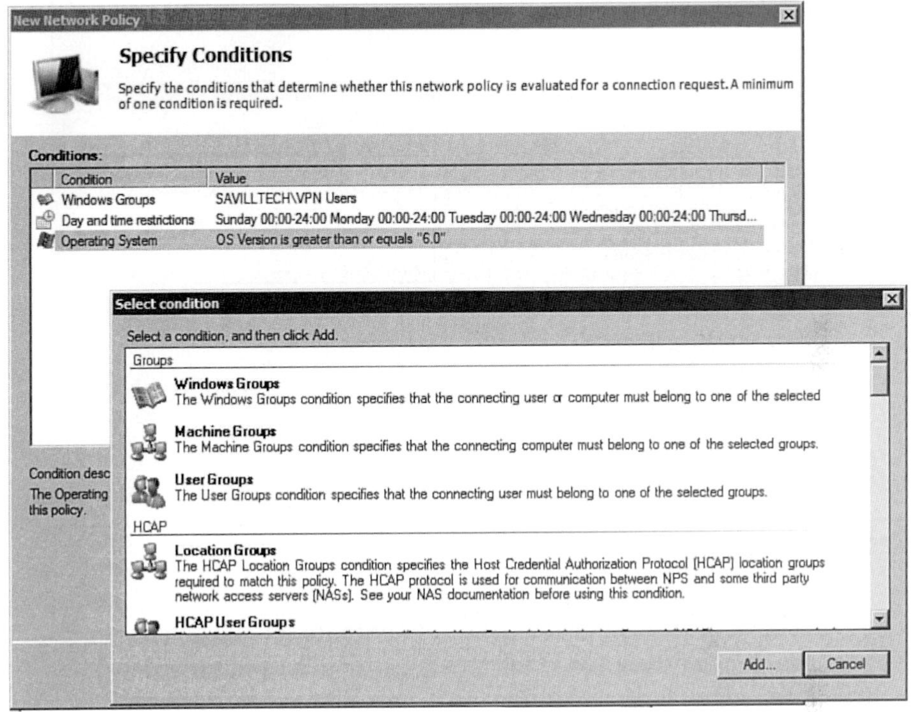

FIGURE 8-22 Additional conditions to a network policy.

The next stage of the configuration confirms the action to take if the policy matches. The actions include grant access, deny access, or use the setting defined in the user properties and override the network policy.

Next, set the authentication methods allowed for the connection as shown in Figure 8-23. Older authentication methods are listed and MS-CHAP 1 and 2 are enabled by default. However, the Add button adds other methods such as Protected EAP and smart card/certificate-based authentication.

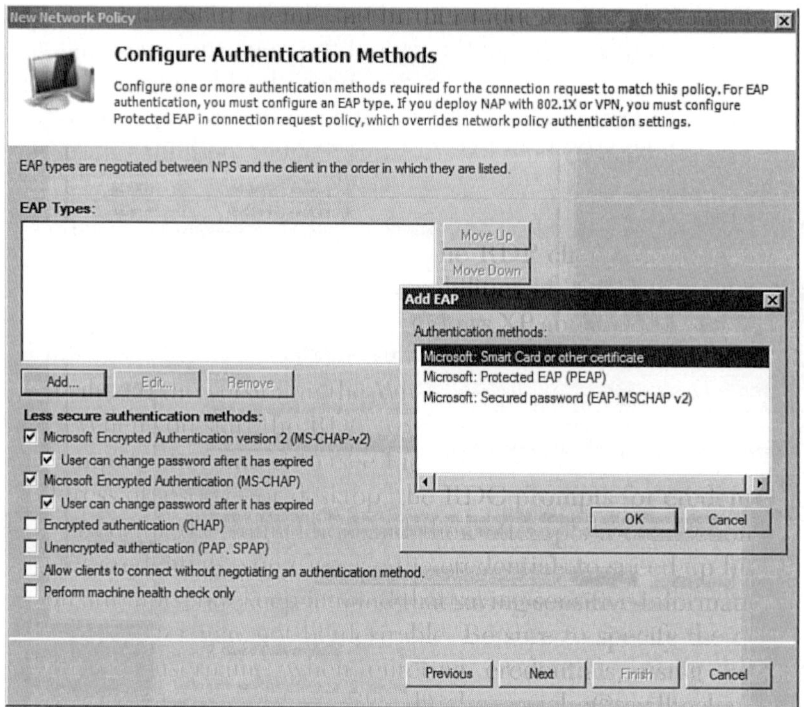

FIGURE 8-23 Configuring authentication methods.

The next stage enables the configuration of constraints for the policy. The constraints include idle time out and maximum session duration in addition to configuring the type of medium used for the connectivity (see Figure 8-24).

Next, enable settings for information given to the client, including many different types of RADIUS attributes, plus vendor-specific, custom attributes. NAP can be considered during the access, enabling various levels of access based on NAP status, plus configurations related to bandwidth allocation, multilink options, and encryption.

Finally, a summary is displayed of the conditions defined to meet the policy and then the settings of the policy. Confirm all the information and click Finish to create.

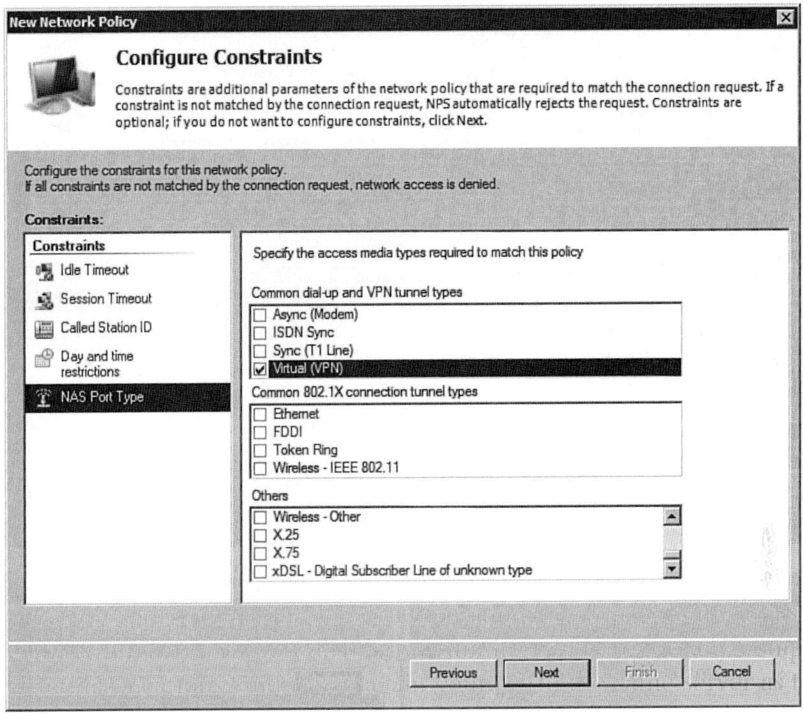

FIGURE 8-24 Specifying the port connection type constraints.

The new policy displays in the list of network policies (by default, you also have deny policies for all connections). The built-in deny policies have the lowest possible processing order (999999 and 999998), so any policies you create process first. When a matching policy is found, no other policies are processed. So, if you create an allow access policy that processes first and matches a user/computer, that user/computer has access. Likewise, if you have a deny policy before an allow policy and both match a user/computer, the deny policy matches first and the connection is denied. So, it is important that you have policies in the right order. Modify them via the Move Up and Move Down actions for a policy, as shown in Figure 8-25.

This ordering of policies is vital because, for example, you might have a general policy to allow access to all users during working hours but want IT support to have access 24 hours a day. So, you would create an allow access policy for members of the IT support group for all hours access and have a higher processing order than the general user access policy.

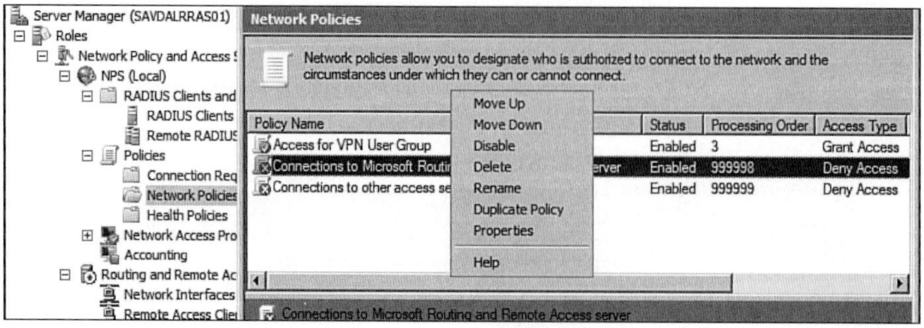

FIGURE 8-25 Setting the order of policies.

Modify existing network policies via the Properties action, which breaks down the policy into the four types of configuration. First is the overview, which is the name of the policy, whether the policy is enabled, its access permission, and the connection method. You then have the conditions that must be met to match the policy, the constraints for the policy, and the settings that apply to the client and connection. You might want to create a general type of network policy and then use the Duplicate Policy action, which creates a copy of the policy with a lower processing order that is disabled by default. You can then access the properties of the copy, change the name, enable and modify settings such as the hour constraints, medium of connection, and conditions to apply, such as group memberships.

The network policies are powerful for managing configuration properties for the environment. If you want to enable/disable particular users outside of policy, modify the user's properties directly.

The Connection Request Policy Wizard configures how incoming authentication requests are handled. By default a connection request policy exists that is configured to authenticate requests locally on the server for all hours and clients. However, additional policies can be created using the Create Connection Request Policy Wizard, which works in the same basic way as the network policy wizard—you have a set of conditions for when the policy is used and then the settings that the policy defines.

Logging

Errors related to remote access are written in the Event log. However, additional information is written to the C:\Windows\System32\LogFiles folder in a comma-separated log file format that gives additional information, as shown in the following listing. The name of the file is INyymm.log where yy is the year and mm is the month, assuming that you have performed no other naming configuration. You can easily import this file into Excel and specify the comma as the separator to make it easily readable:

```
"SAVDALNPS01","RAS",01/18/2008,14:51:44,1,"SAVILLTECH\john",
"savilltech.net/Users/John Savill",,"10.1.1.20",,,
"SAVDALNPS01","192.168.1.142",256,,"192.168.1.142",
"SAVDALNPS01",,,5,,1,2,4,"Access for VPN User Group",0,"311 1
fe80::48aa:cc3a:980e:2444 01/15/2008 20:19:32
25",,,,,,,,,"15",,,,,,,,,1,1,"10.1.1.20",,,,,,,,"MSRASV5.20",31
1,,,,,"Microsoft Routing and Remote Access Service
Policy",1,,,"MSRAS-0-SAVDALSAND01","MSRASV5.20"
"SAVDALNPS01","RAS",01/18/2008,14:51:44,2,,"savilltech.net/
Users/John Savill",,,,,,,,,,,,,,,1,2,4,"Access for VPN User
Group",0,"311 1 fe80::48aa:cc3a:980e:2444 01/15/2008 20:19:32
25",,1800,,,,,,,"15",,,,,,,,,,,,,,,,,,,,,,"0x00534156494C4C5445
4348",,,"Microsoft Routing and Remote Access Service
Policy",1,,,,
"SAVDALNPS01","RAS",01/18/2008,14:51:46,4,"SAVILLTECH\john",,,"
10.1.1.20",,"192.168.1.58",
"SAVDALNPS01","192.168.1.142",256,,"192.168.1.142",
"SAVDALNPS01",1200689506,,5,,1,2,,,0,"311 1
fe80::48aa:cc3a:980e:2444 01/15/2008 20:19:32
25",,1800,,,1,,,,"15",3,,,,,"27",1,,1,1,"10.1.1.20",,,,,,,,
"MSRASV5.20",311,,"0x00534156494C4C54454348",4,,"Microsoft
Routing and Remote Access Service Policy",1,,,"MSRAS-0-SAVDAL-
SAND01","MSRASV5.20"
```

Logging is configured via the Accounting console tree item under NPS and enables configuration of two types of logging. By default, you have the file-based logging that was covered earlier which you can configure via the Configure Local File Logging link. This enables configuration of the information to log, which includes individual accounts and authentication requests, along with periodic account and authentication status. Some access servers use that information during sessions to obtain accounting data.

The Log File tab enables configuration of where to create the log file, how often to create a new log file (which can be based on time or file size), and whether to automatically delete older log files as needed if the disk fills. The format of the output can also be configured between database-compatible, which is comma-separated format, or Internet Authentication

Service (IAS) format, which logs data in its own format. The following listing shows an example of the IAS format:

```
192.168.1.142,SAVILLTECH\john,01/18/2008,15:24:59,RAS,SAVDALNPS
01,32,SAVDALNPS01,4,192.168.1.142,6,2,7,1,5,256,61,5,64,1,65,1,
31,10.1.1.20,66,10.1.1.20,25,311 1 fe80::48aa:cc3a:980e:2444
01/15/2008 20:19:32
26,44,16,8,192.168.1.57,12,1400,28,1800,50,29,51,1,55,120069149
7,45,3,46,67,43,2329,42,7344,48,30,47,114,49,1,40,2,4108,192.16
8.1.142,4128,SAVDALNPS01,4147,311,4148,MSRASV5.20,4160,MSRASV5.
20,4159,MSRAS-0-SAVDALSAND01,8158,{271C5170-220D-4FE3-A5BC-
6AFA7099F3D0},8132,2,4120,0x00534156494C4C54454348,4294967206,4
,4154,Microsoft Routing and Remote Access Service
Policy,4155,1,4136,4,4142,0
```

If you change log file formats, a new log file is not created. Instead, the log just switches format mid-file. You can optionally output the logging information to a SQL database with the same information logged, which can be local or remote, and a specific database instance on the server can be specified along with the credentials needed to connect.

Configuration Backup

The easiest way to export the configuration is via the `NETSH` command and output to a file; for example, `netsh nps show config > npsconfig.txt`.

Routing

You covered some routing aspects earlier, and there is little configuration to perform. If you access the NPS server properties, the General tab gives you insight into the types of IP routing that the server performs, as shown in Figure 8-26.

RRAS works great where multiple network interface cards are present on different networks and route traffic between the networks per the configuration. Detail on the NICs present in a server can be viewed via the Network Interfaces area, but the main area is protocol specific via the IPv4 and IPv6 console tree areas.

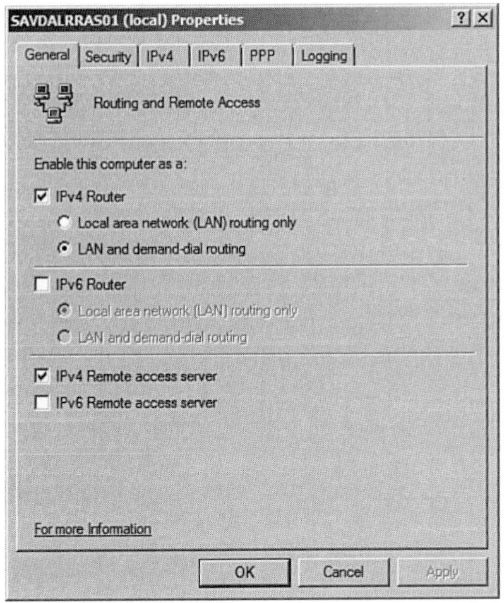

FIGURE 8-26 The General tab for an NPS server's properties.

If you take IPv4 you have a General area that shows you the interfaces on the server, their type, and information related to the connection including address, amount of data, and status. The Static Routes area enables you to define specific routes on the server based on the interface to use for the route and the destination information along with a metric, as shown in Figure 8-27. Static routes are useful if you have firewalls or restrictions in place and you want to ensure that traffic is routed via a specific gateway to a particular subnet.

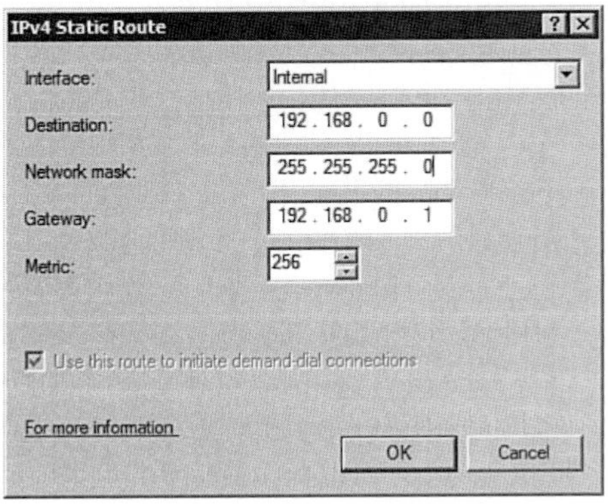

IPv4 Static Route

Interface: Internal

Destination: 192 . 168 . 0 . 0

Network mask: 255 . 255 . 255 . 0

Gateway: 192 . 168 . 0 . 1

Metric: 256

Use this route to initiate demand-dial connections

For more information

OK Cancel

FIGURE 8-27 Configuring a static route.

Network Access Protection (NAP)

NAP is a major feature of Windows Server 2008 and addresses the problem of clients connected to the network that don't meet the organization's health requirements.

Many of the defenses you place on your servers and desktop systems are based on firewalls, anti-malware, and policies to lock down aspects of the environment, to protect you from harmful software. However, you can place the most advanced firewall and malware checking on the planet at your company's perimeter, but that does zero good if someone brings a laptop into the company and plugs it in via the wired or wireless network. If that laptop has a virus, it quickly spreads. Likewise, you have problems if a user VPNs into your organization or even remotes in via Terminal Services.

You want to be able to state a healthiness level that a client must meet to connect to your network. That level could be defined in terms of Windows updates, firewall configurations, antivirus definition files, and so forth.

Under Windows Server 2003, you had a limited ability like this for VPN connections. Microsoft provided sample VPN Quarantine scripts (available at www.microsoft.com/downloads/details.aspx?FamilyID=a290f2ee-0b55-491e-bc4c-8161671b2462&displaylang=en) that were used in conjunction with the Connection Manager Administration Kit (CMAK) to perform checks on incoming connections to ensure that they met certain criteria. If the script passed the client, the VPN connection was allowed with full access. If the script failed the client, the connection was either refused, or it was allowed but the client was placed in a quarantine network. The quarantine network had limited routes to the rest of the network, so it could access only specific resources; for example, an update server to get the client to a state so that it can pass the script. But this was only for VPNs. Wired and wireless networks still had no capability to limit connectivity based on the health of a client.

With NAP you can now request a statement of health (SoH) from a client when connectivity is attempted. Based on the SoH and the requirements defined in policies, connection can be allowed, refused, or the client can, as with the VPN, be placed in a quarantine network to be made healthy. This NAP not only performs initial checks on clients and helps enforce a level of health but enforces the health requirement over the long term when computers connect, ensuring ongoing compliance. It is not a "pass once and you're good to go forever" system. When you look at virus attacks, the computers attacked are typically those that have not had recent patches applied, that don't have a firewall enabled, and that don't have recent virus definition files.

NAP supports Windows Vista and Windows XP SP3 as clients. A Windows Server 2008 server is required as the policy server to validate the health of clients. It's important to understand that NAP provides the platform to provide the enforcement of health. However, many other companies will write components for NAP particularly for the system health agents (SHAs) that report elements of health. A full API is available to integrate those components. Also understand that NAP is a method to report on the health of a computer and, based on that health, enforce levels of access, but it is not a replacement for any firewall, anti-malware, and patch processes you have in place. Those solutions are all still needed, and NAP just communicates with those solutions to understand the overall health of the computer and provide health enforcement. For example, Windows Update is still needed to obtain patches for a computer. The missing piece with Windows Update is that if a computer has not had the latest patches applied, there is no way to enforce a level of access. With NAP you can check the patches applied. If the latest patches are not applied, you can enforce limited access and instruct the client to use Windows Update to get the latest fixes. The client has only limited access until compliant.

When a client first connects to the network, a health policy validation is performed, which causes the computer to be validated against the health requirement policies that have been defined using the various available SHAs and system health validators (SHVs). If a computer is compliant, unrestricted access is given via a number of methods, such as an IP address with routes to the entire network or certificates that enable secure communication with the computers in the environment. A noncompliant computer, one that does not meet your health requirements, might be quarantined into a limited access, restricted network. This is typically the case when you are using NAP to enforce a restricted access environment. Another option is to allow the computer full access but log the fact that the computer is not compliant—this is the approach taken when you use NAP in a monitoring-only environment. You likely used a phased approach when implementing NAP, which involves both types of implementation as you see later in this section. The limited access network that you can define for noncompliant computers can be limited access in terms of connectivity and/or a specific amount of connection time. If you enable a restricted network, you would do this primarily so that the clients can gain access to resources to update their health from a remediation server or health update resources. That means those servers/resources (for example, a Windows Server Update Services [WSUS] server or antivirus definition server) must be accessible from the restricted network.

A couple of questions might occur to you at this point. What about my older computers? What about my non-Microsoft clients? As stated earlier, the NAP client is supported, at least initially, on Windows Vista, Windows XP SP3, and of course, Windows Server 2008. Older operating systems do not support NAP nor do non-Microsoft OSs such as Linux and those pesky Macintosh computers—at least support will not come from Microsoft. A NAP client is available for Linux already from http://unetsystem.co.kr/nap/ and you can expect more NAP clients to come as NAP grows in popularity. There is currently no support for Windows CE/Mobile/PDAs and printers as NAP clients.

Microsoft is forming partnerships, and NAP clients are being developed for other platforms. A partnership has also been created with Cisco, which has its own NAP solution, known as Network Access Control (NAC), to enable NAP to fully interoperate with NAC installations. Look at www.microsoft.com/windowsserver2008/nap-partners.mspx, which lists all the partners Microsoft has for NAP. It's pretty big and gives an indication of how many different systems can participate in the health validation of clients and the enforcement of access. However, it is possible to configure exceptions for certain types of clients so that they can get access if their platform does not support NAP.

If a client does support NAP and is noncompliant, you want to make it compliant. If you are using that monitoring-only NAP mode, the client is given full access. However, you can still send the client updates to get it compliant, whereas if you are in the restricted-access NAP mode, the client won't get full access until after you have updated it. However, it is important that you don't consider NAP the method to update clients. You need solutions such as System Center Configuration Manager (SCCM) or Group Policy and WSUS in place to automatically update clients as you get patches, malware definitions, virus definition updates, and so forth.

In Figure 8-28, you see all the components that are involved in the NAP process. On the client, you have a number of SHAs of which Microsoft provides a base agent to report on core items used by the Windows Server 2008 System Health Validator. The included Windows SHA can report on the following:

- Whether firewall software is installed and enabled
- Whether antivirus software is installed, enabled, and its definition files are current
- Whether antispyware software is installed, enabled, and whether definition files are current
- Whether Automatic Updates is enabled

Other SHAs may be present including ones by third parties and other Microsoft solutions, such as the SCCM agent. You then have the core NAP agent and a number of enforcement agents. The client has a number of Microsoft-provided enforcement clients such as DHCP, IPsec, 802.1x, and VPN, and others can be provided by third parties, such as other VPN solutions.

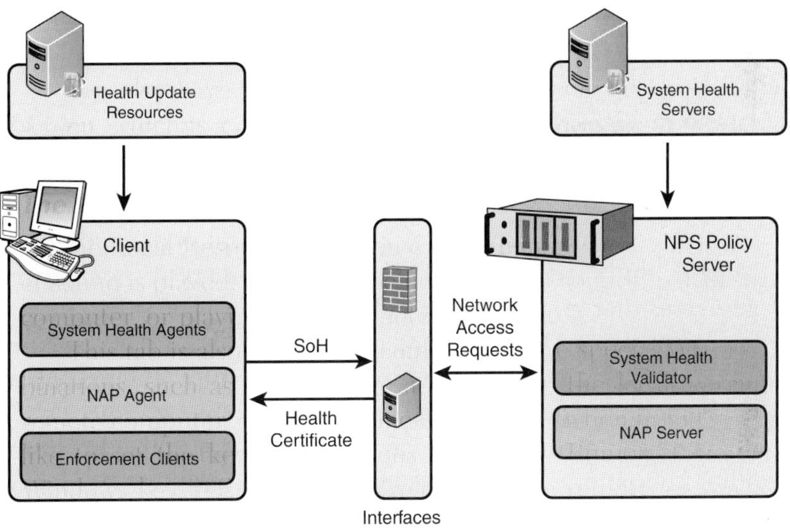

FIGURE 8-28 The overall NAP architecture.

Health update resources in their quarantine network are available to your clients if compliance was not met. On the server side is the NAP server component running on your NPS policy server, along with SHV components that communicate with system health servers. The NPS holds the system health policies defined by the administrators and performs the validation of health against the configured policies.

Between the client and the NPS policy server are various network access technologies that need to communicate with the NAP server to control access. For example, you use the Windows Server 2008 DHCP service and VPN, which understand NAP and include an enforcement server to use DHCP and VPN enforcement. Other network access components can use NAP without new versions because for access control they rely on RADIUS, of which NPS is an implementation. All these components act as RADIUS clients that communicate with NPS (the RADIUS server) to have the health of the clients requesting access validated, and the RADIUS responses control the access given.

NAP Enforcement

You've heard about enforcement a number of times now, but what are your enforcement options and which should you use? The actual enforcement you use depends on your environment and requirements. DHCP is easy to implement but is the easiest to bypass, whereas IPsec is probably the hardest to implement but provides the most secure environment.

DHCP Quarantine Enforcement

In nearly all environments DHCP enables a client to connect to the network and automatically receive an IP address. However, this service is friendly to almost anyone. Any computer placed on the network can request an IP address, and the DHCP servers respond with offers of addresses that give the client full access to the network.

When using DHCP enforcement with NAP, a DHCP server no longer just gives out a normal IP address. Noncompliant computers receive IP configuration with limited access, which is an IP address with a 32-bit subnet mask and no default gateway defined. This means communication with other computers is not possible and static routes are configured for the machine allowing limited communication. They can communicate with only the servers needed for updating their health status.

You are limited, though. You cannot specify different subnets to use for compliant and noncompliant systems. You can just define different scope options and restrict system access for restricted clients via routing table entries. If you want the ability to have clients made members of different networks or VLANs, you need to use 802.1x-style enforcement, which has the capability to move systems between VLANs/subnets.

The DHCP enforcement is weak because all it controls is IP addresses from DHCP servers. Any moderately capable user can just give a computer a static IP address, which circumvents the entire NAP protection. Or a user could manually update the routing table to enable other communication. The DHCP enforcement network is isolation rather than network quarantine because of the existence of these enforcement workarounds. Using DHCP on its own is a start. But you need to use either IPsec or 802.1x for real protection.

To use NAP with DHCP, the Network Policy Server Role service must be installed on the DHCP server with local policies configured or configured as a RADIUS client to forward authentication requests to a different NPS server that contains the policies.

Internet Protocol Security (IPsec)

With IPsec enforcement, any incoming connection attempts for computers must be protected with IPsec, and to use IPsec the computer must have the necessary certificate. That certificate is a X.509 certificate, which is returned to compliant computers during the NAP process. This means only healthy computers can receive the certificate necessary for IPsec communication and can therefore talk to the other computers. Nonhealthy computers do not have the X.509 certificate and therefore cannot talk to any computer other than those servers that you do allow non-IPsec communication with, which are the health update resource servers.

Because of this IPsec foundation, IPsec enforcement is the strongest NAP enforcement available—use it where possible. Unlike DHCP enforcement, with IPsec, computers get IP addresses. However, this just allows communication over the network. If all communication with computers and servers must be encrypted with IPsec, the IP address does not benefit the computer. This overcomes the weakness with DHCP where a computer can just give itself a static IP address.

How do computers know to use IPsec? After all, with DHCP the enforcement is done when an IP address is requested, but with IPsec the computer has an IP address and now just can't talk to anyone. Health registration authorities (HRAs) grant the X.509 health certificate to clients in conjunction with the NPS, and clients can find an HRA in a number of ways. The NAP client sends its health status to the HRA (also known as the health certificate server), which then sends it to the NPS for validity checking. The HRA is a role service that is part of Network Policy and Access Services.

For domain-joined machines, use Group Policy to configure the HRA for the client's location, which requires the Group Policy Object (GPO) to be linked at a site level. A better option is the following: The NAP client supports auto-discovery by checking DNS service (SRV) records with a name of _hra, which contain the name of the HRA server in their data. Clients look first for an _hra service record in the DNS zone for their local site (such as _hra._tcp.Dallas._sites.savilltech.com), followed by the Active Directory domain general zone (_tcp.savilltech.com), and then the DNS zone for the host computer (if different from the AD domain zone name). This auto-discovery is enabled by creating the Registry DWORD value HKEY_LOCAL_MACHINE\SYSTEM\CurrentControlSet\Services\napagent\LocalConfig\Enroll\HcsGroups\EnableDiscovery and setting it to 1.

IPsec is the best method to use to protect your environment but has the downside of requiring a public key infrastructure (PKI) implementation in your environment. However, after you configure the PKI and get past the initial pain involved in an organizationwide PKI, you quickly find many other uses for the new encryption capabilities you now have available.

IEEE 802.1x Authenticated Network Connection AKA EAP Quarantine

802.1x enforcement is used for the wireless large area network (LAN) and authenticated switches environment. Noncompliant computers have limited access, which is achieved via either a set of IP packet filters or linking the user's connection with a limited virtual LAN (VLAN). This limited communication again allows a client access to limited resources.

802.1x is a great enforcement solution but is applicable only for 802.1x connections. It is not likely to cover most companies' wired networks, so although you may use this solution, it is only part of your overall NAP solution.

The hardware must support dynamic VLAN, which means dynamically moving from one VLAN to another. During the boot process, dynamic VLAN switching can be an issue—imagine group policy is being applied and then the client switches networks. The group policy does not know the client has switched, which could mean some scripts might be applied but not others. This also requires the Windows 1x supplicant to use (third parties don't understand NAP). You need multiple VLANs just for the purpose of health remediation. NAP can use passwords or certificates for the credential (passwords are good if an organization doesn't want to deploy PKI).

Remote Access Quarantine

Like 802.1x, this enforcement is for VPN access only, and once again a restricted network is defined via a set of IP packet filters that are sent to the VPN server by the NPS server for a noncompliant computer. You need the VPN server to be running on Windows Server 2008 and have the RRAS role service (which is needed for VPN) installed.

The NAP VPN enforcement requires a computer certificate on the VPN server to enable Protected EAP (PEAP) authentication of VPN clients, so a PKI infrastructure is required in the environment. However, there are no complex certificate requirements to manage as with IPsec. You need just a computer certificate for the VPN server.

Terminal Services Gateway

TS Gateway enforcement can quarantine Terminal Server connection requests via the gateway based on the health of the requesting client. However, you cannot remediate a client via the TS Gateway enforcement. You can only allow access or quarantine. For example, imagine you enable redirected drives for Terminal Server connections, which effectively opens up the file system of a client onto the server being connected to via remote desktop. With NAP you can check that the requesting computer meets your health requirements, such as having current antivirus updates, before letting those redirected drives be mapped.

How NAP Works

Let's walk through a sample NAP connection for a VPN connection, as shown in Figure 8-29. The process, however, is almost the same for all connectivity types. For example, for 802.1x enforcement, replace the VPN server with an `802.1x` switch.

Before any connection attempt, the system health servers are constantly passing policy updates to the NPS Policy server (which could be the same physical box).

In step 1, a client requests VPN access to the Windows 2008 VPN server, which also has the NAP role service installed. The VPN server's NAP server (also known as the enforcement server) informs the NAP agent (also known as the enforcement client) on the client that an SoH is needed, so an SoH is sent along with the authentication credentials. It is generated by the NAP agent on the client PC with information from the SHAs installed.

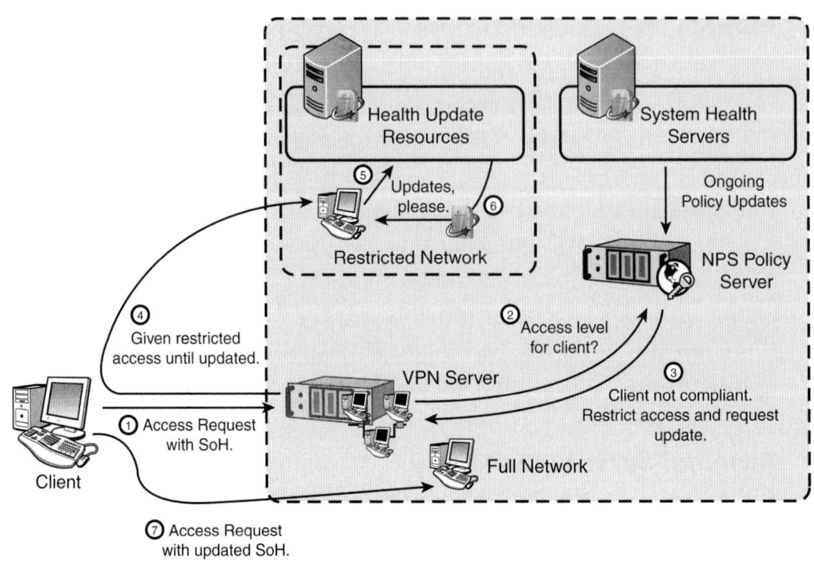

FIGURE 8-29 NAP process for a VPN connection.

In step 2, the SoH from the client is sent via the RADIUS protocol to the NPS policy server to be checked by the SHVs against the policy information stored. If one of the SHVs returns noncompliance, the area of noncompliance is noted in the statement of health response (SoHR), which is generated by all SHVs. You might ask, "Is the VPN server forwarding the SoH of the client?" The answer is no. For VPN, after a tunnel to the VPN server is established, a separate EAS tunnel from the client to NPS is created, so the SoH is sent directly from client to NPS. The same process applies for 802.1x enforcement. For DHCP the broadcast is met by a health request broadcast response. SoH communication never occurs via a middle point except for IPsec, which communicates via the HRA.

In step 3, all the SoHRs are combined into a single system statement of health response (SSoHR), which returns an overall status of noncompliance. So, connectivity is restricted. This SSoHR is then returned to the VPN server.

In step 4, the NAP server on the VPN server processes the SSoHR and constructs a packet filter, which restricts the client to the restricted network, and then notifies the NAP agent on the client of the SoHRs.

In step 5, the SoHRs are passed to each SHA, which processes the SoHR. If autoremediation is enabled, the SHA either contacts the health update resources where necessary (for example, to download updates as shown in step 6), or just performs system changes to be compliant (for example, enabling the firewall).

In step 7, when the SHAs now report the client has remediated all the items in the SoHRs, connectivity is attempted again with an updated SoH. The VPN server once again communicates with the NPS policy server, which performs the checks. This time no problems are found, so a clean SSoHR is generated, informing the system that it can give full access to the client. The VPN server grants the client access to the full network. Steps 2 and 3 are repeated, but this time with a healthy status.

NAP Deployment Process

It would be a bad idea to just enable NAP in your environment in restricted-access mode because there is a good chance many computers are noncompliant. You cause major productivity issues, which then might cause you major issues related to job-seeking.

The best way to implement NAP is via a staged approach using the various modes possible with NAP. Additionally, as with any other technology implementation, first perform a proof of concept (PoC) in a lab environment, followed by a pilot test. A pilot test is a live implementation in your production environment, but it is limited to a small group of users and computers who are typically IT savvy, such as your IT department. Then you expand the pilot to include users from all the various divisions and business units of the company to ensure that the technology is tested in all the possible ways it might be used. Someone in Accounting, for example, might use the infrastructure in a way someone in the IT department or another department does not. When the pilot is complete and all the business units have signed off, you can deploy NAP to the organization in a controlled manner, such as by floor, building, or business unit. The type of technology dictates how deployment can be broken up into units of implementation. For something like enabling NAP on DHCP, the most logical implementation method is probably by subnet.

A number of early adopters choose to implement DHCP enforcement initially because of its easy implementation and good information on the compliance state of an environment. Many companies find that after implementing DHCP enforcement, they reach a satisfactory compliance state and don't use further enforcement options. Obviously, however, you still have the inherent weakness of DHCP enforcement, which is circumvented by just using a static IP address.

Remember to test how you handle exceptions. For example, for the Linux clients or the Windows 2000 boxes, you can't just lock out machines that don't support NAP. You can define exceptions with NAP that could be based on your rules. You could have a rule that says if a machine is not NAP-capable, exclude it and give it full access. You could also have rules for guest machines (such as those of visiting clients), and those rules could be based on whether the machine is part of the corporate domain or you could base the rules on specific machine MAC addresses. For internal machine exceptions, you could also base exceptions on group membership—all the criteria supported by the policies that are used.

Here are some general design considerations. The list summarizes some of what you have already learned and some other things to consider.

- Is every machine or device in the environment NAP capable? Third parties are creating Linux, UNIX, and other NAP agents but what about Windows 2000 and NT 4? Also consider the criticality of systems. Would you want to risk quarantining machines in a manufacturing line?
- Who is exempted? To the previous point, manufacturing production line machines are one example. In financial institutions, make sure you don't risk disconnecting important systems such as mainframes. Or imagine a hospital. Consider what is vital to your organization and don't risk breaking it, don't stop the money, don't risk lives, and never upset the senior executives. Consider the effect on business in all cases. Even with automatic remediation, there might still be downtime.
- What are the most important security settings? Out of the five possible settings included "in box" via the security center or additional settings, which might be needed and could be available via third parties? Start simply, maybe check firewall status and antivirus up-to-date status. You can create custom system health agents and validators if necessary. For example, clients want to detect whether removable media that could remove confidential information is installed. This detection is possible via a Globally Unique Identifier (GUID) written in the Registry. So, using the NAP software development kit (SDK), if the GUID is written in the Registry, the machine is locked out of the network automatically and then beaten by security. (That would require some human intervention; the Microsoft Robotics SDK has no good "beating" actions at present.)

- What about guests to the environment? Many different types (partners, vendors, visitors, and so on) exist. Different types may control types of access. For 802.1x, you would need to create multiple VLANs. For IPsec, you would have to create multiple extranets.
- Auto or manual remediation? Initially you might just let clients fix themselves by notifying clients that they are not compliant, which normally drives compliancy up. Auto remediation is generally the best option.
- Can remediation servers be reached by unhealthy clients? Otherwise they are stuck in quarantine.
- What entities do you need to identify? Consider IP printers, for example. If you were using 802.1x and had a printer on a port, you can't just open up the port and exclude it from policy because someone could plug a computer into that port. In this case, you can (on the switch) configure that only a certain MAC can connect via the port.
- What is the process in place to handle exemptions on the fly? You have quarantined the CEO and need to get him out instantly or you'll be out instantly.

After you have planned out the NAP implementation, and done lab testing and PoC, begin the live rollout. The typical stages of NAP functionality are usually implemented as follows:

- **Stage 1—Reporting mode**. NAP is deployed to only report on compliance levels with no information displayed to the connecting user and no restriction of access being done but with automatic remediation used where possible. This stage gives the IT department insight into the compliance state of the enterprise in an ongoing manner. Thanks to the automatic remediation, compliance improves as clients connect.
- **Stage 2—Deferred enforcement**. In this stage users are now notified of areas of noncompliance that could not be automatically remediated. However, access is still not restricted, at least not for a set amount of time. The goal is to get users to act on the notifications and address compliance issues. For example, you might notify users of compliance problems and allow them to connect for two weeks without remediation until you restrict them. This stage provides insight into the impact on the infrastructure as clients start updating themselves, making the manual changes, and then calling

the help desk when stuck, which is an important aspect of any implementation. The worst thing you can do is implement a new technology that affects users and then not have the manpower available to address user problems. This is another major reason for implementing technologies in small units. Stay in this mode until about 90 percent of the company meets compliance, which you can see via the NAP reporting.

- **Stage 3—Enforcement mode**. When you reach an agreed upon percentage of compliance in your systems (for example, the 90 percent just cited), NAP is switched to enforcement mode where noncompliant systems are placed into restricted networks or denied access. You now are protecting your networks from noncompliant systems.

Implementing NAP

After all that, let's configure a NAP enforcement. Microsoft has produced amazingly detailed step-by-step guides for all the various enforcement methods. It is recommended that you read them before implementing NAP. The coverage in general for NAP on Microsoft is amazing. The TechNet Network Access Protection page at http://technet.microsoft.com/en-us/network/bb545879.aspx is a great start. It has links to the step-by-step guides. However, this section walks through an implementation of NAP to show you both the process and how to configure NAP to match various roll-out stages.

Because you learned about VPNs, let's walk through enabling NAP for VPN. The implementation differences for DHCP are covered later to show there is no difference from a health and network policy perspective. The only differences are in calling those policies and how restricted access is governed.

First, ensure that Network Policy Server Role service is enabled on your NPS server. Because you use NAP on your VPN, you also need a computer certificate from your enterprise CA in the domain via the Certificates MMC snap-in. No other questions are asked, and the certificate is saved into the Personal container of the computer account, as shown in Figure 8-30.

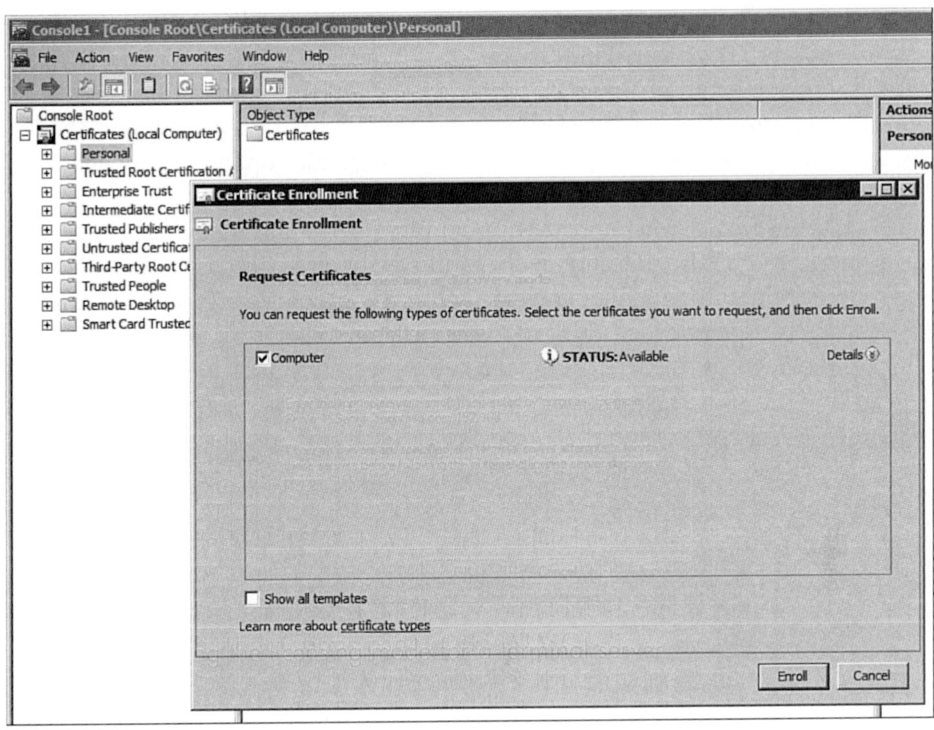

Figure 8-30 Requesting a certificate.

The certificate is necessary because NAP with VPN requires PEAP, which enables quarantine checking. It is enabled by default as an authentication option, but verify this via the properties of the RRAS server. Under the Security tab, click the EAP Methods button (which is checked along with MS-CHAP v2) and ensure that PEAP is listed.

If NAP and the VPN server are not on the same box, you need to configure the VPN server as a RADIUS client of the NPS, as discussed in the "Radius Configuration" section. Also, create a connection request policy on the NPS server to configure it to authenticate connection requests from the VPN server.

Configuring System Health Validators and Policies

A default Windows Server 2008 NPS has only one SHV: the Windows Security Health Validator. Navigate to System Health Validators under the

Network Access Protection console tree item within NPS and select the properties of the Windows Security Health Validator. When the dialog is open, click the Configure button to enable configuration of the properties you want to check for as shown in Figure 8-31. In this example, check that the firewall is enabled and that automatic updates are enabled for Windows Vista/2008 clients. Notice all the options available: checks for firewall, antivirus, antispyware, automatic updating, and security updates within a defined amount of time. Concerning that last item, set things so that they must have checked within the last 22 hours for Important and above updates (see the grayed-out options in Figure 8-31). You could set the Security Update protection to Critical Only or to Moderate and Above.

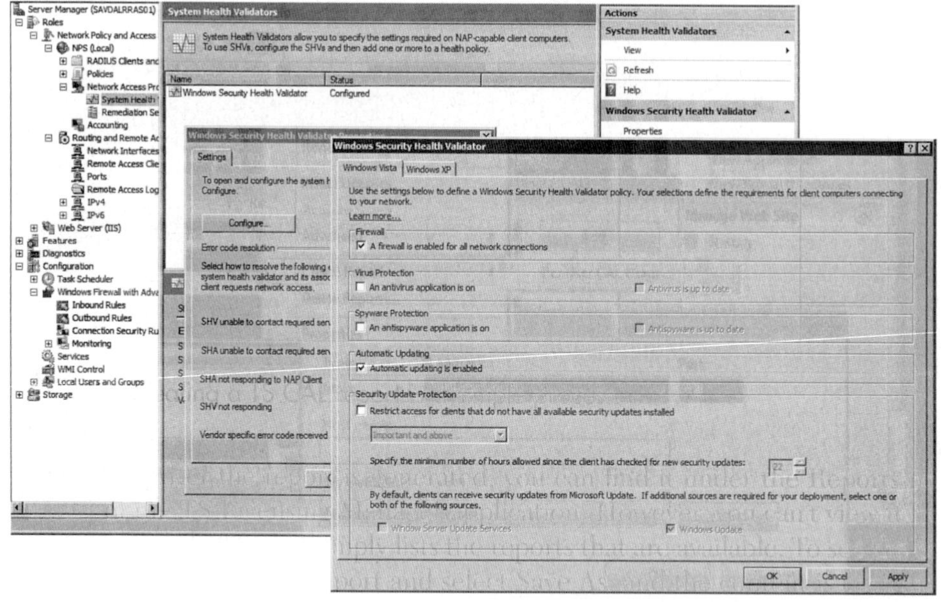

FIGURE 8-31 Configuring the elements checked by the Windows Security Health Validator.

For the main settings of the SHV, configure the results for the errors that might occur, such as the health agent or validator being unable to contact required services. By default such errors result in the client being treated as noncompliant.

Now that you have defined the SHV, create a health policy that uses it. Under the Policies console tree item is a Health Polices area where you create a new policy. Select the New action to create a new policy, which requires you to select a name for the health policy, choose the SHVs checked in the policy, and define which check is performed. In most circumstances you want to check the Client Passes All SHV Checks option, as shown in Figure 8-32. There are also options in which the client passes at least one SHV check, the client fails all, and the client fails at least one, in addition to checks whether an SHV reports a client as infected, transitional, or unknown.

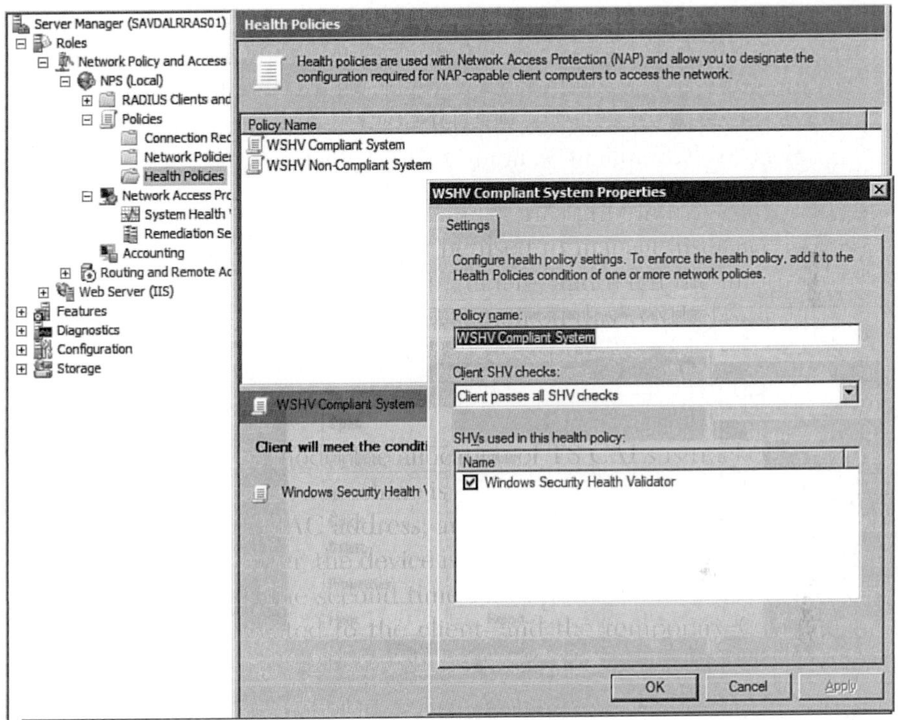

FIGURE 8-32 Configuring a health policy to use the available SHV.

Now repeat the process, but this time create a health policy if a client fails one or more SHV checks. Name the policy WASH Noncompliant System, and check the Windows Security Health Validator again, but select Client Fails One or More SHV Checks. You now have two separate health policies: one for a client that passes the checks and one for a client that does not.

Configuring Network Policies to Use the Health Policy

You previously created a network policy based on group membership and the time of day. All you do now is add conditions that check the health policy matches to control levels of access. For this, assume that you don't have any existing policies and start from scratch.

Select the Network Policies node under Policies and select the New action from within Server Manager in the Network Policy and Access – NPS area. First create a network policy for clients that meet compliance—name the policy Compliant Client with Full Access, and leave the type of network access blank. Now add conditions. You still want a check that the user is a member of your VPN Users group, so add a User Group condition check and a Health Policies check. From the list of health policies, select My Compliant System Health Check because it is your full access policy, as shown in Figure 8-33.

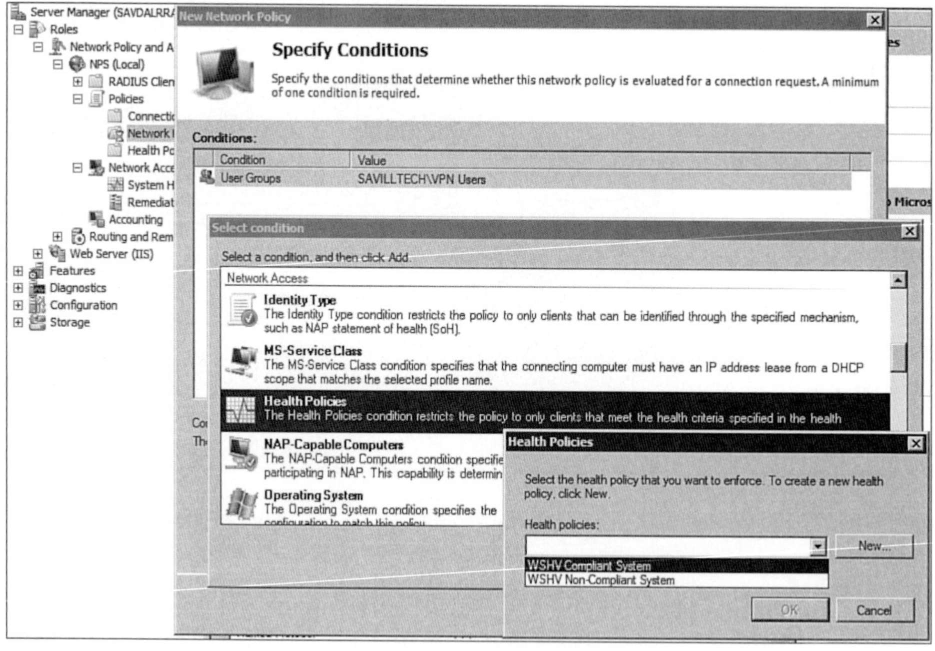

FIGURE 8-33 Enabling a health policy check.

In the next stage for access, select the Access Granted option and Use My Standard Authentication Methods for the Environment and

Constraints (If Any). On the Configure Settings stage, select NAP Enforcement and ensure that the Allow Full Network Access option is selected because this is a healthy client, as shown in Figure 8-34. You also have options to give full access for a limited time in addition to limited access, which are the options you use for a phased implementation of NAP.

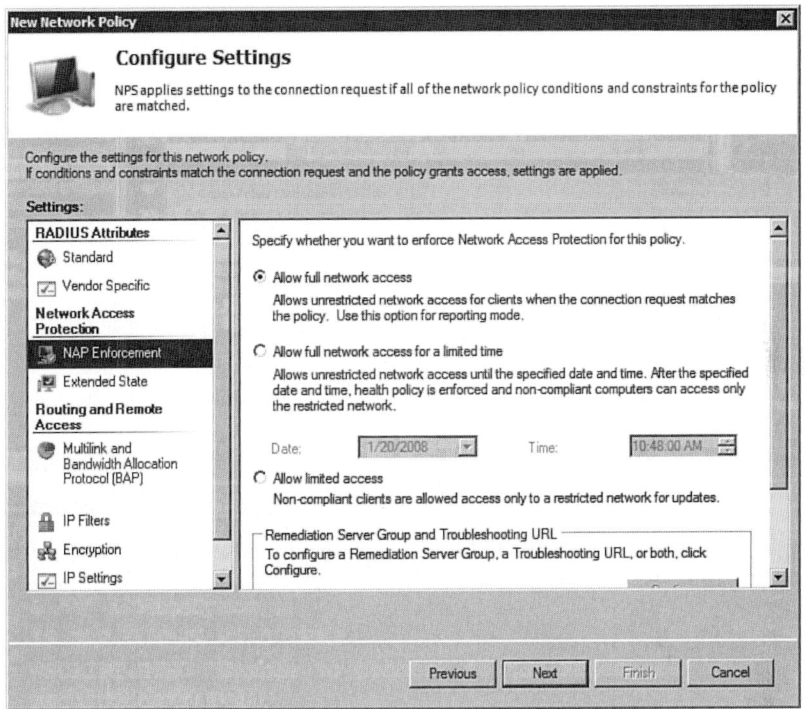

Figure 8-34 Configure NAP enforcement options.

A summary of the new network policy is displayed. Click Finish to create the policy. Repeat these steps and create a new policy, but this time for a noncompliant system. Configure the policy to grant limited access for noncompliant systems with an IP filter to allow access only to a server that has updates. Select the New action under Network Policies and name it Non-compliant Client with Limited Access. For conditions, specify the user checks and any others, but for the health policies, select the WSHV Non-Compliant System health policy. For the access permission, select Access Granted because you want the client to have access, but you use filters as part of the constraints to control what actual access the client gets.

Continue with the authentication and constraints as usual until you get to the Configure Settings stage. This time, for NAP Enforcement, select Allow Limited Access, and check the Enable Auto-Remediation of Client Computers option. Don't click Next yet. Select the IP Filters setting option. Under IPv4, select Input Filters, and click New to create a new filter. At this point, you enter details to lock down access to specific computers or subnets. For example, if you want to allow access only to server 192.168.1.10, add a filter for this address with a 32-bit subnet mask so that only that server can be contacted, as shown in Figure 8-35.

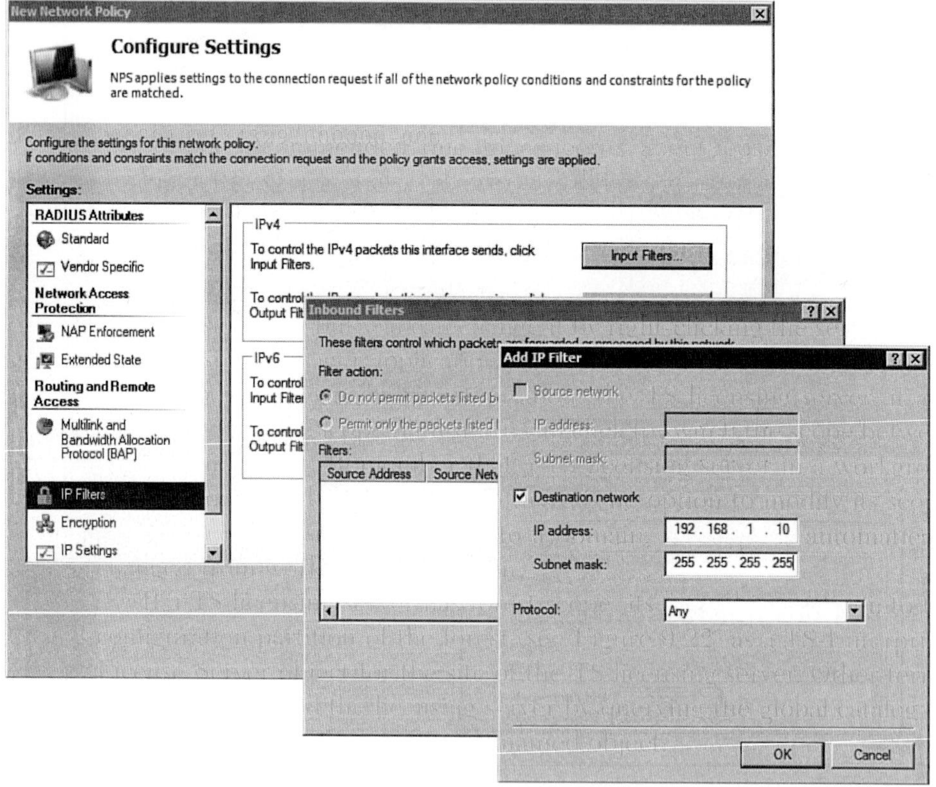

FIGURE 8-35 Creating a limited access network via IP filters.

When the details are added, change the filter action to Permit Only the Packets Listed Below because the default is to not permit the packets listed, which would hamper what you are trying to do. If you did not change it, you would let the clients access everything except the systems that can update them. Repeat this process for an outbound filter for the same addresses and again ensure that you change the filter action to permit only the IPs selected. You can add multiple IP filters for both IPv4 and IPv6. In this case you have one inbound IPv4 filter for 192.168.1.10 and one outbound IPv4 filter for 192.168.1.10, both with a subnet mask of 255.255.255.255, which limits the restricted access to sending and receiving to 192.168.1.10 only. Click Next and then click Finish to create the policy. If you want to allow access to multiple nodes, use a subnet other than 255.255.255.255 and instead use a mask that allows access to the required nodes (assuming the nodes are contiguous in IP address). After creating the network polices, use the Move Up action to ensure that both your policies are above the built-in deny access policies.

You could create an additional policy that would use the NAP-Capable condition and set it to apply only to NAP-incapable clients, as shown in Figure 8-36. The settings for these noncapable clients could be to allow full network access or configure access to a limited set of resources. Or configure them for access only to the Internet by placing them on a separate VLAN if the enforcement agent supports this type of functionality (for example, 802.1x but not DHCP).

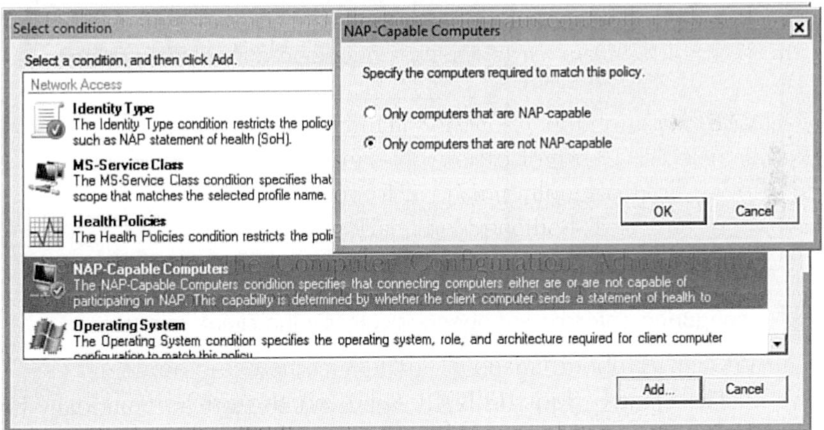

FIGURE 8-36 A policy for clients that are not NAP-capable.

Client Configuration

You have some requirements on the client. The Security Center is necessary to monitor the status required to run the Windows SHA, which is what you used for your policies. This can be enabled through Group Policy using Computer Configuration, Administrative Templates, Windows Components, Security Center and setting the option Turn on Security Center (Domain PCs Only) to Enabled. You can also set this directly on the local policy of a computer by running gpedit.msc on the computer and accessing the same setting. Once enabled, this is used by the Windows SHA to check whether the firewall is enabled, the state of antivirus protection, and so on.

The enforcement agents to enable on the client must also be configured via the NAP Client Configuration utility, which is accessed via napclcfg.msc. It enables you to select the enforcement clients as shown in Figure 8-37. In this case, enable the Remote Access Quarantine Enforcement Client.

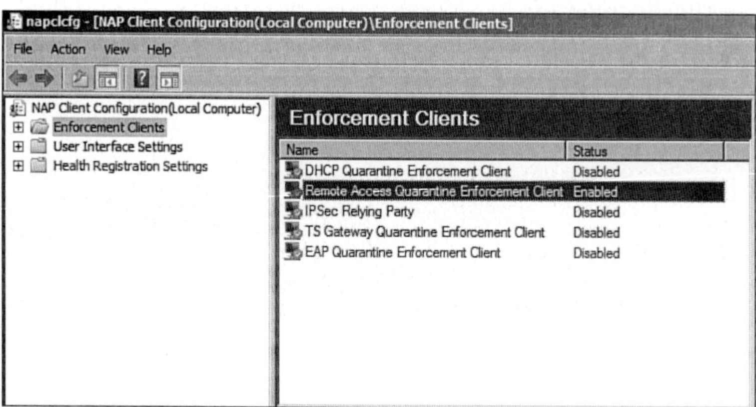

FIGURE 8-37 Configuring enforcement agents locally on the client.

The clients need the NAP Agent set to start automatically instead of the default, which is manual and is done via the Services Administrative Tool. To start from the command line, use the command `net start napagent`.

Perform all these configurations via Group Policy. For the NAP enforcements, go to Computer Configuration, Policies, Windows Settings, Security Settings, Network Access Protection in the GPO. The NAP Agent service can be controlled via the Windows Settings, Security Settings, System Settings GPO area (see Figure 8-38).

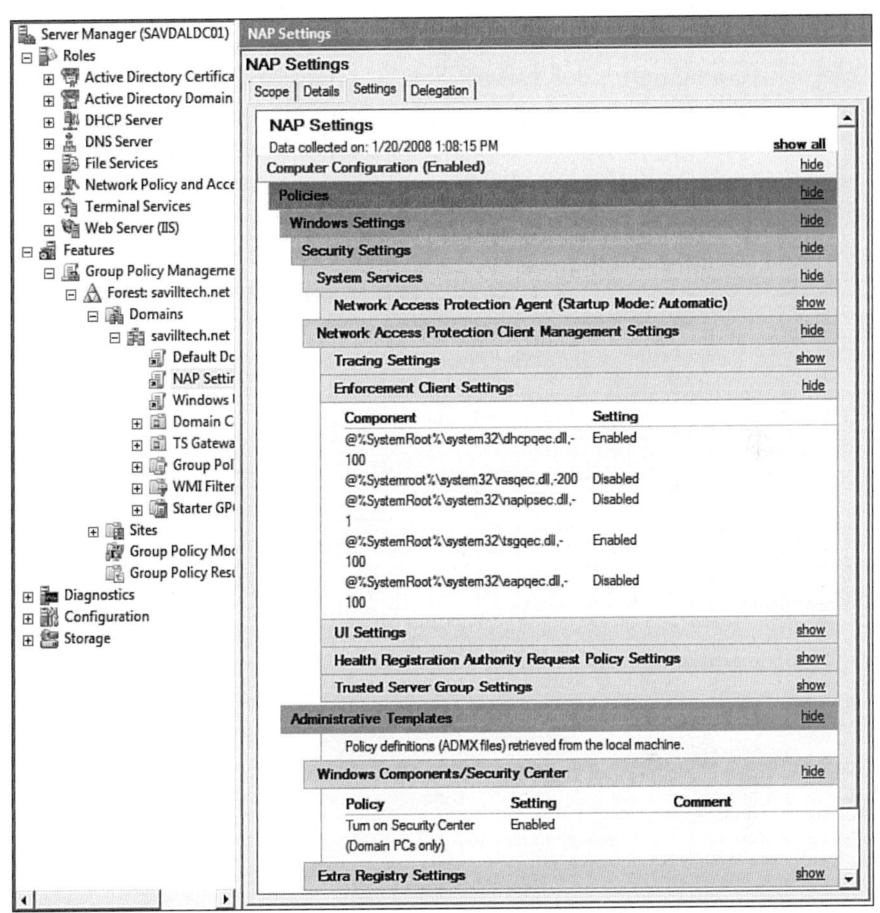

FIGURE 8-38 Configuring client NAP settings via GPO.

For the VPN connection on the client, use the Advanced options of the Security tab for the VPN connection properties. Select Use Extensible Authentication Protocol (EAP) and choose PEAP (Encryption Enabled). Then select Properties for the PEAP and select the Validate Server Certificate check box. Clear the Connect to These Servers check box, and then select Secured Password (EAP-MSCHAP v2) under Select Authentication Method. Clear the Enable Fast Reconnect check box, and then select the Enable Quarantine Checks check box. You are now ready for NAP-enabled VPN connections.

DHCP Configuration

The configuration for DHCP NAP is almost the same as with VPN. The same health policies and network policies are created: one for compliant and one for noncompliant. However, this time, for the authentication methods in both your policies, unselect everything except for Perform Machine Health Check Only, as shown in Figure 8-39.

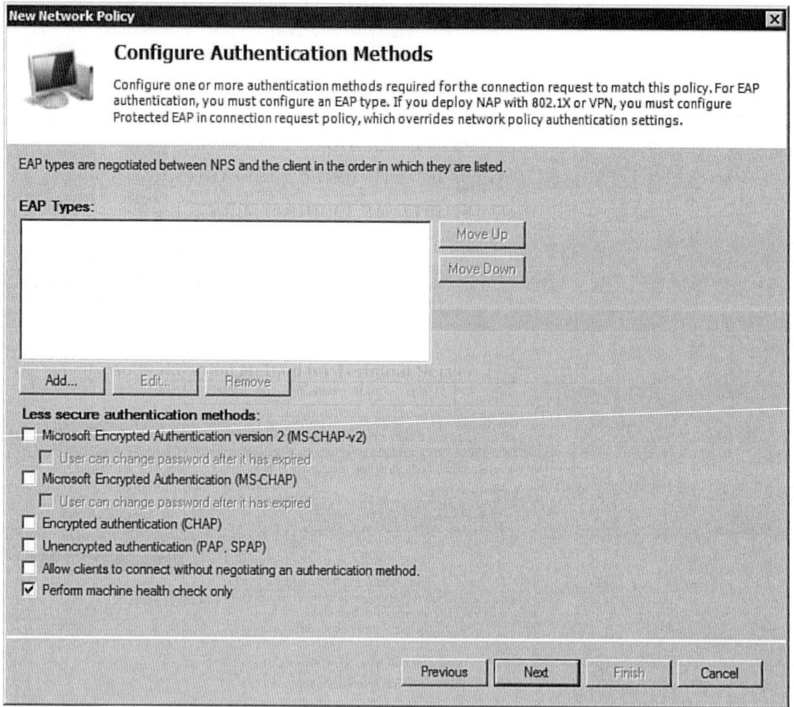

FIGURE 8-39 Authentication when used for DHCP checking.

For your noncompliant policy, NAP Enforcement is set to Allow Limited Access. Make sure Enable Auto-Remediation of Client Computers is turned on. You now have two DHCP policies: one using the compliant health policy and one using the noncompliant health policy that provides limited access.

For the noncompliant network policy, you can also define a remediation group that the noncompliant network policy allows the client to access. Other than with the DHCP server itself, no communication is allowed. First, use the Remediation Servers node to define a new group of servers that contains the IP addresses of servers that clients can connect to. In the network policy, click the Configure button for the remediation servers, as shown in Figure 8-40, and configure the group to which to allow access.

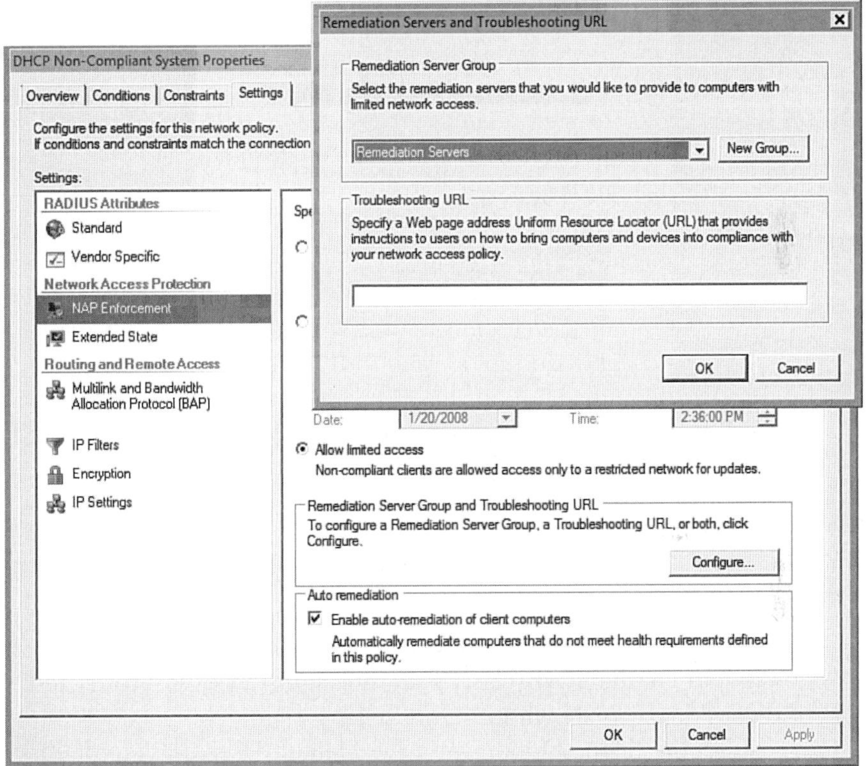

FIGURE 8-40 Allowing access to additional servers needed for remediation.

The next stage is to configure DHCP to use these policies. You enable for a specific scope, so select the scope you want to use NAP on and select its properties. Select the Network Access Protection tab, check the Enable for This Scope option, and select the Use Default Network Access

Protection profile options, as shown in Figure 8-41. Specify a custom profile name instead of using the default and check it against the MS-Service Class condition within a network policy to enable the use of different network policies based on which DHCP scope the client is requesting an address from. The custom value for the scope in the NAP dialog is compared against an MS-Service Class condition in a policy.

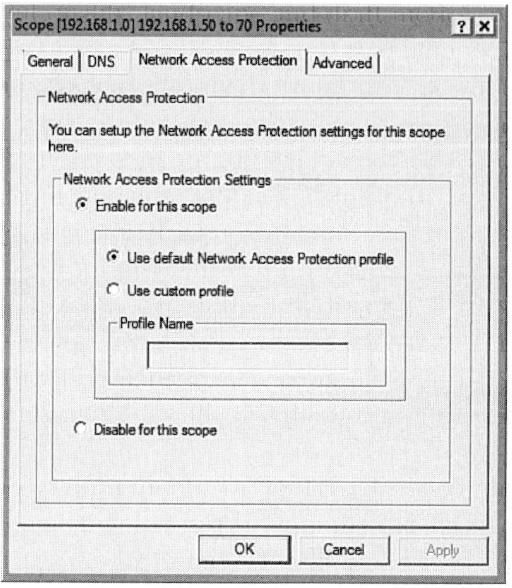

FIGURE 8-41 Configuring a DHCP scope to use NAP.

When enabled, select Properties of the Scope Options, where you can define different properties for whether the client is a full access NAP client or is part of the NAP class. For the latter, access is restricted via the Advanced tab, as shown in Figure 8-42.

With the Scope Options, use the Default User Class to define options for clients that meet compliance, and use the Default Network Access Protection Class to define settings for clients that failed compliance.

There is no client configuration for DHCP NAP other than the requirement to enable NAP support, including the DHCP quarantine enforcement agent. However, this entire configuration was covered by the GPO you created.

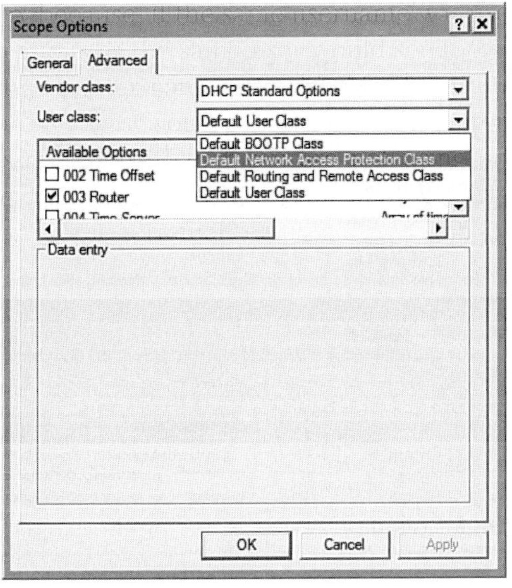

Figure 8-42 Configuring options for NAP class.

Client Experience

On the client side, if you initiate a VPN connection or regular network connectivity and you fail compliance, depending on the enforcement you have used, you are initially notified via a pop-up in your system tray, as shown in Figure 8-43. You can always force a display of the NAP status by running the `napstat` command.

Figure 8-43 The NAP failure initial pop-up.

If you select the pop-up or the NAP client icon, you see why you do not meet the requirements of the network. For example, as shown in Figure 8-44, antivirus is not enabled.

FIGURE 8-44 NAP client notification.

While you're in this noncompliance state, your IP functionality is limited. For example, if you run `IPCONFIG /ALL`, you see in multiple places that your system quarantine state is set to restricted. Depending on the enforcement, you have different options. For example, for DHCP enforcement, you have a different DNS suffix (restricted.savilltech.net) and no default gateway, as shown in the following listing. These are the DHCP settings you defined for the NAP class.

```
E:\>ipconfig /all

Windows IP Configuration

   Host Name . . . . . . . . . . . . : savdalvst5
   Primary Dns Suffix  . . . . . . . : savilltech.net
   Node Type . . . . . . . . . . . . : Hybrid
   IP Routing Enabled. . . . . . . . : No
   WINS Proxy Enabled. . . . . . . . : No
   DNS Suffix Search List. . . . . . : savilltech.net
                                       restricted.savilltech.net
   System Quarantine State . . . . . : Restricted


Ethernet adapter Local Area Connection:

   Connection-specific DNS Suffix  . : restricted.savilltech.net
   Description . . . . . . . . . . . : Intel 21140-Based PCI Fast
```

```
Ethernet Adapter (Emulated)
   Physical Address. . . . . . . . . : 00-03-FF-77-E9-2B
   DHCP Enabled. . . . . . . . . . . : Yes
   Autoconfiguration Enabled . . . .  : Yes
   IPv4 Address. . . . . . . . . . . : 192.168.1.62(Preferred)
   Subnet Mask . . . . . . . . . . . : 255.255.255.255
   Lease Obtained. . . . . . . . . . : Sunday, January 20, 2008
2:24:38 PM
   Lease Expires . . . . . . . . . . : Saturday, January 26, 2008
2:26:44 PM
   Default Gateway . . . . . . . . . :
   DHCP Server . . . . . . . . . . . : 192.168.1.10
   DNS Servers . . . . . . . . . . . : 192.168.1.10
   Quarantine State. . . . . . . . . : Restricted
   NetBIOS over Tcpip. . . . . . . . : Enabled
```

If you try to communicate with a server on the network, it fails. And if you run PING, it fails with a 1231 error code. The only servers you can communicate with are those defined in the remediation group selected for the limited connectivity.

A look at the routing table shows why. You have routes only for the servers in the remediation group and the DHCP server itself, as shown in the following listing. You have two routes for 192.168.1.10, which is the DHCP/NPS server, and one for 192.168.1.30, which is the server in my remediation group, both with 255.255.255.255 subnet masks. You have no other routes available to communicate. If you're an administrator, you could add a route to gain access to other networks, which is why DHCP is the weakest of the enforcements. Normally, you would have a route to the gateway for 0.0.0.0 and a mask of 0.0.0.0—almost everything.

```
E:\>route print
===========================================================================
Interface List
  8 ...00 03 ff 77 e9 2b ...... Intel 21140-Based PCI Fast Ethernet Adapter
(Emulated)
  1 ........................... Software Loopback Interface 1
  9 ...02 00 54 55 4e 01 ...... Teredo Tunneling Pseudo-Interface
 10 ...00 00 00 00 00 00 00 e0  Microsoft ISATAP Adapter
===========================================================================
```

```
IPv4 Route Table
===========================================================================
Active Routes:
Network Destination        Netmask          Gateway       Interface  Metric
        127.0.0.0        255.0.0.0         On-link         127.0.0.1    306
        127.0.0.1  255.255.255.255         On-link         127.0.0.1    306
  127.255.255.255  255.255.255.255         On-link         127.0.0.1    306
     192.168.1.10  255.255.255.255         On-link      192.168.1.62     21
     192.168.1.30  255.255.255.255         On-link      192.168.1.62     21
     192.168.1.62  255.255.255.255         On-link      192.168.1.62    276
        224.0.0.0        240.0.0.0         On-link         127.0.0.1    306
        224.0.0.0        240.0.0.0         On-link      192.168.1.62    276
  255.255.255.255  255.255.255.255         On-link         127.0.0.1    306
  255.255.255.255  255.255.255.255         On-link      192.168.1.62    276
===========================================================================
```

If the problem can be automatically remediated, the NAP dialog tells you, as shown in Figure 8-45. Alternatively, after you manually correct the problem by installing antivirus, click Try Again to force a reevaluation of your health assessment.

FIGURE 8-45 NAP client notification when healthy.

If the IP configuration is examined when healthy, the System Quarantine State shows as Not Restricted.

```
E:\>ipconfig /all

Windows IP Configuration

   Host Name . . . . . . . . . . . . : savdalvst5
   Primary Dns Suffix  . . . . . . . : savilltech.net
   Node Type . . . . . . . . . . . . : Hybrid
   IP Routing Enabled. . . . . . . . : No
   WINS Proxy Enabled. . . . . . . . : No
   DNS Suffix Search List. . . . . . : savilltech.net
   System Quarantine State . . . . . : Not Restricted
```

You can also use the netsh `nap client show state` command to view the current NAP restrictions, a list of the SHAs installed, and their states. In addition to the NAP client dialogs, this can help you see why compliance failed.

As the following listing shows, the Operational NAP event log contains troubleshooting information. Access this via the Event Viewer (eventvwr.msc). Navigate to the Applications and Logs, Microsoft, Windows, Network Access Protection, Operational area.

```
Log Name:      Microsoft-Windows-NetworkAccessProtection/
Operational
Source:        Microsoft-Windows-NetworkAccessProtection
Date:          1/20/2008 2:39:08 PM
Event ID:      29
Task Category: None
Level:         Information
Keywords:
User:          NETWORK SERVICE
Computer:      savdalvst5.savilltech.net
Description:
A Statement of Health Response with correlation ID {4B9ACF1C-
F93D-4DA6-96A3-581C11F6E476} - 2008-01-20 20:39:00.659Z was
received from the enforcement client 79617.
 The current client state is Restricted Access.
 The following SHAs report this client non-compliant: 79744,
 The following error categories were encountered:
FailureCategory None,
 The probation expiration time is:
 The help URL is:
 The duration of health check was 7430 ms.
```

8. REMOTE ACCESS AND SECURING AND OPTIMIZING THE NETWORK

The event log on the NAP server also shows information concerning quarantine events. For example, event ID 6276 shows a user was quarantined. That information is written to the Security log as shown here:

```
Log Name:      Security
Source:        Microsoft-Windows-Security-Auditing
Date:          1/20/2008 2:39:03 PM
Event ID:      6276
Task Category: Network Policy Server
Level:         Information
Keywords:      Audit Success
User:          N/A
Computer:      savdaldc01.savilltech.net
Description:
Network Policy Server quarantined a user.

Contact the Network Policy Server administrator for more
information.

User:
  Security ID:          NULL SID
  Account Name:         -
  Account Domain:             -
  Fully Qualified Account Name: -

Client Machine:
  Security ID:          SAVILLTECH\SAVDALVST5$
  Account Name:         savdalvst5.savilltech.net
  Fully Qualified Account Name: SAVILLTECH\SAVDALVST5$
  OS-Version:     6.0.6001 1.0 x86 Domain Controller
  Called Station Identifier:          192.168.1.0
  Calling Station Identifier:         0003FF77E92B

NAS:
  NAS IPv4 Address:             192.168.1.10
  NAS IPv6 Address:             -
  NAS Identifier:               SAVDALDC01
  NAS Port-Type:                Ethernet
  NAS Port:                     -

RADIUS Client:
  Client Friendly Name:         -
  Client IP Address:                  -
```

```
Authentication Details:
  Proxy Policy Name:            Use Windows authentication for
all users
  Network Policy Name:          DHCP Non-Compliant System
  Authentication Provider:              Windows
  Authentication Server:        savdaldc01.savilltech.net
  Authentication Type:          Unauthenticated
  EAP Type:     -
  Account Session Identifier:           31333834313236383637

Quarantine Information:
  Result:          Quarantined
  Extended-Result:                      -
  Session Identifier:                   {4B9ACF1C-F93D-4DA6-96A3-
581C11F6E476} - 2008-01-20 20:39:00.659Z
      Help URL:                -
      System Health Validator Result(s):
Windows Security Health Validator..
      NonCompliant
      No Data
      None
      (0x0 - )
      (0xc0ff0002 - A system health component is not
installed...)
      (0x0 - )
      (0x0 - )
      (0x0 - )
      (0x0 - )
      (0x0 - )
      (0x0 - )
```

When you put together these two event logs at both the client and the server, you have plenty of information to troubleshoot almost any problem.

Summary

The Remote Access capabilities and quarantine in Windows Server 2008 are a great leap forward compared to what you had before, especially when you consider the industry partnerships concerning the NAP technology based around RADIUS. Compatibility is not a limiting factor in implementing NAP.

Given the effects of NAP, take care when using it. From a remediation perspective, products such as SCCM are fully integrated with NAP and provide the capability to remediate all aspects of a client. SCCM provides its own SHV/SHA pair, which you access by installing the SCCM SHV role on the NPS server that hosts the NAP services.

For resources, you explored the TechNet NAP area. Check out the NAP blog at http://blogs.technet.com/nap/default.aspx. It has good information, and a detailed discussion of various enforcement options and their pros and cons.

CHAPTER 9

TERMINAL SERVICES

Technology has a weird habit of looping around. When I started in technology 14 years ago, my first job was at Logica, where I was a VAX/VMS systems manager. At that point, my computing experience had been based on PCs and Amiga 500s, so imagine my disappointment when this huge multinational computer company sat me in front of something that looked like an old black-and-white TV. It turns out I was on a VT320 terminal, which mapped via a Local Area Transport (LAT) port to a server that performed all the processing and passed back the output of commands entered via the keyboard to the VT320's screen. My VT320 was a dumb terminal; it was just an input/output device, and the main server did all the processing.

As I worked in the industry longer and moved to other technology areas, of course I used desktop computers that performed the processing locally via locally installed applications. However, locally installed applications have issues, including the following:

- **Installation**. Any locally installed piece of software has to be installed, well, locally. This can be simplified via group policy, System Center Configuration Manager (SCCM), or other deployment solutions, but this is still an issue. The application may require large amounts of configuration that cannot be automated.
- **Access to data**. Some applications require access to data that is available in a database or other resource. A large amount of data may be required for the application to function, and sending that data over the network might be a problem. Ideally, the application would run on the same box where the data resides.
- **Maintenance**. Some applications have frequent updates, and deploying frequent updates to large numbers of desktops can be a major effort.
- **Compatibility**. Some applications have many prerequisites that make deployment a hassle or cannot be deployed with other applications.

- **Performance**. There may be instances in which an application has great processing or hardware requirements that make them unsuitable for desktops.
- **Hardware requirements**. In order to function, some applications need hardware components or dongles that may be too expensive to have on each user's desktop.
- **Anywhere access**. A locally installed application is great, but if many people have to access the application infrequently or people have to access it from many different computers and want a consistent experience, a roaming capability has to be introduced, which can be complex or even impossible.

The solution to all these problems is to go back to the good old days and enable a user to remotely interact with a session that runs on a server via a special client application on the remote client. As with my VT320 terminal, today my keyboard and mouse actions are sent to the server for processing, and the screen output is sent back to my computer. The result is that I see a full session with Start menu, Task Manager, and so on, with multiple remote clients as well as the local console connection supported concurrently (see Figure 9-1). This is known as presentation virtualization, and it is part of Microsoft's virtualization story. Chapter 19, "Virtualization and Resource Management," covers this topic.

A number of other factors make Terminal Services (TS) an attractive option:

- **Increasing core capacity**. Per Moore's law, hardware power is increasing, and now with more cores on each physical processor, we can run a lot of computing on a single physical box.
- **Green computing**. Thin clients use less power than fat clients. With thin clients, we have more power usage on the server side, but not enough to outweigh the savings at the client side.
- **Connectivity**. Connectivity is increasing, in terms of both speed and availability, which facilitates centralized computing even outside the traditional workplace via wireless/broadband. You hear about Internet access on planes, and eventually there will be no place you can't get a connection. Previously, the lack of Internet access was a common barrier to Terminal Services.

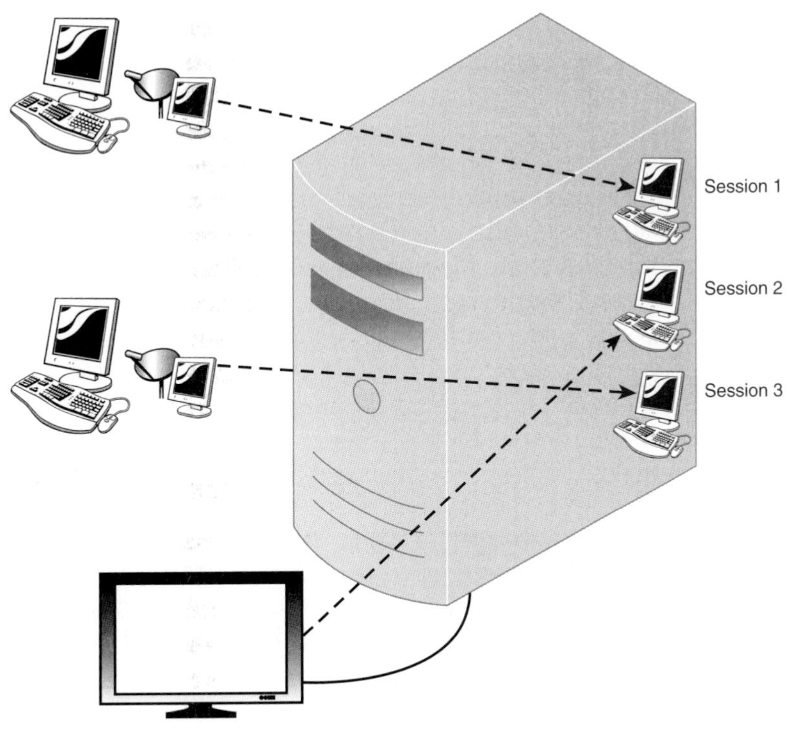

FIGURE 9-1 Three sessions running on the server, with one of them the local console session, which is treated no differently from a remote session.

- **Contingency**. Centralized information is easier to replicate to a disaster recovery (DR) location. In addition, by using terminal servers, users can access the DR location from their desk or from home, which is useful in disaster situations or when the user cannot get to the office, such as during bad weather. (Although this does ruin users getting a snow day and enjoying themselves so you may want to delay implementing Terminal Services for this reason or expedite depending on if you like the users.)
- **Compliance**. Data on clients is difficult to control. Data placed on a central server is easier to control.
- **Cost**. Thin clients require less maintenance and are less expensive than a full operating system (OS) computer, so cost containment is an advantage for a terminal server–based environment. Obviously, system center helps make running fat computers cheaper, so balance these factors.

There may not be one best answer. Some users might fit well into a terminal server situation, such as phone operators, or people who run only one or two applications. Power users and developers will probably need fat clients, but that's the great thing: You don't have to make a 100% choice. You have options and can choose the best one in each circumstance.

From the user desktop perspective, multiple remote sessions can run at the same time. As shown in Figure 9-2, I have my local Start menu and processes in addition to the full environment and processes on the remote server. You may already have used this. With Windows XP, and enhanced with Windows Vista, you have the capability for Remote Desktop, which enables remote access to your Vista machine from another computer. The XP/Vista Remote Desktop uses the same technology as TS. You just redirect the screen output for a session and send it to the Remote Desktop client, and, in turn, send the keyboard and mouse strokes to the session.

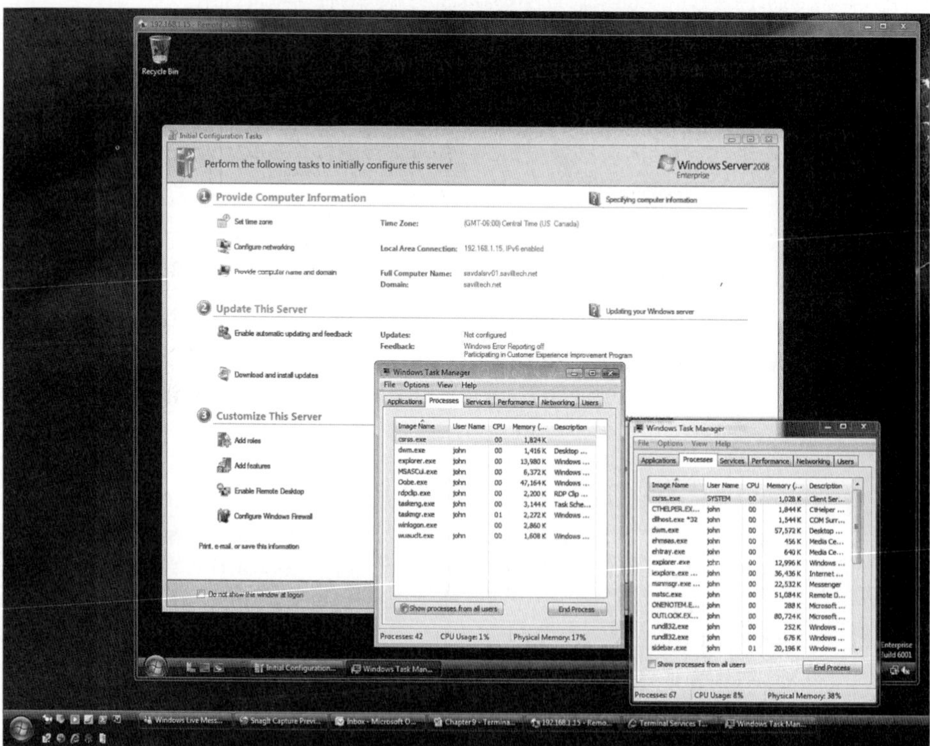

FIGURE 9-2 The remote session looks like a normal desktop experience but is running on a remote server.

A *thin client* is nothing more than a Remote Desktop Protocol (RDP) client, and it saves the cost and management of using a full Windows installation as an RDP client. If you have a lot of older machines, you can also use them as RDP clients, but running a basic Linux shell or Windows Fundamentals for legacy PCs is another good option. RDP 6.1 is the latest RDP version, and thin client vendors are currently working on thin clients that support RDP 6.1 to allow all the functionality of Windows Server 2008 TS.

Why use TS instead of application virtualization or just install the application locally? Imagine a program that has a huge local component that could be gigabytes in size and updated frequently. TS is great for this because the application and data are on a single terminal server (or possibly a group of terminal servers that collectively offer a service that provides high availability). Imagine an application that constantly communicates with a database over the network. It would generate huge amounts of traffic. Even for normal applications, maintaining 5 copies of an application on 5 terminal servers is better than maintaining 500 copies on 500 desktops.

There are obviously trade-offs. You have a powerful desktop PC; using it for every application as a dumb terminal client is a waste of resources. And the terminal server solution requires a powerful terminal server farm to host many sessions, so you should have specific reasons for installing an application in a terminal server farm. There should be clear business reasons, or the terminal server option should offer clear technical or cost advantages.

There are two modes of operation for the TS capability. The first is Remote Desktop for Administration, which involves a server that facilitates remote administration through a full-session environment but which is limited to two concurrent connections. Remote Desktop for Administration does not enable some useful experience elements such as the TS Easy Printing capability for a full printing experience and the enhanced Vista theme. The other mode is the full TS role, which enables all the terminal server functionality and is designed to be used when the server will be accessed by users for remote session and application execution. This topic is fully explored in this chapter. Let's start with the easy one: Remote Desktop. This will get you using TS quickly, so you can see the basic features.

Windows Server 2008 is far more scalable than Windows Server 2003. A Windows Server 2003 maxes out at 800 concurrent users on 16 processor cores. With Windows Server 2008, additional cores are used, and with a 32-core x64 system, you can have nearly 1,200 concurrent connections.

In testing, this seems to be about the maximum number on a single server, but many more could be supported in a terminal server farm configuration. This is not to say that 1,200 concurrent users would be recommended, but it gives an indication about what is possible and how Windows Server 2008 makes full use of the available hardware.

Enabling Remote Desktop

By default, Remote Desktop is disabled on a newly installed server. However, you can enable it via Initial Configuration Tasks in the Customize This Server section, as discussed in Chapter 3, "Installing and Upgrading Windows Server 2008." Or you can modify it at any time via the System Control Panel applet's Remote tab. When you enable Remote Desktop, you can choose to allow connections from any version of the Remote Desktop client or choose the more secure option of allowing connection only from clients with Network Level Authentication (NLA). When either of the Remote Desktop options is selected, you are notified that an exception in the firewall will be enabled to allow the remote sessions, which by default will be for all known interfaces, as shown in Figure 9-3. You can modify this as required via the Windows Firewall management interface. By default, the local administrator has rights for Remote Desktop access. You can give additional users rights by clicking the Select Users button and adding them.

NLA enables the credentials used for authentication with the terminal server to be entered before the full connection is established. With the lack of NLA in previous OSs, NLA today is more secure and less prone to credential hijacking and denial of service attacks because until the credentials are verified, the full session is not created and thus is not using resources. Without NLA in previous OSs, as soon as you clicked Connect, the session was created and then the credentials were entered, and they were vulnerable to theft as they were entered over the network. As an additional security level, Server Authentication is used with RDP 6.0, and it uses Transport Level Security (TLS) to verify that the server the user thinks he is connecting to is the target server and not an imposter server trying to harvest credentials or other information. By default, you are warned if Server Authentication fails. However, via the Advanced tab of the Remote Desktop Connection (RDC) tool, you can modify the behavior to warn you to refuse to connect.

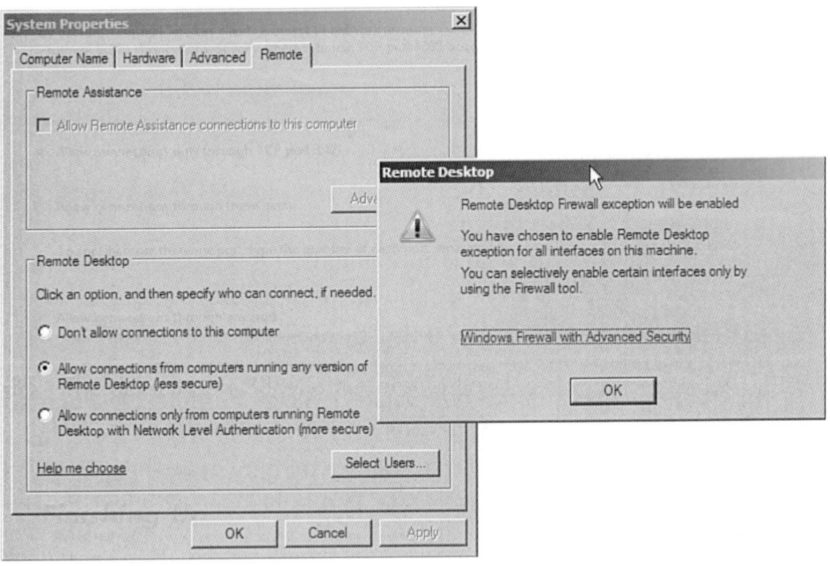

FIGURE 9-3 With Windows Server 2008, Windows Firewall is enabled by default, and any feature that requires an exception will bring up a prompt to ensure that functionality is not compromised.

If you are unsure whether a Remote Desktop machine supports NLA view, open the About dialog by clicking the top-left corner icon of Remote Desktop and selecting About. If NLA is supported, it appears in the dialog, as shown in Figure 9-4 (which was taken from a Vista client).

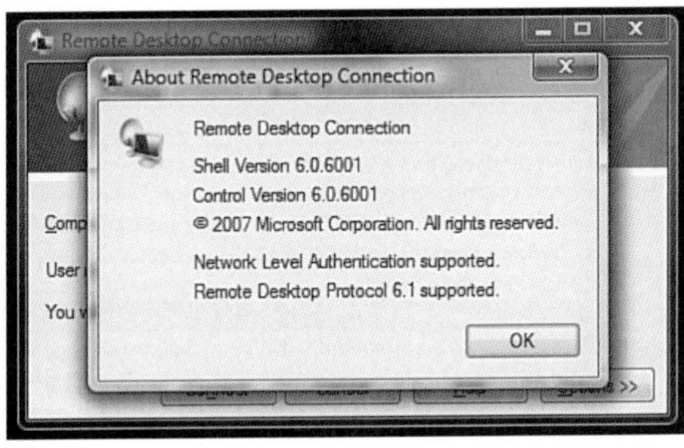

FIGURE 9-4 The Remote Desktop client in Vista and above includes NLA support.

If all Remote Desktop clients will be Windows Vista or above, you can choose to allow connections only from NLA-capable clients. Microsoft has released an RDP 6.0 client for Windows Server 2003 Service Pack 1 and above and Windows XP Service Pack 2 (see KB925876 at www.microsoft.com) that adds NLA capabilities. If you are not sure of the client's NLA capability, you should allow connections from any version of the Remote Desktop client.

The Windows Firewall component that is accessed via Server Manager provides a detailed view of the firewall configuration. If you navigate through Configuration, Windows Firewall with Advanced Security, Inbound Rules, you can see all the various inbound rules, and the ones that are enabled have a green checkmark. When Remote Desktop is enabled, the Remote Desktop (TCP-In) rule is enabled for any profile, which includes private, public, and domain-type networks.

To look at the details of a rule, right-click it and select Properties. On some computers, you may see two rules for Remote Desktop (see Figure 9-5): One rule that applies to public and private profiles and another for domains. This can happen after an upgrade from Windows Server 2003. If the server is part of a domain and is on a network that has access to the domain, it is important that the Domain Profile scope inbound rule be enabled, or Remote Desktop connections will fail. If you are unsure of what type of network your server thinks it is on, open the Network and Sharing Center in the Control Panel; next to the name of your network, you see the type of network in brackets (for example, [Domain network]).

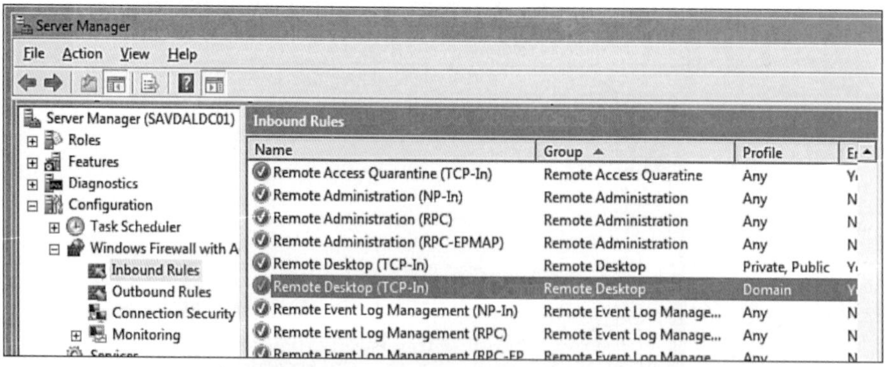

FIGURE 9-5 When Remote Desktop is enabled, this inbound rule is automatically enabled.

Remote Desktop is fully configurable via unattended installation, as is the method of authentication (with or without NLA). The following example shows a basic section that is used to enable Remote Desktop, which also includes enabling the exception in Windows Firewall for Remote Desktop. The default NLA configuration is Allow without NLA. However, enable this by selecting Microsoft, Windows, TerminalServices, RDP, WinStationExtensions and setting UserAuthentication.

```
<settings pass="specialize">
- <component name="Microsoft-Windows-TerminalServices-
LocalSessionManager" processorArchitecture="x86"
publicKeyToken="31bf3856ad364e35" language="neutral"
versionScope="nonSxS"
xmlns:wcm="http://schemas.microsoft.com/WMIConfig/2002/State"
xmlns:xsi="http://www.w3.org/2001/XMLSchema-instance">
  <fDenyTSConnections>false</fDenyTSConnections>
  </component>
- <component name="Networking-MPSSVC-Svc"
processorArchitecture="x86" publicKeyToken="31bf3856ad364e35"
language="neutral" versionScope="nonSxS"
xmlns:wcm="http://schemas.microsoft.com/WMIConfig/2002/State"
xmlns:xsi="http://www.w3.org/2001/XMLSchema-instance">
- <FirewallGroups>
- <FirewallGroup wcm:action="add" wcm:keyValue="rd1">
  <Active>true</Active>
  <Group>Remote Desktop</Group>
  <Profile>all</Profile>
  </FirewallGroup>
  </FirewallGroups>
  </component>
  </settings>
```

Now that you have Remote Desktop enabled, let's look at connecting to it.

Initiating a Remote Desktop Connection

Windows XP, Windows Server 2003, Windows Vista, and Windows Server 2008 all contain the RDC tool, mstsc.exe, which is found in the Accessories group of the Start menu (and further hidden in the Communications subfolder in Windows XP and Windows Server 2003).

NOTE *MSTSC* in the filename mstsc.exe stands for Microsoft Terminal Services Client.

There are various versions of the RDP client, each of which exposes additional functionality to the capabilities of TS at the time of the RDC release. The base version with Windows XP and Windows Server 2003 was Version 5.x; Version 6.1 is available as a download that matches the functionality to the version in the Windows Server 2008 release.

When you start the RDC, you see a basic dialog that asks the name of a computer to connect to (see Figure 9-6). After you enter the name or IP address of a server or desktop, the RDC prompts for credentials that will be used for the connection and then attempts a connection. When you enter credentials, you can save the credentials to speed up future connection attempts, but keep in mind that saving sensitive information locally on the computer may not be desirable. Be sure to specify the domain name with the username when entering credentials, using *<domain>*\ or *@domain* (for example, savilltech\john or john@savilltech.net), or RDC will try to use the local account database of the terminal server, which will not be correct in a domain environment.

The remote connection is full screen on your computer, running at the maximum color quality supported by your local machine (32-bit, if possible), and it maps your Clipboard and printers. By default, RDC sessions are "old style" looking; you won't see a desktop background or any font smoothing, contents aren't shown when a window is dragged, and you don't see the menu and window animation you've grown to know and love. This is because by default the RDC thinks it's running over a 56Kbps modem.

FIGURE 9-6 The RDC tool has a basic initial interface and requires only a name.

When you run RDC in full-screen mode, an RDC bar—known as the connection bar or the "b bar" internally at Microsoft—appears at the top of the screen and stays there. However, you can configure it to hide itself by clicking the little pushpin icon on the far left of the bar, as shown in Figure 9-7. If you want to see the bar, you just move the mouse pointer to the top center of the screen, and the bar lowers itself down. Next to the pin is a padlock icon, and if you select, it, you see how the server's identity was verified (for example, via Kerberos). You see this icon only if you are running an RDC that supports RDP 6.0 or higher, which is the version needed for Server Authentication. This has nothing to do with user authentication; it just confirms how the client and the server mutually authenticated.

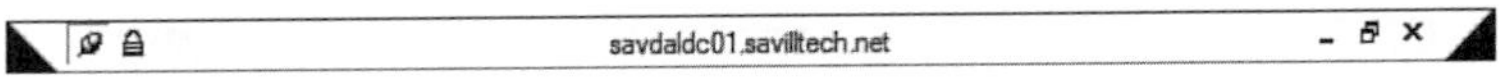

FIGURE 9-7 The RDC bar tells the name of the server to which you are connecting.

You can now work away happily on the session. When you want to disconnect, click the close cross on the connection bar. When you disconnect, the session is not closed. It stays running, carrying on any computations and applications, and if you again connect to the same server as the same user, you are reconnected to that session, with all open windows and applications still there. If you want to close the session, log off via the Start menu. For the user, it's normally better to disconnect the session than to log off because the next connection goes faster without the logging on, processing of group policy, and so on. When the user has disconnected rather than logged off, the sessions are already running; the user is just connecting to it. For an administrator (and the terminal server), all those disconnected sessions are just like someone logged on, still taking up resources, and with too many disconnected sessions, the performance of the server may start to be affected. However, as an administrator, you do have some control.

If you selected Clipboard sharing, you quickly find that you have way more power than in previous RDP clients. With RDP 6, you can cut and paste objects (including files) between the remote session and the local session.

With Windows Server 2003, you sometimes needed to use a switch if you wanted to connect to the console of the server (that is, the session used for the keyboard, mouse, and monitor physically connected to the server). If you had been logged on to the console of a server and then wanted to connect to that console session remotely, you had to add `/console` to the end of the `mstsc` command. There was no graphical way in the Remote Desktop client GUI to say "connect to the console," so you had to run the following command:

```
mstsc /console
```

The rest of the RDC experience was the same as in Windows Server 2008, but when you connected, you would connect to the console session, which was always Session 0.

Do I still use `/console` when connecting to a Windows Server 2008 server if I want the special console session? No, there is none. In Windows Server 2008 and Windows Vista, Session 0 is reserved for services, and there is no special logon session reserved for the console anymore. The reason that Session 0 is no longer used for the console session is that many kernel services ran in Session 0, so if a user logged on to the console, it was possible that the user would be able to get access to high-privileged processes. This is commonly achieved by services that send an alert or error to the user interface, which would now be the logged-on user's session that allows the user to interact with high-privilege service. This is known as a shatter attack. If you are a software writer and your software relies on being run/installed in Session 0, you have some changes to make!

In Figure 9-1, the local console is not Session 0 or anything special; it is just a session in the middle of the remote sessions. There is one downside to this; in Windows Server 2003, you could have two remote sessions in Remote Administration mode (which is where Remote Desktop is enabled but TS is not installed) and one session locally on the console, so you could have three in total. In Windows Server 2008, you can have only two concurrent session in total because the physical console session is just lumped in with remote sessions. There is still a session named console that is the one that's physically connected to the server, but its session number changes as people log on and log off the server. When a session ends on the console, another session is automatically created, waiting for the secure attention sequence. The `/console` switch is still supported in the latest RDC, however, so you can connect the console session to Windows Server 2003 servers.

If you are running in Remote Desktop mode and can have only two sessions, what happens if both sessions are in use? In Windows Server 2003, you just got a message that the maximum number of sessions had been reached and to please go away. In Windows Server 2008, a list of the currently open sessions is displayed (see Figure 9-8), and you have the option of disconnecting one. Notice that the session must be *disconnected*, not closed; so the session won't lose any work. If you don't check Force Disconnect of This User, a dialog is displayed in the session, as shown in Figure 9-9, giving you 30 seconds to click OK and be disconnected or to reject the takeover bid by clicking Cancel. If you check the Force Disconnect box, users will be disconnected immediately, with no notification. The Force Disconnect option is available only to administrators, not to normal users.

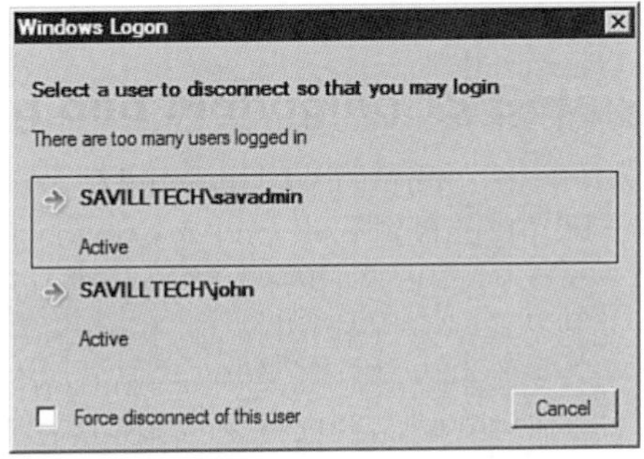

FIGURE 9-8 Even if a server is full, you can now connect by disconnecting an existing session.

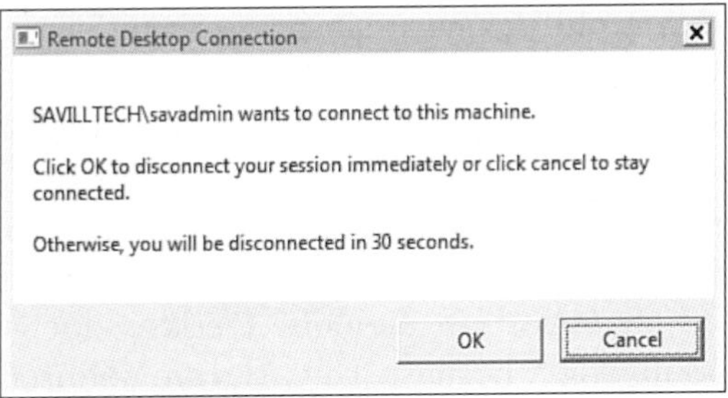

FIGURE 9-9 This dialog is shown for the session that is being disconnected.

This may seem like a drop in functionality. If you have a session running on the physical console, how do you get to it now? Remember that there is no console session; if you connect remotely with the same username as the session that is disconnected on the console, you will just resume the session that was previously used locally at the console. If the session is not disconnected on the console, you will probably also get reconnected. But you may not. If you have a brand-new Windows Server 2008 installation, then TS is configured to limit every user to only one session. This means when you log on remotely, you're allowed only one session, so you're forced to take over the session that was running locally. If, however, you upgraded from Windows Server 2003, this one-session restriction is not enabled. So if the session is active at the console, you get a second, new session as the same user. If the session at the console was disconnected, you could connect to it.

To control this session restriction, use the Terminal Services Configuration Microsoft Management Console (MMC) snap-in, which is found in the Terminal Services folder under Administrative Tools. (You learn more details about this snap-in later in this chapter.) For now, you just need to know that when you're in Remote Desktop for Administration mode, you still have a few configuration options. The important setting for now, Restrict Each User to a Single Session, is on the General tab, shown in Figure 9-10. If you double-click the setting, the server properties are opened, and you can change the configuration. In this case, the server was currently not restricting a user to a single session, so after opening the properties, you can check the restriction option so in the future each user will have one session.

There is, however, the concept of connecting to an administrative session. Although you don't use `/console` anymore, because the console session is no different from any other session, you have a new option, `/admin`, that you can add to your `mstsc` call (that is, `mstsc /admin`). You use the `/admin` option when you want to initiate an administrative session. This is important when you connect to a server with the TS role installed and therefore connections use TS Client Access Licenses (CALs), discussed later in this chapter. If you use the `/admin` switch, the connection does not consume a TS CAL. (In Remote Desktop for Administration mode, `/admin` has no effect because TS CALs are not used anyway.)

Only two concurrent sessions on a terminal server can use the `/admin` switch, which emulates the restrictions when using Remote Desktop for Administration mode. If you try to connect a third session by using the `/admin` switch, a list of the current sessions that are in Administration mode are displayed, and you have the option to disconnect one within 30 seconds (unless Force Disconnect is enabled).

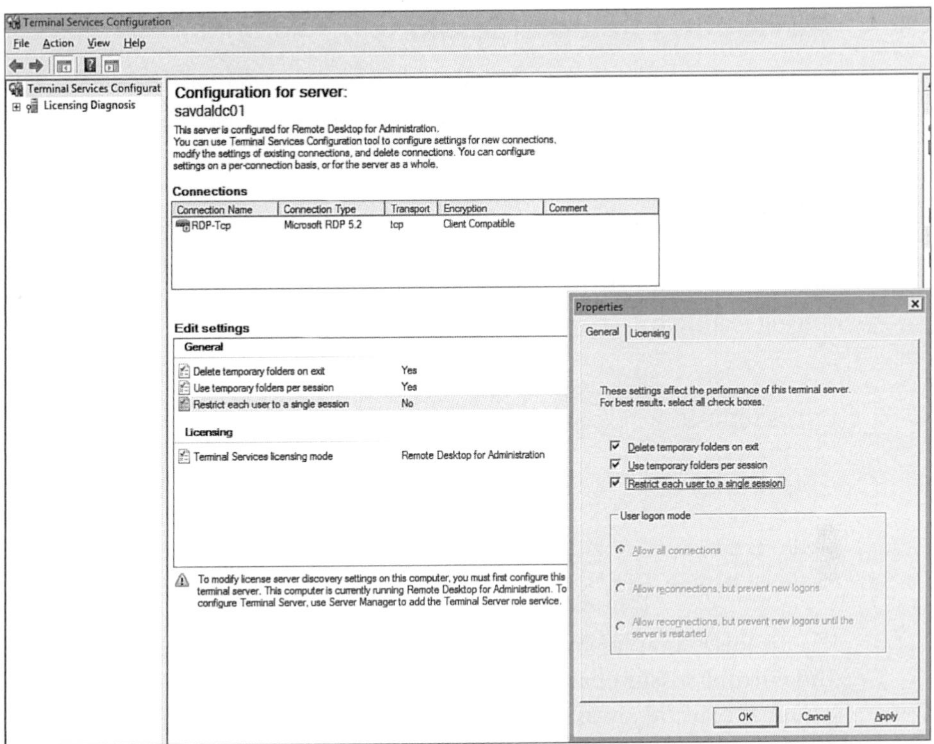

FIGURE 9-10 You have three general server-based configuration items in Remote Desktop for Administration mode.

Only users who are part of the Remote Desktop users group and listed in the SD_CONSOLE Access Control List (ACL) can connect with an `/admin` session. By default, SD_CONSOLE contains only administrators and should not need to be modified.

Sessions connected with `/admin` have some special rights. Even if a user has been marked with Deny Users Permissions to Log on to Terminal Server, if she has the authority to use the `/admin` switch (that is, the user is an administrator), that user will be able to connect as long as she uses `mstsc /admin`. Also, if a terminal server is in drain mode, which means no new sessions are accepted, then an `/admin` session can be created. Finally, `/admin` sessions do not count toward the session limit that may be configured on a terminal server.

If you are connecting to a server with the TS role installed, and you are an administrator and don't want to consume a TS CAL, use the `/admin` switch.

Navigating Remote Sessions

In some cases, one-session-per-user restrictions may not be enabled on a server, or you may want to connect to someone else's session. In such a case, you can use the Terminal Services Manager to see all the sessions/users connected to a terminal server and then from the properties of the user/session entry, you can choose to connect to the session. However, let's be old-school right now and look at the `qwinsta` command-line tool, which lists the current sessions on a server, as shown in the following example.

```
C:\Users\savadmin>qwinsta
 SESSIONNAME       USERNAME                 ID  STATE   TYPE DEVICE
 services                                        0  Disc
>rdp-tcp#1         savadmin                  7  Active  rdpwd
 console                                     8  Conn
 rdp-tcp#0         john                      9  Active  rdpwd
 rdp-tcp                                 65536  Listen
```

In this example, you can see that session ID 9 is user John. Notice that the current session has a greater-than arrow at the far left. Notice that the physical console always has a session connected, which is the security dialog waiting for a logon. You can connect to the console session; it just is no longer Session 0. If you do not have limits on the number of sessions per user and want to connect to your console session, you use `tscon console`. To connect to another session, you can use the `tscon` command and pass the session ID. For example, if you want to take over John's session, you need to pass the session ID, plus you need the `/PASSWORD` switch to pass John's password (it would be a huge security issue to not have to pass the password of another user's session). This would all look something like the following:

```
tscon 9 /password:thepassword
```

Configuring the RDC Client

Let's look at some of the interesting options of the RDC client. If you click the Options button, you are presented with a far fuller dialog that has six tabs in the RDP 6.x version of RDC: General, Display, Local Resources,

Programs, Experience, and Advanced. For RDP 5.x clients, the Advanced tab is missing.

The General Tab

The General tab enables you to configure a username for the connection, as well as the credentials to be saved for a connection. You also see options to save and open RDP files, which are files that contain a set of configuration items related to a specific connection. As you walk through the tabs of the RDC, you see that there are many options that you may want to set in different ways for different target servers. Instead of reconfiguring the options every time you connect, you can just configure the connection and then save it as an RDP file (for example, savdaldc01.rdp for a customized connection to the savdaldc01 server). By default, RDP files are saved to the Documents folder of your home path, but you can browse and save them anywhere. RDP files are associated with the RDC application, so you can place them on your desktop, put shortcuts to them in your Quick Launch bar, or just double-click them in Explorer to automatically connect to the target.

The Display Tab

The Display tab enables you to configure the size of the display in the remote session, as shown in Figure 9-11. To have a session fill the entire screen, you slide the bar all the way to the right. All the various combinations and ratios of screen sizes are now available such as widescreen-type resolutions.

The largest possible resolution is 4096×2048, which seems beyond any human-made monitor, but not when you consider that multiple-monitor configurations are now supported. You access multiple-monitor configuration by passing `/span` to the `mstsc` command. Both monitors must run the same resolution and must be configured as side-by-side. To pass a resolution from the command line, you can use the `/w:` and `/h:` parameters for width and height, respectively, as in this example:

```
mstsc /w:1680 /h:1050
```

FIGURE 9-11 The Display tab property sheet.

You also have the option to use 32-bit color. However, by default, Windows Server 2008 may limit the color depth of sessions to 24-bit, so to get the full 32-bit, use the Terminal Services Configuration MMC snap-in and uncheck the Limit Maximum Color Depth option under Client Settings for the RDP connection properties. (This is discussed further later in the chapter.) Because of the encryption used in RDP 6.x, 32-bit color uses less bandwidth than 24-bit color, thanks to the new bitmap compression scheme, so consider 24-bit as a last resort. Graphics are much improved in RDP 6, which sets aside 70% of the bandwidth just for video via its flow control. However, you can modify this, if required, to more or less of the bandwidth, and if that percentage is pre/postcompression, you can just disable flow control totally and make it a free-for-all. This 70% was introduced to ensure no drop in quality of responsiveness; previously, printing a large document would use up a lot of bandwidth and cause the session to crawl. You use four registry values to set this behavior, and they're all found at HKEY_LOCAL_MACHINE\SYSTEM\Current ControlSet\Services\TermDD:

- **FlowControlDisable**. When set to 1, this value will disable the new flow control algorithm, making RDP work as in Windows Server 2003.

- **FlowControlDisplayBandwidth**. You can set a value between 0 and 255 for the amount of bandwidth for display.
- **FlowControlChannelBandwidth**. You can set a value between 0 and 255 for the amount of bandwidth for everything that's not video. This number and the FlowControlDisplayBandwidth value are used to portion bandwidth between video and everything else. Setting FlowControlDisplayBandwidth to 200 and FlowControlChannelBandwidth to 100 would mean FlowControlChannelBandwidth would use 33% of the bandwidth, with the rest reserved for display. If you change these values, making sure they add up to 100 can preserve your sanity.
- **FlowControlChargePostCompression**. If this is set to 1, it bases the bandwidth allocation on postcompression bandwidth usage, and if it is set to 0, the bandwidth distribution is applied on precompressed data.

You also have the option to display the connection bar when in full screen, which is a good idea because it offers easy disconnection.

The Local Resources Tab

On the Local Resources tab, you can configure where the remote computer sound is played, which can be no playing of sounds, playing at your local computer, or playing at the remote computer.

This tab is also where you configure where special Windows key combinations, such as Alt+Tab, are activated: on the local computer, on the remote computer, or on the remote computer when in full-screen mode. I like to set the key combinations to On the Remote Computer so that Windows key + E brings up Explorer on the remote session when it has focus instead of on the local machine.

The final part of this tab deals with local devices and resources. You have basic options to share printers and the Clipboard with your remote sessions. (Printing is covered later in this chapter.) If you click the More button, you also get options to share smart cards, serial ports, your drives, and supported plug-and-play devices, as shown in Figure 9-12.

If you map drives, then in the RDP session, your local drives are shown as *<drive letter>* on *<client computer name>* under the actual terminal server drives.

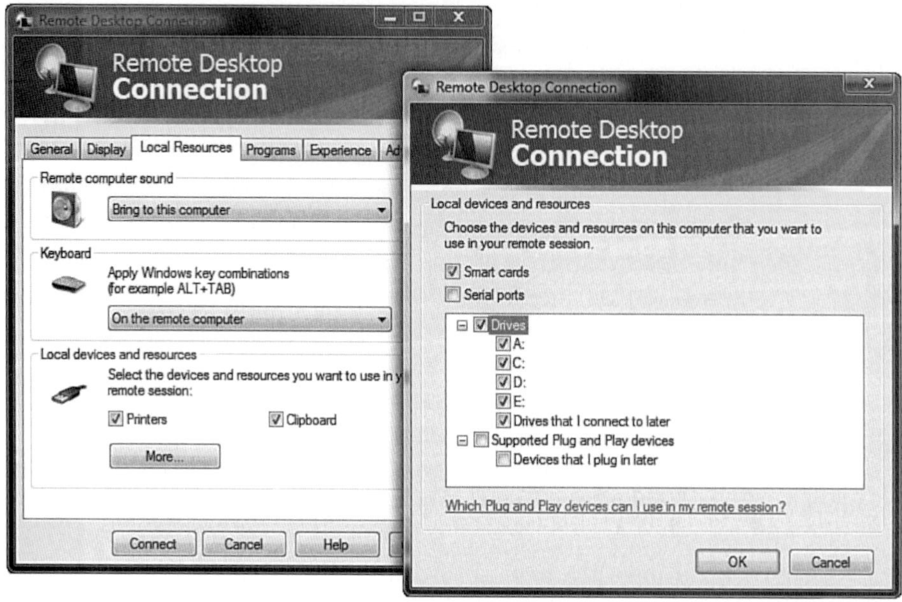

FIGURE 9-12 Mapping drives to your RDP sessions can be an easy way to share information.

One new feature with Windows Vista RDP is Plug and Play redirection, which you configure here. With Plug and Play device redirection, you can plug a camera into a desktop and launch a remote application or session, and the remote auto-play launches for the locally connected device and allows full access. Currently audio capture redirection does not work, but it will in Windows 7. There are no plans for video capture (for example, webcams) currently, but Windows 7 RDP will have much-improved video playback.

For RDP to work with the device, the Plug and Play driver must follow the user mode driver framework and other rules set in the Device Logo Program specific to TS.

In Windows Server 2008, as in Windows Server 2003, disk drives, smart cards, serial ports, and printers can be redirected. Vista added support for Plug and Play devices such as media players and digital still cameras. Windows Server 2008 adds point–of-service devices (bar code and check scanners) that are based on Microsoft Point of Sale (POS) for .NET 1.11. Currently, biometric devices are not supported because the vendor drivers don't support TS, but that may change. No scanners or multifunction devices, such as fax machines, can be redirected currently. Redirection works only with devices that have an inbox (such as a camera).

The Programs Tab

You use the Programs tab to configure a program to be started when the session initiates on the remote server, and you also use it to set an initial working folder. This is useful if you want a program, such as Word or Internet Explorer, to start when you connect to the terminal server. You can only specify programs that have been shared via RemoteApp, which is discussed later in this chapter. When you enable this option, when the application specified closes, the session also closes.

The Experience Tab

A number of Experience tab elements are new to RDP 6.x. The most notable of these are font smoothing and desktop composition. By default, you can set one of the included configurations: LAN (10Mbps or higher), Broadband (128Kbps–1.5Mbps), or Modem (56Kbps and 28.8Kbps). For each of these template connection types, different elements of the experience are enabled, as shown in Figure 9-13. With LAN, you get all the options available for the best experience. However, you can create a custom configuration by selecting various elements.

FIGURE 9-13 A variety of experience elements are available.

Some of these elements require Windows Server 2008/Vista targets, such as Vista/font smoothing, and are ignored by earlier RDP targets. Most of the options speak for themselves. However, let's talk briefly about font smoothing and desktop composition.

Font smoothing sounds great, and with today's LCD monitors, it is important for a nice look. However, it has a negative effect: RDP is efficient with normal font rendering and uses a minimal amount of bandwidth. To use font smoothing, however, the rendering has to be performed on the RDP target via Graphics Device Interface (GDI) and then sent back to the client via RDP as bitmaps. This process works fine, but it uses up a lot of bandwidth. Be aware that a session that uses font smoothing could use up to ten times more bandwidth than a non-font-smoothed session. Test it in your environment and see what the performance is like.

Desktop composition enables an RDP session to be rendered locally on the client, using the Desktop Windows Manager, which allows remote sessions to be Aero themed. That's right: You can have Flip 3D, Aero windows, and so on. There are requirements for this, though, and some restrictions. In the Windows Server 2008 Release To Manufacture (RTM), the full Aero experience is disabled, but if you are connecting to a Windows Vista box, and the Vista box and your local machine support Aero, as long as your color depth is 32-bit and desktop composition is enabled, you will have an Aero session.

As of Windows Server 2008 RC0 and with the RTM, the full Aero experience has been removed. For Beta 3, you performed the following to get full Aero theme for terminal server sessions. Your local machine must support Aero, and the TS client must be configured with 32-bit and Desktop Composition, and you also need to make some changes on the server. First, install the Desktop Experience feature. Then start the Themes service by selecting Server Manager, Configuration, Services. Next, right-click Themes, set the startup to Automatic, and click the Start button.

The server also needs the TS role installed; you don't get this theme support with Remote Desktop for Administration. Finally, ensure that your RDP session is not limited to 24-bit by the Terminal Services Configuration MMC snap-in, so you have to open the Terminal Services Configuration MMC snap-in and on the RDP properties page, under Client settings, ensure that the Limit Maximum Color Depth option is not configured, as shown in Figure 9-14.

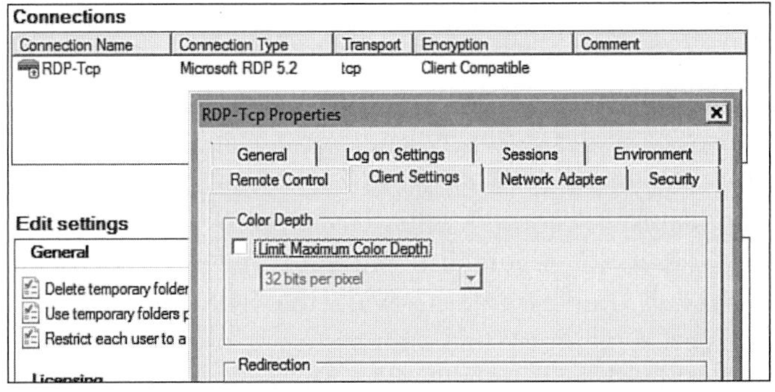

FIGURE 9-14 You may find that your server is configured as 24-bit color by default.

When all these changes are done, you have an Aero-themed session. Because Aero was removed in the RTM, instead of Aero you get Vista Basic theme, and you still need to perform all the above except for the 32-bit color setting. The full Aero experience was removed for quality testing purposes and will hopefully make a future update. The previous steps enable the full Aero.

Finally, by default, if the connection is dropped, the client attempts automatic reconnection. You can change this setting on the Experience tab if you like.

The Advanced Tab

With the Advanced tab, you can configure the Server Authentication component of the RDC, which verifies that you are connecting to the server you think you are connecting to. As discussed earlier in this chapter, you can configure the RDC to warn you in the event of server authentication failure, connect and don't warn, or not connect. Windows Server 2003 Service Pack 1 and earlier OSs cannot provide identity verification, so if you need to connect to one of those earlier OSs, ensure that you don't configure the option to not connect in the event of server authentication failure. Also on the Advanced tab are the Connect from Anywhere settings, which relate to the new 2008 TS Gateway feature.

Terminal Server Licensing

Now that we have examined the RDP client in depth and connected to various types of systems, let's look at the licensing requirements for TS. If you are running in Remote Desktop for Administration mode, there are no special licensing requirements. However, if you intend to install the TS role on servers for general use, purchase Terminal Server CALs in two possible models: per user and per device. The licensing server tracks per-device CALs, whereas the honor system is used for per-user CALs. A user or device needs only one TS CAL to connect to any number of terminal servers in the infrastructure for which they are licensed. As with all other CALs, a TS CAL cannot be used across infrastructures.

Keep in mind that a TS CAL is permanently assigned to a specific user. While TS does return a CAL to the pool after 59 days, this fact must not be used to effect concurrent licensing. TS CALs can be transferred only when a customer reasonably expects a user/device to never come back onto its system.

If you choose the per-device licensing model, the actual computer or device that connects to the terminal server receives a TS CAL. Any user using the client with the TS per-device CAL has rights to access the terminal server, so this is a good model if lots of users use the same physical machine. With the per-user model, the user account is granted the TS CAL and can connect to the terminal server from any computer or device, so this is a good model if you have select users who use many different machines.

To facilitate the checking and tracking of licenses, you must install a licensing server in the environment within 120 days of the first client session logon to the terminal server, or that terminal server stops servicing user session requests unless the requesting client has a TS CAL that has been issued. You get a 120-day grace period to get TS Licensing configured.

If you want to use a combination of per-device and per-user CALs, choose Per User TS CAL mode, but keep tracking usage correctly in your environment. Also remember that the licensing is per named device or named user. If you have 20 shift workers all using the same Active Directory (AD) account, you need 20 per-user TS CALs, not 1. It's important not to confuse what the licensing server may see compared to your end-user-license agreement.

TS Licensing is part of the TS role, and in small environments, the TS licensing server can be installed on the same box as a terminal server. However, the best practice is to place it on a separate box. There are advantages to installing the TS Licensing server on a domain controller: Terminal servers within the forest find the licensing server automatically, without any configuration. It is not a best practice to enable TS on a domain controller, however, due to the security changes that are required for users to connect to a server. Typically, you want only domain administrators logging on to a domain controller.

Installing TS Licensing

You install TS Licensing as you install any other role component: via Server Manager Roles, clicking Add Roles. After you select Terminal Services, enable only the TS Licensing role service (unless you are installing other parts of TS at this point), as shown in Figure 9-15.

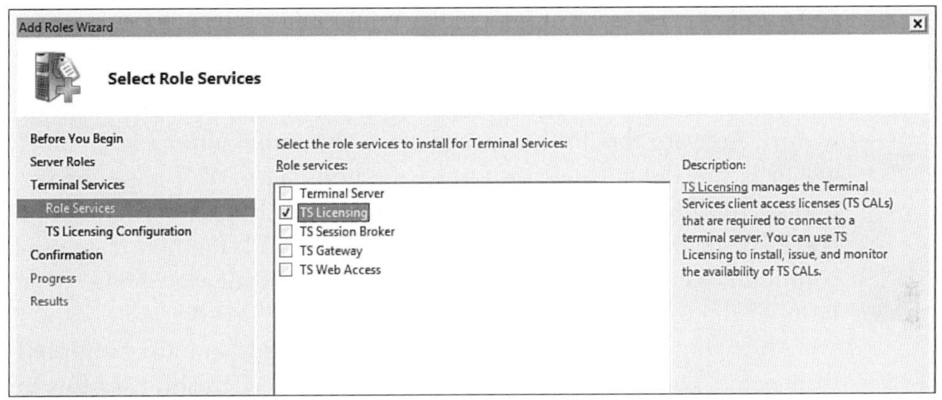

FIGURE 9-15 Installing just the TS Licensing component.

If you are installing the TS Licensing component on a computer in a domain, set the options for the discovery scope of the TS licensing server to the domain. This means any terminal server in the same domain can discover the license server. If the scope of the TS Licensing component is set to the forest, then terminal servers from any domain in the forest can discover the license server. For domain scope, you must be logged on as a domain administrator, and for forest scope, you must be logged on as an enterprise administrator. If you're installing TS Licensing on a non-domain server, the only option is for the scope to be the workgroup the TS Licensing server is in.

By default, the TS Licensing database is located in the C:\Windows\system32\LServer folder. However, you can change this on the licensing configuration screen. After the licensing configuration is performed and you click Next, a summary is displayed. Click Install to complete the installation.

Managing TS Licensing

Manage TS Licensing by using the TS Licensing Manager application. This is not an MMC snap-in but the file LicMgr.exe, which means it does not integrate with Server Manager, which is MMC based. A shortcut also exists in the Terminal Services folder, under Administrative Tools. After you install the TS Licensing server, activate it with the Microsoft licensing clearinghouse before you can start adding licenses to the server.

Activating a TS Licensing Server

To activate a TS Licensing server, right-click and select Activate to launch the Active Server Wizard. Click Next in the initial welcome page of the wizard. Activate the TS Licensing server by using automatic connection, which is the default and preferred method, via a Web page, or via the phone (see Figure 9-16). However, if connectivity prohibits the port 443 (HTTPS) connection that is required, use the Web method from another computer, using a URL that the wizard displays, or via phone, with the number the wizard displays.

After your connection to Microsoft is verified, you are prompted for your name, company name, and country/region. Microsoft uses this information for support purposes and also to verify that you are not in a region that has export restrictions. The next screen asks for optional information such as e-mail address and physical address. Leave this all blank and just click Next. After activation, a summary shows that the license server was successfully activated and also displays the option to start the Install Licenses Wizard, which is discussed in the next section.

You can now see in the TS Licensing Manager that the server is activated and the information you entered during activation is now part of the info for the server.

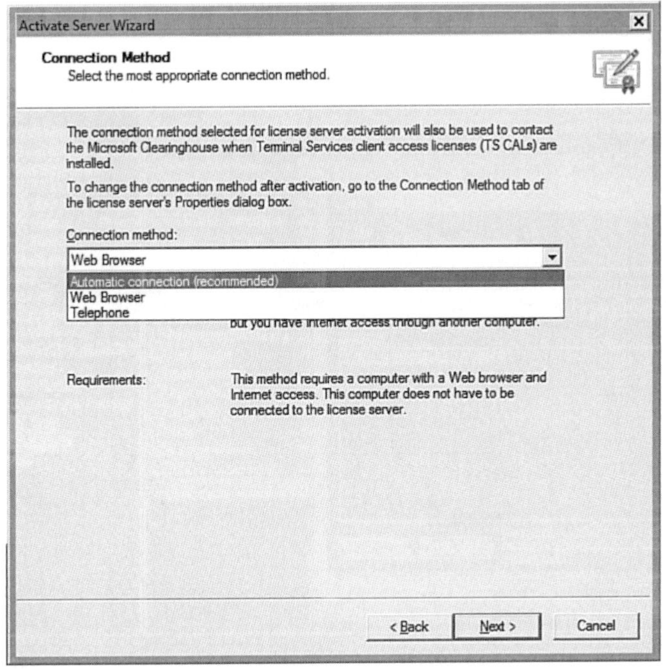

FIGURE 9-16 Selecting the connection method for activation.

Installing Licenses

A license server without licenses is not highly functional, so install TS CALs that you have purchased from Microsoft or a reseller. To add licenses, select Install Licenses from the context menu of the server, which launches the Install Licenses Wizard. As usual, the first page is the welcome page—click Next to skip over it.

The next dialog asks for the license program you are using. If you have purchased retail licenses, you select License Pack (Retail Purchase). However, many other programs are available, such as Enterprise Agreement and Select Agreement, which have different formats for entering the license information. After clicking Next, enter the code for the license, as shown in Figure 9-17. If you want to add multiple license packs, enter a code and then click Add to enter the next one. After you enter all the codes, click Next to contact Microsoft and install the licenses.

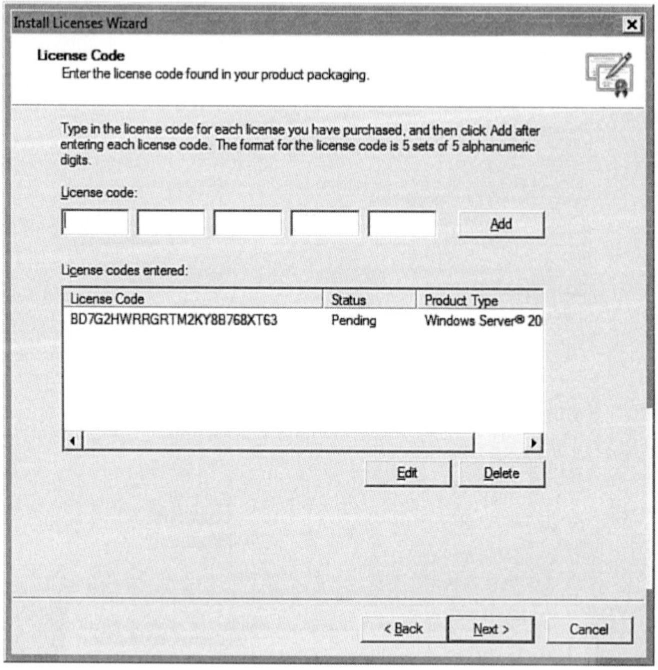

FIGURE 9-17 This is a per-client license pack.

You can install both user and device CALs on a TS Licensing server. However, it is not the TS Licensing server that gives a CAL to a user or devices; it's the terminal server. The TS Licensing just acts as a broker, storing the licenses that a terminal server can request.

Configuring the Licensing Mode

On each terminal server, configure the mode that is used, either per device or per user. You do this by using the Terminal Services Configuration MMC snap-in and double-clicking the settings of the server. By using the Licensing tab as shown in Figure 9-18, you can configure the type of licensing mode to use. In the example shown here, Per User is selected. You can select whether the licensing server is automatically discovered, or you can name a specific server or servers to use. You can change the licensing mode at any time in the terminal server's lifetime. However, if you keep changing licensing modes, you have a mix of device and user TS CALs issued, which potentially wastes your per-device TS CALs that are tracked because you are likely to end up with a device and the user on the device each with a TS CAL.

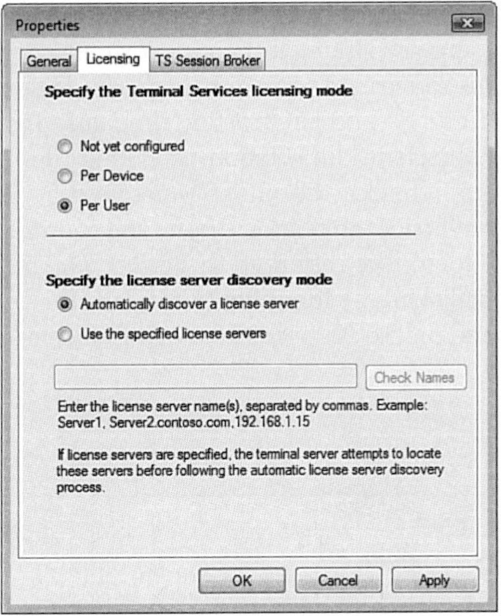

FIGURE 9-18 Selecting the licensing mode for a terminal server.

When the licensing server is selected, the terminal server starts requesting TS CALs from the licensing server and giving them to the device or user, based on the licensing mode selected.

Per-User Mode

As discussed earlier, if you select per-user mode, the licensing server does not track the number of per-user TS CALs that have been allocated. Remember that the TS CAL in per-user mode is on the named user, not the AD account used to connect, although ideally this would be a one-to-one match. It is quite possible that one user uses multiple user accounts or that multiple users use one AD account, so hard tracking of TS CALs per user is not practical. This does not mean you can't see who is using the TS CALs.

You can create a report to list all the current users of TS CALs by selecting Create Report, Per User CAL Usage from the context menu of a server from the TS Licensing Manager application, as shown in Figure 9-19. A dialog appears, asking if the report should be run for the entire local domain of the licensing server, for a specific organizational unit (OU), or for the entire forest and any trusting domains. This report scans through all the user objects in the locations specified (domain, OU, or all trusted domains) and checks the msTSManagingLS, msTSExpireDate, and msTSLicenseVersion attributes (there are four sets of these, allowing a user to have up to four different TS CALs). The msTSManagingLS values are the Globally Unique Identifier (GUID) of the licensing server instance, which is found on the properties dialog of a licensing server.

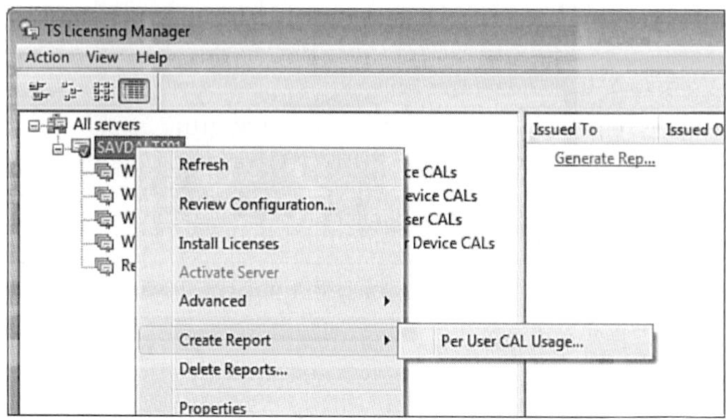

FIGURE 9-19 Creating a TS CAL report is a simple process.

After the report is generated, you can find it under the Reports node of the TS Licensing Manager application. However, you can't view it from this tab; this node simply lists the reports that are available. To see the content, right-click a report and select Save As, and the content is then saved to a comma-separated value (.csv) file. You then read the file in a text editor or another program that understands .csv files, such as Excel. The following example shows sample output from the report, including the per-user allocation. Notice that the user account using the CAL is shown, along with its expiration. A user CAL is returned to the pool after 59 days. However, as discussed earlier, this does not affect concurrent licensing. It's one TS CAL per user. You can't move them around unless you are sure a user or device is not coming back.

```
TS CAL Usage Report
TS License Server:      SAVDALTS01
TS CAL Type:       Per User
Report Date:       11/4/2007 8:14
Report Scope:      Domain
Installed TS CALs:      20
TS CALs in Use:   2
TS CAL Availability:   Available

Issued to User    TS CAL Version    Expires On
TS\john      Windows Server (R) 2008 Thursday January 03 2008
08:13:34
TS\Bruce     Windows Server 2008     Thursday January 03 2008
08:13:52
```

A Windows Management Instrumentation (WMI) class, Win32_TSLicenseReport, can be used to manage user license reports. It has three interfaces to generate, delete, and fetch the information from a report. Microsoft provides information on this WMI class at http://msdn2.microsoft.com/en-us/library/aa383515.aspx.

Per-Device Mode

With per-device mode, the allocation of TS CALs is tracked. This tracking is possible because a machine is a definable and identifiable entity: It has a unique GUID, MAC address, and so on. When a computer first connects to a terminal server, the device is given a temporary license so as to not use a full TS CAL. The second time a computer contacts a terminal server, a TS CAL is allocated to the client, and the temporary CAL is removed. Figures 9-20 and 9-21 show these two CALs.

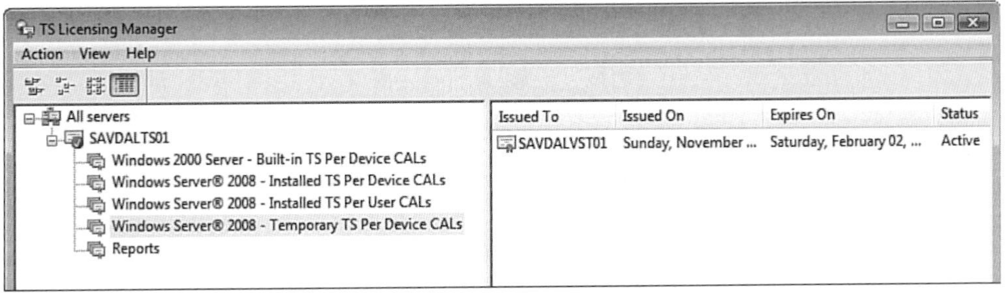

FIGURE 9-20 A temporary TS per-device CAL is initially used.

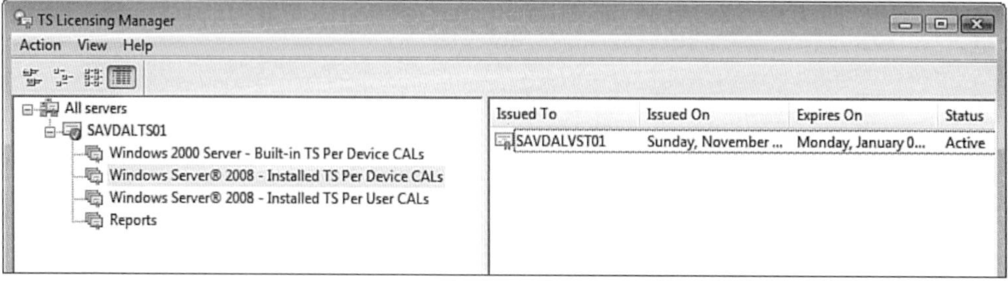

FIGURE 9-21 The temporary TS per-device CAL is missing here because a full TS CAL has been allocated, and the temporary CAL is no longer required.

If you need to revoke a CAL for a device, right-click its entry and select Revoke TS CAL.

There is no report for per-device TS CAL usage. However, the TS team posted the following script on its blog, and you can use it to determine usage.

```
'--------------------------------------------------------------
' Script to generate TS Per-Device license usage report.
' Requires Administrator privilege on the license server.
' Works only with WS08 TS License Server, as there is no WMI
' interface for TS Licensing on earlier versions.
'--------------------------------------------------------------
-
SET Args = WScript.Arguments
NameSpace = "root\cimv2"
ClassName = "Win32_TSIssuedLicense"
IF Args.Length > 2 THEN
Help
WSCRIPT.QUIT(1)
END IF
IF Args.Length = 1 THEN
Help
WSCRIPT.QUIT(1)
END IF
IF Args.Length = 2 THEN
' Checking if Server Name has been provided
CompResult = strComp(Args(0), "-server",1)
IF CompResult = 0 THEN
```

```
ServerName = Args(1)
ELSE
Help
WSCRIPT.QUIT(1)
END IF
ELSE
' if argc.length = 0, no arg supplied
ServerName = "."
END IF
GeneratePerDeviceReport
WSCRIPT.QUIT
'--------------------------------------------------------------
-
' FUNCTIONS
'--------------------------------------------------------------
SUB Help()
WSCRIPT.ECHO "Usage: GeneratePerDeviceReport.vbs
[-Server ServerName]"
WSCRIPT.ECHO " If no ServerName is provided, then report
generation"
WSCRIPT.ECHO " is attempted at host machine"
END SUB
SUB GeneratePerDeviceReport()
Err.Clear
Set ObjWMIService = GetObject("winmgmts:\\" & ServerName
& "\" & NameSpace )
IF ERR.NUMBER <> 0 THEN
WSCRIPT.ECHO "Unable to connect to the Namespace"
WSCRIPT.QUIT(2)
END IF
Set ObjectSet = ObjWMIService.ExecQuery ("Select * from
Win32_TSIssuedLicense")
ReportCountBefore = ObjectSet.Count
' No Reports are present
IF ObjectSet.Count = 0 THEN
WSCRIPT.ECHO "No Per Device license issued"
WScript.Quit(5)
END IF
WSCRIPT.ECHO "KeyPackID,LicenseID,IssuedToMachine,HWID,
ExpiryDate"
FOR EACH ObjectClass IN ObjectSet
```

```
WSCRIPT.ECHO ObjectClass.KeyPackId & "," & ObjectClass.
LicenseId
& "," & ObjectClass.sIssuedToComputer & "," &
ObjectClass.sHardwareId & "," & ObjectClass.ExpirationDate
NEXT
END SUB
```

The following example shows the script running:

```
C:\temp>cscript listdevicerep.vbs
Microsoft (R) Windows Script Host Version 5.7
Copyright (C) Microsoft Corporation. All rights reserved.

KeyPackID,LicenseID,IssuedToMachine,HWID,ExpiryDate
3,6,SAVDALVST01,00027dc5dac165cbe6db6478747d6c05d080,
20080107134329.000000-000
```

Changing the Discovery Mode of the Licensing Server

The discovery mode of the licensing server is selected when you install the TS Licensing role, but you can change it by right-clicking the server in the TS Licensing Manager application and selecting Review Configuration. A screen opens, showing information about the TS licensing server; it also includes a Change Scope button you can click to switch the scope between domain and forest. Remember that a TS licensing server in a workgroup can have only workgroup scope, so there is no option to modify its scope. If a TS licensing server is joined to a domain, its scope is automatically changed from workgroup to domain.

If a TS licensing server has forest scope, its record is written into the configuration partition of the forest (see Figure 9-22) as a TS-Enterprise-License-Server object for the site of the TS licensing server. Other terminal servers can find the licensing server by querying the global catalog for the TS-Enterprise-License-Server named object.

NOTE If you have Windows 2000/Windows Server 2003 terminal servers, there is a known issue where the search of the global catalog searches for the wrong name. Microsoft provides a solution in KB895151.

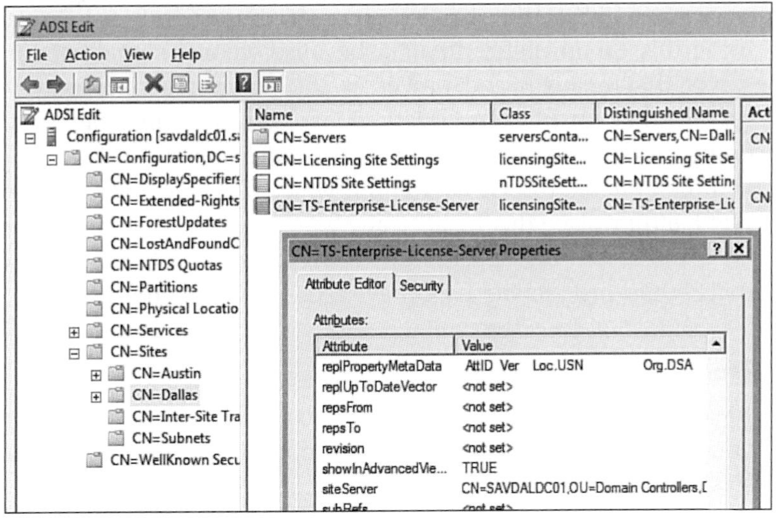

FIGURE 9-22 The attributes of the object identify the name of the server in the siteServer attribute.

If a TS licensing server has domain scope, it is not published in AD and will be found automatically by terminal servers in the domain only if the TS licensing server is installed on a domain controller. The other way a terminal server finds a licensing server is if it's installed locally on the terminal server.

You can use the Terminal Services Configuration MMC snap-in to specify a specific license server (refer to Figure 9-18). You can use Group Policy for the configuration of licensing, along with all the other configuration items, by enabling Use the Specified Terminal Services License Servers under the Computer Configuration, Administrative Templates, Windows Components, Terminal Services, Terminal Server, Licensing. When this is enabled, just enter the names of the licensing servers to use. In this same area you can set the licensing mode for any terminal server that has the Group Policy Object (GPO) applied as well.

By default, a TS licensing server responds to any terminal server in the environment. However, you can configure TS licensing servers to respond only to specific terminal servers by enabling the Computer Configuration, Administrative Templates, Windows Components, Terminal Services, TS Licensing, License Server Security group policy and then populating the local group Terminal Server Computers with the terminal servers in the environment that the TS licensing server responds to. Be careful with using this group policy, though, because when it's enabled, any terminal server that receives and processes the policy responds only to terminal servers that have been added to its local Terminal Server Computers group. So test populate the local Terminal Server Computers group first and then enable the GPO. To limit which TS licensing servers receive the GPO, either place the TS licensing computer object in an OU and link the GPO to the OU or use a security ACL on the GPO so only the computers that should process the GPO have read and apply permissions.

Troubleshooting Licensing

Ideally your terminal server automatically locates the licensing servers. If not, you can use group policy or manual configuration so that terminal servers can obtain TS CALs and give them to the clients.

To help troubleshoot TS configuration, the Terminal Services Configuration MMC snap-in has a Licensing Diagnosis node that lists any problems it finds in its licensing configuration as well as possible resolutions. Even when there are no problems, the Licensing Diagnostics node is useful. You can see which TS Licensing Server you are using and how it was found in addition to the credentials it has available (see Figure 9-23).

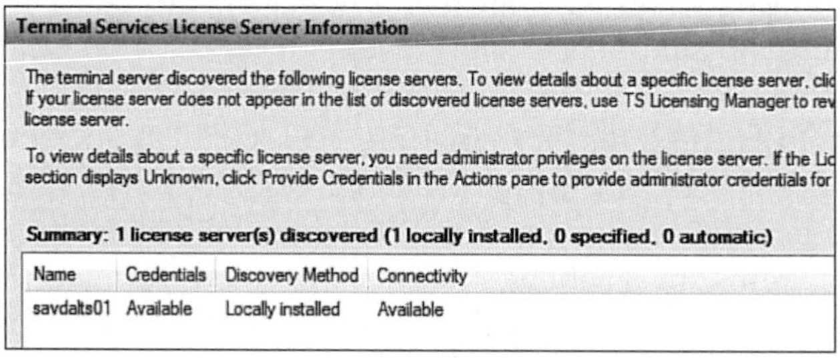

FIGURE 9-23 In this example, TS licensing is installed on this terminal server, making location easy.

Common issues that the Licensing Diagnosis node identifies include the following:

- Any configuration problems on the terminal server side, such as the 120-day grace mode ending.

- A list of license servers that the terminal server contacts for licenses. This list includes both auto-discovered license servers and manually configured license servers.
- A list of configuration problems with the license servers known to the terminal server in addition to the type and number of TS CALs available.

Always make sure you have the correct TS CALs for the type of clients. If you have Windows Server 2003 TS CALs, they will not work for clients connecting to Windows Server 2008 terminal servers. In addition, a Windows Server 2008 terminal server cannot talk to a Windows Server 2003 licensing server, only a Windows Server 2008 TS licensing server, although a Windows Server 2003 terminal server can talk to a Windows Server 2008 TS licensing server. If you have Windows Server 2003 TS CALs, you need to buy new Windows Server 2008 TS CALs unless you are lucky enough to have software assurance.

Backing Up Licensing Information and Ensuring High Availability

Your licensing information is important, and so when you are considering your availability and recovery plan, ensure that you are backing up the correct information. At a minimum, back up the following items:

- The system state of the TS licensing server via Windows Backup
- The TS licensing folder, which by default is C:\Windows\System32\lserver

If you perform a restore to a rebuilt server, the unissued servers are not available. However, you can reactivate them by contacting the clearinghouse via telephone.

For high availability of TS licensing, the best option is to install at least two TS Licensing instances with Enterprise scope, which tells the licensing servers to advertise themselves in AD. The TS CALs you have in your environment should be spread out over the available TS licensing servers that are installed in the environment.

As with a DHCP lease, a client tries to renew its license seven days before its expiration, so if a TS licensing server is unavailable, there would only be an impact on clients connecting for the first time. If the TS licensing server is unavailable for more than seven days, existing clients who were on the verge of the expiration would be denied connections.

Installing Terminal Services

If you want to use a server for more than two administrators, enable the Terminal Server role, which you enable via the Add Roles Wizard. If you have already configured terminal service licensing, as discussed earlier, install the Terminal Server role service.

There is not a large amount of configuration to perform during the installation of the TS component. You are notified that any existing applications installed on the terminal server may need to be reinstalled and asked if you want to require NLA for clients connecting, as shown in Figure 9-24. You can change this at a later time, and if you are unsure of all the clients that connect to your terminal server, select the Do Not Require Network Level Authentication option.

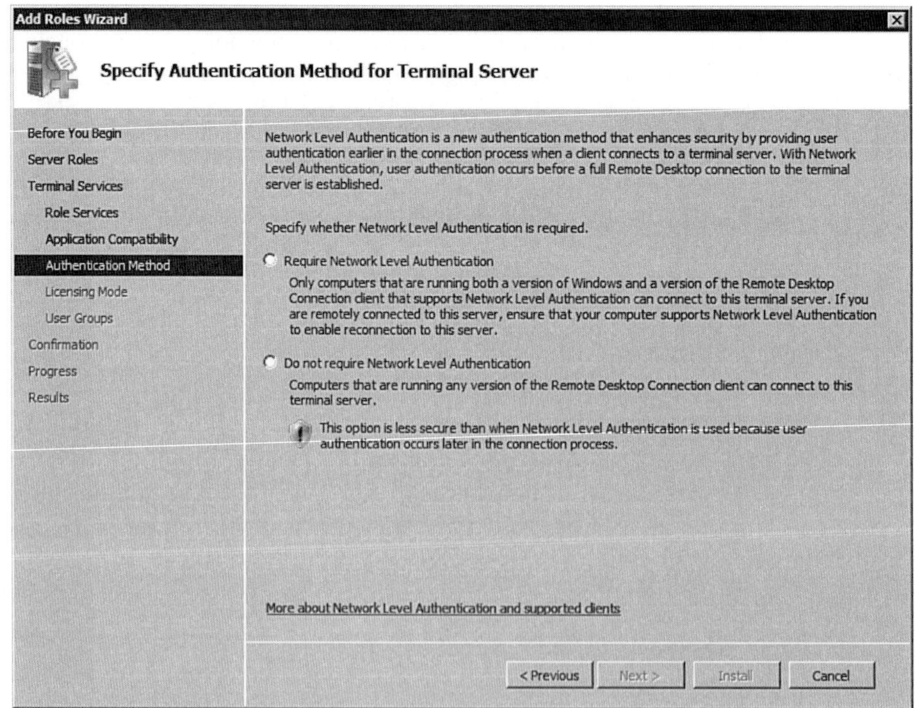

FIGURE 9-24 Configuring the initial Network Level Authentication requirements.

Next, select the licensing method to be used by the terminal server, which is based on the client access license types purchased, or select to configure the TS CAL type later. Finally, you are prompted to select the users and groups that are allowed to create remote sessions to the terminal server, which by default is just the Administrators group.

When the installation is complete, you now have a fully functional terminal server, which supports all the Windows Server 2008 advanced capabilities related to remote sessions. This leads us nicely into the first of these cool new features: TS Easy Print.

TS Easy Print

For you and your users' day-to-day existence, printers are mapped on the desktops to facilitate printing data to paper. When you connect to a TS session, you are running a totally different session on another server, and your printers don't exist there. Solutions in the past tried to remap the locally mapped printers in your terminal server sessions. However, this type of solution has been hit-and-miss and has required printer drivers to be installed locally on the terminal server boxes. Even then, there is no guarantee that printers that exist locally on the client computer are seen in terminal server sessions from the client. One of the biggest problems has been when a printer driver does not even exist for the Windows Server 2003 platform because the printer is considered "desktop class."

The TS Easy Print Driver

TS Easy Print is a new universal V4 printer driver solution in Windows Server 2008 that aims to provide a consistent printing experience between your desktop remote sessions. This new printer driver means the Windows Server 2008 terminal server no longer requires any printer driver installation or even configuration to enable client printers to map to their terminal sessions. The default behavior when connecting from the Vista Service Pack 1 and above RDC client that supports RDP 6.1 is to map locally known printers (which can be locally connected via USB/LPT or over the network) via the new TS Easy Print driver. This means any printer, old or new, is shown in the TS sessions, local and remote. For Windows XP, install Service Pack 3 (although a stand-alone RDP 6.1 client for Windows XP Service Pack 2 may be made available) for TS Easy Print functionality. This new process means both 32- and 64-bit drivers are fully supported because nothing is installed on the actual terminal server.

TS Easy Print maps all the printer properties of the local printer to the terminal server session. It accomplishes this by redirecting all user interface calls to display the printer properties to the local client machine instead of trying to emulate the properties on the actual terminal server. Previously, it was common that default settings—for example, paper orientation, print quality, landscape and draft mode—were configured on the local desktop. But when the printer was mapped in a TS session, the remote terminal server installed printer drivers, which would revert to the defaults for the terminal server printer driver. This situation was even worse with Windows Server 2003 Service Pack 1 and above servers, which had limited-functionality fallback printer drivers. These were lowest-common-denominator drivers with only the most basic of configuration. They were there to just "print the thing" and had none of the bells and whistles that were present in the full driver. With TS Easy Print, this is not the case. Any configurations and defaults performed locally are passed through to the terminal server version of the printer. Every property and configuration from the locally installed printer driver is available in the TS session.

There are requirements for TS Easy Print to function. First, the server you are connecting to must be running the TS role; TS Easy Print is not available for servers in Remote Desktop mode. The client has to be running a client that supports RDP 6.1. You can verify this by viewing the About box of the client (refer to Figure 9-4). Inventory solutions such as SCCM could also collect this type of information.

For printers to be mapped from the client to the TS session, select the appropriate setting on the RDP client in the Local Resources tab of the Options dialog. Ensure that in the Local Devices and Resources section, Printers is checked to be used in the remote sessions.

If you are running RDC 6.1 or above and connecting to a Windows Server 2008 server running the Terminal Server role, your printers are available in your remote session. Figure 9-25 shows two Printer Control Panel applets. The lower one is the native Windows Vista printers content and shows two custom printers, both Hewlett-Packard printers using non-out-of-the-box drivers. The upper Printer Control Panel applet is the view from my terminal server session. Notice that the printers from my local machine have "(redirected 2)" next to the name. This indicates that they are redirected from a client computer, and 2 is the session number. Under Windows Server 2003, the client computer name was also shown, and this was necessary because, if the same username was used from multiple computers, all sessions as the same user would see the sum of all the printers, so the client computer name was added to the printer to make it easier to tell which printer was "yours." Now that the printers are per session, this is not necessary. Note that if you are not using an RDP 6.1 client, the Windows Server 2003 behavior occurs, and printers show only if the driver is installed on the terminal server for the printer.

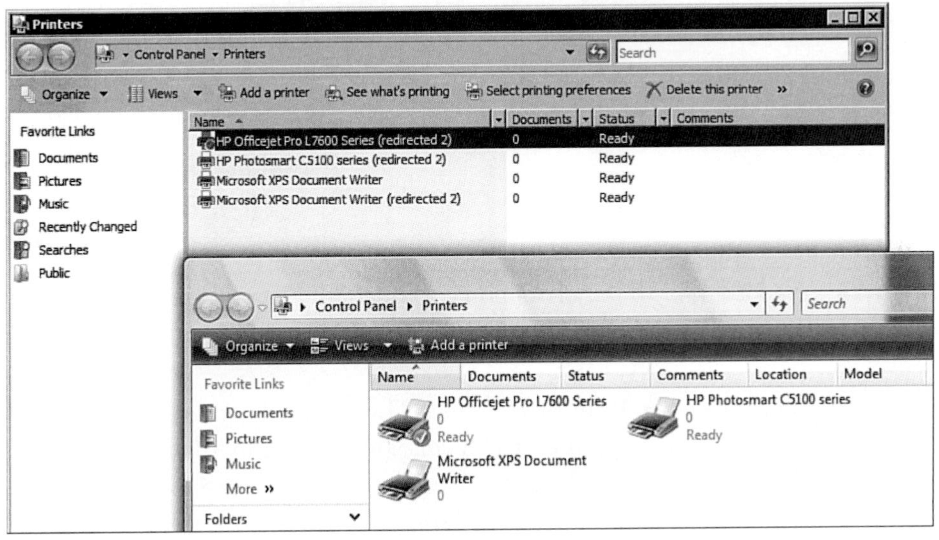

FIGURE 9-25 The local printers are available in the remote session.

When you look at one of these printers, it looks just like a normal one. Even if the driver for the printer is installed on the terminal server, TS Easy Print is still used because it gives a better client experience, thanks to the configuration and so on being carried through into the terminal server session. You can see this in a number of different ways. The left side of Figure 9-26 shows a printer as it is seen in the TS session, and the right side shows the same properties as shown from the local machine. The major difference is the model; notice that the redirected version of the printer in the terminal server session has the model as Terminal Services Easy Print, which shows that the printer is being redirected via TS Easy Print.

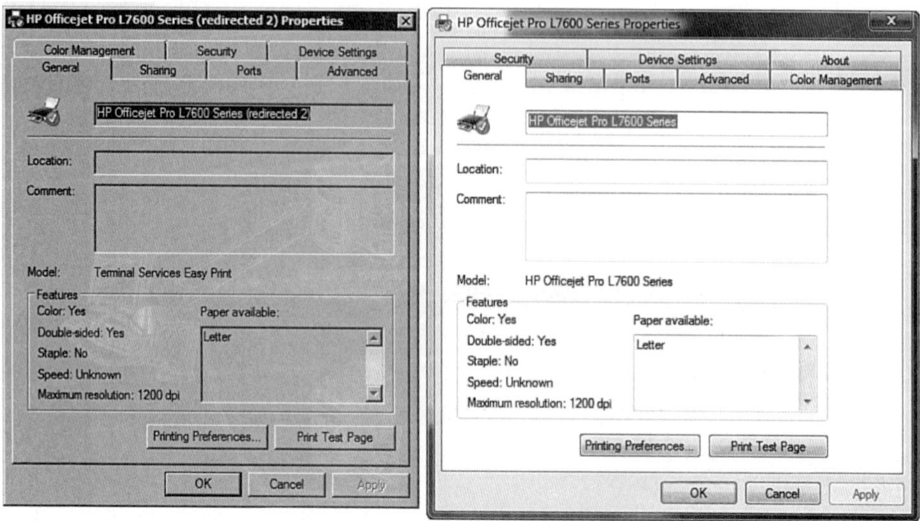

FIGURE 9-26 The local and TS Easy Print printer properties: Notice the model on the TS session is just TS Easy Print.

The TS Easy Print driver is used by default even when a local printer driver exists on the server. However, you can modify this behavior through group policy by disabling the Use Terminal Services Easy Print Printer Driver First policy under Computer Configuration, Administrative Templates, Windows Components, Terminal Services, Terminal Server, Printer Redirection.

Everything else about the printer looks similar; it provides the printing preferences and the capability to print a test page (which on the terminal server session also shows TS Easy Print as the driver). This is key, again, to reinforcing the TS Easy Print message: It is a universal print driver solution, and the terminal server knows nothing about the actual physical printer, and it shows the default printer properties that are available to all printers. But something does not sound right. Remember that the big deal with TS Easy Print was that it's a fully functional solution; if it knows nothing about the printer, then the configuration you can perform through the properties of the printer are only the generic properties, available to all printers, right? No. This is a TS session, so a little reverse magic happens. When you select a button or property that would be specific to the actual printer driver, the session uses RDP to open the driver-specific dialog on your local computer instead of on the RDP session, which is then using the full local driver capabilities (see Figure 9-27). Figure 9-27 shows that Printing Preferences was selected on the General tab; but in the session, a dialog opened saying that it was actually opened to the client; then the actual properties are seen on the client. Notice also that the properties of the printer are using the graphical theme of the local client (Aero) instead of the Windows Standard theme of the RDP session. This is because of the redirection.

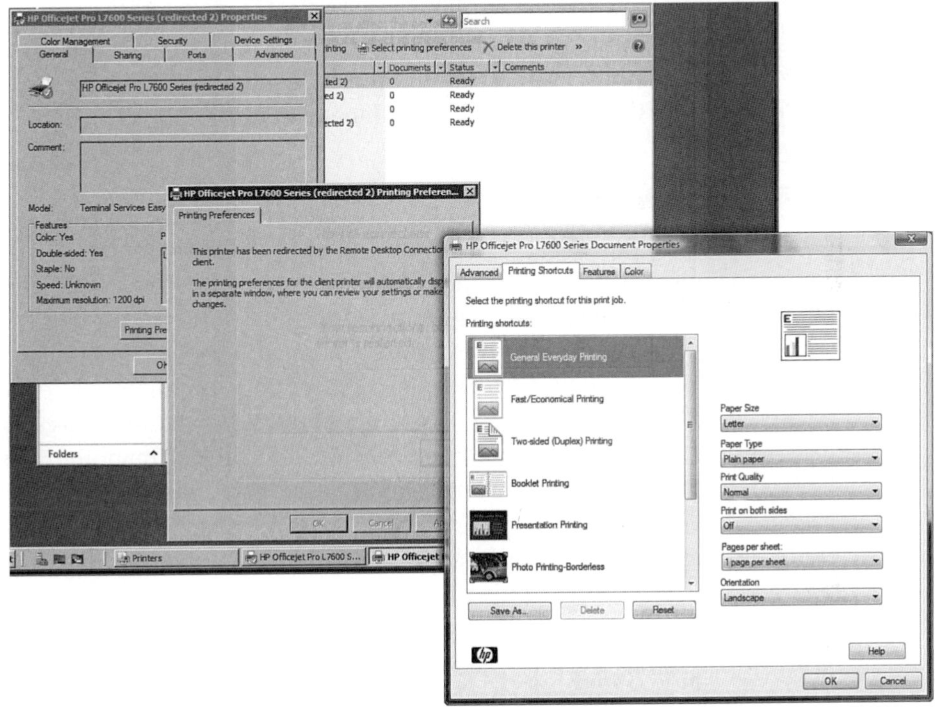

FIGURE 9-27 You can tell by the Hewlett-Packard logo that this is the full local driver.

Anything changed is used by the TS version of the printer because it's just using the configuration of the local printer. This works in your favor in a number of ways. If you change your page orientation to landscape locally on your client, then the printing on your RDP sessions is also landscape. There is only one configuration, so there is no duplication of effort. The Printer Preferences button is not the only place that properties are redirected to the local RDP client. Some drivers add extra tabs, such as an

About tab or a Complex Device Settings tab. Access these tabs by selecting the Device Settings tab on the RDP session, which then opens a redirected dialog on the RDP client, with all the additional driver configuration and information.

The actual mechanics of TS Easy Print are facilitated by the new XPS document type that is native to Vista and Windows Server 2008. When you print a document, the TS Easy Print driver creates an XPS document, which is then sent via RDP to your local print processor for processing as if it were generated locally on the client and printed. Anything printed is just sent to an XPS file and then everything to physically print is performed on your local computer. (You can find more details about the XPS process in Chapter 5, "File System and Print Management Features.")

Printer Mapping

Another major change in the Windows Server 2008 architecture is that printer mapping is now performed at the session level. Previously, if multiple client computers connected to a terminal server with the same account, each session saw all the printers mapped from any computer that is using the same account. (Sadly, anyone running administrator sessions could see *all* the printers from any session on the terminal server, as shown in Figure 9-28.) With Windows Server 2008, the printer mapping is performed at the session level, so if multiple sessions use the same user account, the printers seen are only those that are mapped from the session's desktop computer. The scoping of printers is now consistent with how all other resource mapping is performed, which is per session.

In Figure 9-28, user John would see only 1 printer in each session, the printer local to his machine, and the administrator would see no printers. This does not just solve the usability issue of users having trouble finding the printer they want among all the printers displayed from other sessions. This session-level scoping of printers addresses a scalability and performance problem that administrators experienced when they could see printers for all sessions. Imagine having 50 users on a terminal server, each with 2 printers mapped; that would be 100 printers that administrator sessions would have to enumerate through the print spooler, which takes a significant amount of time.

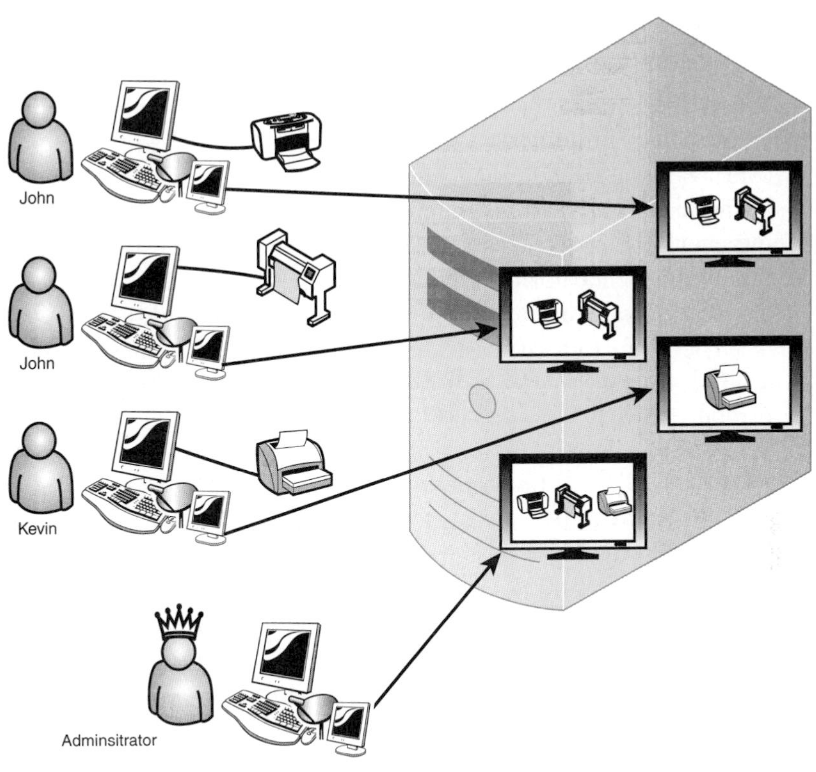

Figure 9-28 Under the previous architecture, the two sessions for user John saw the printers from both desktop computers, while the poor administrator session saw all the mapped printers for any session on the server.

One nice touch with Windows Server 2008 is that previously all printers were redirected from the clients' computers to their TS sessions. However, a group policy in Windows Server 2008 allows only the user's default printer to be mapped in her TS session, giving a much more usable terminal session environment, with only the printer the user needs made available. You can enable the Redirect Only the Default Client Printer policy under Computer Configuration, Administrative Templates, Windows Components, Terminal Services, Terminal Server, Printer Redirection. After this is enabled and group policy is refreshed, only the user's default printer is redirected, which in most cases is the only one she needs.

TS Gateway

When you connect to a terminal server for a full session or a remote program, you communicate over TCP port 3389, and sound tries to stream over a separate UDP connection. But if such a connection is unavailable, sound also uses a virtual channel in RDP, which means also communicating over port 3389. This is only one port to open in your firewall, but in reality this is not normally allowed; to use Remote Desktop for a computer, you normally use a VPN to your network first and then use RDP.

There are some workarounds to this port problem. Some people work around firewalls at clients that normally only allow outbound traffic through ports 80 and 443 (HTTP and HTTPS traffic). They reconfigure a machine on their network to RDP over port 443 instead, modifying the RDP listening port by changing the value of HKEY_LOCAL_MACHINE\SYSTEM\CurrentControlSet\Control\Terminal Server\WinStations\RDP-Tcp\PortNumber to the new port number. When they connect to a machine that is running on a nonstandard RDP port, they add the port number to the end of the server name/IP address (for example, savdalts01.savilltech.net:443). This is not a good solution because it means just running RDP over the Internet, which, while it has some encryption, is not great.

TS Gateway introduces a capability that users of Outlook 2003 with Exchange 2003 will be familiar with: communication over the Internet by encapsulating the RPC calls used between Outlook and Exchange in HTTPS traffic, allowing all communication to take place over port 443. TS Gateway acts as a gateway point for RDP traffic to be encapsulated in HTTPS. You configure the RDP client with TS Gateway from your various connections, and through a single TS Gateway server, you can then communicate with the various terminal servers that the TS Gateway server can communicate with. TS Gateway is responsible for extracting the RDP data from the HTTPS encapsulation and passing it to the terminal servers and then encapsulating the responses from the terminal servers in HTTPS and sending them back to the RDP clients.

You have granular control and can configure TS Gateway to only allow communication to specific terminal servers on the internal network, such as allowing only connections from specific users, groups, or computers; setting what authentication method is required (password or smart card); and setting what device redirection is allowed.

In addition, you can leverage other technologies, such as ISA Server, to sit on the perimeter network to receive and authenticate the incoming

HTTPS connections before TS Gateway is ever contacted; this means no terminal server component has to exist in the perimeter/DMZ network. ISA is just an example, and any SSL terminator implementation should suffice. If you don't use ISA, normally the TS Gateway server would sit in the perimeter network, as Internet-facing servers are not normally placed on the internal network due to the security risk that poses.

You can leverage Network Access Protection (NAP) to perform health checks on the client requesting the connection, and if the client does not meet the health requirements, the connection is refused. You cannot bring a client up to health requirements with TS Gateway. You can only accept or refuse based on the statement of health. But this is useful to help protect your infrastructure from clients that would expose you to malware or other problems.

Figure 9-29 shows two deployment options for TS Gateway. The top flow shows the TS Gateway in the DMZ, which has RDP over SSL sent to the TS Gateway, which then strips out the RDP and sends the traffic to the Internet network. The firewall in the DMZ needs the RDP port (3389) open and needs the ports required for the TS Gateway to talk to the domain controller. The TS Gateway server is a member of the domain and performs checks based on the requesting user and computer. So domain controller communication is necessary. The communication between the TS Gateway server and the domain controller can be locked to specific source and target machines to limit the exposure created by opening the communication.

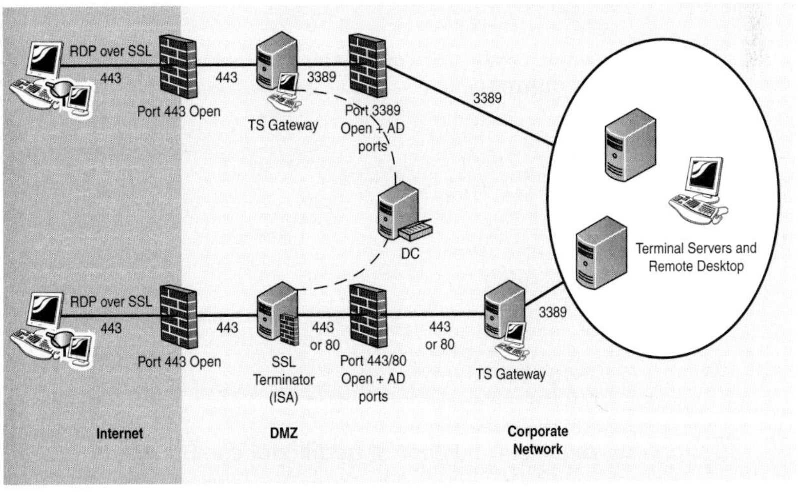

FIGURE 9-29 In these two placement scenarios for TS Gateway, the top one does not have an SSL terminator, and the bottom one does.

The bottom flow in the figure uses an ISA server in the DMZ, which acts as the SSL terminator and then forwards the traffic to the TS Gateway server. However, it can send with the SSL removed, which reduces the workload on the TS Gateway server so its RDP is encapsulated in unencrypted HTTP. Then the TS Gateway server strips out the RDP inside the network and forwards things on to the terminal servers and Remote Desktop–enabled machines inside the network. If you choose to use HTTPS–HTTP bridging with an SSL terminator, check the Use HTTPS–HTTP bridging option on the SSL Bridging tab of the TS Gateway Server dialog.

Installing TS Gateway

The TS Gateway functionality is a role service of the TS role. To install it, select the TS role and then add the TS Gateway role service via the Server Manager.

TS Gateway has a number of requirements because of its HTTP encapsulation capabilities, which utilize the RPC over HTTP Proxy feature, which in turn needs the Web Server role service, which in turn needs the Windows Process Activation Service. The Network Policy Server is also required for the connection request authentication and authorization. You get quite a number of components added when you install TS Gateway, as shown in Figure 9-30. These are all mandatory, and you have to click the Add Required Role Services button to continue the installation.

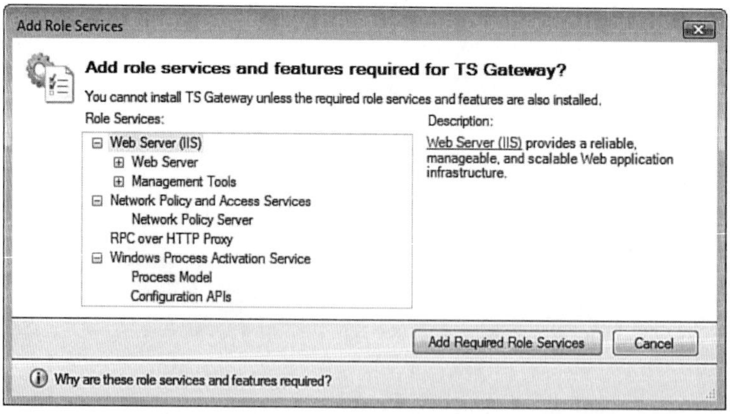

FIGURE 9-30 TS Gateway requires a number of additional components.

The first step in configuration is to select the certificate that is used for the SSL encryption. Ideally, this certificate is issued by a trusted certificate authority (CA) such as VeriSign or RapidSSL. The certificate used must be trusted by the client. You do not get the option in the RDP client to accept a certificate you don't trust, so you need either a certificate issued by an industry-trusted public CA or a certificate issued by an enterprise CA that your computer trusts (for example, a company-hosted enterprise CA that is trusted by all clients of the domain), or you need to manually import the certificate onto all clients.

It's vital that the certificate name (CN) match the full DNS name the client uses to communicate with TS Gateway (for example, ts.savilltech.net), and it must be a computer certificate for SSL-specific use. A wildcard certificate is now fully supported by the TS Gateway role, as well as all the TS roles. This is a great new addition to Windows Server 2008.

TS Gateway can create a self-signed certificate, which is useful for testing, but you have to import it to any client computers that are involved in the testing. For now, you can use a self-signed certificate, as shown in Figure 9-31. However, later you can change it to a trusted public CA certificate.

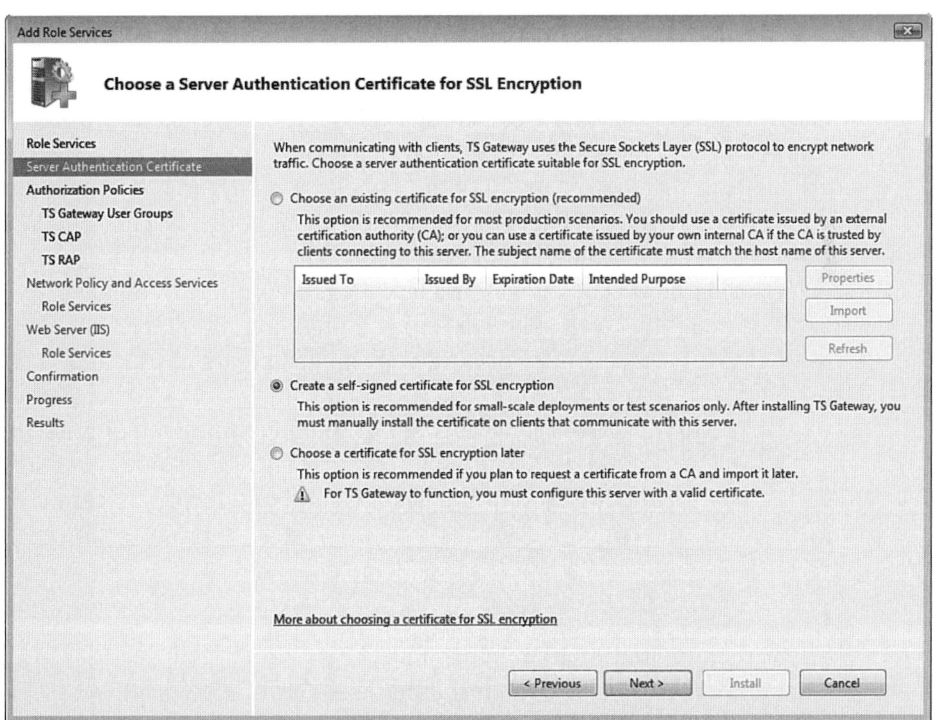

FIGURE 9-31 Manually importing a self-signed certificate onto all clients who use the gateway requires some effort.

The next phase of the installation gives the option to configure authorization policies for TS Gateway. This consists of a TS Connection Authorization Policy (CAP) that says which users, and, optionally, which computers can connect to the TS Gateway server and a TS Resource Authorization Policy (RAP), which controls which server's identified user groups can connect to via the gateway. You can elect to create these later so you can see how to manage them via the TS Gateway interface.

You can leave the rest of the pages of the installation wizard at their defaults. Just click Next all the way through the installation wizard until you get to the installation stage. Review the summary. If you opted to create the TS CAP and RAP later, you should see a warning that no one is able to access it. That's fine. Click Install.

Creating Authorization Policies

Before users and computers can connect, define the connection and resource authorization policies via the TS Gateway Manager MMC snap-in.

Create the Connection Authorization Policy (CAP) and Resource Authorization Policy (RAP) at the same time via the wizard to select which user groups and, optionally, computer groups can connect via TS Gateway Manager and to where.

Expand the TS Gateway server in the navigation node of the TS Gateway Manager MMC snap-in, select Policies, and click the Create New Authorization Policies link in the Actions pane (or you can select the same option from the context menu of the Policies item in the Navigation pane). You can create the CAP and RAP individually in both a wizard and custom format by selecting the CAP or RAP node. The wizard is similar to the one you're using here. The custom mode opens the properties dialog of a CAP or RAP, enabling you to directly enter the configuration items. You'll see these dialogs in a second. For now, you can just create a CAP and RAP via the wizard.

On the first page of the wizard, select the recommended option Create a TS CAP and a TS RAP and click Next. The wizard now runs in two stages, one for the creation of the TS CAP and one for the creation of the TS RAP.

TS CAP

The first configuration item in the TS CAP portion of the wizard is to enter a name for the TS CAP, which should be something descriptive that helps identify the TS CAP.

On the next page, specify the details of the CAP. The default authentication method is Password, but you can instead enable Smartcard.

Use groups to control who can access the TS Gateway; in the User Group Membership area, add all the groups that contain the users who are allowed to connect via TS Gateway. You can add multiple groups from multiple domains by repeating the Add Group process via the Add Group button. As shown in Figure 9-32, you can add additional constraints related to the fact that the client computer on which the RDP client is running must also be a member of a group. However, this is optional, and if you have users connecting from non-domain-joined machines, do not enable this option. In this example, it is enabled so only specific machines can use the TS Gateway as an additional security measure. When you create the group that contains the computers, select the Computer object type when adding members to the group, or you won't be able to browse the computer objects.

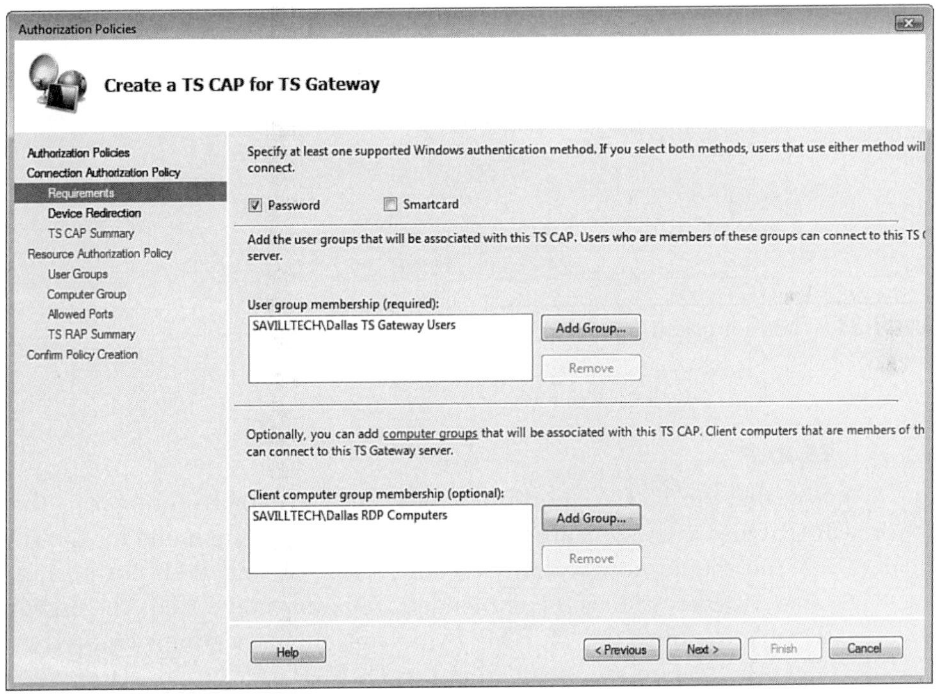

FIGURE 9-32 In this example, a user must be a member of the Dallas TS Gateway Users group, and the computer account on which the RDP client is running must be a member of the Dallas RDP Computers group.

In the next screen in the TS CAP wizard, configure the level of device redirection that is supported. By default, all device redirection is allowed, and which specific devices are redirected is dictated by the options specified in the RDP client. Another option is to disable all redirection, or you can elect to disable specific types of redirection. In Figure 9-33, all types of redirection are allowed except for serial ports and supported Plug and Play devices. A summary of the TS CAP is then displayed, and you can click Next to move on to creating the RAP.

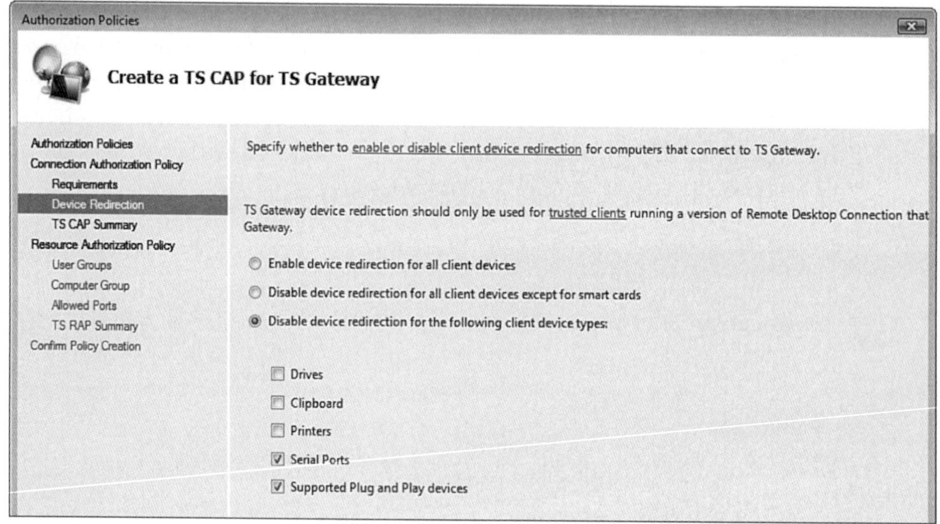

FIGURE 9-33 The redirection option screen for a TS CAP.

TS RAP

Now that the TS CAP portion is complete, move on to configuring the TS RAP. Once again, you are prompted for a meaningful name for the RAP.

You should now see why creating the CAP and RAP portions in the same wizard session is recommended. You must now specify the users who are able to utilize the TS RAP. By default, the user groups entered in the TS CAP creation are included in the TS RAP user groups. However, you can modify this by adding or removing additional groups. When the user groups are specified, click Next.

Now configure the computers that the clients can connect to; these are the target terminal servers and/or remote desktops. This group is not the same group you used when creating the TS CAP, which dictated which computer accounts the client could connect from. You have three options here for what you can connect to:

- You can select an AD security group, which contains the computer objects that users can connect to.
- Another option is members of an existing TS Gateway–managed computer group or create a new one, which you have to use if you are connecting to members of a terminal server farm (which you are getting to in this case). If you use a TS Gateway–managed computer group, ensure that you enter all the names that a user may use to specify a terminal server or remote desktop. For example, a user may use the NetBIOS name or the full DNS name, in which case you need both. The reason for this group type is that when you use a farm of terminal servers, the farm has a name that would not exist as a computer object. So if you used an AD group, the server farm would not be found, and therefore access would be denied. The TS Gateway–managed computer group checks the name specified against a list of names. Hence you can add names for a farm and allow access.
- Finally, you can choose to allow access to any resource on the network so there is no restriction. If you have a highly changeable set of computers, you may use this option. However, if you have a stricter set of servers, use the AD or TS Gateway–managed computer group option.

You use a TS Gateway–managed computer group, so click Next to create the TS Gateway–managed computer group.

As shown in Figure 9-34, no TS Gateway–managed computer groups exist, so you have to create a new one. Then you add numerous names for the computers that can be connected to. Figure 9-34 shows both NetBIOS and fully qualified domain name (FQDN) entered for the savdalsrv01 server, so either name can be used.

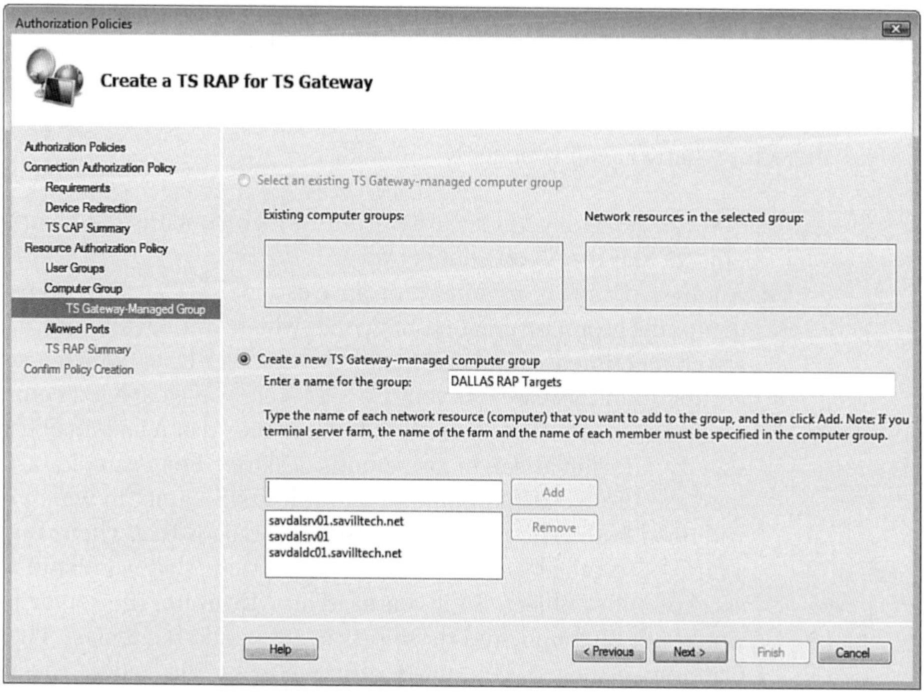

FIGURE 9-34 In this example, you can use either the FQDN or the NetBIOS name for savdalsrv01 but only the FQDN for savdaldc01.savilltech.net.

On the final configuration screen, set the ports that can be used. By default, your terminal servers and remote desktops listen on port 3389, and so the default configuration of allowing connections only through port 3389 works. However, you can select additional ports for RDP connections or allow connection through any port, as shown in Figure 9-35. Again, this is a security consideration; allowing connections over other ports may expose the server to attack, so ideally you should limit the connections to a locked-down port or set of ports.

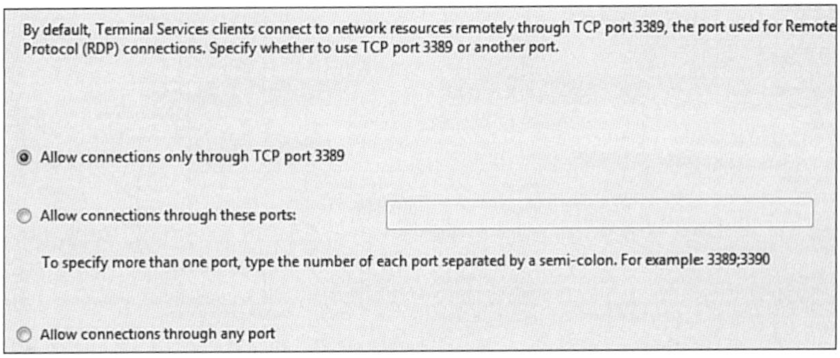

By default, Terminal Services clients connect to network resources remotely through TCP port 3389, the port used for Remote Protocol (RDP) connections. Specify whether to use TCP port 3389 or another port.

- Allow connections only through TCP port 3389
- Allow connections through these ports:

To specify more than one port, type the number of each port separated by a semi-colon. For example: 3389;3390

- Allow connections through any port

FIGURE 9-35 The default port 3389 is the best option for a secure environment.

Finishing Up

After you finish configuring the ports, a summary of the TS RAP configuration is displayed. Click Finish to complete the TS RAP creation, and click Close when the TS CAP and TS RAP are created.

If you now navigate the CAP and RAP child nodes of the Policies node in the Navigation pane, you can see the new policies. Modify a policy's properties by right-clicking and selecting Properties. Notice that all the options available are the same as those configured through the wizard.

Remember that you could run either part of this wizard independently. Anytime you need to add a new set of clients or computers or need access to resources, you can run the wizard to create a new TS CAP or TS RAP.

If you want to change what computers can be accessed and you specified an AD or a local group, you don't need to make any change to the TS RAP. Just edit the group with the required computers. If you used a TS Gateway–managed computer group, edit the group membership. You don't need a new TS RAP. To modify the content of a TS Gateway–managed computer group, select Resource Authorization Policies in the navigation node of the TS Gateway Manager MMC snap-in and select Manage Local Computer Groups from the Actions pane. Figure 9-36 shows all the groups controlled by TS Gateway. You can create new groups or modify existing groups that have full access to the entries in a group, and you can add new members or remove existing ones.

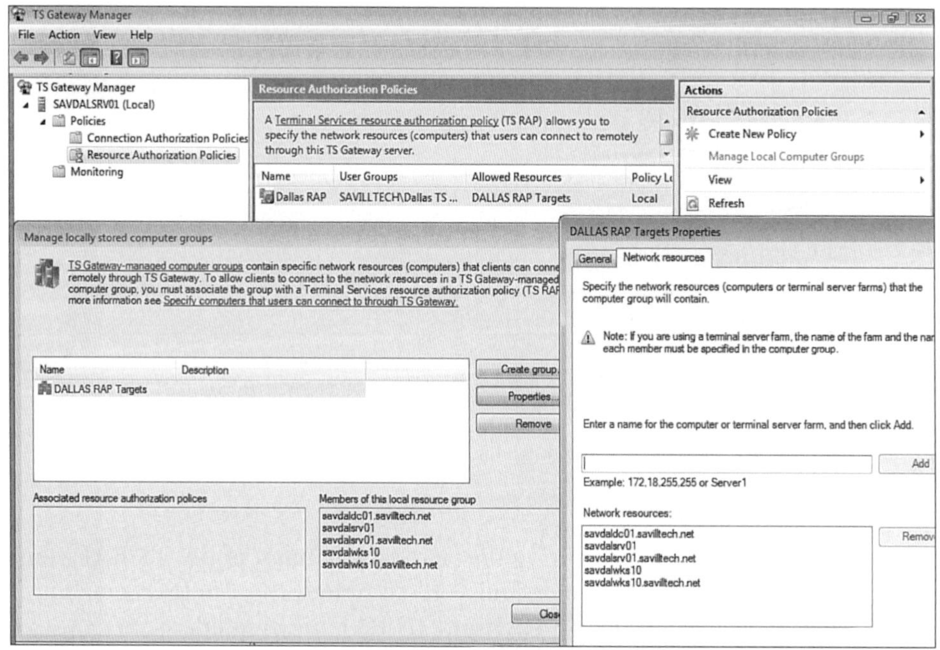

FIGURE 9-36 This busy page shows how to manage TS Gateway–managed groups.

Certificate Management

Now that TS CAP and TS RAP are configured, you're ready to connect, right? That depends. If you selected a certificate issued by a trusted public CA or an enterprise CA that your computer trusts, you are ready to connect now. If you used a self-signed certificate on the TS Gateway, you have to export out that certificate and import it onto the client computers that access through the TS Gateway. To view the certificate that is being used, view the properties of the TS Gateway server via the TS Gateway Manager MMC snap-in and select the SSL Certificate tab. You can use the Certificates MMC snap-in with the Computer account focused to view the certificates, which include the self-signed certificate, as shown in Figure 9-37. You can export this self-signed certificate and then import it into your clients. Notice that the self-signed certificate is issued to and by the local computer, making the certificate easy to spot.

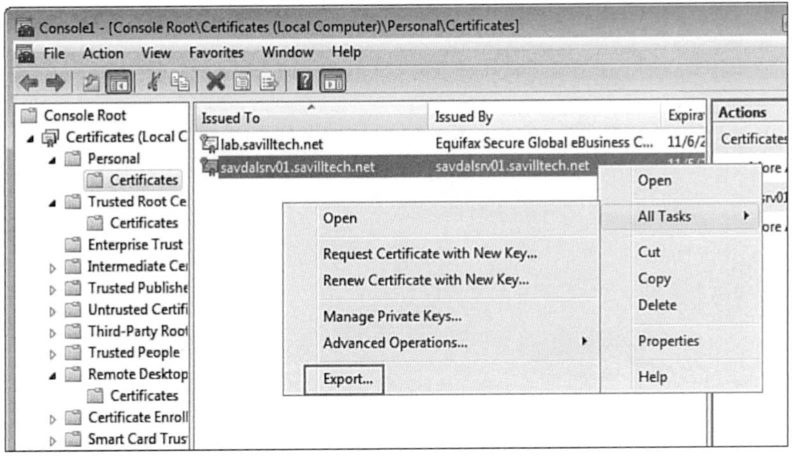

FIGURE 9-37 Exporting a certificate to enable importing into a client.

By default, the self-signed certificate was created with the name of the server. You were not asked for a common name. If you use a different external name on the Internet DNS servers—for example, ts.savilltech.net—then that default self-signed certificate is no use because it names the Internet network name for the server. Instead, you can access the SSL Certificate tab of the TS Gateways server's properties and select Create Certificate, and then you can enter a new common name, such as ts.savilltech.net. And even better, this wizard creates an export of the certificate to a file that can then be imported into clients, as shown in Figure 9-38.

Say that you go out and buy a certificate from RapidSSL so you have a publically available certificate (which is quite rapid even with the spam filter deleting the certificate on first try!). You then use IIS to request a certificate for the externally visible DNS name of the environment because the certificate name must match the DNS name unless you purchase a wildcard certificate. After you have the certificate imported on your TS Gateway server, from the same SSL Certificate tab, select the Select an Existing Certificate for SSL Encryption option and click the Browse Certificates button. You can then select the certificate you want to use and click Install, as shown in Figure 9-39. The certificate is issued by a trusted CA, so no certificates need to be imported into clients. The best practice is to use a trusted Internet CA for the certificate; a self-signed certificate should be used for internal testing only. At this point, provided that the company firewall and routers are configured to allow inbound 443 and forward to the TS Gateway for the name of the certificate, you are ready to connect via the client using TS Gateway.

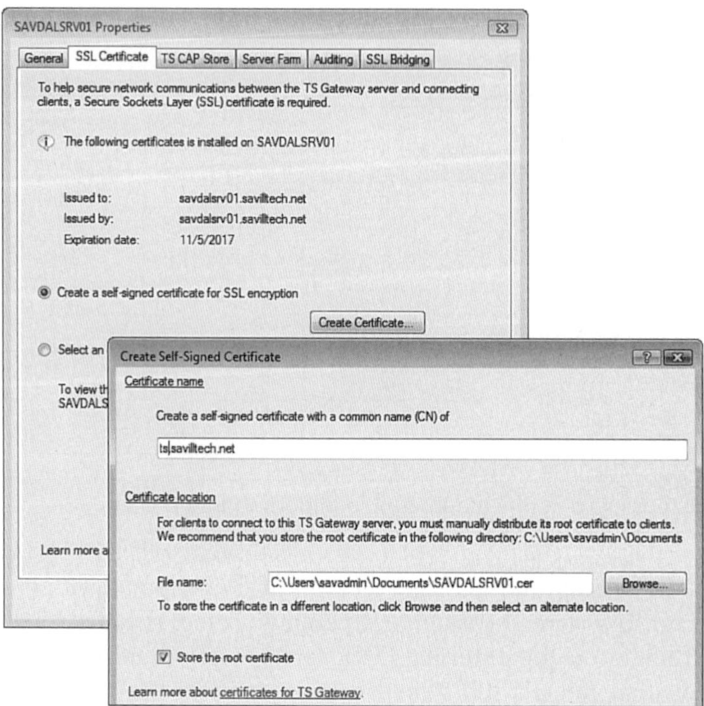

FIGURE 9-38 This self-signed certificate can be used to import into Internet clients and allow this TS Gateway server to be accessed using its external name, ts.savilltech.net.

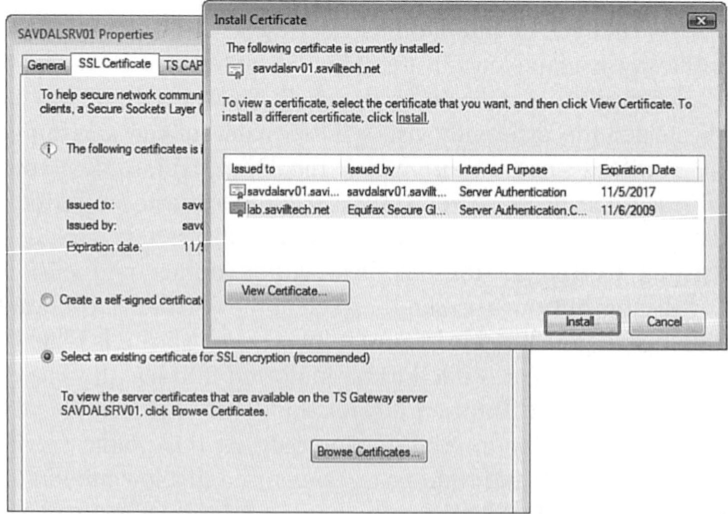

FIGURE 9-39 Using a public certificate issued by a trusted CA is the best option, where it is available.

Connecting via a TS Gateway Server

To connect via a TS Gateway server, you don't need to do much configuration. Access the Advanced tab of the RDC and click the Settings button in the Connect from Anywhere section.

In the TS Gateway configuration, specify the name of the TS Gateway server and a logon method, such as NTLM or Smartcard. Or you can allow credentials to be chosen when the connection is initiated. As you can see in Figure 9-40, you can configure the TS Gateway server to be bypassed for connections to local addresses, and notice that you can configure the same credential you use to connect to the TS Gateway server to be used for the connection to the destination terminal server or remote desktop target. If you want to be able to use different credentials, you should not enable this option. You might have a credential that is in the TS CAP but other credentials that are in the TS RAP for multiple-user logon testing.

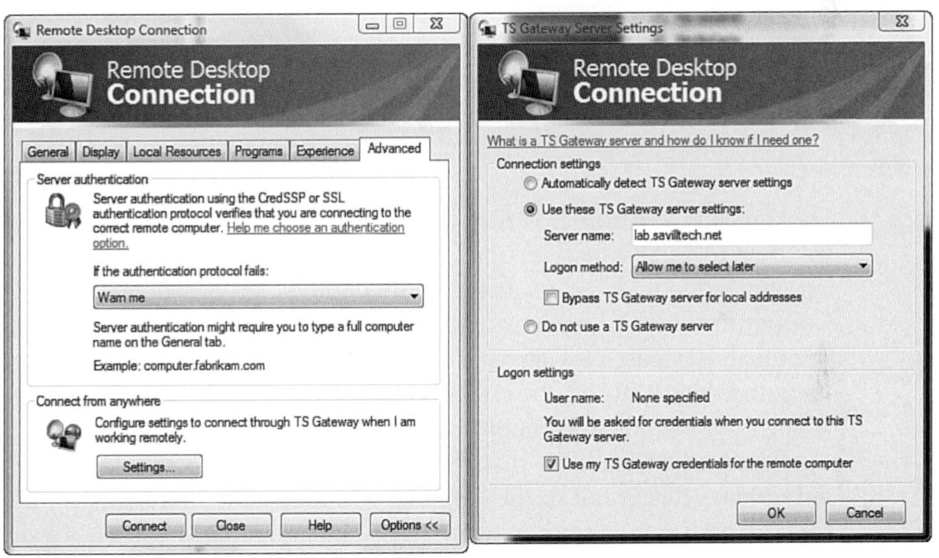

FIGURE 9-40 Configuring for TS Gateway connectivity.

You've completed the configuration. You probably want to save these new settings in the RDP configuration file to avoid having to re-enter them at each logon.

When you click Connect, you see the normal credential dialog. However, if you look closely, you see that it is prompting you for the credentials used to connect to the TS Gateway server and to connect to the target RDP system, as shown in Figure 9-41.

Windows Security

Enter your credentials

These credentials will be used to connect to the following computers:
1. lab.savilltech.net (TS Gateway server)
2. savdaldc01.savilltech.net (remote computer)

User name

Password

Domain: SAVILLTECH

Insert a smart card

Remember my credentials

OK Cancel

FIGURE 9-41 The gateway and server for which the credentials are used.

You can use group policy to configure the use of a TS Gateway server, whether to enable connections through the TS Gateway server or the authentication method to use. These options are available under User Configuration, Administrative Templates, Windows Components, Terminal Services, TS Gateway. If the TS Gateway group policy is configured, then the RDC can be configured to automatically detect TS Gateway settings, which tells the client to use group policy configuration.

Error reporting from the TS Gateway is good. If you specify a computer name that is not in the TS RAP or a username that is not in the TS CAP or RAP, you get an error message. For example, Figure 9-42 shows the error message that is sent when you try to pass the NetBIOS name for one of the servers for which you configured only the FQDN in the TS Managed group.

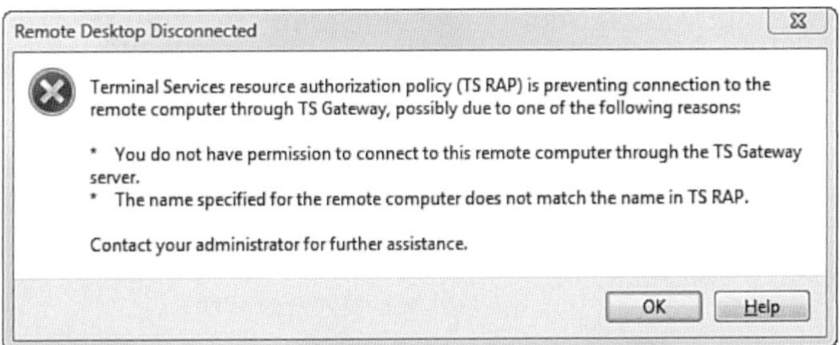

FIGURE 9-42 A descriptive error helps you troubleshoot any problems.

Monitoring and Managing TS Gateway

The TS Gateway Manager has a monitoring component that you launch from the server overview page by clicking the Monitor Active Connections link, as shown in Figure 9-43. Notice that this screen shows the number of connections, the number of distinct user accounts, and the number of different target resources that are being accessed via the gateway. The overview also shows the TS CAP and TS RAP policies that are defined.

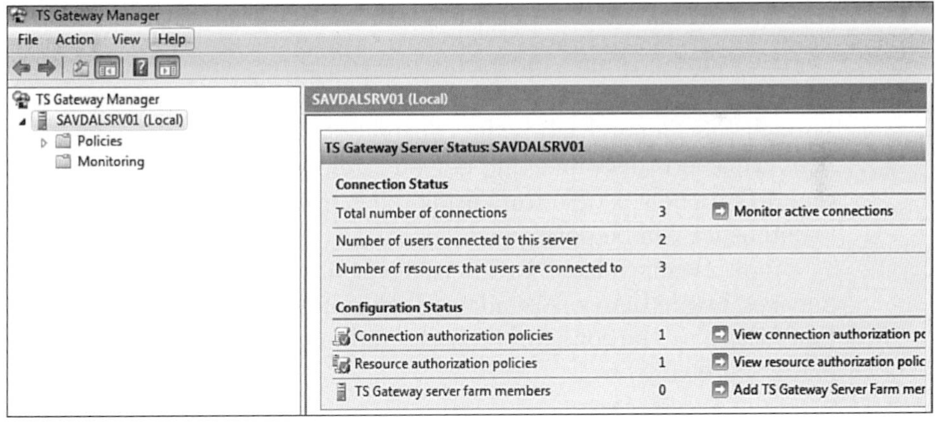

FIGURE 9-43 Three connections via the gateway.

Monitoring the active connections gives details on all the connections, including details on the user, client IP address, target computer, connection duration, idle time, connection time, and session ID. If you select any connection, you see more detail, including the kilobytes sent and received with all the sessions for the selected user shown. Figure 9-44 shows this monitoring.

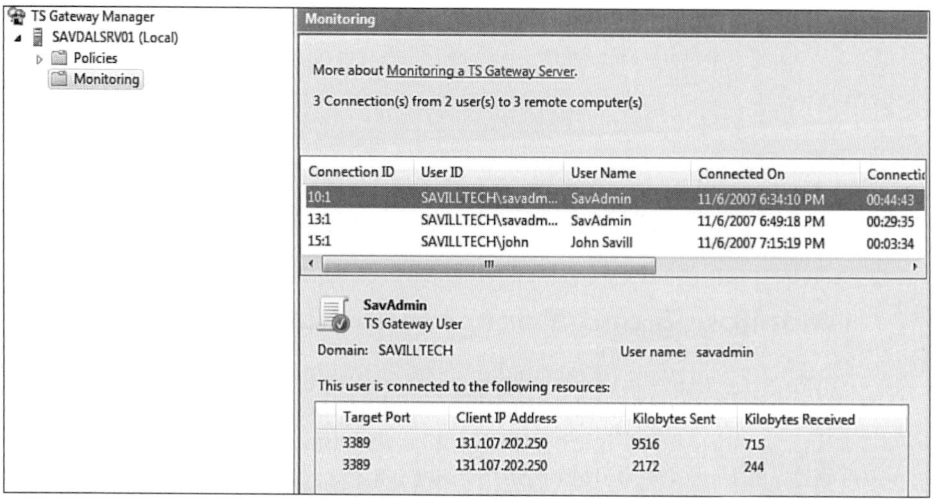

Figure 9-44 TS Gateway Manager's detailed monitoring gives useful connection information.

If you want to limit the number of concurrent connections, do so via the General tab of the TS Gateway server's properties. Also available through this General tab is the capability to stop new incoming connections while not disconnecting current connections. This is useful if you want to stop new people from using the gateway so it can be shut down or maintenance can be performed.

Audit events related to TS Gateway are written to Application and Services Logs\Microsoft\Windows\Terminal Services-Gateway. The exact logs written can be configured via the Auditing tab of the TS Gateway server's properties.

NOTE Look around the TS Gateway interface. It offers many more features than could be described here, such as using a central Network Policy Server for a statement of health processing. Also notice that you can export and import the policy settings for a TS Gateway server by selecting the server in the Navigation pane and selecting the import/export actions from the Actions pane. The configuration is stored in an XML file, so it is readable.

Scaling TS Gateway

A single TS Gateway box on pretty basic hardware can handle a lot of concurrent sessions. Microsoft has some numbers indicating that on a dual-processor box with 2.2GHz AMD Opteron processors and 4GB of RAM, 700 concurrent connections were handled pretty comfortably, and many more were possible (1,300 was found to be the real maximum); however, for availability or just sheer volume, you might need multiple TS Gateway servers.

You can install multiple TS Gateway servers and then use load balancing across them. If you have only a couple nodes, use the built-in Windows load balancing. If you need more nodes, the recommendation is to use a hardware load balancer; with more than 1,500 concurrent connections, it's time to load balance your hardware. The easiest way to manage multiple TS Gateway servers is to configure one of them, export its configuration, and import that configuration into the others.

There is a slight problem: Each RDP session over HTTPS consists of two SSL connections. Now imagine if one SSL connection went to one TS Gateway server and the other to a different TS Gateway server: That would be a problem. You therefore need to tell each TS Gateway server about the other TS Gateway servers that exist so they form a farm, and if a TS Gateway server gets the second SSL connection, it redirects it to the TS Gateway server that got the first connection. Access the properties of the TS Gateway server, and on the Server Farm tab, add the names of the other TS Gateway servers. Perform this step on each TS Gateway server or on one server, export the configuration, and then import the configuration to the others.

NOTE Microsoft provides a document on scaling TS Gateway, which you can find at http://download.microsoft.com/download/d/3/3/d339869e-1291-4733-acb9-294ec793d0b5/Win2008TSTWP.doc.

Remote Applications

So far, we have discussed enabling users to run a session on a terminal server with an entire desktop. While this entire desktop is sometimes required, it is also burdensome and requires the users to understand what is going on. Just running the application remotely in a seamless experience would be preferable. Users should not need to know whether something is running locally, virtualized, or remotely; it should just be there. How you choose to facilitate the services needed for the users is your decision but should not affect them. It's important to remember that while administrators tend to like technology (except when it's not cooperating at 3 a.m., when you're just installing a driver), users see technology as something that facilitates their jobs. The more time they spend having to work out how to use technology, the less time they have to do what they are paid to do.

Windows Server 2008 TS now provides seamless window application usage. Previously, this feature was available only via third-party products such as Citrix Metaframe. However, now you can run RDP programs that appear seamless on the client's desktop.

There is little to do to enable remote applications, known as RemoteApp within TS. By default, a server does not make any programs available via RemoteApp, and the default policy is to not allow unlisted programs to be started. Most of your actions are related to enabling the remote applications and getting to the client.

From the client perspective, the only requirement is that the client run a client that supports RDP 6.0 or above, and if accessing via TS Web Access, the client must support RDP 6.1 or above.

There are some behavioral quirks with remote applications that you probably need to make users aware of, or they will think there is something wrong. Drag and drop between applications is not currently supported (not even if the remote applications are running in the same session), nor is it available between a remote application and a local application. Users can tell remote applications because the end of the application name says "(Remote)," but you probably need to do a little education to avoid floods of support calls. Server–to-client application execution is also not possible. For example, if a user is running Outlook on a terminal server and it contains a Web link, if the user clicks the link, Internet Explorer launches on the terminal server and not the user's local version of Internet Explorer. This cannot be changed currently.

Installing Applications

Let's have a quick refresher on installing applications on a terminal server. If you install a software package from a Windows Installer package (.msi file), the terminal server install mode is automatically enabled to make the application usable in bulk remote session modes. If the application is not in a Windows Installer package, put the server in terminal server install mode before installing the application by running the command `change user /install`. After the application is installed, switch back to execute mode via the command `change user /execute`.

You can also install via the Install Application on Terminal Server Control Panel applet, which places the server in the correct install mode.

The terminal server install mode is required to ensure that the correct Registry and configuration files are created during installation to support running the application in a multiple-user environment mode. If you have applications installed on the server prior to installing the terminal server role, you might need to uninstall and reinstall them.

If you're installing some applications on a terminal server, you need special versions. For example, Office 2007 must be the volume license edition to run on a terminal server.

SoftGrid, known as Microsoft Application Virtualization, has a special version for TS (see Chapter 19). Obviously, installing multiple applications on a single terminal server may cause compatibility problems between the applications. When you use SoftGrid, each application is placed in its own sandbox and is unable to see the others, essentially cocooned, which does away with any application compatibility problems.

Enabling RemoteApp

To enable RemoteApp, from the Action menu or the Actions pane, select Add RemoteApp Program to launch the RemoteApp Wizard. Click Next to proceed past the welcome screen. This wizard displays a list of all the programs it knows about, and you can click Browse to add additional programs that are not displayed in the list. Select the programs you want to share, as shown in Figure 9-45. For each application, click the Properties button to enable some additional configuration options, including enabling the configuration of an alternate icon to be used for the remote app, specifying any default command-line arguments, and specifying whether users are allowed to specify command-line arguments. The default is to not allow command-line arguments.

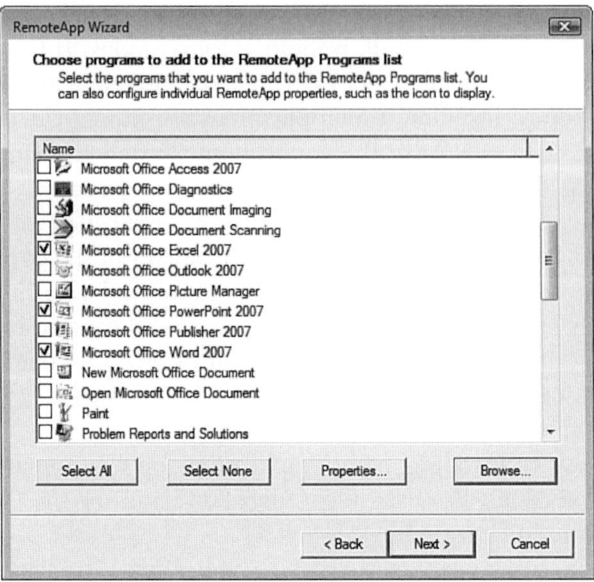

FIGURE 9-45 Selecting the programs that are available as remote applications.

The wizard displays a summary that lists the programs that will be made available and the settings for each program. Click Finish to complete the configuration. The programs are now displayed in the RemoteApp Programs section, and you can select a program to view is distribution options, as shown in Figure 9-46.

Before you try to deploy a remote application, let's take a quick look at some of the configuration you can perform to set defaults for the remote applications. You want to configure this now because when you distribute the remote applications, you have to configure these options; configuring the defaults now saves effort when distributing because you can accept the defaults, which are read from the server configuration.

Notice that the Overview section of the TS RemoteApp Manager provides links to change elements related to terminal server, TS Gateway, digital signature, and RDP Settings. Each of these links opens a specific tab of the properties page of the TS RemoteApp server, so let's walk through them.

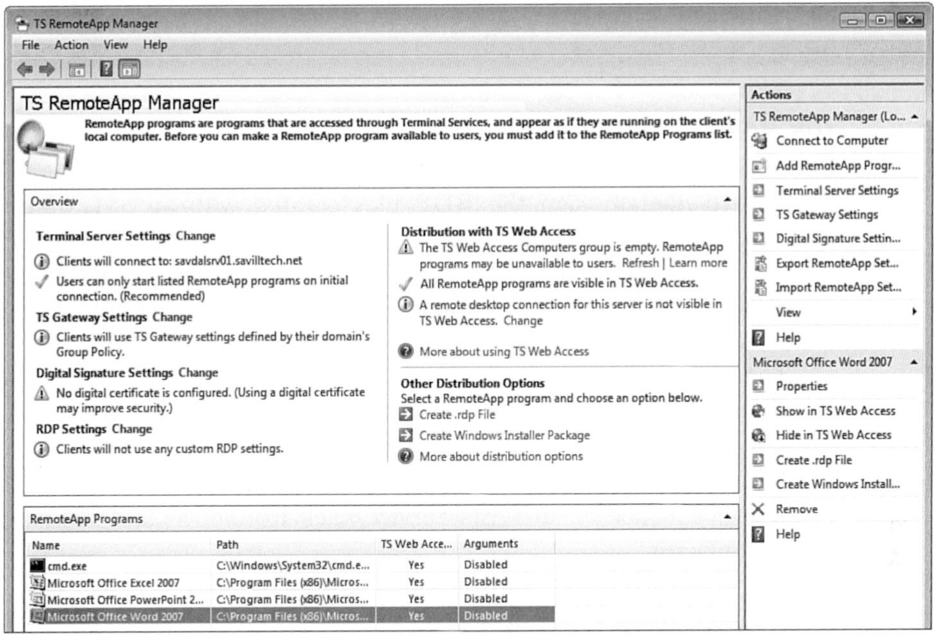

FIGURE 9-46 TS RemoteApp Manager makes it easy to deploy applications.

The Terminal Server Tab

The Terminal Server tab enables configuration of the connection settings, including the server name and RDP port in addition to whether server authentication is required.

Also on this tab is the option to show (in the remote programs section of the TS Web interface) a remote desktop connection to the local terminal server when TS Web Access is enabled.

Finally, this tab provides an option to allow users to start listed and unlisted programs. However, this is not recommended and may expose the terminal server to attack, either deliberate or unintentional. The default setting of not allowing a user to start an unlisted program is the recommended setting.

The TS Gateway Tab

The TS Gateway tab shows the same information as the RDC tab. You can set whether the TS Gateway server settings should be automatically detected, which means using the values from group policy, and you can specify a TS Gateway server, as well as the options having to do with credentials for TS Gateway access and the terminal server and whether to use a TS Gateway server at all.

The Digital Signature Tab

Because you may be using remote applications on many types of clients, it's possible to digitally sign the RDP files created with an SSL or code-signing certificate. This certificate can be the same one you're using for TS or TS Gateway. However, if it will be used on computers not in the enterprise, the certificate must be from or cosigned by a public CA that participates in the Microsoft Root Certificate Program.

The digital signature configuration here is also used by the applications showing via TS Web Access, so if you want the applications to be signed via TS Web Access, configure a certificate here.

If you digitally sign your RDP files, your clients must be running RDC 6.1 or above, which means Vista Service Pack 1 or above, and this may be a limiting factor.

The Custom RDP Settings Tab

The common RDP settings enable the configuration of device and resource redirection in addition to font smoothing and maximum color configuration, as shown in Figure 9-47.

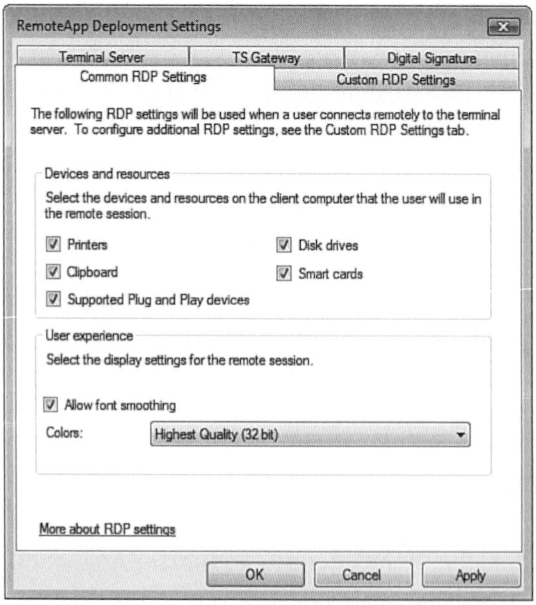

FIGURE 9-47 The common RDP settings.

The Custom RDP Settings tab enables you to configure additional RDP settings, such as audio redirection. This tab is just a text-entry page, and to get the correct format, save an RDP file from the RDC with the required settings and then copy and paste the entries required by opening the generated RDP in Notepad.

Distributing a Remote Application

One of the main ways to access RemoteApp is via TS Web (discussed in the next section), which makes things much easier because TS Web always has the latest list of applications and saves deployment problems. However, you can also generate RDP files that clients can just execute, or create an .msi file that contains the RDP and icon to enable the RDP RemoteApp shortcut to be deployed to clients via group policy or SCCM and placed on the desktop or in the Start menu. It can even be associated with file types.

Creating an RDP is a basic option and is nothing more than the same RDP configuration you can configure via the RDC with a program configured. You simply place some different settings in the RDP to make the application window seamless (for example, remoteapplicationmode:i:1 instead of the normal remoteapplicationmode:i:0).

To create an RDP file, select an application from the RemoteApp Programs list and click the Create .rdp File link in the Other Distribution options. As usual, click Next at the welcome screen of the wizard.

The main package settings dialog, shown in Figure 9-48, uses the settings that are configured as the defaults for the TS RemoteApp manager (which is why you changed them first). You can change any of these settings for this specific publishing, so modify as required and then click Next. A summary is displayed, and when you click Finish, the RDP file is saved to the C:\Program Files\Packaged Programs directory by default. That folder is opened so the RDP file can be seen.

Click the RDP file to execute it. If it is not digitally signed, you receive a warning that the publisher is unknown. You can ignore this and even check an option to not be asked again for connections to the computer. You are then prompted for credentials to be used to communicate with the terminal server and, potentially, a TS Gateway server. The application then launches, as shown in Figure 9-49, and then opens. If you click the Details button, you can see the initial connection taking place, which is the user logon process, preparation of the desktop, and so on. It is hidden when the application starts.

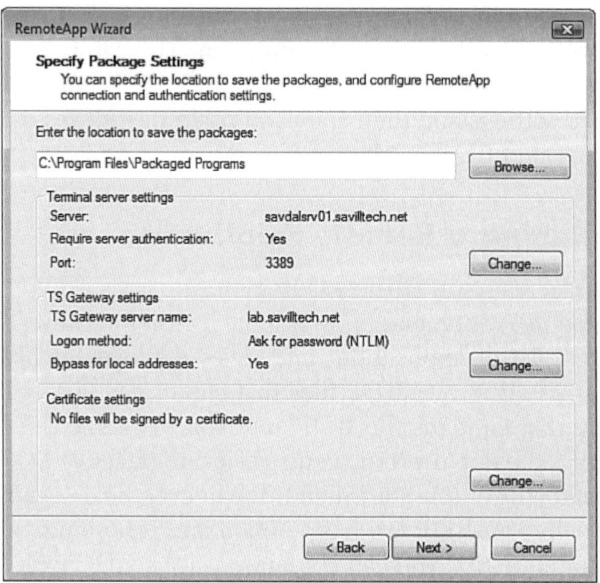

FIGURE 9-48 The values are the ones defined in the Overview section of the TS RemoteApp Manager MMC snap-in.

FIGURE 9-49 Office Word 2007 starting remotely.

Before looking more at the application running, create an .msi file of an RDP file. Select Create Windows Installer Package from the Other Distribution options. The wizard goes through the same process as for creating an RDP file; the second page asks about all the same options, TS Gateway, and so on. However, you have an additional page after that, as shown in Figure 9-50, where you can configure the distribution settings that control where the shortcuts are displayed. By default, the programs are placed in a special Remote Programs Start menu group to make it obvious that they are running remotely. However, you can change this and place the shortcuts in any location. You can also enable the client extensions for the program to be associated with the RemoteApp program. A summary is displayed that shows any extensions that are associated. You now have an .msi file in the Packed Programs folder that you can execute manually or deploy with group policy or by using any other distribution mechanism.

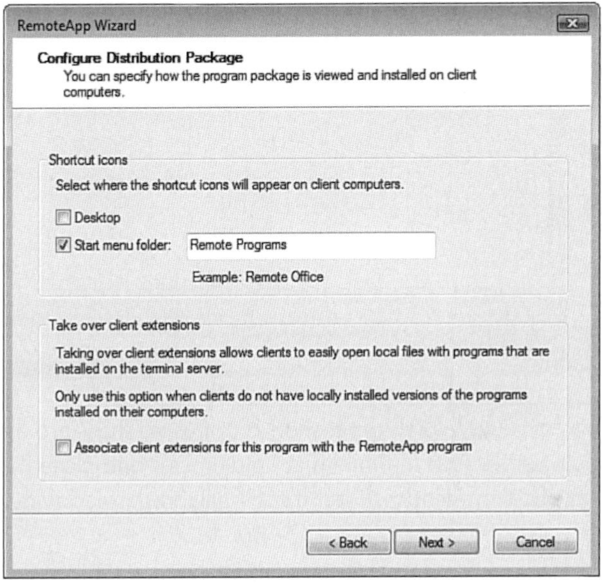

FIGURE 9-50 By default, the remote programs are stored in a special Remote Programs Start menu folder.

Figure 9-51 shows two instances of Word running: one locally and one on the terminal server. Can you spot the difference? The theme of the remote is just Vista Basic because Windows Server 2008 does not support Aero. The system tray icons for the applications integrate with the standard system tray, and you get only the icons related to the application and not icons that relate to a normal session.

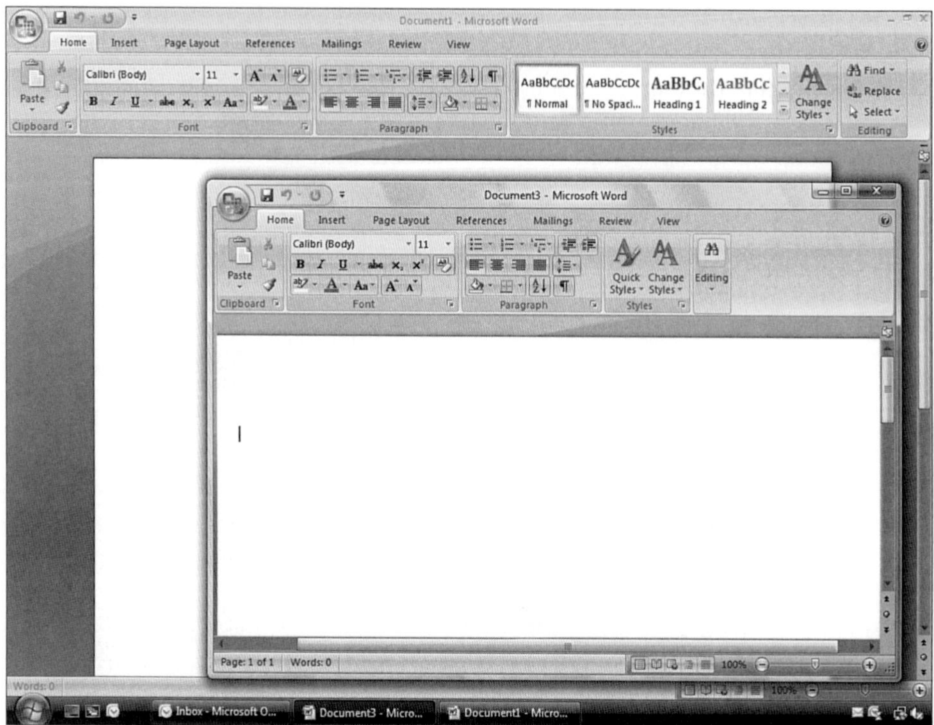

FIGURE 9-51 The background Word application is not using the Aero theme because it's running on the remote server (see the minimize, maximize, and close buttons in the top-right corner of the application window), but it's still fully integrated with the Start menu.

If you run a second remote program to the same terminal server, you are not prompted for credentials; the existing session is used. If you run Task Manager, as shown in Figure 9-52, you can see the running programs. If you right-click a remote program and select Go to Process, you see the process is `mstsc`. This process is shared between all remote programs going to the same terminal server.

Note that with a full session, you can disconnect or log off, which controls whether the session is left open, just disconnected, or logged out. With a remote application, you can only exit the application; so what does that do? There is some clever logic that goes on in the background to check whether the session can be disconnected at all, which involves checking if there are any RemoteApp windows or RemoteApp system tray icons. If there are not, the session can be disconnected, but if there are, the process waits 20 seconds and then checks again, and it repeats every 20 seconds.

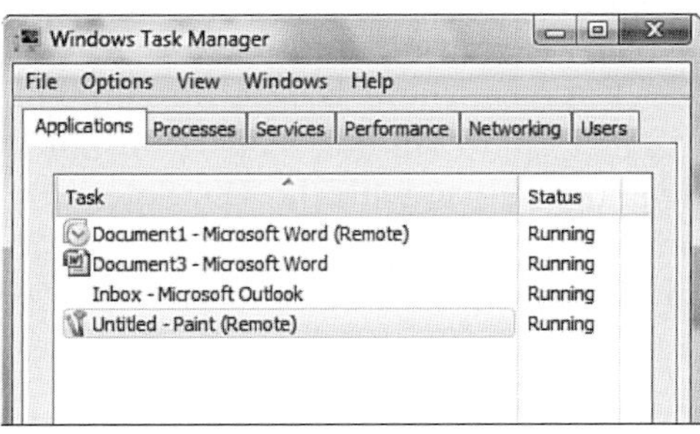

Figure 9-52 The remote programs are identified with "(Remote)."

The next step is when to log off disconnected RemoteApp sessions. By default, RemoteApp sessions are never logged off and will stay open (but disconnected) indefinitely. This provides a good end-user experience because starting an application is far faster than having to process a logon, which is required when no session exists for a remote application starting on a server. You can enable disconnected sessions to time out and log off by setting the group policy Computer or User Configuration\Administrative Templates\Windows Components\Terminal Services\Terminal Server\Session Time Limits\Set Time Limit for Logoff of RemoteApp Sessions. Be aware, however, that the application is never left running. What is left open is a session that can be used by the application. When a remote application is closed, the application process is terminated. You can't have work open, start typing, and not save your work. When you close Word, the process is stopped.

One useful option here, which is discussed in Chapter 14, "Server Core," is making the `cmd` process or `powershell` a remote application, which then allows it to be run on remote machines. It's running locally on the server in question, and because the terminal server role is not required on the server, it can be used on any of your servers.

One final consideration is that TS remote applications do not run all the normal startup options that are associated with a full, entire desktop session. Items in the Startup group are not run, nor are applications in the Run or RunOnce Registry keys. If you want something to run for TS remote applications, consider calling it via group policy in the form of a logon action.

TS Web Access

TS Web Access creates a Web page that acts as an interface into the remote applications that are available on a server and standard Remote Desktop–style sessions. There is little to configure for TS Web Access. However, it does require IIS 7.0, so if IIS is not installed, the IIS role is automatically added, along with the Windows Process Activation Service that IIS requires.

To install TS Web Access, add the TS Web Access role service that is part of TS in the same way as all the other TS roles you have installed (that is, via Server Manager, Roles, Terminal Services). There are no configuration items to select during the role installation of TS Web Access. It just installs silently.

After the installation, update the TS Web Access Computers local group on the terminal server from which TS Web Access offers remote applications (or potentially multiple servers, if you have two identical servers that could be linked via TS Web Access) with the computer name of the TS Web Access server. The easiest way to do this is to open the Local Users and Computers snap-in via the Configuration node in Server Manager. Double-click the TS Web Access Computers group and click Add (see Figure 9-53). Change the object type from Users and Groups to Computers and enter the name of the TS Web Access server, and then click OK. This step is not necessary if TS Web Access is installed on the same server as the terminal server it's using as the source of its application listing.

You can now use the TS Web Access Administration page, which is a Web page under the new TS web site that has been added to the Default web site in IIS. It is available if you log on to the http://<*ts web access server*>/ts page as an administrator or someone who is a member of the TS Web Access Administrators local group on the server and click the Configuration button, as shown in Figure 9-54. The only configuration item is the name of the terminal server to read RemoteApp from.

You can configure TS Web Access to read from a terminal server farm instead of a server, which gives you a load-balanced TS Web Access experience. However, there are restrictions here: The servers in the farm being pointed to all need to be identically configured (same OS, same apps installed, same domain, same security model, and so on) and using Session Broker.

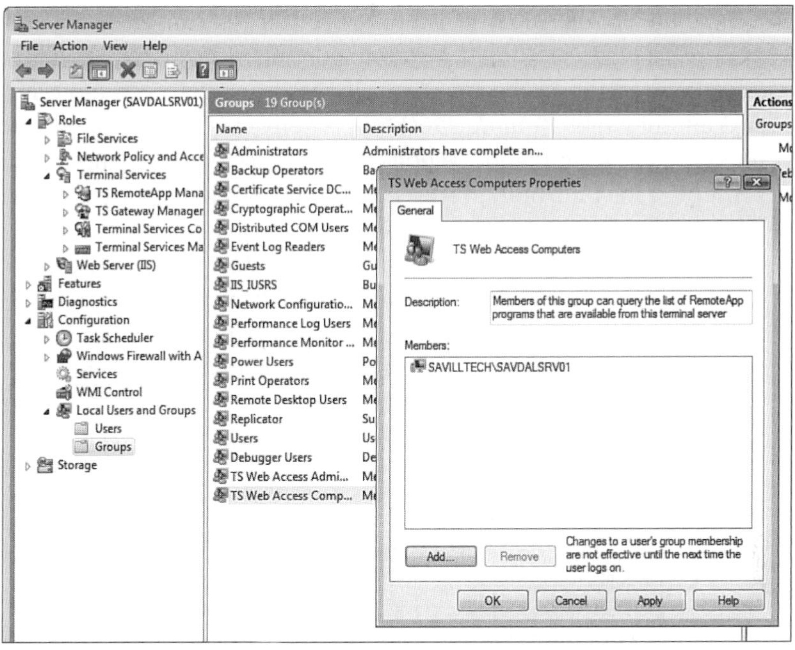

Figure 9-53 Add the TS Web Access server to the group containing the servers that are allowed to offer remote applications.

Figure 9-54 The sum of the configuration available for TS Web Access: the server from which to read applications.

When TS Web Access is configured, users can navigate to http://<*TS web access server*>/ts (for example, http://savdalsrv01.savilltech.net/ts), and they see the Web page that allows access to the remote applications and another tab, Remote Desktop, where you can enable a remote connection to be initiated. When the user selects an application, she is prompted to confirm the redirection of resources that are configured, such as drives and printers. If you configure the Digital Signature Settings for the TS RemoteApp Manager with a certificate, the application accessed via TS Web Access are digitally signed. The advantage of this digital signature is that normally when an application is launched via the website, you get a warning that redirection of resources will take place that shows every time. If a certificate is configured, an extra check box is shown to not prompt again for remote connections from the publisher, as shown in Figure 9-55. This is useful for the end-user experience.

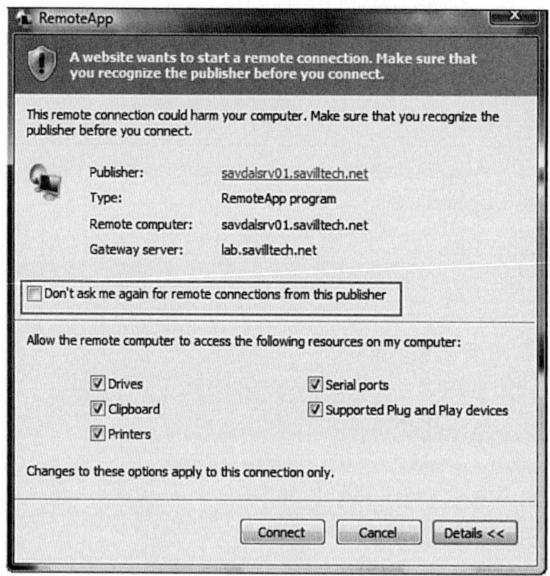

FIGURE 9-55 This option is available only if the Digital Signature settings are configured on the TS RemoteApp server.

The user must then enter the credentials used to connect to the terminal server as a normal remote app. The application runs in the normal seamless manner (that is, it is not enclosed in the Web browser but looks like any normal application).

There is a change here from previous Web access methods for terminal servers. Previously, an ActiveX component had to be installed on the client accessing the Web page. This was problematic in some locked-down environments. With Windows Server 2008, provided that the client computer is running RDC 6.1, the ActiveX component required by TS Web Access is part of the RDC, so no additional ActiveX component needs to be installed. If you are running RDC 6.1 and you cannot load the ActiveX component, ensure that the add-on is enabled via the Tools, Manage Add-ons option in Internet Explorer.

When a user who has an older version of the RDC client tries to use TS Web Access, he receives an error message with a URL that points to more information. You can modify this URL as follows:

1. Open IIS Manager on the server that hosts the TS Web Access web site, which is found in the Administrative Tools folder.
2. In the Navigation pane of IIS Manager, expand the server name, expand Sites, expand Default Web Site, and then click TS. (By default, TS Web Access is installed to this location. If you installed TS Web Access to a different site, locate and then click the site name.)
3. Under the ASP.NET section, double-click Application Settings.
4. In the Actions pane of the MMC, click Add.
5. In the Add Application Setting dialog box, set the name to rdcInstallUrl, and set the value to the URL to which you want the older clients to be redirected, as shown in Figure 9-56.

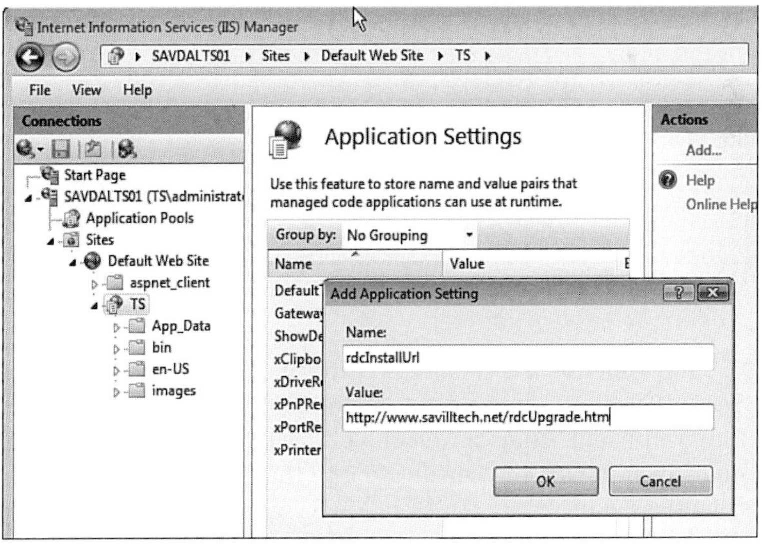

FIGURE 9-56 In this example, older RDC clients are forwarded to an internal page that tells them why they cannot get access and giving them links to where to get the updated RDC 6.1 or above client.

Secure Access to TS Web

If you want to securely connect to your TS site, assign a certificate to https in the IIS Manager for the TS site. Select the Bindings action for the web site that contains the TS site (normally Default Web Site). When the bindings are open, select https and click Edit. In the Edit Site Binding dialog, choose the certificate to use for SSL (see Figure 9-57) and click the View button to get the full details of the certificate.

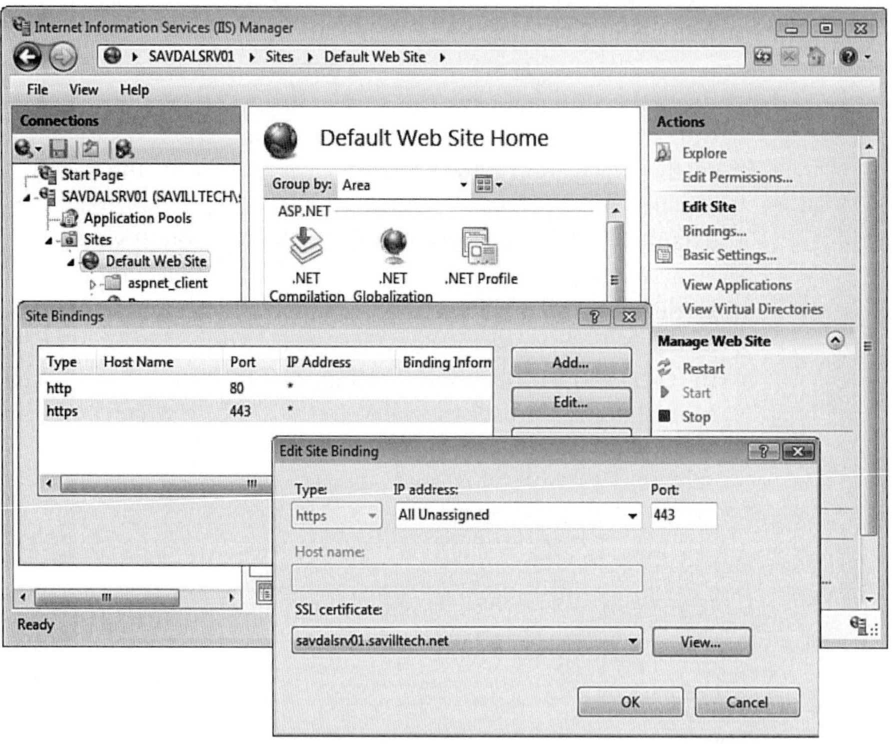

Figure 9-57 Selecting a certificate for HTTPS.

You can use a self-signed certificate, which you can create via the Server Certificate link for the features of the actual IIS server. However, the Web client issues an error, stating that the certificate is not trusted unless you import the certificate into the clients. To export the certificate from the server, create a custom MMC with the Certificates snap-in loaded for the Computer account store. Then navigate to Personal, Certificates;

right-click; and select All Tasks, Export for the certificate, as shown in Figure 9-58. You only need to export the public key to a file and export it to a DER-encoded binary X.509 format (this is a wizard option), so don't panic. When the certificate is exported, just double-click the export file on the client and select Install Certificate, but do not let the wizard choose where to install the certificate. Instead, choose to place the certificate in a store and select Trusted Root Certificate Authorities. You get a warning that the certificate could not be verified, but ignore it. This is not normally advisable, but for testing machines, it is fine. You should not do this in a production environment because you now totally trust the server. Using a public trusted CA or an enterprise CA eliminates this problem. When the SSL is in place, you can use https: instead of http: to connect to the web site.

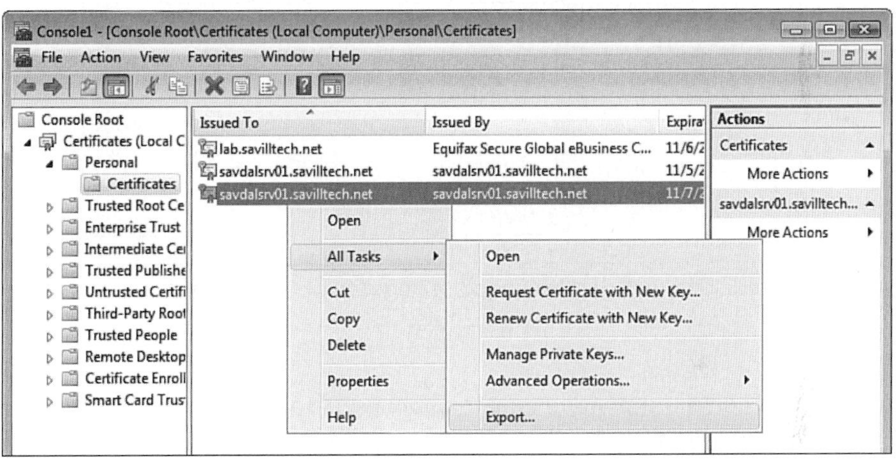

FIGURE 9-58 Exporting the certificate.

If you receive a prompt to enter a username and password when accessing the site from your local network and prompts to run the ActiveX component, make sure the site is in your Local Intranet list of sites (Tools, Internet Options, Security in IE). When accessing the site externally from your network, add it to the Trusted Sites list.

Granting Users Logon Rights to a Terminal Server

By default, administrators have rights to log on to a terminal server. Both the Administrators and the Remote Desktop Users groups are configured to have the Allow Log on Through Terminal Services user right assignment. View this via the Local Security Policy administrative tool and navigate to Local Policies, User Rights Assignment, as shown in Figure 9-59.

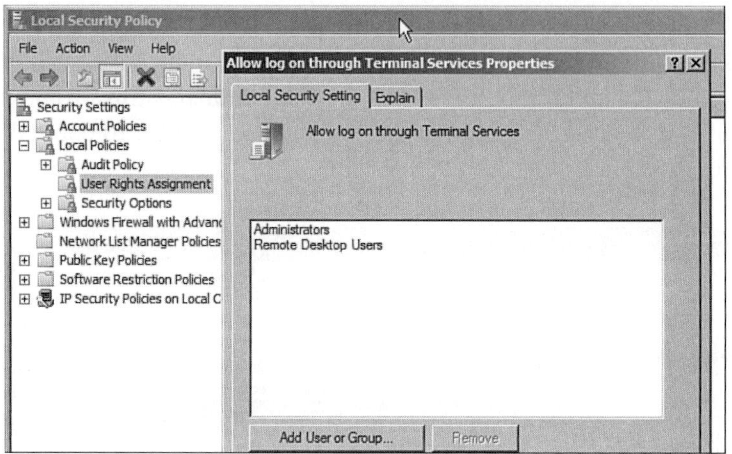

FIGURE 9-59 The default and recommended settings for the people with rights to log on through TS.

The recommended way to allow users to connect to a terminal server is to add them to the Remote Desktop Users group. This is the group that is updated when you add users via the Remote Settings part of the System Control Panel applet.

If you install TS on a domain controller, adding users to the Remote Desktop Users group still does not give them permission to log on. This is because a domain controller is locked down. If you want to enable other nonadministrators to log on, which is not a good idea, use group policy to modify the domain controller to allow the Remote Domain Users group to be given the Allow Log on Through Terminal Services right. Figure 9-60 shows a basic GPO defined that is linked to the Domain Controllers OU. Notice that you need to include the Remote Desktop Users and Administrators groups, or administrators can't use Remote Desktop to access the domain controller (which would be bad). If you only wanted certain domain controllers to allow the Remote Desktop Users group to have the Allow Log on Through Terminal Services right, you could place a security filter on the GPO and only grant the domain controllers that should process the policy read and apply permissions.

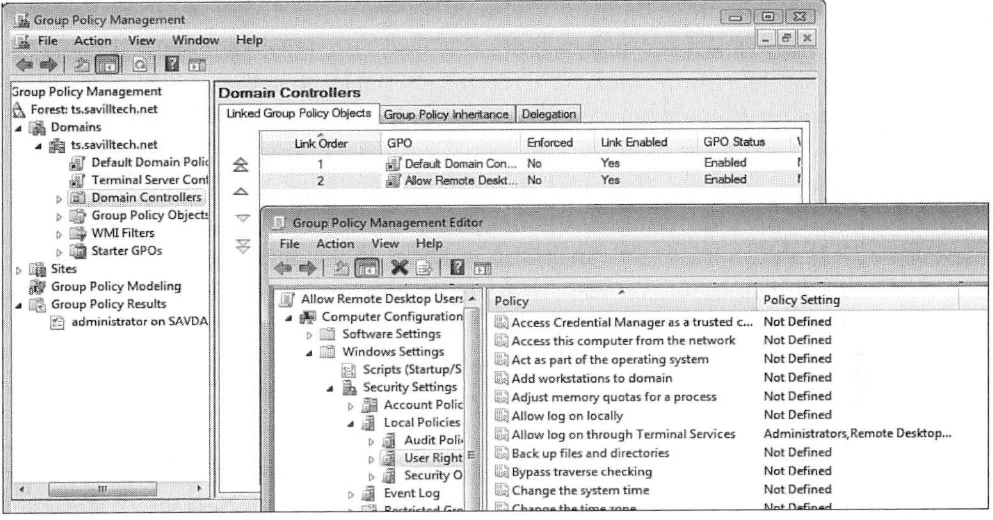

FIGURE 9-60 With this policy, members of the Remote Desktop Users group are able to connect to a domain controller.

Single Sign-on

Up to this point, for every connection, you have had to enter credentials, but chances are you are logged on to the client computer with the same account you want to use for the remote server connection.

To allow the current credentials to be sent to a terminal server, use group policy (or the local policy on a machine) to set the terminal server as an allowed target for credential delegation. This has to be controlled via policy. If applications could just hook into your credentials, they could forward them all over the place (for example, to locations where they can harvest credentials).

In this example, you use local policy to specify that your terminal server can be a target for credential delegation. However, you could also use a group policy by linking a group policy to a location that contains the computers of the users who want to use single sign-on, or you could just link at the domain level to enable this for all computers in the domain. If you use group policy, run `gpupdate` after making the change on the client so the new policy is used.

As shown in Figure 9-61, you navigate to Computer Configuration, Administrative Templates, System, Credentials Delegation and enable the Allow Delegating Default Credentials policy. Click the Show button to open the dialog where you enter the destinations for credential delegation. You must enter them in the form TERMSRV/*<server name>*/. (Note the forward slashes.) You need an entry for each way you may type the server name; for example, if sometimes you use the FQDN and sometimes the NetBIOS name, you need both entries. To enable all terminal servers in the domain, you can use *.*<domain>* (for example, *.savilltech.net), but this is not recommended due to concerns about possible illegitimate servers getting credentials. Likewise, to allow access to any terminal server, just use TERMSRV/*.

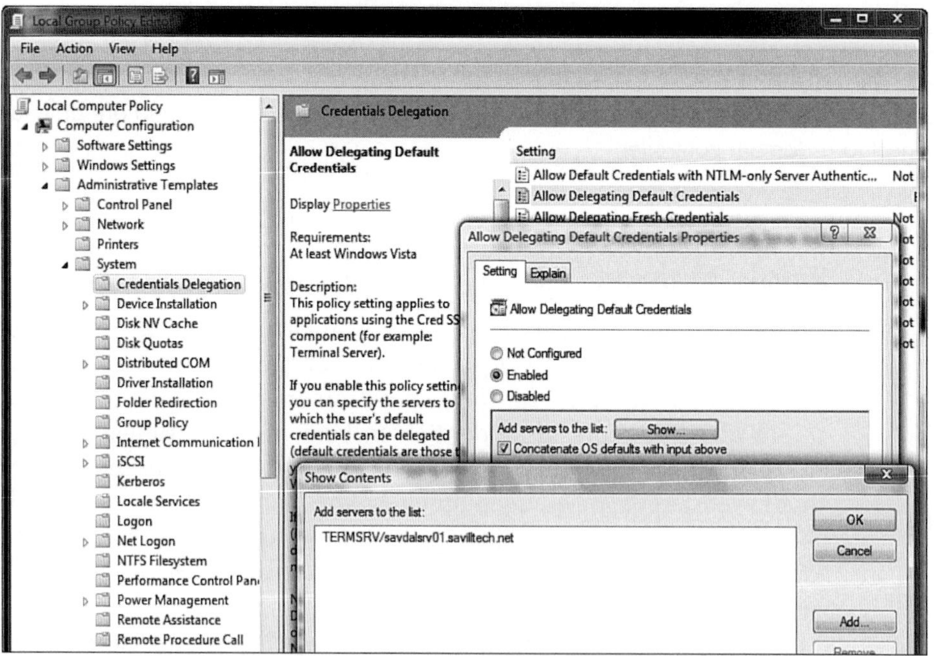

FIGURE 9-61 In this case, credentials are delegated to only one server.

You can also support single sign-on at the TS Gateway server by making another policy change on the local client via the computer's local policy or via group policy. Navigate to User Configuration, Administrative Templates, Windows Components, Terminal Services, TS Gateway and set the Set TS Gateway Server authentication method to Enabled. Set the authentication method to Use Locally Logged-on Credentials, but if you want to let users override this, check the Allow Users to Change This Setting box. Single sign-on is now enabled all the way through the process. If you ever want to be asked for credentials, open the Options in the Microsoft TS client and check the Always Ask for Credentials box that is displayed in place of the Allow Me to Save Credentials box, as shown in Figure 9-62. The utility detects a hostname with which it's allowed to use delegated credentials.

FIGURE 9-62 If you do not see the Always Ask for Credentials option, the computer name entered is not trusted for credential delegation.

TIP Consider putting TS Web Access on your TS Gateway servers. This is a best practice, not a requirement.

TS Session Broker

If you adopt TS for any of your technology needs, you will be impressed with how scalable Windows Server 2008 is with it. Unlike Windows Server 2003, which peaked at 800 users on 16 cores and saw no additional benefit as additional cores were added, Windows Server 2008 continues to scale, supporting nearly 1,200 users on a 32-core box. This does not necessarily mean you can make do with only 1 terminal server in your environment. Depending on the applications and the work being done, sessions may use a lot of processor or memory, which may limit the number of real users that can be supported. More importantly, you can't put all your eggs in one basket. You need multiple terminal servers, known as a farm, for redundancy and load-balancing purposes. You don't want to have to give the users multiple terminal servers to connect to, with instructions that if one is not available, go to a different one.

As shown in Chapter 18, "Highly Available Windows Server 2008," there are various options for high availability, one of which, network load balancing, would seem to be a good fit. It enables a single IP address and name to point to multiple servers. In this case, you could have a name such as tsfarm.savilltech.net that could point clients to savdalts01.savilltech.net, savdalts02.savilltech.net, or savdalts03.savilltech.net, and if a server was unavailable, the network load balancer would stop pointing clients to the unavailable terminal server. This is a fine solution with nothing else needed if users logged on and logged off. However, that is not always the case with terminal servers. Users often log on to a terminal server, disconnect, and then reconnect to their sessions. If the users connect to a farm of terminal servers via a network load balancing solution, they are connected to one of the available terminal servers. If they disconnect and reconnect, the network load balancing might connect them to a different terminal server than the one they were originally connected to, so they would have lost their session and any open work. They may keep reconnecting, hoping to eventually get put back through to the original terminal server.

The solution is to have a directory of the sessions that are active on the farm, so if a user disconnects, when he connects to the farm again, the sessions says, "Hey, John had a session on savdalts01, so I'll put him back to that terminal server." Windows Server 2003 had this functionality, but it had issues. In fact, Windows Server 2003 had farming issues in general. Network load balancing is complicated, not easy to set up, and difficult to troubleshoot. You needed to run the Enterprise edition on all servers in the farm, which is pricey. In addition, if you imagine that a user may connect to any one of the servers in the farm, the user should not have to worry about which server the user is using. Normally the user would have to configure their profile on each terminal server, unless roaming user profiles were used. However, the use of roaming profiles on terminal servers had problems.

Windows Server 2008 no longer has to use network load balancing, but it can. You can use network load balancing or another load-balancing component, but it has its own TS Session Broker and balancing technology that is easy to use and configure. In addition, TS Session Broker has no requirements for Enterprise edition. A TS Session Broker server can support multiple farms. You don't need one TS Session Broker per farm.

NOTE For information on configuration when using network load balancing, see www.microsoft.com/windowsserver2003/techinfo/overview/sessiondirectory.mspx for a document that was written for Windows Server 2003 but that still applies for Windows Server 2008.

The algorithm used to balance the sessions is dependent on the number of sessions on the server, which includes connected and disconnected sessions. The algorithm doesn't include CPU, resources, and so on; it uses only the number of sessions plus the weight of the server, as discussed later in this chapter. There are some additional logic steps applied. For example, if a single user launches two sessions, Session Broker attempts to map both sessions to the same terminal server.

If you need high availability for your TS Session Broker server, install into a Microsoft cluster.

TS Session Broker Installation and Configuration

To install TS Session Broker, add it via the Role Services area of the TS role. No configuration is required for the installation; the configuration is done after installation. You don't need to install the TS Session Broker service on all terminal servers because only one server acts as the TS Session Broker for each farm. TS Session Broker does not have to be installed on a server with the terminal server role installed nor even have Remote Desktop enabled.

When TS Session Broker is installed, the group Session Directory Computers is created, and it is normally a local group, unless you installed the role on a domain controller, in which case it becomes a domain global group. You must add the computer objects of all the terminal servers that use the TS Session Broker service. Remember to set the object type to Computers, as shown in Figure 9-63.

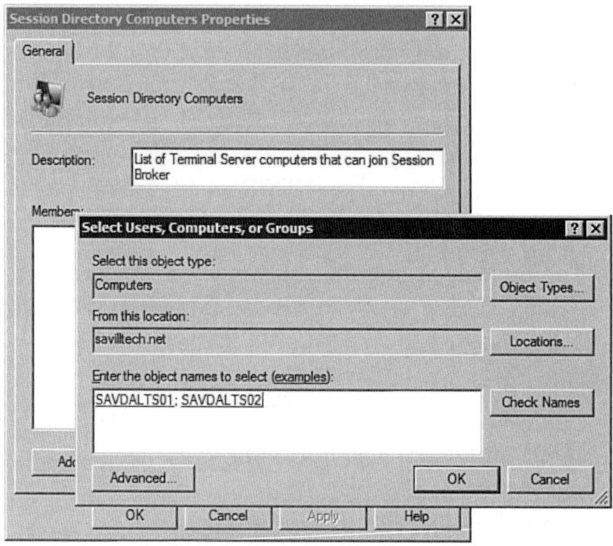

FIGURE 9-63 Set the object type to Computers.

You can now use the Terminal Services Configuration MMC snap-in to enable TS Session Broker integration. All the nodes in the terminal server farm need TS installed and should be configured with the same applications; otherwise, users do not get a consistent experience when using the farm.

In the Terminal Services Configuration MMC snap-in, double-click the Member of Farm in TS Session Broker Text in the TS Session Broker area of the server overview. The properties page of the server opens, with the TS Session Broker tab selected.

As shown in Figure 9-64, check the Join a Farm in TS Session Broker box. For the TS Session Broker server name or IP address, enter the details for the server that is hosting the TS Session Broker service. The farm name should be the DNS name that clients use to access the farm (for example, tsfarm.savilltech.net). Each server in the farm enters the same details for the farm name. This is how they know they are in the same farm. A terminal server cannot be a member of more than one farm.

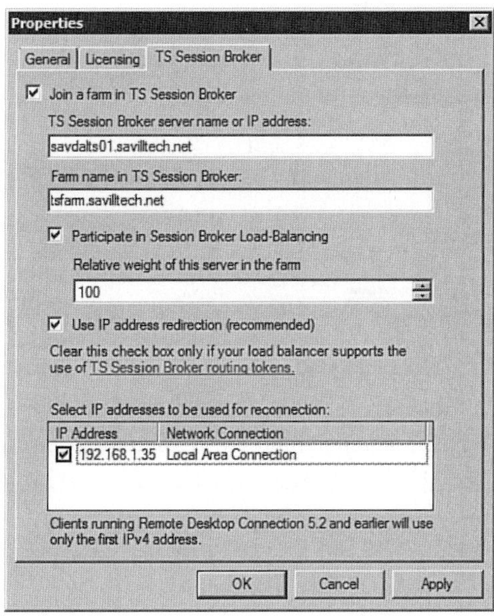

FIGURE 9-64 This terminal server is now a member of tsfarm.savilltech.net.

Check the Participate in Session Broker Load-Balancing option if TS Session Broker balancing will be used, and optionally, assign a weight. By default, each member has a weight of 100, but if you give a server a weight of 50, it receives only half the number of sessions as members with a weight of 100.

By default, IP address redirection is used, which is required if TS load balancing with DNS round-robin or network load balancing is used or if you use a hardware load balancer that does not use routing tokens. If you clear this check box, then token redirection is used, which sends the terminal server client a token that contains the IP address. On reconnection, the token is automatically used to reconnect to the correct box.

Finally, the IP address and connection to be used for the redirection is selected. Remember that the Session Broker server is not a gateway; it performs redirection. The client must be able to directly contact the terminal servers via IP. Repeat this configuration on each terminal server in the farm, remembering to use the same Session Broker server and farm name.

The final configuration is to create a DNS record containing the name of the farm with all the IP addresses of the terminal servers participating. To do this, you run the DNS MMC snap-in on a server that is responsible for the domain (or running the tools remotely) and create a new Host (A or AAAA) type record with the name of the farm for every terminal server. Figure 9-65 shows a test environment with two terminal servers that both have entries for tsfarm.

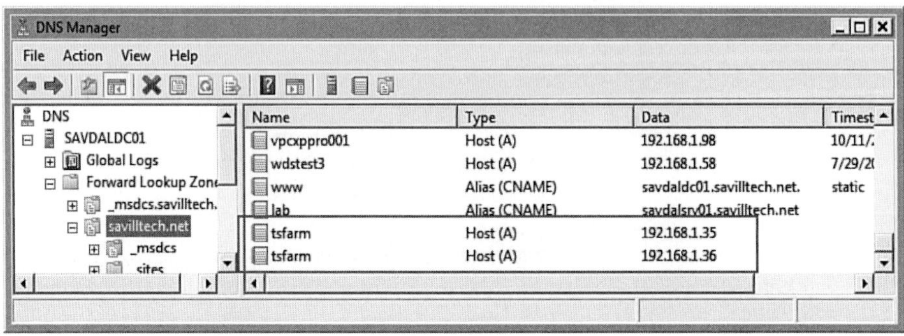

Figure 9-65 In this example, there are two host records for tsfarm in the savilltech.net zone.

If you run `nslookup` for tsfarm.savilltech.net, both records are returned. The following example shows `nslookup` being run three times to show how the order of the IP addresses rotates:

```
C:\Users\john>nslookup tsfarm.savilltech.net
Server:  savdaldc01.savilltech.net
Address:  192.168.1.10:53

Name:    tsfarm.savilltech.net
Addresses:  192.168.1.35, 192.168.1.36


C:\Users\john>nslookup tsfarm.savilltech.net
Server:  savdaldc01.savilltech.net
Address:  192.168.1.10:53
```

```
Name:    tsfarm.savilltech.net
Addresses:  192.168.1.36, 192.168.1.35


C:\Users\john>nslookup tsfarm.savilltech.net
Server:  savdaldc01.savilltech.net
Address:  192.168.1.10:53

Name:    tsfarm.savilltech.net
Addresses:  192.168.1.35, 192.168.1.36
```

Now you are ready to connect to the terminal server farm from a client. The client specifies the DNS name of the farm (for example, tsfarm.savilltech.net), which causes a DNS lookup to be performed. The DNS lookup returns all the IP addresses in round-robin order, which means the DNS server alternates which IP address is first in the return list to provide an initial kind of load balancing. The TS client then attempts communication, and if no response is returned within 20 seconds, the next IP address that was in the DNS return is tried.

When the client makes contact with a terminal server, the terminal server communicates with the TS Session Broker server to find out if the client already has a disconnected session. If there is an existing session, the client is redirected to the original terminal server. If there is no disconnected session, the user is redirected to the terminal server with the fewest number of sessions, considering the terminal servers' weights.

If you ever add additional nodes, remember to do the following:

1. Add the terminal server's computer account to the Session Directory Computers group.
2. Update the DNS record for the farm with the IP address of the new terminal server.

For large deployments, you can use one or more dedicated redirectors. These are terminal servers that are put in a special mode that stops them from accepting user connections. The clients contact them initially because the DNS records for the farm only point to the redirectors. The redirectors communicate with the TS Session Broker server and then redirect the client to one of the terminal servers, based on load. The usage of a dedicated redirector is dependent on the number of clients in the environment, which is illustrated in Figure 9-66.

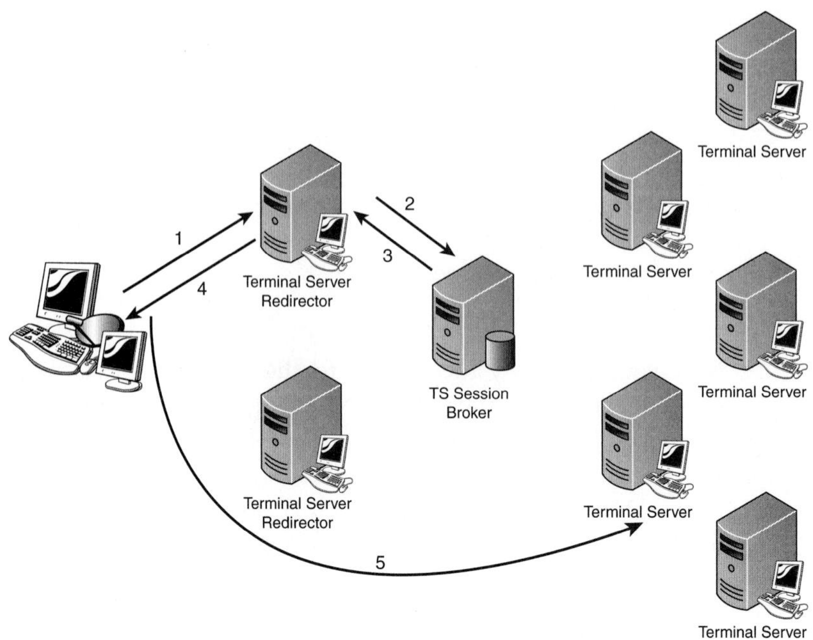

FIGURE 9-66 An example of using a dedicated redirector.

Draining a Server

The preceding section discusses putting redirectors into a special mode where new sessions are not accepted. This is called drain mode, and you can use it on any terminal server.

Drain mode is a useful function that allows existing sessions to stay connected while stopping new people from connecting unless they use the `/admin` switch. The goal is to reach no users. New users can no longer connect, and eventually the server will have no sessions running, so you can perform maintenance on it, reboot it, and then bring it back into service by turning off drain mode.

If you have ten servers in a farm that need to be updated, use drain mode to stop sessions to one of the servers, maintain it, and restart it. Repeat this on the next server until all ten are done. Using this method, the end user never knows servers have been taken out of action because their sessions are not affected.

The Terminal Services Configuration MMC snap-in is used to enable drain mode by changing the user logon mode to Allow reconnections, but to prevent new logons, as shown in Figure 9-67. This option stays in effect only until a server restart.

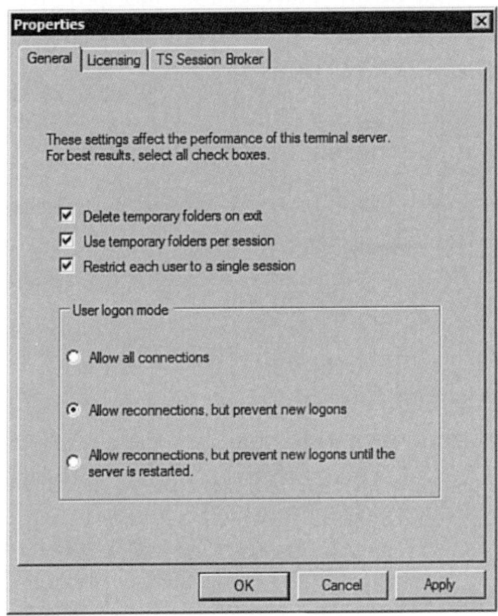

Figure 9-67 Placing a server in drain mode.

You can also place a server in drain mode from the command line by using the `chglogon.exe` command. The `/query` switch allows you to see the current mode of the server, as in the following example:

```
C:\Users\john>chglogon /query
New user logons are DISABLED, but reconnections to
existing sessions are ENABLED.
```

To put the server in drain mode, use the `/drain` switch. To place the server in drain mode until restart, use the `/drainuntilrestart` switch. To not allow any logons, even if a session exists, use `/disable`, and to enable all sessions, use `/enable`.

When a server is in drain mode, users who attempt to connect receive a message that remote logons are currently disabled. If a server is part of a farm, then user sessions are not sent to the terminal server in drain mode.

Management and Maintenance

So far, this chapter has explored the major features of TS, such as enhanced printing capabilities and encapsulation of RDP traffic in SSL. This section looks at the more day-to-day activities needed regarding TS, such as configuring user settings that are pertinent to TS and managing the actual terminal server services.

User Configuration

Users have some terminal server–specific attributes in their AD object in the form of the Environment, Sessions, Remote Control, and Terminal Services Profile tabs in Active Directory Users and Computers MMC snap-in.

The Environment Tab

Use the Environment tab to specify whether a particular program should be started when the user logs on via TS and whether client drives and printers should be connected at a TS logon.

The Sessions Tab

As shown in Figure 9-68, use the Sessions tab to configure how long a disconnected session can stay disconnected before it is ended. This means the session is permanently deleted, and any open processes in the session are closed.

In addition, with this tab, you can configure how long an active and idle session can stay connected; this is used to restrict the length of time someone can stay connected to a session. In active timeout, there is client activity; with idle, there is no client activity. When one of the session limits is reached, you can choose to disconnect the session, which leaves the session running on the server, or to end the session, which logs off the user. The Allow Reconnection setting controls whether a reconnection has to take place from the original client or can take place from any client.

It is most likely that you would not want to do the configuration on the user object; it would be painful to update many users this way. The best option is to configure items on the terminal server itself or via group policy.

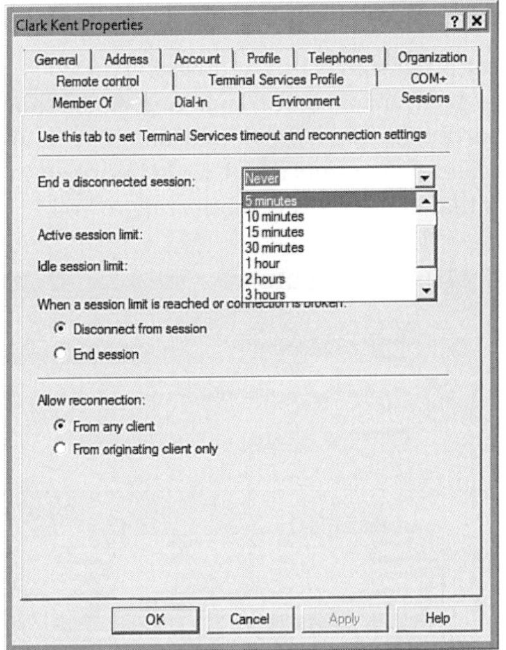

FIGURE 9-68 Session configuration for a user.

The Remote Control Tab

The Remote Control tab enables you to configure whether remote control of a user's session is allowed and, if it is, whether the user's permission is needed. You can also configure whether you can interact with a user's session or just view it.

The Terminal Services Profile Tab

It's likely that the profile a user uses on a terminal server is different from one she uses on a normal desktop. In addition, if you have many terminal servers a user would have a separate profile for each terminal server she used, so you can configure a terminal-server-only roaming profile location that is used on all terminal server sessions.

You can set up a home folder for TS that can be a path or a mapped driver letter. Finally, the option Deny This User Permissions to Log on to Terminal Server is available.

TS Management Tools

As with most other things in Windows Server 2008, the Server Manager is the place to go to manage Terminal Server. As shown in Figure 9-69, the Terminal Server role page provides a summary of all the event logs related to TS. You can select events to get more information or apply filters to view only events that are especially interesting to you.

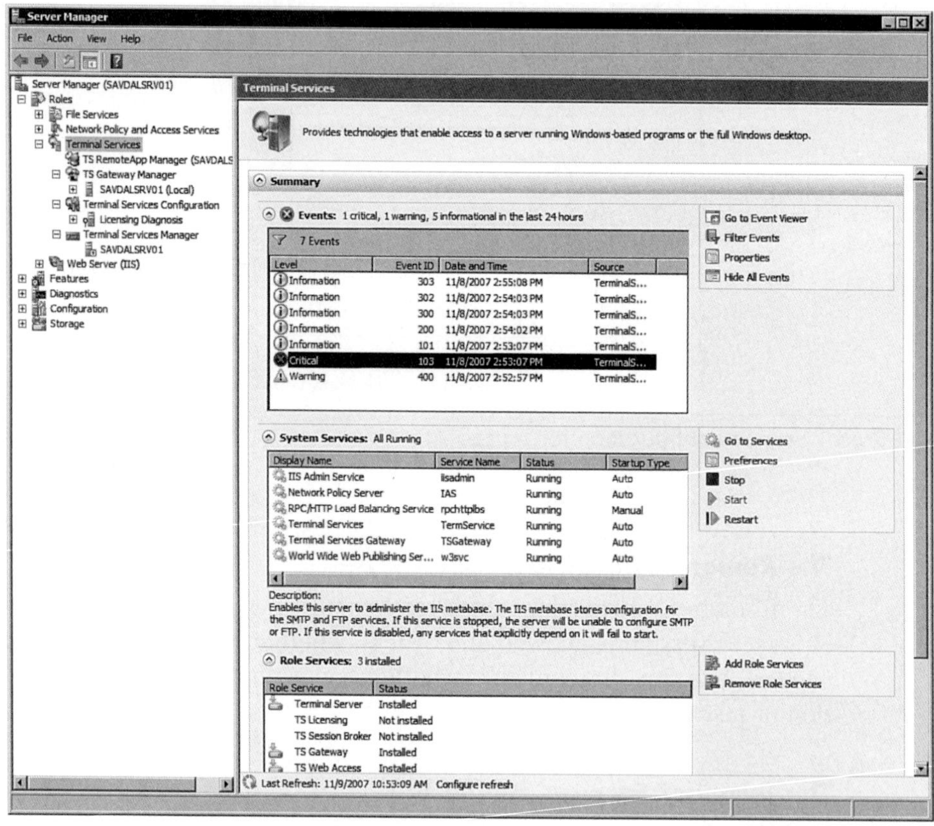

FIGURE 9-69 The summary section gives insight into the overall health of the Terminal Services.

One big plus with Windows Server 2008 is that the event logs give good information. For nearly all logs, the More Information option is displayed as part of the event log and provides a link to the Microsoft Web site, which gives more detailed and potentially more up-to-date information, with useful actions and additional information to help resolve any warning or error events.

Also the Summary section shows all services that TS needs in order to function. That is the key point here: It's not just TS that is shown but also any services that it uses. For example, the state of the World Wide Web Publishing Service is shown because IIS is used, and you control all these services from this one location.

The Role Services section shows the roles currently installed and enables you to add additional role services related to TS or remove roles that are no longer required.

At the bottom of the page is a Resources and Support section. This section contains a list of recommendations to ensure that the terminal server is functioning correctly and configured according to best practices.

Expand the Terminal Services node to see all the TS tools. You can select these tools to manage various aspects of TS. The one exception is the TS Licensing tool, which is not an MMC snap-in but a stand-alone application.

Now, let's look at the details of the configuration and maintenance of sessions.

TS Configuration

The Connections section in the Terminal Services Configuration MMC snap-in by default shows a single connection, RDP-Tcp, which for Windows Server 2008 RTM is of type Microsoft RDP 6.1. A user connects to the terminal server via this RDP-Tcp connection.

Right-click on this connection and select Properties to make changes to the attributes of this connection, some of which are the same as those for user objects such as Sessions, Environment, and Remote Control, with the option to override the settings configured for the user.

The other tabs are Client Settings, Network Adapter, General, and Logon on Settings. There is an additional Security tab. However, do not do configuration via this tab. Instead, set logon rights to the terminal server by adding users to the Remote Desktop Users group.

The Client Settings tab enables you to configure the client experience, which includes whether the color depth of the client session is limited and what types of redirection are not allowed. For example, you can block audio redirection, as shown in Figure 9-70. The configuration settings here override those set in the RDC, which means if a user chooses to redirect audio but it's blocked in the connection, no audio is redirected.

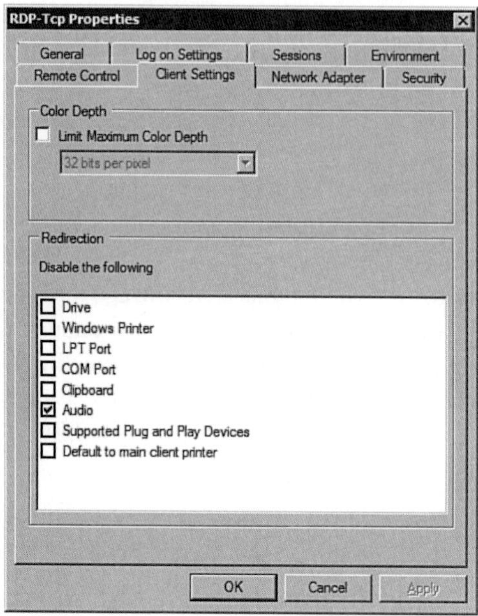

FIGURE 9-70 Controlling the redirection for client sessions.

Use the Network Adapter tab to configure the connection's binding to network adapter cards. By default, the connection binds, and therefore, accepts, connections on any network card that supports the protocol, such as TCP. However, you can instead select a specific NIC. In addition, you can set the maximum number of connections; by default an unlimited number of connections are allowed.

The Log on Settings tab enables you to allow a user account to be used for any session request. By default, the client-provided logon information is used. However, you can configure all inbound connections to use a specific account. This tab also includes Always Prompt for Password.

The final tab, the General tab, has the greatest number of interesting configurations. As shown in Figure 9-71, you can set a comment for the connection. However, the Security section is really interesting.

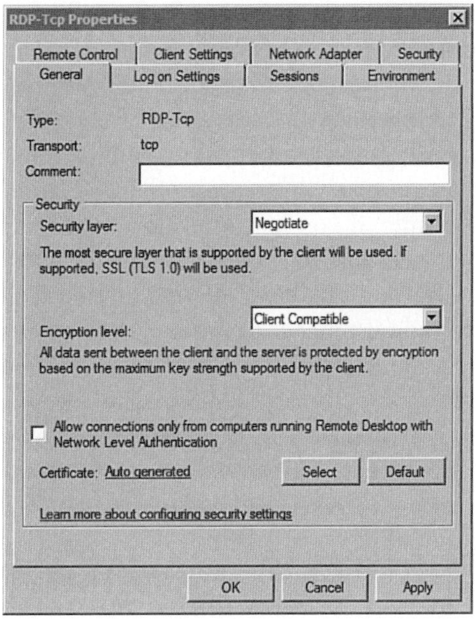

FIGURE 9-71 The General tab of a connection.

By default, Security Layer is set to Negotiate, which causes the client and server to agree on the highest form of security that's mutually supported, such as SSL, which uses Transport Layer Security (TLS) 1.0. TLS has two layers: a handshake protocol layer that verifies that the server is who it says it is and a record protocol layer for the encryption of the data sent and received.

You can change Security Layer to only allow TLS 1.0 to authenticate the server by changing to SSL (TLS 1.0). If you use SSL, ensure that a certificate is configured on the terminal server, and you can do this via the Select button at the bottom of the dialog. If the certificate is not issued by a public trusted CA or an enterprise CA, import the certificate onto the client because the client must have the CA that issued the certificate in its Trusted Root Certification Authorities store. RDP encryption can also be used to secure communications between the client and the server. However, this protocol does not support authenticating the server. To use RDP, select RDP Security Layer.

By default, Encryption Level is set to Client Compatible, which means it uses the highest encryption possible, based on the client's capabilities. Or it can be forced to Low (56-bit encryption), High (128-bit encryption), or Federal Information Processing Standard (FIPS). (For information on FIPS, see www.microsoft.com/technet/archive/security/topics/issues/fipseval.mspx?mfr=true.)

You have an option to only allow connections from RDC clients that support NLA or to turn this option off. You can create additional connections. For example, if you had multiple network adapters, you could map each network adapter to a different RDP-Tcp connection, each of which could have different attributes. Depending on which IP address was used to connect to the terminal server, the client experience might be different. For example, on one connection, the color depth may be limited to 16 bits per pixel, and on the other connection, there might be no limits. Different connections have to have unique attributes—for example, a different network adapter, connection type, or transport type—because there has to be a clear way for the terminal server to know which connection an incoming connection should be connected to. When you create a new connection, a wizard prompts for the details of the new connection and the adapter that are used.

Terminal Services Manager

You may want to manage your sessions, starting by seeing which ones are running and which processes are running on the server. On an idle server, you always see three connections, as shown in Figure 9-72. These sessions are the Services session, which is what used to be Session 0; a Console session, which has no specific session ID; and a Listener session, which is Session ID 65536 and listens for incoming session requests. Figure 9-72 shows an additional session: mine. Notice also the icons that are used and that for Services and Console, the icons show that they are part of the actual server.

Right-click a session to connect to the session, as discussed early in the chapter, or send a message. You can send a message to multiple sessions, which is useful if you want to notify the users of the terminal server that an action is about to be performed (for example, that the server will be shut down in an hour). The messages pop up in the center of the screen on the selected sessions, with an OK button to close the message.

You also have options to remotely control a session, and depending on the configuration of the user, this might prompt the user to accept the remote control session.

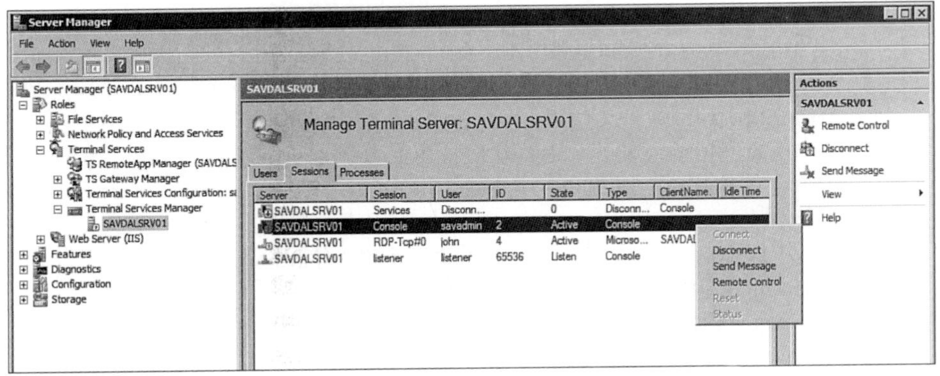

Figure 9-72 The TS Manager interface.

Details of status can be displayed via the Status context menu option, which shows information about the local client, including the client build number. The build number identifies the OS (e.g., 6000 is Windows Vista), client name, encryption used, color depth, resolution, and input/out status (such as bytes in and out). Because the inbound bytes are mouse moves and keypresses, this is normally quite small compared to the outgoing count, which is the screen updates.

If you reset a session, the session is closed and the user logged out. Disconnecting a session just disconnects the user from the session but leaves the session intact, enabling the user to reconnect in the future.

The Users tab presents the same basic options but from a user perspective, so you also have an option to log off. The Processes tab lists all the processes on the system, along with the user and session ID that owns the process. You can select a process and end it if required (for example, if it is using up a lot of resources on the server).

Command-Line Management

A large number of command-line tools are available for interfacing with TS. Some of them have been covered, such as `qwinsta`, `mstsc`, `tscon`, `tskill`, and `chglogon`. However, there are many others.

Sending a message to users was discussed in the previous section. You can do this from the command line, with the `msg` command. For example, to send a message to all users on a server, type the following:

```
msg * /server:savdalsrv01.savilltech.net Get off the server.
```

A number of other command-line tools are discussed in Microsoft help. However, aside from the ones mentioned so far, most of the configuration takes place via the graphical user interface or via Group Policy, which is discussed next. Given that TS is graphical by nature, the development of command-lines tools was not high on the developers' priority list. What was high on the list was WMI integration, which provides access from most scripting languages and, interestingly, PowerShell.

You can use WMI for nearly everything possible in TS, so if you are looking to automate actions and configuration (if Group Policy is not the answer), WMI might be the way to go. For example, you could write a WMI script to monitor and provide an alert about whether everyone has ended their sessions from a terminal server or whether your TS CAL license thresholds are met.

Group Policy Management of TS

Throughout this chapter, Group Policy has been discussed as an option for many of the configuration elements of the environment, and this section sums up that information. Windows Server 2008 help often talks about setting the configuration in the Terminal Services Configuration MMC snap-in and the relevant settings in Group Policy.

The configuration areas related to server configuration are in Computer Configuration, Administrative Templates, Windows Components, Terminal Services; the bulk of the configuration is under the subarea Terminal Server, as shown in Figure 9-73. There are areas for each major part of terminal server configuration. For example, you can configure the time that disconnected sessions are ended via the policy. If you have 100 terminal servers using Group Policy for the configuration, this makes a lot more sense than manually configuring each one. And if you decide to change a setting, you can change it once in Group Policy instead of on 100 machines. Placing TS in a specific OU makes it easy to link terminal server–specific GPOs.

In general, any configuration you can perform via the graphical interface is also possible via Group Policy. So consider the fact that if you need to make a configuration to more than one server, it is probably best to use Group Policy.

The other major configuration area is in User Configuration, Administrative Templates, Windows Components, Terminal Services. However, this has basic settings that relate mostly to the client experience, such as redirection. It also has settings related to user session timeouts.

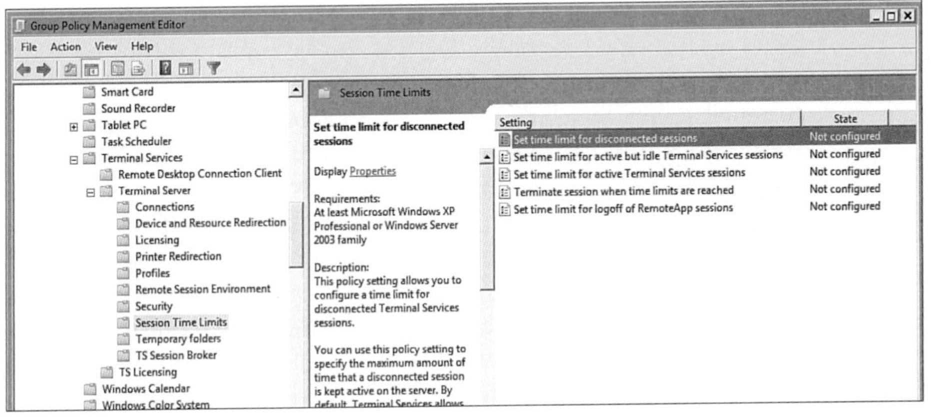

FIGURE 9-73 Using Group Policy is a great way to configure both servers and clients.

Summary

This is a big chapter, but it only scratches the surface of TS in Windows Server 2008. TS is a huge functionality area that is now fully integrated with the product such that sessions that are physically connected to the server have no more rights or privileges or capabilities than those that are connected remotely.

Originally, Microsoft did not plan to create a remote administrative tool pack for Windows Server 2008. The plan was that administrators would use Remote Desktop to connect to the servers. However, clients said they wanted this functionality, so Microsoft created a local tools management set. The preferred method is still to use Remote Desktop to a server.

Many of the features in terminal servers are useful in both large and small offices. For example, TS Gateway is a fantastic feature that I now use to remote to my lab environment. Doing this was difficult previously because many clients blocked the ports for RDP. Now I just connect over HTTPS.

One thing not discussed here, but discussed in Chapter 19, is Windows Server Resource Manager (WSRM). It's great having a shared server for all your sessions, but you are now at the mercy of the "greedy user" who may run applications that use up a lot of CPU or memory on the server, degrading the performance of others. WSRM can be used to throttle sessions to a particular amount of CPU usage. By default, when you install WSRM on a terminal server, you have the option to automatically set up a policy to either allocate CPU so it's divided equally on a per-user basis (Equal_Per_User) or on a per-session basis (Equal_Per_Session). The advantage of the Equal_Per_User basis is that if user John logs on five times and user Kevin logs on only once, user Kevin's one session has the same amount of CPU time as all of John's five sessions put together, meaning there is no resource advantage for John's connecting five times. If you chose the Equal_Per_Session option, each of John's sessions would have the same amount of CPU as Kevin's one, which would make John very happy. Windows Server 2008 has a practical TS solution now, and while Independent Software Vendor (ISV) solutions such as Citrix still provide some additional features, the in-box solution is now highly compelling and is only going to get better. Microsoft recently purchased Calisto, which is being integrated into Windows 7 and will provide high-speed media playback over RDP sessions.

When you consider Microsoft's virtualization roadmap, TS as the presentation virtualization piece makes great sense and will be key to virtualization going forward.

CHAPTER 10

Active Directory Domain Services Introduction

Active Directory (AD) is often used the same way the Security Accounts Manager (SAM) domains were used: to perform authentication for users and authorization to access resources and not much else. Many of the features that AD has as a full-fledged directory service are not used. In the next few chapters, you look at what AD enables and how to best implement and use it. But let's start at the beginning.

Workgroups Versus Domains

Windows for Workgroups was the first version of Windows that introduced a portioning scheme called a workgroup to the peer-to-peer type networking concept. This enabled the sharing of files and printers over the network. Sharing was not granular; you had two options: access could be read-only or full, with some limited password restrictions. Before the advent of the workgroup, users browsed every machine which was cumbersome and time-consuming. However, a workgroup enabled a machine to belong to a particular set of computers, and browsing could therefore be limited initially to just the machines in the same workgroup. The browsing scope could expand as required.

There were no controls on membership to a workgroup; you simply typed in the name of the workgroup you wanted to be a part of. There was no central account repository. Every member of the workgroup had its own account database. For users to share resources, every account had to be manually created and managed on each machine in the workgroup as shown in Figure 10-1. This was a major restriction of a workgroup: As it approached double-digit membership, managing the workgroup became too cumbersome. However, even in the latest operating systems, a workgroup is still an option for a computer's membership. Workgroups are unlikely to go away.

FIGURE 10-1 All computers in a workgroup have their own local accounts database, which requires manual updating of each account's database synchronized with the workgroup peer machines.

The Microsoft LAN Manager product offered the concept of a domain, which remained when LAN Manager was relabeled and packaged as Windows NT Advanced Server version 3.1. This domain concept has remained unchanged since then. However, its implementation changed radically from Windows NT 4.0 to Windows 2000 with the introduction of AD.

Think of a domain as a group of computers configured to use a centralized account database for authentication and authorization. That is different from a workgroup where every machine had its own accounts database, although it's important to remember that each computer always has its own local SAM database even if it's a member of a domain (unless the machine is a domain controller). It just doesn't use the SAM to authenticate. The server holding the domain database is as the primary domain controller (PDC).

If a computer is a member of a domain, when the user logs on, he authenticates against a domain controller. When resource access is attempted, domain credentials are used instead of entries in the local database (see Figure 10-2). Up to and including Windows NT 4.0, the SAM was used for the domain database, but was replaced with Windows 2000 and AD.

Within the SAM database, each user has one account that can be used to log on to any machine that is part of that domain. There is no need to maintain multiple accounts on each machine. Therefore, this approach implements a centralized security model. Because all machines share a centralized account database, a user can log on to any machine that is a member of the domain (assuming that the user has permission), and any machine in the domain can easily grant any user from the domain access to resources thanks to the single, shared security database.

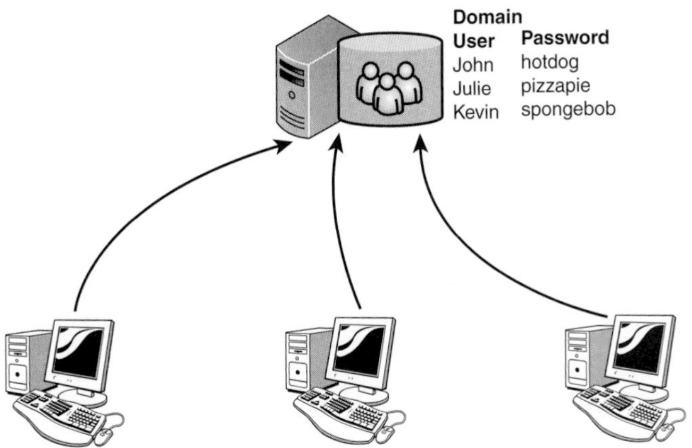

FIGURE 10-2 In a domain environment, the user accounts are defined and maintained in the domain database, removing the management redundancy associated with maintaining every account on each machine in the workgroup.

The idea of a centralized security database sounds great, but it also introduces a single point of failure. Microsoft reduced this risk by creating the role of backup domain controller (BDC), one or more machines that hold a read-only copy of the database, which replicates from the PDC. If the PDC becomes unavailable, the read-only copy of the database can be promoted to a writeable copy by making the hosting BDC the new PDC. You can have only one PDC in a domain, so if the original PDC comes back online, it sees that a PDC already exists and stops its netlogon service, which is responsible for service logon and authentication requests. This single writeable copy of the database is known as a single master model. The Local Security Authority (LSA) database, which contains the secrets used for domain controller computer account passwords, account policy settings, and trust relationships, is also replicated. However, the LSA is replicated with the SAM and does not require further consideration.

The BDCs provide fault tolerance and load balancing: Clients can authenticate against a BDC because no changes need to be made to the database to authenticate, although changes are always sent to the PDC for action and commitment to the security database. It is common to place at least one BDC in the same location as the PDC, and additional BDCs at each physical location to provide localized authentication services and to stop remote clients from having to send all authentication requests over potentially slow WAN links (see Figure 10-3).

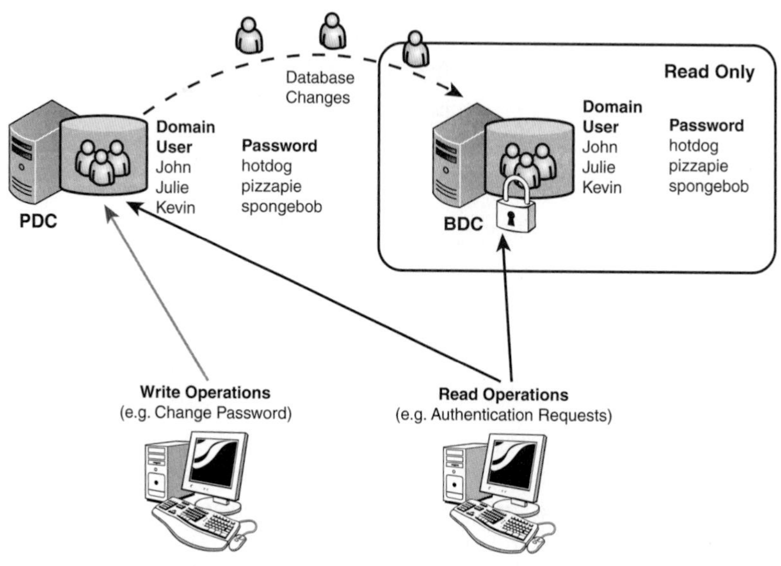

Figure 10-3 The BDC pulls all changes from the PDC. Clients can authenticate against a PDC or BDC but have to direct all write changes to the PDC, which is the only domain controller holding a writeable copy of the database.

The frequency of change replication had limited configuration possibilities, however. By default the PDC checked for changes every 5 minutes and would notify up to ten BDCs at a time. The notified BDCs would then wait a random amount of time before contacting the PDC and asking for replication. The random wait was to stop all ten BDCs from pulling the changes at the same time, thus overloading the PDC and potentially flooding the network with replication traffic.

There are three types of replication between the PDC and the BDC, and the replication is at an object level for all types. This means the entire object is replicated, not just the attribute that changed, resulting in greater network usage.

- **Full**. Used when a new BDC is added or when the number of changes since the last replication is greater than the size of the PDC's change log file, %systemroot%\Netlogon.chg. By default this file is configured to a maximum size of 65,536 bytes, which is normally 2,000 changes, although this can be adjusted via a Registry change. Once the file reaches the maximum size, it starts overwriting the oldest entry.

- **Partial**. Used to replicate changes since the last replication.
- **Urgent**. Used to replicate when an account is locked out, a modification has been made to the account lockout or domain password policy, a machine account password changes, or a modification has been made to an LSA secret.

Replication could be forced using the various available tools. For example, there was the Server Manager application, net accounts /sync, and nltest, which was a resource kit utility.

Exclusive Membership

The domain is a corporate concept, and not many home users are expected to have the infrastructure to support a domain. So, although all versions of Windows can be members of a workgroup, to become a member of a domain requires specific versions of Windows. Before AD, a domain's administrator had to allow a computer to be added to the domain. Table 10-1 shows the various versions of the Windows operating system and their domain compatibility. For computers that cannot be a member of a domain, one way to ease the integration is to set the computer's workgroup to the same name as the domain and create a local user with the same name as the domain account and with the same password. This enables easier resource access.

Table 10-1 Versions of the Windows Operating System and Their Domain Compatibility

Operating System	Domain Compatible
Windows 95	No
Windows 98/98se	No
Windows Me	No
Windows NT 4 Workstation	Yes
Windows NT 4 Server	Yes

(continues)

Table 10-1 Versions of the Windows Operating System and Their Domain Compatibility *(continued)*

Operating System	Domain Compatible
Windows 2000 Professional	Yes
Windows 2000 Server (all versions)	Yes
Windows XP Home Edition	No
Windows XP Professional	Yes
Windows 2003 Server (all versions)	Yes
Windows Vista Starter, Home Basic and Home Premium	No
Windows Vista Business, Enterprise, and Ultimate Edition	Yes
Windows Server 2008 (all versions)	Yes

Domain names prior to AD (and even AD maintains an old style, legacy-compatible name) were in Network Basic Input/Output System (NetBIOS) format, which has a maximum length of 16 characters although only the first 15 characters are usable. NetBIOS separates the details of the network from an application by enabling the application to specify a destination for a request. NetBIOS is network independent and although it originally ran over NetBEUI, it was modified to run over Transmission Control Protocol/Internet Protocol (TCP/IP) also.

As mentioned previously, although NetBIOS names can be up to 16 characters, the maximum length for a domain name is actually 15 characters because the sixteenth character specifies the type of resource. For example, <1C> specifies the resource is a domain controller. See a full list of the NetBIOS suffixes in Knowledge Base article Q163409 at http://support.microsoft.com. Limit domain names to using characters A–Z, 1–9, and the hyphen character. Other legal characters are ! @ # $ % ^ & ( ) - _ ' { } . ~ although these characters can cause complications in other areas.

When a client needed to locate a domain controller, it had the NetBIOS name of the domain and knew its NetBIOS type was 1C. These two bits of information could be used in three ways to locate a domain controller depending on the client configuration and services installed on the network (e.g., WINS Request, Broadcast, or the LMHOSTS file). The actual order in which WINS request or broadcast occurs depends on the configuration node type of the client, as covered in Chapter 7, "Advanced Networking Services."

The Windows NT 4.0 model had some significant problems that limited its capability to compete against other directory services:

- **40MB maximum practical database size**. With a normal account taking up around 1KB and a computer account around .5KB, and adding additional objects such as groups, a domain was realistically limited to 25,000 users per domain.
- **Replication limitations**. Little control was available over the replication of the database between the PDC and the BDCs. Some Registry modifications could be made to change the period between pulses (how often BDCs are notified of changes), the number of BDCs notified at a time, and other settings, but these were generic and domain controllers that connected over slow WAN links could run into numerous issues.
- **No way to delegate control**. Two types of users existed from a domain administration perspective: domain administrators who could do everything and everyone else who could do nothing, except for limited changes to their own account such as changing passwords. A classic limitation was that of help desk staff that needed to reset user passwords; they had to become domain administrators to perform this task, giving them a lot of power and exposing the domain to unnecessary risk.
- **No concept of physical location**. Domain controllers and clients have no idea of where they physically reside, so clients could authenticate against any domain controller (although a workaround is possible by the use of the LMHOSTS file and the #PRE #DOM qualifiers).
- **No expandability**. The SAM contained set fields, username, full name, and not much else. There was no way to add extra information. If services had to store additional information, they had to maintain their own separate database. For example, Exchange 5.5 maintained a separate directory service for mail information.

These factors and others drove organizations to create multiple domains. For example, if you have an office in London and one in Dallas, you create a domain in London for the London users and computers and one in Dallas for the Dallas users and computers. Although one domain might have been possible, the large distance between the locations would have made data replication slow due to poor connectivity speeds.

You are now back to some of the problems with a workgroup because each domain has its own account database, and you now have multiple account databases to share resources between users in separate domains. You would need multiple accounts for a user, one in each domain, right? Thankfully, no, you just need to trust.

Trusts

The big advantage of a domain was its shared account database, making it easy to grant access to resources among all members of a domain. However, if you have multiple domains, there is no way to grant access to users in other domains; they do not show as targets for resource permissions by default. A trust is a mechanism that allows objects in one domain to be granted access to resources in another domain. The domain that held the resources trusted the domain that held the accounts requiring access to the resources. The trusting domain (where the resources existed) was effectively trusting that the domain with the user accounts (the trusted domain) was properly authorizing users and securing their credentials. This one-way trust is known as a unidirectional trust (see Figure 10-4). However, if resources and people existed in both domains needing access to each other's resources, a two-way or bidirectional trust (two separate unidirectional trusts) was used. The creation of a trust was secured by each domain's use of a single password that had to be entered to enable that domain's end of the trust.

Once a trust is established, another benefit is any user that resides in a domain that is trusted by another domain could sit down at a workstation belonging to the trusting domain and log on to his local domain. At the main logon screen, the domain list includes the domain the workstation is a member of and all domains its local domain trusts for pre-Vista operating systems; Windows Vista does not have this domain drop-down list. If a user from the trusted domain sits down at a workstation belonging to the trusting domain, the drop-down domain list would show both the machine's local domain and the trusted domain.

It is important to note that trust relationships are not transitive, which means only the two domains that are part of the trust can share resources. If you have three domains, A, B, and C, and domain A trusts domain B and domain B trusts domain C, there is no relationship between A and C. Domain A does not implicitly trust domain C and users in domain C would not be able to be granted access to resources in domain A (see Figure 10-5).

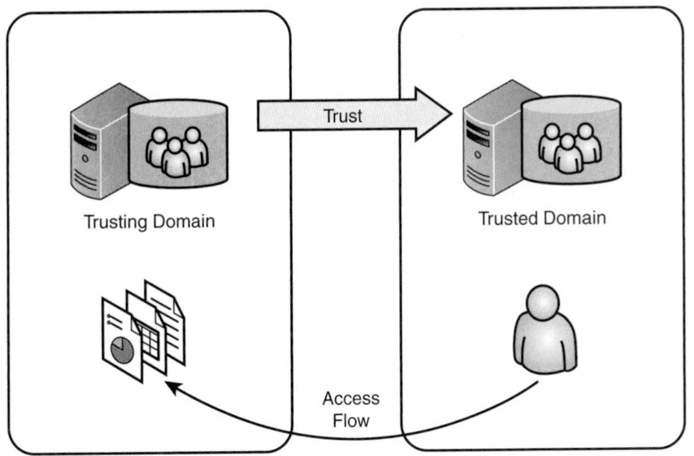

Figure 10-4 The trusting domain that contains the resources the users in the trusted domain want to access trusts the trusted domain, allowing users in the trusted domain to be granted access to resources in the trusting domain.

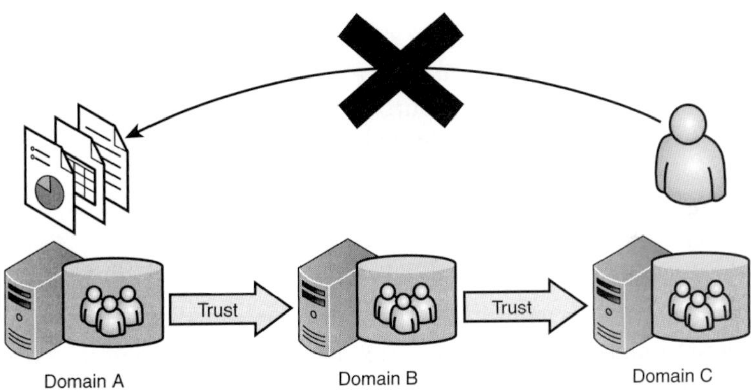

Figure 10-5 Trusts have to be explicitly defined between domains, so for users in domain C to access resources in domain A, a separate trust would have to be created.

Trust relationships opened up a number of models in the NT 3 and 4 days that you might have heard of. The single-domain model had only a single domain; the single-master domain model had one domain holding the account and other domains that trusted the account domain holding the resources; the multimaster master model had multiple account domains trusted by multiple resource domains; and the complete trust model where every domain trusts every domain (which is messy).

The information in these first three sections relates to the domain model up to Windows NT 4.0. However, with Windows 2000, Microsoft enabled its other services (such as messaging) to integrate with the OS more cleanly. Windows 2000 also offered a single sign-on environment where users just needed one set of credentials. A true directory service was finally available on the Windows platform.

Active Directory

Even though the SAM-based domains of NT 4.0 had a single centralized database, the limitations surrounding the domain implementation often governed the design of the infrastructure as opposed to designing the infrastructure to meet the goals of the business.

Microsoft recognized that to compete with other network operating systems, it had to offer a real directory service—something with the following characteristics:

- Could be accessed via standard methods such as LDAP
- Could store information about all aspects of a business including applications and resources, not just users
- Could be modified to include custom attributes
- Would be fully searchable
- Would enable granular delegation of duties
- Would be scalable

One option would have been to upgrade the current domain implementation, but in truth it was not a good foundation and its upgrade probably would have been more work than starting from scratch. Exchange had its own directory service for storing mailbox and distribution list information that supported some industry standards for its interface, so Microsoft took this directory service as a starting point.

The Directory Service Implementation

A directory service has to store the data and provide an interface to access the data, the same as a telephone directory service; it has a big database of all the numbers and then provides a phone number or Internet page you can use to access the data. A directory service is comprised of three things:

- A method to store and arrange the data
- A method to locate the data
- A method to access the data

The concept of a directory service was not new, so Microsoft could implement many industry standards that had been tried and tested in other implementations. Adhering to industry standards also provided a benefit to the customer who might already have directory service tools, enabling a far simpler migration to AD.

For AD's storage model, the common X.500 standard was chosen as a base. X.500 provides a hierarchical structure (see Figure 10-6) named the directory information tree (DIT) that contains a number of objects, and each object comprises one or more attributes (the actual objects and applicable attributes are described in the schema). One important component of X.500 is the organizational unit (OU), which can contain other objects and even other OUs; this component is crucial in creating a directory service that can mimic your business model.

Each object in the DIT has two names. One is an unambiguous name that defines the name and exact location of the object, the distinguished name (DN). The other name is the relative distinguished name (RDN) that contains only the name of the object relative to its position in the tree.

An example of a distinguished name is

```
CN=John Savill, OU=Dallas, DC=savilltech, DC=net
```

This shows an object of name John Savill, in an OU called Dallas, in a domain called savilltech.net. Its RDN is John Savill.

The actual data for the domain is stored in a file called NTDS.DIT, which is stored in the %systemroot%\NTDS folder by default, and this file is based on the Microsoft Extensible Storage Engine (ESE), which is what Exchange uses. This new implementation throws away the old 40MB limit, and a single domain can now hold millions of objects. In fact, testing has shown that AD can hold nearly as many as the 2^31 theoretical maximum number of objects, which would be 2,147,483,648 objects. Just below this number you receive an error indicating that you have run out of distinguished name tags (DNTs), which are the row numbers for each object within the database. But I doubt you'll ever get close to this!

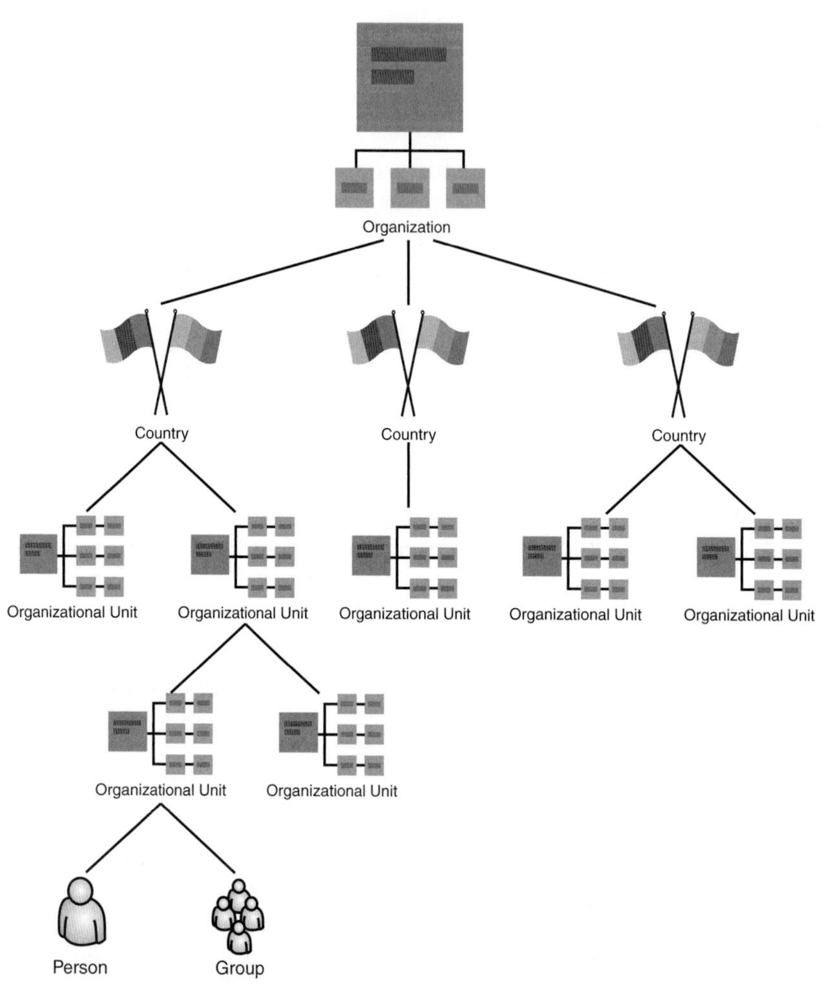

FIGURE 10-6 The X.500 model enables a customizable structure for the organization of objects that goes beyond just the placement of objects. These organization components can be used as the targets for delegation of administration and policy application.

The next issue is how to access the data in the directory. X.500 has its own directory access protocol (DAP). However, it is large and cumbersome to implement. For this reason, another standard access protocol was created, the Lightweight Directory Access Protocol (LDAP), which contains a subset of the full X.500 protocol.

There have been a number of versions of LDAP. However, AD implements version 3 of the LDAP although it also provides backward compatibility for version 2. The use of an industry standard for the access mechanism enables access to the information from practically any network-enabled environment. Another advantage is that unlike X.500 (which is based on the OSI model), LDAP has full support for TCP/IP, which is essential for any network component running in a modern infrastructure. Microsoft also implemented some enhancements to LDAP 3 that are also Internet standards and are add-ons for LDAP 3. Those add-ons include the following:

- Dynamic store entries, which enable entries in the directory to have Time to Live (TTL) values so that they can be automatically deleted (RFC 2589).
- Transport Layer Security (TLS) connection support over LDAP (RFC 2830).
- Digest Authentication (RFC 2829), which enables connection to AD to be authenticated using the DIGEST-MD5 Simple Authentication and Security Layer (SASL) authentication mechanism.
- Virtual list views (VLV) that enable clients to pull down a subset or window of results when the total result set is too large for the client to handle.
- Support for the inetOrgPerson class (RFC 2798 which is available at http://www.ietf.org/rfc.html). Passwords can also be set on inetOrgPerson objects under Windows 2003 implementations.
- Use of domains in LDAP distinguished names (RFC 2247).
- Server-side sorting of search results (RFC 2891).
- Concurrent LDAP binds that enable an application to bind to LDAP multiple times via one connection.

LDAP operates over two main ports, port 389 for standard LDAP and port 636 for secure LDAP, and because AD now provides an LDAP server, it operates over both ports. Early on, this caused trouble if you tried to run Exchange 5.5 on an AD domain controller because AD reserved the 389 port and Exchange tried it use to for its own native LDAP service. AD always won!

There are numerous interfaces to LDAP, including an application programming interface (API) for the C programming language. Because LDAP is a standard, communication between directory services is possible: between a NetWare Directory Service and an AD implementation, for example. Microsoft also offers its Active Directory Services Interface (ADSI), which offers a simple interface to aid in communication with AD.

The final aspect is how to locate the servers involved in AD. Windows NT 4.0 was based on NetBIOS names, so it relied on the WINS service, local subnet broadcasts, or LMHOSTS entries. However, NetBIOS is a legacy naming scheme and is flat in structure, which does not fit well into the hierarchical namespace that is crucial to a directory service.

AD uses domain name system (DNS) as the location mechanism for clients to find domain controllers on the network through service (SRV) and address (A) resource records. If you need a refresher on how DNS functions, refer to Chapter 7. Two important refresher points are necessary at this point because the Microsoft DNS implementation supports two crucial standards:

- **RFC 2782**. Details the service type record, which is essential for AD to function in an environment because it enables domain controllers to advertise the services they offer and the ports they operate over. For example, the LDAP service interfaces with the directory service or Kerberos for authentication.
- **RFC 2136**. Details dynamic update, which is the process by which DNS clients can register their own records and, in the case of AD, enables domain controllers to register all the records (including service records) required for clients to locate the services offered on the network.

The service record is essential for AD operation, whereas the dynamic update is just extremely useful. Although it might be possible to manually create all the records each domain controller registers and then manually update them if any changes occur to a domain controller (changing site scope, global catalog [GC] status, and so on), in reality it would be a horrendous task. Dynamic DNS is necessary unless you have a lot of free time.

After you install an AD domain, you see a large number of service records added to DNS that provide the clients on the network a way to find the domain controllers by, for example, searching for the LDAP service (the actual record is of the form `_ldap._tcp.<domain name>`).

The lines in the following example show the DNS records added when creating a domain (these values are stored in the netlogon.dns file created when a domain controller is promoted and stored in the %systemroot%\system32\config file).

```
adds.test. 600 IN A 192.168.1.150
_ldap._tcp.adds.test. 600 IN SRV 0 100 389 dalsrvdc01.adds.test.
_ldap._tcp.Default-First-Site-Name._sites.adds.test. 600 IN SRV 0 100
389 dalsrvdc01.adds.test.
_ldap._tcp.pdc._msdcs.adds.test. 600 IN SRV 0 100 389
dalsrvdc01.adds.test.
_ldap._tcp.gc._msdcs.adds.test. 600 IN SRV 0 100 3268
dalsrvdc01.adds.test.
_ldap._tcp.Default-First-Site-Name._sites.gc._msdcs.adds.test. 600 IN
SRV 0 100 3268 dalsrvdc01.adds.test.
_ldap._tcp.2d617542-87a2-4440-a892-
9625c528ba3c.domains._msdcs.adds.test. 600 IN SRV 0 100 389 dal-
srvdc01.adds.test.
gc._msdcs.adds.test. 600 IN A 192.168.1.150
30db4a8a-aa35-4f1e-a59c-c158dfbf74f6._msdcs.adds.test. 600 IN CNAME
dalsrvdc01.adds.test.
_ldap._tcp.dc._msdcs.adds.test. 600 IN SRV 0 100 389
dalsrvdc01.adds.test.
_ldap._tcp.Default-First-Site-Name._sites.dc._msdcs.adds.test. 600 IN
SRV 0 100 389 dalsrvdc01.adds.test.
_gc._tcp.adds.test. 600 IN SRV 0 100 3268 dalsrvdc01.adds.test.
_gc._tcp.Default-First-Site-Name._sites.adds.test. 600 IN SRV 0 100
3268 dalsrvdc01.adds.test.
```

Schema

AD is a service designed to hold information about all parts of your organization, so it needs to have an extensible structure because it is impossible to create in advance all possible fields that might be needed by any application or service in the future. The AD schema enables this extensible structure by providing a definition of the objects (or classes) available and the attributes the objects have. These attributes are defined separately from the objects and are then linked to the object definitions, enabling objects to be defined using any attribute described in the schema. Because the schema is extensible, you can add new attributes and classes during the lifetime of AD, enabling support for data not originally implemented with a newly installed AD instance. A warning is in order though; updating the schema is not to be taken lightly. While some services such as Exchange and System Center Configuration Manager update the schema with new attributes and classes, thoroughly plan out and test any change to the schema. During the early days of AD, a Microsoft program manager gave this warning:

> If you find you need to update the schema, look again for another method; if you find you still need to update the schema, look one more time. If you are still sure you need to update the schema, make sure you get buy-in from the highest levels because there is no going back.

To be fair, things are not as severe now as they were with the original AD implementation. Better facilities exist now to turn off changes you made to the schema. However, you have to take care when making changes.

Only one domain controller in your entire organization (assuming that you have one forest) can modify the schema, and the user trying to modify the schema needs to have certain permissions. Also, be sure to restrict normal administrators' ability to change the schema. Only high level administrators should have schema modification abilities.

Now that you have seen some of AD functionality, let's look at its major building blocks.

Domains

With the SAM model, a domain was a boundary of replication, and this remains true with an AD domain. Each domain has a unique naming context in which various objects exist such as users, computers, and groups that replicate only to domain controllers that are part of the same domain. A major change in the domain controller role with AD moves away from the Windows NT 4.0–style single-master model, where only one domain controller held a writeable copy of the database. With AD, every domain controller holds a writeable copy of the database, and multimaster replication keeps all the domain controllers synchronized. This new replication is crucial to the success of AD and is why a well designed infrastructure is vital to AD functioning correctly.

The primary name for a domain with AD is now a DNS name, which enables a hierarchical namespace. As you will see in the rest of this chapter, this is important to the more advanced directory service concepts. Valid names for an AD domain are, therefore, names such as savilltech.net, acme.com, ads.savilltech.com—any valid DNS domain name—which is where some confusion can creep in. In DNS, the discrete namespaces where records reside are known as a DNS domain or zone; with AD a database replication boundary is also known as a domain. Because domains rely on DNS as the locator service for every AD domain, an equivalent DNS zone must exist that supports the service type record and, ideally, dynamic updates. However, if a DNS zone that correlates to an AD domain name does not already exist, the domain creation process installs and configures DNS for you.

In addition to the DNS name for each AD domain, a legacy NetBIOS name is also maintained. If you upgrade from Windows NT 4, the NetBIOS name carries over from the NT 4.0 domain. However, for a clean, pristine AD, the NetBIOS name, by default, will be the first 15 characters of the leftmost component of the DNS name (up to the first period). For example, if your AD DNS name is savilltech.net, by default your NetBIOS name is savilltech, although this can be changed.

Creating a Domain

During the installation of Windows NT 4 Server, you were asked whether the server would be a PDC, BDC, or standalone server. When you install Windows 2008 Server (or even Windows 2000/2003), you are no longer asked this question.

This was always a major problem with NT 4 servers. Having to define the server's role at installation time was a pain, and this has now been resolved. Rather than defining a server's roles during installation, you run a wizard after the operating system installation is complete to change the server to a domain controller or to change a domain controller to a normal server.

This wizard is known as Active Directory Domain Services (ADDS) Installation Wizard, and it is implemented by the dcpromo.exe image (Domain Controller Promotion). It has a step-by-step approach to guide the whole process. To initiate the ADDS Installation Wizard, you can run the dcpromo.exe application from the Run dialog, from the Server

Manager MMC snap-in, or from the Initial Configuration Tasks interface you can select Add Roles and select ADDS (see Figure 10-7).

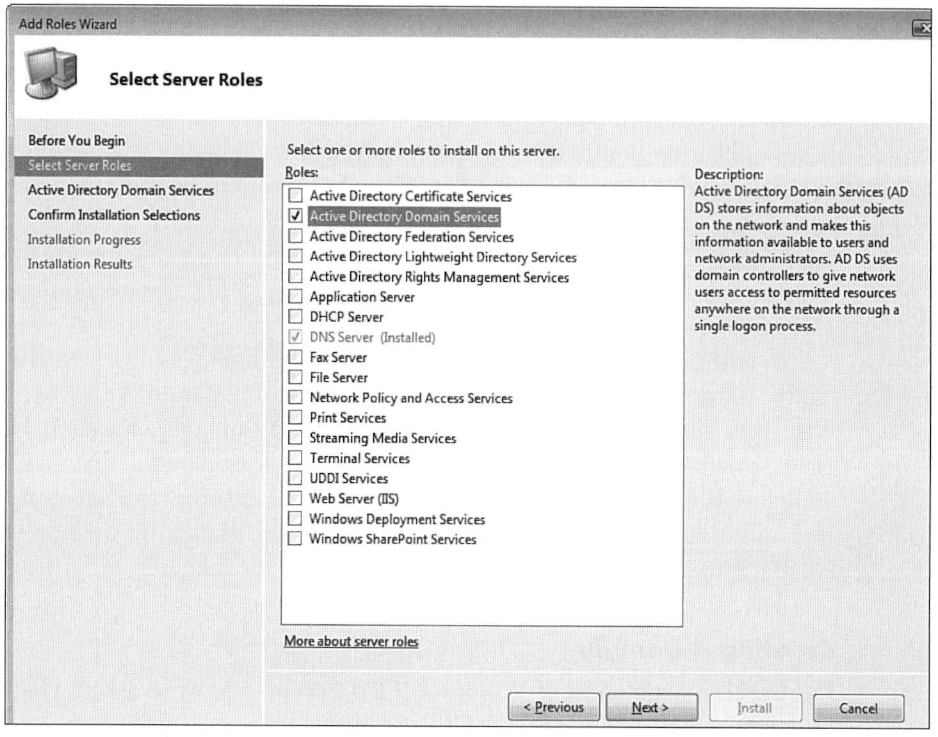

FIGURE 10-7 Installing the ADDS role.

The overview providing information about the domain process displays. Click Next, which displays a final information screen about the actions to initiate. After you click the Install button, the DCPROMO process starts. The screen has links to information on domain controllers, a checklist for deploying domain controllers, and information on managing the directory service (see Figure 10-8).

The first step in starting the installation process is to install the binaries needed for ADDS (if you cancel the installation wizard, the binaries will be uninstalled). At this stage, the domain creation process begins if you directly execute DCPROMO (see Figure 10-9).

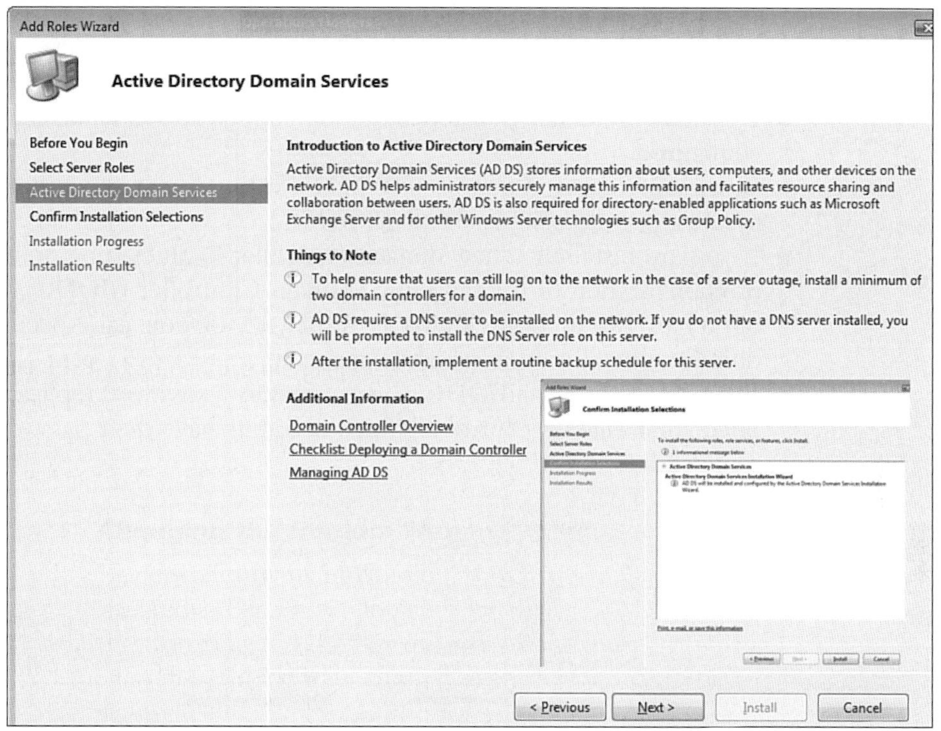

FIGURE 10-8 Introduction screen for the ADDS role.

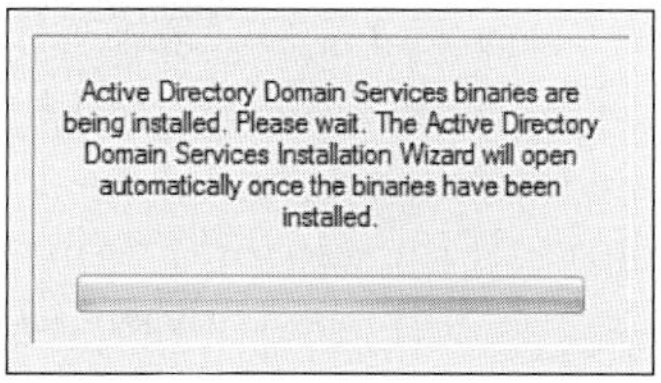

Active Directory Domain Services binaries are being installed. Please wait. The Active Directory Domain Services Installation Wizard will open automatically once the binaries have been installed.

FIGURE 10-9 Installing ADDS binaries.

When the domain controller binaries are installed, the ADDS Installation Wizard starts, and the first option is whether the domain creation is in advanced mode. You enable advanced mode by checking the Use Advanced Mode Installation box (see Figure 10-10). This is the same as passing `/adv` to the `dcpromo` command if started via command line. You are creating your first domain controller with basic options, so you don't require advanced mode. However, if advanced mode is selected, additional installation options are available, including the following:

- If you are creating a new forest, the domain NetBIOS name can be configured.
- If you are creating a new domain in an existing forest, the option to create a new domain tree is displayed.
- If you are installing a new domain controller in an existing domain or configuration of a Read Only Domain Controller (RODC), the option to Install from Media is displayed, or you can specify a domain controller from which to replicate.
- If you are creating an RODC, you can specify a password replication policy that enables control of which accounts have their passwords replicated to the RODC.

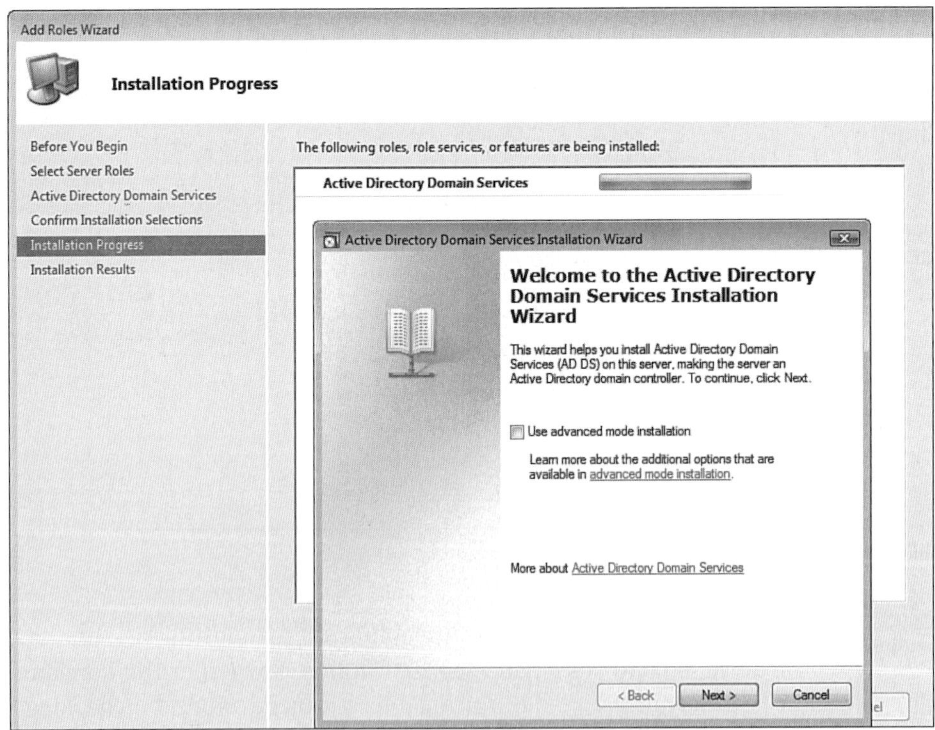

FIGURE 10-10 The promotion wizard main dialog.

The type of deployment must be selected. For the first domain in the organization, select Create a New Domain in a New Forest (see Figure 10-11). However, if this is not the first domain controller in the organization, select Existing Forest, which opens options to add a domain controller to an existing domain or create a new domain in the existing forest. You don't have the option to create a new tree; that option is exposed only during an advanced ADDS installation process.

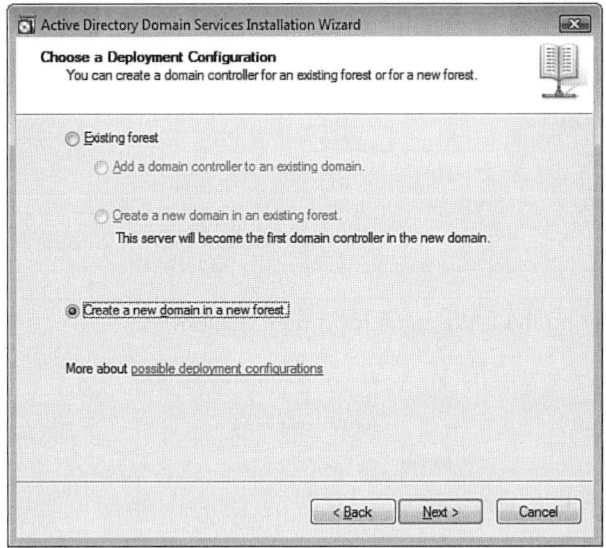

FIGURE 10-11 Creating a new domain.

After you click Next, the name of the domain (the DNS name) is entered, as shown in Figure 10-12. When the domain name is entered, the name is checked on the network to ensure that it does not already exist and is eligible for creation (see Figure 10-13).

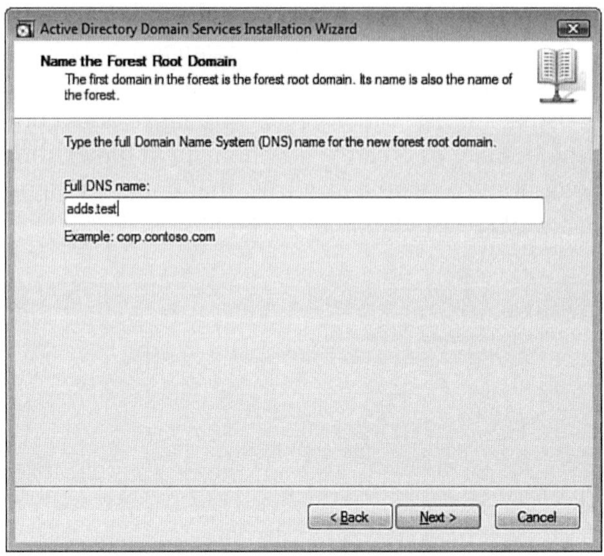

FIGURE 10-12 Entering the DNS name for a new domain.

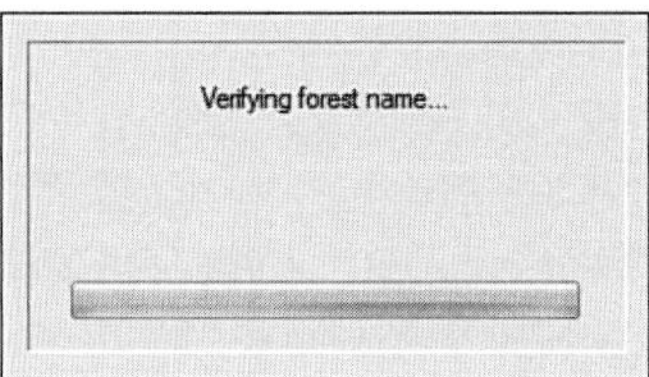

FIGURE 10-13 Verification is performed for the specified name.

The forest level mode can be selected if this is a new domain in a new forest (see Figure 10-14). The forest modes are described at the end of this chapter.

Depending on the forest level, the domain level is selected (see Figure 10-15). The domain modes are discussed at the end of this chapter.

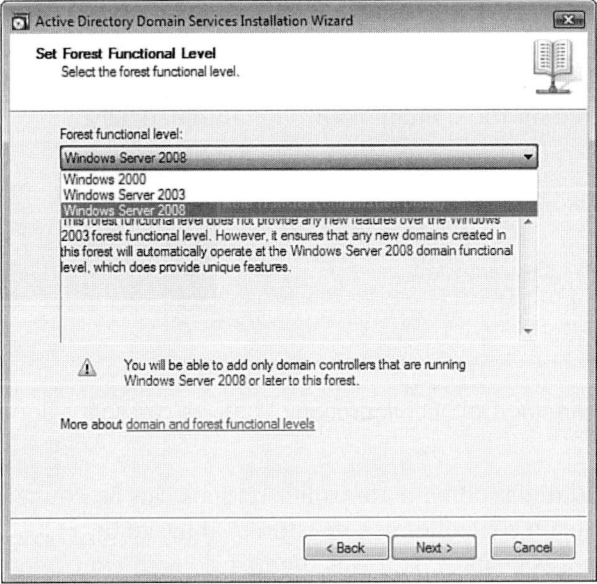

FIGURE 10-14 Setting the forest functional level.

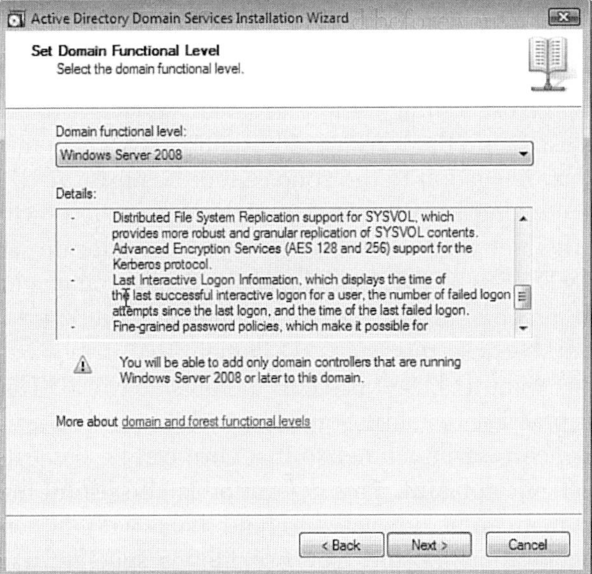

FIGURE 10-15 Setting the domain functional level.

A check on the DNS configuration is performed based on the name of the domain entered (see Figure 10-16). This checks whether a DNS zone exists for the domain name specified, and if it does not exist, by default it is created on the domain controller automatically.

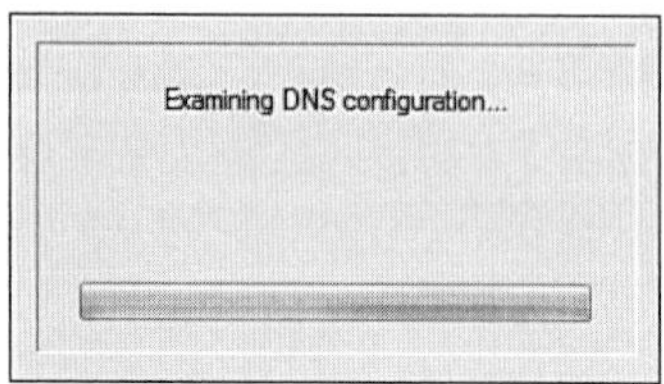

FIGURE 10-16 Confirming DNS configuration.

Additional domain controller options can be configured. If this is the first domain controller in a new forest, it has to be a GC, which is explained later in this chapter. If this is the first domain controller in a new domain, it cannot be an RODC (see Figure 10-17). The domain controller can also be specified to host the DNS service (which is mandatory if DNS services were not found for the domain name specified and are installed locally). You might also receive a warning if the machine has any dynamically assigned Internet Protocol (IP) addresses (IPv4 or IPv6). The best practice is to have static IP addresses for IPv6 and not just IPv4. If you are using Dynamic Host Configuration Protocol (DHCP) to assign reserved IP addresses, ignore the warning. If installing DNS, you might also receive an error that delegation to the zone cannot be performed. This is common if you are creating a new second-level domain such as savilltech.net, which is saying the .net zone cannot be contacted to delegate savilltech records to this new DNS server. You might think, ideally, you would already have delegation records in the top-level domain pointing to this new DNS. However, because this is an AD domain that is internal to your network, you don't want its DNS visible to the outside world. This is one reason it's a good practice to make your AD a child of your company's DNS (for example, corp.savilltech.net so that corp can be delegated from the main savilltech.net domain). This delegation is also useful for child domains in the AD that can be delegated to hold their own DNS child domain zone.

The location for the database files is specified (see Figure 10-18). Chapter 11, "Designing and Installing Active Directory," covers best practices concerning their location.

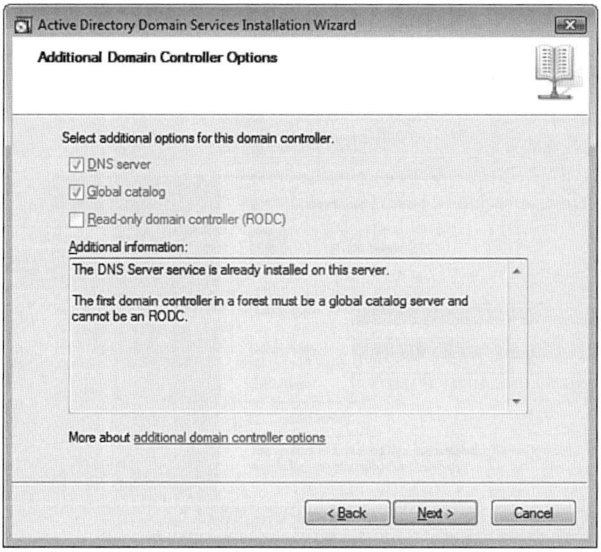

FIGURE 10-17 Additional options for a domain controller.

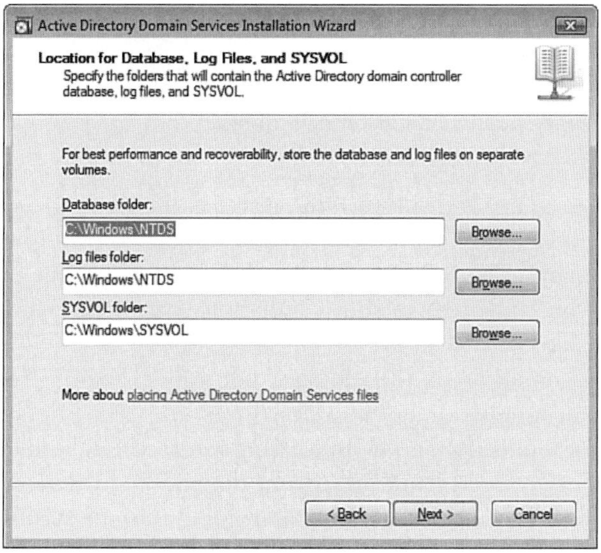

FIGURE 10-18 Specifying locations for the AD files.

Next the Directory Services Restore Mode password is configured (see Figure 10-19), which is used when the domain controller is rebooted into a special safe mode used to perform certain AD functions such as restorations.

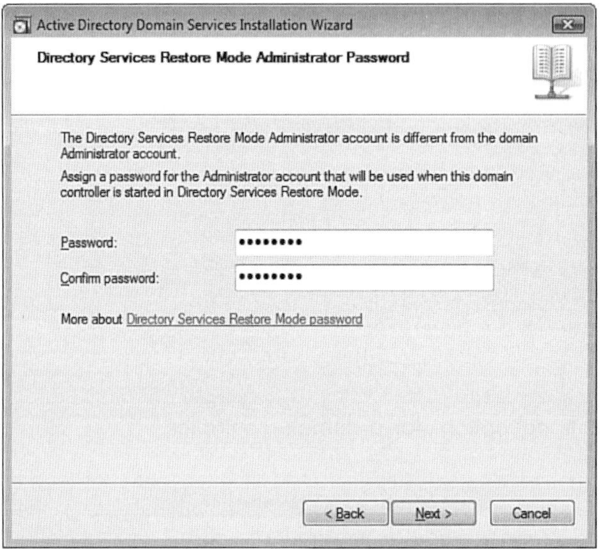

FIGURE 10-19 Recovery password for the new domain.

A summary is displayed that also has the option to export the settings specified to a file (see Figure 10-20), which can then be used to perform the domain creation in an unattended fashion. At this point, exit the wizard if you want to use the installation wizard to create the unattended answer file.

The creation of the domain controller begins (see Figure 10-21), which for a new domain in a new forest imports a default schema definition. For a new domain in an existing forest, the schema and configuration partitions are read from the parent domain and the new domain database is created. For a domain controller going into an existing domain, all the partitions replicate from a domain controller for the specified domain.

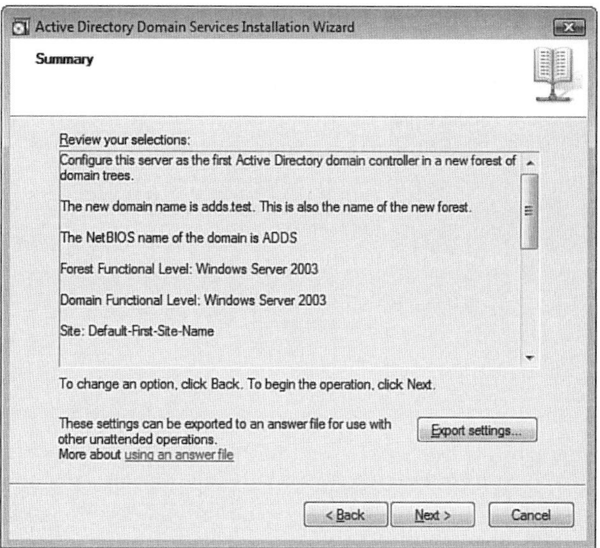

FIGURE 10-20 Summary of select wizard configurations.

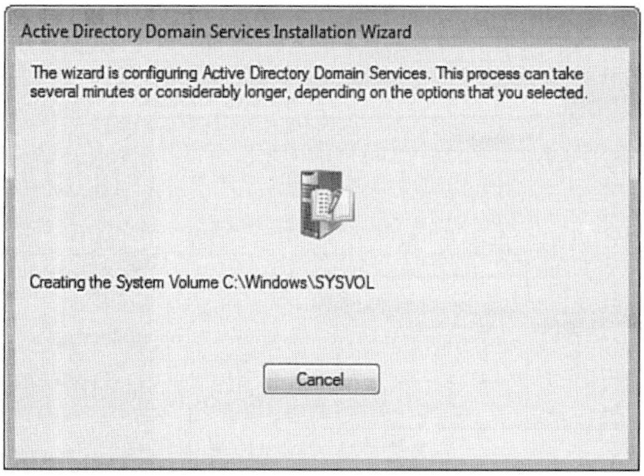

FIGURE 10-21 The promotion process.

When the domain controller promotion has completed, a summary is displayed (see Figure 10-22). Click Finish.

If you initiated the installation wizard from a roles dialog, a summary of the results is displayed and you need to reboot the server (see Figure 10-23). When the server reboots, it will be running directory services.

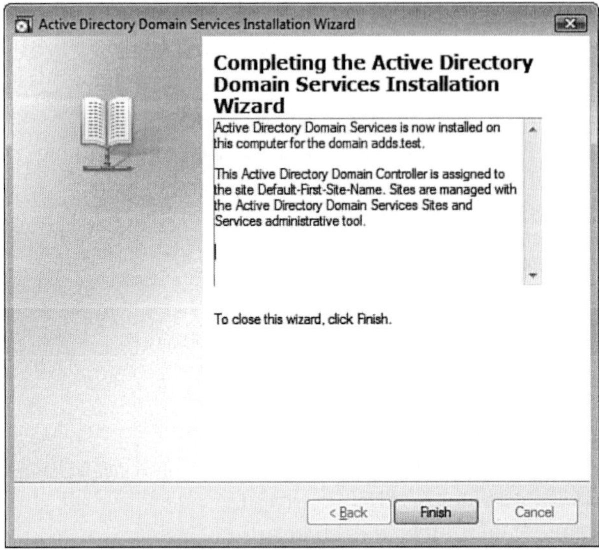

Figure 10-22 Summary of the domain creation.

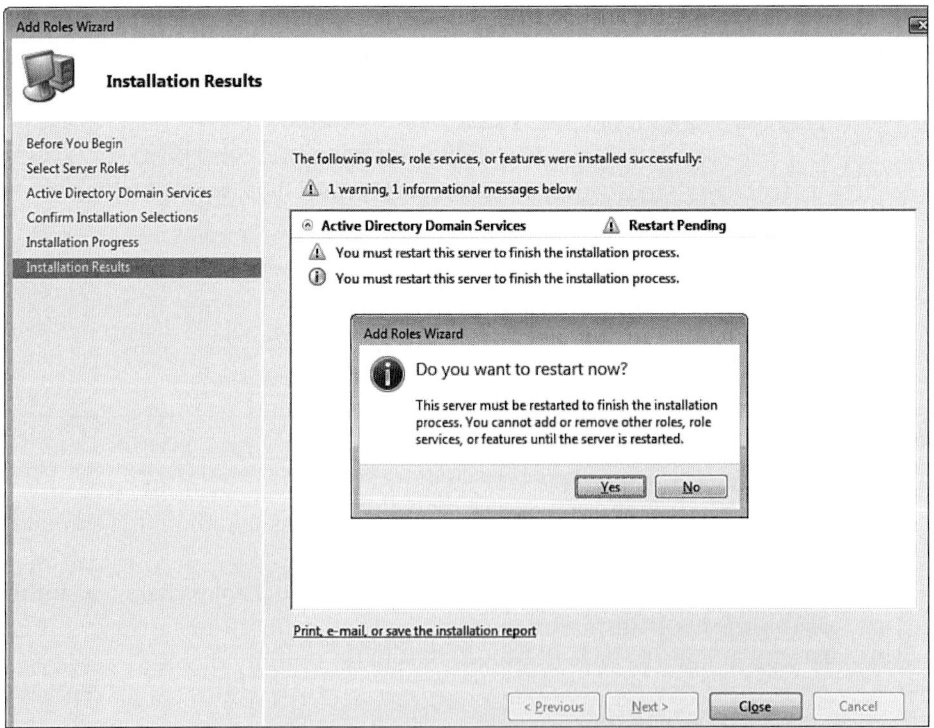

Figure 10-23 Restarting the server after promotion to a domain controller.

Windows NT 4.0 BDCs are still supported in Windows 2000 and Windows 2003 AD domains (but not an NT 4.0 PDC; if you upgrade, it has to be a PDC first), and these BDCs do not support multimaster replication. They pull updates from only one domain controller: the PDC. Windows Server 2008–based domains no longer support NT 4.0 BDCs, and they must be removed prior to removing the last Windows 2000/2003 domain controller from a domain.

Trees

One of the big changes with AD is the fact that the primary name is a DNS name, which enables a hierarchical structure. If you think back to the Windows NT 4.0 domain structure, trusts could be created between domains. With AD, when a domain is created it is possible to specify a parent for the new domain that automatically creates a bidirectional, transitive trust between the newly created domain and the nominated parent (more on this in a second). When a parent domain is specified, the DNS name of the parent automatically becomes part of the child domain name, with the child name adding a lower-level name to that of the parent so that it has a unique name. For example, if the parent domain is savilltech.net, you could specify the child's name as dallas.savilltech.net or anything else; it just has to have "savilltech.net" as the last part of the DNS name. This parent-child structure creates a hierarchy of domains with the key feature of a tree being a contiguous namespace. Every domain in a tree has the parent's DNS name as part of its own, as shown later. The name of the domain at the root of the tree is the also the name of the tree. In Figure 10-24, the root domain is savilltech.net, so the name of the tree is savilltech.net.

This is different from before; a bidirectional, *transitive* trust is created automatically between the parent and child domain. This is a change from NT 4.0 domains, where if domain A trusted domain B, and domain B trusted domain C, domain A did NOT trust domain C. Under AD's transitive trust, A would implicitly trust C. This is possible because of the Kerberos protocol, discussed later in the chapter.

So, what does this transitive trust mean for this domain tree? Because every domain in a tree has a transitive trust with its parent, it means every domain in a tree implicitly trusts every other domain (see Figure 10-25). Any security principal (that is, a user, group, or computer) in any domain in the entire tree can be granted access to any resource in any domain in the entire tree. As the example shows, a user in the london.savilltech.net domain can be granted access to resources in the it.dallas.savilltech.net.

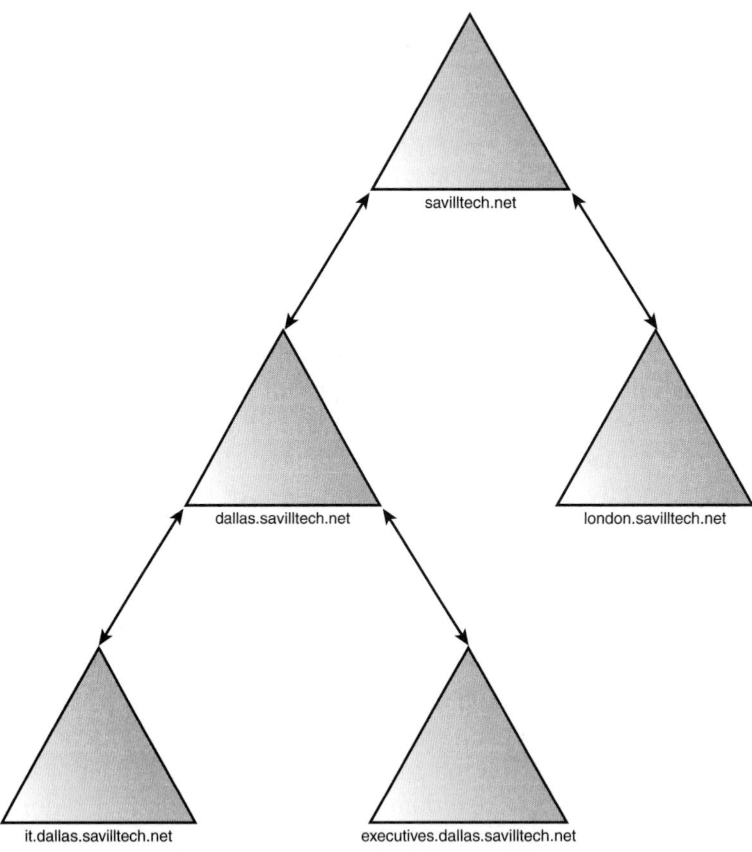

FIGURE 10-24 Notice that the domain tree features a contiguous namespace; it would not be possible for domain london.savilltech.net to have the child domain name boots.othertech.net because this would not be a contiguous namespace.

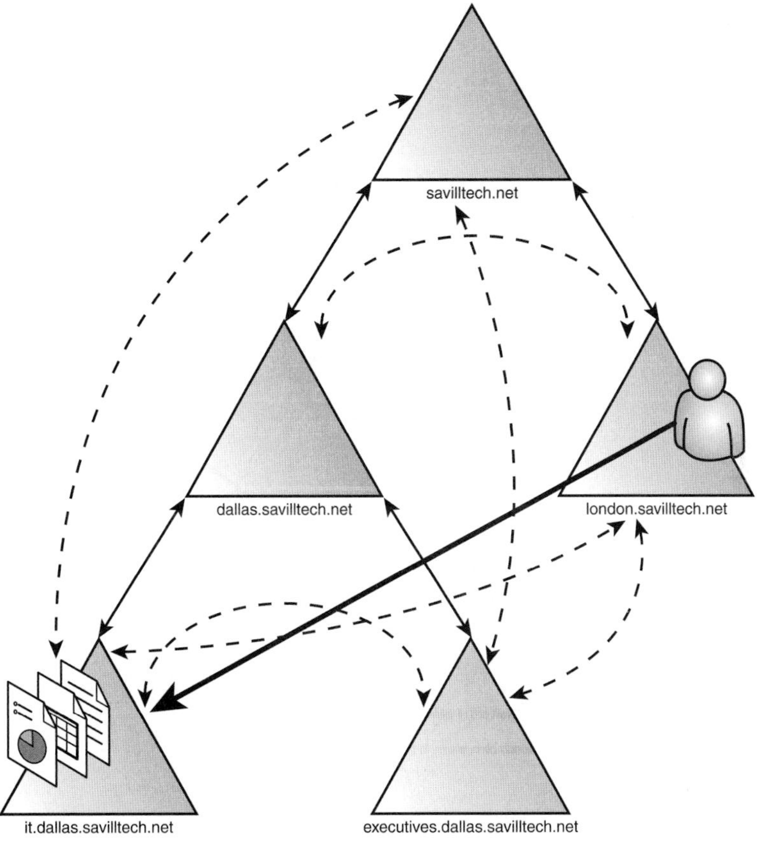

FIGURE 10-25 Although trusts exist between only the parent and the child domains, because they are transitive, every domain trusts every other domain as if the dashed line trusts exist.

Forests

A forest is one or more trees connected at the tree roots by a Kerberos bidirectional transitive trust. As with a tree, this now means that every single domain in a forest trusts every other domain in the forest, even those domains in other trees. Why would you need more than one tree in the first place? Remember, a tree is a contiguous namespace. If you needed a separate namespace, maybe you wanted a domain to be named savtech.org, you could not place this into the existing savilltech.net tree. Instead, when you created this new domain you would specify that you wanted to join an existing forest and give the name of the existing tree. For example, you would give the name savilltech.net, and as with domains in a tree, a trust between the two tree roots would be created as shown in Figure 10-26.

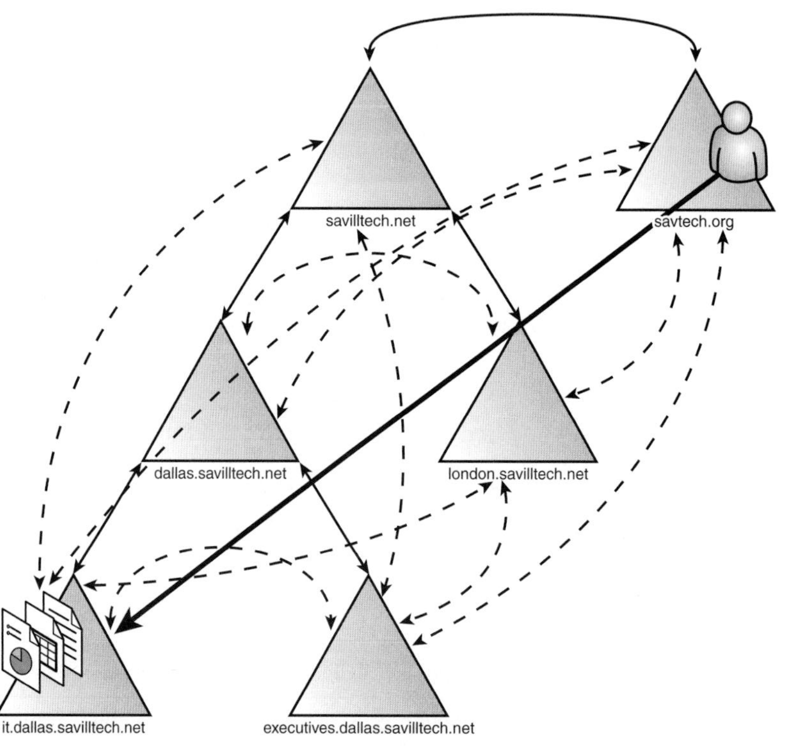

FIGURE 10-26 With all the domains in a forest implicitly trusting each other, users in a completely different tree can still access resources anywhere in the forest.

So, trees and forests give an automatic set of trusts enabling full resource sharing between all domains in the forest. Do they have any other connection? You previously saw how domains acted as a boundary of replication. Each domain contained the information about the objects in the domain. This is known as the domain partition (the partition of AD containing the domain's information). Every domain has a separate domain partition, and every domain controller in a domain contains a full replica of its domain's domain partition (also known as a naming context).

Other partitions within AD are common to all domains in the forest. In other words, they all contain the same information, and this is also what gives the domains in a forest a common structure. Although each domain is a separate security partition, they share many common features because they share these other partitions:

- **Schema partition**. As you previously saw, the schema is the blueprint for your AD and the schema partition contains that blueprint definition. The fact that this schema partition is common to all domains in a forest means every domain in a forest has the same schema, which is why if you change the schema for one domain in a forest, you change the schema for every domain in the forest. It is because of this that if you want to create a test domain, you often create it in its own separate forest so that you can perform testing and experiments concerning schema changes without modifying your production domains. Every domain controller in the forest has a replica of the same schema partition.
- **Configuration partition**. This partition contains the replication topology and other configuration information common to the entire tree. This includes information about the domains in the tree, domain controllers, and sites. Every domain controller in the forest has a replica of the same schema partition.

This gives three partitions. The domain partition is domain specific, whereas the schema and configuration partitions are common to the entire forest. Additionally, Windows 2003 introduced a new directory partition type, the Application Directory partition. The Application Directory partition stores dynamic application-specific data in AD, but rather than replicate to all domain controllers in a domain or tree, the data replicates only to domain controllers specified by the administrator. Application Directory partitions can contain any type of object except security principals. The data contained can be configured to replicate to any domain controller in any domain within the tree or every domain controller in the tree. All the domain controllers configured to host the application directory partition hold a replica of the information. However, only Windows 2003/2008 domain controllers can host a replica of an application directory partition.

Windows 2008 (and previously Windows 2003) creates a number of application partitions to enable the capability to replicate DNS information stored in AD to only specific domain controllers. As you saw in

Chapter 7, DNS information can be stored in AD. This is useful given the criticality of DNS to AD infrastructure. However, because not all domain controllers may host the DNS service, replicating the DNS zones to them would be wasteful. So, with Windows 2003 and above, it is possible to replicate DNS information to only domain controllers that host the DNS service. Two application partitions are created automatically: a DomainDNSZones partition that is created for each domain and hosts the domain context specific for each domain, and a ForestDNSZones partition that exists once in a forest and holds forestwide DNS information, such as the GC type data. The DomainDNSZones partition is replicated to every domain controller hosting the DNS service in the domain, whereas the ForestDNSZones is replicated to every domain controller in the entire forest that hosts the DNS service.

Organizational Units

Organizational units (OUs) are one of the most useful administrative features of AD and offer an organization's architect a lot of flexibility in how the organization is managed. OUs are containers that can hold nearly any other type of object, including other OUs, to form a hierarchy. OUs are used to organize objects into logical groupings for administrative purposes. They are *not* security principals, however. You cannot give an OU access to files or printers, and unlike a group, an OU is an actual container in which objects reside. An object cannot be in more than one OU.

OUs are an administrative tool; users do not see them. Create and design your OUs to meet administrative needs. They are normally used for the following:

- **Delegation of authority**. It is possible to assign people/groups with administrative permissions over OUs. These permissions are far more granular than under NT 4.0 domains. Rather than just being a full administrator, it's now possible to delegate, for example, just the ability to reset users' passwords or to modify only the telephone number attribute of users. Delegation is also possible at other levels; for example, at the domain level. But an OU is the smallest scope at which delegation can occur (you cannot, for example, delegate at a group level).
- **Group Policy application**. Group Policy replaced the old system policies and can be assigned at multiple levels, one of which is OUs.

Because OUs can be nested, Group Policy could be applied at all levels of the OU, nesting providing a lot of flexibility in the resultant policy applied to the computer or user.

- **Hiding objects**. If you have some resources that should not be visible when browsing, you can place them in an OU and then configure the OU so that certain groups of users cannot view the content.
- **Logical grouping of resources to aid administration**. It's possible to perform administrative functions on more than one object at a time. To make this object selection easier, you could place objects in OUs based on how they are typically administered. Take care in this case, however; base your OU creation primarily on the three previously mentioned uses because this use could lead to a large number of OUs which can eventually increase the complexity of an environment and adversely affect performance.

It's important to understand the difference in implementation of groups and OUs. When a user is placed in a group, the actual user object is not moved, only a reference is placed in the group to show membership. When an object is placed in an OU, it is moved inside the OU container. Therefore, you cannot place an object in more than one OU. The exception is that because OUs can be nested, if an object is placed in OU B, and OU B is in OU A, that object would inherit settings (including delegation and group policy) applied to the OUs A and B.

OUs are just another type of object and are stored in the domain partition. Any OU structures you create are localized to the domain, not shared among domains in a forest.

Sites

The preceding sections have dealt with logical components; that is, components not limited by physical constraints. You can create as many domains, trees, forests, and OUs as you want with no regard for physical infrastructure. However, there are also physical components based around the real world, and you need to design based on reality in the most efficient manner.

One of the biggest problems with the Windows NT 4.0 domain implementation was the replication of data between domain controllers and the fact that clients had no concept of physical geography. A client could just as likely attempt to authenticate with a domain controller on the other side of the world instead of one the other side of the room, and likewise, domain controllers would just replicate whenever they wanted. There was no concept of replicating to the closest domain controller. AD uses the concept of sites, which allows you to document the physical infrastructure of your organization in terms that AD can understand. A big change from NT 4.0 is that for intrasite and intersite replication, only the modified attribute is replicated. Previously if a single attribute changed, the whole object replicated. Now only the modified attribute replicates, saving a lot of bandwidth and replication-processing resources.

Given that TCP/IP is mandatory for AD (because you use DNS and LDAP along with other things) and the nature of IP, your physical environment is likely to be broken up, with different locations using different IP subnets. An AD site is denoted by one or more IP subnets, and the site is given a name to reflect the location of those subnets.

In the real world, each of your locations connect to each other by a variety of connectivity types; for example, T1 lines, ISDN, frame relay, and xDSL, each of which has associated network speeds. AD documents these connectivities as site links, which have a number of attributes; the most important is the site's cost. This cost relates to the site's available bandwidth; the lower the cost, the faster the link. In other words, it costs less to use the link. The availability of the link can also be defined. For example, there might be some links that are not available at night, so this needs to be documented as a property of the link. This site and site link information is stored in the Configuration partition, which is replicated to all domain controllers in the forest. Therefore, sites are common to all domains in the forest and do not have to be defined for each domain.

The actual process is fairly straightforward. First create site links for all the connections you have between locations (for example, DallasToLondon). Then create all your sites, and during the site creation, specify which site link it belongs to (you can change the site link at a later time if required and even add to multiple site links, which is the case for hub-type locations). Then define the IP subnets linked to a site. When deciding which IP subnets to place in a site, as long as the subnets are geographically within the same area and are connected via a LAN, over 10Mbps for example (although a speed as low as 512Kbps can be adequate), they can be configured as a site. A site is defined as a group of computers communicating via high-speed, reliable connectivity. Putting this together, you get a site topology similar to that shown in Figure 10-27.

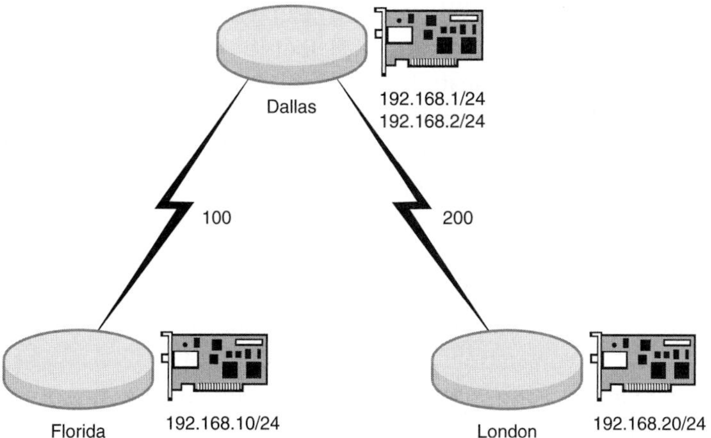

Figure 10-27 In your environment, you have three locations with Dallas as the hub location to which the other locations have connectivity.

Let's walk through creating the sites and site links described earlier. The first action is to create the actual site, which you achieve by right-clicking Sites and selecting the New Site context menu item. Enter the name of the site and select a site link. Don't worry that it's not the final site link, just select any site link (such as, DEFAULTIPSITELINK) as shown in Figure 10-28. Repeat this process for all the sites you want to add.

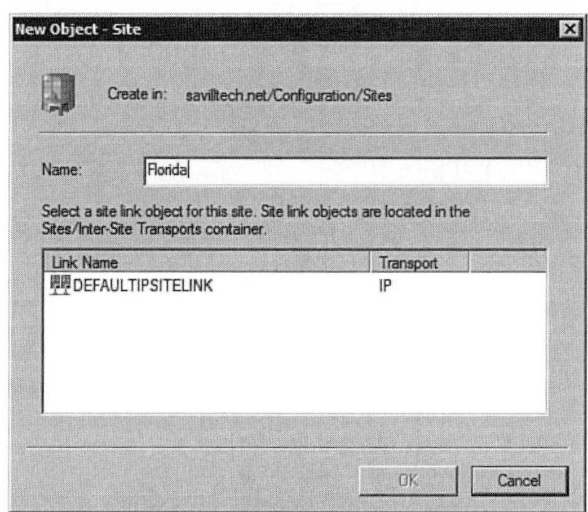

Figure 10-28 Creating a new site is a simple procedure.

When you have the sites, you can add site links that control how the actual replication is performed. Select the transport you want to configure for the intersite replication, which is always IP, and select New Site Link. You are prompted for a name for the site link, so make it something logical (e.g., Dallas to London), select the sites connected by the new site link, and select Add as shown in Figure 10-29. You always need at least two sites in any site link. Once the site link is created, its properties can be modified to set items such as the cost of the site link and how often it replicates, as shown in Figure 10-30. If you click the Change Schedule button, you can configure the hours of the week that replication can occur, which allows you to stop replication occurring at times when you might want to save bandwidth for other uses or if, perhaps, the link was unavailable. After you have created site links, ensure that you either remove all the sites from the DEFAULTIPSITELINK or simply delete DEFAULTIPSITELINK because it's no longer needed.

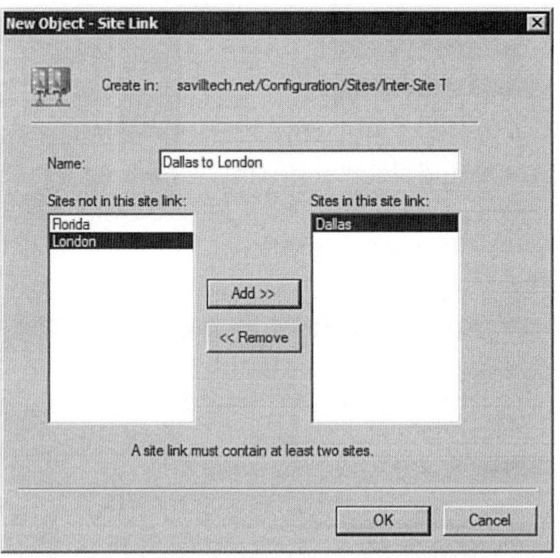

FIGURE 10-29 Creating a new site link.

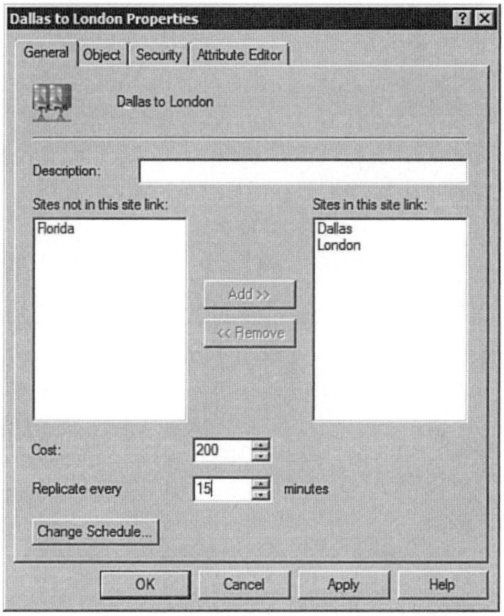

FIGURE 10-30 Modifying a new site link's properties.

Finally, create the IP subnets and link them to the correct sites by selecting New Subnet from the Subnets node context menu. Enter the subnet in the format of subnet ID followed by the number of bits in the mask. For example, 192.168.20/24 would refer to the 192.168.20.0 subnet and the 24 means a mask of 255.255.255.0. Also select the site from the list of configured sites as shown in Figure 10-31.

With the sites defined, AD is aware of where the domain controllers are physically located and the network connectivity between them. The Knowledge Consistency Checker (KCC) uses this knowledge to create connection objects between domain controllers to define a replication topology used for the replication of AD data in the most efficient manner.

Additionally, clients now know which physical location they reside in. Instead of randomly selecting a domain controller, for example, the client can be told to use a domain controller in its local location (or the closest location if no domain controller is available in its local site). This is known as site awareness. Most major AD services are site aware, minimizing traffic sent over slower WAN type links by sending clients to services in its local site where possible. In fact, if a domain controller receives authentication requests from a client and the domain controller is not the client's closest domain controller, it instructs the client to find a domain controller in its site instead. It does this by querying DNS for a domain controller in a specific site.

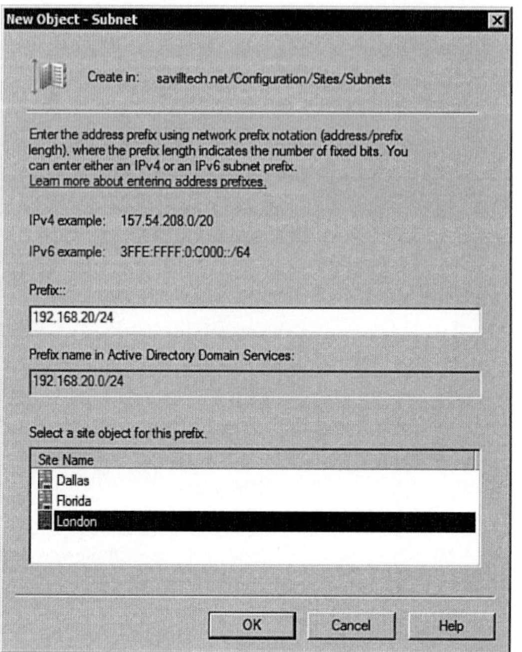

FIGURE 10-31 Creating a new subnet.

By default, the KCC component runs every 15 minutes, checking whether the topology generated is the most efficient. The KCC runs on every domain controller, which might lead you to believe it would be possible for domain controllers to create different topologies leading to problems with the replication. However, because each domain controller uses the same algorithm to create the topology and each domain controller has a replica of the common configuration partition that contains the site information, the output is the same result.

The actual connection objects created by the KCC vary depending on whether the connection objects are created within (intra) a site or between (inter) sites. Remember that within a site, by definition, all the computers are connected by a high bandwidth network, a LAN. So, it is assumed that network bandwidth is plentiful and replication can be based on the fastest update of all the domain controllers in the site. The traffic generated is not a concern.

To achieve this fast replication, domain controllers within a site use a ring topology to replicate information. Every domain controller has at least two connections to other domain controllers within the site, its neighbors in the ring. However, in a site with a lot of domain controllers, additional replication objects are created between certain domain controllers to ensure that there are never more than three hops between any two domain controllers (see Figure 10-32). This ensures that changes do not take excessive time to replicate throughout a site because a change replicates to the domain controller's replication partners, and then on the next replication, the domain controller, which then replicates the newly found change to its replication partners, and so on. If there were 10 hops between domain controllers, the change would take 10 replication cycles to reach the furthest domain controller.

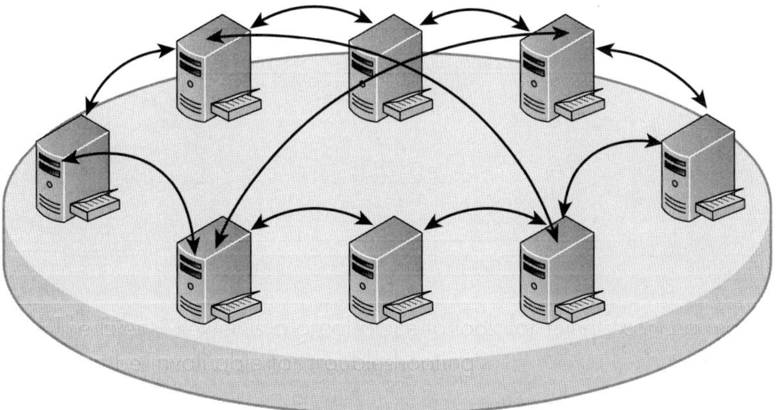

Figure 10-32 In a site with a large number of domain controllers, additional replication objects have to be created to ensure that there are never more than three hops between any two domain controllers.

Replication within a site is trigger based; whenever a change is made within a defined time (5 minutes for Windows 2000, reduced to 15 seconds for Windows 2003 mode forests), the domain controller with a change notifies its replication partners, and they pull the change. No compression is used when sending the data. The CPU time required to perform the compress/decompress is more expensive in terms of resources than the additional network use.

The network might not be as fast and reliable between sites, so the number of connections and replication traffic are minimized. To achieve this, instead of a ring, a least cost spanning tree is used, which ensures that all sites are connected in the cheapest way possible (see Figure 10-33). This means replication traffic is sent only once between domain controllers in different sites. The domain controllers nominated for the replication of changes between sites are known as bridgehead servers. Because the network is slower, replication is based on a schedule. For example, replication might take place every 15 minutes rather than replicating based on notifications of changes (although notification-based replication can be enabled if desired). To save network bandwidth, the information is compressed if it is larger than 32KB.

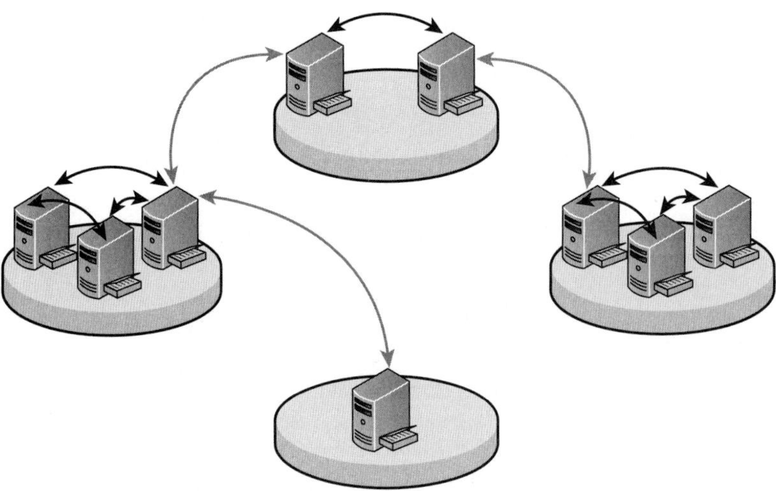

Figure 10-33 Each site has an intrasite replication ring with a single intersite replication object between the sites ensuring changes flow through the entire infrastructure but in the most efficient manner.

There is one more site component known as a bridge. A setting, Bridge All Site Links, is enabled by default, which means all site links are transitive, so even if two sites do not have a direct site link between them the KCC can still create a replication object between domain controllers in them. This won't normally happen because replication objects always take the cheapest approach, but there might be times you have domain controllers for domains in sites that are not directly connected. So, they have to create replication objects between domain controllers in these sites via another site's links.

Bridging of all site links is fine as long as you have a fully routable IP network, which means an IP route exists from any site in your company to every other site. This would allow domain controllers to replicate. If, however, this is not that case, and you do not have a fully routable network, turn off this default bridging behavior as follows:

1. Start Active Directory Sites and Services MMC snap-in (Start, Programs, Administrative Tools, Active Directory Sites and Services).
2. Expand the Sites branch and then expand Inter-Site Transports.
3. Right-click IP and select Properties.
4. Uncheck the Bridge All Site Links option and click OK, as shown in Figure 10-34.

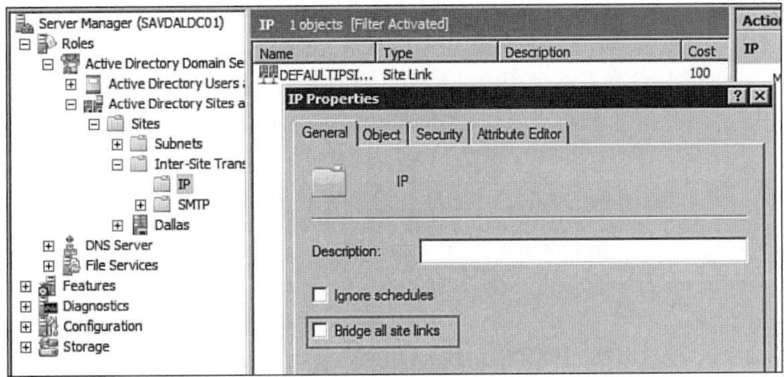

FIGURE 10-34 Removing the Bridge All Site Links option for the IP transport.

5. Close the Sites and Services MMC snap-in.

Once bridging of all site links is disabled, replication connections are created only between domain controllers in directly connected sites. But what happens if you have a particular combination of sites that requires replication between domain controllers but they do not have a direct site link and physically connectivity does not exist?

You could add a site link with a combined cost of the site links that exist, but a better option is to create what is known as a "site link bridge." A site link bridge is two or more sites logically joined, and it enables replication connections to be created between DCs in any sites connected via site links that are grouped within a site link bridge. Site links within a site link bridge are transitive.

FSMO Roles

The other physical components are the domain controllers themselves. As you have seen in AD, all the domain controllers are equal, although to paraphrase George Orwell, some domain controllers are created more equal than others. There is no PDC or BDC role. All the controllers are equal in performing multimaster replication except for a new Windows Server 2008 domain controller type known as a RODC, but you'll cover that in Chapter 11. You have also seen that NT 4.0 BDCs can participate in an AD domain: But how? NT 4.0 BDCs have to pull information from the PDC, which no longer exists.

Certain domain controllers hold five special roles to perform functions that cannot work in a multimaster fashion. These are known as Flexible Single Master Operation (FSMO) roles. The first of these relates to handling NT 4.0 BDCs. That's not all it does, but it's a start.

PDC Emulator FSMO Role

A single domain controller in each domain holds the PDC FSMO role, never more, never fewer. You always have one PDC FSMO role per domain in the same way you used to have one PDC per NT 4.0 domain. The PDC FSMO performs a number of functions:

- Provides the replication point for NT 4.0 BDCs in the domain.
- Each PDC FSMO in the forest synchronizes its time with the other PDC FSMOs within the forest. The PDC FSMO in the root domain of the forest is the source of the time synchronization and is normally configured to synchronize its time with an external time source. All clients and servers within each domain synchronize their time with their domain's PDC FSMO.
- Provides down-level clients support for password updates. Because non–AD–aware clients know BDCs are for read-only purposes, they would always attempt to change passwords with the PDC.
- Acts as the master domain browser if the service is enabled.
- Password changes at any DC always replicate to the PDC FSMO first because replication can take time to propagate the password

change. If a user has just changed his password and attempts to authenticate again against a different domain controller, the new password might not have replicated, so the authentication attempt would fail. If the authentication fails at a domain controller, instead of rejecting the request, the domain controller first contacts the PDC FSMO role holder to attempt a second authentication before passing back a failure to the user.

- Due the criticality of locking out an account, this is always processed at the PDC FSMO to provide a central location for checking the status of accounts.
- Group Policy focus. Where possible, the PDC FSMO is contacted for Group Policy maintenance (edit/create). However, other DCs can be used via configuration.

Even when there are no NT 4.0 BDCs or non–AD clients, the PDC FSMO role is still required. However, in that situation its workload would be reduced.

RID Master FSMO Role

Every object in the domain has a security identifier (SID). The SID comprises the SID of the domain the object resides in and a relative identifier (RID) that is unique in each domain.

Because these RIDs have to be unique in the domain, if each domain controller in the domain made up its own there is a chance a RID would clash with one created by another domain controller. So, a single domain controller in each domain, the RID FSMO, gives batches of 500 RIDs to each domain controller. When a domain controller has only 100 RIDs left (20%), it requests another batch of 500 from the RID FSMO. However, with Windows 2000 Service Pack 4 and above (including 2003 and 2008), a new batch is requested when 50% of the number of RIDs are left (250), improving resilience if the RID FSMO is not available.

The RID Master is also used when moving an object between domains (this is now done easily thanks to some tools supplied with Windows; for example, the movetree.exe utility). Even though you might not specifically run the utility on the RID server, it is automatically contacted by the utility and used. This role is also per domain, so every domain has a RID Master FSMO server.

Infrastructure FSMO Role

It is possible for an object in one domain to be referenced by another domain; for example, when a user from domain A is placed in a local group in domain B. The reference information stored in the domain B group is as follows:

- The Globally Unique Identifier (GUID) of the object, which never changes during the object's lifetime, even if it is moved between domains.
- The SID of the object (which changes if moved between domains).
- The distinguished name (DN) of the object (which changes if the object moves in any way).

This information is stored in a record known as a phantom record.

The Infrastructure FSMO is responsible for ensuring that the SID and DN of the phantom records of objects referenced from other domains are kept up-to-date by comparing the content of its database with that of the GC. If the information it has stored for the GUID of the object is different from that of the GC, the new information is taken and the phantom record updated. This checking process runs periodically, and sometimes you might view a group and see icons with gray hair. This simply means the object with the DN cannot be found at present. It has likely moved, and the infrastructure master has just not updated the phantom record yet. It's not a problem and would not affect the working of the group.

It is vital the Infrastructure FSMO role is not a GC if you have more than one domain because its database never sees anything different from the GC (because it is one). If you have only one domain, it does not matter because you do not have any objects from other domains referenced. This role is also limited to one per domain.

Schema Master FSMO Role

You learned about the schema being the blueprint for every class and attribute within the entire forest, and that it was policed so that only certain users could request a change (members of the Schema Admins group) and changes could be requested only through a particular domain controller: the Schema Master. This time, however, because the schema is forestwide, only one domain controller in the entire forest has the role. Only this machine has the capability to write to the schema, which is replicated to every other domain controller in the entire forest.

Domain Naming Master FSMO Role

During the DCPROMO process, domains can be added to a tree or forest by selecting a parent domain. You need to ensure that the same domain name is not used and that every domain name is unique in the forest. This is the Domain Naming Master FSMO's job. It has to be contacted before any domain can be added to or removed from the forest. With Windows Server 2008, it is also used when moving domains around the forest structure. This is known as "prune and graft" because you are pruning a domain from one position and grafting it onto another. But this is available only in a Windows 2003–mode forest and above.

All the domain specific roles are, by default, held by the first domain controller created in each domain. The roles can be moved to any domain controller within the domain (but not to a NT 4.0 BDC), and can exist on the same server or be split across multiple domain controllers. Some best practices for their placement, in addition to moving the FSMO roles, are examined in more detail later in Chapter 11.

The forest-specific roles are, by default, held by the first domain controller ever created in the forest (which is in the forest root domain). These roles can also be moved. These domain and forest specific roles are summarized in Figure 10-35.

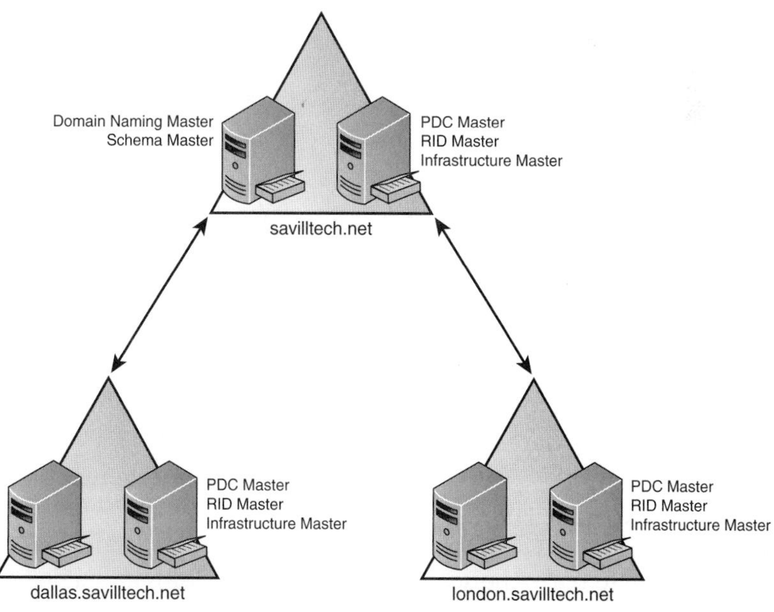

FIGURE 10-35 A forest has one of the domain naming and schema master roles whereas each domain has its own PDC, RID, and Infrastructure Master roles.

These roles do not move automatically. If the server machine running one of these servers goes down, the functions it performs will not be available. For example, if the RID FSMO is unavailable for an extended time, you might no longer be able to create new objects in a domain.

Global Catalog

A GC server is a special domain controller that not only holds a full replica of its local domain partition but also a read-only copy of a subset of attributes of every object in every other domain in its forest (see Figure 10-36).

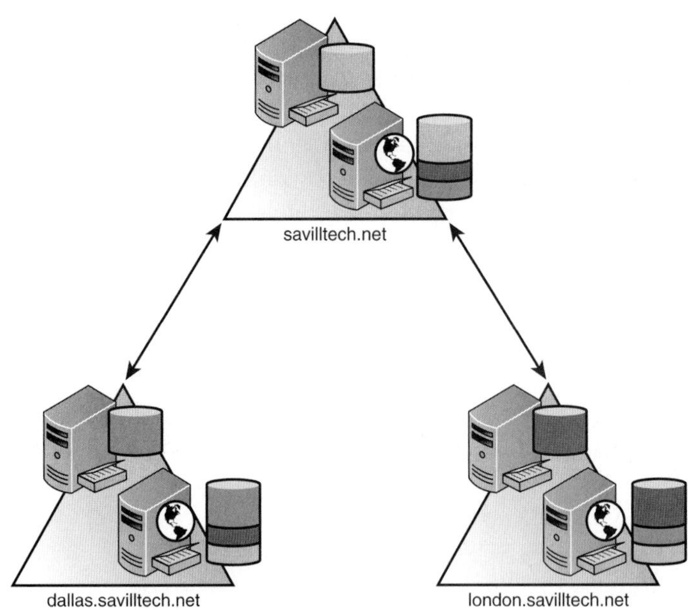

FIGURE 10-36 Each domain's domain controllers hold a full replica of the local domain's partition, and the GCs also contain a subset of every other domain's partition.

By default, the first domain controller created is a GC. However, any domain controller can be configured as a GC, and there are a number of best practices regarding this configuration that are examined in Chapter 11. During the DCPROMO process on Windows 2008 domain controllers, the option to make the server a domain controller is available and checked by default.

The attributes stored in the GC are defined as the Partial Attribute Set (PAS) which can be modified by marking or unmarking attributes in the schema as replicated in the GC. The GC locates resources within the enterprise. A domain contains full information about resources in its domain, but trying to find resources in the rest of the forest would be time-consuming if a domain controller in each domain had to be located and queried for any search. Instead, enterprise queries are directed at a GC.

In addition to providing an enterprise search ability, the GC stores a specific type of group that is accessible from any server in the forest and can contain users for any domain in the forest: the Universal Group. A GC is queried during logon to check for Universal Group membership. If a GC cannot be contacted, users cannot log on unless a feature originally introduced in Windows 2003 is used: the capability of sites to cache Universal Group membership (although domain administrators can log on even without GCs).

Obviously, the GC content has to replicated between every GC in the entire forest. (There is only one "version" of the GC; they all share the same content, assuming that replication was instant. However, obviously there are some minor differences due to replication latency.) The KCC creates additional connection objects for this GC replication. It also creates connection objects to domain controllers in other domains to ensure that a subset of every domain's partition content is available in the GC.

When a user performs a query to the GC, he first asks the DNS server for a GC. Once a GC is returned, he performs the query via port 3268 on the server (normally port 389 is used for a standard LDAP query). If the GC does not have the attribute being queried as part of the PAS, the query is instead referred to the normal LDAP AD service.

GC servers do not return any data stored in an application directory partition that they hold a replica of. Only information originating from domain partitions is returned via GCs.

Domain and Forest Modes

When you first install AD, it's possible to have NT 4.0 BDCs participate in the domain, but obviously AD can offer far more than what was possible previously. To keep compatibility with the older NT 4.0 BDCs, some of this functionality has to be disabled, known as running in mixed mode.

When all domain controllers are Windows 2000 or above, enable this new functionality by switching to an AD native mode. With Windows 2000, there were two domain options: mixed mode and native mode.

Windows 2003 AD introduced more capabilities that are available in Windows Server 2008. When all domain controllers in a domain are running Windows 2003 or above, a Windows Server 2003 mode enables the new capabilities. Once every domain in the entire forest is running Windows 2003, you can switch to a Windows 2003 forest mode.

Windows 2003 also introduced another domain and forest mode, known as Windows 2003 interim mode. This mode is available when upgrading from NT 4.0 to Windows 2003 directly and overcomes some of the limitations of the Windows 2000 AD implementation.

Windows Server 2008 continues this tradition with new features available with a domain containing only Windows Server 2008 domain controllers while maintaining all the new features that were introduced with Windows Server 2003.

Next is a brief overview of the changes between the various domain and forest modes. You go into more detail as you use these modes in later scenarios. It is important to remember that switching to a higher-domain mode is a one-way operation. You can never downgrade your mode. For example, you cannot go from native to mixed mode.

Domain Modes

Between the various versions of Windows Server, there are a number of different modes.

Mixed Mode

Mixed mode is the default domain mode when performing a fresh installation of AD or when performing an upgrade. It enables Windows 2000 and Windows 2003 domain controllers (but not Windows 2008 domain controllers) as well as NT 4.0 BDCs.

Windows 2000 Native Mode

In native mode, only Windows 2000 and Windows 2003 domain controllers can be present. There can be no NT 4.0 BDCs. This mode has additional functionality including nesting groups, Universal groups, support for SID history, and group conversions.

Windows Server 2003 Interim Mode

In Windows Server 2003 interim mode, you can have only Windows 2003 domain controllers and NT 4 BDCs (no Windows 2000 domain controllers) in the domain. You don't have this mode in a Windows 2008–only domain, but I'm including the information for completeness.

This mode does not add any real extra functionality; it is used for the Windows Server 2003 interim forest mode, which fixed some problems with groups over certain sizes and site connectivity. It can be set only when upgrading from Windows NT 4.0 to Windows 2003 and is set while running the DCPROMO utility on the first domain controller to be upgraded.

Windows Server 2003 Mode

Windows Server 2003 mode can have only Windows 2003 domain controllers. It has additional functionality over Windows 2000 native mode, including the following:

- Domain controller rename
- Password on InetOrgPerson objects
- Ability to redirect the default Users and Computers container
- Last logon timestamp attribute

Windows Server 2008 Mode

Windows Server 2008 mode can only have Windows 2008 domain controllers. It has additional functionality over Windows Server 2003 mode, including the following:

- Distributed File System Replication support for SYSVOL, which provides more robust and granular replication of SYSVOL contents.
- Advanced Encryption Services (AES 128 and 256) support for the Kerberos protocol.
- Last interactive logon information, which displays the time of the last successful interactive logon for a user, from what workstation, and the number of failed logon attempts since the last logon.
- Fine-grained password policies allowing multiple password policies to be created within a single domain and applied based on user group memberships.

To change the domain mode, use the AD Users and Computers MMC snap-in and select Raise Domain Functional Level from the domain's context menu item as shown in Figure 10-37. You can now select our new domain mode, as shown in Figure 10-38. But remember that you cannot undo this change. If you still had Windows 2000 domain controllers, you would be unable to change to Windows Server 2003 native mode; if you have 2003 domain controllers, you cannot switch to Windows Server 2008 domain mode.

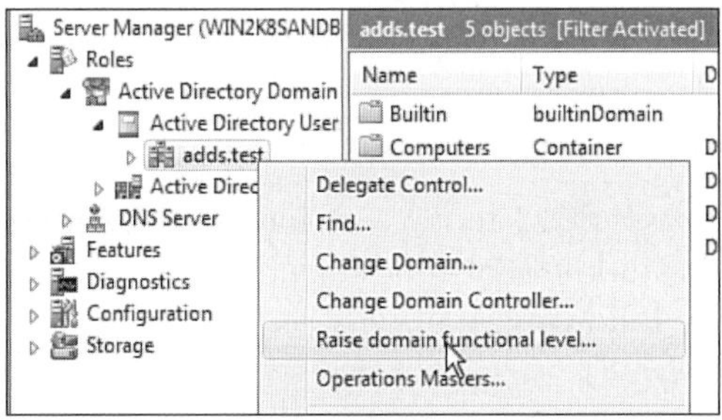

FIGURE 10-37 Raising the domain mode, Part 1.

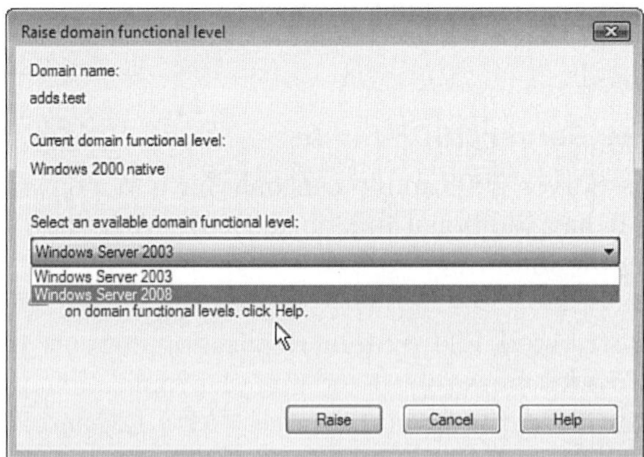

FIGURE 10-38 Raising the domain mode, Part 2.

Forest Modes

The changes in the various versions of Windows Server that have included AD make for various forest modes as well.

Windows 2000

Windows 2000 forest mode allows all versions of domains and therefore all types of domain controllers (NT 4 BDC, 2000/2003 DC). This is the default forest mode.

Windows Server 2003 Interim Mode

Windows Server 2003 interim mode can have only Windows 2003 and NT 4 domain controllers. It was available in the Windows Server 2003 product but is not available in Windows Server 2008 because NT 4 domain controllers are not supported. It has additional functionality over the Windows 2000 mode, including the following:

- More than 5,000 users in a group via linked value replication (LVR)
- Improved Intersite Topology Generator (ISTG), which is responsible for creating the replication topology between different locations
- Additional attributes added to GC Windows Server 2003 Mode

Windows Server 2003 Mode

Windows Server 2003 mode can have only Windows 2003 domain controllers or above. It has additional functionality over 2003 interim mode, including the following:

- Dynamic aux classes that enable the creation of objects with an associated TTL, which are automatically removed once that time has expired.
- The ability to convert user objects to INetOrgPerson (and vice versa).
- Schema de-/reactivation.
- Domain rename.
- Forest trusts.
- Basic and query-based groups.
- 15-second intra-site replication frequency (with a 3-second offset).
- LVR. This now enables individual elements of a multivalued attribute to be replicated instead of the whole value. This is a great improvement for universal group replication, which currently requires the replication of the entire group content each time a single change to its membership occurs. It also reduces the chances of

normal group membership changes within a group occurring, which can happen if administrators on different domain controllers modify the same group. One overwrites the other. Now the changes would be merged.

Windows Server 2008 Mode

Windows Server 2008 mode can have only Windows 2008 domain controllers. It has no additional functionality over Windows Server 2003 mode. All domains subsequently added to the forest, however, operate at the Windows Server 2008 domain functional level by default.

To change the forest mode, use the Active Directory Domains and Trusts MMC snap-in and use the Raise Forest Functional Level root context menu option then select the new forest mode, as shown in Figures 10-39 and 10-40.

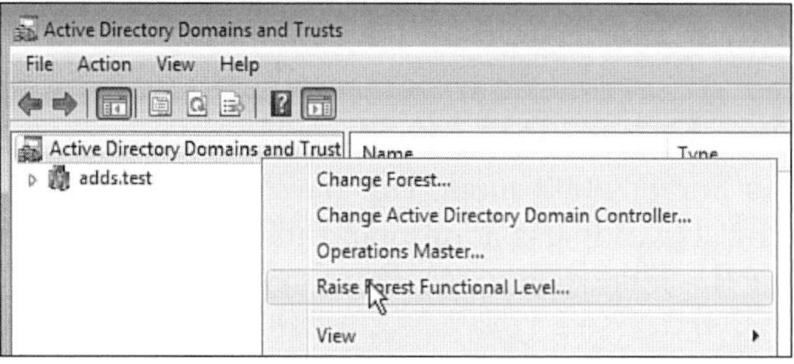

FIGURE 10-39 Raising the forest level, Part 1.

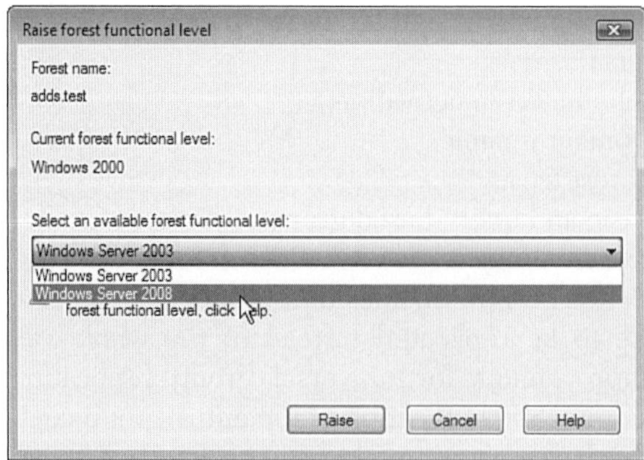

FIGURE 10-40 Raising the forest level, Part 2.

The overall goal of your environment is to get to Windows Server 2008 domain and forest modes, which opens up all functionality in the most efficient way.

Forest mode restricts what versions of domain controllers can participate in the domain, *not* normal member servers or workstations. Even in a Windows Server 2008 mode domain, you can still have NT 4.0 member servers and clients. The modes are used only to restrict the participating DCs to ensure that all DCs can support the newly enabled functionality in order to stop any corruption of the database or variation in the service clients receive.

Summary

The AD is the cornerstone of your entire infrastructure. In this chapter, you looked at its main building blocks and how to create a new domain but right now you only have a single domain controller. This gives you no resiliency to a domain controller failure, which is vital. The next chapter covers this along with more guidance around the best practices for the actual design of your AD environment.

Although understanding the building blocks of the AD is critical, it is equally important to use a sound design for your AD to avoid future modification exercises, which can be complex, and to ensure that the AD serves as an asset to the organization as opposed to something you need to work around.

CHAPTER 11

Designing and Installing Active Directory

In Chapter 10, "Active Directory Domain Services Introduction," you created a domain and learned some of the high-level concepts related to Active Directory (AD). This chapter covers creating additional domain controllers for a domain and creating additional domains in the forest, along with creating answer files to automate the creation of domain controllers.

Adding a Replica Domain Controller

Let's start this chapter by creating a second domain controller. The site that the domain controller joins is based on the Internet Protocol (IP) address and the subnets and sites defined in the configuration partition of the forest. As a best practice, you should normally have at least two domain controllers in your main location, which is typically where the Flexible Single Master Operations (FSMO) role domain controllers are based.

To create a new domain controller in an existing domain, follow the same process as when creating a new domain, with a few modifications to the options selecting during Active Directory Domain Services (ADDS; formally just referred to as Active Directory or AD in Windows Server 2003) installation process. If the domain controller is going to act as a domain name system (DNS) server, installation should be done with the ADDS role to prevent complications with the new domain controller replicating all the partitions related to DNS in the forest and domain. However, when you select the Active Directory Domain Services role, no others can be selected. Don't worry; you get a chance to install DNS in a second. For now, ensure that the server being added as a domain controller has the correct IP address for the site it belongs to and has access to a DNS server that can be used to locate domain controllers for the domain being joined.

After you select the ADDS role from Server Manager and complete the Active Directory Domain Services Installation Wizard, dcpromo.exe launches (or you can launch it by running `dcpromo` from the Run menu).

The first page of the wizard prompts you to choose whether to use the advanced mode. The advanced mode is not required unless you want to install from media or select a specific domain controller from which to replicate, so leave the advanced mode option unselected and click Next.

For this sample deployment configuration, you want to add to an existing domain, so choose the options for an existing forest and adding a domain controller to an existing domain (see Figure 11-1).

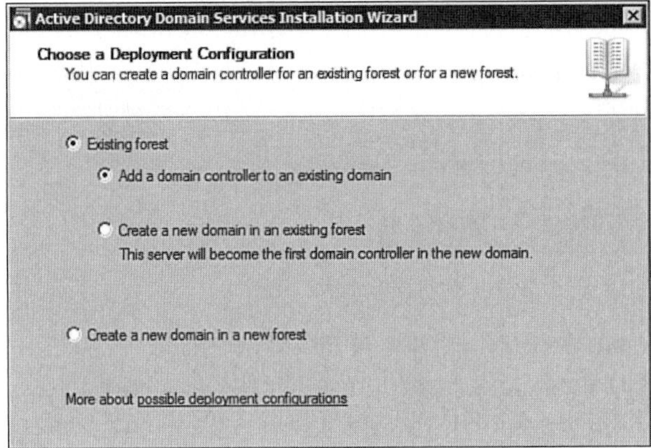

FIGURE 11-1 Select the options to use an existing forest and to add a domain controller to an existing domain.

Enter the credentials that are used to join the domain and the name of the domain to join (see Figure 11-2). Note that when you enter the credentials and domain name, the forest of the domain entered is scanned, and a list is displayed. In either case, after you enter the necessary information, click Next.

A list of domains in the forest is displayed, as shown in Figure 11-3. Select the domain for which this server should become a domain controller and click Next.

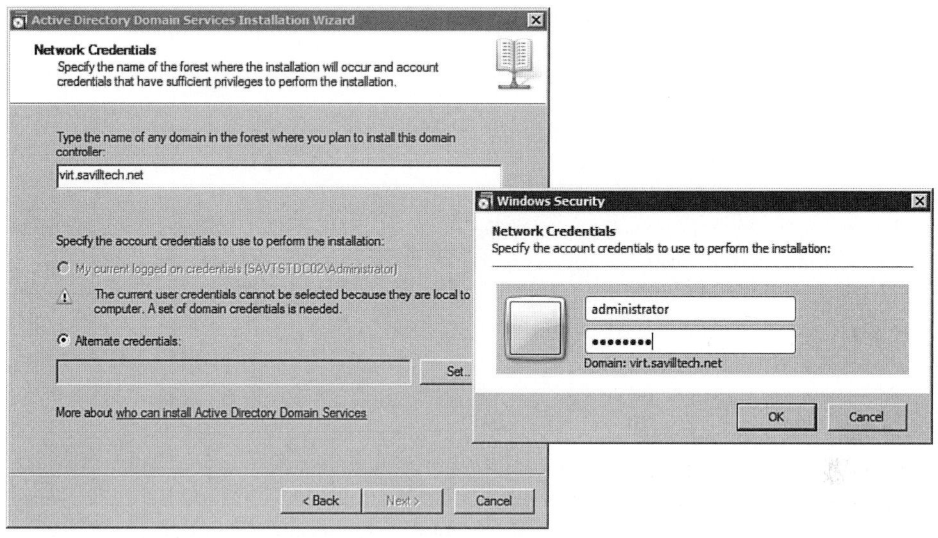

FIGURE 11-2 Any domain in the forest is sufficient for this checking.

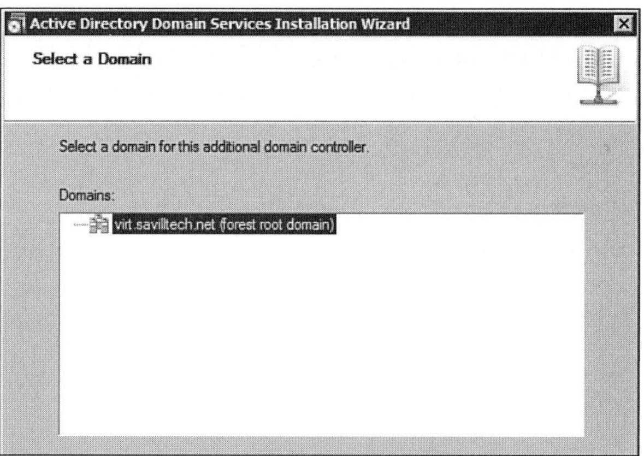

FIGURE 11-3 In this case, the forest has only one domain.

The wizard displays a list of sites the domain controller can join. Select a specific site or leave the default, Use the Site That Corresponds to the IP Address of This Computer, as shown in Figure 11-4. If you choose the default option, the site is determined by comparing the new domain controller's IP address to the subnets defined in the forest configuration and their mapping to defined sites.

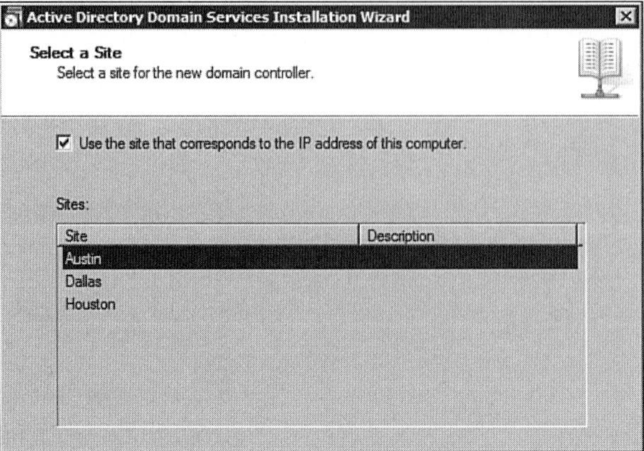

FIGURE 11-4 Normally, you should have configured the new domain controller's IP address to match that of the site where it is located, but this option may be useful when you need to provision a domain controller at another location and then ship it to the final destination.

The next screen (see Figure 11-5) enables you to select additional roles for the domain controller. One of them is DNS Server, and another is Global Catalog (GC). You can also select Read-Only Domain Controller (RODC), which is discussed later.

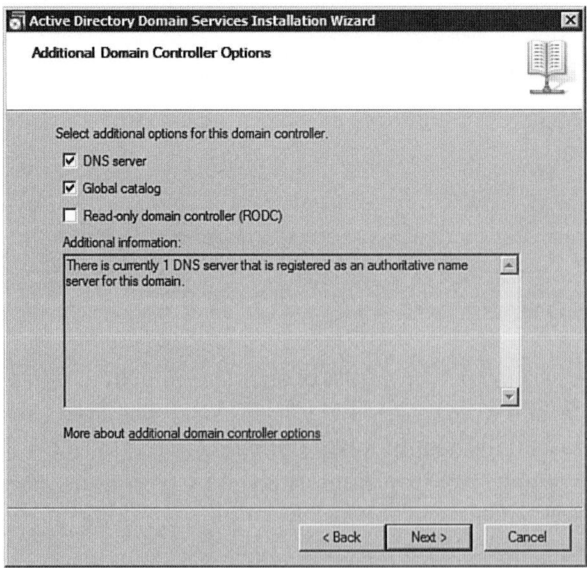

FIGURE 11-5 The capability to make the server a DNS server is a useful option.

You may get a warning if you have an adapter configured without a static IP address (this applies to both IPv4 and IPv6). If DNS has been delegated for the zone in which this domain controller participates and is hosting the DNS service, you are prompted if the DNS delegation for the zone should be updated to also include this new domain controller. At this prompt, leave the default answer, which is yes. The next screen asks you to select the location for the database, log files, and SYSVOL, which by default is under the C:\Windows folder, as with the first domain controller. Be sure to provide a password for Directory Services restore mode.

The final screen of the wizard displays a summary of the settings in addition to an Export settings button. Click Next to begin the promotion process.

Unattended Installation

The answer file for a domain controller promotion contains basic text. Use the Domain Controller Wizard to produce an answer file based on the settings you configure during wizard execution via the Export Settings button on the Summary screen. The output from the Add Replica Domain Controller Wizard is shown in the following example. The password for the domain it is joining is shown as an asterisk, as is the password for `DNSDelegationPassword`, so the passwords are requested interactively when the `dcpromo` process is executed. If you don't want to be prompted, add the password to the unattended answer file. You must also populate `SafeModeAdminPassword`, as this is not prompted for, but a blank password fails the minimum password checking. You may also want to modify `SiteName` to select the correct site for the domain controller or comment it out and have it automatically selected based on IP address.

```
; DCPROMO unattend file
; Usage:
;   dcpromo.exe /unattend:C:\temp\adddctovirt.txt
;
; You may need to fill in password fields prior to using
; the unattend file.
; If you leave the values for "Password" and/or
; "DNSDelegationPassword"
; as "*", then you will be asked for credentials at runtime.
;
[DCInstall]
```

```
; Replica DC promotion
ReplicaOrNewDomain=Replica
ReplicaDomainDNSName=virt.savilltech.net
SiteName=Austin
InstallDNS=Yes
ConfirmGc=Yes
DNSDelegation=Yes
DNSDelegationUserName=virt.savilltech.net\administrator
DNSDelegationPassword=*
UserDomain=virt.savilltech.net
UserName=virt.savilltech.net\administrator
Password=*
DatabasePath="C:\Windows\NTDS"
LogPath="C:\Windows\NTDS"
SYSVOLPath="C:\Windows\SYSVOL"
; Set SafeModeAdminPassword to the correct value prior
; to using the unattend file
SafeModeAdminPassword=Pa55word
; Run-time flags (optional)
; CriticalReplicationOnly=Yes
; RebootOnCompletion=Yes
```

A full list of unattended settings can be found in the Microsoft Active Directory Domain Services Installation and Removal Getting Started Guide on the Windows Server 2008 Technical library site on Technet at http://technet2.microsoft.com/windowsserver2008/en/library/246aa651-6858-4dc9-aade-6806065d0ea21033.mspx?mfr=true.

A sample execution is shown in Figure 11-6. Notice that you are prompted for the administrator password and the DNS delegation information.

Use this same answer file on a Server Core installation to create a domain controller. One of the easiest ways to do so is to run through the wizard on a normal server and then save the unattended answer settings. If you ran the settings shown earlier on a Server Core, the following components are installed:

- DirectoryServices-DomainController-ServerFoundation
- DNS-Server-Core-Role

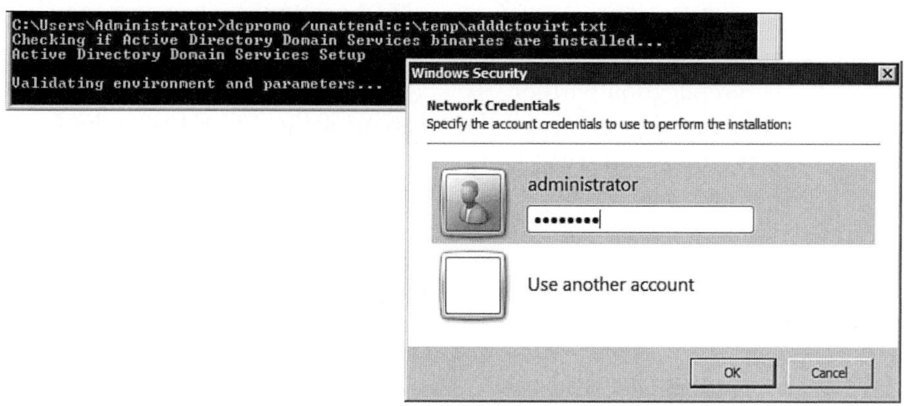

Figure 11-6 When performing the unattended installation of a domain controller, enter the administrator password.

Moving FSMO Roles

Now that you have two domain controllers, you could move the FSMO roles around, but let's first look at some best practices concerning the placement of the FSMO role holders:

- **Best Practice 1**. The PDC (primary domain controller) Emulator and RID (relative identifier) Master role should be placed on the same domain controller. Although all domain controllers are supposed to be equal, the PDC Emulator Master role is contacted more than any other domain controller. This means it performs more actions and uses more RIDs, so placing the PDC with the RID Master role makes the most sense.
- **Best Practice 2**. The Infrastructure Master role must not be on a GC unless there is only one domain in the forest or every domain controller in the domain is a GC.
- **Best Practice 3**. Unless the domain controllers are not heavily utilized, try to avoid placing the PDC/RID FSMOs on a GC because a GC typically gets high usage. Obviously, in smaller environments, you are likely to have only two domain controllers, and both are GCs.
- **Best Practice 4**. Typically, the Schema Master and Domain Naming Master roles are placed on the same domain controller, which is also a GC, given the forest-wide nature of the roles.

For all the FSMO role holders, there should always be another domain controller in the same site so the roles can easily be transferred with an up-to-date replication partner.

You can quickly check the location of the FSMO roles by using the `netdom` command with the `query fsmo` argument, as shown in the following example.

```
C:\Users\Administrator>netdom query fsmo
Schema master               savtstdc01.virt.savilltech.net
Domain naming master        savtstdc01.virt.savilltech.net
PDC                         savtstdc01.virt.savilltech.net
RID pool manager            savtstdc01.virt.savilltech.net
Infrastructure master       savtstdc01.virt.savilltech.net
The command completed successfully.
```

Now that you understand the best practices for role placement, you can move the roles. But why would you want to do that? Some of the roles must be more available than others. If a specific FSMO is unavailable, you may see the following problems:

- **PDC Emulator Master**. This is probably the most important role to have available. If it's unavailable, clocks may become unsynchronized (which would last a *long* period of time) because the PDC is responsible for time sync in its domain. Well before that became a problem, there would be bigger issues, such as users being unable to change their passwords because password changes are always sent to the PDC FSMO. Any account lockouts would also fail. It would also not be possible to raise the mode of the domain.
- **RID Master**. Each domain controller has a cache of 500 relative identifiers to use in the creation of objects, and this cache is renewed when half the identifiers are used up. If the RID Master role were unavailable, a domain controller would be unable to create new objects when its cache was exhausted. This means a domain controller would have to create more objects than its RID cache number (at least 250 objects, but depending on the last time it renewed with the RID Master role, up to 500 objects) while the RID Master role was unavailable before the domain controller would be affected and unable to create new objects.
- **Infrastructure Master**. You'd see effects of this role being missing only if you had more than one domain, and even then the worst

effect would be that attempts to view group memberships would show some grayed-out icons. And this simply reflects the fact that the Infrastructure Master role has not updated across domain group memberships; the group itself would still function.

- **Domain Naming Master**. You cannot add or remove domains or domain controllers without the Domain Naming Master role.
- **Schema Master**. Without the Schema Master role, the schema is not modifiable, and the forest mode cannot be raised.

The only two roles that have an operational impact are PDC Emulator Master and RID Master. Therefore, if FSMO role holders are down for a limited amount of time, you only need to worry about moving the PDC Emulator Master and RID Master roles to ensure their continued availability. That being said, you can move them all. For each domain controller, the following sections describe the graphical way to move the role and a corresponding method from the command line.

Changing the RID, PDC, and Infrastructure FSMO Servers Graphically

You can transfer the RID, PDC, and Infrastructure FSMO roles via the Active Directory Users and Computers Microsoft Management Console (MMC) snap-in by right-clicking on the domain and selecting Operations Masters. This makes sense, considering that these roles are all domain specific. Now when you perform the action from the MMC snap-in, the transference is from the current role to the domain controller that has focus for the MMC snap-in. So before you try to transfer the role, first switch the MMC focus to the domain controller to which you want to transfer the role by right-clicking the root of the MMC navigation node and selecting Change Domain Controller, as shown in Figure 11-7.

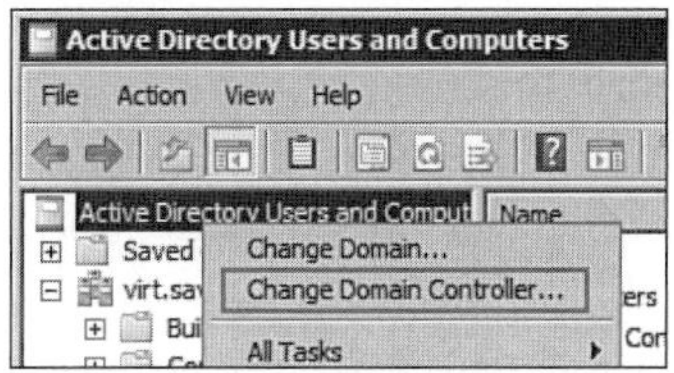

Figure 11-7 All role transfer actions are performed in the MMC.

In the Change Domain Controller dialog box, you can select from the list of the domain controllers in the domain. In this case, select the other domain controller for the domain, as shown in Figure 11-8.

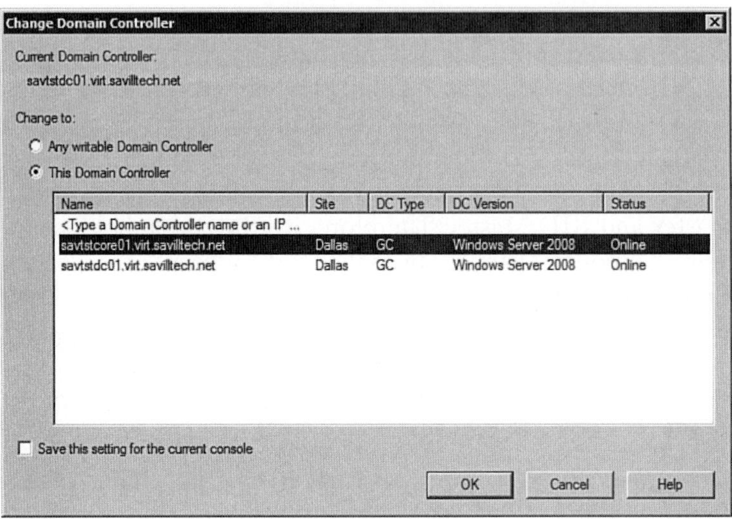

FIGURE 11-8 You can select the domain controller to be used or find any writeable domain controller.

After you select a domain controller to which the role is transferred, right-click and select Operations Masters. The Operations Masters dialog displays three tabs, one for each of the domain roles. Each tab shows the current operations master and the domain controller that is transferred to the roll if the Change button is clicked, as shown in Figure 11-9. If you transfer the Infrastructure Master role to a GC, you are warned that the infrastructure role should not be on a GC. However, if there is only one domain or all domain controllers are GCs, ignore this. Note that although while you can ignore this, if in the future another domain were added to the forest or a domain controller were added that was not a GC, you would have problems. So ensure that you have good change management procedures and checklists in place if additional domains/domain controllers are added, the infrastructure placement still adheres to best practices. That might mean moving the Infrastructure Master role to a non-GC server.

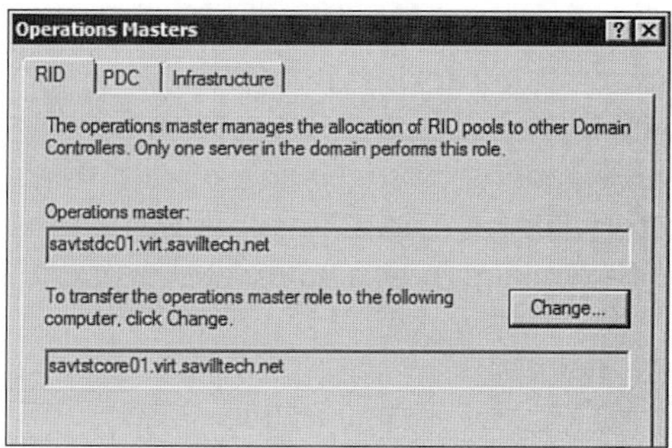

FIGURE 11-9 You can use the graphical interface to change the FSMO role holder for the domain roles.

Changing the Domain Naming FSMO Server Graphically

Because the Domain Naming Master role is a forest role, change it using the Active Directory Domains and Trusts MMC snap-in. In the same way that you changed the domain roles, you must first change the focus of the snap-in to the domain controller to which you want to transfer the role by right-clicking the root of the Navigation pane and selecting Change Active Directory Domain Controller and then selecting the domain controller that is transferred by the Domain Naming FSMO role.

When the new server is selected, right-click again on Active Directory Domains and Trusts root and select Operations Master. A dialog is displayed (see Figure 11-10) that enables you to change the Domain Naming FSMO role. There is no tab in this dialog because the Domains and Trusts MMC snap-in can move only one FSMO role.

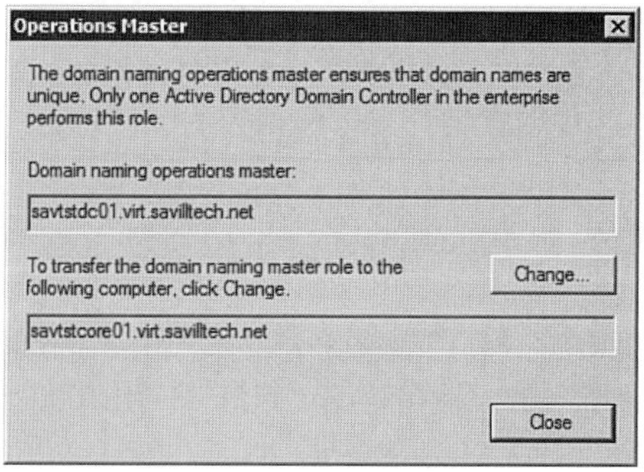

Operations Master

The domain naming operations master ensures that domain names are unique. Only one Active Directory Domain Controller in the enterprise performs this role.

Domain naming operations master:

savtstdc01.virt.savilltech.net

To transfer the domain naming master role to the following computer, click Change.

Change...

savtstcore01.virt.savilltech.net

Close

FIGURE 11-10 Transferring the Domain Naming Operations Master role.

Changing the Schema Master FSMO Server Graphically

Schema Master is the trickiest role to move graphically because the tools associated with it are hidden to prevent you from accidentally causing mass corruption and generally having a bad day. First, enable access to the Active Directory Schema MMC snap-in. To do this, run the following command in the Run dialog or at a command prompt:

```
regsvr32 schmmgmt.dll
```

A dialog notifies you that the DllRegisterServer in schmmgmt.dll succeeded. You are now able to see the Schema Management MMC snap-in in a custom console, so start an MMC console instance (Start, Run, MMC) and select File, Add/Remove Snap-in. The Active Directory Schema snap-in is now available, so add it to the selected snap-ins, as shown in Figure 11-11 and click OK.

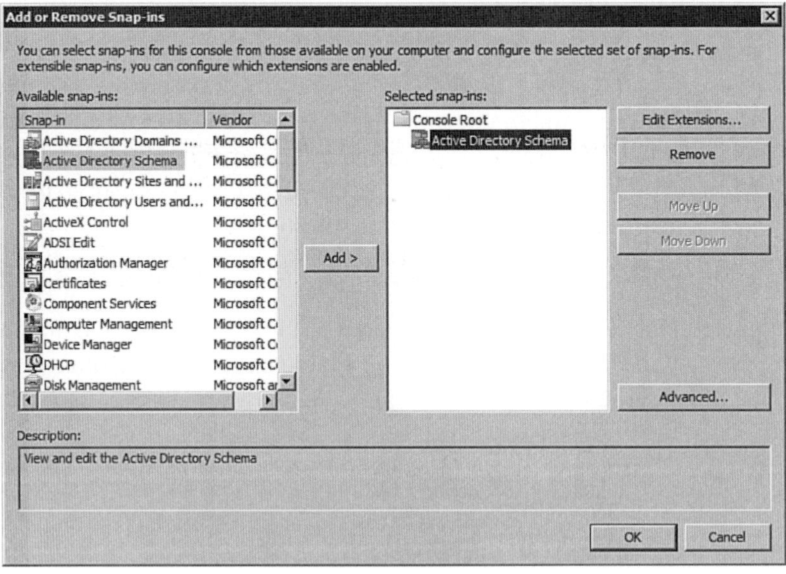

FIGURE 11-11 You can now see the hidden Active Directory Schema snap-in.

When the snap-in is loaded, change the focus to the domain controller to which the role is to be transferred by right-clicking the Active Directory Schema Navigation pane node and selecting Change Active Directory

Domain Controller. Then select Operations Master to move the Schema Master role, as shown in Figure 11-12. A confirmation dialog is displayed; click OK, and the FSMO role is moved.

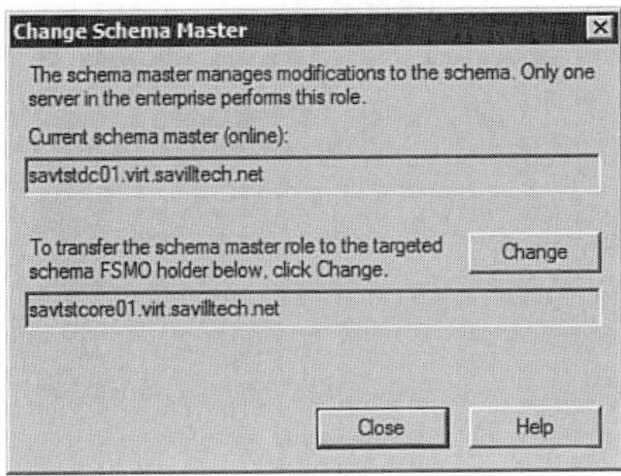

FIGURE 11-12 The Change Schema Master dialog.

Moving FSMO Roles from the Command Line

A command, `ntdsutil`, is mentioned a lot with AD. As its name implies, `ntdsutil` is a utility for the management of the NT Directory Service (NTDS). In this case, use it to move FSMO roles, but it does much, much more.

To start the utility, just run the `ntdsutil` command. A new prompt appears. You can then access the roles portion of the `ntdsutil` functionality and then connect to the domain controller that transfers the FSMO role. Next, use the `transfer` command with the role to be transferred, which can be Schema Master, RID Master, PDC, Infrastructure Master, or Domain Naming Master. The following example moves the Schema Master and Infrastructure Master roles back to savtstdc01 (the selected server). Type **`quit`** at each prompt to exit the utility.

```
C:\Users\Administrator>ntdsutil
ntdsutil: roles
fsmo maintenance: connections
server connections: connect to server
➥savtstdc01.virt.savilltech.net
Binding to savtstdc01.virt.savilltech.net ...
Connected to savtstdc01.virt.savilltech.net using
```

```
credentials of locally logged
on user.
server connections: quit

fsmo maintenance: transfer schema master
Server "savtstdc01.virt.savilltech.net" knows about 5 roles
Schema - CN=NTDS Settings,CN=SAVTSTDC01,CN=Servers,CN=Dallas,
CN=Sites,CN=Configuration,DC=virt,DC=savilltech,DC=net
Naming Master - CN=NTDS
Settings,CN=SAVTSTDC01,CN=Servers,CN=Dallas,CN=Sites,CN=
Configuration,DC=virt,DC=savilltech,DC=net
PDC - CN=NTDS Settings,CN=SAVTSTDC01,CN=Servers,CN=Dallas,
CN=Sites,CN=Configuration,DC=virt,DC=savilltech,DC=net
RID - CN=NTDS Settings,CN=SAVTSTDC01,CN=Servers,CN=Dallas,
CN=Sites,CN=Configurat

ion,DC=virt,DC=savilltech,DC=net
Infrastructure - CN=NTDS
Settings,CN=SAVTSTCORE01,CN=Servers,CN=Dallas,CN=Sites,
CN=Configuration,DC=virt,DC=savilltech,DC=net

fsmo maintenance: transfer infrastructure master
Server "savtstdc01.virt.savilltech.net" knows about 5 roles
Schema - CN=NTDS Settings,CN=SAVTSTDC01,CN=Servers,CN=Dallas,
CN=Sites,CN=Configuration,DC=virt,DC=savilltech,DC=net
Naming Master - CN=NTDS
Settings,CN=SAVTSTDC01,CN=Servers,CN=Dallas,CN=Sites,CN=
Configuration,DC=virt,DC=savilltech,DC=net
PDC - CN=NTDS Settings,CN=SAVTSTDC01,CN=Servers,CN=Dallas,
CN=Sites,CN=Configuration,DC=virt,DC=savilltech,DC=net
RID - CN=NTDS Settings,CN=SAVTSTDC01,CN=Servers,CN=Dallas,
CN=Sites,CN=Configuration,DC=virt,DC=savilltech,DC=net
Infrastructure - CN=NTDS
Settings,CN=SAVTSTDC01,CN=Servers,CN=Dallas,CN=Sites,CN
=Configuration,DC=virt,DC=savilltech,DC=net

fsmo maintenance: quit
ntdsutil: quit
```

When you transfer the FSMO roles from within `ntdsutil`, you get a graphical confirmation prompt, as shown in Figure 11-13.

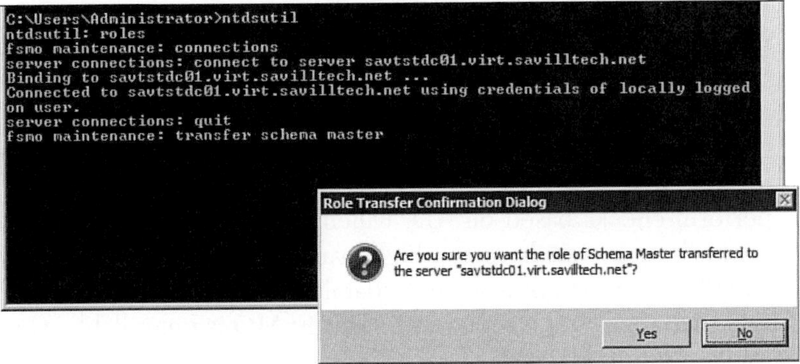
C:\Users\Administrator>ntdsutil
ntdsutil: roles
fsmo maintenance: connections
server connections: connect to server savtstdc01.virt.savilltech.net
Binding to savtstdc01.virt.savilltech.net ...
Connected to savtstdc01.virt.savilltech.net using credentials of locally logged on user.
server connections: quit
fsmo maintenance: transfer schema master
Role Transfer Confirmation Dialog
Are you sure you want the role of Schema Master transferred to the server "savtstdc01.virt.savilltech.net"?
Yes
No

FIGURE 11-13 A graphical prompt is used for `ntdsutil` command-line actions.

Seizing a Role

As you have seen, you can transfer FSMO roles by using the graphical interface utilities or the `ntdsutil` command. However, if the existing FSMO role cannot be contacted, force the FSMO role transfer by using the `ntdsutil` utility and the `seize` switch. This would be necessary if the server hosting the FSMO role crashed before you were able to transfer the role using a normal method.

To use this option, perform the same actions you normally perform when transferring a role with `ntdsutil`, but when you come to move the role, instead of doing this:

```
fsmo maintenance: transfer <role>
```

enter the following command:

```
fsmo maintenance: seize <role>
```

The `seize` option tries to transfer the role gracefully first, and if that fails, it forcefully takes it.

Use `seize` only in circumstances in which the current role holder is not going to be coming back online soon and you can't have its functionality unavailable for the length of time it is offline. This is because `seize` forces the move without requiring communication between the old role holder and the new one, which means some information may not be transferred cleanly. The other situation in which you might have to use it is if the role holder is never coming back. Keep in mind that there is only ever one FSMO per domain or forest (depending on whether the FSMO is domain or forest based). There is no such concept of a mirror of an FSMO for high availability. Remember that the FSMO roles give information or perform checks based on AD, which is already replicated to all domain controllers, so you have the high availability of the information handled already. There is not a separate database of information for each FSMO role that needs to be replicated. If an FSMO is unavailable, you seize the role as described earlier.

GC Setting

When you run the `dcpromo` process, one of the options is to set the new domain controller as a GC. However, you can also do this outside the domain controller promotion process.

As an administrator, you use three main graphical tools for AD management: Active Directory Sites and Services, Active Directory Users and Computers, and Active Directory Domains and Trusts. The Active Directory Sites and Services tool is useful for the management of physical AD elements such as locations, the IP subnets in them, and the links connecting locations. Also with the Active Directory Sites and Services tool you can see the connection objects that have been created by the Knowledge Consistency Checker (KCC) to enable replication of AD data based on these sites and site links, including those used to replicate GC data and logically set whether a domain controller is a GC.

To set a domain controller as a Global Catalog, right-click the NTDS Settings object for the server you want to enable as a GC under its site within the Active Directory Sites and Services MMC snap-in, as shown in Figure 11-14 and check/uncheck the Global Catalog check box.

While setting whether a domain controller is a GC is a simple affair, the background about whether it should be a GC is a different story. In a single-domain forest, it is common to make all domain controllers GC servers. This is generally okay, unless you have specific domain controllers that handle a lot of replication traffic or specific FSMO roles, in which case you may not want them performing the additional GC workload.

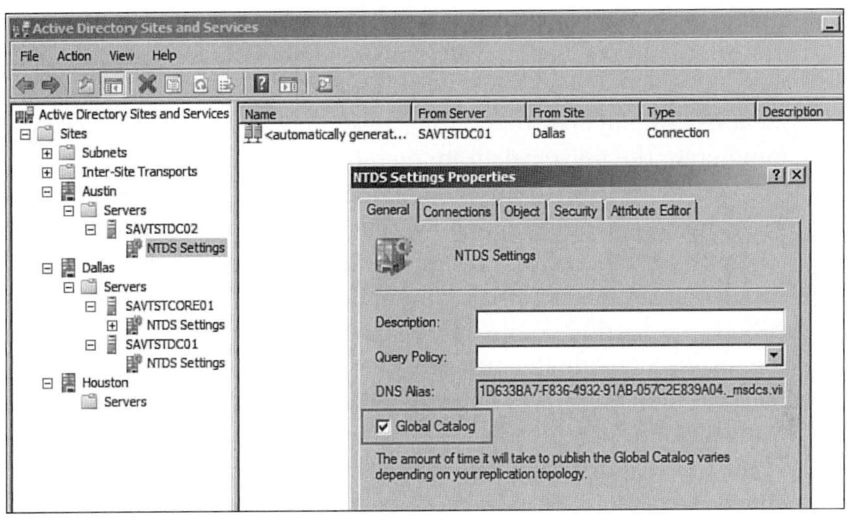

FIGURE 11-14 After the new GC is set, it does not advertise a GC until replication of all partial partitions is complete.

For forests with multiple domains, the decision to make a domain controller a GC is a more complex proposition due to the additional replication traffic involved. The decision normally comes down to the following:

- The number of users at a location
- The quality of the WAN link from the location to a location with a GC
- The applications running at the location

Remember that a GC is used any time a user performs a search for users or printers, during logon to enumerate universal groups, and, of course, the newer versions of Outlook communicate directly with a GC.

Generally, if a location has more than 100 users or has a lot of roaming users, you want a GC at the location. If the location has a good WAN link that is 100% available and has fewer than 100 users, you can probably skip the GC and just have a normal domain controller. But what if you have fewer than 100 users but not a great WAN link? You don't want all the replication traffic associated with a GC, which can be large, especially if the local domain controller is a member of a smaller-volume child domain for a specific region. The GC content from the rest of the forest may be much larger than that of its local domain partition. There is a middle option. Windows Server 2003 introduced universal group membership caching, which helps with the logon problem associated with not having a local GC. Remember that during a user logon, a GC must be contacted to enumerate the universal group memberships of a user.

When universal group membership caching is enabled, the user's universal group membership is stored in the msDS-Cached-Membership attribute of the user's account, and the current time is written to the msDS-Cached-Membership-Time-Stamp value, along with msDS-Site-Affinity to identify the site of the logon the first time the user logs on. Only the msDS-Site-Affinity attribute is replicated between domain controllers; the timestamp and list of group security identifiers (SIDs) are not replicated but are stored only on the authenticating domain controller (see Figure 11-15). The highlighted portion is the SID of a universal group (JLeague), and notice also that you can see the time stamp, which indicates when the caching took place.

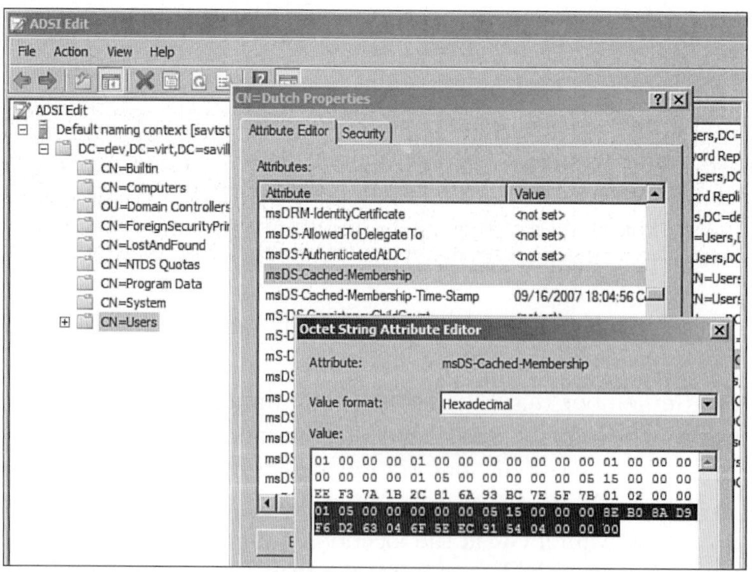

FIGURE 11-15 Use the ADSI Edit tool for advanced viewing and configuration of directory data. It provides insight into information that's not normally available.

The next time the user logs on, the SIDs are read from the msDS-Cached-Membership attribute instead of a GC being consulted, assuming that the msDS-Cached-Membership-Time-Stamp is within the staleness time period (seven days, by default). If the cached membership information is stale, a GC is consulted for universal group membership information, and the msDS-Cached-Membership and msDS-Cached-Membership-Time-Stamp attributes are updated. The cached information is updated every eight hours by default, and up to 500 accounts are refreshed in each refresh cycle.

To enable universal group membership caching, perform the following steps:

1. Start the Active Directory Sites and Services MMC snap-in.
2. Select the site for which you want to enable caching.
3. In the right-hand pane, right-click NTDS Site Settings and select Properties.
4. Check Enable Universal Group Membership Caching and click OK (see Figure 11-16).

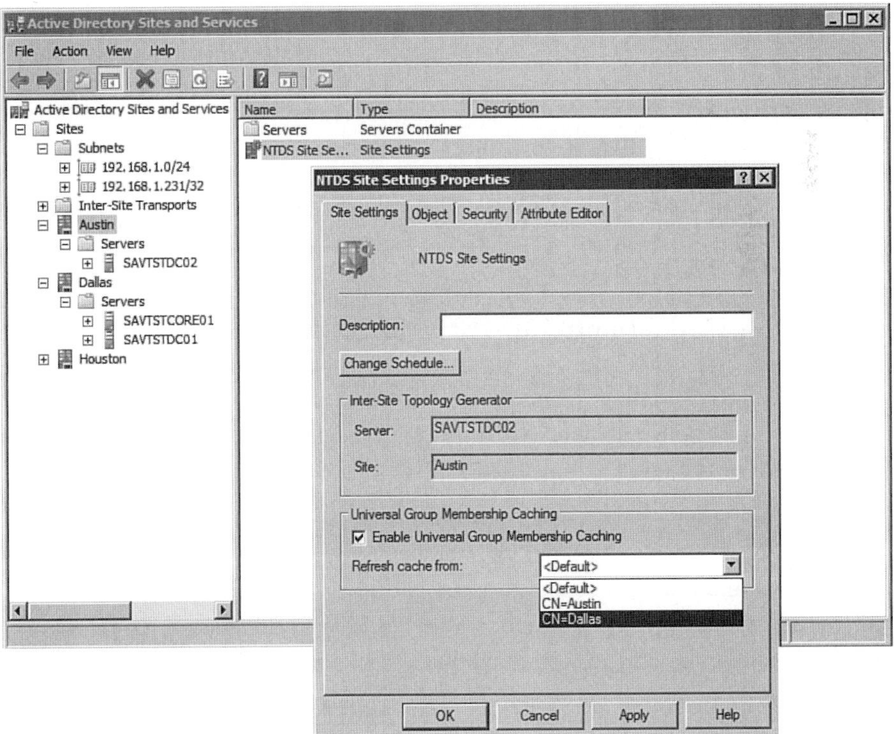

FIGURE 11-16 Enabling universal group membership caching, like enabling a GC, is easy.

Notice in Figure 11-16 that you can select from where the cache should be refreshed (other sites) or leave the default to have it selected automatically.

To modify the default values associated with cached universal groups edit (or create them, if they're missing) the DWORD values shown in Table 11-1 under the Registry key HKEY_LOCAL_MACHINE\SYSTEM\CurrentControlSet\Services\NTDS\Parameters\.

Table 11-1 DWORD Values in the Registry for Cached Universal Groups

Value Name	Purpose
Cached Membership Staleness (minutes)	How long (in minutes) cached information can be used before it is considered stale. The default is 10080, which is 1 week.
Cached Membership Refresh Interval (minutes)	How frequently (in minutes) cached information is refreshed from a GC. The default is 480 (8 hours).
Cached Membership Refresh Limit	The maximum number of accounts that are refreshed in a refresh cycle. If you need to increase this beyond the default 500, consider using a local GC at the site.

Creating a New Domain

There are times when an organizational unit (OU) does not meet the needs of the AD design process, and a separate domain is needed in the forest. Don't take this lightly: A new domain means additional hardware for the domain controllers needed for the domain, more data replicated in the GC, and generally more administrative effort. So why would you want a new domain, and when is a whole separate forest needed?

NOTE Notice that I don't talk about what would drive a separate tree; this is because a tree is the same as another domain in the forest. It just has a separate, noncontiguous namespace from the existing domains in the forest. Therefore, the only reason to create a separate tree is for a new namespace. There is no other difference in the functionality.

Reasons for Creating a New Domain

There are a number of reasons for creating a new domain, although with Windows Server 2008, some of them are no longer such a big issue. An obvious reason for creating a new domain is simply to replicate the data. Replication has gotten more efficient as AD has evolved. Just the changes to groups are replicated now instead of the entire group. This is possible through linked value replication (LVR). In Windows 2000, attributes were the lowest level of replication. For a group, all the members were stored in one attribute, so if the membership of a group changed, the entire group membership had to be re-replicated. This was annoying in the case of a 4,000-member group that had to be re-replicated just because 1 user was added. LVR, which was introduced with Windows Server 2003 AD, replicates only the changes to the group.

However, there is still a lot of data in a domain partition that has to be replicated to all the domain controllers in the domain. If the data changes frequently and your office has a slow connection, the replication of the domain partition may not be practical. Therefore, you might want to create another domain in the forest for its local resources. Remember that although AD has granular replication and uses good compression, it would be possible to configure the replication to occur only overnight, when the link is not in use. So don't jump too quickly to add another domain.

Along the same lines as a poor-quality connection (although this is becoming a non-issue), if the link between locations is so poor as to not support Remote Procedure Call (RPC) over IP, the locations cannot be part of the same domain. A domain partition can only do replication via RPC over IP, and therefore a separate domain would be needed. The other partitions—for example, the configuration, schema, and GC content partitions—can replicate via Simple Mail Transfer Protocol (SMTP).

In previous versions of AD, the security policy related to passwords could be set only at the domain level, which meant that if different groups of users required different password policies, separate domains had to be used. That was a terrible reason. There were third-party applications that enabled more granular password policies, but with Windows Server 2008, a more granular password scheme is now built in, so this is no longer a driver for multiple domains, provided that you are running only Windows Server 2008 domain controllers.

There are other reasons for adding a domain. However, a lot of them may also mean not just a new domain is required but a whole separate forest:

- A common domain administrator is not acceptable. This is often the case due to certain compliance regulations, such as the Health Insurance Portability and Accountability Act (HIPAA). However, because all the domains in the forest have a common Enterprise Administrator group, if no common administrators are needed, a totally separate forest is required.
- If various groups function independently, with no central IT team, then multiple domains may arise. But this is a problem, still assuming that the domains are part of the same forest via a top-level placeholder domain that would have been created. Each department would then create its own domain as a child, which at least keeps one forest with shared configuration, schema, and GC. An even worse scenario would be one in which each department creates its own forest, meaning no shared configuration or GC.
- Some organizations prefer an empty root domain that contains the schema and domain master roles. However, this setup is not widely used today.
- A separate domain for a demilitarized zone may be required for Internet-facing applications. However, to provide high security, a separate forest may be required.

There are additional reasons a separate forest may be required. For example, a schema is forest-wide, and so if you want to have a development domain to test schema changes, you would create a separate development forest. Some services, such as Exchange, also store their configuration in the Configuration partition and can have only one instance per forest. So if multiple Exchange organizations were required, multiple forests would be needed. But that is not a good reason!

How to Create a New Domain

So how do you create a new domain? In this section, you create a child domain in an existing tree. However, the procedure to create a new tree is the same, and this section notes when you would select a different option. Remember that a new tree just enables a noncontiguous namespace. So if you have domain virt.savilltech.net and you want a new domain dev, then as a child domain, its name would be dev.virt.savilltech.net. However, if you want the name of dev.test, then you need a new tree in the forest.

To create a new domain, follow these steps:

1. Start the ADDS installation via the ADDS role and leave the Use Advanced Mode Installation option unchecked. Click Next if this is a child domain. If this is a new tree, check the Use Advanced Mode Installation option.
2. Select Existing Forest and select Create a New Domain in an Existing Forest. If you selected advanced mode, an option to create a new domain tree root instead of a new child domain is available; select it to create a new tree, as shown in Figure 11-17.

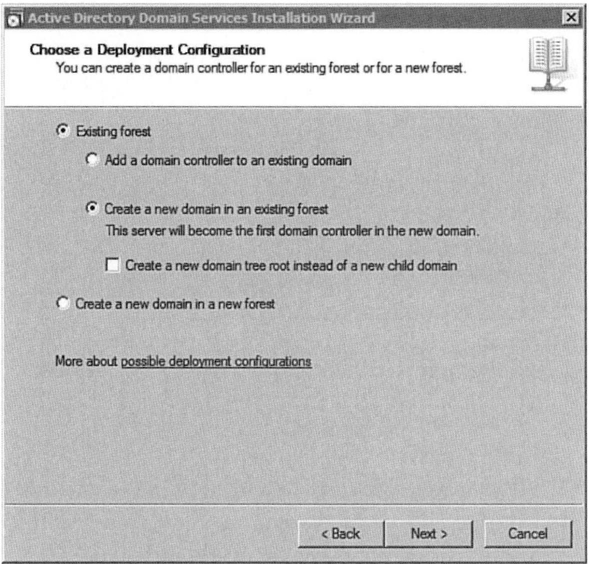

Figure 11-17 Adding a new domain to an existing forest.

3. Enter the name of a domain in the forest in which you make a new domain and click the Set button to set the credentials to use for the domain enumeration. Click Next.
4. In the next screen, name the new domain (see Figure 11-18). Click the Browse button to select the domain that is the parent of the

new domain and then enter the child portion of the name (for example, dev) and click Next. The full name of the new domain is shown in the Fully Qualified Domain Name (FQDN) area of the dialog, and the child portion of the name is added to the parent. If a new tree is being created, you are prompted for the new FQDN of the domain (for example, dev.test).

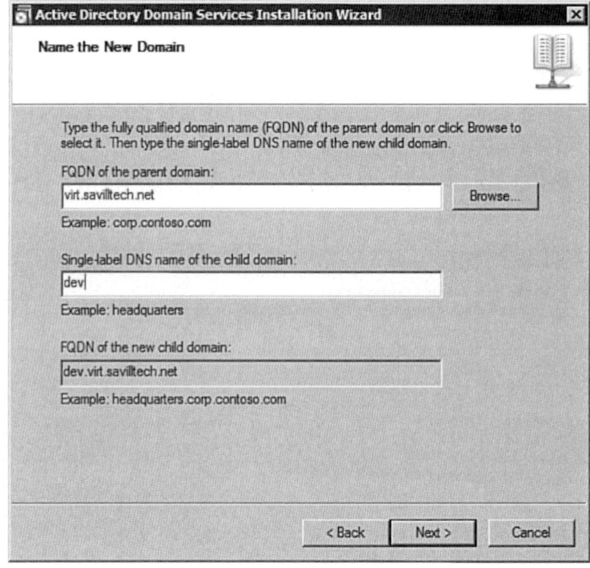

FIGURE 11-18 Specifying the name for the new domain and the parent of the new domain.

5. If advanced mode was selected, you see a dialog that prompts you to change the NetBIOS name. You also see this dialog if a normal mode promotion was selected and a conflict was found during checks on the name specified. Enter the site name.
6. Select options for DNS Server and GC. Note that a new domain's first domain controller cannot be an RODC, so this option is not available. Click Next.
7. With the advanced mode for a new tree, you are prompted to select a domain controller for replication, but leave this as the default, Let the Wizard Choose an Appropriate Domain Controller, and click Next (see Figure 11-19). This is a useful option for locations with constrained firewall rules, so you can control where initial replication is performed.

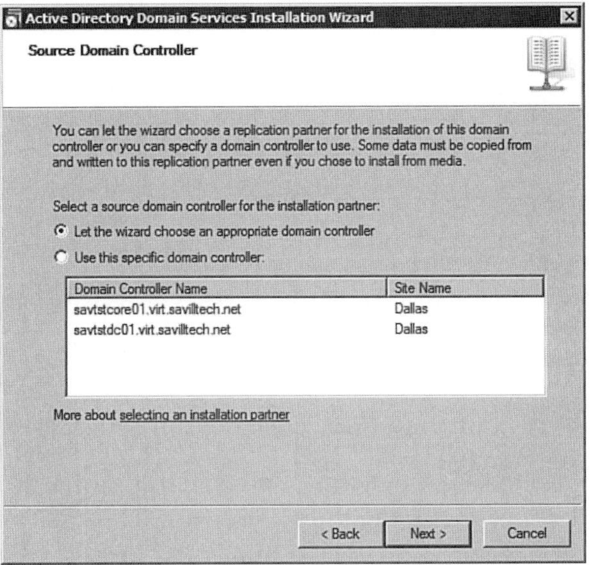

FIGURE 11-19 Select a source domain controller for initial replication.

8. Select locations for the NTDS database and SYSVOL and set the recovery password, as per a normal installation.
9. Check the settings and export them to create an unattended installation file. Click Next to begin the ADDS installation.
10. Click Finish and allow the reboot of the server.

The unattended installation of either a new tree or a new child domain is the same as for a new domain controller. The following example shows a new tree unattended promotion file. It does not have DNS delegation because in this case the made-up domain can't be delegated because the .test DNS zone cannot be located.

```
[DCInstall]
; New tree promotion
ReplicaOrNewDomain=Domain
NewDomain=Tree
NewDomainDNSName=dev.test
DomainNetbiosName=DEV
DomainLevel=3
SiteName=Austin
```

```
InstallDNS=Yes
ConfirmGc=Yes
DNSDelegation=No
UserDomain=virt.savilltech.net
UserName=virt.savilltech.net\administrator
Password=*
DatabasePath="C:\Windows\NTDS"
LogPath="C:\Windows\NTDS"
SYSVOLPath="C:\Windows\SYSVOL"
; Set SafeModeAdminPassword to the correct value
; prior to using the unattend file
SafeModeAdminPassword=
```

The only difference for a child domain is that the first three lines are changed to the following:

```
ReplicaOrNewDomain=Domain
NewDomain=Child
ParentDomainDNSName=virt.savilltech.net
ChildName=dev
```

In addition, because for a child domain the DNS parent zone is available and running Windows DNS, most likely the DNS can be delegated via the following entry:

```
DNSDelegation=Yes
DNSDelegationUserName=virt.savilltech.net\administrator
DNSDelegationPassword=*
```

DNS Delegation

A DNS namespace can be big, and serving from one group of servers makes no sense and would use up a lot of space in AD. This would create a lot of replication data, especially when you throw in dynamic DNS, which has records updating a lot. Because, in the case of child domains, you have a separate set of domain controllers with a separate domain partition, it makes sense for those child domains' domain controllers to store and host the DNS namespace for the domain controllers' local domains. By storing portions of the DNS namespace in different domains, you divide up the replication of the DNS data into smaller chunks and enable DNS to be more available to objects that are local to the domain.

When you choose to install a DNS server on child domains, DNS delegation is automatic. You can see this if you examine the DNS zone of the parent domain, as in Figure 11-20.

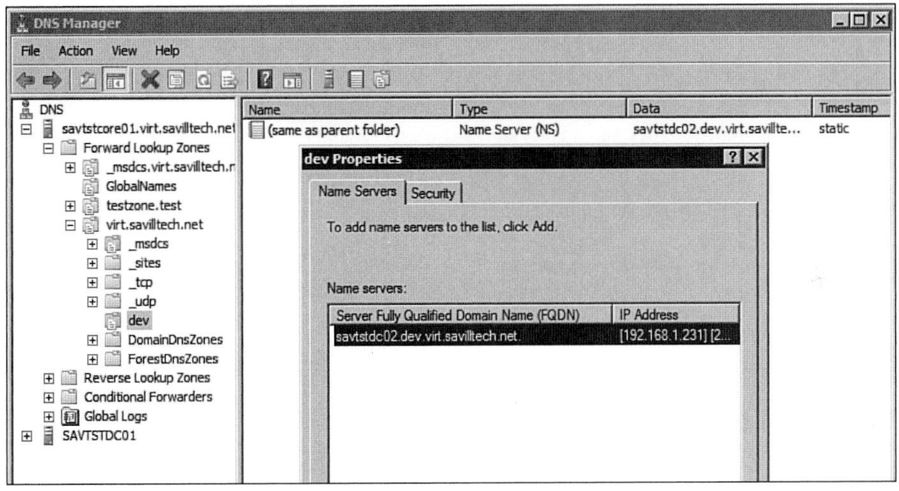

FIGURE 11-20 You can create DNS delegation records manually, using the DNS MMC snap-in. However, the automated fashion is much nicer!

Verifying Domain Controller Operation

You now have multiple domain controllers and potentially multiple domains, so ensure that they are functioning correctly. The first hint of a successful domain controller, and thereby domain creation, is that the Active Directory Domain Services Installation Wizard completed successfully, rebooted, and allowed you to log on as a member of the domain.

After you log in, if you can run Active Directory Users and Computers, Sites and Services, and Domains and Trusts, and if you have data, things are okay. But you can look in detail at the `dcpromo` process. In the %windir%\debug file you should see dcpromo.log, which has every item performed as part of the ADDS installation and labels each entry as informational (INFO), a warning, or an error. You can scan the file for errors and then determine whether they are problems. The following example is a section for a new domain creation.

```
09/15/2007 08:54:53 [INFO] Promotion request for domain
controller of new domain
09/15/2007 08:54:53 [INFO] DnsDomainName
dev.virt.savilltech.net
09/15/2007 08:54:53 [INFO]    FlatDomainName  DEV
09/15/2007 08:54:53 [INFO]    SiteName  Austin
09/15/2007 08:54:53 [INFO]    SystemVolumeRootPath
C:\Windows\SYSVOL
09/15/2007 08:54:53 [INFO]    DsDatabasePath  C:\Windows\NTDS,
DsLogPath  C:\Windows\NTDS
09/15/2007 08:54:53 [INFO]    ParentDnsDomainName
virt.savilltech.net
09/15/2007 08:54:53 [INFO]    ParentServer  (NULL)
09/15/2007 08:54:53 [INFO]    Account
virt.savilltech.net\administrator
09/15/2007 08:54:53 [INFO]    Options  5243072
09/15/2007 08:54:53 [INFO] Validate supplied paths
09/15/2007 08:54:53 [INFO] Validating path C:\Windows\NTDS.
09/15/2007 08:54:53 [INFO]    Path is a directory
09/15/2007 08:54:53 [INFO]    Path is on a fixed disk drive.
09/15/2007 08:54:53 [INFO] Validating path C:\Windows\NTDS.
09/15/2007 08:54:53 [INFO]    Path is a directory
09/15/2007 08:54:53 [INFO]    Path is on a fixed disk drive.
09/15/2007 08:54:53 [INFO] Validating path C:\Windows\SYSVOL.
09/15/2007 08:54:53 [INFO]    Path is on a fixed disk drive.
09/15/2007 08:54:53 [INFO]    Path is on an NTFS volume
09/15/2007 08:54:53 [INFO] Child domain creation -
check the new domain name is child of parent domain name.
09/15/2007 08:54:53 [INFO] Domain Creation -
check that the flat name is unique.
09/15/2007 08:54:58 [INFO] Start the worker task
09/15/2007 08:54:58 [INFO] Request for promotion returning 0
09/15/2007 08:54:58 [INFO] No source DC or no site name
specified. Searching for dc in domain virt.savilltech.net:
( DS_REQUIRED | WRITABLE )
09/15/2007 08:54:58 [INFO] Searching for a domain controller
for the domain virt.savilltech.net
09/15/2007 08:54:58 [INFO] Located domain controller
virt.savilltech.net for domain (null)
```

```
09/15/2007 08:54:58 [INFO] No user specified source DC
09/15/2007 08:54:58 [INFO] Using site Austin for server
virt.savilltech.net
09/15/2007 08:54:58 [INFO] Forcing time sync
```

If everything looks okay, with no warnings or errors, ensure that the domain controller is in the right site, based on its IP address. Open the AD Sites and Services MMC snap-in and ensure that the server shows up in the correct site. If you want it to belong to an alternate site, just drag the domain controller to another site via drag and drop.

MOVING A DOMAIN CONTROLLER TO ANOTHER SITE

Before you move a domain controller to another site, think through the move. Sites are physical constructs, and domain controllers have physical locations and IP addresses. Moving a domain controller to a site it does not physically reside in may have consequences, as users in that location may access a domain controller remote to their actual location.

In the AD Sites and Services snap-in, select the domain controller's NTDS Settings object in the Details pane to see actual connection objects, and if you select them (see Figure 11-21), they show what data is replicated, both fully and partially. It is replicating the ForestDnsZones naming context that is common to all domains in the forest (that are DNS servers); scroll right to see that it is replicating Schema and Configuration (the two forest-wide partitions). This is because this domain controller is from another domain, so it is not replicating the actual domain partition, which would be virt.savilltech.net.

Look at the partially replicated naming context to see an entry for dev.virt.savilltech.net, which is the domain for which the replication partner domain controller is responsible. Why is this being replicated? The server is a GC, which means it has partial information for all domains in the forest. So how does it get this information? It replicates partial information from a domain controller in each of the other domains. In this case, it pulls the partial information for dev.virt.savilltech.net from the SAVTSTDC02 domain controller (which is not a GC in this case). Look at the replication object of another domain controller in the same domain to see the local domain partition listed in the replicated naming contexts. Figure 11-22 shows the domain name as a replicated naming context, and because it's a DNS server, you see another naming context for DomainDnsZones.<*domain*>.

Notice All Other Domains under partially replicated naming contexts. The other domain controller is a GC, so your domain controller is populating the partner domain controller's GC content with the information it gathers from domain controllers in other domains. It makes no sense for each domain controller to replicate with domain controllers in other domains within one site; it's better for one domain controller to do it and then spread the knowledge.

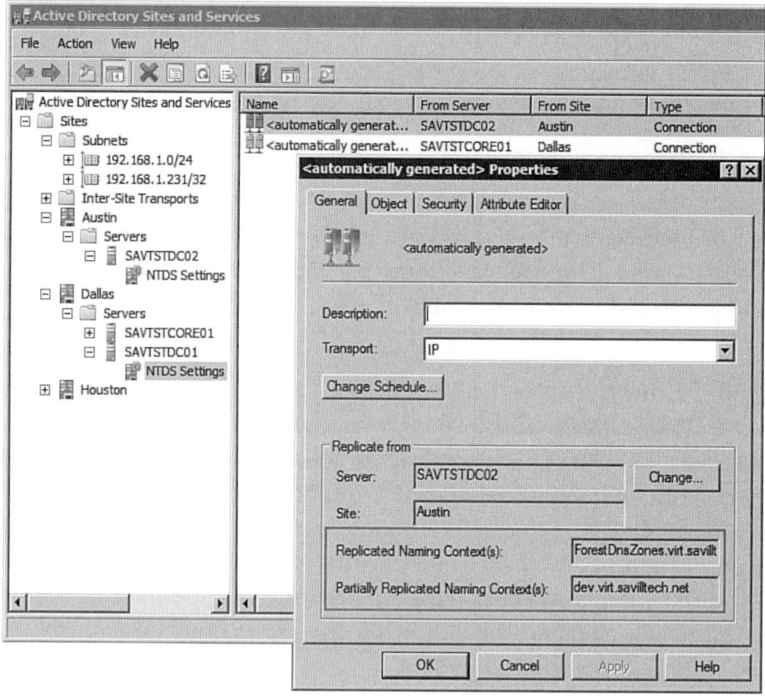

FIGURE 11-21 The SAVTSTDC01 server is a GC, and this shows that it replicates with SAVTSTDC02, a domain controller for a child domain.

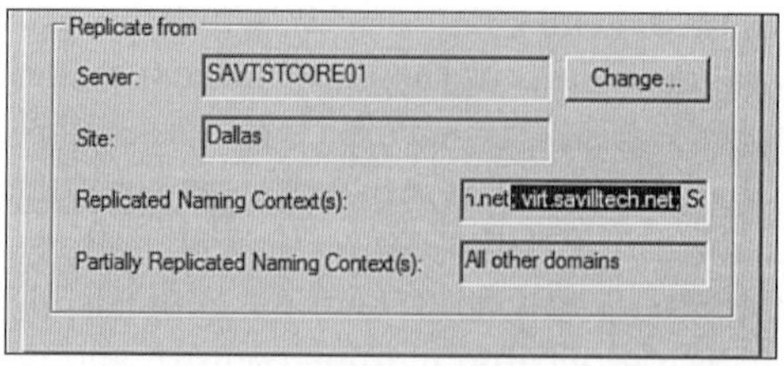

Replicate from
Server: SAVTSTCORE01
Change...
Site: Dallas
Replicated Naming Context(s): n.net; virt.savilltech.net; Sc
Partially Replicated Naming Context(s): All other domains

FIGURE 11-22 This replication is to a domain controller in the same domain that is also a GC.

At this point, you have your domain controller in a site and some replication objects, but is the replication working? The `repadmin` tool is useful for the management of replication in terms of forcing replication to take place (via the `/syncall` switch) and for checking on the state of replication with all partners (via the `/showreps` switch), as shown in the following example. For each partner and the various namespaces, it shows when the last replication occurred and whether it was successful. Notice that for the domain-specific namespaces (virt.savilltech.com and DomainDnsZones), replication takes place only with the savtstcore01 server, which is a domain controller for the virt.savilltech.com domain. The other zones, which are forest-wide, replicate from all domain controllers.

```
C:\Users\Administrator>repadmin /showreps
Dallas\SAVTSTDC01
DSA Options: IS_GC
Site Options: (none)
DSA object GUID: 6286b660-163a-4297-9f71-1ee274a4af38
DSA invocationID: 6286b660-163a-4297-9f71-1ee274a4af38

==== INBOUND NEIGHBORS ======================================

DC=virt,DC=savilltech,DC=net
    Dallas\SAVTSTCORE01 via RPC
        DSA object GUID: 4ae37f1a-7ab6-4e8b-a603-208997ea6e79
        Last attempt @ 2007-09-17 08:23:40 was successful.

CN=Configuration,DC=virt,DC=savilltech,DC=net
    Dallas\SAVTSTCORE01 via RPC
        DSA object GUID: 4ae37f1a-7ab6-4e8b-a603-208997ea6e79
        Last attempt @ 2007-09-17 07:58:39 was successful.
    Austin\SAVTSTDC02 via RPC
        DSA object GUID: 1d633ba7-f836-4932-91ab-057c2e839a04
        Last attempt @ 2007-09-17 07:58:40 was successful.

CN=Schema,CN=Configuration,DC=virt,DC=savilltech,DC=net
    Dallas\SAVTSTCORE01 via RPC
        DSA object GUID: 4ae37f1a-7ab6-4e8b-a603-208997ea6e79
        Last attempt @ 2007-09-17 07:58:39 was successful.
    Austin\SAVTSTDC02 via RPC
        DSA object GUID: 1d633ba7-f836-4932-91ab-057c2e839a04
        Last attempt @ 2007-09-17 07:58:40 was successful.
```

```
DC=DomainDnsZones,DC=virt,DC=savilltech,DC=net
    Dallas\SAVTSTCORE01 via RPC
        DSA object GUID: 4ae37f1a-7ab6-4e8b-a603-208997ea6e79
        Last attempt @ 2007-09-17 07:58:39 was successful.

DC=ForestDnsZones,DC=virt,DC=savilltech,DC=net
    Dallas\SAVTSTCORE01 via RPC
        DSA object GUID: 4ae37f1a-7ab6-4e8b-a603-208997ea6e79
        Last attempt @ 2007-09-17 07:58:40 was successful.
    Austin\SAVTSTDC02 via RPC
        DSA object GUID: 1d633ba7-f836-4932-91ab-057c2e839a04
        Last attempt @ 2007-09-17 07:58:40 was successful.

DC=dev,DC=virt,DC=savilltech,DC=net
    Dallas\SAVTSTCORE01 via RPC
        DSA object GUID: 4ae37f1a-7ab6-4e8b-a603-208997ea6e79
        Last attempt @ 2007-09-17 07:58:40 was successful.
    Austin\SAVTSTDC02 via RPC
        DSA object GUID: 1d633ba7-f836-4932-91ab-057c2e839a04
        Last attempt @ 2007-09-17 07:58:40 was successful.
```

The event logs are another great place to look for problems. Remember that a domain is replicated mainly via the directory service, but SYSVOL is also replicated via the File Replication Service, or Distributed File System Replication (DFSR) in a Windows Server 2008 mode domain. Look at the DFS Replication, Directory Service, DNS Server, and general System event logs to find any problems that may be affecting the health of your domain controller. They are all available via the Computer Management MMC snap-in, under System Tools, Event Viewer, as shown in Figure 11-23.

If you are running File Replication Service because you have non-Windows Server 2008 domain controllers, check the File Replication Service node of Event Viewer.

To view the DFSR SYSVOL configuration, use the DFS Management MMC snap-in (which can be installed without Distributed File System [DFS] via Remote Server Administration Tools, Role Administration Tools, File Services Tools, Distributed File System Tools). When this is installed, view the Replication portion of the DFS Management console, and Domain System Volume is shown with all the members of the SYSVOL replica set. However, unlike with a normal DFSR replica set, no changes can be made, as this is controlled by the directory service.

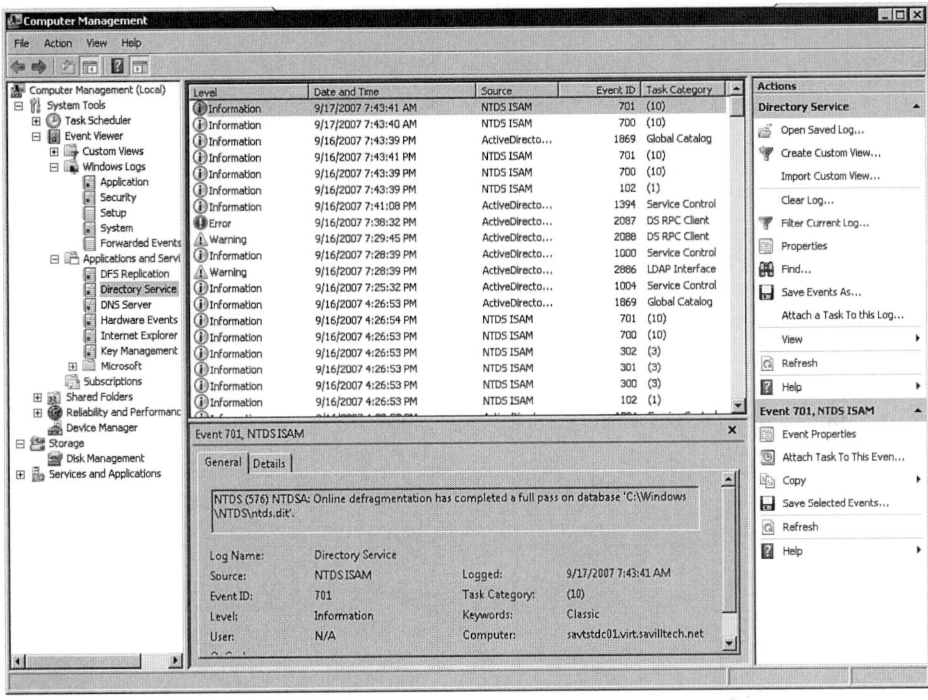

Figure 11-23 The Event Viewer is a great place to look for events concerning all aspects of a server and can be invaluable for troubleshooting.

To make sure SYSVOL is being shared correctly, run `net share` at a command prompt, which lists all shares, and you see an entry for SYSVOL that points to C:\Windows\SYSVOL\sysvol.

For a better all-round health check, run the `dcdiag` utility for domain controller diagnostics, which performs a number of tests, checks event logs, checks replication, and gives a pass/fail on the elements affecting a domain controller. An example of its execution is shown in the following example; when you view the output of the execution, look for failed tests. However, if you are running all Windows Server 2008 domain controllers, you can ignore the failed FrsEvent test because the File Replication Service is not used. Another good command is `netdiag /test:dns`, which confirms DNS functionality.

```
C:\Users\Administrator>dcdiag

Directory Server Diagnosis
```

```
Performing initial setup:
   Trying to find home server...
   Home Server = savtstdc01
   * Identified AD Forest.
   Done gathering initial info.

Doing initial required tests

   Testing server: Dallas\SAVTSTDC01
      Starting test: Connectivity
         Warning during resolution of hostname
savtstdc01.virt.savilltech.net through IPv6 stack.
         *** Warning: could not confirm the identity of
this server in the directory versus the names returned by DNS
servers.
If there are problems accessing this directory server then you
may need to check that this server is correctly registered with
DNS.
         ......................... SAVTSTDC01 passed test
Connectivity

Doing primary tests

   Testing server: Dallas\SAVTSTDC01
      Starting test: Advertising
         ......................... SAVTSTDC01 passed test
Advertising
      Starting test: FrsEvent
         The event log File Replication Service on server
         savtstdc01.virt.savilltech.net could not be queried,
error 0x3a9f
         "The specified channel could not be found. Check
channel configuration."

         ......................... SAVTSTDC01 failed test
FrsEvent
      Starting test: SysVolCheck
         ......................... SAVTSTDC01 passed test
SysVolCheck
      Starting test: KccEvent
         ......................... SAVTSTDC01 passed test
```

```
KccEvent
      Starting test: KnowsOfRoleHolders
         ......................... SAVTSTDC01 passed test
KnowsOfRoleHolders
      Starting test: MachineAccount
         ......................... SAVTSTDC01 passed test
MachineAccount
      Starting test: NCSecDesc
         ......................... SAVTSTDC01 passed test
NCSecDesc
      Starting test: NetLogons
         ......................... SAVTSTDC01 passed test
NetLogons
      Starting test: ObjectsReplicated
         ......................... SAVTSTDC01 passed test
ObjectsReplicated
      Starting test: Replications
         ......................... SAVTSTDC01 passed test
Replications
      Starting test: RidManager
         ......................... SAVTSTDC01 passed test
RidManager
      Starting test: Services
         ......................... SAVTSTDC01 passed test
Services
      Starting test: SystemLog
         ......................... SAVTSTDC01 passed test
SystemLog
      Starting test: VerifyReferences
         ......................... SAVTSTDC01 passed test
VerifyReferences


   Running partition tests on : ForestDnsZones
      Starting test: CheckSDRefDom
         ......................... ForestDnsZones passed test
CheckSDRefDom
      Starting test: CrossRefValidation
         ......................... ForestDnsZones passed test
         CrossRefValidation

   Running partition tests on : DomainDnsZones
```

```
      Starting test: CheckSDRefDom
         ......................... DomainDnsZones passed test
CheckSDRefDom
      Starting test: CrossRefValidation
         ......................... DomainDnsZones passed test
         CrossRefValidation

   Running partition tests on : Schema
      Starting test: CheckSDRefDom
         ......................... Schema passed test
CheckSDRefDom
      Starting test: CrossRefValidation
         ......................... Schema passed test
CrossRefValidation

   Running partition tests on : Configuration
      Starting test: CheckSDRefDom
         ......................... Configuration passed test
CheckSDRefDom
      Starting test: CrossRefValidation
         ......................... Configuration passed test
CrossRefValidation

   Running partition tests on : virt
      Starting test: CheckSDRefDom
         ......................... virt passed test
CheckSDRefDom
      Starting test: CrossRefValidation
         ......................... virt passed test
CrossRefValidation

   Running enterprise tests on : virt.savilltech.net
      Starting test: FsmoCheck
         ......................... virt.savilltech.net
passed test FsmoCheck
      Starting test: Intersite
         ......................... virt.savilltech.net
passed test Intersite
```

You can also run individual tests. For example, to just run the replication tests, use the command `dcdiag /test:replications`. You can get verbose output by adding the `/v` switch. However, do this only with specific tests because it provides a lot of extra information.

If you have not already done so, now is a good time to configure time synchronization. Kerberos is sensitive to time, and by default, all the domain controllers in a domain synchronize their time with the PDC Emulator and clients sync with the authenticating domain controller. If you have multiple domains in a forest, the PDC Emulator of the child domains syncs time with the parent domain's PDC Emulator, and so on. At the top of the forest, ideally, the PDC FSMO should sync with an external Simple Network Time Protocol (SNTP) server. Microsoft lists external SNTP servers at http://support.microsoft.com/kb/262680; use this list to find one that's local to you.

```
C:\Users\Administrator>net time /setsntp:ntp.fnbhs.com
The command completed successfully.

C:\Users\Administrator>net time /querysntp
The current SNTP value is: ntp.fnbhs.com

The command completed successfully.
```

Creating a Domain Controller from Media

So far, the domain creation process has been a simple affair. When a new domain controller is created for a domain, it contacts its closest domain controller and downloads all the information about the domain. The amount of time this process takes depends on the size of AD. Remember, AD databases can be many gigabits in size. If you're creating a new domain controller in a remote office that has poor network speed, copying over the multi-gigabit AD database may not be realistic. So what options do you have?

You could build the domain controller initially at a central, well-connected location and then ship it to the remote office. As long as it's delivered and connected within a short period of time, this works okay, but you still face some logistical challenges. (For example, it may not be possible when trying to ship to certain countries.)

A technical solution is available. Windows Server 2003 allowed a promotion of a domain controller to be performed, with the initial data used having been taken from a system state backup of another domain controller in the same domain. This works because the system state contains the complete AD database information. If the new server is to be a GC, then the system state should be from a domain controller that is also a GC server, to ensure that all data is available. This "install from media" worked great, and when a new server was promoted on a recent system state backup, the only data sent over the network was changes between when the system state backup was taken and the present. To have the option to install from media, pass the `/adv` switch to `dcpromo`. After you select the new domain controller as an additional domain controller for an existing domain, `dcpromo` opens a dialog that enabled replication to occur from a domain controller on the network or from a folder containing the restored system state of a domain controller.

Windows Server 2008 provides a new concept: the RODC, which has some AD information missing. You therefore can now create four types of media to be used for another domain controller promotion via the `ntdsutil ifm` command. Table 11-2 outlines the four types of media and also includes their parameters and a brief description.

Table 11-2 Installation Media

Type of Installation Medium	Parameter	Description
Full domain controller	`create sysvol full` *<path>*	Creates installation media for a writeable domain controller or an Active Directory Lightweight Directory Services (AD LDS) instance in the location specified.
Full domain controller without SYSVOL data	`create full` *<path>*	Creates installation media without SYSVOL for a writeable domain controller or an AD LDS instance in the location specified.
RODC without SYSVOL data	`create RODC` *<path>*	Creates installation media without SYSVOL for an RODC in the location specified.
RODC	`create sysvol RODC` *<path>*	Creates installation media for an RODC in the location specified.

You can run this on any Windows Server 2008 domain controller, but if you run it on an RODC, then only the RODC types of installation media can be created. If you don't create the domain with the SYSVOL data, then the new domain controller populates its AD database via the IFM, but its SYSVOL replicates from an online domain controller. If SYSVOL is included in the IFM, then only changes to SYSVOL need to be replicated from an existing domain controller.

In this case, you'll create a full backup for a new domain controller with SYSVOL, so use the `create sysvol full <path>` option. Remember that the first command activates the NTDS instance for `ntdsutil` to run actions against:

```
C:\Users\Administrator>ntdsutil
ntdsutil: activate instance ntds
Active instance set to "ntds".
ntdsutil: ifm
ifm: create sysvol full c:\temp\ifmfull
Creating snapshot...
Snapshot set {3fb090ef-f878-443e-968f-6448abfd3ec1}
generated successfully.
Snapshot {1f4eb2d3-8aec-4613-9f87-e1173c328cc4} mounted
as C:\$SNAP_200709171456
_VOLUMEC$\
Snapshot {1f4eb2d3-8aec-4613-9f87-e1173c328cc4} is
already mounted.
Initiating DEFRAGMENTATION mode...
     Source Database:
C:\$SNAP_200709171456_VOLUMEC$\Windows\NTDS\ntds.dit
     Target Database: c:\temp\ifmfull\Active Directory\ntds.dit

                  Defragmentation  Status (% complete)

          0    10    20    30    40    50    60    70    80    90  100
          |----|----|----|----|----|----|----|----|----|----|
          ...................................................

Copying registry files...
Copying c:\temp\ifmfull\registry\SYSTEM
Copying c:\temp\ifmfull\registry\SECURITY
Copying SYSVOL...
Copying c:\temp\ifmfull\SYSVOL
```

```
Copying c:\temp\ifmfull\SYSVOL\virt.savilltech.net
Copying c:\temp\ifmfull\SYSVOL\virt.savilltech.net\Policies
..
LOTS of files copied
..
Snapshot {1f4eb2d3-8aec-4613-9f87-e1173c328cc4} unmounted.
IFM media created successfully in c:\temp\ifmfull
ifm: quit
ntdsutil: quit
```

In the destination folder selected, three subfolders are created: Active Directory, which contains ntds.dit (the AD database); Registry, which contains exports of the Security and System portions of the Registry; and SYSVOL, which contains the SYSVOL content (if SYSVOL was specified to be exported). These folders should be copied to media (such as a DVD or a USB drive) and sent to the new server that is a domain controller. (Accessing the server over the network is probably not an option because you do this to avoid replicating over the network.) When the data is available on the new domain controller to be, start `dcpromo` with the `/adv` switch (or just check the Advanced box on the welcome dialog box). Then select Add a Domain Controller to an Existing Domain and follow all the normal dialogs. Just before you select where to store the AD database, you see the Install from Media dialog (see Figure 11-24). By default, this dialog shows the database as replicating from an existing domain controller, but you should instead select Use Data from Media at the Following Location and select the path of the IFM copy. When done, click Next. You are still prompted for a source domain controller, as per a normal advanced installation. This is normal and is required to replicate any changes to AD because the IFM was created on the source domain controller. The domain controller you select (if you select one) does not have to be the same domain controller from which the IFM was created.

To perform this as an unattended installation, the only change to a normal promotion answer file is a one-line addition that specifies the location from which to replicate via the ReplicationSourcePath attribute:

```
ReplicationSourcePath="C:\temp\ifmfull"
```

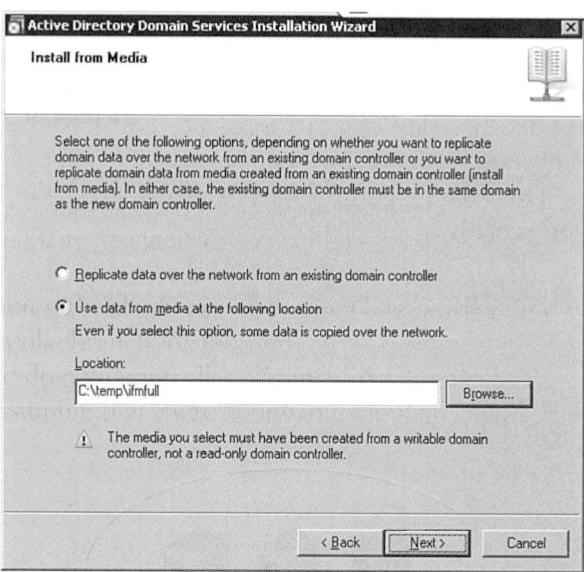

FIGURE 11-24 The initial load of AD is read from the location specified.

Removing Domain Controllers and Domains

There will be times when you want to remove a domain controller from a domain because it is being replaced with newer hardware, or perhaps as part of a swing-type upgrade, or even to move a domain controller from one domain to another. The process to demote a domain controller is simple. Execute the Active Directory Domain Services Installation Wizard (dcpromo), which detects that it is running on an existing domain controller and gives the option to demote the server to a member server. The wizard asks if this domain controller is the last in the domain, and if it is, whether the domain should be deleted, as shown in Figure 11-25. Select this only if this is the last domain controller in a domain and you want to delete the domain. For a normal domain controller demotion, leave the Delete the Domain Because This Server Is the Last Domain Controller in the Domain unchecked.

If the server is a GC, a dialog asks for confirmation that you are removing a GC that may affect servicing of applications and users. If you are removing the last domain controller in a domain, you may also receive notification that domain-hosted application partitions are lost. The most common application would be DomainDnsZones, which is a domain-specific hosted application partition that is used to start DNS information for replication between DNS-serving domain controllers in a domain. You are also prompted for a new password for the local administrator account after the demotion process is complete.

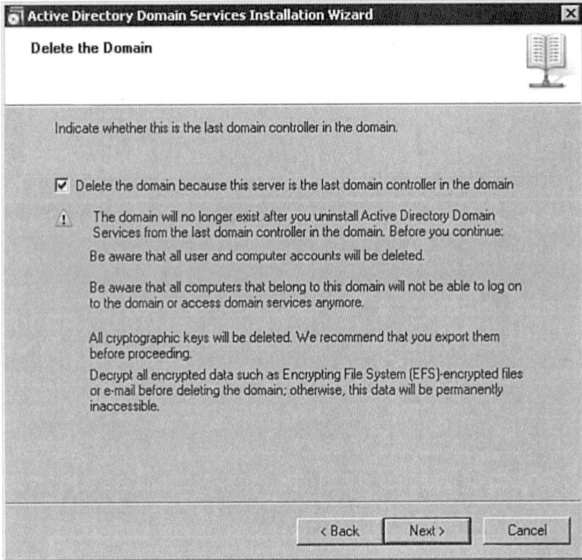

FIGURE 11-25 Checking this box causes the domain and all data associated with it to be removed.

As with the promotion process, you can export these settings to a file, as shown in the following example. Notice that there are no configurations other than the new local password and an option to retain the domain controller's metadata. Set RetainDcMetadata to No unless the demotion is for an RODC and you want to keep the information about the domain controller stored in the directory service.

```
; DCPROMO unattend file
; Usage:
;   dcpromo.exe /unattend:C:\temp\demote.txt
;
```

```
;
[DCInstall]
; Demotion
RetainDcMetadata=No
AdministratorPassword=Pa55word
```

You can run this and see the demotion process from the command line, as demonstrated in the following example. Each part of the demotion process is logged.

```
C:\Users\administrator.VIRT>dcpromo /unattend:demote.txt
Checking if Active Directory Domain Services binaries are
installed...
Active Directory Domain Services Setup

Validating environment and parameters...

----------------------------------------
The following actions will be performed:
Remove Active Directory Domain Services from this computer.

When the process is complete, this server will be a member
of the domain virt.savilltech.net


----------------------------------------

Starting...

Active Directory Domain Services successfully transferred
the remaining data in directory partition
DC=ForestDnsZones,DC=virt,DC=savilltech,DC=net to Active
Directory Domain Controller \\savtstdc01.virt.savilltech.net.
.
Stopping service NETLOGON

.
Stopping service IsmServ


Removing LDAP and remote procedure call (RPC) access to
Active Directory Domain Services...
```

```
.
Completing removal of Active Directory Domain Services,
SAM and LSA...
.
```

Even after this removal, the binaries are still installed on the server, however, and if you want them totally removed, remove the ADDS role from the server. If you plan to promote the server to a domain controller again, leave the binaries in place. Otherwise, remove them.

Read-Only Domain Controllers (RODCs)

Technology is wonderfully cyclical in nature. In the beginning, you had a PDC that had a writeable copy of the security accounts database, which could be replicated to one or more read-only backup domain controllers (BDCs) that could service logons via the read-only database but could make no changes. Windows 2000 and AD moved into a great multi-master, all-writeable world, where every domain controller held a writeable copy of AD. New to Windows Server 2008 is the ability to have RODCs again.

Features

The RODC is geared toward branch offices where there may be a domain controller that is not physically secured as a domain controller should be or you would like to place a domain controller but can't due to lack of security. Often, at a branch office there is not a secure room for servers, and often, any servers sit in a broom closet or similar location. Because a domain controller has a copy of the entire directory for the domain, containing sensitive information and all passwords, if the server is compromised or stolen, you may have a big security problem. Consider not having a local domain controller; if users all logged on with Kerberos tickets, then a lack of network would not stop them from accessing local servers they had tickets for, but if a user has to log out, she would lose all access. Also, branch locations typically have slow connections, and while authentication traffic is not sizable and typically would not take long, the application of Group Policy can be time-consuming over slower links, so a local domain controller speeds up logon times considerably.

Obviously, being read-only does not protect the data (we'll get to why read-only shortly). One of the other features of an RODC is that passwords are not replicated to an RODC. So if an RODC is compromised, the passwords for domain users are not available from the RODC, although it is possible to configure the RODC to cache credentials for the users who are local to the location in which the RODC is situated. A compromise of the RODC would only expose the users at the RODC location. This caching of certain user attributes is known as the Password Replication Policy, and it is specific to a particular RODC. When a user logs on via an RODC and is included in the Password Replication Policy, the RODC requests all credentials for the user from a writeable domain controller and caches them. This enables the RODC to service future logon requests for the user/computer until the credentials change. If a user changes her password via the Security Accounts Manager (SAM) interface (that is, the Windows Security dialog), this change is passed to a writeable domain controller. But then the RODC attempts to pull the new password immediately so its cache is up-to-date. Consider not caching passwords at all and just using the RODC to speed up logon times by being a local Group Policy source location. This depends on the security of the environment.

In addition to configuring passwords, it is possible to configure other attributes that should not be replicated to RODCs. An application might store sensitive data in AD, which also needs to be protected. For example, a human resources application might store Social Security numbers (SSNs) in the AD. You do not want them replicated to RODCs, which are not physically secure. These nonreplicated attributes are known as the RODC filtered attribute set and cannot be replicated to any RODC within the entire forest. This is because the filtered attribute set is configured on the actual schema, which is forest-wide. The filtered attribute set is designed to be defined by application teams because the application needs to know if it needs to go to a Read-Write Domain Controller (RWDC) for a certain attribute instead of to an RODC. Just removing an attribute outside the application knowledge could cause the application to fail if it cannot find the value it's looking for on an RODC.

A malicious user may try to hack the local RODC to modify the filtered attribute set to receive the blocked attributes. If the RODC is replicating from a Windows Server 2008 writeable domain controller, the attribute is still not replicated. However, if the RODC is replicating from a Windows Server 2003 domain controller, because it does not understand the concept of the filtered attribute set, it would replicate the filtered attribute.

However, this would require substantial hacking because an RODC cannot normally replicate from a Windows Server 2003 server. Therefore, if you intend to use the filtered attribute set, make sure the domain controllers replicating to the RODCs are all running Windows Server 2008. You cannot add system-critical attributes (such as schemaFlagsEx attribute value & 0x1 = TRUE) to the filtered attribute set, such as anything needed by the Local Security Authority (LSA), SAM, or the directory service itself. You get "unwillingToPerform" errors if you try to add these attributes on a Windows Server 2008 schema master. The system lets you add them on a Windows Server 2003 schema master, but it ignores you and does not make the update.

The read-only nature of an RODC is based on simplifying the replication of the environment, but it is mostly based on protecting the main AD database from possible corruption from a change made on an RODC. Because nothing is replicated from an RODC, any changes made on an RODC via malicious tools/hacking would not be replicated to any other domain controllers, protecting the integrity of the directory. The replication is unidirectional from a normal writeable domain controller to an RODC of both the AD Directory Service and SYSVOL via DFSR. In terms of simplifying replication, this is simply because if the bridgehead servers (the domain controllers performing replication to other domain controllers) that are responsible for communicating with the branch offices only have to push changes and don't have to receive changes, there is substantially less work involved in calculating what is being replicated. So there is less stress on the bridgehead. In addition, RODC replication links to bridgeheads are automatically reevaluated by the KCC to ensure load balancing, and the ADLB tool is not needed for RODCs. If a client just needs to read data (except passwords) from the AD, the RODC can service the request. However, any write operation via Lightweight Directory Access Protocol (LDAP) is referred to a writeable domain controller in another location, such as a hub.

In reality, there are some attributes an RODC can write to its copy of AD, in addition to passing them on to an RWDC. These attributes are all related to failed logon attempts (for example, LastLogon, BadPwdCount), and this is to protect against brute-force password attacks. If an RODC could not contact an RWDC and someone were trying to brute-force hack a password, no failed logon attempts could be written, and the account could be hacked. With the RODC writing limited attributes around password attempts, even without a RWDC contactable, the RODC can still protect accounts from hacking. The attributes the RODC writes are not replicated; the RODC forwards the information to an RWDC for long-term storage and replication throughout the domain.

Someone hacking the local RODC implies that someone is logging on to it. Often, this is an issue; on a domain controller, you don't want to give some local branch office IT administrator logon rights that may require domain administrator credentials. With an RODC, role separation is possible, and it enables any domain-based user or group to be delegated local administrator rights on the RODC without implying any other domain-based rights. This enables the local IT team to manage the box in terms of backups, updates, and driver maintenance.

The final feature of an RODC is that it is common for a domain controller to host DNS, which is normally dynamic in nature and stored in AD. Because the RODC has only a read copy of AD, it has only a read copy of the DNS zone. The RODC therefore has read-only DNS, which enables clients to query the RODC DNS server to resolve names, but any attempt of a client to write to DNS results in the RODC referring the client to a writeable DNS server. In the background, it would replicate down the new DNS record to its read-only database.

In summary, to answer the question "What does an RODC get you?" consider the following:

- A read-only copy of AD
- Unidirectional replication, which protects the integrity of the directory service
- The filtered attribute set, which removes sensitive information, such as passwords, from the local RODC copy of the database
- Credential caching based on Password Replication Policy, which allows credentials for local users/computers to be cached and serviced by the RODC
- Administrator role separation, which enables local users/groups to be given administrator permissions on RODC without domain administrator powers
- Read-only DNS

RODC Restrictions

Because an RODC is read only, an RODC cannot host any of the FSMO roles because they require the domain controller hosting the role to be able to write to AD.

In addition, because the RODC does only unidirectional replication, it cannot replicate changes to other domain controllers, either locally in the site or to domain controllers in other sites. This means it cannot be a bridgehead server.

An RODC can only replicate a domain partition from a Windows Server 2008 domain controller, although it can replicate other partitions from a Windows Server 2003 domain controller, such as the Schema, Configuration, Application (for example, DomainDnsZones, ForestDnsZones), and Global Catalog (Partial Attribute set of other domains) partitions.

The requirement that the RODC must be able to replicate from a Windows Server 2008 writeable domain controller affects domain controller deployment. Ensure that an RODC can always replicate directly with a writeable Windows Server 2008 domain controller for the same domain, by ensuring that either a Windows Server 2008 domain controller is in an adjacent hub site or that all site links are bridged or a specific bridge is created between the various links (more on this in Chapter 12, "Managing Active Directory and Advanced Concepts"). RODCs use the same replication as normal domain controllers, which means replication is based on sites and site links. In general, the RODCs are placed on the edge of the network (spoke locations), and Windows Server 2008 is in the hub location. Figure 11-26 shows an example of this deployment, which includes the domain controllers that can't replicate the domain partition to an RODC, namely another RODC or a Windows Server 2003 domain controller.

You may have issues with applications that interface with AD. You may have LDAP applications that write to the AD and don't understand what an RODC is. You may get errors and failures when you try to write against an RODC. Applications fall into one of three categories:

- The application does not understand the referral it receives from an RODC when it attempts to write to an RODC and therefore just fails the write request and so the application is not RODC compatible.
- If an application does understand a referral to a RWDC from a write request to an RODC, the application is RODC compatible.

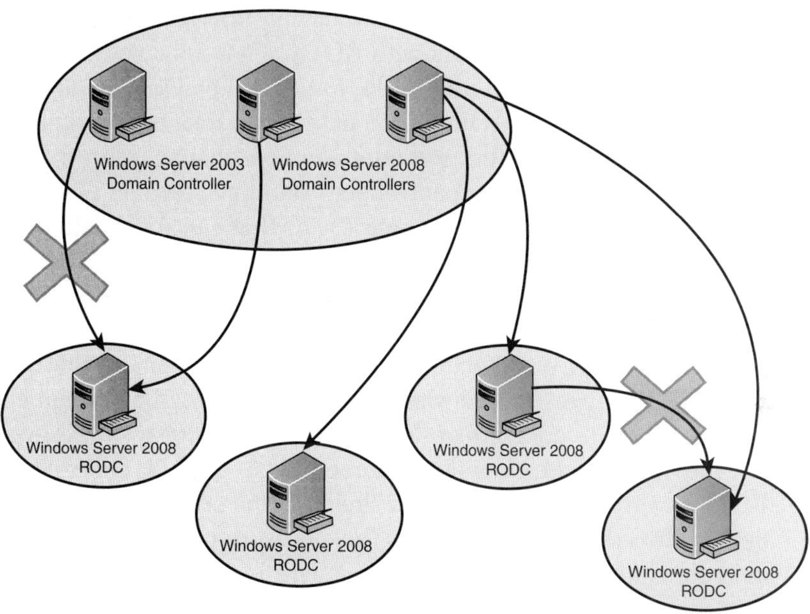

FIGURE 11-26 The domain partition can only be replicated from Windows Server 2008 domain controllers. The Schema, Configuration, Application, and GC partitions could be replicated from a Windows Server 2003 domain controller (but not another RODC).

- The best type of application is one designed with RODCs in mind that makes read requests to the RODC and write requests directly to an RWDC. The application can pass the DS_WRITABLE_REQUIRED flag to a DsGetDcName request to get a list of writeable domain controllers, enabling differentiation between RODCs and RWDCs.

By default, RODCs cannot enroll for domain controller certificates, so an RODC cannot authenticate a logon by a client using a smartcard. To resolve this, add Enroll permissions for the Enterprise Read-Only Domain Controllers (ERODC) group on the Domain Controller certificate template. On the Domain Controller Authentication and Directory E-Mail Replication certificate templates, set Enroll and Auto enroll permissions for the ERODC group. Also, set Read permission for the Authenticated Users group.

There is another issue related to having Windows Server 2003 domain controllers in an environment with RODCs; it is not a restriction but something to be aware of that affects the functionality. Domain controllers register site-specific records for their local site in DNS, enabling clients to easily find domain controllers and other services that are closest to them. If a site contains no domain controllers, Windows Server 2003 and above domain controllers in the sites closest to that site (calculated by site link costs) register site-specific records for that unserviced site and help clients find a domain controller as close as possible. This is known as automatic site coverage.

Windows Server 2008 domain controllers understand the RODC, and if an RODC is present in a site, Windows Server 2008 domain controllers consider the site covered so do not attempt to register their own records for the remote site. Windows Server 2003 domain controllers are not RODC aware, however, and if a site contains only RODCs, if a Windows Server 2003 domain controller is the closest domain controller, it registers its records for the remote site as well. This is not desirable and defeats the purpose of the RODC in the location.

There are numerous solutions. Ideally, if you ensure that only Windows Server 2008 domain controllers are present in the sites closest to RODC services sites, there is no issue. Also, Microsoft may come out with a fix for Windows Server 2003 to be able to detect the RODCs. If there is no fix available, and you can't replace the Windows Server 2003 domain controllers, turn off the automatic site coverage on particular Windows Server 2003 domain controllers by creating a DWORD value of AutoSiteCoverage under the key HKEY_LOCAL_MACHINE\SYSTEM\CurrentControlSet\Services\Netlogon\Parameters and setting it to 0. This affects any remote site for which the domain controller previously registered records, so be sure to consider the full effects of this. You may potentially have to make additional changes to specify sites for Windows Server 2003 domain controllers to register records via a Group Policy Object (GPO). Start by setting the Net Logon service Group Policy Sites Covered by the domain controller locator DNS SRV Records found at Computer Configuration, Administrative Templates, System, Net Logon, DC Locator DNS Records, and then list all the sites the domain controller registers for, separated by spaces. Obviously, if you use Group Policy, ensure that the GPO applies only to the domain controllers you want to register, and you could apply a security filter to the GPO so that only specific domain controllers read the policy. You can also set this via the

Registry by updating the value SiteCoverage under the HKEY_LOCAL_MACHINE\SYSTEM\CurrentControlSet\Services\Netlogon\Parameters key. Each entry should be on its own line on individual domain controllers.

Another option is to modify the weight of the DNS records registered by the RODCs to be higher than those registered by the remote Windows Server 2003. However, this can cause problems if other writeable domain controllers exist in the same site as the RODC, and it makes the RODC chosen over the more functionally writeable domain controllers. This is fun but not recommended!

Prerequisites for RODC Deployment

Before an RODC can be deployed in your environment, in addition to having Windows Server 2008 domain controllers for the same domain as the RODC that are eligible replication partners (via site links or by bridging multiple site links), you must also have performed the following:

- To allow the LVR used by the RODC, the forest functional level must be Windows Server 2003 mode or above.
- The domains containing RODCs must be running Windows Server 2003 domain mode or above, as Kerberos-constrained delegation is required for communication between the RODC and normal domain controllers.
- If this is not a new Windows Server 2008 forest, update the schema to enable the RODC to replicate DNS application partitions by copying the \sources\adprep folder from the Windows Server 2008 DVD and running the command `adprep /rodcprep`.
- If RODCs are GC servers, run `adprep /domainprep` from Windows Server 2008 on *all* domains in the forest, even if a particular domain does not have RODCs.

Installing an RODC

You install an RODC the same way you install a normal domain controller—by running `dcpromo` on a server as a domain administrator—and the only difference at a minimum level is checking the option Read-Only Domain Controller (RODC), as shown in Figure 11-27.

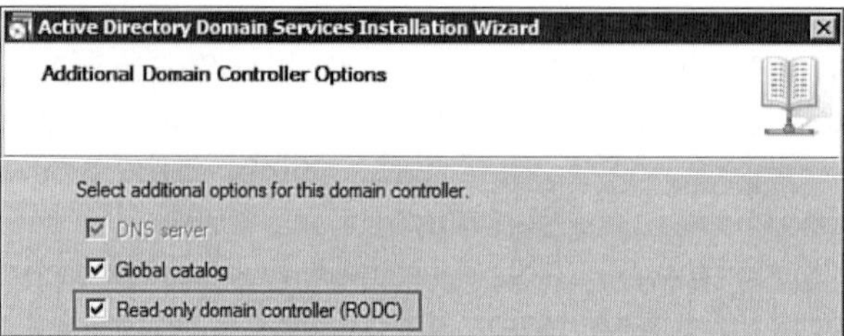

FIGURE 11-27 Making an RODC does not need to be a complex affair.

If you select the option for the domain controller to be an RODC, then an additional dialog box is displayed, asking you to specify a user or group that is delegated administrative permissions on the specific RODC. Remember that this is just local access to the RODC; the users or group members get no domain administrator privileges, as shown in Figure 11-28. All other selections that are part of `dcpromo` are the same.

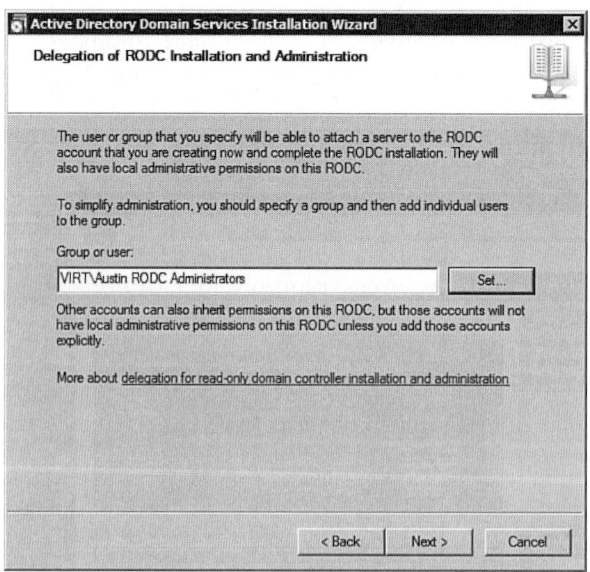

FIGURE 11-28 In this case, members of the Austin RODC Administrators group are able to manage the RODC without having AD permissions.

From an unattended installation perspective, only one extra line is needed to specify the user/group that is delegated permission, and the type of the new domain controller is set to a read-only replica, as shown in the following example:

```
ReplicaOrNewDomain=ReadOnlyReplica
DelegatedAdmin="VIRT\Austin RODC Administrators"
```

If you run `dcpromo` in advanced mode, you also receive an additional dialog, as shown in Figure 11-29, that enables you to configure the initial Password Replication Policy. This policy specifies which accounts can have their credentials cached on the RODC after first authentication, which means their password is stored on the RODC. Note that a deny always takes precedence over an allow, so if a user is a member of an allowed group and a denied group, then his password is not cached on an RODC. If a user is not part of a group mentioned in the policy, his password is not cached. Only explicit allows are cached.

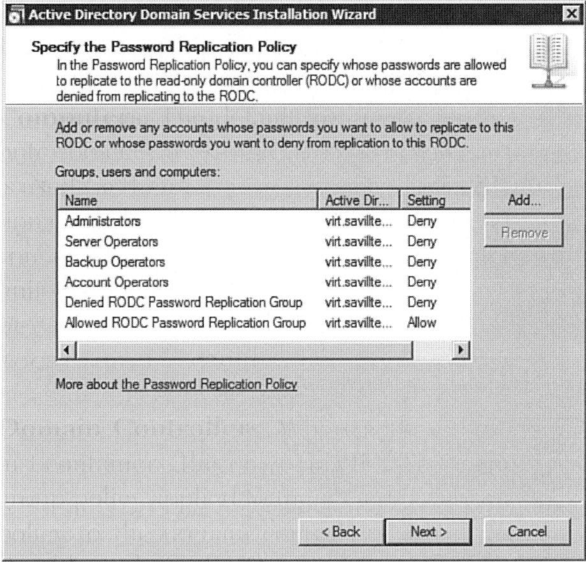

FIGURE 11-29 Default settings for the Password Replication Policy, which can be changed later.

By default, Allowed RODC Password Replication Group is empty. Denied RODC Password Replication Group contains the following:

- Cert Publishers
- Domain Admins
- Enterprise Admins
- Enterprise Domain Controllers
- Enterprise Read-Only Domain Controllers
- Group Policy Creator Owners
- Krbtgt
- Schema Admins

Remember, the more groups you allow to be cached, the more group members whose authentication the RODC can facilitate. But if the RODC is compromised, then all those cached passwords may be cracked and more users exposed. It's a balancing decision. It is common to create groups for each location, with the users for the location as members, and set that group as Allowed for credential caching.

When you do an unattended install, list all allows and denies as either PasswordReplicationDenied or PasswordReplicationAllowed. The default list is shown in the following example, along with an extra allow for the Austin Local Users group, which contains all users in the Austin site. In this example, you want the Austin-based RODC to cache the passwords for the local Austin users:

```
PasswordReplicationDenied="BUILTIN\Administrators"
PasswordReplicationDenied="BUILTIN\Server Operators"
PasswordReplicationDenied="BUILTIN\Backup Operators"
PasswordReplicationDenied="BUILTIN\Account Operators"
PasswordReplicationDenied="VIRT\Denied RODC Password
Replication Group"
PasswordReplicationAllowed="VIRT\Allowed RODC Password
Replication Group"
PasswordReplicationAllowed="VIRT\Austin Local Users"
```

Why do I care so much about unattended installations? Because the RODC is a branch office concept, chances are you are running the RODC on a Server Core environment to reduce the amount of management needed and the overhead involved. This means you have to run the RODC promotion via an unattended answer file. In addition, for the branch locations, you probably also want to look at using BitLocker drive encryption to add another layer of security to the most vulnerable branch office servers. A complete unattend file is shown in the following example.

```
; Usage:
;   dcpromo.exe /unattend:C:\temp\rodcwithcustomprp.txt
[DCInstall]
; Read-Only Replica DC promotion
ReplicaOrNewDomain=ReadOnlyReplica
ReplicaDomainDNSName=virt.savilltech.net
; RODC Password Replication Policy
PasswordReplicationDenied="BUILTIN\Administrators"
PasswordReplicationDenied="BUILTIN\Server Operators"
PasswordReplicationDenied="BUILTIN\Backup Operators"
PasswordReplicationDenied="BUILTIN\Account Operators"
PasswordReplicationDenied="VIRT\Denied RODC Password
➥Replication Group"
PasswordReplicationAllowed="VIRT\Allowed RODC Password
➥Replication Group"
PasswordReplicationAllowed="VIRT\Austin Local Users"
SiteName=Austin
InstallDNS=Yes
ConfirmGc=Yes
DNSDelegation=No
UserDomain=virt.savilltech.net
UserName=virt.savilltech.com\administrator
Password=*
DatabasePath="C:\Windows\NTDS"
LogPath="C:\Windows\NTDS"
SYSVOLPath="C:\Windows\SYSVOL"
; Set SafeModeAdminPassword to the correct value prior
; to using the unattend file
SafeModeAdminPassword=Pa55word
```

The other option is to delegate the RODC creation to a branch office user, which enables the server to be created locally and the server to be promoted to an RODC by the local IT administrator, without requiring the normal domain administrator rights needed for a domain controller promotion. This is accomplished by precreating the account for the new RODC via the Active Directory Users and Computers MMC snap-in. Before trying this, make sure the server is not a member server of the domain for which it becomes an RODC. A computer account cannot already exist for the name of the RODC being provisioned.

First, via the Active Directory Users and Computers MMC snap-in, right-click the Domain Controllers container and select Pre-create Read-only Domain Controller Account, as shown in Figure 11-30.

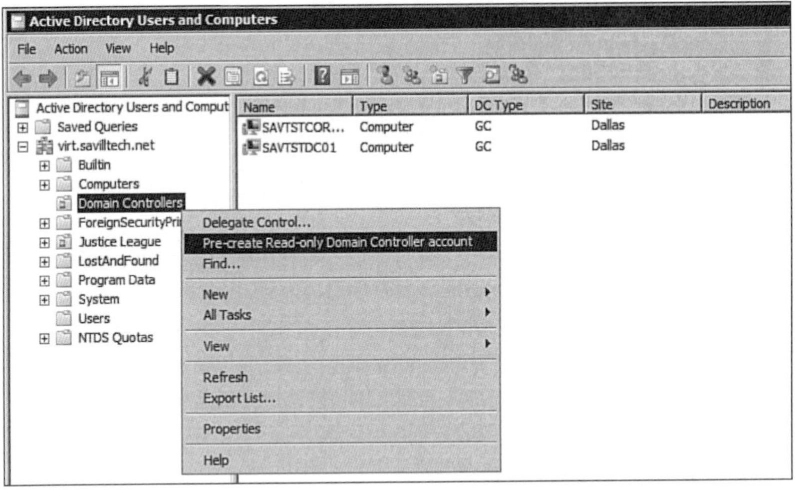

FIGURE 11-30 Precreating an RODC account.

The Active Directory Domain Services Installation Wizard launches, enabling configuration related to the RODC to be configured. As usual, check the Use Advanced Mode Installation option to set the Password Replication Policy for the RODC. Click Next.

Because you are prestaging the RODC account, you cannot choose a domain of which the RODC is a member. It is an RODC for the domain for which you are prestaging the RODC account. Choose the account performing the actual join, which needs to be a domain administrator for the domain. By default, this is the account running the preprovisioning, as shown in Figure 11-31.

The next screen of the wizard asks for the name of the new RODC (for example, savtstdc02). This is used when the promotion is performed on the RODC, and it checks to see if its name already has an RODC account precreated, so the name needs to match.

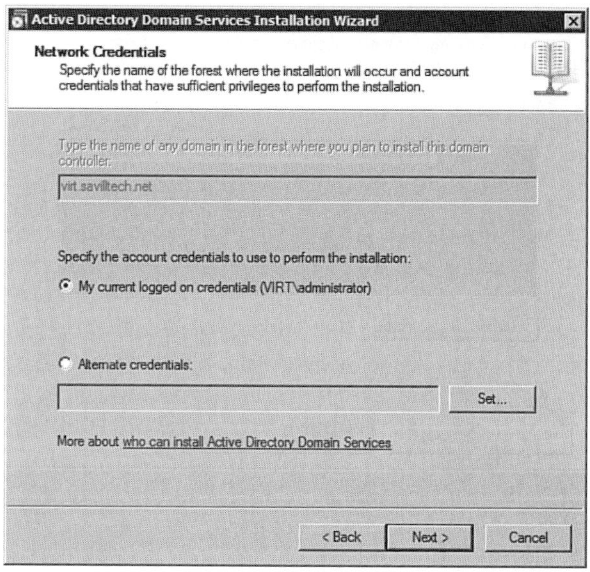

FIGURE 11-31 By default, the membership is determined based on the account of the person preprovisioning.

You are then prompted to select a site, as you would with the Directory Services Installation Wizard, and then you're prompted for the additional roles the RODC performs, which can be GC or DNS. If advanced mode was selected, you can fine-tune the Password Replication Policy.

The delegation of the RODC Installation and Administration is displayed, and the user/group is selected. The user or group specified contains the users who are able to promote the server to be an RODC in the domain. For example, if it's the Austin RODC, you could select the Austin RODC Administration group you created, containing the normal users who have administrator rights on the RODC.

You can export the settings as usual to enable provisioning via an unattended installation. Click Next to create the account and then click Finish at the summary screen. The following example shows output for the unattended file, but notice that when calling via `dcpromo`, you pass switches to tell it to create a domain controller account and the replica DNS name.

```
; DCPROMO unattend file (automatically generated by dcpromo)
; Usage:
;   dcpromo.exe /CreateDCAccount
```

```
;/ReplicaDomainDNSName:virt.savilltech.net
;/unattend:C:\temp\prestageaustinrodc.txt
;
[DCInstall]
; Read-Only Replica DC promotion (stage 1)
DCAccountName=savtstdc02
; RODC Password Replication Policy
PasswordReplicationDenied="BUILTIN\Administrators"
PasswordReplicationDenied="BUILTIN\Server Operators"
PasswordReplicationDenied="BUILTIN\Backup Operators"
PasswordReplicationDenied="BUILTIN\Account Operators"
PasswordReplicationDenied="VIRT\Denied RODC Password
➥Replication Group"
PasswordReplicationAllowed="VIRT\Allowed RODC Password
➥Replication Group"
DelegatedAdmin="VIRT\Austin RODC Administrators"
SiteName=Austin
InstallDNS=Yes
ConfirmGc=Yes
ReplicationSourceDC=savtstdc01.virt.savilltech.net
```

After the account is created, promote the RODC, but use the `UseExistingAccount:Attach` switch so the wizard knows to connect to an existing account:

```
dcpromo /UseExistingAccount:Attach
```

Remember that at this point, the computer must be part of a workgroup and not in the domain.

The wizard starts as usual, and you can select the advanced mode to install from media or specify a domain controller from which to replicate. You see the usual dialog prompt for the domain to join and the credentials to use to join the RODC to the domain, but the credentials do not need to be those of a domain administrator. They just need to be an account that was delegated permission to install/manage the RODC. Figure 11-32 shows an example of using a regular account named Dutch. A check is performed in the domain, and a list of matching prestaged RODC accounts is displayed, as shown in Figure 11-33.

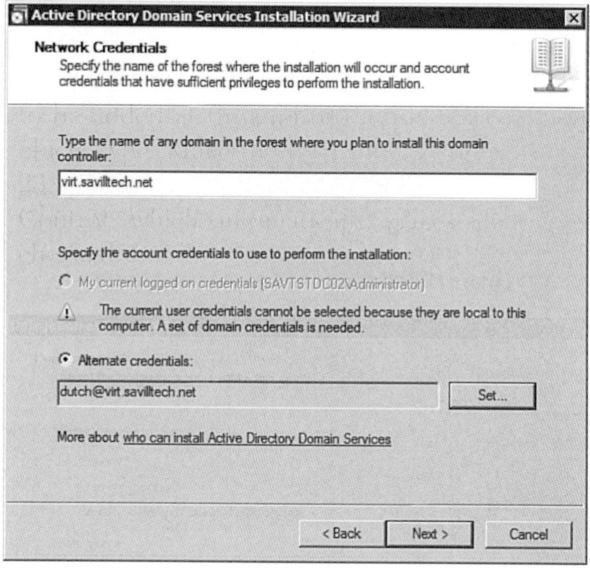

FIGURE 11-32 For the first time, you can promote without being a domain administrator.

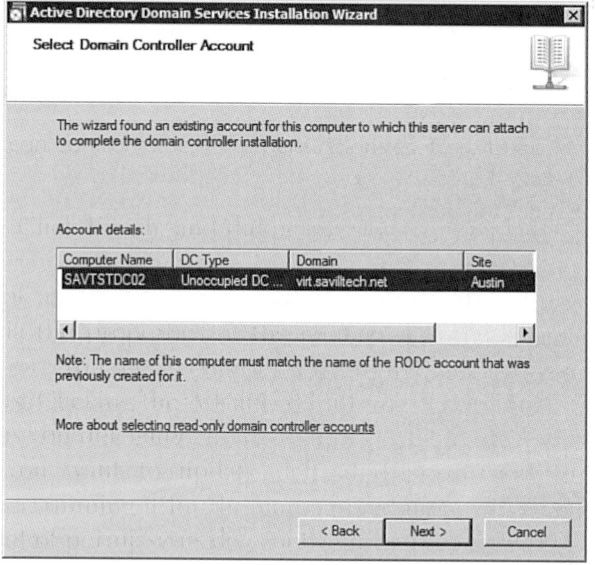

FIGURE 11-33 An unoccupied account is found.

The rest of the wizard runs as usual, allowing you to select the log location and so on. Once again, you can export the configuration to a file for unattended installation, as in the following example. When you run the unattended installation, remember the `/UseExistingAccount:Attach` switch.

```
; DCPROMO unattend file (automatically generated by dcpromo)
; Usage:
;   dcpromo.exe /UseExistingAccount:Attach
; /unattend:C:\temp\rodcviaprestaged.txt
;
; You may need to fill in password fields prior to using
; the unattend file.
; If you leave the values for "Password" and/or
; "DNSDelegationPassword"
; as "*", then you will be asked for credentials at runtime.
;
[DCInstall]
; Read-Only Replica DC promotion (stage 2)
ReplicaDomainDNSName=virt.savilltech.net
UserDomain=virt.savilltech.net
UserName=dutch@virt.savilltech.net
Password=*
DatabasePath="C:\Windows\NTDS"
LogPath="C:\Windows\NTDS"
SYSVOLPath="C:\Windows\SYSVOL"
; Set SafeModeAdminPassword to the correct value prior
; to using the unattend file
SafeModeAdminPassword=Pa55word
; Run-time flags (optional)
; CriticalReplicationOnly=Yes
; RebootOnCompletion=Yes
```

Once the RODC is rebooted, you can manage it as you would any other server, via the local administrators who were delegated permissions. They just won't be able to affect the directory service. The only special maintenance you, as domain administrators, may want to possibly perform on the RODC is to modify who is delegated to manage the server and to modify the Password Replication Policy. Access these configuration items by selecting the properties of the RODC in the Active Directory Users and Computers MMC snap-in. The Managed By tab shows who can manage the server. Again, use a group, and just add/remove people in the group without having to modify the RODC configuration. On the Password

Replication Policy tab, as shown in Figure 11-34, make changes to the accounts that have passwords cached via the Add button, which then enables you to specify whether you are adding a Deny or Allow entry.

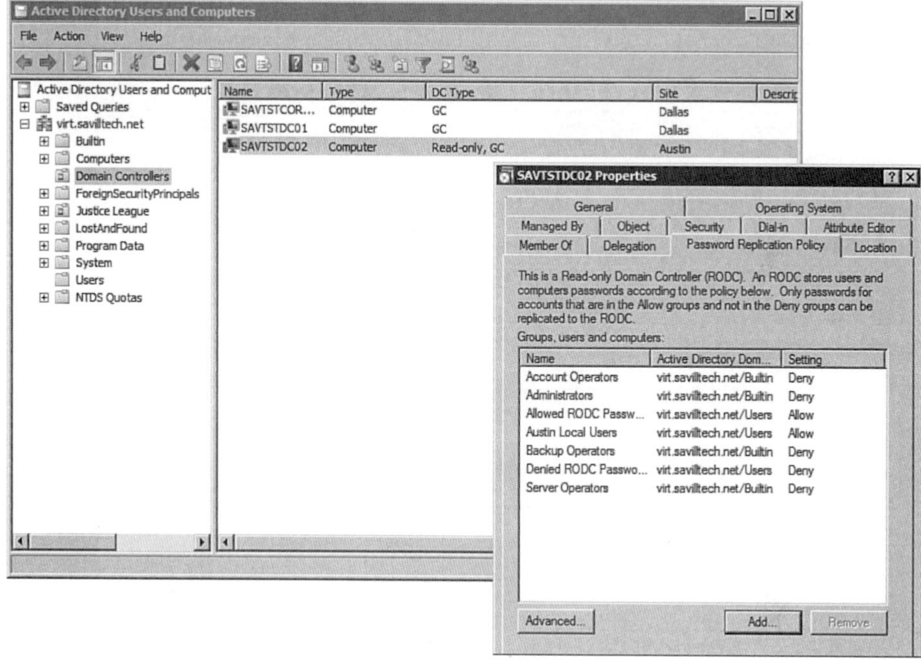

FIGURE 11-34 The Austin Local Users group added to cache accounts.

Click the Advanced button to display a dialog listing all the accounts that have passwords cached on the server, as shown in Figure 11-35. If you are unsure whether a user's password is cached, check the Resultant Policy tab.

Advanced Password Replication Policy for SAVTSTDC02

Policy Usage | Resultant Policy

Display users and computers that meet the following criteria:

Accounts whose passwords are stored on this Read-only Domain Controller

Users and computers: Objects retrieved: 3

Name	Domain Services Folder	Type	Password Last Changed	Password Ex
Dutch	virt.savilltech.net/Users	user	9/18/2007 6:48:47 PM	Never Expire
krbtgt_37708	virt.savilltech.net/Users	user	9/19/2007 4:08:10 PM	10/31/2007
SAVTSTDC02	virt.savilltech.net/Dom...	computer	9/19/2007 4:30:35 PM	Never Expire

FIGURE 11-35 The Kerberos ticket for the RODC and its computer account are cached. Here the user Dutch is also cached, as he is a member of the Austin Local Users group and has an explicit Allow in the Password Replication Policy.

So is it really working? Download Proactive Password Auditor and run it on the RODC to get a result similar to that shown in Figure 11-36. The passwords for the domain users are all empty except for those that are set to Allow in the Password Replication Policy.

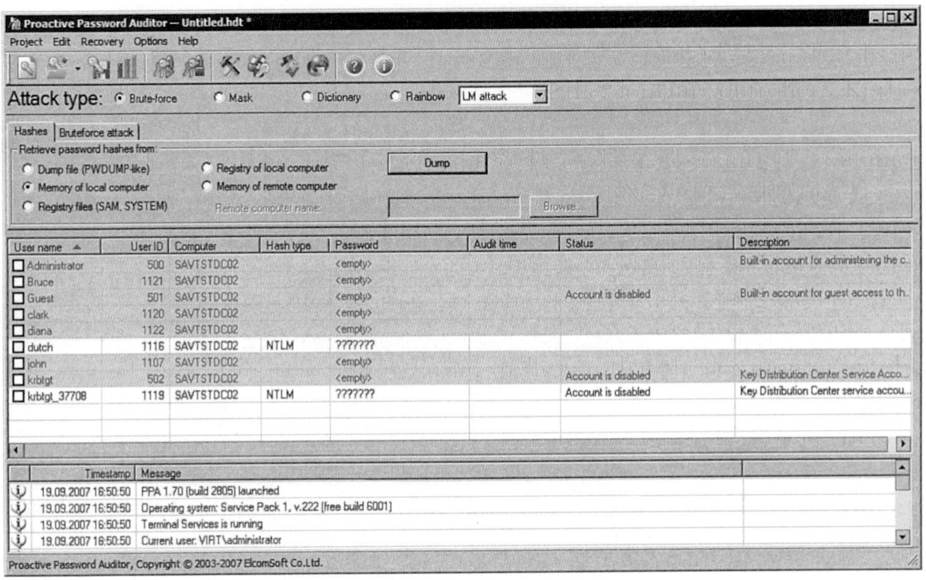

FIGURE 11-36 If this RODC is compromised, only the accounts that are cached are exposed; all the rest don't have the passwords stored on the RODC.

One other cool feature is that if you delete the computer object for an RODC, a special dialog appears, allowing you to reset passwords for the accounts that had their passwords stored on the RODC.

Trust Relationships

Directory Services of today is different from Directory Services of Windows NT 4.0, when a lot of manual trust relationships had to be created between the various domains in an organization, sometimes leading to a complex and difficult-to-maintain set of relationships. Within an AD forest, a number of automatically created trust relationships are maintained that enable resources to be shared between any domains in the forest. You never create a trust relationship that you know of; the Active Directory Domain Services Installation Wizard does it for you.

Trust Relationship 101

If you have more than one domain, it is highly likely that you want to be able to securely grant users/computers/groups from one domain access to resources in another domain. For example, user Bob in domain development needs access to a set of files in the marketing domain. By default, the Access Control List of an object cannot have entries for accounts in other domains; they won't be visible. To resolve this, create a trust between the two domains.

The domain that holds the resources has to trust that the domain containing the user accounts requiring access performs proper authorization. You are trusting that the domain is secured and is not going to expose your resources. This logical view of a trust is how it is technically implemented: A trust relationship is created where one domain would trust the other domain. The domain holding the resources would be the trusting domain (it trusts the domain with the accounts), and the domain holding the accounts would be the trusted domain (see Figure 11-37).

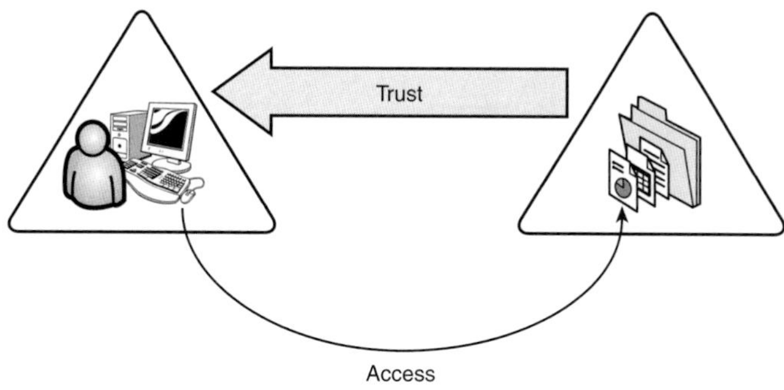

FIGURE 11-37 The trust runs in the opposite direction of the resource requirement. To access a resource in another domain, that other domain has to trust your domain.

If both the domains involved need to trust each other, allowing users from either domain to be assigned access to resources in either domain, then a bidirectional trust would be created, which is two unidirectional trusts.

To create a trust, an administrator in the trusted domain creates a trust relationship with a password, and then an administrator in the trusting domain completes the relationship by specifying the password set by the trusted domain administrator. This ensures that trust relationships are managed and cannot be created without input from administrators from both domains.

Another side effect of the trust relationship is that any user who resides in a domain trusted by another domain can sit down at a workstation that belongs to the trusting domain and log on to his local domain. In the pre-Vista operating systems, the trusted domain would be listed as a selection in the domain drop-down.

Now what if you have three domains in the picture, and Domain A trusts Domain B, and Domain B trusts Domain C, as shown in Figure 11-38? Does Domain A trust Domain C? It depends on the type of trust; by default, trusts are not transitive, and you may need to create a trust between Domain A and Domain C. However, because AD uses Kerberos, a transitive type of trust is possible, which is how the domains within a forest function.

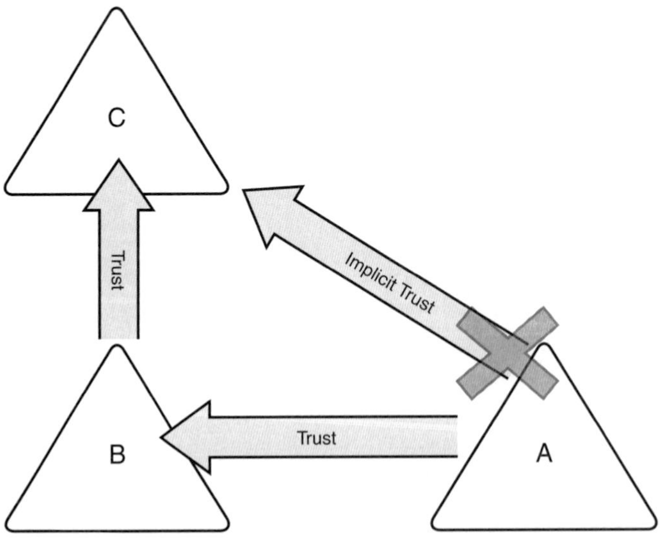

FIGURE 11-38 This shows the behavior without Kerberos transitive trusts. If the trusts used Kerberos, then implicit trust would exist.

With AD, there are six different types of trust, each with particular scenarios for when they should be used:

- Parent–child trust
- Tree–root trust
- Forest trust
- Shortcut trust
- External trust
- Realm trust

Parent–Child Trust

A parent–child trust is used to connect child domains to their parent—that is, the domain that was specified as the parent domain during the child domain's creation via ADDS installation process. Parent–child trusts are created automatically when a domain is created. You do not have to create or maintain these trusts; they are a feature of the AD tree mechanism and are put in place between the domain being created (for example, dev.virt.savilltech.com) and the parent domain specified (for example, virt.savilltech.com).

Parent–child trusts are two-way trusts, which means the parent trusts the child, and the child trusts the parent. These trusts are also transitive in nature, which means that every domain in a tree trusts every other domain in the tree (because every domain in a tree has a trust path to every other domain in the tree). View a domain's properties via the Active Directory Domains and Trusts MMC snap-in. Figure 11-39, for example, shows the trusts for the virt.savilltech.net domain, including a transitive trust, both trusting and trusted, to its child domain, dev. These two trusts make up a bidirectional transitive relationship.

Because every domain in a tree has a parent–child bidirectional trust that is transitive (remember that a transitive trust means any domain that trusts a domain implicitly also trusts any domains trusted by the domain it is trusting), every domain in a tree implicitly trusts all the other domains in the tree.

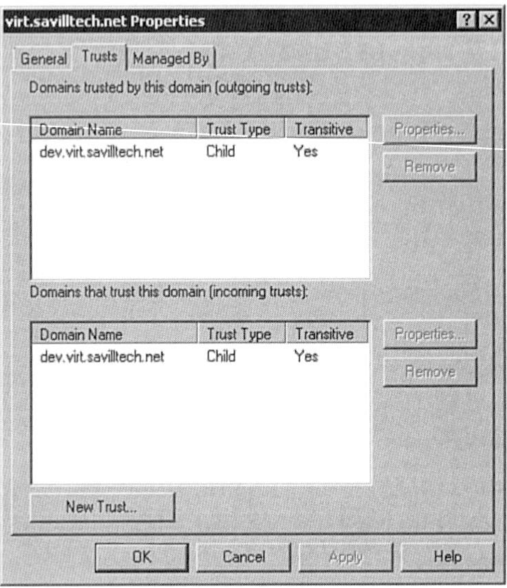

FIGURE 11-39 The trusts shown here were automatically created during the domain creation process and require no manual management.

Tree–Root Trust

The parent–child trust explains how every domain in a tree trusts each other, but if every domain in a forest trusts each other, even if in separate trees, how does this function? When you create additional trees within a forest via the Active Directory Domain Services Installation Wizard, specify the name of the forest in which to create a new tree. When you add a new tree, a tree–root trust is created between the new tree's root domain and the existing forest root domain. This is known as a tree–root trust, as it is used to join the roots of the separate trees within a forest.

Like the parent–child trust, tree–root trusts are two-way and transitive, and their transitive nature means all the trees trust each other, which in turn enables every domain in every tree to trust each other.

Forest Trust

The forest trust, introduced in Windows Server 2003, is available only if the forest is running in at least Windows Server 2003 mode. The forest trust enables a transitive trust between two separate forests, which means every domain in both forests implicitly trusts each other. This transitive nature is not like that of a tree–root trust, however; if you have more than two forests, then every forest needs a forest trust to every other forest (as with a non-Kerberos trust). If you had three forests, create trusts from Forest 1 to Forest 3, Forest 1 to Forest 2, and Forest 2 to Forest 3.

Forest trusts can be either one-way or two-way trusts, and there is some configuration required in addition to just setting up the forest trust. The forests have to be able to locate each other via DNS, which means the DNS server in a forest needs to know about the DNS server for the other forest to resolve the forest with which it is trying to create a trust relationship. This is accomplished via DNS conditional forwarding (covered in Chapter 7, "Advanced Networking Services").

Shortcut Trust

While every domain in a forest trusts the others implicitly, the only actual trusts that exist are between the parent and child domains and between the various tree roots in a forest. For authentication between domains in the forest, Kerberos referral tickets have to be created and passed between each set of trusted domains that are in the path between the two domains trying to communicate.

As shown in Figure 11-40, the request for authentication to the required resource needs to pass through every domain along the path. This is due to the nature of the Kerberos implementation. Why is this important?

Tickets for access to a resource in a domain can come only from a domain that hosts the resource. That way, a user gets a ticket from another domain if he is referred by his local domain via a referral ticket to a domain trusted by the user's domain. Notice that you can only refer to domains that are explicitly trusted.

Only a domain controller in the domain of the target resource/server can issue a ticket for access. Therefore, if a user in a different domain wants a ticket, he needs to be "referred" by his home domain, thus proving the user is who he says and can be trusted to be given a ticket.

These referrals are possible because each pair of domains that are connected by a transitive trust (parent–child, tree–root, and so on) share an interdomain key that is based on the trust password used when creating the trust relationship. This key can be used for encryption to create the referral tickets that a domain controller creates for a user, which can then be given to the target domain. Because the target domain can decrypt the ticket, it knows the user must have received it from a domain controller in the source domain that would have authenticated the user requesting service.

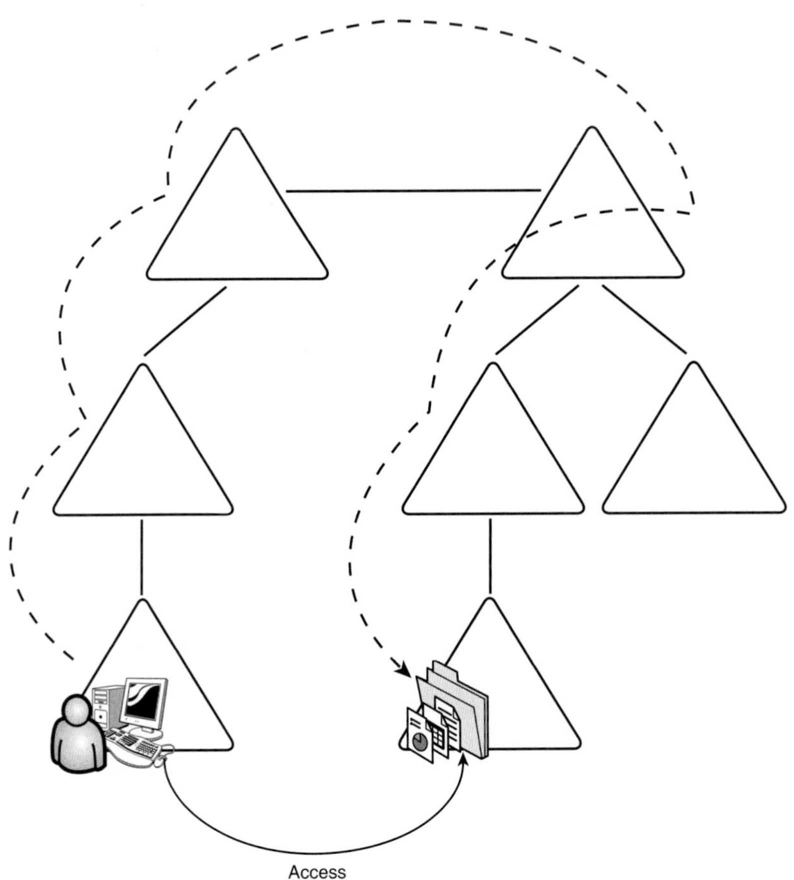

FIGURE 11-40 To access the resource, the user has to go through five referrals to get to the resource domain to be granted a ticket to gain access.

All these hops are required because no direct trusts exist between the domains and thus there are no shared passwords that could be used to encrypt referral tickets. A shortcut trust is a trust that is manually created by an administrator between two domains within a forest to provide this direct path, thus removing the need for multiple hops of referrals by Key Distribution Centers (KDCs) that are required if the normal parent–child and tree–root trust route is used. This provides faster authentication.

Shortcut trusts are transitive trusts that can be either one-way or two-way trusts, depending on the administrator's needs. Do not create shortcut trusts unless you have an issue with authentication lag between domains. Shortcut trusts are also referred to as *cross-link trusts*.

External Trust

External trusts are familiar to any NT 4 administrators, as they were used between NT 4 and earlier domains. An external trust is an intransitive trust as it is non-Kerberos in nature and is used to connect to NT 4.0 domains still in the environment.

Realm Trust

A realm trust is used to connect an AD domain to a non-Windows Kerberos realm, such as a UNIX or MIT Kerberos Version 5 implementation. Realm trusts are one-way or two-way trusts and can be transitive or intransitive.

Trust Management

Figure 11-41 shows a summary of all the various trusts you may use. You manage all the trusts via the Active Directory Domains and Trusts MMC by right-clicking the domain that contains the trust, selecting Properties, and selecting the Trusts tab.

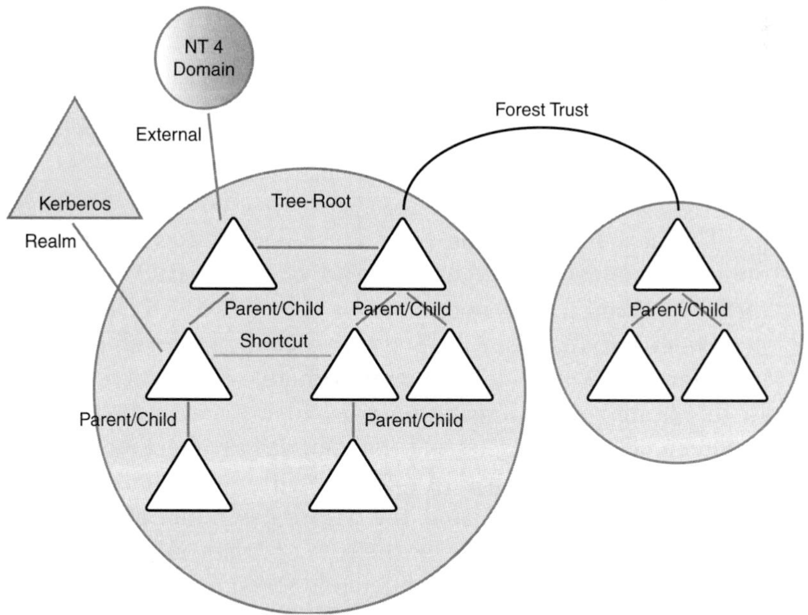

Figure 11-41 The various trust types: the two large circles are forest trusts.

Notice that the Trusts tab contains a New Trust button. It is used to create new trust relationships. If you select the forest root domain, you have the option to create a shortcut (another domain in the forest), external, realm, or forest trust. No other domain allows the option to create a forest trust. The whole process is wizard driven, as shown in Figure 11-42.

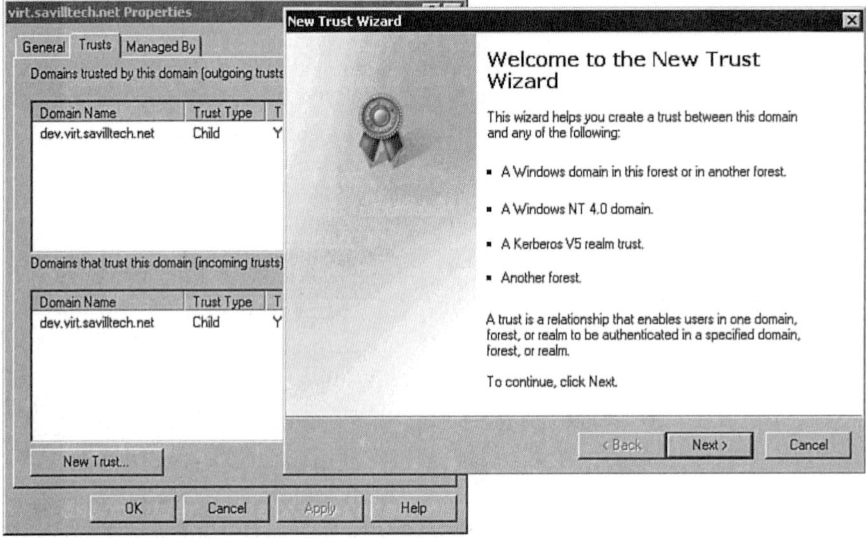

FIGURE 11-42 The New Trust Wizard checks on the domain selected and displays the list of possible trusts available.

The next screen of the New Trust Wizard asks for the name of the domain to connect to, which can be a DNS or NetBIOS name. Remember that if you want to connect to another forest or DNS named domain, you need to ensure that your DNS server is configured with a conditional forward for the DNS zone to the authoritative name servers for that zone. In this example, I'm creating a trust to my main lab domain, which is savilltech.net, from my testing domain, virt.savilltech.net, so I've already created a conditional forward rule from virt.savilltech.net to savilltech.net.

After you enter the name, the wizard communicates with the entered name and gives you options for the type of trust you can create. Figure 11-43 shows a Windows Server 2003 mode forest detected, so you can create a forest trust or an old-style external trust.

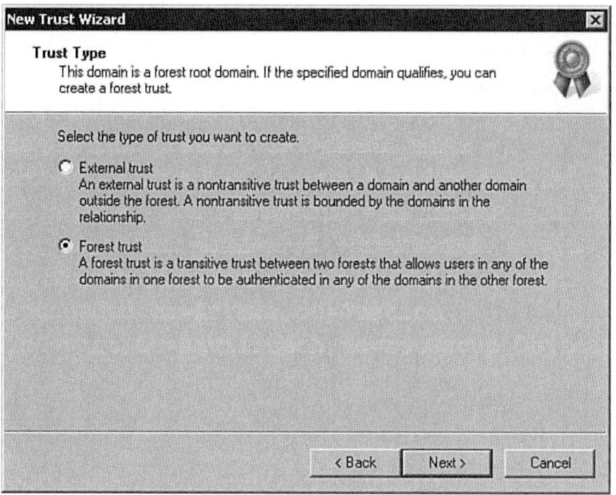

FIGURE 11-43 For another forest, you can create a transitive enabled forest trust or an old-style external trust.

Depending on the type of trust you select, select options concerning the trust direction. The direction can be two-way (two trusts are created, one incoming and one outgoing) or single direction (incoming or outgoing).

The wizard also allows you to create the trust on both sides, avoiding the need for this to be a two-step process (see Figure 11-44). If you are the administrator for both sides of the trust, you can elect to create both the local domain and the specified domain. If different administrative groups govern the domains, each needs to create its side separately. If you opt to create both sides, you are prompted for credentials in the other domain that has permissions to create the trust.

If you selected a Kerberos trust, you are prompted about whether the trust should allow forest-wide authentication capabilities for anyone in the trust or only for selected users. This option is also displayed for the other forest if this is a forest trust type. Finally, a summary screen appears. Click Next to create the trust, and it is listed for the domain. You can now grant access to resources from the other side of the trust, as shown in Figure 11-45. If you ever remove the trust, any permissions given no longer function.

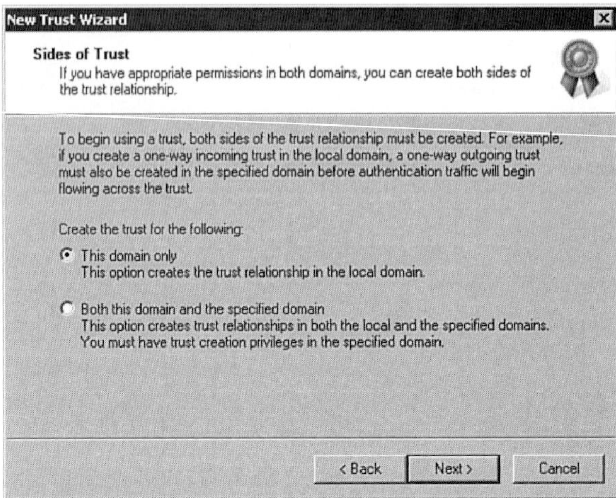

FIGURE 11-44 If you are an administrator and have credentials for both sides of the trust, you can elect to create the trust on both domains.

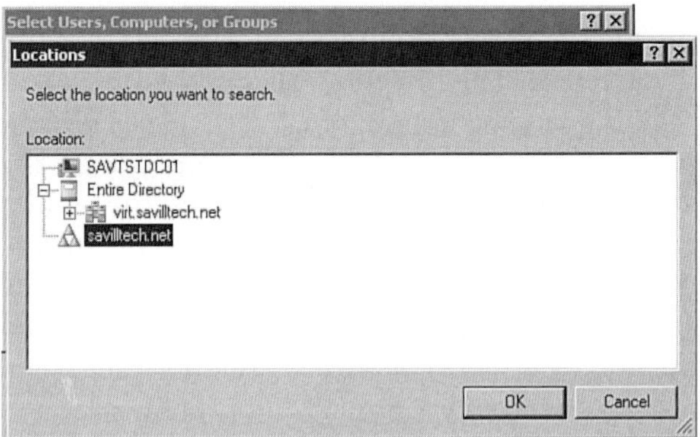

FIGURE 11-45 With the forest trust set to savilltech.net, I can now grant its users/groups/computers access to resources.

To remove a trust, select it from the list of trusts and click Remove. If it is a bidirectional trust, you are prompted to indicate whether to remove both sides, in which case you must enter credentials for the other domain if it is an outgoing trust (see Figure 11-46).

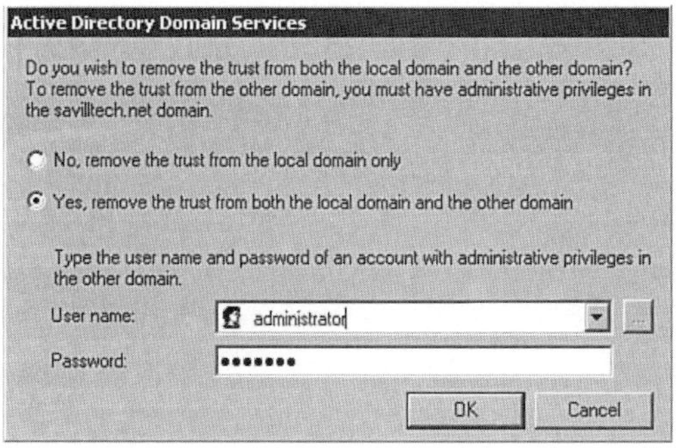

Active Directory Domain Services

Do you wish to remove the trust from both the local domain and the other domain? To remove the trust from the other domain, you must have administrative privileges in the savilltech.net domain.

No, remove the trust from the local domain only

Yes, remove the trust from both the local domain and the other domain

Type the user name and password of an account with administrative privileges in the other domain.

User name: administrator

Password: •••••••

OK Cancel

FIGURE 11-46 You can easily remove a trust.

Note that you cannot create or remove trusts established by the AD creation process (that is, parent–child and tree–root trusts). AD maintains these trusts, and although you can see them, you cannot change them—nor should you want to. To move domains, use another technique (described in Chapter 12), referred to as prune and graft, but it's not nice!

You can create trusts from the command line by using the `netdom trust` command as part of command-line management of AD (see Chapter 12).

Summary

The AD creation process is powerful, and it provides full unattended capabilities. This chapter looks at decision criteria and best practices related to the design of AD. It also examines the features that allow for more flexible and more secure deployments, such as improved deployment of domain controllers from media and secure domain controllers via the RODC functionality.

This chapter also examines more complex domain features related to vital roles required to keep AD running, such as the FSMO roles and how you should manage those roles in addition to sharing resources between separate domains and forests via the trust capability. When you combine all the AD features, it is clear that AD is not a limiting factor that has to be considered in your designs but rather acts as a facilitator of business and technical requirements.

Chapter 12 looks at more of what you can do with AD and how to manage and maintain it.

CHAPTER 12

MANAGING ACTIVE DIRECTORY AND ADVANCED CONCEPTS

This chapter closes out this book's look at Active Directory (AD) by examining some of the advanced concepts related to AD design and implementation. In this chapter, you learn about the main tools and techniques you use to manage AD and its migration from previous versions of AD.

Customizing Site Connectivity

So far you have created domain controllers. You have also seen that you can create sites, which are just names you give to the physical grouping aspects of the network (for example, Dallas, Austin), and then you can define the IP subnets in your environment. You left the environment as all the sites belonging to a single site link, and unless you have a cloud-type WAN infrastructure, this is unrealistic. In any case, it is normally good to have a hub location to act as the center of replication, which then replicates any changes to the other spoke locations. This enables replication to reach all domain controllers in the environment more quickly.

This chapter concentrates on Internet Protocol (IP) site links. Although Simple Mail Transfer Protocol (SMTP) is supported, it is not commonly used, mainly because it cannot be used to replicate a domain partition. SMTP can be used only with forestwide partitions, such as

Configuration and Schema, to enable physically separate domains to still be part of a single forest.

Remember that you care about sites and site links in particular to help AD make the right decisions about how to replicate information. If you lay out a good site and site link design, then the Knowledge Consistency Checker has the right information to create connection objects over the most logical path where the best connectivity exists.

By default, a single DEFAULTIPSITELINK exists, and also by default, all sites are linked to it via the site link. As discussed in the previous chapter, "Designing and Installing Active Directory," you don't want that.

If you have a traditional type of infrastructure with T1 lines and so on between specific locations, you can easily see where to create the site links and costs of these links by looking at tables that show you what values to use. If you have a cloud of connectivity with no direct connections, then the speed of the links are based on the "cloud," but where the links are from is based on the physical sites. For example, you are likely to have one or more major data centers, and they would form the major locations, with the "spoke" locations having site links into one or more of the hubs. Why? To control and make replication efficient. If replication between sites occurs every 15 minutes, and if you implement a central location, changes are replicated to this central site and then replicated out to the other locations, giving 30 minutes max for changes to propagate through the entire infrastructure. Also, in large locations, there are likely to be more domain controllers, which are better suited to handle the replication overhead.

So what do you need to consider for a site link; what attributes do site links have? There are three attributes you need to consider for a site link (aside from the protocol, which in this chapter we assume is IP). Figure 12-1 shows a screen of DEFAULTIPSITELINK. All site links are located under Inter-Site Transports, IP in the Active Directory Sites and Services Microsoft Management Console (MMC) snap-in. Remember that, sites are forestwide and stored in the Configuration partition, so they need to be configured only once for the entire forest. They ascertain the replication topology for all domains.

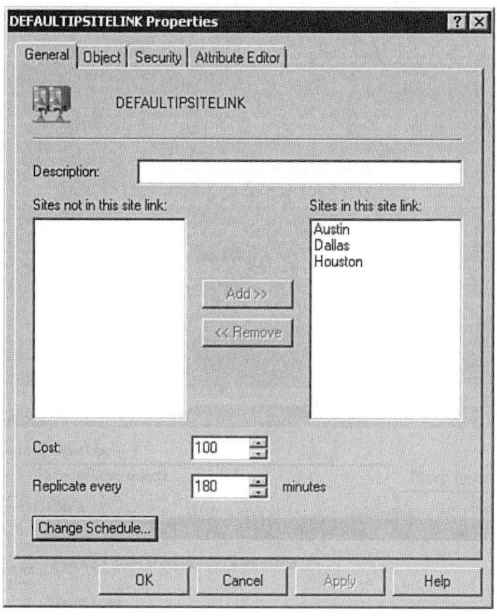

FIGURE 12-1 All new forests have this single IP site link, and all sites are joined to it by default.

Core Site Link Attributes

The three attributes of the core site link are the sites that are connected via the site link, cost, and replication interval.

Sites Connected Via the Link

The most basic attribute of the core site link is the sites that are connected via the site link. All sites are displayed; sites that are not currently in the site link are shown in the left box, and those that are in the site link are in the right box. You can move sites into and out of the site link via the Add/Remove buttons.

Cost

Cost is one of the most vital settings for replication. The cost tells AD the speed of the link that is connecting the sites or, more accurately, the available speed of the link that can be used for replication. The lower the cost, the more preferred the link, and the faster the link, the lower the cost. So what values should you use for the site link costs, based on speed? There are two main schools of thoughts. One is based on the following algorithm:

$$Cost = \frac{1024}{\log(Available\ Bandwidth\ [Kb])}$$

Table 12-1 presents common network speeds and the costs the algorithm would yield for them.

Table 12-1 Input and Outputs of Cost Algorithm

Available Bandwidth (Kbps)	Cost
56	586
128	486
256	425
512	378
1,024	340
2,048	309
4,096	283

These values are a little difficult to work with. Another version of these values, shown in Table 12-2, is not as accurate but uses whole numbers and so is nicer to use. If you have big differences in link speeds, then the simplified version works well, but if the links are closer in speed, the algorithm gives better values.

Table 12-2 Simplified Version of the Cost Algorithm

Available Bandwidth	Cost
>10Mbps	10
10Mbps to 1.544Mbps	100
1.544Mbps to 512Kbps	200
512Kbps to 128Kbps	400
128Kbps to 56Kbps	800
<56Kbps	2,000

So now, based on the speed of the link—or, more accurately, the bandwidth available—you can ascertain a cost for a link.

Replication Interval

By default, the site link replicates every 180 minutes, which is 3 hours. This may be okay in some circumstances, but in other scenarios, replication between sites needs to happen more frequently. The exact frequency depends on the requirements of the sites. If a location is fairly isolated in terms of object creation and resource access, it may not need to replicate frequently. However, if a site is managed via the central location and changes need to reach the client more frequently, the replication interval should be reduced. Fifteen minutes is the minimum replication interval. Remember that password changes are handled outside this replication because password changes are pushed to the PDC (primary domain controller) FSMO emulator. In the event of a password authentication failure, the DC asks the PDC FSMO to verify that the password is wrong.

Notice that the site link properties page includes a Change Schedule button. Press it and a dialog appears, showing a grid for all the various hours of the days of the week, as shown in Figure 12-2. By default, all hours of the week are available for replication. However, hours can be unselected, which means replication cannot occur over those hours. This would be useful for locations where the bandwidth at certain times should not be used for replication. For example, the link could be configured to be unavailable between 9 a.m. and 5 p.m., and then replication would occur during the evening hours.

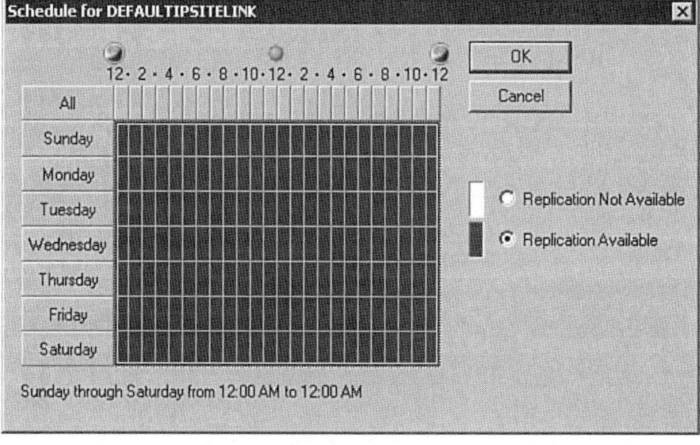

FIGURE 12-2 There is a box for every hour of each day of the week.

Managing Site Topology

After you have decided on the site links you want in your environment, first rename DEFAULTIPSITELINK to something more meaningful. Ensure that only the sites you want are in the site link and that the cost, schedule, and so on are correct. Another option is to get all the sites you want in the environment and then just delete DEFAULTIPSITELINK; either way, just make sure it's gone.

For now, create the site links you want and then delete DEFAULTIPSITELINK. It's important to get the site topology up and running before you start adding domain controllers to the environment. Until the site links are defined correctly and the replication schedule is configured, by default, replication occurs only every three hours.

To create a new site link, right-click IP under Inter-Site Transports and select New Site Link. The New Object - Site Link dialog appears. Initially, the only configuration item is to select the sites that are connected via the site link. Because it's a site link, select at least two sites to be part of the site link. Select the links from the left side of the dialog, as shown in Figure 12-3, and click the Add button to make them part of the site link. Also provide a name for the site link; make it something that's easily distinguishable for the sites that are part of the link, such as *SiteA-SiteB*, and then click OK.

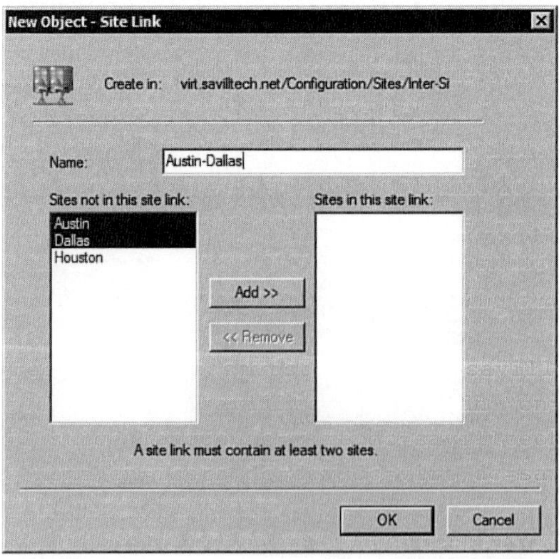

FIGURE 12-3 You can configure some basic properties via the New Object - Site Link dialog.

Repeat this process for all the site links you need. Create a Houston-Dallas link, as shown in Figure 12-3. In this environment, Dallas is the hub location, so all other sites replicate via Dallas. Because Dallas is the hub, place its name second, so it's easier to see which site is part of the link when just glancing, as the "other" site's name is first.

Now select each site link and change its cost and replication frequency by right-clicking the site link object and selecting Properties. In this example, the sites are well connected, so you can leave the cost as the default 100, but replicate every 15 minutes instead of 180 minutes, so changes spread more quickly. There is the downside of having a shorter replication interval: Replication traffic between sites is compressed if larger than 32KB using high compression, resulting in data possibly being only 10% of the original size. So the more you replicate, the less chance the data is larger than 32KB, so you lose the compression feature. However, on modern networks of 1.5Mbps and above, this may not be an issue. The other potential reason for replicating frequently may be that objects might have attributes changing value frequently, so replicating every 15 minutes may replicate a new value every 15 minutes instead of just getting a value once an hour or less. Remember that you can also use the Change Schedule option to set specific hours during which replication does not occur.

When the site links are all created, right-click DEFAULTIPSITE and delete it. The next time the knowledge consistency checker runs, new connection objects are generated based on the new site links. Or speed this up by right-clicking a server's NTDS Settings object and selecting All Tasks, Check Replication Topology, as shown in Figure 12-4.

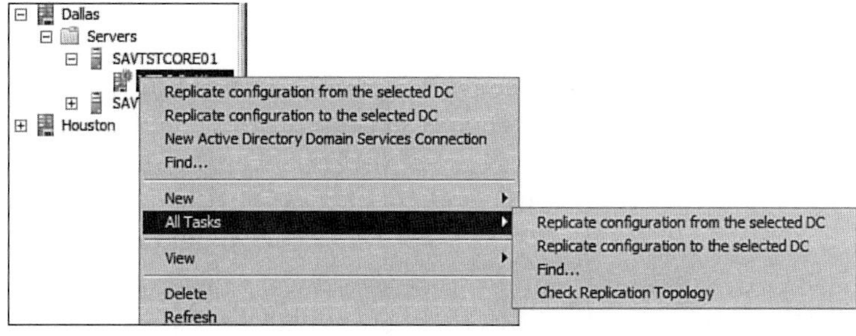

FIGURE 12-4 Force a KCC execution via the Check Replication Topology option.

There are additional considerations. The previous chapter discussed disabling the Bridge All Site Links option as part of the IP Inter-Site Transport properties, which means only sites directly connected via a site link can replicate. But what if you need domain controllers in sites that are not directly connected to replicate? Perhaps you have a scenario like the one illustrated in Figure 12-5, where a domain controller for the domain of the DCs in the sites on either side does not exist in the central site. There would be no way to replicate between them because a domain controller for another domain cannot replicate the domain partition for another domain.

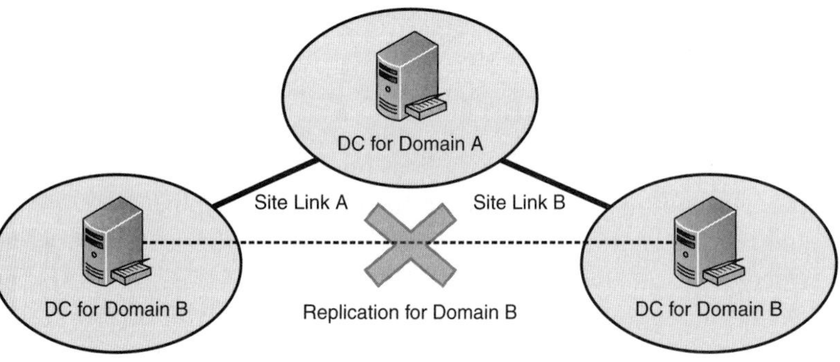

Figure 12-5 Without a direct site link, the sites containing the domain controllers for Domain B cannot replicate.

One option would be to turn on the Bridge All Site Links setting, but there is a neater option: You can bridge specific site links, which enables replication to occur between domain controllers linked by the bridge. In this case, add a site link bridge to connect Site Link A and Site Link B, which would look as shown in Figure 12-6. This would then enable the two domain controllers to replicate because it would let AD know that network connectivity between the two nondirectly connected locations is possible. The central site routes the traffic.

Using a site link bridge is a good way of controlling how replication can occur. Use a site link bridge at locations that may have multiple-hub sites. If the major central site becomes unavailable in a disaster, you want the spoke sites to replicate with the other hub location. If Bridge All Site Links is turned off and the spokes only have site links to the now-offline hub location, then that would not be possible. The solution is to create a site link bridge between each spoke site link and the site link between the two hub locations, giving the spoke domain controllers a way to connect to the other hub location. Under normal circumstances, the KCC would create replication objects only to the spokes directly connected to the hub because the least cost is used. But in a disaster, the higher-cost route could be used.

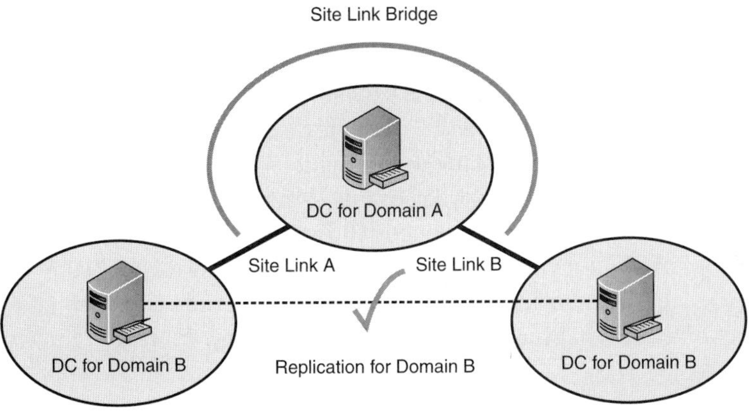

FIGURE 12-6 With the site link bridge connecting Site Link A and Site Link B, the domain controllers for Domain B can now replicate.

To create a site link bridge, right-click the IP Inter-Site Transports container and select New Site Link Bridge. Like a site link, a site link bridge needs to contain at least two site links. Don't specify sites; specify site links, which is what you are bridging, as shown in Figure 12-7.

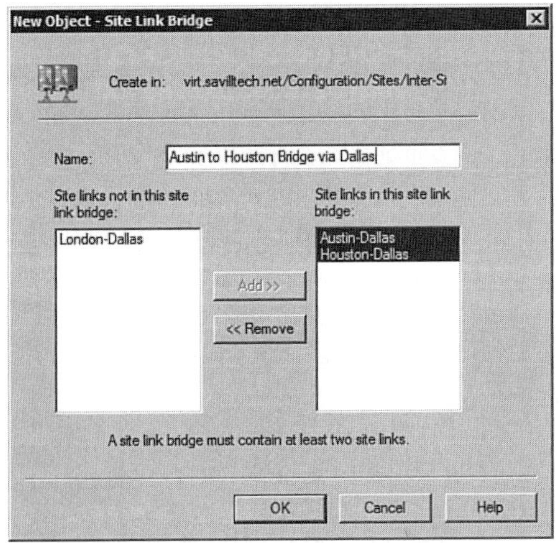

FIGURE 12-7 Domain controllers in Austin and Houston could now have replication objects created between them.

The Preferred Bridgehead

The bridgehead server is a server that is involved in the replication of data between two sites. In Windows 2000, only one domain controller per naming context per site could act as a bridgehead server. This was an issue. If there many sites were replicating from a single site, such as in a hub-and-spoke model, that one domain controller could get heavily overloaded. In Windows Server 2003, this was changed so multiple domain controllers per site can act as bridgehead servers for a single partition/naming context.

There may be instances in which you want to specify a particular domain controller(s) to act as the bridgehead(s) for a site. Perhaps you have specified particular boxes to better handle large amounts of replication, or you may have strict traffic policies/firewalls between locations, and you need to ensure that replication occurs only between specific domain controllers that have rules in the firewall or a router to allow communication.

NOTE For information on ports used for replication, see http://technet.microsoft.com/en-us/library/f9733398-a21e-4b40-8601-cfb452da82ad.aspx.

To set a server as a preferred bridgehead server, access the server's properties page in the Active Directory Sites and Services MMC snap-in. At the bottom of the General tab, as shown in Figure 12-8, set the transports for which the server should act as a bridgehead by selecting them and clicking the Add button. To remove a server from the role as a preferred bridgehead server, select the transport and click the Remove button.

CAUTION When you set one or more domain controllers as preferred, then *only* those domain controllers can perform intersite replication. If they are unavailable, then intersite replication stops because the Inter Site Topology Generator (ISTG) has no domain controllers it can use to perform replication. Where possible, do not configure preferred bridgehead servers as it adds complexity to the environment.

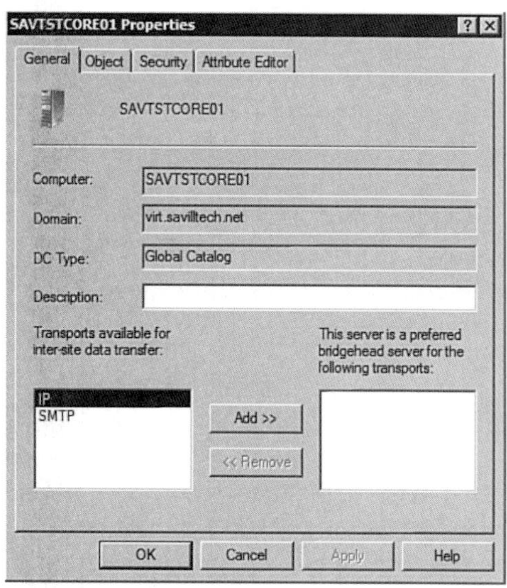

FIGURE 12-8 Although making a server a preferred bridgehead is easy, it does not mean you should do it.

If you decide to go the preferred bridgehead server route, define a preferred bridgehead for all domains/partitions in a particular site. For example, if you have domain controllers for Domain A and Domain B in a site, then a preferred bridgehead must be set on a DC from both domains. If you don't do this, then the partitions that are not stored on any preferred domain controllers cannot be replicated intersite. The KCC logs an event to the event log, notifying that the replication topology is not complete, and then set a preferred bridgehead server for the directory partition that cannot currently be replicated. The KCC does this only when partitions have no preferred domain controllers set, but preferred domain controllers have been set for other partitions in a site.

If you want to view the domain controllers acting as bridgeheads, use the `repadmin` tool with the `/bridgeheads` parameter, as shown in the following example. Notice that it shows the bridgeheads for each site and the partitions of the forest it is replicating.

```
C:\Users\Administrator.VIRT>repadmin /bridgeheads

Repadmin: running command /bridgeheads against full DC local-
host
```

```
Gathering topology from site Dallas
(savdaldc01.virt.savilltech.net):

Bridgeheads for site Austin
(savtstdc02.dev.virt.savilltech.net):
             Source Site    Local Bridge  Trns         Fail.
Time    #    Status

         ===============  ==============  ====  ==========
=======   ===  =======
=
                  Dallas      SAVTSTDC02    IP
(never)   0   The operation completed successfully.
                 ForestDnsZones Configuration virt

Bridgeheads for site Houston (savtstdc03.virt.savilltech.net):
             Source Site    Local Bridge  Trns         Fail.
Time    #    Status

         ===============  ==============  ====  ===========
======   ===  =======
=
                  Dallas      SAVTSTDC03    IP
(never)   0   The operation completed successfully.
                 Configuration dev DomainDnsZones ForestDnsZones
virt

Bridgeheads for site Dallas (savtstcore01.virt.savilltech.net):
             Source Site    Local Bridge  Trns         Fail.
Time    #    Status

         ===============  ==============  ====  ===========
======   ===  =======
=
                 Houston    SAVTSTCORE01    IP
    (never)   0   The operation completed successfully.
                 DomainDnsZones ForestDnsZones Configuration
virt
                  Austin    SAVTSTCORE01    IP
       (never)   0   The operation completed successfully.
                 Configuration dev ForestDnsZones
```

Advanced Replication Options

For most environments, the automatic replication objects created by the KCC are the most efficient for an organization, assuming that the sites, site links, and so on have all been correctly documented via the Active Directory Sites and Services MMC snap-in. After all, garbage in, garbage out. There are some circumstances in which you may want to fine-tune the connection object behavior.

This chapter doesn't cover manual creation of replication objects because it's a messy process. Although in Windows 2000 it was sometimes necessary, it is not needed for Windows Server 2003 and above. If you configure a site's topology correctly, the KCC generates a logical set of replication objects. If it does not, your site topology is probably not correctly defined. So go back and check whether you have missed a site link or whether you have Bridge All Site Links turned on. If you manually create replication objects, disable the KCC.

However, instead of manually creating replication objects, you can massage the replication objects in two ways. The first massage applies when you have a lot of spoke sites connected to a central hub (20, 30, or hundreds of spoke sites all replicating to the hub).

This chapter has already talked about how intersite replication is load balanced with Windows Server 2003 and above over the available domain controllers in a location. However, this load balancing is performed only initially when a domain controller at a spoke site is added. If a new domain controller is added at the hub location, existing connections are not reevaluated and spread more evenly among the domain controllers. The Active Directory Load Balancer (ADLB) tool solves this problem. It looks at the connection objects and load balances them among the available domain controllers. ADLB is not part of the operating system (OS) but is part of the Windows Server Resource Kit. It is also provided with the Active Directory Branch Office Deployment Kit. The ADLB tool runs in three phases: It gathers data about the sites and connection objects, calculates the new replication connection object design, and writes the updated connection object properties.

Load balancing of connection objects among the domain controllers is useful, but ADLB also staggers when replication occurs within the replication interval. By default, all replication takes place in the first 15 minutes of a replication cycle with the replication partners. With ADLB, that replication is staggered. For example, Site A replicates between minutes 0 and

15 of the replication time, Site B replicates between minutes 16 and 30, and Site C replicates between minutes 31 and 45. This is a great feature that spreads the load experienced by the hub domain controllers even further, enabling them to support more branch sites.

The ADLB tool does not have to modify all the connection objects at once. Tell it to run in batches of 10 (or any other number) modifications to reduce the number of changes occurring at any one time. In its most basic use, just specify a server to process the connection objects and the site to balance, as follows:

```
adlb /server:savtstdc01 /site:DALLAS
```

A full ADLB walkthrough is provided in the Active Directory Branch Office Deployment Kit.

In addition to staggering when replication happens, you have another option. This option, redundant connection mode, and ADLB are mutually exclusive; if you use ADLB, you can't use redundant connection mode. Normally, only one replication object is created per namespace between sites. This is how you achieve the most efficient replication using a least-cost spanning tree.

With a hub-and-spoke model that has many spoke/branch locations all connecting to a hub location, if a domain controller at the hub goes down, all the remote locations have to recalculate replication objects. This results in a huge number of changes at the connection object to the domain controller that is now unavailable. In addition, when the domain controller is back, the connection objects do not fail back. To solve this problem, use redundant connection mode. The configuration of redundant connection mode requires two steps. First, enable the redundant connection mode, which tells the ISTG to have two connection objects to the hub location. Second, disable detection of failed connection objects because you assume that a failed domain controller is coming back. So there is no need to modify the connection objects.

Run the commands for redundant connection mode on all remote locations that require the redundant connections. The following is an example:

```
C:\>repadmin /siteoptions /site:Austin
➥+IS_REDUNDANT_SERVER_TOPOLOGY_ENABLED
➥Austin
```

```
Current Site Options: (none)
New Site Options: IS_REDUNDANT_SERVER_TOPOLOGY_ENABLED
C:\>repadmin /siteoptions /site:Austin +IS_TOPL_DETECT_
➥STALE_DISABLED
Austin
Current Site Options: IS_REDUNDANT_SERVER_TOPOLOGY_ENABLED
New Site Options: IS_TOPL_DETECT_STALE_DISABLED
IS_REDUNDANT_SERVER_TOPOLOGY_ENABLED
```

When redundant connection mode is enabled, the domain controllers in the spoke/branch locations create two connection objects to the hub to separate domain controllers. Your replication looks something like Figure 12-9, assuming that there is only one domain.

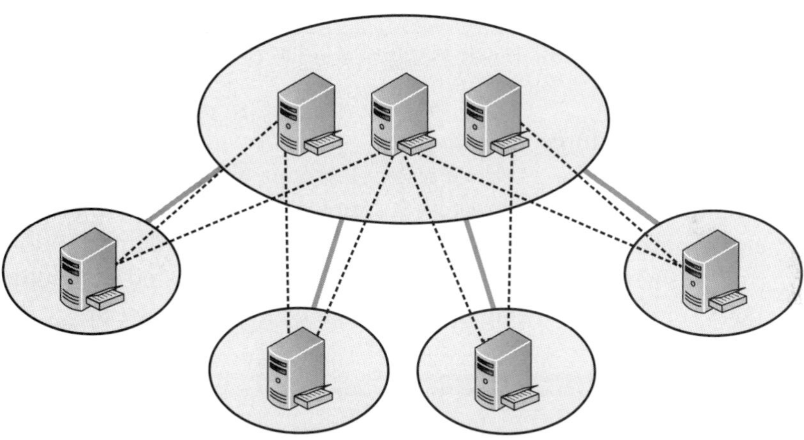

FIGURE 12-9 The dotted lines show the replication objects created, and with the redundant server topology enabled in each of the sites, two objects are created from each site to the hub.

Forcing a Demotion

When you demote a domain controller via `dcpromo`, checks are performed to ensure that the Domain Naming Master role can be contacted, along with other domain controllers for the local domain. The checks ensure that the domain controller, and possibly the domain (if you remove the last DC in the domain), is cleanly removed.

There may be times when you need to demote a domain controller without these checks, such as when connectivity is not available. This is not advisable at all because it leaves a large amount of data in the directory service metadata that requires cleaning. You receive errors if you try a normal demotion, for example, where the forest root domain cannot be contacted (see Figure 12-10).

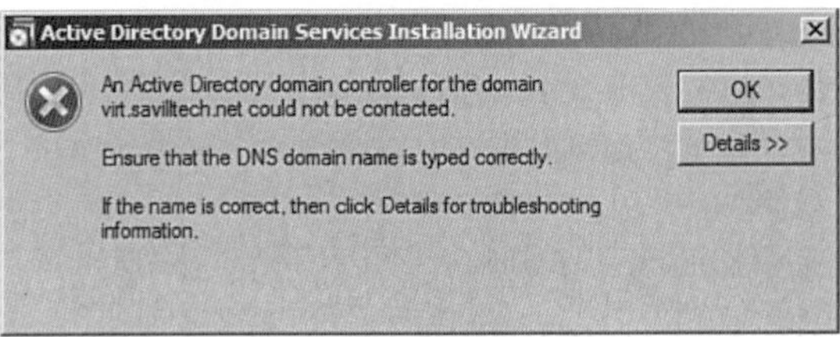

FIGURE 12-10 Connectivity to the forest root is needed to demote a domain controller.

You can force the removal of a domain controller by running `dcpromo` with the `/forceremoval` switch. When you do this, you bypass the normal checks and receive a series of errors, as shown in Figure 12-11 and Figure 12-12, stating that you are forcefully killing the domain controller; saying that any FSMO roles it holds are listed, in addition to any DNS service; and listing whether it's a Global Catalog (GC).

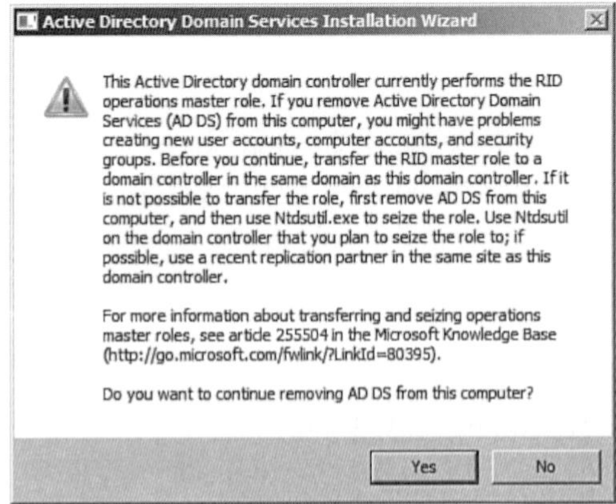

FIGURE 12-11 Forced removal can be dangerous and potentially lead to loss of data.

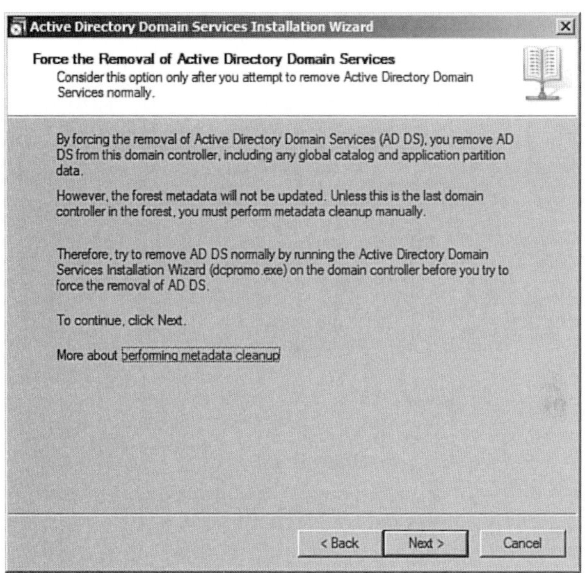

FIGURE 12-12 In addition to the warnings about the FSMO, DNS, and GC roles, the wizard does not "think" this is a good idea!

You can, as usual, perform this unattended. There are no entries in the unattended file except for the new local administrator password, as shown here:

```
[DCInstall]
AdministratorPassword=
```

Execute this as follows:

```
dcpromo /forceremoval /unattend:<unattend file name>.txt
```

Cleaning Up the Metadata

If a domain controller crashed and cannot be restored or if you performed a `forceremoval` demotion, there are metadata left in the directory service. Clean it up by using `ntdsutil`.

Removing a Defunct Domain Controller

The first step in cleaning up the metadata is to activate the NT Directory Service (NTDS) instance, as in the following example:

```
C:\Users\Administrator>ntdsutil
ntdsutil: activate instance ntds
Active instance set to "ntds".
```

Then access the metadata cleanup portion of `ntdsutil` and connect to your Domain Naming FSMO role holder, as shown in the following example:

```
ntdsutil: metadata cleanup
metadata cleanup: connections
server connections: connect to server savtstdc01
Binding to savtstdc01 ...
Connected to savtstdc01 using credentials of locally logged on
user.
server connections: quit
```

When you connect to a server, select the target of your command. To do this, first list the domains and then select the number for the domain that contains the domain controller you want to remove. In this case, it is domain it.dev.virt.savilltech.net, as shown in the following example:

```
metadata cleanup: select operation target
select operation target: list domains
Found 3 domain(s)
0 - DC=virt,DC=savilltech,DC=net
1 - DC=dev,DC=virt,DC=savilltech,DC=net
2 - DC=it,DC=dev,DC=virt,DC=savilltech,DC=net
select operation target: select domain 2
No current site
Domain - DC=it,DC=dev,DC=virt,DC=savilltech,DC=net
No current server
No current Naming Context
```

When the domain is selected, select the site that contains the domain controller you want to delete, as shown in the following example:

```
select operation target: list sites
Found 3 site(s)
0 - CN=Dallas,CN=Sites,CN=Configuration,DC=virt,DC=savilltech,
DC=net
1 - CN=Austin,CN=Sites,CN=Configuration,DC=virt,DC=savilltech,
DC=net
2 - CN=Houston,CN=Sites,CN=Configuration,DC=virt,
DC=savilltech,DC=net
select operation target: select site 2
Site - CN=Houston,CN=Sites,CN=Configuration,DC=virt,
DC=savilltech,DC=net
Domain - DC=it,DC=dev,DC=virt,DC=savilltech,DC=net
No current server
No current Naming Context
```

Then list the servers in the site, select the server, and then exit the `select` operation target area of ntdsutil, as shown in the following example:

```
select operation target: list servers in site
Found 1 server(s)
0 - CN=SAVTSTDC03,CN=Servers,CN=Houston,CN=Sites,
CN=Configuration,DC=virt,DC=savilltech,DC=net
select operation target: select server 0
Site - CN=Houston,CN=Sites,CN=Configuration,DC=virt,
DC=savilltech,DC=net
Domain - DC=it,DC=dev,DC=virt,DC=savilltech,DC=net
Server - CN=SAVTSTDC03,CN=Servers,CN=Houston,CN=Sites,
CN=Configuration,DC=virt,D
C=savilltech,DC=net
        DSA object - CN=NTDS
Settings,CN=SAVTSTDC03,CN=Servers,CN=Houston,CN=Sites,
CN=Configuration,DC=virt,DC=savilltech,DC=net
        DNS host name - savtstdc03.it.dev.virt.savilltech.net
        Computer object - CN=SAVTSTDC03,OU=Domain
        Controllers,DC=it,DC=dev,DC=virt,DC=savilltech,DC=net
No current Naming Context
select operation target: quit
```

Finally, enter the command to remove the selected server, as shown in the following example, and exit the utility:

```
metadata cleanup: remove selected server
Transferring / Seizing FSMO roles off the selected server.
Unable to determine FRS owner for role PDC.
Unable to determine FRS owner for role Rid Master.
Unable to determine FRS owner for role Infrastructure Master.
"CN=SAVTSTDC03,CN=Servers,CN=Houston,CN=Sites,
CN=Configuration,DC=virt,DC=savilltech,DC=net"
removed from server "savtstdc01"
```

During this procedure, confirm whether you want to delete the entry (see the dialog shown in Figure 12-13). If the domain controller is the last in the domain, you get another dialog, in which you confirm whether the domain controller can never be brought back online (see Figure 12-14). In both of these dialogs, click Yes.

FIGURE 12-13 When confirming the delete option, be sure.

In addition to cleaning up the metadata, do some tidying at both the DNS and domain controller object levels. There should be no need to manually delete replication connections because the KCC sees that the domain controller is gone from the metadata and automatically removes the connections.

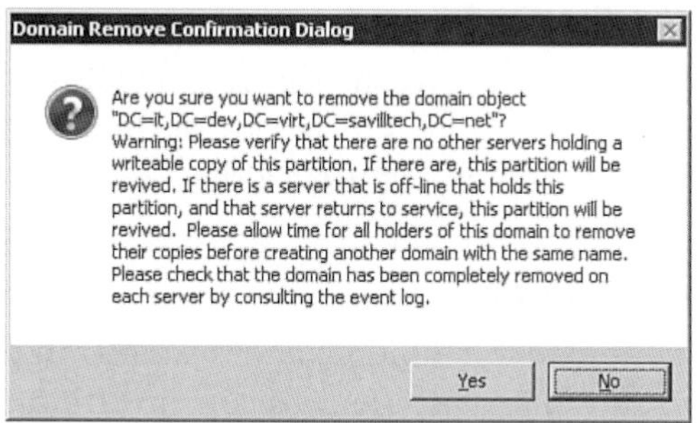

FIGURE 12-14 Click Yes to remove the last domain controller.

Cleaning DNS

After you remove the defunct domain controller, clean DNS. Open the DNS Management MMC snap-in, select _msdcs.<*forest root domain*>, and delete any records related to the deleted domain controller, such as any cname (alias) or A (host) records. If the domain controller was a DNS server, also remove the name server record, as shown in Figure 12-15.

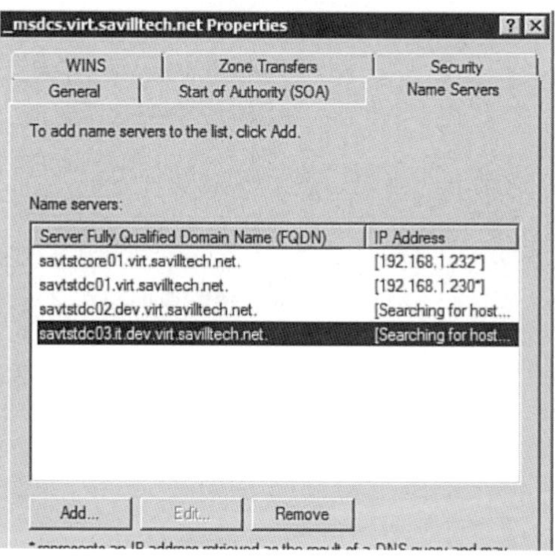

FIGURE 12-15 Remove the name server record to avoid having the nonexistent domain controller accessed.

Cleaning the Server Record

To clean the server record, in the Active Directory Sites and Services MMC snap-in, expand the site where the server previously resided and under the Servers branch, right-click the server and select Delete.

Removing a Domain

Deleting a nonexistent child domain is a similar process to deleting a nonexistent domain controller. Once again, use `ntdsutil`, connect to the NTDS instance, select the metadata cleanup, and select a server to which to connect. The following is an example:

```
C:\Users\Administrator>ntdsutil
ntdsutil: activate instance ntds
Active instance set to "ntds".
ntdsutil: metadata cleanup
metadata cleanup: connections
server connections: connect to server savtstdc01
Binding to savtstdc01 ...
Connected to savtstdc01 using credentials of locally logged on
user.
server connections: quit
We now select the domain and select to delete it.
metadata cleanup: select operation target
select operation target: list domains
Found 3 domain(s)
0 - DC=virt,DC=savilltech,DC=net
1 - DC=dev,DC=virt,DC=savilltech,DC=net
2 - DC=it,DC=dev,DC=virt,DC=savilltech,DC=net
select operation target: select domain 2
Site -
CN=Houston,CN=Sites,CN=Configuration,DC=virt,DC=savilltech,DC=net
Domain - DC=it,DC=dev,DC=virt,DC=savilltech,DC=net
Server -
CN=SAVTSTDC03,CN=Servers,CN=Houston,CN=Sites,
CN=Configuration,DC=virt,D
C=savilltech,DC=net
        DSA object - CN=NTDS
Settings,CN=SAVTSTDC03,CN=Servers,CN=Houston,CN=Sites,
CN=Configuration,DC=virt,DC=savilltech,DC=net
        DNS host name - savtstdc03.it.dev.virt.savilltech.net
        Computer object - CN=SAVTSTDC03,OU=Domain
Controllers,DC=it,DC=dev,DC=virt,DC=savilltech,DC=net
```

```
No current Naming Context
select operation target: quit
metadata cleanup: remove selected domain
DsRemoveDsDomainW error 0x2015(The directory service can per-
form the requested operation only on a leaf object.)
```

Why is there an error in this example? It's telling you that you are trying to delete a domain while it still contains information. Normally, that information is an application partition, such as DomainDnsZones, so check by listing all the partitions (in previous versions of `ntdsutil`, this was domain management instead of partition management) and delete it if you find it, as in the following example:

```
C:\Users\Administrator>ntdsutil
ntdsutil: activate instance ntds
Active instance set to "ntds".
ntdsutil: partition management
partition management: connections
server connections: connect to server savtstdc01
Binding to savtstdc01 ...
Connected to savtstdc01 using credentials of locally logged on
  user.
server connections: quit
partition management: list
Note: Directory partition names with International/Unicode
  characters will only display correctly if appropriate fonts
and language support are loaded
Found 9 Naming Context(s)
0 - CN=Configuration,DC=virt,DC=savilltech,DC=net
1 - DC=virt,DC=savilltech,DC=net
2 - CN=Schema,CN=Configuration,DC=virt,DC=savilltech,DC=net
3 - DC=DomainDnsZones,DC=virt,DC=savilltech,DC=net
4 - DC=ForestDnsZones,DC=virt,DC=savilltech,DC=net
5 - DC=dev,DC=virt,DC=savilltech,DC=net
6 - DC=DomainDnsZones,DC=dev,DC=virt,DC=savilltech,DC=net
7 - DC=it,DC=dev,DC=virt,DC=savilltech,DC=net
8 - DC=DomainDnsZones,DC=it,DC=dev,DC=virt,DC=savilltech,DC=net
```

Notice the last entry; it's the DomainDnsZones application partition for the domain you deleted, so delete it first, as in the following example:

```
partition management: delete nc
➥DC=DomainDnsZones,DC=it,DC=dev,DC=virt,DC=savilltech,DC=net
The operation was successful. The partition has been marked
for removal from the enterprise. It will be removed over time
in the background.

Note: Please do not create another partition with the same
name until the servers which hold this partition have had an
opportunity to remove it. This will occur when knowledge of
the deletion of this partition has replicated throughout the
forest, and the servers which held the partition have removed
all the objects within that partition. Complete removal of the
partition can be verified by consulting the Directory event log
on each server.
partition management: quit
```

You can now perform the same domain deletion initially discussed, and the removal works as shown in the following example:

```
metadata cleanup: remove selected domain
"DC=it,DC=dev,DC=virt,DC=savilltech,DC=net" removed from
server "savtstdc01"
```

Finally, delete the trust from the parent domain to the child domain by performing the following steps:

1. Start adsiedit.msc.
2. Open the Domain Naming Context (NC) for the parent domain and expand the System container.
3. Right-click the trustDomain object for the deleted child domain and select Delete, as shown in Figure 12-16.

If the child domain DNS was delegated to the child domain, then access the parent domain's DNS server and delete the delegation record in the zone for the child. You now know how to clean up the metadata from a failed domain/domain controller demotion.

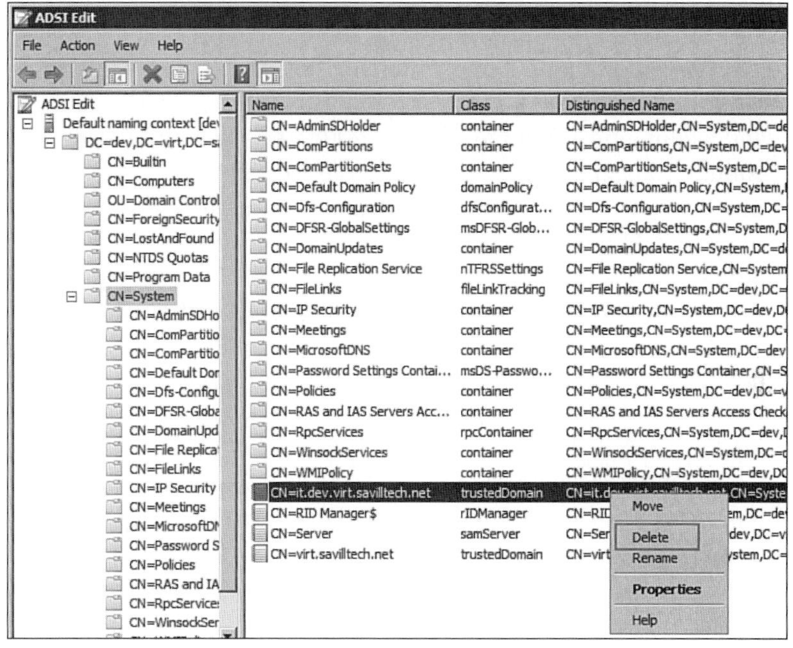

FIGURE 12-16 Delete the trust object for the nonexistent child domain.

Managing AD

We've already covered most of the tools used to manage AD. The major tools are Active Directory Domains and Trusts, Active Directory Sites and Services, and Active Directory Users and Computers. These are the main graphical tools for day-to-day use. There are other utilities. For example, you used `ntdsutil` in this chapter for a number of AD-related actions, and ADSIEDIT.msc gives you direct access to all information stored in AD. To this point, we haven't discussed the Active Directory Users and Computers MMC snap-in, so let's stop and take a look at that. There is reasoning I saved this snap-in for now: It's important that you understand the design aspects of AD and best practices before rushing to create and use it. Now that you understand the various aspects of a good AD design you're ready to start some object creation inside AD.

Server Manager

To access tools, go to Administrative Tools and launch the Active Directory Users and Computers MMC snap-in. But as seen in Chapter 17, "Managing and Maintaining Windows Server 2008," the Server Manager includes the common interfaces related to the roles installed on a server. Open Server Manager and access the Active Directory Domain Services Role node to see the Active Directory Users and Computers snap-in, along with the Sites and Services MMC snap-in. Notice that the Domains and Trust tool is not listed because it's used far less frequently than the other snap-ins.

As shown in Figure 12-17, the main Active Directory Domain Services node shows general information related to domain services, which in this case are the most recent events (in the past 24 hours) and services that relate to Active Directory Domain Services (ADDS).

Scroll down the page to see that it has an Advanced Tools section with links to all the utilities used for other AD tasks. For example, there are links to the AD Domains and Trusts MMC snap-in, ADSI Edit, `ntdsutil`, and `repamin`—all tools discussed in this book for managing AD. This shows what a great job the Server Manager and management teams in general have done in making this the go-to point for managing Windows Server 2008.

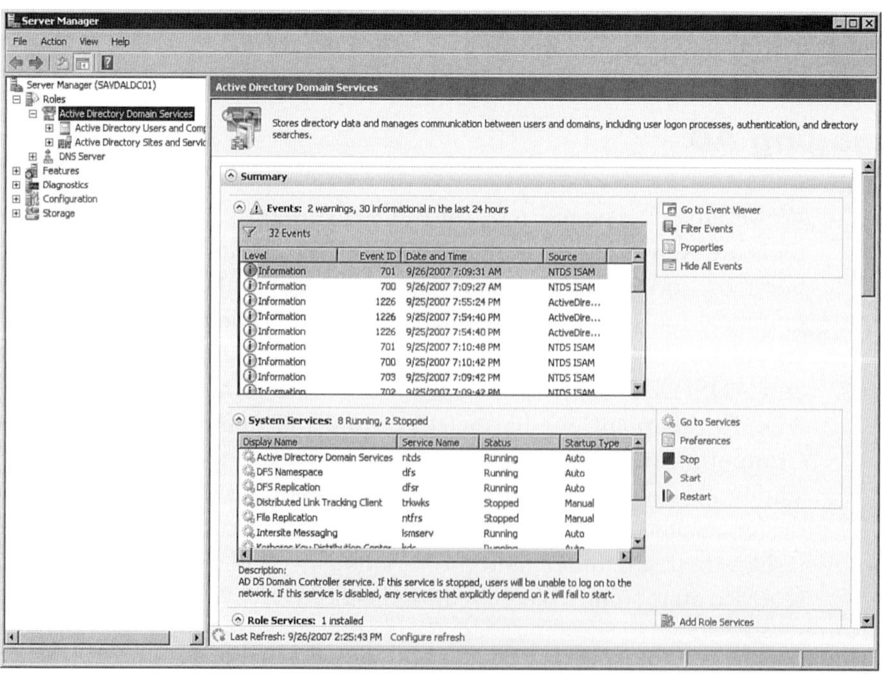

FIGURE 12-17 Server Manager is a great starting point for managing AD and, indeed, all the roles and features available in Windows Server 2008.

Keep scrolling down to the Resources and Support section, which lists best practices associated with AD, such as adding domain controllers, using Read-Only Domain Controllers (RODCs) in branch locations, and using security groups. Take a look; there may be things you have not thought of that will undoubtedly help your environment.

Active Directory Users and Computers

By default, the local domain of the computer running the Active Directory Users and Computers MMC snap-in is displayed. Remember that, as with the other management tools, these can be run on other computers besides the Windows Server 2008 server.

Change the domain or domain controller you are connected to via the context menu of the root Active Directory Users and Computers navigation node. The domain controller you are currently connected to is displayed in square brackets.

By default, there are several child containers for the domain. At a minimum, you see the following:

- **Builtin**. Contains groups that are core parts of the OS and should not be deleted.
- **Computers**. The default location where new domain-joined computer objects are stored. However, you can modify which container is used via the `redircmp` command, provided that the domain functional level is at least Windows Server 2003. By using `redircmp`, you can redirect computers to be created in any organizational unit (OU) in the domain; the syntax is `redircmp` *`<FQDN of new default location>`*, where *`<FQDN of new default location>`*. could be `ou=newcomp,ou=use,dc=virt,dc=savilltech,dc=net`.
- **Domain Controllers**. Whereas the other standard containers are just containers, this one is an OU. Why is this special? OUs can have group policy applied to them, and it's normal to apply special group policy to the domain controllers, which are the only objects that should reside in the Domain Controllers OU and are placed there by default.
- **ForeignSecurityPrincipals**. Is empty by default but can contain Foreign Security Principals (FSPs). FSPs are common when you have trusts to foreign domains and place users/groups from the foreign domain into groups in the local domain. The names of the object are in security identifier (SID) format.

- **Users**. The default location for new User objects to be created, which, like computers, can be changed via the `redirusr` command.

In the most basic of environments, you may leave this structure alone, but it is more common to create an OU structure. As discussed in Chapter 10, "Active Directory Domain Services Introduction," there are a number of reasons, including the capability to delegate authority, apply Group Policy Objects (GPOs), and match your organization's actual structure. OUs can be nested, which means an OU can exist inside other OUs. Best practice is to keep this to a maximum depth of four levels, and seven levels should be the absolute deepest nesting.

To create an OU, right-click a domain or an existing OU and select New Organizational Unit from the context menu. You can create an OU only at the root domain level or inside another OU. You can't create OUs in normal container objects, such as the Computers or Users container that exist in domains by default.

Enter a name for the OU. A new feature in Windows Server 2008 is the Protect Container from Accidental Deletion option, as shown in Figure 12-18. A big human error problem is that administrators would often delete an OU by mistake, which is a huge issue because normally an OU contains a large amount of important objects, such as users and computers. When this kind of deletion happened, a painful process known as an authoritative restore had to be performed. When the Protect Container from Accidental Deletion option is selected, the security descriptor of the OU is updated so no users or administrators have the right to delete the object. Use this protection on any object by selecting the Object tab and enabling the Protect Object from Accidental Deletion option, which performs the same Access Control List (ACL) changes.

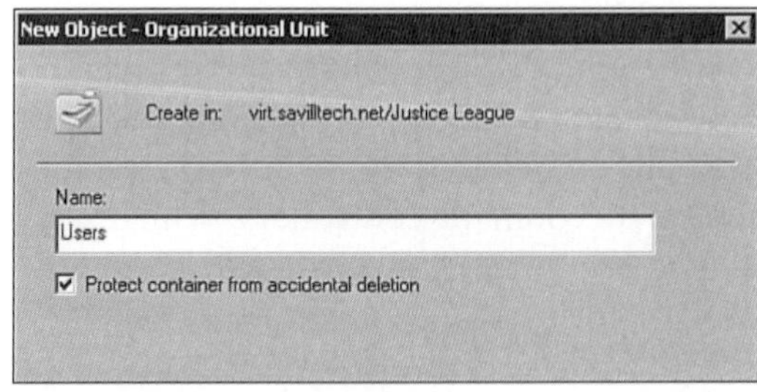

FIGURE 12-18 By default, the Protect Container from Accidental Deletion setting is enabled.

Right now if you right-click an OU and select its properties, the Security tab is hidden from you. To view the Security tab, and indeed some more advanced information, in the Active Directory Users and Computers MMC snap-in, enable the Advanced Features view by selecting View, Advanced Features. When this is enabled, you see a few extra containers that weren't previously visible, such as LostAndFound, Program Data, System, and NTDS Quotas. But the big item is that you see a Security tab for your OU. Enabling the Protect Container from Accidental Deletion setting works in two ways—well, three if you include not using it at all. The first way is to protect all OUs from accidental deletion. This causes a special Access Control Entry (ACE) to be written to the OU for the Everyone group that has explicit deny permissions for Delete and Delete Subtree. Remember that a deny always takes precedence over an allow, which means no one can delete the OU. If additional OUs are created inside an OU that is protected, those new OUs have the everyone deny rule. The parent OU is also updated with an everyone rule denying the capability to delete child OU objects. So what does this protection mean? If you try to delete a protected OU, you are asked for confirmation and then given an access denied message. If you attempt to delete an unprotected OU that has child OUs that are protected, a separate dialog is displayed, as shown in Figure 12-19. As the figure shows, check Use Delete Subtree Server Control, which overrides the protected objects and allows them to be deleted.

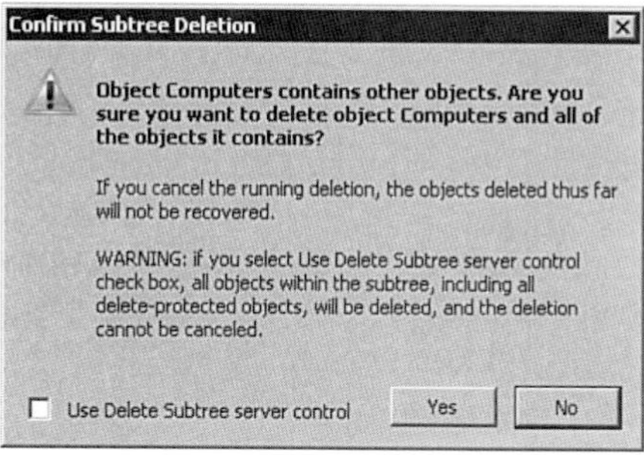

FIGURE 12-19 For the deletion of a protected OU to succeed, check Use Delete Subtree Server Control.

To delete a protected OU directly and not an unprotected OU with protected child OUs, first remove the explicit deny ACE via the Security tab of the OU and remove the Everyone entry.

Delegating Permissions

As discussed in Chapter 10, one of the major reasons AD in Windows Server 2008 is such a great improvement over previous versions is that you no longer have just domain administrators and then everyone else. With AD in Windows Server 2008, you now have granular control over delegation of authority and can give specific users or groups the ability to manage certain aspects of the directory or part of the directory, such as an OU.

The most common use of delegation of authority is where you have local IT administrators for an office, so an OU is created containing all the users, computers, groups, and resources for that office. Delegate permission to manage the content of the OU to a local administrators group that contains the local IT administrators. It's a good idea to use a group instead of individual users because undoing delegation is not as easy as it should be. It's much easier to add/remove people in a group than to run the delegation wizard and try to remove delegated permissions. Removing delegated permissions requires a lot of manual effort, however, `dsrevoke` helps somewhat.

Say that you delegated permission for an OU and granted the local OU administrators group full permissions over the OU. However, more granular delegation is possible. Also, if granular permissions were required at the domain level, you perform the same process but select the Delegate Control context menu option at the domain object instead of an OU. To delegate permissions for an OU, perform the following steps:

1. Right-click the Organizational Unit to be delegated permissions and select Delegate Control.
2. When the welcome screen of the Delegation of Control Wizard is displayed, click Next.
3. Select the users or groups to which you're delegating permissions. Again, use a group here rather than individual users. Create a group for the delegation if one does not exist and click Next, as shown in Figure 12-20.

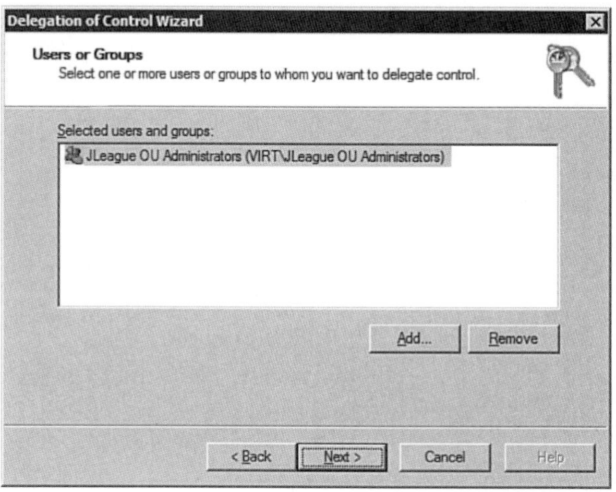

FIGURE 12-20 Here you have selected to delegate control to the JLeague OU Administrators group. Note that naming groups according to their role helps in your management of an environment.

4. A list of common tasks is displayed, and they are all unselected by default. Check the rights you want to delegate and click Next, as shown in Figure 12-21. At this point, a confirmation dialog appears. If you're ready to delegate the permissions, click Finish and skip the rest of the steps. If you want a more complex delegation, select the Create a Custom Task to Delegate option, click Next, and continue to the next step.
5. The type of objects on which you are delegating permissions is displayed, which by default is the object being delegated and any type of object stored within it. However, you can select only specific objects by selecting Only the Following Objects in the Folder and then specifying whether the delegated group (or user, if you're ignoring my recommendations to delegate to groups) can also create and/or delete the objects in the container. Make your selections and click Next, as shown in Figure 12-22. If you're using this level of detail, you must have some goal in mind, so you know the objects you want to modify.

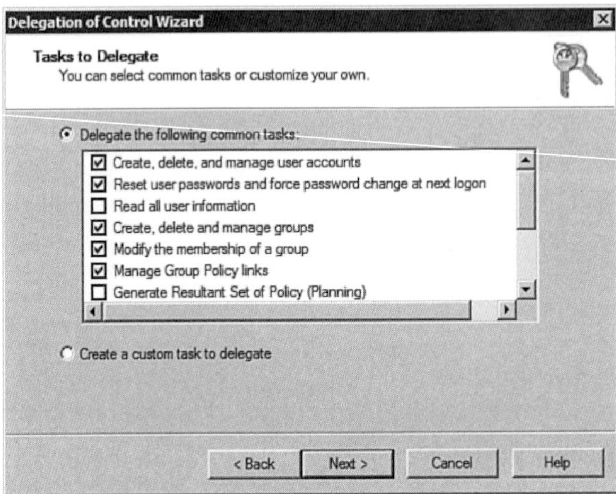

FIGURE 12-21 Selecting the tasks that are delegated to the authorized users/groups.

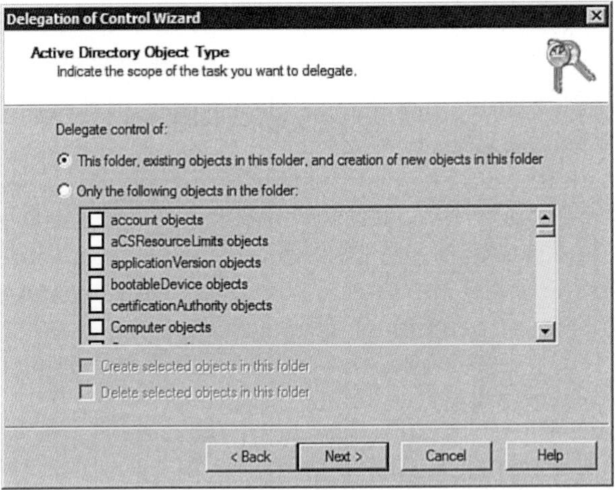

FIGURE 12-22 Configuring the scope of the delegation.

6. The next screen shows the permissions being delegated. By default, only the general permissions are shown, such as Full Control, Read, Write, and so on. However, you can check the Property-specific option to allow control over specific settings being delegated. For example, you can control being able to read

or write a user's telephone number or address attributes. In other words, the control can be detailed. Check the Creation/ Deletion of Specific Child Objects option for a list of object types to be added at the end of the permissions to create/delete each object type. Make the relevant selections, as shown in Figure 12-23, and click Next. Figure 12-23 shows an example of granting Full Control, which automatically makes all the other option boxes checked.

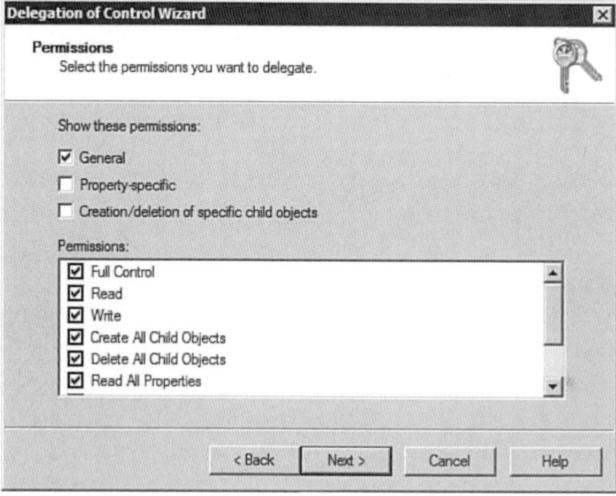

FIGURE 12-23 You can control exactly the permissions that are being delegated.

7. Click Finish, and the permissions are applied.

Look at the security of the container on which you delegated permissions via the properties of the container (with Advanced Features view turned on): You see an entry for the group that has been delegated the permissions. Clicking the Advanced button gives you full insight into the permissions you delegated.

If you want to update delegated permissions, rerun the wizard. However, running it for the same group already delegated and selecting a lower set of permissions does not remove the existing delegations given. It just adds delegations. So how do you remove delegations?

Manually delete entries for the group in question via the Security tab of the properties page. However, you have a better option. Microsoft provides a tool, dsrevoke, that is available at www.microsoft.com/downloads/details.aspx?FamilyID=77744807-c403-4bda-b0e4-c2093b8d6383&displaylang=en for use on any genuine Windows installation. The first of the two capabilities of dsrevoke is to show delegations for a given group (the tool works best with groups, another reason not to use users for delegations) via the report switch, and the second is to pass a root to search through. The following example shows a search of an entire domain for the JLeague OU Administrators group:

```
C:\Tools>dsrevoke /report /root:dc=virt,
➥dc=savilltech,dc=net "virt\JLeague OU Administrators"


ACE #1
Object: OU=Justice League,DC=virt,DC=savilltech,DC=net
Security Principal: VIRT\JLeague OU Administrators

Permissions:
  READ PROPERTY
ACE Type: ALLOW

ACE does not apply to this object
ACE inherited by all child objects of class User


ACE #2
Object: OU=Justice League,DC=virt,DC=savilltech,DC=net
Security Principal: VIRT\JLeague OU Administrators

Permissions:
  DELETE
  READ CONTROL
  WRITE DAC
  WRITE OWNER
  CREATE CHILD
  DELETE CHILD
  LIST CONTENTS
  VALIDATED WRITE ACCESS
  READ PROPERTY
  WRITE PROPERTY
  DELETE TREE
```

```
  LIST OBJECT
  EXTENDED ACCESS
ACE Type: ALLOW

ACE inherited by all child objects


# of ACEs for virt\JLeague OU Administrators = 2
```

Notice that there are two entries in the output. The latter is Full Permissions, which is what you delegated in the sample delegation walkthrough. The former is a second delegation you ran, granting read permissions for the same group. This demonstrates how a second delegation does not remove the first; it only adds to it.

You can also revoke delegation via the `/remove` switch. However, this is not granular. Specify a root path as before, which could be a specific OU and the group/user. The problem is that it removes all delegations; you cannot be specific. The following is an example:

```
C:\Tools>dsrevoke /remove /root:dc=virt,dc=savilltech,
➥dc=net "virt\JLeague OU Administrators"


ACE #1
Object: OU=Justice League,DC=virt,DC=savilltech,DC=net
..
..
<listed as with report>


# of ACEs for virt\JLeague OU Administrators = 2

Do you want to remove the above listed ACEs (y/n): y
All ACEs successfully removed

C:\Tools>dsrevoke /report /root:dc=virt,
➥dc=savilltech,dc=net "virt\JLeague OU Administrators"

No ACEs for virt\JLeague OU Administrators
```

If you want to be more specific than this, update via the Security tab of the container's permissions.

User Objects

In the domain you've been creating, you already have at least three accounts without having done anything, and you can see them in the Users container of the domain. Administrator, which is the account you're probably logged on as, if in the forest root domain, is also an enterprise administrator. At a minimum, it is a domain administrator. You also have a disabled Guest account (which you should leave disabled) and a disabled krbtgt account, which is used as part of the domain controller's Kerberos role. So leave that alone as well.

To create a new User account, right-click the domain/OU/container in which you want to create the user and select New, User. If you ever want to move an object, simply select the object by holding down the mouse button and dragging and dropping the object to the new location. You receive a notification that moving objects may cause things to not work as expected; click Yes, and you can disable the notification for future drag-and-drop operations. The warning tells you that the location of an object affects the GPOs that are potentially applied to it (because they are applied at OU levels) in addition to delegation of managing the object. Just moving an object may affect all this.

Create a new User account, and you get the dialog displayed in Figure 12-24. You are prompted for a first name, last name, middle initial, and logon name for the user. The logon name is the name the user uses during a logon, and the full name is used as the user's relative distinguished name (RDN), which is applied to the user's location in the domain to construct the distinguished name (DN). In our example, Wally West would be the RDN (relative to where the object is created), and because the user is being created in the Justice League OU in the virt.savilltech.net domain, the DN would be `cn=wally west, ou=justice league,dc=virt, dc=savilltech,dc=net`.

When the basic user information is entered, click Next to access the security parts of the user creation, which include setting the user's initial password by entering it twice. In addition, four check boxes are available. By default, User Must Change Password at Next Logon is selected (see Figure 12-25), which is a best practice because you are setting an initial password for the user but you should not know the users' passwords. So the first time the user logs on to the system, he is forced to change the password.

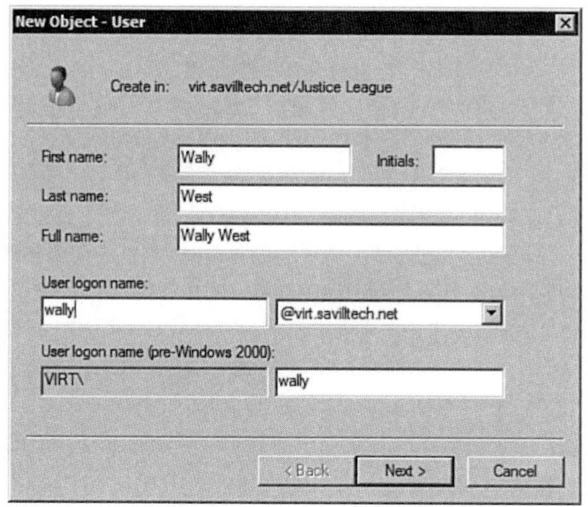

FIGURE 12-24 Fill in basic identity information on this screen.

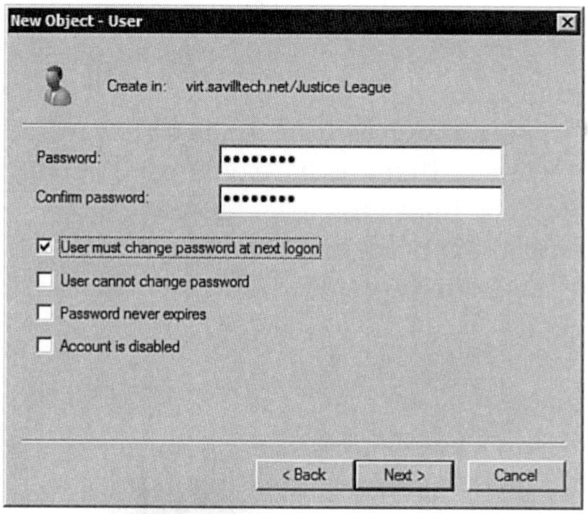

FIGURE 12-25 Avoid the Password Never Expires option.

The second check box is User Cannot Change Password, and it specifies that the user cannot change the password. This may be useful for a shared account. However, in general, you don't want an account shared by multiple people. Account sharing makes security and auditing changes impossible because more than one person knows the credentials and could have used the account. This is the same reason you should never give someone else your password or allow users to share theirs.

The third check box is Password Never Expires, and it is used to override security policies that are set on the domain. Normally, you use group policy to force a user to change her password. However, if you have accounts whose passwords should not be forced to change, enable this option. This is common on service accounts. However, it's is dangerous because service accounts typically have high privileges, and coupling that with a password that never changes makes for a great hacking target. The use of service accounts is being minimized in newer software via the system accounts, but they still may be needed. If you enable Password Never Expires, you can't force the user to change her password at the next logon.

Finally, Account Is Disabled creates the account but sets it as disabled, which means it cannot be logged into or used. This is useful for provisioning accounts that are needed in the future but that you don't want active yet.

After clicking Next, you may be prompted for additional information if you have custom plug-ins. For example, if Exchange 2000/2003 is in the organization, and the Exchange version of the Active Directory Users and Computers MMC snap-in is in use, you are prompted about whether to mail enable the user and which server, storage group, and store on which to create the mailbox. This changed in Exchange 2007 to being separate and not integrated. After you have entered all the information, a summary is displayed. Click Finish to create the user.

If you access the properties page of a user object, you see a large number of tabs related to the details of the user. These are described in the following sections.

The General Tab

Use the General tab to add to the user object additional identification information, such as a description, an office location, telephone numbers, an e-mail address, and Web pages.

The Address Tab

Use the Address tab to configure a physical address for the user, including street address, post office box, city, state, zip/postal code, and country region.

The Account Tab

The Account tab is the tab you probably use the most. In addition to allowing the user logon name to be modified, as shown in Figure 12-26, it provides the options Logon Hours and Log On To.

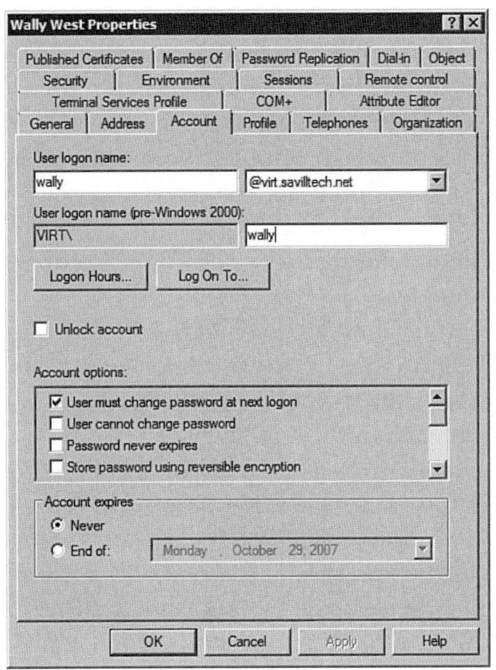

FIGURE 12-26 Spend time in this dialog for users in the domain.

Clicking the Logon Hours button opens up a dialog that shows every hour for each day of the week, and by default it has all hours available for logon. However, you can select hours during which you deny logon for the user. This is useful if you want to restrict when an account can be used. Perhaps the user is a shift worker who should not be allowed to log on outside his shift hours. By default, if a user is already logged on and the time changes to when logon is not permitted, he is not logged out but simply blocked from logging on again. However, you can use group policy to force the logoff via Computer Configuration, Windows Settings, Security Settings, Local Policies, Security Options, Network security: Force logoff When Logon Hours Expire. Click the Log On To button to limit a user to logging on to a defined set of machines identified by DNS or NetBIOS name.

One of the security features of Windows is that if a user account fails a logon attempt a configurable number of times, the user account is locked out. This is designed to prevent the account from being hacked by an attacker who is entering different possible passwords, normally via an automatic tool. In the real world of administrative life, most of the time, a lockout occurs because a user forgot his password or just mistyped it. When an account is locked out, the account can be unlocked by someone with account unlock permissions for the user by checking the Unlock Account box. If the account is locked out, the text says "Unlock account. This account is currently locked out on this Active Directory Domain Controller," assuming that the locked-out status is known to the domain controller.

The Account Options area allows some of the functionality that was available when the account was created, such as forcing the user to change the password at next logon, stopping the user from being able to change the password, configuring the password to never expire, and setting the account as disabled. There are additional options, such as storing the password using reversible encryption, which is required for some protocols/applications. Using reversible encryption, however, means storing the password in plain-text. There is an option to stop the account from having its management delegated, and there are security options concerned with encryption and Kerberos options, which are discussed in more detail later in this chapter.

Finally, by default, an account never expires, but if you're dealing with an account that's for a contractor or just a limited lifetime, enable an expiration so that the account becomes unusable at a defined date.

The Profile Tab

When a user logs on to a machine for the first time, a folder is locally created on the machine to store the user's preferences, such as desktop background, shortcuts, and Outlook cache. This is the user's local profile. Under Windows Vista and above, this profile is stored under the C:\Users folder, previously C:\Documents and Settings. It's possible to also store a copy of this profile on the network and configure it to be downloaded when the user logs on to a machine from the network copied back up to the server with any updates when the user logs off. This is known as a roaming profile, and it enable the configuration of settings and preferences to be available no matter which computer the user logs on to.

To enable roaming profiles, you need a share on the network onto which to store the profiles; enter that location in the profile path on the user's properties page. One neat trick is to use *%username% variable*, so if you set the path to *<server>**<share>**%username%*, it is automatically set to the user's logon name and is created with the right permissions so only that user can read the profile the first time she logs on. Not even administrators can read the profile; only SYSTEM and the user have access. The local copy of the profile is still left on the computers the user logs on to. To stop this, set Registry value HKEY_LOCAL_MACHINE\SOFTWARE\Microsoft\Windows NT\CurrentVersion\Winlogon\DeleteRoamingCache to 1.

You can specify a logon script via the Logon Script area, and you can also configure scripts by using group policy. The Logon Script area should be used only for something like a special activity account that needs commands to run at logon time. It should not be used for general users. That's what group policy is for.

By default, a user has a home path, which is normally her profile. It is the default location for most types of file open/save operations. You can change this to an alternate local path or redirect it to a network location by specifying the Connect option in the Home Folder section, as shown in Figure 12-27, and specifying the drive letter to use. The example shows the H: drive specified, which means you can then use H: from the command line and the Explorer shell. Again, if you use the *%username%* environment variable, the folder is automatically created under the share with permissions so that only administrators and the user can see the content.

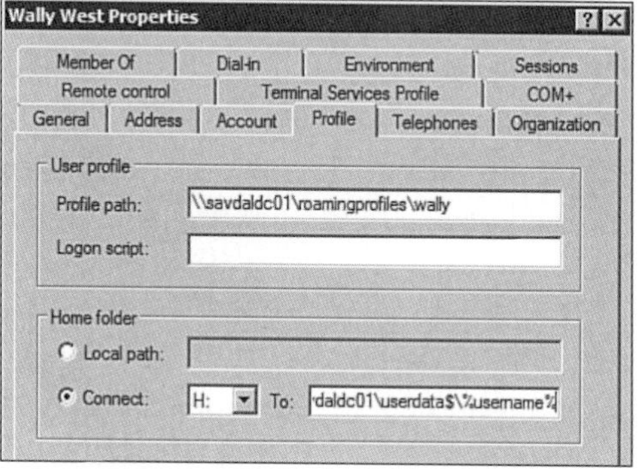

FIGURE 12-27 In this case, the user's home drive changes to H, which is mapped to a network location.

The Telephones Tab

On the Telephones tab, you can enter various phone numbers for the user, such as home, pager, mobile, fax, and IP.

The Organization Tab

Use the Organization tab to enter the user's job title, department, and company. You can also set a manager for the user and show any users for whom the user is configured as the manager (see Figure 12-28). This is updated automatically when a user is set as the manager for another user.

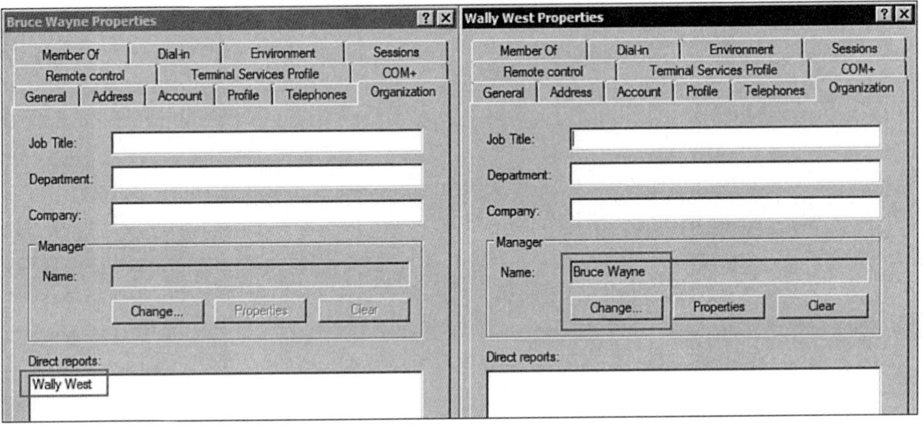

FIGURE 12-28 This type of functionality is closer to helping manage the organizational-type roles of a directory service.

The Member Of Tab

The Member Of tab displays the groups to which a user belongs. Use the Add and Remove buttons to modify the user's memberships.

The COM+ Tab

A COM+ partition is a container user for storing the configuration of a COM application that enables one application to run multiple times. Use the COM+ tab to associate a user with a particular COM+ partition set and therefore a certain COM+ application configuration. This is mainly used for Web-based applications.

Other User Properties

A few more properties are covered in other chapters: the Dial-in tab is covered in Chapter 8, "Remote Access and Securing and Optimizing the Network," and environment, sessions, remote control, and Terminal Services profile properties in Chapter 9, "Terminal Services."

Right-click a user object to get a variety of context menu options. Some are obvious; for example, Copy enables you to duplicate a user object.

Select Copy and a dialog appears, as if you're creating a brand-new user, asking for name, logon name, and so on. However, the rest of the properties of the original user are copied to the new target user. A cool feature of Copy is that properties that were user-specific, such as the user profile roaming path or home locations, are replaced with the new user's name, provided that the last part of the path matches the logon name. Using the Add to a Group option is a quick way to add a user to a group, and the Disable Account option just disables the account. You will probably use Reset Password quite a lot. Other options are available for moving the user to a new location, but you can do this most easily by just dragging and dropping the object to put it in its new location.

Select the All Tasks menu options to perform group policy configuration to see Resultant Set of Policy (RSOP), which is explored fully in Chapter 21, "Group Policy."

When you select the properties for a user, select multiple objects at once by holding down Shift to select a contiguous set of objects or Ctrl to select individual objects. While you select the multiple objects, some context menu items are available, such as Move, Disable/Enable, Add to Group, and Delete. Select Properties to modify some attributes of the users en masse. Not all attributes are available, but most of the General, Account, Address, Profile, and Organizational tab options are available, as shown in Figure 12-29. On the Profile tab, use *%username%* to set a home folder location or roaming profile for multiple users.

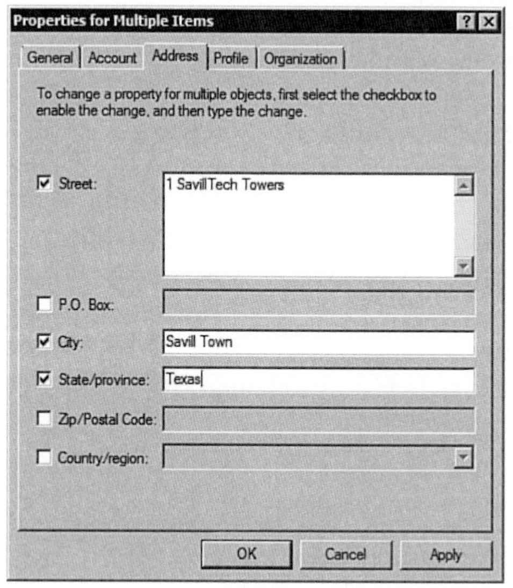

FIGURE 12-29 Check the box for the attribute you want to set en masse and then enter the value.

All these fields are stored as attributes for the user object; using the Active Directory Users and Computers MMC snap-in is an easy way to manipulate the object. You can also use tools such as ADSIEDIT.MSC to directly access the attributes, but be careful because you can cause damage if you don't know what you are changing.

You can do a lot of user management from the command line. At the most basic level, you can add a user via the `net user /add` command. However, you can't set many options. You can set the user's logon name, a password, a full name, and a few other settings but not much more. The following is an example:

```
C:\Users\Administrator.VIRT>net user hal Pa55word!
➥/add /fullname:"Hal Jordan" /domain
The command completed successfully.
```

The user in this example is created in the default Users container. If you want to set other settings, go in and work with them later. By using ADSI, you can set any option for the user. However, aside from scripting, you probably want to use the `dsadd` command the most; it's basic syntax is as follows:

```
dsadd user <distinguished name of user> -samid <username> -
pwd <new password>
```

The following example creates a user, Arthur Curry, in the Justice League OU. Notice that for anything that includes a space, put the whole component into quotes.

```
C:\Users\Administrator.VIRT>dsadd user "cn=Arthur,ou=Justice
➥League,dc=virt,dc=savilltech,dc=net" -samid Arthur -pwd
➥Pa55word!
dsadd succeeded:cn=Arthur,ou=Justice League,dc=virt,
dc=savilltech,dc=net
```

Use the `/?` switch with `dsadd` to see a full list of options. The following example creates the same user with more options. First, it deletes the user by passing the DN to the `dsrm` command, and then it creates the user again.

```
C:\Users\Administrator.VIRT>dsrm "cn=Arthur,ou=Justice
➥League,dc=virt,dc=savilltech,dc=net"
```

```
Are you sure you wish to delete cn=Arthur,ou=Justice
League,dc=virt,dc=savilltech,dc=net (Y/N)? y
dsrm succeeded:cn=Arthur,ou=Justice League,dc=virt,
dc=savilltech,dc=net
C:\Users\Administrator.VIRT>dsadd user
➥"cn=Arthur,ou=Justice League,dc=virt,dc=savilltech,dc=net"
➥-samid Arthur -pwd Pa55word! -fn Arthur -ln Curry
➥-display Aquaman -memberof "CN=JLeague,ou=justice
➥league,dc=virt,dc=savilltech,dc=net" -mustchpwd yes
dsadd succeeded:cn=Arthur,ou=Justice
League,dc=virt,dc=savilltech,dc=netGroup Objects
```

Groups

OUs are used for the organization of AD objects. An object such as a user or computer can reside only in a single OU, and OUs cannot be used for security permissions; for example, you can't assign an OU access to a file. Instead, use groups, which can contain objects such as users, computers, or other groups. Then give the groups access to resources.

There are two main types of groups: security and distribution groups. A security group is used to assign authorization to a resource, whereas a distribution group cannot be assigned access to a resource and is typically used as a target for messaging systems. So, if you're familiar with Exchange 5.5, you see that this is like a distribution list. It is possible to "mail enable" a security group so you can use it as a target for messaging applications, giving the same functionality as a distribution group, and also use it as part of a discretionary ACL.

After you determine the type of group, select the scope of the group. The scope defines where the group can be used and where objects in the group can reside. There are three scopes for groups:

- **Domain local**. Domain local groups have visibility only in the domain where the local group exists. However, accounts and any group scope from any trusted domain can be members.
- **Global**. Global groups are visible in any domain that trusts the local domain of the global group and can contain as members accounts and global groups from the local domain of the global group.
- **Universal**. Available only in Windows 2000 native mode or above, universal groups are domains of the security type (the distribution

type can be created in mixed mode) and are visible in the entire forest. They can have accounts from any domain in the forest of the universal group in addition to global and universal groups from any domain in the forest.

It is possible to perform group scope conversions. For example, you can convert a universal group to a domain local group, which would then allow it to only be granted access in the same domain as the domain local group. You can also convert a universal group to a global group, but only if the universal group does not contain as members another universal groups because global groups cannot contain universal groups. You can convert a global group to a universal group, provided that the global group is not a member of another global group, again, because global groups cannot have as members a universal group. So if Global Group A were in Global Group B and you converted Global Group A to Universal Group A, then Global Group B would not have Universal Group A in it because that's not allowed. Finally, you can convert a domain local group to a universal group as long as the domain local group does not have as a member another domain local group because universal groups cannot have domain local groups as members. Phew!

You may have heard that you should not use universal groups much because of replication problems, and this was true in Windows 2000. In the "old" days, replication occurred at an attribute level (we've talked about this previously), so when the membership of a universal group changed, the entire membership had to be re-replicated. Why is this a big deal for universal groups? Universal groups are forestwide and are replicated as part of the GC, so they are replicated throughout the entire enterprise any time they change. This could have a major performance impact. To combat this, the best practice was to place global groups into a universal group so the direct membership never really changed. Windows Server 2003 introduced Link Value Replication (LVR), but this best practice still remains.

The following mnemonic can help you remember a greater best practice: "**A**ll **G**ood **U**sers **D**o **L**ove **P**ermissions." Here's what it means:

- **A**ccounts—user/computer or even other groups—are placed into global groups.
- These **G**lobal groups are then placed into universal groups that are forestwide.

- The **U**niversal groups are placed into domain local groups
- The **D**omain **L**ocal groups are assigned **P**ermissions to resources.

If you are running a single-domain forest, you are less likely to use the domain local or universal groups than to directly assign global groups access to resources, but the bigger model works well in larger environments.

To create a group, right-click the OU or container in which you want to create the group and select New, Group. A dialog is displayed, as shown in Figure 12-30, in which you specify the group name and the type and scope of the group.

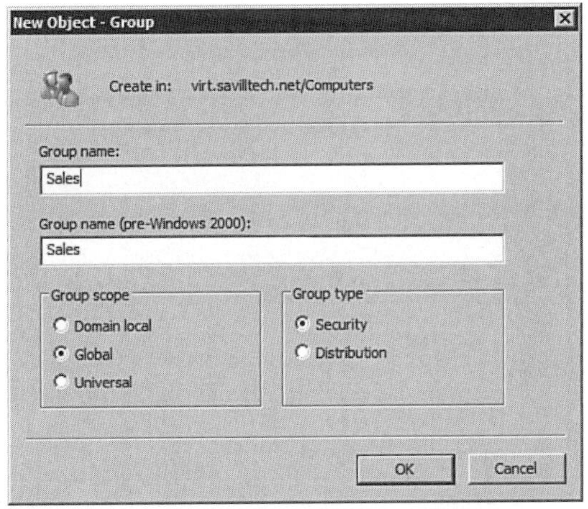

FIGURE 12-30 The default type of group is security with a global scope.

When the group is created, you can see its properties by double-clicking the group object or right-clicking and selecting Properties. On the General tab of the properties page, you can specify a description of the group along with an e-mail address, and then the group can be used as a target for messaging. The General tab also allows you to set options for valid conversions in the Group Type and Scope sections, as shown in Figure 12-31. You can also include notes about the groups.

On the Members tab, you can add users/computers/groups as members. Only valid objects are displayed; for example, when you're adding members to a global group and perform a search for objects, universal and domain local groups are not listed.

The Member Of tab enables you to add this group to other groups. Again, if you search, only groups that can contain the group type and scope are displayed.

On the Managed By tab, you can link a user object to the group as it's managed, along with contact information. You can also allow the user to update the membership of the group by selecting the Manager Can Update Membership List option.

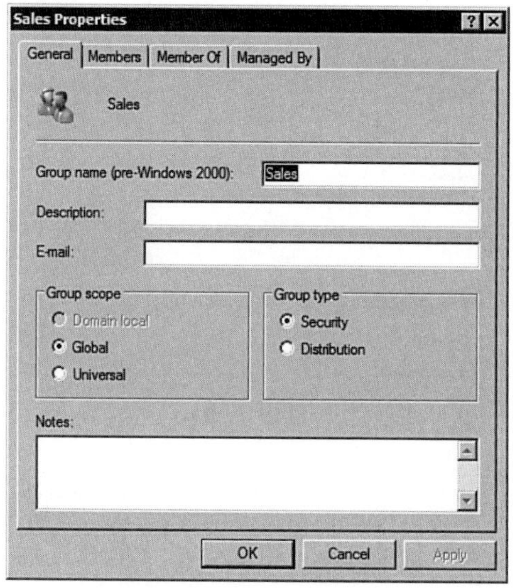

FIGURE 12-31 The option to convert to a domain local group is not available for this global group.

If you are using the Advanced Features view, then an additional three tabs are displayed on the properties page. The Object tab gives detailed information about the group, such as when it was created, when it was last modified, and its update sequence numbers, which are used for replication purposes. This tab also provides the check box Protect Object from Accidental Deletion, which you can use to set an everyone deny rule for Delete, as with OUs.

The Security tab enables detailed configuration of the object. If you set Managed By and gave permission to update the group membership, you see an entry for that user, who has only one right, Write Members, as shown in Figure 12-32. If you wanted other users to be able to add members to the group, give them the Write Members permission, too.

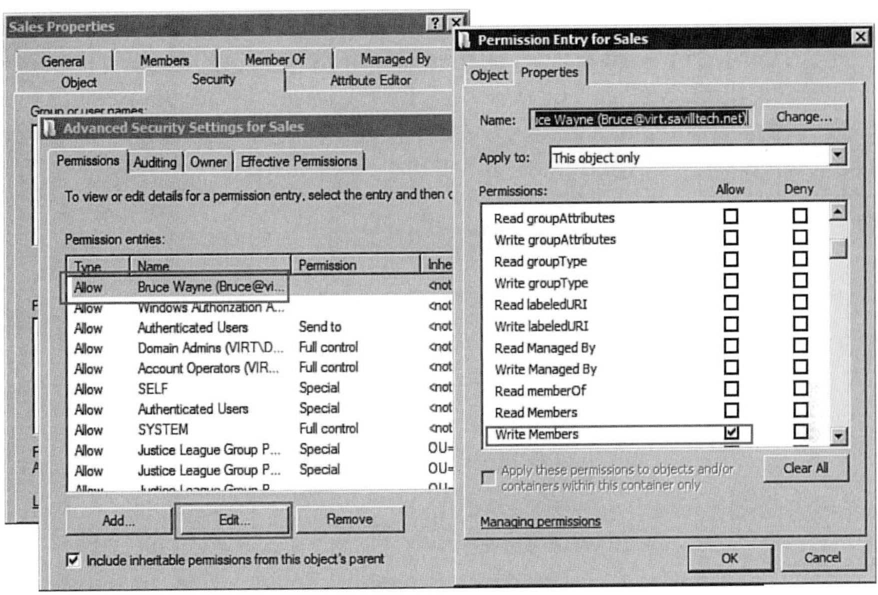

FIGURE 12-32 Accessing the advanced security settings and then clicking the Edit button for Managed By User shows the Write Members permission.

The Attribute Editor tab is available for all objects in the Advanced Features view. To add a user to a group by using the command line, you can use `net group <group> <user> /add /domain`. For example, to add user Bruce to domain group JLeague, use the following:

```
C:\Users\Administrator.VIRT>net group JLeague Bruce
➥/add /domain
The command completed successfully.
```

To remove a user, use the same command but with `/delete` instead of `/add`. You can also remove a user by using the `dsadd` command or by using `adsi` in a script. For example, the following example adds user Clark to the domain group JLeague. Notice that you use the DNs of the user and group.

```
Set grp = GetObject("LDAP://cn=jleague,ou=justice
league,dc=virt,dc=savilltech,dc=net")
Set oUser = GetObject("LDAP://cn=clark kent,ou=justice
league,dc=virt,dc=savilltech,dc=net")
grp.Add(oUser.AdsPath)
grp.SetInfo
```

Contacts

A contact is an object in AD that is normally just used as a recipient for an e-mail message but does not exist as a person in the company. When you create a contact via New, Contact, you only have options to enter the contact's name attributes, as shown in Figure 12-33.

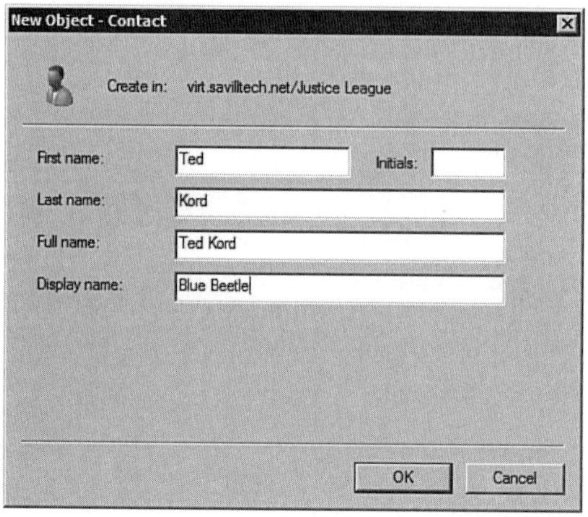

FIGURE 12-33 You don't have many options in the New Object - Contact dialog.

After the contact is created, you can access its properties, and you can see some tabs similar to those you see for a user: General, Address, Telephones, Organization, and Member Of. What is Member Of for? Why does a contact need to be a member of a group? Consider that you can give a contact an e-mail address, and one use of groups is for mail transmission to multiple recipients, so a mail-enabled contact (a contact with an e-mail address) in a group would be sent any messages sent to the contact's group.

Computer Objects

In Chapter 17, we look at pre-creating computer objects to provision them for OS deployment. However, a computer object still has attributes after installation. A computer object can be moved around the domain for the purposes of organization, group policy application, and management via delegation.

A computer object's properties page has a General tab that shows the name and type of the computer, where the type distinguishes between whether the computer is a normal member workstation/server or a domain controller and, if it is a domain controller, whether it's an RODC and/or a GC.

The Operating System tab contains details about the computer's OS, and the Member Of tab allows you to set group membership for a computer. Normally, when you look at adding members to a group by browsing, computers are not displayed, but this is just because, by default, only users, groups, and other objects are displayed. Click the Object Types button to check the Computers option to allow computer objects to also be shown (see Figure 12-34).

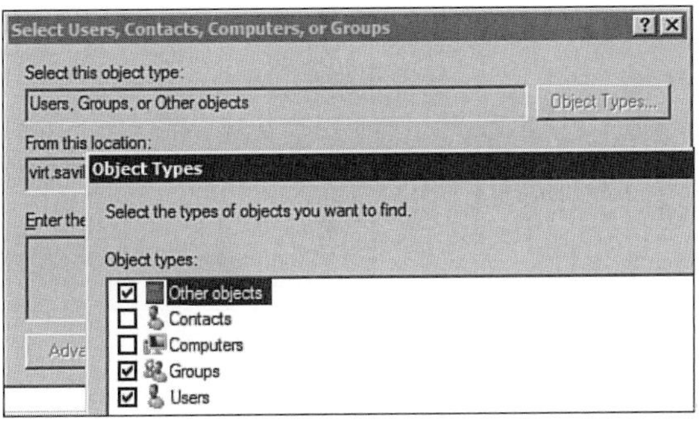

FIGURE 12-34 Checking the Computers option causes computer objects to be shown.

The other interesting tab is the Delegation tab, which you use to manage the delegation of authentication permissions; this allows a service to impersonate another user or computer account for the purpose of accessing network resources. You can use the Delegation tab, as shown in Figure 12-35, to allow the computer to delegate credentials to any service via Kerberos, which means any service on the computer can access any network resource by impersonating a connected user or the preferred option, constrained delegation, in which delegation is for only specified services. Constrained delegation is the more secure option because the administrator controls which service principal names (SPNs) the account is able to delegate to.

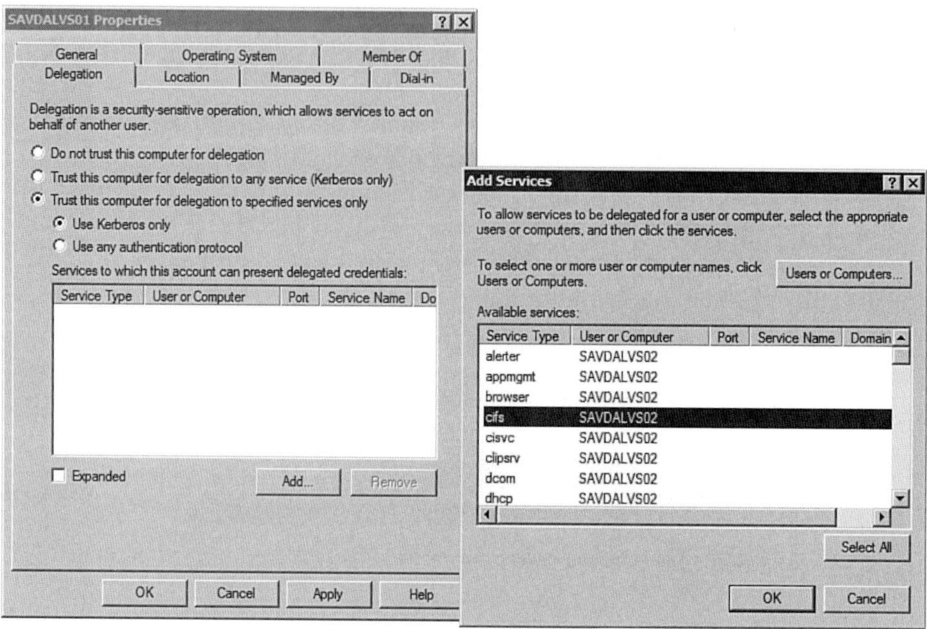

Figure 12-35 Restricted delegation to specific users or computers.

Delegation is commonly used when a user accessed a service on a computer and the service then needs to access resources on another network resource, and that access is possible only if the user's credentials are used instead of the computer's local system credentials. Figure 12-35 shows a remote server selected. You can then choose the services that will be delegated permission to the remote computer. For example, if on the VS01 server you are running a service, such as a web site, that accesses file services on VS02 but needs to access them as the user that is logged on to the web site, delegate permission to the cifs service that is running on VS02.

Command-Line Management

In Chapters 10 and 11, as well as earlier in this chapter, you saw some examples of command-line options for AD. Some of the most useful commands besides those for scripting AD object management are the DS line of utilities. You've seen `dsadd`, which you use to create user objects. In fact, you can use `dsadd` to create computers, contacts, groups, OUs, and quotas in addition to user objects. For each type of object, find the available switches and uses by using the `/?` switch (for example, `dsadd computer /?`). Notice in the switches that are common to all the DS commands that you can pass a server (`-s`) or another domain (`-d`) to run the commands on. To pass different credentials, use the `-u` *<username>* and `-p` *<password>* switches.

You've also seen `dsrm`, which deletes an object via its DN. Just as the `del` command for files has the `/s` switch to delete the content and subfolders of a selected folder, `dsrm` can be configured to delete all the contents of a passed container object. For example, it can delete an OU and all its content. To delete your Justice League OU and all its content, use the following command:

```
C:\>dsrm "ou=Justice League,dc=virt,
➥dc=savilltech,dc=net" -subtree
Are you sure you wish to delete ou=Justice
League,dc=virt,dc=savilltech,dc=net (Y/N)? n
```

In this example, don't want to delete all the test objects. But later on you can delete them if you want to.

You can use `dsmod` to modify existing computers, contacts, groups, OUs, servers, users, quotas, and partitions. Again, to see full help for the options on each type of object, run `dsmod` *<object>* `/?`. Let's look at an example of modifying a user object. The following example shows a common change: A user needs his password modified and account unlocked.

```
C:\>dsmod user "cn=Arthur,ou=Justice League,dc=virt,
➥dc=savilltech,dc=net" -pwd Pa55word -disabled no
dsmod succeeded:cn=Arthur,ou=Justice League,dc=virt,
dc=savilltech,dc=net
```

You can specify multiple users with one command by separating them with spaces. The following example sets up users with a new Web page:

```
C:\>dsmod user "cn=Arthur,ou=Justice League,dc=virt,
➥dc=savilltech,dc=net" "cn=clark kent,ou=Justice League,
➥dc=virt,dc=savilltech,dc=net" -webpg http://www.savilltech.com
dsmod succeeded:cn=Arthur,ou=Justice League,dc=virt,
dc=savilltech,dc=net
dsmod succeeded:cn=clark kent,ou=Justice
League,dc=virt,dc=savilltech,dc=net
```

To move an object from a domain or rename it in place, use the dsmove command. dsmove deals only with the object location and does not care about the object type. The only parameters you need with it are the DN of the object and, optionally, the new name for the object and its new parent container. In the following example, Lois Lane marries Clark Kent, and, forgetting about modern practices, she decides to take his name and so will now be Lois Kent:

```
C:\>dsmove "cn=lois lane,cn=users,dc=virt,
➥dc=savilltech,dc=net" -newname "Lois Kent"
dsmove succeeded:cn=lois lane,cn=users,dc=virt,dc=savilltech,
dc=net
```

Well, now Lois is married to Clark. She gets to be part of the Justice League OU group policies and management, so move her object from the Users container to the Justice League OU. The following example shows how:

```
C:\>dsmove "cn=lois kent,cn=users,dc=virt,
➥dc=savilltech,dc=net" -newparent "ou=Justice
➥League,dc=virt,dc=savilltech,dc=net"
dsmove succeeded:cn=lois
kent,cn=users,dc=virt,dc=savilltech,dc=net
```

In this example, you could have combined the two commands by having -newname and -newparent used together.

Both the Active Directory Users and Computers snap-in and dsmove are limited to moving objects within a domain. To move an object or an entire OU structure and its content, use the movetree support tools. Despite its name, movetree moves not only entire trees but individual objects. The basic usage is shown in the following example:

```
C:\>movetree /start /s savtstdc01.virt.savilltech.net /d
➥savtstdc02.dev.virt.savilltech.net /sdn "cn=lois
➥kent,ou=justice league,dc=virt,dc=savilltech,dc=net" /ddn
➥"cn=lois kent,cn=users,dc=dev,dc=virt,dc=savilltech,dc=net"
MOVETREE PRE-CHECK FINISHED.
MOVETREE IS READY TO START THE MOVE OPERATION.
MOVETREE FINISHED SUCCESSFULLY.
```

In this example, the first item starts a new `movetree` operation via the `/start` switch. Then pass an authoritative source server for the place from which the objects are being moved by using `/s` and an authoritative server to where the objects are being moved by using `/d`.

The `/sdn` is the object or path being moved and is the full DN. In this case, you moved an individual object. However, you could just as easily have moved the entire Justice League OU. The `/ddn` is the destination DN of the object/collection being moved. The `ddn` is the new DN and not the new parent location, so it needs to be a full DN, such s `cn=Lois Kent, cn=Users`, not just the DN of the Users container.

If `movetree` has errors, it writes them to the movetree.err file. To check for potential errors instead of performing a move, use `/check` instead of `/start`.

To move users/objects between forests, you need either the Active Directory Migration Tool (ADMT), which is designed for the migration of resources, or a third-party utility such as those made by Quest. For information on ADMT, check the Microsoft web site.

The next important action you may want to perform is to find information about objects in the domain, and this is where `dsquery` is useful. It returns the DN, RDN, or SAMid for any matching objects for the query given. The `dsquery` command is object type-specific and can operate on computers, contacts, groups, OUs, sites, servers, users, quotas, partitions, and generic object type searches via the `*` type. Again, use the `/?` switch for full help on what can be done for each object type. The basic usage is `dsquery` *<object type> <root DN to query from> <attributes to search on>*. The following example looks for all users in the Justice League who have not changed their passwords in the last two days:

```
C:\>dsquery user "ou=justice league,dc=virt,
➥dc=savilltech,dc=net" -stalepwd 2
"CN=Clark Kent,OU=Justice League,DC=virt,DC=savilltech,DC=net"
"CN=Bruce Wayne,OU=Justice League,DC=virt,DC=savilltech,DC=net"
"CN=Diana Prince,OU=Justice League,DC=virt,DC=savilltech,DC=net"
```

`dsquery` is far more powerful than its few command-line switches suggest. If you use the `*` object type, you can then use LDAP filters as part of the command. This enables you to query on any attribute of the objects in AD. However, it requires more in-depth knowledge of AD. For example, to find all mail-enabled users, find all user object types with a non-blank mail attribute, as in the following example:

```
C:\>dsquery * "ou=justice league,dc=virt,
➥dc=savilltech,dc=net" -filter "(&(objectcategory=user)(mail=*))"
➥-limit 20 -attr displayname mail
  displayname    mail
  Bruce Wayne    batman@savilltech.net
  Wally West     flash@savilltech.net
  Clark Kent     superman@savilltech.net
```

Notice that in addition to specifying a more complex filter, you can specify the attributes you want returned from `dsquery`. The additional information you got from `dsquery` is also possible using the `dsget` command, which returns information on a passed object. The following example uses `dsget` on a group object instead of a user and looks at its members:

```
C:\>dsget group "cn=jleague,ou=justice league,dc=virt,
➥dc=savilltech,dc=net" -members
"CN=Arthur,OU=Justice League,DC=virt,DC=savilltech,DC=net"
"CN=hal,OU=Justice League,DC=virt,DC=savilltech,DC=net"
"CN=Wally West,OU=Justice League,DC=virt,DC=savilltech,DC=net"
"CN=Diana Prince,OU=Justice League,DC=virt,DC=savilltech,DC=net"
"CN=Bruce Wayne,OU=Justice League,DC=virt,DC=savilltech,DC=net"
"CN=Clark Kent,OU=Justice League,DC=virt,DC=savilltech,DC=net"
```

The real power is that you can chain these commands together. In Chapter 22, "The Command Prompt and PowerShell," you see how to pipe the output of one command as the input of another. The following example takes the original state password `dsquery` command and sends its output to `dsget` for more information on each object, such as its full name and DN:

```
C:\>dsquery user "ou=justice league,dc=virt,
➥dc=savilltech,dc=net" -stalepwd 2 |dsget user -display -dn
  dn
display
```

```
  CN=Clark Kent,OU=Justice League,DC=virt,DC=savilltech,DC=net
Clark Kent
  CN=Bruce Wayne,OU=Justice League,DC=virt,DC=savilltech,DC=net
Bruce Wayne
  CN=Diana Prince,OU=Justice League,DC=virt,DC=savilltech,
DC=net
Diana Prince
dsget succeeded
```

You can even combine commands to perform actions, such as searching for all the users in an OU and updating their address, details, and even password. Obviously, you probably want to set only passwords en masse in a lab-type environment!

```
C:\>dsquery user "ou=justice league,dc=virt,
➥dc=savilltech,dc=net" | dsmod user -pwd Pa55word
dsmod succeeded:CN=Wally West,OU=Justice
League,DC=virt,DC=savilltech,DC=net
dsmod succeeded:CN=test,OU=Justice League,DC=virt,
  DC=savilltech,DC=net
dsmod succeeded:CN=hal,OU=Justice League,DC=virt,
  DC=savilltech,DC=net
dsmod succeeded:CN=Arthur,OU=Justice League,DC=virt,
  DC=savilltech,DC=net
dsmod succeeded:CN=Clark Kent,OU=Justice
League,DC=virt,DC=savilltech,DC=net
dsmod succeeded:CN=Bruce Wayne,OU=Justice
League,DC=virt,DC=savilltech,DC=net
dsmod succeeded:CN=Diana Prince,OU=Justice
League,DC=virt,DC=savilltech,DC=net
```

There is one other big area of object manipulation: bulk import and export of objects. (We discuss backing up AD in the next section.) In some cases, you may want to mass export and/or import objects. There are two tools for bulk import/export: `csvde` and `ldifde`. `csvde` operates via comma-separated value files, which you can edit in any spreadsheet-type utility, such as Excel. `ldifde` uses the LDAP Data Interchange Format, which is defined at www.ietf.org/rfc/rfc2849.txt. Although `ldifde` t is rather complex, it has one big advantage: Unlike with `csvde`, you can use it to set passwords. You'll want to use these tools more if you use Active Directory Lightweight Directory Services (ADAM in its old name) because it has far fewer graphical management tools.

When using `csvde` to export the contents of a container, pass the file

(-f) to write the content to the DN from which to export (-d), and you can limit the type of objects to export via -r, using an LDAP filter. The following example exports all users and groups from the Justice League OU, running the commands for the users and for the groups:

```
C:\>csvde -f jleaguegrpout.csv -d "ou=justice league,dc=virt,
➥dc=savilltech,dc=net" -r "(objectcategory=group)"
Connecting to "(null)"
Logging in as current user using SSPI
Exporting directory to file jleaguegrpout.csv
Searching for entries...
Writing out entries
........
Export Completed. Post-processing in progress...
8 entries exported

The command has completed successfully
C:\>csvde -f jleagueusrout.csv -d "ou=justice league,dc=virt,
➥dc=savilltech,dc=net" -r "(objectclass=user)"
Connecting to "(null)"
Logging in as current user using SSPI
Exporting directory to file jleagueusrout.csv
Searching for entries...
Writing out entries
.......
Export Completed. Post-processing in progress...
7 entries exported

The command has completed successfully
```

You now have two files that you can manipulate. To import, use the -i switch with csvde, and identify the file to import. Normally, you want the verbose mode (-v) and want to ignore import errors (-k). For the import file, the first line tells the attributes for the objects being created. There can be a *lot* of attributes. The easiest way to work out these column headings is to perform a full export first and then use that as the format. However, some attributes cannot be imported. For example, the GUID is created when the object is made by AD, so you can't include that. But the information that is available gives a good idea of the attributes populated for the in-scope objects. At a basic level, to import some users, you could have a CSV file, as shown in the following example, that contains just the usernames and e-mails for the users:

```
DN,objectClass,name,samaccountname,mail
"cn=Zatanna Zatara,ou=justice
league,dc=virt,dc=savilltech,dc=net",user,Zatanna,Zatanna,zata
nna@savilltech.com
"cn=Ralph Dibny,ou=justice
league,dc=virt,dc=savilltech,dc=net",user,Ralph,Ralph,
  elongatedman@savilltech.com
To import you would use the following.
C:\>csvde -i -f newusers.csv -v -k
Connecting to "(null)"
Logging in as current user using SSPI
Importing directory from file "newusers.csv"
Loading entries
2: cn=Zatanna Zatara,ou=justice league,dc=virt,dc=savilltech,
dc=net
Entry modified successfully.
3: cn=Ralph Dibny,ou=justice league,dc=virt,dc=savilltech,dc=net
Entry modified successfully.
2 entries modified successfully.

The command has completed successfully
```

By default, the new users need their passwords set and enabled.

Backing Up and Restoring AD

The notion of backing up AD may seem pointless. If you have multiple domain controllers running multimaster replication with, potentially, multiple domain controllers over multiple sites, the idea of a total loss of all the domain controllers seems unlikely. If your eight locations spread over the whole United States suddenly disappeared, it's unlikely you're still here anyway. Create backups to recover from data loss or corruption, and in reality, most of this is from accidental deletion of objects. In Windows Server 2008, you have the option to enable a Prevent Accidental Deletion option when creating a new OU. That option is not an accident. It is common for an administrator to accidentally delete an entire OU and all its content with a single click. What happens if an OU or an object is deleted? Restore it. From where do you restore? The backup.

NOTE If you delete a user, it may be tempting to just re-create him. That won't work. The user object has a security identifier, which is what is given access to resources. Just creating a new user with the same name as the old user doesn't re-create the user; the new user won't be able to access his old resources.

Backing up AD is simple, using the Windows Backup feature, which is not installed by default. Initially, the plans for Windows Server 2008 were to do only volume-level backups, which would have meant you would have to ensure that the system volume, the boot volume, the volume containing SYSVOL, and the volume containing the NTDS.DIT AD database were all backed up. But due to customer feedback, the option to perform a system state backup was put back into the product. You cannot back up the system state on its own using the graphical Windows Server Backup interface, but you can back up the system state by using the command-line tool `wbadmin`. As part of normal scheduled automatic backups, back up the four volumes mentioned; although they could all be the same volume, such as C:.

The system state backup target can only be a volume letter, not a file, so you need a partition that is not a critical volume (not system or boot) as the target of the backup. The following example backs up the system state to the E: drive. In all honesty, the system state backup in Windows Server 2008 is ugly. Because the system state backup was added at the end of the product cycle and the Windows Server 2008 backup is based on volume backups from volume snapshots and the various VSS writers, you get an overblown system state backup. It takes about 30 minutes to perform a system state backup of a directory service with about 20 extra objects in it.

```
C:\>wbadmin start systemstatebackup -backupTarget:E:
wbadmin 1.0 - Backup command-line tool
(C) Copyright 2004 Microsoft Corp.

If you have already created backups of this server using
Windows Server Backup, you might lose access to them
if you do not restore the catalog first.
Do you want to proceed without restoring the catalog?
```

```
Select C if this is the first backup of this server or
you do not need to access earlier backups.

Select E if you have already created backups of this
server and want to restore the catalog for those backups before
you proceed.
To recover the catalog and access the earlier backups, type the
following command,where <Backup Location> is the location con-
taining latest backup of the server:
WBADMIN RESTORE CATALOG -backuptarget:<Backup Location>

[C] Continue [E] Exit c

Starting System State Backup [9/30/2007 3:53 PM]
Retrieving volume information...

This would backup the system state from volume(s)
Local Disk(C:) to E:.
Do you want to start the backup operation?
[Y] Yes [N] No y

Creating the shadow copy of volumes requested for backup.
Identifying system state files to backup (This may
take a few minutes)...
Found (2281) files
Found (45379) files
Search for system state files complete
Starting backup of files
Overall progress - 0% (Currently backing up files
reported by 'System Writer')
Overall progress - 1% (Currently backing up files
reported by 'System Writer')
Overall progress - 1% (Currently backing up files
reported by 'System Writer')
Overall progress - 3% (Currently backing up files
reported by 'System Writer')
Overall progress - 4% (Currently backing up files
reported by 'System Writer')
Overall progress - 5% (Currently backing up files
```

```
reported by 'System Writer')
Overall progress - 96% (Currently backing up files
reported by 'System Writer')
Overall progress - 97% (Currently backing up files
reported by 'System Writer')
Backup of files reported by 'System Writer' completed
Backup of files reported by 'DFS Replication service
writer' completed
Backup of files reported by 'Registry Writer' completed
Backup of files reported by 'COM+ REGDB Writer' completed
Overall progress - 99% (Currently backing up files
reported by 'WMI Writer')
Backup of files reported by 'WMI Writer' completed
Backup of files reported by 'NTDS' completed
Overall progress - 99% (Currently backing up additional
system state files)

Summary of backup:
------------------

Backup of system state completed successfully [9/30/2007 4:14
PM]

Log of files successfully backed up
'C:\Windows\Logs\WindowsServerBackup\SystemStateBackup
30-09-2007 15-53-51.log'
```

When the backup is complete, you have a folder on the destination drive, E:\WindowsImageBackup\<*server name*>\SystemStateBackup\Backup <*date of backup*> 205351, which contains a .vhd file, which is the backup. Mount this file in a virtual machine and view it. (To give you an idea of how overblown this process is, my backup of the tiny domain with an ntds.dit file of 16MB was 6GB!)

When you have the backup, you can restore the data. There are two types of restore: authoritative and nonauthoritative restores.

For a nonauthoritative restore, restore a backup of a domain controller. However, the data you restore may have been updated since the backup, and so while the data is restored at replication time, the restored data can be overwritten by data replicated to it.

Use an authoritative restore when the data you restore from backup, or (more likely) a part of it, needs to be considered authoritative. Even though there may be newer data on other domain controllers, this domain controller's restore data should be considered absolute and should overwrite the other data stored. This is normally the case if something is deleted. Perform a restore and mark the deleted objects as authoritative. Why?

When you delete an object, it's not deleted straight away. It's marked as deleted via a tombstone flag, which is replicated to all the other domain controllers in the domain, and after a certain tombstone lifetime, the object is deleted. If this didn't happen, the deleted object might just be recreated at replication time. If the object were just deleted, another DC could say, "Hey, you're missing this, here you go."

To restore AD, boot the domain controller into the Directory Services Restore Mode (DSRM), which you select by rebooting the domain controller, pressing F8, and selecting Directory Services Restore Mode. When you boot to this mode, the domain controller leaves its database offline, and you log on as the administrator account, with the password you set for the DSRM during the `dcpromo` process.

If you don't remember the DSRM password, reset it using `ntdsutil`. In the following example, use `null` for the server, which means the local server is the target, or you can pass an actual server name:

```
C:\Users\Administrator.VIRT>ntdsutil
ntdsutil: set dsrm password
Reset DSRM Administrator Password: reset password on server
null
Please type password for DS Restore Mode Administrator Account:
********
Please confirm new password: ********
Password has been set successfully.

Reset DSRM Administrator Password: quit
ntdsutil: quit
```

Reboot to the DSRM and press F8 to access the DSRM, as shown in Figure 12-36. The OS boots in Safe DSRM mode. At logon, select Switch User. For username enter .\administrator and the DSRM administrator password, as shown in Figure 12-37. At this point, the machine is standalone, not even a domain member, so no domain account can be used.

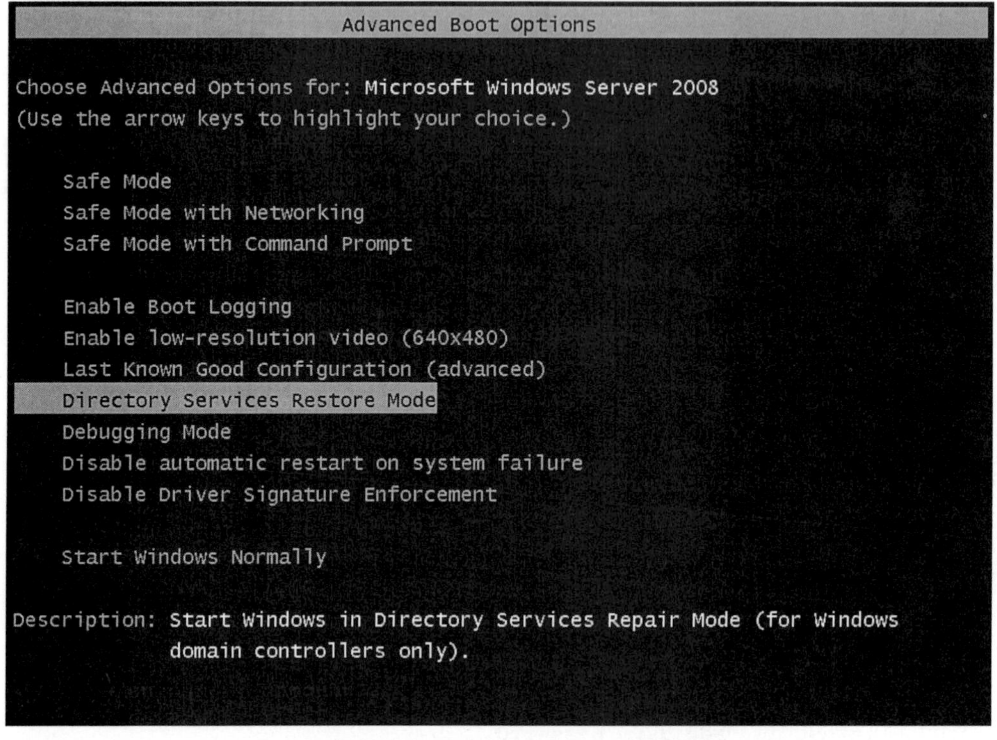

FIGURE 12-36 Press Enter to enable DSRM after selecting the menu option.

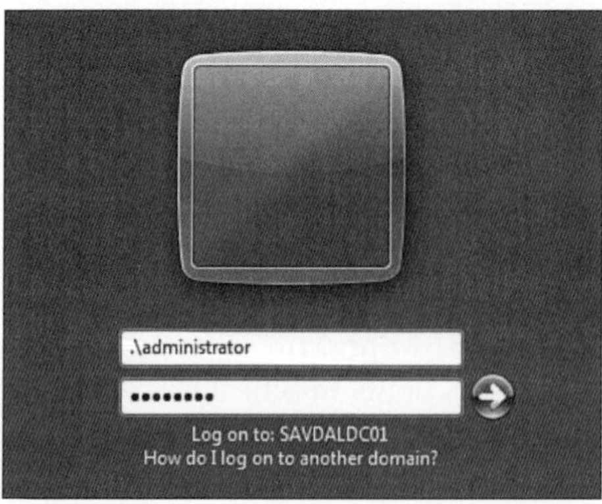

FIGURE 12-37 The .\ tells the system to use the local account database for logon.

You can now restore the system state backup. Remember that DSRM command that you didn't run to delete the entire Justice League OU? You ran it just before the reboot, so now the OU and all the users and groups in it are gone. To check the backups available on a backup target, use this command:

```
Wbadmin get versions -backuptarget:<drive>:
-machine:<server name>
```

Figure 12-38 shows a single backup available, and it is a system state backup.

```
C:\>wbadmin get versions -backuptarget:e: -machine:savdaldc01
wbadmin 1.0 - Backup command-line tool
(C) Copyright 2004 Microsoft Corp.

Backup time: 9/30/2007 3:53 PM
Backup target: Fixed Disk labeled E:
Version identifier: 09/30/2007-20:53
Can Recover: Application(s), System State
```

FIGURE 12-38 One system state backup is available on the E: drive.

To restore from the system state backup, use the following command:

```
Wbadmin start systemstaterecovery -version:09/30/2007-20:53
-backuptarget:e: -machine:savdaldc01
```

You are notified that the replication engine was Distributed File System Replication (DFSR) or NTFRS and that the technology has changed since the system state backup, so you shouldn't use a system state backup. At this point, if this was a nonauthoritative restore, just reboot the server. However, when you perform replication with other servers, anything restored is overwritten if newer versions exist, deleting any objects you've just restored.

The next step is to set the objects you want to bring back from the authoritative backup, and use `ntdsutil`. First, activate the NTDS instance and then select the authoritative restore mode. At this point, to mark the entire database as authoritative, issue the following command:

```
authoritative restore: restore database
```

You can mark only a certain object as authoritative; for example, you could mark an OU, or you could also do an individual user or group. The following is an example:

```
authoritative restore: restore subtree
<distinguished name of subtree,
e.g. "ou=justice league,dc=virt,dc=savilltech,dc=net">
```

Quit `ntdsutil` after confirming that you want to perform the authoritative restore (see Figure 12-39).

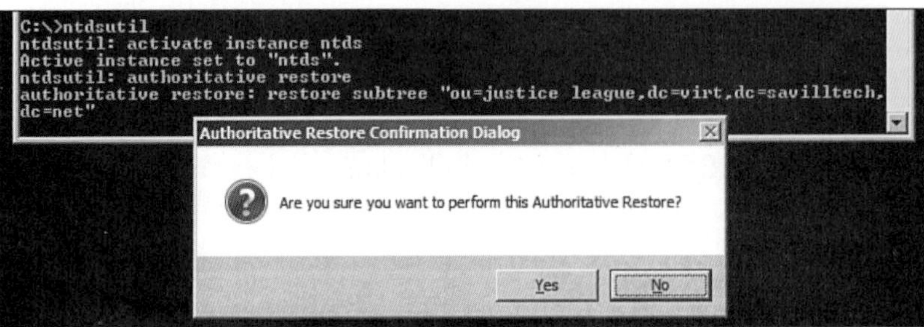

FIGURE 12-39 Confirm whether to perform an authoritative restore.

Notice that Figure 12-40 provides information at the end regarding back-links. Back-links are important relationships between objects if some groups are of the Windows 2000 type, which don't use LVR. The LDIF file created needs to be run on a domain controller in each domain in the forest, using the following command:

```
ldifde -i -k -f <generated ldf file>
```

```
Administrator: C:\Windows\system32\cmd.exe - ntdsutil
Records found: 0000000045
Done.

Found 45 records to update.

Updating records...
Records remaining: 0000000000
Done.

Successfully updated 45 records.

The following text file with a list of authoritatively restored objects has been
 created in the current working directory:
        ar_20070930-165321_objects.txt

One or more specified objects have back-links in this domain. The following LDIF
 files with link restore operations have been created in the current working dir
ectory:
        ar_20070930-165321_links_virt.savilltech.net.ldf

Authoritative Restore completed successfully.

authoritative restore:
```

FIGURE 12-40 Information is given at the end of an authoritative restore.

When all objects are marked as authoritative, reboot the server normally. When replication has taken place, the objects are available again.

Displaying Last Logon Information

One of the new features of Windows Server 2008 that is enabled when Windows Server 2008 domain mode is enabled is Last Interactive Logon Information, which goes beyond what was available in previous versions of Windows. While Windows 2000 AD had a lastLogon attribute, that value was not replicated between the domain controllers within a domain, and to check the last time a user logged on, you had to query every domain controller in the domain and use the latest date/time. Windows Server 2003 provided the lastLogonTimestamp attribute, which was replicated between domain controllers—but only every 14 days, so it was not useful for accurate information. The lastLogonTimestamp attribute was designed to identify stale accounts that had not been used for a long time.

With Windows Server 2008, you now have multiple values that are replicated between domain controllers per the normal Windows replication cycles and that give you not just the last time you logged on but also information on failed logon attempts, which is obviously important information for a user to see and report on if he did not personally experience the failed logons. Find this setting by navigating Computer Configuration, Policies, Administrative Templates, Windows Components, Windows Logon Options and enabling the Display Information About Previous Logons During User Logon, as shown in Figure 12-41. This setting must be applied to both domain controllers and the client machines for which you want to display last logon information. If you enable only for the computers and not the domain controllers, clients receive an error that last logon information is not available and are not able to log in.

The first time a user logs on after you enable this policy, she is notified that it is the first time she has interactively logged on with the account. On subsequent logons, the user sees more detailed information, as shown in Figure 12-42.

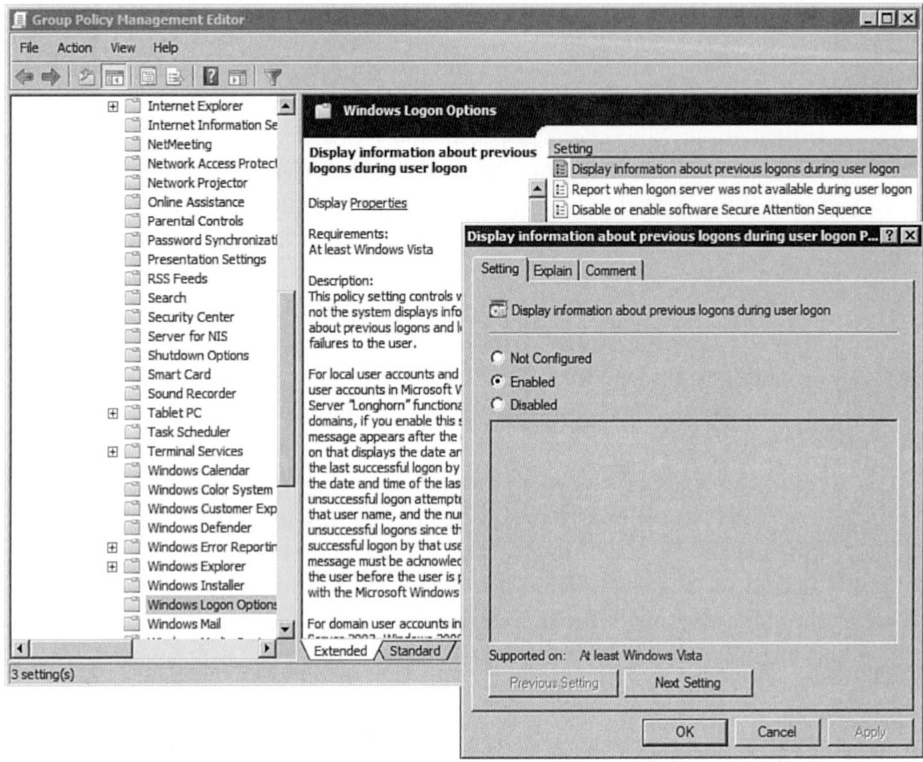

FIGURE 12-41 Use this group policy setting to enable the display of last logon information.

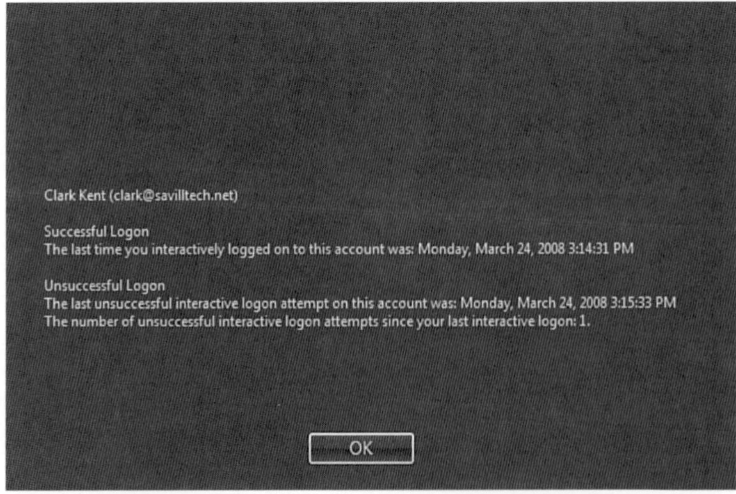

FIGURE 12-42 An example output for a user who has had previous failed logon attempts.

The information is stored as information in each user object, as shown in Figure 12-43, which exposes the information via ADSI Edit.

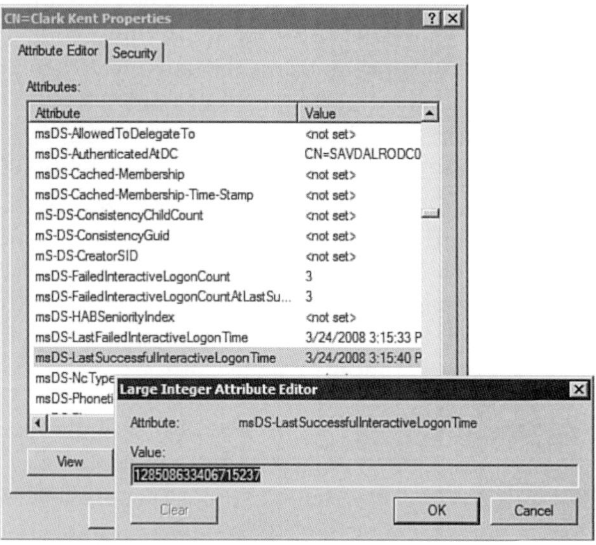

FIGURE 12-43 When you view the last interactive logon time via ADSI Edit, notice the other values in the main window are also visible, such as failed interactive logon count.

The values used are:

- **msDS-LastSuccessfulInteractiveLogonTime**. The last successful interactive logon
- **msDS-LastFailedInteractiveLogonTime**. The last failed interactive logon
- **msDS-FailedInteractiveLogonCount**. The total number of failed interactive logons recorded since the time logon logging was enabled
- **msDS-FailedInteractiveLogonCountAtLastSuccessfulLogon**. The total number of failed interactive logons recorded since the last successful interactive logon

If you have an RODC, the changes are written to the RODC and to the closest writeable DC (because RODCs cannot replicate information outwardly).

AD Snapshots

As you saw when backing up the system state, the whole process works on snapshots of the system. Windows Server 2008 has a new capability to use these snapshots of the volumes containing the AD database and log files, mount a historical snapshot using the new AD database mounting tool (Dsamain.exe), and view AD as it was at points in time in the past, whenever a snapshot was taken.

To create a new snapshot, use the `ntdsutil` tool, and you must be logged on as a domain administrator or an enterprise administrator. The following example shows the creation and listing of a snapshot:

```
C:\Users\Administrator.VIRT>ntdsutil
ntdsutil: snapshot
snapshot: activate instance ntds
Active instance set to "ntds".
snapshot: create
Creating snapshot...
Snapshot set {99fc172f-15e6-4379-b502-e849edb5fb66}
generated successfully.
snapshot: mount {99fc172f-15e6-4379-b502-e849edb5fb66}
Snapshot {ff4febf7-de9a-4353-ac5e-dccc273e0b96}
mounted as C:\$SNAP_200710010815
_VOLUMEC$\
snapshot: list mounted
 1: 2007/10/01:08:15 {99fc172f-15e6-4379-b502-e849edb5fb66}
 2:    C: {ff4febf7-de9a-4353-ac5e-dccc273e0b96}
C:\$SNAP_200710010815_VOLUMEC$\

snapshot: unmount 2
Snapshot {ff4febf7-de9a-4353-ac5e-dccc273e0b96} unmounted.
snapshot: delete 2
Snapshot {ff4febf7-de9a-4353-ac5e-dccc273e0b96} deleted.
snapshot: list mounted
No snapshots found.
snapshot: create
Creating snapshot...
Snapshot set {224cba54-b5c7-48de-bb96-25e9f06c4aef}
generated successfully.
snapshot: list all
 1: 2007/10/01:08:17 {224cba54-b5c7-48de-bb96-25e9f06c4aef}
 2:    C: {6d0c98fc-df48-417c-b508-4b2770b5f670}
```

```
C:\$SNAP_200710010817_VOLUMEC$\
snapshot: mount {224cba54-b5c7-48de-bb96-25e9f06c4aef}
Snapshot {6d0c98fc-df48-417c-b508-4b2770b5f670} mounted
as C:\$SNAP_200710010817
_VOLUMEC$\
snapshot: list mounted
 1: 2007/10/01:08:17 {224cba54-b5c7-48de-bb96-25e9f06c4aef}
 2:    C: {6d0c98fc-df48-417c-b508-4b2770b5f670}
C:\$SNAP_200710010817_VOLUMEC$\

snapshot: quit
ntdsutil: quit
```

Notice how when you create a snapshot, you are told the GUID of the snapshot that was created, which you use to mount. When you mount a snapshot, list those that are mounted, which are two mounts. Likewise, unmount and delete snapshots you no longer need.

To use the Task Scheduler to automate snapshot creation at periodic intervals, such as every day, set the following command to execute. You can even just run this normally from the command line to quickly create a snapshot:

```
ntdsutil "activate instance ntds" snapshot create quit quit
```

When a snapshot is created, mount the snapshot by using the `dsamain` tool and give the mounted ntds.dit file a new LDAP port to allow this snapshot to be accessed via LDAP tools such as LDP.exe and the Active Directory Users and Computers MMC snap-in.

```
C:\>dsamain /dbpath C:\$SNAP_200710010817_VOLUMEC$\
➥Windows\NTDS\ntds.dit /ldapport 51389
EVENTLOG (Informational): NTDS General / Service Control :
1000
Microsoft Active Directory Domain Services startup complete,
version 6.0.6001.16
659
```

The snapshot must be available as a mount, which means it must be mounted via `ntdsutil` first, with a folder assigned to the snapshot, as shown in Figure 12-44. Mount/unmount/delete a snapshot via its GUID or its index number.

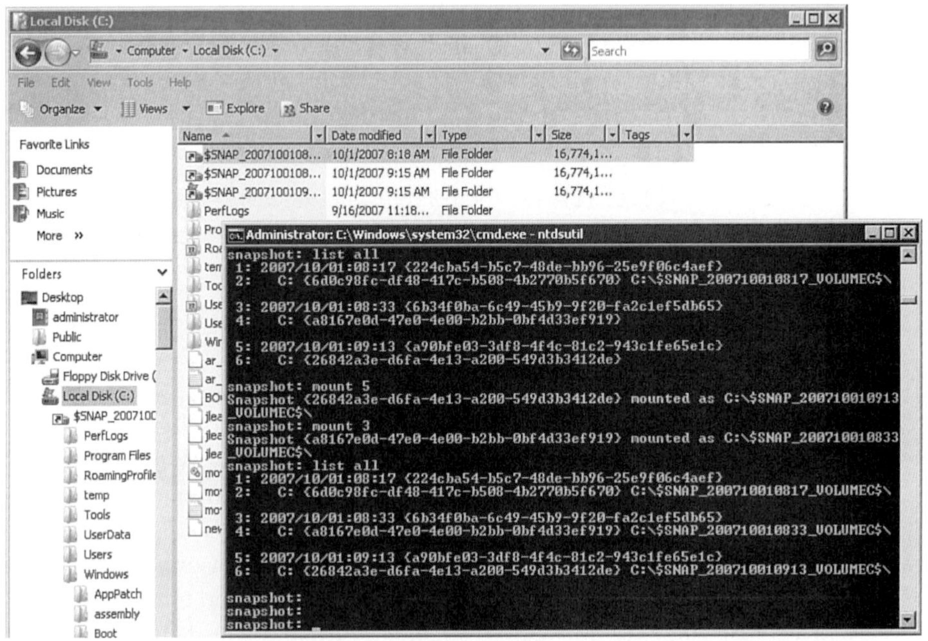

Figure 12-44 After you mount the snapshots, a file path is allocated to them, which is visible in Explorer and available to dsamain.

Leave the command prompt running because it owns the mount of the snapshot. You can now access it. For example, by using the Active Directory Users and Computers snap-in, you elect to change the domain controller, and in the dialog, select the option to enter a new domain controller, and port and specify the server and the LDAP port at which it was mounted (see Figure 12-45). When mounted, the data can be viewed. When you're done, close the Active Directory Users and Computers MMC snap-in.

Change Directory Server

Current Directory Server:
savdaldc01.virt.savilltech.net

Change to:

- Any writable Domain Controller
- This Domain Controller or AD LDS instance

Name	Site	DC Type	DC Version	Status
savdaldc01:51389				
savdaldc01.virt.savilltech.net	Dallas	GC	W2K8	Online
savtstcore01.virt.savilltech.net	Dallas	GC	W2K8	Online
savtstdc03.virt.savilltech.net	Houston	GC	W2K8	Online

Figure 12-45 You can view the snapshot you have mounted.

To close the mounted snapshot, press Ctrl+C in the command window that's running `dsamain`:

```
EVENTLOG (Informational): NTDS General / Service Control : 1004
Active Directory Domain Services was shut down successfully.
```

Why is this useful? It's a great way to quickly see the state of AD at various points in time before performing an actual recovery. For example, if an object was deleted, mount the snapshot and check whether it has the data you want before you try to recover. In addition, in the case of a deleted object, use the snapshot to get information about the object for the purpose of tombstone re-animation. Remember that when an object is deleted, it's not deleted; it's just marked as deleted via a tombstone. You can undo that tombstone and bring back the object. The size of the snapshot depends on the size of the data in AD.

Deleted Object Recovery

A great article in the September 2007 edition of *TechNet* magazine talks about the tombstone and re-animation process. However, for the purposes of this chapter, use the `adrestore` tool, which is available at http://microsoft.com/technet/sysinternals/utilities/AdRestore.mspx (and can be saved to the %windir%\system32 folder).

Run `adrestore` with no parameters to list all known deleted objects in the domain, or you can narrow the search by passing a search string, such as HAL. If you also use the `-r` switch for each object found, you have the option to restore. If you want to restore user Hal, run the code in the following example:

```
C:\>adrestore -r hal

AdRestore v1.1
by Mark Russinovich
Sysinternals - www.sysinternals.com

Enumerating domain deleted objects:
cn: hal
DEL:b94b6d3c-73cc-4311-b853-03047261daaf
distinguishedName: CN=hal\0ADEL:b94b6d3c-73cc-
4311-b853-03047261daaf,CN=Deleted
Objects,DC=virt,DC=savilltech,DC=net
lastKnownParent: OU=Justice
```

```
League,DC=virt,DC=savilltech,DC=net

Do you want to restore this object (y/n)? y
Restore succeeded.
Found 1 item matching search criteria.
```

When Hal is restored, the user is disabled and should be enabled and checked to make sure it has the right attributes and so on. You can verify any settings you are unsure about by looking at a snapshot. Remember that this may work fine for a small number of objects, but an authoritative restore is generally a good solution.

Restartable Directory Service

One of the new features of Windows Server 2008 is the capability to stop and start the directory service. In previous versions, to perform any maintenance-type actions on the database, the domain controller had to be rebooted in DSRM, which we looked at in the previous section.

With Windows Server 2008, you have the option to stop the ADDS, and while it is stopped, the server acts like a member server, provided that there are other domain controllers for the domain available. Otherwise, the DSRM administrator password can be used.

While the directory service is stopped, you cannot use `dcpromo` to demote the domain controller normally. However, the `/forceremoval` switch works. To stop the directory service, use the Services node of Server Manager and control the Active Directory Domain Services entry by stopping and starting it, as shown in Figure 12-46.

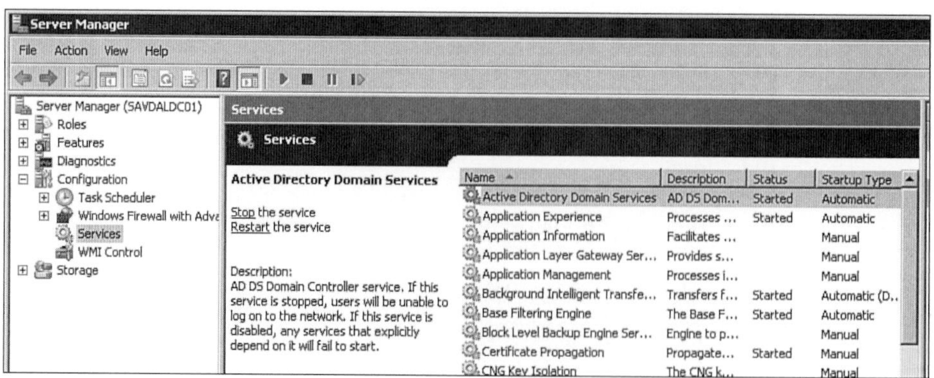

FIGURE 12-46 Stopping and starting the Active Directory Domain Services service.

Services that are not dependent on ADDS continue to run while ADDS is stopped. However, ADDS-dependent services shut down before ADDS shuts down: File Replication service (FRS), Kerberos Key Distribution Center (KDC), and Intersite Messaging all stop before ADDS is stopped. If these dependent services are running, they restart when ADDS restarts.

You can also control NTDS via the command line, by using `net stop/start`, as in the following example:

```
C:\Users\Administrator.VIRT>net stop ntds
The following services are dependent on the Active
Directory Domain Services service.
Stopping the Active Directory Domain Services service
will also stop these services.

   Kerberos Key Distribution Center
   Intersite Messaging
   DNS Server
   DFS Replication

Do you want to continue this operation? (Y/N) [N]: y
.
The Kerberos Key Distribution Center service was
stopped successfully.

The Intersite Messaging service is stopping.
The Intersite Messaging service was stopped successfully.


The DNS Server service was stopped successfully.


The DFS Replication service was stopped successfully.

The Active Directory Domain Services service is stopping.
The Active Directory Domain Services service was
stopped successfully.
```

While the directory service is stopped, you can perform maintenance operations. For example, you can check the integrity of the database by using `ntdsutil`, as shown in the following example. With the second set of actions, compact the AD database to an alternative location and then copy it over the original directory database. Again, all these commands normally had to be done when booted to DSRM, but in Windows Server 2008, you can just stop ADDS.

```
C:\Users\Administrator.VIRT>ntdsutil
ntdsutil: activate instance ntds
Active instance set to "ntds".
ntdsutil: files
file maintenance: integrity
Doing Integrity Check for db: C:\Windows\NTDS\ntds.dit.

Checking database integrity.

                     Scanning  Status (% complete)
```

```
Integrity check successful.

It is recommended you run semantic database analysis
to ensure semantic database consistency as well.


file maintenance: compact to e:\ntdscompress
Initiating DEFRAGMENTATION mode...
     Source Database: C:\Windows\NTDS\ntds.dit
     Target Database: e:\ntdscompress\ntds.dit

                  Defragmentation  Status (% complete)
```

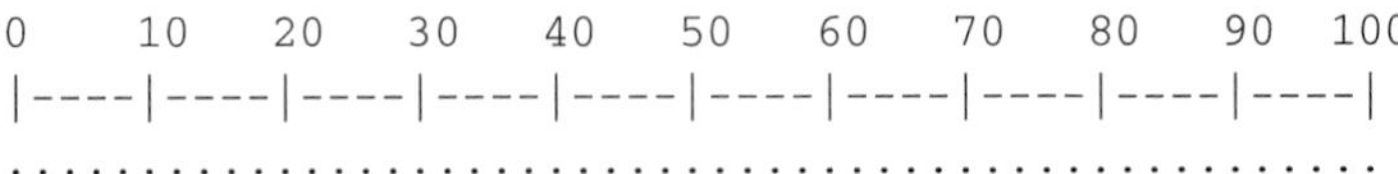


```
It is recommended that you immediately perform a full backup
of this database. If you restore a backup made before the
defragmentation, the database will be rolled back to the state
it was in at the time of that backup.
```

```
Compaction is successful. You need to:
   copy "e:\ntdscompress\ntds.dit" "C:\Windows\NTDS\ntds.dit"
and delete the old log files:
   del C:\Windows\NTDS\*.log


file maintenance: quit
ntdsutil: quit

C:\Users\Administrator.VIRT>copy
➥"e:\ntdscompress\ntds.dit" "C:\Windows\NTDS\ntds.dit"
Overwrite C:\Windows\NTDS\ntds.dit? (Yes/No/All): y
        1 file(s) copied.

C:\Users\Administrator.VIRT> del C:\Windows\NTDS\*.log
```

When you finish, start the directory service via Services or by using the command `net start ntds`.

Auditing AD

Windows Server 2008 allows new value-based auditing. It logs information about before and after values of object manipulation, whereas in previous versions of AD, the only information logged was who made changes and to what objects.

This section doesn't go into a lot of the reasons for why you would want to audit. That's the job of Chapter 8. In your environment, you have requirements for a certain amount of forensic capability after a change or an event, in addition to using tools that may trigger off events being generated.

With Windows Server 2008 AD, you have granular control concerning the actions that are audited in four main groupings:

- Access
- Changes
- Replication
- Detailed replication

There are two parts to auditing. The first is to update the Global Audit Policy, which controls the type of auditing that can be enabled on objects.

The second is that the System Access Control List (SACL) is updated to control which actual objects and attributes should be audited. Setting the Global Audit Policy on its own for items such as write actions do not result in any audit logs unless the SACL is enabled accordingly.

To set the Global Audit Policy, edit the Default Domain Controllers Policy (one of the few times you edit a default) object via the Group Policy Management Editor. Open the policy and navigate to the Computer Configuration, Windows Settings, Security Settings, Local Polices, Audit Policy. In this case, enable change audit tracking. Double-click Audit Directory Service Access, check Define These Policy Settings, and select to audit success attempts, as shown in Figure 12-47. This enables all categories of audit to be available.

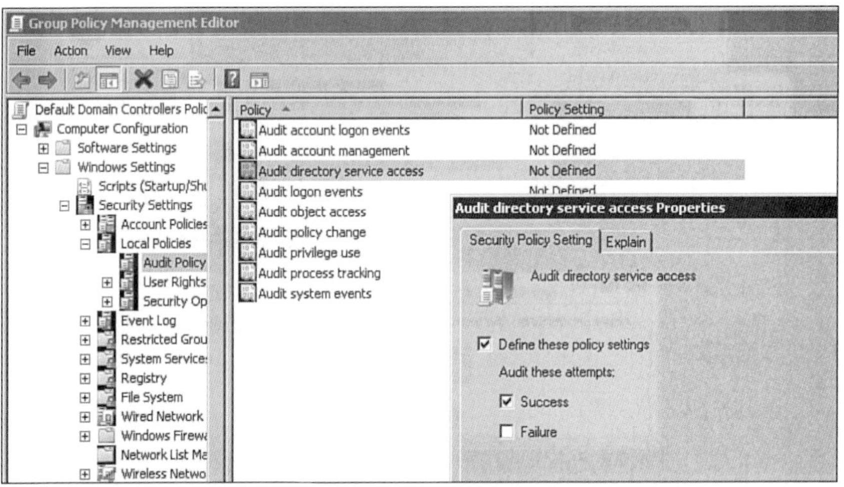

FIGURE 12-47 Enable general auditing for changes via the Default Domain Controllers Policy GPO because all changes occur on domain controllers.

After making the change, ensure that the GPO Editor is closed to save the GPO changes and then refresh group policy on the domain controllers by running GPUPDATE.

The next step is to set up the SACLs to generate the audit logs you want. Enable them based on an OU. However, you could also do so at a domain level or an individual object level. Open the Active Directory Users and Computers MMC snap-in and select View, Advanced Features to enable the Advanced Features view. Access the properties of the

OU/object for which you want to enable auditing. Select the Security tab, click the Advanced button, and then select the Auditing tab. Click the Add button to create a new audit criterion. You are prompted for a group to be within the scope of the audit; normally Authenticated Users is selected. However, you can choose any security principal.

If the audit is being performed on an OU and the contents should be audited, change the Apply Onto value to All Descendant Objects. However, note that other options are available, such as This Object Only. You want to audit any changes to the properties of objects in the OU, so enable Successful for Write All Properties on the Properties tab, as shown in Figure 12-48. Click OK to all dialogs to save your changes.

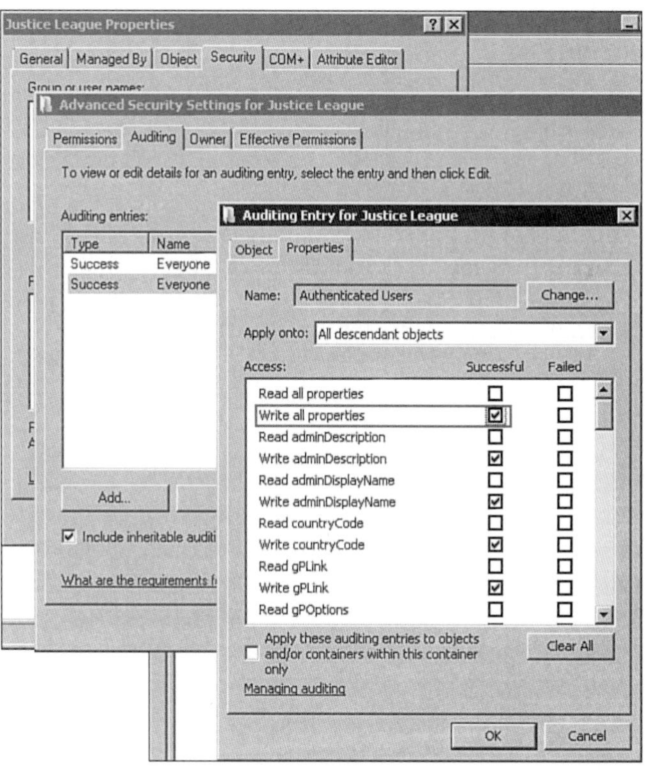

FIGURE 12-48 When Write All Properties is enabled, any changes are logged to the Security log with before and after settings.

The following is an example of a Security event log series after the description of an object was changed. It shows only the non-XML version—otherwise, there is a *lot* of information—but this shows the data it captures. There are two logs, one with the before value and one with the after value.

NOTE A 5137 event is generated with information entered when you create an object, a 5138 when you undelete an object, and a 5139 when you move an object.

```
Log Name:      Security
Source:        Microsoft-Windows-Security-Auditing
Date:          10/1/2007 3:24:44 PM
Event ID:      5136
Task Category: Directory Service Changes
Level:         Information
Keywords:      Audit Success
User:          N/A
Computer:      savdaldc01.virt.savilltech.net
Description:
A directory service object was modified.

Subject:
      Security ID:       VIRT\administrator
      Account Name:      administrator
      Account Domain:    VIRT
      Logon ID:          0x27e4f

Directory Service:
      Name: virt.savilltech.net
      Type: Active Directory Domain Services

Object:
      DN:CN=Clark Kent,OU=Justice League,DC=virt,
DC=savilltech,DC=net
      GUID: CN=Clark Kent,OU=Justice League,DC=virt,
DC=savilltech,DC=net
      Class:    user
```

```
Attribute:
      LDAP Display Name:  description
      Syntax (OID):       2.5.5.12
      Value:              Mild Mannered Reporter

Operation:
      Type: Value Deleted
      Correlation ID:    {316be7d4-73c5-417a-91d1-e1adf204d51d}
 Application Correlation ID:   -



Log Name:      Security
Source:        Microsoft-Windows-Security-Auditing
Date:          10/1/2007 3:24:44 PM
Event ID:      5136
Task Category: Directory Service Changes
Level:         Information
Keywords:      Audit Success
User:          N/A
Computer:      savdaldc01.virt.savilltech.net
Description:
A directory service object was modified.

Subject:
      Security ID:       VIRT\administrator
      Account Name:      administrator
      Account Domain:    VIRT
      Logon ID:          0x27e4f

Directory Service:
      Name:             virt.savilltech.net
      Type:             Active Directory Domain Services

Object:
      DN: CN=Clark Kent,OU=Justice League,DC=virt,
DC=savilltech,DC=net
      GUID: CN=Clark Kent,OU=Justice League,DC=virt,
DC=savilltech,DC=net
      Class: user
```

```
Attribute:
      LDAP Display Name: description
      Syntax (OID):      2.5.5.12
      Value:             Superman

Operation:
      Type: Value Added
      Correlation ID:   {316be7d4-73c5-417a-91d1-e1adf204d51d}
      Application Correlation ID:  -
```

This example shows the granularity of the auditing available, and Chapter 8 goes into more detail on auditing in general. Auditing is useful, but auditing too many actions may affect performance. So you need to balance the level of auditing accordingly.

Advanced Password Policies

One of the big problems with AD regarding passwords has been that only one password policy was possible per domain, which does not always meet the requirements of an organization. Windows Server 2008 makes possible more granular password policies, enabling different policies to be set for various groups of users.

To facilitate the fine-grained password policies, two new types of object classes are used that are part of the Windows Server 2008 schema changes: Password Settings Container and Password Settings. The fine-grained password policies can be applied only to user objects, iNetOrgPerson objects, and global security groups.

Create a Password Setting Object via ADSIEDIT.msc. There is no integration with the Active Directory Users and Computers MMC snap-in, but hopefully, this will come in the future. However, the ADSIEDIT.msc creation is wizard-driven and walks through the various settings available.

Microsoft describes the entire process for the advanced password policies in a thorough step-by-step format, at http://technet2.microsoft.com/windowsserver2008/en/library/2199dcf7-68fd-4315-87cc-ade35f8978ea1033.mspx?mfr=true. Be sure to target only global group types, iNetOrgPerson objects, or users; the process doesn't work for other types of groups. When you set the precedence values, the lower the precedence, the higher its priority, so a fine-grained password policy with a preference of 5 wins over a policy with a preference of 10.

Figure 12-49 shows a PasswordSettings object named BasicPassword. (To view Password Settings Container, you need to be in Advanced Features view.) The normal domain in this case requires a six-character password minimum with complexity. However, let's say you have some executives who want a basic password with different password lifetimes. Although this is unsafe, it is now possible in Windows Server 2008. Figure 12-49 shows that this basic policy does not require complexity (msDS-PasswordComplexityEnabled) and has a minimum length of four characters (msDS-MinimumPasswordLength). You can modify who the policy applies to by modifying the msDS-PSOAppliesTo attribute and the other settings. The great thing is that the people in the JLeague global group can now have four-character basic passwords, whereas anyone not in the group has to follow the domain password policies. To inspect the fine-grained password policy that applies to a user, view the user's msDS-ResultantPSO; if it is blank, the domain password policy, not the fine-grained password policy, applies to the user. The msDS-PSOApplied attribute shows the password policy directly linked to a group or user.

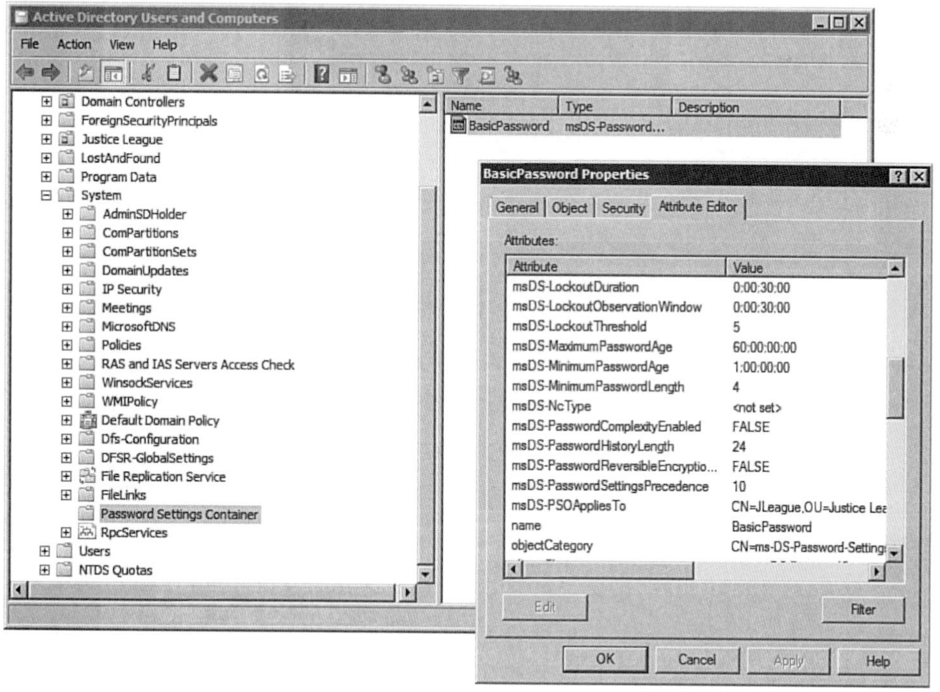

Figure 12-49 An example of a password policy created to enforce only a basic password.

Manage a fine-grained password policy via the Active Directory Users and Computers snap-in when in the Advanced Features View mode. System, Password Settings Container is where you view and change the attributes of the fine-grained password policy.

Prune and Graft

With Windows 2000, after you created domains in a forest, you could not restructure them. For example, you could not move a domain that was a child of one domain and make it a child of another. There was no capability to prune domains from one place in the forest and graft them to another.

Windows Server 2003 introduced prune and graft functionality, which enables you to both move the location of a domain in the forest and to rename the domain. However, this capability is not to be taken lightly. Performing these actions isn't a simple procedure. It is vital to use proper planning in your AD design, and the need to rename or move domains is not a requirement.

Why is prune and graft such a problem? Let's ignore for a second the actual complexity of the task, which requires actions to be taken on every domain controller in the entire forest and for them all to be restarted. Prune and graft is also a problem with services that depend on AD supporting a rename (for example, group policy, Exchange). For some of these products, there are separate utilities to run to help them handle a domain rename. Others require manual effort.

Upgrading AD

We have been dealing only with a new installation of AD. It's highly probable that you have an existing Windows 2000 or Windows Server 2003 AD in place. An in-place upgrade is possible only from Windows Server 2003, but ideally your Windows Server 2008 domain controllers are new servers and `dcpromo`'d into the existing domain. Before you can introduce a Windows Server 2008 domain controller into a domain, prepare both the forest and the domain. There must also be no NT 4 domain controllers in the domain, and the domain must be running at least Windows 2000 in native mode.

If you are installing new Windows Server 2008 domain controllers, don't forget to move the five FSMO roles onto Windows Server 2008 domain controllers and then demote the existing Windows 2000/2003 domain controllers as soon as possible, which enables you to move to Windows Server 2008 domain and forest modes and also allows you to move to DFSR for SYSVOL replication.

You can only "upgrade" Windows Server 2003 servers; there is no upgrade from NT 4.0 to Windows Server 2008 because you cannot upgrade the NT 4.0 PDC. You would have to go via Windows 2000 or Windows Server 2003 to create a new, clean domain and migrate the objects.

To prepare, copy the \sources\adprep folder from the Windows Server 2008 DVD and run the various `adprep` commands. If the new domain controller is the first Windows Server 2008 domain controller in the forest, prepare the forest for Windows Server 2008 by extending the schema with the Windows Server 2008 schema changes by using the `adprep /forestprep` command on the schema operations master. Perform this step even if this is a new Windows Server 2008 domain being upgraded into an existing Windows 2000/Windows Server 2003 forest.

Although this upgrade is part of the OS, you should ideally test this schema update in a test environment prior to running it in your production environment. You can facilitate this by restoring a backup of a domain controller onto a test box, seizing all the FSMO roles to make it functional, and then executing the `adprep` commands. It's a good best practice to always have a test environment that matches production, albeit scaled down, for the testing of any changes, such as upgrading or introducing new software.

If the domain controller is the first Windows Server 2008 domain controller in a Windows 2000 Server domain, you must prepare the domain by running `adprep /domainprep /gpprep` on the infrastructure master. If this domain controller is the first Windows Server 2008 domain controller in a Windows Server 2003 domain, prepare the domain by running `adprep /domainprep` on the infrastructure master.

As discussed in Chapter 11, to install a Windows Server 2008 RODC into an upgraded Windows 2000/Windows Server 2003 forest, first run `adprep /rodcprep` on any computer in the forest. You can run it multiple times if necessary, as some application partitions may not be accessible (in which case you get a message notifying you that this is the case). At that point, run `adprep /rodcprep` on another domain controller that has access to other partitions.

Even if you are performing an in-place upgrade from Windows Server 2003 to Windows Server 2008 on a domain controller, you must still run the adprep steps, or the option to upgrade is not available, as shown in Figure 12-50. When the adprep operations have been run and are in place, upgrading is possible.

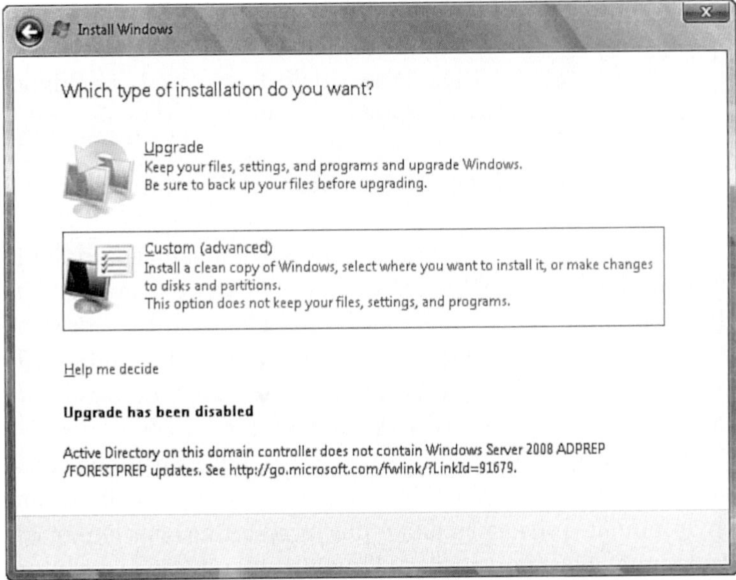

Figure 12-50 Because adprep has not been executed, the option to upgrade is not available.

The following is an example of the execution of upgrades on a Windows Server 2003 forest and domain. The contents of the sources\adprep folder from the Windows Server 2008 media have been copied to the c:\2008adprep folder on the Windows Server 2003 domain controller.

```
C:\2008adprep>adprep /forestprep

ADPREP WARNING:

Before running adprep, all Windows 2000 Active Directory Domain
Controllers in the forest should be upgraded to
Windows 2000 Service Pack 4 (SP4) or later.
```

```
[User Action]
If ALL your existing Windows 2000 Active Directory Domain
Controllers meet this
requirement, type C and then press ENTER to continue.
Otherwise, type any other
key and press ENTER to quit.
```

C

```
Opened Connection to SAVTST2K3DC
SSPI Bind succeeded
Current Schema Version is 30
Upgrading schema to version 44
Connecting to "SAVTST2K3DC"
Logging in as current user using SSPI
Importing directory from file "C:\WINDOWS\system32\sch31.ldf"
Loading entries..........................................
.........................................................
...................................
139 entries modified successfully.

The command has completed successfully
Connecting to "SAVTST2K3DC"
Logging in as current user using SSPI
Importing directory from file "C:\WINDOWS\system32\sch32.ldf"
Loading entries..................
18 entries modified successfully.

The command has completed successfully
Connecting to "SAVTST2K3DC"
Logging in as current user using SSPI
Importing directory from file "C:\WINDOWS\system32\sch33.ldf"
Loading entries.................
17 entries modified successfully.

The command has completed successfully
Connecting to "SAVTST2K3DC"
Logging in as current user using SSPI
Importing directory from file "C:\WINDOWS\system32\sch34.ldf"
Loading entries.........................................
................
60 entries modified successfully.

The command has completed successfully
Connecting to "SAVTST2K3DC"
```

```
Logging in as current user using SSPI
Importing directory from file "C:\WINDOWS\system32\sch35.ldf"
Loading entries........
7 entries modified successfully.

The command has completed successfully
Connecting to "SAVTST2K3DC"
Logging in as current user using SSPI
Importing directory from file "C:\WINDOWS\system32\sch36.ldf"
Loading entries...........................
26 entries modified successfully.

The command has completed successfully
Connecting to "SAVTST2K3DC"
Logging in as current user using SSPI
Importing directory from file "C:\WINDOWS\system32\sch37.ldf"
Loading entries.............................................
.............
56 entries modified successfully.

The command has completed successfully
Connecting to "SAVTST2K3DC"
Logging in as current user using SSPI
Importing directory from file "C:\WINDOWS\system32\sch38.ldf"
Loading entries....
3 entries modified successfully.

The command has completed successfully
Connecting to "SAVTST2K3DC"
Logging in as current user using SSPI
Importing directory from file "C:\WINDOWS\system32\sch39.ldf"
Loading entries...............
14 entries modified successfully.

The command has completed successfully
Connecting to "SAVTST2K3DC"
Logging in as current user using SSPI
Importing directory from file "C:\WINDOWS\system32\sch40.ldf"
Loading entries.............................................
..........................
```

```
69 entries modified successfully.

The command has completed successfully
Connecting to "SAVTST2K3DC"
Logging in as current user using SSPI
Importing directory from file "C:\WINDOWS\system32\sch41.ldf"
Loading entries..........
9 entries modified successfully.

The command has completed successfully
Connecting to "SAVTST2K3DC"
Logging in as current user using SSPI
Importing directory from file "C:\WINDOWS\system32\sch42.ldf"
Loading entries................................................
...............................................................
...............................................................
...............................................................
...............................................................
...............................................................
..
364 entries modified successfully.

The command has completed successfully
Connecting to "SAVTST2K3DC"
Logging in as current user using SSPI
Importing directory from file "C:\WINDOWS\system32\sch43.ldf"
Loading entries.........................
24 entries modified successfully.

The command has completed successfully
Connecting to "SAVTST2K3DC"
Logging in as current user using SSPI
Importing directory from file "C:\WINDOWS\system32\sch44.ldf"
Loading entries............
11 entries modified successfully.

The command has completed successfully
...............................................................
...............................................................
..................................
```

```
Adprep successfully updated the forest-wide information.

C:\2008adprep>adprep /domainprep
Running domainprep ...

Adprep successfully updated the domain-wide information.

The new cross domain planning functionality for Group Policy,
RSOP Planning Mode, requires file system and Active Directory
Domain Services permissions to be updated for existing Group
Policy Objects (GPOs). You can enable this functionality at any
time by running "adprep.exe /domainprep /gpprep" on the
Active Directory Domain Controller that holds the infrastruc-
ture operations master role.
This operation will cause all GPOs located in the policies
folder of the SYSVOL to be replicated once between the AD DCs
in this domain.
Microsoft recommends reading KB Q324392, particularly if you
have a large number of Group policy Objects.

C:\2008adprep>adprep /rodcprep
Adprep connected to the domain FSMO: SAVTST2K3DC.2003dom.local.

============================================================

Adprep found partition DC=ForestDnsZones,DC=2003dom,DC=local,
and is about to up date the permissions.

Adprep connected to a replica DC SAVTST2K3DC.2003dom.local
that holds partition
DC=ForestDnsZones,DC=2003dom,DC=local.

The operation on partition
DC=ForestDnsZones,DC=2003dom,DC=local
was successful.

============================================================

============================================================
```

```
Adprep found partition DC=2003dom,DC=local, and is about to
update the permissions.

Adprep connected to the Infrastructure FSMO:
SAVTST2K3DC.2003dom.local.

The operation on partition DC=2003dom,DC=local was successful.
============================================================

============================================================
Adprep found partition DC=DomainDnsZones,DC=2003dom,DC=local,
and is about to update the permissions.

Adprep connected to a replica DC SAVTST2K3DC.2003dom.local that
holds partition DC=DomainDnsZones,DC=2003dom,DC=local.

The operation on partition DC=DomainDnsZones,DC=2003dom,
DC=local was successful.

============================================================

Adprep completed without errors. All partitions are updated.
See the ADPrep.login directory C:\WINDOWS\debug\adprep\logs\
20071001182053 for more information.
```

The schema preparation takes the longest, but the domain and RODC finish almost instantly.

Migrating from FRS to DFSR for SYSVOL Replication

If you create a new AD domain in Windows Server 2008 mode, then DFSR is used for the replication of SYSVOL. However, if you install in any other mode or if you upgrade, NTFRS is used for SYSVOL replication, even if all servers are running Windows Server 2008.

Microsoft provides a utility, `dfsrmig`, that was written to migrate all the domain controllers in a domain from using FRS to DFSR. It works by creating a second copy of SYSVOL, which DFSR replicates, and then eventually the DFSR copy of SYSVOL is made primary. Run the `dfsrmig` tool in stages, setting a stage for the tool. The stages are as follows:

- **Stage 0: Start**. FRS is only responsible for replicating SYSVOL.
- **Stage 1: Prepared**. FRS is primarily responsible for SYSVOL replication. However, DFSR has taken a copy of SYSVOL and is replicating it between peer Windows Server 2008 domain controllers.
- **Stage 2: Redirected**. DFSR is now the primary SYSVOL replication engine, and NetLogon points to the DFSR version of SYSVOL. FRS is still replicating the old SYSVOL, but it is now not the primary.
- **Stage 3: Eliminated**. DFSR is solely responsible for replicating SYSVOL, and the FRS is retired.

By default, the domain is in the Start mode; view this via the `/getglobalstate` switch, which reads what state the domain controllers should be getting to.

```
C:\Users\john>dfsrmig /getglobalstate
Current DFSR global state: 'Start'
Succeeded.
```

To check the state of each domain controller in the domain, use the `/getmigrationstate` switch, which lists any domain controllers whose local state does not match the global desired state.

```
C:\Users\john>dfsrmig /getmigrationstate
All Domain Controllers have migrated successfully to
Global state ('Start').
Migration has reached a consistent state on all Domain
Controllers.
Succeeded.
```

To set a new desired global state that all domain controllers should try to reach, use the `/setglobalstate <state>` switch. You do not have to go from 0 to 1 to 2 to 3; specify your desired end state, and the tool takes care of going through the various stages of preparing a new DFSR set for SYSVOL, switching to DFSR for primary, and then retiring the NTFRS replica set.

Let's try jumping straight to stage 2. Remember that when you do so, set the global state so all domain controllers try to get to the redirected state, but it takes time for all domain controllers to see the new desired level. You can run `/getmigrationstate` to track the progress of the migration, as shown in the following example. Take note of the information given, especially around `robocopy`. If you make changes to the "old" SYSVOL location after this step, manually `robocopy` the content to the new SYSVOL_DFSR folder, or it is lost.

```
C:\Users\john>dfsrmig /setglobalstate 2

Current DFSR global state: 'Start'
New DFSR global state: 'Redirected'

Migration will proceed to 'Prepared' state. DFSR service will
copy the contents of SYSVOL to SYSVOL_DFSR folder.

Migration will proceed to 'Redirected' state. The SYSVOL share
will be changed to SYSVOL_DFSR folder.

If any changes have been made to the SYSVOL share during the
state transition from 'Prepared' to 'Redirected',
please robocopy the changes from SYSVOL to SYSVOL_DFSR
on any replicated RWDC.
Succeeded.

C:\Users\john>dfsrmig /getglobalstate

Current DFSR global state: 'Redirected'
Succeeded.

C:\Users\john>dfsrmig /getmigrationstate

The following Domain Controllers are not in sync with Global
state ('Redirected'):
```

```
Domain Controller (Local Migration State) - DC Type
====================================================

SAVDALDC01 ('Start') - Primary DC
SAVDALDC02 ('Start') - Writable DC

Migration has not yet reached a consistent state on all
Domain Controllers.
State information might be stale due to AD latency.

C:\Users\john>
C:\Users\john>dfsrmig /getmigrationstate

The following Domain Controllers are not in sync with Global
state ('Redirected'):

Domain Controller (Local Migration State) - DC Type
====================================================

SAVDALDC02 ('Waiting For Initial Sync') - Writable DC

Migration has not yet reached a consistent state on all
Domain Controllers.
State information might be stale due to AD latency.

C:\Users\john>dfsrmig /getmigrationstate

All Domain Controllers have migrated successfully to Global
state ('Redirected').
Migration has reached a consistent state on all Domain
Controllers.
Succeeded.
```

To remove the NTFRS, set the global state to 3 and wait for that change to take effect, as shown in the following example:

```
C:\Users\john>dfsrmig /setglobalstate 3
```

```
Current DFSR global state: 'Redirected'
New DFSR global state: 'Eliminated'

Migration will proceed to 'Eliminated' state. It is not possi-
ble to revert this step.

If any RODC is stuck in the 'Eliminating' state for too long
then run with option /DeleteRoNtfrsMembers.
Succeeded.

C:\Users\john>dfsrmig /getmigrationstate

The following Domain Controllers are not in sync with Global
state ('Eliminated'):

Domain Controller (Local Migration State) - DC Type
===================================================

SAVDALDC01 ('Redirected') - Primary DC
SAVDALDC02 ('Redirected') - Writable DC

Migration has not yet reached a consistent state on all
Domain Controllers.
State information might be stale due to AD latency.

C:\Users\john>dfsrmig /getmigrationstate

All Domain Controllers have migrated successfully to Global
state ('Eliminated').
Migration has reached a consistent state on all Domain
Controllers.
Succeeded.
```

At this point, you are able to see that the domain controllers are now part of a new Domain System Volume replica group for DFSR, which you can see in the DFS Management snap-in (see Figure 12-51).

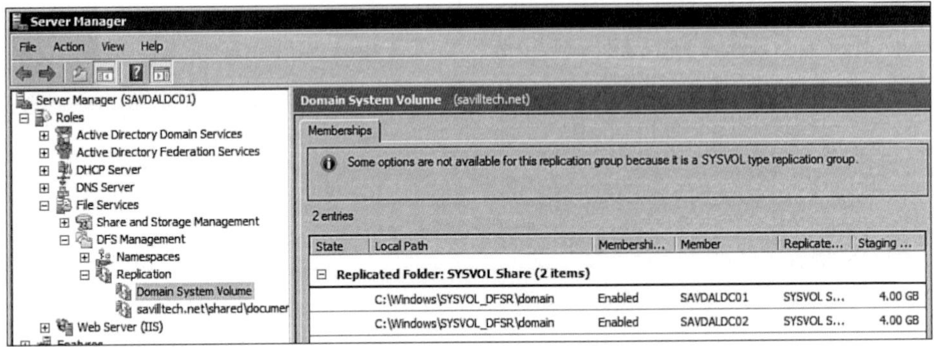

FIGURE 12-51 The domain system volume as part of the new SYSVOL_DFSR structure.

In addition, as shown in the following example, run the `ntfrsutl sets` command to see that the old SYSVOL share replica set is now stopped:

```
C:\Users\john>ntfrsutl sets
ACTIVE REPLICA SETS
DOMAIN SYSTEM VOLUME (SYSVOL SHARE) in state STOPPED

DELETED REPLICA SETS
```

When possible, reboot the domain controllers to complete the process and have the old SYSVOL deleted. Until a reboot, services.exe has the old SYSVOL locked, and you see an 8021 event log trying to delete SYSVOL. After the reboot, the migration can fully complete. Look at event ID 8004 (showing the NTFRS member object deletion) and also look at event IDs 8008, 8018, and 8019. You see multiple event ID 8008s for each move of the local state to the next phase toward eliminated SYSVOL global state. The event ID 8018 shows that the domain controller is moving to the eliminated state, and 8019 confirms that the DC has moved to eliminated state. The easiest way to see these is to set an event log filter on the DFSR application event log for event IDs 8004, 8008, 8018, and 8019.

You are now running your domain SYSVOL using pure DFSR. The SYSVOL share now points to the SYSVOL_DFSR structure. To see what is going on under the covers, head to http://blogs.technet.com/filecab/archive/2008/02/08/sysvol-migration-series-part-1-introduction-to-the-sysvol-migration-process.aspx for a great blog series on the internals of the FRS-to-DFSR migration.

Summary

Now that you've read Chapters 10 and 11 as well as this one, you understand that AD is vital to the entire infrastructure and that its design is important. It was difficult deciding what *not* to include in these chapters, as an entire book this size could cover AD alone. However, these three chapters concentrate on the items you need to design and manage your AD environment.

CHAPTER 13

Active Directory Federated Services, Lightweight Directory Services, and Rights Management

The last few chapters discussed Active Directory (AD), which provides a huge amount of functionality centered on the directory infrastructure. This chapter looks at additional AD capabilities for maintaining, protecting, and sharing sensitive information by both securing the rights to data and enabling secure access to it. This is done both within an organization and between organizations, without having to maintain multiple sets of credentials.

The identity and access (IDA) space is concerned with managing identities, authenticating users, reducing cost and risk, enabling a single-sign-on experience for users to avoid the problems associated with users having to manage multiple sets of credentials, and allowing this access from outside your organization. You need to ensure that only the correct people have access to the correct information and use it in the way in which you intend. "Correct people" means people in your company and partner organizations with whom you want to share information in a controlled fashion.

Before getting to the meat of this chapter, which is protecting data and sharing credentials between organizations, let's look at a way to store data in a directory service without filling up AD, which is closely tied to the core Active Directory Domain Services (ADDS).

Active Directory Lightweight Directory Services

You have probably already heard of this component but under its old name, Active Directory Application Mode (ADAM). It has been renamed under Windows Server 2008 to Active Directory Lightweight Directory Services (AD LDS), but it's the same component. The only difference is that previously ADAM was available as a download from Microsoft as an out-of-band release, with the exception of Windows 2003 R2, which included ADAM on its second additional feature CD.

ADAM, in its downloadable form, is available for the following platforms:

- Windows Server 2003, Standard Edition (not Web Edition)
- Windows Server 2003, Enterprise Edition
- Windows Server 2003, Datacenter Edition
- Windows XP Professional Service Pack 1 (SP1)

Windows XP, Windows Server 2003, Enterprise Edition, and Windows Server 2003, Datacenter Edition also have 64-bit support. If you want to download for these platforms, just search Microsoft for ADAM.

Why do you have AD LDS/ADAM? AD LDS addresses the requirements of directory-enabled applications that need to store their data and configuration in a directory service, but one that does not have to be AD and yet still offers the option to take advantage of the security and authentication AD can offer. The AD LDS uses the same technology and database format as AD but does not store security principals such as user or computer accounts. It can hold user and computer objects; they just can't be security principals. The interface to the AD LDS is via the same directory service as AD: dsmain.exe. However, an AD LDS–specific dynamic link library is used for communication to the AD LDS database instance, which is named Adamntds.dit instead of the normal AD name of ntds.dit.

AD LDS does not include logical components such as domain controllers (although it has servers hosting the AD LDS instance), Group Policy, trees and forests, and so forth. That is not its intended use. It comes into play in situations such as the following. Suppose that you have a large amount of custom data you want to store about users in your company. Instead of extending the schema, create an AD LDS instance to store the additional information and link to the AD user object.

Just like AD, AD LDS has a schema that can have new object classes and attributes added, and can store many different types of objects based on the schema configuration of the AD LDS. It can then integrate with AD as the basis for controlling what objects in the AD LDS instance a requesting user can access. With AD, be careful about modifying the schema due to the scope of the change and the possible implications. With AD LDS you need not have the same concern; the AD LDS is a separate directory instance.

For example, an application might want to store a large amount of information that is not globally of interest or that you might not want replicated to every domain controller. AD LDS uses a totally separate database from AD, which means you can have a separate schema for each ADAM instance. That can be useful for testing. In this arrangement, all your user accounts, computer accounts, policies, and so on reside in AD. You could create an AD LDS instance and import a schema definition that describes the attributes and object classes used by the application. Then the application can communicate with the AD LDS for application-specific information. This is why the original name of AD LDS was AD Application Mode; it's for use by applications.

Figure 13-1 shows an example with a domain for a company that sells many different clothing items. This company has just branched out into a special custom hat solution, so it purchased a hat application that has to store details about the various hat configurations and the clients in a directory service. The application has a special hat object class and user objects for its customers. The central IT team had no desire to add the hat object to the AD used globally or to store customer details for one part of the company. So, it created an AD LDS instance to hold information related to the application. However, there can still be integration, and you can create links between AD users and objects in AD LDS.

FIGURE 13-1 Poor AD LDS usage example involving hats.

Other services and applications use ADAM/AD LDS as a way to store information from AD without having access to a domain controller. For example, Exchange 2007 Edge servers are placed in the demilitarized zone (DMZ) of the network and are not members of the domain. However, they need information about the AD configuration and recipient information to perform lookups on incoming mail to ensure that it should be accepted. To solve this, place an ADAM instance in the DMZ and, using an Exchange component called EdgeSync, perform a one-way replication from AD to replication configuration and recipient information to the ADAM instance to which the Edge server has access.

Just because AD LDS is not AD does not mean you cannot make it highly available. It has many of the capabilities of AD including multimaster replication and its own site configuration. There are complexities, however. AD LDS does not use the same graphical tools as AD. You cannot use AD Users and Computers. However, with AD LDS you can use the AD Sites and Services Microsoft Management Console (MMC) snap-in to manage an AD LDS instance if you import certain schema definitions. Where no graphical tools exist, it's because AD LDS is designed to be configured and accessed via the application using the AD LDS instance. For manual configuration, you can use the adsiedit.msc application, which has the capability to access all the data within the AD LDS instance, including its configuration partition. There you can create site and site link objects to control replication if you don't want to import the MS-AD LDS-DisplaySpecifiers.LDF schema definition needed to use AD Sites and Services.

By default, as with AD, all the servers that are servicing the AD LDS exist in the same Default-First-Site-Name site. You can add replicas of an AD LDS instance, making it highly available. The tools you use to troubleshoot replication, such as REPADMIN, are the same tools you use for AD LDS replication. You also have a separate version of ntdsutil just for AD LDS: DSDBUTIL.

AD LDS, like AD, offers a Lightweight Directory Access Protocol (LDAP) interface, both secure and insecure, enabling LDAP- and AD-based applications to seamlessly use AD LDS without even knowing it is communicating with AD LDS and not AD. Multiple instances of AD LDS can run on a server, although each instance could not listen on the same LDAP ports. For example, 389 and 636 could be used by only one instance unless you install AD LDS on a domain controller, in which case those ports are already being used by AD LDS. Each instance of AD LDS is unique, can use different schemas, and is unrelated to the others running on the same box in any way.

Installing AD LDS

Install AD LDS via the normal roles method in Server Manager, and there are no questions to answer. A separate wizard creates the actual AD LDS instances after you install the role.

The AD LDS Setup Wizard is available via the Administrative Tools group. Or you can access it via the AD LDS Role area within Server Manager through the AD LDS Setup Wizard link in the Advanced Tools area.

Creating an AD LDS Instance

Let's create an AD LDS instance. Initiate the wizard. The first welcome screen informs you how powerful the directory service you are about to install is. Click Next.

The next screen allows you to create a new unique instance of AD LDS. Think of it like creating a new domain in a new forest with AD. (Because it has a separate schema, it's a new "forest" instead of a new "domain.") Or you can add a replica of an existing instance, which is like adding a new DC to an existing domain in AD terms, as shown in Figure 13-2.

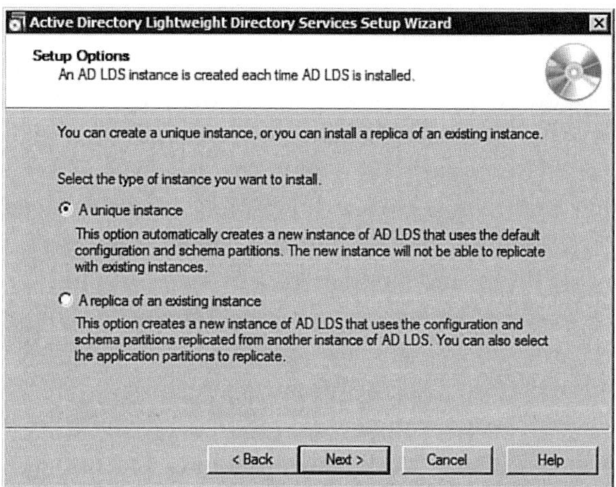

FIGURE 13-2 Create a new AD LDS instance.

Now enter a unique AD LDS instance name for this server. This becomes the name of the AD LDS instance service name. (Although in

Figure 13-3 it still has ADAM_ prefixed to the name, not AD LDS.) Make this a meaningful name (for example, CRMApp), especially if you will be running multiple AD LDS instances.

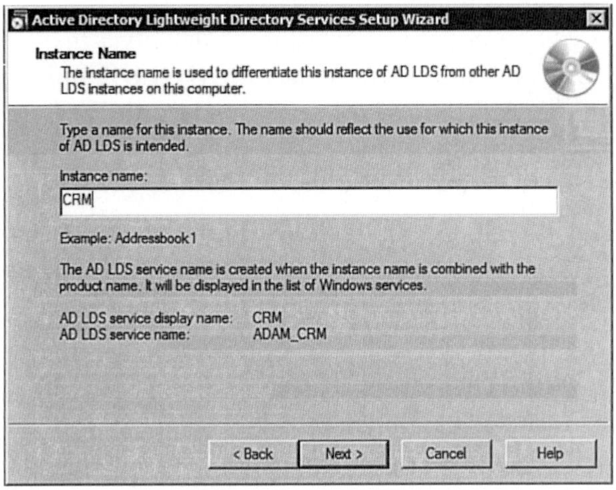

FIGURE 13-3 Naming the AD LDS instance.

The next screen asks for the port to use for LDAP and SSL communication. By default the ports are 389 and 636, respectively, which are the correct ports for these services. However, you cannot use these ports if the server is a domain controller (because the AD already uses these ports), or if you have another AD LDS instance already using the ports. Each AD LDS instance must use unique LDAP and SSL port numbers. If you are not using the default 389 and 636 ports, you must pick unique numbers between 1025 and 65535. Numbers below 1025 are reserved for other services to listen and operate on. In this example, configure the CRM instance to listen for LDAP on port 5000 and SSL on port 5001, as shown in Figure 13-4.

The next dialog asks whether to create an application partition. This depends on the application that will be using the AD LDS instance. Some applications create their own directory partitions and configure the schema; in that case you select No to creating an application directory partition, which is the default. Alternatively you can select Yes and enter the distinguished name for the partition, which must be unique in the AD LDS instance. It can be the same name as other application partitions in other instances, although this is not recommended. In this case, create a CRM application partition in the savilltech.net namespace (for example,

CN=CRM,DC=Savilltech,DC=net) as shown in Figure 13-5. Remember, this is just a name; it is not linked to savilltech.net in any way. It just gives the environment a coherent namespace.

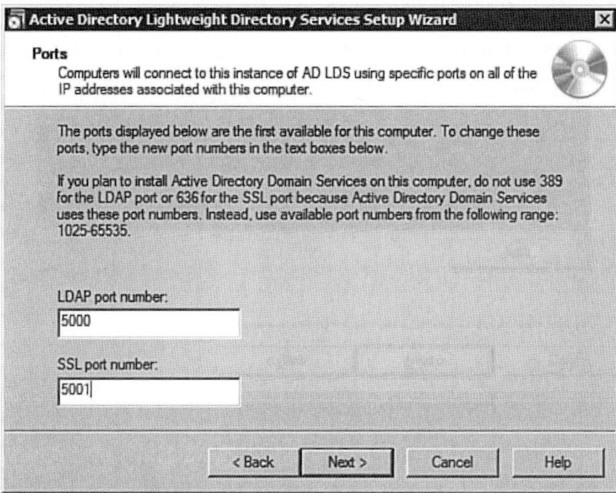

FIGURE 13-4 Customizing the LDAP and SSL ports.

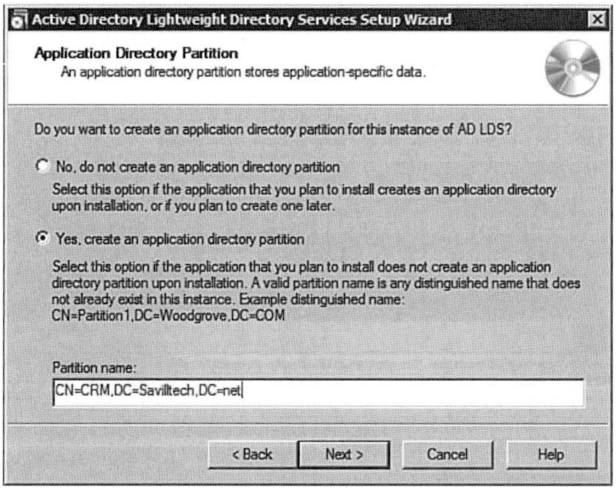

Active Directory Lightweight Directory Services Setup Wizard
Application Directory Partition
An application directory partition stores application-specific data.
Do you want to create an application directory partition for this instance of AD LDS?
No, do not create an application directory partition
Select this option if the application that you plan to install creates an application directory upon installation, or if you plan to create one later.
Yes, create an application directory partition
Select this option if the application that you plan to install does not create an application directory partition upon installation. A valid partition name is any distinguished name that does not already exist in this instance. Example distinguished name: CN=Partition1,DC=Woodgrove,DC=COM
Partition name:
CN=CRM,DC=Savilltech,DC=net
< Back
Next >
Cancel
Help

FIGURE 13-5 Creating an application directory partition in your AD LDS instance.

The next dialog is the location for the AD LDS instance, which by default is location C:\Program Files\Microsoft ADAM\<AD LDS instance name (for example, CRM)>\data. However, you can change the paths as required. If this AD LDS instance will be heavily used, move the locations off the system partition and separate the data and recovery files onto different volumes.

The next dialog prompts for the service under which to run the AD LDS instance. The default is to use the Network service account, which is a built-in account with authority like a normal authenticated user. If special permission or access is necessary, specify an alternative account to run the AD LDS instance.

The next screen selects who has administrative permissions for the AD LDS instance. By default, the logged-on user receives administrative permissions. You can select an alternative user (or, more likely, a group) to have administrative permissions.

The last configuration dialog enables you to select which LDAP Data Interchange Format (LDIF) files to import. They define the schema configuration. Select these files even if you elected not to create a directory partition. Load schema definitions for InetOrgPerson types, users, and other types, as shown in Figure 13-6. If you want to use the AD Sites and Services MMC snap-in, load in the MS-ADLDS-DisplaySpecifiers-0409.LDF file. If you need to add custom object classes and attributes, use the `ldifde` command with the `-i` switch to import and the `-f` switch to pass the LDIF file that contains the new schema configuration to be imported. Look at the help on `ldifde` for full information on modifying the schema. You can also use the normal schema management MMC snap-in.

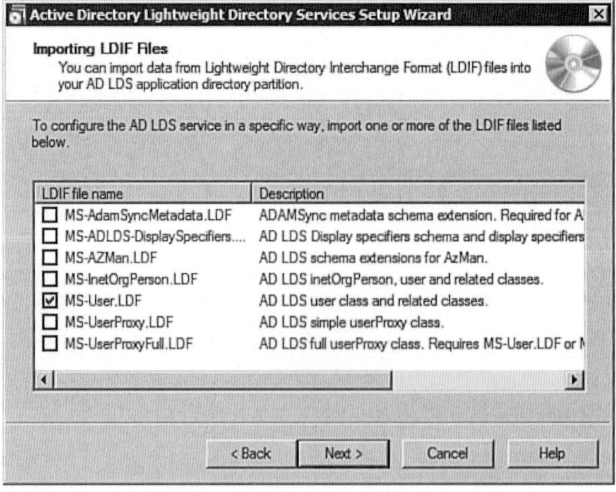

FIGURE 13-6 Configuring the schema definitions to use in the directory partition.

A summary of your selections now displays. Click Next to create the partition, which copies the required files, imports the schema, and starts the instance. Click Finish when creation of the partition ends. After the instance is created, you can access the information using tools such as adsiedit.msc and ldp.exe.

Administering AD LDS

Let's first look at using the AD Sites and Services MMC snap-in, which is installed when the AD LDS role is installed. By default when you start the AD Sites and Services snap-in, the forest that your server belongs to is connected, and the sites for your forest are shown. Change this to connect to your AD LDS instance. Right-click the root of Active Directory Sites and Services and select Change Domain Controller from the context menu. As shown in Figure 13-7, enter a custom server and port. This needs to be the name or IP address of the AD LDS server hosting the AD LDS instance you want to connect to and the LDAP port that the instance you want to connect to is using. You receive a prompt that you are changing the administered forest. Click Yes.

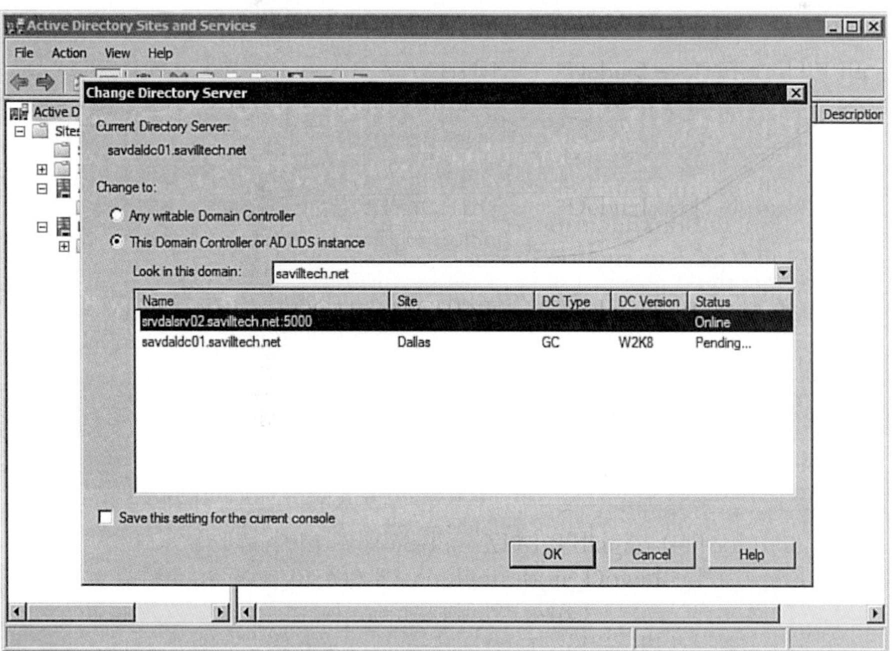

FIGURE 13-7 Enter the server name hosted, the AD LDS instance, and then the LDAP port number of the instance to which you want to connect.

When you view the sites, you see a default site, Default-First-Site-Name, with a server in the form of <server name>$<AD LDS instance name>. The object looks the same as with a normal domain controller except the type of the NTDS Settings, object is nTDSDSA instead of Domain Controller Settings and the nTDSDSA instance has no configuration properties, unlike a normal domain controller NTDS Settings object. If you have replicas of an instance, there are multiple server records, as shown in Figure 13-8.

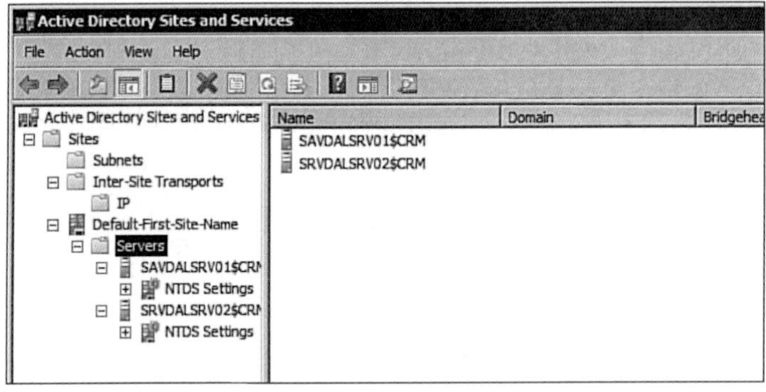

FIGURE 13-8 Viewing the sites using AD Sites and Services.

You can create additional sites and map subnets to sites as with a normal AD forest. Right-click AD LDS servers and move them between sites with the `Move` command. This helps you control the replication where multiple servers are hosting a copy of an AD LDS instance.

To add a replica, run the wizard to create an instance as usual. However, select the A Replica of an Existing Instance option for your instance installation. Select an instance name and ports as usual, but instead of entering for an application directory partition name, enter the name of the server hosting the AD LDS replica you want to replicate and the LDAP port for the AD LDS listener, as shown on the top in Figure 13-9. Select the application directory partitions hosted in the AD LDS instance that you want to replicate, as shown on the bottom in Figure 13-9.

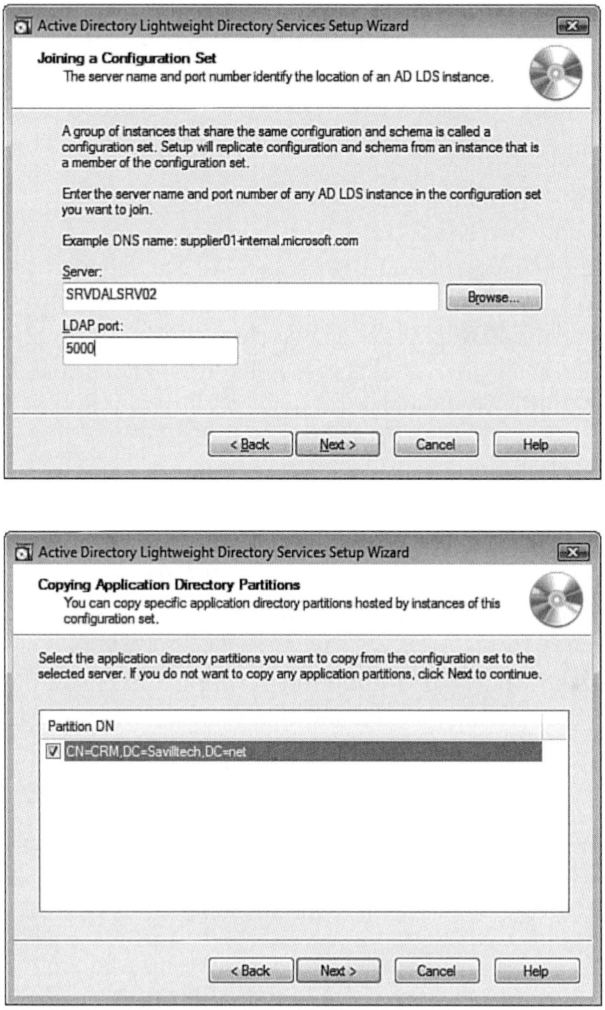

Figure 13-9 Selecting the source for the replication.

Use the normal `repadmin` command to troubleshoot replication with AD LDS. For example, to force a replication, use the `/syncall` command or any of the other replication switches:

```
C:\>repadmin /syncall localhost:5000
cn=crm,dc=savilltech,dc=net
Syncing partition: cn=crm,dc=savilltech,dc=net
CALLBACK MESSAGE: The following replication is in progress:
    From: SRVDALSRV02.savilltech.net:5000
```

```
    To  : savdalsrv01.savilltech.net:5000
CALLBACK MESSAGE: The following replication completed success-
fully:
    From: SRVDALSRV02.savilltech.net:5000
    To  : savdalsrv01.savilltech.net:5000
CALLBACK MESSAGE: SyncAll Finished.
SyncAll terminated with no errors.
```

The data side of AD LDS is beyond the scope of this chapter because it is typically an application writing to AD LDS. However, the same tools that can import/export to AD (for example, `csvde` and `ldifde`) can be used. Refer to the AD chapters (Chapters 10, 11, and 12) for information on these utilities. As a general point of illustration, let's look at using ADSI Edit.

Start ADSI Edit as usual (Start, Run, adsiedit.msc or via the shortcut under Advanced Tools in Server Manager in the AD LDS role section). When ADSI Edit opens, right-click the root and select Connect To from the context menu. As shown in Figure 13-10, enter a friendly name for the connection, enter the application directory partition name, and specify the server and LDAP port for the AD LDS instance that hosts the partition. You can now navigate around the partition and create new objects depending on the schema defined and that controls the object classes available.

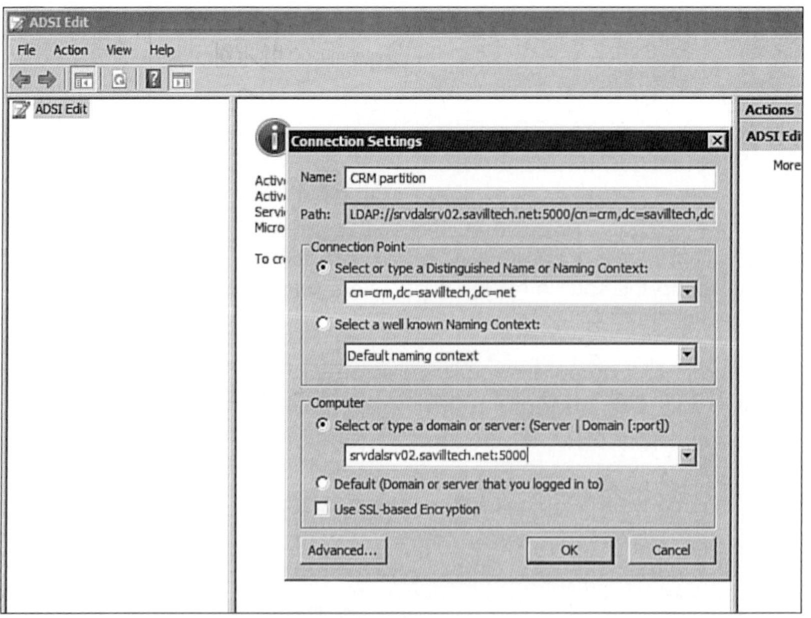

FIGURE 13-10 Connecting to your AD LDS instance.

If you want to view the configuration partition, select Configuration Naming Context from the Well Known Naming Context drop-down in the Connection Settings dialog and select the server name and LDAP port of the AD LDS instance. From the configuration naming context, you can also manage the sites and replication by editing the properties of the site links and changing attributes such as cost and replInterval, as shown in Figure 13-11. Right-click the site link and select Schedule to get the graphical interface to set the availability of the link for replication.

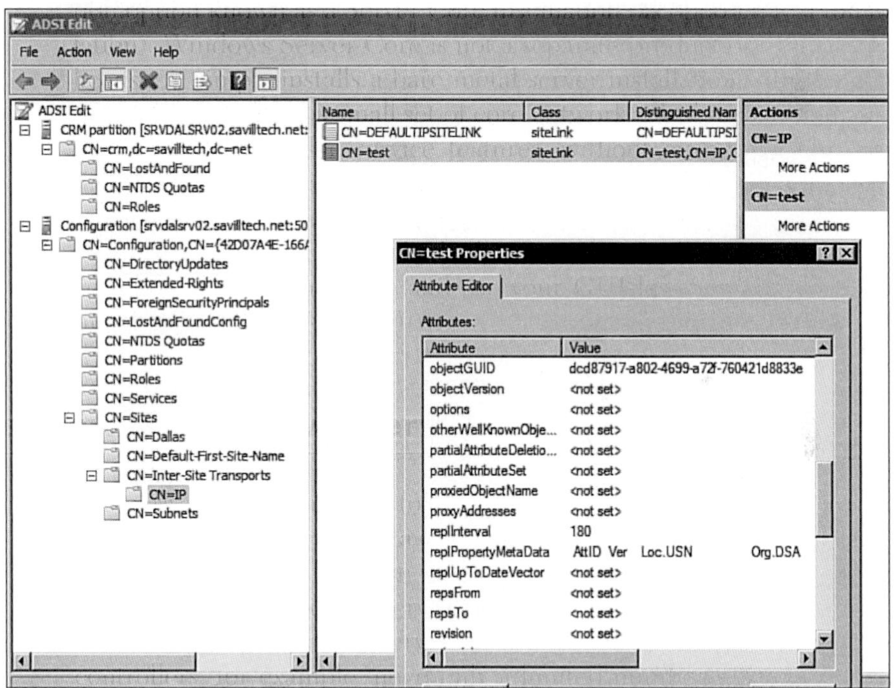

Figure 13-11 Modifying site data via ADSI Edit.

To remove an AD LDS instance, use the Programs and Features Control Panel applet, which displays all the AD LDS instances. Right-click the instance you want to remove and select Uninstall. If you are removing the last instance/replica of an application partition, you receive a prompt to confirm you understand you are deleting the last copy of the partition.

To back up and restore AD LDS instances, use the Windows Server Backup component and ensure that the volumes containing the AD LDS database and log files are selected. If you want to back up only AD LDS instance information and not entire volumes, use `dsdbutil` and utilize the install from media function (`ifm`) to create a snapshot. The only commands needed are to select the instance of AD LDS to back up and then a destination:

```
C:\>dsdbutil
dsdbutil: activate instance crm
Active instance set to "crm".
dsdbutil: ifm
ifm: create full c:\temp\crmbackup
Creating snapshot...
Snapshot set {cd45a7a7-4a83-42d9-b32d-c0cc55a79693} generated
successfully.
Snapshot {6696fbee-8aff-4b8a-a0fe-561582d485a1} mounted as
C:\$SNAP_200711162022
_VOLUMEC$\
Initiating DEFRAGMENTATION mode...
     Source Database: C:\$SNAP_200711162022_VOLUMEC$\Program
Files\Microsoft ADA
M\CRM\data\adamntds.dit
     Target Database: c:\temp\crmbackup\adamntds.dit

                 Defragmentation  Status (% complete)

          0    10   20   30   40   50   60   70   80   90  100
          |----|----|----|----|----|----|----|----|----|----|
          ...................................................

Snapshot {6696fbee-8aff-4b8a-a0fe-561582d485a1} unmounted.
IFM media created successfully in c:\temp\crmbackup
ifm: quit
dsdbutil: quit
```

The media you just created can be used to install AD LDS instance replicas using the same kind of install from media capability you have with AD. Access that capability via the `%windir%\adam\adaminstall /adv` command, which adds an additional dialog to the instance creation process. That dialog enables you to specify a restored backup location for the initial replica population to be sourced from.

AD LDS is a great alternative to populating your AD with information that is not appropriate for storing in the enterprise directory. Its actual use will be determined by the applications and services in use within your organization and their support of AD LDS/ADAM. Now when you hear of a service needing a directory service, you can offer an alternative to filling up the AD.

Active Directory Rights Management Services

Data is what infrastructure is there to take care of—making it available, making it secure, and manipulating it. An organization's data is a key asset. If an organization loses data and parties who should not have the information obtain it, numerous problems might result. Such problems include financial, legal, and regulatory compliance; image and credibility, if you have to disclose the information loss (such is the case in certain United States locales). It's even worse if parties come forward to say that they have the data.

Information can be shared in countless ways. You can put data onto a file share, post it on a web site, collaborate on it via SharePoint, send it as an e-mail or attachment, or copy it to a universal serial bus (USB) key, and strap it to a carrier pigeon. (If you choose the latter, you need Rights Management Services [RMS].) But there might be times you need to restrict who can view data and what they can do with the data. In early computing days, you protected data via walls, data was on servers inside your company, and only people that were connected in the company could view it. As connectivity has grown, the walls have disappeared because of the technologies just mentioned (such as e-mail and removable devices), so you need to move the protection to the data itself.

Existing solutions are available to protect data. When you think of data protection, you probably think of BitLocker, which encrypts an entire file system, and the Encrypting File System (EFS), which can be used to encrypt individual files on a file system. Both are good encryption options and should not be discounted, but they protect the data only when it's on that machine, on the file system.

Neither of these technologies travels with the data, nor are they granular. If users can read the data, they can do anything they want: forward it on to their friends, print it out, modify it, and so forth. Active Directory Rights Management Services (AD RMS) solves this problem by attaching a policy directly to the document considered sensitive by the organization, either in terms of who can access it or how the data can be used. Because the policy is part of the document, even if a user forwards the document to another user, that policy is still in place and in effect. This is the main difference between AD RMS and a technology such as EFS. After a file is attached to an e-mail or copied to another medium such as a USB key, the EFS encryption stops. With AD RMS, that protection is always with the document.

AD RMS has had a major promotion in Windows Server 2008 in many ways. Previously AD RMS was available as an out-of-band download for Windows Server 2003 and was managed through a combination of a basic, nonintuitive Web interface and a collection of tools to make sense of the logs generated by RMS and other management actions. This is no longer the case in Windows Server 2008. Microsoft is serious about protecting and controlling access to data, so RMS is now a core role within the 2008 product. It has an MMC plug-in for management and log viewing, a scriptable administrative interface, and a neat health model that details all the events that AD RMS can generate, with next steps on what to do when you receive each event. You also get Active Directory Federation Services (AD FS) integration, which allows you to protect content for users in other organizations without having to use a Windows Live ID.

To access an AD RMS–protected document, you need the RMS client installed (which is built into Windows Vista), and applications need to understand the RMS policies. For example, if you protect a Word document, you need Office 2003 or 2007 to be able to access the protected document. For readers running older versions of Office, an RMS add-on for Internet Explorer that provides view-only access to the document is available at www.microsoft.com/downloads/details.aspx?FamilyId=B48F920B-5AF0-46B4-994F-2F62582CC86F&displaylang=en. A good practice for non-Vista deployments is to bundle the RMS client into the Office deployment package so that all computers that have Office get RMS client as well.

Windows Mobile 6 also has support for RMS-protected documents but can only consume (that is, view) RMS content. A Mobile 6 client cannot publish RMS-protected documents but can consume and publish RMS-protected e-mail. The RMS application programming interface (API) for mobile devices is part of the Windows Mobile software development kit (SDK), if you want to create your own mobile application.

So, how does this work? Within the organization, install the AD RMS server, which stores its policies and logs in a SQL Server database. This SQL instance is not part of the AD RMS role, so you need to install SQL Server in advance of installing AD RMS. AD is the authority for which users can be given access to protected data, and the Mail attribute of the user accounts needs to be configured with their e-mail addresses. Because the e-mail address is the basis of RMS protection, never reuse e-mail addresses for different users. If user John Savill, who had e-mail address john@savilltech.com leaves the company, and John Smith joins and is given John's old e-mail address, Smith might be able to get access to RMS-protected information to which only John Savill should have access. One option to stop e-mail addresses from being reused is to disable users who have left, but not to delete them.

The first time a user wants to protect a document with RMS, he communicates with the RMS server, which is found by the client in the enterprise by querying for the Service Connection Point (SCP) created during the AD RMS role installation. An alternative is manually specifying the AD RMS server at the client.

After contacting the AD RMS server, the user receives two pieces of information. The first is a Rights Account Certificate (RAC), which is a public/private key pair for the user's account encrypted with the client machine's public key. Each machine with the RMS client has a key pair with the RMS server as well. The key pair is based on the hardware ID of the client that is hidden away in the %allusersprofile%\Application Data\Microsoft\DRM location. The second piece of information is a Client Licensor Certificate (CLC), which is a copy of the RMS server's public key. It allows content to be protected offline. The CLC enables the client machine to define usage rights and rules for the files. These certificates, which are in eXtensible Rights Markup Language (XrML) format, are stored in the %USERPROFILE%\AppData\Local\Microsoft\DRM location in Vista or %USERPROFILE%\Local Settings\Application Data\Microsoft\DRM\ in older operating systems. These keys are strongly protected and form the RMS "lock box," which is the protected store for RMS and is part of the RMS client. The last stage is that the application used to author the data creates a publishing license (PL), which attaches to the document and then encrypts the content of the file. The operating system handles all this automatically.

When a recipient receives the RMS-protected file and opens the document, the RMS client on the receiver's machine opens the PL in the document and contacts the RMS server identified in the PL. The recipient sends the RMS server the PL from the document and the user's RAC. If the user does not have a RAC, the user is enrolled with RMS so that the user has a RAC before access to the document is initiated. Based on the PL and the user's RAC, the RMS server issues the user a use license (UL) that consists of a content key so that the client can access the content. It is encrypted with the user's public key and signed by the server. If the user does not have rights, the document is not decrypted, which is the strongest piece of protection in RMS. If the user has rights to the file, the application then processes the UL, renders the file, and enforces the rights detailed in the PL that travels with the encrypted file. For example, the PL might state that the document contents cannot be cut and pasted. Obviously there are ways around this, but they are not easy. You could retype the content of a document or use a camera to take a picture of the screen. The normal Windows Print Screen, however, does not function while a rights-protected document is open. However, third-party screen capture utilities might still work.

If the receiving user does not have the RMS client, she receives notification that the document is protected with RMS and is directed to download and install the RMS client. If you use RMS in your organization, ensure that you use Windows Vista or have the RMS client deployed. There are numerous ways to deploy the RMS client to pre-Vista clients. You can deploy with Group Policy, make the client available on a file share, or even package with Office so that any machine that gets Office installed automatically gets the RMS client.

Mobile devices are a special consideration because to read protected content, they need to contact the RMS server, which they might be unable to do. There are some workarounds. If the protected document is read on a PC and then synchronized to the mobile device, the document already has the RMS license in the document, so the mobile device can read it. Another option is to use Exchange 2007 SP1's capability to prelicense an RMS e-mail.

Exchange 2007 SP1 can contact RMS as it sees protected content going to a user's mailbox and contact RMS on behalf of the user and get the required RMS license. This avoids users having to communicate with RMS as they try to read protected content. This is useful for mobile clients that might not be easily connected to RMS because Exchange is prelicensing; then no call is needed to RMS because the license is already put into the data. This is also useful if you send out a protected e-mail to 50,000 employees. Normally every user would try to contact RMS at the same time. With Exchange 2007 prelicensing, this is done in batches by Exchange (resulting in fewer calls to RMS), and the users aren't required to directly contact RMS.

Applications that support RMS include Office 2003/2007 applications with support for the main Word, PowerPoint, Excel and InfoPath (2007 office only) formats. Additionally the XML Paper Specification (XPS) format is RMS-aware as part of Windows Presentation Foundation RMS support. SharePoint is also RMS-aware, allowing you to configure RMS for sites and documents within SharePoint with a few clicks of the mouse. You will see additional applications add in support for RMS, and this support is expected to grow over time.

One action you can't do today, but that some clients ask for, is to force RMS protection on certain users. For example, you don't trust the sales team and want any mail they send to be RMS-protected so that they can't send sensitive information of a technical nature outside the company. Microsoft is aware that forcing RMS protection is a requested feature from companies and are looking at it as a future option.

Installing AD RMS

Before going any further, let's get AD RMS up and running, which is a little more involved than a normal role installation. With all other roles, all the necessary components for the role to function are part of the operating system and are just installed normally. With the AD RMS role, you require additional operating system components, which are parts of Web Server (IIS), Windows Process Activation Service, and Message Queuing roles. In addition you need SQL Server available if you ever want more than one server in the AD RMS cluster. SQL should not be installed on the same server as AD RMS, but it obviously needs to be contactable during the AD RMS role installation and during AD RMS functioning hours. If this will always be a single-instance AD RMS implementation, you can choose to use an internal Windows database. However, doing so is not a best practice.

AD RMS is tied to the domain that the server belongs to. After you install AD RMS, you cannot move the server to another domain. The AD RMS service can run as either the local system or as a named domain account, which requires only normal user rights. The best practice is to run AD RMS under a domain user account, so before installing AD RMS, create a new user in the domain (for example, ADRMS_SVC). You might want to set the account so that the password never expires. This does introduce a potential security risk: an account with a static password. You can opt to let the password expire. Just make sure you have procedures in place to regularly modify the password for the user account and update the AD RMS service to have the correct password. Also remember that all users who use AD RMS must have their Mail attribute populated in AD. If you assign RMS rights to groups, those groups also need their Mail attribute populated.

The account used to install the AD RMS role must be different from the service account used by AD RMS and needs to be a member of the System Administrators role on the SQL Server with permission to create new databases. Ideally the installation account is an enterprise administrator so that an SCP can be created during installation.

When you install the AD RMS role via Server Manager, you receive a prompt to add additional role services and features that are required, as shown in Figure 13-12. Accept or the AD RMS role cannot be installed.

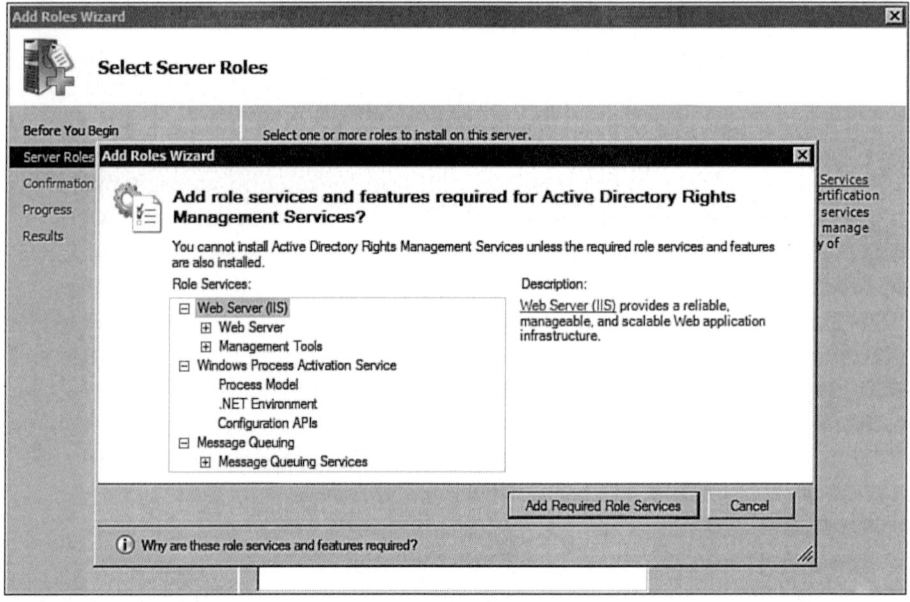

Figure 13-12 AD RMS requires a number of extra components to function, not just those in the operating system.

Remember that AD RMS was previously a complex stand-alone component, and you have a number of configuration choices to make that you deduce when you see the nine subinstallation parts of the AD RMS cluster. The AD RMS installation is cluster-aware. RMS is effectively stateless (because a request is made by a client and fulfilled straight away via a response), so you can use clustering or load balancing to make AD RMS highly available. If you are making AD RMS highly available, ensure that SQL Server is also highly available via SQL clustering because SQL is core to the functionality of AD RMS.

Click Next and an introduction to AD RMS is shown with some helpful links on scaling and securing your AD RMS environment that are certainly beneficial. However, you can look at this later. Click Next again to display the list of role services that can be installed. By default the AD RMS role service is selected. However, note that another option for identity federation support is also available but don't select this for now. This component integrates AD RMS with AD FS, which you get to at the end of this chapter.

The next screen, shown in Figure 13-13, presents the option to create a new AD RMS cluster or join an existing cluster. If an existing AD RMS cluster is detected by the wizard, the option to join is available. Otherwise it is grayed out, as in your installation. Adding additional AD RMS servers to the cluster increases availability by removing dependence on a single server and increases scalability by having more servers processing AD RMS requests.

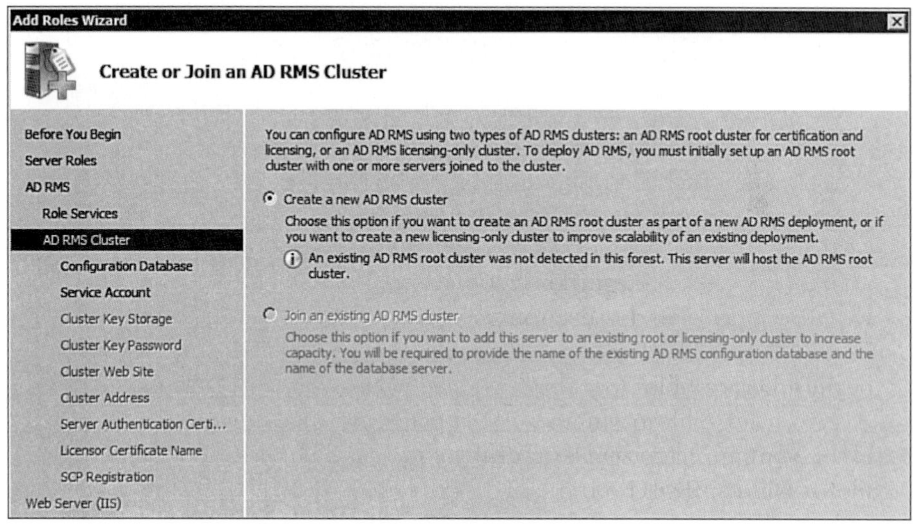

Figure 13-13 Creating a new AD RMS installation.

The next screen enables you to select a SQL server to use for storage of AD RMS logs, configuration, and policy. By default, an internal Windows database can be used. However, this limits future growth of the AD RMS environment and does not yield the same performance as that of a full SQL installation. After selecting the SQL server and the database instance, validate that the database can be contacted and configured by clicking the Validate button. AD RMS communicates via named pipes, which are disabled on a default SQL Server (version 2005 or higher) instance. To enable named pipes, use the SQL Server 2005 Surface Area Configuration utility and under Database Engine, Remote Connections, enable Using Both TCP/IP and Named Pipes, as shown in Figure 13-14. Also using the SQL Server Surface Area Configuration tool, enable the SQL Server Browser service and set its start type to Automatic. After making this change, stop and start the SQL Server installation via the Microsoft SQL Server Management Studio.

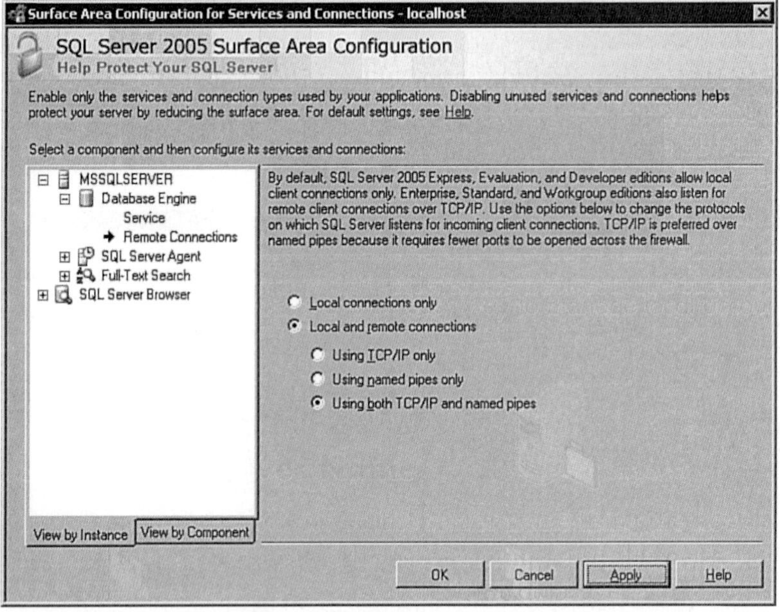

FIGURE 13-14 Allowing named pipe connections to your SQL Server 2005 installation.

The next dialog requests the domain account under which AD RMS runs. This is the account you created earlier. Select Specify, enter the user account and password, and then click Next.

The next screen enables configuration of the RMS cluster key storage. By default the cluster key is stored within the AD RMS installation on the server and managed automatically. The cluster key is vital to RMS and provides the foundation of the security used in all the other facets of RMS, so protect it. If you stick with the default of using AD RMS to secure the key, enter the password used for the encryption. Make the password complex.

The best practice is to use a software- or hardware-based cryptographic service provider (CSP) instead of the AD RMS service for the cluster key storage. If using a CSP, manually distribute the key if other servers join the AD RMS cluster.

A password is now required to encrypt the cluster key. Choose a complex password, but don't lose it. You need the password to add other servers to the AD RMS cluster or to restore the AD RMS cluster from a backup. A big safe would be handy right about now, or you could just write the password on a post-it note and stick it on your monitor. (I'm joking!)

The next stage of the wizard is to select the web site under which the AD RMS exists; this is the default web site. After you select the web site, the option to encrypt the connection is available, which is mandatory if you want to use AD FS later. You also need to specify the address that the clients use to communicate with the AD RMS server, as shown in Figure 13-15. This uniform resource locator (URL) cannot be changed, so choose carefully. If you intend to add additional servers in the future, select an alias name such as RMS.savilltech.net. However, you cannot then use a self-signed certificate.

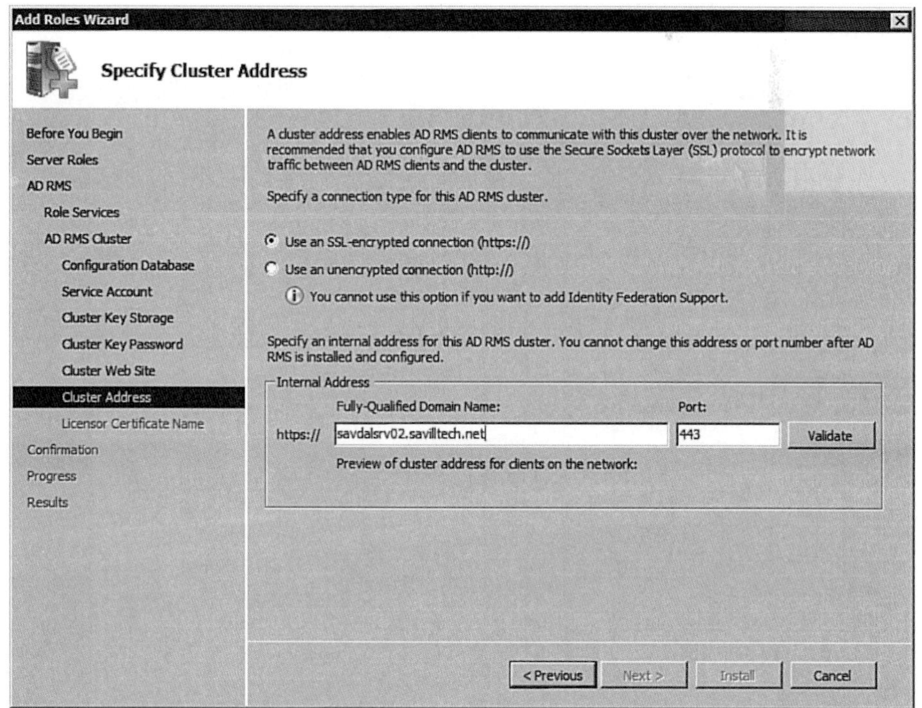

FIGURE 13-15 The configuration of the Web cluster address.

If you selected SSL, the next screen enables the configuration of the certificate. The best option is to use an existing certificate that is enterprise-trusted or a publicly trusted certificate authority. If a certificate is not available now, choose the certificate for SSL encryption later or use a self-signed certificate. Using a self-signed certificate is not a good solution and requires the certificate to be imported into each computer that communicates with the AD RMS server, but it is okay for testing environments. Enter a name for the certificate if a self-signed certificate is used.

The last question is whether to configure the AD RMS service to register an SCP. If you are logged on as an enterprise administrator, you can elect to create the SCP, which is a good idea and saves future work.

Installation of AD RMS commences. When it finishes, log out of the server and log on again to start administering and using RMS.

If you uninstall AD RMS from a server, information stored in the domain, such as the SCP, is not removed. You can manually view and remote this information via the ADSI Edit tool, by opening the Configuration partition and navigating to CN=RightsManagementServices,CN=Services,CN=Configuration, <domain>. As shown in Figure 13-16, the SCP information is present, and you can modify it if required (such as installing a new alternative SCP). However, managing the SCP via the AD RMS MMC snap-in is a better choice.

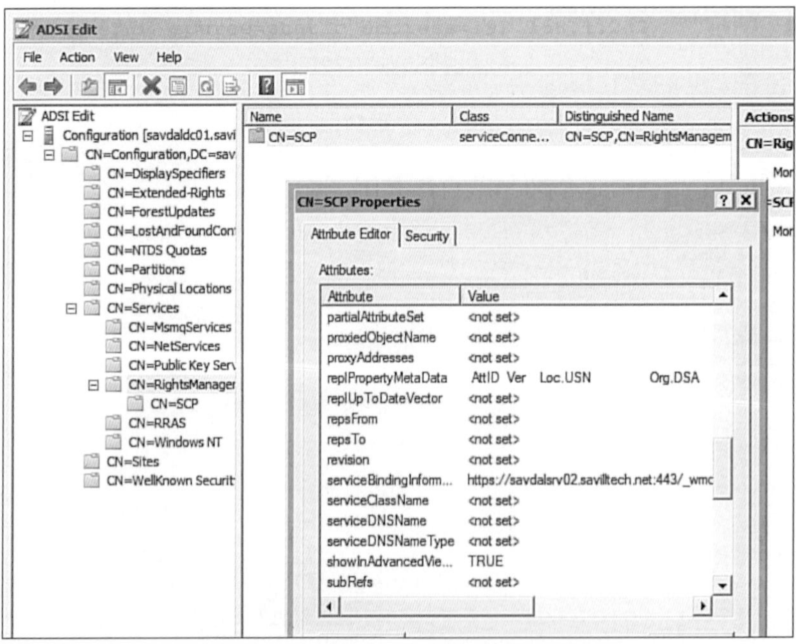

FIGURE 13-16 Manually viewing the information written by AD RMS installation and SCP registration.

Using AD RMS

If you chose to use a self-signed certificate, the first time you try to access the AD RMS, you see a warning that the security certificate was issued by an untrusted authority. You can ignore this error, but let's fix it.

Start a new MMC instance (Start, Run, MMC), add the Certificates snap-in, and when prompted select the option to Manage Certificates for the Computer Account on the Local Computer.

If you expand the Personal and Trusted Root Certification Authorities nodes, each has a Certificates child node. Under Personal, right-click the self-signed certificate generated during AD RMS installation and select Copy, as shown in Figure 13-17. Paste this in the Trusted Root Certification Authorities, Certificates store by right-clicking Certificates and selecting Paste.

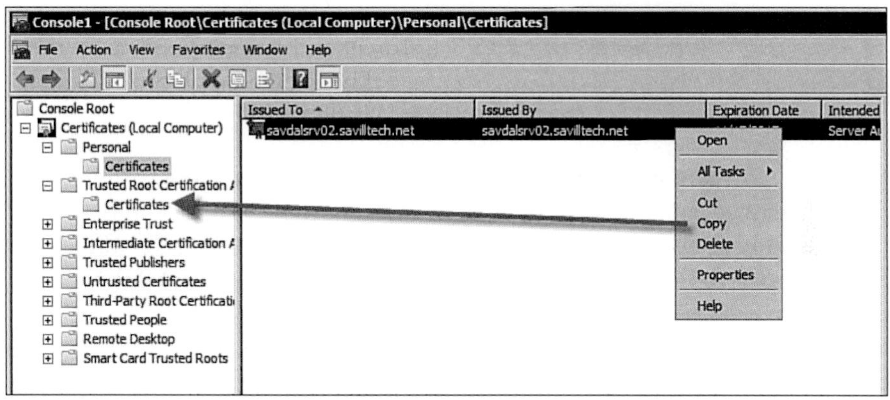

FIGURE 13-17 After copying the certificate, select the paste option from the context menu of the Trusted Root Certification Authority\Certificates.

While you are in the certificates store and because you chose to use a self-signed certificate, you need to import this into your AD RMS client computers. Refer to Chapter 9, "Terminal Services," for instructions on exporting and importing a certificate. Use the Certificates MMC snap-in with the computer account selected as you did in the last paragraph and import the certificate you copied from the RMS server. To export from the RMS server, select Export from the All Tasks menu and export the certificate to a file in DER encoded in binary X.509 (.CER) format. The private key does not need to be exported. Then import the certificate onto the clients by right-clicking the generated DER file and selecting Install

Certificate. Choose to install the certificate into the Trusted Root Certificate Authority store and not to let the import wizard decide where to place the certificate, as shown in Figure 13-18. You get a warning that the certificate cannot be validated. Click Yes to install the certificate anyway. After importing it, you can navigate to https://<server name> without certificate warnings.

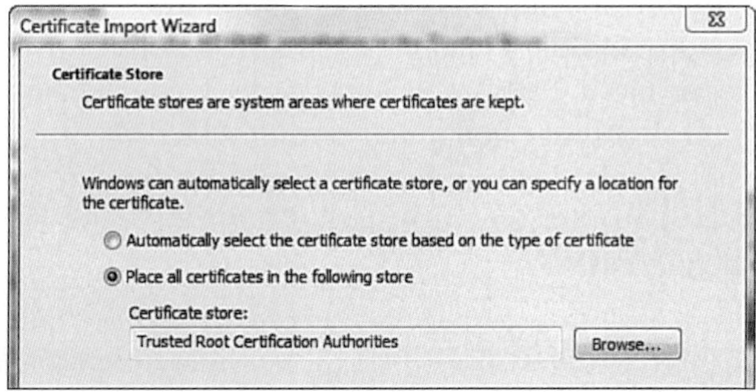

FIGURE 13-18 Importing the certificate into clients.

You can now launch the AD RMS management tool without any errors about certificates. As shown in Figure 13-19, you see the trusted user domains, which in this case is the Enterprise, and easily add support for Windows Live ID by clicking the Trust Windows Live ID link in the Actions pane. This is a fast way of giving access to nondomain users. However, external users still have to be able to communicate with the RMS server, which requires an externally facing name for the server and exceptions in the firewall. Clients do not communicate directly with the SQL server, so no exceptions are required for client-to-SQL communication.

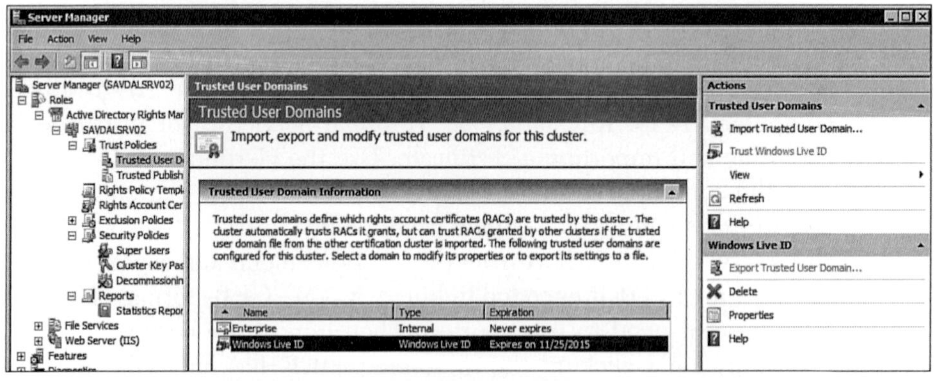

FIGURE 13-19 Quickly enabling Live ID integration but only for inside the organization.

Right-click the server to see the properties, which include the certificates used, URLs for access, and an SCP tab that enables you to modify the SCP you previously saw via ADSI Edit.

Restricting Access

The best way to see AD RMS is to restrict something, so let's restrict a Word 2007 document. There is an additional step here to avoid prompting users to enter credentials for the RMS server. Communication with AD RMS occurs over HyperText Transfer Protocol (HTTP) or HyperText Transfer Protocol over Secure Sockets Layer (HTTPS). To enable your logged on credentials to be passed automatically, you need the AD RMS URL added to your Local Intranet zone. From the IE Tools menu, select Internet Options. Select the Security tab and select the Local Intranet zone. Click the Sites button and click the Advanced button in the Local Intranet dialog. Add the URL of the AD RMS server, as shown in Figure 13-20, and click Add. Click Close and OK in all dialogs. If you don't want to perform this setting on all machines, use Group Policy to set the sites in the Local Intranet zone via the User Configuration, Policies, Windows Settings, Internet Explorer Maintenance, Security, Security Zones, and Content Ratings policy.

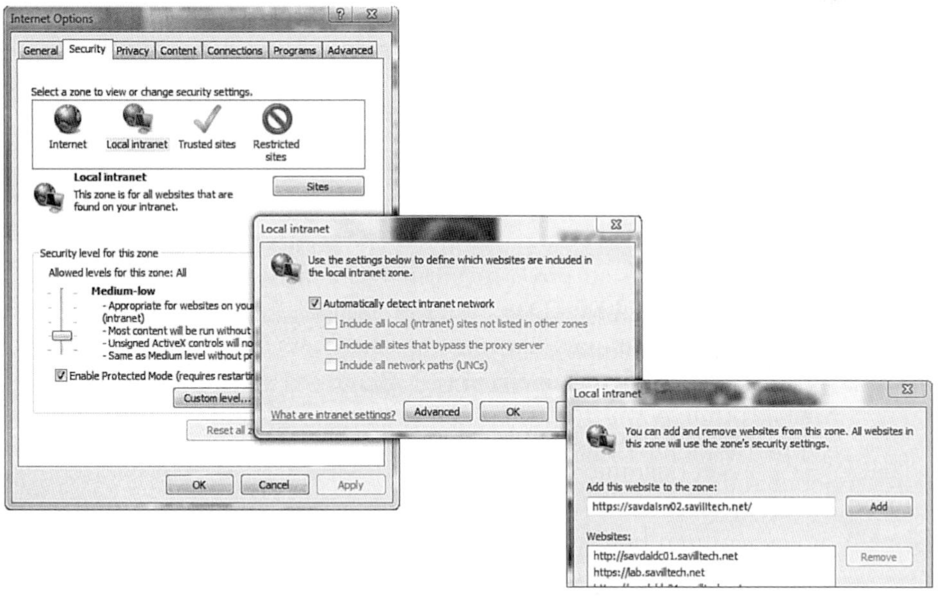

FIGURE 13-20 Adding the RMS server to the Local Intranet zone.

Start Word, and open and create a document on a Vista client or on XP with the RMS client installed. Access the restricted permissions via the Prepare, Restrict Permissions, Restricted Access menu item, as shown in Figure 13-21, which verifies your logon information with the RMS server.

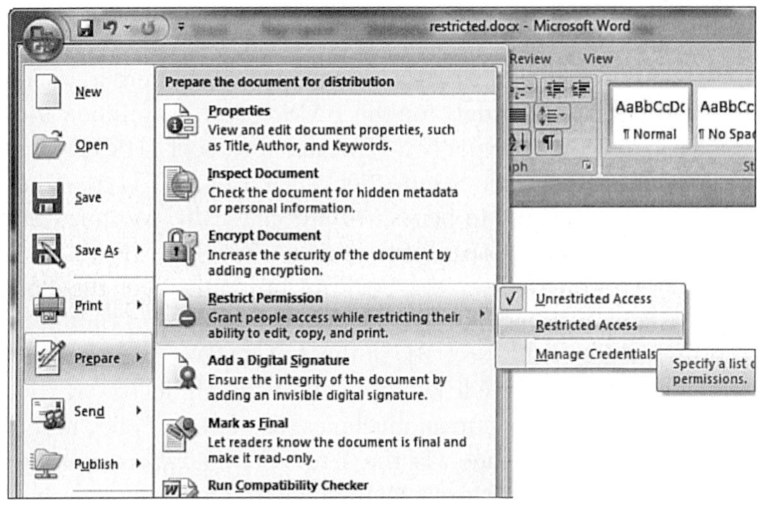

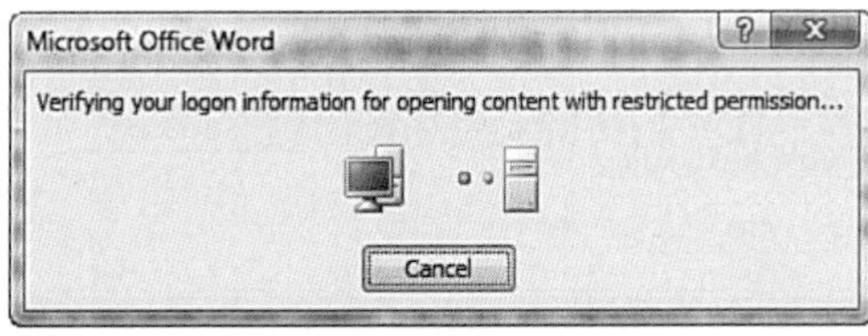

FIGURE 13-21 Restricting access with Word 2007 and RMS.

If you receive an error regarding your account or are prompted to select a Windows Live ID or other credential, go to the AD RMS server and look at the summary of events, which shows an error. If you see Event ID 139, it probably means the user account you are using does not have its Mail attribute populated, so set the Mail attribute and try again. Following is a partial dump of a log when the user does not have the Mail attribute populated:

```
Log Name:      Application
Source:        Active Directory Rights Management Services
Date:          11/18/2007 8:37:43 AM
```

```
Event ID:      139
Task Category: Certification
Level:         Error
Keywords:      Classic
User:          N/A
Computer:      savdalsrv02.savilltech.net
Description:
Active Directory Rights Management Services (AD RMS) failed to
query Active Directory Domain Services (AD DS).

Parameter Reference
Context: Pipeline[CertificationPipeline._GetPrincipalIdentifier]
RequestId: {d322adef-c5d8-46c5-8cf9-962253b0e557}.6:1
principal: id=S-1-5-21-1659785588-4139460291-2490238386-1110
desiredIdentifier: primarymail
result: null

Microsoft.DigitalRightsManagement.Utilities.ADEntrySearch-
FailedException
        Message: Failed to find an entry in the Active Direc-
tory: id=S-1-5-21-1659785588-4139460291-2490238386-1110.
        Context: CertificationPipeline._GetPrincipalIdentifier
        principal: id=S-1-5-21-1659785588-4139460291-
2490238386-1110
        desiredIdentifier: primarymail
        result: null
```

If the user has the Mail attribute populated, a dialog displays, as shown in Figure 13-22, that enables you to restrict the document. By default, enter the e-mail addresses for those who should have Read and Change permissions. However, clicking the More Options button enables you to place an expiry on the document, as well as to give users the ability to print the content, to grant permission for users with Read access to be able to copy content from it, and to access the content programmatically. There are also options for users to contact the owner to get more permissions and to require a connection each time the document is opened. By default, the UL is cached, and after the user has access, she can continue to open the document. By requiring a connection each time the document is opened, you can increase the security on the document. By default, as the owner setting the permissions, you have Full Control over the document.

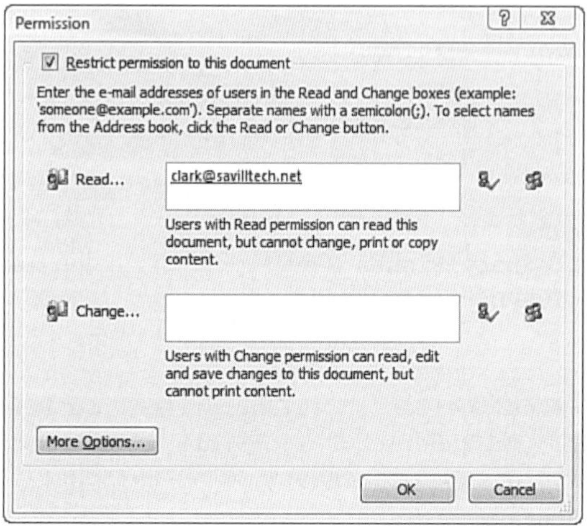

FIGURE 13-22 Restricting access to a document.

After the permissions are set, you can let someone else try to open the document. The reader is notified that the document is restricted and asked to confirm it is okay for the application (such as Word) to communicate with the RMS server, to which the user needs to click OK. Also present on the dialog is an option not to display the prompt to connect again, which is a good idea.

If the user has permissions on the file, the document opens with the UL applied. For example, it may be opened in a read-only mode, and cut and paste may be disabled. The exact restrictions for the user display at the top of the dialog, where a bar highlights Restricted Access. The user can click View Permissions to see exactly what his abilities are, as shown in Figure 13-23. All the options around cut, copy, and formatting are grayed out because the user has no permissions to do any of these. The main menu also has options concerning save disabling. However, the user can print the document because you granted that permission.

If you try to access the protected document from an account that does not have permissions, you receive notification you don't have permission and are asked whether you want to request permission. You can also opt to change the user, as shown in Figure 13-24.

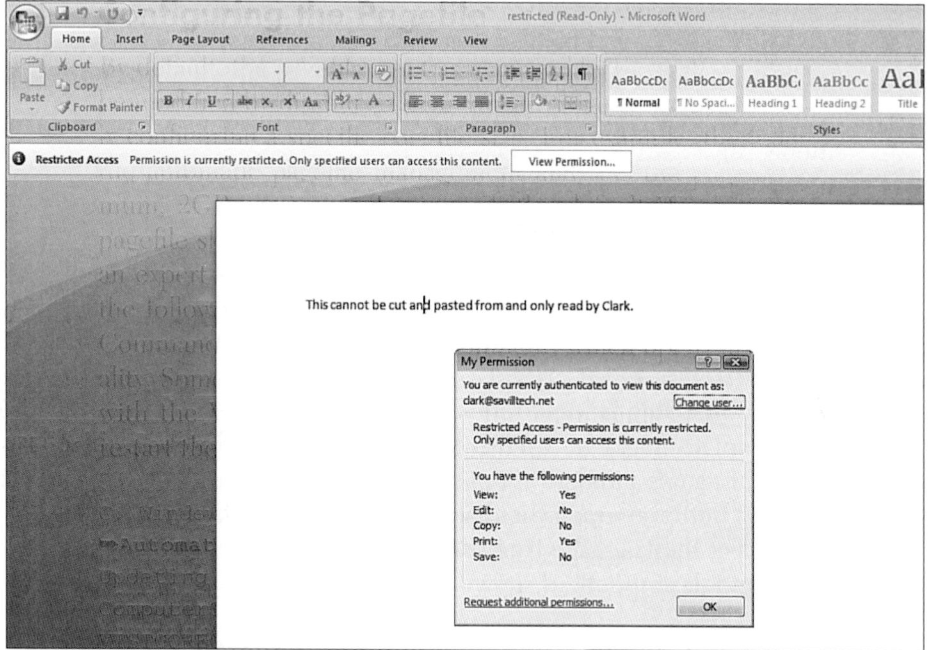

FIGURE 13-23 Not many permissions for Clark.

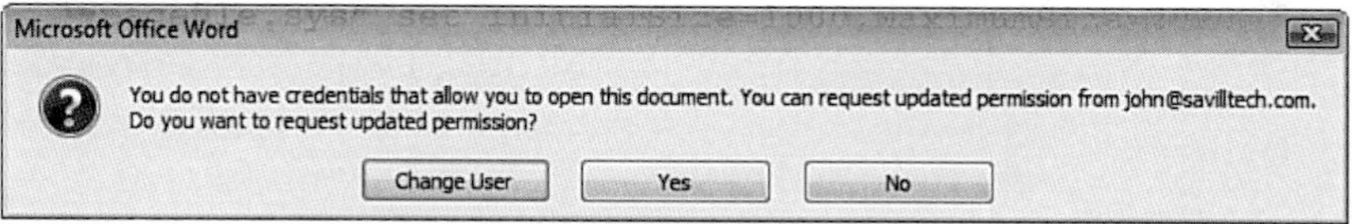

FIGURE 13-24 No access for Barry.

That is all there is to using RMS for the user. It's easy to use and powerful. There are additional capabilities. For example, with the latest version of SharePoint, you can set rights management permissions on a SharePoint library that enforces certain restrictions for any documents contained in the library.

Template Creation

While protecting your document, you had the option to enable Restricted Access and then set the various restriction options. Instead of having to set these options each time, it is possible to create a number of templates. For example, you could create a template to automatically give a group read only permissions or a quick option to disable Reply All for mail messages, which would be useful if you work in a company where everyone loves to Reply All.

Creating a New Template

To create a new template, navigate to the Rights Policy Templates node of the AD RMS server with the AD RMS snap-in. There is a link in the Actions pane to Create Distributed Rights Policy Template; click it to start the Add Template Wizard.

The first step is to add identifications for the new template. Because the template might be used by clients running different languages, give different names and descriptions based on the language of the client. Click the Add button to open the dialog for selection of the language and naming. Select the language from the Language drop-down list and provide a name and description, as shown in Figure 13-25.

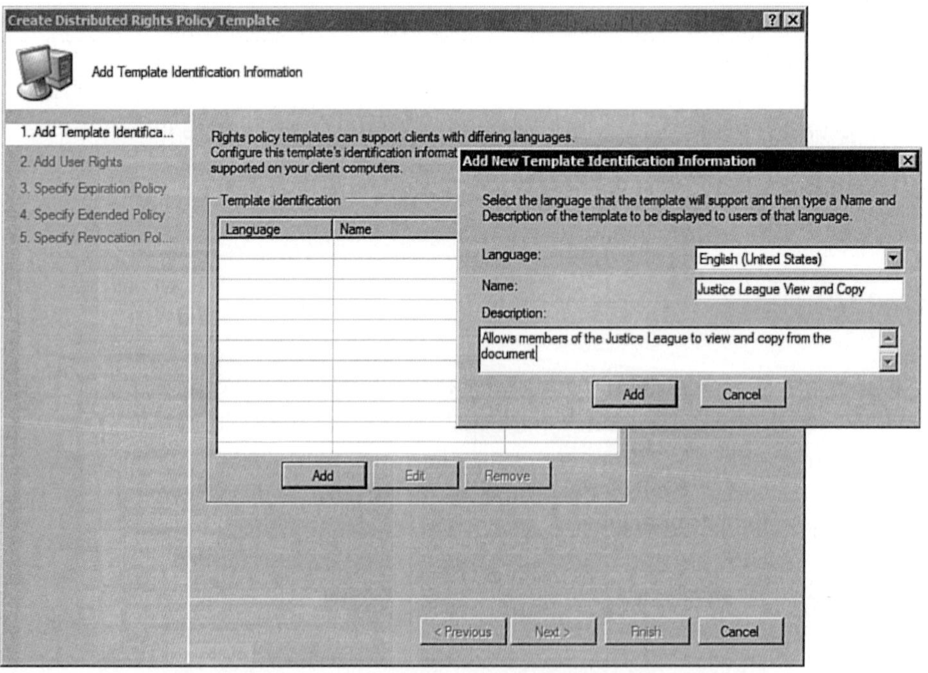

FIGURE 13-25 Specifying the template identification for the English language.

After adding all the languages that need access to the template, click Next to enable configuration of the actual rights that are configured for the template. Click the Add button to add the users or groups who have restricted access, as shown in Figure 13-26. You can browse for users and groups or just enter the user or group e-mail address. The Anyone option is a special group that gives any RMS user the access specified. You can also create custom rights, which are just text strings. These must mean something to the application consuming the RMS settings.

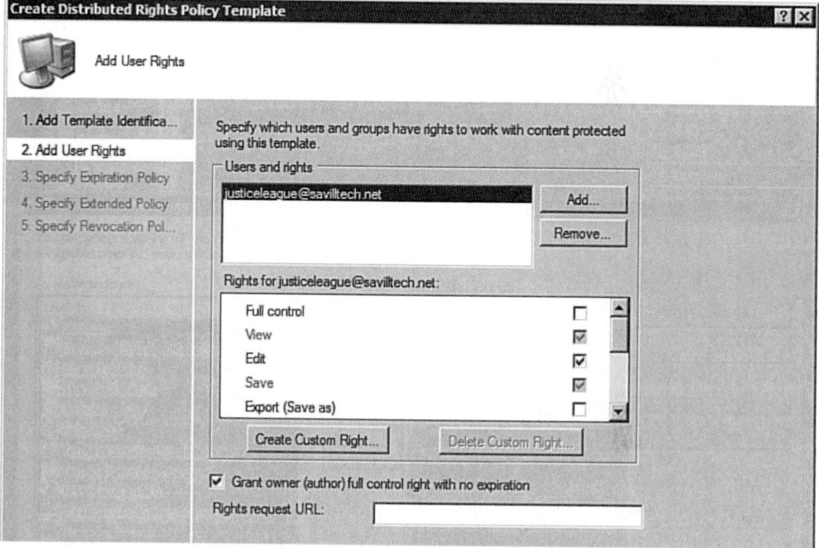

FIGURE 13-26 Specifying the permissions.

Table 13-1 shows the full permissions.

Table 13-1 Rights for an RMS-Protected Document

Right	Description
Full Control	Gives the user every right listed here, and the right to make changes to permissions associated with content. Expiration does not apply to users with Full Control.
View	Allows the user to open IRM content. This corresponds to Read Access in the Office user interface.

continues

Table 13-1 Rights for an RMS-Protected Document *(continued)*

Right	Description
Edit	Allows the user to edit the IRM content.
Save	Allows the user to save a file.
Extract	Allows the user to make a copy of any portion of a file and paste that portion of the file into the work area of another application.
Export	Allows the user to save content in another location or format that may or may not support IRM.
Print	Allows the user to print the contents of a file.
Allow Macros	Allows the user to run macros against the contents of a file.
Forward	Allows e-mail recipients to forward an IRM e-mail message.
Reply	Allows e-mail recipients to reply to an IRM e-mail message.
Reply All	Allows e-mail recipients to reply to all users on the To: and Cc: lines of an IRM e-mail message.
View Rights	Gives the user permission to view the rights associated with a file. Office ignores this right.

Click Next to set other options in the template such as expiration options in terms of the whole document or just the Use License, extended policy items that force a new Use License each time the content is consumed, and revocation options. However, for now click Finish because you are setting only permissions.

Edit templates by selecting the template and selecting Properties from the action or context menu. All the dialogs displayed during the creation of the template are available as tabs in the Properties dialog. You can change permissions, add languages, and make any other changes. You can also copy templates to create new templates based on existing template settings.

An Archived Rights Policy Template option is for templates not used at a point in time. For example, some templates are required at only certain times of the year (for example, year end options). When the template is not needed, move it to the Archived Rights Managements Templates area via the Archive This Rights Policy Template option. Likewise, you might want to create a template in advance of its actual deployment. Create it into the Archived Rights Policy Template area and then move it into the Distributed Rights Policy Template area when ready for roll out via the Distribute This Rights Policy Template action.

Enabling Clients to Use Templates

Creating the actual templates is easy. However, you also need to distribute the templates to the client's computers. The templates' current file location is Not Set, which means you have no way of getting the templates to the clients.

First create a share on the network to store the templates. This share needs to be readable by anyone in the organization who uses RMS and writeable by the RMS service account (for example, ADRMS_SVC). After you create this share, make a note of its Universal Naming Convention (UNC); for example, \\savdalsrv02.savilltech.net\templates.

To tell RMS to use this template location, right-click the Rights Policy Templates node and select Properties. In the dialog, check the Enable Export option and enter the UNC of the share created, as shown in Figure 13-27.

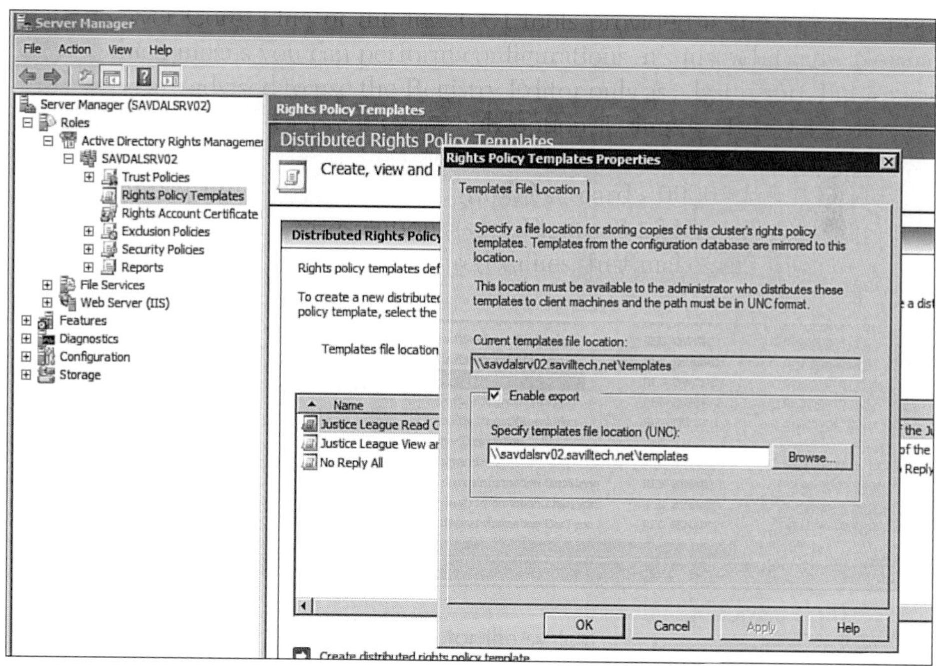

Figure 13-27 Specifying the export location.

Browse the specified folder when the export finishes to see a number of eXtensible Markup Language (XML) documents that detail the RMS templates you created.

The last step is telling the RMS clients how to find the templates. You can use Group Policy, which requires you to download the Office 2007 templates from http://go.microsoft.com/fwlink/?LinkId=80639 and import the Office12.adm into a group policy. The other option is to copy the office12.admx and its adml into the PolicyDefinitions folder of the client editing the group policy, and then set the Specify Permission Policy Path under the Manage Restricted Permissions area setting to that of the template UNC, as shown in Figure 13-28.

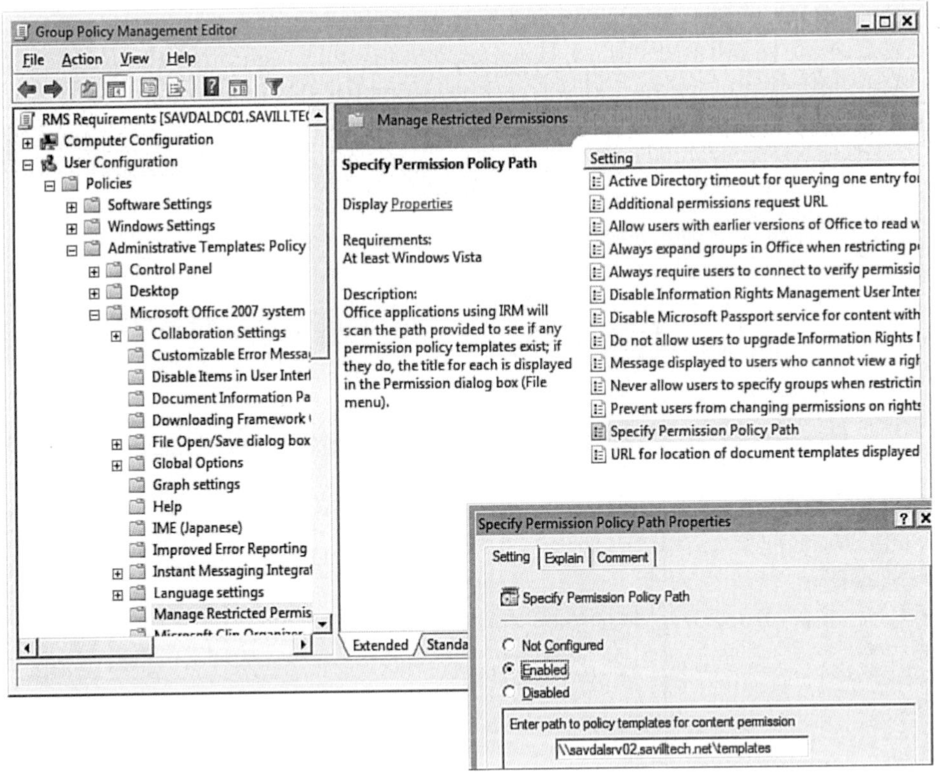

FIGURE 13-28 Configuring the locations for the RMS templates.

When set with the Group Policy update, the policy on the client (gpupdate) and the new templates are available. You can check the application by viewing the Registry value AdminTemplatePath at HKEY_CURRENT_USER\Software\Policies\Microsoft\Office\12.0\Common\DRM. You can manually set this value to the correct location if you don't want to use Group

Policy by editing the AdminTemplatePath value at location DRMHKEY_CURRENT_USER\Software\Microsoft\Office\12.0\Common\DRM. (Note it's not part of the policy path.)

Word must be restarted and the templates become usable, as shown in Figure 13-29. When a policy is applied, the name of the policy and its description are shown in the restricted permissions bar within the application, as shown in Figure 13-30.

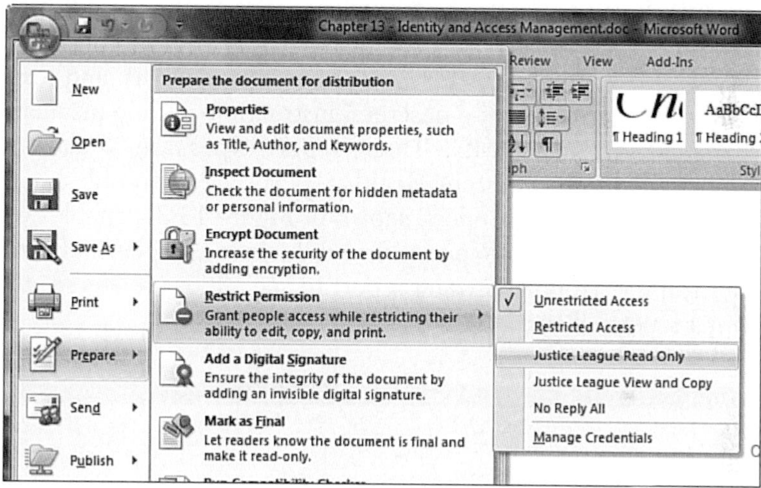

FIGURE 13-29 Using templates is far easier than manually configuring permissions each time.

FIGURE 13-30 Information bar showing the name and description of the template.

Licensing for AD RMS

Although AD RMS is part of the Windows Server 2008 product, in the same way users need Client Access Licenses (CALs) to use certain services of the operating system, a separate CAL is required for users of RMS. Any user, either internal or external, must have an RMS CAL. If you use federated services to allow users from other organizations to access RMS-protected content, those external users need RMS CALs.

NOTE For more detailed information on licensing, see www.microsoft.com/windowsserver2003/techinfo/overview/rmsoverview.

Reporting

When you select the Reports node of the AD RMS, you might notice that by default you only see a high-level statistics report and a link to download the ReportViewer control, a redistributable package available from the Microsoft web site. After you have downloaded and executed the ReportViewer, follow the onscreen instructions. When installation is complete, restart the MMC. Three report types are available: the basic Statistics report, a System Health report, and a Troubleshooting report. The Troubleshooting report, shown in Figure 13-31, enables you to select a user and a time range and is useful if a user complains of problems. You can run the Troubleshooting report to see all logs related to that user. To run a report, click the View Report action link.

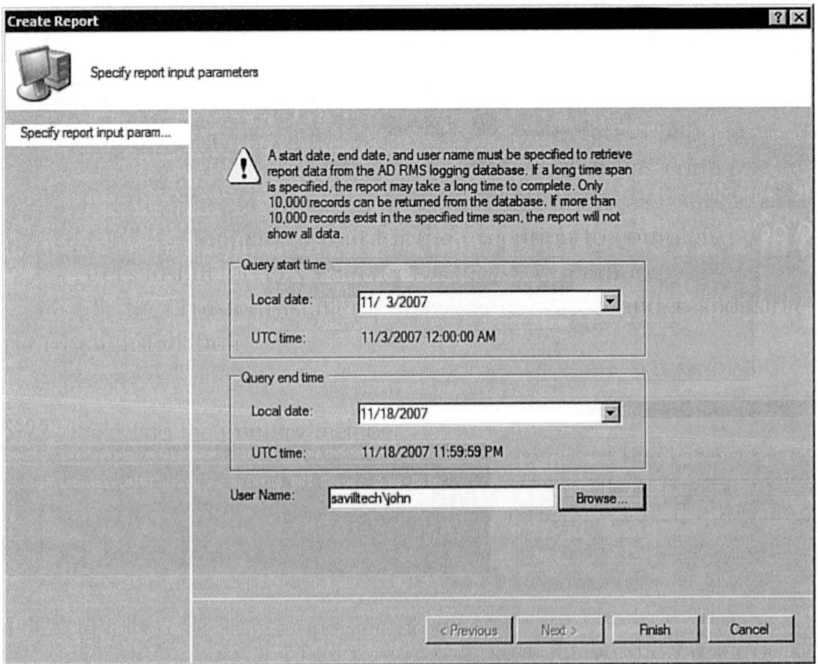

FIGURE 13-31 Running a report for a user between times.

After viewing the report, you see a summary of counts for the number of Certify, Find Service Locations for User, and Get Client Licensor Certificate requests. Each of the options can then be selected to get more detail, and that more detailed report can provide full detail if you choose each item as shown in Figure 13-32.

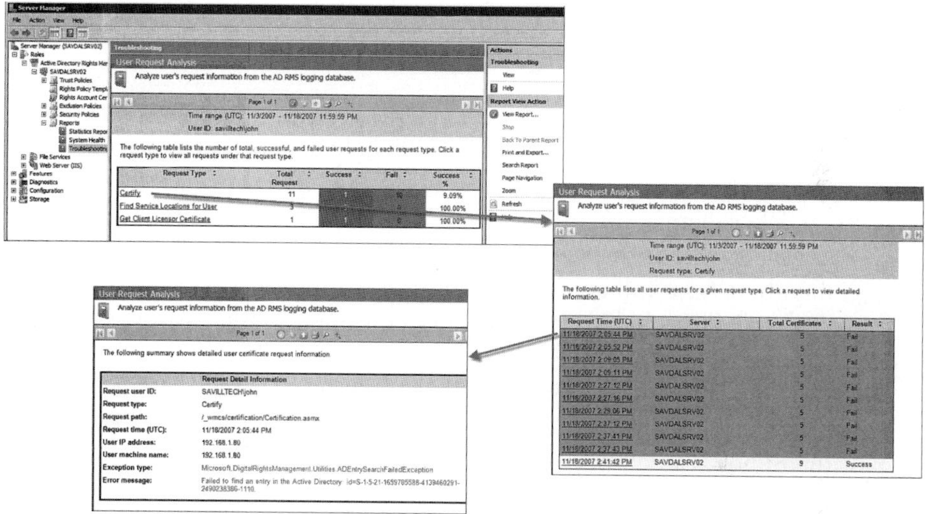

Figure 13-32 The reports visible for troubleshooting.

The System Health report works in the same way as the Troubleshooting report except that you select a time range. The report produces a report of the types of requests during that period. As in the Troubleshooting report, you can drill down into it.

High Availability

If AD RMS is heavily used in your environment, ensure that AD RMS is highly available because users cannot view protected materials without access to the AD RMS infrastructure. Because users have the CRC for offline protecting of documents, they can continue to protect documents with the RMS infrastructure offline.

The SQL database is a vital component that you must back up. It exists in SQL as three separate databases: DRMS_Config_rmsxx_80, DRMS_DirectoryServices_rmsxx_80, and DRMS_Logging_rms01_80. As a best practice, ensure that the transaction logs for SQL are on a separate disk from the database.

In the event of a server failure, reinstall the server using the same server name and RMS options. In the event of a corrupt database, restore the database backup and restore the transaction logs. If you have problems adding the new server, it is because it is detecting the ServiceConnectionPoint in AD. Manually delete that via ADSI Edit, as you saw earlier in this chapter.

Advanced Features

AD RMS is far more powerful than 20 pages can cover. Read through the help on RMS in Windows Server 2008 help center that is part of the product. However, let's briefly look at other capabilities of the RMS.

What happens if someone leaves the company and protected all his documents? You have the option to create a Super Users group whose members have full control over all rights-protected material. This is obviously not desirable under normal circumstances. Rights-protected material should be visible only to its owner and those who have been given access to it. By default, the Super Users group is disabled and has no group assigned. If you find the need to view protected materials, you can enable the Super Users group and assign a universal group whose members have the full privileges to access protected content. If you do, enable the Super Users group via Security Policies, Super Users, and turn off the Super Users group when you finish retrieving the required information.

By default, anyone can use the RMS environment. However, you can add exclusions to block certain users, certain versions of Windows, certain applications, and certain versions of the RMS client via the Exclusion Policies tab of the RMS MMC snap-in. For example, a vulnerability in a version of RMS might have been found, so you can choose to block clients not running an updated version.

The final item for discussion is a licensing-only RMS cluster. You can add it as a subordinate to a root cluster, which can only give out licenses. The reason for using a separate licensing-only cluster is primarily to isolate different departments within an organization. A department could be allocated to a separate licensing-only RMS cluster, which would then have its own rights templates, separate Super Users groups, separate logging, and separate exclusion policies.

As you have seen, AD RMS is an attractive technology for applications that have RMS support. Today, that is primarily the Microsoft office suite, but this will expand in the future. As you increase the usage of RMS in your organization, ensure that you scale your RMS infrastructure accordingly with additional RMS servers in the RMS cluster.

Microsoft has step-by-step guides for configuring RMS in an extranet environment and another for integrating RMS with SharePoint available on Microsoft.com. Follow them if you use RMS in these environments.

Active Directory Federated Services

AD FS was introduced in Windows Server 2003 R2 as a way to allow credentials from partner domains to be used on Web-based applications within your organization. For example, user Bob at widgets.com can be granted specific permissions on a Web-based application at SavillTech. Why would you even want this? Imagine your typical users. Those users, in their day-to-day job, might have to access 20 different web sites—each one hosted by a different organization. One could be a site someone uses to buy a component that your company needs to make its product. There might be another site used to upload inventory. Every one of these sites is authenticated, so your user could potentially have 20 different sets of credentials to remember. There are multiple problems with this.

First, the users have to remember 20 sets of credentials, which means they either write them down, a potential security risk, or they don't write them down, forget passwords for various sites, and cause the administrative teams at the partner organizations effort in resetting. Second, if a user leaves your company, for whatever reason, the user still has 20 active accounts at your partners. That's 20 phone calls, asking for access to be terminated with various delays and problems that occur.

A far better solution would be for all your partner web sites to grant the users access based on their AD accounts in your organization. That means only one account for each user to remember and only one account for you to disable when a user leaves.

To facilitate this, create a special type of trust relationship between the organizations to allow secure tokens that describe information about the user to be passed by a client. The token is signed in such a way that the receiving organization knows it is valid and comes from the user's trusted organization. You are enabling cross forest single sign-on, and you can use either ADDS or AD LDS Services as the source of the accounts that the Web application uses for authentication and authorization. AD FS is not an account repository; it is only a method to extend the reach of an existing account store.

This is not like a normal trust in which domain controllers from each domain communicate with each other and can browse the security directory. With a federation trust, the two organizations never communicate directly; all authentication and validation uses Web protocols and redirections, as you will see when you walk through it. You are extending the visibility of your accounts in a controlled manner. Your partner organizations cannot see any information you don't explicitly allow as part of the token content, and the partner organization cannot directly ask for information in any way.

The actual communication between the client and the Web application and the AD FS servers is via HTTPS, so only port 443 needs to be opened between the client who uses AD FS to gain access to a web site and the AD FS front end services.

Although AD FS was present in Windows 2003 R2, there are changes in the Windows Server 2008 implementation. Along with now being a role in Windows Server 2008, which means all the other requirements for AD FS are automatically installed, the Windows Server 2008 AD FS has a much simpler process for establishing the federated trusts with other organizations. Previously there were many steps and configurations involved that were often done incorrectly causing problems. Now a simple import and export process is performed, circumventing most issues.

There is also another neat feature with Windows Server 2008. Previously, only specially written Web applications that could consume the AD FS–generated tokens could take advantage of the federated trusts between organizations. However, with Windows Server 2008, both Microsoft Office SharePoint Server 2007 and AD RMS have tight integration with AD FS, allowing credentials from trusted organizations to access resources.

AD FS Components

There are three components to AD FS that are described in this section: the Federation Service (FS), the Federation Service Proxy (FS-P), and the Web Server SSO Agent. AD is not discussed here, but it is also important as the source of the user objects that contain the attributes used to populate the claim tokens.

The FS is a token-granting service facilitated by the Security Token Service (STS), which populates the claims in the security tokens. The FS also maintains the federation trusts with other organizations. One or more federated servers that share a common trust policy host the FS; that is, all the AD FS servers know of the same federated trusts. The FS is the brains behind AD FS.

The FS-P acts as a proxy for the FS, which can be placed in a perimeter network such as a DMZ. The FS-P communicates with Web clients via the WS-Federation Passive Requestor Profile (WS-F PRP) protocols over HTTPS and then forwards requests to FSs hosted safely in the internal network. When the FS generates the required tokens, the FS-P communicates the token back to the requesting client. An FS-P is not mandatory; clients can communicate directly to the FS. The FS-P and FS cannot be installed on the same server.

The final component is the Web Server SSO Agent. Web applications use it to query the AD FS security token claims. An alternative version exists that can use Windows NT tokens. Web applications must be specially developed to use the AD FS claims.

Let's focus on claims. The FS can have a list of mappings for each federated trust it maintains that it uses to decide which information to place in the token based on the user attributes requesting access or any other criteria. For example, a federated trust with a supplier of components probably cares only about how much a user has authorization to spend. You can therefore configure the FS to populate a spending cap, based on the grade of the user, in the token it creates to send to the supplier company. For example, if the AD says the user is a Manager, it could populate a token with a spending cap of $50,000. If it sees the user is a Director, it could populate the token with a spending cap of $100,000. The FS digitally signs the token with a key that the two organizations agree on. When the AD FS in the partner company receives it, it knows the token is from the user's organization and trusts the claims. Think of a claim as a statement made by the users' organization about the user for the trusting organization's consumption. There are three types of information in a claim: identity of the user by UPN, e-mail or common name; group memberships; and custom attributes. A good write-up on claims is at http://technet2.microsoft.com/windowsserver/en/library/a4ed50a7-dbbc-4d01-898f-f90de19b82531033.mspx?mfr=true.

AD FS in Action

The easiest way to understand AD FS is to step through the process. Figure 13-33 presents a complete AD FS flow. When the user is redirected, that user's Web browser is redirected to another URL. This communication is Web-browser-based and forwards the user around different servers.

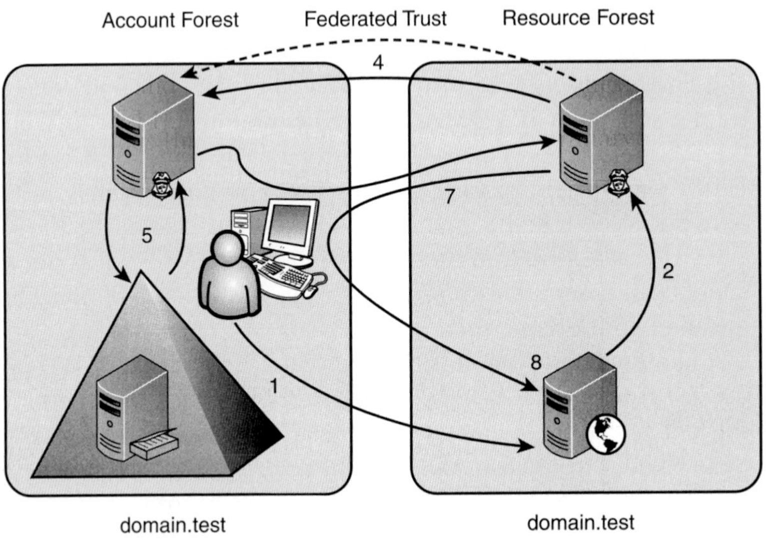

Figure 13-33 ADFS in action.

Let's unpack this:

1. The user in the account forest tries to access a Web server in another organization's forest connected to the account forest via a federated trust. The AD FS Web agent on the Web server checks for a security token for the user, which at this point does not exist.
2. Because the user has no security token, no access is given to the application, and the user is redirected to the federation server in the resource forest.
3. The resource forest federation server performs a home realm discovery in which the server ascertains the home forest of the user by prompting the user via a Web page that by default displays in a drop-down fashion all the forests trusted by the federation server. Or it does so by inspecting a persistent cookie if it exists; it is placed on the client by the resource federated server after the first communication to save future requests from being prompted for a home realm.
4. After identifying the home forest of the requesting user, the resource federation server redirects the user to the user's local federation server to continue processing.
5. Authentication then takes place with the user's local FS, which in turn authenticates via the AD and pulls information from the AD

pertinent to the token it will create for transmission to the resource forest currently attempting access. (Different information might be designated for the different resource forests trusting the account federation.)

6. The local federation server then issues the client a token specifically for the resource forest and redirects the user back to the federation server in the resource forest.
7. The resource federation server checks the passed token and confirms it is digitally signed with the correct certificate, creates its own local token for the user to use when communicating with the Web application, and then redirects the user to the Web application server. This might remind you of referral tickets in a multiple domain forest; it works in a similar fashion.
8. The Web application then checks the passed token. This is a Security Assertions Markup Language (SAML) token, version 1.1 format, which is an industry standard format enabling maximum support from different Web applications. The Web application reads the SAML token and allows authorization to the application and its content dependent on the access limitations specified in the token.

In essence, the user asks for access to a partner site, but the user has no permissions, so the web site passes the user to a federation server in its forest. The federation server has no clue what to do with the user, so it forwards the user back to a federation server in the user's home forest. The federation server checks out the user and provides a token to give to the resource federated server that it trusts and that the resource federated server trusts. It then gives the user a local token to talk to the Web server based on the content of the user's token from his home FSs. The user finally gets to see the requested Web page (assuming that the tokens gave permission).

Installing AD FS

One of the big pluses with Windows Server 2008 AD FS is that it's easier to install and easier to establish trusts than it was with Windows Server 2003. Let's walk through this process.

In a normal live environment, you probably have the AD FS service running on dedicated servers that are not domain controllers, with separate servers running FS-P. However, in this example, you run the FS and can install it on a domain controller.

If you are performing this installation in a test environment, your test Internet Explorer client has to be able to resolve the names of the resource forest. So, create a conditional forwarder in DNS for the zone name of the resource forest pointing to a DNS server in that resource forest.

The first item is to secure the certificates you will be using for the SSL encryption for each organization. Although you can generate a self-signed certificate and then copy it into the trusted root certification area of the involved computers in AD FS, doing so is practical only in a lab environment. In a production environment, you must be using trusted certification authority certificates for your servers. These SSL certificates should be associated with the default web sites on the FS in both organizations and on the Web server in the resource forest. Additionally, token signing certificates are also required, one for each FS.

To install AD FS, use Server Manager to add the AD FS role. In the Role Services list, select only the FS, as shown in Figure 13-34, on the FSs in both organizations. You also receive a prompt to install the Web Server (IIS) role if it is not already installed on the server.

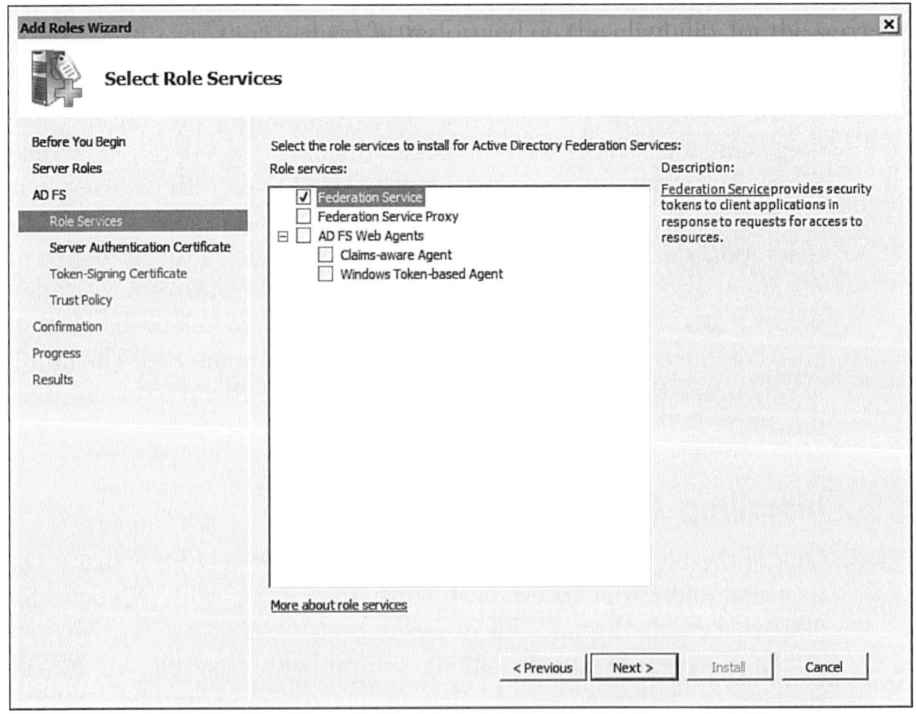

FIGURE 13-34 Installing the FS.

The next phase of the FS installation is the selection of the certificate to use for the SSL encryption used for communication between the FS and clients. A certificate installed on the server can be selected, or you can create a self-signed certificate by selecting the Create a Self-Signed Certificate for SSL Encryption option and clicking Next. The next dialog enables the selection of the certificate to use for the token signing. Again, a certificate can be selected or self-signed.

The last configuration item is to select the trust policy. By default a new trust policy is created to the C:\Windows\systemdata\adfs\trustpolicy.xml file. However, an existing policy can be opened if one exists within the organization. The policy defines the parameters that the FS uses. If multiple federated services are configured to use the same policy file by placing it in a shared folder, and each server has the public key of all the other FS servers, the FSs form a farm. If this is a new installation, select a new trust policy. Finally, click Install to complete the FS installation.

After the FS is installed on the federated services in each organization, the default web site on the servers will also have been modified to support HTTPS and bound to the certificate specified during the FS installation. If you selected self-signed certificates, export the certificates to files on both federated servers, both the server authentication (SSL) and the token-signing certificates. Then import the SSL certificate from the resource forest into the trusted root certification authorities on the Web servers in the resource forest.

You must also configure the web site to use SSL using a trusted certificate or self-signed certificate. Export the certificate and import it on any clients that communicate with the server. On the Web server, install the relevant AD FS Web agent, either claims-aware or the Windows token–based agent. This depends on the Web application that uses FS. In this case you are using a claims-based application, so the claims-aware agent is installed (see Figure 13-35).

For the client, you need to import the SSL certificates from all three servers on to any clients if the certificates were not generated by a trusted root authority into the Trusted Root Certificate Authorities container. The next step is to create the federation trust. After the FS is installed, a new snap-in is available, the AD FS snap-in, which is used in the FS Management.

The first step in creating the federation trust is to configure the federation properties in each organization. On each federation server, right-click the Trust Policy navigation node item and select Properties. The FS uniform resource identifier (URI) is a unique name for the federation realm that identifies the federation. It can be an HTTP URL, a uniform resource name (URN) as shown in Figure 13-36, or any format you choose. Notice the FS endpoint URL, which is the location that the Web-based clients connect to for FSs.

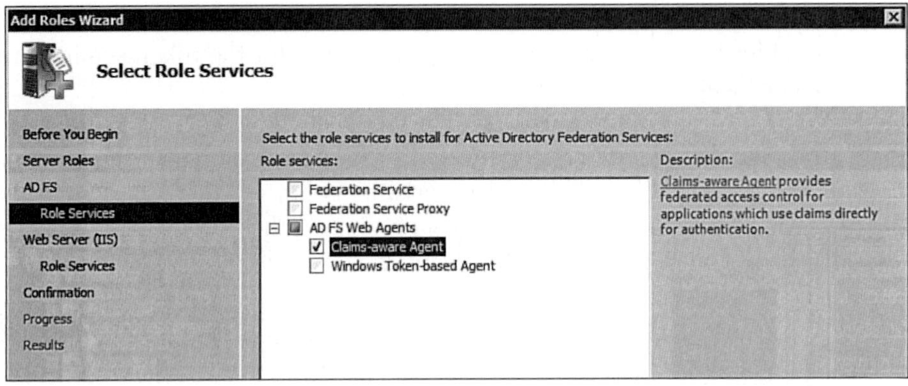

FIGURE 13-35 In this case, you install the claims-aware agent.

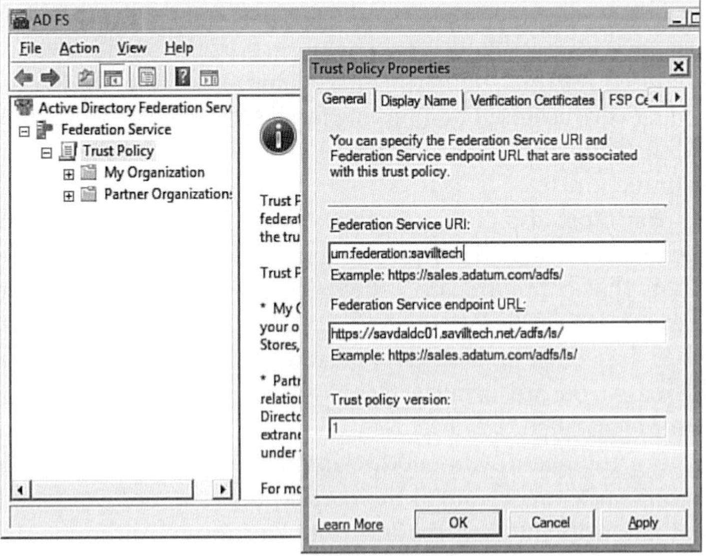

FIGURE 13-36 Specifying the local federation details.

Click the Display Name tab and change from the fully qualified domain name (FQDN) of the server to the organization name, and then click OK.

The next step is to create an Organization Claim in the account forest. Expand the My Organization node, right-click Organization Claims, and select New, Organization Claim. The claim name should relate to the application that consumes the claim in the partner resource forest. For example, you are connecting to the Microsoft ClaimApp in the Widget forest, so name the claim Widget ClaimApp Claim. Make sure the claim type is Group Claim, and click OK, as shown in Figure 13-37.

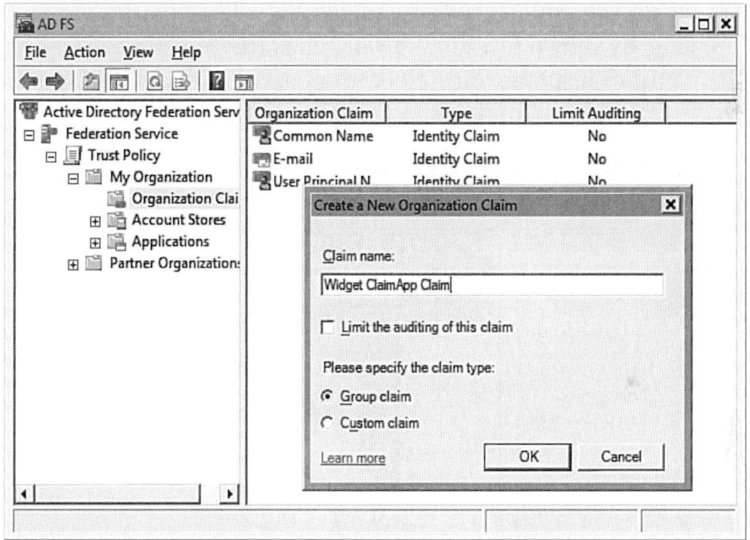

FIGURE 13-37 Creating a new claim.

Now tell the FS which account repository to use; remember you can use ADDS or an AD LDS instance. Even if you install the FS on a domain controller, you still need to configure the account store to use. Right-click the Account Stores navigation node item and select New, Account Store to launch the Add Account Store Wizard. The option to add an AD DS or AD LDS is available, although you can have only one AD DS account store association per FS. If you select an AD LDS, you must enter the name of the AD LDS and then the LDAP path to the AD LDS instance. If you select AD DS, the local forest is used and no configuration is required. Just leave checked the default option, Enable This Account Store.

You must perform all three preceding steps on both federations. Even though you might be accessing services in only one federation, you have to map an organization claim name from one federation to the other. So, modifying the trust policy properties, adding an organization claim, and specifying the account store are complete in both federations.

You now need to map an AD DS global group to the claim you have created on the account federation forest. You should create a group using the AD Users and Computers MMC snap-in and populate it with the users who have access to the Web application in the resource forest. To map the global group to the claim, right-click the AD or AD LDS instance you added to Account Stores and select New, Group Claim Extraction. After opening, as shown in Figure 13-38, click the Add button to browse the AD or AD LDS instance and select users and groups that link to the claim.

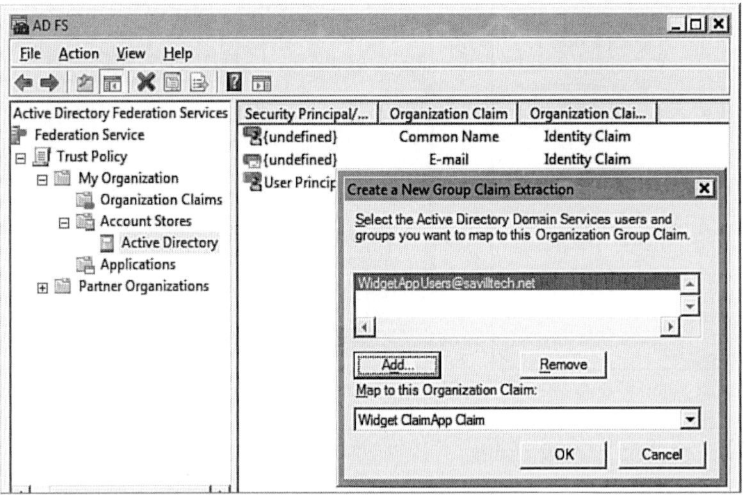

FIGURE 13-38 Mapping a group to an organizational claim.

The next phase is to configure the federation on the resource side as to who has the application that needs to be accessed. You already configured the federation server on the resource side with a unique URI and name. The next step is to add the claims-aware application.

A sample application is installed that displays the claim information provided by Microsoft. You could also use SharePoint 2007 or Windows Server 2008 AD RMS, both of which are documented by Microsoft with step-by-step guides. Microsoft makes this demo available as part of its AD FS walkthrough.

Right-click the Applications navigation node and select New, Application. For the application type, select Claims-Aware Application, and then on the next screen, enter a name for the application and the URL, as shown in Figure 13-39. You *must* have a trailing slash on the application URL or the federation server does not match the application. For instance, https://widgetweb01.widget.local/claimapp does not work. It must be https://widgetweb01.widget.local/claimapp/. The next screen enables configuration of the types of identity to accept; for example, User Principal Name (UPN), E-mail, or Common Name. The selections depend on the application consuming the tokens. Ensure that the Enable Application option is checked and click Finish.

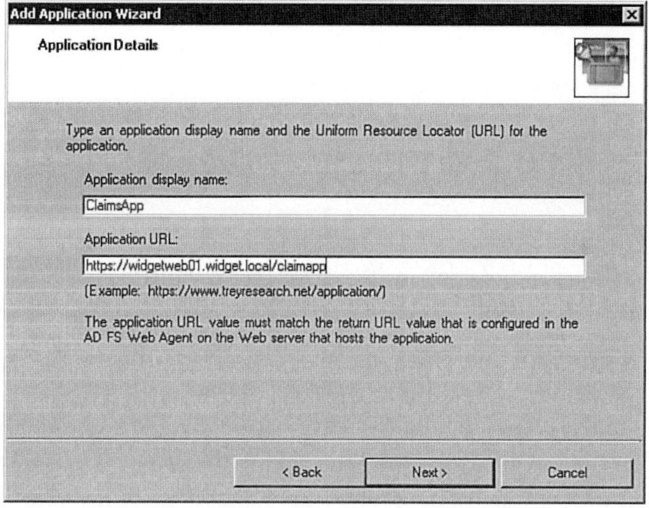

FIGURE 13-39 Adding a claims application to AD FS—don't forget to add the trailing slash.

You are now ready to link the two federations. The first step is to export the basic settings from one side of the forest. On the account side, right-click Trust Policy and select Export Basic Partner Policy. This enables you to select a path and filename for the XML that contains the basic information about the federation.

You now need to get this XML file to the other organization. Do this in a secure fashion and, ideally, not over the Internet. On the resource forest, import the XML file. Via the AD FS MMC snap-in, navigate to Trust Policy, Partner Organizations and right-click Account Partners. Select New, Account Partner from the context menu. This starts the Add Account

Partner Wizard, which asks whether you have an account partner policy file to import. That is what you just exported, so choose Yes and browse to the XML file, as shown in Figure 13-40.

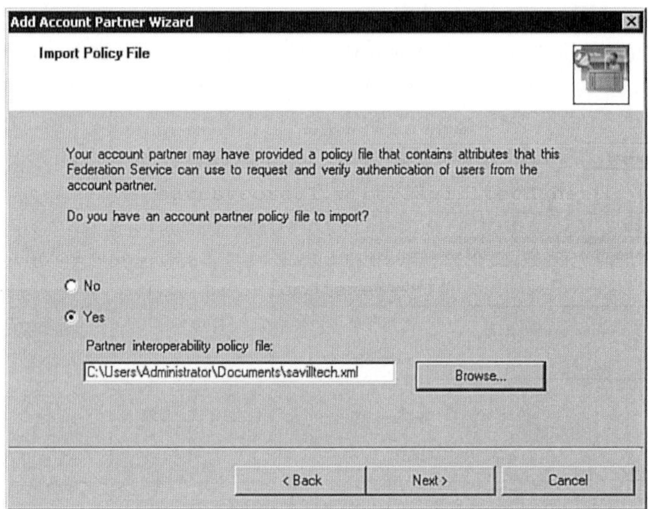

FIGURE 13-40 The XML file that contains the details from the account forest.

A summary of details displays that are read from the XML file, including the display name, the URI of the FS, and the URL of the FS endpoint. Click Next when you confirm these are correct. You receive a prompt as to where the verification certificate is for the trust. It is part of the imported XML file, so leave selected the default setting, Use the Verification Certificate in the Import Policy File, and click Next.

Next select the type of federation. By default it is a Federated Web SSO. However, if the two forests involved also have an AD forest trust, select the Federated Web SSO with Forest Trust option.

The types of account partner identity claims are displayed, which by default have UPN Claim and E-mail Claim enabled but also include an option for Common Name Claim. The values enabled depend on the services being exposed for the federation and how the tokens are consumed. For each type of identity, you receive a prompt for the suffix (for example, UPN and e-mail), which would be the DNS domain name (such as savilltech.net).

When all details are complete, ensure that the check box to enable the partner now is activated and click Finish to complete the relationship creation.

You can now create a mapping from the group claim from the account federation to a group claim in the resource federation. Right-click the account partner and select New, Incoming Group Claim Mapping, as shown in Figure 13-41. You receive a prompt from a group claim name that must exactly match the name of the outgoing group claim mapping. However, this is not a problem because the outgoing group claim mapping is created automatically when you import the configuration from the resource federation. But if you were using other technologies to create federations, make sure you get the case and name correct. When the name is entered, click OK.

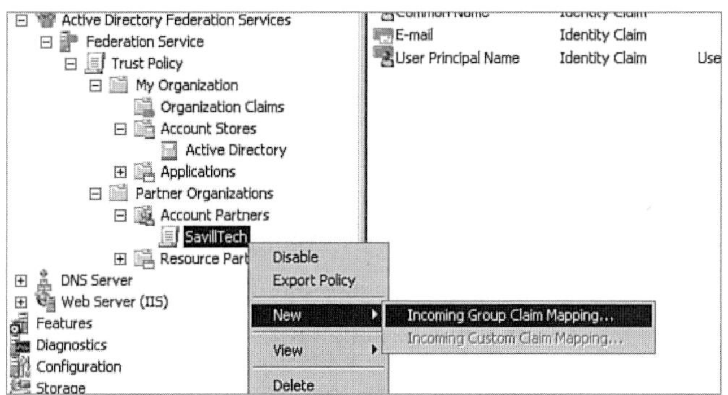

Figure 13-41 Creating a claim mapping.

Now export the configuration from the resource forest by right-clicking the partner organization under Trust Policy, Partner Organizations, Account Partners, <partner> and selecting Export Policy. Enter a name and location for the output XML to be created and save.

Again take this file and securely get it to the other organization via offline media by using a server such as a courier company.

Now repeat the process, but on the account federation. Select New, Resource Partner from the Trust Policy, Partner Organizations, Resource Partners node. You receive a prompt for the XML file again, and when selected, click Next to import the content of the XML.

A summary of the content is displayed, as shown in Figure 13-42. Confirm that all the information is correct. You are prompted for the type of federation. Again, this is a Federated Web SSO. You receive a prompt for the identity claims, which by default are UPN and E-mail. For each identity, you are prompted for what to replace the suffix with. This updates automatically; for example, to savilltech.net.

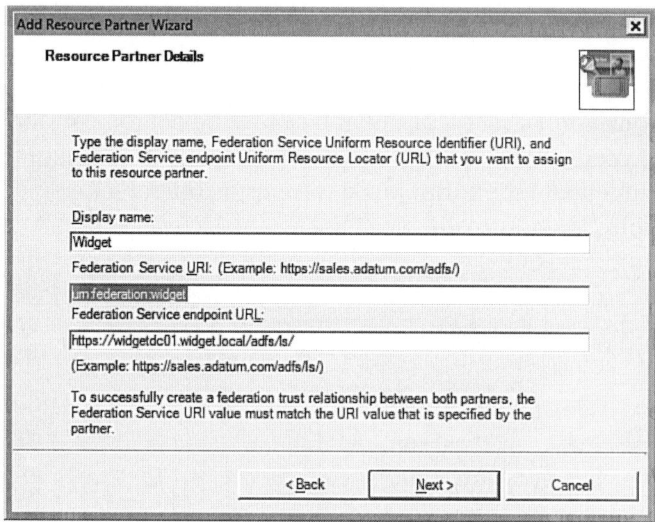

FIGURE 13-42 Importing the federation information.

The final configuration is to map the claim transformation to the claim you created on the account federation, as shown in Figure 13-43. Click Next, ensure that the resource partner is enabled, and click Finish.

You are now ready to access the Web-based service. The only other thing to do beforehand is ensure that the AD FS server is in your Local Intranet zone in Internet Explorer. When your client communicates with a federated server in your environment, you want to be sure that the AD FS server is in your Local Intranet zone. This can be done in Internet Explorer via the Tools, Internet Options, Security tab, Local Intranet option or via Group Policy for a large scale configuration as you saw in the "AD RMS" section of this chapter. The reason you want the AD FS server in your Local Intranet zone is so that your credentials can be passed to the server. Also, if you did not use a trusted root CA for the SSL certificates, the clients need the SSL certificates from the AD FS servers and Web server imported into their trust root certification authorities store.

Let's connect. Type the URL of the service that you want to access. For example, if you are using the Microsoft test application, use https://<server>/claimapp.

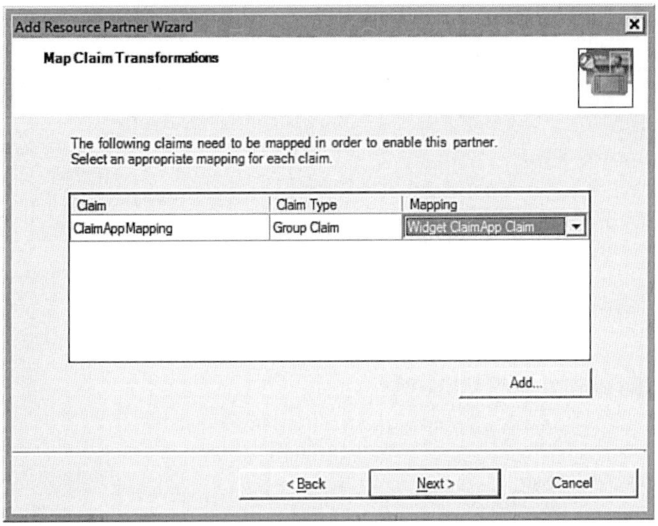

FIGURE 13-43 Configuring the mapping.

What do users see? Nothing. The only visible clue to users is a prompt for their home realm the first time they connect to another organization. This is because the federation server in the forest of the Web application needs to know where to redirect the user so that a SAML token can be created, as shown in Figure 13-44. After the realm is selected, the user's Web browser redirects to the AD FS server in the user's home realm, which was specified as the end point for the user's federation as part of the federation trust. The user redirects to the application realm and then to the application. As you see in Figure 13-45, success! You just used a credential in your home forest for a Web service in a separate forest.

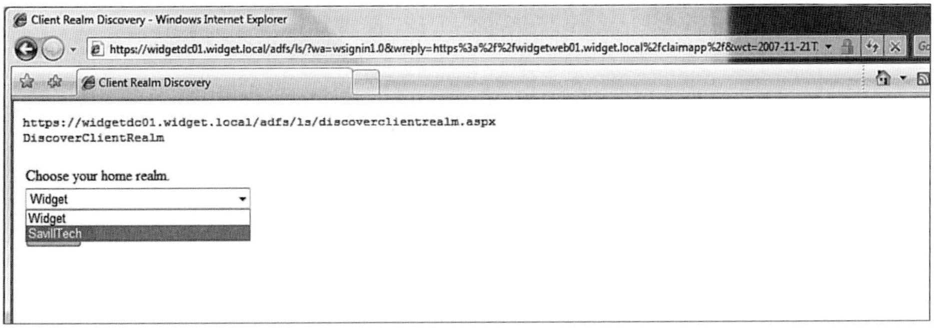

FIGURE 13-44 Selecting the realm for the user.

FIGURE 13-45 The output from the Microsoft sample application that shows the federation in action.

If you view your cookie files, you notice one for the application realm FS server; its content looks something like the following:

```
_LSRealm
urn:federation:savilltech
widgetdc01.widget.local/adfs/ls/
```

```
9729
479644544
29901836
614995904
29895801
*
```

The next time a user is sent to the federation server, it can read the cookie to know the user is from the savilltech federation and not prompt the user. Instead it sends the user directly to the FS endpoint it has for its account relationship with SavillTech.

Troubleshooting

You can enable a number of logs, which are written to the %systemdrive%\ADFS\logs folder. Logs can be enabled for the various components of FS by configuring Registry keys. See Table 13-2 for more information.

Table 13-2 Log Components, Registry Keys, and Values

Component	Registry Key	Value
Account Federation Server	HKEY_LOCAL_MACHINE\SYSTEM\CurrentControlSet\Control\Lsa\WebSso\Parameters	"DebugLevel"=dword:ffffffff
ADFS Web Agent Authentication Package	HKEY_LOCAL_MACHINE\SYSTEM\CurrentControlSet\Control\Lsa\WebSso\Parameters	"DebugLevel"=dword:ffffffff
ADFS Web Agent ISAPI Extension	HKEY_LOCAL_MACHINE\SOFTWARE\Microsoft\ADFS\WebServerAgent	"DebugPrintLevel"=dword:ffffffff
ADFS Web Agent Authentication Service	HKEY_LOCAL_MACHINE\SYSTEM\CurrentControlSet\Services\IFSSVC\Parameters	"DebugPrintLevel"=dword:ffffffff

Microsoft has also released an AD FS diagnostic tool that helps identify problems in your AD FS configuration. Download it from http://blogs.technet.com/adfs/attachment/2305228.ashx.

The tool is simple to use via its GUI and works by exporting its configuration on one server that is part of the federation trust. That configuration is used as the import for the tool for another server in the federation trust.

There is no order needed. When you run the utility, tell the user interface what roles are running on the server and select a data file for the output.

For example, you can first install the tool on your account server, specify a data file, and then run the diagnostic. A report displays, confirming the status of the tests. Now install and run the tool on the resource federation server, specifying the output file generated on the account FS server. The tool detects that it has data related to other FS roles and performs additional checks, as shown in Figure 13-46. You can then take the output file, which now has more information, and use it on the Web server. After running on all three servers, the report can give a complete picture of the health of the entire federation.

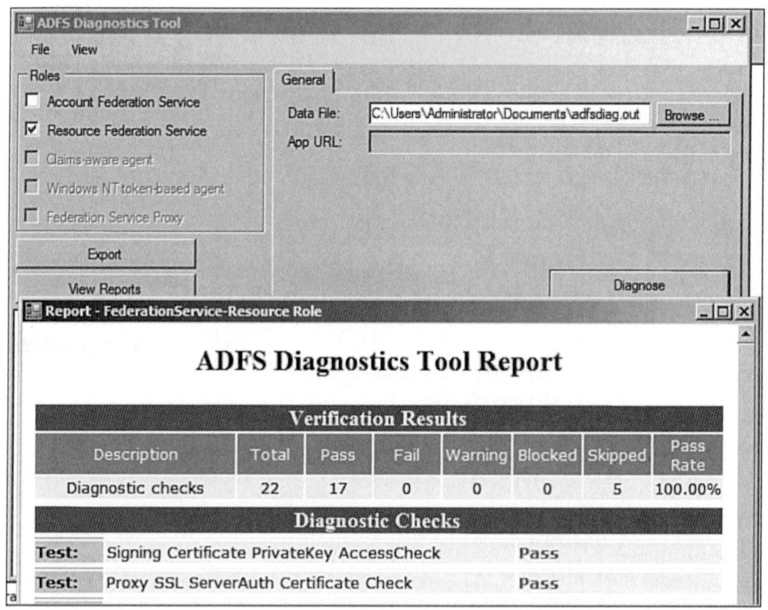

FIGURE 13-46 Using the ADFS diagnostic tool.

This is a high-level look at AD FS. Microsoft has a number of useful AD FS walk-throughs. Review the Microsoft AD FS blog at http://blogs.technet.com/adfs/ if you are interested in AD FS.

Summary

In this chapter, you looked at the vital services that focus on enabling information to be globally accessible while keeping it secure. It's easy to make data available everywhere, but facilitating that sharing in a controlled and secure way is vital, and that is exactly what AD FS and AD RMS provide.

AD LDS is great for protecting your ADDS from pollution of data that is not of enterprise interest but is still useful for specific applications. It gives that application a separate directory service in which it can store its own data with its own schema that can link to objects in the main organization's AD if necessary.

With AD FS, you have a single account that, through federation, is trusted by other organizations. You can gain access to web sites with access controlled by the partner organization but based on information that your company has decided to provide in the form of claims. This single account means no loss in productivity, which is common as you wait days for accounts to be created, and no compliance problems because you have just one account that must be disabled.

AD RMS provides security that travels with the data, which means you are secure in knowing that people cannot share or use information in a way you did not intend. After RMS is available in an organization, everyone wants to use it. Although there are some workarounds, such as using an application like snag-it to capture a screen and then running it through an optical character reader, RMS is protecting the original data. If someone is determined enough, he could type the whole content again or phone someone up and read it out, but with RMS you can stop at least the casual or accidental sharing of information. Obviously you could use Group Policy to block screen capture utilities if you wanted to address that particular vulnerability.

AD is fantastic, and these add-on services make it even more so.

CHAPTER 14

SERVER CORE

This chapter looks at a new feature in Windows Server 2008, an installation option known as a Server Core installation (as opposed to a full installation). Windows Server Core is not a separate product or even a separate license; it simply installs a bare metal server installation with the components needed to run a small set of core network roles, such as domain controller service and file service features, without everything else...which includes the exclusion of the familiar Windows Explorer GUI. You start with a detailed overview of Windows Server Core, which details the roles that it can fulfill, and then you look at ways to install Server Core. Finally, you learn how to configure and use your GUI-less Server Core environment.

Overview of Windows Server Core

In nearly all environments today, servers are designated for a single purpose. Often when you go to a client's site, the conversation is "these are the domain controllers, here are the file servers" and so on. Microsoft recognizes this specialization of servers. This recognition can be seen in the role-based nature of Windows Server 2008. However, even though your domain controllers, for example, need only a limited number of services to function (and maybe domain name system [DNS]), the server has a plethora of unneeded components. These components bloat the server, requiring the server to have more resources to function than are needed for its main function. Most importantly, the more components the system has installed, the more possible vulnerabilities it has. The more components there are, the greater the attack surface and the more patches required, resulting in more management overhead.

The typical server has the full .NET Framework, Internet Explorer, Media Player, and Outlook Express, all of which will likely never be used but still have to be managed.

With Windows Server Core, the "extra" parts of Windows Server 2008 have been removed, leaving a much thinner core operating system than with a normal Windows Server 2008 full installation. Because it has far fewer components, you benefit from having a reduced attack surface and less to manage and maintain. Server Core has only the critical components of the operating system necessary to support the various roles and features made available on a Windows Server Core installation. Many of the non-value-add legacy and client components are missing from Server Core.

This much smaller footprint, and optimized installation based around specific roles such as a domain controller or file server, means the following:

- As already discussed, Server Core presents less attack surface because it involves fewer components with less possible vulnerabilities.
- Because you have fewer components installed, fewer patches apply to a Server Core installation than to a normal full installation. You often hear of an urgent patch related to an Internet Explorer vulnerability. If Internet Explorer is not installed, you don't need to apply that patch. Microsoft believes there will be a large reduction in the number of patches needed for a Server Core install compared to a full installation. It's not possible to know how many patches will be released for Windows Server 2008 or what components the patches will be applicable to. But if a core version had been available for Windows 2000, it would have required 60 percent fewer patches than a full installation, and if available for Windows 2003 there would have been a 40 percent reduction in patches. The servicing stack in Windows Server 2008 downloads and applies only fixes that apply to components installed on the system. No actions or special Windows Update site is required that is Server-Core-specific.
- Administrators can focus more on their technology area without having to be so worried about general Windows knowledge because all the extra parts are no longer installed.
- With fewer components running, the installation uses fewer system resources and becomes more reliable because the fewer different components executing, the less chance of problems occurring.
- Less disk space. A typical core installation uses 1GB of disk space for the install and additional disk space for its actual operation. In

terms of other resources, there is not a great deal of difference, although obviously with fewer components, fewer resources are used overall. But remember: A Windows 2008 install alone requires 512MB of RAM.

The Server Core is available as an installation option for the Standard, Enterprise, and Datacenter editions of Windows Server 2008 and is available on both the x86 and x64 architectures.

Because the Server Core is a minimal installation of Windows, not all the full Windows Server components can run. For example, because the .NET Framework is not present in Server Core, which in turn means no Common Language Runtime (CLR), no managed code can run. That means no PowerShell. A Server Core installation has many "nots":

- There is no Explorer-based shell, so the Start button, taskbar notification area (system tray), and taskbar are eliminated. There are no fancy wall papers, screen savers (a default screen saver shows the Windows Server 2008 logo), and no Aero Glass. Explorer itself is not available, which means no My Computer. Because you have no system tray, you get no balloon notifications, which also means no password prompts because they are balloon notifications.
- No Explorer means no Internet Explorer, no Search, no Run, and no Help, but you do get Notepad.
- No .NET Framework. This is because the .NET Framework is monolithic, meaning all or nothing. And .NET has a lot of multimedia-related code and other components that do not fit the Server Core model. However, a "core" version of the .NET Framework is expected for the Windows Server 2008 R2 timeframe. This means no managed code, which requires .NET.
- No Microsoft Management Console (MMC), which means no snap-ins either. That is an issue because nearly everything is managed with the MMC.
- Only two Control Panel applets.

So let's get it clear. With Server Core, there is no graphical interface, no management tools, no Explorer, no Control Panel applets? Before you get freaked, this is a great feature. The advantages of the reduced overhead are worth a little hardship. You do have a shell, but it's the command prompt. However, if you think about it, nearly every MMC snap-in you have today can connect to a remote computer, which helps you manage your GUI-less Server Core installation.

What do you get? Much more than in the early builds of Longhorn when the only roles available were Active Directory Domain Servers (a domain controller), DNS, DHCP and File Servers. You are a lot further than that now. As you've seen, with Windows Server you have roles, which are important components of Windows Server 2008, and features, which are less important than their older, driving Role brothers. Table 14-1 provides a list of the roles and features available in Windows Server Core. Note there are no relationships between the roles and features; they are in a table only to save space.

Table 14-1 Windows Server Core Roles and Features

Server Core Roles	Server Core Features
Active Directory Domain Services (ADDS)	BitLocker Drive Encryption (and remote admin tools)
Active Directory Lightweight Directory Services (formally known as ADAM)	Failover Clustering
DHCP Server	Multipath I/O
DNS Server	NAP Client
File Services	QoS (Qwave)
Internet Information Services (IIS)	Removable Storage Management
Print Services	Simple Network Management Protocol (SNMP) Services
Streaming Media Services	Subsystem for UNIX-based applications
Windows Server Virtualization (Hyper-V)	Telnet Clients
	Windows Process Activation Service
	Windows Server Backup
	WINS Server

Don't forget that Server Core is not a separate operating system. It just takes advantage of the highly componentized nature of Windows Server and deploys only the most critical components. Core still has the same kernel as a normal installation in addition to other core components such as the Hardware Abstraction Layer (HAL), memory manager, security subsystem, Winlogon, file systems, networking subsystem, Windows File Protection, Distributed Component Object Model (DCOM), and remote procedure call (RPC), and device drivers for NIC, disk, and basic video. Many of the other drivers have been removed from Core, such as audio drivers and modem drivers. However, you can add them manually. Imagine a print server, however; print drivers are also not included with Server Core because Windows Server 2008 has nearly 1GB of printer drivers. Instead of including drivers in Server Core for a role that might not be used, the print drivers are not included. When you enable the Print Server role, the spooler starts, and drivers need to be manually added using the Print Management Console remotely from a Windows Vista/Windows 2008 machine.

Also included are features such as the event log, which is critical to nearly all components of Windows, performance counters, WS-Management for remote management, and Windows Management Instrumentation (WMI).

Think of Server Core as a subset of the full Windows installation. If a core kernel patch is released, the same patch for Windows Server is applicable to a Server Core installation. How do you use this? What do you get to manage this Server Core environment? Let's look at installing Server Core, and then you can see the usable environment.

Installation

Server Core installation does not warrant its own section because it's the same as a normal installation of Windows Server 2008. The install media is placed into the server or the server boots over the network, and a product key is entered that identifies the particular edition of Windows Server 2008. In this case, it needs to be Standard, Enterprise, or Datacenter. The only difference is during the actual installation, after entering the product key, you select the type of Windows Server 2008 installation, full or core, as shown in Figure 14-1.

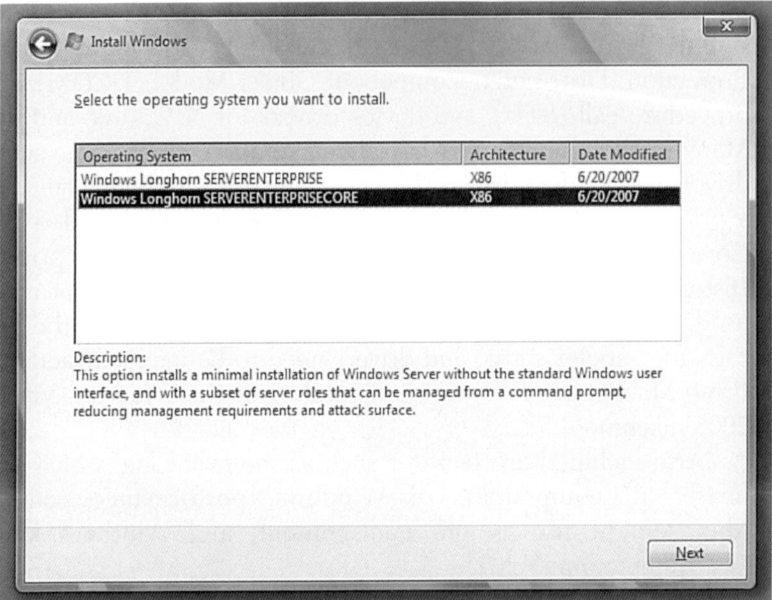

FIGURE 14-1 The description is your first clue that your command-line skills are about to get much better.

When the installation is complete, you get the familiar and comfortable Press Ctrl+Alt+Del to Log On dialog with the pretty Windows Server logo at the bottom. If you press the secure attention sequence, you are prompted to enter logon credentials, so for now all you can do is log on with the administrator account with a blank password.

So far, this is looking great, as Figure 14-2 shows. After clicking the logon button, you are prompted to change the password as normal, and you set a new administrator account password. The normal process of applying local policy and preparing the desktop takes place, and then your Server Core desktop loads, as shown in Figure 14-3.

Note that you cannot upgrade from Windows Server 2003 to Server Core; only fresh installations of Server Core are supported. You also cannot upgrade from Server Core to the full Windows Server 2008 product, nor can you downgrade from Windows Server 2008 to Server Core. If you need to switch between versions, perform a clean installation.

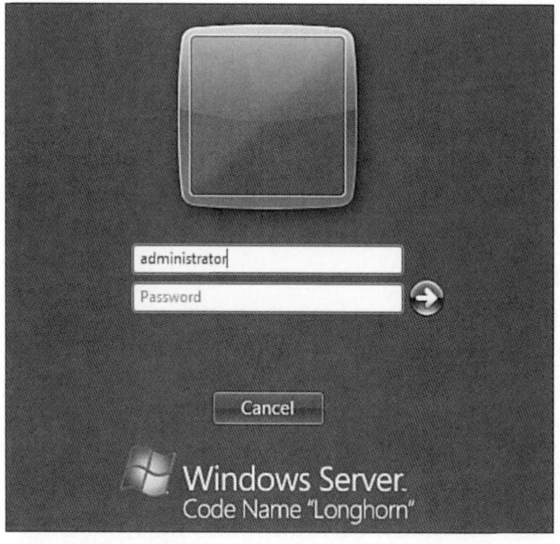

FIGURE 14-2 So far this Server Core environment looks familiar.

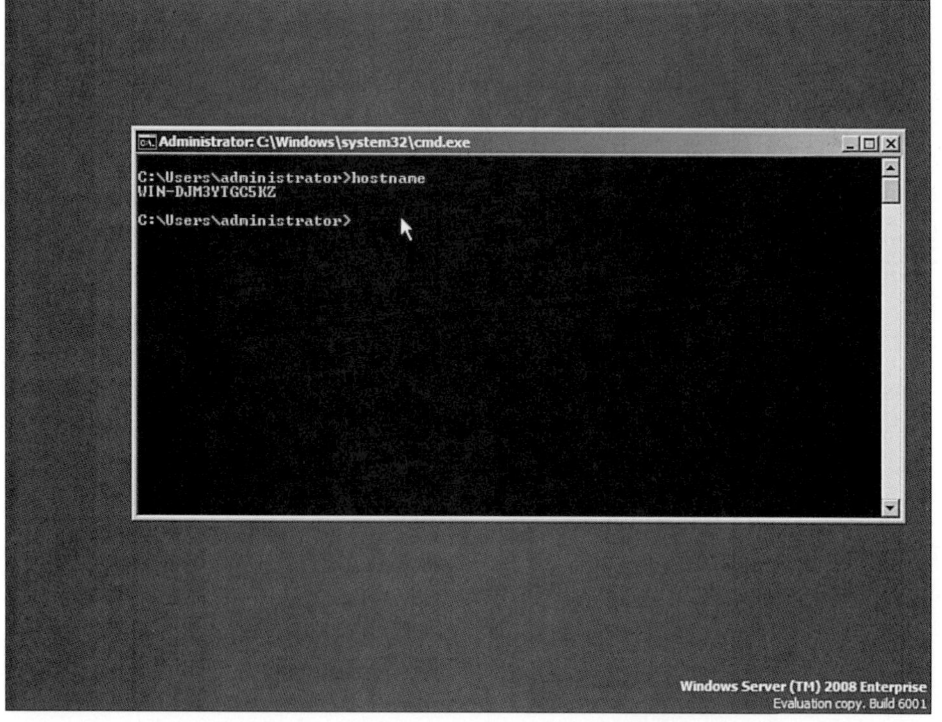

FIGURE 14-3 In keeping with trends from server-based computer to client/server back to server-based, you are now back to a command prompt server environment.

Server Core Configuration

Now that Server Core is installed, first you need to configure it. Without the normal graphical elements, you don't have the nice Initial Configuration Tasks (ICT) interface that you would normally use to configure Windows Server 2008 server, so you have two options:

- Manually configure the server using command-line tools.
- Automate the configuration using answer files during the actual installation.

The second option is the way to go for any sizable deployment. One of the big pushes of the latest operating system has been zero-touch deployments, so you can automate the install and configuration of all the main components. However, this does take up-front effort and planning but is definitely an option. Other areas of the book talk about unattended installations, so for now concentrate on the manual configuration of the server. However, if you go the unattended route, Server Core uses the same unattended syntax as Windows Vista and a normal server. Use the Windows System Image Manager from the Windows Automated Installation Kit (WAIK) to help create the unattended eXtensible Markup Language (XML) answer file. There are some advantages to using the unattended XML, however, because some items are quite hard to configure in Server Core. For example, configuring screen resolution is quite complex without the Display Control Panel applet! The display options are part of the Microsoft-Windows-Shell-Setup component, and a sample code extract for an unattend.xml is shown here:

```
<settings pass="oobeSystem">
    <component name="Microsoft-Windows-Shell-Setup"
processorArchitecture="x86" publicKeyToken="31bf3856ad364e35"
language="neutral" versionScope="nonSxS"
xmlns:wcm="http://schemas.microsoft.com/WMIConfig/2002/State"
xmlns:xsi="http://www.w3.org/2001/XMLSchema-instance">
        <Display>
            <HorizontalResolution>1280</HorizontalResolution>
            <VerticalResolution>1024</VerticalResolution>
            <ColorDepth>16</ColorDepth>
        </Display>
    </component>
</settings>"
```

If you examine the content of the install.wim file for Windows Server 2008, you see that a CORE version exists for each operating system. If you are using Windows Deployment Services (WDS) or any other XML installation, select the CORE post-fixed version, as shown in Figure 14-4.

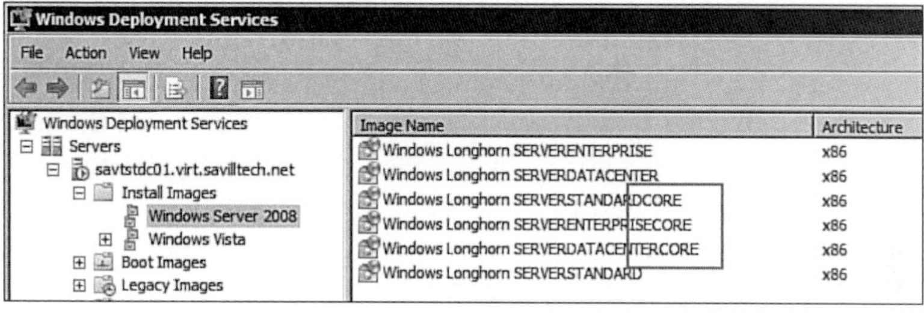

FIGURE 14-4 The core versions of the main Server 2008 editions.

Let's look at the main things you normally do when you configure a new server:

- Set the administrator password.
- Set the machine name.
- Set static TCP/IP v4 details.
- Set the time zone.
- Join a domain.
- Set keyboard and international settings.
- Set the default scripting engine.
- Activate the server.
- Install patches.
- Configure the firewall.
- Configure the server pagefile.
- Enable Remote Desktop.
- Configure hardware.
- Add roles and features.

You would normally do all this via GUI interfaces. For example, you would use Network and Sharing Center to configure IP settings, Windows Update for patches, and so on, but none of these interfaces are available. You can still set all of these things using the command line and some Server Core–specific commands. However, most of these are standard commands and can be used on normal installations for configuration and for scripted communication.

Setting the Administrator Password

The Winlogon and security subsystem in Core is the same as in a standard installation of Windows Server 2008, so to change the password of the logged-on account, just press Ctrl+Alt+Delete as you would normally do. Select the Change a Password link from the menu, and the normal change password dialog displays.

Passwords can also be changed via the `net user` command as on any other Windows installation by passing the username and the new password or passing the wildcard (*) character to be prompted for the new password, as shown in Figure 14-5. To change a domain account password, add the `/domain` switch.

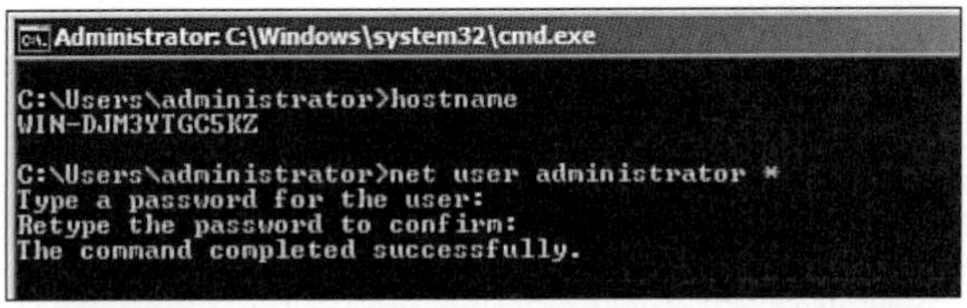

```
Administrator: C:\Windows\system32\cmd.exe

C:\Users\administrator>hostname
WIN-DJM3YTGC5KZ

C:\Users\administrator>net user administrator *
Type a password for the user:
Retype the password to confirm:
The command completed successfully.
```

FIGURE 14-5 The `net user` command is an easy way to manage local account passwords.

Setting the Server Name

In the first screen, you viewed the server name using the `hostname` command. However, to change the server name, use the `netdom` command with the `renamecomputer` switch. To avoid having to type in the long default computer name, use the `%computername%` environment variable and then pass the new server name with the `/NewName` switch:

```
C:\Windows\System32>netdom renamecomputer %computername% /New
➥Name:savtstcore01
This operation will rename the computer WIN-DJM3YTGC5KZ
to savtstcore01.

Certain services, such as the Certificate Authority, rely on a
fixed machine name. If any services of this type are running on
WIN-DJM3YTGC5KZ, then a computer name change would have an
adverse impact.
```

```
Do you want to proceed (Y or N)?
Y
The computer needs to be restarted in order to complete the
operation.

The command completed successfully.
```

This change does not take immediate effect; a reboot is required by selecting the Restart option from the Ctrl+Alt+Del screen shutdown options as shown in Figure 14-6 or by using the `shutdown /r /t 0` command. When the reboot is complete, the server has taken the new name, which you can verify by rerunning the `hostname` command.

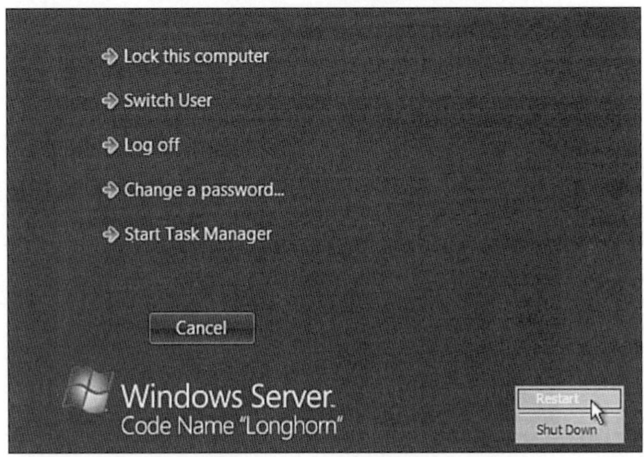

FIGURE 14-6 Although you don't have a Start menu, access shutdown options via the Ctrl+Alt+Del menu.

Setting Static TCP/IP v4 Information

By default, the new installation has been dynamically allocated an IP address. However, in most cases a server needs static IPv4 information, which can be seen with the `ipconfig /all` command. It will show `DHCP Enabled` set to `Yes`.

Because you can't use the normal Network interface to set the IP properties, instead use the `netsh` command. However, before you can set the

IP properties, check which interface you are configuring. By default your server has two network interfaces: the "real physical" interface and a second IntraSite Automatic Tunnel Addressing Protocol (ISATAP) tunneling interface, which sends IPv6 packets over an IPv4 network by encapsulating the IPv6 packet in the IPv4 header. You need to configure the physical connection and not the ISATAP one, so list your interfaces to identify the index of the physical adapter.

```
C:\Users\administrator>netsh interface ipv4 show interfaces

Idx  Met   MTU   State        Name
---  ---  -----  -----------  -------------------
  2   10   1500  connected    Local Area Connection
  1   50 4294967295  connected    Loopback Pseudo-Interface 1
```

When the adapter is identified, which in this case is index 2, the IP details can be set. They most likely consist of an IP address, a subnet mask, a gateway, and one, possibly two, DNS servers.

To set the IP address, subnet mask, and gateway, run the following and change the information for your environment:

```
C:\Users\administrator>netsh interface ipv4 set address
➥name="2" source=static address=192.168.1.232
➥mask=255.255.255.0 gateway=192.168.1.1
```

You can now add the DNS servers. The primary DNS server gets an index of 1, the secondary DNS server gets an index of 2.

```
C:\Users\administrator>netsh interface ipv4 add dnsserver
➥name="2" address=192.168.1.230 index=1


C:\Users\administrator>netsh interface ipv4 add dnsserver
➥name="2" address=192.168.1.10 index=2
```

If you need to configure primary and secondary Windows Internet Name Service (WINS) servers, use the same syntax as for adding DNS servers but use `winsserver` instead of `dnsserver`. The first index would be the primary WINS server and the second index the secondary WINS server.

If you now examine the IP information with `ipconfig/all`, the configured settings are displayed, as shown in the following example:

```
C:\Users\administrator>ipconfig /all

Windows IP Configuration

   Host Name . . . . . . . . . . . . : savtstcore01
   Primary Dns Suffix  . . . . . . . :
   Node Type . . . . . . . . . . . . : Hybrid
   IP Routing Enabled. . . . . . . . : No
   WINS Proxy Enabled. . . . . . . . : No

Ethernet adapter Local Area Connection:

   Connection-specific DNS Suffix  . . :
   Description . . . . . . . . . . . : Intel 21140-Based PCI
Fast Ethernet Adapter (Emulated)
   Physical Address. . . . . . . . . : 00-03-FF-0E-0D-F9
   DHCP Enabled. . . . . . . . . . . : No
   Autoconfiguration Enabled . . . .  : Yes
   Link-local IPv6 Address . . . . . :
fe80::c49a:b729:8c8b:471e%2(Preferred)
   IPv4 Address. . . . . . . . . . . : 192.168.1.232(Preferred)
   Subnet Mask . . . . . . . . . . . : 255.255.255.0
   Default Gateway . . . . . . . . . : 192.168.1.1
   DNS Servers . . . . . . . . . . . : 192.168.1.230
                                       192.168.1.10
   NetBIOS over Tcpip. . . . . . . . : Enabled
```

If you need to remove a DNS server, or more likely a WINS server, after you finally get it killed off, use the `del` keyword instead of `add`. For example:

```
Netsh interface ipv4 del winsserver name="2"
address=192.168.1.10
```

Setting the Time Zone

The date and time are easy to set using the `date` and `time` command lines, but using a command-line method to set the time zone is trickier. There are Registry areas for the time zone. However it's not necessary to use the Registry. Remember that Control Panel is unavailable in Server Core except for two applets. The Date and Time Control Panel applet is one of them; start it via the following command:

```
control timedate.cpl
```

14. SERVER CORE

After loading the applet, perform the normal date/time and time zone configurations, as shown in Figure 14-7. Note that in a domain environment, the time synchronizes; however, you might need to set the time zone.

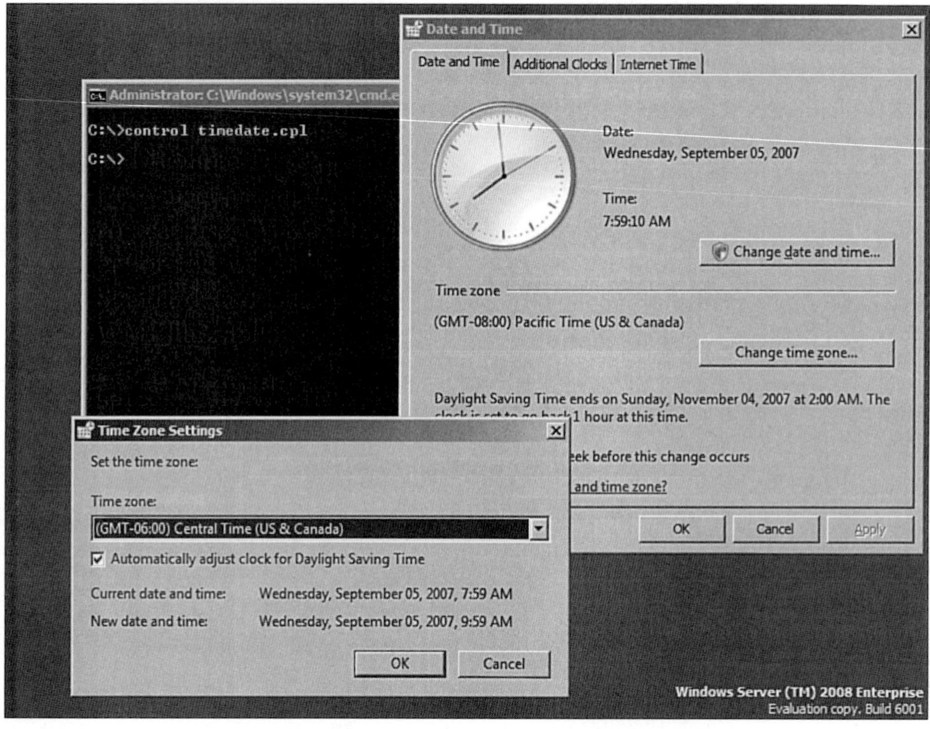

FIGURE 14-7 At last, a graphical way to configure something.

Joining a Domain

It is most likely your servers are part of a domain, and unless the server was preprovisioned during deployment or used an answer file, you need to configure your server to join a domain. After the IP configuration is configured with the correct DNS servers, the computer name is set, and the time configuration is correct, you can join the domain.

To join a domain, use the same command that you used to rename the computer: `netdom`. Full help can be seen by running `netdom join /?`, which gives information on specifying a specific organizational unit (OU) to place the computer into. However, at the most basic level, pass the domain you want to join, the account to use to perform the join, and its password:

```
C:\>netdom join %computername% /domain:virt.savilltech.net
➥/userd:administrator /passwordd:*
Type the password associated with the domain user:
*******
The computer needs to be restarted in order to complete the
operation.

The command completed successfully.
```

Replace the domain name with your domain, and then restart the server. After the reboot, you can log on as a domain user, which confirms the domain join operation worked successfully. You can also verify your connectivity to the domain using the `netdom /verify` command as in the following example:

```
C:\Users\administrator.VIRT>netdom verify %computername%
➥/domain:virt.savilltech.net
The secure channel from SAVTSTCORE01 to the domain VIRT.
SAVILLTECH.NET has been verified.  The connection
is with the machine \\SAVTSTDC01.VIRT.SAVILLTECH.NET.

The command completed successfully.
```


Configuring International Settings

The second Control Panel applet available in Server Core is the Regional and Language Options applet. It enables the configuration of the keyboard layouts, languages, and location. To launch the applet, run the following command and configure as a normal installation:

```
Control intl.cpl
```

Setting the Default Scripting Engine

With Server Core, you do a lot via various scripts executed by the Windows Scripting Host, which has a GUI and a command-line engine. By default the GUI engine is the preferred tool, which goes against the idea of managing Server Core from the command line and requires you to remember to put `cscript` at the start of your scripts to process the script using the command-line interpreter.

To change the Windows Scripting Host to use the command-line interpreter by default, use the following command:

```
C:\Windows>cscript //H:CScript //NOLOGO //s
Command line options are saved.
The default script host is now set to "cscript.exe".
```

If you've enabled `cscript` as the default engine, you don't need to type it every time.

Activating the Server

Server Core includes the Slmgr.vbs script, which when passed with the `-ato` switch, performs an automated activation of the operating system. Slmgr.vbs is not a Server Core feature; it is present in Windows Vista and full Windows Server 2008 deployments and is the main license manager for the Vista/2008 products.

Because Server Core has no taskbar or system tray, you do not receive any prompts to activate the server, so remember to do so shortly after the installation of Server Core.

Before you activate, check your status to see how far into your initial 30-day grace period you are by using the `-xpr` switch as shown here:

```
C:\Windows\System32>cscript slmgr.vbs -xpr
Microsoft (R) Windows Script Host Version 5.7
Copyright (C) Microsoft Corporation. All rights reserved.

Initial grace period ends 10/4/2007 2:48:10 PM
```

There is also more information available via the `-dli` switch or the `-dlv` switch to get detailed info.

```
C:\Windows\System32>cscript slmgr.vbs -dli
Microsoft (R) Windows Script Host Version 5.7
Copyright (C) Microsoft Corporation. All rights reserved.

Name: Windows(TM) Server code name "Longhorn",
ServerEnterpriseCore edition
Description: Windows Operating System - Server code name
"Longhorn", RETAIL channel
Partial Product Key: 2T9PJ
License Status: Initial grace period
Time remaining: 42000 minute(s) (29 day(s))
```

If you have a normal license key or Multiple Activation Key (MAK) that activates with Microsoft, you can go ahead and just activate. However, if you have a local Key Management Service (KMS), tell the activation to use it via the `-skms <KMS server>` switch. If you need to clear the configured KMS server, use the `-ckms` switch. If you are using an enterprise license key, use the `-ipk <key>` switch.

To activate, use the `-ato` switch as previously mentioned. Rerun the display of license information to see the status is now licensed with no time remaining.

```
C:\Windows\System32>cscript slmgr.vbs -ato
Microsoft (R) Windows Script Host Version 5.7
Copyright (C) Microsoft Corporation. All rights reserved.

Activating Windows(TM) Server code name "Longhorn",
ServerEnterpriseCore edition
 (f00d81ce-df2c-47cb-a359-36d652296e56) ...
Product activated successfully.


C:\Windows\System32>cscript slmgr.vbs -dli
Microsoft (R) Windows Script Host Version 5.7
Copyright (C) Microsoft Corporation. All rights reserved.

Name: Windows(TM) Server code name "Longhorn",
ServerEnterpriseCore edition
Description: Windows Operating System - Server code name
"Longhorn", RETAIL channel
Partial Product Key: 2T9PJ
License Status: Licensed
```


Installing Patches and Configuring Auto-Update

You can use various methods to patch Server Core. You can push patches with Group Policy or System Center Configuration Manager or any other deployment-type product. You can use Windows Update, which is disabled by default. (You can confirm that with the `/au /v` switches with scregedit.wsf.) To enable Windows Update to perform the normal 3 a.m. checks, run the following commands. The scregedit.wsf script is Server Core–specific and was written to help perform the functions that are otherwise difficult to do from the command line. The script is installed automatically on all Server Core installations.

```
C:\Windows\System32>cscript scregedit.wsf /au 4
Microsoft (R) Windows Script Host Version 5.7
Copyright (C) Microsoft Corporation. All rights reserved.

Registry has been updated.

C:\Windows\System32>net stop wuauserv
The Windows Update service is stopping.
The Windows Update service was stopped successfully.


C:\Windows\System32>net start wuauserv
The Windows Update service is starting.
The Windows Update service was started successfully.
```

You can force an update pass to run using the following command:

```
C:\Windows\System32>wuauclt /detectnow
```

You can't configure options to download patches and prompt for installation. You can either enable automatic download and application of patches or have automatic update turned off: There is no in-between configuration. You can always check the state of patch installations via the `wmic qfe list` command.

You can manually install patches using the `wusa` command, as in the following example:

```
wusa <patch name>.msu /quiet
```

Remember the patches all have applicability rules, so they won't install if the patch does not apply. If you want to check whether a patch applies, run the command without the `/quiet` switch. If you are prompted to install, it means the patch applies; if you are not prompted, it means the patch does not apply to Server Core and has been ignored. You learn more detail about patching in Chapter 17, "Managing and Maintaining Windows Server 2008."

Configuring the Pagefile

By default, the pagefile is set as managed by the system. This behavior can be modified by disabling the automatic pagefile management and manually configuring a specific pagefile size. For example, the following disables the automatic pagefile management and sets the pagefile to 1GB minimum, 2GB maximum. In general, the default Windows settings for the pagefile should not be changed—do so only if given specific guidance by an expert or vendor of an application being installed. Notice the code in the following listing is using the Windows Management Instrumentation Command-Line (WMIC) environment, which opens up a lot of functionality. Some of the other commands you performed could have been done with the WMIC. After running the commands in this listing, you must restart the server for the changes to take effect.

```
C:\Windows\System32>wmic computersystem set
➥AutomaticManagedPagefile=false
Updating property(s) of '\\SAVTSTCORE01\ROOT\CIMV2:Win32_
ComputerSystem.Name="SA
VTSTCORE01"'
Property(s) update successful.

C:\Windows\System32>wmic pagefileset where name="C:\\
➥pagefile.sys" set InitialSize=1000,MaximumSize=2000
Updating property(s) of '\\SAVTSTCORE01\ROOT\CIMV2:Win32_
PageFileSetting.Name="C
:\\pagefile.sys"'
Property(s) update successful.
```


Configuring the Firewall

On a new Server Core installation, the firewall is enabled by default and blocking almost everything. You can turn off the firewall by using the following command, which opens up the ports and allows Remote Desktop, SNMP, and so forth. You can enable the firewall again by changing `disable` to `enable`.

```
Netsh firewall set opmode disable
```

You can configure the firewall elements using the `netsh` command and its various components. For example, to enable the Remote Desktop, use the following command:

```
C:\Windows\System32>netsh firewall set service
➥type=remotedesktop mode=enable
```

There is an easier way, however. The Windows Firewall MMC snap-in can connect to a remote machine, so let's try that approach as opposed to working out the hundreds of possible `netsh` commands. If you are configuring many servers, however, it would be worth creating a script with the `netsh` commands, or configuring the firewall using Group Policy. If you want to use Group Policy, the firewall is available as part of Computer Configuration, Windows Settings, Security Settings, Windows Firewall with Advanced Security. Right-click Inbound Rules (see Figure 14-8) and select a new rule, and you can use the predefined Remote Administration and Remote Desktop rules. It might not be practical to place the Server Core machines in their own OU for the application of the Group Policy, so you can use a WMI filter to check the `OperatingSystemSKU` of the server for the values 12, 13, and 14, which correspond to the Datacenter, Standard, and Enterprise Server Core installations, respectively. A sample WMI filter follows:

```
select * from Win32_OperatingSystem where OperatingSystemSKU=12
or OperatingSystemSKU=13 or OperatingSystemSKU=14
```

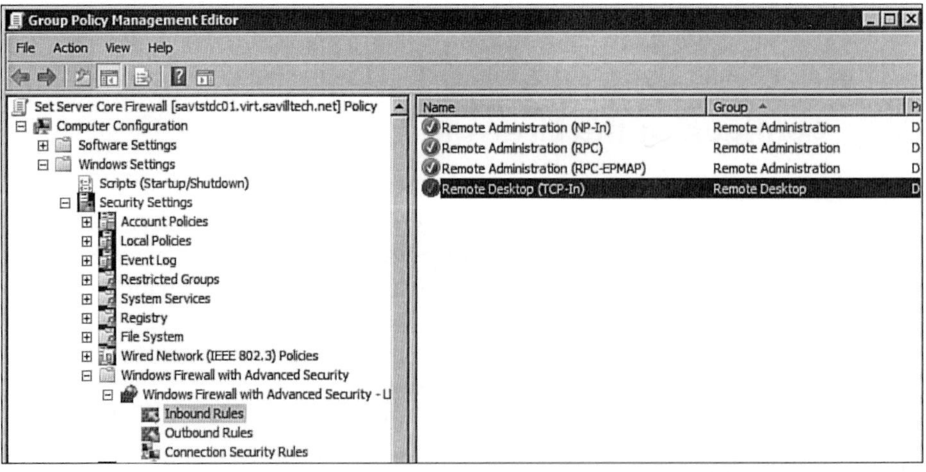

FIGURE 14-8 Using Group Policy to configure the firewall is a good option for larger deployments.

Before you try this, you get an error when you launch the remote firewall snap-in because the firewall you are trying to configure blocks remote management by default. So, you need one more `netsh` command to enable the remote management capability:

```
C:\Windows\System32>netsh firewall set service
➥type=remoteadmin mode=enable
```

Now let's manage remotely:

1. Open a new MMC instance (Start, Run, MMC).
2. From the File menu, select Add/Remove Snap-In.
3. Select Windows Firewall with Advanced Security, and click the Add button (see Figure 14-9).

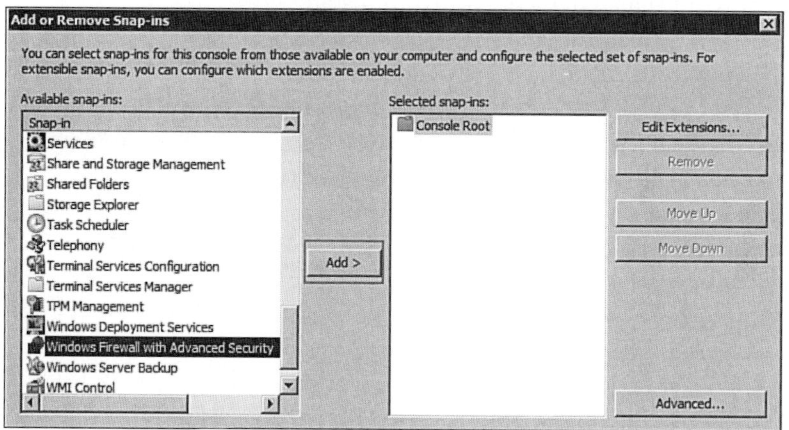

FIGURE 14-9 Select Windows Firewall with Advanced Security.

4. You are prompted to indicate whether the computer is the local computer or another computer. Check Another Computer (see Figure 14-10), specify the name of your Server Core computer, and click Finish.
5. Click OK to close the Add or Remove Snap-Ins dialog box.

Now configure the firewall remotely and enable exceptions as required.

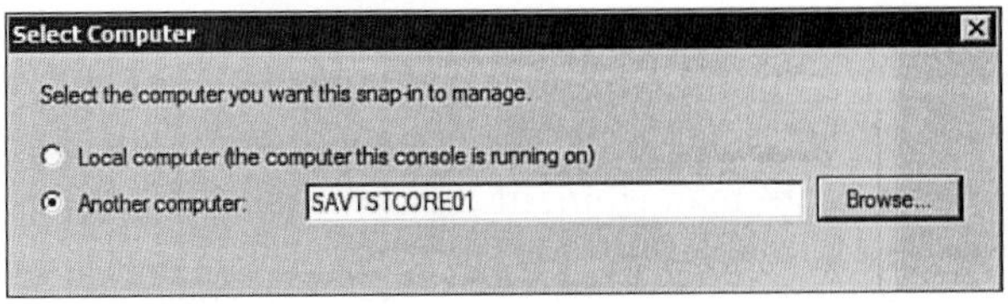

FIGURE 14-10 Check Another Computer.

Enabling Remote Desktop

Server Core contains the Remote Desktop component, which can be a useful way to manage a Server Core environment. But due to its mainly command prompt–based interface nature, there are less resource-greedy ways of managing a Server Core install.

To check the current state of Remote Desktop, use the scregedit.wsf script with the `/ar /v` switches, as shown in the following listing. In this case, by default, the Remote Desktop is disabled because the Deny Terminal Server Connections setting is set to true. You must be in the Windows\System32 folder to run the script:

```
C:\Windows\System32>cscript scregedit.wsf /ar /v
Microsoft (R) Windows Script Host Version 5.7
Copyright (C) Microsoft Corporation. All rights reserved.

System\CurrentControlSet\Control\Terminal Server
fDenyTSConnections
View Registry setting.
1
```

To enable Remote Desktop, use the `/ar 0` switch:

```
C:\Windows\System32>cscript scregedit.wsf /ar 0
Microsoft (R) Windows Script Host Version 5.7
Copyright (C) Microsoft Corporation. All rights reserved.

Registry has been updated.

C:\Windows\System32>cscript scregedit.wsf /ar /v
Microsoft (R) Windows Script Host Version 5.7
```

```
Copyright (C) Microsoft Corporation. All rights reserved.

System\CurrentControlSet\Control\Terminal Server
  fDenyTSConnections
View Registry setting.
0
```

Additionally, by default, only connections from the newest Remote Desktop Protocol (RDP) clients that support the Credential Security Service Provider (CredSSP) are accepted, which allows the user's current credentials to be automatically passed to the target server. However, you can change this behavior using the `/CS 0` switch with scregedit.wsf.

Configuring Hardware

Some things, such as screen resolution, are difficult to configure from Server Core. One of the few GUI tools provided is the Registry Editor, which means you can perform configurations; it's just a bit ugly. Normally, you are advised to use the Registry Editor only as a last resort, but for some things in Server Core it's your only option. Using the Registry Editor, navigate to the HKEY_LOCAL_MACHINE\SYSTEM\CurrentControlSet\Control\Video\<GUID of graphics card>\0000 key. Modify the DefaultSettings.XResolution (see Figure 14-11) and DefaultSettings.YResolution values to the desired values. Just make sure they are right.

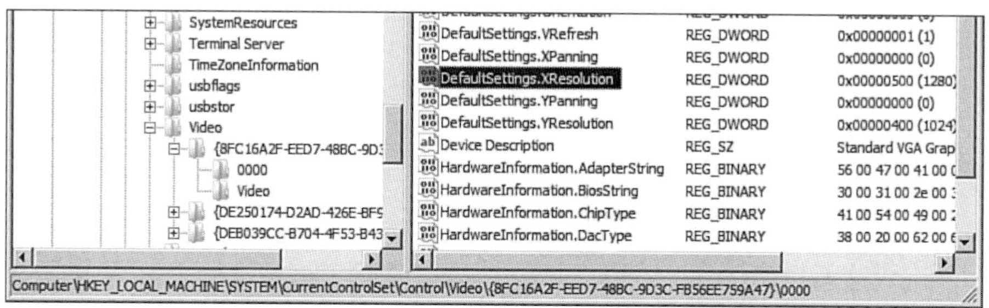

FIGURE 14-11 Setting the screen resolution for the system.

If you want to modify screen saver values, for example, do it in the Registry as well. By default, the screen saver kicks in after 10 minutes and uses the logon screen saver (logon.scr), requiring a password when the screen saver is deactivated. To modify this, use the Registry Editor again and move to the HKEY_CURRENT_USER\Control Panel\Desktop key. The following values can be changed:

- **ScreenSaveActive**. 1 means screen saver is turned on, 0 disables.
- **ScreenSaverIsSecure**. 1 means password is required, 0 no password needed.
- **ScreenSaveTimeOut**. Time in seconds of inactivity before screensaver starts.
- **SCRNSAVE.EXE**. The name of the screen saver. Logon.scr or scrnsave.scr for the blank screen saver.

You can also specify a background wallpaper by creating a string value named WallPaper under the same key with the full name and path of the image to use as the background.

In terms of adding hardware, if you need to install drivers, you are not prompted to install a driver for new hardware as in a normal Windows Server installation. Instead you need to manually install the driver and then, depending on the hardware, reboot the server for the new driver to be used with the hardware. Copy the driver files to a location on the server and then run the following command to load the driver:

```
Pnputil -i -a <driver>.inf
```

You can list all drivers on the system via the `sc query type= driver` command (note the space between `type=` and `driver`). When you have the service name of the driver, uninstall with the `sc delete <service_name>` command.

Adding Roles and Features

So far everything you have done configures the server. So far it does not do anything; it's not running any roles or features that are the cornerstone of Windows Server 2008.

You don't have access to the normal Server Manager interface to add roles and features, and all the features, except ADDS, are added via the

`Ocsetup` command. `Ocsetup` is a case-sensitive command and is part of all Windows Server 2008 installations. Active Directory installation is installed via the `dcpromo` command, which installs the binaries and configures things via an unattended answer file. You can't use DCPROMO GUI. You have to use an unattended answer file or command-line switches. See the Active Directory chapters for examples of unattended Active Directory installations.

To uninstall roles and features, use the same command but add `/uninstall` at the end. The exception again is ADDS, which once again uses DCPROMO.

Tables 14-2 and 14-3 list the names of the components and what they correspond to in features and roles. However, you can run `oclist` for a complete list; `oclist` is a Server Core–specific command. New roles and features will be added to Server Core in the future. For example, WDS support is expected in the Windows Server 2008 R2 timeframe.

Table 14-2 Server Roles and `Ocsetup` Names

Server Role	Ocsetup Name
Active Directory Lightweight Directory Services (ADAM)	DirectoryServices-ADAM-ServerCore
DHCP	DHCPServerCore
DNS	DNS-Server-Core-Role
Distributed File System Service	DFSN-Server
Distributed File System Replication (DFSR)	DFSR-Infrastructure-ServerEdition
File Services	File-Server-Core-Role
File Replication Service (FRS)	FRS-Infrastructure
IIS (no ASP.NET)	IIS-WebServerRole (plus subcomponents visible via oxlist)
Network File System (NFS)	ServerForNFS-Base
Media Server	MediaServer
Hyper-V	Microsoft-Hyper-V

Table 14-3 Server Features and `Ocsetup` Names

Server Feature	Ocsetup Name
Backup	WindowsServerBackup
BitLocker Drive Encryption	BitLocker
BitLocker Remote Admin Tool	BitLocker-RemoteAdminTool
Failover Cluster	FailoverCluster-Core
Multipath IO	Microsoft-Windows-MultipathIO
NFS Client	ClientForNFS-Base
Network Load Balancing	NetworkLoadBalancingHeadlessServer
Quality of Service	QWAVE
Removable Storage Management	Microsoft-Windows-RemovableStorageManagementCore
SNMP	SNMP-SC
Subsystem for UNIX-bases applications	SUACore
Telnet Client	TelnetClient
Windows Activation Service (WAS)	WAS-WindowsActivationService
WINS	WINS-SC

By default, if you execute `Ocsetup` with a package to install, the command prompt returns instantly while the installation happens in the background, and you will not know when the install has completed. To work around this, run the `Ocsetup` command after a `start /w` to tell the command to execute and to wait for the execution to complete.

Let's install the DNS Server role, as shown in Figure 14-12. During the install, the TrustedInstaller process is activated and responsible for the actual installation.

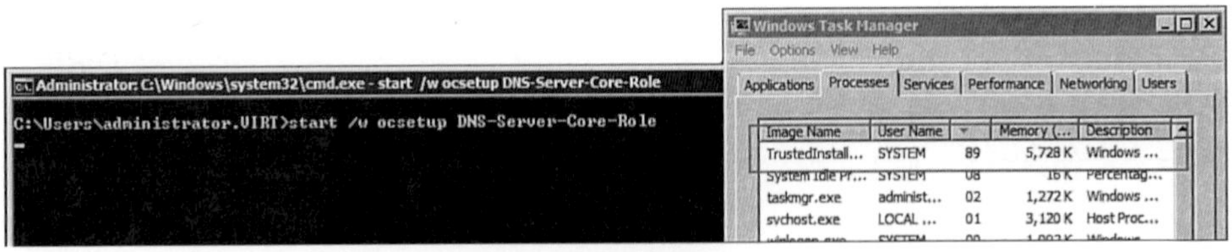

FIGURE 14-12 Installing a role is a one-step process.

After you install the role, it is marked as installed in the Optional Component listing, as shown in the following:

```
C:\Users\administrator.VIRT>oclist
Use the listed update names with Ocsetup.exe to install/unin-
stall a server role or optional feature.

Adding or removing the Active Directory role with OCSetup.exe
is not supported.
It can leave your server in an unstable state. Always use
DCPromo to install or uninstall Active Directory.

==============================================================
Microsoft-Windows-ServerCore-Package
Not Installed:BitLocker
Not Installed:BitLocker-RemoteAdminTool
Not Installed:ClientForNFS-Base
Not Installed:DFSN-Server
Not Installed:DFSR-Infrastructure-ServerEdition
Not Installed:DHCPServerCore
Not Installed:DirectoryServices-ADAM-ServerCore
Not Installed:DirectoryServices-DomainController-ServerFounda-
tion
    Installed:DNS-Server-Core-Role
Not Installed:FailoverCluster-Core
Not Installed:FRS-Infrastructure
```

In the DNS case, the service could be managed locally via DNSCMD, which is a standard part of the DNS role to facilitate command-line management, or more likely you can run the DNS MMC snap-in on a Vista/2008 box and remotely connect and manage the DNS service on the core installation. For example, in Figure 14-13, the root of the DNS navigation node is right-clicked and the Server Core installation is added, which you can now manage with the GUI remotely.

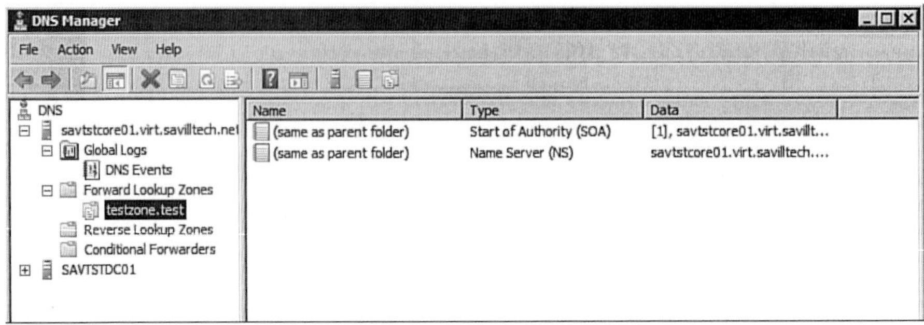

FIGURE 14-13 In reality, you remotely control most of the server core areas of functionality.

As with all the remote GUI tools, if you receive an Access Denied error, solve it by performing a `net use` to the machine before remotely connecting. The command establishes an authenticated session:

```
C:\Users\john>net use * \\savtstcore01.virt.savilltech.net\c$
➥/user:virt\administrator *
Type the password for \\savtstcore01.virt.savilltech.net\c$:
*****
Drive Z: is now connected to
\\savtstcore01.virt.savilltech.net\c$.

The command completed successfully.
```

A better way is to use `cmdkey`, which allows credentials to be set for various target systems:

```
C:\Users\john>cmdkey /add:savtstcore01.virt.savilltech.net
➥/user:virt\administrator /pass:********

CMDKEY: Credential added successfully.
```

Installing Applications

For the Windows Server 2008 release, Server Core is designed to run in-the-box functions, that is, the supported server roles and features and not additional applications.

None of the major products are supported on Server Core; for example, Exchange, SharePoint, SQL, and so on. For additional applications, there is some planning for the future when managed code support is added to Server Core. However, there are limits to what can be added to Server Core; otherwise, it becomes a normal Windows installation.

Agents should be installable and supportable under Server Core, for example, backup agents, Microsoft Operations Manager (MOM), Systems Management Server (SMS) agents, and so on, which are managed via a remote administrative console function. You can install antivirus agents on Server Core installations and manage them remotely. For example, ForeFront runs on Server Core. Virtual machine additions can be installed and they run fine; in fact, they are recommended. The general rule of thumb is that agents have no shell or GUI dependencies and do not require managed code; if all these are true, the agent runs under Server Core.

To install additional software, execute the setup executables or manually install the MSI files using this command:

```
Msiexec /i <application>.msi
```

To check the installed applications, use the `wmic` command and the production function as shown in the following:

```
C:\Windows\System32>wmic
wmic:root\cli>product
AssignmentType  Caption                     Description
1               Virtual Machine Additions   Virtual Machine
Additions
```

This output is long, so you need to scroll to see everything.

To uninstall an application, use the `wmic` command by checking the name of the application and then calling uninstall for it, for example:

```
C:\Windows\System32>wmic product get name /value
Name=Virtual Machine Additions

C:\Windows\System32>wmic product where name="Virtual Machine
➥Additions" call uninstall
```

In the short term, the only installations you do will likely be agents and antivirus, but who knows what the future will bring?

Performing Common Actions Using Server Core

One quick way to get information about your environment is with the systeminfo command, as shown executing in the following listing:

```
C:\Windows\System32>systeminfo.exe

Host Name:                 SAVTSTCORE01
OS Name:                   Microsoftr Windows Serverr 2008
Enterprise
OS Version:                6.0.6001 Service Pack 1, v.222 Build
6001
OS Manufacturer:           Microsoft Corporation
OS Configuration:          Member Server
OS Build Type:             Multiprocessor Free
Registered Owner:          Windows User
Registered Organization:
Product ID:                78440-034-0066664-70918
Original Install Date:     9/4/2007, 4:05:28 PM
System Boot Time:          9/9/2007, 6:46:54 PM
System Manufacturer:       Microsoft Corporation
System Model:              Virtual Machine
System Type:               X86-based PC
Processor(s):              1 Processor(s) Installed.
                           [01]: x86 Family 6 Model 15 Stepping
6 GenuineIntel ~
4 Mhz
BIOS Version:              American Megatrends Inc. 080002 ,
2/22/2006
Windows Directory:         C:\Windows
System Directory:          C:\Windows\system32
Boot Device:               \Device\HarddiskVolume1
System Locale:             en-us;English (United States)
Input Locale:              en-us;English (United States)
Time Zone:                 (GMT-06:00) Central Time (US &
Canada)
Total Physical Memory:     1,023 MB
Available Physical Memory: 778 MB
Page File: Max Size:       2,299 MB
Page File: Available:      2,092 MB
Page File: In Use:         207 MB
```

```
Page File Location(s):       C:\pagefile.sys
Domain:                      virt.savilltech.net
Logon Server:                \\SAVTSTDC01
Hotfix(s):                   N/A
Network Card(s):             N/A
```

One item many users struggle with is no system clock, which they get used to in the System Tray. You can update your prompt to include the time with the following prompt command:

```
C:\Windows\System32>prompt [$T]$S$P$G

[10:50:03.26] C:\Windows\System32>
[10:50:04.50] C:\Windows\System32>
```

What else do you normally use on a system? The Task Manager. Its keyboard shortcut still works in Server Core, so press Ctrl+Shift+Esc to open the Windows Task Manager or access it via the Windows Security Dialog by pressing Ctrl+Alt+Del. There is no Windows Task Manager help, however, because the help is based on HTML, which is not included in the Server Core.

What about rebooting, shutting down, and logging off? You can access the Windows Security dialog and elect to shut down or reboot, or you can use the Windows standard shutdown command. The key switches you use are as follows, but you can find full information by running `shutdown /?`.

- `/s`. Shutdown.
- `/r`. Reboot.
- `/t 0`. Wait 0 seconds to perform the action.
- `/a`. Abort a shutdown. This is usable only if you had a time other than 0, so you can type before the reboot/shutdown occurs.

For example, to reboot the computer immediately, use this command:

```
Shutdown /r /t 0
```

To log out, you can use the logoff command-line utility or the Windows Security dialog.

From a utility perspective, both Notepad and Regedit are included in Server Core, RegEdit because you need it and Notepad because customers demanded it. However, neither has help because the help has dependencies on HTML. As noted previously, HTML is not included. However, the basic Copy, Paste, Find, and other commands all function. The Open and Save dialogs might look familiar, but not in a good way (see Figure 14-14).

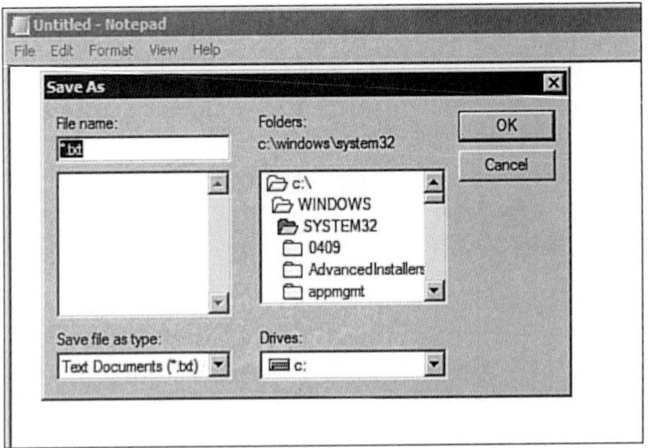

FIGURE 14-14 The days before the new operating system dialogs.

Remotely Managing Server Core

You have seen that you can use the command line for many configuration items, and nearly all Windows components come with command-line tools for management. So, you could manage Server Core locally. However, that is far from ideal, and you turned on the remote admin mode of Terminal Services so that you could remote to the box and access Server Core as if logged on locally. You have also seen how the MMC snap-ins can run on other computers and remotely manage the services on a Server Core installation. For example, the DNS MMC snap-in is probably the most-used remote management method. There are other options which give you the ability to remotely run commands on the Server Core installation—thanks to the inclusion of RPC and DCOM on Server Core, which facilitate the remote administration. Remember to enable the RemoteManage firewall rule.

Three of the MMC snap-ins require additional configuration on the Server Core installation:

- For Device Manager, enable the PnP policy. Even when enabled, Device Manager runs in a read-only mode, which is useful for checking hardware and device driver info. Load the local policy on the Server Core box (or create a Group Policy Object [GPO] that applies to Server Core) and enable the Allow Remote Access to the PnP Interface policy under Computer Configuration, Administrative Templates, System, Device Installation and reboot the Server Core computer, as shown in Figure 14-15.
- The Disk Management MMC snap-in requires two changes. Enable a firewall group on the server core installation and on the machine performing the remote management: `netsh advfirewall firewall set rule group="Remote Volume Management" new enable=yes`
  In addition, run the Virtual Disk Service via this command:
  `net start VDS`
- Enable Remote IPsec Monitor management using the SCRegEdit.wsf script:

```
C:\Windows\System32> cscript scregedit.wsf /IM 1
```


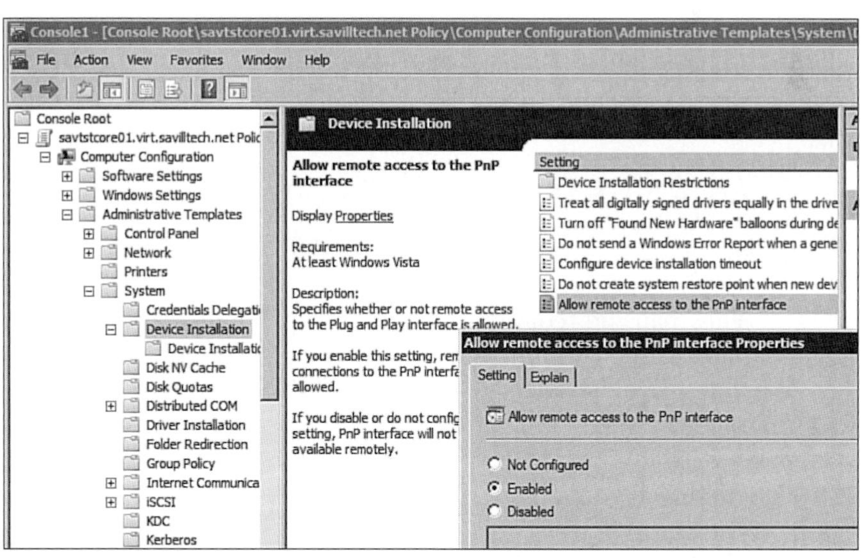

FIGURE 14-15 Enable the Allow Remote Access to the PnP Interface policy.

Another command-line option is the WS-Management and Windows Remote Shell. However, this runs the command, remotely catches the output, and sends it back. The advantage of WS-Management is that it operates over HyperText Transfer Protocol (HTTP) or HyperText Transfer Protocol over Secure Sockets Layer (HTTPS), so there are no additional port requirements for WS-Management to function because the HTTP ports are normally open by default. However, you can change this port if required.

When you enable WS-Management on the server using the quick configuration, the best security method available to the installation is used. For example, on a domain-joined machine, Kerberos is selected. Run the `winrm quickconfig` command as shown in the following listing:

```
C:\Users\administrator.VIRT>winrm quickconfig
WinRM is not set up to allow remote access to this machine for
management.
The following changes must be made:

Create a WinRM listener on HTTP://* to accept WS-Man requests
to any IP on this machine.
Enable the WinRM firewall exception.

Make these changes [y/n]? y

WinRM has been updated for remote management.

Created a WinRM listener on HTTP://* to accept WS-Man requests
to any IP on this machine.
WinRM firewall exception enabled.
```

This can be configured via Group Policy through Computer Configuration, Administrative Templates, Windows Components, Windows Remote Management, WinRM Service and enabling Allow Automatic Configuration of Listeners. There are other options in the same policy location regarding the use of Kerberos/Basic authentication.

On the client side, use the `WinRS` command in the following format:

```
WinRS -r:<remote system> command
```

For the remote system, type in the name of the remote computer or enter it in the form of a URL; for example, http://ip address:port or http://fqdn; http://192.168.1.232:80 or http://savtstcore01.virt.savilltech.com. By default, your existing credentials are used. Credentials are passed using the /domain, /userd and /password arguments. Some sample uses are shown in the following listing:

```
C:\Users\Administrator>winrs -r:savtstcore01 ipconfig

Windows IP Configuration



Ethernet adapter Local Area Connection:

   Connection-specific DNS Suffix  . . :
   Link-local IPv6 Address . . . . . :
fe80::c49a:b729:8c8b:471e%2
   IPv4 Address. . . . . . . . . . . : 192.168.1.232
   Subnet Mask . . . . . . . . . . . : 255.255.255.0
   Default Gateway . . . . . . . . . : 192.168.1.1

Tunnel adapter Local Area Connection*:

   Media State . . . . . . . . . . . : Media disconnected
   Connection-specific DNS Suffix  . . :

Tunnel adapter Local Area Connection* 2:

   Media State . . . . . . . . . . . : Media disconnected
   Connection-specific DNS Suffix  . . :

C:\Users\Administrator>winrs -r:savtstcore01 cscript
➥c:\windows\system32\scregedit.wsf /AR /v
Microsoft (R) Windows Script Host Version 5.7
Copyright (C) Microsoft Corporation. All rights reserved.

System\CurrentControlSet\Control\Terminal Server
  fDenyTSConnections
View Registry setting.
0
```

You can use the Task Scheduler as in a normal Windows installation, as items such as event logging/forwarding and performance counters, which you can fully access via the Computer Management MMC running remotely, as shown in Figure 14-16. You can use the reliability interface against Server Core. Note that you can access both the Task Scheduler and Event Viewer through the Computer Management MMC snap-in. You have full access to the local users and groups. (Although you could use the `net user` and `net localgroup` commands to perform user/group management locally.)

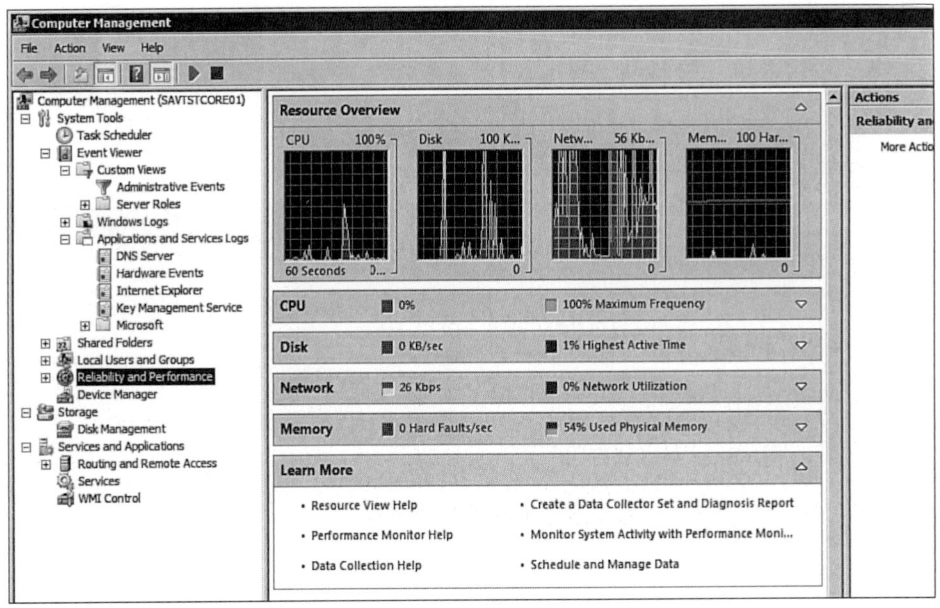

FIGURE 14-16 The remote capabilities of RPC and DCOM give the GUI-less Server Core a great remote GUI experience.

If you want to view the event log locally on a Server Core installation, use the `Wevtutil.exe` command. For example, to view the five most recent event logs in text format from the SYSTEM log, use the following command:

```
C:\Windows\System32>wevtutil qe system /rd:true /c:5 /f:text
Event[0]:
  Log Name: System
  Source: Virtual Disk Service
  Date: 2007-09-09T19:04:09.000
```

```
  Event ID: 4
  Task: N/A
  Level: Information
  Opcode: N/A
  Keyword: Classic
  User: N/A
  User Name: N/A
  Computer: savtstcore01.virt.savilltech.net
  Description:
Service stopped.
```

You can also search for specific event IDs. For example, to search for reboots, which are event ID 1074, use the following command:

```
wevtutil qe system /q:*[System[(EventID=1074)]] /f:text
```

SNMP can be enabled on Server Core to allow management by your management tools if they are SNMP-based. SNMP is enabled by installing the SNMP feature. Both SNMPv1 and SNMPv2c are supported. Normal WMI scripting can be used both locally and, more likely, from a remote station.

Let's look back at the Remote Desktop option. Maybe you want a remote command prompt without a full session. With the new application publishing features of Windows Server 2008, you can publish a command prompt by performing the following actions.

You need to use the Terminal Services (TS) RemoteApp Manager, which is available on a full Windows 2008 installation with the Terminal Server Role installed. So, on a full Windows Server installation, add the Terminal Server role. Notice you need Terminal Server only because you want access to the RemoteApp Manager. Alternatively, you can add the Remote Server Administration Tools feature and select only the Terminal Server Tools option if you don't want to install the Terminal Server role on any server, as shown in Figure 14-17. This latter option avoids installing TS and allows configuration from any platform supporting Remote Server Administration Tools; for example, Windows Vista.

After the TS RemoteApp Manager is running, change the server that the client connects to so that the Server Core machine is selected via the Connect to Computer option in the Action menu of the Actions pane. In the Actions pane, click the Add RemoteApp Programs link, which starts the RemoteApp Wizard (covered in detail in Chapter 9, "Terminal Services"). After clicking Next at the Introduction screen of the wizard, a list of programs that can be published is displayed. Click the Browse button, navigate to the Windows\System32 folder, and select cmd.exe. Click Next, as shown in Figure 14-18, and then click Finish.

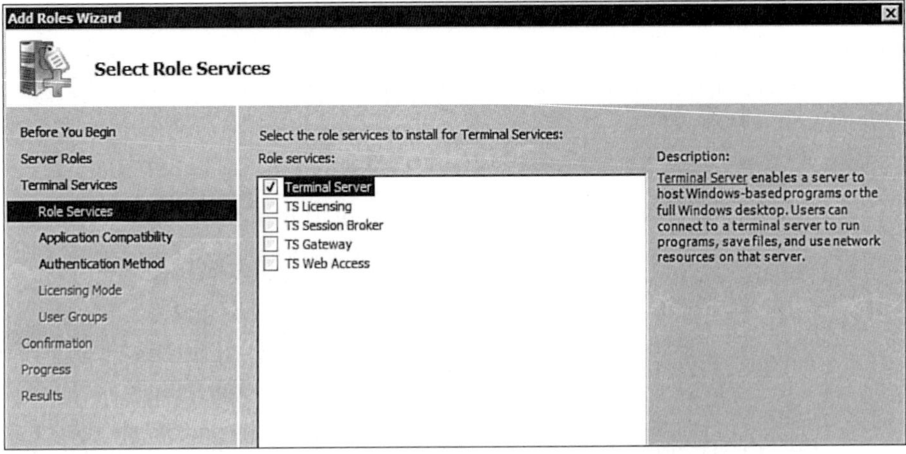

FIGURE 14-17 Adding the Terminal Server role to a server. There's no need for the other components.

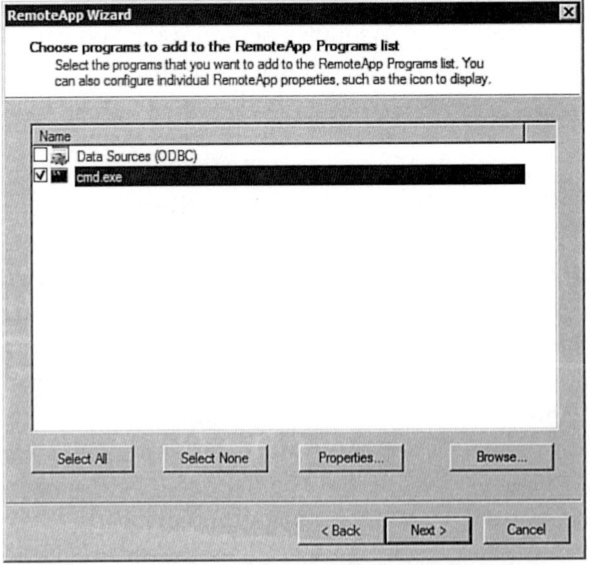

FIGURE 14-18 Publishing the cmd.exe application.

Finally, as shown in Figure 14-19, click the Create .rdp File link. Figure 14-19 shows the options for connecting to a computer and starting the Add RemoteApp Program Wizard.

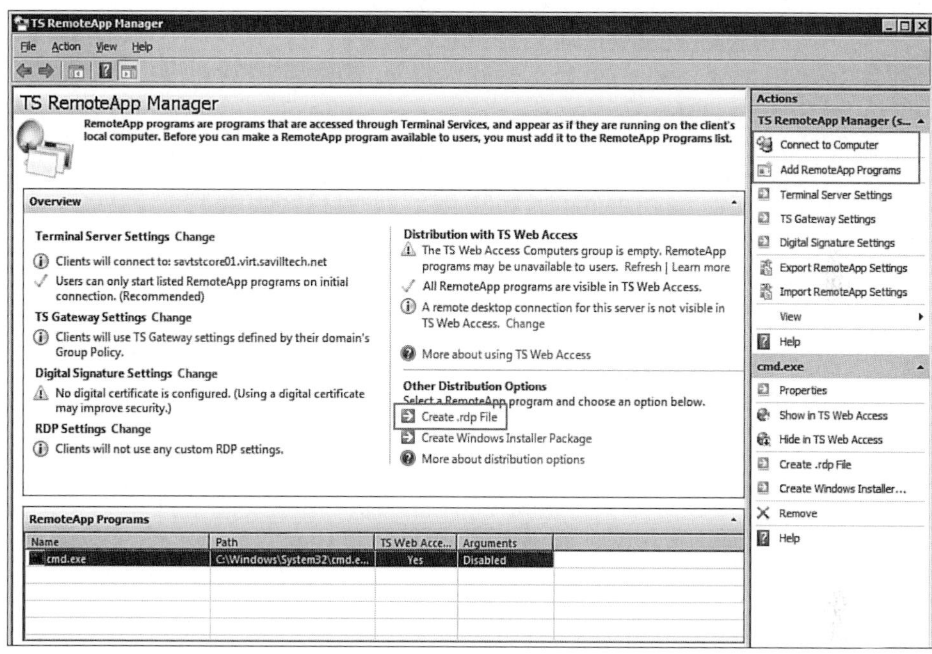

FIGURE 14-19 Creating a published application RDP for the cmd prompt.

You can take the generated RDP file and run it from any Vista/Windows Server 2008 client to open a seamless command window that is running on the Server Core installation. The following listing shows the content of the generated RDP that can be modified with an updated server name:

```
disableclipboardredirection:i:0
redirectposdevices:i:0
redirectprinters:i:1
redirectcomports:i:1
redirectsmartcards:i:1
devicestoredirect:s:*
drivestoredirect:s:*
redirectdrives:i:1
```

```
session bpp:i:32
span monitors:i:1
remoteapplicationmode:i:1
server port:i:3389
allow font smoothing:i:1
promptcredentialonce:i:0
authentication level:i:0
gatewayusagemethod:i:2
gatewayprofileusagemethod:i:0
gatewaycredentialssource:i:0
full address:s:savtstcore01.virt.savilltech.net
alternate shell:s:||cmd
gatewayhostname:s:
remoteapplicationname:s:cmd.exe
remoteapplicationcmdline:s:
screen mode id:i:2
winposstr:s:0,1,424,117,835,356
compression:i:1
smart sizing:i:1
keyboardhook:i:2
audiomode:i:0
redirectclipboard:i:1
displayconnectionbar:i:1
autoreconnection enabled:i:1
prompt for credentials:i:0
negotiate security layer:i:1
remoteapplicationicon:s:
shell working directory:s:
disable wallpaper:i:1
disable full window drag:i:1
allow desktop composition:i:0
disable menu anims:i:1
disable themes:i:0
disable cursor setting:i:0
bitmapcachepersistenable:i:1
```

When using a terminal server connection with the Terminal Server Client (`mstsc`), ensure that disk drives are available from the client machine by selecting the drives as available under the Local Resources tab (you have to click the More button) or as an option, as shown in Figure 14-20. The local client drives are accessible as \\tsclient\<drive> on the remote system. You can then map to these drives to get full access as in the following example:

```
C:\Windows\System32>net use * \\tsclient\d
Drive Y: is now connected to \\tsclient\d.

The command completed successfully.
```

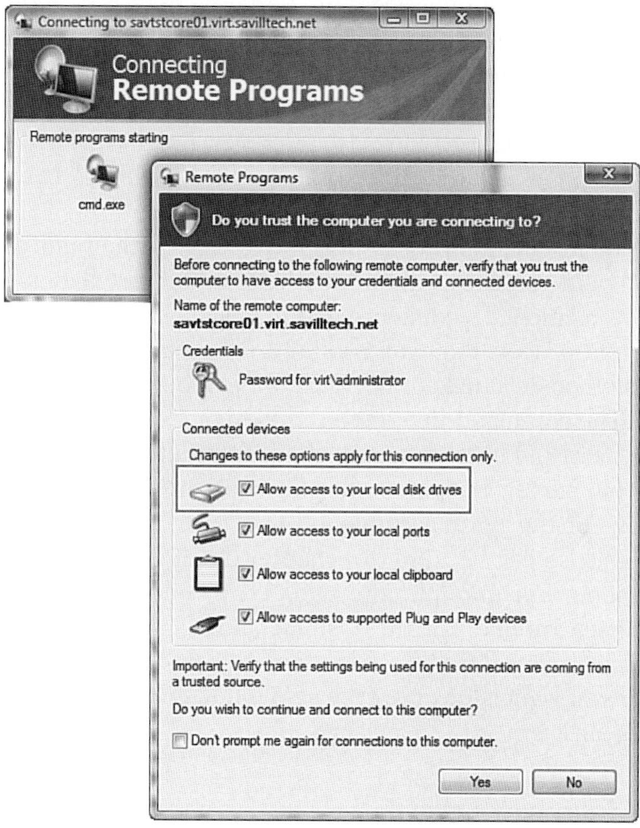

FIGURE 14-20 The Remote Programs client gives easy access to controlling the local resource access.

Summary

Server Core is a great addition to the Windows Server family. If the estimate of Server Core needing only one-third the patches required by a full Windows installation is accurate, Server Core will be much easier to manage. Resource usage is lower, with around two-thirds of the normal number of services both installed and running.

So far the top uses for Server Core are expected to be domain controllers (and Server Core also supports Read Only Domain Controllers [RODC]) making it ideal for branch office locations, IIS Web servers, and file/print servers.

The installation process for Server Core is the same as for a full installation, and you can use the same automated installation methods as for a full installation. To configure and manage a core installation, use a slightly different process than you use for a full installation, even though many of the methods you use for Server Core can be used on a full server installation. The command-line options in Server Core give you the ability to perform nearly all functions, and where they fall short you can remotely manage your server. But remember that Server Core is still a Windows installation. All the normal command-line tools and scripting capabilities are available, so just because this chapter didn't cover it does not mean it's not an option. For example, the `tasklist` command is great for seeing the processes running on the system, and `taskkill` is great for stopping them!

If you want a lower overhead Windows installation, Server Core might be the answer.

CHAPTER 15

DISTRIBUTED FILE SYSTEM

Most environments today have some elements of a distributed infrastructure, the exact scale of which depends on the company and the business performed. This distributed environment could range from a single head office with a few branch locations to a global organization with multiple main locations in each country, with branch locations acting as spokes from the regional hubs.

There are numerous challenges with a distributed environment in terms of maintaining a consistent deployment of servers and clients among the enterprise, sharing information between the locations in a bandwidth-efficient manner while not adversely affecting the end-user experience, and managing the distributed environment.

This book looks at a large number of services that relate to distributed environments and best practices. This chapter recaps some of the key areas that are critical to distributed environments. You've already spent a lot of time on the availability of file servers. So what else is important?

The decision about whether to have a local file server depends on the amount of data accessed by the users and the network connectivity speed between the location and the central hub/data center locations. Ideally, the more you can consolidate servers to a central location, the easier the management and the lower the IT costs. However, there will be times when you need local servers for performance/bandwidth reasons. Just make sure you always consider the additional costs for hardware, software, licensing, and the complexities of managing remote systems, including patching and backups.

Security is always an important consideration; any servers should be physically secure, if possible. Definitely consider using BitLocker to encrypt the drives of any servers.

Distribution of Other Services

Let's take a look at distributed services for some of the key services in an environment.

Domain Controllers

Chapters 10, "Active Directory Domain Services Introduction," through 13, "Active Directory Federated Services, Lightweight Directory Services, and Rights Management," talk about placement of domain controllers. However, it is likely that you will need domain controllers in most locations that have any sizable user population—say, more than 20 people. A local domain controller is important if you have any resources at a location that a user may need to access even if network connectivity to the hub locations is down. Without a local domain controller, if network connectivity to the hub locations is down, the users cannot authenticate. That means even if resources are in the same location as the user, without authentication, no access is possible.

If a location does not have good security, use the new Windows Server 2008 Read-Only Domain Controller (RODC) functionality to minimize potential security risks.

Networking Services

Most branch locations have some limited network hardware that could support a dedicated line between the branch and the hub location or a simple router to run a virtual private network (VPN) over the Internet to the central location. In some cases, for small environments, this hardware could act as a Dynamic Host Configuration Protocol (DHCP) server to give out Internet Protocol (IP) addresses. However, your IP configuration is closely tied to the Windows environment, so where possible, the DHCP services should be located on a Windows server. They could be on a local server in the environment, or a DHCP relay agent could be used to forward address requests to a DHCP server in another location over a wide area network (WAN) link via configuration on a router or via a DHCP relay agent.

For other services, such as domain name system (DNS), if a location has a local domain controller, the best option is to enable DNS on the domain controller, which clients can access locally, with a central location DNS server as the secondary.

Remote access should be accomplished via the central location. Do not configure separate remote access interfaces at branch locations. This should be prohibited because if local branch people set up their own remote access systems that do not meet the corporate standards, you have a serious security breach.

Print Management

If a location has printers, it makes sense to have a local print server for the management of printing. Although a remote print server in another location could theoretically be used, this does not make sense from a bandwidth perspective. If a user prints a document, the print data has to be sent across the WAN link from the branch to the hub from the printer client to the print server and then back over the WAN link from the print server to the actual printer.

The management of remote print servers has always been problematic. However, with the Print Management Console in Windows Server 2008, it's much easier to remotely manage print servers and the connections to remote print servers. Review Chapter 5, "File System and Print Management Features," to learn about the Print Management Console.

Management

The biggest challenge in a remote environment is the management of the servers and clients. From a basic administration perspective, most of the Microsoft Management Console (MMC) snap-ins can remotely connect to a server and then perform actions as normal. Another option is to use Remote Desktop to access the servers or options such as Windows Remote Management (WinRM). You can also use scripts to manage multiple remote servers, especially with Windows Management Instrumentation (WMI). Microsoft provides remote server administration tools that you can install on Windows Vista Service Pack 1 to enable easy management both locally and remotely from normal client machines.

Aside from just the administration, there are other factors. Servers require patching, which can be a challenge for remote servers. A partial solution is to use Server Core at remote, and even local, locations because it has a much smaller footprint and requires less patching than a full installation. For the actual patching, use Windows Server auto update or, ideally, a centralized solution that enables administrators to approve patches prior to deployment, such as Windows Server Update Services (WSUS) or System Center Configuration Manager (SCCM) 2007.

Backup is another challenge because most remote locations do not have full backup solutions. Although Distributed File System Replication (DFSR) can be used to replicate information from the branches to a central location for backup, there are other options, such as System Center Data Protection Manager, that can replicate data from remote locations to a centralized disk-based backup solution, which can then export to tape.

Deploying remote servers and desktops is challenging. If you have a solution such as SCCM, then any local file servers can be used to distribute applications and operating systems (OSs). Other options would be to use group policy for application deployment, specifying installation from a path at the local location or from a Distributed File System (DFS) target that redirects to a local installation source. For the installation of OSs, a common model is to ship hardware to a central location for buildout and then ship it to the remote locations.

For desktop and server configuration at all locations, use both central and distributed group policy; avoid trying to use Registry modifications to set configuration because doing so is not scalable.

There is one technology that stands out and deserves its own chapter when it comes to providing simple and efficient access to data in a distributed environment: DFS. One of the toughest aspects of a distributed environment is providing access to file-based information. Although a solution would be to store the information once in a central location and then allow other offices access over the links to the central location, this does not work well if the link speed between the central office and the remote offices is slow or has high latency. For usability purposes, the data needs to exist locally at the larger locations. However, this introduces other problems:

- How do users know which copy of the data to use if it exists in multiple locations?
- How do you know where the data is?
- How is the data in each location kept in sync with the other copies?
- What happens if a file is edited in multiple locations at the same time?

Fortunately, one solution, DFS, addresses all these problems. Although DFS has been around a long time (initially as an optional download for Windows NT 4.0 Server), the technology has continued to evolve. With Windows Server 2008, there is finally an implementation that is a realistic option for maintaining copies of data between multiple locations.

Although DFS is a solution to the problem of sharing and replicating data between multiple locations, you have two separate technologies in play. The first is Distributed File System Namespace (DFSN), which is used to provide the user with a single, abstracted view of all the data in the environment in a logical namespace that is totally separate from where the data physically resides. The second is Distributed File System Replication (DFSR), which was new to Windows Server 2003 Release 2 and is part of Windows Server 2008. It provides the replication technology to keep multiple copies of data synchronized. Let's look at each part separately.

Distributed File System Namespace

Think about how users normally access data. Normally, you map a letter to a share on a server as part of a logon script or other policy. If users have to access multiple shares on a server, they have multiple mapped drives, until their Explorer interface looks like a can of alphabet soup. This is not usable. Alternatively, the users may know the Universal Naming Convention (UNC) path of a share (for example, *<server>**<share>*) and use it to access less data that are used relatively infrequently. However, this is difficult for the average user. Finally, users can search for shares by browsing the network, clicking a server, and viewing the shares that are available. Now this browsing of shares is made a little easier by publishing shares in Active Directory (AD), but it's still a flat structure of shares. The more shares you have, the harder it is to find the data you want to find.

DFSN enables you to create a hierarchical namespace for the data that users can navigate. Although DFSN gives the impression of being a single share with a number of folders, it is a series of pointers that redirect the users to the location of data without the users' knowledge. With DFS, the user sees a single share to connect to, which has a hierarchical layout that makes navigation of the data available and intuitive. Think of DFSN as a share virtualization service, with all the shares as virtual names within the namespace.

A DFSN Example

Figure 15-1 shows an example of three file servers with two shares each. Under normal circumstances, users would have six mapped drive letters for each of the shares or a combination of mapped drive letters and the use of UNC paths. Instead, a single share is used, which provides a single view of all the shares that are available but of which the user is unaware. The user thinks she is navigating a single share where all the information resides (see Figure 15-2), which is what the end user sees when viewing a domain-based namespace. The only clue that the user isn't browsing a normal server share is that instead of a server name, there's a domain name (for example, savilltech.net). That is, of course, because the user is viewing a domain-based DFSN. If the user were viewing a stand-alone server namespace, the name of the DFSN server would be used. Notice that the user has no idea where these folders point to; the redirection is all done behind the scenes, unknown to the client.

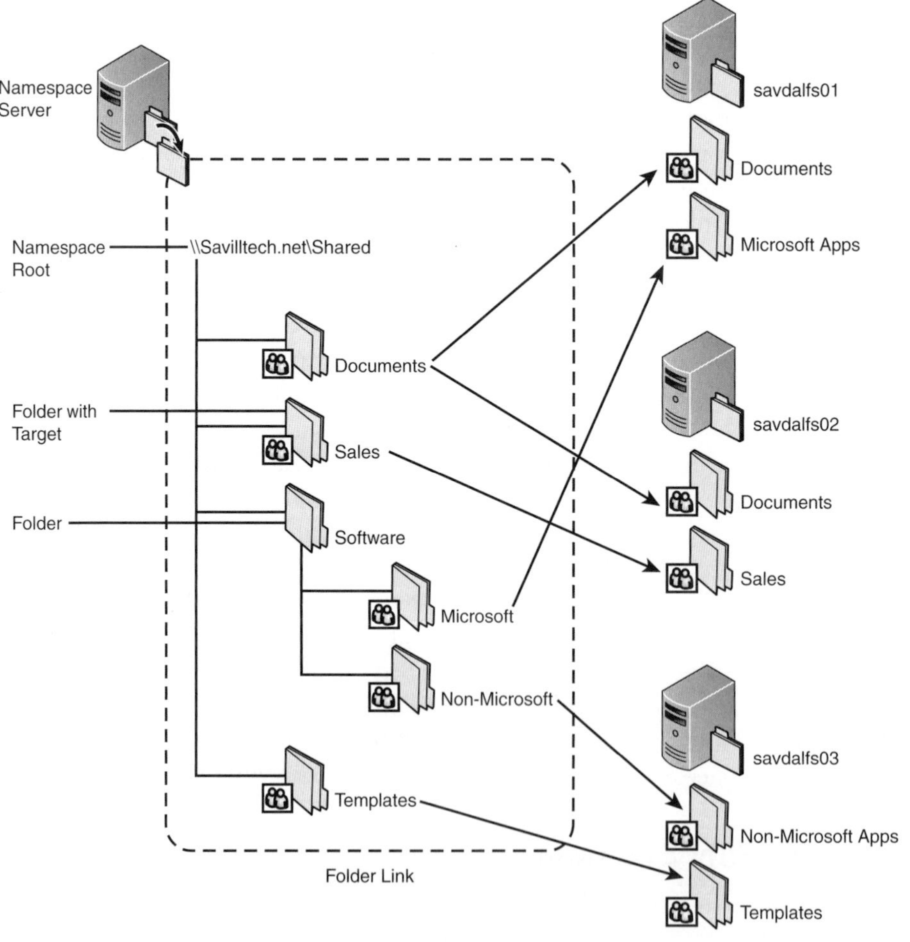

FIGURE 15-1 An overview of a DFSN.

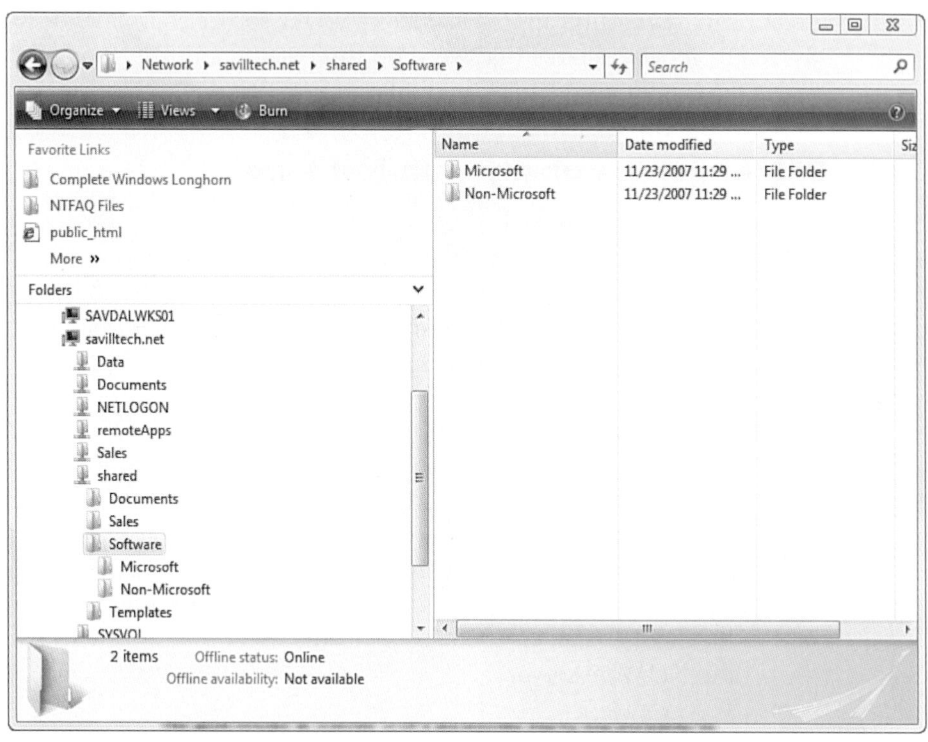

FIGURE 15-2 The client view of a DFSN.

It is possible to create multiple namespaces. Doing so may be desirable in environments with different sets of information that are viewed, to avoid showing users large numbers of "folders" that are of no interest to them.

Further Applications of DFSN

This DFSN view simplifies the end user's experience but can also help administrators. Imagine that you want to decommission server savdalfs03 and replace it with savdalfs04. If users are using direct UNC paths to savdalfs03 or mapped drives, after you migrate the data, the users must update any paths containing savdalfs03 to, say, savdafs04, which may include going through many documents that contain embedded links. With DFS, update the folder target to point to savdafs04 instead of savdalfs03, and the end user will never know. Where the information resides does not affect users. The same approach is possible for server consolidation. Let's say you're moving shares that were on three servers down to one server. With DFSN, you just change the folder target; the client never knows.

DFSN Interoperability with NetWare

The preceding section looked at migrating data. You can also use that approach to move data from other OSs, such as NetWare, to Windows. Performing a migration would normally be complex and troublesome. It would involve trying to move the data and update the client paths at the right times. Instead, simply perform the following:

1. Create a DFSN with folders that have targets on the NetWare OS.
2. Update all user paths from \\netwareserver\share to the path via DFS. Do this over a period of weeks because the NetWare path and DFS path both work and point to the same location.
3. When all clients are accessing NetWare via DFS, migrate the contents of a NetWare share to a Windows-based server and update the DFS folder target to point to the Windows server instead of the NetWare server.

With this approach, you don't have to try to make sure all paths that point to NetWare are updated at the time you migrate the actual data. Instead, take your time and update all paths to the DFSN weeks in advance of the actual move. DFS links can point to virtually any file share that the client OS can communicate with. Remember that DFS redirects the user. It does not act as a protocol or communication gateway. DFS has been tested with and used to connect to not only Server Message Block (SMB) shares but also Network File System (NFS) and Distributed Authoring and Versioning (DAV) shares.

DFSN Components and Mechanics

A number of components in DFSN are core to the functionality of DFS. For example, the namespace server is a server with the DFSN service that stores the actual namespace for the DFSN instance. Clients use DFSN servers to navigate and view the logical namespaces. The namespace root is the starting point in a DFSN logical namespace. The actual namespace can be stored in a stand-alone mode, where the namespace is written to the Registry and cached in memory, or in a domain mode, which uses AD to store the namespace, enabling multiple servers to host the namespace, providing greater availability and scalability by spreading the client requests to navigate the namespace across multiple servers.

With DFSN, there are two types of folder: a plain folder and a folder with a target/link. Folder target and folder link are used interchangeably in the OS. Both of these folder types, with or without targets, are created the same way, using the DFS Management MMC snap-in. However, a folder without a target is configured without any links to target shares on other servers and can contain other folders with or without links. You would typically create folders without links for the purpose of adding hierarchy to the namespace—for example, grouping other types of links. The earlier example shows a folder named software that was created with no links, and it contained two subfolders, both with links to Microsoft and non-Microsoft software. A folder with a target has a target share where actual content is stored. You cannot add folders in the DFSN to a folder that has targets. A folder that has targets is considered a boundary point for the DFSN. When a user is redirected to a DFS target, that target share can have a folder hierarchy, but it does not link back to DFS or have other DFS links. It is possible to have folder links pointing to another DFSN. This allows you to create embedded namespaces and large DFS environments.

Folder targets can point to any share, and you can point to more than one share for a DFS folder, as is the case with documents in Figure 15-1. Why? Typically, there are two reasons. First, do this to provide redundancy so if one server that hosts the data goes down, clients can be redirected to another folder target that should host the same content. The second reason is to allow regionally distributed environments to host copies of a folder on servers at each location without the clients having to worry about which copy of the data to use. The users are automatically redirected to the folder target that is closest. This is determined by checking the AD site that the client IP address belongs in and the AD sites of the various servers that are folder targets for a specific folder. This process is shown in Figure 15-3. This figure shows the same DFS configuration as Figure 15-1, but now the servers hosting documents are in two different AD sites, and clients in each site are directed to the folder target in their local site. DFS is an AD site-aware application, and this is another reason why getting your AD sites properly defined is vital.

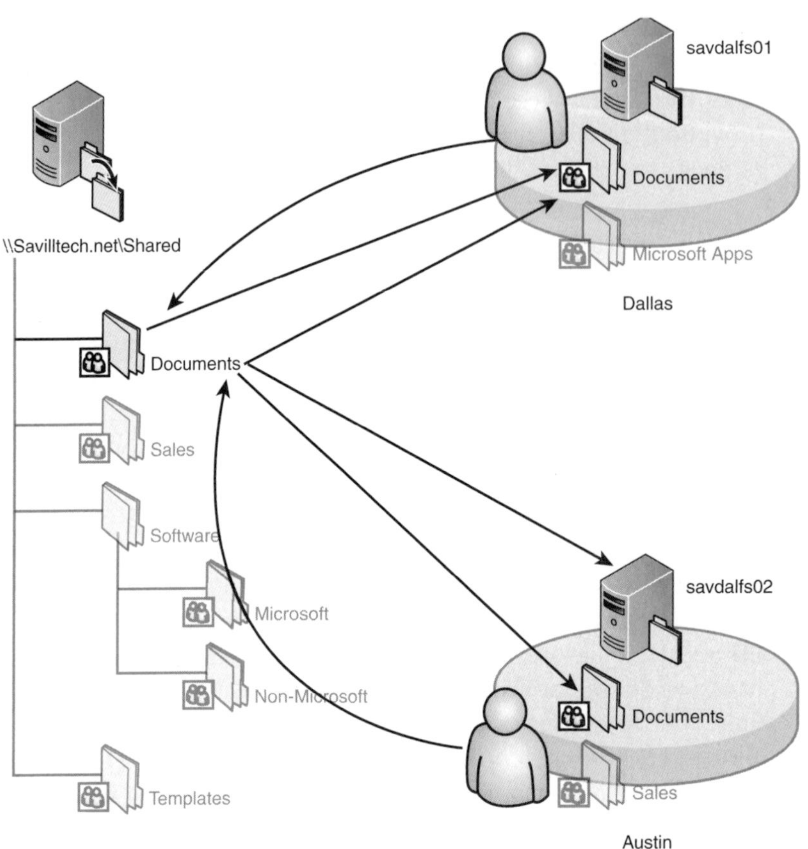

FIGURE 15-3 The site awareness of namespaces.

This single namespace folder that redirects users to a target that is closest to them is useful. Imagine how it could be used in software deployment. Today, when deploying software, you may need to perform checks on where the user is and run a separate script. With DFS, just deploy the software from a DFSN path, and the user automatically downloads and installs the software from the closest folder target.

So what is required for clients to be able to use DFS? Any computer running Windows NT 4.0 with Service Pack 6a or above supports namespaces (with Windows Preinstallation Environment [PE] supporting standalone namespaces only). However, the following OSs also support client failback to a preferred folder target:

- Windows Server 2008
- Windows Vista Business, Windows Vista Enterprise, Windows Vista Ultimate
- Windows Server 2003 Release 2
- Windows Storage Server 2003 Release 2
- Windows Server 2003 with Service Pack 2, or Service Pack 1 and the Windows Server 2003 client failback hotfix (KB898900)
- Windows XP Professional with Service Pack 3 or Service Pack 2 and the Windows XP client failback hotfix (KB898900)

Client failback enables a client who was redirected to another folder target because his preferred target was not available (for example, because the server crashed) to be redirected to the preferred target when the target is available again and the client's referral Time to Live (TTL) has expired, which causes the client to ask the DFS server which folder target it should use.

The configuration of sites is covered in more detail later in this chapter, but for now you at least understand the idea behind DFSN.

Windows Server 2008 DFSN Changes

There are some major differences between the Windows Server 2008 implementation of DFSN and those of previous versions:

- Prior to Windows Server 2008, a maximum number of links could exist within a single namespace; this maximum number was 5,000 for a domain-based DFSN and 50,000 for a stand-alone DFSN. Because of this limitation, it was sometimes necessary for companies to chain together multiple namespaces. With Windows Server 2008, there is no limit imposed by DFSN. However, there are still performance issues that may limit the number of links you can have in a namespace, but this will be much higher than the old limits. To avoid the limits, all domain controllers must be running Windows Server 2008 and the domain must be running in Windows Server 2008 mode, which means the new metadata and schema changes must have been propagated into the domain.
- In terms of performance, the internal workings of DFS have been improved, providing much better performance than with previous DFS implementations, enabling faster link additions and the DFS server to start faster with large namespaces.

- Command-line tools are supplied as part of the DFS role, including `dfsutil` and `dfsdiag`, which can be used to completely manage DFS from the command line or scripts.
- There is now a single MMC snap-in that manages both DFSN and replication.
- Cluster support for stand-alone namespaces now enables a stand-alone namespace to be made highly available. However, this is possible only on Windows Server 2008 cluster members. For a domain-based namespace, a cluster is not required because the namespace is stored in AD, and high availability is added via multiple DFSN servers configured to read from AD.

These changes do not affect the clients, however, only how you manage the DFS servers.

We have talked about having multiple targets for a DFSN folder. However, there are challenges with this, which is where the second component of DFS—DFSR—comes into play.

Distributed File System Replication

Although having multiple targets for a folder is great in concept, it's a problem when a client may travel and be redirected to different servers that are all targets for a DFSN folder if the content is not kept consistent. Imagine that you're in Dallas and save a proposal to the documents folder of the DFSN. It saves to a Dallas file server as the target. You then drive to Austin and navigate to the same documents folder, but this time you're redirected to a file server in Austin, and your document is not there because the two copies of the folder are not synchronized.

This was a major problem with DFS prior to Windows Server 2003 Release 2, which finally introduced a technology to successfully keep the various folder targets synchronized. The previous "in box" solution was to use File Replication Service (FRS), which had been designed to synchronize the SYSVOL shares between domain controllers in a domain, a relatively small volume of data that did not change frequently. FRS replicated at the file level; a file was the smallest unit of replicable data; if you had a 10MB file with 20KB of changes, FRS would replicate the entire 10MB file and not the 20KB of changes. This used up a lot of bandwidth on the network, and there were also other problems with FRS.

FRS relied entirely on the NTFS Update Sequence Number (USN) journal, which is a fixed-size file that records all changes that are made to an NTFS-formatted partition. The FRS would monitor the NTFS USN journal for closed files in the folders that were replicated by FRS. Because the NTFS journal is a fixed size, at a certain point, the file wraps around and starts overwriting previous journal entries. This is where the problem creeps in. With a large NTFS partition that has lots of files and lots of changes, the journal log could wrap before all the changes were replicated, at which point FRS would break, and manual intervention would be needed.

Due to the problems with the NTFS journaling and the file-level replication, many environments could not use the DFS replication. Instead, they had to use other replication technologies, such as a manual copy using the robust file copy (`robocopy`) utility at periodic intervals, or even `xcopy`.

Microsoft finally addressed these problems by introducing DFSR technology, which uses a new replication process known as Remote Differential Compression (RDC) that performs compression and delta-based replication. Only the changes in a file are replicated, which means if 20KB of a 10MB file changes, only the 20KB of changes are replicated. This saves bandwidth and enables all the various replica members to be kept in sync faster. This process is shown in Figure 15-4, where only the changed portion of the file is copied to the other replica member.

NOTE FRS and DFSR are not compatible; all replicas in a set must be replicated via FRS or DFSR. While a server can run both FRS and DFSR, they must be used to replicate separate folder structures.

DFSR has been tested with terabytes of data, consisting of millions of files, and can support up to 4,000 members in each replication group, with a number of topologies available for the replication. For example, you can use a full mesh where every member of the replica set replicates to every other member of the set; this would work fine for smaller environments. Or you can nominate several members as hub locations and then link the other members to a particular hub to create a hub-and-spoke model, which is great for larger environments. This is particularly the case where locations in the environment are geographically spread out. Limit the number of times data is sent over slower WAN links. Each server can be a member of 256 different replication groups, with a total of 256 replication folders.

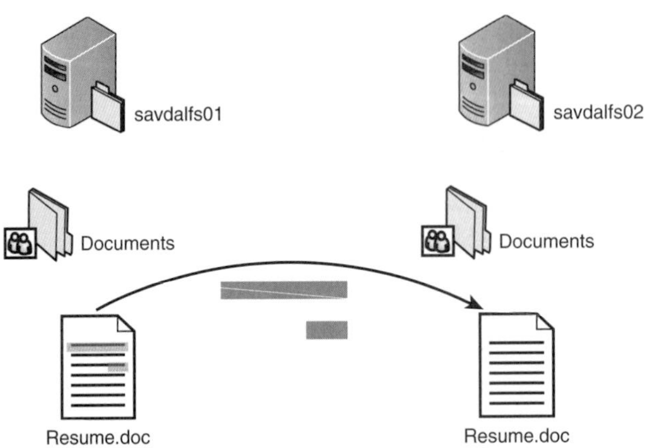

FIGURE 15-4 This example shows DFSR in action.

In addition to the use of RDC, the overall performance of DFSR has improved. For example, instead of 4 threads used to copy data, 16 threads are now used. The replication also sends its data as low priority, so it doesn't interfere with existing traffic on a link.

The new DFSR requires little management; it has a intuitive GUI and wizards to help create DFSR sets, which you can have created automatically when you create a DFS folder with multiple targets. A management pack is available for System Center Operations Manager so the health of DFSR can be automatically monitored and alerts can be generated as needed. The old problem with the NTFS journal wrapping does not break DFSR. Instead, DFSR automatically realizes that the NTFS transaction log has wrapped and performs a check of each side of the replication set and continues replicating changes, normally taking less than 60 seconds to recover automatically. The DFSR process goes like this:

1. A change is made to a file and is reflected in the NTFS USN journal log.
2. DFSR subscribes to the NTFS USN journal log, and any changes go through a filter so files that are not being replicated are ignored.
3. For a file that is being replicated, when the file is closed (if the file had a lock; otherwise, files opened with a read-share access by an application can be replicated while still open) an entry is written to the internal DFSR ID table to track the change.
4. The changes between the saved file and its previous contents are calculated, and the changes are sent to the replication partner.

5. The replication partner's sync engine receives the update and uses its own database to compare the changes and, via hash values (MD4), computes the changes.
6. A copy of the file being changed is copied to a private DFSR staging area.
7. The updated file is created from the existing content in the staging area and the changes that were received from the replication partner, and then it is placed in the DFSR private preinstall folder.
8. The new version of the file is copied to the file's normal location, overwriting the old content.

DFSR is a multimaster technology, so it could be possible that a file changes at the same time on members of a replica set, in which case the last writer wins. The version of the file that lost is stored in a conflict folder in the DFSR private area. It is important to remember this limitation; DFSR does not lock files while they are open over a distributed environment. If you intend for files to be edited in multiple locations at the same time, DFSR is not the right solution. For example, if you have a marketing team in Dallas editing documents on a local DFSR replica and a marketing team in London editing the same documents on their local DFSR replica, you could lose data. Consider using Windows SharePoint Server, which allows files to be checked out for editing. DFSR works best for replicating copies of data out to branch locations, where users only view the data or, in reverse, to take data from branch locations and store it in a central location for backup purposes. Other great uses are if you have a network load-balanced Web farm where each server is presenting the same content; instead of having to manually copy the Web content between each server, just use DFSR to keep all the Web root folders synchronized. Some organizations use DFSR to replicate roaming profiles for users. However, this is not recommended because if a user logs on at multiple workstations at the same time, data may be lost due to the DFSR conflict resolution. If you know a user will never log on more than once simultaneously, and the time it would take the user to travel to another location where another copy of the roaming profile would be used is much longer than the replication time to update the other roaming profile copies, use DFSR.

DFSR does not support the idea of a one-way replica. Although a one-way replica is technically possible, the recommended approach is to train administrators to update only a primary server with new data or set the share permissions on the destination servers to read-only so changes cannot be made. The exception to this is a situation in which you are running Windows Server 2008 in domain mode, and SYSVOL is being replicated via DFSR; then, if a domain controller is an RODC, any changes to its SYSVOL are not replicated but are rolled back at each replication cycle.

RDC uses additional CPU cycles to calculate changes to a file but saves bandwidth, which is generally the scarcest of resources. If a file is small, however, calculating the changes to the file does not make sense, so any file smaller than 64KB RDC is not used, and the file is just sent whole to the replication partners. Adjust this size, or even disable RDC use if you have fast network links.

The final DFSR-related feature is a feature known as Cross-file RDC. Imagine that you have a 10MB PowerPoint presentation and save it under a new filename with a different client name on it. So you have client1.ppt and now a new client2.ppt with a difference of only 10Kb. It's a brand-new file, so all 10MB is copied to the replication partners, right? Not if at least one member of the replication partnership is running Windows Server 2008 Enterprise edition. Enterprise edition supports cross-file RDC, which means when a new file is created, instead of replicating the entire file, the sync engine looks for files that are similar to the new file and then sends just the differences between the existing file and the new file. As shown in Figure 15-5, when a new file is created, a heuristic is used to identify that client2.ppt is similar to client1.ppt, so the replication partner savdalfs02 is told to apply the differences between the files to a copy of client1.ppt, which it has already done.

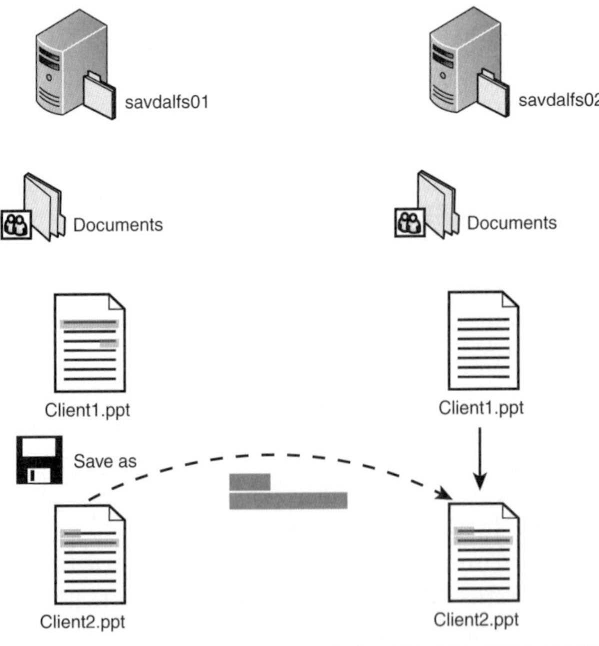

FIGURE 15-5 Cross-file RDC.

Installing and Configuring DFS

Before you can use DFSR, install the Windows Server 2008 schema changes and make sure they have been applied by using the `adprep /forestprep` command.

Install DFS via the normal Server Manager role approach, with DFS a part of the File Server role. You probably already have the File Server role installed to enable file sharing, so to install DFS, select the File Server role and select the Add Role Services link, as shown in Figure 15-6.

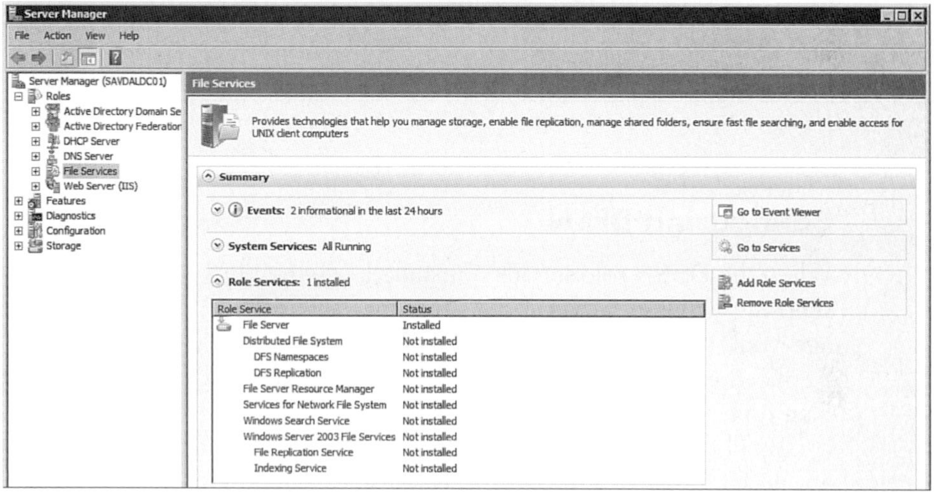

Figure 15-6 Adding the DFS role service to a server.

Although you can add the DFSN and DFSR services separately, if this server acts as a DFSN server and contains shares whose content is replicated, you want both the DFSN and DFSR services. Check the components that are required and click Next in the Select Role Services dialog.

If you selected only to install DFSR, no further questions are asked because you are only installing the replication engine, which is managed separately. If the DFSN service is installed, you are offered the option of creating a namespace as part of the role installation, as shown in Figure 15-7. However, for now, select the option Create a Namespace Later Using the DFS Management Snap-in in Server Manager, which stops any further questions and causes the services selected to be installed.

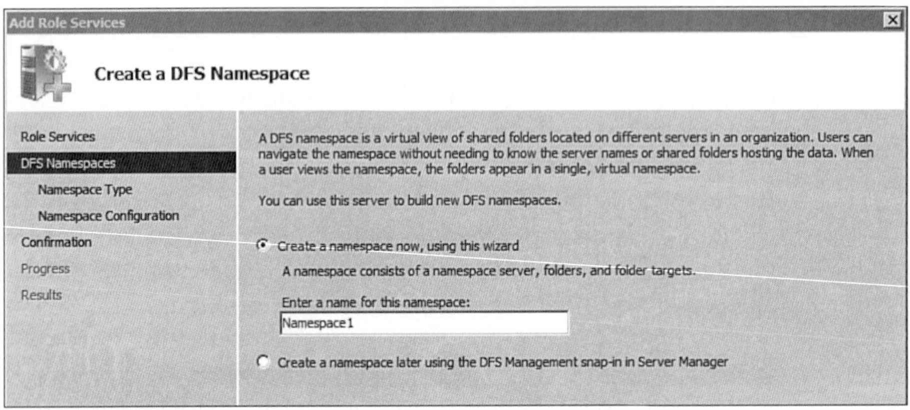

FIGURE 15-7 Creating a namespace during the service installation.

Configuring DFSN

When the DFSN role service is installed, use the DFS Management MMC snap-in (which in Server Manager is located under File Services) to manage your namespaces in DFS. You see nodes for Namespaces and for Replication. Initially, configure the namespace so you focus on the Namespaces node.

By default, if a namespace were not created during installation, there are no namespaces listed in the Namespaces area. However, you can create them via the New Namespace Wizard, or you can add existing namespaces that may be stored within AD. As discussed earlier in this chapter, with a domain-based namespace, the information for the namespace is stored in the domain partition to which the DFS server belongs. Select the Add Namespace to Display link and the DFS Management snap-in scans the domain selected under the CN=Dfs-Configuration, CN=System, <*domain*> area of the domain partition. You can fire up ADSIEdit.msc and open the domain partition and navigate to the Dfs-Configuration container, where you see containers for each domain-based DFSN. Under the namespace are msDFS-Linkv2 objects, which are the actual links within the namespace, as shown in Figure 15-8. You can also use the Active Directory Users and Computers snap-in to view the same data if you enable the Advanced Features view.

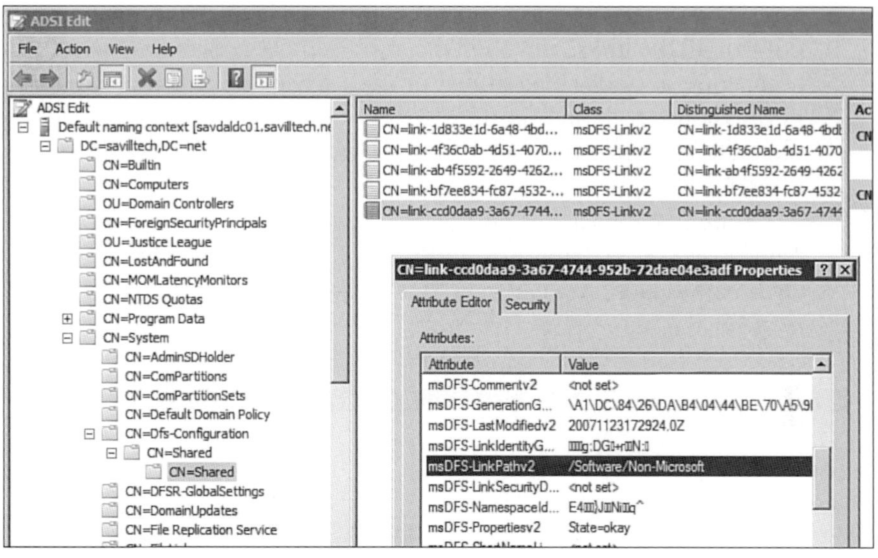

FIGURE 15-8 Viewing a DFS link via its data in the AD.

Let's create a new namespace. Select the Namespaces navigation/console tree item and select the New Namespace action to launch the New Namespace Wizard. The first task in the wizard is to select the server that hosts the namespace. This does not have to be a Windows Server 2008 server. However, if you want to use the new Windows Server 2008 namespace features—for example, because you want no limit on the number of links—it needs to be a Windows Server 2008 server. (We won't concern ourselves with Windows 2000 here, but a Windows 2000 server can host only a single namespace. This is not a limit with Windows Server 2003, although Standard needs a hotfix, or Windows Server 2008.) Select a server that hosts the namespace and click the Next button.

The next page in the wizard asks you to select the name for the namespace. This is equivalent to the share name and is used by clients as the component after the server or domain name, depending on the namespace type you select. This name should reflect the content that is linked under it. If it's going to contain everything in the company, you can just name it public or shared. By default, the namespace is configured as a read-only root. However, you can modify this by clicking the Edit Settings button, as shown in Figure 15-9, and setting permissions as needed. You do not need to change this permission in most instances, though. Just because the DFS root is read-only does not limit the users navigating the structure to read-only for all the links; only the DFS root is limited. You don't want users creating content under it anyway. For each share the user is redirected to, the permissions are based on the share the user is redirected to and the local file system permissions, as if the user were accessing the file server share directly.

Note that a local path is created on the server as a launch point for the namespace. By default, it is under the C:\DFSRoots folder. After you create a namespace, you can view this location by using Explorer, and folders exist for the namespace structure.

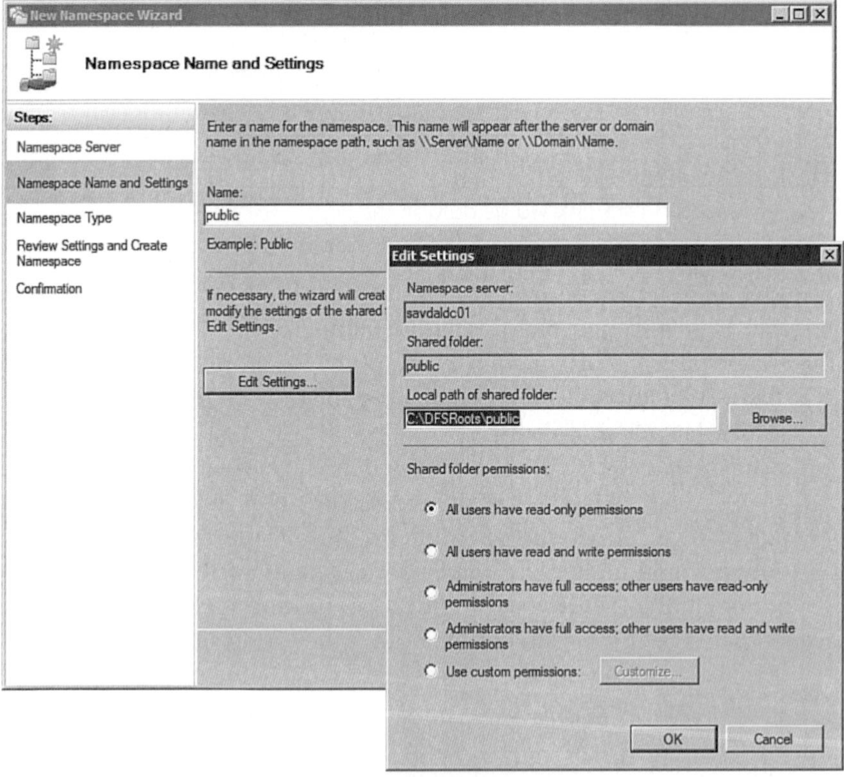

FIGURE 15-9 Naming the namespace and advanced options.

The next setting in the wizard to be configured is the type of namespace. It can be either domain-based or stand-alone. As discussed earlier in this chapter, a domain-based namespace enables higher availability by having multiple servers host the namespace by reading from AD; this is generally the best option. However, with Windows Server 2008, a stand-alone namespace can now be hosted on a cluster. In addition, if the namespace is being hosted on Windows Server 2008 servers only, the Windows Server 2008 mode can be enabled, as shown in Figure 15-10.

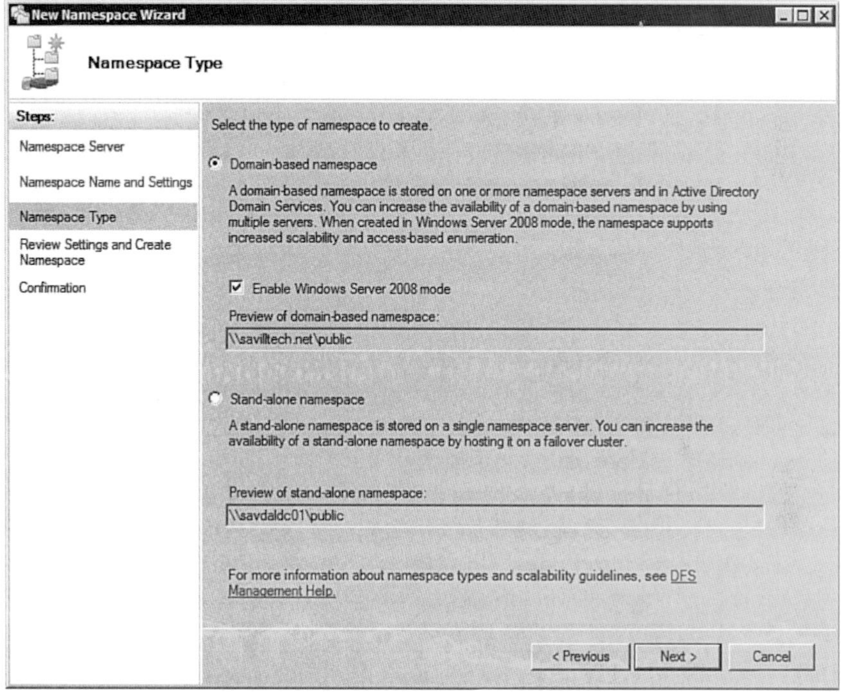

FIGURE 15-10 Configuring the namespace type.

The wizard displays a review of the settings. Click Create to create the new namespace, and when creation is complete, click the Close button to close the wizard. You now have an empty namespace. Navigate to it by using *<domain name>**<namespace>* for a domain-based namespace or *<server name>**<namespace>* for a server-based namespace.

Adding Additional DFSN Servers

If you create a domain-based namespace and you intend to use it for production purposes, add additional name servers now before you start doing much with the namespace or giving users access. Adding an additional name server is easy; select the namespace in the DFS Management snap-in and you see four tabs:Namespace, Delegation, Search, and Namespace Servers (which lists the name servers for the namespace). With the namespace selected, select the option Add Namespace Server. Enter the new server that acts as a namespace server. Then click OK, as shown in Figure 15-11. The Add Namespace Server Wizard performs checks on the new server and remotely configures it as needed, as shown in Figure 15-12. When the configuration is complete, you have an additional server that is servicing the namespace.

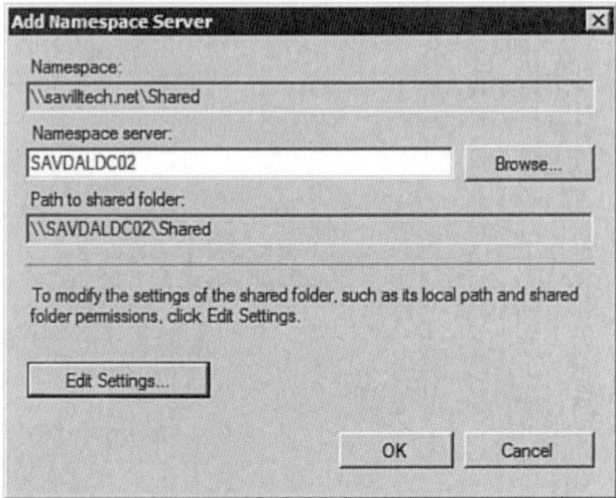

FIGURE 15-11 Adding an additional name server for a namespace.

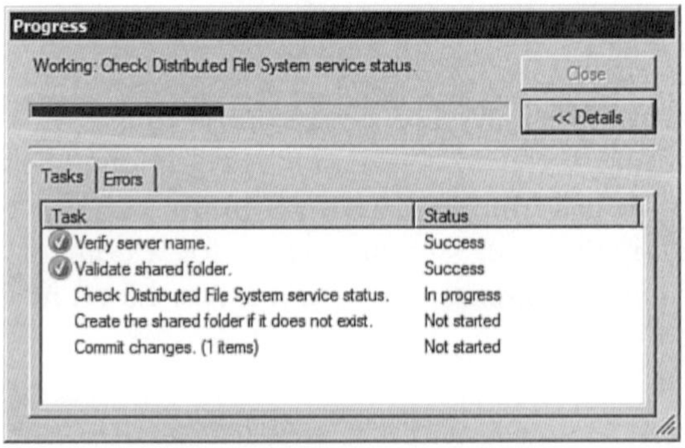

FIGURE 15-12 The validation check.

Configuring Advanced Namespace Options

By default, the domain-based namespaces read the DFSN configuration from the primary domain controller (PDC) Emulator FSMO role holder. This ensures consistency among all the DFSN servers because if all DFS servers are reading and writing to a single domain controller, there is no chance of consistency problems. Each server could see a different configuration if DFS servers read the information from their closest domain controllers. If the closest domain controller were used, the information on the local domain controller shared with the DFS server would be affected by the time AD information takes to replicate between sites. That amount of time could be significant, depending on the site link topology and replication interval. If you have many name servers, it may become impractical for all of them to poll the PDC FSMO, so instead configure the polling to take place on the closest domain controller via the Advanced tab of the namespace properties page (see Figure 15-13), which you access by right-clicking the namespace and selecting Properties. If you enable the closest domain controller polling, take into account the time it takes for AD to replicate throughout the enterprise to ensure a consistent DNS namespace experience.

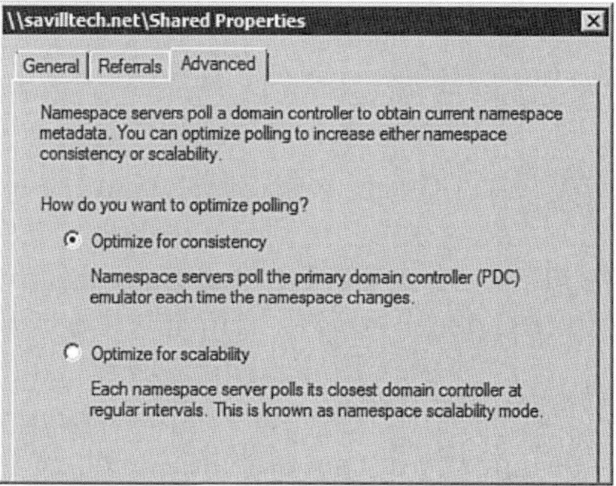

FIGURE 15-13 Setting the polling for the DNS namespace.

The other major item at a namespace level is delegating who can manage the namespace. By default, the Domain Admins and Enterprise Admins groups have management permissions on the namespace. However, you can also delegate other users and groups with namespace management permissions to allow those users to modify the folders and folder targets that make up the namespace.

You can see which people currently have management permissions by selecting a namespace and selecting the Delegation tab in the Details pane, as shown in Figure 15-14. Notice that there are Explicit and Inherited permissions. Inherited rights cannot be removed via the console and are taken from AD for a domain-based namespace (for example, Enterprise Admins). Explicit rights are DFSN-specific and can be removed via the console. Click the Delegate Management Permissions action to give additional users and groups management rights, which are Explicit grants.

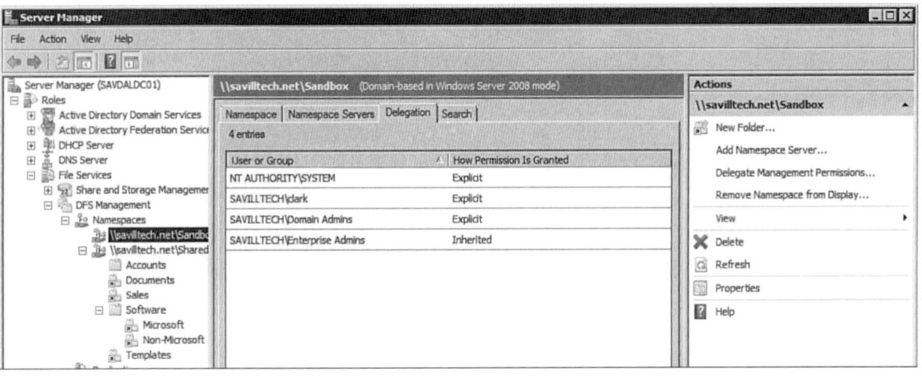

FIGURE 15-14 Viewing the users and groups with management rights on a namespace.

Before you can delegate a user or group to create a namespace, the user or group must be configured as a member of the local administrators group on the DFS server. In addition, the user/group needs AD rights to create domain-based namespaces, which is accomplished by right-clicking the Namespaces Navigation pane item and selecting Delegate Management Permissions. You see a list of the groups and users that currently have rights, and you can add additional users and groups.

In the Search tab for a namespace, type in a string, and the management interface searches the namespace and displays a list of folders that contain it. Select Go to DFS Folder from the search item results context menu item, as shown in Figure 15-15, and the management interface switches to showing the relevant folder in focus in the normal namespace management structure. This gets more useful as you namespaces grow larger.

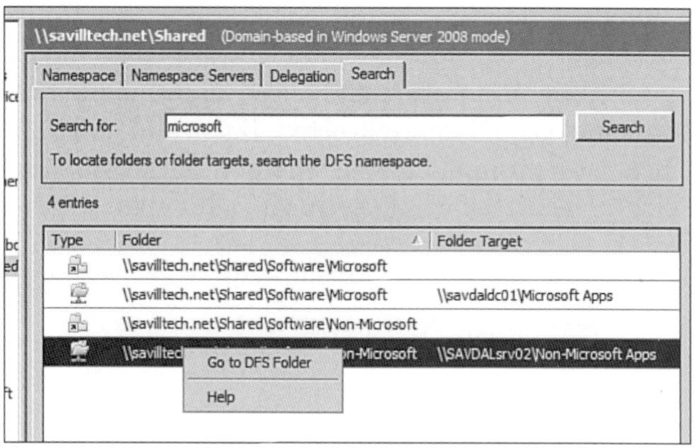

FIGURE 15-15 Performing a search of the DFSN.

It is recommended for domain-based namespaces that a client be able to access the namespace via the name of the domain (for example, \\savilltech.net\shared) or the server name of the DFS server (for example, \\savdaldc01\shared). However, accessing the namespace via a server name is a bad habit. If clients access the namespace via the server name and the server is unavailable, the clients do not use another name server for the namespace. One feature that was being discussed for Windows Server 2008 was to configure the namespace to be accessible only via the domain name instead of the server name; however, this feature never made the Release To Manufacture (RTM).

Managing Folders in the DFSN

When a namespace exists, you can give it some use by adding folders with links to shares containing the content or empty folders to give some structure to the namespace hierarchy.

As discussed earlier in this chapter, you can add folders and folders with targets. The process to create both types of folder is exactly the same; the only difference is that for an empty folder that is created for hierarchy structure purposes only, you do not specify any folder targets.

Right-click the namespace and select New Folder or open the Actions menu, and you are prompted for a new folder name and given a list of possible folder targets, as shown in Figure 15-16. The name of the folder is the name shown in DFSN when navigated to from a client. This folder name does not have to match the share names of the servers that the namespace folder may target; the name just has to be unique in DFSN. To create an empty folder in DFSN for the purpose of hierarchy (for example, the Software folder), stop now and click OK. To make the folder a link to file servers, click the Add button and enter shares on file servers to which the users browsing DFSN are redirected. If you add more than one folder target, you are also prompted about whether to configure replication between the folder targets. That would automatically create a DFSR replica set. For now, say no.

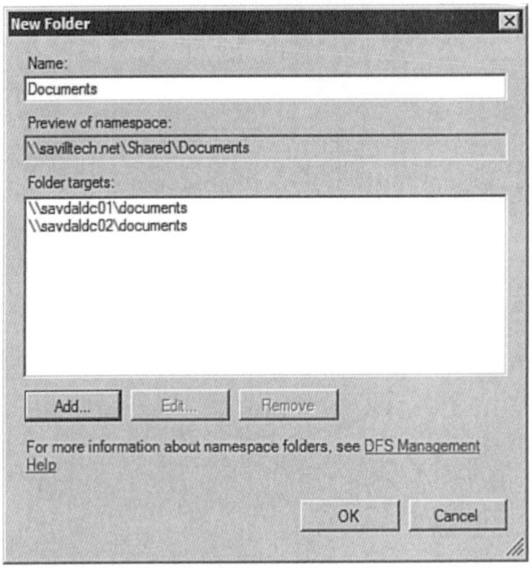

FIGURE 15-16 Creating a new folder under DFSN.

If you right-click a folder that has targets, you cannot add additional folders in the structure; you have no New Folder option. If you right-click a folder that does not have folder targets, you can add child folders that can have targets. Figure 15-17 shows the structure that was described in the overview of DFS earlier in this chapter. Notice that the Software folder does not have an arrow over it, showing it has no folder targets and is a normal folder that contains folders with targets.

Add folder targets by right-clicking a folder and selecting Add Folder Target. This enables you to specify the UNC path of a file share, to which you might want to redirect clients. You cannot add folder targets to a folder that has no targets and has child folders under it; the option to add a folder target is not available for such folders.

Select a folder in the Details pane of the MMC, and the Folder Targets tab shows the targets you can enable or disable via the target's context menu. Disabling a target is a good option if a target server is being taken out of service for routine maintenance and you want to stop clients from being redirected to it, but you don't want to delete the server as a target because it is brought back at some point. If a target server has been deleted, delete it as a folder target for the folder.

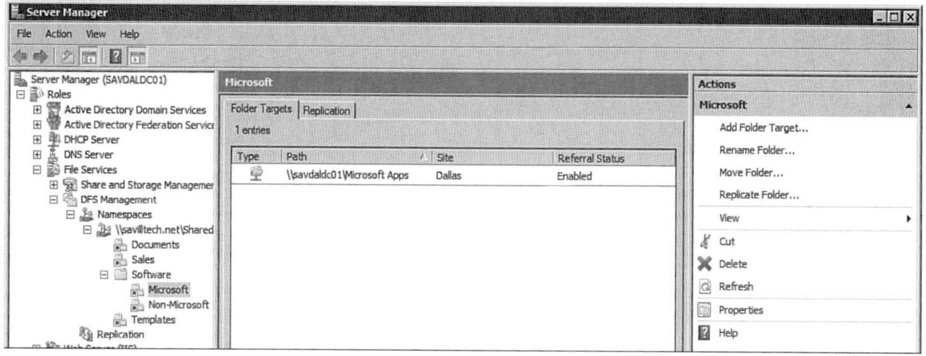

FIGURE 15-17 Your DFSN implementation.

If you select the properties of a folder target, you can modify the share permissions (which you generally do not want to do), and if you click the Advanced tab, you can modify how this folder target is referred to clients, as shown in Figure 15-18. In general, you don't want to do this. DFS works out the referral based on cost. However, there may be times when you want to give certain servers preferential treatment. Normally, clients are given a random-order list of all the targets that are in the same site as the client and then a list sorted by site link cost, with lowest cost first.

As shown in Figure 15-18, you can set a server to be first or last among all targets. Either would be dangerous as it would ignore the site placement of DFS servers and would potentially send users to a copy of the data in a remote location, even if a site were local to their office. The other options are First Among Targets of Equal Cost and Last Among Targets of Equal Cost. These are a lot safer and would only come into effect if a client had multiple referral targets in its local site or if it had no servers in its local site, only multiple options in sites that were all accessible over site links with the same cost. The best situation in which to use this setting is when you have a server that you don't want used under normal circumstances. For example, for a disaster recovery server, you could override its referral order so it's always last.

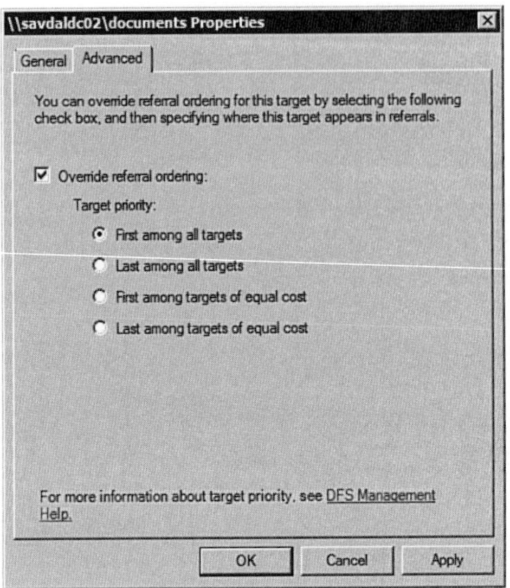

FIGURE 15-18 Modifying the referral priority of a target.

In addition to the referral setting of a folder target, you can also set referral preferences on the folder itself. To do this, open the folder's properties page and access the Referrals tab. Then you can configure how long, in seconds, clients cache the referral to a folder target. In addition, you can configure clients to be referred to folder targets only in their local site by checking Exclude Targets Outside of the Client's Site, as shown in Figure 15-19. You can also enable client failback to preferred targets by checking the Clients Fail Back to Preferred Targets option.

You can set global options for a namespace by selecting the properties of a namespace and modifying the configuration under the Referrals tab, which gives you three options for client referrals:

- **Random order**. With this setting, folder targets in the client's site are sent first and then all other targets in a random order.
- **Lowest cost**. With this setting, folder targets in the client's site are sent first and then all other targets, in least-cost-first order.
- **Exclude targets outside of the client's site**. With this setting, folder targets only in the client's site are sent.

You can also configure these settings with the `dfsutil property` command. For example to enable lowest-cost order, use `dfsutil property sitecosting enable` *`<namespace>`*.

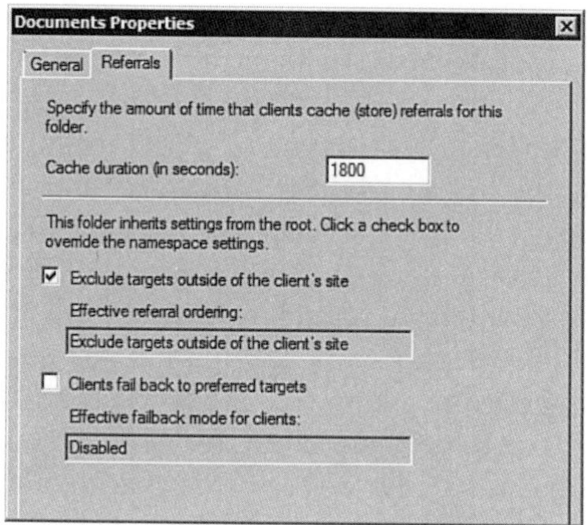

FIGURE 15-19 With this configuration, clients are not referred to any folder target outside the client's local site.

Access-Based Enumeration (ABE)

Access-based enumeration (ABE) is a familiar concept in the NetWare world and was introduced with Windows Server 2003 for file shares. With Windows Server 2008 domain mode DFSN, you can now enable ABE for the actual namespace. BE displays only folders and files for which a user has permissions. Use the `dfsutil` command to enable access based enumeration:

```
dfsutil property abde enable \\<domain>\<namespace>
```

You can also use ABE on a stand-alone namespace running on a Windows Server 2008 server.

Configuring DFSR

Using DFSN is a fantastic way to get a virtualized view of the file services in an environment, and the user doesn't have to worry about where data physically exists or which copy of data is closest. DFSN takes care of those things by enabling multiple targets for a single folder in the namespace. The challenge is keeping those multiple targets consistent, and that's where DFSR comes in. But what do you do to configure it?

DFSR is not compatible with FRS, and you cannot have a combination of DFSR and FRS for a single replica group. While both DFSR and FRS can run on one server, the content replicated must be in separate groups, and different tools are used to manage FRS. It is highly recommended that you migrate away from FRS and use DFSR. There is no supported way to upgrade from FRS to DFSR; you need to break the replication group and create a new one by using DFSR. However, there is an unsupported script at https://blogs.technet.com/filecab/articles/420952.aspx, which you may want to take a look at if you have a complicated FRS configuration that you don't want to create from scratch.

As mentioned earlier in this chapter, if you select multiple targets for a folder, the wizard prompts you about whether to configure replication. Let's now choose to do that. (Note that DFSR does not have to be tied to a DFSN folder. You can use DFSR to replicate any set of folders, provided that the servers all support DFSR [for example, Windows Server 2003 Release 2 or Windows Server 2008]). Also, only content stored on NTFS volumes can be replicated with DFSR because of the reliance on the NTFS change journal, although you probably don't have FAT on your server systems anyway, right?

The easiest way to configure DFSR is via a namespace folder that has multiple targets because the DFSR Wizard can automatically ascertain what folders need to be replicated, based on the targets for the folder. However, the only difference in creating a replica group separate from a namespace is that if you select New Replication Group from the Replication node in the DFS Management snap-in, you are prompted to select what the replication group is used for: multipurpose or data collection. Your choice here affects the replication topology, and if you select data collection, then hub-and-spoke is automatically chosen as the topology. You are also asked to select the servers that are in the replication group, but all other questions about the replication group are the same as when creating from DFSN.

To create from a DFSN, right-click a folder that has one or more folder targets (probably more) and select the Replicate Folder option, as shown in Figure 15-20. Notice that this folder has three targets, which make for interesting replication options.

An initial collection of the folder targets is completed, which involves ascertaining the server's capability to participate in a DFSR replica set, and then the Replicate Folder Wizard launches. It initially asks for a name for the replication group (which, by default, is the folder's namespace path, for example, \\savilltech.net\shared\documents) and a name for the replicated folder (for example, Documents).

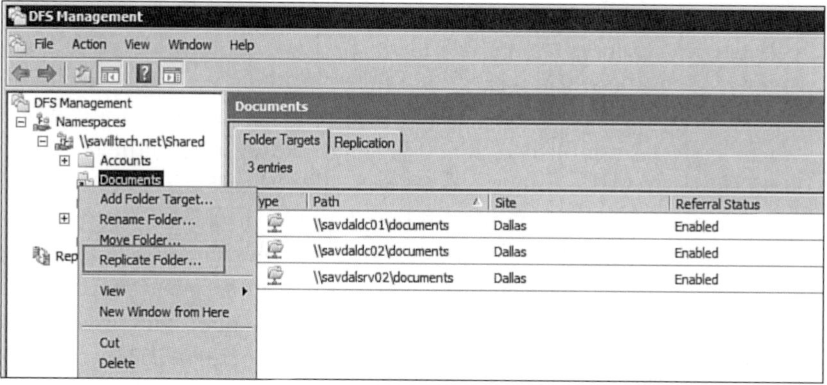

FIGURE 15-20 Creating a new DFSR replica set based on folder targets.

The next page of the wizard shows the eligibility of the servers to participate in the replica set, and if a server is not eligible, the reason is displayed. (If the reason scrolls off the screen, select it and press Ctrl+C to copy and then paste it into Notepad to see the full explanation.) Such a reason is shown in Figure 15-21; in this case, DFSR is not installed on the savdalsrv02 server. If you have an eligibility issue, you can exit the wizard, fix the issue, and restart the wizard. If you have a server that is not eligible and you want to continue, that's fine; that server just won't participate in the replica set. Don't think the wizard is completely lazy. If it finds a server with DFSR installed but not started, it prompts you and then starts the DFSR service and automatically sets it to start.

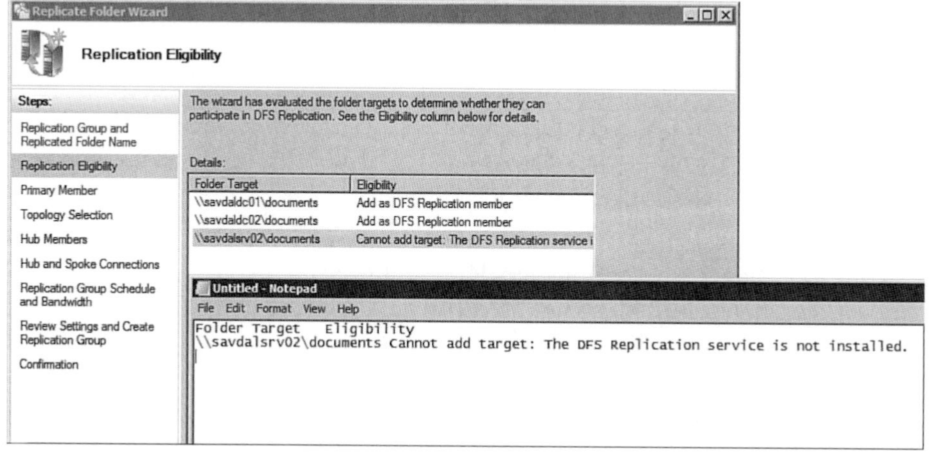

FIGURE 15-21 Viewing the eligibility.

The next page of the wizard asks you to select a primary member for the replication, as shown in Figure 15-22. Although DFSR is a multimaster engine, there still has to be one server that is considered the definitive version for the initial replication pass only in the case of a conflict. When replication is established, it is strictly last writer wins in the event of a clash. At the end of the initial replication, all replication partners look like the primary member. If other members had files in the folder that were not in the primary members' folder, then those files are deleted. You can prestage the other members with data if you want to speed up the initial replication, but if you do that, it is recommended that you use `robocopy` (don't use the `/copyall` or `/copy:s` switches), `xcopy` with the `/O` switch, or Windows Backup. Any of these three methods copies the content correctly and preserves the correct Access Control Lists (ACLs) on the files. Although you don't need to prestage files, it may be beneficial if you have large amounts of data because the initial sync with DFSR considers every file new. That causes a lot of work in the internal DFSR database, which in turn may slow down that initial replication. In addition, you don't want users modifying the files during this initial replication, so schedule the first replication to take place after-hours.

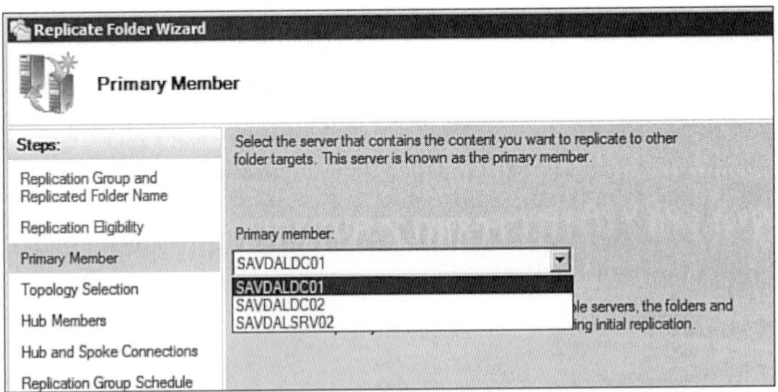

FIGURE 15-22 Selecting the primary member.

The next page of the wizard enables you to select the topology for the replication. The options are Hub and Spoke (if you have three or more members), Full Mesh, and No Topology, as shown in Figure 15-23. If you choose the No Topology option, you have to create it. If you select Full Mesh, then all the members replicate with each other, which is okay with a small number of servers but does not make a lot of sense. The better option is to select Hub and Spoke, so you can define a core set of major location servers to replicate to each other and then have smaller sites replicate with one of the large locations, much the same way that AD replication works between sites. Consider the major locations that have the highest bandwidth and can then replicate out to the smaller locations.

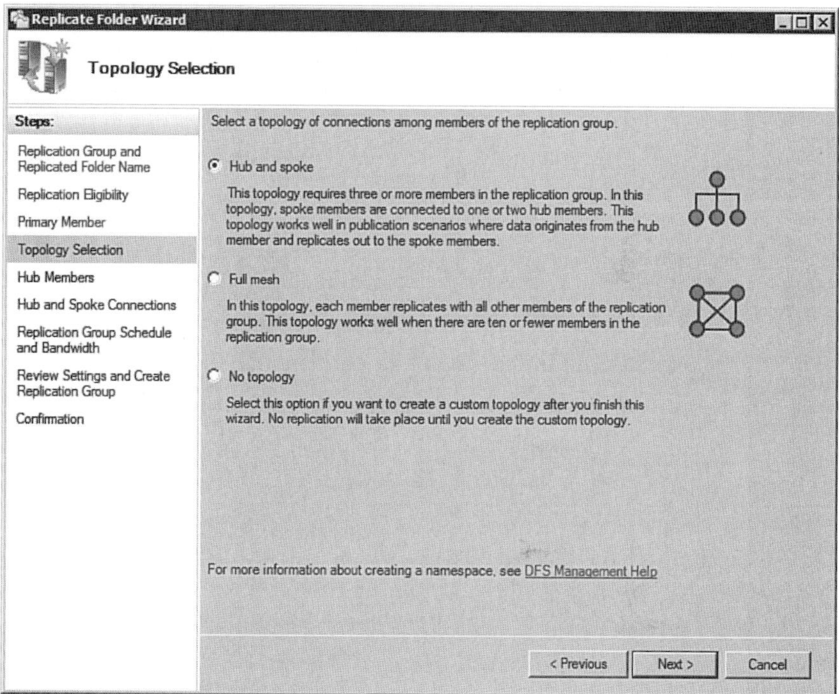

FIGURE 15-23 The topology options.

If you selected Hub and Spoke, next select which of the servers are hubs by selecting the hub servers and clicking the Add button, which moves them into the hub member area of the wizard. The next stage of the wizard enables each spoke server (servers that were not made hubs) to be linked to a specific hub server, and if there is more than one hub, an optional hub server, as shown in Figure 15-24. When all the connections are configured, click Next to move on to the replication schedule.

When you select either Full Mesh or Hub and Spoke, next configure the bandwidth that can be used for replication. By default, all the available bandwidth can be used at any time, or you can elect to use only increments from 16Kbps through to 256Mbps. You can be even more granular and select amounts of replication to use on an hourly basis throughout the entire week, as shown in Figure 15-25. The "by hour" schedule is great if you want to reduce the replication that DFSR uses during business hours by limiting DFSR to a small or zero-bandwidth amount during the working hours and then allowing it higher bandwidth during the night and weekend to catch up on synchronization. Be aware that if you do this, files may not complete replication during the day. Therefore, users may see different content, depending on which replica they look at. If you built in a schedule to update the content at 7 p.m. each day and then had replication starting at 8 p.m. each day, that would be a great way to push out content to servers on a controlled schedule.

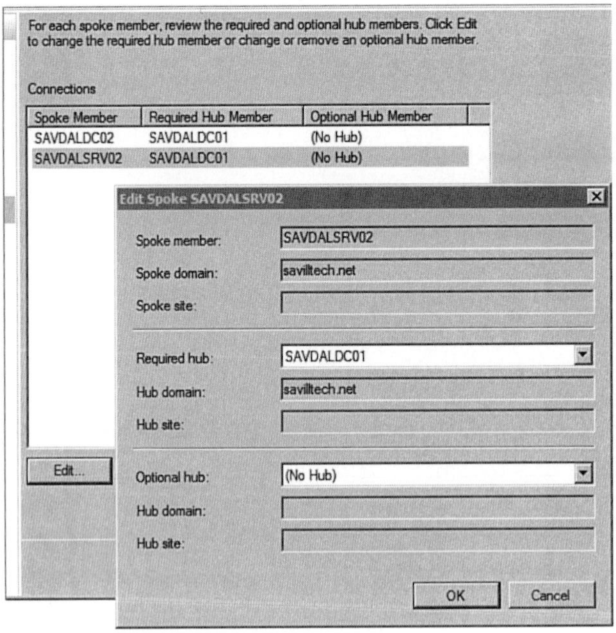

For each spoke member, review the required and optional hub members. Click Edit to change the required hub member or change or remove an optional hub member.

Connections

Spoke Member	Required Hub Member	Optional Hub Member
SAVDALDC02	SAVDALDC01	(No Hub)
SAVDALSRV02	SAVDALDC01	(No Hub)

Edit...

Edit Spoke SAVDALSRV02

Spoke member: SAVDALSRV02

Spoke domain: savilltech.net

Spoke site:

Required hub: SAVDALDC01

Hub domain: savilltech.net

Hub site:

Optional hub: (No Hub)

Hub domain:

Hub site:

OK Cancel

FIGURE 15-24 Modifying the hub for each spoke server.

The last page of the wizard displays a summary of the replica set configuration. Click Create to create the replica set, which displays a status as each action is performed. Then click Close when the replica set is created; you then see a warning that replication does not start instantly and that the DFS servers have to poll to see the new replica set information. The polling period is 60 minutes by default, and if you are polling their local domain controller, then AD replication also factors in.

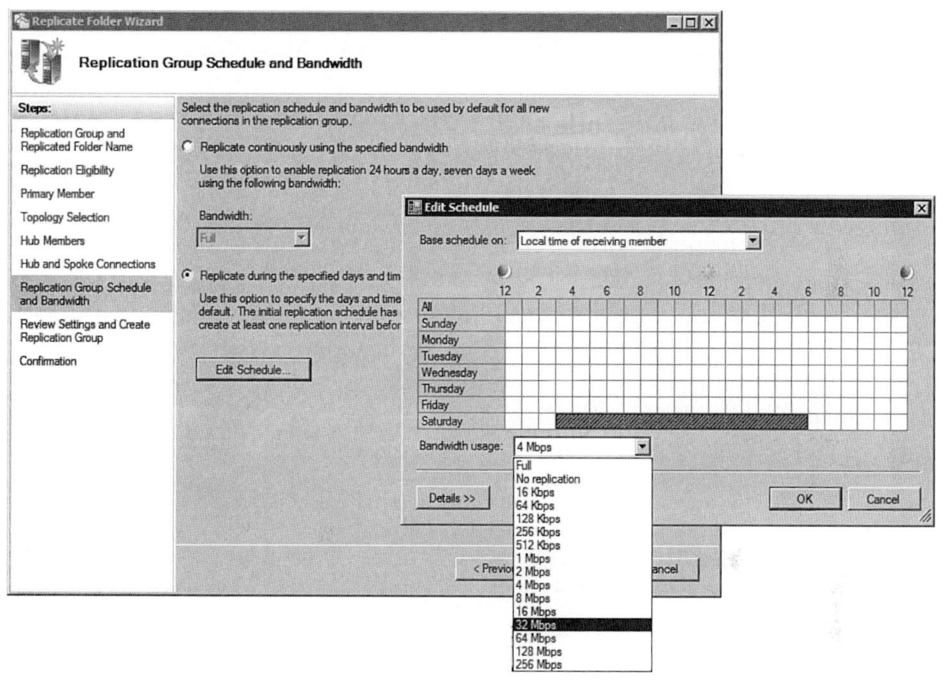

FIGURE 15-25 Very granular replication.

If you are impatient, you can force the DFSR service to poll via the `dfsrdiag pollad` command, as shown in the following example. This triggers an immediate poll, and when the DFSR service sees it is part of a replica set, it begins replication:

```
C:\Users\john>dfsrdiag pollad

Operation Succeeded
```

If you have a hub-and-spoke model, when the primary server has replicated to its receiving replication partners, those partners then replicate files to their receiving partners and so on until the data replicates throughout the replica set.

You now have a DFSR replica set that you can see. Set yourself as a member of it with the `dfsradmin` command, as shown in the following example:

```
C:\Windows>dfsradmin membership list
➥/computer:savilltech\savdaldc01
```

```
MembershipGuid                        LocalPath
e826692a-9357-4c59-bba4-d2257827f144  E:\Documents

Command completed successfully.
```

You can also now use the Replicate node in the Navigation pane of the DFS Management snap-in, which has four tabs, as shown in Figure 15-26, to see your replication group. The Memberships tab shows the replica set members, if it's enabled, and the folder. The Connections tab shows each individual replication connection that was created, based on your topology, and enables you to fine-tune each replication connection, if required. The Replicated Folders tab shows the replicated folder in the set, because you can have more than one folder replicated in a DFSR replica set. The Delegation tab enables delegation of who can manage the replica set instance.

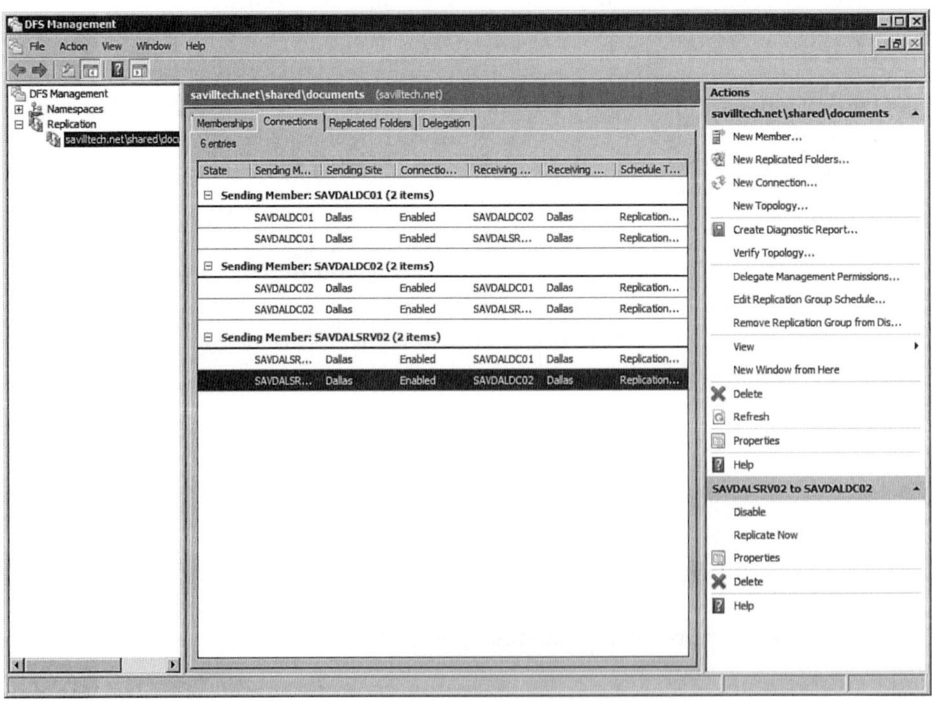

FIGURE 15-26 Viewing the replication connections for a DFSR set.

Let's first look at what exactly has happened to the replicated folder. You saw that there was a primary member, and its content is absolute. At the end of the initial replication cycle, all replicas look the same as the primary server. (After that replication cycle, the primary member tab is removed, and all replica members are equal.) If a file already exists on a member server, and it is identical, based on a hash value, to that on the primary member, then the file is not copied. But what about the conflicted or additional files that may have been on other servers?

Open the folder that was designated as the folder for replication to see a new child folder, DfsrPrivate, whose contents administrators can view but normal users cannot. You see this folder only if you have the Explorer option set to show protected OS files. There are four (sometimes five) subfolders in this special folder:

- ConflictAndDeleted
- Deleted, Installing
- PreExisting (maybe)
- Staging

DFSR uses these subfolders. Two of them relate to your initial replication. PreExisting contains any files that were in a replication member on initial replication and were not on the primary member and were, therefore, moved to it. It also contains a PreExistingManifest.xml file that is updated to reflect where the file used to be located and its new name, as shown in the following example. This folder is created only if any files existed on nonprimary replica servers that are not part of the primary member's folder content.

```
<?xml version="1.0" encoding="UTF-8" ?>
- <PreExistingManifest>
- <Resource>
  <Path>\\.\C:\documents\test.txt</Path>
  <Uid>{60DC626C-F71A-4907-BD15-2E7C040B1CAC}-v11</Uid>
  <Gvsn>{60DC626C-F71A-4907-BD15-2E7C040B1CAC}-v11</Gvsn>
  <PartnerGuid>{00000000-0000-0000-0000-000000000000}
</PartnerGuid>
  <Attributes>20</Attributes>
  <NewName>test-{60DC626C-F71A-4907-BD15-2E7C040B1CAC}
-v11.txt</NewName>
  <Time>GMT 2007:12:1-0:50:48</Time>
- <Type>
  <FileNotExistOnPartner />
  </Type>
  <Files>1</Files>
```

```
<Size>12</Size>
</Resource>
</PreExistingManifest>
```

Any files that conflicted with files on the primary member are moved to the ConflictAndDeleted folder, and again, a manifest file is created, ConflictAndDeletedManifest.xml, detailing the original filename and its new name in the ConflictAndDeleted folder. This is the same folder that is used during normal operation of DFSR for conflicted files. If two files are updated at the same time on different servers, the oldest written file is moved to ConflictAndDeleted. An administrator can then view the file and take action as needed.

The other folders are used internally by DFSR. For example, the Deleted folder holds files that have been deleted from the folder. DFSR keeps them in case new files are created that are similar to the deleted files, which can then be used as the basis for the new files, thus saving replication bandwidth. DFSR uses the Staging and Installing folders as part of the replication to piece together modified files from existing content and the information received via the RDC protocol and then ready the files for installation into the replicated folder.

Managing Connections

The Connections tab for a replica set shows all the connections that are used for the replication of a DFSR set. You can use the context menu of each connection object to individually disable the object or force replication. Use the Replicate Now option to ignore the replication schedule defined for the connection object, which may be useful to replicate outside the normal replication schedule. You can also force a replication by using the `dfsrdiag syncnow` command or using the WMI method `ForceReplicate()`. For example, to ignore the replication schedule for five minutes and replicate immediately, use the following command:

```
C:\Windows>dfsrdiag syncnow /partner:savdalsrv02
➥/rgname:savilltech.net\shared\documents /time:5

Operation Succeeded
```

Remember that this command is only to override the schedule; it does not force replication of unchanged or identical files. Use this command to stop replication to avoid bandwidth use for a period of time and then replicate afterward.

Select the Properties tab of a replication connection object, and a Schedule tab is displayed that enables you to configure a replication schedule for the specific connection object. You also see a General tab, which has the option Enable the Replication on This Connection and an option to disable the use of RDC by unselecting Use Remote Differential Compression (RDC), as shown in Figure 15-27. Disabling RDC can reduce CPU utilization and replication latency where you have fast network connections and where the files in a replica set are all small (less than 64 KB).

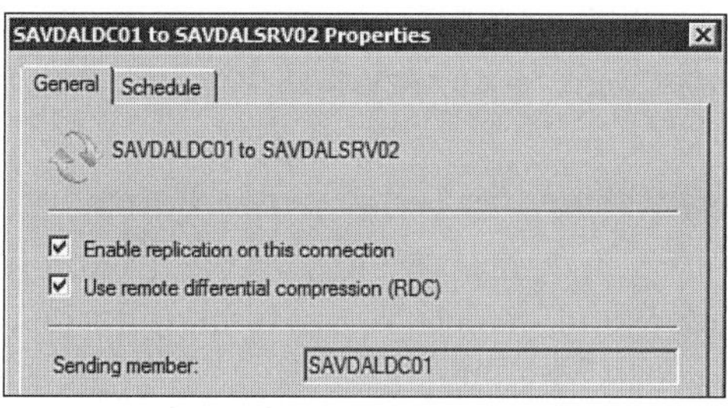

FIGURE 15-27 The connection object properties.

By default, the minimum file size that is required for RDC to be used is 64KB; smaller files are not compressed. However, you can change this minimum by using the `dfsradmin` command to modify the connection. Include the replica group name and the sending and receiving server to identify the connection. Set the new minimum file size required for RDC via the `/ConnRdcMinFileSize` parameter. The following example sets a minimum size of 128KB for RDC to be used for replication for files sent from savdaldc01 to savdaldc02:

```
C:\Windows>dfsradmin connection set
➥/rgname:savilltech.net\shared\documents
➥/sendmem:savdaldc01 /recvmem:savdaldc02
➥/ConnRdcMinFileSize:128

Command completed successfully.
```

If you want to verify that the connections in place support full replication of the data between all replication members, select Verify Topology from the Actions pane with the replica group selected. This is useful if you have manually created and deleted connections to ensure that when you modified connections, you didn't leave a replication member on an island without partners. As mentioned earlier, ideally, you would use the wizards for connection object management, but you can manually create new connections via the New Connection action, which allows you to specify the sending and receiving server. Remove existing connections by using the Delete action.

To change the topology, run the New Topology action. It deletes all existing connection objects and creates new connection objects based on the options selected in the wizard, which asks the same questions that are asked when you create the replica set for the replication topology. This is especially useful if you add a new member to the replica set and need to modify the topology; so let's try that now.

Adding and Removing Replica Members

To add a new replica group member, select the replica group to which the server is added and select New Member from the Actions pane. This launches the New Member Wizard.

On the first page of the wizard, select the server to add to the replica group, and then a check is performed on the eligibility for the server to be part of a DFSR group. Assuming that the server has the DFSR service installed, the wizard continues to the connections stage. This stage enables you to configure which servers replicate to the new server, as shown in Figure 15-28. Notice that you no longer have the option of which topology to use. Adding servers to the replica group after creation requires you to manually define the connections. However, after adding the server, run the New Topology action to use the Topology Wizard to automatically generate the connections for a certain model, such as full mesh or hub-and-spoke.

Next, configure a replication schedule for this new set of connections (sending and receiving). You can either make this schedule match the rest of the replication group or select a unique schedule for the connection. When you have configured the replication, click Next to proceed and define which replicated folders replicate to the new member. As shown in Figure 15-29, by default the new replica member is not configured to replicate existing folders. However, selecting the folder and selecting Edit enables you to select a folder to replicate to/from on the new member.

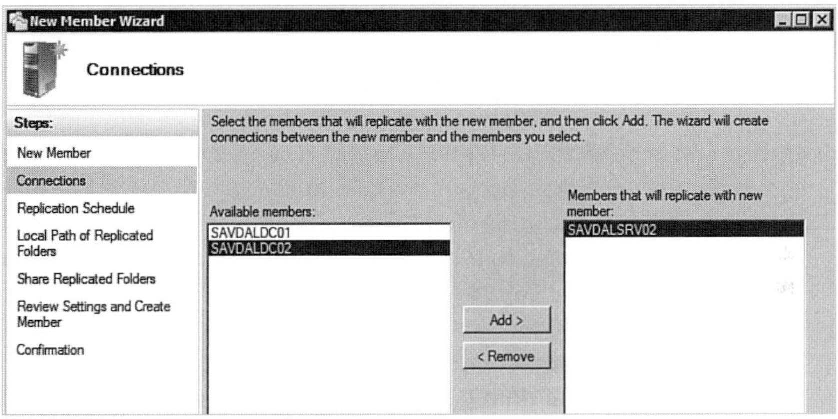

FIGURE 15-28 Selecting the servers with which the new server replicates.

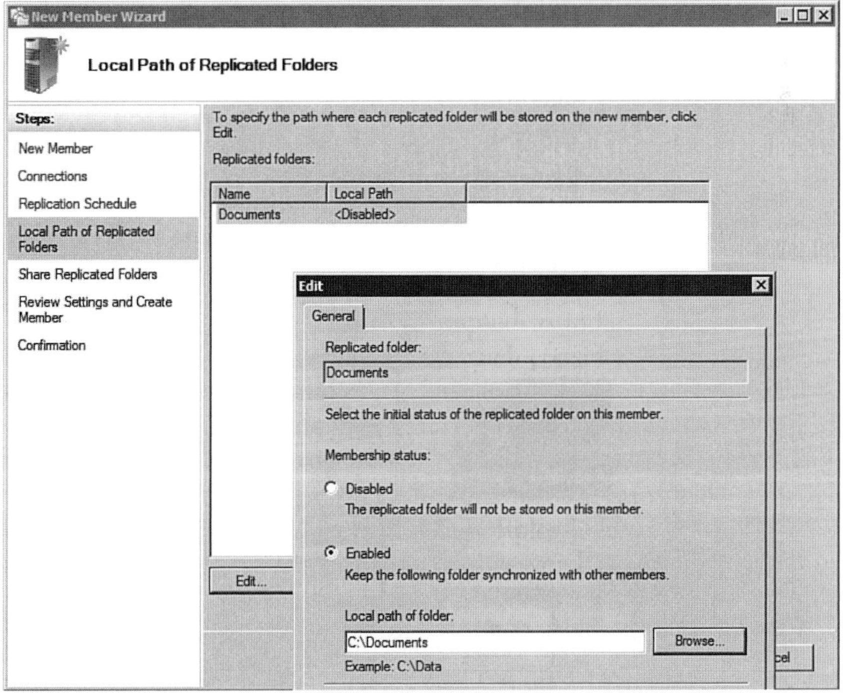

FIGURE 15-29 Selecting the folder for the replicated folder.

If the replica group is also a target of a DFSN, you receive a request to create a share for the folder to enable the namespace to be updated with this folder as a target. If a share already exists for the folder, then no action is required. Otherwise, the wizard prompts you to create a new share. Finally, a summary is displayed, and the new server is added to the replica group. If this were part of a namespace folder target, the DFSN has also been updated with a new folder target. The whole process is totally integrated and works the opposite way if you added a new folder target in the namespace: You are prompted to also update the replica group by selecting a server with which to replicate with or use a custom set of connections. To force replication, run the `dfsrdiag pollad` command on the server that is replicating to the new member first, so that it knows about its new replication partner, and then run the `dfsrdiag pollad` command on the new replication group server. If you run the AD poll only on the new server, you are likely to get an error in the event log, informing you that the replication partner politely told your new server to go away because it knows nothing about the new replica group. This situation is exemplified in the following example:

```
Log Name:      DFS Replication
Source:        DFSR
Date:          12/1/2007 6:02:12 AM
Event ID:      5012
Task Category: None
Level:         Error
Keywords:      Classic
User:          N/A
Computer:      SAVDALSRV03.savilltech.net
Description:
The DFS Replication service failed to communicate with partner
SAVDALSRV02 for replication group
savilltech.net\shared\documents. The partner did not recognize
the connection or the replication group configuration.

Partner DNS Address: savdalsrv02.savilltech.net

Optional data if available:
Partner WINS Address: savdalsrv02
Partner IP Address: 192.168.1.40


The service will retry the connection periodically.

Additional Information:
Error: 9026 (The connection is invalid)
```

```
Connection ID: 976967B2-DC83-4838-BDEE-D39E734E594A
Replication Group ID: 4D33543B-3BFC-4435-95A3-983DE4AA7C31


Adding a new folder to replicate
Diagnostics report
```

Let's remove a member from the replica set and remove the SAVDALSRV02 server. It is in a unique position because right now it's the only server replicating to SAVDALSRV03. That is what you configured during the addition of SRV03, as shown in the replication summary in Figure 15-30. When you remove SAVDALSRV02, the SRV03 server no longer has any replication partners, so the integrity of the replication is lost.

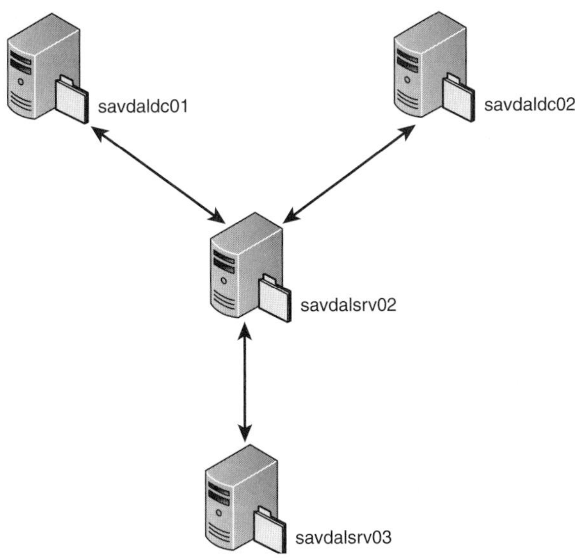

FIGURE 15-30 Replication connections.

To remove a member from the replica group, right-click the member and select Delete Member. If the replica group is part of a DFSN, a dialog appears, asking if the server should be removed from the replica group or the replica group and the namespace (see Figure 15-31). If the replica group is part of a namespace, then remove it from the namespace because the content on the target is no longer synchronized, causing end-user consistency issues.

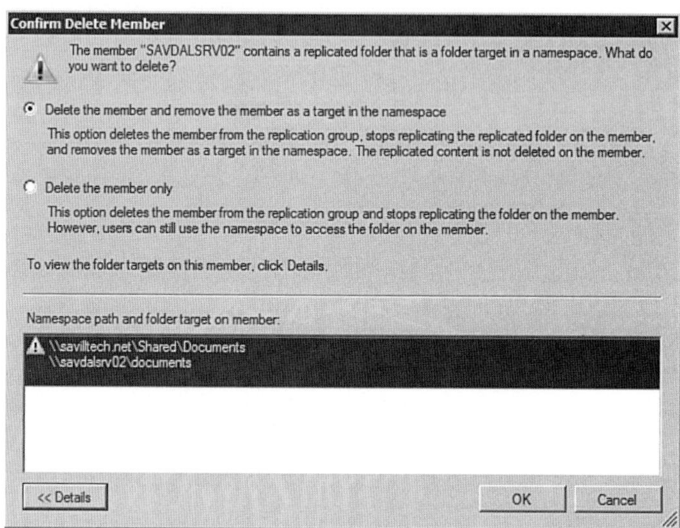

FIGURE 15-31 Removing a replica group member.

After it's deleted, if this server were critical in replication, as in this case, if you select the Connections tab for the replica group, a warning appears, informing you that the topology is not fully connected, and you can click a link to get more details, as shown in Figure 15-32. This is the same output that's displayed if the Verify Topology action was executed. You have several options. You can manually create a connection object to connect the server or run the New Topology action to let the wizard work out the connections. Which option you choose should depend on the number of members in the replica group. If you have fewer than 10 members, running the New Topology action is probably the best option: Just reselect the hubs and join the spokes to a specific hub. However, if you have many members, then reconfiguring all the hubs and spokes again takes a lot of effort, and it is easier to just manually create a connection object between the new member and an existing member.

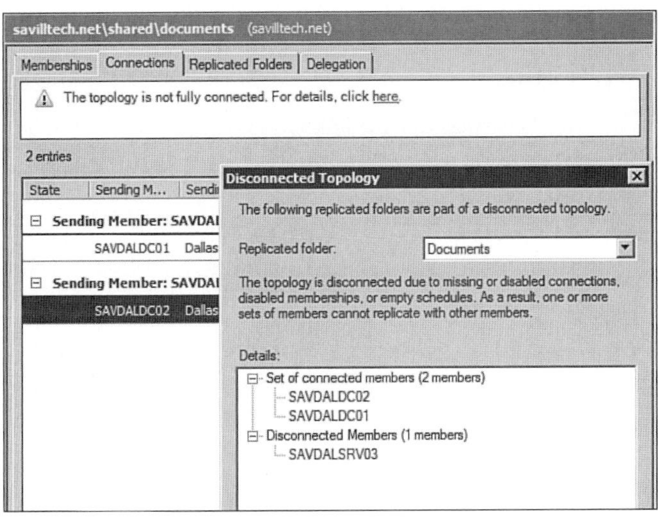

FIGURE 15-32 A disconnected replica set.

Folder Management

You can add and remove the folders being replicated that are part of a replica group. To add a new folder, select the replica group and then select Actions, New Replicated Folders. The New Replicated Folders Wizard launches. On initialization, you are prompted to indicate which server is the primary member, because again, on the first replication, one server is considered primary, and all other members' folder contents are synchronized to match the primary member's folder content.

The next page of the wizard asks for the folder to replicate, the folder on the primary member to replicate, and a name for the new replicated folder. The new replicated folder is, by default, based on the folder name, although you can configure a custom name, as shown in Figure 15-33. You can add multiple folders by repeating the Add process. When all folders are added, click Next to continue configuring the other members of the replica group.

For each folder added, specify the folder to be used on each of the other replica members. By default, the local path is disabled on all members. Select each member in the wizard and click Edit to set a local path where the content is replicated. Note that the option to create a new folder is available. You do not have to replicate to all members of the replica group. Just leave the local folder as <Not Defined> for any server that should not replicate the new folder.

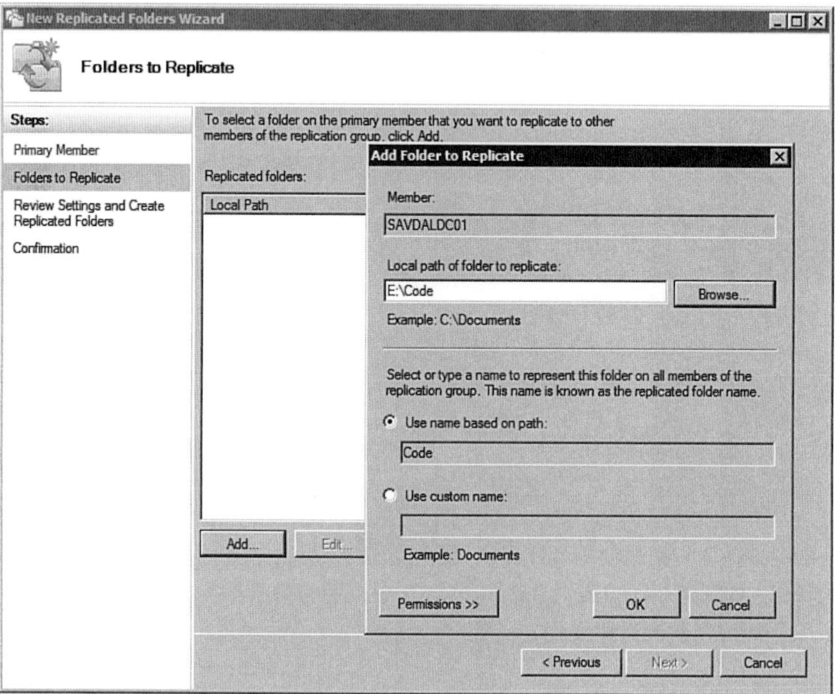

FIGURE 15-33 Adding a new folder to a replica group.

When you add a new folder, you can share and add it to DFSN via the Share and Publish in Namespace action. Selecting this action launches a wizard that guides you through creating shares and a name in DFSN.

Removing a folder is a matter of selecting the folder and selecting Delete, and if the replicated folder is in the namespace, you also have the option to remove the folder from the namespace.

Upgrading to Windows Server 2008 Mode DFSN

Currently, no in-place upgrade is supported from existing namespaces to the Windows Server 2008 mode DFSN. At release time, you must either re-create a new DFSN and populate the links from scratch or delete the existing DFSN and re-create it. Microsoft is working on a more automated solution. Meanwhile, use `dfsutil` to export the namespace and then import it back again. That would be much better than re-creating it from scratch. For example, such a process would work as follows:

1. dfsutil root export \\<*domain*>\<*namespace name*> <*path*>\filename.xml
2. dfsutil root remove \\<*domain*>\<*namespace name*>
3. dfsutil root adddom \\<*domain*>\<*namespace name*> v2
4. dfsutil root import merge <*path*>\filename.xml \\<*domain*>\<*namespace name*>

Troubleshooting

FRS provides the Sonar and Ultrasound troubleshooting tools. DFSR doesn't have these tools. Instead, DFSR has its own troubleshooting tool, `dfsrdiag`, in addition to integrated diagnostic reporting and event logging.

Initially, most people complain that replication doesn't start right away after you tell it to start. The DFS servers poll AD every 60 minutes by default to find out about any new replica groups they belong to and changes in configuration. This means replication may not start for 60 minutes. In addition, if the DFS servers are configured to use their local domain controllers instead of the PDC Emulator domain controller, then the time for the changes of DFSR configuration to replicate through the AD is added to that 60 minutes. The AD replication time depends on the sites where the replica members are located and the replication schedule between the sites. Be patient initially, but remember that you can force a poll by using the `dfsrdiag pollad` command.

If your problem is not just that replication has not started, the next best place to go is the File Services area of Server Manager. It provides a great summary of all the events that relate to the file services, including DFSR, as shown in Figure 15-34. This screen shows a summary of the number of errors, warnings, and information events; select each event to see the full details. It is common for the Error and Warning event logs to give indications of the cause for the problems; the details there are good and normally can help you resolve the problems. Make sure to look at both servers involved in replication for any errors or warnings. Also shown in the Summary section is the status of the file services, including DFSR.

The next place to go if you are experiencing problems is the diagnostic report, which you can run for each replication group by selecting the replication group you are experiencing problems with and selecting Actions, Create Diagnostic Report. This gives you two ways to diagnose problems. The first is to run a health report, which is generally the first course of action, and the second is a two-phase propagation test, which tests the replication of data by placing a test file in the replica group, monitoring its process, and then running a report. Run the health report first, so select the Health Report option and click Next. This enables the path and filename for the report to be selected, and by default this information is stored in the C:\DFSReports folder.

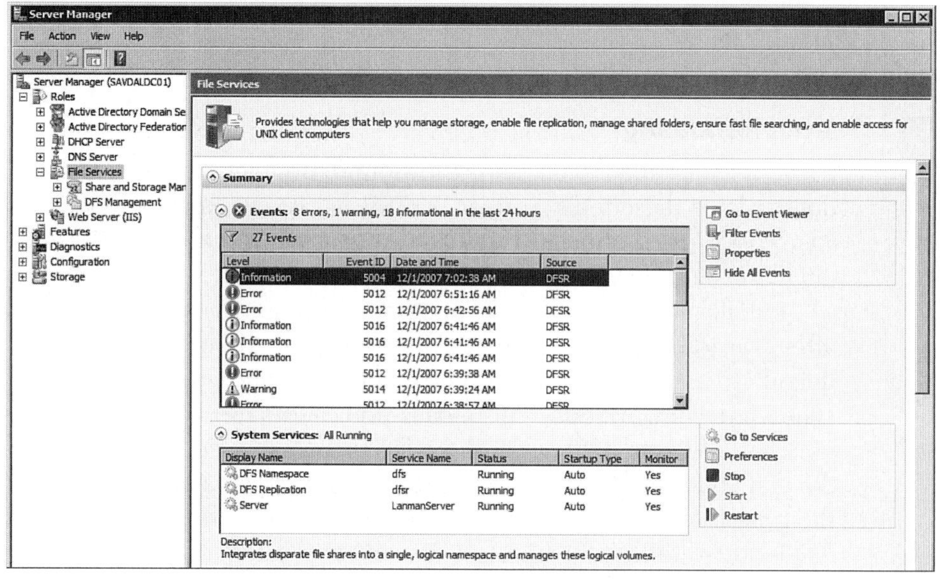

FIGURE 15-34 DFSR status information in Server Manager.

The next page of the Diagnostic Report Wizard requests which members of the replica group to include in the health report, as shown in Figure 15-35. By default, all members are included. However, you can modify this by selecting members and clicking the Remove button.

The final configuration is to select whether backlogged files (that is, files that have not replicated yet) should be calculated and whether a count of replicated files and their sizes should be performed (see Figure 15-35). Running the count takes a significant amount of time if a large number of files are present, so take care when selecting this option. Finally, a summary of the options is displayed. Click Create to begin the report generation process. The report generation may take a significant amount of time, depending on the number of members in the replica set and the amount of data. Microsoft recommends not running a report for more than 50 servers at a time.

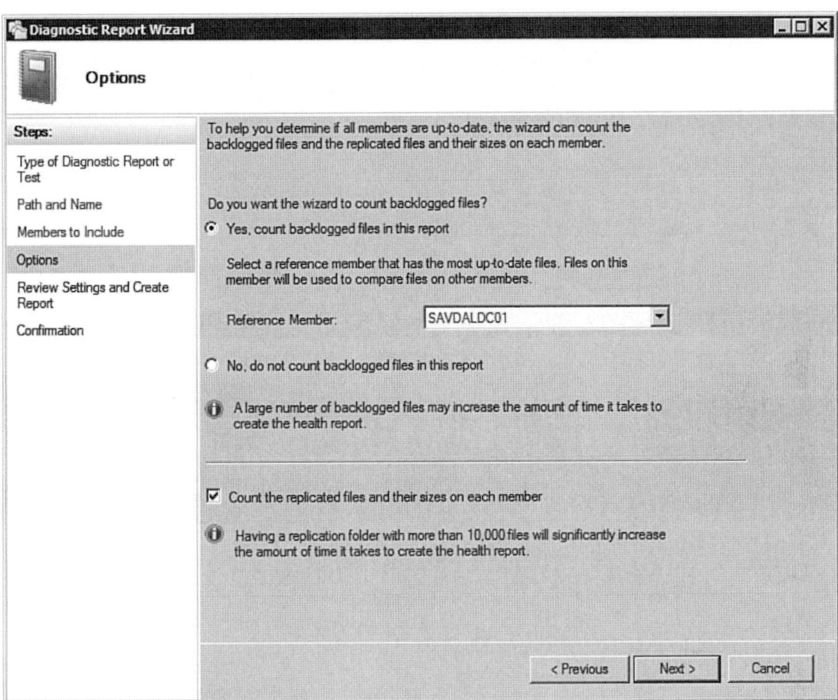

FIGURE 15-35 Specifying options for a health report.

When the report is complete, it is displayed. The report in Figure 15-36 shows the bandwidth saved by using DFSR, along with information on servers with errors, servers with warnings, and servers that are unavailable and then a details section about the servers. If you have errors, select an error to link to the server details section, where you can see an explanation of the problem.

The second test, a propagation test, works in a similar fashion to a health report, but you have to run it in two parts. To start, launch the Create Diagnostic Report action, but this time select the Propagation Test option. Select a replicated folder from the replica group under which to place the test file and the server from which the file is initially propagated. You also have the option to delete any test files older than a configurable number of days (90 is the default), as shown in Figure 15-37. Finally, you see a summary. Click Create to begin the file propagation.

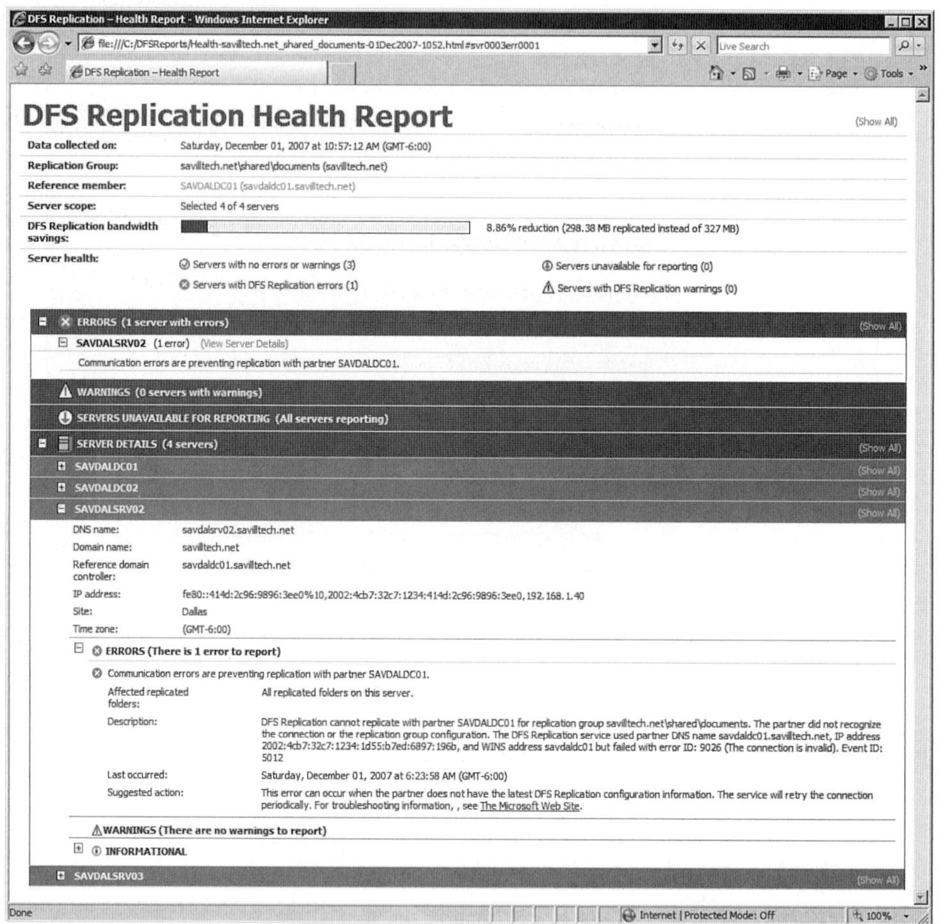

FIGURE 15-36 Sample health report.

A new folder, named __DFSR_DIAGNOSTICS_TEST_FOLDER__, is created under the folder selected, and under this new folder is a new XML test file for this propagation test with a long name that contains the name of the server, a Globally Unique Identifier (GUID), the DFSR replica group name, and the folder name (for example, SAVDALDC01@301428A2-14C9-4E34-AC17-F5B0F665C1F8@savilltech.net_shared_documents-Documents.xml).

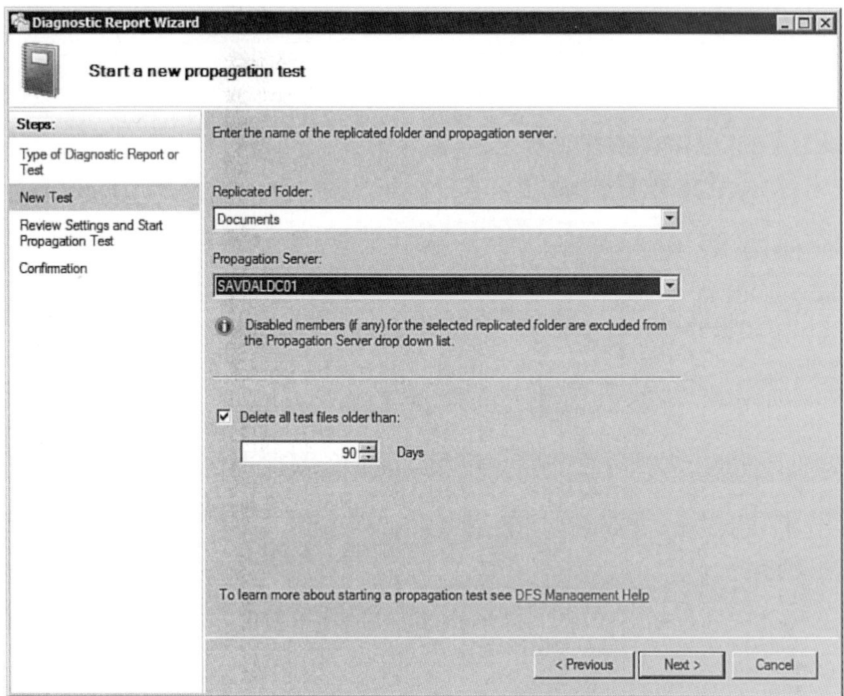

FIGURE 15-37 Selecting the test file options.

Based on your replication schedule for the DFSR group and the bandwidth available, the test file replicates throughout the replica group. When you have waited enough time for the file to replicate throughout the replica group, launch the Create Diagnostic Report option again. This time, select the Propagation Report option, and you are asked for the folder to use to look for test files. It should be the same one to which you propagated a file. You're also asked for the maximum number of test files to include in the report and to provide a path for the report and a name. Finally, the report is generated, as shown in Figure 15-38. Notice in the report a list of all the tests run (in this case only one), and for each test, details concerning how long the file took to replicate to all the members, along with options to show a graph of the replication time. Obviously, in this case, you would be happy. Replicating data within one second is good. You can feel satisfied with the replication, but the goal would be to run the propagation tests at different times of the day over a period of time to get a feel for how replication is performing at different times of the day.

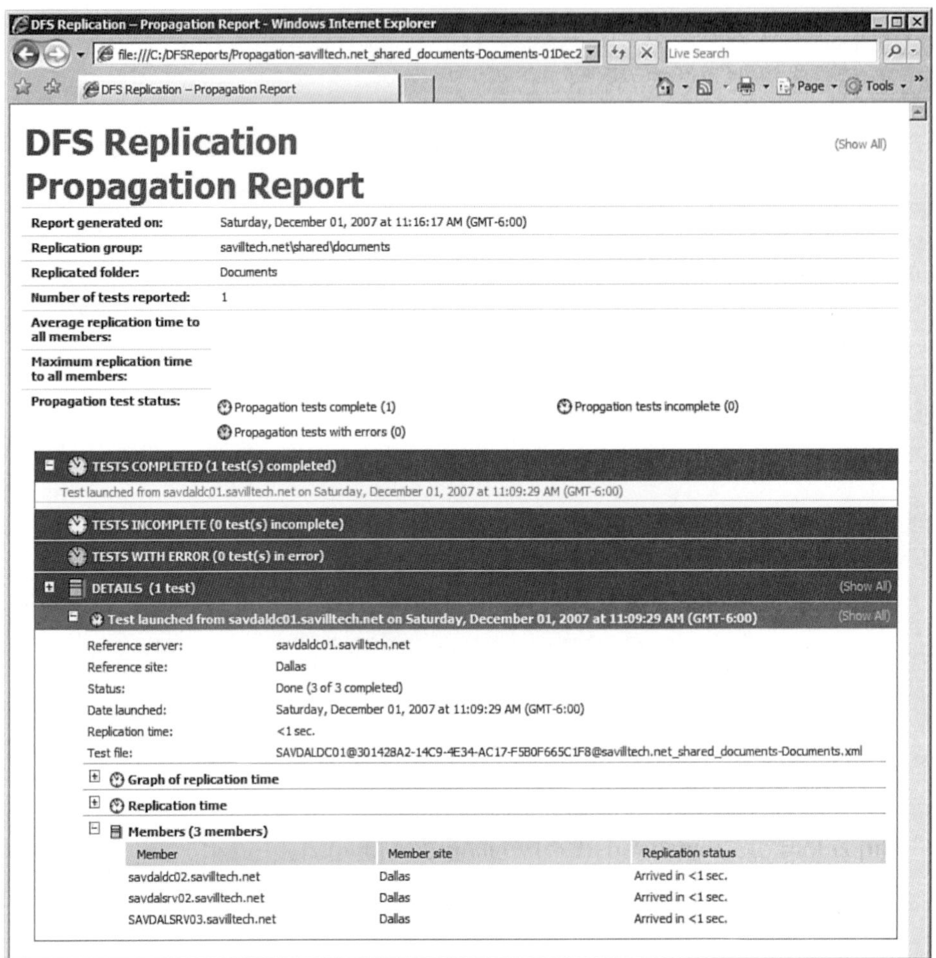

FIGURE 15-38 The output of a propagation report.

You can also initiate and report on propagation via the `dfsrdiag propagationtest` and `propagationreport` commands, which enable you to select a filename to use for the test. The text is still placed in the __DFSR_DIAGNOSTICS_TEST_FOLDER__ folder. A sample test is shown in the following command-line example. When the test is run, open the XML file specified on the command line to see more details about the times of the test by viewing the `CreateTime` and `UpdateTime` values, which are in FILETIME format (which you can convert by using the `w32tm /ntte` command). The `CreateTime` value indicates the time the file was created on the propagation folder, and `UpdateTime` is the time it was created on each of the servers in the replica group. So the difference between the values is the time replication took:

```
C:\Windows>dfsrdiag propagationtest
➥/rgname:savilltech.net\shared\documents
➥/rfname:documents /testfile:proptest5

Operation Succeeded

C:\Windows>dfsrdiag propagationreport
➥/rgname:savilltech.net\shared\documents
➥/rfname:documents /testfile:proptest5
➥/reportfile:c:\dfsreports\proptest5.xml

PROCESSING MEMBER SAVDALSRV03 [1 OUT OF 4]

PROCESSING MEMBER SAVDALSRV02 [2 OUT OF 4]

PROCESSING MEMBER SAVDALDC02 [3 OUT OF 4]

PROCESSING MEMBER SAVDALDC01 [4 OUT OF 4]

Total number of members              : 4
Number of disabled members           : 0
Number of unsubscribed members       : 0
Number of invalid AD member objects  : 0
Test file access failures            : 0
WMI access failures                  : 0
ID record search failures            : 0
Test file mismatches                 : 0
Members with valid test file         : 4


Operation Succeeded
```

Next, use the `dfsrdiag` command-line tool, which gives you more options for troubleshooting. For example, to view a list of backlog files between servers in a replica group, use the `backlog` argument to see up to 100 backlog files in addition to a backlog count, as shown in the following example. Notice that you pass the replica group, the replication folder to check for backlog files, and the sending and receiving servers:

```
C:\Windows>dfsrdiag backlog
➥/rgname:savilltech.net\shared\documents
➥/rfname:documents
➥/sendingmember:savdaldc01 /receivingmember:savdalsrv03

Member <savdalsrv03> Backlog File Count: 5
Backlog File Names (first 5 files)
     1. File name: en_system_center_configuration_manager_2007
_50571.iso
     2. File name: install.wim
     3. File name: Windows6.0-KB936330-
X64_wave1_SPInstaller.exe
     4. File name: Windows6.0-KB936330-
X86_wave1_SPInstaller.exe
     5. File name: en_office_project_server_2007_X13-38790.iso

Operation Succeeded
```

Other causes of problems can include such things as having a large number of changes, the 4GB staging quota not being enough, and the rest of the replication waiting until there is space in the staging area. You get event ID 4202, notifying you of staging quota issues as the space used reaches a certain percentage of the quota. If this is common, increase the staging quota by selecting the properties of the replica group server and changing it via the Staging tab, as shown in Figure 15-39. You can also modify the quota used for conflicts and deletions via the Advanced tab.

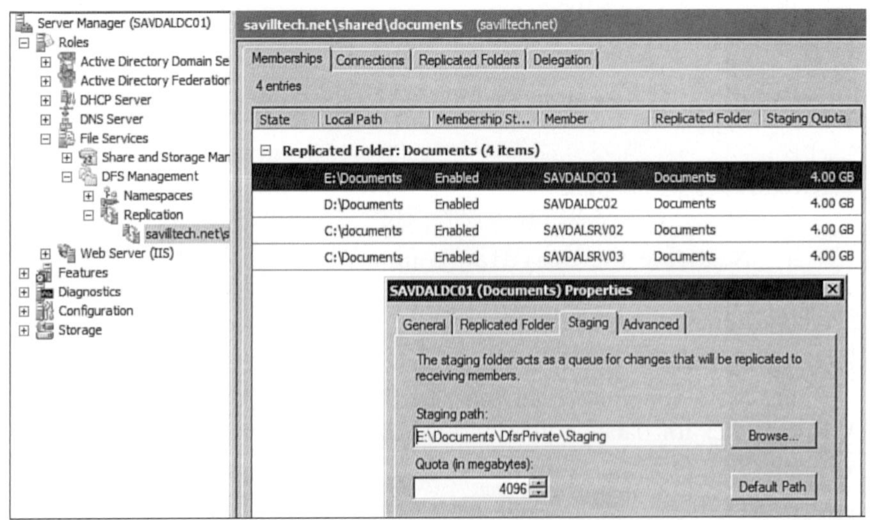

FIGURE 15-39 Modifying the staging quota.

Another common problem is that the bandwidth restrictions are too restrictive, which is indicated by a backlog of files while the actual available bandwidth is plentiful. Remember that you can change the replication schedule via the Edit Replication Group Schedule action for a replica group, and you can also change it on an individual replication connection level, if required. Ensure that you have not turned off RDC on a connection object, which would also use a lot more bandwidth because delta replication is not performed. However, this may deliberately not have been set on a fast network where the bandwidth is fast enough to warrant copying the whole file instead of performing the calculations needed for RDC replication.

Remember that for a file to be replicated, it has to be closed. DFSR cannot replicate open files, so if you are using DFSR to copy a database for backup purposes that is always open, you are going to be disappointed. Most organizations use DFSR primarily to replicate read-only materials such as human resources information and marketing materials, but with the right controls, it can be used for much more.

Finally, remember that you can block certain types of files from replicating, and you configure this, at the level of a replicated folder. By default, you don't replicate any files that match ~*, *.bak, or *.tmp; however, you can modify this, as shown in Figure 15-40. Also notice that you can configure a particular subfolder, such as a local subtemp folder, to not be replicated. Similarly, remember that in Windows Server 2008 you can use file screening, which can, in real time, block certain types of file. If you don't have consistent file screens across all the servers, one server may allow a certain type of file that is blocked on another server, which causes replication issues and access-denied errors in the DFSR debug logs. You can find those logs in `%systemroot%\debug\` and in the format dfsr*nnnnn*.log, where *nnnnn* is a sequential number.

In general, DFSR functions well if you use the wizards and follow the practices outlined in this chapter. DFSR is far more resilient and self-healing than NTFRS was, and you'll see far fewer problems than were encountered in the past with replication. That being said, if you want the best in monitoring, look at System Center Operations Manager, which has a dedicated DFSR management pack to track the health of your DFSR environment.

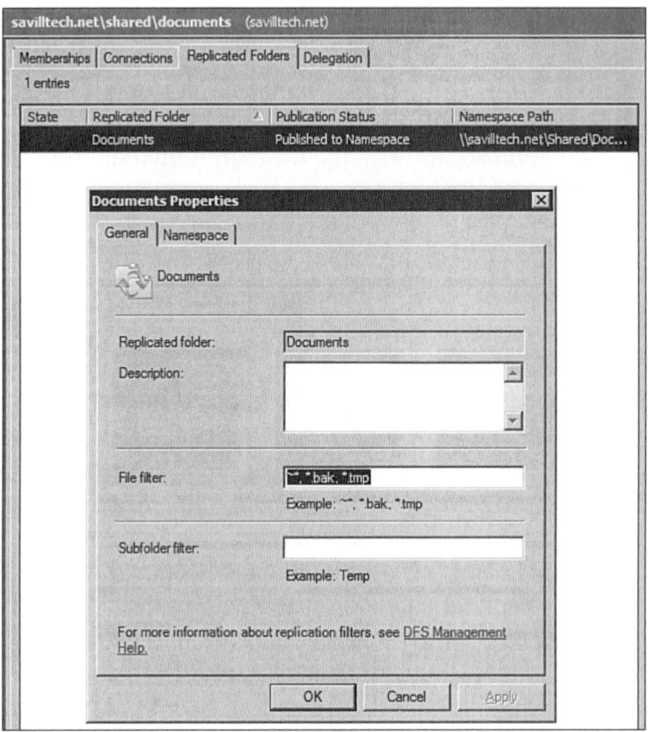

FIGURE 15-40 Setting the excluded files filter.

Summary

A distributed environment is always a challenge. However, with proper planning and by using the facilities provided by Windows Server 2008, you can enable all the offices of an organization, both central and remote locations, to enjoy full functionality without an administrative nightmare.

Microsoft is still working on DFS, and you can look forward to numerous improvements in future versions that includes reduced management for large namespaces and a more automated experience when you move shares between servers. In that more automated experience, you will see the DFS Management snap-in taking care of replicating the data, modifying the share, updating the namespace, and reconfiguring DFSR. And all this will be done in such a way that there will be no interruption to the end user, who can enjoy 24/7 availability. The full life cycle of share management is on the agenda, with various levels of storage class being available and with DFS deciding where the shares should physically reside. This virtualization of where storage exists via the DFSN follows Microsoft's strategy with server virtualization, which sees the System Center Virtual Machine Manager solution able to provision and move virtual instances to best suit the load of the virtual instance and where resources are available.

In terms of replication, although DFSR is great, there are still improvements on the agenda, which focus on using even less bandwidth for replication, adding cluster support for DFSR, and allowing read-only capabilities for replicas. You should also see the capability for DFSR to replicate open files.

You may hear conversations about which should be used, SharePoint or DFSR. These are two different solutions. DFSR has no distributed locking mechanism, which means there are complications if the same file is edited at the same time on different replicas of the folder, whereas SharePoint has a powerful checking out process. DFSR is good for replicating data between locations that are primarily edited only in a single location at any one time.

CHAPTER 16

DEPLOYING WINDOWS

In the early days of operating systems (OSs), there were not many configurations to perform during an installation; most desktop OSs were installed manually, and an operator answered minor questions as needed. As OSs grew in complexity, however, the number of components needed for installation also grew, thus increasing the questions asked during the installation process. To help in the deployment of newer OSs, both desktop and server solutions were created.

Microsoft introduced Remote Installation Services (RIS), which enabled a computer to boot over the network via a Preboot Execution Environment (PXE) that downloaded a minimal operating environment to the computer. This enabled the computer to pull down the OS installation files and perform the install. In addition to providing the OS installation files, an answer file could be specified that removed the need for an operator to answer questions during the install process—for example, unattend.txt. RIS was a free solution. However, the RIS installation process performed a full installation of the OS file by file; as the OSs grew, the installation times grew accordingly, making this an increasingly less attractive option. Third-party vendors worked on their own installation options for Windows OSs, which were based on images of an already-installed OS.

This chapter examines how Windows Server 2008 solves deployment problems with its own imaging solution.

Image Deployment

The most time-consuming part of installing an OS is not copying files from media or a network source to the local machine's hard disk. The various configurations and installations performed for each component of the OS take the most time. To avoid a lengthy installation process, some vendors introduced image-based deployments, which followed this process:

1. Install Windows on a single workstation using traditional media-based installation.
2. Configure the workstation as required in the enterprise, along with other software that is desired, such as antivirus and office applications like word processing.
3. Shut down the workstation.
4. Boot the workstation from a floppy disk or CD that has a capture utility, which replicates the workstation's hard disk content sector by sector to a capture file on a network location.
5. Machines that require installation boot from the network, floppy, or CD, and the capture file of the source workstations is applied to them. The disk content is "restored" sector by sector to their local hard disk.

This process is a disk duplication—all the machines that restore the capture of the source machine's hard drive, when booted, have the same software and configuration as the source machine. Because it is a disk duplication, however, the target machines must have the same hardware as the source machine. This led to many organizations having a large number of images for each hardware configuration present in the environment.

An additional problem with this approach (aside from the hard disk sizes often having to match due to the sector-based nature of the capture) was because the disk was effectively duplicated, there were multiple instances of one OS installation running at the same time. Why is it a problem to have multiple instances of one OS installation?

When Windows is installed as part of the OS configuration, the installation generates a unique identifier for the machine that goes beyond user-settable attributes, such as computer name or IP address. This unique identifier is known as the machine's security identifier (SID), and it is a core part of security in a Windows environment; every object has a unique SID. If you install Windows on one machine and then copy it many times, every machine would have the same SID; this would cause many security problems because all machines would seem to be the same. It is, in fact, unworkable in an Active Directory environment, which relies on the machine's SID. In addition to its SID, a computer also has a Globally Unique Identifier (GUID), which is a 128-bit value that is guaranteed to be unique across the entire world and not just an organization. If you copy a machine, however, this GUID would also be duplicated. That's a problem.

To combat the issue of non-uniqueness in duplicated machines, solutions were created to modify the SID and GUID of copied machines, which would run as part of the duplication process; this enabled the duplication technique of a machine to be a viable option. Disk imaging became the prevalent method of OS deployment to such an extent that Microsoft provided a supported tool to enable the duplication of machines, while ensuring uniqueness was maintained.

System Preparation (SYSPREP) Tool

If you have a computer made in the last five years, it is likely that, when you turn it on for the first time, you are prompted for a few basic pieces of information, such as registered user and organization. This mini-setup is part of the SYSPREP process, which demonstrates how SYSPREP is now the standard for all disk-imaging processes used today. Let's look at the process in more detail.

Previously, SYSPREP was available in various ways. It was available as a download from Microsoft, with each OS having its own version of the tool; it was vital to never use SYSPREP with different OS versions, even to the extent that each service pack update to an OS would have an accompanying SYSPREP version. SYSPREP was made available as part of the deployment tools that were bundled on the OS installation media with Windows 2000 and later in the support\tools folder. With Windows Vista and Server 2008, SYSPREP is now installed as standard and can be found in the %systemroot%\system32\sysprep folder.

SYSPREP has various usage options but one main role: It's designed to take a system you have tailored to your organization's requirements and duplicate it to other machines. SYSPREP is executed after the customization has been done. This execution can work in various modes, including the following:

- Removing system-specific configuration and information, such as the SID.
- Configuring the installation to boot to Windows Welcome after reboot; this is useful for capturing an image that will be written to computers being sent to customers who want to see the mini-setup stages to enable customization.

- Boot to an audit mode, enabling third-party application and driver installation.
- Product Activation reset up to three times.

SYSPREP has a full graphical interface that is launched by running SYSPREP with no arguments (see Figure 16-1), or the command-line version can be used by passing the options as command-line arguments.

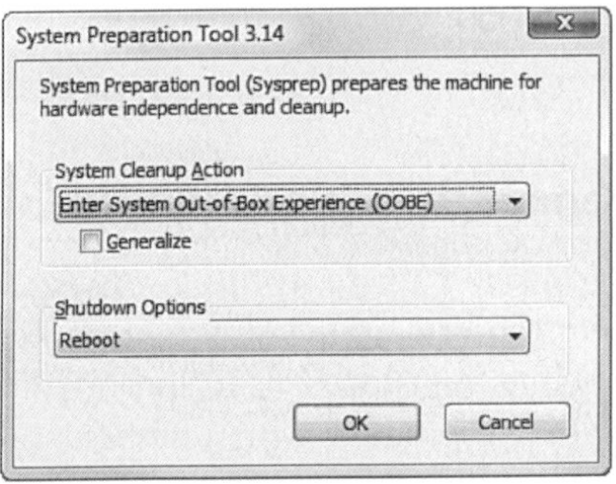

FIGURE 16-1 The graphical interface to SYSPREP gives easy access to the various SYSPREP options.

Let's look at the command-line options. They will explain the detailed capabilities of SYSPREP, which are easily located in the graphical version:

- **`/quiet`**. Stops any on-screen display, which is useful when running in an automated fashion.
- **`/generalize`**. Prepares the computer for duplication by removing all unique system information, including system restore points deleted, event logs cleared, and the SID reset.
- **`/audit`**. Restarts the computer in audit mode, which enables additional drivers and applications to be added to an installation of Windows and also enables performance testing before duplication or delivery to an end-user. auditSystem and auditUser configuration passes are processed if configured, which control the drivers and applications to install.
- **`/oobe`**. Runs the Out Of Box Experience (oobe) on restart, which displays the Windows Welcome enabling end-user customization, such as creating a user and naming the computer. Settings in the answer XML file that make up the oobe system configuration pass are processed once the Windows Welcome is shown.

- **/reboot or /shutdown or /quit**. Configures the machine to reboot, shut down, or simply exit SYSPREP once it has completed its system changes.
- **/unattend:<file>**. Specifies the answer XML file to be used during the Windows unattended installation to complete configuration of the OS.

A common execution you will use for sysprep looks like the following:

```
c:\windows\system32\sysprep\sysprep.exe /oobe /generalize
/shutdown
```

This command removes the unique information from the machine, configures the Windows Welcome to run on next boot-up, and shuts down the OS ready to be duplicated.

Although SYSPREP solved the problems associated with duplicating an image of an installation, the actual method of creating and using an image was provided by third parties. Microsoft's first foray into image deployment was with Automated Deployment Services (ADS), which was available as a feature pack for Windows 2003 Enterprise edition. It was designed with the deployment of server OSs in mind and not client OSs. ADS used a new image format that was able to capture a machine at either the hard disk-sector level or the actual files the OS installation consisted of. The capture and deployment of an OS was facilitated via the ADS deployment agent; this was a highly scaled-down version of Windows 2003 (similar to Windows Pre-Execution Environment [PE]) that contained the components for network and disk access required for image-based installations. The deployment agent enabled virtual floppy disks to be used during an installation, which enabled steps such as updating the BIOS of a server or performing hardware RAID configuration. This enabled the entire process of standing up a server in an environment to be automated through a sophisticated set of actions, which are configured via an XML-based task sequence.

ADS was a great technology, but it was for server OSs only—it did not catch on in many environments, as its initial setup and configuration was not considered a great time investment when the OS could be manually installed fairly quickly. Of course, this ignored the advantages of automated installations, one of which—consistency—is crucial when supporting larger environments.

A parallel installation methodology was being investigated at Microsoft; the company realized that as the OS grew in size, complexity, and number of components, the traditional installation method—installing the OS one component at a time, with each component having its own set of configuration steps—was going to result in extremely long installation times for Windows Vista. It was decided instead to first perform the installation of Windows Vista at Microsoft, and then a SYSPREP installation would be captured to an image. An image-based installation would then be performed for end users and businesses. This meant Microsoft needed an image format of its own and a method to distribute the image for both home and business users.

Microsoft created the Windows Imaging Format (WIM) that, unlike many other technologies, was a file-based format for storing information in a single cabinet format-type structure. This enabled the format to use single-instance storage, which saved space by storing any duplicate files found in an installation only once instead of multiple times. This may not seem to be a big deal. However, consider the Windows Resource Protection that Windows Vista employs to protect the OS (the replacement for Windows File Protection present in Windows 2000 and XP). It includes the duplication of key files needed to boot Windows Vista that are stored in the %Windir%\winsxs\Backup folder and take up around 500MB. With single-instance storage, this duplicated 500MB is not stored twice, saving 500MB from the size of the image. Coupled with compression technologies, a WIM file of an OS is typically one third the size of the partition it is capturing.

This single-instance storage enables another cool feature. Over the years, the number of editions of Windows has grown. However, these different versions share mostly the same core set of files, and so Microsoft now ships all versions of Windows Vista on one media, with all sharing a single WIM file.

Because the Windows media now contains all the versions of the OS, Microsoft can enable another interesting feature: Anytime Upgrade. If initially you install a "lower" version of Vista and want to upgrade, all you need is a new product key; the Vista DVD and the components that are part of the upgrade Vista will be installed. This new key is available via the Windows Anytime Upgrade component of Vista. The Windows Anytime Upgrade (as with any upgrade) performs a full Vista upgrade in the same way as upgrading XP to Vista; new components are not just installed, but the entire OS is redeployed to the machine, with the previous settings and programs migrated to the "new" OS.

The first support for the WIM format was via the System Management Server OS Deployment Feature Pack, which used an early 0.9 version of the WIM format, but utilized PE-based wizards to capture and deploy

WIM-based OSs. These were principally custom Windows XP and Windows 2000 OSs because, although server OSs were supported, SMS OSD lacked features typically needed to deploy server OSs. One problem was that the SMS OSD PE environment was based on Windows XP, and many server drivers for storage devices and network interface cards are not supported under XP. When booting from the PE environment, there was no way to access the physical storage on the server. This problem has been resolved with the new deployment technologies, as the PE environment is based on the Windows Server 2008 code base.

As an interim step to the release of Windows 2008, Microsoft released an update for Windows 2003 SP1 that included the new OS deployment technology, Windows Deployment Services (WDS), as part of the Windows Automated Installation Kit (WAIK). WAIK was a suite of tools and information to help with the deployment of Windows Vista. Because Windows Vista and Windows Server 2008 were so far apart in release schedules, Microsoft had to find a way to roll out Windows Vista. RIS was not an option, because Windows Vista was entirely WIM based. RIS was totally replaced as part of Windows 2003 SP2, and any RIS installation on a 2003 box was converted to WDS as part of the standard service pack installation.

WDS is a set of services and management tools to handle the deployment of Microsoft's next generation of OSs, Windows Vista and Windows Server 2008, over the network. Although WDS is designed with Vista and 2008 as the focus, older OSs such as Windows XP and 2003 can be captured to an image and deployed using WDS. WDS includes PXE boot services, transport mechanisms to transmit the image data, multicast support, and an intuitive management interface. WDS is one-half of the puzzle that is deploying Vista and 2008. As previously mentioned, WAIK is still needed to customize and automate installations.

The next section discusses WDS installation, including relevant areas of the product in reference to other technologies.

Installing Windows Deployment Services

Like all Windows Server 2008 components, WDS is installed as a role for the server (it was not shamed by being called a "feature," unlike poor old WINS). Via the Server Manager MMC snap-in, select the Roles node of the navigation pane and click the Add Roles link. Within the roles, check the Windows Deployment Services entry (see Figure 16-2) and click Next.

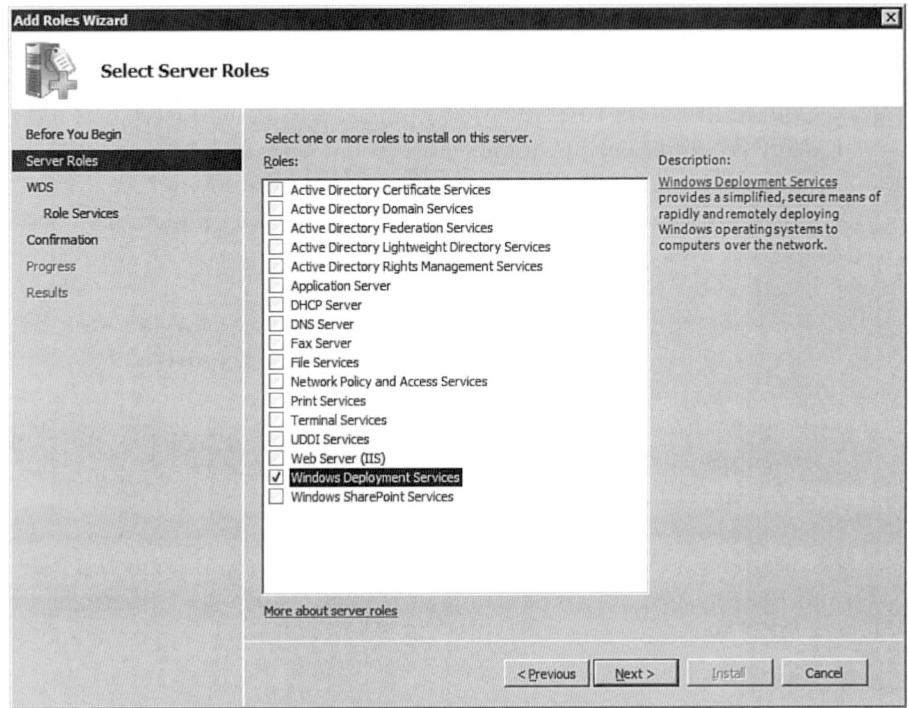

FIGURE 16-2 Windows Deployment Services falls into one of the coveted "roles."

The next screen in the installation of the WDS role confirms the network requirements for WDS to work: Active Directory Domain Services, DNS, and, of course, DHCP, to give addresses to clients booting PXE to download the OS. The other requirement is an NTFS partition for image storage. After reading the information about the requirements, click Next, and the components of WDS to install are displayed:

- **Deployment Server**. This is the main full-functionality component of WDS, including PXE server for network boot, a store for the images, management tools, and so on.
- **Transport Server**. This is the networking part of WDS—for example, TFP, multicast server, and the base PXE server (but not the PXE provider that does business logic/AD interaction). If you want to use multicast to send other types of media such as VHD files, install the transport server and use other tools to connect to the transmission. For example, you could use the Wdsmcast tool that is part of the WAIK.

Normally, you install both components for the full WDS functionality. After the WDS role is installed, the next task is to configure it. That can be performed by the WDS MMC snap-in or the command-line interface, `wdsutil`. First, use the graphical interface and then look at the command line.

Configuring Windows Deployment Services

After installation, the WDS server will first be displayed in the WDS MMC snap-in with a warning symbol, indicating that it needs to be configured (see Figure 16-3).

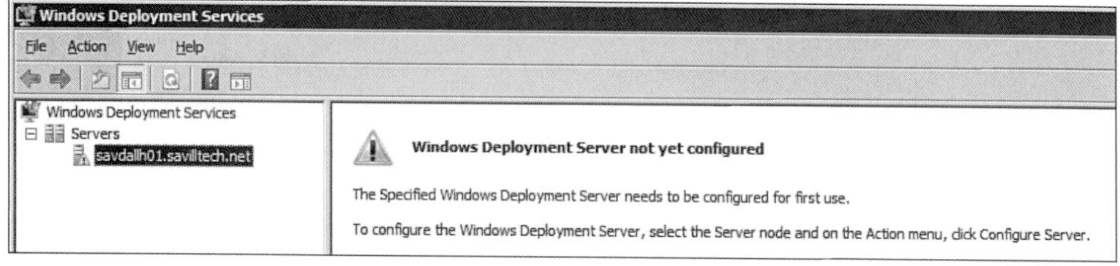

Figure 16-3 A newly installed WDS server initially has no functionality and requires configuration.

To configure the server, right-click it and select Configure Server from its displayed context menu. During the configuration, initially an installation image and a boot image will be requested to enable WDS to provide installation services to requesting clients. These can be from the Windows Vista media or customized images, but have one of each image type handy.

The welcome page, as shown in Figure 16-4, confirms the requirements for full deployment service use, as previously described. Click Next to proceed to the next wizard page. The next dialog, shown in Figure 16-5, prompts for a path for the root of the storage of the images used by WDS, which by default is %systemdrive%\RemoteInstall (for example, C:\RemoteInstall). This is a change from the previous Windows deployment technology—namely RIS—that, while also requiring an NTFS partition, insisted on the partition used *not* being the system or boot partition. This was due to its use of single-instance storage to minimize the amount of space used when hosting multiple versions of the same or similar OS. The best practice, however, is to place RemoteInstall onto a volume that is not the Windows system volume and, ideally for IO performance purposes, an entirely separate physical drive.

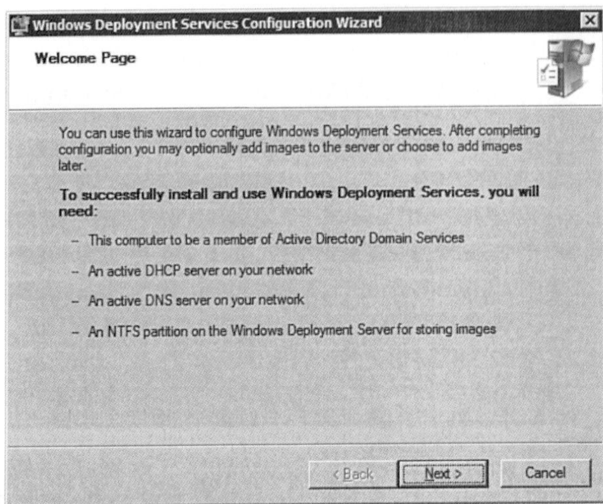

FIGURE 16-4 The basic requirements for using WDS infrastructure.

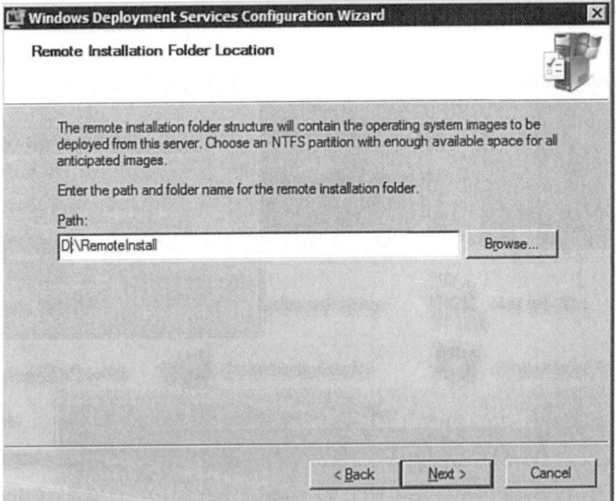

FIGURE 16-5 Unlike with RIS, the image store can be on the system/boot partition.

Single Instance Storage

Let's take a quick look at Single Instance Storage (SIS). In previous versions of Windows (such as Windows XP and Windows 2003, and even Windows 2000 and NT), it was common to have multiple versions of the same OS in an organization. This was to cater to the different physical hardware types within an organization (drivers and, at a minimum, one version for each Hardware Abstraction Layer [HAL] type), as well as to the various uses of a machine, such as an accounting installation or a sales installation (with all functions except Solitaire and a calculator removed). Full versions of the OS were stored five, ten, or more times, with all of them gigabytes in size and all essentially identical except for a different HAL file.

Therefore, SIS is used, which has a groveler agent process that runs at times of low processor usage, identifies duplicate instances of the same file, and removes all duplicates with a link to a singularly stored version of the file in the SIS Common Store. These links are known as *junction points*. SIS ensures space isn't wasted by storing a file only once on a partition. You don't need to run this with WDS because installations are now a single file, which will look different. Thus, SIS would not do anything, and, most importantly, WIM files have built-in SIS, as discussed previously.

This is not to discount the use of SIS. In a file server environment, SIS is useful for saving disk space—in many organizations, people save similar data, taking up space. With SIS, the data is stored only once, effectively consolidating duplicate information. This saves on disk space, cache used by a server, and, perhaps most importantly, data to back up, which enables faster backup and restore times. In Windows 2003, SIS was available only for non-RIS purposes, as part of the Windows Server 2003 R2 Storage Server product. In Windows Server 2008, this continues, with SIS only being part of the 2008 Storage Server solution.

The next set of options enable configuration of whom the Windows Deployment Server will respond to (see Figure 16-6). The client support options are as follows:

- To not respond to any computer, which is not useful unless you want to use a WDS server as a central image repository and not respond to client computers. The content of the RemoteInstall folder could then be replicated to other WDS servers via technologies, such as Distributed File System Replication (DFS-R); the target replica WDS servers will automatically monitor their RemoteInstall folder, read in any replicated images, and add to their WDS repository.

- Respond to only known client computers that have been prestaged in the Active Directory via the Active Directory Users and Computers MMC snap-in with the computer's GUID or Media Access Control (MAC) address.
- Respond to all computers (known and unknown) with the option of asking for administrator approval in an unknown computer case.

In many organizations, the option to only respond to known client computers is preferred in order to avoid the chance of a random computer connecting to the network and being given a potentially sensitive OS image. However, this does require a good provisioning process in place for organizations, so new computers are added to the Active Directory prior to their OS installation.

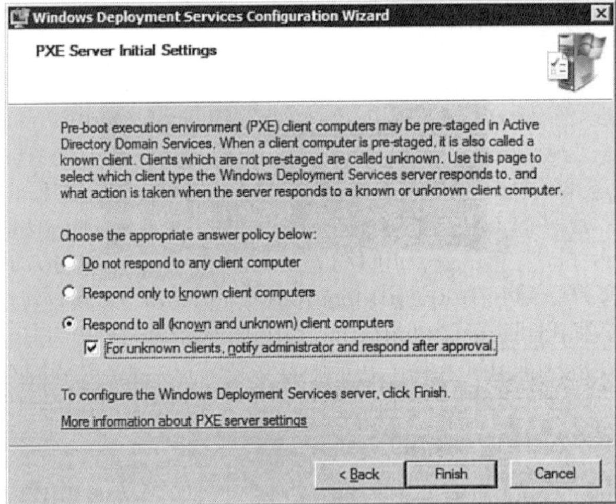

FIGURE 16-6 Depending on the organization, the options for client support may be more or less strict.

After these options are configured, the full WDS configuration will be completed and the required services started. At this point, the WDS configuration wizard gives the option of adding some images to WDS to get you up and running as quickly as possible, as shown in Figure 16-7.

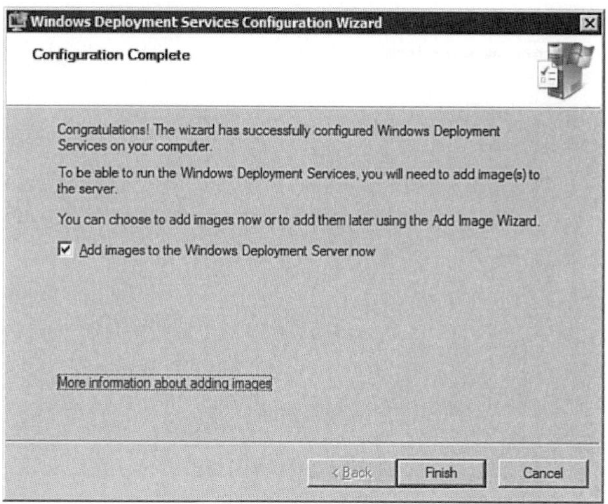

FIGURE 16-7 WDS prompts you to add some images at the start.

Assuming you accept this help, leave the Add images to the Windows Deployment Server now check box selected and click Finish. At this point, the Add Image Wizard will launch, asking for a location where boot and install images can be found (see Figure 16-8). By default, regular Vista media has one of each. However, you can use customized images, Windows Server 2008, and so on, so enter the location of your Vista media or a customized version and click Next. Although the PE version on the Vista media will work with WDS, to get the full functionality, use the boot.wim from the Sources folder of Windows Server 2008 for extra features, such as multicasting support.

A new image group is created, and you should give it a sensible name, as opposed to the default ImageGroup1 (for example, Windows Vista). A summary of what was found in the folder given is shown in Figure 16-9. Click Next and then the images are imported and the status displayed. After the import is complete, click Finish.

After the initial configuration is complete, the main navigation node of the WDS MMC snap-in for the server will become populated and will display five child nodes, exposing the various options for the WDS server:

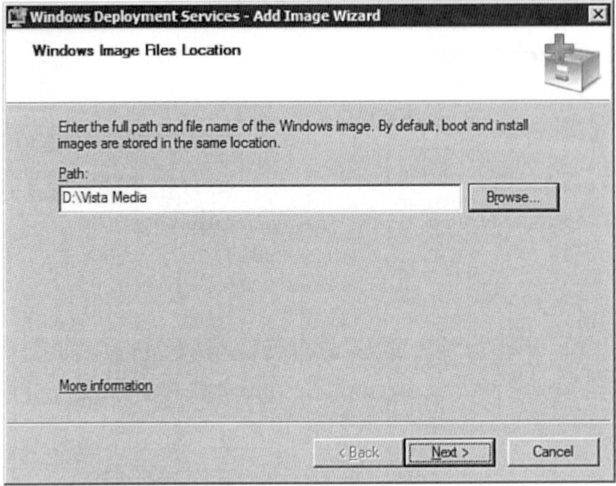

FIGURE 16-8 A Vista (or other WIM OS, for that matter) path should be given.

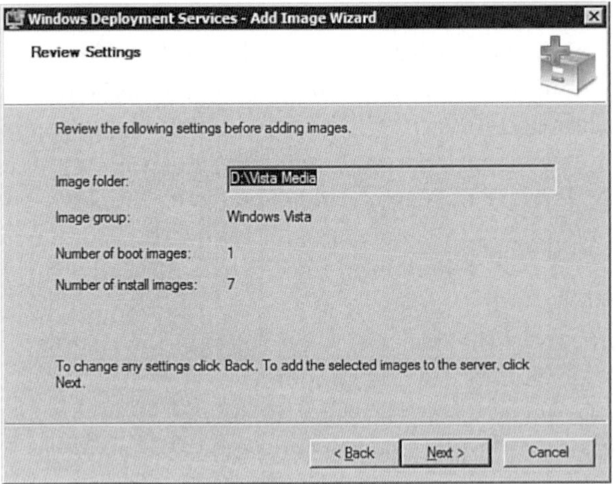

FIGURE 16-9 A normal Windows Vista install.wim contains all versions of Vista except Enterprise—even those strange European –N versions, which have all the fun bits removed. (I'm English, so I can insult Europeans and get away with it.)

- **Install Images**. Lists the various image groups you have defined that contain actual OS images, which has seven versions of Vista (see Figure 16-10).

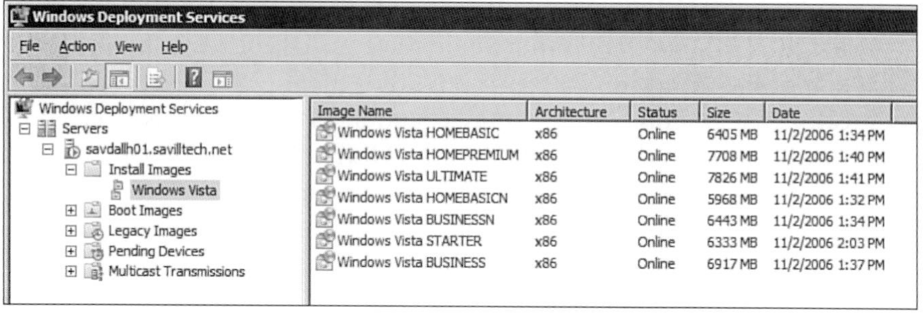

Figure 16-10 The Windows Vista versions included in the Windows Vista basic retail version.

- **Boot Images**. Contains the images used for the actual deployment of an Install image. The boot images are Windows PE instances that can be sent over the network via a PXE boot to a client or written to removable media to enable a boot from media and then launch the install image downloading from a WDS server.
- **Legacy Images**. For Windows Server 2008 servers, this will nearly always be empty since Windows 2008 WDS servers are native mode only and therefore use no RIS-style images. However, if you remotely managed a 2003 server, this shows the older RIS-style image entries. This also shows Remote Installation Preparation (RIPREP) images, where you upgraded a 2003 server to 2008. Although the RIPREP images would be unusable by WDS, they are still shown for information purposes and potential migration to WIM format. If you want to convert a RIPREP to WIM, see the help on the `/convert-RiPrepImage` switch of WDSUTIL.
- **Pending Devices**. Shows any unknown devices (not prestaged in Active Directory) that require authorization prior to being sent a Windows PE environment.
- **Multicast Transmissions**. Used to create and manage multicast transmissions of install images to minimize network traffic used during OS deployment.

These options are discussed later in more detail, in addition to customizing WDS. However, let's first verify how clients find this Windows Deployment Server. When a PXE client starts, it requires two things: an IP address and a Network Boot Program (NBP). The PXE client sends out a DHCP Discover; if the DHCP server and WDS server are on separate boxes, the PXE client receives two offers from the network (there could be multiple DHCP servers or WDS servers): one for an IP address and one for an NBP (the NBP offer would have no IP address). The client accepts one of the IP address offers it received. Ideally, the PXE client accepts an offer that has both an IP address and a NBP, but if this is not offered, it instead accepts the IP address-only offer.

After it has the IP address, it sends out a new DHCP request for a NBP, which uses its new IP address and responds with a boot to use (see Figure 16-11). The PXE client then uses TFTP to download the specified NBP, and the client is prompted to press F12 to network boot (unless the NBP was changed to the non-F12 version).

The story is slightly different if the WDS server is also a DHCP server. In that case, the offer received by the client contains both an IP address and a NBP, which the client requests and is subsequently acknowledged by the server. At that point, the PXE client begins the NBP download.

If DHCP and WDS are on separate boxes, no configuration is required. WDS was designed to work off separate boxes for the IP and NBP (oobe configuration). If WDS does exist on the same box as a DHCP server, some changes are required.

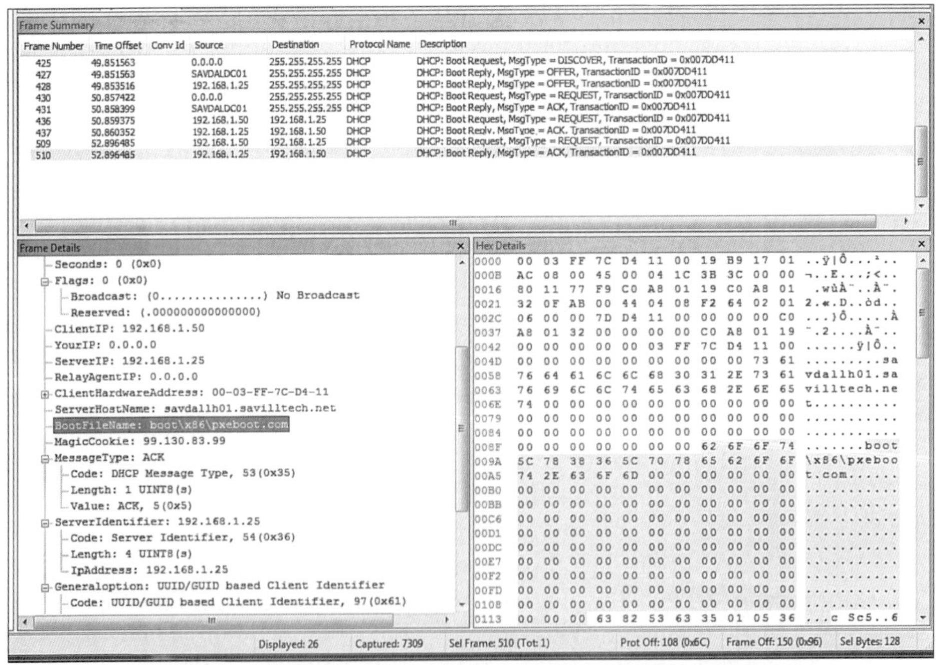

FIGURE 16-11 The packets that are part of a PXE client boot, where 192.168.1.25 is the WDS server, SAVDALDC01 is the DHCP server, and 192.168.1.50 is the IP address given to the PXE client.

Configuring DHCP Options for WDS

If DHCP services and WDS exist on the same box, tell the WDS service to not listen on UDP port 67, as this is used by the DHCP service and also to configure the local DHCP server option 60 to PXEClient.

1. Right-click the server in the navigation pane of the Windows Deployment Services MMC snap-in and select Properties.
2. Select the DHCP tab (see Figure 16-12).
3. Check both boxes and click OK.

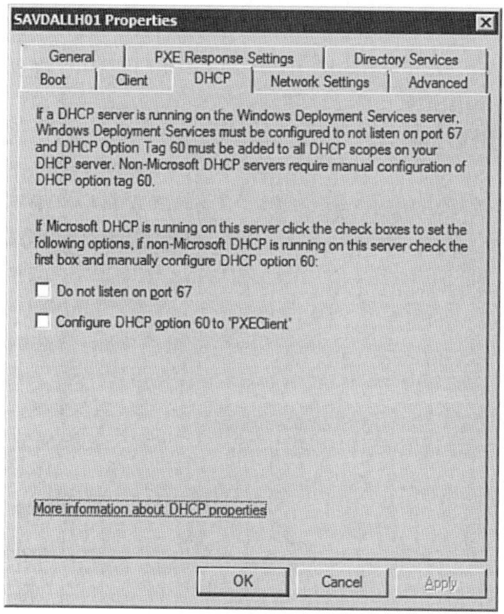

FIGURE 16-12 Both boxes should be checked if the WDS and DHCP are on the same box.

These changes can also be made via the command line locally on the WDS server, as follows:

```
WDSUTIL /set-server /DHCPoption60:yes /UseDHCPPorts:no
```

Additional configuration may be required if the client machines are not on the same subnet as the DHCP/WDS server, in which case a DHCP relay agent or router may be used. If the DHCP relay agent or router is used, you may need to update the IP helper tables to ensure requests are sent to both the DHCP and WDS servers (recommended). An alternative to updating the IP helper tables is to configure options 66 and 67 on the DHCP server. Those options are the boot server host name and boot file name, respectively; an example is shown in the network trace in the previous pages—for example, the boot server name would be the fully qualified host name, savdallh01.savilltech.net, and the boot file name would be the architecture and file, boot\x86\pxeboot.com. Using the 66 and 67 options can cause problems for some PXE BIOSs, which is why the IP helper tables is preferred.

Configuring WDS from the Command Line

As mentioned previously, in addition to the graphical configuration of WDS, the same configuration is possible from the command line (although this is not as intuitive as a GUI).

WDSUTIL help is complete, and you can pass a `/?` to any of the WDSUTIL switches to get information on how to use it. To see the complete list of top-level commands, run `WDSUTIL /AllHelp`.

To perform the initial configuration to initialize the server and specify the Remote Installation folder, use the following command:

```
WDSUTIL /initialize-sever /reminst:"<drive and path, e.g.
d:\REMINST>"
```

The next task is to set the options to which clients are to answer: all, known (only), or none. The following example sets the option to known:

```
WDSUTIL /set-server /answerclients:known
```

Additionally, if you want the unknown clients to be placed in pending first, this is part of the Automatic Add Policy for the server and can be set as follows: The first option requires administrator approval, while the second automatically enables.

```
WDSUTIL /set-server /autoaddpolicy /policy:adminapproval
```

Or

```
WDSUTIL /set-server /autoaddpolicy /policy:disabled
```

You have already seen how to set the DHCP options via the `/DHCPoption60` and `/UseDHCPPorts` options. The other tasks involve adding images, and the WDS server is configured.

Prestaging a Computer in Active Directory

The options for handling PXE clients were discussed previously; one of these options was to respond only to known or prestaged computers. In WDS terms, a computer is known by its MAC address or GUID. You can prestage a computer using the Active Directory Users and Computers MMC snap-in. Create a new Computer object and name the computer (for example, wdstest01); click Next to display the managed computer dialog (see Figure 16-13). Check the This is a managed computer box and enter the GUID or the MAC address of the computer. If you enter the MAC address, then the MAC must have 20 preceding 0s.

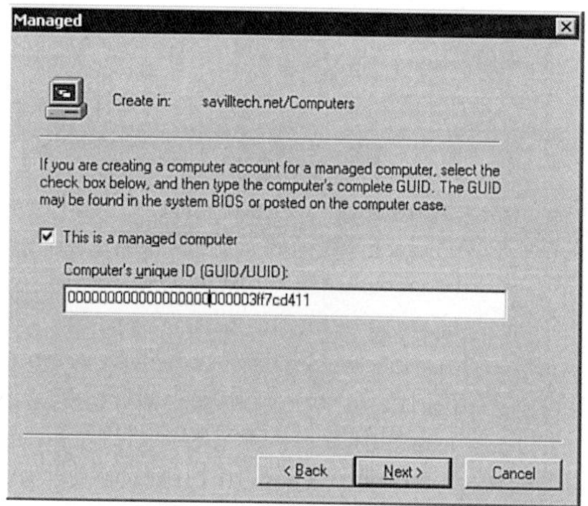

FIGURE 16-13 In this case, the computer's MAC address has been entered instead of the GUID. The Next button will not be clickable until the correct number of digits has been entered.

After clicking Next, you are prompted to select a specific remote installation server to respond to the client or leave the default of any available remote installation server and click Next. A summary is displayed. Click Finish to create the new computer object. If you had a client waiting to be approved, then within 10 seconds of creating the object, the client proceeds and downloads the Network Boot Program. By default, the clients check every 10 seconds.

You can also prestage clients with the `/add-device` option of WDSUTIL using the format outlined next. This creates a computer object in the Active Directory in the configured container for computer objects:

```
wdsutil /add-device /device:<computer name> /id:<GUID or MAC
with 20 zero's preceding>
```

Authorizing Unknown Clients

If you configured the PXE response settings to enable unknown computers, but required them to be approved, then unknown computers will boot to the network and then wait to be approved. Every 10 seconds, they will send out a new DHCP request for a NBP (see Figure 16-14).

```
Argon PXE Boot Agent v2.00 (BIOS Integrated)
(C) Copyright 2004 Argon Technology Corporation
All rights reserved. www.ArgonTechnology.com


CLIENT MAC ADDR: 00 03 FF 7C D4 11  GUID: 928DCA05-4C77-9649-8EE4-21DB92186DCB
CLIENT IP: 192.168.1.50  MASK: 255.255.255.0  DHCP IP: 192.168.1.10
GATEWAY IP: 192.168.1.1

Downloaded WDSNBP...

Architecture: x86

The details below show the information relating to the PXE boot request for
this computer. Please provide these details to your Windows Deployment Services
Administrator so that this request can be approved.

Pending Request ID: 1

Message from Administrator:


Contacting Server: 192.168.1.25......
```

FIGURE 16-14 In this instance, the client is unknown and waits until it has an object created in the Active Directory.

To enable the computer to continue, create an object in the Active Directory with its GUID/MAC, as discussed in the previous section. You can also view the computers pending approval via the WDS management interface under the Pending Devices section. If you right-click on a device, options to approve the device, name and approve the device, or reject the device are displayed (see Figure 16-15).

Figure 16-15 Naming and approving is the best option unless you are setting the names using another process.

Without making any changes when you attempt to approve a computer, you will get an access denied message (unless WDS is also a domain controller); the deployment service does not have permissions on the Active Directory where it is attempting to create the object. To resolve this, grant the computer account of the WDS server rights to create computer objects in the Computers container in the Active Directory (the default location where computer objects are created):

1. Start the Active Directory Users and Computers MMC snap-in.
2. Right-click on the container where the computer accounts are created (Computers by default) and select Delegate Control.
3. Click Next on the welcome screen of the delegation of control wizard.
4. You are prompted for the user or group to add permissions for. Click Add.
5. Click the Object Types button and ensure Computers is selected (see Figure 16-16); ensure all other types are not selected and then click OK.
6. In the selection dialog, enter the name of the WDS server and click OK (see Figure 16-17).
7. After the server is selected, click Next.
8. Under the tasks to delegate, select Create a custom task to delegate.

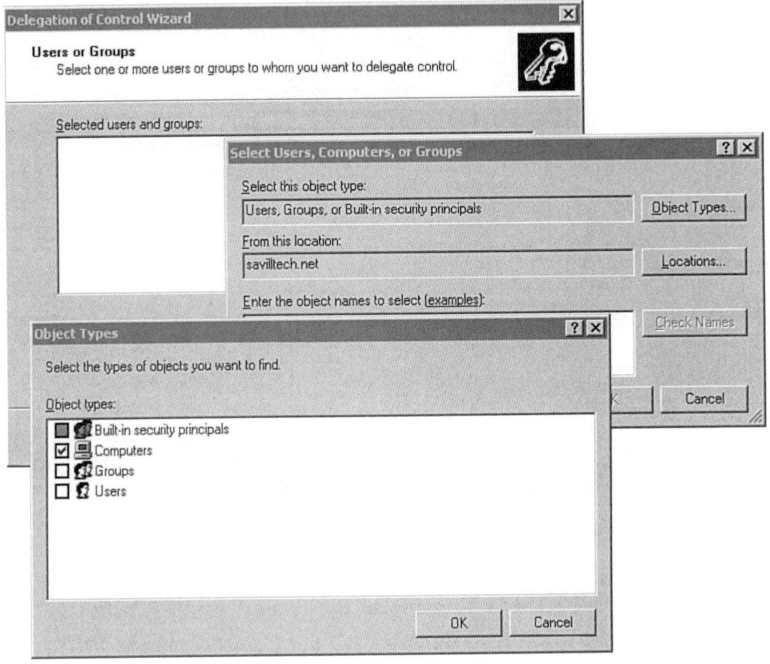

FIGURE 16-16 Ensure the Computers object type is selected.

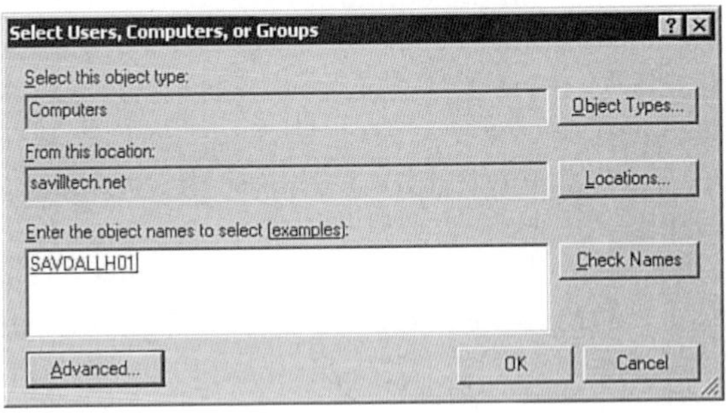

FIGURE 16-17 Enter the name of the WDS server to be given permissions.

9. Select the Only the following objects in the folder, check the Computer objects type, and ensure Create selected objects in this folder is checked before clicking Next (see Figure 16-18).

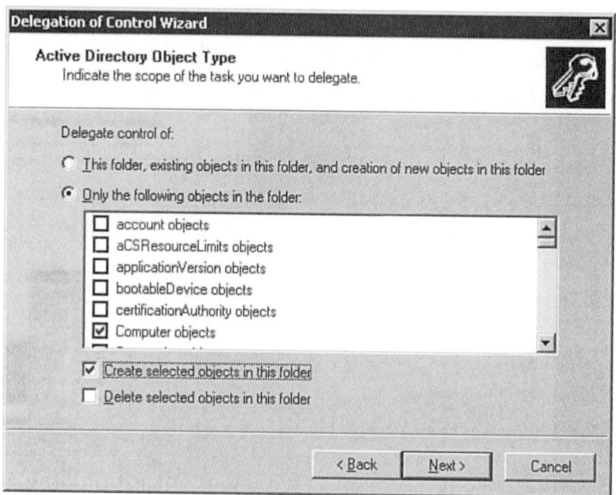

FIGURE 16-18 The WDS server needs to be able to create Computer objects only.

10. Under permissions, give the server Read and Write permissions and click Next.
11. Click Finish on the summary dialog.

Now if you select Approve, a computer account is created automatically, per the selected naming scheme (for example, DomainAdmins1), if the default naming scheme (username) has been left unmodified, followed by an increasing number. If you select Name and Approve, you are prompted to also enter the name of the new computer. Rejecting the pending device results in an abort NBP being sent to the client, and the client will attempt to boot from the next boot device.

If you do reject devices and then attempt to boot the rejected computer again, it will not work correctly. To fix this, right-click on Pending Devices and select Delete Rejected Devices, which resets the WDS internal table and enables the device to be marked as pending again. If you're interested, WDS has a database in the Mgmt folder of the Remote Installation folder, binlsvcdb.mdb, which keeps track of the pending devices. You can purge this database of pending, approved, and rejected computers via `WDSUTIL /Delete-AutoAddDevices /DeviceType:<PendingDevices|RejectedDevices|ApprovedDevices>`.

You can optionally configure the location of where to create the computer objects via the Directory Services tab of the server properties or from the command line with the `wdsutil /NewMachineOU` switch and configuring the object to be created in the WDS domain, the users' domain, the same OU as the user, or a custom OU location. For example, to set creation to a custom root OU, WDSComputers in the savilltech.net domain, use the following command:

```
C:\Users\Administrator.SAVILLTECH>wdsutil /set-server
➥/newmachineou /type:custom /ou:ou=WDSComputers,
➥dc=savilltech,dc=net

Windows Deployment Services Management Utility [Version
6.0.6001.16606]
Copyright (C) Microsoft Corporation. All rights reserved.

The command completed successfully.
```

Remember, if you change where computer accounts are to be created, the computer account of the WDS server must be delegated permission to create computer objects in that location.

You can also manage the pending clients from the command line. Using the `WDSUTIL /get-autoadddevices` command, you can view devices that are pending, approved, or rejected, for example:

```
C:\Users\Administrator.SAVILLTECH>wdsutil /get-autoadddevices
➥/devicetype:pendingdevices

Windows Deployment Services Management Utility [Version
6.0.6001.16606]
Copyright (C) Microsoft Corporation. All rights reserved.

Request ID: 4
MAC address: 0000000000000000000000003FF7BD411
UUID/GUID: C8F945657061D547B81A7C75D899F316
Architecture: x86
Referral server:
Boot program:
WDS client unattend file:
Boot image:
User: Domain Admins
Join rights: Full
Join domain: Yes

Total 1 device(s) returned.

The command completed successfully.
```

The approval or rejection is also possible using the `/Approve-AutoAddDevices` switch and passing a `/RequestId:<number>` for a specific device to approve or `/RequestId:ALL` to approve all pending devices. This command-line interface also opens up far greater possibilities, enabling you to specify a particular unattended answer script for a particular client in addition to setting a name (`/MachineName`) and even a particular OU (`/OU`).

Customizing the Server

Although basic options were set during the WDS initialization, these can be modified via the server's properties. Access the server's properties by right-clicking on the server and selecting properties under the Windows Deployment Services MMC snap-in. This reveals eight tabs, each showing different aspects of the server's configuration. The DHCP tab was discussed previously. The Client tab will be considered separately as part of unattended installations, but the others are covered next.

General

The General tab shows the name of the WDS server, the path for its Remote Installation Folder, and the server's mode. With a WDS server, its mode is always native. However, the version running on Windows 2003 had three modes, as follows:

- **Legacy**. In legacy mode, only RIS-style images can be deployed. Legacy mode is achieved by installing and configuring RIS-style images, and installing WDS on 2003, but not performing a WDS configuration via the GUI or command line. The RIS images are managed using the WDS Legacy application, and the new WDS Management MMC snap-in is not used.
- **Mixed**. With mixed mode, both image formats are supported; RIS-style images can be deployed and maintained, in addition to the new WIM image format. Clients are presented with a boot manager screen, which enables them to select booting to the RIS OS Loader or the Windows PE environment used by WDS. Mixed mode is achieved by configuring WDS on a RIS server that has existing RIS images.
- **Native**. Only WIM images can be managed and deployed in native mode. This is achieved by installing and configuring WDS on a server with RIS installed but not configured (no RIS images). If RIS has previously been configured, uninstall RIS and then reinstall prior to

installing WDS. It is also possible to force native mode using the `WDSUTIL /set-server /ForceNative` command.

Because no RIS images are supported in Windows Server 2008, these will relate only to 2003 servers you may manage.

PXE Response Settings

This dialog enables configuration of how the server will respond to the PXE clients, which matches the same options as those during initial installation, plus one optional setting: a PXE Response Delay value in increments of one second. By default, the delay is set to 0. However, if you had multiple servers and other servers were higher in preference, you could add a delay to a server so clients would first receive responses from the more preferred servers.

Directory Services

The Directory Services tab enables configuration of two key aspects of the automated creation of computer accounts: the name of the computer account and where to create the client computer object, as shown in Figure 16-19.

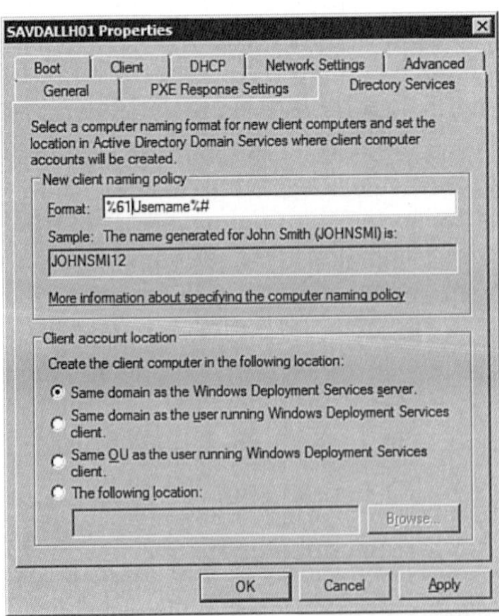

FIGURE 16-19 The naming scheme used for the computer and the computer object's creation location.

The client naming can be any static text, plus a combination of certain special variables, as shown in Table 16-1.

Table 16-1 Client-Naming Variables

Variable	Result
%First	The user's first name.
%Last	The user's last name.
%Username	The user name.
%MAC	The network adapter MAC address.
%[0][n]#	An incremental number containing n digits. To include zero-padding in the incremental number, type a zero as shown. For example, if you use %04#, a four-digit number in the range from 0001 through 9999 is used. If you use %#, then just a number is used in the computer name.

A great part of the dialog is that it has an example username that, as you type your new format, changes the output of the computer name. This dynamically updates it in the Sample area of the dialog so you can see if what you are configuring will generate the desired computer names.

The Client account location enables configuration of where the computer account objects will be created. The default is the default computer container for the WDS server's domain. However, there are options to create the computer object in the default computer container for the user's domain or the actual same OU as the WDS user. The OU option is also configurable via the `/NewMachingOU` switch of `WDSUTIL`.

The interesting point here is what the username actually is. To use the WDS client, a username is entered to control which images a computer can choose from (see Figure 16-20). It is that account that is used for the username.

Boot

The Boot tab enables configuration of the boot program to send to PXE clients, with one for each of the supported architectures: x86, ia64, and x64 (see Figure 16-21).

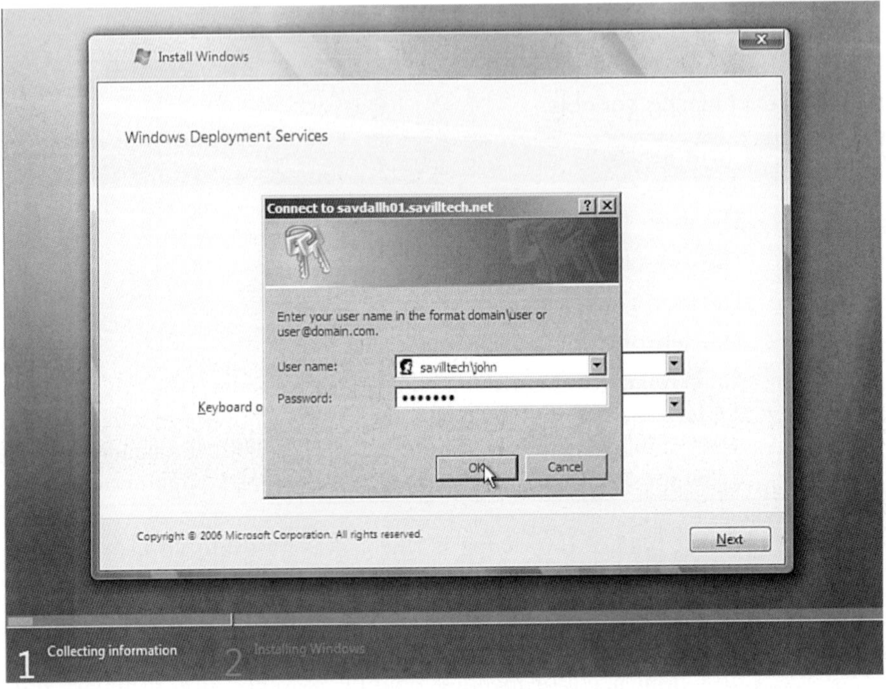

Figure 16-20 For non–prestaged computers, or where an unattended answer file is not specified, the client will be prompted for credentials.

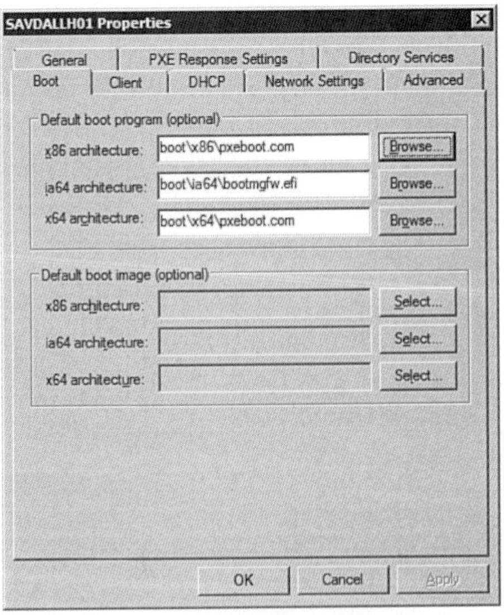

SAVDALLH01 Properties

General | PXE Response Settings | Directory Services

Boot | Client | DHCP | Network Settings | Advanced

Default boot program (optional)

x86 architecture: boot\x86\pxeboot.com Browse...

ia64 architecture: boot\ia64\bootmgfw.efi Browse...

x64 architecture: boot\x64\pxeboot.com Browse...

Default boot image (optional)

x86 architecture: Select...

ia64 architecture: Select...

x64 architecture: Select...

OK Cancel Apply

Figure 16-21 The Boot tab enables configuration of the boot information.

Removing the Need to Press F12 During Network Boot

It can be frustrating that F12 must be pressed to complete the network boot for PXE clients. If you click browse for each architecture, you find a .n12 version, which does not require the client to press F12—for example, for the x86 architecture, change this from boot\x86\pxeboot.com to boot\x86\pxeboot.n12.

You can also optionally set a default boot image for each architecture, which avoids clients specifying which boot image they want to use if more than one is available for them.

Network Settings

The Network Settings tab (see Figure 16-22) enables configuration of the IP address used for multicast transmissions (discussed in the "Deploying Multiple Machines Simultaneously" section later in the chapter). Ideally, you will have a Multicast Address Dynamic Client Allocation Protocol (MADCAP) DHCP-compatible server on your network that can give out multicast compatible addresses. However, many environments do not, so select the option Use IP address from the following range. It is precompleted for you from the 239.0.0.0 network, which is reserved for multicast transmissions.

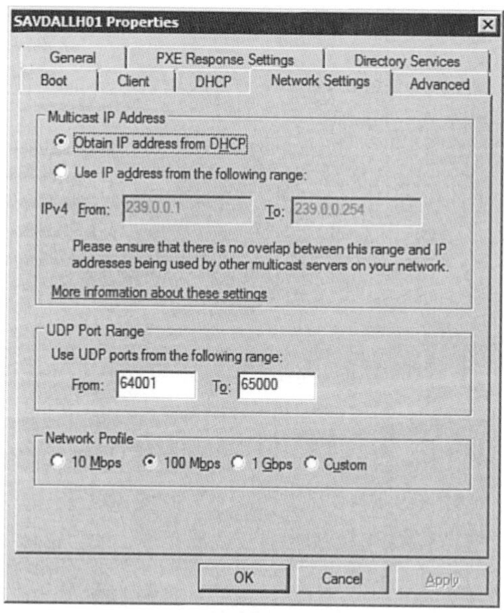

Figure 16-22 The Network Settings tab enables multicast settings to be configured, in addition to UDP ports used and the type of network that is present.

The UDP Port Range will ideally not be modified and is used by the multicast and TFTP. By default, 1000 ports are available to handle 1000 concurrent TFTP sessions (single client download of OS/NBP) and multicast transmissions (each multicast uses only one port per network adapter). If you need to change this, ensure that you enable at least as many ports as current connections will ever exist.

The final option is the Network Profile, which should reflect the network speed at which your clients will communicate with the WDS server and not that of your server backbone network. Your server backbone network may be gigabit per second, while the rest of the network is 100Mbps. Choose the right network speed, as this affects items such as the maximum transport window size, transport cache size, and block size.

Advanced

By default, WDS will choose the domain controller and global catalog it uses by normal lookup methods (DNS service lookups). However, the Advanced tab enables you to specify a specific domain controller and global catalog if, for example, you had internal firewalls and wanted to restrict communication to only that between specific servers (see Figure 16-23).

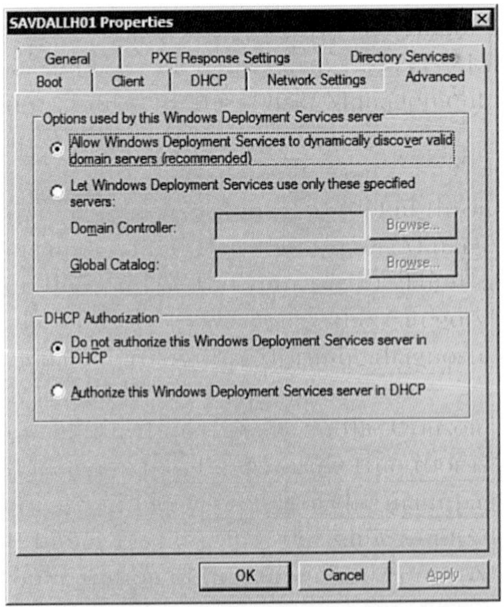

FIGURE 16-23 The Advanced tab gives <sarcasm> incredibly useful options of restricting communication to a specific DC and authorizing the DHCP for no extra features </sarcasm>.

Normally, Windows-based DHCP servers have to be authorized in Active Directory to function, which stops rogue DHCP servers from performing services on the network. WDS can also be authorized in the Active Directory by selecting the Authorize this Windows Deployment Services server in DHCP. What new features does authorizing enable? None. Authorizing changes nothing about WDS functionality; it's only there to help you identify all servers that can respond to DHCP requests by having it authorized and therefore listed to enforce a corporate policy.

Customizing the Windows Vista Deployment Process

At this point, you have a functioning Windows Vista deployment environment for new installations performed over the network. With this current configuration, Figure 16-24 displays a high-level view of what the user would see to help identify other actions you need to remedy.

Figure 16-24 Although user entry is required, you can now fully deploy an OS. This will be discussed in more detail when how to automate the deployment is discussed. (Work counterclockwise from the top inward.)

What are the problems with the current process? The main issue is that questions still need to be answered, such as which OS to install and what settings should be used for that OS. Before we go any further, however, let's answer another question: How many images do you need?

Image Requirements for Windows Vista and Windows Server 2008

Previously, one OS required multiple images for various reasons. Let's look at each of these reasons and assess whether they still apply in the Windows Vista world:

- **Applications**. It's common for organizations to have different configurations and applications based on the role of the computer. A good example is a finance computer that would have Outlook, Excel, and accounting applications, whereas an operator machine might allow access to an ordering application and Internet Explorer for Web-based mail. No other access to the OS or applications is possible. Windows Vista does not do anything major to change how this should be done—there are two areas: the applications and the configuration of the desktop. For the applications, the best practice is always to keep the OS image lean. No applications should be included. Rather, they should be installed after OS installation via technologies such as group policy software installation or, even better, the System Center Configuration Manager. Removing applications from an image cuts down on the number of images *and* makes the images far less likely to become dated as new application versions come out requiring updates to the images. The second part, the desired configuration, is not well suited to image configuration anyway. Setting a configuration initially is not a good idea since once a user changes it, that configuration is gone. The best practice is to use group policy for configuration of the desktop, including lockdown. This applies to XP and Vista equally, although Vista does have some advantages, especially concerning the lack of requirements for users to be local administrators due to improvements in the OS.
- **Language**. For global organizations that require multiple language versions of Windows, separate images were required with previous versions of Windows. However, this was partially addressed with the Multilingual User Interface (MUI) version of XP that enabled multiple language versions of XP to be installed on one instance. Windows Vista has language neutrality, so multi-language versions

are not required. This is accomplished through storing the language resources for the user interface separately from the actual OS binaries, which contain no language information. Language packs are installed onto the OS, which contains the information needed to display localized language user interface elements without any changes to the underlying OS code.

- **Hardware Abstraction Layer (HAL).** Windows XP required one image for each HAL in use. Windows Vista has HAL independence, and the HAL is selected at startup time. The only requirement that still exists for multiple images is 32- versus 64-bit images.

When you use group policy or system center for desired configuration and the same technologies for software deployment, you need only two images for each OS version: one 32- and one 64-bit. For different versions of the OS, you can use one WIM for each architecture that contains all required versions (for example, Business and Ultimate).

64-Bit Support

As mentioned previously, separate images are required for different architectures—for example, 32- and 64-bit. Because 64-bit is the future direction, WDS has full support for 64-bit.

To send the initial Windows PE version to a computer, the BIOS of the client should identify to the WDS server which architecture it is running so it gets the right PE. However, if the BIOS is not identifying the architecture correctly, WDS can be configured to perform auto-detection via the following command:

```
WDSUTIL /set-server /architecturediscovery:yes
```

Additionally, because x64-based computers can also run x86 OSs by default, WDS will offer both x64 and x86 type images to x64 clients. However, this behavior can be changed using the following command:

```
WDSUTIL /Set-Server /Defaultx86x64ImageType:{x86|x64|both}
```

This command enables you to configure if 64-bit clients see x86 type images only, x64 type images only, or the default of both image types.

When using the Windows 2008 Server version of the boot environment, it's no problem to deploy a 64-bit architecture OS from the x86 version of Windows PE; you don't have to use the x64 version of PE to deploy an x64 OS.

Image Management

If you want to support a new OS or architecture, what do you need to do? Image management with WDS is fairly straightforward. There are two types of images: the boot image, which is the Windows PE environment used in the deployment (and capture) of a WIM image, and install images, which contain an actual OS.

Adding a New Image

To install a new image, use the same process for both boot and install images. However, with install images, you can create an image group; the install images are placed in this group to ease the management of multiple images of one OS family (for example, Windows Vista).

Let's add a new boot image first. For most people, this is definitely something you need to do—it is likely that you took the boot.wim from the sources folder of the Windows Vista media. Although it is based on the Longhorn environment, the build is an earlier version than the Windows Server 2008 media version and lacks a number of features, including the following:

- Multicast support
- Support for x64 EFI boot
- Enhanced TFTP performance
- Capability to deploy a 64-bit OS from a 32-bit boot.wim

Let's import the boot.wim from the Windows Server 2008 media (you may want to repeat this for both the 64-bit and 32-bit versions of boot.wim):

1. Right-click the Boot Images node of the navigation pane and select Add Boot Image from the displayed context menu.
2. In the image file dialog, click the Browse button and select the boot.wim file from the sources folder of the Windows Server 2008 media or from a location you have copied the file to, and click Next (see Figure 16-25).
3. The next dialog prompts for a name for the image and a description, which by default is read from the XML embedded in the WIM file. You can change this as needed. The image name is shown to clients only when they first boot to the WDS Network Boot Program. It's unlikely you will need multiple versions of the PE unless one is customized for troubleshooting, for example. The

architecture of the image will also be displayed. Make changes, if required, to the name and/or description, and click Next.

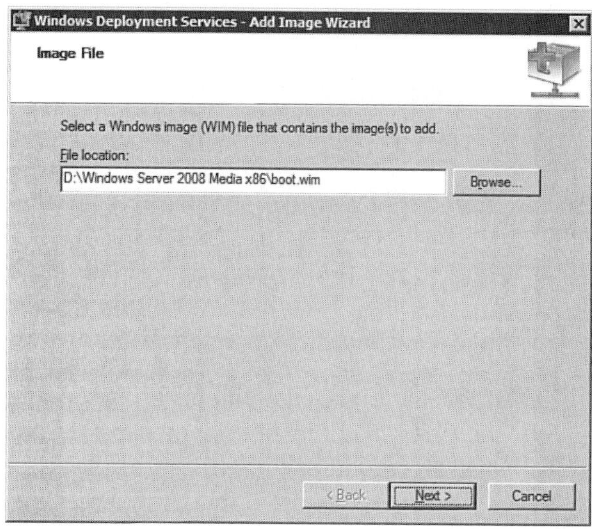

Figure 16-25 Adding the Windows Server 2008 version of boot.wim is important to get the most out of WDS.

4. A summary is displayed of the images to be imported. Click Next to begin the import, and once the import is complete, click Finish.

Your list of images is now displayed in the details pane along with the OS version. As shown in Figure 16-26, the version contained on the 2008 media is distinguished by the OS version of 6.0.6001 instead of 6.0.6000, which is the version on the Windows Vista media.

Image Name	Architecture	Status	Size	Date	OS Version
Microsoft Windows Longhorn Setup (x86)	x86	Online	319 MB	11/2/2006 11:50 AM	6.0.6000
Microsoft Windows Longhorn Setup (x64)	x64	Online	398 MB	6/20/2007 10:12 AM	6.0.6001
Microsoft Windows Longhorn Setup (x86)	x86	Online	345 MB	6/20/2007 8:27 AM	6.0.6001

Figure 16-26 The 6.0.6000 life expectancy will be short on this server now that its new, improved model is sitting right next to it, unless you want to run with reduced functionality and poorer performance.

The steps to add an install image is the same process; however, if it's a new OS family or group, right-click on Install Images and select Add Image Group, enter the new group name, and click OK (see Figure 16-27).

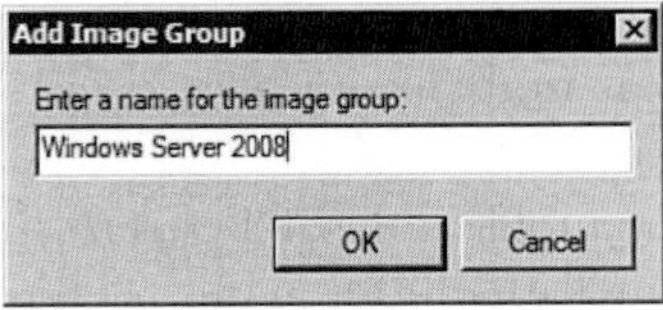

FIGURE 16-27 Using groups helps keep images organized and makes it easier to find them when browsing.

To install an image, right-click the image group and select Add Install Image. After the WIM file has been selected in the same fashion as a boot image, the images list found in the WIM is displayed, as shown in Figure 16-28. After the images to import have been selected, the images are imported in the same fashion as a boot image. The only difference is, because install images are much larger than boot images, the process takes significantly longer.

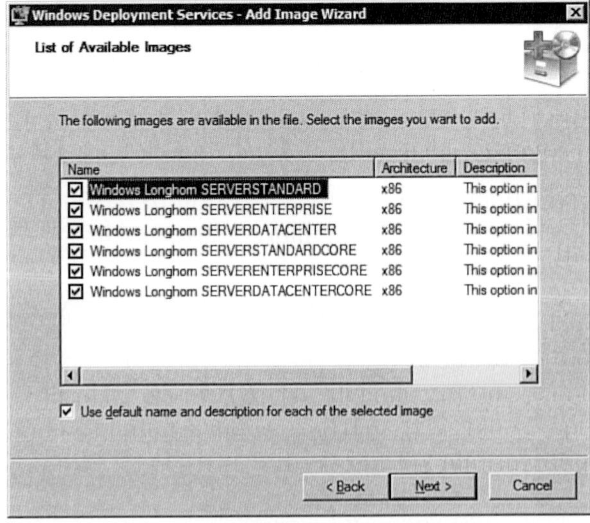

FIGURE 16-28 There are only six versions on the Windows Server 2008 media. Vista was far more generous.

To add images via the WDSUTIL command, use the following commands for boot and install, respectively:

```
WDSUTIL /add-image
/imagefile:\\<server>\<share>\sources\boot.wim /imagetype:boot
```

```
WDSUTIL /add-image
/imagefile:\\<server>\<share>\sources\install.wim /image
type:install
```

Managing Images

After the images are imported, there is not much management required in WDS. You might want to add updates, services packs, drivers, language packs, and so on, but that is not done within WDS. If you have an image with a service pack integrated, import it in the same manner as an image without a service pack—that is all outside. The only item that you have to do inside WDS is if an image is updated, you have to re-import it. Let's get rid of that Windows Vista-supplied boot.wim content. Right-click on the image under Boot Images and select Delete. However, to play it safe, select Disable which puts the image into Offline status, and it will no longer be offered to clients.

There are other properties. If you right-click a boot image, you can see its properties but can't change anything other than its name and description—everything else is informational only. This is not the same for install images, which expose additional options.

On the General tab for an install image at the bottom, there is an option to enable an unattended installation. For now, let's pretend you have not seen the unattended option. Notice the Security tab which enables you to control which OSs various users can see. To see an OS as an option to install, the user must have read and execute permission on the image. By default, these permissions are granted to the Authenticated Users group, as shown in Figure 16-29. To restrict OS deployability, restrict the read and execute permission to the users/groups that should see the OS.

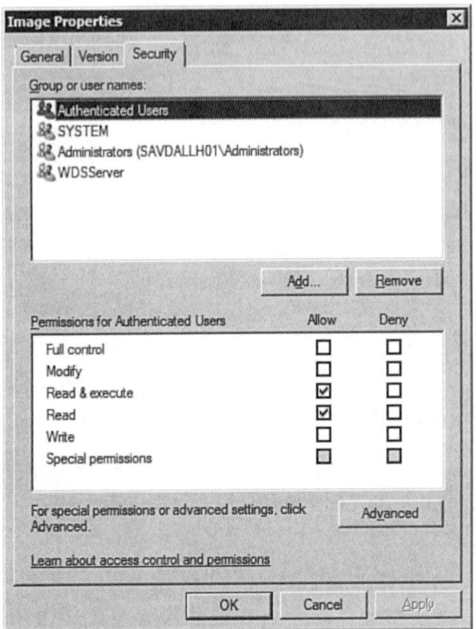

FIGURE 16-29 By default, any authenticated user is able to install any of the OSs imported into WDS; however, you can restrict who has the read and execute permissions.

When you right-clicked on both the boot and install images, you saw options to Export Image and Replace Image. The export option is used to create a new WIM file on the local file system from the images stored within WDS. This is useful if you no longer have the original source WIM you used to import into WDS and want to update the WIM with a fix or other update. If you export, you are prompted for a file name, and once selected, the export is executed and a new WIM file will be created on the file system. After the WIM is updated and you want to read back into WDS, you could import an image as a brand-new WIM file. However, it's better to select the Replace Image option from the context menu of the image you want to replace (see Figure 16-30). Select the WIM file that contains the image you want to use to replace the current image, and your image is updated with new content.

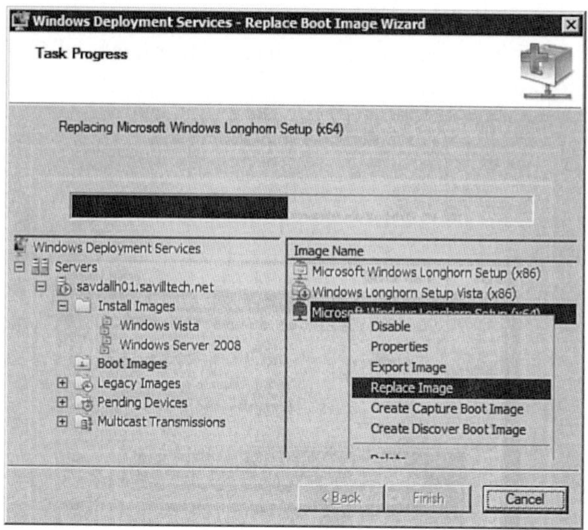

FIGURE 16-30 The Replace dialog, created in PaintShop. The menu where you select Replace Image has been put on the dialog's empty space to save space.

Automating the Installation

Remember, install the WDS role, pop in the Vista DVD, ideally pop in the 2008 media, and replace the boot image (although you don't have to); without doing anything else, you can deploy Vista with the deployer by only having to give minimal input. It might be overkill to have a whole chapter for something so simple, but let's look at removing that human interaction altogether for a number of reasons, as follows:

1. Human interaction limits the number of concurrent installations that can be performed at any one time.
2. Manually inputting information and configuration may lead to misconfigurations, which lead to an inconsistent environment that is harder to support.
3. It's no fun.
4. See #3.

Remember your original picture of the OS installation with a barebones WDS installation? There were two phases of OS installation where user intervention was required (ignore the need to press F12; remove that by selecting the .n12 version of the PXE ROM, as already discussed). The following is the first phase:

1. First, the installer had to select the locale and keyboard type of the PE environment.
2. The installer had to enter credentials that were used to check which install images had read and execute permissions for the credential entered (and were the same architecture as the client being installed).
3. An install image had to be selected from the list displayed.
4. The disk had to be selected to install the image to, and potentially complex portioning may have been required.

At this point, the installation went off to install the install image. Then the installer was once again prompted for information related to the installation of the actual OS:

1. Enter the locale, keyboard, and country.
2. Enter the serial number (which is never fun to type in).
3. Accept the license agreement.
4. Create a local user (even if the computer will be part of a domain, which is required—under Vista, the local administrator is disabled, and you should always have one local account).
5. Configure how Windows will update.
6. Set the time zone.
7. Set the network location.

If you preprovisioned the computer's account in a domain, it automatically joins the domain. Otherwise, it's now part of a workgroup, and you have to manually add it to the domain.

An answer file can be specified for each of these groups of questions. However, those questions are the bare minimum. Many other options are available for the various components of Windows Vista and Windows Server 2008, and that is the key point. Vista and 2008 are modular, with each component installed and serviced independently. Each component is self describing via an XML format that describes the Registry items, configurable properties, files, and dependencies that the component has. This sounds great, but with all these components and options, how do you know what to do? Microsoft provides a great tool that enables you to look at the SKU XML manifests for a product that defines the components, which is discussed later.

Although this looks like two phases where configuration is possible, there are actually seven phases to interact with that correspond to various points of the OS installation described next. Each of the setup phases can have actions involving different components of the OS:

- **WinPE**. Corresponds to the initial Windows PE boot, where the OS is chosen, languages are set, and the disk is partitioned.
- **offlineServicing**. Used to perform offline changes of settings and packages to an offline Windows image—for example, adding a language pack, service pack, and so on; performed on a WIM file that is not currently in use.
- **Generalize**. Used to create a Windows image reference template that can be used throughout a company or, commonly, to be placed on computers that are being sold. This is the removal of system-specific information such as the SID and other hardware-specific information, and this phase only runs if the `/generalize` switch was used with the `SYSPREP` command.
- **Specialize**. Used to apply machine-specific updates, such as applying different Internet Explorer home pages for the various departments within an organization or setting domain membership information. It would overwrite any settings made as part of the Generalize phase.
- **auditSystem**. An optional pass used by OEMs and corporations to add additional device drivers and applications to an image. This mode enables changes to be made to an installation under the guise of an Administrator account as part of the system context. These settings are made before a user logs in. auditSystem only runs if you boot the computer into Audit mode, as discussed later in the section, "Customizing an Image."
- **auditUser**. Processes unattended settings after a user logs into the system in Audit mode. It also requires the computer to be booted into Audit mode.
- **oobeSystem**. Applies settings to Windows before the Windows Welcome dialog as part of the oobe.

Note that you don't create an answer file for offlineServicing. It's a logical phase updating a WIM file but not something that you perform via the OS deployment. However, the other six phases can be automated via an answer file.

How do you create the answer files that interact at one of the seven phases with one of hundreds of components? The answer is WAIK. WAIK was originally made available at the Windows Vista launch time as a method to deploy Windows Vista and has been updated for Windows Server 2008 to take advantage of some of the newer technologies available. To download it, go to the Microsoft site and search for WAIK. Make sure you download the version designed for Windows Server 2008. WAIK consists of a number of components, as follows:

- WDS for Windows 2003 SP1.
- Whitepapers and documents on the use of WAIK and WDS.
- Windows Vista-based Windows PE environments, which are useful for creating bootable media to manually capture and deploy images.
- The Windows System Image Manager, which is used to create the automated answer XML files that can be configured to be used with WDS and adding/modifying components in the images, such as new drivers.
- An API is supplied, WIMGAPI, that can be used by any application to capture, apply, and modify WIM files. This will be used by third-party utilities to support WIM.
- Various tools including imagex.exe. The imagex.exe tool is probably the most useful tool. It is used to capture and deploy WIM images, in addition to mounting WIM images as part of the file system to enable easy manipulation of the WIM content.

To install WAIK, insert the media, and the tools can be installed on Windows XP SP2, Windows Server 2003, or Windows Vista. Select the Windows AIK Setup link on the main WAIK dialog, and answer the questions about where to install. All the components will be installed. First look at the documentation from the installation, which contains useful information, particularly the Unattended Windows Setup Reference.chm file. It discusses details on the settings needed to perform a full installation and also details on every setting that can be configured. The WAIK Kit User's Guide.chm file contains the overall process of deployment and has walkthroughs and information on the deployment tools. The Windows PE

User's Guide.chm file discusses all elements relevant to PE, including its customization and troubleshooting.

The first tool is the Windows System Image Manager; although you can manually create the unattended answer file for use with WDS deployments, unattend.xml (yes, it's XML-based now), it's better to use a tool, as provided by Windows System Image Manager (see Figure 16-31).

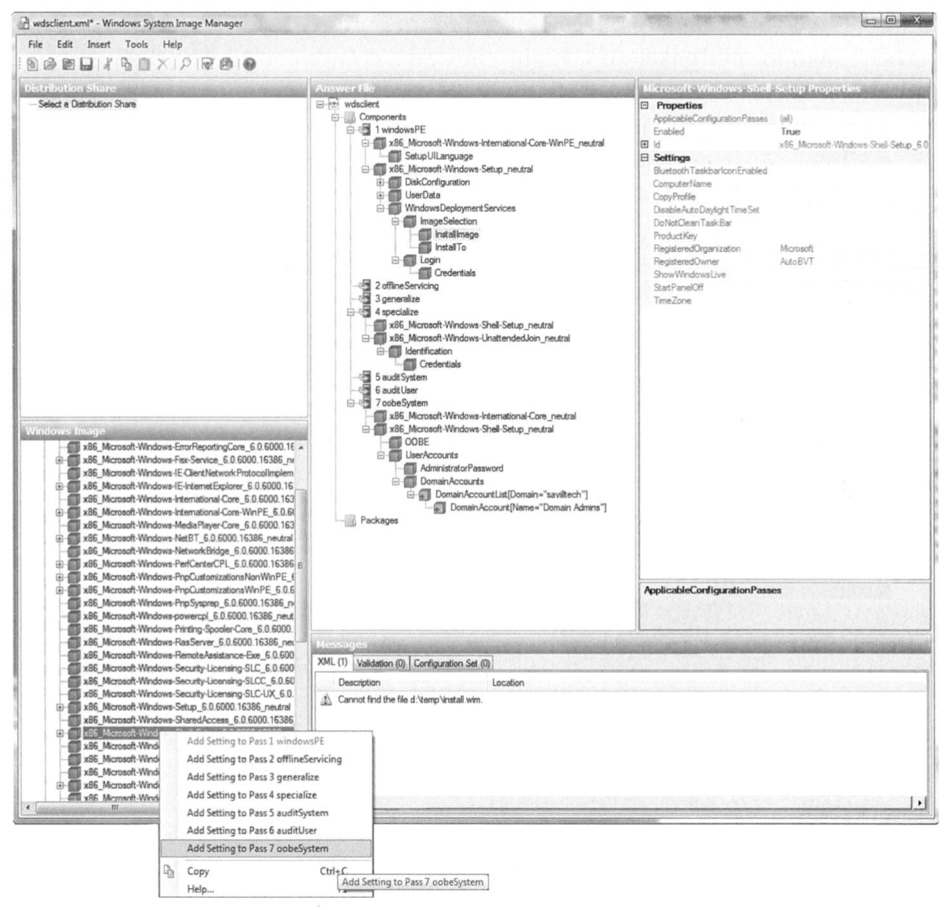

FIGURE 16-31 The Windows System Image Manager is your new best friend when it comes to automating Windows installations.

When you first open the tool, you see five panes, but they are blank. First open a Windows image to see a list of the components and packages that are available—it's these components and packages that have settings that can be configured. To open a Windows image, right-click on the Select a Windows image or catalog file and choose Select Windows Image from the displayed context menu. Navigate to the WIM file you want to open, select it, and click Open. If the WIM contains multiple images, select the image you want to open. After the image is opened, two child nodes will be displayed: Components and Packages. If you expand the Components leaf, you see all the components that are available for the OS. Notice that some of them expand to contain more options, such as the x86_Microsoft-Windows-Shell-Setup. Right-click on a component to see the phases available. However, you need to create an answer file onto which to apply the settings. Right-click Create or open an answer file, and select the option New Answer File (notice also the option to open an existing one). When you create the new answer file, the Components section is expanded and the seven phases of installation are displayed, ready to have settings from components added. For example, expand the x86_Microsoft-Windows-Setup component, expand UserData, and right-click on Product Key. Notice that you get the option to set this only at the stage 1, Windows PE phase. If selected, it now shows as part of the answer file and can then have values set as required. After you start making settings, save the answer file via the File menu. Select a name and a location to save to.

The WAIK documentation gives great detail on the components from which to read in settings. However, look at the following XML file that results in a complete unattended installation, which you can use as a reference when you create your own:

```
 <?xml version="1.0" encoding="utf-8"?>
<unattend xmlns="urn:schemas-microsoft-com:unattend">
    <servicing></servicing>
    <settings pass="windowsPE">
        <component name="Microsoft-Windows-Setup"
publicKeyToken="31bf3856ad364e35" language="neutral"
versionScope="nonSxS" processorArchitecture="x86">
            <WindowsDeploymentServices>
                <Login>
                    <WillShowUI>Never</WillShowUI>
                    <Credentials>
                        <Username>administrator</Username>
                        <Domain>savilltech</Domain>
                        <Password>password</Password>
                    </Credentials>
                </Login>
```

```
                <ImageSelection>
                    <WillShowUI>Never</WillShowUI>
                    <InstallImage>
                        <ImageName>Windows Vista BUSINESS
                        </ImageName>
                        <ImageGroup>Windows Vista</ImageGroup>
                        <Filename>Install.wim</Filename>
                    </InstallImage>
                    <InstallTo>
                        <DiskID>0</DiskID>
                        <PartitionID>1</PartitionID>
                    </InstallTo>
                </ImageSelection>
            </WindowsDeploymentServices>
            <DiskConfiguration>
                <WillShowUI>OnError</WillShowUI>
                <Disk>
                    <DiskID>0</DiskID>
                    <WillWipeDisk>true</WillWipeDisk>
                    <CreatePartitions>
                        <CreatePartition>
                            <Order>1</Order>
                            <Type>Primary</Type>
                            <Size>20000</Size>
                        </CreatePartition>
                    </CreatePartitions>
                </Disk>
            </DiskConfiguration>
            <UserData>
                <ProductKey>
                    <Key>XXXXX-XXXXX-XXXXX-XXXXX-XXXXX</Key>
                    <WillShowUI>OnError</WillShowUI>
                </ProductKey>
                <AcceptEula>true</AcceptEula>
                <FullName>SavillTech IT</FullName>
                <Organization>SavillTech</Organization>
            </UserData>
        </component>
        <component name="Microsoft-Windows-International-Core-
WinPE" processorArchitecture="x86" publicKeyToken=
"31bf3856ad364e35" language="neutral" versionScope="nonSxS"
xmlns:wcm="http://schemas.microsoft.com/WMIConfig/2002/State"
xmlns:xsi="http://www.w3.org/2001/XMLSchema-instance">
            <SetupUILanguage>
                <UILanguage>en-US</UILanguage>
```

```
            </SetupUILanguage>
        </component>
    </settings>
    <settings pass="oobeSystem">
        <component name="Microsoft-Windows-Shell-Setup"
processorArchitecture="x86" publicKeyToken="31bf3856ad364e35"
language="neutral" versionScope="nonSxS"
xmlns:wcm="http://schemas.microsoft.com/WMIConfig/2002/State"
xmlns:xsi="http://www.w3.org/2001/XMLSchema-instance">
            <OOBE>
                <HideEULAPage>true</HideEULAPage>
                <NetworkLocation>Work</NetworkLocation>
                <ProtectYourPC>1</ProtectYourPC>
            </OOBE>
            <RegisteredOrganization>SavillTech
            </RegisteredOrganization>
            <RegisteredOwner>IT</RegisteredOwner>
            <TimeZone>Central Standard Time</TimeZone>
            <UserAccounts>
                <AdministratorPassword>

<Value>UABhADUANQB3AG8AcgBkACEAIQBBAGQAbQBpAG4AaQBzAHQAcgB-
hAHQAbwByAFAAYQBzAHMAdwBvAHIAZAA=</Value>
                    <PlainText>false</PlainText>
                </AdministratorPassword>
                <DomainAccounts>
                    <DomainAccountList wcm:action="add">
                        <DomainAccount wcm:action="add">
                            <Group>Administrators</Group>
                            <Name>Domain Admins</Name>
                        </DomainAccount>
                        <Domain>savilltech</Domain>
                    </DomainAccountList>
                </DomainAccounts>
            </UserAccounts>
        </component>
        <component name="Microsoft-Windows-International-Core"
processorArchitecture="x86" publicKeyToken="31bf3856ad364e35"
language="neutral" versionScope="nonSxS"
xmlns:wcm="http://schemas.microsoft.com/WMIConfig/2002/State"
xmlns:xsi="http://www.w3.org/2001/XMLSchema-instance">
            <InputLocale>en-US</InputLocale>
            <SystemLocale>en-US</SystemLocale>
            <UILanguage>en-US</UILanguage>
            <UserLocale>en-US</UserLocale>
```

```
        </component>
    </settings>
    <settings pass="specialize">
        <component name="Microsoft-Windows-Shell-Setup"
processorArchitecture="x86" publicKeyToken="31bf3856ad364e35"
language="neutral" versionScope="nonSxS"
xmlns:wcm="http://schemas.microsoft.com/WMIConfig/2002/State"
xmlns:xsi="http://www.w3.org/2001/XMLSchema-instance">
            <ProductKey>XXXXX-XXXXX-XXXXX-XXXXX-XXXXX
</ProductKey>
            <RegisteredOrganization>SavillTech
Ltd</RegisteredOrganization>
            <RegisteredOwner>SavillTech Ltd</RegisteredOwner>
            <ComputerName>*</ComputerName>
        </component>
        <component name="Microsoft-Windows-UnattendedJoin"
processorArchitecture="x86" publicKeyToken="31bf3856ad364e35"
language="neutral" versionScope="nonSxS"
xmlns:wcm="http://schemas.microsoft.com/WMIConfig/2002/State"
xmlns:xsi="http://www.w3.org/2001/XMLSchema-instance">
            <Identification>
                <Credentials>
                    <Domain>savilltech</Domain>
                    <Password>password</Password>
                    <Username>administrator</Username>
                </Credentials>
                <JoinDomain>savilltech</JoinDomain>
            </Identification>
        </component>
    </settings>
    <cpi:offlineImage
cpi:source="wim:d:/vista%20media/install.wim#Windows Vista
BUSINESS" xmlns:cpi="urn:schemas-microsoft-com:cpi" />
</unattend>
```

Figure 16-32 shows how those same settings look in the System Image Manager application.

For a complete listing of the values at each level, look at the WAIK documentation. In particular, look at the Unattended Windows Setup Reference, which has details under the Overview of the Unattended Windows Setup Reference—Settings to Use for an Unattended Installation section (see Figure 16-33).

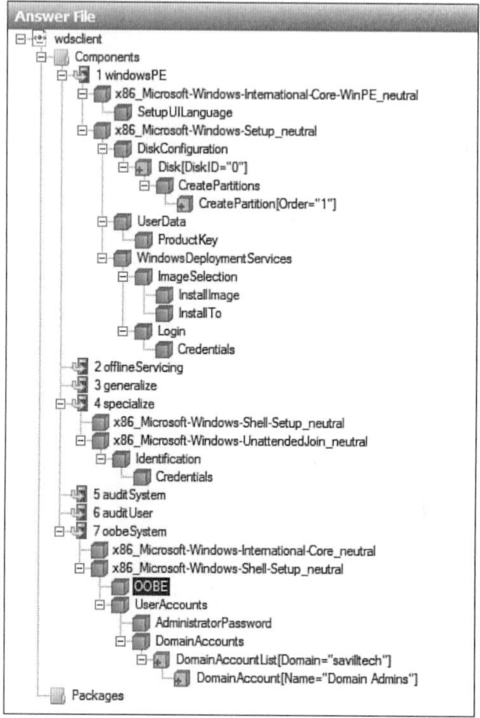

FIGURE 16-32 All the component parts required for an unattended installation. The actual values are described in the WAIK documentation or view the XML.

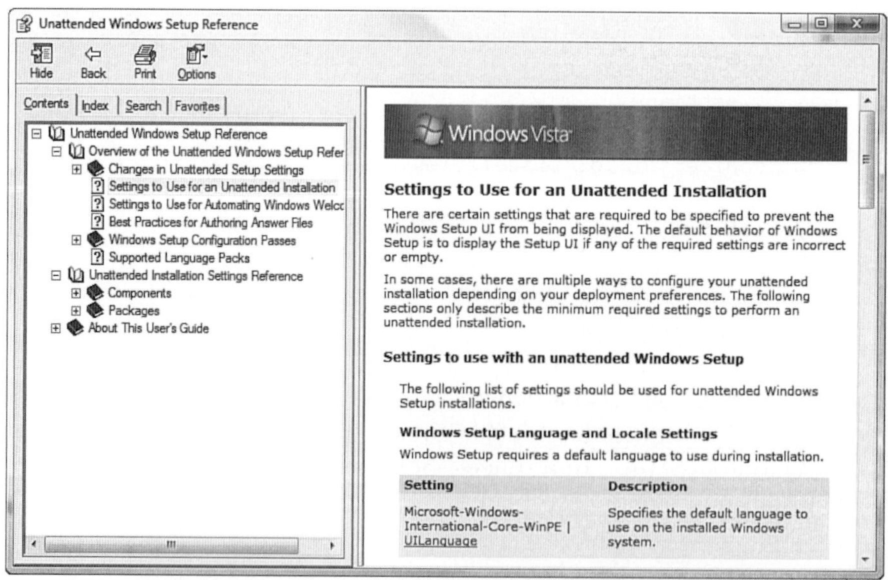

FIGURE 16-33 The WAIK documentation for an unattended installation.

Let's walk through adding one setting together so the process makes sense. After you have an image loaded and an answer file created, add a step to erase the current partitions on the first disk and create a new partition:

1. Expand the x86_Microsoft-Windows-Setup_xxxx component.
2. Expand DiskConfiguration, Disk, CreatePartitions, CreatePartition.
3. Right-click on Create Partition, and select the option Add Setting to Pass 1 windowsPE (see Figure 16-34).

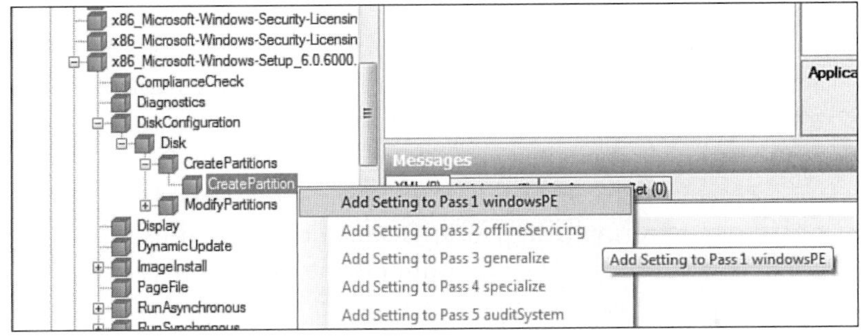

FIGURE 16-34 Adding a stage to an unattended answer file.

4. Under the windowsPE part of the answer file, the disk configuration is now shown. First configure any existing partitions to be wiped. Select the Disk element of the tree, as shown in Figure 16-35, and in the properties pane, change WillWipeDisk to true.

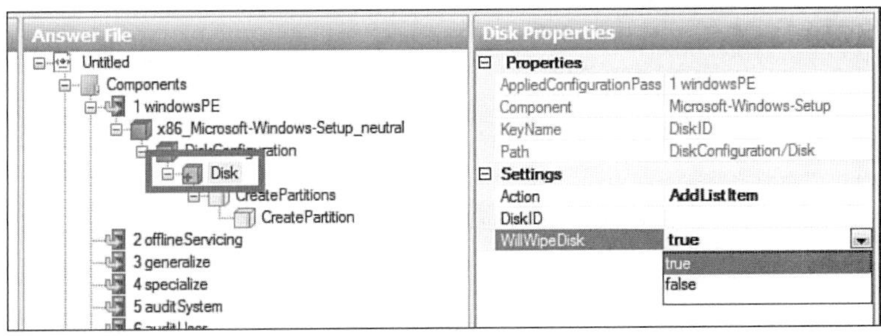

FIGURE 16-35 This setting wipes any existing partitions on the disk.

5. Select the CreatePartition item at the end of the tree, and in the properties pane, set the Order value to 1, the size in MB (for example, 20000 for a 20GB partition), and the type of the partition, such as Primary (see Figure 16-36).

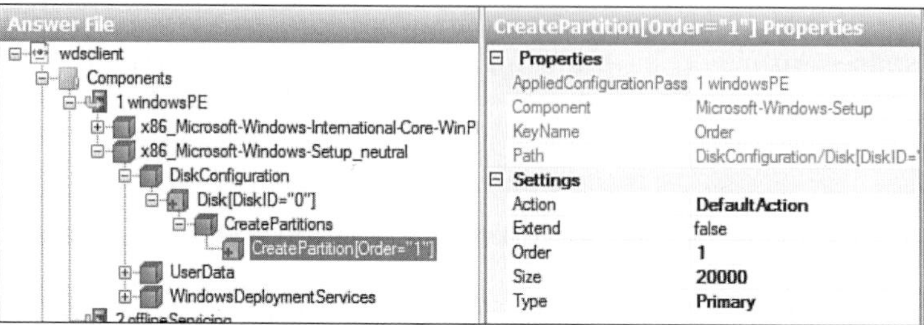

FIGURE 16-36 This creates a 20GB primary partition on disk 0.

Right-click the CreatePartitions item, and there is an option to add additional CreatePartition insertions which enables you to tune the partitions you have on your system. Then follow this process for the other items required for your customized unattended installations.

Let's briefly discuss removing the need to create a user during the installation. Normally in a Vista installation, a local user account must be created because the default Administrator account is disabled. To avoid having the end user prompted to create a local user during the Vista installation, you can create a local user or add a domain account/group to a local group. The latter is preferred for machines joining a domain. Add the Domain Admins group to the local Administrators group via the Microsoft-Windows-Shell-Setup_neutral–UserAccounts–DomainAccounts, as shown in Figure 16-37.

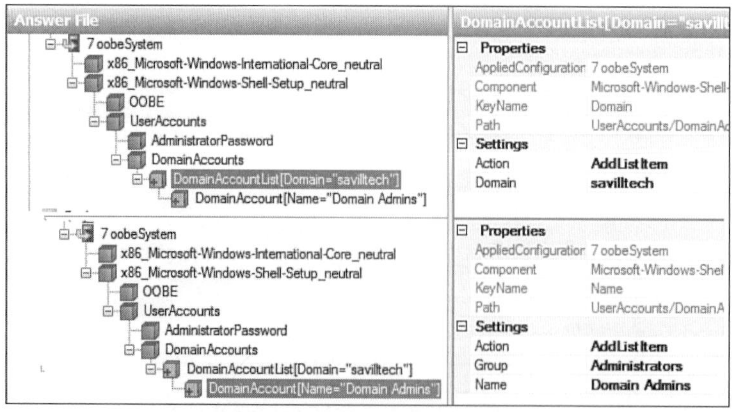

FIGURE 16-37 The two values add the Domain Admins account from the savilltech domain to the local Administrators group. Another approach is to add Domains Users to the local Users group.

After you have all the settings, save your unattended answer file and copy it to the WDSClientUnattend folder under your RemoteInstall folder (for example, c:\RemoteInstall). Now that the unattended answer file is available on the server, link it to the PXE boot stage to automatically select the OS, language, disk configuration, and so on, and then link the answer file to each actual OS image that may be selected.

To assign the answer file for the initial WDS stage where the OS is selected, select the Properties of the WDS server, and under the Client tab, check the Enable unattended installation option and select the answer XML file for the architecture (see Figure 16-38).

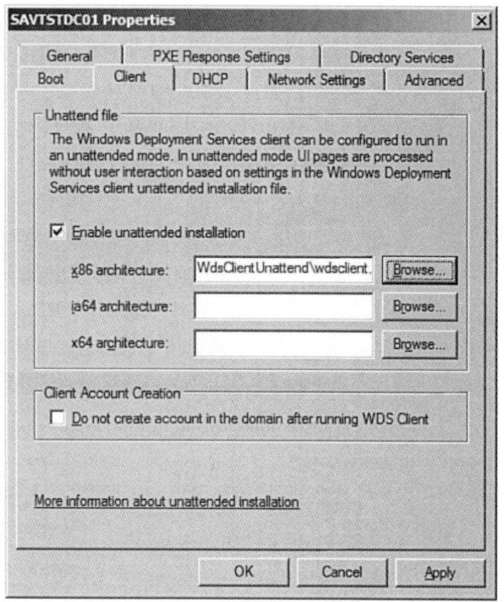

FIGURE 16-38 Different unattended files can be specified for each architecture.

To select the answer file for a particular image, right-click on the image and select Properties from the Install Images–Image group section. Under the General tab, check the Enable image to install in unattended mode and select the XML install file to use (which must be part of the RemoteInstall folder structure where images are stored), as shown in Figure 16-39. For images, the unattended answer file is copied to the install\Unattend sub-folder of the group (for example, C:\RemoteInstall\Images\Windows Vista\install\Unattend). If you update the unattended

XML file, reselect it within the WDS GUI so it is copied to the right location and used. You can use one answer file for multiple images if required. For example, you may have different images with different content, but all require the same configuration.

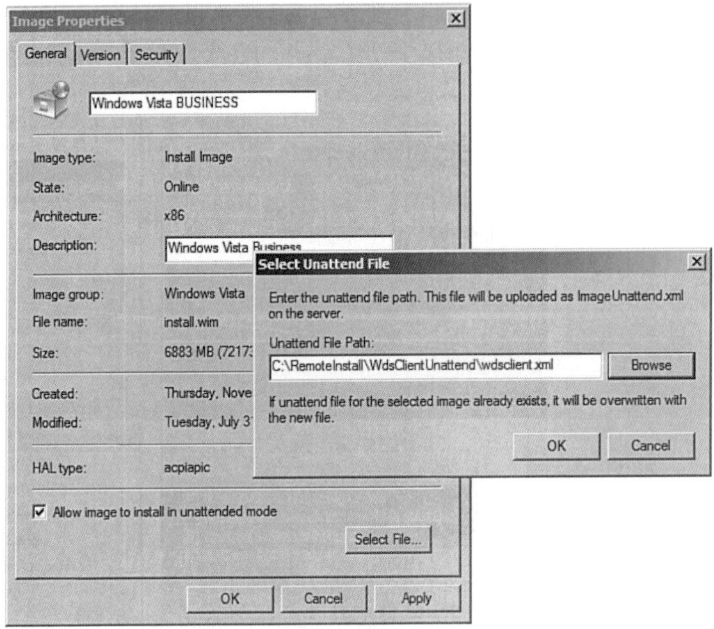

FIGURE 16-39 Each image can have separate default unattended answer files configured.

Remember that individual, per-client answer files can be assigned to particular clients via the `wdsutil` command when a client is authorized with the `/approve-autoadddevices` switch, as in the following example:

```
WDSUTIL /Approve-AutoAddDevices /RequestId:12
/MachineName:wdstest5
/BootProgram:boot\x86\pxeboot.n12
/WdsClientUnattend:WDSClientUnattend\Unattend.xml
/BootImagePath:boot\x86\images\boot.wim
```

Assuming you configure the no-F12 version of the PXE ROM, you should be able to connect a computer to the network, and it is installed automatically now without any user intervention.

Media-Based Windows Deployment Environment

If a client does not support PXE, or perhaps you just want to save on the 80MB or so of PE being sent over the network, you can place the WDS PE environment on media and boot from that.

Like RIS's RBFG utility that created a floppy disk from which non-PXE clients could boot, WDS has bootable media for machines that don't natively support booting over the network. However, it's much larger than the floppy disk-sized image RIS created since it's essentially a Windows PE environment. You can still use the RIS floppy for just PXE boot capability, but that will still pull the Windows PE over the network; when using the WDS Discover boot image, the PE load over the network is avoided. To create a Discover boot image, right-click on the Longhorn-based Windows PE under the Boot Images section of the Windows Deployment Services Management snap-in and select Create Discover Boot Image. Use a Longhorn and not a Vista-based boot image, as the Vista-based PE does not contain the WDS agent. A location and filename for the new WIM file that will be created is requested, along with the WDS server that is contacted for actual OS images (see Figure 16-40).

After you have the WIM file, convert it to an ISO file so it can be burned to a CD to enable bootable deployment by following these steps:

1. Open the Windows PE Tools Command Prompt (Start, Programs, Microsoft Windows AIK, Windows PE Tools Command Prompt).
2. Create a WinPE build environment:

   ```
   CopyPE <architecture, e.g. x86> C:\Winpetemp
   ```

3. To copy the discover image created in the previous procedure, save it as boot.wim to replace the default one that exists already (created by CopyPE); type the following:

   ```
   Copy /y c:\images\discover.wim
   c:\Winpetemp\ISO\Sources\boot.wim
   ```

4. Change back to the PETools folder:

   ```
   Cd C:\Program Files\Windows AIK\Tools\PETools
   ```

5. To create the bootable ISO image, type the following:

   ```
   oscdimg -n -bc:\winpetemp\iso\boot\etfsboot.com
   c:\winpetemp\iso c:\winpediscover.iso
   ```

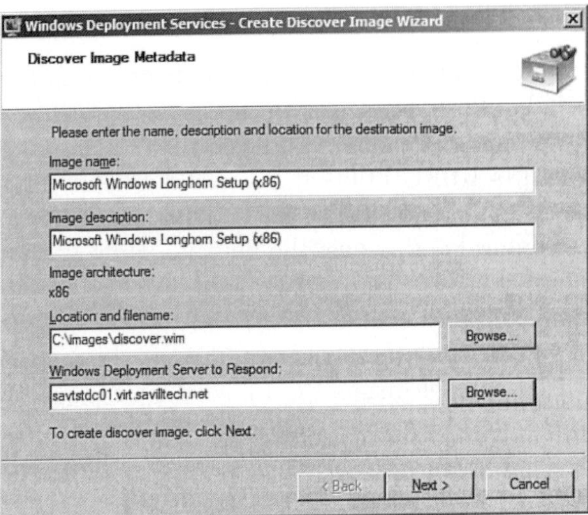

FIGURE 16-40 The Discover image is used to create a media-based PE environment to replace the process of pulling the PE over the network.

You now have an ISO file that can be burned to a CD or DVD (or used directly from a virtual machine for testing purposes), which loads the PE environment from media and then proceeds with WDS-based OS deployment.

Capturing New Images

In the same way you could create a discover media from the boot images on your WDS server, you can also create a capture image that you would boot to on a prepared computer (that has been SYSPREPed). This launches the capture wizard and captures the content of the computer to a new WIM file. Right-click on a boot image and select Create Capture Boot Image. Figure 16-41 shows the first screen of the WDS image capture wizard.

In addition to the wizard-driven method, you can use WAIK to create a bootable Windows PE environment that could be sent via WDS. It also could be done via a CD or even USB thumb drive that contains the imagex utility. The imagex utility has a huge number of uses when it comes to the manipulation of WIM files, but one of them is the capture and deployment of WIM files. To create an imagex PE environment, perform the following:

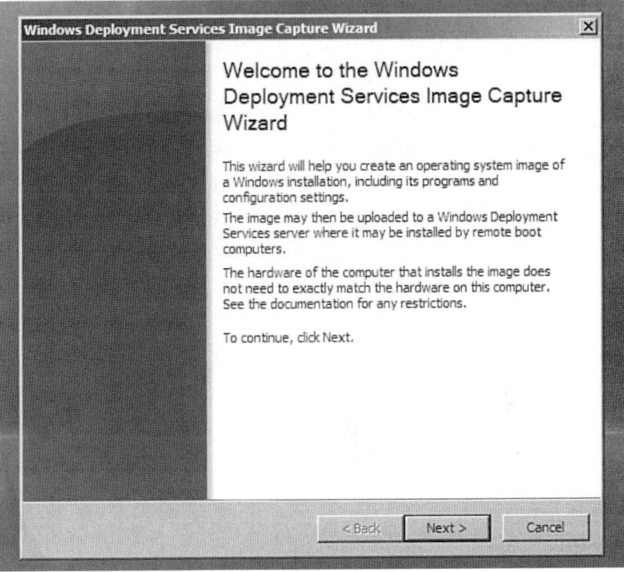

FIGURE 16-41 The first dialog of the image capture wizard.

1. Start a command prompt (Start - Run - cmd.exe) on the machine with WAIK installed.
2. Navigate to the C:\Program Files\Windows AIK\Tools\PETools folder (the default install path for WAIK).
3. Use the copype.cmd to create a PE folder structure on disk using the following format:

   ```
   copype.cmd <arch> <destination>
   ```

4. `<arch>` can be x86, amd64, or ia64, and `<destination>` is a path to the local directory. An example would look something like this:

   ```
   copype.cmd x86 c:\winpe_x86
   ```

   A large number of file copies are displayed to the screen, and the path for the command prompt is modified to enable simpler copying of the PE tools by adding the PETools folder to the path.
5. Copy the `imagex.exe` command into the ISO folder (c:\winpe_x86\ISO) of the PE build from c:\program files\Windows AIK\Tools\x86\.
6. Also in the ISO folder, place the content from the following listing into a file named wimscript.ini, which is used to instruct the `imagex` command when executed to ignore certain files from the capture. Don't capture the NTFS log file, the hibernation file or

the pagefile, any of the System Volume Information, deleted files, or the Windows offline files cache. Don't waste processor cycles trying to compress data that is already compressed. Imagex automatically detects the presence of the file if it is in the same folder. If you want to place the imagex configuration file in another location, pass the `/config` switch with the location and the name of the file during any capture or append operations (for example, `/config c:\imaging\imagexconfig.ini`).

```
[ExclusionList]
ntfs.log
hiberfil.sys
pagefile.sys
"System Volume Information"
RECYCLER
Windows\CSC

[CompressionExclusionList]
*.mp3
*.zip
*.cab
\WINDOWS\inf\*.pnf
```

7. You could also place other files in the ISO folder, such as malware tools, but this is optional.
8. Create an image (.iso) file by using the `oscdimg` tool, which should take a few minutes. For example, from a command prompt, run the following:

```
C:\>cd \program files\Windows AIK\Tools\PETools\
C:\program files\Windows AIK\Tools\PETools\>oscdimg -n
➥-bc:\winpe_x86\etfsboot.com c:\winpe_x86\ISO
➥c:\winpe_x86\winpe_x86.iso

OSCDIMG 2.45 CD-ROM and DVD-ROM Premastering Utility
Copyright (C) Microsoft, 1993-2000. All rights reserved.
For Microsoft internal use only.


Scanning source tree complete (20 files in 8 directories)

Computing directory information complete

Image file is 192546816 bytes

Writing 20 files in 8 directories to
```

```
c:\winpe_x86\winpe_x86.iso

100% complete

Final image file is 192546816 bytes

Done.
```

Now that you have an ISO image with the PE environment, you can burn a CD and capture an installed system by booting to the media and then capturing the content of the C: drive using the following command:

```
d:\imagex.exe /compress fast /capture c:
c:\vistawithoff2007.wim "Custom Vista Install with Office 2007"
/verify
```

In this case, boot to a Vista with Office installation, and capture it locally to a WIM file. The amount of time taken to capture will depend on the hardware of the machine being captured and the size of the data being captured. It could take 20 minutes, or it could take hours. However, this could also have been a network location. Likewise, you could apply a WIM file to a computer using the following command:

```
d:\imagex.exe /apply c:\vistawithoff2007.wim 1 c:
```

If you're creating custom images, the installation of the OS must have been prepared with SYSPREP. For example, a typical `SYSPREP` command to run on an OS to prepare it for imaging is shown next. It strips away its uniqueness and shuts down the OS ready to be booted to a capture environment. After you reboot the captured machine, it has to be reconfigured since it has been stripped of its configuration.

```
c:\windows\system32\sysprep\sysprep.exe /oobe /generalize
➥/shutdown
```

Customizing an Image

As previously mentioned, you can capture anything to a WIM. You can install an OS, install applications onto it that you want to be part of the image (this is not best practice, but it is certainly possible), and then run SYSPREP to ready the computer to be captured for deployment to multiple target machines.

In addition, a special audit mode is available that enables access to a Windows Vista installation after a fresh install without having to create accounts before getting access to the interface, keeping the image as clean as possible. To access this special mode, press Ctrl-Shift-F3 when prompted to create a new account. When you press Ctrl-Shift-F3, the computer reboots, and you are automatically logged on as the local administrator (see Figure 16-42). At this point, install applications and drivers; once changes are made, click OK at the SYSPREP window that will be waiting to execute to prepare the computer for duplication.

Other changes you can make to the OS include placing the installation files onto the local disk instead of installing them. That makes it easier to update the applications on the image in the future by just updating install files, as opposed to having to deal with uninstalling actual components that will be part of the OS.

FIGURE 16-42 The special audit mode gives you an administrator-credentialed environment that enables customization with the SYSPREP tool, which is loaded and ready to be executed when changes are complete.

Manipulating WIM Files

The imagex file for capturing and deploying WIM files from a PE environment was discussed previously. However, the same utility can be used to mount WIM files. Its first use is to see what images are contained within a WIM, as in the following example:

```
D:\Temp>imagex /info install.wim

ImageX Tool for Windows
Copyright (C) Microsoft Corp. 1981-2005. All rights reserved.



WIM Information:
----------------
GUID:         {c7fbd5c6-f4ad-4bb1-b6fd-b8f0e8e77716}
Image Count: 1
Compression: LZX
Part Number: 1/1
Attributes:  0xc
             Integrity info
             Relative path junction


Available Image Choices:
------------------------
<WIM>
  <TOTALBYTES>1808206323</TOTALBYTES>
  <IMAGE INDEX="1">
    <NAME>Windows Vista ENTERPRISE</NAME>
    <DESCRIPTION>Windows Vista Enterprise VL</DESCRIPTION>
    <FLAGS>ENTERPRISE</FLAGS>
    <WINDOWS>
      <ARCH>0</ARCH>
      <PRODUCTNAME>Microsoft« Windows« operating system
</PRODUCTNAME>
      <HAL>acpiapic</HAL>
      <PRODUCTTYPE>WinNT</PRODUCTTYPE>
      <PRODUCTSUITE>Terminal Server</PRODUCTSUITE>
      <LANGUAGES>
        <LANGUAGE>en-US</LANGUAGE>
        <DEFAULT>en-US</DEFAULT>
```

The best functionality comes from mounting a WIM file, which is accomplished with the `/mount` switch passing the name of the WIM file, the image number from the WIM to load, and the folder to mount the WIM as (the folder must already exist). For example, to mount the first image (1) from the d:\temp\install.wim to folder d:\temp\imgmount, use the following command:

```
D:\Temp>mkdir imgmount

D:\Temp>imagex /mount d:\temp\install.wim 1 d:\temp\imgmount

ImageX Tool for Windows
Copyright (C) Microsoft Corp. 1981-2005. All rights reserved.


Mounting: [d:\temp\install.wim, 1] ->
          [d:\temp\imgmount]

Successfully mounted image.
```

This mount was read-only, so you can view the content through any normal tool that enumerates a folder—for example, command line or Explorer. If you want to be able to modify the WIM, use the `/mountrw` switch instead of the `/mount` switch. The rest of the command is identical, as when you apply a patch to a WIM file.

When you are finished looking at the content of a WIM, the `/unmount` command is used along with the path that was mounted. If you had opened the WIM file in its read/write version and wanted to commit the changes, you would also add the `/commit` switch to the command shown:

```
D:\Temp>imagex /unmount d:\temp\imgmount

ImageX Tool for Windows
Copyright (C) Microsoft Corp. 1981-2005. All rights reserved.


Unmounting: [d:\temp\imgmount]...

Successfully unmounted image.
```

Applying an Update to a WIM File

One of the great features of WIM is that you are able to add components, drivers, updates, and even service packs using (almost) normal install methods via the `pkgmgr` command, which is part of WAIK. Updates from

Microsoft are supplied in the new MSU format. WAIK has documentation on applying drivers, language packs, and updates, but let's look at the process to apply an update to the WIM file.

After you download the updates from http://www.microsoft.com/downloads and select the Windows Vista family, extract the content of the MSU to a folder (the folder must be created in advance), as in the following example:

```
D:\temp>mkdir kb935806-x86

D:\temp>expand -f:* Windows6.0-KB935807-x86.msu
➥d:\temp\kb935806-x86
Microsoft (R) File Expansion Utility Version 6.0.6000.16386
Copyright (c) Microsoft Corporation. All rights reserved.

Adding d:\temp\kb935806-x86\WSUSSCAN.cab to Extraction Queue
Adding d:\temp\kb935806-x86\Windows6.0-KB935807-x86.cab to
Extraction Queue
Adding d:\temp\kb935806-x86\Windows6.0-KB935807-x86-
pkgProperties.txt to Extraction Queue
Adding d:\temp\kb935806-x86\Windows6.0-KB935807-x86.xml to
Extraction Queue

Expanding Files ....

Expanding Files Complete ...
4 files total.
```

After the files are extracted, mount your WIM file using `imagex` in read/write mode:

```
C:\Program Files\Windows AIK\Tools\PETools>imagex /mountrw
➥"d:\OS Images\Windows Vista\install.wim" 1 d:\temp\vista

ImageX Tool for Windows
Copyright (C) Microsoft Corp. 1981-2005. All rights reserved.


Mounting (RW): [d:\OS Images\Windows Vista Final English DVD
Images (x86 and x64)\install.wim, 1] ->
[d:\temp\vista]

Successfully mounted image (RW).
```

After mounting, apply the update extracted using the package manager utility, pkgmgr. Ensure you use the correct architecture version. For example, don't use the PETools folder version, but instead use the `<processor>\Servicing` version:

```
C:\Program Files\Windows AIK\Tools\x86\Servicing>start
➥/w pkgmgr /n:"D:\temp\update\Windows6.0-KB932246-x86.xml"
➥/o:"d:temp\vista;d:\temp\vista\windows" /l:d:temp\insert.log
```

After the update is installed, check the log text file for return status 0x0:

```
Pkgmgr: return code: 0x0
```

After the update is complete, unmount the WIM file with the `commit` option:

```
C:\Program Files\Windows AIK\Tools\x86\Servicing>imagex
➥/unmount /commit d:\temp\vista

ImageX Tool for Windows
Copyright (C) Microsoft Corp. 1981-2005. All rights reserved.


Unmounting: [d:\temp\vista]...

Successfully unmounted image.
```

This has updated the image mounted from the WIM file. Remember, if a WIM file contains multiple images (the default install.wim on the Vista media contains seven), mount each image separately, apply the patch, and commit the change. To patch all seven, the previous process is repeated seven times. If you do patch every image in a WIM file, then the files that have been replaced by the newer versions will remain in the WIM file, and it is larger than it needs to be. To purge the excess, unused files, export the images from the WIM file into a new WIM file that contains only the files referenced by the exported images, therefore removing the unused files. The `/export` switch for `imagex` enables a specific image to be exported into a new WIM file, or you can export all images (which is what you would want to do) by specifying * for the image number, as in the following example:

```
Imagex /export d:\vista\install.wim * d:\vista\leaninstall.wim
"Windows Vista 2"
```


Adding Drivers to a WIM Image

Injecting drivers into an offline WIM file works in a similar fashion, but this time use the System Image Manager to create an unattended answer file to just inject the driver and then read the answer file into the image via the pkgmgr utility. Open the System Image Manager and then open the image you want to inject the driver into (for example, Windows Vista Enterprise). Create a new answer file, right-click on x86_Microsoft-Windows-PnpCustomizationsNonWinPE, and select the Add Setting to Pass 2 offlineServicing. As shown in Figure 16-43, right-click DriverPaths and select Insert New PathAndCredentials.

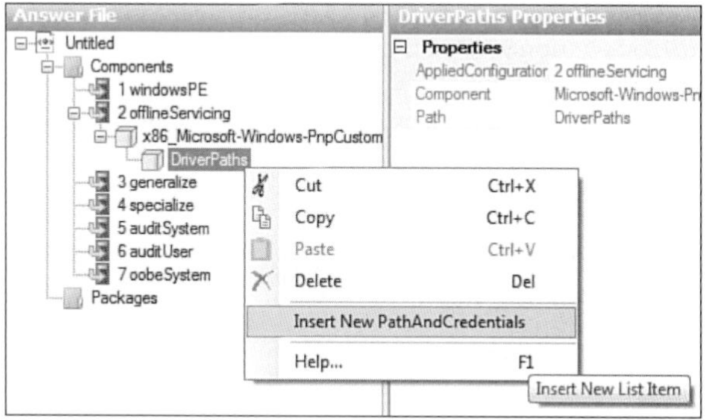

FIGURE 16-43 Insert New PathAndCredentials enables you to add a path to additional drivers.

Select the new PathAndCredentials node, and in the properties area of the console, enter a unique ID for the key (for example, 1) and then a path to the drivers (for example, \\server1\share\driversfolder or c:\drivers), as shown in Figure 16-44. Select the Credentials child node, and in the properties, enter the domain, username, and password that have the credentials to access. If you are accessing a network location, this credential element is not needed for a local path. Save this answer file. This is why offlineServicing existed in the Image Manager tool, since it would never be used while installing an OS.

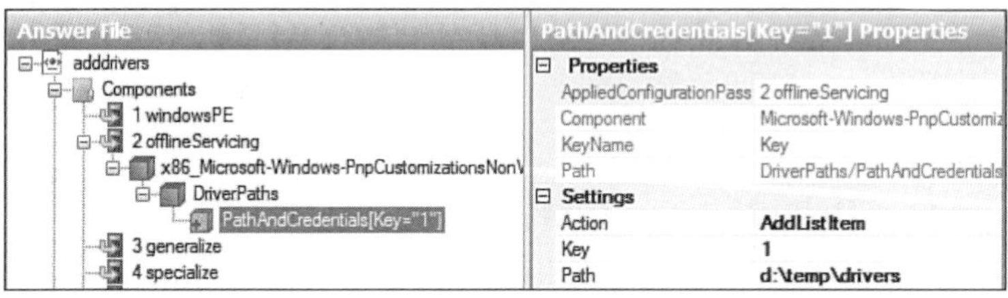

FIGURE 16-44 An example driver path entry.

The following listing presents example XML to add a locally based driver:

```
<settings pass="offlineServicing">
        <component name="Microsoft-Windows-
PnpCustomizationsNonWinPE" processorArchitecture="x86"
publicKeyToken="31bf3856ad364e35" language="neutral"
versionScope="nonSxS" xmlns:wcm="http://schemas.microsoft.com/
WMIConfig/2002/State"
xmlns:xsi="http://www.w3.org/2001/XMLSchema-instance">
            <DriverPaths>
                <PathAndCredentials wcm:action="add"
wcm:keyValue="1">
                    <PathAndCredentials>
                    <Path>d:\temp\drivers</Path>
                </PathAndCredentials>
            </DriverPaths>
        </component>
    </settings>
```

Now that you have the XML answer file, use it to inject drivers into the WIM. Mount the WIM file with `/mountrw` in the same way as you mounted the WIM to apply an update—for example, `imagex /mountrw "h:\OS Images\Windows Vista\install.wim" 1 d:\temp\imgmount`.

Make sure the drivers you want to import are in the path specified in the answer file. The driver folder can contain subfolders, which will all be searched. Then inject into the mounted WIM using the following command, where `d:\temp\imgmount` is where the WIM is mounted and `d:\temp\adddirvers.xml` is the name of the answer file:

```
C:\Program Files\Windows AIK\Tools\x86\Servicing>pkgmgr
➥/o:"d:\temp\imgmount;d:\temp\imgmount\windows"
➥/n:"d:\temp\adddrivers.xml" /l:d:\temp\unattend
```

No output will be given; instead, check the txt version of the log file. The important item is the return code 0x0 at the end, but also look at all the files and drivers found to confirm it added what was needed. The following is an example of some parts of the file:

```
2007-08-01 11:08:27, Info                  CBS    Pkgmgr: called with:
"pkgmgr  /o:"d:\temp\imgmount;d:\temp\imgmount\windows"
/n:"d:\temp\adddrivers.xml" /l:d:\temp\unattend"
2007-08-01 11:08:30, Info                  CBS    Pkgmgr: Install Dri-
vers Offline Callback: INFO:   ENTER InstallDriversOffline (Error code
(HRESULT) 0x0.)
2007-08-01 11:08:30, Info                  CBS    Pkgmgr: Install Dri-
vers Offline Callback: INFO:   Parameter Offline Windows Directory Path:
'd:\temp\imgmount\windows' (Error code (HRESULT) 0x0.)
Callback: INFO:   Path = 'd:\temp\drivers' (Error code (HRESULT) 0x0.)
2007-08-01 11:08:30, Info                  CBS    Pkgmgr: Install Dri-
vers Offline Callback: WARNING:No credentials provided (Error code
(HRESULT) 0x0.)
2007-08-01 11:08:30, Info                  CBS    Pkgmgr: Install Dri-
vers Offline
2007-08-01 11:08:30, Info                  CBS    Pkgmgr: Install Dri-
vers Offline Callback: INFO:   Searching for drivers at 'd:\temp\driv-
ers'... (Error code (HRESULT) 0x0.)
2007-08-01 11:08:30, Info                  CBS    Pkgmgr: Install Dri-
vers Offline Callback: INFO:   Locating INFs in 'd:\temp\drivers' (Error
code (HRESULT) 0x0.)
2007-08-01 11:08:30, Info                  CBS    Pkgmgr: Install Dri-
vers Offline Callback: INFO:   Found directory crystal under search path
(Error code (HRESULT) 0x0.)
2007-08-01 11:08:30, Info                  CBS    Pkgmgr: Install Dri-
vers Offline Callback: INFO:   Found file caliaud.sys (Error code
(HRESULT) 0x0.)
2007-08-01 11:08:30, Info                  CBS    Pkgmgr: Install Dri-
vers Offline
….
```

```
2007-08-01 11:08:30, Info                 CBS    Pkgmgr: Install Dri-
vers Offline Callback: INFO:   Found directory nvidia under search path
(Error code (HRESULT) 0x0.)
2007-08-01 11:08:30, Info                 CBS    Pkgmgr: Install Dri-
vers Offline Callback: INFO:   Found file data1.cab (Error code (HRESULT)
0x0.)
..
2007-08-01 11:08:30, Info                 CBS    Pkgmgr: Install Dri-
vers Offline Callback: INFO:   Found 2 driver package(s) at
'd:\temp\drivers'. (Error code (HRESULT) 0x0.)
2007-08-01 11:08:30, Info                 CBS    Pkgmgr: Install Dri-
vers Offline Callback: INFO:      Driver Package 'd:\temp\drivers\
crystal\hpa0850.inf' (Error code (HRESULT) 0x0.)
2007-08-01 11:08:30, Info                 CBS    Pkgmgr: Install Dri-
vers Offline Callback: INFO:      Driver Package
'd:\temp\drivers\nvidia\nv_disp.inf' (Error code (HRESULT) 0x0.)
2007-08-01 11:08:30, Info                 CBS    Pkgmgr: Install Dri-
vers Offline Callback: INFO:   Installing driver package 'd:\temp\driv-
ers\crystal\hpa0850.inf' to the currently offline OS ... (Error code
(HRESULT) 0x0.)
2007-08-01 11:08:30, Info                 CBS    Pkgmgr: Install Dri-
vers Offline Callback: INFO:   'd:\temp\drivers\crystal\hpa0850.inf' is
not a boot critical driver. (Error code (HRESULT) 0x0.)
2007-08-01 11:08:31, Info                 CBS    Pkgmgr: Install Dri-
vers Offline Callback: SUCCESS:Added
'd:\temp\drivers\crystal\hpa0850.inf' to offline driver store at
'd:\temp\imgmount\windows\system32\DriverStore\FileRepository\hpa0850.i
nf_b2f23504\hpa0850.inf'. (Error code (HRESULT) 0x0.)
2007-08-01 11:08:31, Info                 CBS    Pkgmgr: Install Dri-
vers Offline Callback: SUCCESS:Added driver
'd:\temp\drivers\crystal\hpa0850.inf' to the offline Windows image at
'd:\temp\imgmount\windows\system32\DriverStore\FileRepository\hpa0850.i
nf_b2f23504\hpa0850.inf'. (Error code (HRESULT) 0x0.)
2007-08-01 11:08:31, Info                 CBS    Pkgmgr: Install Dri-
vers Offline Callback: SUCCESS:Driver package
'd:\temp\drivers\crystal\hpa0850.inf' installed! (Error code (HRESULT)
0x0.)
2007-08-01 11:08:49, Info                 CBS    Pkgmgr: Install Dri-
vers Offline Callback: SUCCESS:Added
'd:\temp\drivers\nvidia\nv_disp.inf' to offline driver store at
'd:\temp\imgmount\windows\system32\DriverStore\FileRepository\nv_disp.i
nf_30e3ba63\nv_disp.inf'. (Error code (HRESULT) 0x0.)
```

```
2007-08-01 11:08:49, Info                  CBS    Pkgmgr: Install Dri-
vers Offline Callback: SUCCESS:Added driver
'd:\temp\drivers\nvidia\nv_disp.inf' to the offline Windows image at
'd:\temp\imgmount\windows\system32\DriverStore\FileRepository\nv_disp.i
nf_30e3ba63\nv_disp.inf'. (Error code (HRESULT) 0x0.)
2007-08-01 11:08:49, Info                  CBS    Pkgmgr: Install Dri-
vers Offline Callback: SUCCESS:Driver package
'd:\temp\drivers\nvidia\nv_disp.inf' installed! (Error code (HRESULT)
0x0.)
2007-08-01 11:08:49, Info                  CBS    Pkgmgr: Install Dri-
vers Offline Callback: INFO:   Installed '2' drivers. (Error code
(HRESULT) 0x0.)
2007-08-01 11:08:49, Info                  CBS    Pkgmgr: Install Dri-
vers Offline Callback: INFO:   RETURN InstallDriversOffline (0) (Error
code (HRESULT) 0x0.)
2007-08-01 11:08:49, Info                  CBS    Pkgmgr: return code:
0x0
```

After you have made changes, unmount with the `commit` command—for example, `imagex /unmount /commit d:\temp\imgmount`. Note that the size of the WIM file will increase due to the new files contained in it.

For Windows PE, use the `peimg` command, and then use the `/inf` switch passing the folder that contains the INF files for the driver being inserted, as well as the location of the mounted Windows PE WIM file (again, must be mounted in read and write mode). The folder containing the INF files can have multiple INFs for multiple drivers, and the wildcard character can be used, for example:

```
peimg /inf=C:\Temp\Driver\*.inf /image=C:\Temp\Mount
```

After the drivers are added to the mount, perform a commit unmount.

Some devices require multiple drivers that are needed for the device to function. For example, the Broadcom network driver has a normal NIC driver and a BUS driver that are both needed for the NIC to function; after extracting the content of the files from the installation file (msiexec /a <file>.msi), ensure that you copy both the NIC driver and the bus driver (for example, in the VBD folder) to the driver path that will be injected into the WIM file.

In international organizations, you could install language packs into an OS image. If you search www.microsoft.com for "Windows Server 2008 Multilingual User Interface Language Packs," you can download language packs for Windows Server. Search Technet.microsoft.com for "Language Interface Packs" for instructions on adding language packs into an image. It's the same process as for adding drivers. Create an answer file that performs a package install in the Servicing section of the XML file, and then use PKGMGR to apply the answer file to a mounted image. An additional step is required, however, which uses intlcfg.exe to recreate the language configuration file (lang.ini). At the time of this writing, detailed steps can be found at http://technet2.microsoft.com/WindowsVista/en/library/a7ac8143-9162-4fc0-928d-1c45b321b3261033.mspx?mfr=true.

Vista Reduced-Functionality Mode

Before going any further, a quick digression on Windows Vista reduced activation and how to reset it as part of your testing is in order. If Vista isn't activated within 30 days after installation for the retail release of Vista or within three days of changing a major hardware component, the built-in Windows Genuine Advantage (WGA) feature will place the computer in out-of-grace reduced-functionality mode, which will enable access to Vista for a period of one hour. During that one hour, you can perform most functions, including the following:

- Activating the Vista product key
- Using Windows Management Instrumentation (WMI) to run scripts on the computer from a remote location
- Changing the product key
- Using most of the features that are available in Vista
- Remotely accessing a shared network location
- Running Vista in safe mode for data access purposes

You can't run any of the built-in games or run premium features such as the Aero UI, Windows ReadyBoost, or BitLocker Drive Encryption. If you attempt to log on when Vista is in reduced-functionality mode, you receive a message: "Activate Windows Now. Your activation period has expired and Windows is no longer working. To use Windows, you must activate this copy of Windows." You can extend this three times for 30 days each, giving a total of 120 days use with the command:

```
Cscript \windows\system32\slmgr.vbs -rearm
```

Windows Vista Service Pack 1 removed reduced-functionality mode and replaced it with a notification mode that nags users until they activate the installation. This does not mean you should forget about activating, however.

Deploying Multiple Machines Simultaneously

It's highly likely that you will want to deploy multiple clients at the same time; although it is possible to run 10 deployments at the same time, this means the image is pulled down over the network 10 times, slowing all the deployments as they fight for network bandwidth. Windows Server 2008 WDS introduces multicast support, which enables multiple clients to subscribe to a single transmission of data. That means you send the image of the OS over the network once, and up to 1000 clients can download that single transmission, providing a fast deploy time.

There is little needed to get multicast running. By default, WDS is configured to use its own multicast DHCP scope, but if you have a MADCAP server, then that can be used instead, as discussed via the Network Settings tab of the WDS server properties. The clients need to be running the Windows Server 2008 boot image for multicast support, and no other configuration is required. If you configure a client to install Windows Vista Business, and a multicast session exists for that image, it automatically joins the multicast session. Nothing else is needed.

The easiest way to create a new multicast transmission is to right-click on the install image you want to multicast and select Create Multicast Transmission from its context menu. You are prompted for a friendly name for the transmission, such as "Windows Vista Business MCT," and when you click Next, you are prompted for the multicast type (see Figure 16-45).

If you want a multicast to start whenever needed, leave the default setting of Auto-Cast, which starts a transmission as soon as a client needs the image. However, you may prefer to use a Scheduled-Cast, which is where clients will see that the multicast transmission exists and will wait for it to start. A WDS administrator via the WDS MMC interface can perform the actual starting of the multicast by right-clicking on a Multicast Transmission and selecting Start. Or check one or both of the auto-start options, which are based on starting the transmission after you have *x* number of clients waiting for the image—for example, start only after 10 clients are waiting for Windows Vista Business—or schedule to start at a certain date and time, which would be useful if you wanted to turn on machines during the day but not start the install until after-hours. After the setting is made, click Next and Finish at the summary display.

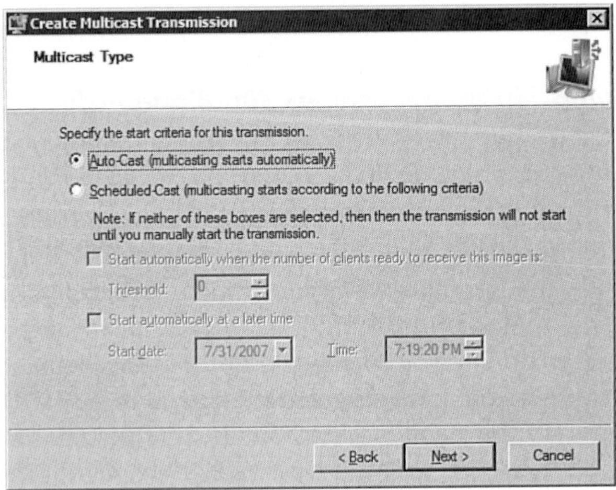

FIGURE 16-45 Multicast transmission can be Auto-Cast or Scheduled-Cast.

While clients are waiting for an image, they are in a "Waiting for server" status, as shown in Figure 16-46. Also shown is the Administrator console—the clients waiting for the transmission. If you want to, right-click on a multicast client and start them outside the multicast, and they would download the image via SMB, which is the normal transmission method. Clients will wait up to 72 hours for the multicast transmission to start—after 72 hours, Windows PE reboots to stop people trying to use it as a proper OS.

During the multicast session, selecting Deactivate enables existing multicast clients to complete but stops new computers from joining the multicast session. Or you can just Delete, which will stop any sessions.

Clients can join in halfway through a multicast transmission. When a multicast transmission first starts, the transmission broadcasts to all multicast clients what blocks are needed by them. The clients respond by saying "need whole file," so the server starts sending out all the data of the image. If someone joins halfway through the process, then they get the second half of the transmission only. After the data has been sent, the server sends out another packet, asking "what else do you need;" all the clients that were there at the start say "nothing else." However, the one that joined halfway through says "I need the first half," and the server sends out that data again.

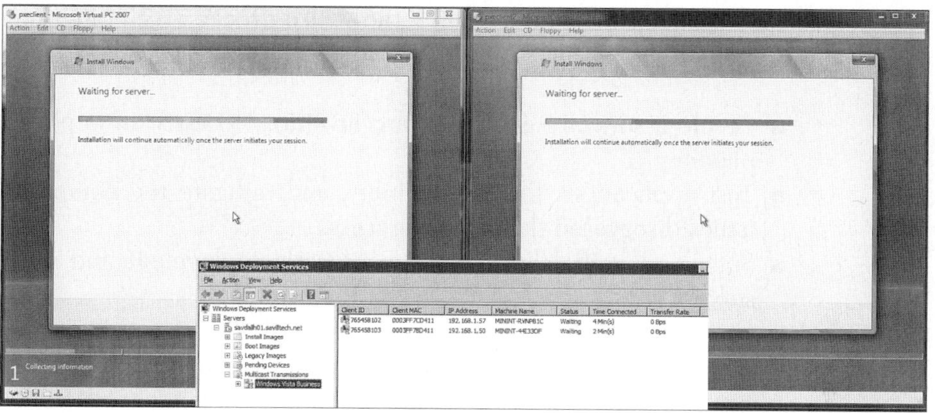

FIGURE 16-46 Clients waiting for the multicast to initiate pause in the PE phase with a "Waiting for server" status and are awaiting initiation from the server.

Other Technologies for Deployment

WDS is a powerful technology, and hopefully you now have a better understanding of how to use it. However, there are still some functions that are missing. For example, you cannot upgrade a client with WDS—it has no client agent that can be used to tell an existing OS to capture computer state and user data, store it, and then restore after the new OS is deployed. Also, drivers are still somewhat of an issue. Yes, you can insert drivers into a WIM file using PKGMGR. However, it would be far nicer for computers being installed to dynamically pull down drivers from a central repository on the network, keeping the image far leaner and requiring fewer updates. There are two complementary technologies Microsoft provides for OS deployment.

The Microsoft Solution Accelerator for Business Desktop Deployment 2007, a free download available at http://www.microsoft.com/technet/desktopdeployment/bdd/2007/default.mspx, is a huge add-on for WDS. It adds a full workbench interface that facilitates upgrades of an existing OS and online driver libraries, plus the capability to inject drivers and languages via a graphical interface and a lot more. The Windows System Image Manager allowed you to customize and automate the deployment of the OS and only that aspect of deployment. The BDD is a solution for the entire deployment of your desktop, so it's not just a technology solution. It includes best practices for planning the entire process, including the following:

- Create a software and hardware inventory to assist in deployment planning.
- Test applications for compatibility, and mitigate the compatibility issues discovered during the process.
- Set up an initial lab environment with deployment and imaging servers.
- Customize and package applications.
- Automate desktop image creation and deployment.
- Ensure that the desktop is hardened to improve security within the environment.
- Manage processes and technologies to produce a comprehensive and integrated deployment.

It is recommended that you add the BDD to your deployment planning to simplify the process of deployment and take advantage of the BDD-enhanced functionality. WAIK was designed with BDD in mind, and the Windows System Image Manager had a Distribution Share window. This is something used by the BDD as part of its dynamic driver and component deployment.

The other Microsoft-provided option for OS deployment is System Center Configuration Manager. It is a product from Microsoft that requires both server and client licensing but offers a rich OS deployment environment that supports upgrades of machines, dynamic driver library management including driver packages for different brands of hardware, and sophisticated task sequences that enable Configuration Manager built-in actions to be executed, in addition to custom actions such as command lines, VBScripts, and executables. All of these capabilities are backed up by great reports, as shown in Figure 16-47. Additionally, System Center enables media to be created containing the entire image via a wizard, although this could also be achieved with WAIK by creating a custom PE with `imagex` and including the WIM file on the DVD. The System Center Configuration Manager goes much further because an entire sequence of actions can be placed on media, such as deploying an image and then deploying services such as Exchange; anything configured in a task sequence is written to the media for offline application. The System Center Configuration Manager still uses WDS for its PXE boot capability, but aside from that, you definitely want to use the System Center Configuration Manager for OS deployment if you already have it in your organization or can justify its introduction.

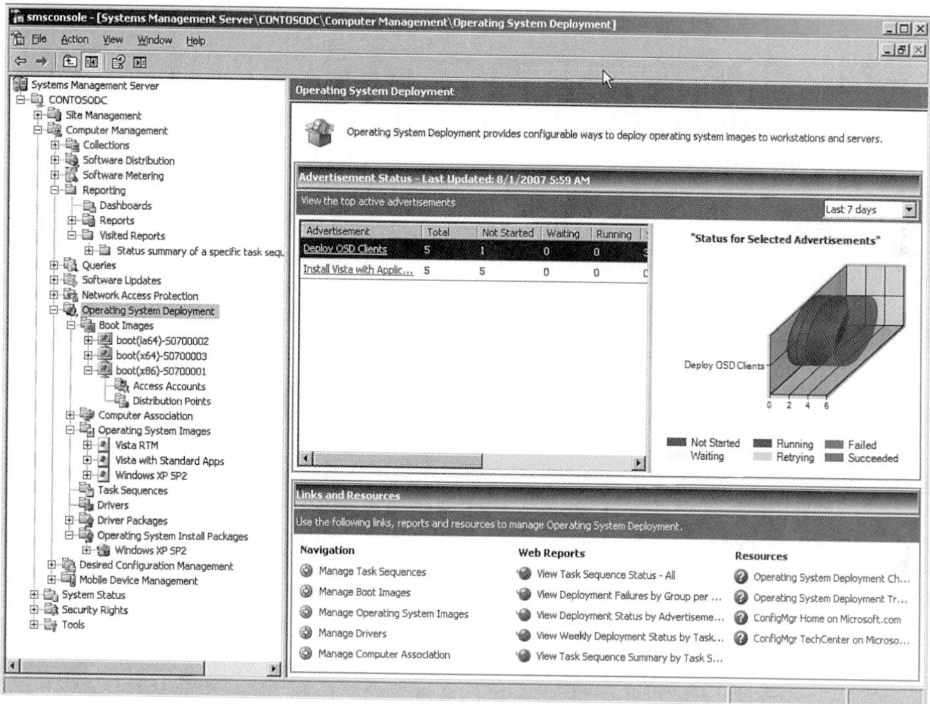

FIGURE 16-47 The SMS interface gives a nice overview of the OS deployment status, and clicking the items loads a full report.

Summary

This chapter has discussed the possibilities of WDS and its deployment capabilities. Some of the technologies are carried over from previous deployment solutions such as SYSPREP, but WDS is definitely a next-generation solution. Both Windows Vista and Windows Server 2008 share the same deployment mechanism and component-based structure, and anything concerning deploying Windows Vista also applies to Windows

Server 2008. In terms of raw deployment of an OS, WDS can also be used to push Windows XP, for example.

Good planning is key to success with deploying any environment, so take time to document the right content for your images, both desktop and server. After the WDS environment is configured to meet your needs, as discussed in the "Installing Windows Deployment Services" section, you can customize your images and create automated deployments using the new XML-based answer format, which is facilitated via the Windows System Image Manager tool that is part of the essential WAIK. Consider your network environment in your planning. If you are using any kind of network protection—for example, Network Access Protection, which stops network access until machines have a certain level of health—you need to make sure your newly deployed servers either meet initial health requirements or can access servers while quarantined that can resolve any health deficiencies.

There are plenty of third-party solutions for deployment, but Windows Server 2008 provides a great in-box solution that does an awesome job of deploying OS images, especially when paired up with WAIK. For larger environments, the add-on capabilities of a solution such as SCCM add network-based driver management, task sequences containing "next steps" such as software deployment, and offline deployment facilities that can do almost anything.

CHAPTER 17

Managing and Maintaining Windows Server 2008

With an operating system as large, complex, and functionally rich as Windows Server 2008, the operating system is only as good as the tools available to expose this functionality, configure it, and manage it on a day-to-day level.

Chapter 3, "Installing and Upgrading Windows Server 2008," showed how the Initial Configuration Tasks (ICT) interface helps perform the initial configuration on a server, but this is designed to assist with the questions that are no longer asked as part of the installation process. It is just more setup; it does not help with the day-to-day running of Windows Server. Thankfully, however, there is something even better for day to day.

Although this chapter discusses the many snap-ins available via Server Manager, the functionality of Server Manager is available as part of the stand-alone snap-ins; these snap-ins are often found in the Administrative Tools folder. Access management tools outside of Server Manager if you want to manage another server, which most snap-ins allow via a connect-to-computer action. This functionality is disabled inside Server Manager because it can manage only the local server.

Server Manager

Server Manager is the biggest factor in effectively managing your Windows Server 2008 environment. Prior to Windows Server 2008, administrators had a tough time installing, configuring, and administrating the various components of Windows Server and the underlying operating system itself.

With Windows Server 2003, when an administrator installed a Windows feature, there were always issues. These concerns included what other components were required for proper functionality, what tools were used to manage the features, where the troubleshooting information was stored, how configuration could be automated—and that is just scratching the surface.

Server Manager brings together the entire process of managing a server operating system into a single interface; this interface is designed around the functionality a server provides, instead of being designed around individual components. Somewhat similar to this was the Computer Management console, which collected a large number of individual snap-ins that provided a good overview of the computer configuration in terms of event logs, services, resources, and so on. However, this console but did not provide any real focus on what a server does.

As previously discussed in this book, the guiding principle for Server Manager is how administrators think about their servers. If you ask an administrator to show you their server room, they don't point to "my Windows Server 2003 box, my Windows 2003 box, and my Windows 2000 box." Instead, they say "that's my domain controller; that's my File and Print server." Administrators think of servers by their role, or what they do, and not by the server operating system.

Windows Server Manager works the same way, with a server running both roles, which are major services offered, and features, which help the server perform its main role purpose. For example, Windows Backup is a feature, as it helps keep a server maintained by providing backup and recovery. That is the only way to add components to Windows Server 2008: by role or by feature. You no longer use Add/Remove Programs and add Windows Components. Simply tell the server a role or feature you need it to perform/use, and the operating system components are automatically added; this includes any pre-requisite services that are needed. This is made possible by the Component-Based Servicing (CBS) foundation that both Windows Vista and Windows Server 2008 are built on. The CBS helps track all dependencies across binaries, system resources, and configurations. This process also includes any changes to configuration of the operating system. For example, enable the Dynamic Host Configuration Protocol (DHCP) role, and the firewall is automatically updated to allow DHCP traffic to flow. If you remove the role from a server, the firewall exception is removed (unless this exception could be used by other roles and features). For example, the Domain Name System (DNS) port is used only by the DNS role; if the DNS role is removed, the firewall exception for DNS would be closed. However, a role that uses port 80 (Hypertext Transfer Protocol [HTTP]) might not exclusively use that port, and so uninstalling IIS might not close the firewall exception.

Server Manager is your primary interface to managing Windows Server 2008. If you already installed Windows Server 2008 and used the

ICT, after you have completed the ICT, Server Manager automatically runs and launches at each Administrator logon. A shortcut to Server Manager is also placed in the Quick Launch toolbar on the taskbar, as well as being available in the Administrative Tools group.

In the Windows 2008 final release, Server Manager cannot connect to remote servers. It can manage only the local server. Future versions will support remote server management.

Navigating Server Manager

When Server Manager is launched, initially it runs as a two-pane Microsoft Management Console (MMC) environment with the Console/Navigation tree pane and the Details pane, as shown in Figure 17-1.

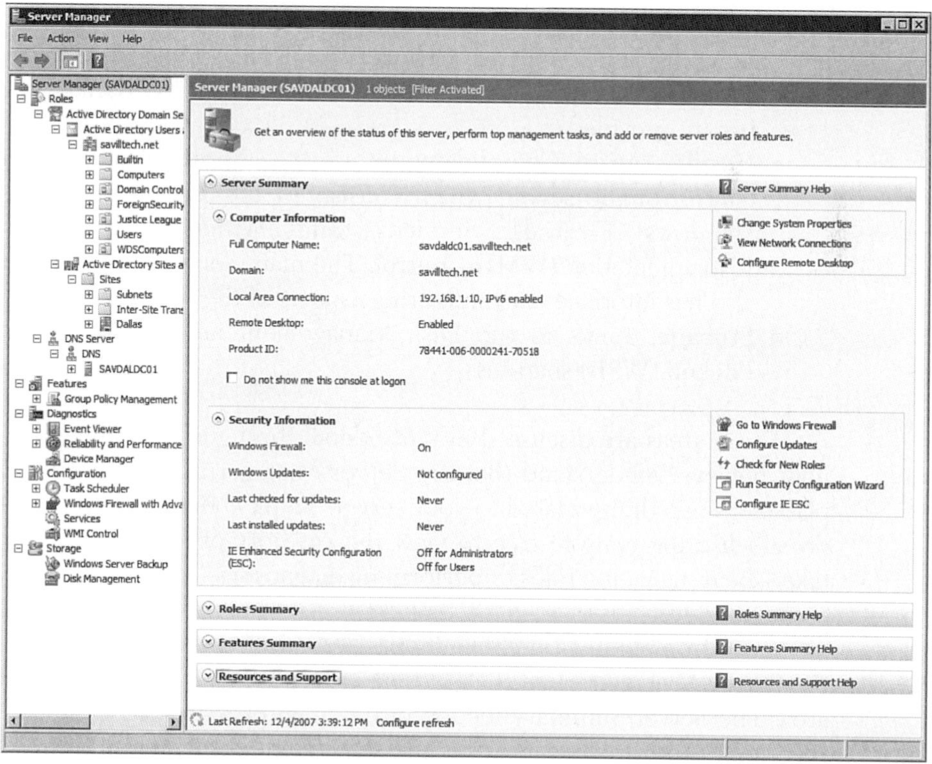

FIGURE 17-1 The main Server Manager home screen.

The Console tree pane breaks the functionality of the Server Manager into five main areas:

- **Roles**. Enables the administrator to install, remove, and manage roles for the server. Contained within roles is a child node for each role; this in turn has child links to the MMC snap-ins used to manage the Role functionality. For example, the Active Directory Domain Services (ADDS) role has links to the Active Directory Users and Computers MMC snap-in and the Active Directory Sites and Services MMC snap-in.
- **Features**. Enables the administrator to install, remove, and manage features for the server. As with roles, there is a child node for each installed feature, which in turn has child links to the MMC snap-ins used to manage the Feature functionality.
- **Diagnostics**. Links to the snap-ins used to troubleshoot and diagnose problems, such as performance issues. Links to the Event Viewer, Reliability and Performance, and the Device Manager snap-ins are provided.
- **Configuration**. Consolidated interface to the snap-ins for granular control of the server, which consists of the Tasks Configuration, Windows Firewall, Services, and Windows Management Instrumentation (WMI) Control. The main Server Manager screen also has interfaces to configuring aspects of the server.
- **Storage**. Links to the Disk Management and Windows Server Backup (WSB) snap-ins.

These areas are discussed in more detail throughout this chapter; for now, however, understand that the Server Manager is your central go-to place for everything related to your server. Think about what you want to do and use the console tree to view the category of action you want to take—be it managing roles or performing diagnostics—and the tools needed are readily available.

Aside from all this functionality in the Console tree, the main page of the Server Manager, when the Console tree root is selected, is a powerful area. The Server Summary section of the main page looks a little like the ICT content; this is because it is the same content. After you've finished your initial configuration of the server, use Server Manager to configure, so the main screen has easy access to those features you most want to configure or view.

The Server Summary is broken into two areas: Computer Information and Security Information. The Computer Information area provides detail on the fully qualified domain name of the computer if it is part of a domain or just the NetBIOS name if it is only in a workgroup. The domain or workgroup that the server is joined to is displayed, along with the network adapters in the server and the IP address information for both IPv4 and IPv6. It shows either the actual IP address, if statically assigned, or a notification that the address was assigned via DHCP. The enablement state of Remote Desktop is displayed along with the Product ID and, if the product is not activated, the number of days left in the grace period. An option to not display the Server Manager at logon is also available by selecting Do Not Show Me This Console at Logon.

Displaying this information is fine, but what if you want to change it? To the right of the displayed information are three links to control panel applets that enable the configuration of the attributes displayed. The applets are the System control panel applet (to modify the computer name and domain/workgroup membership via the Computer Name tab), the Remote Desktop via the Remote tab, and the Network Connections control panel applet for the LAN connection configuration.

The second area of the Server Summary is the Security Information, which gives critical information relating to the security of the server. For Server Manager, that means whether the Firewall is turned on or off, how the server is being updated, when updates were last checked for, and when updates were last installed. The state of the Internet Explorer Enhanced Security Configuration is also shown, which you probably remember from Windows Server 2003. This is that great bit of functionality. Whenever you look at a Web page, you are prompted to indicate whether you want to mark the web site as safe or ignore such considerations for now.

Similar to the Computer Information area, to the right of the Security Information section are links to configure the Windows Firewall, configure the automatic updating of the server, run the Security Configuration Wizard, and turn the IE ESC on or off for users and administrators. Additionally, run the Check for New Roles link, which looks for any new roles that might be available for the server based on any updates made. The security aspects of Windows Server 2008 are covered in Chapter 4, "Securing Your Windows Server 2008 Deployment," so they are not discussed here.

The next section of the main Server Manager is a summary of the roles, which displays each role installed on the server and a summary of its status for the past 24 hours (see Figure 17-2). Do not confuse this status with the health of the role. Although it is an indication, it shows the worst type of event that is in the log for the services related to the role in the past 24 hours. In the example, there was an error event logged in the past 24 hours for both ADDS and DNS. However, both issues were resolved many hours before, and the services are now both running healthily. Additionally, if a monitored server is stopped, the role also shows as having encountered an error. The icon can show the role in Error, Warning, or Information event log state. Click one of the roles to open the Roles main status page to get more information and see the Event logs that are being summarized. On the right side of the Roles Summary are links to navigate to the Roles area of Server Manager and to Add or Remove Roles.

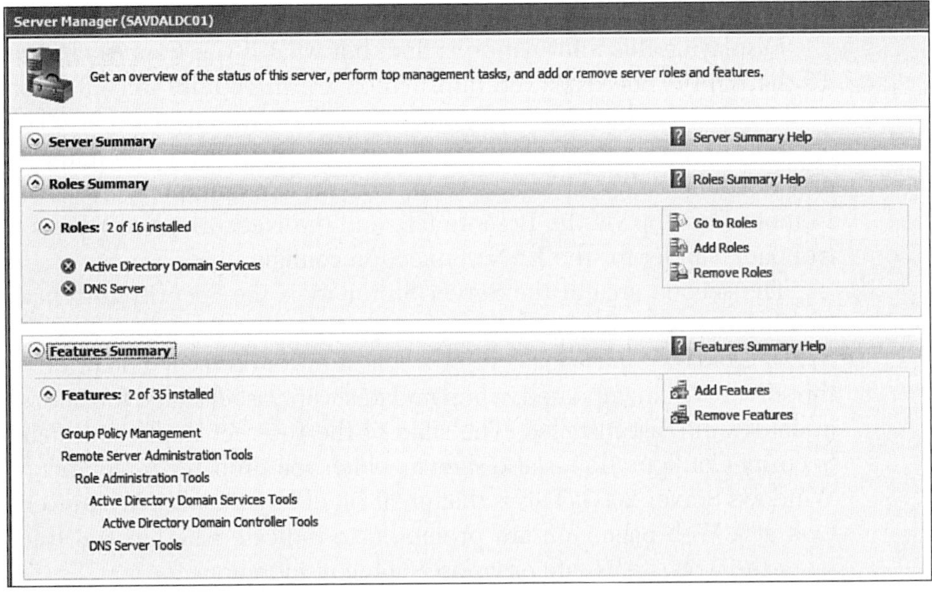

FIGURE 17-2 The Roles and Features area of the Server Manager overview page.

The Features Summary section lists the features that are installed and has links to Add or Remove Features. No status is given for the features because typically they help facilitate a role's duties and do not, on their own, provide a service. There are exceptions to this. Windows Internet Name Service (WINS), for example, provides a direct service. However, the experience for features is not as integrated as with roles, and no summary information is given about the state of a feature. You simply see which features are installed.

The final section of the main Server Manager page is the Resources and Support section, as shown in Figure 17-3; this is a common theme throughout Server Manager. As you walk through the roles in Server Manager, each role has its own resources section.

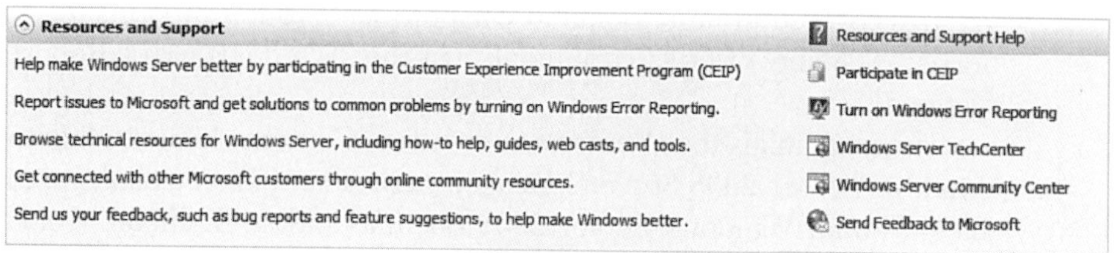

FIGURE 17-3 The Resources and Support section of the Server Manager main page.

The first area of configuration is the participation in the Customer Experience Improvement Program (CEIP); this is used by Microsoft to gather information about the usage of the Microsoft products installed and problems encountered. No identifiable information is sent to Microsoft. However, you can optionally give information about the number of servers and desktops in your organization and the type of industry in which your company operates. More information on CEIP can be found at http://www.microsoft.com/products/ceip/EN-US/default.mspx. By default, CEIP is not enabled, but there is no harm in enabling it; the information gathered helps shape future releases and helps Microsoft better address how the products are used.

The next item is Windows Error Reporting (WER), which enables configuration of what to do when an error occurs. There are four levels of participation:

- Send detailed reports to Microsoft for errors
- Send summary reports to Microsoft for errors
- Request permission before sending a report to Microsoft for errors
- Never send a report to Microsoft

If a report is sent to Microsoft, and it is a known issue, a response is returned that notifies you of potential fixes or workarounds. For this reason, it is recommended that you enable WER. If Microsoft does not know the problem, the information contained in the error report helps them start working on a fix. Many different products have WER support, including Windows XP, Vista, and Office. If you belong to a larger organization, use Corporate Error Reporting (CER), which is an error-reporting server locally installed in the organization. It receives the error reports generated in the company that would normally be sent to Microsoft via a Group Policy configuration. IT administrators can see an overview of the crashes in their environment, including problem trends, and then forward selected crash dumps to Microsoft (manually and automatically) as appropriate.

WER is covered in more detail in Chapter 20, "Troubleshooting Windows Server 2008 and Vista Environments," in the "Windows Error Reporting" section.

The next link is the Windows Server TechCenter, which is a link to the Windows Server 2008 Server Manager page. That page has links to information on all Windows Server 2008 documentation, TechNet Webcasts, step-by-step guides, and much more. It's a great resource center.

The next link is to the Microsoft Communities web site, where you can find information from blogs, newsgroups, user groups, and other community type resources at http://www.microsoft.com/communities/default.mspx.

The final link is to the Windows Server 2008 feedback web site at http://connect.microsoft.com/WindowsServerFeedback, which enables you to log feature suggestions and bug reports.

The last configuration item, which applies to all aspects of Server Manager, is a refresh of the information displayed. By default, Server Manager refreshes information every two minutes, which includes the event logs displayed in role summaries and the overall information. This refresh can be modified by clicking the Configure Refresh link at the bottom of the details pane of Server Manager, which opens the Refresh Options dialog (see Figure 17-4). The refresh interval can be disabled or set to an interval in units of minutes, hours, or even days (not sure how useful a day refresh would be, but it is an option). You can always force a refresh by pressing F5 or selecting Refresh from the Server Manager context menu.

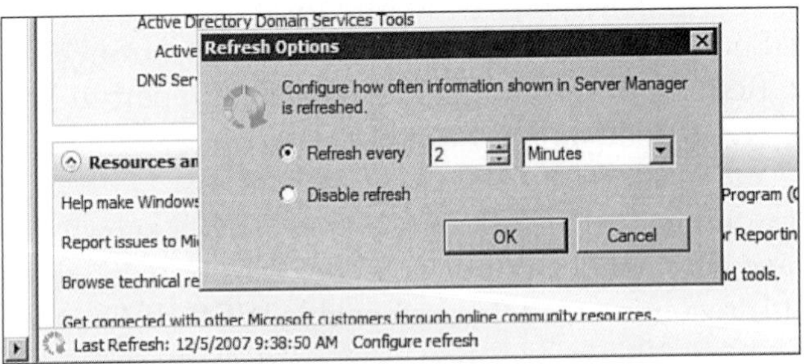

FIGURE 17-4 Configuring the Server Manager refresh.

Managing Roles

The main role of Server Manager is being the interface that manages what your server does, and what your server does is controlled by what roles the server has—that is, "that's my domain controller, that's my DNS server, that's my file server," and so on.

On the Server Manager main page, the Roles Summary displays a list of roles that are installed on the server and the role's health state based on event logs and monitored services for the role. Click on one of those roles to be redirected to the actual Roles entry under the Roles console tree item. However, before looking at a particular role, let's look at the main Roles page. Like the Server Manager main page, the Roles main page has the same Roles Summary section; this shows the installed roles and their event log status over the past 24 hours, plus the option to Add and Remove Roles.

Role Summary

After the Summary section is a section for each installed role, which includes an icon to set the Role information to be shown or hidden. In Figure 17-5, everything has been collapsed (the arrow points down, but clicking the arrow "drops down" the information to display it), except for ADDS.

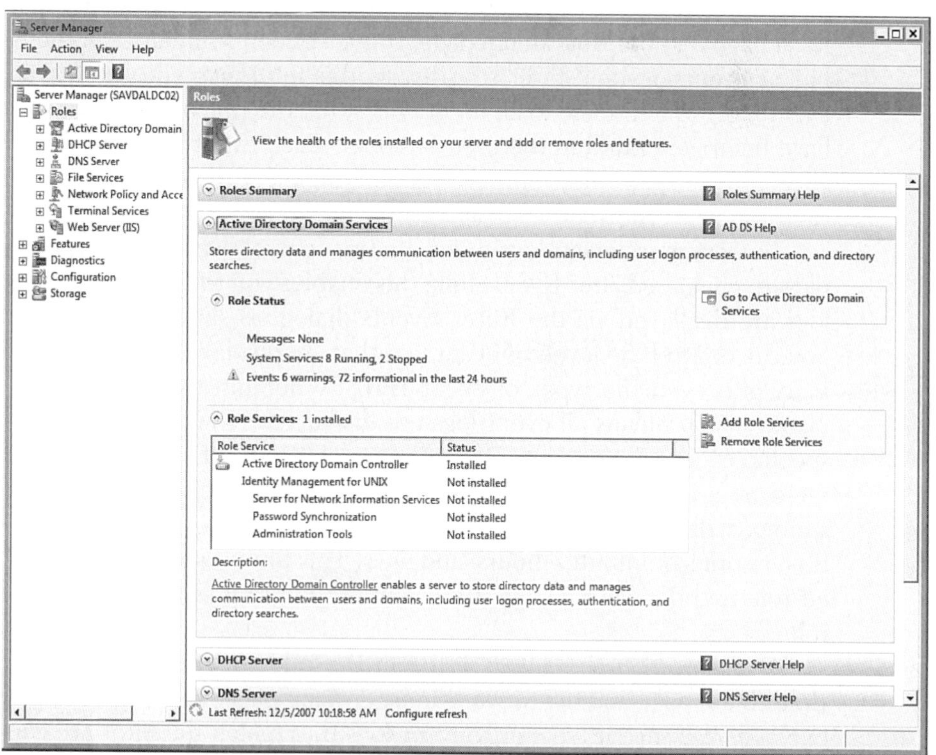

Figure 17-5 The main Roles page with only ADDS displayed.

Each Role section displays the status of the role; this includes an overview of any messages conveyed via the role, the status of all the services that are related to the role, and a summary of the event logs related to the service in the last 24 hours (grouped by event severity type).

Role services is also displayed for ADDS, which takes a little bit of explaining. Several roles for Windows Server 2008 are major duties that a server performs. However, some of those roles have multiple sub-roles, which are known as role services for the role. For example, ADDS has a core role service of Active Directory Domain Controller and an optional role service centered on integration with Unix (refer to Figure 17-5). If a role is already installed, and you want to modify the role services for the role, use the Add Role Services and Remove Role Services links that are part of the Role Services section.

The real power of the Server Manager and the knowledge it conveys comes to the forefront when you select a specific role. By selecting a role, you instantly get insight into the health of the role and guidance on how to manage it.

As shown in Figure 17-6, the Summary section for the role gives information on the three critical areas around a role. In the Server Manager main page and the Roles main page, you have seen summaries of the number of event logs and their severity. In this interface, you see the actual event logs, which relate to all the services that the role owns or utilizes that have been generated in the past 24 hours. Each event log can be double-clicked to see the full event information, or select the event log and click the Properties shortcut.

To view more event logs or have more control over the event logs displayed, click the Filter Events link; this enables you to control which event logs are displayed via the Filter Events dialog, as shown in Figure 17-7. You can control the levels of event logs that are displayed in the event summary and even the types of event IDs. By default, the event ID box is blank, which means all event logs are displayed. However, to check for a specific event ID or event IDs, enter the IDs in the Event IDs box, separated by a comma. You can also change the time period over which the summary displays event IDs. The default 24 hours can be changed to any time in units of minutes, hours, and days. This filter is specific to the selected role and does not change the event log filtering of any other installed role.

Also note that the events listed in the role summary filter up to the Roles main page and the Server Manager main page. If you filter to display only a certain event type, only event logs that match the filter are considered for the overall count in the Roles main page; this also applies to the "worse" event log type in the Server Manager main page. For example, filter to only show information events; even if you had many error or critical event logs for your service, the Roles main page shows that only your role has had *x* number of information events. The main Server Manager page shows the role as an information state only, which might be misleading. So, take care in filtering.

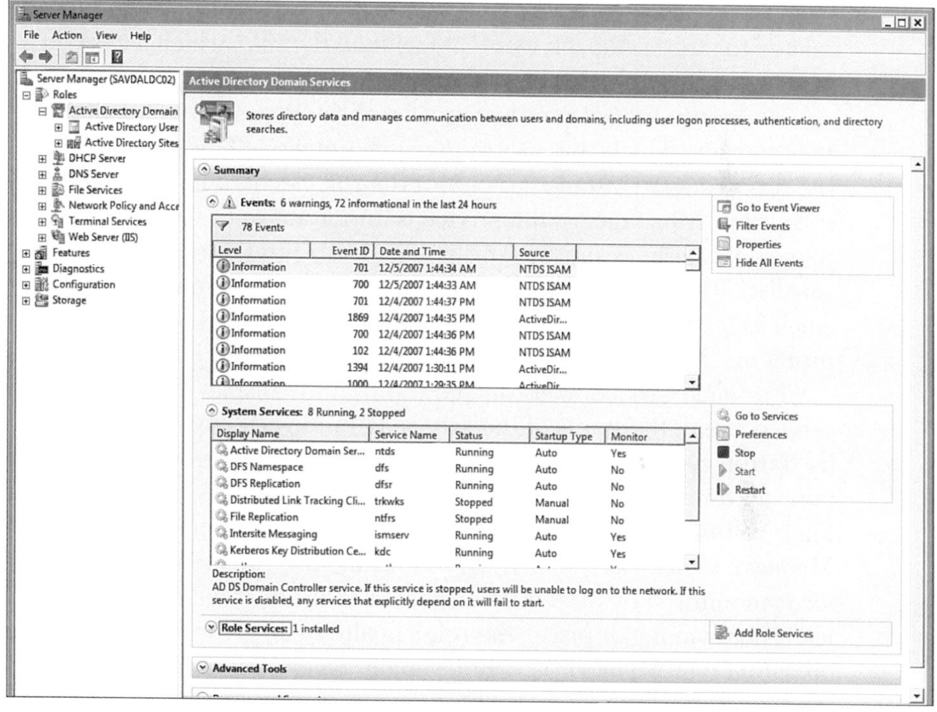

FIGURE 17-6 The ADDS role summary.

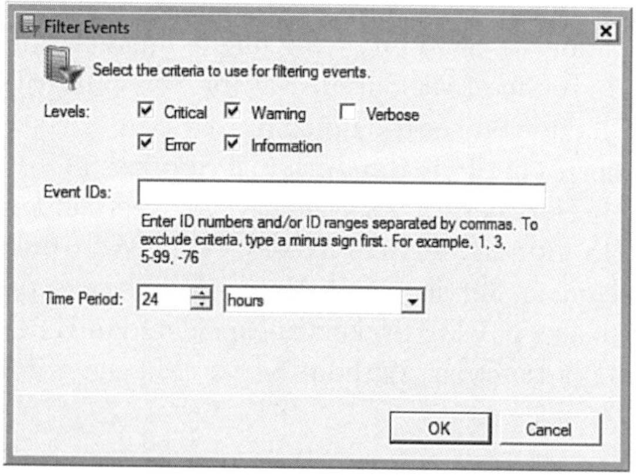

Filter Events

Select the criteria to use for filtering events.

Levels: ☑ Critical ☑ Warning ☐ Verbose

☑ Error ☑ Information

Event IDs:

Enter ID numbers and/or ID ranges separated by commas. To exclude criteria, type a minus sign first. For example, 1, 3, 5-99, -76

Time Period: 24 hours

OK Cancel

FIGURE 17-7 Controlling the event logs.

To view the events related to other services, select those roles or click the Go to Event Viewer link to be redirected to the Event Viewer snap-in under Diagnostics. This Events summary is fantastic. Previously, when there was a problem, you checked the event log; among the huge number of events listed, you might have been able to identify events that relate to the service problem you were having. With the Server Manager, navigate to the role you are experiencing problems with; you see a list of events related to the various services that facilitate the role, which leads you to the next important information.

Under the Events summary is a list of the System Services that provide functionality, which the role requires to function. This does not mean all the services were installed as part of the role; some might be used by multiple roles. It just means the service is important to the functionality of the role, so its status is shown. This is also useful. In the example, the ADDS role lists 10 separate services. If people were having trouble with a process (such as logging on), after you see there are no event IDs that relate to that problem, check if any services are stopped that should be running.

For each service, you can see the friendly display name, the internal service name, the status of the service (Running, Stopped, and so on), and its startup type (which controls whether the service starts automatically at boot-up time, if it has to be manually started, or if it's just disabled). The final column indicates whether the service is monitored by System Manager, which can be changed by clicking the Preferences link. If a service is monitored by System Manager for the role, it means that if the service is not running, it places the role's health in an error status (as displayed on the Server Manager and Roles main pages). By default, only the core services for a service are monitored—those that, if not running, prevent the role from functioning. The Preferences dialog enables you to set other services as monitored that affect the status of the role's health (see Figure 17-8). For example, if you have migrated your domain using DFSR for replication of SYSVOL, you might enable monitoring of the DFS Replication service. Without DFSR, the SYSVOL will not replicate, which impacts functionality of the domain.

Another example is the Terminal Services (TS) Gateway role. If you examine the services for TS Gateway, you see that key monitored services include IIS Admin Service, World Wide Web publishing, RPC/HTTP Load Balancing Service, and Network Policy Server. All of these are required to accept RDP packets encapsulated in HTTP traffic, which is the TS Gateway's function. Without Server Manager, if TS Gateway was not functioning, you might be trying to work out what the dependencies are. With Server Manager, select the role and see the state of all services that the role requires.

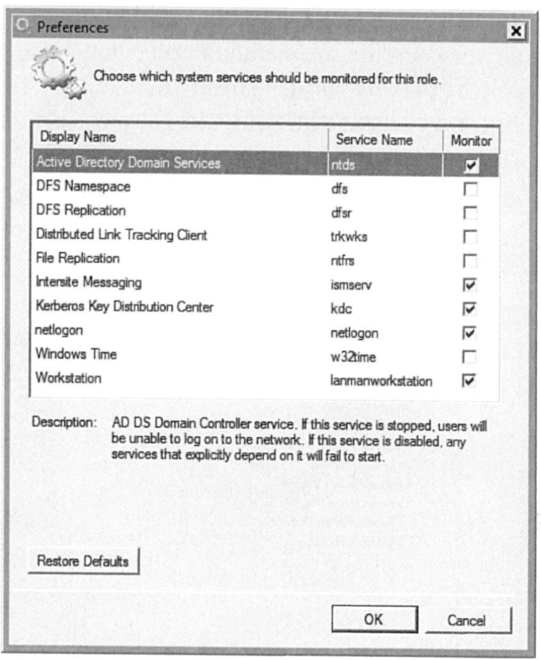

FIGURE 17-8 Modifying the services to monitor.

The final element of the role summary is the Role Services element, which enables you to add and remove role services for installed roles. The particular role services vary depending on the role. Figure 17-9 shows the main Add Role Services page for the File Services role. As role services are added, the main wizard navigation display on the left side of the dialog updates to show if any configuration is required for the role services. As shown in the figure, when Distributed File System role service was selected, a new stage in the Add Role Services was added, which comprises multiple steps. This dynamically updating stage and progress display is designed to make sure administrators are fully aware of where in the install process they are. This is the same format for installing roles. It's frustrating to be installing something with no idea where in the install process you are. With the progress dynamically updating and showing all the role service installation stages, it's always clear where in the install process you are.

The navigation area can be used to jump between configuration pages by clicking the various entries, so you don't have to keep clicking Previous or Next to jump around in the role services configuration. If you're at the Confirmation stage of the wizard and want to add another role service, click the Role Services entry in the navigation pane. Just remember that to modify role services for an installed role, you have to use the Add and Remove Role Services wizards. These are accessed via the Roles summary page, as opposed to using the Add and Remove Role wizards.

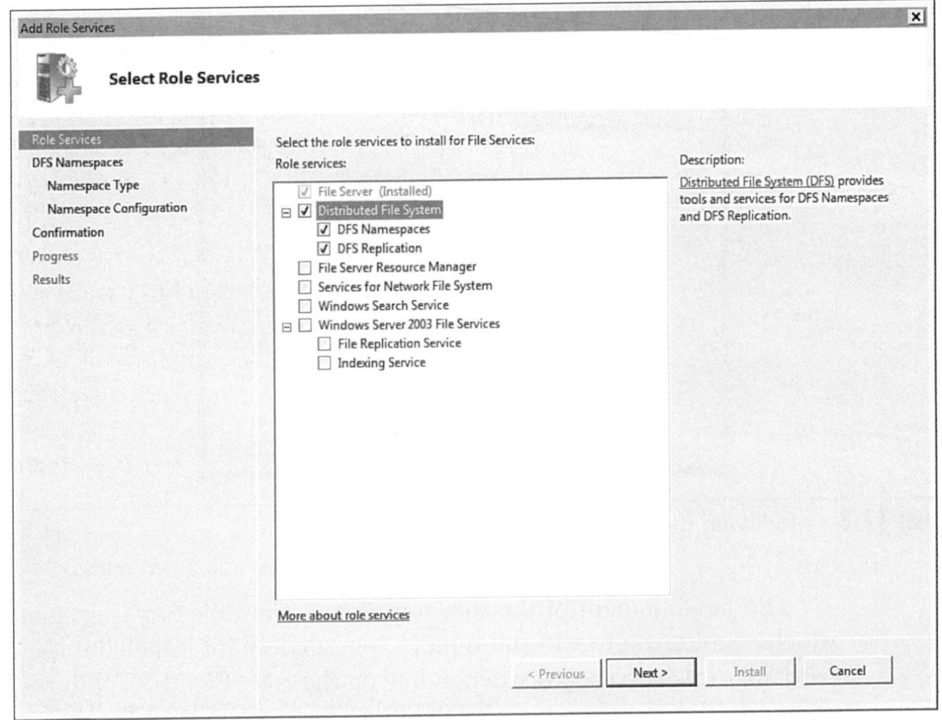

FIGURE 17-9 Adding role services for a role.

So, that is the Summary components of a role. The console tree/navigation pane area has links to the core MMC snap-ins that expose the functionality of the installed roles required for managing the role day to day. Figure 17-10 shows the navigation pane for Server Manager with several roles installed.

Those of you familiar with Active Directory (AD) are probably asking, "Where is AD Domains and Trusts?" The explanation from Microsoft is the AD Domains and Trusts tool is a management tool for AD, but it is not considered a component that adds new functionality to the server role. So, the snap-in is installed when the role is installed and available via the Administrative Tools, but is not exposed as a functional component tool in the console tree. It's a fine line, but don't worry about it too much—Microsoft still links you to the tool in a different way. They expose the snap-ins used the most to manage the role; the typical administrator uses AD Users and Computers and even AD Sites and Services, but infrequently accesses AD Domains and Trusts. It's not just a shortcut to the snap-in. Each snap-in can be expanded, and the full navigation options are available. They are all fully integrated via the Server Manager.

FIGURE 17-10 The snap-ins for various installed roles.

Advanced Tools

The core MMC snap-ins that are used to manage the role day to day were just discussed. However, there are other tools that could be used less frequently or are not MMC snap-ins (for example, the licensing management tool for TS). The Advanced Tools section lists other tools that are used to manage, configure, and troubleshoot the selected role. Not all roles have an Advanced Tools section if there are not additional tools needed for the role.

AD has a great Advanced Tools section, which is broken down into three groupings. The first grouping is that of tools related to ADDS, which includes links to AD Domains and Trusts, the ADSI Edit tool, DCPromo, ldp, netdom, ntdsutil, and repadmin (see Figure 17-11). These are all the tools used to manage and troubleshoot an AD domain (except for dcdiag, which is cool). The next grouping includes more generic directory services tools that work with AD, but would also work with other directory services via LDAP—for example, tools to add/remove/query objects in a directory service. Finally, a group of networking tools are listed, such as nslookup and nltest. For tools that are command-line–based, select the tool, and a command-line window is opened with the help for the tool displayed.

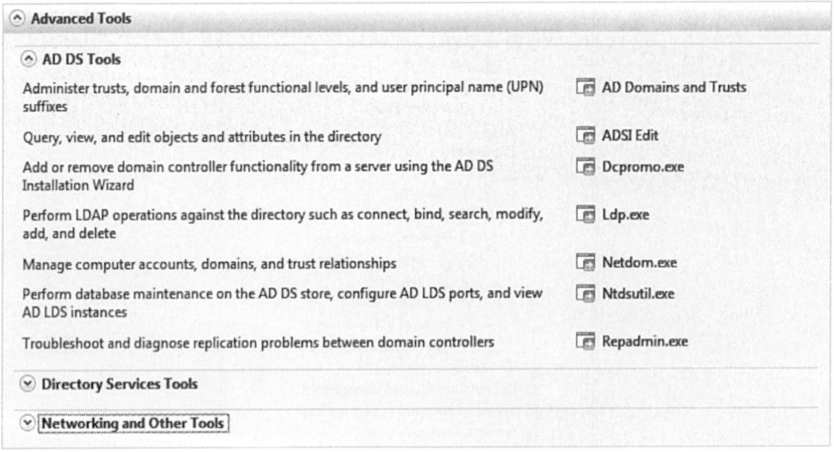

Advanced Tools

AD DS Tools

Administer trusts, domain and forest functional levels, and user principal name (UPN) suffixes	AD Domains and Trusts
Query, view, and edit objects and attributes in the directory	ADSI Edit
Add or remove domain controller functionality from a server using the AD DS Installation Wizard	Dcpromo.exe
Perform LDAP operations against the directory such as connect, bind, search, modify, add, and delete	Ldp.exe
Manage computer accounts, domains, and trust relationships	Netdom.exe
Perform database maintenance on the AD DS store, configure AD LDS ports, and view AD LDS instances	Ntdsutil.exe
Troubleshoot and diagnose replication problems between domain controllers	Repadmin.exe

Directory Services Tools

Networking and Other Tools

Figure 17-11 The Advanced Tools area for the ADDS role.

Resources and Support

The final area of a role's main page is the Resources and Support section, as shown in Figure 17-12 for the File Services role. Resources and Support contain a list of next steps and recommendations that are related to the role. However, they are high level and are not based on the actual role services installed. Instead, they offer guidance concerning subjects related to the role; they might encourage the installation and configuration of role services not currently installed. They even affect roles or features that are separate from the selected role, but would have a positive impact on the role. In the File Services case, many of the recommendations relate to other roles; for example, configuring a fail-over cluster for file service high availability and extending disk volumes. Each recommendation can be selected and a description shown at the bottom of the section with a hyperlink to more detailed information about implementing the suggestion.

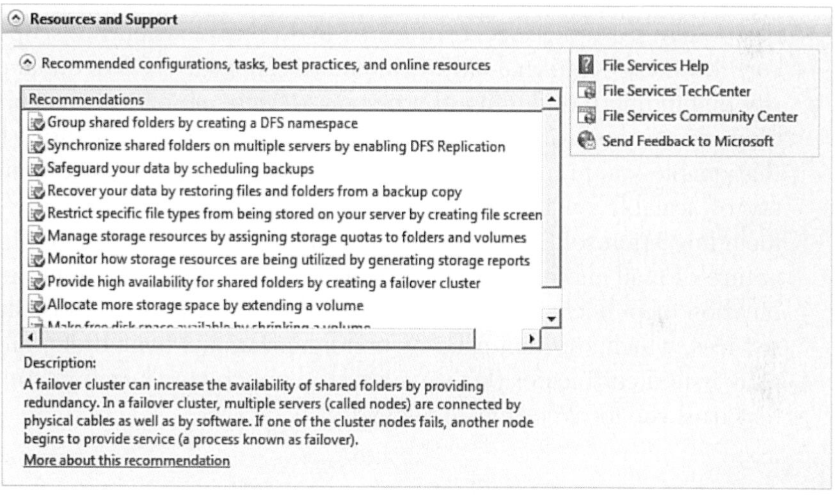

FIGURE 17-12 Resources and Support for File Services.

One of the great items next to the recommendations is a list of resource pointers that are the go-to places for information on the role—for example, TechCenter specialist areas and community areas.

In a nutshell, this is the main page for a role. It gives great insight into the status of a role via its event logs and service information; it also provides easy access to the common and advanced tools that relate to the role, plus recommendations and resources to get the most out of the role.

Available Roles

Throughout this book, the various roles that can be installed are discussed in great detail; this includes any configuration options specific to the role when installing. A walkthrough of installing each role and the configuration options is thus not included here. Instead, let's quickly review all the roles that are available with a brief description.

Active Directory Certificate Services (ADCS)

ADCS provides the services for creating and managing public key certificates used in most aspects of security today; this includes HTTP encryption (HTTPS) that is vital to many Windows roles, wireless network security, VPNs, IPsec, Encrypting File System (EFS), and other software security systems that require encryption or digital signatures. Although publicly trusted certificate authorities exist, such as Verisign and RapidSSL, the use of publicly trusted issued certificates is expensive when the scope of the certificate use is internal only. Companies can use ADCS to enhance security by binding the identity of a person, device, or service to a corresponding private key within their organization. ADCS also includes features that enable you to manage certificate enrollment and revocation in a variety of scalable environments. Other products can leverage the ADCS, including Microsoft Exchange, which can use the certificates for digital signature of mail and encryption. In many environments, it might be a combination of publicly issued certificates (that are used for externally facing services, which are then used by nonorganizational computers) and internally issued certificates (for services used only by organizational machines that trust the local certificate authority).

Active Directory Domain Services (ADDS)

ADDS stores information about users, computers, and other devices on the network in a security boundary known as a domain. With resources and users, members of a domain or trusted hierarchy of domains (known as a *forest*), access to company-wide information is secure and no burden on the user. ADDS is required on the network to install directory-enabled applications, such as Microsoft Exchange Server, and for applying other Windows Server technologies, such as Group Policy.

Active Directory Federation Services (AD FS)

AD FS provides Web single-sign-on (SSO) capabilities across separate organizations, enabling authentication across multiple Web applications in various companies using a single user account. AD FS accomplishes this by securely federating, or sharing, user identities and access rights, in the form of digital claims, between partner organizations after a federation trust has been established.

Active Directory Lightweight Directory Services (AD LDS)

Previously known as Active Directory Application Mode (ADAM), AD LDS provides a directory service that organizations can use to store information specific to an application that is separate from the organization's main AD. AD LDS runs as a non-operating-system service and does not require deployment on a domain controller. Multiple AD LDS instances are supported on a single server. AD LDS supports key features of ADDS, including multi-replication of AD LDS instances, providing a highly available environment.

Active Directory Rights Management Services (AD RMS)

AD RMS provides granular protection on supported documents via AD RMS-enabled applications to not just protect documents and other digital information, but also to control the actions that authorized consumers of the information can take. For example, an RMS-protected document can be configured so certain recipients can view the document but not print or copy from it.

Application Server

Application Server comprises several components that are responsible for the deployment and managing of .NET Framework 3.0 applications. These components include the .NET Framework, Web Server (IIS) Support, Message Queuing, COM+ Network Access, TCP Port Sharing, and Distributed Transactions. Application Server also includes the Windows Process Activation Service Support, which enables the invocation of applications remotely via protocols such as TCP, HTTP, and named pipes; this is used by several components in Windows Server 2008.

Dynamic Host Configuration Protocol (DHCP) Server

The DHCP enables servers to assign, or lease, IP addresses to computers and other devices that are enabled as DHCP clients on the network. DHCP servers can also configure other aspects of IP including DNS servers, WINS servers, domain names, routers, and many other options.

DNS Server

DNS resolves host names to Internet Protocol addresses, both IPv4 and IPv6. Services that use host names make a request to a DNS server to resolve the name to an IP address to enable IP-based communication. Reverse lookups can also be performed, allowing a host name to be found from an IP address if the DNS server is configured with the necessary zones.

DNS in the Windows server operating system was originally a statically maintained configuration, with administrators adding records to DNS for various types of hosts and services. This changed with Windows 2000, enabling dynamic updating of DNS via server and client requests. Integration with DHCP was also added, enabling DHCP servers to register records on behalf of clients that cannot register for themselves.

Fax Server

Fax Server sends and receives faxes and enables you to manage fax resources, such as jobs, settings, reports, and fax devices, on the server or on the network.

File Services

File Services provides technologies for storage management, which includes control of the types of files stored on a server via file screens and powerful quotas, file replication, distributed namespace management, Network File System, and support for UNIX clients.

Hyper-V

Formally known as Windows Server Virtualization, Hyper-V provides the services to create and manage virtual machines and their resources. Each virtual machine is a virtualized, sandboxed computer system that operates in an isolated execution environment with an allocated amount of memory and CPU utilization. File systems of virtual environments are enabled via virtual disks, which are files on the file system of the Hyper-V server. Because each environment is totally isolated from the other environments in physical terms, multiple operating systems can exist on a single physical server. Hyper-V requires 64-bit, virtualization-enabled processors. Hyper-V ships out of band, and the latest version needs to be downloaded from Microsoft; the version supplied with Windows 2008 is just a beta version.

Network Policy and Access Services

Network Policy and Access Services delivers a variety of methods to provide users with local and remote network connectivity, to connect network segments, and to allow network administrators to centrally manage network access and client health policies. With Network Access Services, you can deploy VPN servers, dial-up servers, routers, and 802.11-protected wireless access. You can also deploy RADIUS servers and proxies and use the Connection Manager Administration Kit (CMAK) to create remote access profiles that enable client computers to connect to your network.

Print Services

Print Services enables the management of print servers and printers. A print server reduces administrative and management workload by centralizing printer management tasks. Also part of Print Services is the Print Management Console, which streamlines the management of all aspects of printer server management, including the capability to remotely scan a subnet for printers and automatically create the necessary print queues and shares.

Terminal Services (TS)

TS enables users to access Windows-based programs that are installed on a terminal server or to access the Windows desktop itself, from almost any computing device that supports the RDP protocol. Users can connect to a terminal server to run programs and to use network resources on that server. Windows Server 2008 has technologies that allow the RDP traffic necessary for communication with a terminal server from a client to be encapsulated in HTTPS packets. That means all communication is via port 443, meaning no special holes are required in the firewall for access to terminal servers within an organization from the Internet.

Universal Description, Discovery, and Integration (UDDI) Services

UDDI Services provides Universal Description, Discovery, and Integration (UDDI) capabilities for sharing information about Web services within an organization's intranet, between business partners on an extranet, or on the Internet. UDDI Services can help improve the productivity of developers and IT professionals with more reliable and manageable applications. With UDDI Services, you can prevent duplication of effort by promoting reuse of existing development work.

Web Server (IIS)

Web Server (IIS) enables sharing of information on the Internet, an intranet, or an extranet. It is a unified Web platform that integrates IIS 7.0, ASP.NET, and Windows Communication Foundation. IIS 7.0 also features enhanced security, simplified diagnostics, and delegated administration.

Windows Deployment Services

Use Windows Deployment Services to install and configure Microsoft Windows operating systems, which are stored in the Windows Imaging format remotely on computers via Pre-boot Execution Environment (PXE) boot ROMs. Windows Deployment Services provides a great way to not only deploy Vista and Windows Server 2008 but also older operating systems by creating a custom Windows image containing a reference installation. For example, you could deploy an XP installation that has been prepared for duplication via SYSPREP.

Other Facets of Roles

Many of the roles discussed in this section also have several role services, as described earlier in the chapter. There are also often dependencies between roles. However, that is not a worry because the entire role structure is built on the CBS that understands dependencies. So, if a role is selected that requires other role services to be installed, those additional role services are automatically selected for installation.

Installing and Removing Roles

With Windows Server 2003, there was an optional concept of a role for some types of services. However, most people still used the Add/Remove Windows Components feature of the Add or Remove Programs control panel applet. That is no longer an option with Windows Server 2008; you can only use Server Manager. Run the Programs and Features control panel applet in Windows Server 2008, click the Turn Windows features on or off link, and then Server Manager is started.

Microsoft received a lot of feedback that a server often has more than one role, and so it is possible to install multiple roles at once with the exception of ADDS. The other feedback was that the installation of roles should be intelligent, and the roles and configuration offered should be pertinent to the state of a server. For example, installing DFS Namespace does not enable the creation of a domain-based namespace if the server is in a workgroup.

With Windows Server 2008, the installation media is not needed after you install the operating system. Disk space is cheap, so all the install files for the various components of Windows Server 2008 are stored locally within the Windows installation structure, namely the winsxs folder, which contains all manifests and optional components of the operating system. In fact, the files never leave the winsxs folder. All the files in system32 are hard links to the file stored in the winsxs folder.

Server Manager uses a wizard for the installation of roles that has a dynamic navigation area on the left side to show where in the installation process you currently are; this is in addition to enabling you to instantly select stages of the install without having to use the Previous and Next buttons multiple times. In addition to installing the role, the Server Manager often prompts you to perform basic configuration to get the role up and running. It's rare that an administrator just wants to install a role. The administrator wants the service that the role enables, so to save the initial fact finding to learn how to configure a role, the Server Manager allows basic configuration to be performed during the Role installation.

To install a new role, select the Roles item in the navigation/console tree pane of Server Manager and click the Add Roles link, which launches the Add Roles Wizard. The first page of the Add Roles Wizard is a Before You Begin page; this displays some key server settings to perform before you start hosting roles on the server:

- Ensuring the Administrator account has a strong password; once you start exposing services on a server, ensure it is secure and cannot be easily compromised. This is especially important if a server is Internet facing.
- Configuring the correct IP settings, which should include configuring static IP addresses to enable clients to consistently access servers and allow IP-specific firewall rules to be configured.
- Ensuring the server has the latest security updates.

After ensuring these, check the Skip This Page By Default option so you are not prompted again and click the Next button.

The main Server Roles page is displayed, as shown in Figure 17-13. The existing installed roles are shown in gray and cannot be modified. That means you cannot uninstall the role (run the Remove Roles wizard for that), nor can you change the role services for that role (run the Add Role Services wizard from the Roles page to do that).

As you select a role, the navigation pane on the left side changes to reflect both the selections available/required for the selected role and the configuration choices. You also find additional stages to the role installation are added after you select specific role services and even when certain configurations are made that lead to other configuration choices. The stages that are in black can be selected to jump to that stage, while those in gray cannot yet be selected. In Figure 17-14, the navigation pane changes as multiple roles are selected. After all roles have been selected, click Next to move to the next stage of the Role installation wizard. Hyper-V is not listed as a role because this poor server does not have a processor that supports virtualization. So the Hyper-V update that enables the installation of the role cannot be installed.

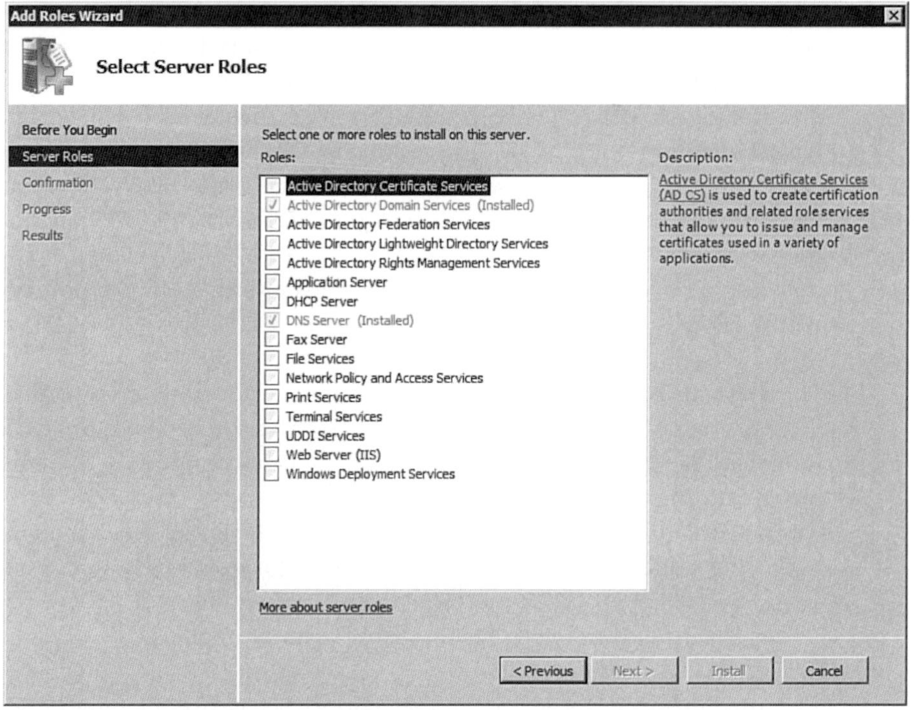

FIGURE 17-13 The main roles page.

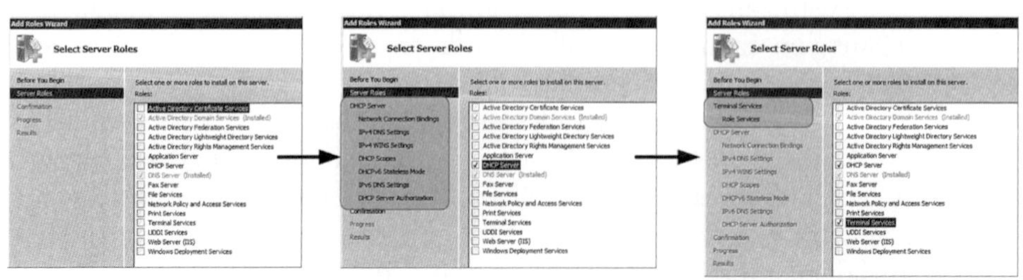

FIGURE 17-14 The changing navigation pane, showing the stages of the wizard.

The rest of the wizard now depends on the roles selected. Let's walk through part of it. The first stage of a specific role is an introduction to the role, which explains what the role does and provides any special notes. For example, the terminal services introduction page tells you that you don't need the role if all you want is to remote into the server for administrative purposes; you just need to enable Remote Desktop. In addition, one or more links might be provided for further information on the role. After you have read the introduction information, click Next; if there are no configuration or role service options, this moves you to the next role introduction. If there are more choices, the wizard continues with the role configuration.

For TS, there are several role services that comprise the role. For example, install the TS Gateway role to access your servers from outside the lab without opening up RDP ports. Click the TS Gateway role, and you get a pop-up, as shown in Figure 17-15. This is where the power of the roles comes into play. The TS Gateway role knows it has dependencies on other roles and features, so a check is performed as to which of those are already installed. Any missing roles or features are displayed, asking the installer to say OK to adding these additional role services. If you click Cancel, the role cannot be installed. If you click the Why Are These Role Services and Features Required? text at the bottom of the dialog, the Windows Server help opens to a page that lists all the various role services and any antecedents the role service depends on (an *antecedent* is a program that another program depends on).

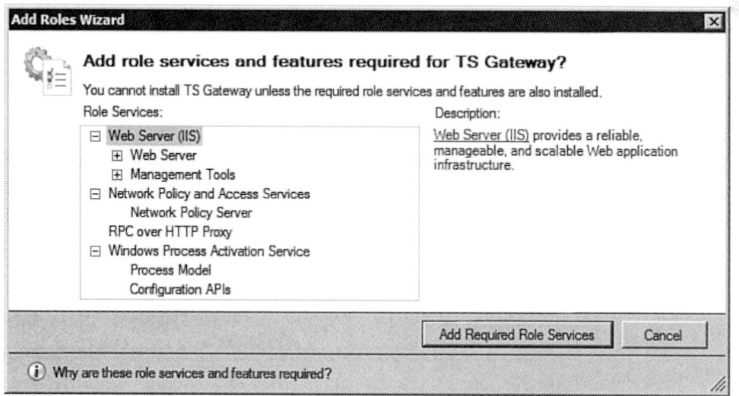

Figure 17-15 Additional roles and features required for a role service.

If additional roles are added, the navigation pane grows, with even more stages. TS now has more configuration stages because a role service has been selected, as shown in Figure 17-16. The rest of the stages are now role service-specific, which is discussed in those chapters specific to the role. If roles were added as part of a requirement of a role selected, although configuration and Role Service selection screens might be shown, click through them. The right role services are automatically enabled for you.

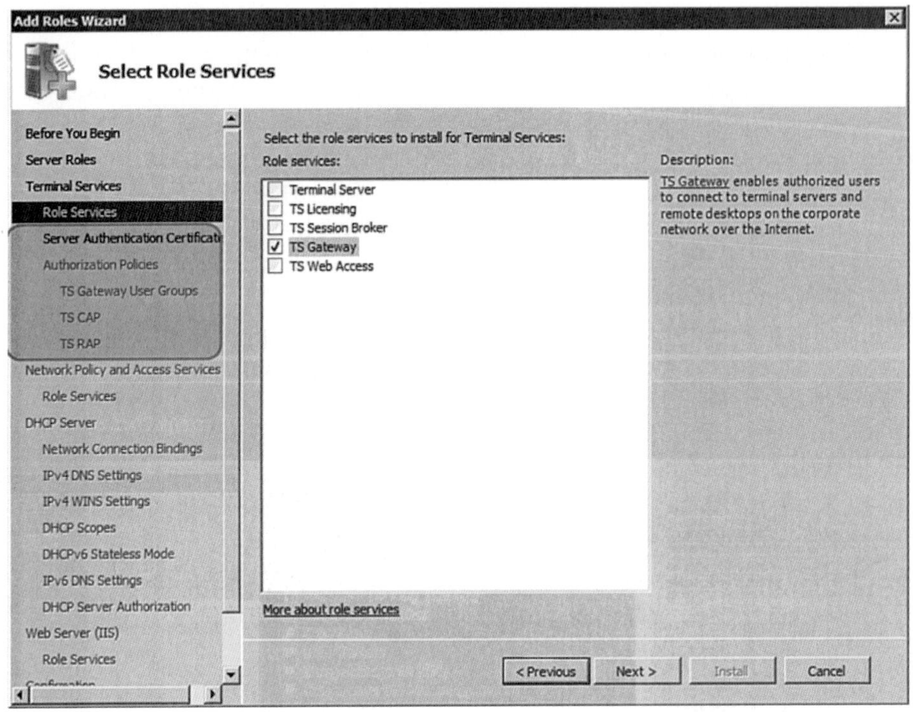

FIGURE 17-16 The role services for a role and new stages for the role installation.

At the end of the role service selections and configurations, a confirmation screen is displayed, confirming all the choices you made (see Figure 17-17). All the items in the navigation menu are black; this means if there is a setting in the summary that is not correct, you can click that stage in the navigation to jump right to it. To change your Server Authentication Certificate, you don't have to click Previous 14 times! There are several warnings. This is because you chose not to configure TS Gateway via the Add Roles wizard; you have an exported configuration file to import after the wizard finishes. The wizard sees that it's not configured and won't work, so it is letting you know users won't be able to use the feature until you configure it.

To save the summary information, click the Print, e-mail, or save this information link; this converts the information shown in the HTML, saves it as ServerManagerInstallationLog.html in the %windir%\Logs folder, and then opens it in IE for browsing.

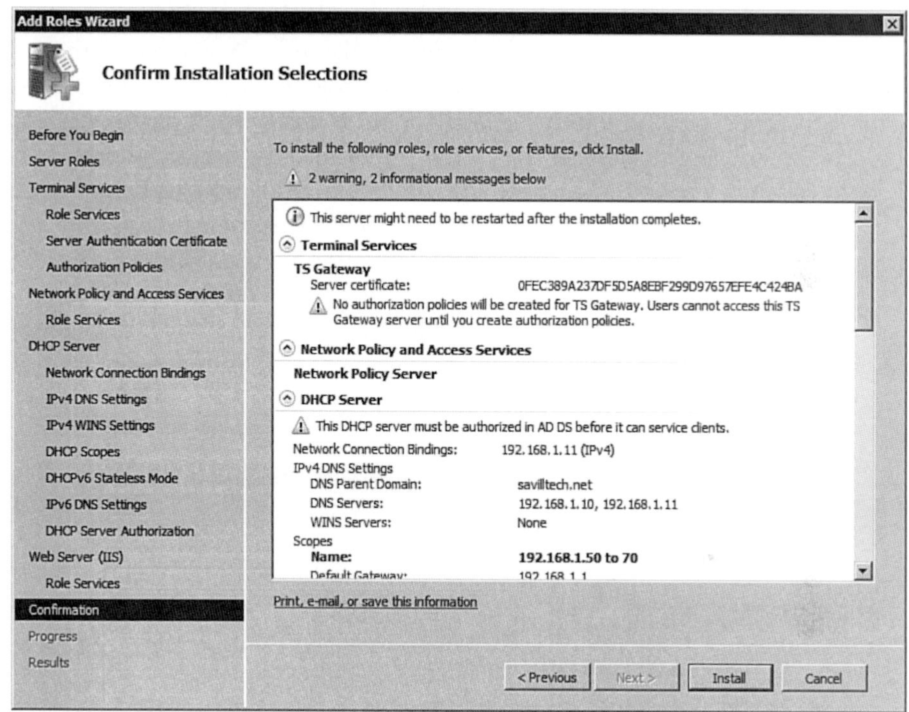

FIGURE 17-17 The confirmation screen for role installation.

After the settings are confirmed, click the Install button, and a Progress page shows the installation progress of each of the roles being installed. Now would be another good time to go get a drink—exactly for how long depends on the role being installed. After you come back, the wizard is on the Results page (hopefully) with a summary of the installation for each stage. You might have a warning about automatic updates not being enabled, which is just Microsoft pushing you to enable automatic updating and does not reflect a problem with the installation of roles. Once again, you can save the results to HTML via the Print, e-mail, or save the installation report link. Depending on the roles installed, you might need to reboot; after the reboot, when you log on, the Add Roles wizard launches to complete the installation.

Also behind the scenes as you add role services, any requirements of the system for the role are automatically performed. For example, if exceptions are needed in the firewall for a role service to function, the exception is automatically enabled.

Removing a role is the same process, except you run the Remove Role wizard. It has the same list of roles, but only the installed roles are selected and can be unchecked to remove the role. Note that if the role is checked, it stays installed. Unselect the role if you want it removed, so in the end, only the roles still checked are installed. In Figure 17-18, DHCP Server is unselected, so this role is removed. The rest of the process is the same, except you won't be asked for configuration options because you are removing. If you unselect a role that had dependencies on other role services, those antecedent role services are not removed. This is because those antecedent role services might be used directly on their own or by other roles, so it's not safe to remove them just because one role no longer needs them. If you are sure other role services are not required, manually remove them.

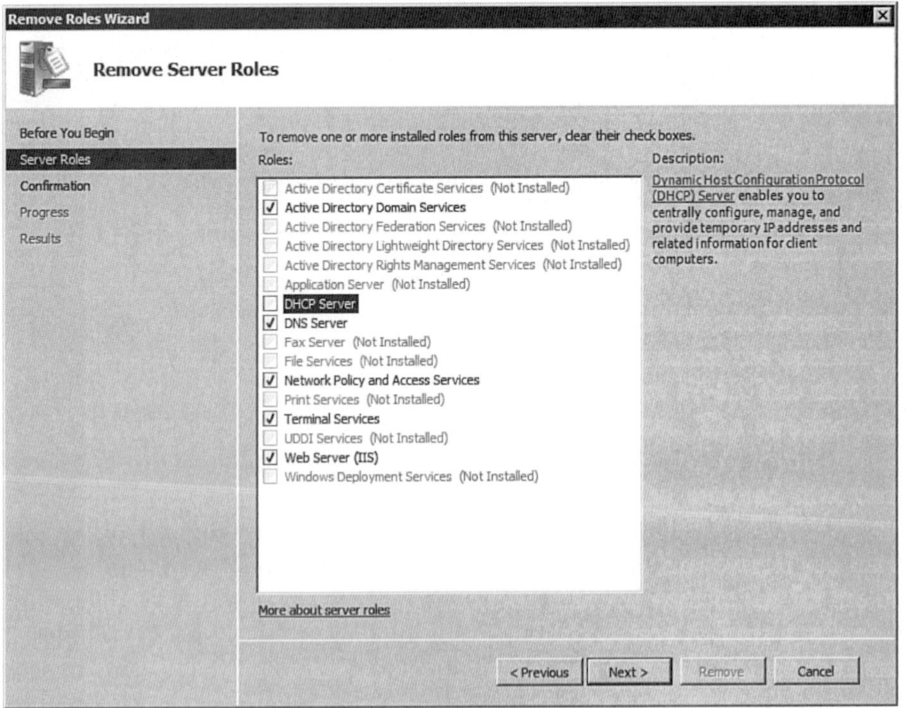

FIGURE 17-18 Removing the DHCP Server role.

Managing Features

If roles are the quarterbacks, then features are the offensive linemen. Although roles are the core purpose of a server, a feature helps the role do its job better or improves the functionality of a server. For example, Windows Backup helps manage a server and keep it available, clustering helps keep a service available through planned and unplanned outages, and the Desktop Experience helps administrators listen to music on a server while working. The next section is a breakdown of all the various features that are available.

Available Features

The available features include the following:

- **Microsoft .NET Framework 3.0**. Combines the key features of the .NET Framework 2.0 APIs with newer technologies for building applications, and this is used by several other roles and features. Also available as options for this feature are the XPS Viewer for viewing XML Paper Specification documents and the Windows Communication Foundation Activation components.
- **BitLocker Drive Encryption**. Helps to protect data on lost, stolen, or inappropriately decommissioned computers by encrypting the entire volume and checking the integrity of early boot components. Data is only decrypted if those components are successfully verified and the encrypted drive is located in the original computer. Integrity checking requires a compatible trusted platform module (TPM) or, with additional configuration, USB keys or passwords can be used.
- **Background Intelligent Transfer Service (BITS) Server Extensions**. Enable a server to perform file transfers using BITS, which exploits unused bandwidth on a network and enables resumable downloads from the last data received. If a 50MB file is downloading via BITS and the connection stops at 25MB, when the client reconnects, the download starts from the twenty-sixth megabyte.
- **Connection Manager Administration Kit (CMAK)**. Generates Connection Manager profiles.
- **Desktop Experience**. Includes features of Windows Vista, such as Windows Media Player, desktop themes, and photo management. Desktop Experience does not enable any of the Windows Vista features by default; you must manually enable them, and for some features, other services must be enabled. For example, to activate the Windows Aero theme, start the Themes service.

- **Failover Clustering**. Enables multiple servers to work together to provide high availability of services and applications. Failover clustering is often used for file and print services, and database and mail applications, in addition to other services like Exchange and SQL.
- **Group Policy Management**. Makes it easier to understand, deploy, manage, and troubleshoot Group Policy implementations. The standard tool is Group Policy Management Console (GPMC), a scriptable MMC snap-in that provides a single administrative tool for managing Group Policy across the enterprise. This is installed automatically when a server is promoted to a domain controller.
- **Internet Printing Client**. Enables you to use HTTP to connect to and use printers that are on Web print servers. Internet printing enables connections between users and printers that are not on the same domain or network. Examples of uses include a traveling employee at a remote office site or a remote employee in a coffee shop equipped with Wi-Fi access.
- **Internet Storage Name Server (iSNS)**. Provides discovery services for Internet Small Computer System Interface (iSCSI) storage area networks. iSNS processes registration requests, deregistration requests, and queries from iSNS clients.
- **Line Printer Remote (LPR) Port Monitor**. Enables users who have access to UNIX-based computers to print on devices attached to them.
- **Message Queuing**. Provides guaranteed message delivery, efficient routing, security, and priority-based messaging between applications. Message Queuing also accommodates message delivery between applications that run on different operating systems, use dissimilar network infrastructures, are temporarily offline, or that are running at different times. Message Queuing contains the Message Queuing Services (MSMQ) feature, support for Windows 2000 client features, and a DCOM proxy.
- **Microsoft Multipath I/O (MPIO)**. Along with the Microsoft Device Specific Module (DSM) or a third-party DSM, provides support for using multiple data paths to a storage device on Microsoft Windows.
- **Network Load Balancing (NLB)**. Distributes traffic across several servers, using the TCP/IP networking protocol. NLB is particularly useful for ensuring that stateless applications, such as a Web server running Internet Information Services (IIS), are scalable by adding additional servers as the load increases. If an application requires state maintained, then fail-over clustering should be considered.

- **Peer Name Resolution Protocol (PNRP)**. Enables applications to register on and resolve names from your computer, so other computers can communicate with the applications.
- **Quality Windows Audio Video Experience (qWave)**. A networking platform for audio and video (AV) streaming applications on IP home networks. qWave enhances AV streaming performance and reliability by ensuring network quality-of-service for AV applications. It provides admission control, run time monitoring and enforcement, application feedback, and traffic prioritization. On Windows Server platforms, qWave provides only rate-of-flow and prioritization services.
- **Remote Assistance**. Enables you (or a support person) to offer assistance to users with computer issues or questions. Remote Assistance enables you to view and share control of the user's desktop in order to troubleshoot and fix the issues. Users can also ask for help from friends or co-workers.
- **Remote Differential Compression**. Used as part of replication technologies to replicate only delta information in a compressed format so as to use minimal amounts of bandwidth.
- **Remote Server Administration Tools (RSAT)**. Enables remote management of Windows Server 2003 and Windows Server 2008 from a computer running Windows Server 2008 by enabling you to run some of the management tools for roles, role services, and features on a remote computer. Normally tools are installed as roles and features are installed. However, if you have a server that you want to use to administer other servers that have roles not locally installed, add the administration tools via RSAT. To manage from a client computer, download and install RSAT for Windows Vista SP1.
- **Removable Storage Manager (RSM)**. Manages and catalogs removable media and operates automated removable media devices.
- **Remote Procedure Calls (RPC) Over HTTP Proxy**. Used by objects that receive RPCs over HTTP. This proxy enables clients to discover these objects even if the objects are moved between servers or even if they exist in discrete areas of the network (usually for security reasons).
- **Simple TCP/IP Services**. Supports the following TCP/IP services: Character Generator, Daytime, Discard, Echo, and Quote of the Day. Simple TCP/IP Services is provided for backward compatibility and should not be installed unless it is required.
- **SMTP Server**. Supports the transfer of e-mail messages between e-mail systems.

system because of its features, with the number one being Hyper-V for virtualization to enable easier testing through virtualization. The Desktop Experience packs make 2008 more friendly and homey as a desktop OS.

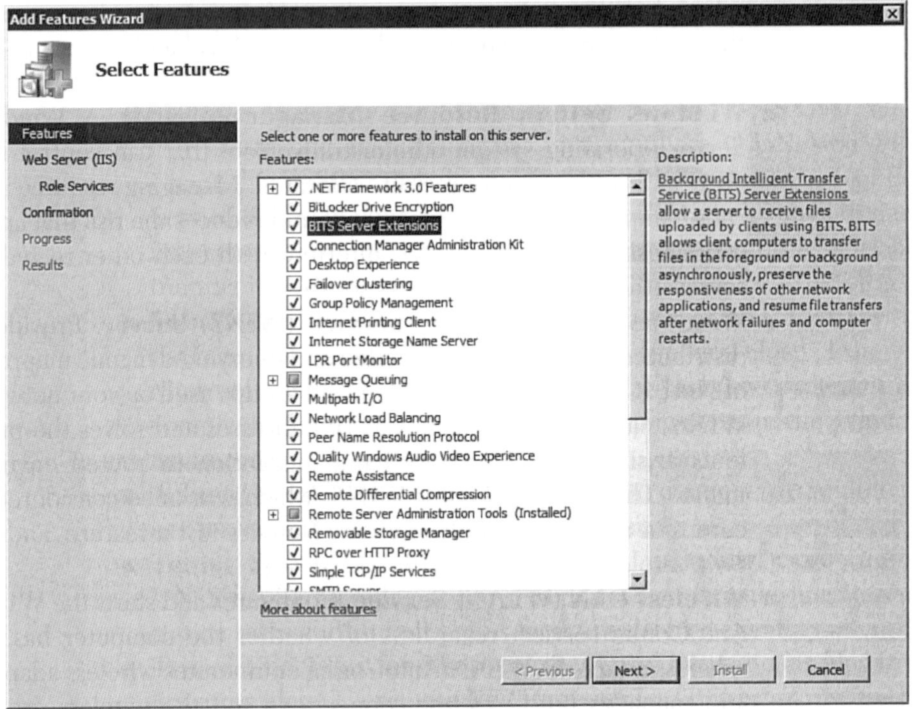

FIGURE 17-19 Adding features.

Click Next, and a confirmation of the features to be installed is shown; clicking Install completes the installation. In this case, Desktop Experience is installed, which requires a reboot (see Figure 17-20). Click Close, and you are prompted to reboot; it's a good idea to let it reboot, so click Yes. After the machine reboots and you log on as the same user that started the install of the feature, the wizard launches automatically and displays the completion of the feature installation in a Resuming Configuration mode. It then displays the final installation result.

To remove a feature, use the Remove Features wizard and unselect the features you no longer want installed, much in the same way as removing roles. If the feature is checked, then it will not be removed. You cannot have multiple Add or Remove Role or Feature wizards running at the same time, not even across different user sessions.

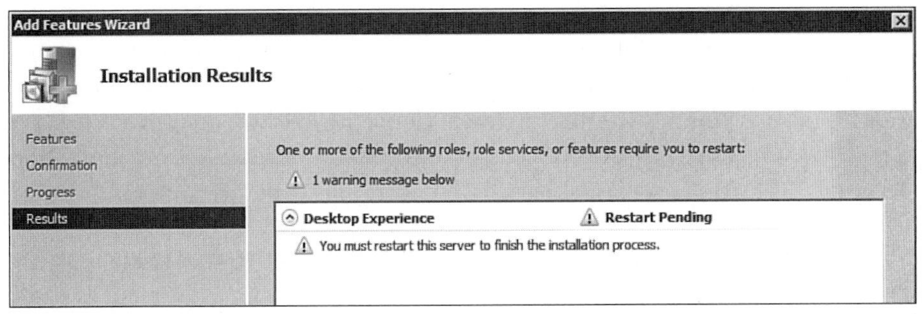

FIGURE 17-20 Reboot required.

Viewing Server Information

Server Manager is a central portal for managing the server, and is the quick-start place for all things server, including troubleshooting. Chapter 20 discusses the tools available, so Resource Monitor or Event Viewer are not covered here; however, let's look, at a high level, at the Diagnostics console tree item.

The Diagnostics node does not have a main summary page. It is just a grouping of the main tools that are used for Diagnostics, so there are no summaries of machine problems or links to resources. For diagnosing problems, look at Events, which are readily available now via the main page of a role. However, there are other times when you want to look at other event logs, so Event Viewer is your first item.

The Reliability and Performance MMC snap-in is the second child item for Diagnostics and is a great new feature. As discussed in Chapter 20, previously there was Task Manager, which provided insight into CPU and Memory usage, along with some network stats. Now, Reliability and Performance gives a more complete view of your machine's performance, in addition to a reliability monitor; this displays a score for your server over time, summarizing various types of failure and software uninstalls.

The last item is Device Manager, which groups the various hardware devices known to your system by category such as disk drives, display adapters, processors, and so on (see Figure 17-21).

For each device in Device Manager, select Properties, which exposes varying information. You always see a minimum of three tabs. The first is a General information tab about the device, such as device type, manufacturer, and the device status. A Driver tab displays the current driver installed, who created the driver, its version, and if it's digitally signed. As shown in Figures 17-22 and 17-23, the Driver Details button can be selected to see all the files that form the driver. A button, Update Driver, enables a new driver to be specified for supported types of devices. For example, you can update the driver for a video device but not for a core system resource such as the processor, which uses drivers that are embedded in the OS.

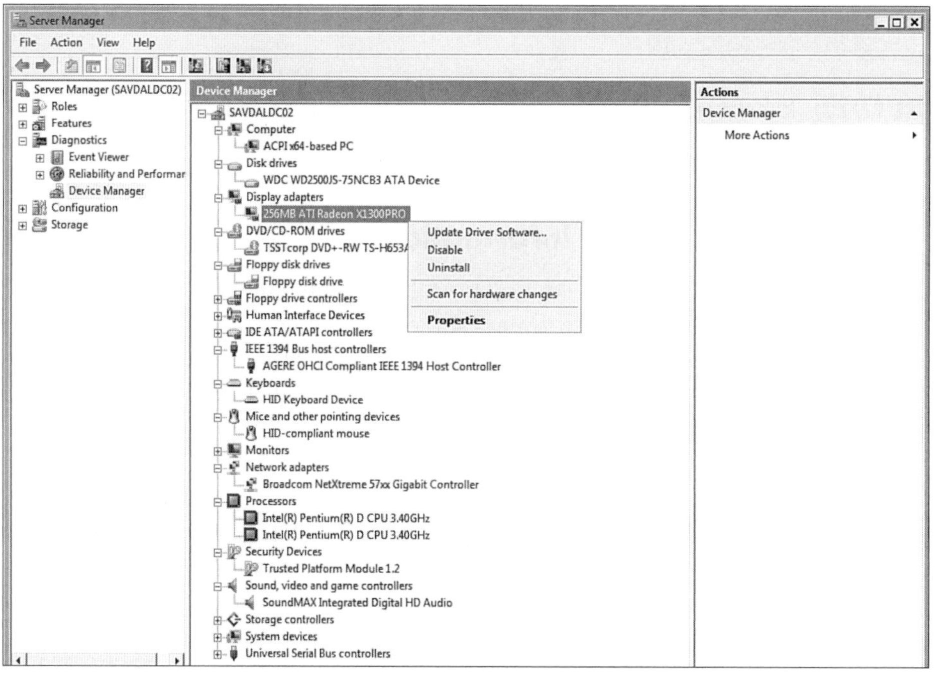

FIGURE 17-21 Device Manager information.

If a new driver is installed for a device, and after the update the device does not function correctly, you can roll back to the previous driver via the Roll Back Driver button. This is a useful feature and saves time and effort scrambling around for the old driver disk when things go wrong.

You also have options to disable the device and to uninstall the driver that is used for the device. That is sometimes necessary if a device has been installed using the wrong driver, and to install things correctly, the device must be detected without a suitable driver. All devices also have a Details tab, which enables you to view various properties of a device.

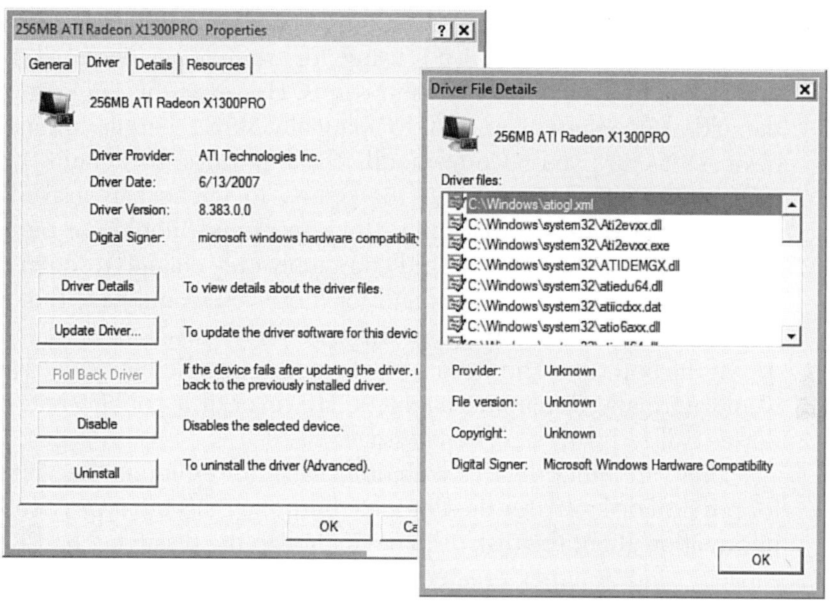

FIGURE 17-22 Device driver information.

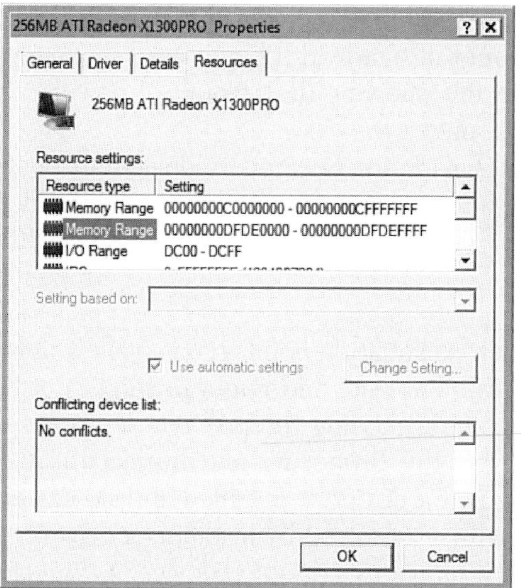

FIGURE 17-23 Resources for a device.

You might see a Resources tab for certain types of devices that displays the various resources a device is using; for example, a video card shows the memory ranges that it uses and interrupts. However, this is a long way from the old days where you had to manually select certain interrupts for devices. It's rare you have to modify these settings; by default, Use automatic settings is selected and the option to uncheck is grayed out, as Windows has detected that the settings work and should not be modified or physically can't be. You would commonly only change resource settings for non-plug and play devices, and for those you would have the option to uncheck the use of automatic settings.

At the bottom of the Resources dialog is a Conflicting device list, which would normally display no conflicts. However, if a conflict is found, the device is listed with an error message.

There are other devices with other tabs (for example, the Volumes tab for physical disks). After the Populate button on this tab is pressed, volume information about the disk displays, including the disk type, partition style, capacity, and volumes created. You see a Regions tab for DVD drives, enabling you to switch region a fixed number of times to watch, for example, Region 2 movies from England. You also see a Power Management tab for devices that support Power Management facilities. For USB hubs, you have an Advanced tab that shows the speed at which the hub is operating and the amount of bandwidth being used by devices on the hub. There is also a Power tab, showing the amount of power each USB device is using in milliamps (mA).

To avoid having to check every device for possible problems, devices that are not functioning normally are automatically made visible when you expand their category. The device is marked with one of the following icons:

- A black exclamation point (!) on a yellow field indicates the device is in a problem state and might or might not be functioning. A problem code explaining the problem is displayed for the device when you view the Properties and inspect the General tab. A common cause is if a device is installed and no driver is present, which can normally be resolved by installing a driver.
- A red X indicates a disabled device. A *disabled device* is a device that is physically present in the computer and is consuming resources, but does not have a protected-mode driver loaded.
- A black down arrow in a white circle indicates a user-disabled device and can be enabled by selecting Enable from the devices context menu.

- A blue i on a white field on a device resource in Computer properties indicates that the Use Automatic Settings feature is not selected for the device and that the resource was manually selected. This is informational only and not a problem.

Normally, when a hardware device is installed, it is automatically detected by the system, and you are prompted to indicate how the device should be installed via the Found New Hardware dialog. If a driver is not locally installed, you are prompted if Windows Update should be checked for a driver, or whether you have a driver on media. However, force a scan for new hardware by right-clicking on the computer name and selecting Scan for hardware changes or clicking the scan for hardware change button (the little computer icon with a magnifying glass over it). For older hardware that is not plug-and-play compatible, select the Add legacy hardware option from the context menu of the server name in device manager; follow the instructions that enable a search to be performed to try to find the device or to manually select the type of device and driver that are needed.

Installing hardware is an interesting topic. By default, you need to be an administrator to install hardware, and for servers, you probably should keep it that way. But for desktop computers, and maybe test servers, use Group Policy to allow certain types of devices to be installed by normal users. See Chapter 5, "File System and Print Management Features," for an example of using Group Policy to allow non-administrators to be delegated rights. To enable this, navigate to the Computer Configuration, Administrative Templates, System, Driver Installation part of a Group Policy Object and enable the Allow Non-Administrators to Install Drivers for These Device Setup Classes policy and enter the device IDs of the device that can be installed.

Adding a Driver to the Driver Store

Windows Server has a driver store that it checks when devices are installed. When a device is installed that requires a new driver, you are prompted to install the driver. To avoid this, pre-stage a driver into the driver store without the device being present via the `PnpUtil` command, as follows. Administrator credentials are needed to modify the driver store unless the driver is digitally signed or the device type for the driver has been allowed via Group Policy:

```
Pnputil -a <path>\<driver name>.inf
```

This command adds the driver specified and its dependent files to the driver store, and it is therefore available for any new hardware. If you don't want to modify the driver store but instead want to add additional paths to be searched when new hardware is added, use the Registry editor to add additional locations to the HKEY_LOCAL_MACHINE\SOFTWARE\Microsoft\Windows\CurrentVersion\DevicePath value. But do NOT remove the existing %SystemRoot%\inf entry. Just add additional paths after it, separated by a semi-colon (;).

Configuring Windows Server

This book looks at configuring the server to offer services. However, there are a few general configuration items exposed by the Server Manager that are covered here; this includes the Configuration console tree items, which consist of the Task Scheduler, Windows Firewall, Services, and WMI Control. Windows Firewall is discussed in Chapter 4, but let's discuss the others.

Task Scheduler

It's common to want to run a task regularly; for example, a backup of the system or a disk defragmentation. Although you can set an alarm clock as a reminder to perform the task every day, a better option is to have the operating system automatically perform tasks at certain times or when certain conditions, or triggers, are met.

In earlier operating systems, the `AT` command allowed you to schedule commands to run at specific times and run under the Schedule service, which ran under the local system context. Although that user account for the service could be changed, it could only be changed at the service level, so all jobs running under the schedule service had to run as the same user.

Windows 2000 introduced the Task Scheduler graphical interface, which offered more granularity, enabled scheduled jobs to run under different security contexts, and had better auditing of the job's execution. Windows XP improved on this with a command-line interface (CLI), `SCHTASKS`.

In Windows Server 2008 and Windows Vista, the Task Scheduler is more powerful than ever and is used a great deal by the operating system to perform many of its actions. Figure 17-24 displays the Task Scheduler environment. There are a lot of scheduled jobs, with many running that you probably have no recollection of creating, which is fine because you didn't—the system did.

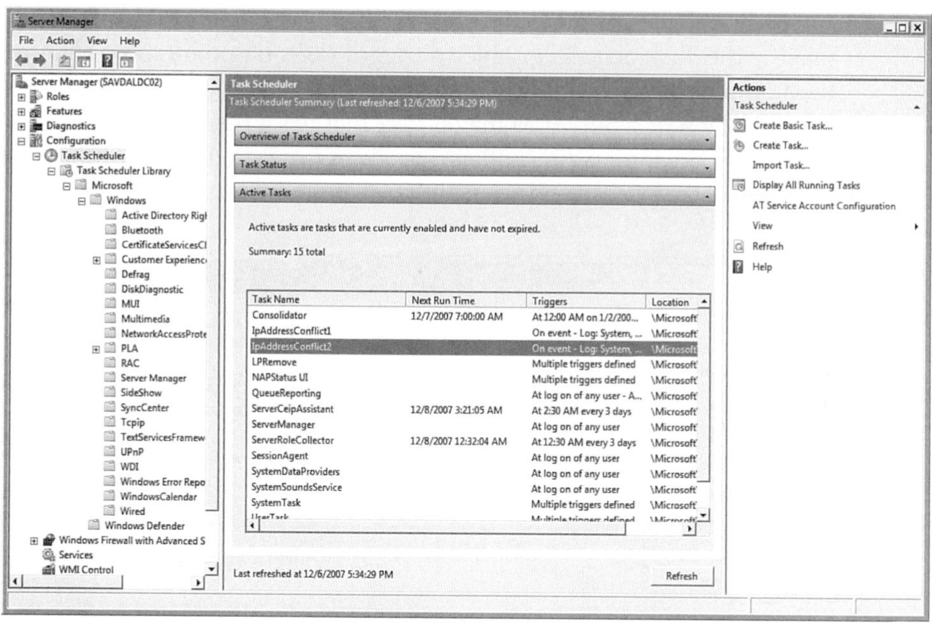

FIGURE 17-24 The main Task Scheduler window.

If you feel brave, select the View action and choose Show Hidden Tasks. The operating system adds many scheduled tasks. It breaks them down into a library of tasks broken down by component. The main details pane has three sections. The first is just an overview of Task Scheduler, which explains what Task Scheduler does. The second is a summary of all the task executions over a certain time period and their status—that is, if the run was successful, and the start and end time. By default, the last 24 hours are displayed, but you can modify this to show the past hour, 24 hours, 7 days, or 30 days.

The third section, which is in the example, shows the Active Tasks. These are tasks that are enabled and have not expired. Some of these might seem familiar. For example, there is an IPAddressConflict. Double-click on this, and you are redirected to the Task Scheduler Library, Microsoft, Windows, Tcpip section, where you see two tasks. Explore the details to see that the task is triggered by a particular event ID, and if the Actions tab is selected, you can see the command that is run (see Figure 17-25). This is the functionality that displays a pop-up on your screen when someone else is using the same IP address as you, which is triggered by an event ID (4198 or 4199) that is written by the TCP/IP component.

Microsoft is smart to consolidate how components trigger actions by making the Task Scheduler able to trigger tasks based on more than just a time. You also see how Server Manager manages to pop up when a user logs on. There is a Server Manager task that has a trigger of "At log on" for any user. Looking at the built-in tasks can be a great way to understand how the system works and what the Task Scheduler is capable of.

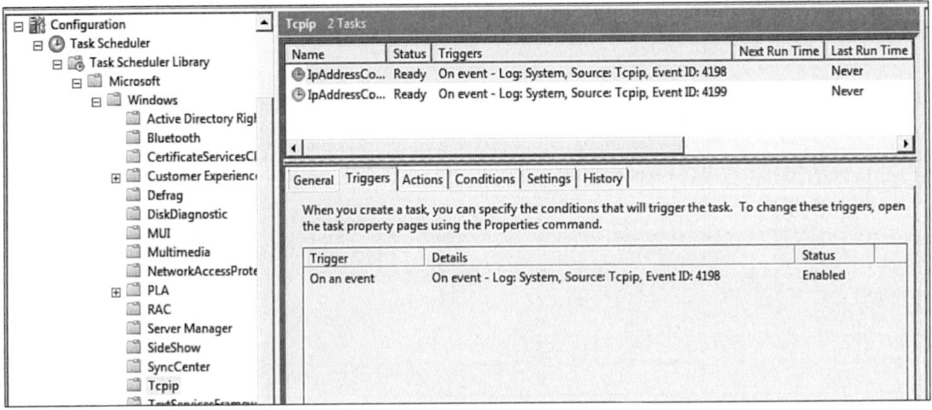

FIGURE 17-25 A built-in task that detects IP conflicts.

Managing the Library

You can create your own folders within the Task Scheduler Library. If you don't expect to create many scheduled tasks, create tasks that exist at the root of the library. However, if scheduled tasks are a larger part of your management, it makes sense to create a folder for custom-created tasks—for example, SavillTech IT with additional child folders to help organize further such as "Disk and Backups" and "Event Triggers."

To create new folders, right-click on the location in the Library in which you want to create a folder and select New Folder from the context menu, in the same way you would with Windows Explorer.

Creating a New Task

There are two different ways to create a scheduled task via the Task Scheduler: a Basic Task wizard, which gives limited options for the scheduled task but covers the most common options, and the regular Create Task, which exposes the full options for a task but is not wizard driven. The Basic Task wizard is covered at a high level, running through the main steps, and then the normal Create Task is covered in more detail.

Creating a Basic Task

Because you can create tasks anywhere in the Task Scheduler Library, select the folder where the new task is created (for example, SavillTech IT), and then select the Create Basic Task action. The Basic Task Wizard has four configuration steps. The first is to give the task a name and an optional description, which is a good idea to complete for someone just browsing the tasks. For example, include information about what the scheduled task does and how it is triggered.

The next stage of the task creation is to pick the trigger for the task to execute, which can be Daily, Weekly, Monthly, a single occurrence, every time the computer starts, when a user logs on, or when a specific event ID is logged. Depending on the trigger selected, you might additionally be prompted to enter a date or time for the trigger or an event ID to trigger on. For example, select Monthly: you can configure to run on the first Wednesday of each month via the interface (see Figure 17-26).

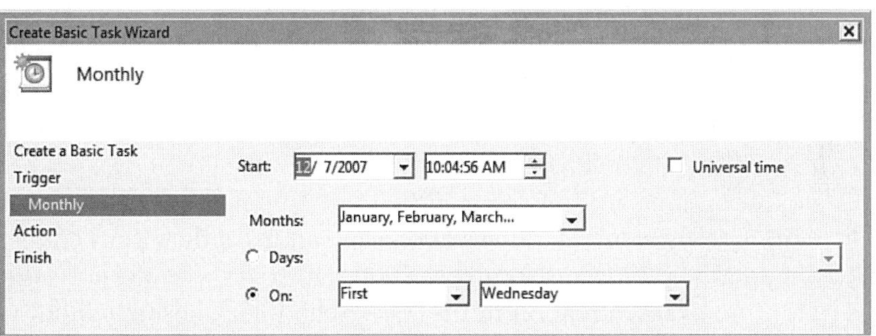

FIGURE 17-26 Setting a monthly trigger for an action.

The last configuration of the task is the actual action to perform: elect to start a program, send an e-mail, or display a message. If you choose to start a program, specify the executable to run with optional arguments and a start folder. To send an e-mail, complete who the mail goes to, who it appears from, and a subject, body, attachment, and supply an SMTP server that the mail is sent via. The attachment capability is useful, as you can configure a report to run on a server and then create another task to mail the report *x* number of minutes after the job should have finished that creates the report.

Finally, a summary is displayed with the option to open the task properties after creation that lets you tweak the configuration further and expose more advanced options. Click Finish to create the scheduled task.

Creating a Standard Task

The basic task wizard normally achieves what you want 99% of the time, especially if you go in and modify any additional settings via the task properties after creation. However, to have full access to all task capabilities as you create the task, use the Create Task action; once again, select the place in the Task Scheduler Library you want the task created.

The Create Task action opens a blank properties dialog for a task that enables you to fill in all the details, so let's walk through the five tabs that are exposed. These five tabs are the same if you choose to modify a task.

The General tab enables a name and description to be specified for the task, in addition to enabling you to modify the security context under which the task runs. By default, the security context is the user account creating the scheduled task. You also have options to run the task only when a user is logged on or regardless of user logon state and whether to run the task with the highest privileges possible. You can choose to hide the task from normal view, plus configure the task for Windows Vista and Windows Server 2008 or for Windows Server 2003, Windows XP, and Windows 2000 (see Figure 17-27). The difference is that the Task Scheduler in Vista and 2008 has more capabilities than those in earlier operating systems, so if a task runs on an older client, choose to configure for Windows 2003/XP/2000. If you select the Windows 2003/XP/2000 choice, options are not selected that are incompatible with the older OS. Windows Vista and Windows 2008 can run tasks that were configured for Windows 2003/XP and Window 2000. However, you do not see the date and time of task creation in the Task Scheduler console window. Why do you care about other operating systems? This is Task Scheduler via Server Manager, which locks the focus to the local server. However, if you run Task Scheduler outside of Server Manager, you can connect to a remote machine to manage tasks—thus, the need to be able to lock facilities to that of a "lower" operating system.

The Triggers tab enables you to create one or more triggers that cause the actions associated with the task to run. You can have multiple triggers for a task by clicking the New button and configuring the options. As shown in Figure 17-28, there are several different options for when to begin the task, ranging from a simple schedule down to idle time and user connect/disconnects. Most of the trigger options can be configured via the New Trigger dialog. However, if you select On idle, access the Conditions tab to set how long the machine needs to have been idle for.

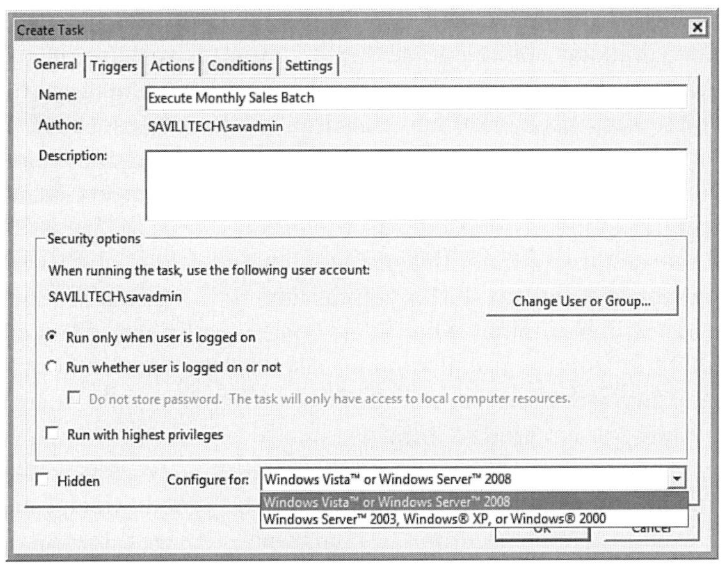

FIGURE 17-27 The General tab of a new task.

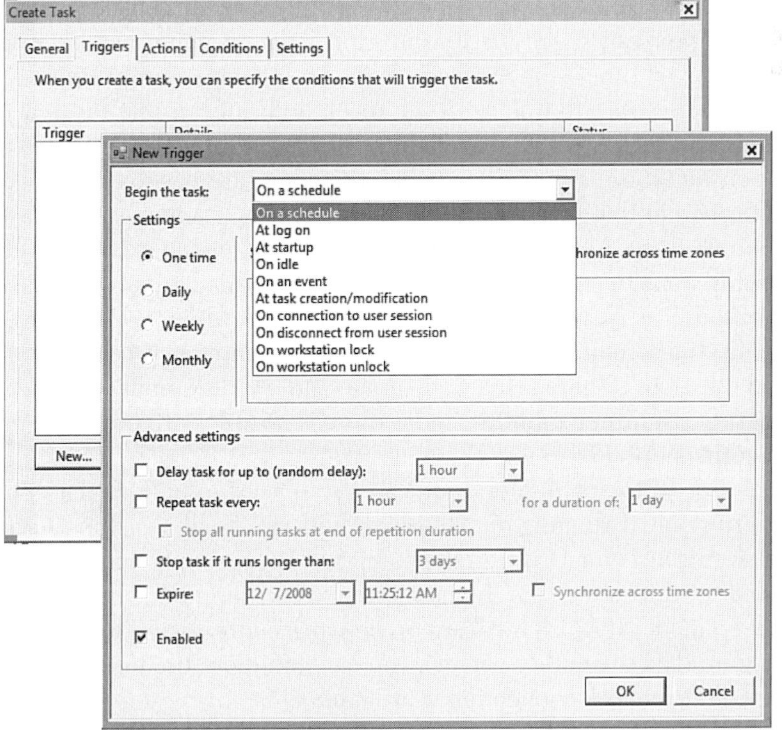

FIGURE 17-28 The options for task triggers.

There are also several advanced settings that enable you to have even more granular configuration. For example, if you fire off multiple tasks, and you want to stagger them slightly, configure an optional random offset, which waits between 0 and the time selected (30 seconds, a minute, 30 minutes, an hour, 8 hours, or a day) before starting the actions associated with the task. Options exist to repeat the task at a certain interval and to stop the actions associated with the task if it runs for longer than a configurable amount of time. Imagine you have a backup job that runs overnight that you schedule to start at 8 p.m. Due to the resources, the backup task cannot still be running when users come in at 8 a.m., so you can enable the option to stop the task if running takes longer than 12 hours. You can set an expiry for regularly occurring tasks so, for example, it could run every morning for a period of three weeks.

The next tab is the Actions tab; as with the Triggers, you can add multiple actions to perform when the task is triggered, which can be combinations of program executions, e-mails, and messages.

The Conditions tab, as shown in Figure 17-29, enables conditions to be applied for the task actions to be executed on top of the triggers. The trigger tells the task to execute, but before the actions are called, the task scheduler makes sure any conditions configured are satisfied. The first condition you can specify is to only run if the machine has been idle for *x* amount of time—for example, 1, 5, 10, 15, 30, or 60 minutes—and an amount of time to wait until the machine has been idle for that length of time. For example, if you set the condition to be idle for 10 minutes, and then wait for idle for an hour, then the computer has to be idle for 10 minutes within that 60 minutes for the task to run. Otherwise, the actions are not executed. You can also configure the task to stop executing if the computer stops being idle and to resume when the computer is idle again. A computer is considered to be in an idle state when a screen saver is running. If a screen saver is not running, the computer is considered to be in an idle state if there is 0% CPU usage and 0% disk input or output for 90% of the past fifteen minutes, and if there is no keyboard or mouse input during this period of time.

For laptop computers, you can also set power options that tell the task to run only if running on AC power and, optionally, to stop the task if the power is disconnected and the computer starts running on battery. You can also set things to wake the computer to run the task if the computer is in sleep mode. If a task is reliant on network connectivity (for example, backing up data to another server), you can configure the task to start only if a specific network connection is available.

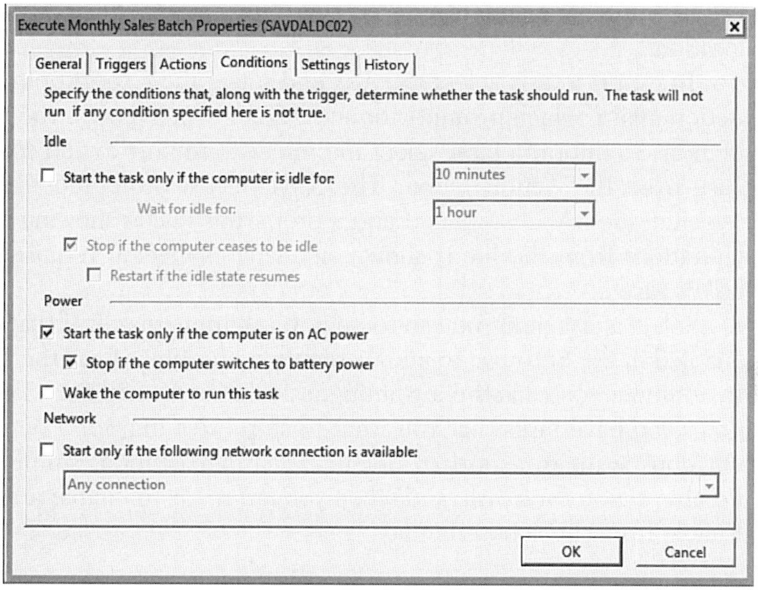

Execute Monthly Sales Batch Properties (SAVDALDC02)

General | Triggers | Actions | Conditions | Settings | History

Specify the conditions that, along with the trigger, determine whether the task should run. The task will not run if any condition specified here is not true.

Idle

Start the task only if the computer is idle for: 10 minutes

Wait for idle for: 1 hour

Stop if the computer ceases to be idle

Restart if the idle state resumes

Power

Start the task only if the computer is on AC power

Stop if the computer switches to battery power

Wake the computer to run this task

Network

Start only if the following network connection is available:

Any connection

OK Cancel

FIGURE 17-29 Conditions for a task.

The final tab is the Settings tab, which enables you to configure granular settings on whether tasks can be run on demand. This should be disabled if executing a task outside of its scheduled time would have negative effects on the environment, such as a backup or disk defragmentation. You can also configure whether a task should be run if its scheduled time has been missed and whether the task should be restarted if it fails execution. You also have a general option to stop the task if it is running for more than a configurable amount of time and to automatically delete the task if it is not scheduled to execute again in the future after a configurable amount of time. This is a good option if you are creating a task that you know you will never use again. However, if you think it might be used again, keeping it around will probably save you work in the future, so at a minimum make sure you export the task to a file before deleting it. An option to configure what to do if the task is already running is available that enables you to configure whether another instance should run, nothing happens, the existing instance running is stopped, or another instance gets queued behind the existing one. Your new task is now available in the library.

Modifying Tasks

The process to modify a task is the same as creating one without the wizard; it's exactly the same dialog and the same tabs. You cannot move a task between folders in the library, but you can export and import into a new location.

To export a task, select the task and select the Export option from the Action menu, which prompts for an XML to which to save the task configuration. To import a task, select the folder to import to and select Import Task from the Action menu. The XML file is prompted for, and once selected, the XML is opened and a properties dialog showing all the configurations from the file is shown, allowing changes if required; then the task is saved.

Select a task, and you can force it to run immediately if that option was enabled in the Settings, to allow execution on-demand via the Run action. In addition, you can stop a running task via the End action. There will be times you have tasks that you want to stop executing for a period of time but don't want to export or delete. To stop execution, simply select the Disable action for a task, and when you are ready to enable it again, select Enable from the action menu.

Viewing Task Execution

To see which tasks are executing at any moment in time, select the Display All Running Tasks action. This shows all running tasks, along with when they were started and for how long they have been running. Any of the running tasks can be selected and stopped by clicking the End Task button. However, the operating system has tasks running that you should not touch. Only stop tasks that you know are custom tasks created by your organization; don't stop the Certificates Services Client tasks!

To view the actual execution of a task, view the properties of a task, which has a History tab that shows all information and logs regarding the task. As shown in Figure 17-30, a fine level of detail is shown for each event ID related to the log. Where do these come from? Notice the Log Name. What the History tab is doing is searching the operating system Microsoft-Windows-TaskScheduler\Operational log for any logs that have the TaskName of the task being viewed in the EventData section of the log. If you delete a task and create a new one with the same name, you see the logs of the old task, as well as logs for your new one.

To view all event logs related to the Task Scheduler, use Event Viewer and navigate to Applications and Services Logs, Microsoft, Windows, Task Scheduler, Operational. Good luck with viewing that log; remember that the OS uses the Task Scheduler for tasks, so the log is very full.

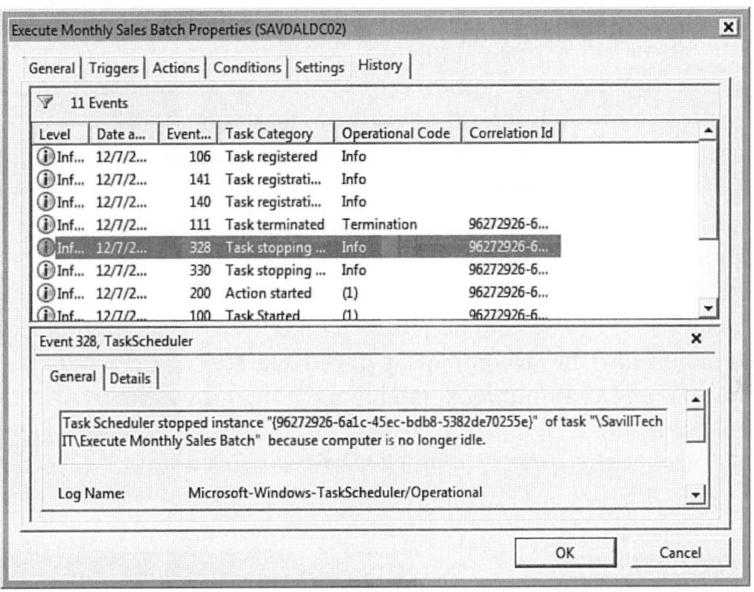

Figure 17-30 Viewing the events for a task.

Command-Line Access

The AT command is still supported. However, it is now obsolete (replaced by schtasks.exe) and is not covered here. If you choose to use AT, modify the user context; the jobs submitted by it run through the "AT Service Account Configuration" action that is available when the root of Task Scheduler is selected.

Use schtasks.exe to schedule jobs; it's a powerful utility. In most cases, for scheduling jobs, use the GUI just because there are so many options available; it is much easier to use and more feature rich. However, you can do most of the same configurations with the command line as you can with the GUI. Let's look at some examples.

Let's create a task to run on the first day of the week (Monday) and start Notepad. The important parameter is /TN, which is the task name. You use it in many of the commands:

```
C:\>schtasks /create /SC monthly /D 1 /TN "Popup first of
➥month" /TR notepad.exe
SUCCESS: The scheduled task "Popup first of month" has
successfully been created.
```

Once created, you can also see the task in the Task Scheduler GUI.

For a full list of parameters, use the `schtasks /create /?` command. Another good option is to use the `/XML` switch and create a new task based on an XML file exported from Task Scheduler.

You can get a list of all scheduler tasks by just running `schtasks` with no switches, or to get output for a specific task, use the `schtasks /query /tn <task name>` command (make sure to put the task name in double quotes if it contains spaces).

To view the detail for a task from the command line, use the `/V` switch for verbose output and an output format (`/FO`) type; in this case, a list. But it could also be a comma-separated file (CSV) or a table (which is the default and does not look good in a command window).

```
C:\>schtasks /query /tn "Popup first of month" /v /fo list

Folder: \
HostName:                              SAVDALDC02
TaskName:                              \Popup first of month
Next Run Time:                         1/1/2008 2:14:00 PM
Status:                                Ready
Logon Mode:                            Interactive only
Last Run Time:                         12/7/2007 2:29:15 PM
Last Result:                           0
Author:                                john
Task To Run:                           notepad.exe
Start In:                              N/A
Comment:                               N/A
Scheduled Task State:                  Enabled
Idle Time:                             Disabled
Power Management:                      Stop On Battery Mode, No
                                       Start On Batteries
Run As User:                           SAVILLTECH\john
Delete Task If Not Rescheduled:        Enabled
Stop Task If Runs X Hours and X Mins: 72:00:00
Schedule:                              Scheduling data is not
                                       available in this format.
Schedule Type:                         Monthly
Start Time:                            2:14:00 PM
Start Date:                            12/7/2007
End Date:                              N/A
Days:                                  01
```

```
Months:                                     Every month
Repeat: Every:                              Disabled
Repeat: Until: Time:                        Disabled
Repeat: Until: Duration:                    Disabled
Repeat: Stop If Still Running:              Disabled
```

To trigger a specific task to run right away, use the `/Run` argument and the `/TN` argument to specify the task name, for example:

```
C:\>schtasks /run /tn "Popup first of month"
SUCCESS: Attempted to run the scheduled task "Popup first of
month".
```

Likewise, to enable or disable a task, use the `/change` argument, the `/tn` argument to specify which task, and then `/enable` or `/disable`. Notice a flow here.

Services

The Services node of Configuration enables you to view all the services on the system. Although the best way to view services is to use the role main page, which groups all services related to the role, there might be times you want to just generally view the services or modify a service that is not related to a role.

The Services node has no structure. It's a flat list of all the services on the system, and shows the name of the service, a description, its status, startup type, and who the service logs on as.

Right-click on a service to see tasks having to do with the control of the service. For example, you can Start, Stop, Pause, Resume, or Restart services, and the options available depend on the current state of the service. You can't start a service that's already started and you can only affect the states a service supports, For example, not all services support being paused.

For more detailed management of a service, select the service and its Properties. This enables you to control all aspects of the service. Figures 17-31 and 17-32 show the General tab and the Recovery tab for a service, which are the two most configurable tabs.

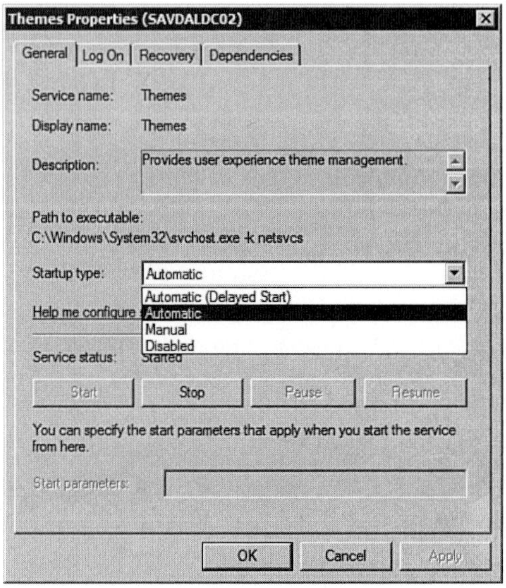

Figures 17-31 The General tab for a service.

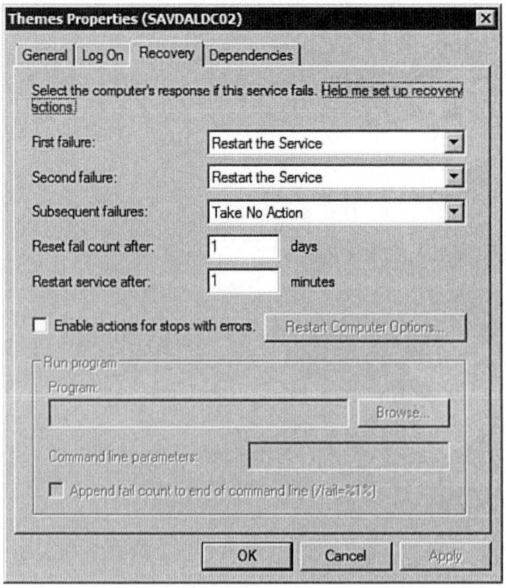

Figure 17-32 The Recovery tab for a service.

The General tab gives control over the current state of the service, but more importantly, it also give control over its Startup type. The Startup type controls whether the service starts at system boot automatically, starts after the boot is complete, whether the service must be started manually, or whether it's disabled, which means it cannot be started.

All services reside under HKEY_LOCAL_MACHINE\SYSTEM\CurrentControlSet\Services, and the startup type updates the Start value to one of the following:

- **0**. Boot time load of device driver.
- **1**. Core part of system kernel initialization.
- **2**. Start automatically.
- **3**. Manual.
- **4**. Disabled.

If you have problems where a computer does not start because of a service, boot to a recovery environment, load the Registry hive, and modify the value to 4 to disable the service. There is not an option for a delayed autostart. A delayed autostart is facilitated by setting the Start value to 2 (for automatic) and creating a separate DWORD value, DelayedAutostart, which is set to 1.

The Type values can be 1 for a kernel device driver, 2 for a file system driver (which is also a kernel driver), 4 for a set of arguments for an adapter, 10 for a program that runs as a service in its own process space, and 20 for a service that can share a process with other services.

The Log On tab configures a service to run under a particular user account. By default, a service runs as the Local System account. However, you can run under a local or domain user account, which might be required where network resource access is required. Care should be taken with the accounts used. If you specify a normal user account that has an expiring password, unless you have good procedures in place, if you change the password on the account and forget to update the service with the new password, the service won't start. Ideally, the accounts have their passwords set to Password Never Expires, so this is not an issue. However, this opens up another security problem because accounts with nonexpiring passwords are generally a bad idea. So, set the Password Never Expires, and set a complex password (or phrase in this case); then have an alert or run book entry (a *run book* is a set of instructions an organization maintains that tell someone how to maintain an environment, tasks to run, and so on) to change this password every *x* number of months in keeping with your normal organizational password standards.

The Recovery tab enables you to specify actions if the service fails. You can specify a different action for the first failure, the second failure, and then all subsequent failures. Your actions can be to do nothing, restart the service, run a program (which can be any executable or script, along with configurable command-line parameters, including the number of times the service has failed), or you can restart the computer. All of these are useful options, and the approach taken depends on the criticality of the service.

By default, most services try to restart twice and then give up. If you have an important service, you could configure the first attempt to restart and then the second attempt to run a program; this could call a script to fire off an SNMP event to your monitoring server, informing it of the failure or perhaps a script that clears some condition on the server that you know can make the server fail. If you have a problem that requires a reboot to resolve, and this service is the most important job of the server, you could configure the server to restart.

The Dependencies tab shows any services that a service depends on to start; that is, they must be running before the service can start. This information is not just used for service startup. If you select a service that has dependencies, you are informed that stopping the service also stops other services that cannot run without it.

For management from the command line, you have several options, such as the old-style `net stop` and `net start` to stop and start services, the WMI, and `sc`. `sc` is great for controlling services from the command line. For example, to quickly see the state of a service from the command line, use the query parameter with the name of the service, as shown:

```
C:\>sc query themes

SERVICE_NAME: themes
        TYPE               : 20  WIN32_SHARE_PROCESS
        STATE              : 4  RUNNING
                                (STOPPABLE, NOT_PAUSABLE,
ACCEPTS_SHUTDOWN)
        WIN32_EXIT_CODE    : 0   (0x0)
        SERVICE_EXIT_CODE  : 0   (0x0)
        CHECKPOINT         : 0x0
        WAIT_HINT          : 0x0
```

Not only do you see the state of the service, but also the allowed states for the service. In this case, the service cannot be paused, which is why the option to pause was grayed out on the Themes services context menu.

To set a services startup type, use the `config` parameter, for example. Notice that there is a space after the equals sign; this is a requirement. `Start=auto` would not work.

```
C:\>sc config themes start= auto
[SC] ChangeServiceConfig SUCCESS
```

You can also change other attributes of the service, including the password use, dependencies, and so on. If you just run `SC` with no parameters, you are given a complete list of everything it can do, which is basically everything, including what happens in failure situations for a service.

WMI Control

The WMI Control is something you probably won't touch. It enables you to manage the WMI settings on your server. The only option is to select the Properties of the WMI Control, which opens a four-tab dialog box.

The General tab displays the version of WMI installed on the server and its location, which is C:\Windows\system32\wbem by default.

The Backup/Restore tab enables the backing up of the WMI repository to a selected location and the capability to restore a backup.

The Security tab enables permissions to be modified on different portions of the namespace, as shown in Figure 17-33.

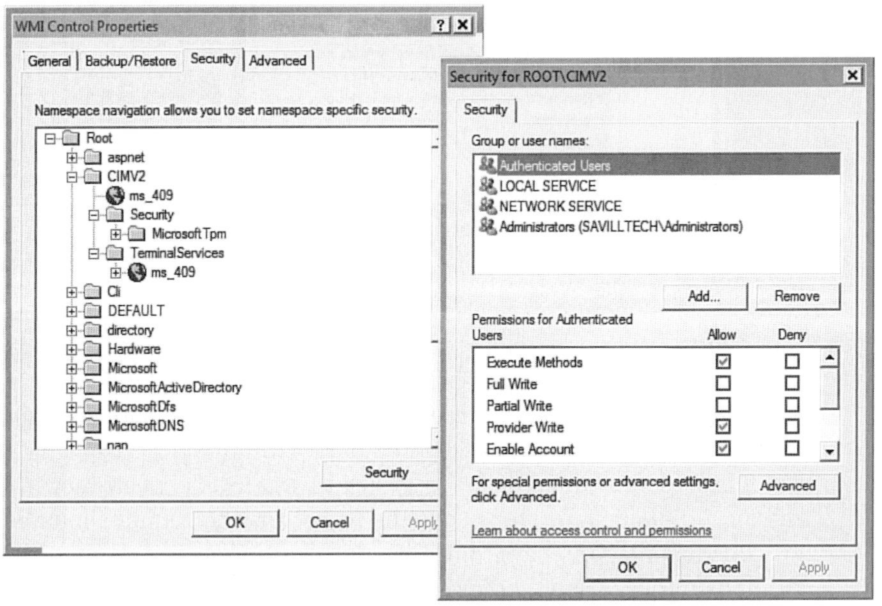

Figure 17-33 Viewing and modifying security on a WMI namespace.

The Advanced tab enables the default WMI namespace used for scripting to be changed from the default root\cimv2. However, most settings you inspect for the operating system are part of the root\cimv2, and modifying this default might cause certain scripts to fail that assume the system is configured to a standard. So, only modify this with good reason.

Local Users and Groups

The Local Users and Groups snap-in is available only under Configuration for nondomain controllers; this enables the management of users and groups contained in the local security database of a server, as shown in Figure 17-34.

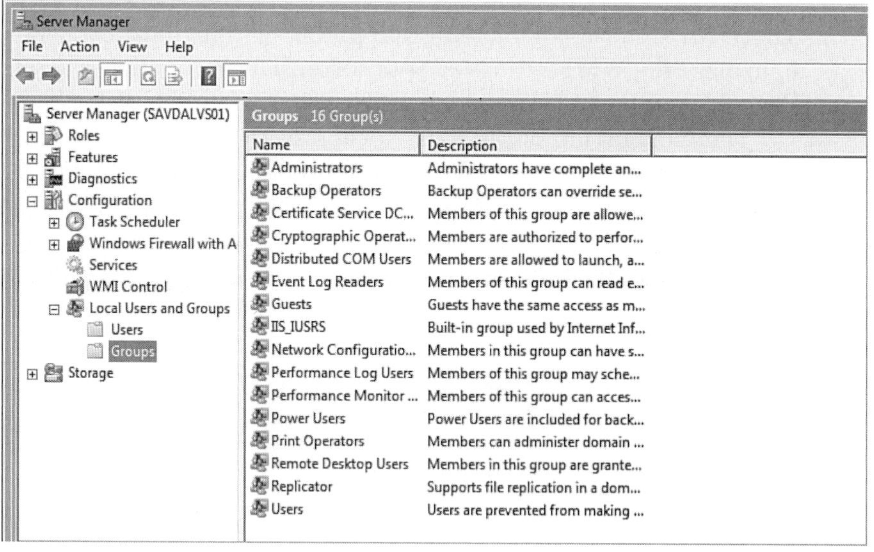

Figure 17-34 The local user and group configuration.

The most common action performed on a domain-joined server is modifying the membership of the local Administrators group to add domain users who might not be domain administrators (and who are automatically made a member of the local Administrators group when the server joins the domain), but need administrative rights over a specific server. To add a user, double click the group to which you need to add a new member, and click Add to specify the new user who requires membership.

By default, you have only two local accounts on your server: the Administrator account and a disabled Guest account. You might see other accounts added when certain roles are installed on the server. However, most services stay away from local accounts where possible.

If you have a server in a workgroup, local accounts are far more important. However, most servers are joined to a domain, with the possible exception of servers in a DMZ/perimeter network, so you should steer clear of using local accounts. The Windows help has a detailed list of the various local groups found on a server, and these are examined throughout the book where appropriate.

Storage Management

The Storage node of Server Manager has access to Disk Management, which was explored in Chapter 5. Disk Management and the WSB link are not covered in this chapter. However, by default, WSB is not installed; install the WSB feature to perform backups in Windows Server. Backup is covered later in this chapter, so for now remember that Storage Management contains the key areas for managing your storage, which is your disks and backups of what is on the disks.

Command Line

To enable interaction with other services, and even for command line management and automation, Server Manager has a CLI that exposes the key tasks that are possible via the Server Manager GUI exclusively. That boils down to the management of roles and features. The CLI is implemented via servermanagercmd.exe, and the full list of options can be seen using the `/?` switch:

```
Servermanagercmd /?
```

The most common use is for the installation of roles and services. To quickly see which roles and features are installed, use the `-query` switch, and optionally specify an XML file name. It contains the output of the command in XML format. What follows is a short excerpt of the output. The selected roles and features are highlighted in green when running the command, which makes them stand out nicely. For each role or feature, the various sub-components/services are displayed within the hierarchy:

```
C:\Users\john>servermanagercmd -query
.

----- Roles -----
```

```
[ ] Active Directory Certificate Services  [AD-Certificate]
    [ ] Certification Authority  [ADCS-Cert-Authority]
    [ ] Certification Authority Web Enrollment  [ADCS-Web-
Enrollment]
    [ ] Online Responder  [ADCS-Online-Cert]
    [ ] Network Device Enrollment Service  [ADCS-Device-
Enrollment]
[X] Active Directory Domain Services
    [X] Active Directory Domain Controller  [ADDS-Domain-
Controller]
    [ ] Identity Management for UNIX  [ADDS-Identity-Mgmt]
        [ ] Server for Network Information Services  [ADDS-NIS]
        [ ] Password Synchronization  [ADDS-Password-Sync]
        [ ] Administration Tools  [ADDS-IDMU-Tools]
[X] Active Directory Federation Services
    [X] Federation Service  [ADFS-Federation]
    [ ] Federation Service Proxy  [ADFS-Proxy]
    [ ] AD FS Web Agents  [ADFS-Web-Agents]
        [ ] Claims-aware Agent  [ADFS-Claims]
```

The same section is displayed in the XML format (`servermanager-cmd -query query.xml`) in the following listing. Notice the Installed attribute to differentiate between installed and noninstalled roles and features:

```
- <ServerManagerConfigurationQuery Time="2007-12-02T09:33:00"
Language="en-US" xmlns="http://schemas.microsoft.com/sdm/
Windows/ServerManager/Configuration/2007/1">
- <Role DisplayName="Active Directory Certificate Services"
Installed="false" Id="AD-Certificate">
  <RoleService DisplayName="Certification Authority"
Installed="false" Id="ADCS-Cert-Authority" Default="true" />
  <RoleService DisplayName="Certification Authority Web
Enrollment" Installed="false" Id="ADCS-Web-Enrollment" />
  <RoleService DisplayName="Online Responder"
Installed="false" Id="ADCS-Online-Cert" />
  <RoleService DisplayName="Network Device Enrollment Service"
Installed="false" Id="ADCS-Device-Enrollment" />
  </Role>
- <Role DisplayName="Active Directory Domain Services"
Installed="true">
  <RoleService DisplayName="Active Directory Domain Controller"
Installed="true" Id="ADDS-Domain-Controller" Default="true" />
- <RoleService DisplayName="Identity Management for UNIX"
```

```
Installed="false" Id="ADDS-Identity-Mgmt">
  <RoleService DisplayName="Server for Network Information
Services" Installed="false" Id="ADDS-NIS" Default="true" />
  <RoleService DisplayName="Password Synchronization"
Installed="false" Id="ADDS-Password-Sync" Default="true" />
  <RoleService DisplayName="Administration Tools"
Installed="false" Id="ADDS-IDMU-Tools" Default="true" />
  </RoleService>
  </Role>
- <Role DisplayName="Active Directory Federation Services"
Installed="true">
  <RoleService DisplayName="Federation Service"
Installed="true" Id="ADFS-Federation" />
  <RoleService DisplayName="Federation Service Proxy"
Installed="false" Id="ADFS-Proxy" />
- <RoleService DisplayName="AD FS Web Agents"
Installed="false" Id="ADFS-Web-Agents">
  <RoleService DisplayName="Claims-aware Agent"
Installed="false" Id="ADFS-Claims" />
```


The XML format is useful, as it gives you information that you don't see on the console, namely the ID (`Id`) of the various role/feature components. The ID installs or removes role and feature components via the `servermanagercmd -install` and `-remove` switches.

Borrowing from PowerShell, the `servermanagercmd` has an optional `-whatIf` switch that shows us what would happen if the command was run without making any actual changes to the system. A detail log file can be created by adding the `-logfile <logfile name>.txt` switch, and an XML output of the actions can be created via the `-resultPath <results file>.xml` switch. If you run the command in `-whatIf` mode, no output is written to the `resultPath` XML file because no actions are taken.

Let's take an example and see what would happen if you installed BITS on your server. After reviewing the ID in the query XML, the ID for Bits is BITS.

```
C:\Users\john>servermanagercmd -install bits -whatif
.
Note: Running in 'WhatIf' Mode.
Specified for installation: [BITS Server Extensions]
Specified for installation: [Web Server (IIS)] Directory
Browsing
Specified for installation: [Web Server (IIS)] HTTP Errors
```

```
Specified for installation: [Web Server (IIS)] HTTP Redirection
Specified for installation: [Web Server (IIS)] Health and
Diagnostics
Specified for installation: [Web Server (IIS)] HTTP Logging
Specified for installation: [Web Server (IIS)] Logging Tools
Specified for installation: [Web Server (IIS)] Request Monitor
Specified for installation: [Web Server (IIS)] Tracing
Specified for installation: [Web Server (IIS)] Performance
Specified for installation: [Web Server (IIS)] Static Content
Compression

This server may need to be restarted after the installation
completes.
```

As this shows, if you install BITS on this server, several additional IIS components are also installed as requirements for BITS. If a reboot was required, you can automate the reboot by adding the `-reboot` switch to our command.

If a role or feature has sub-features, you can individually install each sub-feature via its ID as separate commands, or you can choose to install all sub-features via the `-allsubfeatures` switch. Notice the output that follows with the different features selected when the `-allsubfeatures` switch isn't used and then is used:

```
C:\Users\john>servermanagercmd -install web-server -whatif

Note: Running in 'WhatIf' Mode.

Skipping [Web Server (IIS)] Web Server (IIS) because it is
already installed on this computer.

Specified for installation: [Web Server (IIS)] Health and
Diagnostics
Specified for installation: [Web Server (IIS)] Performance
Specified for installation: [Web Server (IIS)] Request Monitor
Specified for installation: [Web Server (IIS)] Static Content
Compression
Specified for installation: [Web Server (IIS)] Directory
Browsing
Specified for installation: [Web Server (IIS)] HTTP Errors
Specified for installation: [Web Server (IIS)] HTTP Logging

This server may need to be restarted after the installation
completes.
```

```
C:\Users\john>servermanagercmd -install web-server
➥-allsubfeatures -whatif

Note: Running in 'WhatIf' Mode.

Skipping [Web Server (IIS)] Web Server (IIS) because it is
already installed on this computer.

Specified for installation: [Web Server (IIS)] FTP Publishing
Service
Specified for installation: [Web Server (IIS)] Performance
Specified for installation: [Web Server (IIS)] Health and
Diagnostics
Specified for installation: [Web Server (IIS)] IIS Management
Scripts and Tools
Specified for installation: [Web Server (IIS)] Management
Service
Specified for installation: [Web Server (IIS)] FTP Management
Console
Specified for installation: [Web Server (IIS)] FTP Server
Specified for installation: [Web Server (IIS)] URL Authorization
Specified for installation: [Web Server (IIS)] IIS Client
Certificate Mapping Authentication
Specified for installation: [Web Server (IIS)] Client Certificate
Mapping Authentication
Specified for installation: [Web Server (IIS)] IP and Domain
Restrictions
Specified for installation: [Web Server (IIS)] Dynamic Content
Compression
Specified for installation: [Web Server (IIS)] Static Content
Compression
Specified for installation: [Web Server (IIS)] Directory
Browsing
Specified for installation: [Web Server (IIS)] Server Side
Includes
Specified for installation: [Web Server (IIS)] HTTP Logging
Specified for installation: [Web Server (IIS)] Logging Tools
Specified for installation: [Web Server (IIS)] HTTP Errors
Specified for installation: [Web Server (IIS)] HTTP Redirection
Specified for installation: [Web Server (IIS)] ASP
Specified for installation: [Web Server (IIS)] ODBC Logging
Specified for installation: [Web Server (IIS)] Basic
Authentication
Specified for installation: [Web Server (IIS)] Digest
Authentication
```

```
Specified for installation: [Web Server (IIS)] Request Monitor
Specified for installation: [Web Server (IIS)] Tracing
Specified for installation: [Web Server (IIS)] Custom Logging

This server may need to be restarted after the installation
completes.
```

To remove a role or feature, the command is exactly the same, but instead of using `-install`, use `-remove`. Again, use the `-whatif` switch to verify the effect of a removal.

Automated Role/Feature Installation

Using `ServerManagerCmd`, you can perform unattended installations of roles and features via the `-install` switch. However, you are limited to one component at a time. An alternate approach is to use the `-inputPath` parameter and pass an XML file, which lists all the roles and features to install. An example file is shown in the following listing that installs the DNS role and the Desktop Experience feature:

```
<?xml version="1.0" encoding="UTF-8"?>
<ServerManagerConfiguration Action="Install"
xmlns="http://schemas.microsoft.com/sdm/Windows/ServerManager
/Configuration/2007/1">
   <Role Id="DNS"/>
   <Feature Id="Desktop-Experience"/>
</ServerManagerConfiguration>
```

If it's a role, use the `<Role>` tag, and if it's a feature, use the `<Feature>` tag. Take note also that `Action` is set to `Install`. You could just as easily set the action to `Remove` and list the features and roles you want to remove from a server.

Use the install answer file in the following command. The `-reboot` switch was not added, so the reboot could be controlled. But to automate, you would add `-reboot` to the end of the command. You also can use the `resultPath` option to create XML output of the actions performed:

```
C:\temp>servermanagercmd -inputPath install.xml -resultPath
c:\temp\results.xml
.................................

Start Installation...
Warning: [Installation] Succeeded: [Desktop Experience]. You
must restart this server to finish the installation process.
```

```
Warning: [Installation] Succeeded: [DNS Server]. You must
restart this server to finish the installation process.
<100/100>

Success: A restart is required to complete the installation.
```

Although the format of the installation file is quite basic, the format is different from the output generated from the `-query` command. Microsoft has a tool, msxsl.exe, which enables the conversion of one file format to another via an Extensible Stylesheet Language (XSL) transformation format. The utility can be downloaded from http://www.microsoft.com/downloads/details.aspx?familyid=2FB55371-C94E-4373-B0E9-DB4816552E41&displaylang=en. Microsoft has provided three transformation files that convert a query file taken from a server via `servermanagercmd` into an install or remove format file, and even an HTML-formatted file for easier viewing of roles and features installed on a server. The following listing is the XSL to create an installation XML file based on a query, so if you use this, install a server with all the roles and features you want to deploy to other servers. That makes it a template server. Then run a query to XML and run this conversion to create an install XML file on other servers:

```
<xsl:stylesheet
xmlns:xsl="http://www.w3.org/1999/XSL/Transform"
xmlns:sm="http://schemas.microsoft.com/sdm/Windows
/ServerManager/Configuration/2007/1"
version="1.0">

  <!-- Transform to xml that can be used to install all roles,
role services, and features that were discovered as installed
in the output query. -->

  <xsl:output indent="no" />

  <xsl:template match="/">
    <xsl:apply-templates/>
  </xsl:template>

  <xsl:template match="sm:ServerManagerConfigurationQuery">
    <xsl:element name="ServerManagerConfiguration"
namespace="http://schemas.microsoft.com/sdm/Windows
/ServerManager/Configuration/2007/1">
```

```
        <xsl:attribute name="Action">Install</xsl:attribute>
        <xsl:apply-templates/>
      </xsl:element>
    </xsl:template>

    <xsl:template match="sm:Role">
      <xsl:if test="@Id and @Installed='true' and count
(sm:RoleService) = 0">
        <xsl:element name="Role"
namespace="http://schemas.microsoft.com/sdm/Windows
/ServerManager/Configuration/2007/1">
          <xsl:attribute name="Id">
            <xsl:value-of select="@Id"/>
          </xsl:attribute>
        </xsl:element>
      </xsl:if>
      <xsl:apply-templates/>
    </xsl:template>

    <xsl:template match="sm:RoleService">
      <xsl:if test="@Id and @Installed='true' and count
(sm:RoleService) = 0">
        <xsl:element name="RoleService"
namespace="http://schemas.microsoft.com/sdm/Windows
/ServerManager/Configuration/2007/1">
          <xsl:attribute name="Id">
            <xsl:value-of select="@Id"/>
          </xsl:attribute>
        </xsl:element>
      </xsl:if>
      <xsl:apply-templates/>
    </xsl:template>

    <xsl:template match="sm:Feature">
      <xsl:if test="@Id and @Installed='true' and count
(sm:Feature) = 0">
        <xsl:element name="Feature"
namespace="http://schemas.microsoft.com/sdm/Windows
/ServerManager/Configuration/2007/1">
          <xsl:attribute name="Id">
            <xsl:value-of select="@Id"/>
          </xsl:attribute>
        </xsl:element>
      </xsl:if>
```

```
    <xsl:apply-templates/>
  </xsl:template>
</xsl:stylesheet>
```

To use the transform file, pass the name of the query XML output, then transform the XSL file, and then transform the `-o` parameter with the name of the install XML file you want to create:

```
msxsl.exe query.xml install.xsl -o install.xml
```

Open the generated XML file (install.xml), and you see a lot of blank lines. The transformation modifies the header lines of the query XML and then converts any lines that are installed on a server in the query file to an install line in the output file. If the feature or role is not marked as installed in the query file, a blank line is inserted. You can clean up the generated file and remove the blank lines using something like Notepad or leave them in. It works just fine. One thing to watch is if you run the query on a 64-bit computer and want to install on a 32-bit computer. Change the `encoding="UTF-16"` part of the XML header to say `encoding="UTF-8"`, or you receive errors trying to pass the XML file.

To see the other transform files, refer to the Windows Server blog at http://blogs.technet.com/windowsserver/archive/2007/08/16/transforming-servermanagercmd-query-xml-to-input-xml.aspx.

You can use the install and remove capabilities via an XML file to automate the bulk installation of roles and features. It can be built into an unattended build of a server or executed via other applications that require Windows roles or features to function.

Expanding Server Manager

Microsoft is not currently allowing Independent Software Vendors (ISV) to add roles to those available in Server Manager. As of Windows Server 2008, the Server Manager is a closed system. However, in the future, you might see Server Manager allow additional roles and features to be added to the system, and even allow configuration to remove certain roles and features from Server Manager so administrators cannot install them. For example, in a future version, it might be possible to remove the Desktop Experience feature as an available option, making it impossible to install.

Microsoft has internally added some roles to Server Manager in the form of updates. Both Hyper-V (Windows Server Virtualization) and the Windows Software Update Services have updates to Server Manager to allow management via Server Manager, and it is likely this will continue for Microsoft solutions.

This does not mean other applications cannot take advantage of the Server Manager capabilities, however. For example, Exchange Server 2007 uses IIS for its Web-based mail interface, Outlook Web Access. It would be possible for the Exchange Server 2007 install routine to call the command-line Server Manager interface to install IIS automatically without any user intervention. The CLI is currently the method for other applications and services to interface with Server Manager. There is no API available.

It is not currently possible to add additional snap-ins to the Server Manager itself. Server Manager is considered a single MMC snap-in, even though it is comprised of many separate snap-ins and is not a console that could be opened in author mode and modified. The shortcut to Server Manager is an executable, CompMgmtLauncher.exe, which launches an MMC environment with the Server Manager snap-in loaded.

You can create your own MMC console and include the Server Manager snap-in alongside other snap-ins, and you can even select certain Server Manager extensions to not display (see Figure 17-35). As you can see by the grayed-out Install button, you cannot add other extensions into the Server Manager snap-in environment. Any snap-in you add shows below the Server Manager snap-in environment.

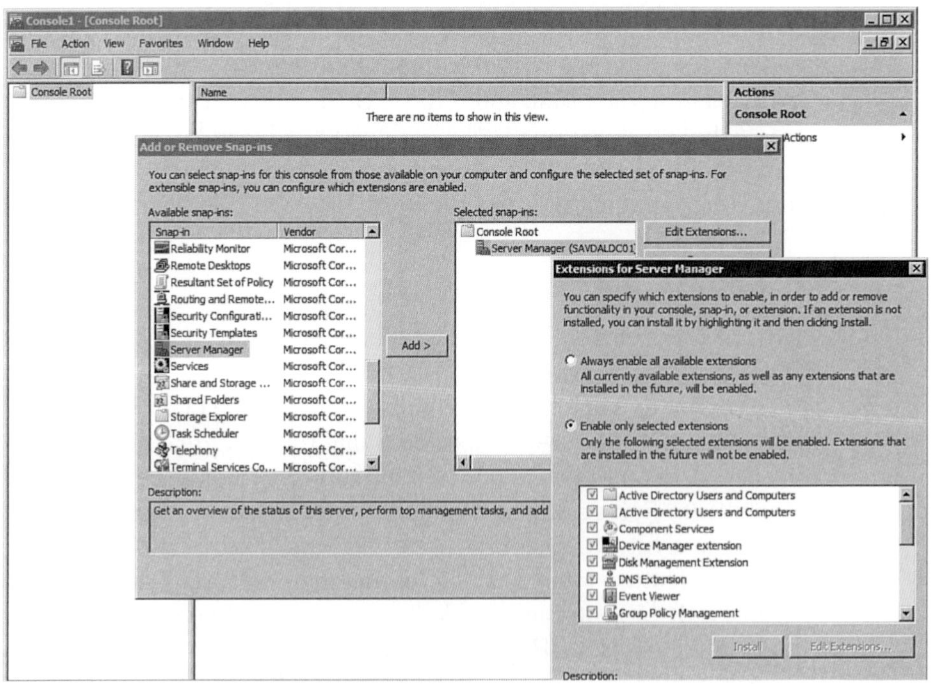

FIGURE 17-35 Customizing the extensions displayed in Server Manager.

Permissions and Delegation

In the final release of Windows Server 2008, there is no delegation possible for individual components of Server Manager; you must be a member of the local Administrators group to access Server Manager. If you attempt to run Server Manager as an account that is not an administrator, you receive the User Access Control dialog, asking for credentials that have the permissions to run Server Manager (see Figure 17-36).

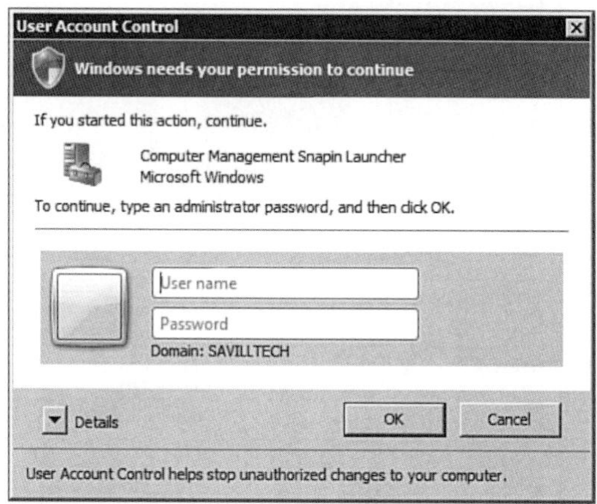

Figure 17-36 The UAC dialog for a non-administrator accessing Server Manager.

Computer Management Console

Server Manager is designed to replace computer management console. However, the computer management console is still supplied with Windows Server 2008 for two primary reasons. First, from a user-familiarity perspective, administrators might want to continue using Computer Manager while they get used to Server Manager. Second, some applications expect to see Computer Manager on the server to function correctly. You can expect that Computer Manager will be removed in the next major version of Windows Server.

There is nothing the computer management console (compmgmt.msc) can do that cannot be done with Server Manager. Computer Manager is focused around tools rather than the roles of a server, but the snap-ins contained are the same as those found in Server Manager. Both Computer

Manager and Server Manager effectively act as portals to the utilities to get the job done; Server Manager is just a much more complete and role-centric solution. Figure 17-37 shows the computer management console and some of the snap-ins it includes.

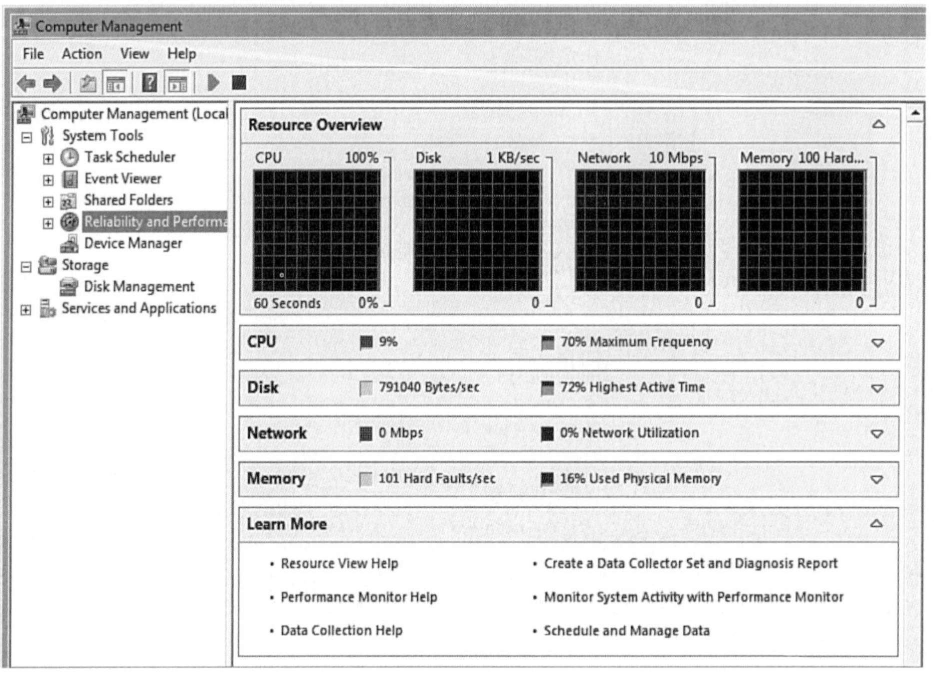

FIGURE 17-37 Computer management snap-ins.

Windows Server Backup (WSB)

With Windows Server 2008, there is a brand-new backup solution that has been written specifically toward smaller organizations, which is indicated by its redesigned architecture and options for an organization. In the early days of backup, you could only back up to tape. Then the capability to back up to media was added, in addition to tape support. Now, with Windows Server 2008, you can only back up to media, including DVDs and external drives. This is a big shift, and the explanation from Microsoft on this removal of tape drive support is it found that customers who use tapes for backup use third-party backup solutions anyway; they wanted to better tailor the backup application to those who use the in-product backup solution: smaller companies. Additionally, with disk storage being so cheap now, it is far more common to back up to disk and then take those disk-based backups and write to tape for offsite storage. Tape drives, tape media, and media changers are still supported in the operating system. However, WSB cannot interface with them.

The model of tiered backup is built into System Center Data Protection Manager (SC DPM). Data from remote machines is backed up to a pool of disks on the DPM server; that disk-based information is output to tape at regular intervals for offsite storage.

WSB was written to address all the backup and recovery needs of a typical organization, which includes backing up the following:

- File-based data, by backing up volumes using Volume Shadow Copy Service (VSS).
- System state information.
- Application data, which is accomplished by hooking into the VSS writer's applications register when installed and the Registry changes that make the VSS writer known to WSB. Examples of applications that provide VSS writers are Exchange, SharePoint, and SQL. If an application does not have a VSS writer, the application would be backed up via the standard block-level volume backup performed by WSB.

Although the backups are at a volume level, you have the capability to restore a full server, restore just the operating system, or restore individual files. In addition, the management of backups has been made easier, which was considered a challenge in earlier Windows backup solutions—that is, NTBackup. It is important to bear in mind that WSB is not a feature-by-feature replacement for NTBackup. It is a rewritten solution working in a different way.

Backup Features

WSB is a VSS-based block-level backup solution. This means backups are faster than under NTBackup, which operated at a file level, and should also be more reliable, given that VSS is a core part of the OS and most major server applications like Exchange and SQL. In addition, after you have taken one full backup, the incremental backup feature of WSB results in only the modified data being backed up and a fast backup time.

When a backup is performed, a snapshot/shadow copy is taken of entire volumes. You cannot select files and folders as part of the backup. Any VSS writers that are registered are utilized to back up application data, so only the volume needs to be backed up and the application VSS writers are automatically called. WSB then reads, block-by-block, the volume being backed up and stores this information inside a Virtual Hard Disk (VHD) file on the target disk. You get one VHD file for each volume being backed up. After the transfer to the VHD is complete, a snapshot is taken of the target disk where the VHD is stored. The next time a backup is performed, the VHD content is overwritten, and a new snapshot taken, which is how multiple versions of the backup are maintained: as snapshots of the backup target disk. The shadow copy on the source disk is deleted after the backup is complete if a full backup is taken. Hardware VSS writers are not used by WSB, only the system VSS writer. Snapshots and VSS are used for everything. The fact you are using VHD files as the backup target also means you can mount the VHD files to look at the content, although they are not bootable.

You can back up to three different media. The first is to back up to DVD, which is designed as an ad-hoc backup. If a backup is needed for offsite storage, the capability is there for a backup to span multiple DVDs. This works fine for a small amount of data, but not for anything sizable. Only ad-hoc backups can be taken to DVD and not a scheduled backup. When you back up to DVD, the data is always compressed.

The second medium is that of a network share, which again is designed for an infrequent backup and also for a redundancy backup. This would commonly be accomplished by, once a week, backing up to a network share. The normal daily backups are written to local disk on a server, which is fine for dealing with data corruption but not good if the server goes bang! As with DVDs, an ad-hoc backup can be taken to a network share but not a scheduled backup. This is because WSB relies on snapshots to maintain the versions of the backups for scheduled backups, and today it is not possible to perform remote snapshots. That means the multiple versions that are required for scheduled backups are not supported. To schedule the backup to a network share, you could use `wbadmin` and call it regularly via the Task Scheduler. However, each backup would be a complete backup, and the savings associated with delta-based snapshots would not be realized.

The final backup medium is the primary one, and that is backup to disk, either internal or external. It is designed as the target for your regular backups. Fixed, nonremovable type USB storage devices are also supported for disk backups, both scheduled and ad-hoc. You cannot use USB flash type devices, which could be removed at any time, for just that reason!

For the types of backup in previous backup solutions, there were various types of backup that could be full, copy, incremental, and so on. However, in WSB, you don't need these. By default, and the best practice, is that every backup is an Optimized Full Backup, which transfers the entire contents of the volume to the target backup disk. However, because of the VSS, delta-based technology, the only space used would be the changed data; even though you are performing a full backup, you only take up the space of an incremental, or differences, backup. The amount of space needed depends on the amount of change that occurs, in addition to the size of original data. By default, after seven days, a full backup is taken and the entire VHD file is rewritten as if it was the first time a backup was ever taken. This is to avoid the possibility of a disk corruption affecting the integrity of a backup; if you wrote the changes only to the VHD, it is quite possible that, over time, blocks on the disk might become corrupt, which would not be noticed by the backup application if the content had not changed. By writing a full backup each week, the WSB can make sure all blocks are still functional and that your backup can be restored when you need it.

Incremental backups are still possible, but are only recommended for low I/O servers; the incremental backup works by leaving the shadow copy of the source disk after a backup in place to use for tracking changes to the disk. This means there is a copy-on-write for every write to the disk, which impacts performance because both the old and new content of the disk are being maintained. When an incremental backup is performed, only the changes to the disk are written to the target, by reading the Shadow copy differences area. Again, if the last full backup taken is more than seven days old, a full backup is taken automatically. Be sure of your server I/O before you consider using incremental backups.

It's important to note, however, that the difference between a full backup and an incremental one is just how the backup is taken. No matter which method you use, the target VHD file is still a complete copy of the source disk; when it comes to restoring the performance optimization that was used to keep the VHD current, the method has no effect. You are choosing between how to keep the VHD backup up-to-date (with a full backup being a slower backup, but not causing day-to-day I/O overhead), whereas incremental backs up faster, but introduces a day-to-day I/O overhead. (This should not have a huge impact on modern systems, but it depends on the amount of change and the type of disk system.)

A system state backup is also possible using the WSB; this was originally not a facility included in WSB, but was requested by testers who wanted to back up the system state without backing up the entire volume. However, a Windows Server 2008 system state is much larger than with 2003. Previously a system state might have been around 1GB; now, with Windows Server 2008, there is a 4GB to 5GB system state.

To perform a complete PC restore, make sure all critical volumes (boot and system) are backed up; WSB helps you do this via a simple switch, discussed later in this section.

One fact that many find troubling is WSB has to have its own disk. That's not a volume—it has to have an entire disk to use for its scheduled backups. This might not be an issue for everyone, but it's definitely something to consider. The disk used for the scheduled backups should be around 1.5 times larger than the data being backed up. However, if the data is frequently changing, this disk should be even bigger. The reason for the insistence on a separate disk is simply one of trying to force a best practice. Storing the backup of a volume on the same disk as the volume is not good resiliency; for your main, scheduled backup, back up to a separate physical disk. The reason you need an entire disk is that you might want to take the disk offsite, and so it should not be used by other data. Second, to avoid backups being deleted or messed with, the disk used for the scheduled backup target is hidden from the OS by default, with no drive letter assigned. A drive letter can be assigned via Disk Manager (such as B for Backup). However, this defeats the purpose of hiding it from the administrators. These same constraints do not apply for nonscheduled backups, which can be written to any of the supported target media types.

The general idea here is that this backup solution is for the basic environment and is designed to force a good backup strategy. At times, though, you might feel too restricted; at that point, look at third-party solutions.

Recovery Features

There are five core recovery scenarios with WSB. The first is recovery of individual files or folders, which generally happens when "the computer lost the file" and never when "the user deleted the file." Technologies like the Volume Shadow Copy Server running on a disk enables a Previous Version tab on shares, which generally allows users to self-service this type of restoration. However, you still might need to restore files and folders from a backup, and that is possible.

The second scenario is an entire data volume is corrupt—not a system or boot volume containing the operating system, but a volume containing non-OS data. In this instance, use WBS to restore the entire volume; this is also useful to restore the contents of a disk to a new server.

You then have system recovery-type scenarios where either the operating system volume is corrupt and needs restoring, or the entire server disk set has crashed and all the volumes need to be restored, in addition to the disks requiring repartitioning. These operating system restores are performed from the Windows Recovery Environment (RE), which is discussed in detail in Chapter 20. This chapter looks at RE with regards to backup restoration. This type of disaster-recovery scenario, where you rebuild the system from the recovery environment, is known as a bare metal recovery (BMR). To replace a server with a new server, use a bare metal recovery to restore a backup from one server to another (assuming their hardware was similar enough).

The final scenario is the recovery of system state information, which is used primarily in AD recovery scenarios where objects are deleted. If a server's Registry becomes corrupt, a system store needs to be rolled back, such as DHCP, DNS, or Certificate Authority, or just to roll back an application or application patch. You cannot use the system state backup to restore information to another computer. For example, you cannot build a brand-new server and restore the system state backup from another server in an attempt to make the new server the old server's replacement. To replace a server, perform a system recovery.

Microsoft has a neat table that summarizes all this (recreated in Table 17-1), showing the types of recovery you can perform, based on the medium you backed up to. You can perform all recovery types for any backup medium except for a DVD, which cannot support file/application/system state recovery.

Table 17-1 Backup Medium Support for the Types of Backup Recovery

Recovery Type Backup Medium	System Recovery	Volume	File/ Application	System State
Local disk	Yes	Yes	Yes	Yes
DVD	Yes	Yes	No	No
Network share	Yes	Yes	Yes	Yes
USB drive	Yes (fixed type only)	Yes (fixed type only)	Yes (fixed type only)	Yes (fixed type only)
USB flash	No	No	No	No

It should be noted that WSB is not compatible with NTBackup from Windows Server 2003. To restore data from a backup set created with NTBackup, download the Windows NT Backup recovery utility from http://www.microsoft.com/downloads/details.aspx?FamilyID=7da725e2-8b69-4c65-afa3-2a53107d54a7&DisplayLang=en.

Installing Windows Server Backup (WSB)

WSB is a feature; to install it, use Server Manager and add the WSB feature, which has two subcomponents. The main WSB component contains the core WSB graphical and CLI (wbadmin.exe) environment. The Command-Line Tools component contains a script for managing backups via PowerShell, as shown in Figure 17-38.

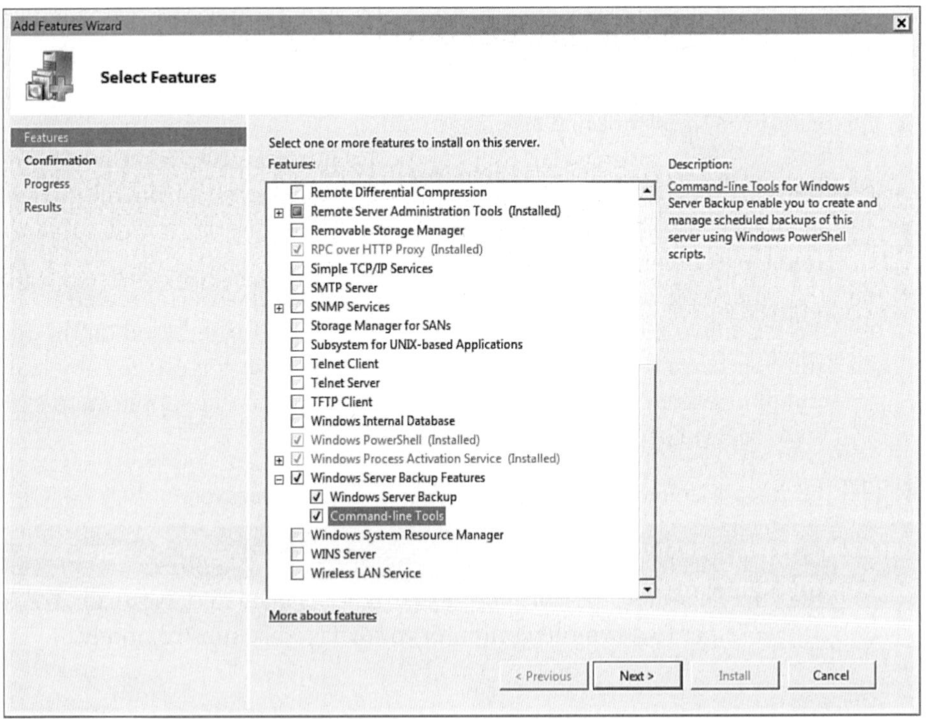

FIGURE 17-38 Installing the WSB features.

Performing a Backup

Performing a backup is simple, which is the point behind WSB. To run the WSB MMC snap-in, you must be an administrator or a member of the backup operators group.

Don't select the type of backup when performing a backup. To switch between performing the full or incremental backup, use the Configure Performance Settings action within the WSB, which lets you configure Full or Incremental. Additionally, you can select different types of backup for each volume if required, as shown in Figure 17-39.

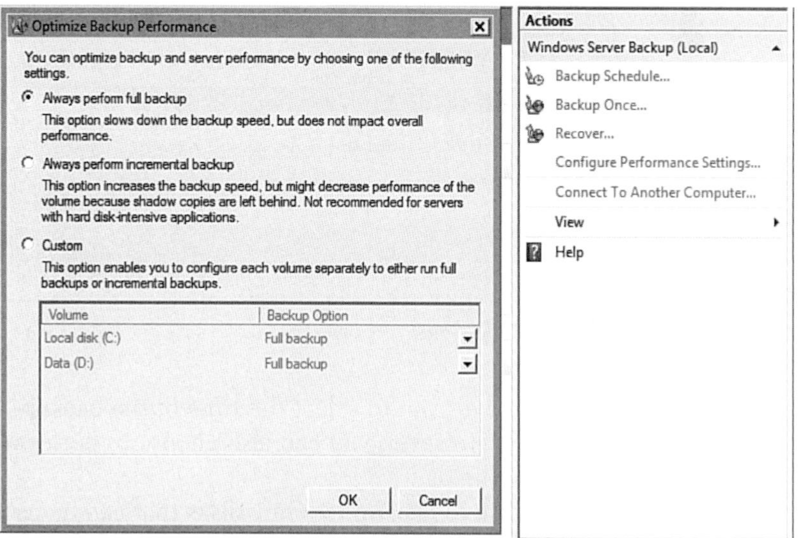

FIGURE 17-39 Configuring the backup optimization to use.

The WSB interface is clean and limits your options to creating a Backup Schedule, performing an ad-hoc backup, and Recover. You can also connect to a remote computer to manage backups remotely.

Schedule a Backup

On most systems, you want to create a regular backup schedule; click the Backup Schedule action to create a scheduled backup task. The first page of the Backup Schedule is a general welcome screen. Click Next to move on through. The next page enables the configuration of what to back up. By default, Full Server is selected, which backs up all volumes on the server. That includes all applications, system state, and data. Alternatively, you can select Custom to perform a more granular backup. You cannot perform a system state backup from the GUI. You must use the command-line tool, `wbadmin`. If you selected a custom backup, you are prompted to select the volumes to back up, as shown in Figure 17-40. Notice you don't have options to back up individual files or folders or VSS writers. The backup only occurs at the volume level.

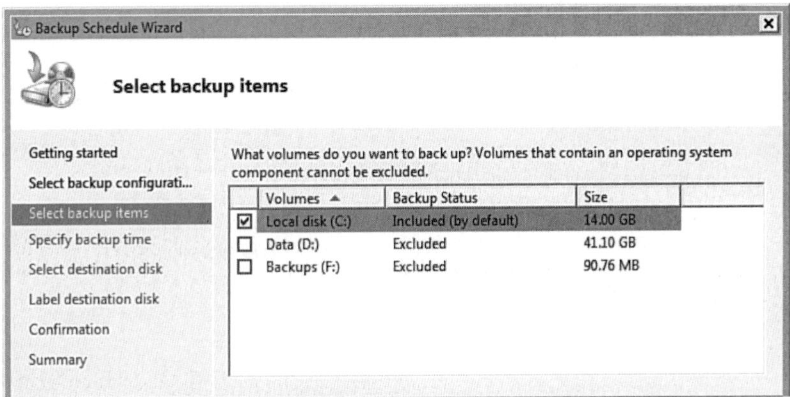

FIGURE 17-40 Performing a custom backup.

The next stage enables you to select the time of the backup, which by default is 9 p.m. daily. However, you can also choose to perform backups multiple times during the day.

Next, select the disk to backup to. Only disks that can be used for the backup are displayed. You cannot use a disk that stores the operating system or data being backed up, as shown in Figure 17-41. The disk that is selected must be dedicated for backup purposes. The selected disk is wiped of all partitions and reformatted once selected, so if you use a disk containing other data, move the data first! The selected disk can be unpartitioned. WSB partitions it automatically.

By default, only external disks are displayed. However, if you have an internal disk that is not being displayed that you want to use for the backup target, click the Show All Available Disks button to force a refresh. You can set the disks to display both internal and external. You are then shown the label allocated for the selected disk in the next stage.

A confirmation screen is displayed. Click Finish to create your scheduled backup job and to format your target disk to be ready for backup. A summary is displayed, confirming when the next backup will take place. To change your selections, run the Backup Schedule action again, and you are given options to modify your scheduled backup or to stop it from running.

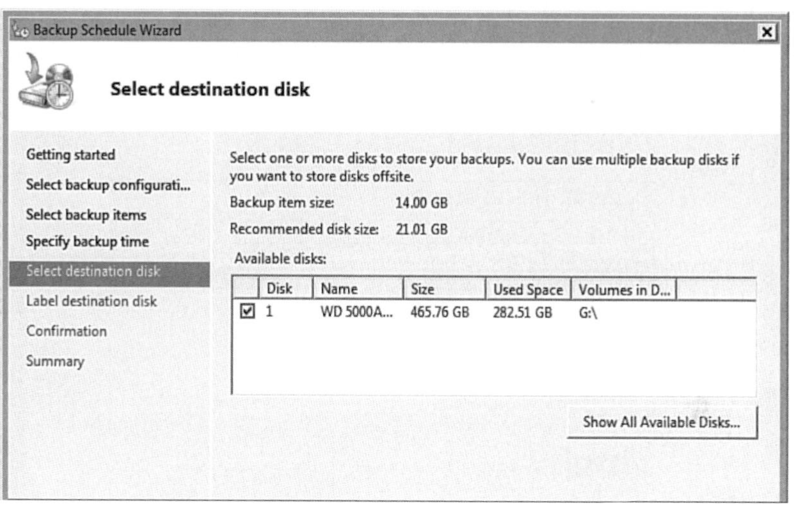

Figure 17-41 Selecting the backup target.

Single-Time Backups

You can also run an ad-hoc backup, which is a one-off backup. When you run this type of backup, you cannot use the same disk as the target that you use for scheduled backups unless you choose to initiate a scheduled backup immediately, or if you added a drive letter to the scheduled backup disk. You can use any other volume on a basic disk with sufficient spare space except for OS volumes. You also can use data volumes and network shares. You cannot write backups to dynamic disks.

Click the Backup Once action to launch an immediate backup job. If you have a scheduled backup configured, you have the option to use the same options as the scheduled backup, or you can select Different options to perform a backup of different volumes and to alternate locations. If you select the same options as the scheduled job, no more configuration is required, and the backup is launched after you click Backup in the configuration screen. This is the only way to back up to the disk reserved for the scheduled backups, unless you have used the Disk Management MMC to assign the scheduled backup target disk a drive letter; however, that is not a best practice.

If you select different options, you can once again perform a Full server backup or a custom backup. That enables you to select specific volumes to back up, which is the same as when you configured a scheduled backup.

You are presented with an option, Enable System Recovery, which automatically checks the disks required to perform a complete PC recovery and prevents you from unchecking the critical volumes. That is why the option is selected, as shown in Figure 17-42.

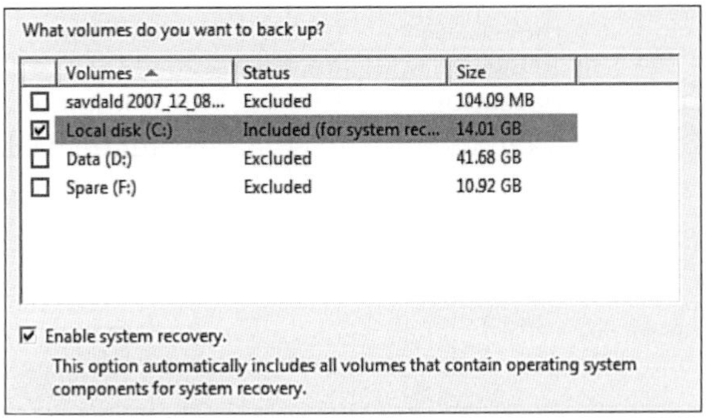

What volumes do you want to back up?

	Volumes	Status	Size
☐	savdald 2007_12_08...	Excluded	104.09 MB
☑	Local disk (C:)	Included (for system rec...	14.01 GB
☐	Data (D:)	Excluded	41.68 GB
☐	Spare (F:)	Excluded	10.92 GB

☑ Enable system recovery.
This option automatically includes all volumes that contain operating system components for system recovery.

FIGURE 17-42 There is an option to ensure that critical volumes for a system recovery are selected.

The next screen enables you to select the target for the backup, which is different from your scheduled job. First, choose if the backup is to a local drive or to a remote shared folder. Select the type of target, and the next stage in the wizard enables you to select either the drive to use or the shared folder target. Figure 17-43 shows a list of the local drives available.

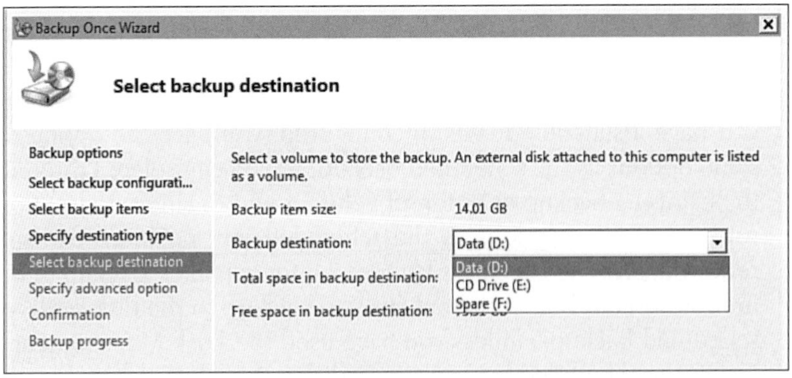

Backup Once Wizard

Select backup destination

Backup options
Select backup configurati...
Select backup items
Specify destination type
Select backup destination
Specify advanced option
Confirmation
Backup progress

Select a volume to store the backup. An external disk attached to this computer is listed as a volume.

Backup item size: 14.01 GB

Backup destination: Data (D:)

Total space in backup destination: Data (D:) / CD Drive (E:) / Spare (F:)

Free space in backup destination:

FIGURE 17-43 Backing up to a local drive.

Your last configuration choice is whether you are performing a VSS copy backup or VSS full backup. The difference is that a copy backup does not clear any log files associated with applications (for example, Exchange transaction logs). Select this if you primarily use another application to back up the application that maintains the log files. If WSB is the only backup solution for an application, use the VSS full backup option to clear the application log files and mark the files as backed up.

After all the options are set, click Backup on the confirmation screen, and the backup progress is displayed, showing the amount of data transferred and the percentage of the backup complete. You can close the progress window, and the backup continues in the background. To inspect it again, double-click the backup entry in the Messages window of the WSB console, as shown in Figure 17-44.

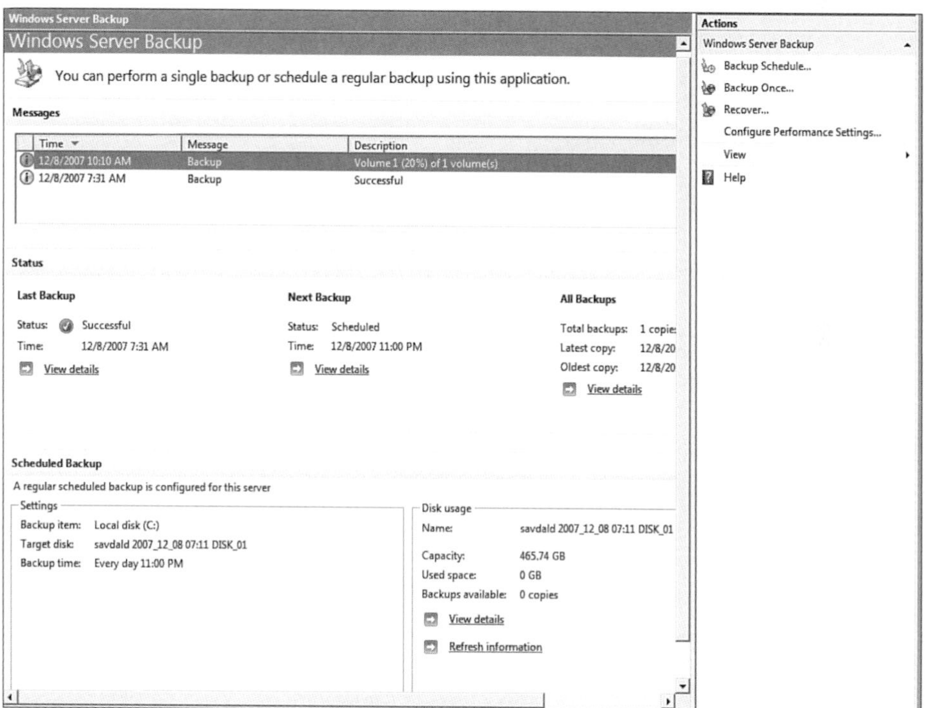

FIGURE 17-44 The WSB console shows the most recent backup status and any current backups.

You can view the actual files for an ad-hoc backup. A root folder on the destination disk is created, WindowsImageBackup, under which a folder with the name of the server is created. Under that folder, a catalog folder to track all the backups taken is created, as well as a folder for each backup that includes the VHD file containing the actual backup and several XML files detailing the content. The files in the catalog folder are used to track the backups taken and are read during a recovery.

The main WSB window displays a list of the most recent backup results, in addition to showing the space available for your scheduled backups and the details of your scheduled backup job. Click the View Details link to see information about the last, next, and all backups.

Backing Up the System State

To back up the system state, use the `wbadmin.exe` command, as follows:

```
wbadmin start systemstatebackup -backupTarget:<VolumeName>
```

For example, to create a system state backup and save it to volume F:, perform the following:

```
C:\>wbadmin start systemstatebackup -backupTarget:F:
wbadmin 1.0 - Backup command-line tool
(C) Copyright 2004 Microsoft Corp.

Starting System State Backup [12/8/2007 10:53 AM]
Retrieving volume information...

This would backup the system state from volume(s) Local
Disk(C:) to F:.
Do you want to start the backup operation?
[Y] Yes [N] No y

Creating the shadow copy of volumes requested for backup.
..
...
LOTS of files to process and % completed shown
...
```

This system state backup is horrendously slow and still leaves you with a large backup file. However, if your main boot volume is large, then backing up the system state might be desirable. On the other hand, given that a full backup finishes so much faster, the system state backup use is limited when you consider that a system state can be restored from a regular backup.

Performing a Recovery

This section covers the various types of recovery to make, including a complete restoration of a computer and selective data restore.

Complete PC Restore

To perform a System Restore, boot from the RE by inserting the Windows 2008 media and booting from the DVD. After making language selections, the screen to install the operating system is displayed. Instead of clicking the Install Now option, select the Repair Your Computer link at the bottom of the screen, which opens a dialog displaying the installed operating systems on the computer. Select the Windows Server 2008 instance you want to recover, and click Next to see your recovery options.

Click the Windows Complete PC Restore option, which performs a scan of all the disks on the system. By default, it gives the option to restore the latest backup taken, as shown in Figure 17-45. However, if a different backup should be restored, select the Restore a Different Backup option to show all known disks containing backups, as shown in Figures 17-45 and 17-46. After a disk is selected, all the backups stored on that backup disk are displayed, including the date and time of the backup and the volumes that are included in the backup. Select a backup to restore and click Next. In general, restore the most recent disk.

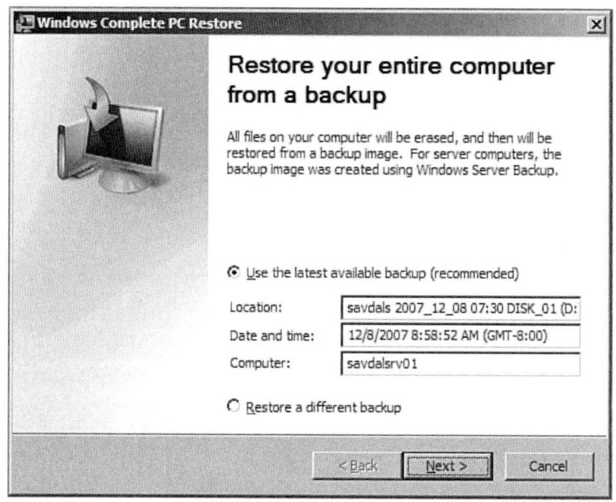

FIGURE 17-45 Performing a system restore.

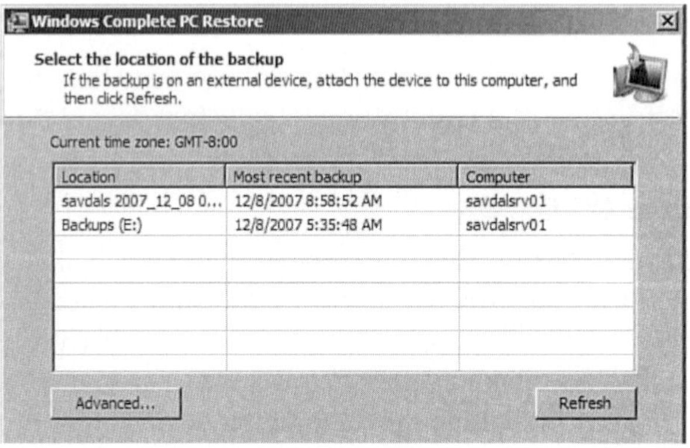

FIGURE 17-46 Selecting the location of the backup.

To restore a backup from a network location, click the Advanced button. It enables a network location to be specified to search for backups; it also includes an option to load additional drivers, which might then expose disks currently unreadable.

After the backup to restore is selected, you are presented with the advanced options, which give you the option to format and repartition disks to match those defined in the backup. This is desirable if you have inserted a new disk to restore to. If your partitions are still intact and you just want to restore the system, leave the option unselected (see Figure 17-47). If you check the option, click the Exclude disks button to prevent disks in the system from being repartitioned. By default, the disk containing the backup being restored is automatically excluded. If you boot from a recovery environment installed locally on the hard drive, the option to format and partition is not available. Click the Advanced button to control the automatic reboot after restoration and the checking of disk error information.

After all settings are confirmed, click Next. A summary is displayed. Click Finish to start the restoration, and if you chose to repartition the disk, another dialog pops up, asking to confirm whether you want to wipe all the volumes on a disk and potentially lose data. The restoration then commences with the progress shown. After reboot, your computer is restored and should be good as new!

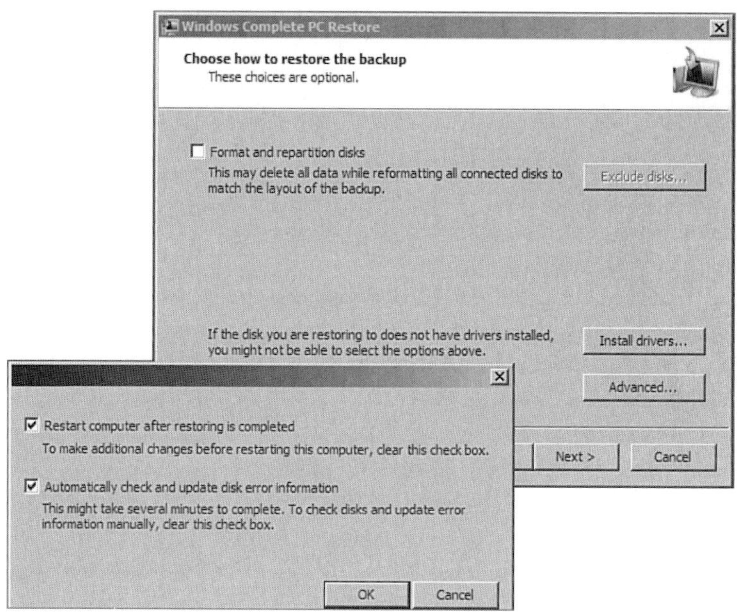

FIGURE 17-47 Selecting advanced restore options.

System State Recovery

To perform a restore of the system state, use the `wbadmin` command:

```
Wbadmin start systemstaterecovery -version:<version of backup
in format mm/dd/yyyy-hh:mm>
```

WSB restores all files/folders reported by "System State Writers" and also the Registry; then the administrator is asked to reboot the server so files that are in use can be replicated, including the Registry. Reboot immediately, and after the reboot, the system state recovery is complete. An example execution is shown in the following listing:

```
C:\>wbadmin start systemstaterecovery
➥-version:12/08/2007-16:58
wbadmin 1.0 - Backup command-line tool
(C) Copyright 2004 Microsoft Corp.

Do you want to start the system state recovery operation?
[Y] Yes [N] No y
```

```
Starting System State Restore [12/8/2007 12:08 PM]
Processing files to restore (This may take a few minutes)...
…
LOTS of files to process and % completed shown
…
Overall progress - 98% (Currently restoring files reported by
'System Writer')

Summary of recovery:
--------------------

Restore of system state completed successfully [12/8/2007
12:21 PM]

Log of files successfully restored
'C:\Windows\Logs\WindowsServerBackup\SystemStateRestore 08-12-
2007 12-08-40.log'

Please restart the machine to complete the operation.
NOTE: When you restart your server, System State Recovery will
attempt to recover many system files which may take several
minutes to complete depending on the number of files that are
getting replaced. The machine might reboot multiple times in
the process. Please be patient and do not interrupt the reboot
process.
```

After the reboot completes and you log on, a command window opens, confirming the system state recovery completed, as shown in the following:

```
wbadmin 1.0 - Backup command-line tool
(C) Copyright 2004 Microsoft Corp.

System State Recovery operation started at 12/8/2007 12:08 PM
completed successfully
Press ENTER to continue...
```

Volume/Files/Folders/Application Data

The final type of restore is that done within the operating system, restoring a subset of the data on a volume. This is the only time you use the WSB interface to restore information. Click the Recover action to launch the recovery wizard.

The first stage of the recovery wizard is to indicate whether data should be recovered from the local server or another server. In this case, select the local server. However, to use backup data from another server, select Another Server and click Next, which enables the backup store location to be chosen, such as a network share location.

After the location to restore from is selected (local computer, drive, or network location), a calendar is displayed, as shown in Figure 17-48, which shows all the available backups with the day shown in bold. The Time field is a drop-down of all available backups for that day.

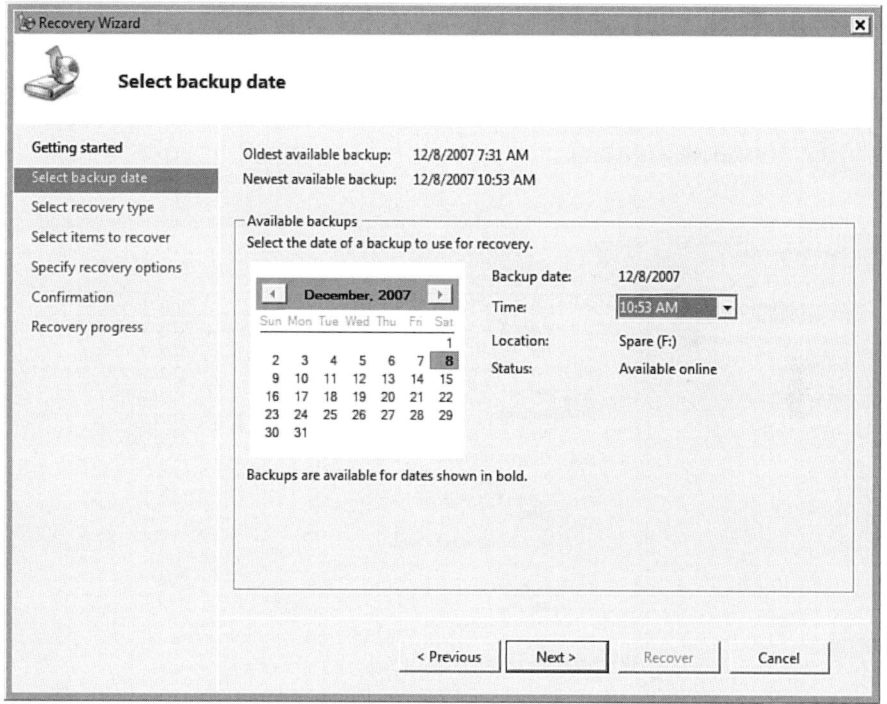

FIGURE 17-48 Selecting the backup to restore.

After the backup has been selected, the type of recovery can be selected:

- **Files and folders**. Enables individual files and folders to be selected for recovery, as shown in Figure 17-49. After the files are chosen, the next stage prompts you to indicate where the data should be restored: to either the original or alternate location. Additionally, options can be set for how restored files behave if a file of the same name already exists. Options include replacing, creating a renamed copy so both files are maintained, or doing nothing. Finally, you can choose whether security settings are restored.

- **Applications**. If application VSS writers are registered on the server and the backup contains data applicable to the application VSS writer, individual application data can be restored. For example, you could restore Exchange message stores if a volume contained an Exchange database and the Exchange VSS writer was installed.
- **Volumes**. Restore an entire volume to a selected volume.

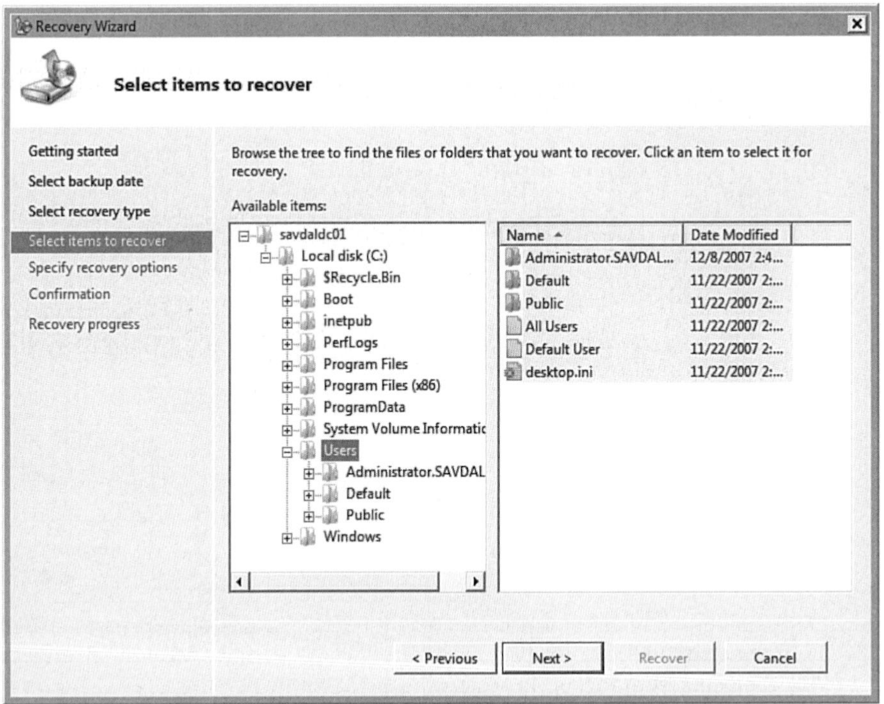

FIGURE 17-49 Selecting files to restore.

Command-Line Interface (CLI) Management

WBADMIN.EXE is provided for CLI-based management of backup. Anything possible via the GUI is possible via WBADMIN. This is useful for your Windows Server Core installations that have to use the CLI tool, unless you remotely manage them.

View all known backups using the `get versions` `wbadmin` command, which is useful when you want to restore from the command line, as you have to pass the version to restore (version identifier). The following listing provides an example:

```
C:\>wbadmin get versions
wbadmin 1.0 - Backup command-line tool
(C) Copyright 2004 Microsoft Corp.

Backup time: 12/8/2007 7:35 AM
Backup target: Fixed Disk labeled Backups(E:)
Version identifier: 12/08/2007-13:35
Can Recover: Volume(s), File(s), Application(s), Bare Metal
Recovery, System State

Backup time: 12/8/2007 10:58 AM
Backup target: Fixed Disk labeled savdals 2007_12_08 07:30
DISK_01(\\?\Volume{44
18d907-a590-11dc-b936-00155d011e01})
Version identifier: 12/08/2007-16:58
Can Recover: Volume(s), File(s), Application(s), Bare Metal
Recovery, System State
```

To perform a backup from the command line, use the `wbadmin start backup` command, which, with no additional parameters, runs an immediate backup using the parameters of the configured schedule backup.

Alternatively, you can perform more granular backups via the `-backupTarget` switch to specify the target volume or network share for the backup and the `-include` switch to specify the volumes to back up. Or you can use the `-allcritical` switch to have `wbadmin` ensure the important volumes on the system are backed up. Plus, via `-vssFull`, you can specify that you want to perform a full VSS backup instead of the default VSS copy.

The command in the following listing performs a full VSS backup of the C: volume (add a colon to the end of the volume) to the E: volume:

```
C:\>wbadmin start backup -backupTarget:E: -include:C: -vssFull
wbadmin 1.0 - Backup command-line tool
(C) Copyright 2004 Microsoft Corp.

Retrieving volume information...
```

```
This would backup volume Local Disk(C:) to E:.

Do you want to start the backup operation?
[Y] Yes [N] No y

Backup to E: is starting.

Creating the shadow copy of volumes requested for backup.
```

To view the content of a backup, use the `wbadmin get items` command, passing the version to inspect.

Restoring from the command line is accomplished using the `wbadmin start recovery` command, passing the version to restore (`-version`) and the type and specifics of the data to recover. For type, indicate volume, applications, or file (`-itemtype:Volume|App|File`), and for the specifics, include the `-items` switch. Run `wbadmin start recovery /?` to see a list of all the options for recovery and examples.

The best policy is to ensure you have a scheduled backup configured to make sure your server has resiliency, and also to ensure you have an offsite backup, in case your location becomes unavailable due to disasters such as fire damage, flood, and so on. The frequency at which an offsite backup should be performed depends on the criticality of the up-to-dateness of the data and the cost required for a frequent offsite backup. There are many services that collect backups each day and store them securely.

Volume Shadow Copy Service (VSS)

No backup conversation could be considered complete until Volume Shadow Copy is explored in a bit more detail. In the old days, pre-Windows 2003, it was cumbersome to get a good backup. Typically, to get a complete backup that was usable, it was important that any files that were required for the service or application were not open; this meant that the service had to be shut down during the backup. For applications with large amounts of data to back up, such as an Exchange database, this could take a long time, so there would be a long service outage. This was not acceptable. Some solutions existed to enable open files to be backed up. However, this did not guarantee the integrity or consistency of the file. For example, a database might not have flushed transactions completely, and to speed up backup times, it was common to back up to disk and then copy the backup from disk to tape.

With Windows Server 2003, Microsoft introduced the VSS, which was a set of APIs and components that enabled point-in-time copies of a unit of data, also known as snapshots and shadow copies. The VSS enabled a consistent copy of a source, such as a database or file system, to be taken in seconds without the application being stopped. Then the snapshot could be backed up to tape while the application was running. To achieve this, the support of the industry was required as VSS breaks down into four components:

- **VSS Requestor**. The VSS requestor makes the initial request for a snapshot to be taken. The Windows Server 2008 Backup solution is a VSS requestor, and nearly all other backup solutions from third parties are VSS requestors.
- **VSS Coordination Service**. This is part of the operating system and coordinates with all the other VSS components to ensure the snapshot is taken correctly.
- **VSS Writer**. The VSS writer is application/service-specific and guarantees that the data captured is consistent. Examples include Exchange and SQL, which both provide VSS writers that are called to take care of flushing transactions to the database and ensuring the database files are in a state suitable for copying for backup.
- **VSS Provider**. The VSS provider keeps shadow copies maintained after they are taken. This might not make sense right now, but read on—there are two types of snapshot, and you are probably wondering how you can copy a 50GB database in seconds. Windows provides us with a copy-on-write (differential) provider, while hardware solutions such as SANs provide clone (full copy) VSS providers.

You have multiple components. How do they play together? The first stage is wanting a backup, so the backup application, for example Windows Backup (VSS requestor), can enumerate the VSS writers on a system to ascertain which data can be backed up via VSS—for example, an Exchange mail database or a NTFS partition—and then communicates to the VSS coordinator that data is to be backed up. The VSS writers are informed that a backup of data that they are responsible for is requested. The VSS writer freezes any write to the data, ensures the data is consistent, and queues up any write requests to the data (read requests are still permitted). The VSS provider then takes a snapshot of the data once informed by the VSS writer that the data is ready. This could be a clone or differential via a hardware or software provider. After the snapshot is complete (it has to be within 10 seconds, or the snapshot is considered to have failed), the VSS writers are informed the snapshot has been taken. The VSS writers write any queued-up writes that were marked while the copy was performed. The VSS requestor, the backup software, is then notified that the snapshot was taken successfully.

The part that baffles most people is the actual VSS provider. How, in under 10 seconds, is a copy of potentially hundreds of gigabytes of data taken? There are two answers. If you are using a SAN that supports VSS, the SAN has a VSS provider that takes advantage of the SAN functionality to copy large amounts of data in a small amount of time. The actual methods depend on the SAN, but might involve caching data or writing data to other areas of disk while a copy finishes. But it's all handled at the hardware level. This hardware provider typically enables either a differential or clone snapshot, with the clone being a complete copy of the data in another location.

For those without a VSS-supported storage solution, such as a locally attached drive, how is that data snapshot-ed in 10 seconds or less? The software VSS providers use takes differential snapshots, also known as *copy-on-write*, which work in a different way.

For a copy-on-write snapshot, no copy of the data is performed. Instead, all the snapshot contains are blocks on the disk, which contain information related to the snapshot. This process is shown in Figure 17-50.

In step 1, you have a disk with data that takes up certain blocks on the disk. A snapshot is taken in step 2, and in step 3, the snapshot is now linked to the blocks on the disk that the data occupied. When a change is attempted on a block that is part of a VSS snapshot, in step 4 the write is intercepted; before the new data is written, the current content of the block is copied into the snapshot area and linked to the snapshot instance, and then the new data is written. In this way, when a point-in-time snapshot needs to be viewed, the system looks at the current blocks on the volume related to the snapshot and then any blocks that have been added to the shadow copy area, as shown in step 5. These shadow copy blocks contain data that has subsequently been overwritten in the original block locations by new data, and the shadow copy blocks are effectively overlaid by whatever new data is in the block. So when the snapshot is viewed, the data is viewed as it was at the time the snapshot was taken.

Remember, this is just the snapshot generation. After the snapshot is generated, it can be exposed to an application, which could then copy the content of the snapshot to another location or disk.

There are advantages to the clone method. Because the clone is a complete copy of the data, that snapshot is generally transportable, which means it could be copied to another server to be read. Some solutions use this capability to perform a clone snapshot, copy the snapshot to another server, and then back up to tape on another server or even restore the snapshot on another server to quickly create a copy of a server for development/testing purposes. Because a copy-on-write snapshot is just changes from the original data on the disk, the snapshot on its own is not complete and cannot be transported to another server for use.

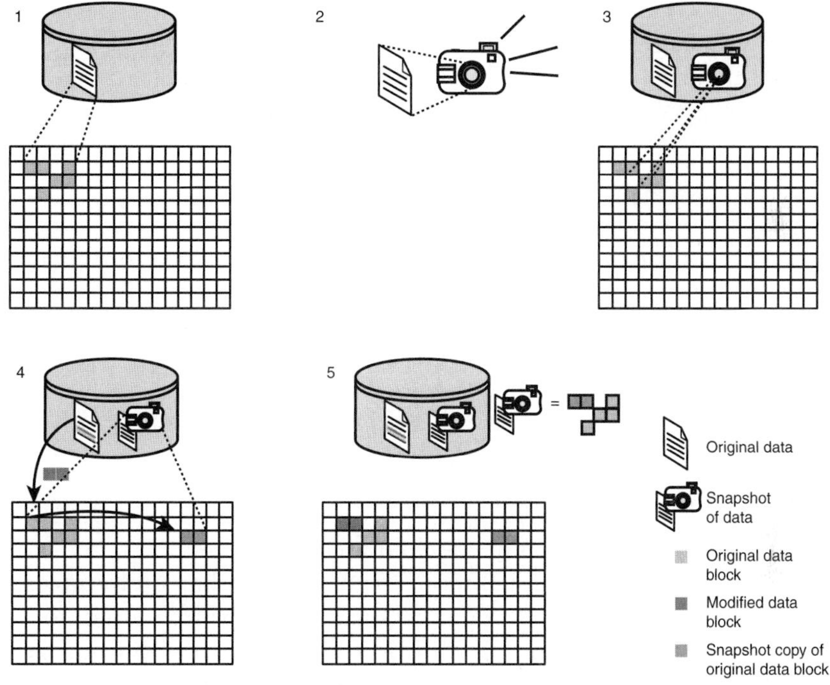

FIGURE 17-50 A copy-on-write snapshot in action.

Additionally, the copy-on-write increases system overhead. Any time a write is performed to disk, if the write is to data covered by a copy-on-write snapshot, the old data first has to be copied to another area before the write can be completed.

New to Windows Server 2008 is Diskshadow, which is an in-box VSS requestor that can be used to request and access volume shadow copies, both hardware and software. This tool runs from the command line and can also be used in scripts to automate VSS processes.

The cool thing about Diskshadow is it's not just used to back up things. In fact, it's more useful as a way to interrogate hardware and software snapshots to check content, list all the VSS writers on a system, enable a shadow copy to be mounted as a drive letter and accessed, import a transportable shadow copy (that is, a clone) into a system, and even revert a volume back to a shadow's copy content.

To view the VSS providers, use the `list providers` command. Notice that `diskshadow` is an environment. Start `diskshadow` first and then enter commands. Unless you have a hardware add-on, you probably just have the Microsoft shadow copy provider, as in the following example:

```
C:\>diskshadow
Microsoft DiskShadow version 1.0
Copyright (C) 2007 Microsoft Corporation
On computer:  SAVDALDC01,  12/20/2007 4:38:32 PM


DISKSHADOW> list providers

        * ProviderID: {b5946137-7b9f-4925-af80-51abd60b20d5}
                Type: [1] VSS_PROV_SYSTEM
                Name: Microsoft Software Shadow Copy provider
1.0
                Version: 1.0.0.7
                CLSID: {65ee1dba-8ff4-4a58-ac1c-3470ee2f376a}

Number of providers registered: 1
```

To view all the writers on your system, use the `list writers` command, which shows much more output. Depending on the roles and features installed on a system, additional writers will be listed; for example, NTDS has a VSS writer (used by ADDS), IIS has a writer, and so on. A list of all known shadow copies can be found via the `list shadows all` command.

Multiple commands can be placed in a script file and passed to `diskshadow` via the `/s` switch. In the following steps, create a snapshot and then expose the snapshot as a drive letter (S:). Notice an environment variable is created, which contains the ID of the shadow copy to make it easy to script actions on an ID that is not known until the shadow copy is created:

```
DISKSHADOW> set context persistent nowriters

DISKSHADOW> set metadata d:\temp\shadowtest.cab

DISKSHADOW> set verbose on

DISKSHADOW> begin backup
```

```
DISKSHADOW> add volume c: alias cdriveshadow

DISKSHADOW> create

Alias cdriveshadow for shadow ID {1ef1939f-42c6-4ddd-a432-
612521909f5e} set as environment variable.
Alias VSS_SHADOW_SET for shadow set ID {e3b47d8a-9c39-4f6a-
bfe0-51182bfe6b5e} set as environment variable.
Inserted file Manifest.xml into .cab file shadowtest.cab
Inserted file Dis7DB8.tmp into .cab file shadowtest.cab

Querying all shadow copies with the shadow copy set ID
{e3b47d8a-9c39-4f6a-bfe0-51182bfe6b5e}

        * Shadow copy ID = {1ef1939f-42c6-4ddd-a432-
612521909f5e}
%cdriveshadow%
                - Shadow copy set: {e3b47d8a-9c39-4f6a-bfe0-
51182bfe6b5e}
%VSS_SHADOW_SET%
                - Original count of shadow copies = 1
                - Original volume name: \\?\Volume{dd30f127-
a399-11dc-bd88-806e6f6e6963}\ [C:\]
                - Creation time: 12/20/2007 4:49:09 PM
                - Shadow copy device name:
\\?\GLOBALROOT\Device\HarddiskVolumeShadowCopy39
                - Originating machine:
savdaldc01.savilltech.net
                - Service machine: savdaldc01.savilltech.net
                - Not exposed
                - Provider ID: {b5946137-7b9f-4925-af80-
51abd60b20d5}
                - Attributes:  No_Auto_Release Persistent
No_Writers Differential

Number of shadow copies listed: 1

DISKSHADOW> expose %cdriveshadow% s:
-> %cdriveshadow% = {1ef1939f-42c6-4ddd-a432-612521909f5e}
The shadow copy was successfully exposed as s:\.

DISKSHADOW> end backup
```

The S: drive is visible on the server and the data in the snapshot is visible and could be copied elsewhere. You know the S: drive is a consistent, reliable copy of the source partition. To unexpose the snapshot as a drive letter, use the `unexpose` command. In the following example, unexpose and then delete the shadow copy.

```
DISKSHADOW> unexpose s:
Shadow copy ID {1ef1939f-42c6-4ddd-a432-612521909f5e} is no
longer exposed.

DISKSHADOW> delete shadows id {1ef1939f-42c6-4ddd-a432-
612521909f5e}
Deleting shadow copy {1ef1939f-42c6-4ddd-a432-612521909f5e}...

1 shadow copy deleted.
```

Patch Management

Keeping your servers patched is important as vulnerabilities are found and then exposed. You need a good method to ensure that the latest updates get applied to your servers in a timely fashion, not *after* the latest vulnerability is found on your network.

Microsoft releases patches on the second Tuesday of each month. A Microsoft Security Bulletin Advance Notification is released three business days prior to the patch day before 10:00 a.m., outlining the security (and other) patches that will be released. On the actual release day, a Security Bulletin Summary is released, finalizing the details about the patches.

The Security Bulletins can be found at http://www.microsoft.com/athome/security/update/bulletins/default.mspx and a summary at http://www.microsoft.com/technet/security/bulletin/summary.mspx. To sign up for the bulletins, go to http://www.microsoft.com/technet/security/Bulletin/advance.mspx.

Urgent patches are rarely released, and only if a vulnerability is sufficiently dangerous that it cannot be left unaddressed; in this case, Microsoft also notifies subscribers. If you are responsible for patching or the security of your organization, sign up for the security bulletins.

One interesting side effect of patch Tuesday is exploit Wednesday. This is caused by hackers viewing the patches released on Tuesday, reverse engineering to ascertain the vulnerability the patch fixed, and then attacking the vulnerability that the patch is intended to fix—all before the patch can be implemented. It is, therefore, important to get patches applied as quickly as possible.

Windows Server 2008 makes the patching of your server a priority task. It is part of the ICT and part of the Security Information section of Server Manager; unless automatic updating is enabled, every time you add roles and features, you receive a warning about the Windows Update configuration.

To configure Windows Update, use the Windows Update control panel applet. It enables the current configuration to be displayed in addition to the update history. It also enables you to change the update settings, as shown in Figure 17-51.

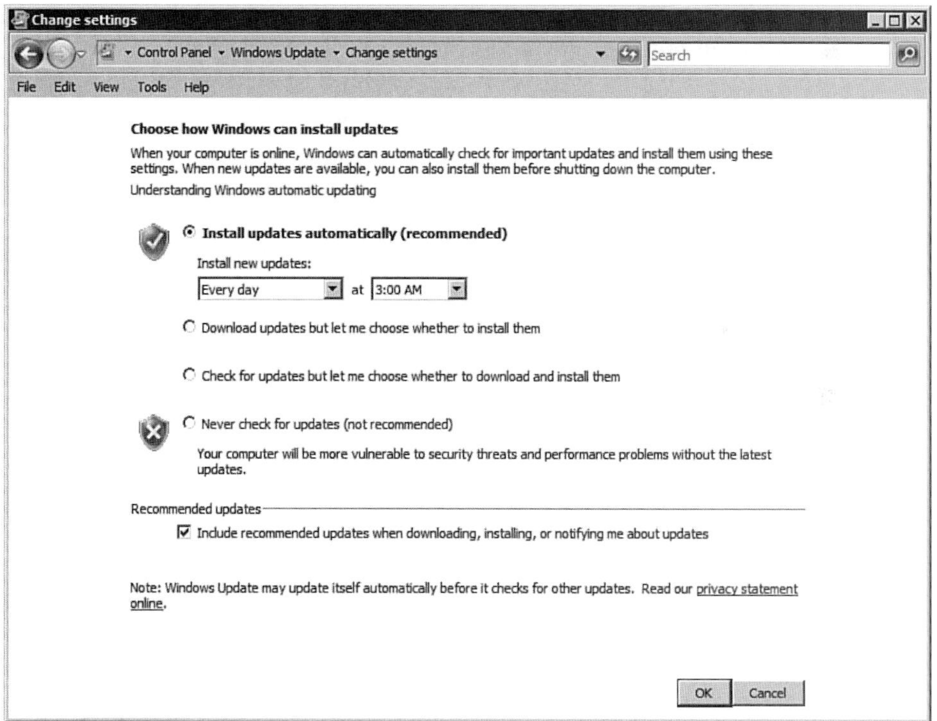

FIGURE 17-51 Configuring the automatic update status.

As shown in the figure, you can configure the settings to automatically install updates and set how often to install patches that are found to be required. The frequency can be every day or once a week on a specific day—for example, on Tuesday after new patches are released. You can set the time to install. The actual process of checking for updates is done in the background every 17.6 to 22 hours (there is a random offset in the checking process).

Alternatively, you can choose to download the patches automatically but to wait for the administrator to allow the patches to be installed. You also can choose to detect patches that are required, but not download or install them until authorized by the administrator. Finally, you can choose to never check for updates, which is not recommended because the server is left totally exposed.

A final configuration enables recommended patches to also be downloaded and installed using the same option as for the important updates. To view additional types of updates such as drivers and options, click the Check for updates link under the main Windows Update dialog; this checks for any type of update that applies to the server.

You can configure Windows Update to automatically pull down applicable drivers via the Hardware tab of the System control panel applet. It has a Windows Update Driver Settings option that enables you to select whether drivers should automatically be pulled from Windows Update, whether the administrator should be prompted to check Windows Update, or to never check Windows Update for drivers.

One big change with Windows Vista and Windows Server 2008 is, thanks to transactional NTFS and the Registry, a patch installation is now done as part of a transaction. If the install of a patch fails, there is no requirement to undo any changes that might have been made. Until the installation of the update is complete and the transaction committed, there are no changes made to the system.

Group Policy Configuration

The best practice to ensure that servers (and workstations) are configured for optimal Windows Updates is to use Group Policy to enforce automatic updating. In previous versions of Windows, you had to load a special administrative template into a Group Policy Object (GPO) to be able to manage Windows Update. However, with Windows Server 2008, this is a core part of the automatically loaded templates.

Create or open a GPO that is linked to the domain or organization units containing computers you want to configure for automatic update and navigate to Computer Configuration, Policies, Administrative Templates, Windows Components, Windows Update; this has several key settings you use to configure updating (see Figure 17-52).

The Configure Automatic Updates setting reflects the values you configure via the Windows Update control panel applet and enables you to set how updates are downloaded and installed, along with the time of installation.

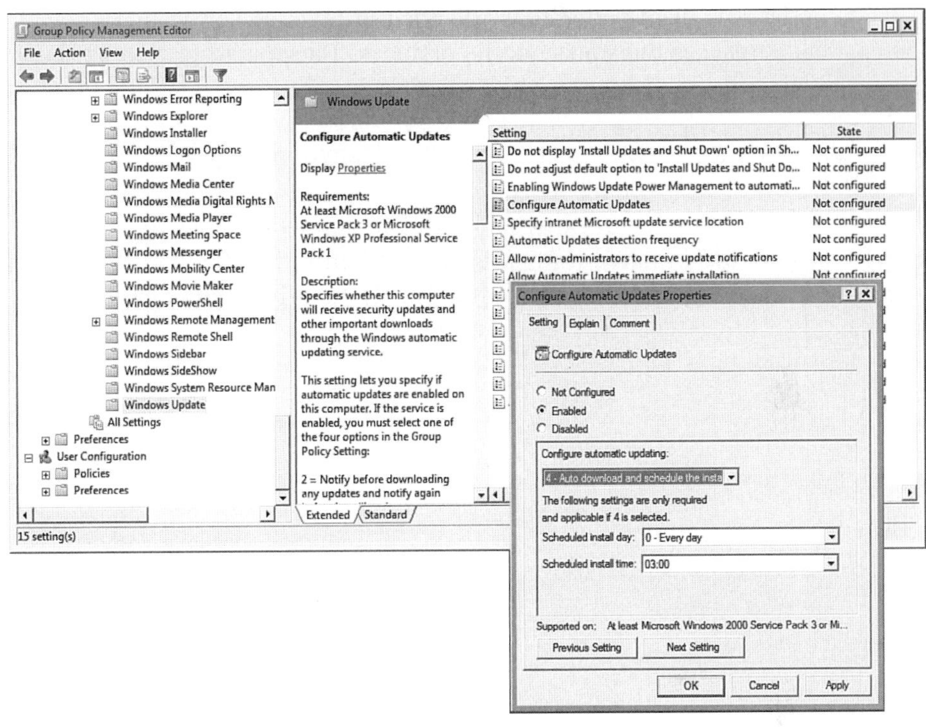

FIGURE 17-52 Managing Windows Update via Group Policy.

Other settings allow you to configure how often to check for updates (Automatic Updates Detection Frequency) and for waking the machine, if sleeping, to install updates (Enabling Windows Update Power Management to Automatically Wake Up the System to Install Scheduled Updates), and more. Take a look at the Windows update policy area. There is a lot of configuration possible concerning all aspects of deployment and system restarts related to patch application.

Microsoft Update Catalog

Microsoft has a catalog web site that downloads updates from update.microsoft.com for local installation. It is available from http://catalog.update.microsoft.com/v7/site/Home.aspx. This catalog has all the updates, drivers, and hotfixes that would normally be available from the Microsoft update web site.

To use the site, enter a search in the search dialog on the main page (for example, "vista 64-bit driver") and click Search. A list of all matching updates is displayed. Click Add for the updates you want to download, which causes the update to be added to the update basket, as shown in Figure 17-53.

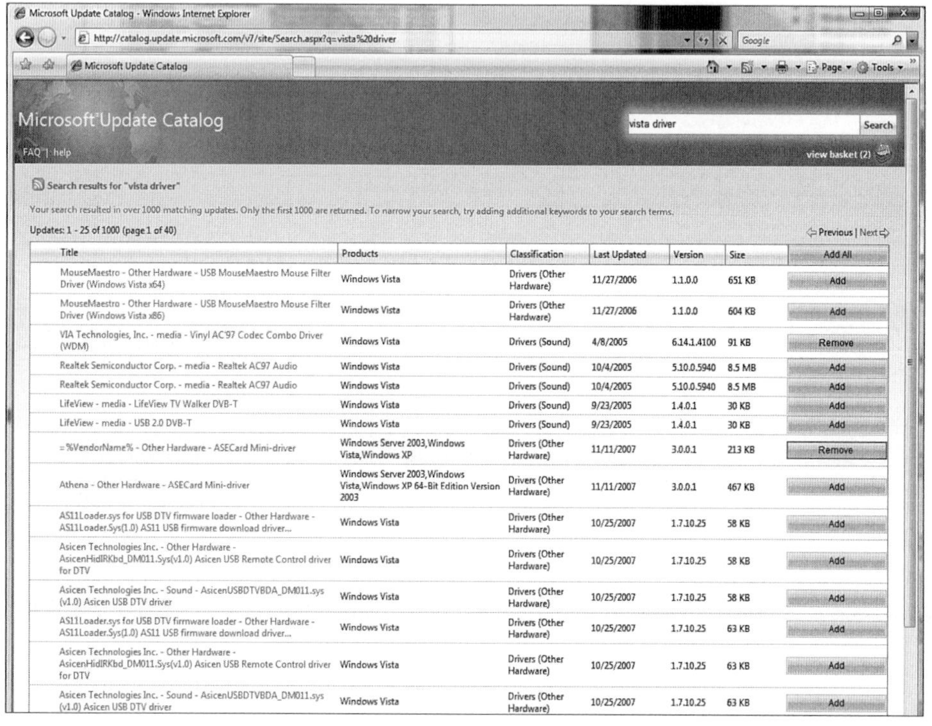

FIGURE 17-53 Adding updates to the download basket.

Multiple searches can be performed and more updates added to the catalog. After all updates are in the catalog, click the view basket link under the search box, which displays all the updates in the update basket. Click the Download button, and you are prompted to confirm a folder to download the updates to and click Continue. The updates download with the download progress displayed and once complete, click Close in the download window.

Each update is placed in its own subfolder of the selected destination folder, which is named the same as the update title. You can then use these downloaded patches to inject them into a Windows Image ready for automatic inclusion in OS deployments or deploy them to your organization via a patch deployment process. What follows is an example folder structure of downloaded updates:

```
D:\temp\Drivers>dir
 Volume in drive D is Data
 Volume Serial Number is 1CA8-B772

 Directory of D:\temp\Drivers

12/09/2007  05:44 AM    <DIR>          .
12/09/2007  05:44 AM    <DIR>          ..
12/09/2007  05:44 AM    <DIR>          nVidia - Video - NVIDIA
GeForce 8800 GTS
12/09/2007  05:45 AM    <DIR>          NVIDIA driver update
for NVIDIA GeForce 8
800 GTS
12/09/2007  05:44 AM    <DIR>          Xbox Peripherals driver
update for Micros
oft Xbox 360 Live Vision Camera
               0 File(s)              0 bytes
               5 Dir(s)  91,184,259,072 bytes free
```


Update Options

Although Automatic Update keeps your servers patched automatically, as an organization, you have no control over the patches applied. This might be an issue for your servers, as in most cases, you would want to test the effects of a patch on a server prior to deploying to production. Therefore, you have options.

Windows Server Update Services (WSUS), which can be downloaded from http://technet.microsoft.com/en-us/wsus/default.aspx, enables a server to be placed within the organization's environment; this synchronizes its own patch database with that of Microsoft. It enables administrators to authorize patches for deployment in the organization prior to clients (desktops and servers) downloading them. The WSUS uses the same process as Windows Update, but instead of the client checking at Microsoft, the client checks the internal WSUS server. This is accomplished via the Specify Intranet Microsoft Update Service Location Group Policy setting, which tells the clients where to look for updates. The same thing is accomplished by updating Registry value WUServer under key HKEY_LOCAL_MACHINE\Software\Policies\Microsoft\Windows\WindowsUpdate\AU. WSUS also has reporting capabilities to track the patch deployment process.

Another option is to use System Center Configuration Manager (SCCM) 2007, which turns off auto update on the clients and sends the updates as packages to the client via SCCM's software deployment process. It enables full reporting on the deployment process. SCCM has full inventory capabilities so it's possible to run reports to see exactly what patches are deployed on each computer and those that are missing.

Note that while WSUS and SCCM are the best options, this applies only if administrators keep those systems up-to-date with approved patches. If the patch deployment solutions are not kept current with the latest approved patches, then clients will not receive updates in a timely fashion, leaving them vulnerable. If you use WSUS or SCCM, ensure you have a good process to approve patches regularly. Figure 17-54 illustrates the three main patch deployment solutions.

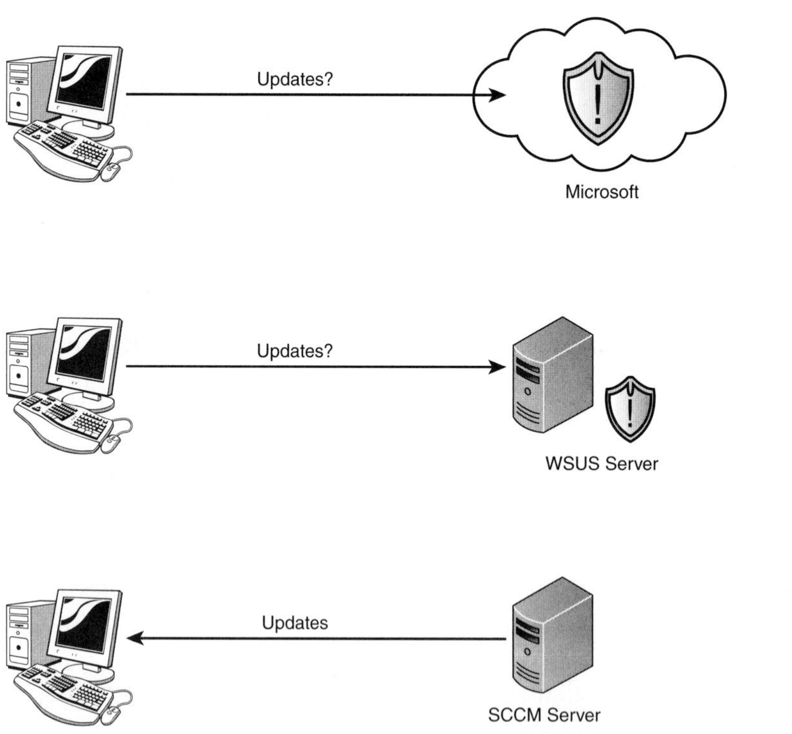

FIGURE 17-54 Update options.

Registry

The Registry is the cornerstone of the operating system and contains most of the configuration of the operating system and many applications. Most Group Policy settings set entries in the Registry, as do most of the control panel applets, and these tools are the best way to configure the system. However, there are times when you might want to directly modify the Registry, especially when there are problems.

The Registry is maintained via the regedit.exe tool, and there are five key Registry areas when the Registry editor is first launched (see Figure 17-55). Not all of these main branches are real branches; some are just links to other areas. HKEY_LOCAL_MACHINE is often referred to as HKLM and HKEY_CURRENT_USER as HKCU.

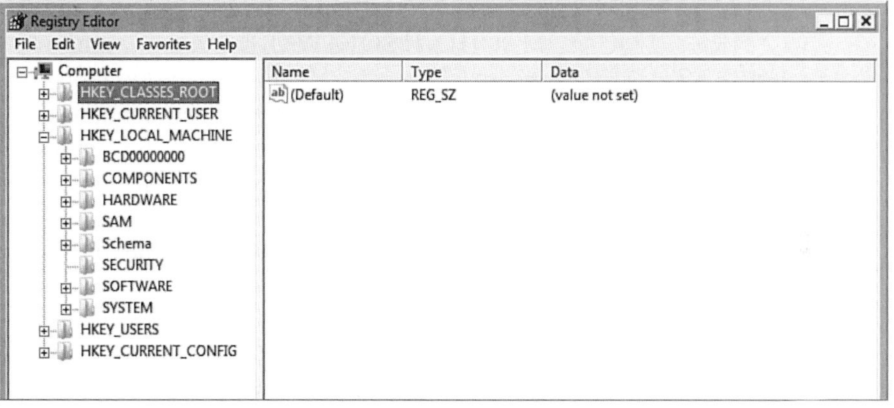

FIGURE 17-55 The Registry editor.

The Registry is stored in several files that are located in the %windir%\System32\config folder, except for each user's ntuser.dat, which is stored in their home profile area (%userprofile%). The Registry is made up of several hives, which are exposed via the Registry editor. The files that make up the hives are shown in Table 17-2. Additionally, each hive has a file with a .log extension, which is the transaction log file of changes to the hive, and a .sav extension file, which is a copy of the hive as it was at the end of the text portion of setup. The system hive also has an additional .alt file extension, which is a backup, as the system Registry hive contains all the most critical system information.

Table 17-2 Registry Hives and Their Supporting Files

Registry Hive	Supporting Files
HKEY_CURRENT_CONFIG	System
HKEY_CURRENT_USER	Ntuser.dat
HKEY_LOCAL_MACHINE\SAM	Sam
HKEY_LOCAL_MACHINE\Security	Security
HKEY_LOCAL_MACHINE\Software	Software
HKEY_LOCAL_MACHINE\System	System
HKEY_USERS\.DEFAULT	Default

Notice the keys in the Registry editor do not directly match those of the Registry hives. One of the root keys in the Registry editor is HKEY_CLASSES_ROOT, which is a merging of the information stored in HKEY_LOCAL_MACHINE\SOFTWARE\Classes and HKEY_CURRENT_USER\Software\Classes. It contains the information about file associations and COM class registration. HKEY_USERS contains a list of all the profiles that have been loaded on the computer, and HKEY_CURRENT_USER contains the information for the currently logged-on user.

The majority of information related to the operating system is contained in the HKEY_LOCAL_MACHINE\SYSTEM\CurrentControlSet key, which is an alias to one of the control sets known to the system storing the system configuration—for example, HKEY_LOCAL_MACHINE\SYSTEM\ControlSet001 and HKEY_LOCAL_MACHINE\SYSTEM\ControlSet003. To view which control set is being used, examine the HKEY_LOCAL_MACHINE\SYSTEM\Select key, which contains a Current value showing the control set that is in use.

The Registry contains a hierarchy of keys to define structure that can be thought of in the same way as folders for the file system; within a key, you have Registry values that can be of different types with the common values described in the following list:

- **String Value (REG_SZ)**. This can contain a fixed length ascii string.
- **Binary Value**. This is a raw binary data value.
- **DWORD (32-bit) Value**. A 32-bit number, 4 bytes.
- **QWORD (64-bit) Value**. Only available on 64-bit operating systems, a 64-bit number, 8 bytes.
- **Multi-String Value**. A value that can contain multiple string values.
- **Expandable String Value**. A variable length data string.

Modifying the Registry

The Registry editor (regedit.exe) is a fairly intuitive tool. The skill it takes to use it is not modifying values, which is accomplished by double-clicking on the value you want to modify, but finding the value in the first place.

Searches can be performed by selecting the key you want to search inside (all sub-keys are searched). Then, select Find from the Edit menu and select what you want to search for and what should be searched—that is, the name of the keys, the name of the values (which are like the attributes), and the data stored within the values (see Figure 17-56). Searches might take a while depending on the speed of the machine and the Registry key being searched. To search the entire Registry, select the root of the Registry, Computer, and run the search. To find the next match, press F3.

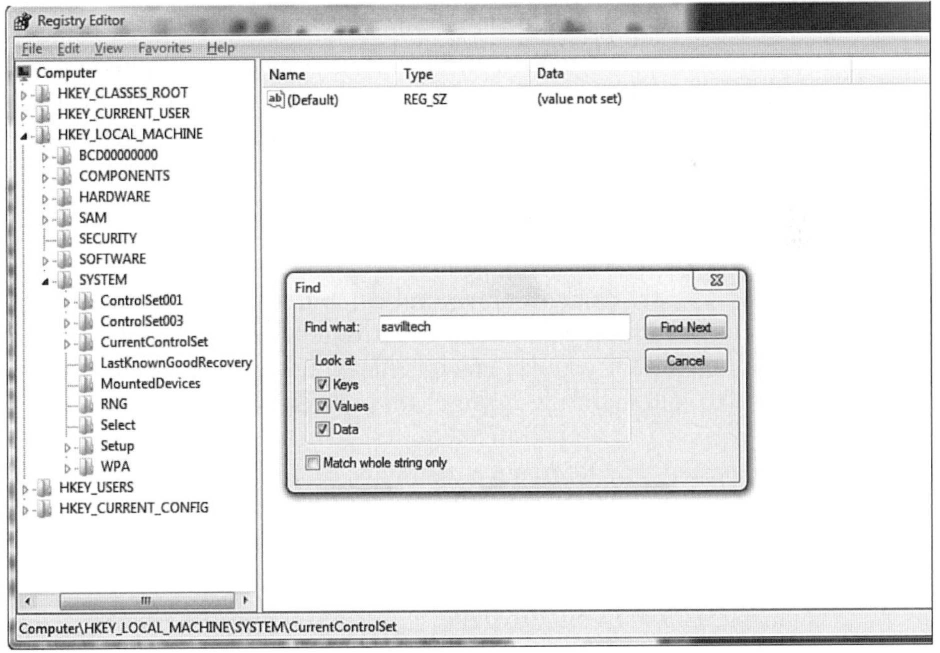

FIGURE 17-56 Searching the Registry.

To create new values or keys, right-click on the key under which the key/value should be created and select New; then select key or the type of value from the New submenu. Then enter a name for the new value. Next, you can double-click the new value and set data for it. If you are editing a

DWORD value, you can choose to enter the value in either hexadecimal or decimal. Make sure you set this correctly, as 5000 in hex is different than 5000 in decimal and could negatively affect your environment.

WARNING It is important to note that you should not be in the Registry without a good reason and a clear objective. Changing the Registry improperly or incorrectly can be damaging—a few poorly chosen values could render your system unbootable. Create a virtual test system and play there or on your workstation, but don't look around in a server's Registry, and only edit when you have to.

Like a file system, the Registry has Access Control Lists for each key and value that can be modified by selecting the key/value and then selecting Permissions from the Edit menu. You can give users general read or full control and, via the Advanced dialog, give individual rights concerning creating child values and keys, setting key values, and so on. The access control on the Registry is highly granular. Once again, the Registry has permissions in place on the important keys, which you should not modify.

Using .reg Files to Modify the Registry

To make Registry changes on several computers, you could create a custom adm/admx group policy administrative template and apply the settings via group policy. Or you can create a file with a .reg extension that can be executed to automatically make changes to the computer the .reg file is executed on.

The easiest way to create a .reg file is to make the changes on a computer that you want to distribute (modified values and new values) and then export out the key containing the values via the Export context menu for a key; this enables a file to be selected for all the values contained in the key to be written to. The following is an example export file:

```
Windows Registry Editor Version 5.00

[HKEY_LOCAL_MACHINE\SOFTWARE\SavillTech]
"DWORD1"=dword:0000002a
"String1"="I am a string"
"Binary1"=hex:10,01,10,10,10
"MultiStr1"=hex(7):4a,00,6f,00,68,00,6e,00,00,00,54,00,65,00,73
,00,74,00,00,00,\
```

```
  46,00,69,00,6c,00,65,00,00,00,00,00
"QWORD1"=hex(b):54,00,00,00,00,00,00,00
```

This same file could be executed (double-clicked); it would create the SavillTech key (if it did not exist) and create all the values contained within. Executing a Registry file prompts you as to whether you want to import the information stored within; click Yes. This is the same as performing an import from the File menu. Do not import a Registry file without first checking the content, though.

The format of a Reg file always contains the Registry editor version for the first line, then a blank line, and then the key for which values will be modified. For multivalue and expandable string values, notate the data as hexadecimal(7) and hexadecimal(2), respectively. The easiest way to do this is to create the values you want to place into a reg file into a Registry and then export out to file. This takes away all the hard work, unless you enjoy converting multivalue strings to hex!

To modify values in multiple keys, just use a blank line, and then the new key name under which to modify, for example:

```
Windows Registry Editor Version 5.00

[Key name]
"value"=dword:aaaaaa
 "value2"="string"

[Key name]
"value"=dword:aaaaaa
```

To delete a key from the Registry, add a hyphen (-) in front of the key. For example, to delete the SavillTech key under software, the Registry file would have the content shown next. Any values contained in the key are also deleted:

```
Windows Registry Editor Version 5.00

[-HKEY_LOCAL_MACHINE\SOFTWARE\SavillTech]
```

To delete an individual value, use the normal format to add/modify, but for the data, use a hyphen. To delete the String1 and MultiStr1 values, use the following code:

```
Windows Registry Editor Version 5.00
```

```
[HKEY_LOCAL_MACHINE\SOFTWARE\SavillTech]
"String1"=-
"MultiStr1"=-
```

There is no rename via a .reg file. To rename, delete the old value and create a new value with the new name.

So far, for all these .reg files, the user is prompted to click Yes to import. To import from a script and avoid user interaction, add `regedit /s` to the name of the Registry file, which performs a silent import:

```
Regedit /s import.reg
```

Command-Line Registry Access

You can access the Registry in several ways from the command line. PowerShell can be used to manage the Registry by accessing the Registry in the same manner as the file system. This is displayed in Chapter 22, "The Command Prompt and PowerShell," by accessing the HKCU: and HKLM: data stores. For example, the following shows the value of the ProductName value (you could just as easily set values by using set-ItemProperty cmdlet):

```
PS C:\Users\Administrator.SAVDALDC02> cd hklm:
PS HKLM:\> cd 'SOFTWARE\Microsoft\Windows NT\CurrentVersion\'
PS HKLM:\SOFTWARE\Microsoft\Windows NT\CurrentVersion>
Get-ItemProperty . -name ProductName


PSPath       :
Microsoft.PowerShell.Core\Registry::HKEY_LOCAL_MACHINE
\SOFTWARE\Microsoft\Windows NT\CurrentVersion
PSParentPath :
Microsoft.PowerShell.Core\Registry::HKEY_LOCAL_MACHINE
\SOFTWARE\Microsoft\Windows NT
PSChildName  : CurrentVersion
PSDrive      : HKLM
PSProvider   : Microsoft.PowerShell.Core\Registry
ProductName  : Windows Server (R) 2008 Enterprise
```

You can use WMI Registry provider methods via the WMI command interface (WMIC), as seen in Chapter 22, in addition to VBScript using the `RegDelete`, `RegRead`, and `RegWrite` methods. However, for the interactive command line, concentrate on the REG command, which can read, write, delete, and pretty much do anything with the Registry.

For a full list of commands, run `reg /?`. However, the codes in Table 17-3 are used for the five main keys of the Registry.

Table 17-3 Codes and Registry Keys

Code	Key
HKCR	HKEY_CLASSES_ROOT
HKCU	HKEY_CURRENT_USER
HKLM	HKEY_LOCAL_MACHINE
HKU	HKEY_USERS
HKCC	HKEY_CURRENT_CONFIG

To query the data in a Registry value, use the `reg query` command, passing the name of the key to inspect, and the `/v` switch with the name of the value whose data you want to view. In the following example, the product name is checked. Notice you use HKLM for HKEY_LOCAL_MACHINE, and HKCU for HKEY_CURRENT_USER:

```
C:\>reg query "HKLM\SOFTWARE\Microsoft\Windows NT
➥\CurrentVersion" /v ProductName

HKEY_LOCAL_MACHINE\SOFTWARE\Microsoft\Windows NT
➥\CurrentVersion
    ProductName    REG_SZ    Windows Server (R) 2008 Enterprise
```

To add a new Registry value, use the `reg add` command, passing the keyname the value to add (`/v`), the Registry value type (`/t`), and the data to store in the value (`/d`). Let's add a new value under the SavillTech software key of type string, storing `"almost done"` as the data (yes, this has been a long chapter!). `reg add` is also used to modify an existing value.

```
reg add HKLM\Software\SavillTech /v testString /t REG_SZ /d
"almost done"
```

If the Registry key has spaces in the path, place it in double quotes, as you did when you queried for a value earlier. For double quotes in the data to store in a value, you can't just type a double quote because you enclose the data in a double quote anyway. Add a back-slash (\) in front of the double quote (which is the escape sequence character).

To delete values, use the `reg del` command with the same format as an add—that is, the keyname with an option value (`/v`) to delete. If only a key is passed, the entire key is deleted. To delete all sub-keys, add the `/va` switch (value all). To avoid being prompted to perform the delete, add the `/f` (force) switch:

```
C:\>reg delete HKLM\Software\SavillTech /v testString /f
The operation completed successfully.
```

There are other commands possible with REG. Refer to the command-line help for the full list of options.

Backing Up the Registry

The Registry can be backed up via the command-line tools previously discussed, but it is also backed up when the system state is backed up or the boot volume is backed up via WSB. This is sufficient to protect the Registry. See the "Windows Server Backup (WSB)" section earlier in the chapter for more information on backing up and restoring the system state.

Performance and Paging File Tuning

The Advanced tab of the System control panel applet gives you the capability to set some important characteristics of the system, including how the system is prioritized regarding background and foreground processes, paging file sizing, and some core data execution protection settings.

Click the Settings button in the Performance section of the Advanced tab content of the System properties to access the Performance Options. They are broken down into three areas: visual effects, processor scheduling and virtual memory, and data execution prevention.

Visual Effects

By default, the visual effects are automatically configured according to some internal metrics used by Windows Server 2008 to decide what works best for the computer. They attempt to achieve a balance between aesthetically pleasing and not using up resources that would be better used servicing the services and applications. That is the main role of the server. This decision is based on the hardware available on the server. For a modern server, this is probably equivalent to choosing the Adjust for Best Appearance option, which enables all visual elements, as shown in Figure 17-57.

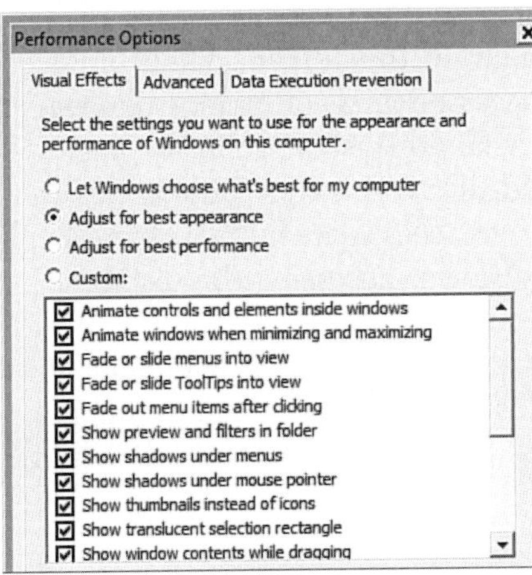

FIGURE 17-57 Visual options in Windows Server 2008.

If you choose Adjust for Best Performance, then none of the visual luxuries are enabled, ensuring no resources are diverted from the core purpose of the server. If you would like more control, select Custom and then enable specific graphical features you want to use—for example, enabling shadows or using thumbnails instead of icons.

Let Windows Choose What's Best for My Computer is a good option; with modern computers, the amount of resources used in many of these visual elements is so small, it will not affect the day-to-day working of the server.

Processor Scheduling and Virtual Memory

The main use for Windows Server 2008 is to run applications and services and not interactive applications; by default, the operating system favors background services for processor scheduling instead of interactive applications running in a user session. This means in the event of processor contention, the background services have priority. If you are using Windows Server 2008 as a workstation, or if the server is running an application that has to run as an interactive program in a session, you can configure Windows Server to give priority to programs via the Advanced tab of the Performance options and change the processor scheduling so that programs are given priority instead of background services.

The next item you can configure is the amount of disk-based virtual memory available to the system; this is an area on disk that subsidizes the physical memory in the machine in times when more memory is needed than is physically in the server. When physical memory is running out, infrequently accessed areas of memory, known as pages, are written to the virtual memory file; this is known as the paging file to make room in physical memory. Ideally, you want as little as possible written to the paging file; when you have to access data in the paging file, known as a page fault, it is multiple times slower accessing the disk-based paging file than accessing information in the physical RAM.

When Windows is installed, by default, the system drive is automatically selected as the location for the paging file, whose size varies dynamically as needed by the system. This is shown in Figure 17-58.

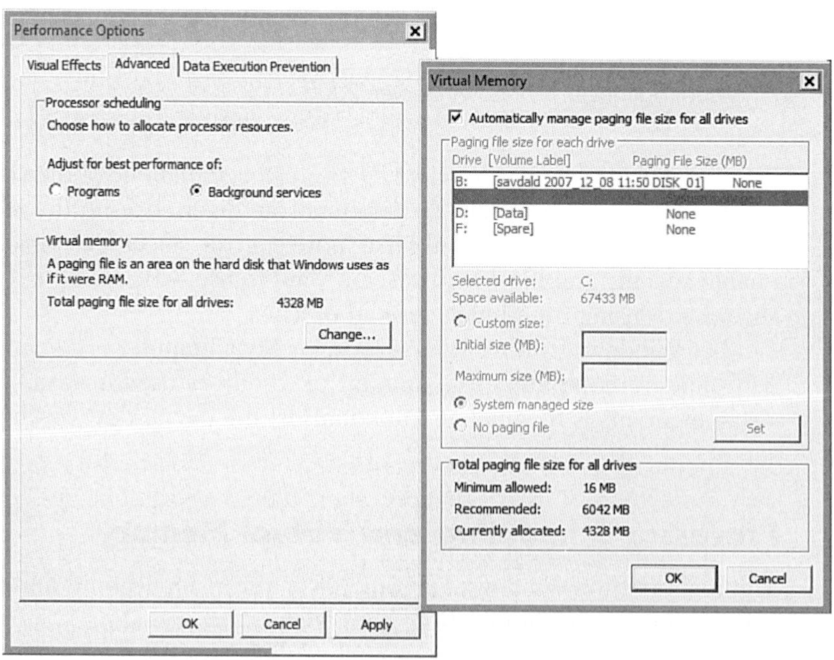

Figure 17-58 Configuring virtual memory for Windows Server 2008.

In most cases, leave the paging file configuration set to letting the operating system automatically manage the paging file sizing across the disks on the system as needed. There might be instances where you want to use different settings. One setting consists of setting a disk with a fixed-size paging file with an initial and maximum file size, or a paging file whose size is decided by the system. Another setting is specifying that the selected disk might not have a paging file.

One problem that creeps in if you have a system-managed paging file size is the paging file might shrink and grow over time, which sounds efficient. However, unless you have a volume dedicated to the paging file, the amount of contiguous space on the disk might not be sufficient to house the paging file. The paging file is then split into multiple parts on the partition and thus becomes fragmented. Because this happens repeatedly, the paging file gets more and more fragmented, hurting performance even more. You can defragment the paging file to help resolve this issue using add-on tools; one common practice is to disable the Automatically Manage Paging File Size for All Drives option and then change the paging file on the system drive to have the same size value for initial and maximum size. The space is allocated initially and does not grow or shrink, thus avoiding fragmentation. Obviously, if you are going to do this, make sure you defragment the disk first.

It is not as bad as it seems, however; when you reboot a server, the paging file shrinks back to the starting value and thus all fragmentation is removed. Another option is to place the paging file on another partition that is on a different disk (different physical spindles) than the operating system to avoid conflict and improve the performance of the paging file. This is a useful technique if you have an application that makes use of the paging file. If you don't have a different physical disk, you might still use a different partition on the same disk as the operating system. This is useful, because if the partition has nothing on it but the paging file, then the paging file has no file system contention and won't fragment. So, how big should the paging file be? A generally accepted guideline is 1.5 times the amount of physical memory in the server, although some people say twice the amount of RAM. If you are running a very high-performance server with more than 8GB of memory, then the vendor might give different guidelines for the amount of paging file to configure.

There is an issue with basing the paging file size on the amount of RAM in the machine. Logically, the more RAM you add to a server, the less likely the server needs to use the paging file. (There's no need to increase its size just because you add more RAM.) A better approach to ascertain the paging file size is to look at the peak commit size when a system runs its various workloads. This displays the total amount of memory used since the computer started including physical RAM and disk-based paging file usage. Set your paging file to this value which covers the eventuality that every page of committed memory has to be written to disk (which is highly unlikely). Sadly, with Windows Server 2008 and Windows Vista, Microsoft removed the Commit Peak value from the Performance tab of Task Manager. The Commit Charge value which is the current total amount of committed pages (RAM or disk-based paging file) is displayed as the first number of the Paging File value in the Performance tab. The Commit Limit, which is the total size of the physical RAM and disk-based paging files, is the second part of the Paging File value and is the maximum amount of memory that can be committed (which makes sense since this value is the total of the RAM and disk paging files). Whereas you can watch the Paging File value in Task Manager while your system is running to get an idea of the Commit Peak, the best options are to either download Process Explorer which shows the Commit Peak or use Performance Monitor to log the Memory \ Committed Bytes counter for a sufficient period of time to capture the most intensive memory usage of a server and use the Peak value for that collection period.

If you decide to move the paging file to another partition, ensure the Automatically Manage Paging File Size for All Drives Option is unselected, and then select the partition that houses the paging file, set the custom size, and click Set. Next, select the system drive that currently houses the paging file, set the No Paging File option, and then click Set. When you click OK in the dialog, you might need to restart the computer for the paging file change to take effect.

Crash Considerations

There is a drawback to not having a paging file on the system partition. In the event of a system crash, the memory is dumped to the paging file for debugging purposes. If the paging file on the system partition is smaller than the amount of physical RAM used by the kernel (assuming you are using the default kernel dump mode, 2GB is a common value to use for the paging file) or there is no paging file, this dump of memory is not possible. This might hamper you in the investigation of why the crash occurred. You can configure how memory is dumped via the Settings option of Startup and Recovery, which has options for debugging information output (see Figure 17-59). You can choose to write the kernel memory dump (very big), write a small 64/128KB memory dump, or don't write out any memory dump.

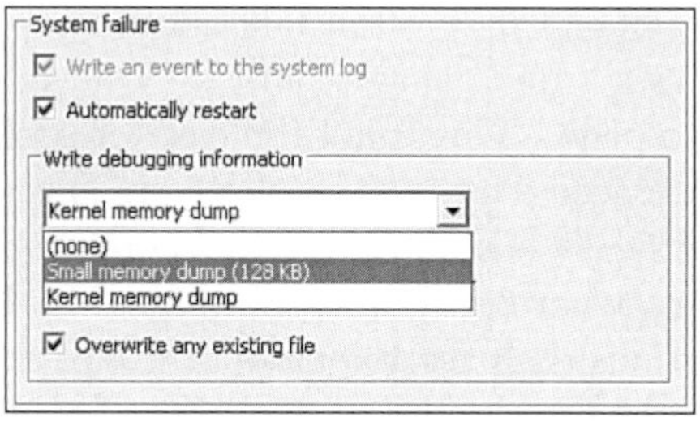

System failure
Write an event to the system log
Automatically restart
Write debugging information
Kernel memory dump
(none)
Small memory dump (128 KB)
Kernel memory dump
Overwrite any existing file

FIGURE 17-59 Configuring the memory dump options.

The Complete Memory Dump option in Windows Server 2003 is removed in Windows Server 2008; when debugging a system crash, the information in the user portion of memory is not typically of interest. Instead, the small memory dump, also known as a minidump or Triage dump, contains only minimal crash data, which is written to a unique file name in the \Windows\Minidump folder after the reboot. This file is 64KB on 32-bit systems or 128KB on 64-bit systems. The kernel dump writes out all operating system memory but not process memory, which is not used for debugging a crash anyway because a process can't crash the operating system.

The actual final crash filename is configurable from the default of memory.dmp. Confused? Earlier it was mentioned that it writes the memory to the paging file. When the crash of the system happens, the memory is dumped to the paging file; at the time of the crash, it's probably too risky to create a new file. When the computer restarts, the Session Manager (smss.exe) checks the paging file and notices it has a crash header. The paging file content related to the crash dump is protected from being overwritten and is moved into the final file location (for example, memory.dmp by the Winlogon process) and a new paging file is created.

Moving the Paging File

You can have multiple paging files on a system, which improve paging performance if the paging files are on different physical drives; it's all about the spindles! If you have a high-availability system, ensure the paging file is on a RAID 5 disk set to ensure high performance and high availability. If your paging file disk dies, the system crashes, because you've just lost a big chunk of memory that had data in it for running processes.

The paging file is an actual file at the root of the volume selected named pagefile.sys. To view it, enable the viewing of hidden files—for example, dir /ah c:\pagefile.sys would show a page file on the C: drive (if it exists).

As a side note, people often talk about simply turning off the paging file because it's so much slower, and they have "lots of RAM so nothing should need to page." This is not the case. A program running on an Intel 386 or later can access up to 4GB of RAM. This is normally far more than a machine physically has; thus, a virtual address space is created known as virtual memory, where programs see their own 4GB memory space (split into 2GB portions: half for the program, half for the operating system). The operating system holds responsibility for allocating and mapping to physical RAM those parts of the program or memory that are currently active.

The RAM of the computer is split into two sections: the nonpaged area, which stores core operating system and can never be paged out to a file, and the paged area, which contains normal program code and data (as well as some file system cache) and which can be written to the paging file if needed (and not currently active).

Although the preceding paragraphs might make you think Windows stores only the active code and data in physical RAM (plus the core operating system), this is not the case. Windows attempts to use nearly all the RAM (because it is so much faster than disk)—if, for nothing else, to cache programs that might have recently been used and closed, so the next time they are used, they can start that much faster. If you have low free RAM, this is not normally a problem. If an application needs physical RAM, then pages of memory that, for example, are just caching recently run programs, can be removed from memory or nonactive data paged to file.

Because you are concerned with removing the paging file, all the information so far leads to the conclusion that if you have lots of RAM, you don't need a paging file. But some applications, when they start, allocate a huge amount of memory, even though they do not use it (hundreds of MBs, which is normally allocated in the Virtual Memory space). The operating system normally leaves this in the paging file. If, however, there was no paging file, it would use up a large chunk of memory and only a few such applications would be needed to bring machines even with a GB of RAM to a halt. Some applications give warnings on startup if no paging file is present (such as Adobe Photoshop, whose warning cannot be disabled).

The advice, then, is to not disable the paging file. Windows only pages if it has to, and there is no performance gain to be made by turning it off. It would be better to set a small initial paging file size (as little as 100MB), but set a higher maximum size, which enables Windows to increase the size if needed. With 1GB of RAM, under normal application loads, it is unlikely the paging file would need to grow.

To stop any of the core operating system being paged, there is a Registry setting at HKEY_LOCAL_MACHINE\SYSTEM\CurrentControlSet\Control\Session Manager\Memory Management\DisablePagingExecutive that, when set to 1, halts paging of the core OS kernel and drivers. This is only done at the request of specific application vendors.

Paging File Usage

To see how many paging files are being used, query the `Win32_PageFileUsage` pagefile object. What follows is a script to show the usage of all paging files on the system:

```
For Each obj in GetObject("winmgmts:\\.\root\cimv2").
ExecQuery(_
    "Select Name, CurrentUsage, PeakUsage, AllocatedBaseSize
from Win32_PageFileUsage",,48)
  WScript.Echo  "Pagefile Physical Location: " & vbtab &
obj.Name
  WScript.Echo  "Current Pagefile Size: " & vbtab &
obj.AllocatedBaseSize & " MB"
  WScript.Echo  "Current Pagefile Usage: " & vbtab &
obj.CurrentUsage & " MB"
  WScript.Echo  "Peak Pagefile Usage: " & vbtab &
obj.PeakUsage & " MB"
Next
```

This listing shows the script in action:

```
D:\temp>cscript getpagefileuse.vbs
Microsoft (R) Windows Script Host Version 5.7
Copyright (C) Microsoft Corporation. All rights reserved.

Pagefile Physical Location:     C:\pagefile.sys
Current Pagefile Size:  4328 MB
Current Pagefile Usage:         0 MB
Peak Pagefile Usage:    0 MB
Pagefile Physical Location:     D:\pagefile.sys
Current Pagefile Size:  4040 MB
Current Pagefile Usage:         0 MB
Peak Pagefile Usage:    0 MB
```

There are two paging files (both 4GB), and neither have been used in the entire time the server has been running. That is because I have run it on my domain controller, which has 4GB of memory and does nothing besides being a domain controller, DNS server, DHCP server, and TS Gateway. It does nothing memory intensive, so no paging has been needed. Running it on my virtual server instead, which has 4GB of memory but runs multiple virtual servers via Hyper-V, results in the following:

```
D:\Temp>cscript getpagefileuse.vbs
Microsoft (R) Windows Script Host Version 5.7
Copyright (C) Microsoft Corporation. All rights reserved.

Pagefile Physical Location:      C:\pagefile.sys
Current Pagefile Size:   4328 MB
Current Pagefile Usage:          0 MB
Peak Pagefile Usage:     10 MB
```

The important thing here is the paging file is used only as needed; so, don't remove the paging file. It's important to the system to be there if needed, and it won't be wastefully used.

Data Execution Prevention

Malicious code (mainly viruses) is a major headache for organizations and home users alike. Data Execution Prevention (DEP) is a technology designed to stop code being executed in areas of memory that have not been designated as containing executable code. Commonly, viruses insert themselves into system memory areas reserved for the operating system and then execute. With DEP, the programs would not be able to execute. The program would be closed and an exception would be raised.

DEP is principally provided by the processor manufacturer and is enforced at a hardware level. AMD provides the no-execute page-protection (NX) processor feature and Intel the Execute Disable Bit (XD) processor feature. If your processor supports hardware-based DEP, this is shown in the Data Execution Prevention page of the Performance Options, as shown in Figure 17-60 at the bottom. If your processor does not support hardware DEP, a software-based DEP is used instead.

By default, DEP is enabled for all programs and services. There is a reliance on the application correctly marking memory as containing executable code. If a program does not correctly mark its memory, the application might not be able to execute correctly. Try to start the program several times. If it yields errors every time, and you know you are not under attack because you have anti-virus applications running with current definition files, check the application vendor for a DEP-compatible version. If a DEP-compatible application is not available, do not disable DEP via the

Turn on DEP for Essential Windows Programs and Services Only option. Instead, add an exception via the Add button for the specific program that is not working with DEP, which is possible with the default mode of DEP.

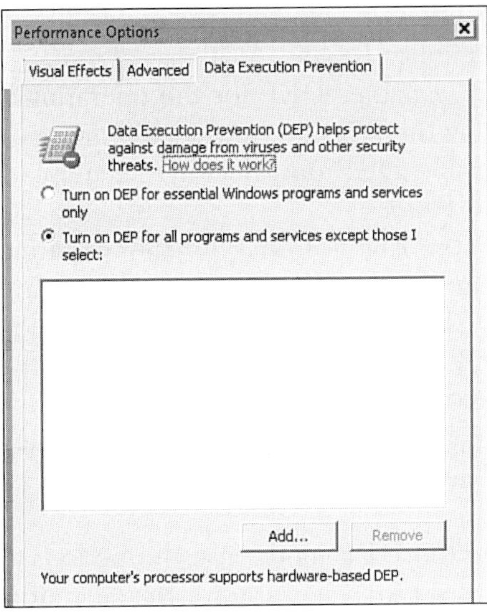

FIGURE 17-60 Configuring Data Execution Prevention.

There are four modes of DEP setting. The current mode for your server is visible as the NX value for the boot loader of the operating system visible via `bcdedit /enum osloader`, as shown here:

```
C:\>bcdedit /enum osloader

Windows Boot Loader
-------------------
identifier              {current}
device                  partition=C:
path                    \Windows\system32\winload.exe
description             Microsoft Windows Server 2008
locale                  en-US
inherit                 {bootloadersettings}
osdevice                partition=C:
systemroot              \Windows
resumeobject            {ca45c967-a399-11dc-8ee6-b4333e3f1935}
nx                      OptOut
```

Notice the last line, `nx` set to `OptOut`. Possible values are as follows:

- **`Optin`**. Enables DEP only for operating system components, including the Windows kernel and drivers. Administrators can enable DEP on selected executable files by using the Application Compatibility Toolkit (ACT).
- **`Optout`**. Enables DEP for the operating system and all processes, including the Windows kernel and drivers. However, administrators can disable DEP on selected executable files by using System in Control Panel.
- **`AlwaysOn`**. Enables DEP for the operating system and all processes, including the Windows kernel and drivers. All attempts to disable DEP are ignored, and the graphical interface is nonfunctional as all DEP configuration options are disabled.
- **`AlwaysOff`**. Disables DEP. Attempts to enable DEP selectively are ignored, and again the graphical interface related to DEP is nonfunctional.

To change the DEP mode, use the `bcdedit /set ns <value>`—for example, to set to `AlwaysOn` for the current operating system, use the following:

```
C:\>bcdedit /set nx AlwaysOn
The operation completed successfully.
```

Once rebooted, notice the options to set DEP on or off or add an exception are not available, because DEP is now always on via the boot `NX` option.

Managing from a Client

The Windows Server 2003 admin pack, which contained the administrative tools for the management of Windows 2003 servers, has been replaced with the Remote Server Administration Tools; these can be installed via the Features capability of Server Manager to add tools for roles not enabled on a server. Additionally, the Remote Server Administration Tools can be downloaded from Microsoft and installed on Windows Vista SP1. However, Server Manager is not part of these tools and neither are the Hyper-V management tools. Another option is to use a remote desktop connection to a Windows Server from your client, which exposes all the management tools, including Server Manager. This was Microsoft's original desire for client management of servers. A great way to remotely install/remove roles and features is via the servermanagercmd.exe. Invoke the command via a remote execution, such as WMI or WinRS, which are explored in Chapter 14, "Server Core."

Summary

Besides the Server Manager, there are many other items that are part of management but are also part of other areas, such as Security Configuration Wizards, performance analyzers, detailed event viewing, or command-line management. All of these areas are covered throughout the book. Everything administrators do can be broken down into the design of the infrastructure and its management—but a book with only two large chapters would be hard to read. This chapter tries to cover only the core aspects of server management and items that are not covered elsewhere in the book.

Much of what was discussed in this chapter is manual management of systems, which often leads to reactive management of systems. It is vital to get a process in place to regularly monitor event logs of servers to ensure no critical problems are occurring and to ensure servers and services are running by doing the following: running tests (including synthetic transactions to check that correct and timely results are returned, such as DNS lookups), cleaning and defragmenting disks, performing backups, and making sure patches are applied. As environments grow, manually monitoring servers becomes impossible. This is where the System Center product line becomes invaluable, especially the System Center Operations Manager product, which has agents running on servers in the environment with product- and service-specific knowledge. This is covered in more detail in Chapter 20.

In summary, Server Manager is a fantastic portal for managing your server; it is the go-to place for checking on initial health of roles via the main pages, which show pertinent events and service status, along with the core tools to manage. What is not shown are the dependencies on other services. For example, AD services could be running just fine, but with DNS not functioning, clients will not be able to communicate with AD. So,

AD would be unavailable. Again, System Center Operations Manager solves this by monitoring services and understanding all the services AD is dependent on that are needed for it to function. This includes monitoring AD servers, DNS servers, and network connectivity as one service for the organization.

CHAPTER 18

Highly Available Windows Server 2008

Services are useful only when they fulfill their role and are accessible. This is the key to high availability—keep services available. There is no point in purchasing a state-of-the-art iSCSI storage area network (SAN) with 30TB of storage for your organization's data storage and then having it accessed via a single file server. If the file server is unavailable, there is no way to get to the data. The file services provided by the file server need to be highly available.

Windows Server 2008 provides two types of high availability: Network Load Balancing (NLB) and failover clustering. This chapter discusses these in detail; each tackles a different type of service that needs high availability.

High-Level Overview of NLB and Failover Clustering

NLB provides a method to distribute TCP/IP traffic among several separate servers running the NLB feature. Clients access a separate IP address and domain name system (DNS) name, which the NLB service owns. It then distributes the traffic through the available members. Because NLB has multiple servers that can respond to a client request, NLB gives higher availability to the service offered over the NLB IP address; however, there is no replication of information or shared storage between the servers in the NLB group.

Services that use NLB tend to be *stateless* (which means requests do not require any link between each other to be maintained by the service) because a client request could be sent to any server in the NLB group. Any prior state the client and server had would be lost if, the next time, the client communicated to the NLB that he was redirected to a different server. Client requests are spread evenly among the servers in the NLB group.

Each server in the NLB has its own installation of the application or service. NLB is, therefore, used for services and applications that require little or no state maintenance (for example, Web services and services with no shared storage, although they can have a common link back to a shared resource, such as a SQL database backend). It is common to have multiple Web servers that all have the same content accessed via NLB, because no state is maintained for Web sessions. Each time the user makes a request via HTTP/HTTPS, all pertinent information is sent as part of the HTTP request; the server does not have to remember anything. If an update to a web site is required, then all sites in the NLB cluster must be updated with the same content to ensure a consistent end-user experience. If a server in the NLB group fails, this is detected, and traffic is no longer sent to the unavailable server; instead, it is redistributed to the other servers. There are facilities in NLB, so a client is redirected to the server who last communicated with the client, if possible. This is useful in cases where some state is desirable (for example, a shopping cart on a web site) through the use of server-side caching.

NLB is fairly easy to manage. If performance starts to become an issue, add an additional server into the NLB group. This will lighten the load on the other servers.

The basic NLB process is displayed in Figure 18-1. The figure shows three Web servers with IP addresses 192.168.1.131 to 133, and they form a NLB group with an address of 192.168.1.130 and an associated DNS name (for example, nlbweb.savilltech.net). A client goes to the Web browser and enters the NLB group DNS name as its target, which is then sent to the NLB group and serviced by one of the three Web servers enabled for NLB. Note that there is no separate NLB server that redirects the requests of clients; the NLB runs on each of the servers and handles updating the DNS record if a member of the NLB group becomes unavailable.

Failover clustering is used when the service being offered needs to maintain a state or when only one server can own the resource being offered and should have shared storage (for example, a file or print server, SQL Server, or Exchange mailbox server). Backend applications and services typically require failover clusters for high availability where the application or service cannot be distributed over multiple servers concurrently. In all the example roles—file/print server, SQL, Exchange—there is a backend data store that can be serviced only by a single server at any one time, given the nature of the service to ensure data consistency. If the server offering the service becomes unavailable, another server in the failover cluster group can take over the service and ownership of the shared resources and provide high availability of the service to the client with no down time in the event of a server failure. Because the shared resource or service instance can be serviced only by a single server in a cluster, there are active nodes that provide a service and passive nodes that are idling in a stand-by state, but ready to take over applications and services should the active node fail or need to be stopped for maintenance. This is known as an *active-passive cluster*, and it is possible to have multiple active and passive nodes in a cluster. Obviously, the passive nodes are effectively doing nothing most of the time, so many organizations will implement a four-node cluster with three active nodes and one passive node (where the passive node can be used to take over the roles of any of the three active nodes).

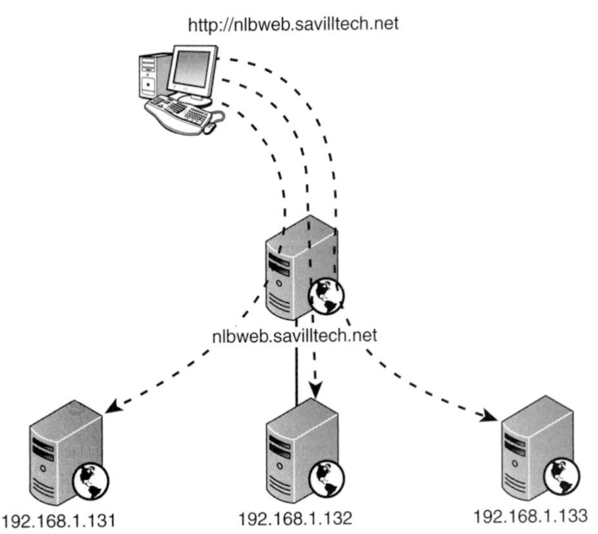

Figure 18-1 The NLB process.

You can also have *active-active clusters*, where all nodes in a cluster are active. Active-active clusters generally mean performance problems are an issue in the event of a node becoming unavailable—the active node has to not only do the work it was already doing, but also that of the unavailable node. It is important to size the nodes correctly if active-active is used to ensure all nodes have sufficient "spare" resources to handle the workload of other nodes in the cluster on top of their own.

Because a cluster offers a service that can be fulfilled only by a single node, it is vital that all nodes in the cluster have a common membership view of the cluster and of which nodes should be active and offer what services. To that end, a cluster has a *quorum*, which is responsible for maintaining a consistent view and agreed state of the cluster. The quorum tells the nodes in the cluster which node(s) are active and, should nodes in the cluster fail to be able to contact each other, the quorum controls who is allowed to still run the application or service. (Only one node can own the quorum.) To facilitate the quorum, certain cluster resources can contribute to determining whether a configuration has a quorum by casting votes. Votes can be assigned to nodes in the cluster, to a shared storage medium (such as a universally accessible SAN via fiber, iSCSI, and so on), and to a file share. In 2008, there is a single quorum model that has four modes (see the "Failover Clustering" section). The voting system governs the active status of a cluster and, with Windows Server 2008 (or 2003 SP1 with update 921181), node majority no longer has a three-node minimum. You can now use a *file share witness*, which is a share on a server in the domain of the cluster that holds a vote for the cluster and helps maintain a quorum in the cluster.

As with NLB, the failover cluster has its own IP address and hostname. After the cluster is configured, cluster resources are added (such as file shares, print shares, disk resources, network names, and addresses) that form the service offered by the cluster. They are the resources that failover when a passive node becomes active. Other services, like Exchange and SQL, which are cluster-aware have specific areas of functionality that are cluster-compatible and are added as cluster resources.

Figure 18-2 shows an example failover cluster for a file server with shared storage via a SAN, which could contain both the data being offered and the quorum. Any client request to a share on the cluster is serviced by the active node, which owns the IP address, name of the cluster, and all the cluster resources for the cluster group it is active for (in this case, a file share).

Only certain versions of Windows Server 2008 support failover cluster, and there are far less restrictions on the type of hardware supported in a cluster and the network and storage configurations. Make sure all components of a cluster are fully tested for cluster usage.

FIGURE 18-2 A basic two-node active-passive file cluster.

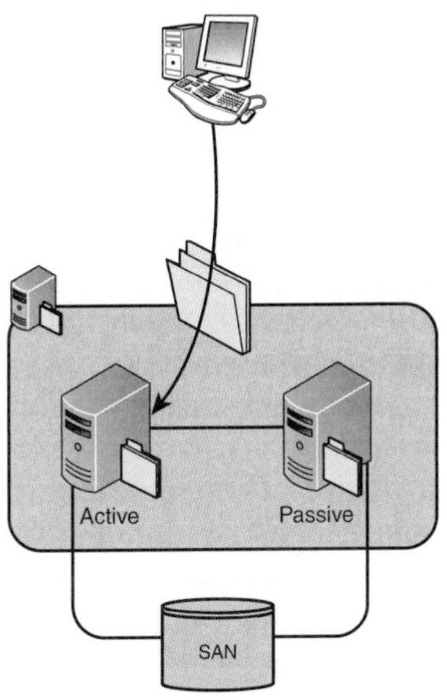

Choosing the Right High-Availability Method

Windows 2008 has two primary high-availability solutions, but where are these used? There are three different ways high availability is achieved for different types of services: services and applications that have high availability built in, those that require Windows clustering to help, and those that rely 100% on Windows clustering.

Some roles within Windows and other services have high availability built into their architecture and do not require additional help to be highly available. A good example is Active Directory Domain Services (ADDS) which has multiple domain controllers that manage their own replication of the directory service content totally independent of the Windows clustering technologies.

Other services need help from Windows cluster technologies. A good example is Exchange 2007, which uses NLB for scalability and availability of its client access servers that service client requests for mail access, both from ActiveSync clients and Web clients. The mailbox servers take advantage of the failover clustering capabilities of Windows servers, as only one server can service a particular mail database. In the event a mailbox server is unavailable, the passive node in the mailbox server cluster takes over the servicing of the mail databases providing clients access to e-mail. With Exchange 2007, there are numerous types of back-end cluster. The most basic is the single copy cluster (SCC) scenario, where the databases exist on shared storage, such as a SAN, and the nodes in the cluster connect to the shared storage. Alternatively, there are technologies, such as Cluster Continuous Replication (CCR), where the mail servers are part of a failover cluster but don't use shared storage; instead, Exchange replication is used to keep a copy of the mail database on both servers synchronized. The failover cluster is used only to control which server is running the mailbox servers on their copy of the database.

Finally, there are services that rely 100% on the windows clustering services, such as file and printer services that use the clustering resources to make their solutions highly available by using shared storage.

There are other ways to make services "more" available or "more" scalable. For example, with DNS, clustering can have multiple records for a single hostname that can point to different servers. DNS will then round-robin requests from clients for the name to one of the servers. This allows multiple servers to be used for a single hostname; however, this works better for some services than others. Imagine that one of the servers is unavailable. If the client component is smart enough to attempt communication, it fails, so it tries the next returned resolution from DNS. In this case, DNS round robin is not a terrible solution; however, if the client tries only the first name returned, there is a big problem if it's unavailable. Active Directory uses DNS for its availability; each domain controller registers records in DNS, and if a DC is unavailable, the client will timeout and try another. Let's look at both technologies in more detail.

Network Load Balancing

With NLB, you add a service to multiple servers that allow them to communicate and to detect if one of them is unavailable. The servers respond to a single IP address and hostname, sharing the load equally between them. The actual services and content have to be managed and maintained outside of NLB. For example, if you are sharing a web site, you need to keep the folder on each Web server updating with the same content via a script or other technology, such as DFS-R.

Each node in a NLB cluster, up to 32, has its own unique IP address, and the NLB cluster has one or more IP addresses that all nodes in the NLB cluster respond to and distribute evenly. It is possible to elect one node in the NLB to receive all traffic by default, such as with the default host or even by assigning weightings to each member of the NLB cluster to control the portion of incoming traffic each node will receive. If you had a server that was twice as powerful as another node, you could configure it to receive twice the number of requests.

The nodes in the NLB cluster exchange heartbeat messages and, if a host fails to send a heartbeat for five seconds, it is considered to have failed. If this happens, the NLB cluster converges and performs a check of the nodes that are still active. It also establishes a default host in the NLB and ensures client requests are sent only to the available hosts. If a new host is added to the NLB, it starts sending heartbeats, and a convergence is performed to add to the servers responding to NLB requests. The convergence process is generally fast, and active nodes continue to respond to client requests, which means little end-user impact.

There are different IP addresses at play in an NLB cluster. Each node in the cluster has its own dedicated IP address that communicates with the server outside of NLB. Additionally, the cluster has its own IP address, which is a virtual IP address specified on all the nodes in the cluster in addition to their own. If the NLB server has only one Network Interface Card (NIC), it is important that the server's unique IP address has a higher priority than the cluster IP address in the network properties; however, this is done for you if you use the NLB Manager.

If you read Chapter 6, "TCP/IP," you know that clients resolve an IP address to a MAC address prior to connecting. So, how does this work with NLB, where there are multiple nodes? The NLB cluster also has its own MAC address that all nodes use in the NLB cluster in one of two ways.

Ideally, the nodes in your NLB will have two NICs. One NIC is used for traffic destined just for the NLB cluster using the cluster IP address (such as the web site requests), and a second NIC is used for host-specific communication and the heartbeat traffic. If two NICs are not an option, one NIC can be used. This brings you to the sticky situation of how to handle the MAC address of the cluster, because you now have the MAC address of the actual server and the cluster MAC address.

Two modes are available in the single NIC instance: unicast and multicast. In unicast mode, which is the default, the adapter's own MAC address is disabled, and the cluster MAC used. This means that both the server's dedicated IP address and the cluster IP address resolve to the same MAC address. You need to use the same mode on all nodes in the NLB cluster. If unicast is used, all the network cards for the servers have the same MAC address, so communication between the NLB nodes is not possible. (Heartbeat traffic is still possible.) Each node has the same MAC address, so any attempt to communicate with another node resolves to its own local MAC address. Similarly, external traffic trying to get to a single node in the NLB generates load on all the members of the NLB—they all receive the traffic and have to ignore the traffic not meant for them. If direct cluster communication is not frequent, then this is not an issue.

Multicast mode allows the NICs in each server to service not only its own local MAC, but also the MAC of the cluster that is converted to a multicast MAC address. This enables direct communication to each node in the NLB, and each node in the NLB can communicate with each other. The downside is that not all routing equipment will support the multicast MAC for the ARP, and some static configuration might be required; otherwise, the NLB will not be accessible outside the local subnet because the routing will not function. Additionally, the Internet Group Management Protocol (IGMP) multicast can be used; this is designed to limit the amount of flooding experienced by networks using multicast by helping the switches on a network send traffic only to ports that it knows have members of the multicast traffic, instead of sending to all ports.

For those experienced with NLB in previous versions of Windows, a number of enhancements have been added with Windows Server 2008:

- IPv6 support for all communication, including the primary cluster IP and dedicated IP addresses.
- Easier cluster creation through the graphical wizard.
- Availability in Windows Server Core.
- WMI support via the MicrosoftNLB namespace for multiple dedicated IP addresses and IPv6.
- Better denial of service (DoS) detection and protection.
- Multiple dedicated IP addresses for the nodes in a NLB cluster.
- Consolidated management using the NLB Manager. You no longer need to separately use Network Connections and manually configure the IP properties, which often caused problems.

Installing and Configuring NLB

The NLB is a feature in Windows Server 2008. It is added via the Add Features Wizard, which is accessible via Server Manager. There are no configurations to perform, and no reboot is required. You can also install NLB via the command line using the following command (which would be required for a server core installation):

```
servermanagercmd.exe -install nlb
```

After NLB is installed, configure NLB via the Network Load Balancing Manager application, nlbmgr.exe—that's right, not an MMC snap-in. To configure an NLB, you must be an administrator on the machine you are configuring NLB. The first step is to create a new NLB cluster. Right-click the Network Load Balancing Clusters node in the console tree and select New Cluster. The configuration of NLB is broken down into three parts, as follows:

- The configuration of host-specific information, such as dedicated IP addresses and the host priority
- The cluster configuration, which consists of the cluster configuration
- The port rules, which define what traffic is distributed among the NLB nodes

A New Cluster dialog is displayed. Enter the name of a host that will be part of the NLB Cluster and click Connect. This displays a list of the interfaces on the server. Select the adapter that will be used to host the cluster virtual IP address and respond to client traffic, as shown in Figure 18-3, and click Next.

The next stage enables a priority to be configured for the cluster node, which has to be unique. The node with the lowest-priority number is the server that responds to traffic targeted for the server IP address that is not covered by a port rule. (A *port rule* allows specific handling of data on specific ports, which is covered in more detail later in this chapter.) This means the node with a priority 1 will receive all traffic not covered by a port rule. Additional dedicated IP addresses can be added, and you can set the initial default state, as shown in Figure 18-4.

FIGURE 18-3 Selecting a server for the NLB cluster to be created on and the interface.

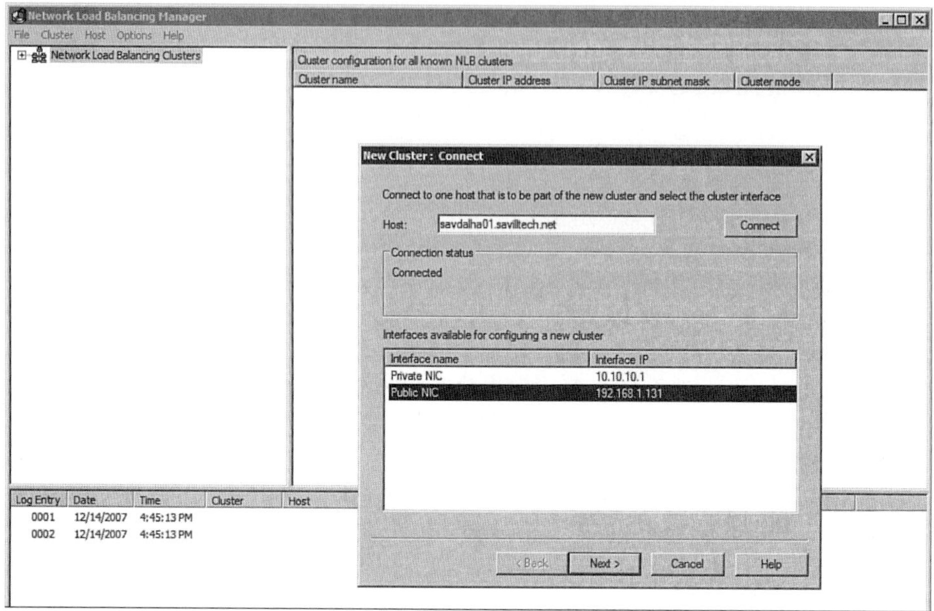

Figure 18-4 More NLB details.

The next stage starts the cluster configuration section. This section allows IP addresses to be added for the cluster, as shown in Figure 18-5. It is possible to configure an IPv4, IPv6, or auto-generated IPv6 link-local, site-local, and global addresses. You can have multiple IP addresses of both IPv4 and IPv6 type. After all addresses are added, click Next.

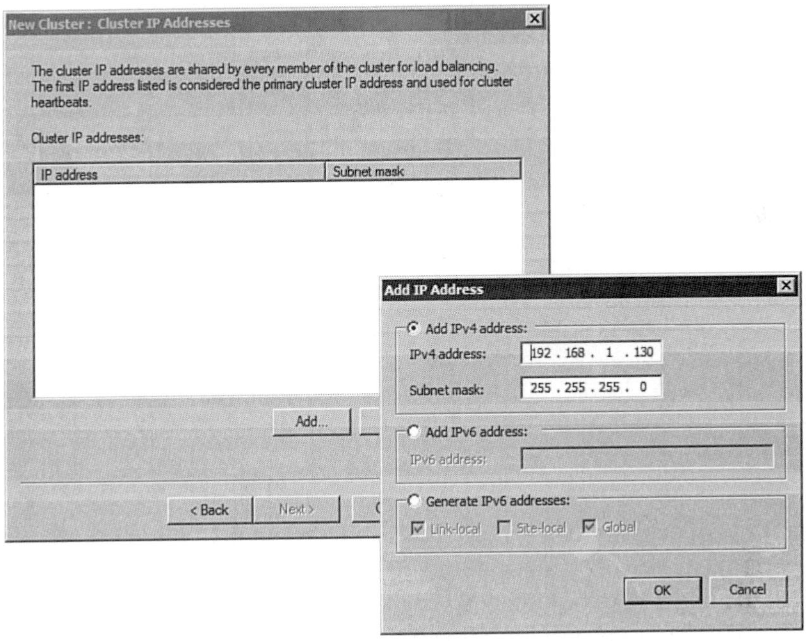

FIGURE 18-5 Configuring the NLB cluster IP address.

As shown in Figure 18-6, the fully qualified hostname of the cluster is configured, along with the cluster operating mode discussed earlier: unicast, multicast, or IGMP multicast (where supported by the network).

The final stage allows configuration of the port rules to be defined, which control how incoming traffic is handled (for example, if it is distributed between all nodes in the NLB cluster or the default host, which has the highest host priority).

By default, a port rule exists for both UDP and TCP protocols across all the ports. This default rule spreads the traffic across all nodes in the NLB cluster. Affinity is set so that multiple requests from a single IP address are redirected to the same node in the NLB cluster. If this default rule meets your requirements, there is no traffic that will target the NLB cluster that needs to be handled by a specific member, and you do not need more granular priorities or loads, you don't need to modify the port rule. For now, remove the rule and create one specifically for HTTP, which is TCP port 80. Disable Affinity so any server can handle connections from the same client machine.

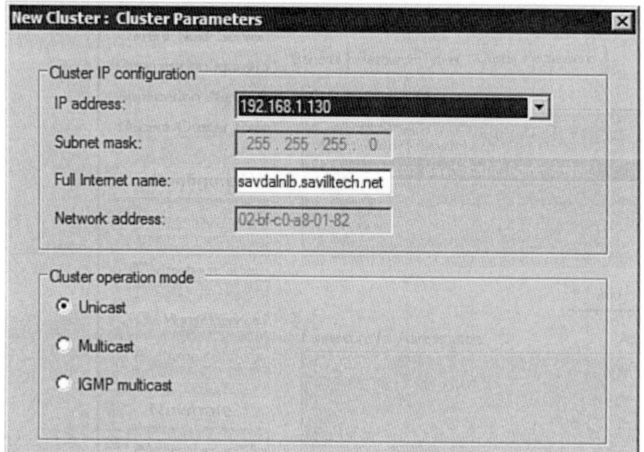

Figure 18-6 The cluster advanced details.

Select the existing All Port and Protocol Role and select Delete to remove the existing rule. Now click the Add button that opens the Add/Edit Port Role dialog, as shown in Figure 18-7. In the example, this port rule is selected to apply to all cluster IP addresses the NLB cluster supports for TCP port 80. The mode is set to send the traffic to multiple hosts in the NLB cluster with no affinity.

There are multiple options for the Filtering mode, as follows:

- **Multiple host**. Traffic is sent to all the hosts in the cluster. When multiple host is selected, the affinity can be chosen, which controls how incoming traffic from an existing client is handled. If affinity is set to None, existing clients can be handled by any node in the NLB cluster; if affinity is set to Single, multiple requests from the same client IP address are sent to the same NLB cluster host. Finally, the affinity can also be set to Network, which directs all requests from the same class C network to the same NLB host; this is useful if clients might use multiple proxy servers for access. If a Web application uses server-based cookies, it is important that affinity is set to single or network. Additionally, technologies such as VPN must have affinity configured.

- **Single host**. All traffic matching the rule is sent to a single host based on the handling priority of each host. The host priority is a setting available via the hosts properties.
- **Disable this port range**. Any traffic matching the port rule is blocked.

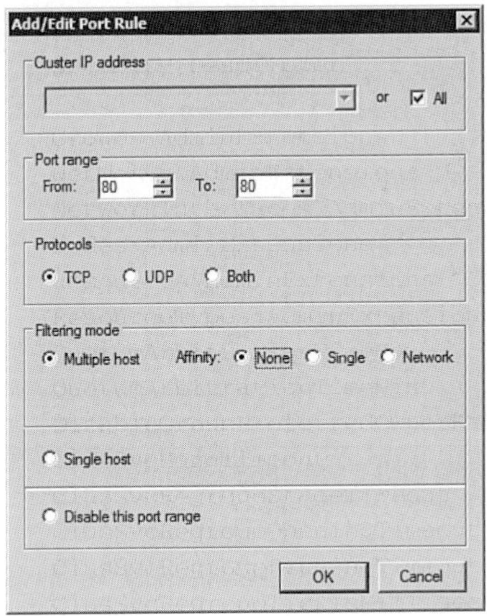

FIGURE 18-7 Port rule creation.

The port rules control how traffic of certain types is handled by the NLB cluster and which nodes receive the traffic.

After the NLB cluster is created, the new IP address for the cluster is added to the TCP/IP network stack of the NLB cluster member; see the Advanced TCP/IP settings, as shown in Figure 18-8. Notice that the cluster IP address (192.168.1.130) is second in priority to the host's own unique IP address. This is vital for outgoing traffic from the server to ensure that its own unique IP address is used by default. If the NLB cluster has multiple IP addresses, all addresses are listed in the TCP/IP properties of the members.

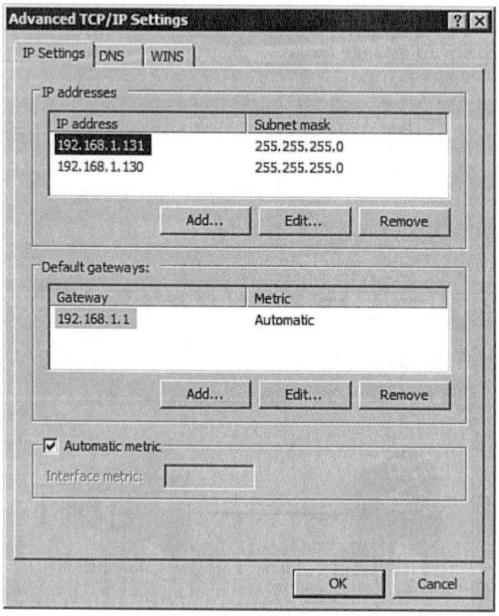

FIGURE 18-8 IP properties of a NLB cluster node member.

Adding Additional Nodes

The next stage is to add additional nodes to the NLB cluster. Right-click on the NLB cluster instance and select Add Host to Cluster. The Add Host to Cluster dialog opens and asks for the host to be added to the NLB cluster. It also wants the interface that is used for the cluster communications. This next stage asks for the host priority of the new host of the NLB cluster (which is 2, in this example)—the higher the host priority number, the lower its actual priority.

After the new node is added, the NLB cluster goes through a convergence process, as shown in Figure 18-9. The log at the bottom of the Network Load Balancing Manager shows the full process and the stages of convergence, with the nodes in the NLB cluster reading the changes and performing the update.

To remove a node from the NLB cluster, right-click on the host and select Delete Host from the context menu. Click Yes to the confirmation dialog.

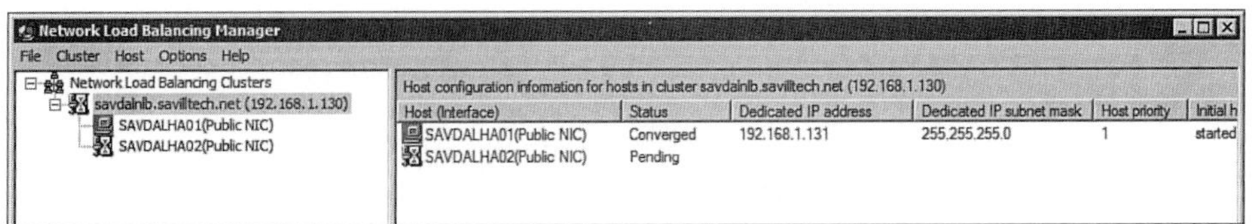

FIGURE 18-9 The convergence of the new NLB node.

Adding a DNS Record

Although the cluster IP address works without any further configuration, add DNS entries for the cluster IP address to enable easier use by clients. Unlike normal hostnames, NLB does not dynamically register a DNS entry for the cluster name and cluster IP address; this must be done manually.

Create a normal host (A) record in DNS so that the fully qualified domain name matches that of the cluster name that was specified during creation. The following command creates a record from the command line:

```
C:\>dnscmd /recordadd savilltech.net savdalnlb A 192.168.1.130

Add A Record for savdalnlb.savilltech.net at savilltech.net
Command completed successfully.
```

The NLB can now be referenced via its IP address or cluster full Internet name.

Accessing the NLB Cluster

You do not have to do anything special to access the NLB cluster. Whatever services have been NLB-enabled via a port rule can be accessed using the cluster IP or full Internet name (assuming the DNS record has been created).

As an example, create a small ASP page that displays the name of the actual physical host. Save this as serverinfo.asp and place it in the wwwroot on both the servers in your NLB cluster (after installing the Web role with ASP support):

```
<html>
<%Set objWSHNetwork = Server.CreateObject("WScript.Network")%>
<head>
```

```
<title><%Response.Write objWSHNetwork.ComputerName%></title>
</head>
<body>
<p class="style1">You are connected to Server <%Response.Write
objWSHNetwork.ComputerName%></p>
<p>You requested access to <%=
Request.ServerVariables("HTTP_HOST")%> </p>
</body>
</html>
```

Start a Web browser and navigate to the name of the NLB cluster (in this case, http://savdalnlb.savilltech.net/serverinfo.asp). As shown in Figure 18-10, the actual name of the server that responds to your request appears. This is a useful script to leave on Web servers for testing because it quickly shows which node is responding to your requests.

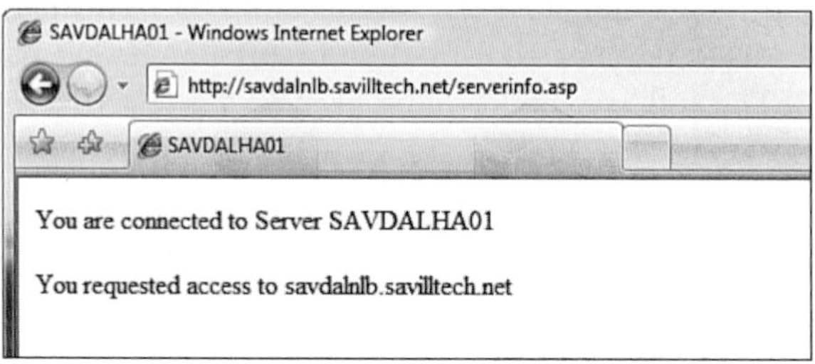

FIGURE 18-10 A test page showing which server handled a request and the URL entered by the user.

Managing NLB

After the NLB is created and you have added additional nodes, you might not need to do anything else. But if you selected port rules that had single node destinations, adjust the priority of the destination nodes because, by default, the priority for the single-mode targets is the node's cluster priority. This might not be the desired order.

Port Rule Management

You have to manage port rules at two levels: at the cluster level to define port rules and at the node level to modify priority and loading for existing port rules. You cannot set priority and loading at the cluster level, and you cannot create new port rules at the node level; you have to interact at both levels.

To modify the port rules, right-click on the NLB cluster in the console tree and select Cluster Properties. Select the Port Rules tab, which displays all the port rules in the same format as when you created the NLB cluster.

New rules can be added via the Add button and removed with the Remove button. If you edit a port rule, you can change all the properties of the rule, including the cluster IP address to respond to, the ports and protocols covered by the rule, and once again the filtering mode (whether it is multiple, single, or disabled, along with affinity required for multiple hosts). This is the place to go to manage port rules.

Within those port rules, you could define a single host as the destination for the port rule, but you had nowhere to configure which host out of the NLB cluster should receive the traffic. Additionally, if the target was multiple hosts, you have no option to load some hosts higher than others. This is where the host-specific properties come into play.

Expand the console tree cluster entry to display the nodes in the cluster. They appear as little computer icons: A green background shows that they are processing requests and are fairly happy; a yellow color means the node is not currently responding to client requests; a gray background means the node is in a suspended state; a red background means the NLB service is not running on the server and is not handling any NLB cluster traffic; and a white X in a red circle means the node is unavailable. An hourglass shows that actions are being taken, such as convergence after a change. Details for each node include the current status of the node, the node's dedicated IP address and subnet mask, host priority, and the initial host state.

If a node is selected, as shown in Figure 18-11, the port rules for the NLB cluster are shown, along with any host-specific attributes. There are two rules, which have a mode of single for telnet and FTP. Each rule has its own priority for the selected node. This is how single host mode rules work. A specific host is not specified as the target; this would not make the availability any better than a normal DNS record because if the node was unavailable, you would have to manually change the host, which should now service the specific port rule. (There would be no Time-To-Live timeouts to wait for like with DNS.) Instead, the nodes in the NLB each have a priority for each specific port rule, which by default is the same as the node's priority within the NLB; however, it can be different. The node with highest priority (the lowest number—for example, 1 is highest priority) for a port rule will service the traffic applicable to the rule. If the node with the highest priority is unavailable, the second-highest priority will service; if that's not available, the third highest will service, and so on. Using this method, only one node services the traffic, but high availability is achieved automatically as lower-priority nodes for each rule can provide service if required.

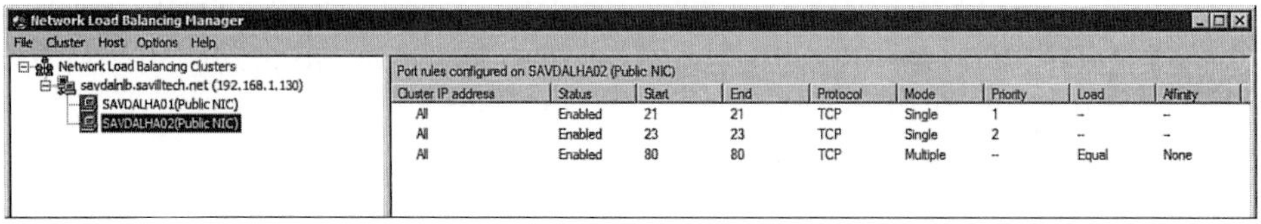

Network Load Balancing Manager

File Cluster Host Options Help

Network Load Balancing Clusters
savdalnlb.savilltech.net (192.168.1.130)
SAVDALHA01(Public NIC)
SAVDALHA02(Public NIC)

Port rules configured on SAVDALHA02 (Public NIC)

Cluster IP address	Status	Start	End	Protocol	Mode	Priority	Load	Affinity
All	Enabled	21	21	TCP	Single	1	-	-
All	Enabled	23	23	TCP	Single	2	-	-
All	Enabled	80	80	TCP	Multiple	-	Equal	None

FIGURE 18-11 The node-specific port rule configurations.

To change these values, right-click on the node in the console tree and select Host Properties from the context menu. This opens up the node-specific information, which allows dedicated IP addresses for the host to be configured via the Host Parameters tab; additionally, the cluster IP and configuration can be viewed but not changed. The last tab shows the Port Rules for the cluster with only the ability to edit the rules enabled; you can't add or remove. After you open a rule, everything is unavailable to change except for the handling priority for a single host mode rule or the Load weight for a multiple host mode rule.

In Figure 18-12, a single host rule is being edited, which allows the handling priority to be modified from 1-32. (You can have 32 nodes in a NLB cluster.) The priorities that are not currently assigned for the port rule to other nodes in the cluster are available. If, for example, you want to make a node number 1 and another node currently has the handling priority of 1, you will first need to change the priority on the existing number 1 node's port rules (to 3, for example, because the node you want to make 1 is probably number 2); then you can set the handling priority to 1 for the new number 1 node.

The other type of configuration is load balancing. If you select a multiple host rule, you can modify the load weight. By default, load weight is set to "Equal," so all nodes process the incoming requests evenly. However, you can assign a load weight between 0 and 100 to enable specific nodes to receive more connections than others. If you give a node a weight of 0, it receives no portion of the traffic; however, a load of 100 does not mean it receives all the traffic. To calculate the amount of traffic a particular node receives, take the configured load weight divided by the sum of all the loads configured across all nodes. So, if in a three-node cluster, each node set the load weight to 100, then each node would receive a third of the traffic, or 100/300. The reason this is not allocated out of 100 is that nodes can be added and removed to the NLB cluster, so having to redefine the load weights every time would be highly cumbersome and inaccurate. You would use higher weighting when you have nodes in the NLB that have differing capabilities, such as a node with more memory and processor power.

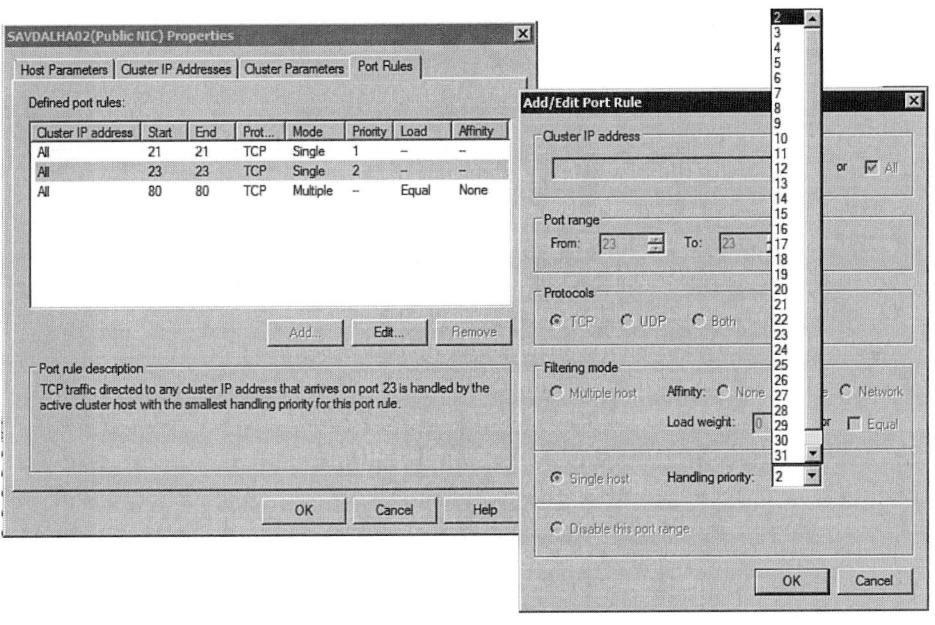

FIGURE 18-12 Configuring the handling priority for a node.

Managing Servers

The worst-case scenario for an NLB cluster is when a node becomes unavailable. When this happens, it's detected via the absence of the heartbeat, and the nodes status changed to Unreachable. Its icon changes to a white X in a red circle, as shown in Figure 18-13. When the server is restarted, it will automatically be detected as available, and the NLB will go through a convergence to reintroduce the now-available service into the NLB cluster. Accelerate the detection of the newly available server by selecting Refresh from the context menu of the NLB cluster item in the console tree.

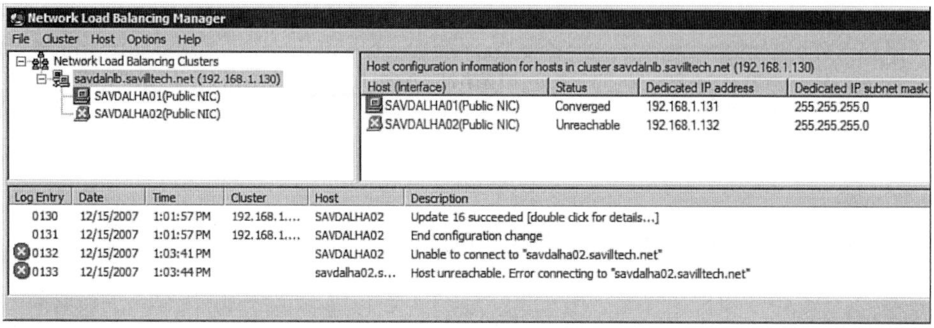

FIGURE 18-13 A node in the NLB cluster is unreachable.

You can still perform configuration changes for an unavailable host; however, they are not be applied to the host until it is restarted and goes through the convergence process. If a node is unavailable and not coming back, remove the node from the NLB cluster via its Delete Host context menu option.

If you want to take down a server for maintenance, place the server you want to remove from service into a drain mode. This stops any new connections but allows active connections to complete. After the server has completed, all active connections to the server are stopped automatically and will no longer service any load-balancing traffic. When a server has its NLB service stopped, it has a red background.

To place a server in drain mode, right-click the server and select the `Drainstop` command from the Control Host menu, as shown in Figure 18-14. The other options on the Control Host menu are as follows:

- **`Start`**. Starts the NLB services on a node, making available to service NLB cluster requests.
- **`Stop`**. Stops the NLB services on a node immediately, which might potentially interrupt active connections. Use `Drainstop` instead, when possible.
- **`Suspend`**. Stops the NLB services on a host and tells it to ignore all cluster control commands except a `Resume`. If you try the `Start` command on a suspended node, the start request fails.
- **`Resume`**. Ends the suspend state of a node and places it in a stopped state, which can then be started via the `Start` command.

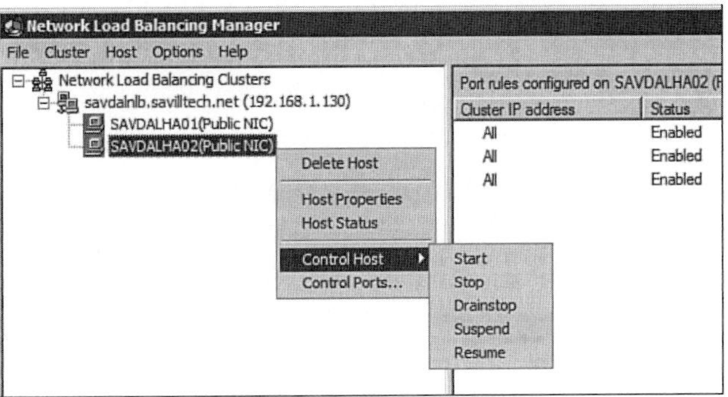

FIGURE 18-14 Control options for a host.

In addition to controlling individual nodes, the entire NLB cluster can be controlled via the Control Hosts context menu option for the actual NLB cluster instance, which performs the same function as the `node` command but for all the nodes in the NLB cluster.

If only a specific port rule needs to be suspended on a node, the Control Ports context menu item should be selected for the node in question. This opens the Control Ports dialog, which allows individual rules to be drained, enabled, or disabled (see Figure 18-15). Once again, a drain places the rule in a state where existing connections can complete but no new connections are allowed. Disable stops all connections, and Enable allows all connections again and is valid from a Drain or Disabled state.

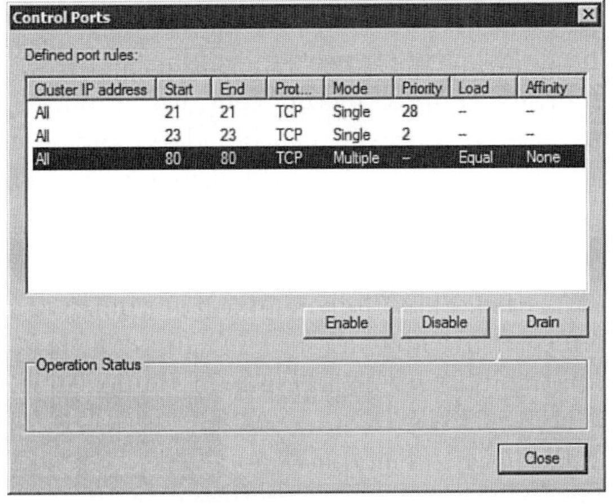

FIGURE 18-15 Controlling port rules on a server.

It is also possible to globally enable, disable, and drain port rules for all nodes in a cluster via the Control Ports context menu for the NLB cluster instance in the console tree.

Cluster Mode and IP Address Management

Adding additional IP addresses to the NLB enables specific traffic to target one node over another. For example, if you are hosting multiple web sites and want one node to be the higher priority for one web site and another node to be the higher priority for another, this would not be possible if the cluster had a single IP address. Because the port rules work based on the IP address, port, and protocol, this would all be the same no matter what web site was used (unless you wanted to host the web sites on different ports). If you give the cluster multiple IP addresses, port rules can be defined for each IP address, allowing nodes to have different priorities for each of the port rules specific to each IP address.

To add a new cluster IP address, select Cluster Properties from the context menu of the NLB cluster entry in the console tree menu; under the Cluster IP Addresses tab, click the Add button to add an IPv4 or IPv6 address. After you click OK, you are prompted to accept this IP address change. (And once the NLB cluster has completed convergence, the new IP address has been added to the IP stack of each node in the NLB cluster.) This new address is now available to be used for port rules by unchecking the All button for the cluster IP address and selecting a specific IP address. To remove an address, perform the same process but select an address and then click the Remove button.

You can also add additional dedicated IP addresses for a particular node in the cluster. This is used for node-specific communication via the Host Properties context menu item for a node. Through the Host Parameters tab, IP addresses can be added and removed as required. If you are using NLB for VPN load-balancing, then the nodes should not have any dedicated IP addresses; they should only have the cluster IP address configured, which means direct node communication is not possible.

If you want to change the cluster operation mode for the NLB cluster (that is, whether it's unicast, multicast, or IGMP multicast), use the Cluster Parameters tab of the Cluster Properties dialog. This also allows the full Internet name of the cluster to be modified, in addition to selecting which IP address is the primary address of the cluster if more than one IP address was added. This change could be made based on the addition or removal of a NIC.

Logging and Credentials

By default, the NLB logs are not written to a file; however, the Log Settings menu item under the Options menu allows logs to be written to a specified file and location. It contains any new log in a basic text format, as shown here:

```
0183  Information  12/15/2007  2:29:19 PM  192.168.1.130
SAVDALHA01  "Drainstop" operation result : SUCCESS, Host State
: Host is Stopped
0184  Information  12/15/2007  2:29:24 PM  192.168.1.130
SAVDALHA02 "Drainstop" operation result : SUCCESS, Host State :
Host is Stopped
0185  Information  12/15/2007  2:29:35 PM  192.168.1.130
SAVDALHA01
      "Start" operation result : SUCCESS, Host State :
       Converging
0186  Information  12/15/2007  2:29:35 PM  192.168.1.130
SAVDALHA02
     "Start" operation result : SUCCESS, Host State :
      Converging
```

If you want to specify alternate credentials for connecting to remote servers, select Credentials from the Options menu. This allows the entry of the credentials to be used in place of the current logged-on credentials.

Command-Line Management

NLB clusters cannot be configured from the command line; however, control is possible using NLB.EXE. Run `nlb /?` to see all options, but let's look at some of them. To see the MAC addresses for a cluster IP address, use the `ip2mac` argument and the IP address of the cluster, for example:

```
C:\>nlb ip2mac 192.168.1.130
NLB Cluster Control Utility V2.5 (c) 1997-2007 Microsoft
Corporation.
Cluster:             192.168.1.130
Unicast MAC:         02-bf-c0-a8-01-82
Multicast MAC:       03-bf-c0-a8-01-82
IGMP Multicast MAC:  01-00-5e-7f-01-82
```

To display all information about a NLB cluster, use `nlb display <cluster name>`, and to query the state, use `nlb query <cluster name>`.

To control the NLB, use the `stop`, `start`, `resume`, `suspend`, and `drainstop` commands, which control the local host NLB is running on, or control all nodes by adding the cluster name and global at the end, as shown here:

```
C:\>nlb stop savdalnlb.savilltech.net global
NLB Cluster Control Utility V2.5 (c) 1997-2007 Microsoft
  Corporation.
The name savdalnlb.savilltech.net was resolved to:
192.168.1.130
Host 1 [savdalha01.savilltech.net] (192.168.1.131) reported:
cluster mode already stopped
Host 2 [savdalha02.savilltech.net] (192.168.1.132) reported:
cluster mode stopped
```

You can also control individual port rules, for example, stop the port rule for all IP addresses for port 21 for the specific node on the cluster:

```
C:\>nlb disable all:21
➥savdalnlb.savilltech.net:savdalha01.savilltech.net
NLB Cluster Control Utility V2.5 (c) 1997-2007 Microsoft
  Corporation.
The name savdalnlb.savilltech.net was resolved to:
192.168.1.130
Host 1 [savdalha01.savilltech.net] (192.168.1.131) reported:
port rule traffic disabled
```

Removing NLB

To remove NLB, use the standard Remove Features Wizard or use the `servermanagecmd.exe`, as shown here:

```
Servermanagercmd.exe -remove nlb
```

Before removing the NLB feature, remove each node from the NLB cluster and then delete the NLB cluster. Otherwise, after removing the NLB cluster feature, you will need to manually remove the cluster IP addresses from the adapters installed in the servers.

Migrating from a Windows Server 2003 NLB

It is possible to have a combination of Windows Server 2003 and Windows Server 2008 nodes in a single NLB cluster; however, until all nodes are running Windows Server 2008, you cannot use 2008 features, such as IPv6, and multiple dedicated IP addresses.

Prior to upgrading a Windows Server 2003 server to 2008, place the NLB in drainstop mode and set its initial host state to Stopped to prevent it from automatically starting after upgrade. After one server is upgraded, use the Windows Server 2008 NLB Manager to manage the NLB cluster because the 2003 version cannot manage 2008 servers. After all nodes are running 2008, you can start using the new features.

Because NLB clusters can have nodes added and removed easily, you can perform clean installations of 2008. Just ensure all the required data and services are enabled and then add 2008 as a new node to the cluster.

Failover Clustering

In Windows Server 2008, failover clustering is the biggest area of change around high availability in terms of ease of use. Although there are technical changes between 2003 and 2008, Windows Server 2008 clustering is being labeled as "clustering for mere mortals." Previously, clustering under 2003 was difficult to set up and maintain, with specialist-level knowledge needed for clustering to truly function reliably. With 2008, an IT generalist can configure and maintain a cluster while providing a more secure and more stable environment. To facilitate this easier configuration, Windows Server 2008 has a more streamlined cluster setup experience; the Windows 2003 cluster setup experience was miserable for most people. Additionally, configuration validation tools are now integrated into the cluster setup and management interfaces instead of being separate tools. The management interface is completely rewritten from Windows Server 2003.

NOTE Failover clustering is formally known as Server Clustering or Microsoft Cluster Service (MSCS), but in this chapter, it is referred to as clustering. Although there are other cluster technologies, this section refers to the Microsoft implementation.

As with Windows Server 2003, only the Enterprise and Datacenter editions of Windows Server 2008 support clustering; however, there are enhancements. The previous limit of 8 nodes to a cluster has been raised to 16 nodes when running on 64-bit Windows Server 2008. The existing eight-node limitation remains in effect for 32-bit and IA64 implementations of 2008.

Failover clustering is suited for many applications, and many of those services give step-by-step guides for configuring the cluster that is required for the application to function. This section examines the concepts around clustering and the various cluster models.

Architecture of a Cluster

A cluster consists of two or more nodes that offer services to the network, which consists of a number of resources such as an IP address, file server, network name, disk, or other back-office component (such as an Exchange 2007 or SQL component) that are collected into a cluster group. To clarify, a one-node cluster is technically possible, which might be used to take advantage of the cluster service capability to restart an application if it fails, but this is uncommon and gives no protection from hardware failures.

Although active and passive nodes have been discussed, in reality, you can configure multiple services and applications within a cluster that can be hosted on different nodes in the cluster. At any time, every node might be running a specific server or application. Ensure that the resources in the cluster nodes are sufficient to run the services and applications from other nodes in the cluster in the event of a planned failover of services and applications for maintenance purposes, or in the event of server failure.

Figure 18-16 shows the basic structure of a cluster: a cluster name, IP address, and a pool of shared storage that is detected as available for all the nodes specified during the cluster creation process. Depending on the quorum model, some of this shared storage might be used as a witness disk.

The nodes in the cluster communicate constantly via a heartbeat to ensure nodes are available. In the event of a change in cluster status, such as a node becoming unavailable or network problems stopping the cluster nodes from communicating, the cluster goes into *quorum arbitration*, where nodes fight for which partition has quorum. Here, the remaining nodes fight out to decide who should be hosting which services and applications to avoid split-brain. *Split-brain* is when multiple nodes in a cluster try to bring online the same service or application, which then causes the nodes to try and bring online the same resources. More importantly, consider that NodeA hosts SQL and is writing to the database on shared storage, and NodeB also hosts SQL and is writing to the same database on the same shared storage; because of this, you can get asynchronous data writing, which means corruption. This is why the quorum is vital to ensuring you always have a majority for the cluster to function, and why you often have a shared disk or file share that can be used in arbitration. If the cluster nodes cannot communicate with each other, they can still communicate with a shared disk or share to help decide where ownership of services and applications should be.

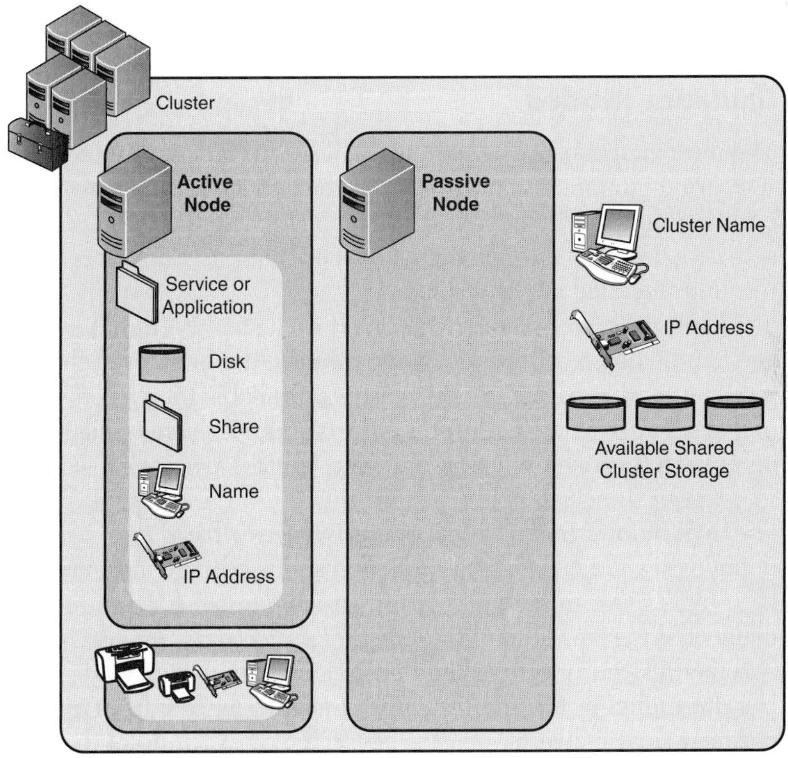

FIGURE 18-16 Basic architecture of a cluster.

Imagine you have a cluster of four nodes without any shared disk or file share that can be used for the quorum and arbitration. If a split occurs, and for some reason, the nodes could only contact the node next to them, then each half of the cluster would have two nodes. This would be a disaster because both halves might decide they should own all the services and applications. That is why all the quorum modes are based on a majority (that is, more than half is needed for the cluster to function). In the example of two nodes on each side, neither side would have majority, so no cluster resources would be serviced. This is far better than multiple nodes trying to service the same resources. As you see in the next section, if you have an even number of nodes, it is recommended to also have a shared disk or file share used as part of the quorum. This shared disk or file share ensures that in this type of split scenario, there is still a resource that can be claimed by only one partition, thanks to locking, thus giving only one side a majority and allowing the cluster to function.

Quorum Modes

The most vital concept needed for a cluster to function is that of a quorum. A quorum guarantees consistency of the services offered by the cluster by ensuring that specific services and applications are offered only by a single active node, and that services and applications are offered only if the resources needed are available.

The quorum configuration tells the cluster the number of failures it can handle before effectively going offline. At a high level, this is achieved by ensuring the majority of the cluster is available to stay active—for example, in a three-node cluster, at least two nodes must be available. However, in practice, you have more granular control over what constitutes the majority of the cluster.

In Windows Server 2003, there were two basic quorum models that defined how the quorum was achieved and used. The most used model was the Single Quorum Device cluster, which consisted of a number of nodes connected to some kind of shared storage (SAN commonly), with a volume specified as the quorum disk that helped the cluster configuration database. As long as the quorum was available with at least one node, the cluster was available, no matter how many nodes in total there were. The problem with this model was if the cluster quorum disk was unavailable, the entire cluster became unavailable; even though SANs are highly available with RAID to protect volumes, there were problems in production, and the loss of the quorum disk was a major threat and a single point of failure. The other model supported in Windows Server 2003 was the

Majority Node Set Cluster, which did not use a shared quorum disk, but instead each node in the cluster held its own copy of the cluster database. To maintain the quorum, over half the nodes had to be available, which meant you had to have a minimum of three nodes in the cluster, which was not commonly the case—in most production environments, a cluster consisted of two nodes. An update for Windows 2003 SP1 also introduced the concept of a file share witness that could be used in place of the shared quorum disk and could have a vote in the cluster; this meant a two-node cluster could stay active as long as either both nodes were running or one node and the file share witness, which is carried on into the 2008.

Windows Server 2008 combines the two main Windows Server 2003 models and gives certain elements of a cluster a vote. To maintain the quorum, the majority of the votes have to be present. Cluster components that could have a vote are the following:

- Cluster nodes.
- A shared disk containing a copy of the cluster configuration Registry, which, instead of being called the quorum disk, is renamed to the witness disk. Only one witness disk per cluster.
- A file share that does not contain a copy of the cluster configuration Registry but can hold a vote. Only one file share witness per cluster.

You cannot have both a file share witness and a witness disk in a cluster. One new feature of Windows Server 2008 is that the witness disk no longer has to have a drive letter assigned, or even a mount point, for that matter.

Windows Server 2008 has one quorum model, the Majority Quorum Model, which allows the removal of dependence on any one aspect of the cluster. It requires the majority of the votes in the cluster to be present. There are four different quorum mode configurations available with Windows Server 2008. Some take advantage of the new majority quorum model capabilities, and others emulate the Windows Server 2003 options in the way votes are allocated.

Node Majority

Node majority does not use any witness disk or file share witness and instead relies on at least half the number of nodes being available. Votes are assigned only to the nodes in the cluster. The cluster must have at least three nodes. To be exact, the number of nodes that must be present is half the total number of nodes rounded down, plus 1—in a four-node cluster, at least three nodes must be present; in a five-node cluster, at least three nodes must be present; in a seven-node cluster, at least four nodes must be present, and so on. This configuration is recommended when there are an odd number of nodes, as shown in Figure 18-17.

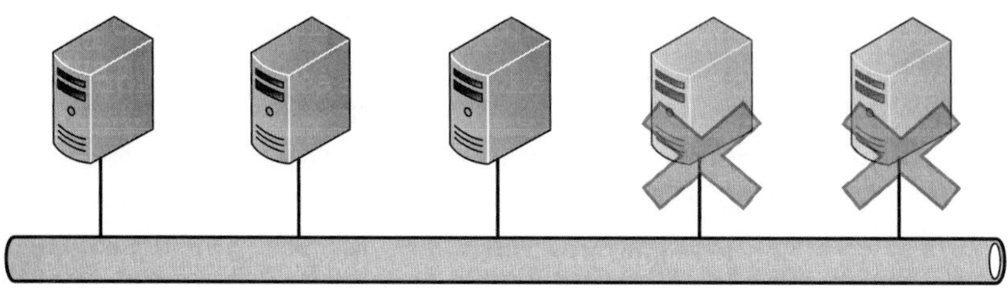

FIGURE 18-17 The cluster can survive if the majority number of nodes are present.

Node and Disk Majority

In node and disk majority configuration, the witness disk and each node have one vote. This configuration can sustain availability if half the nodes fail, providing the witness disk is present. This means a six-node cluster could have three nodes unavailable, providing the witness disk is online.

If the witness disk is not online, the number of supported failures is half the number of nodes (rounded up) minus 1, so a six-node cluster with an unavailable witness disk can support only two nodes being unavailable (shown in Figure 18-18). Notice there are five votes and, in both situations, three votes are present. This configuration is recommended for an even number of nodes where shared storage is available.

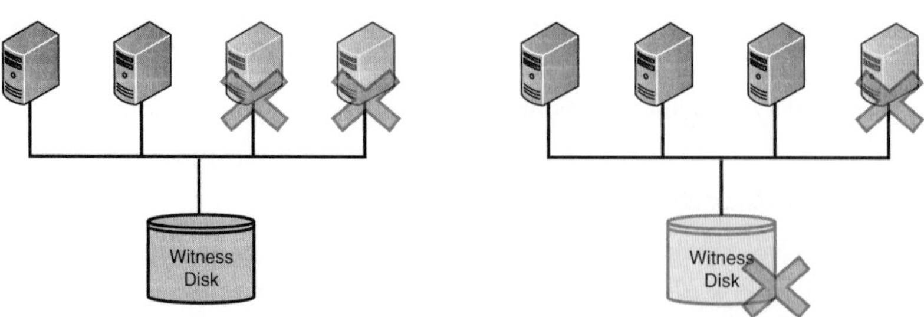

FIGURE 18-18 The cluster can survive if the majority number of nodes are present; either two nodes and the witness disk or three nodes are required with the witness disk unavailable.

Node and File Share Majority

Node and file share majority works the same as Node and Disk Majority, but instead of a shared witness disk holding a copy of the cluster configuration Registry, a file share witness is used containing just a token file, as shown in Figure 18-19. This is recommended for configurations where no shared storage is available, and you have two nodes.

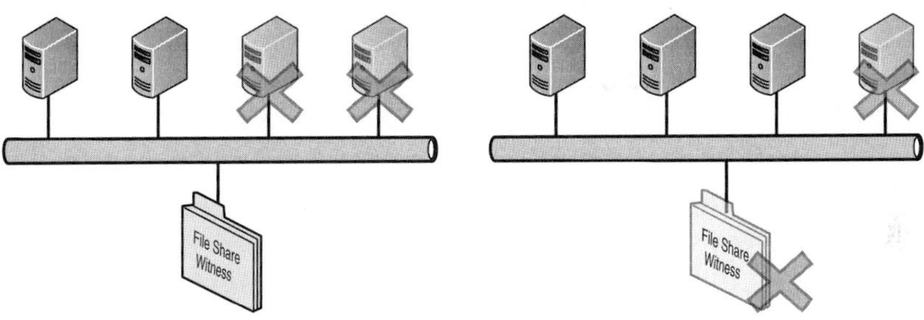

FIGURE 18-19 The cluster can survive if the majority number of nodes are present; either two nodes and the file share witness or three nodes are required with the file share witness unavailable.

No Majority: Disk Only

In the disk-only model, the number of available nodes does not matter, and the cluster can sustain failure of all nodes except 1, as long as the witness disk is available. (The witness disk has the only vote.) This configuration relies 100% on the witness disk, which introduces a single point of failure, as all nodes could be available, but if the witness disk goes offline, the cluster is stopped, as shown in Figure 18-20. This model is never recommended because of the single point of failure that the reliance on the witness disk introduces.

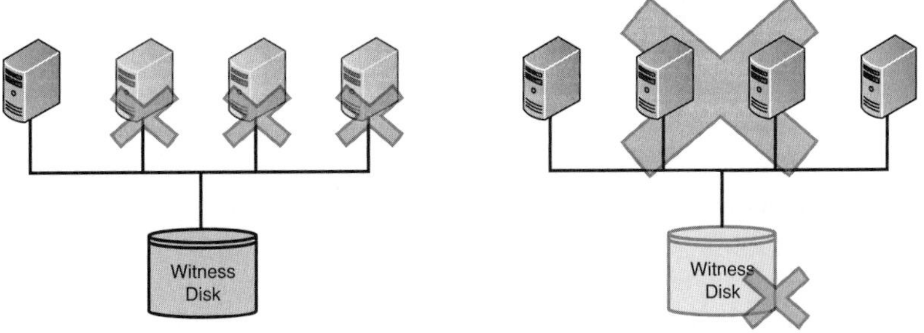

FIGURE 18-20 When using the disk-only model, only one node is required with the witness disk; if the witness disk is unavailable, however, the cluster is unavailable, no matter how many nodes are running (even all, as shown on the right).

Networking and Security Enhancements

A number of network enhancements are introduced for clusters in Windows Server 2008. First, DHCP is now enabled for all IP components of the cluster. Previously, the cluster IP and dedicated IPs had to be statically assigned. With Windows Server 2008, all addresses are DHCP-generated; the default process when creating a cluster is, if the network adapter is configured for DHCP, you are not prompted for an address for the cluster. The cluster also uses DHCP. (Although this can be changed.)

The use of DHCP has good points and bad points. DHCP is an easier configuration for the cluster; however, the cluster then becomes dependent on DHCP being available and effectively introduces a single point of failure due to the DHCP reliance. This depends on your organization, but it's certainly welcome in some environments.

IPv6 is fully supported and can be used for client access to the cluster and for inter-node communication.

The dependency on NetBIOS has been removed with Windows Server 2008 failover clustering. This offers simpler SMB traffic transportation, no more WINS and NetBIOS name resolution broadcasting, and a standardized name resolution on DNS, as with most Windows components.

Kerberos is now mandatory for failover clustering, with NTLM no longer used. When Kerberos is combined with secure TCP session-oriented protocols instead of datagram (UDP) RPC protocols and IPsec improvements, you have a far more secure cluster implementation than with 2003. However, there is no compatibility between 2003 and 2008 clusters. The security changes break compatibility at an API level. A mix of 2003 and 2008 nodes is not possible in a cluster, and the cluster management tools are not interoperable. You can't manage a 2003 cluster from the 2008 failover cluster management MMC snap-in, and you can't manage a 2008 cluster from the 2003 cluster MMC snap-in. Customer feedback to Microsoft indicated that the improvements in security were more important than interoperability.

Clusters can have multiple IP addresses. A cluster can stay up, providing any one of the IP addresses is still available (known as an *OR dependency*), instead of requiring all; this is important when considering the next change in clustering. One of the biggest changes is the new stretched cluster enhancements that allow cluster nodes to be in separate IP subnets, which enables globally dispersed clusters (multisite cluster) with cluster communication operating over network routers. This removes the need for VLANs, which were a common solution under Windows Server 2003. Because of the IP changes for 2008, the cluster can have multiple addresses in different subnets, and as long as one of the IP addresses is available, the cluster name can be available.

With the requirement for the same subnet removed, organizations move cluster nodes further and further apart; to support this, failover clusters can have configurable heartbeat timeouts to avoid failures due to network latency, which effectively removes cluster distance limitations. The old requirement of 500 millisecond round-trip latency between cluster nodes has also been removed, and configuration for heartbeat is configurable for the various groups of nodes in a cluster that are primarily based on location.

When you create a cluster, you no longer have to specify a cluster service account, which used to be a domain account specially created for cluster execution. Under 2008, the local system account is used, so no more manual accounts to worry about!

Supported Hardware

All the nodes in a cluster must have the same or similar hardware, and all components in the nodes are certified for Windows Server 2008; however, with Windows Server 2008, there is no longer a separate Cluster Solution logo program accreditation. The Microsoft Windows Hardware Compatibility Test (HCT) center no longer accepts cluster submissions. However, the cluster test tools, such as the Driver Test Manager (DTM), are still available for manufacturers to internally test components.

It was becoming too complex to track all the different hardware that could be used in a cluster. With 2008, create your cluster using components that are certified under the Windows Logo Program for Windows Server 2008 (see http://www.microsoft.com/whdc/winlogo/default.mspx for more information). For example, ensure you use logoed Host-Based Adapter (HBA), logoed storage, and so on; after the failover cluster feature is installed, a Validation tool must be run, which checks the configuration and components of the server and verifies that the installation is cluster-compatible. If the validation passes all tests, the cluster configuration is now supported. This used to be available as a downloadable tool from Microsoft called ClusPrep—but it is now in its 2.0 version and part of 2008 clustering. The validation tests fall into four categories: Inventory,

Network, Storage, and System Configuration. You must have run all tests on a configuration for the cluster to be supported by Microsoft. It's also a good idea because the validation tests will find problems that will stop the cluster from working correctly. Validate can also be run on a configured cluster to check for any issues, which is a new feature of the 2008 version.

In the Inventory stage, the following information is collected: BIOS information, Environment variables, Fibre Channel, SAS Host Bus and iSCSI Host Bus adapters, memory, operating system (OS), Plug and Play devices, running process, services, software updates, system and unsigned drivers, and general system information (computer model, domain, and so on).

In the Network stage, the cluster network configuration is checked. This check verifies the IP and subnet information on adapters and validates IP configuration, ensuring addresses are unique, multiple adapters are not connected to the same subnet, a default gateway is configured on one adapter, and there are no duplicate MAC addresses (important if you are using virtual machines). Network communication between the nodes is checked and the firewall rules verified to ensure that cluster communication will not be interrupted.

The Storage portion lists all disks and those that are visible to all nodes. Shared disks are then tested for failover suitability, including data that is kept intact.

The System Configuration phase verifies that Active Directory is configured correctly and that all nodes are in the same domain and ideally the same OU. (This is important to ensure consistent group policy application; however, this is not mandatory—only a warning is generated.) A check is performed that all drivers are signed and that the same OS version is installed, as well as the same service pack and same software updates. The required services for clustering are checked to ensure they are running (RPCSs, Remote Registry, Lanmanserver, and WinMgmt). Finally, all nodes are checked to ensure they are running the same architecture.

At this point, there might be readers who are concerned. You don't want to buy components, install them, and run the validation tool, and you still don't have a supported configuration. To combat this, Microsoft has the Failover Cluster Configuration Program (FCCP), which will list entire cluster configurations that have been validated by Microsoft and its partners. Go to http://windowsservercatalog.com/results.aspx?bCatID=1291&cpID=0&avc=10&OR=1 for more information on the FCCP.

There are still requirements around network and storage. Cluster nodes should have a minimum of two network cards: one for the public communication to the clients on the network and one for private, cluster-to-cluster node communication. Additionally, if you are using iSCSI to connect to storage, the iSCSI traffic should be on a separate NIC and ideally on a separate network/switch. As an example, on my cluster nodes (which use iSCSI), I have three network cards, as shown in Figure 18-21. It is a good practice to rename the NICs to a name that reflects their purpose, and only the public NIC will have a gateway IP address defined as the default adapter for the cluster. The private NICs are typically connected to a dedicated switch or VLAN with just the cluster node's communication traffic. This traffic needs to be a different network than the public interface and should use a subnet not used on the network—for example, my public is 192.168.1/24, and I use 10.10.1/24 for my private network because this traffic will never be routed anywhere. I can use any nonpublic subnet, and it's a completely different class than the normal traffic operates over. If you use a dedicated private network, the best practice is to use IPv6 because IPv6 is self-configuring, so there is no network setup to worry about. The Microsoft Failover Cluster Virtual Adapter (NetFT) adapter natively uses IPv6; if you have only IPv4, then the IPv6 is tunneled.

Also, for the NIC that is used for the cluster private communication, disable the client for Microsoft Networks and File and Printer Sharing via the NIC properties dialog. In addition, disable NetBIOS over TCP/IP for the private NIC via the WINS tab of the Advanced properties of TCP/IP.

Ensure that the correct Link Speed and Duplex has been configured for both the public and heartbeat network cards. For example, on the public, you would normally use 100Mbps with full duplex (assuming this is how the switch is connected). You can access the duplex settings via the Advanced tab of the network adapters properties.

The autosense mode of some 10/100 Ethernet adapters might automatically detect the speed of the connected network. However, during the detection process, packets cannot be handled by the adapter and must be queued. Some adapters might inadvertently trigger the auto-detection process to reoccur intermittently. As a result, communications are queued and communication delayed. Delays of this nature might cause cluster nodes not to receive critical packets in a timely fashion and might cause premature failover of cluster resources. It's important to manually set the correct speed and duplex to avoid any possible autosense-related problems if using a cross-over cable.

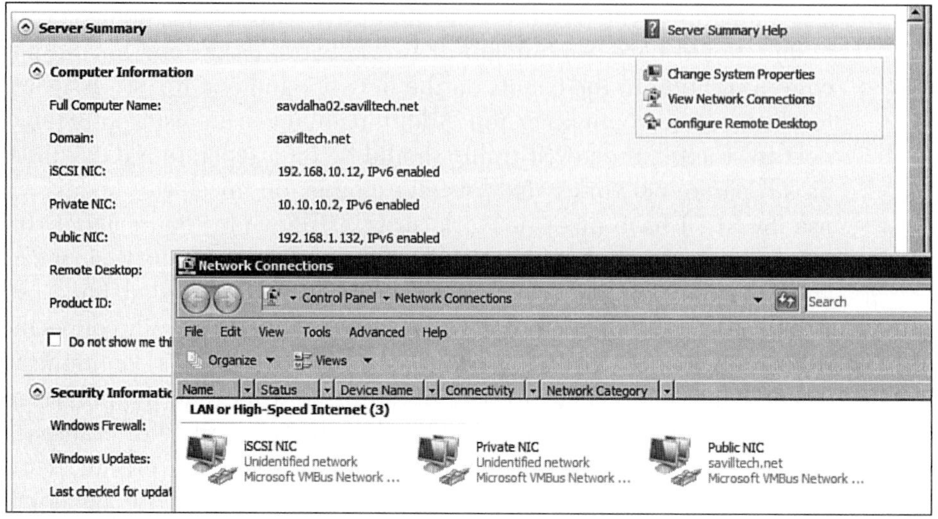

FIGURE 18-21 Networks on a failover cluster.

NOTE You can use DHCP for the configuration of the interfaces used in the cluster; however, if you use a separate switch for the private NIC, a static IP address should be configured because no DHCP server will be contactable.

The iSCSI NIC should also be on a separate network to ensure that iSCSI traffic is sent over the correct NIC; for example, I have a separate network that the iSCSI device and the iSCSI NICs are connected to: 192.168.10/24. All nodes in the cluster should have the same network interfaces defined and ideally the same names; ensure that each adapter has a different IP address.

Make sure that the binding order for the network adapters has the Private NIC last, because you want the public NIC to be used first for normal traffic, as shown in Figure 18-22. This is accessed via the Advanced Settings menu item from the Advanced menu.

One change in Windows Server 2008 is around the supported storage technologies. Parallel SCSI is no longer supported in Windows Server 2008, which means a different approach for virtual environment cluster testing. Instead, you need to use shared storage via Fibre Channel, Serial Attached SCSI (SAS), or iSCSI. In the example, iSCSI is used for the shared storage. Parallel SCSI typically sees many problems due to cable lengths, slow failovers, and termination problems. It is essentially obsolete now, which is why Microsoft dropped support. (Most vendors are moving to SAS and iSCSI.)

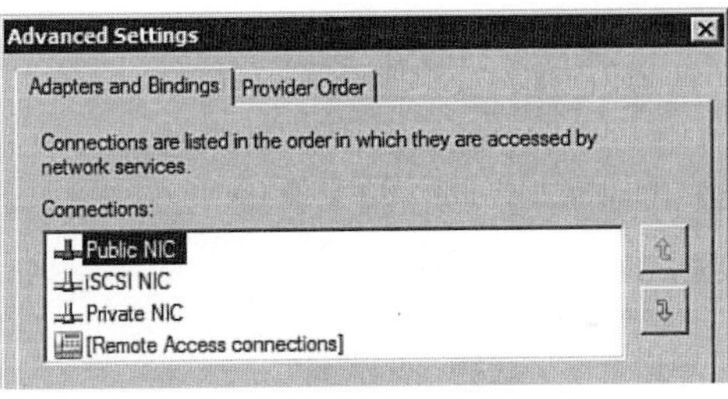

FIGURE 18-22 Ensuring the bindings are correct.

Servers from different clusters must not be able to access the same storage devices. The best solution is that a Logical Unit Number (LUN) that is used for one set of cluster servers should be isolated from all other servers through LUN masking or zoning.

For high-availability connectivity, consider using multipath I/O software if possible. This software allows the use of multiple host bus adapters, so the storage fabric eliminates single points of failure. However, the multipath solution must be based on the Microsoft Multipath I/O that is found in Windows Server 2008; if the Microsoft-provided device-specific modules (DSM) cannot be used, the hardware vendor must supply an MPIO DSM.

There is additional good news for SCSI users. In Windows Server 2003, SCSI bus resets were performed (although less frequently than with Windows 2000 clustering). These were potentially disruptive to the SAN because the reset breaks all reservations on the target device by causing all devices on a bus to reset, which is a problem if a shared bus is used. This is no longer used with Windows failover clustering. Persistent reservations are now used, which means your storage needs to support the SPC-3 standard that is common in many SCSI-3 implementations—SCSI-2 no longer cuts it with 2008.

If you want to test clustering with shared storage and don't have a SAN available to support any of the device controllers or adapters, use iSCSI and a software-based iSCSI target. Windows Server Storage Server has an iSCSI target built in, but there are other options available on the Web. This book uses StarWind from http://www.rocketdivision.com/wind.html. It lets you easily create iSCSI targets using physical drives or image files, as shown in Figure 18-23. As you can see in the example, two devices are created on the iSCSI target: a quorum and a storage device, which are accessible to the iSCSI initiators that are part of Windows Vista and Windows Server 2008. The iSCSI initiator is the client component of iSCSI and allows the connection to resources on the iSCSI target, which is the server piece.

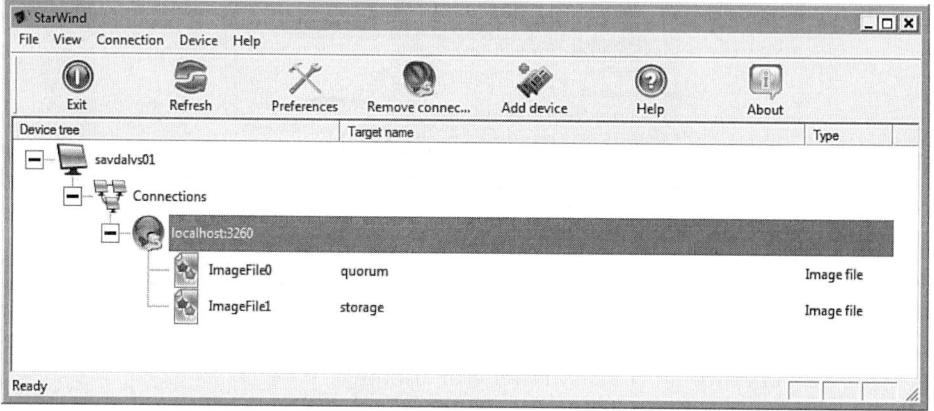

FIGURE 18-23 Using a software-based iSCSI target.

Here's another change from Windows 2003: Storage is now detected when the cluster is created and added to a pool of available storage. Services and applications can then be allocated storage from the available storage instead of having to add for each service/application.

Installing and Creating a Failover Cluster

Failover clustering, like NLB, allows the high availability of a service (for example, file services, print services, and Exchange services). It is improving and making the main role of a server highly available. Failover cluster is a feature of Windows Server 2008, and it is installed via the Add Features Wizard. No configuration is required for the installation, and you don't have to reboot.

When installed, a Cluster folder is added to the `%windir%` of the installation containing the failover cluster components. Before doing anything else, configure the shared storage if needed. If the cluster is used for Exchange, for example, no shared storage is needed, and you can continue past this step.

If you are connected to the storage via SAS or Fibre channel, make the necessary physical connections. From a connectivity perspective, you are done. If you are using iSCSI, however, configure the iSCSI initiator.

Configure the iSCSI Initiator

iSCSI support is part of Windows Server 2008. You can use the native iSCSI Initiator control panel applet to configure it. Select the Discovery tab of the iSCSI Initiator. Under Target Portals, click Add, and add the IP address of the iSCSI target you want to use resources from. If the iSCSI uses credentials, click the Advanced button to add the required authentication. After the iSCSI target has been entered, click the Targets tab. This brings up a list of the storage devices that are available on the iSCSI targets entered. By default, the status will be inactive, because you are not connected, but click the Log On button and ensure you check the Automatically Restore This Connection When the Computer Starts (see Figure 18-24). Clicking the Advanced button allows authentication and IPsec parameters to be configured.

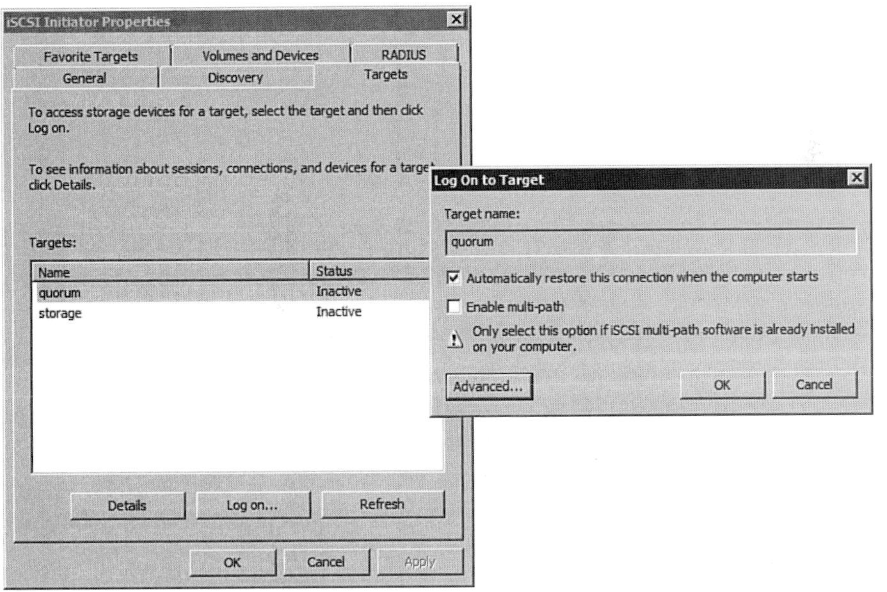

FIGURE 18-24 Attaching to an iSCSI storage device.

After the shared storage is connected, if there are new disks, initialize and format the partitions. Start the Disk Management MMC snap-in (via Computer Manager or Server Manager), and the disk-management process automatically detects whether new disks are present. It prompts you to initialize the disks, as shown in Figure 18-25. Also, it asks if the Master Boot Record (MBR) or Global Partition Table (GPT) partition style should be used. MBR has a limit of 2TB partitions, so you might need to use GPT for large partitions. GPT is the best-practice recommendation to use. Do not convert the disks to dynamic. With Windows Server 2008, you can shrink and grow basic disks anyway, and dynamic disks are not support out of the box. If you want dynamic disk support, look at a third-party product, such as Symantec Storage Foundation for Windows.

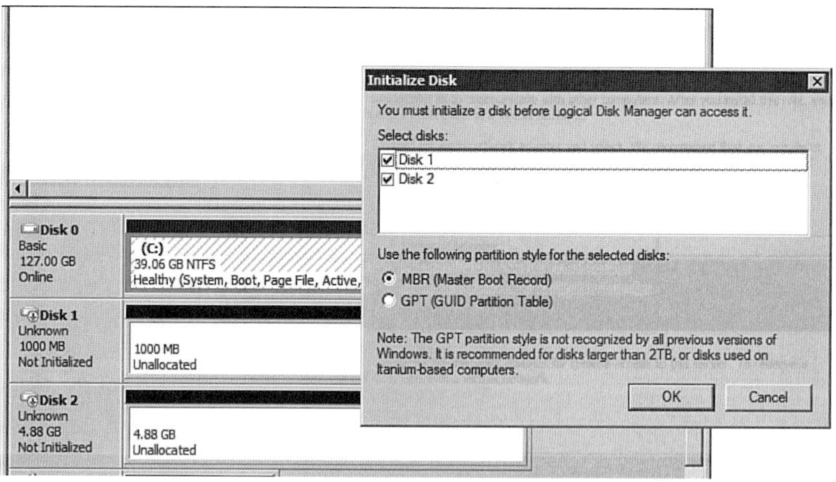

FIGURE 18-25 Initializing the new cluster disks.

After the disks are initialized, create a simple volume and format as NTFS. If you have a witness disk, it is common to give it letter Q and other SAN resources subsequent drive letters (for example, R for storage). It is vital that the drive letters used are consistent across all nodes in the cluster.

After configured, add the connectivity to the other nodes in the cluster; however, the disks will not be online as they can only be active on a single node. When the network and storage configuration is complete, and you are confident all nodes are running the same version of OS, the same updates, and the same features, launch the Failover Cluster Management MMC snap-in via its administrative tools link.

Validating the Cluster Configuration

The Failover Cluster Management interface is driven by the central pane that has three major steps around clustering: validating a configuration, creating a cluster, and managing a cluster. As discussed in the section, "Supported Hardware," the first task is to validate the configuration by running the Validate a Configuration action, which launches the Validate a Configuration Wizard.

The first page of the wizard walks through what the wizard will be performing, so click Next to begin the wizard process. As shown in Figure 18-26, the cluster must be selected, which needs to be verified, or if the cluster has not yet been created, select the nodes that will be added to the cluster. If you are unsure of the node names, click the Browse button to view the Active Directory store or just enter the names and click Add. After all nodes are specified, click Next.

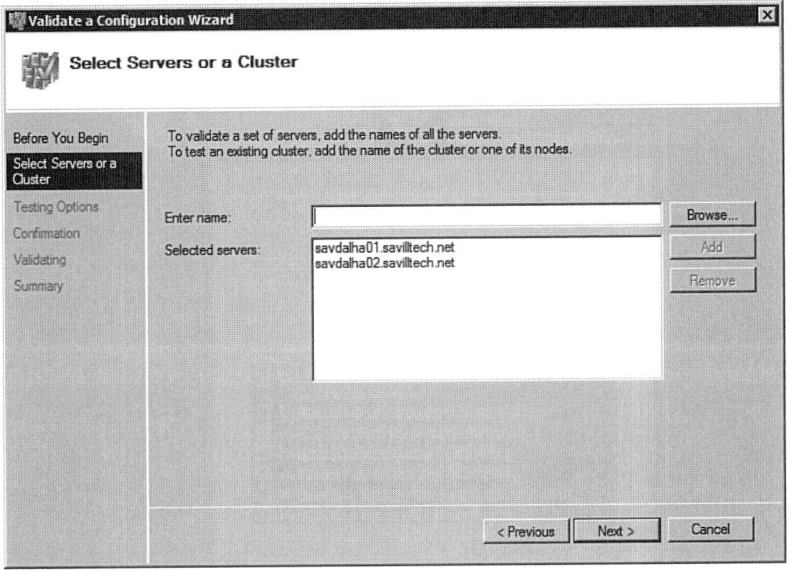

FIGURE 18-26 Specifying the cluster or the hosts in the cluster.

The next page in the dialog allows selection of the tests that will be performed. The default is to run all tests, which is required if you want the cluster configuration to be supported; however, you can also select to run only selected tests, as shown in Figure 18-27.

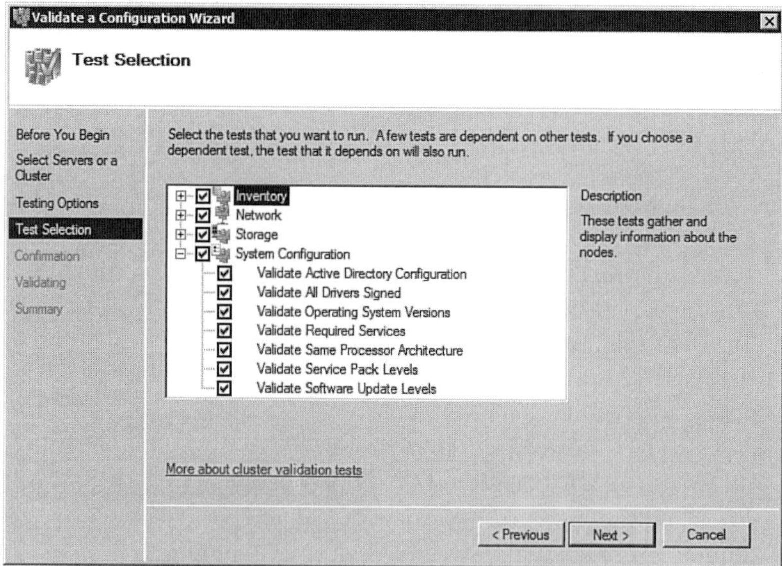

FIGURE 18-27 Selecting a specific validation test.

The confirmation screen displays a list of the validation to be performed, listing the cluster or nodes to be checked and the tests to be performed. Select the Confirmation text and copy via Ctrl+C to paste to a file if needed. Click Next to begin the actual testing, which displays the Validating page of the wizard that shows the percentage complete of each test performed. During the testing, shared disks become unavailable because the validation process tests if they can be failed over between the nodes in the potential cluster. Some tests are skipped and then run after other tests have been completed. For example, the disk arbitration, failover, and simultaneous failover tests run last after the rest of the validation is performed and the actual disks that can be used for clustering have been discovered (see Figure 18-28). The actual tests being performed are displayed; for example, you can see disks being failed over between nodes that are being tested. The testing typically takes between 20 and 30 minutes, with the majority of the time being spent on the disk failure portions of the validation ensuring consistent failover and ownership. The exact time scales exponentially based on the number of disks and nodes.

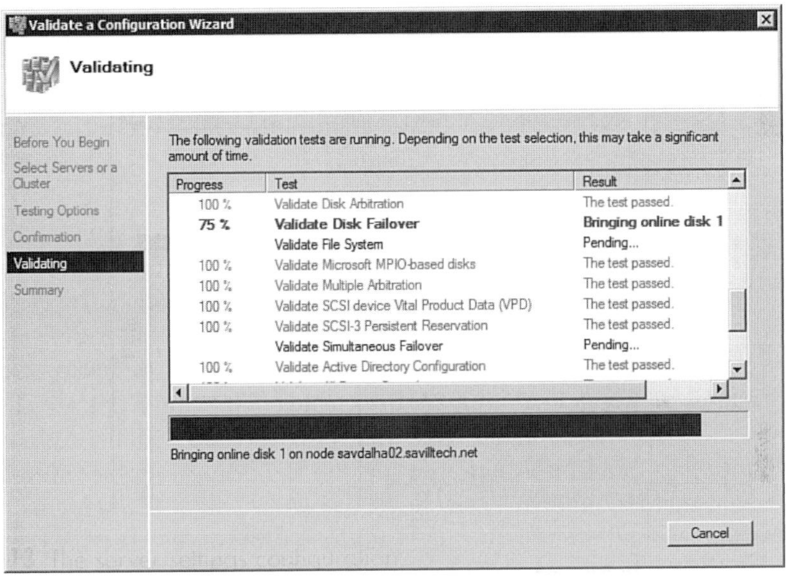

FIGURE 18-28 Disk failover testing by the validation process.

A summary of the testing is displayed. At the bottom of the screen is a result if the environment is suitable for clustering. Save the report to a file by selecting View Report. A generated single file Web archive file (.mht) opens, which can be saved via the Page, Save As command in Internet Explorer. Additionally, the reports are automatically saved in the C:\Windows\Cluster\Reports folder in both Web archive format and XML. This report has a huge amount of data, far more than that displayed in the wizard, and displays all the information that was discovered in the validation; keep this report somewhere safe as the go-to place for information about the cluster validation test and the environment. You can run the Validate at any time through the Cluster Administrator, and it is a useful diagnostics tool if you have cluster problems.

Creating a Cluster

After the nodes that will become part of the cluster have been validated, create the cluster. With previous versions of Windows, you had to create the cluster on one node and then go to each additional node and add it to the cluster. With Windows Server 2008, you run the wizard once on a single node, and it automatically configures the other specified nodes, and the cluster is ready. You can use the old style of cluster creation and can add additional nodes at a later time; however, this is not necessary.

Select the Create a Cluster action to begin the cluster creation. The intro screen of the wizard displays information about cluster creation process; click Next to begin the configuration.

The first step is to add the fully qualified names of the servers that will be part of the cluster. As each node is added, the suitability for cluster membership is checked; once all nodes are added, click the Next button.

The next stage asks for the name of the cluster that will be used for the cluster name resource and the IP address that will be used for communication purposes to administer the cluster. The wizard detects all the NICs on the network, and the NIC that has a gateway configured is displayed with its subnet information; a specific IP address can be entered that will be used for connectivity, as shown in Figure 18-29. If you are using DHCP, then no configuration for the IP address is displayed, as the wizard defaults to the configuration used for the normal IP configuration and simply uses DHCP for the administration address for the cluster; there is a blank area on the dialog. If IPv6 is dynamically configured, you are not prompted for IPv6 information. After the configuration for the administration is complete, click Next. Make sure that the name specified for the cluster does not already exist in DNS, as the cluster creation process dynamically registers the name in DNS automatically and fails if the record exists.

A configuration summary is displayed (which can be copied via Ctrl+C if required, or look at the log that is created in the C:\Windows\Cluster\Reports folder as an .htm file, CreateCluster.htm), as shown here:

```
Cluster:             savdalclus
Node:                savdalha01.savilltech.net
Node:                savdalha02.savilltech.net
IP Address:          IPv6 address on 2002:4cb7:32c7:1234::/64
IP Address:          192.168.1.135
```

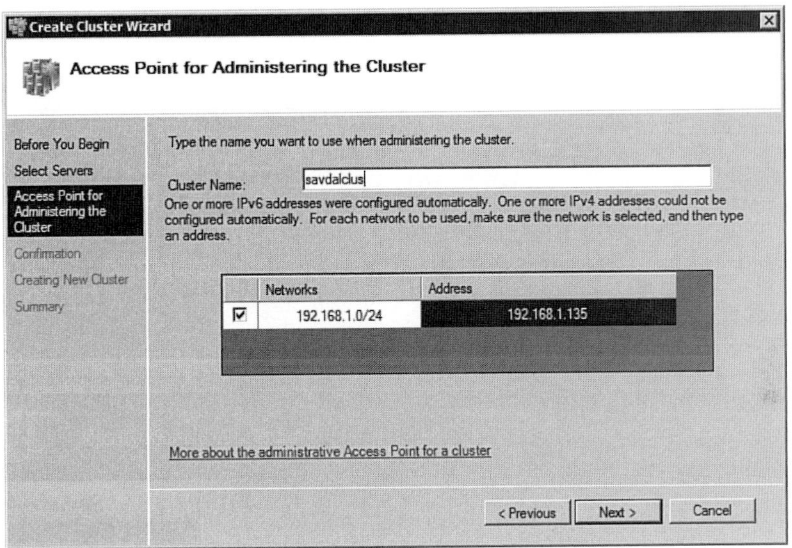

FIGURE 18-29 Administration details for a cluster.

Click Next to create the cluster, and the progress of creating the cluster is displayed, including creating the cluster computer object and configuring the IP properties. A summary is displayed and a full report can be viewed via the View Report button, or a report is saved to the Reports folder. Notice you are not asked about quorum configuration; the wizard decides the best quorum configuration based on your environment.

After the cluster is created, a DNS record is registered for the name specified in the domain's zone, such as savdalclus.savilltech.net for the configured IP addresses (for example, v4 and v6).

Like the Server Roles main page for a role, the Failover Cluster Management main page for a cluster shows a summary of the information about the cluster, showing the number of applications, nodes, quorum information, and the number of errors and warnings (see Figure 18-30). After creating the cluster, look at this area, and if there are any warnings or errors, click the link that opens the Cluster Events node in the Failover Cluster Management snap-in showing all event logs that pertain to failover cluster; if there are problems, resolve them prior to continuing.

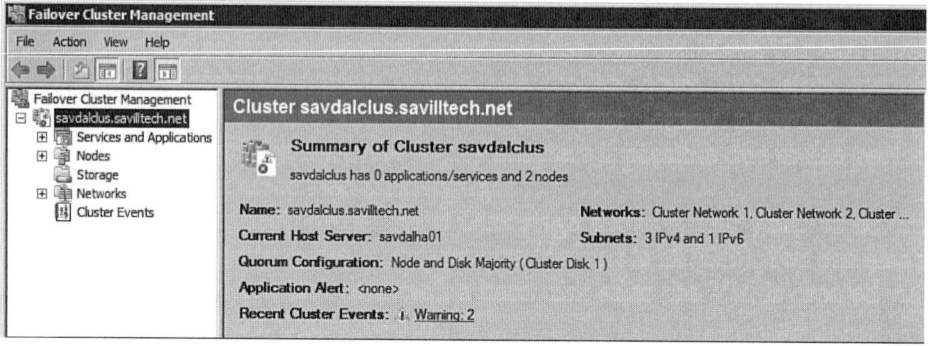

FIGURE 18-30 Cluster summary information.

Configuring the Network Adapters

Each network adapter by default is enabled for use by the cluster, and if the adapter has a gateway, it is also enabled for client communication. If you have a network adapter that should not be used for cluster configuration—for example, if you use iSCSI—then configure the adapter to not be used for cluster configuration.

Expand the cluster within the Failover Cluster Management MMC snap-in and select the Networks console tree item. This shows the networks that exist as part of the cluster. If you select each network, you are shown the actual network name for each node in the details pane, which is a great reason why networks are given useful names.

Right-click the cluster network that corresponds to the network that should not be used for cluster communication and select Properties. As shown in Figure 18-31, the network can then be marked to not be used by the network. Also note that adapters can be configured to be used by the cluster by a separate check box, which has to be selected to allow actual client traffic. If you look through your adapters, you see that the private NIC is marked as allowed to be used by the cluster, but the Allow Clients to Connect Through this Network is not checked.

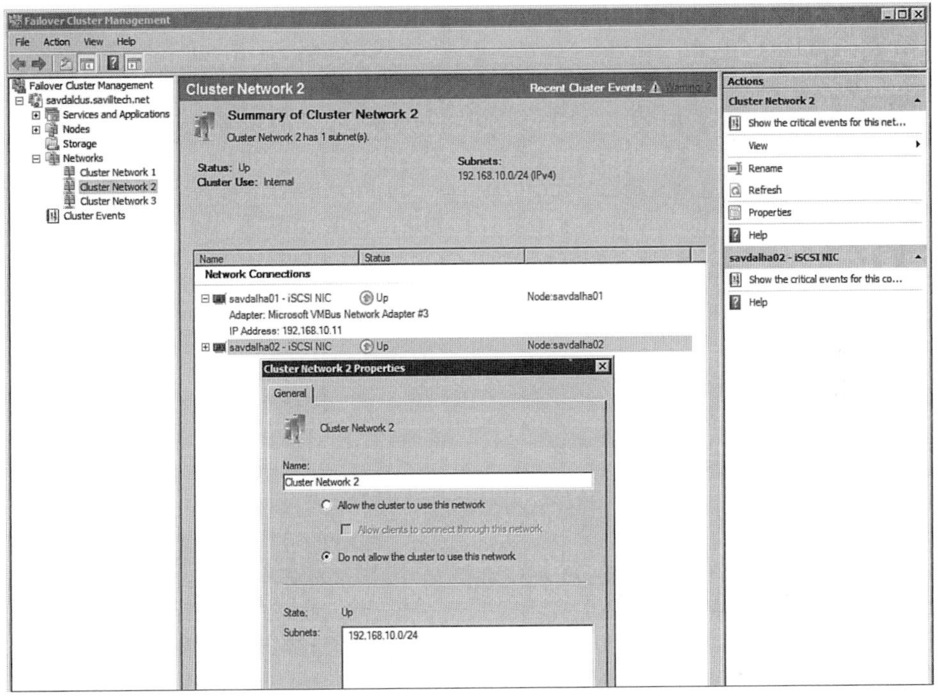

FIGURE 18-31 Configuring the iSCSI network to not be used for cluster communications.

Adding High-Availability Services and Applications

You now have a cluster with no resources, apart from the administrative interface resource and a quorum disk. Well, this is not completely true. A new cluster consists of two core groups: the Cluster group, which contains those core cluster resources, and an Available Storage group, which are covered later. Both of these groups are effectively hidden from the user interface because they are for internal purposes and should not be modified by users directly. Many of their properties are exposed via the interface in controlled ways.

The next step is to create a cluster group, now known as a service or application, which contains resources that will be made highly available. If you are making a non-Windows OS service or application highly available, use the applications management interface to cluster enable (for example, an Exchange 2007 clustered mailbox server); however, for Windows OS components, use the Failover Cluster Management MMC.

Select the Services and Applications console tree item and select the Configure a Service or Application action. This launches the High Availability Wizard, which has an introduction screen that explains making a service or application high availability. Click Next to begin the configuration.

A list of all the services and applications supported out of the box is displayed, as shown in Figure 18-32. Depending on the application or service selected, the next stages of the wizard will vary; however, select File Server, which allows you to make a storage device and one or more shares highly available.

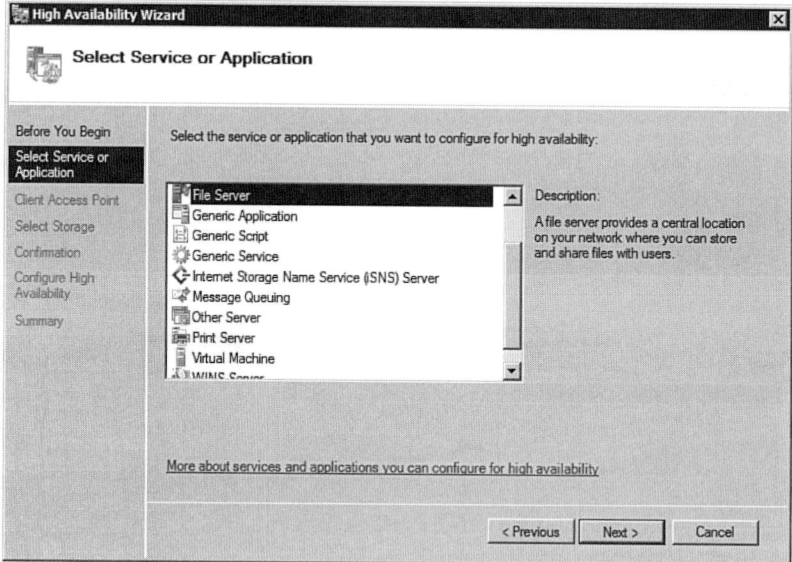

FIGURE 18-32 Selecting the server or application to make highly available.

No matter what the role, a client access point must be configured, which is a name for the new service point and the IP address information if DHCP is not used, as shown in Figure 18-33.

The next stage of the High Availability Wizard varies, but for a file server, you need at least one storage device where the data will be stored; this is read from the cluster's Storage configuration, as shown in Figure 18-34.

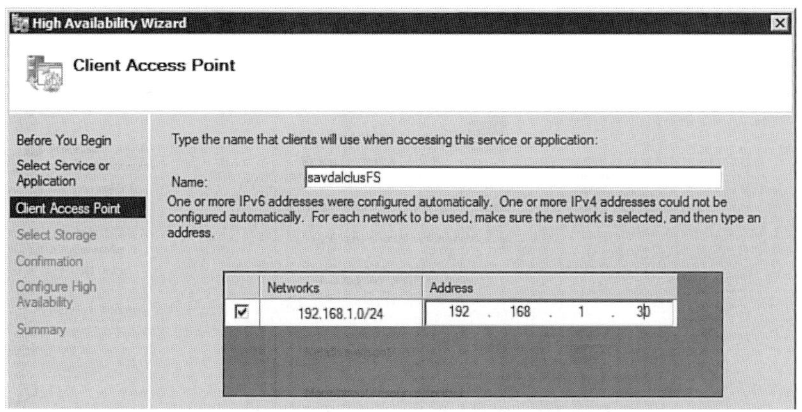

FIGURE 18-33 Setting the name and IP information for the new service or application.

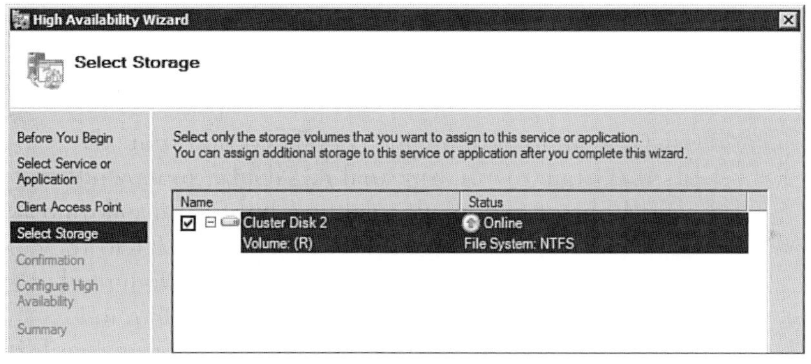

FIGURE 18-34 Selecting the storage to be used.

Finally, a configuration is displayed of the settings to be used. Click Next to begin the installation, and when complete, a summary of the configuration is displayed with a view report option that is also saved to the clusters report folder as usual.

Once again, a dynamic DNS record will be created for the new service name, and your resources can be viewed by selecting the cluster group within the Failover Cluster Management MMC snap-in.

Depending on the type of service, additional resources might be required, which can be added by right-clicking on the cluster group (for example, savdalclusfs) and selecting to add a resource. By default, the context menu has quick links to the resource types that are most common for the application or service; for example, for a file server, a context menu option is added to add a shared folder and storage, as shown in Figure 18-35.

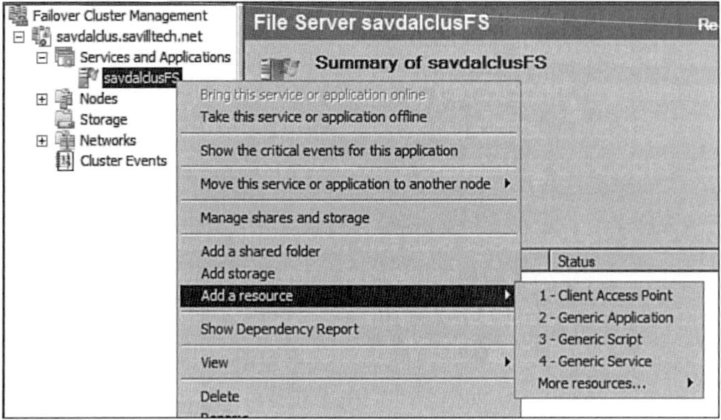

FIGURE 18-35 Adding new resources to a cluster group.

By default, when you add a file server, a hidden share is added. However, you probably want a better named share for use by clients, so select to add a shared folder, which allows a location to be specified on one of the storage devices to be shared (see Figure 18-36). You can additionally create new folders via the Browse dialog. Additional storage can be added via the Provision Storage button if required. The rest of the wizard is self-explanatory and allows NTFS permissions to be changed if required. Although not recommended, the SMB share name can be configured and created, and if Network File System (NFS) is installed, an NFS share is also added. Advanced settings for the SMB can be configured, allowing configuration of the maximum number of users, offline settings, and if access-based enumeration is enabled. The share permissions can also be configured to allow for custom permissions. For example, you can set it up so everyone has only read access, or where administrators have full control and everyone else has only read access, or where administrators have full control and everyone else has read and write permissions.

One great feature of Windows Server 2008 is the total integration of failover clustering with the Windows shell. For example, if you create a share using Explorer on a disk that is owned by the cluster, the share is automatically added to the file server cluster service instead of being defined locally on the server. This is part of the ease of use of clustering. The shell understands the action being performed, decides the share should be created on the cluster, and creates as needed.

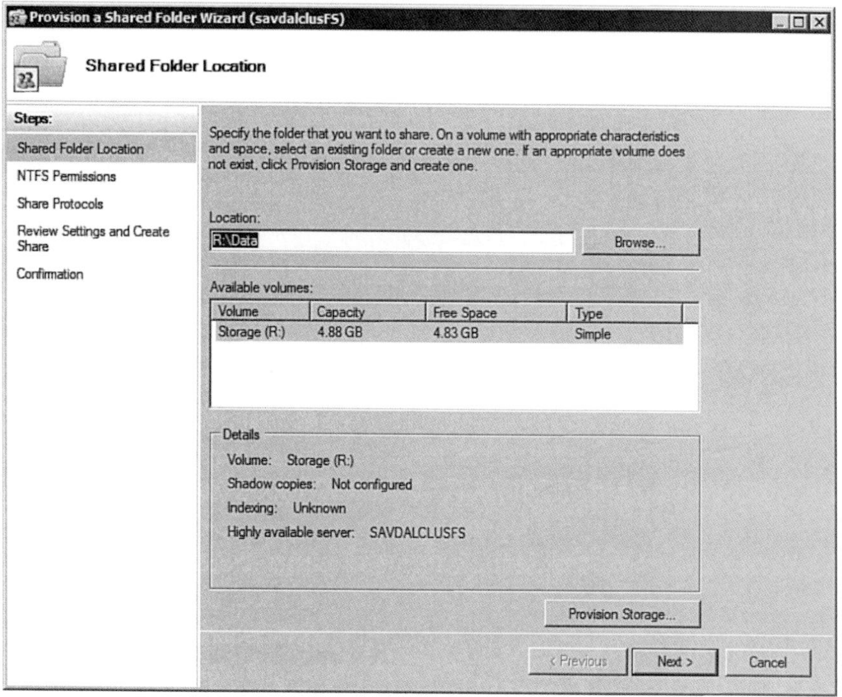

FIGURE 18-36 Creating a new shared folder.

Managing Failover Clustering

There are numerous aspects to managing failover clustering, such as simple day-to-day maintenance tasks, failing resources between nodes in the cluster, and modifying the configuration of the cluster (such as modifying the quorum scheme).

Cluster Failover

After a cluster is created and resource groups exist, you can test moving the resource group to another node in the cluster via the Move This Service or Application to <Node> action; you are prompted to confirm the move operation. The current owner of a resource group is displayed in the summary of the resource group.

When a move operation is initiated, the move process is seen as the resources in the group are taken offline and then brought online on the

new active node for the group, as shown in Figure 18-37. This process is fast and should last for only a few seconds, and users should see only a minor service interruption.

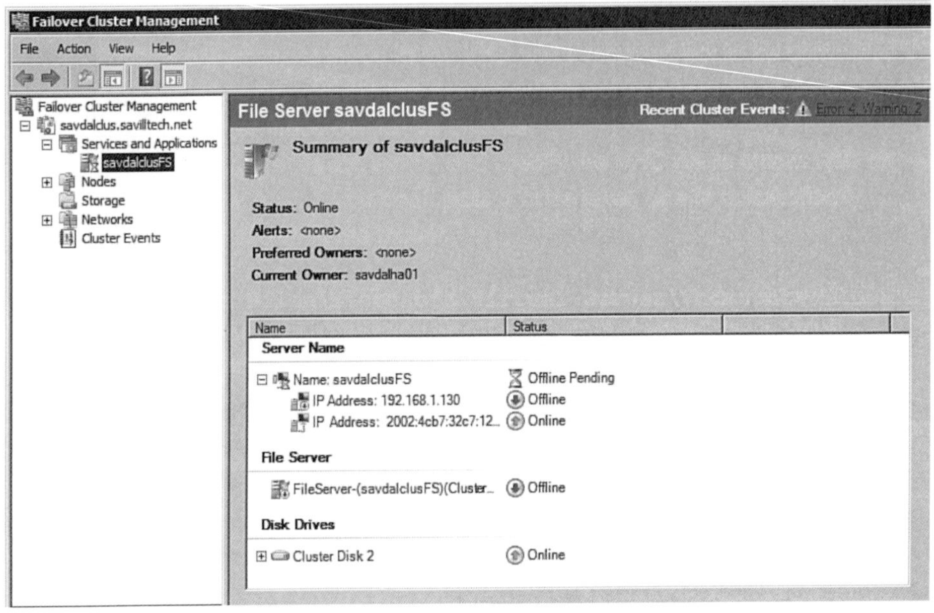

FIGURE 18-37 The move process.

The move process is useful for planned maintenance procedures: Move the resource group to a passive node from an active node, perform maintenance on the now-passive node while it is not running any resource groups, reboot, and then move resource groups back to the now-maintained node.

If a node crashes, the other nodes in the cluster detect the unavailability, and any resource groups that the node owned is transferred to another node in the cluster. A critical event log is written to the System event log of ID 1135. Example event log text content is shown here:

```
Cluster node 'savdalha02' was removed from the
active failover cluster membership. The Cluster
service on this node might have stopped. This
could also be due to the node having lost communi-
cation with other active nodes in the failover
cluster. Run the Validate a Configuration wizard to
check your network configuration. If the condition
```

```
persists, check for hardware or software errors
related to the network adapters on this node. Also
check for failures in any other network components
to which the node is connected such as hubs,
switches, or bridges.
```

You have control over what happens in the event of a failover, both at a cluster and server/application level.

On the main screen for a cluster is a "Cluster Core Resources" section. This section shows the resources owned by the cluster and not a specific application or service. If one of these resources has its properties examined, there is a Policies tab (see Figure 18-38) that gives you the capability to define restart actions if the resource fails. If restart fails, it offers whether a failover to another node should be performed and, optionally, a wait time until attempting to restart the resource again.

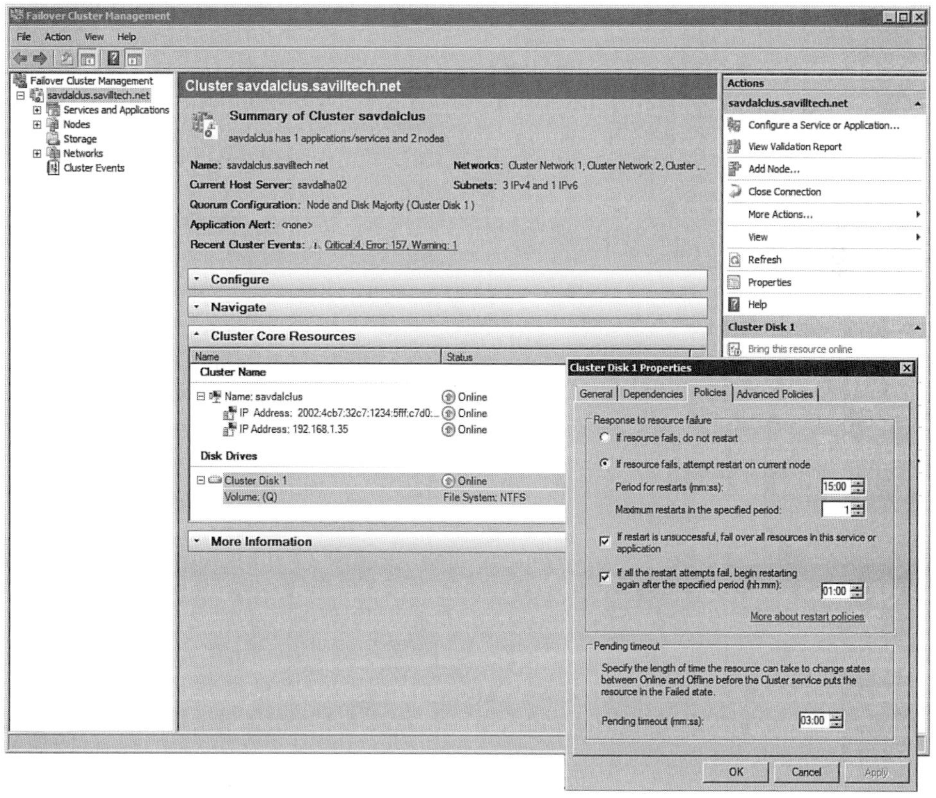

FIGURE 18-38 The policies for resources in the cluster.

If the Advanced Policies tab is selected, all the nodes in the cluster are displayed and must be checked if they are a possible owner for the resource. This is more useful for services and applications, which will be covered shortly. Also in the Advanced Policies is the option to specify the standard heartbeat interval (5 seconds) and the time for a thorough resource health check, which is a more-detailed query of the node health (60 seconds).

For Service and Application, right-click the Service/Application and select Properties. The General tab displays the name of the service/application, and specific nodes in the cluster can be checked to make them the preferred owners for the service or application, as shown in Figure 18-39. After preferred owners are configured, where possible, an application or service will always attempt to fail over to a node that is preferred over other node members. By default, if a service or application is running on a non-preferred node, it will not fall back to a preferred node if one becomes available; however, this can be enabled via the Failover tab of the properties. This allows failback to be performed either immediately or, more likely, to minimize end-user impact between a certain timeframe in the day, as shown in Figure 18-40. Also notice that you can configure a number of failures allowed within a certain time period before the service or application is considered failed.

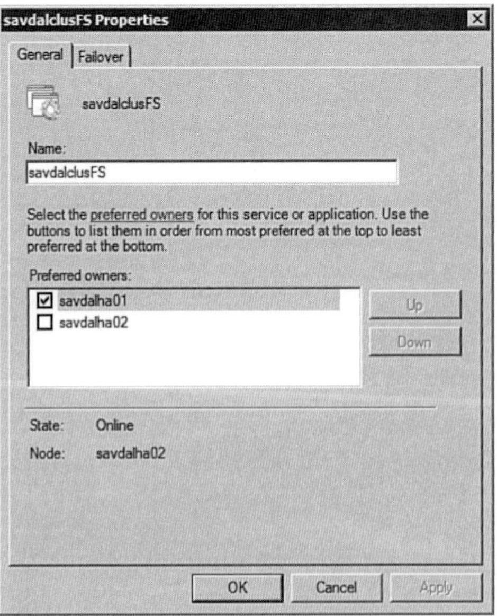

FIGURE 18-39 Failover properties for a service or application: General tab.

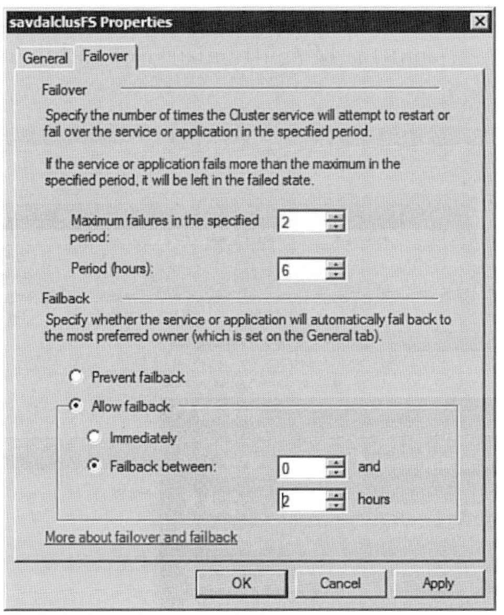

FIGURE 18-40 Failover properties for a service or application: Failover tab.

Modifying the Quorum Mode

The best quorum mode for the nodes available is selected when the cluster is created by the wizard. You are not asked for your input during the cluster creation process, because the wizard is designed for noncluster experts, so it decides for you; however, after the cluster is created, you can modify the quorum mode by selecting Configure Cluster Quorum Settings from the More Actions context menu item for the cluster. If you want a node and file share witness majority, you need to configure this after the cluster creation because the wizard cannot automatically guess which share to use. Instead, it creates a node majority cluster.

This should not be something you need to do. However, as you can see in Figure 18-41, the wizard to change the quorum is straightforward. If you select the node and file share majority option, you will be prompted for the file share to own a vote. If you select Node and Disk Majority or No Majority, you are prompted for the shared disk to own a vote. This wizard could also be used to change the disk that is used for the quorum. You can change the quorum while the cluster is online without affecting availability.

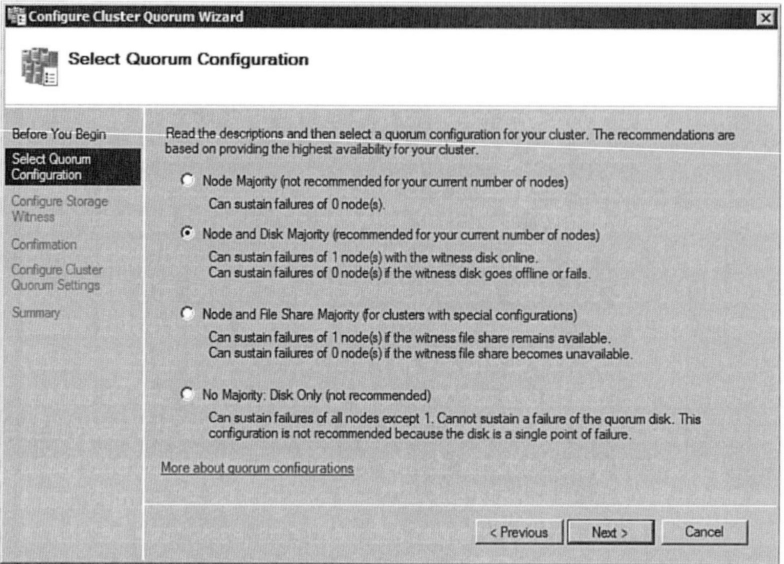

FIGURE 18-41 Selecting the quorum mode.

If you use a file share witness, ensure that share specified is configured as follows:

- Computer objects for the cluster object (not the nodes that make up the cluster, but the actual cluster computer account) should have full control at both the NTFS and share level; however, this is configured via the Quorum Wizard. Ensure the Administrator running the wizard has full permissions on the share and NTFS, and the wizard will give the cluster object the necessary rights.
- The file share can be on a clustered file server for high availability.
- The file share cannot be on DFS because the point of the file share is a single point of arbitration in the event cluster nodes cannot communicate with each other directly. If DFS is used, cluster nodes might be directed to different targets for the file share, which would cause problems and might lead to split-brain clustering, where multiple cluster nodes might try to bring the same resources online.

Managing Nodes

Detail for a node can be viewed by selecting the node from the console tree under the Nodes branch tree item. The node information shows the OS information about the node, processor, system model, memory, and paging. As shown in Figure 18-42, the cluster groups and storage from the cluster that are online on the selected node are also displayed.

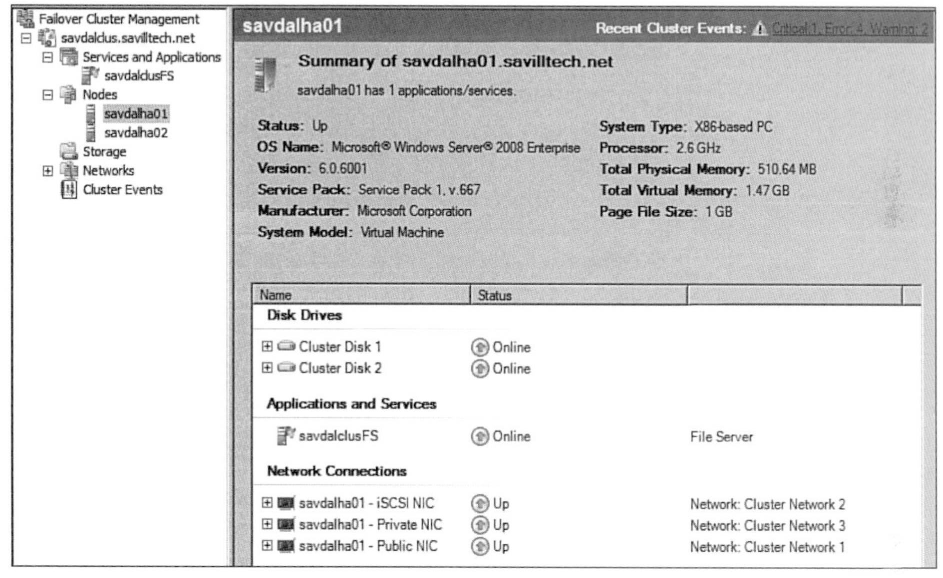

FIGURE 18-42 Cluster node detailed information.

Each resource can be selected, and actions are available to take the resource offline, along with certain resource-specific actions (for example, changing the drive letter of a disk drive). Be careful when changing any cluster-used resource because the resources must be consistent across all nodes in the cluster.

Additional servers can be added to a cluster by selecting the Add Node action from the Nodes action menu. You are prompted for the name of the node, and a verification is performed that the node is suitable to be added to the cluster. After all checks are complete, the new node is added. The cool thing to notice is you are performing all the configuration from the Failover Cluster Management console; you don't have to go to the nodes to configure the cluster, except for items such as configuring any iSCSI and network connections. To manage the cluster, you are single-point entry.

To remove a node from the cluster, move any cluster services or applications that are active on it to another node, and then select the node and select Evict from the Actions menu. You are asked if you're sure that the node should be evicted and that the remaining nodes in the cluster are sufficient to continue servicing the services and applications that the node handles.

Best of the Rest

Clustering is a huge topic, and although we've touched on the major concepts, there are always more options and actions in the event of problems. The first place to go if you encounter issues is to run the cluster validation reports (which highlights problems) and check the cluster event logs (which is your first "best of the rest").

A Cluster Events item is on the console tree for a cluster. By default, it lists all Critical, Error, and Warning level events for the Microsoft-Windows-FailoverClustering/Operational log and the System log for all the nodes in the cluster. However, the events displayed can be changed via the Query action for the log, which allows additional logs to be queried and results displayed. Check this in the event of problems for any problem events. Logs can also be viewed via the Cluster Log command-line tool (new to 2008). For example, to view the cluster logs for a cluster, use the following command, which creates a log file for each node in the cluster in the location specified:

```
C:\>cluster savdalclus.savilltech.net log /gen /copy:"c:\temp"
Generating the cluster log(s) ...
The cluster log has been successfully generated on node 'savdalha02'...
The cluster log has been successfully generated on node 'savdalha01'...
The cluster log has been successfully copied from node 'savdalha02'...
The cluster log has been successfully copied from node 'savdalha01'...

The cluster log(s) have been copied to 'c:\temp'...
```

Another cool item is the dependency report that can be executed via the Actions menu for a service or application or for a storage device. It both textually and graphically shows the dependencies for the services, application, or storage to be available. The storage is not generally interesting, but the report for a service/application can give great insight. An example report is shown in Figure 18-43. To create a report, run the Show Dependency Report action.

As shown in Figure 18-43, both the network name and disk storage are required, in addition to one of the IP addresses required for the file server service to be available.

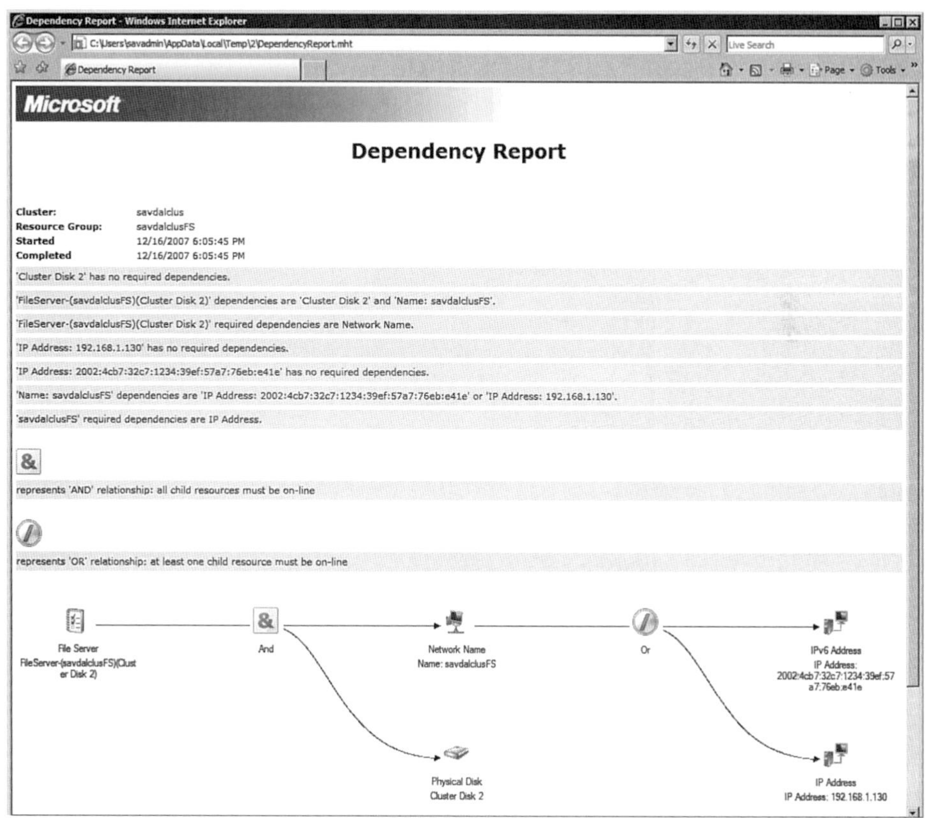

FIGURE 18-43 The dependency report for a file service.

To grant nonadministrators permission to manage a cluster, access the properties of the cluster, select the Cluster Permissions tab, and grant the user to manage the cluster Full Control. To use the Cluster Administrator MMC snap-in (CluAdmin.msc), you have to be a local administrator. You can use cluster.exe with just cluster administrator rights. However, be careful that you do not remove any existing permissions on the cluster. You cannot grant permissions at a more granular level. (For example, you cannot grant a user permission to manage a specific application or service, as shown in Figure 18-44.)

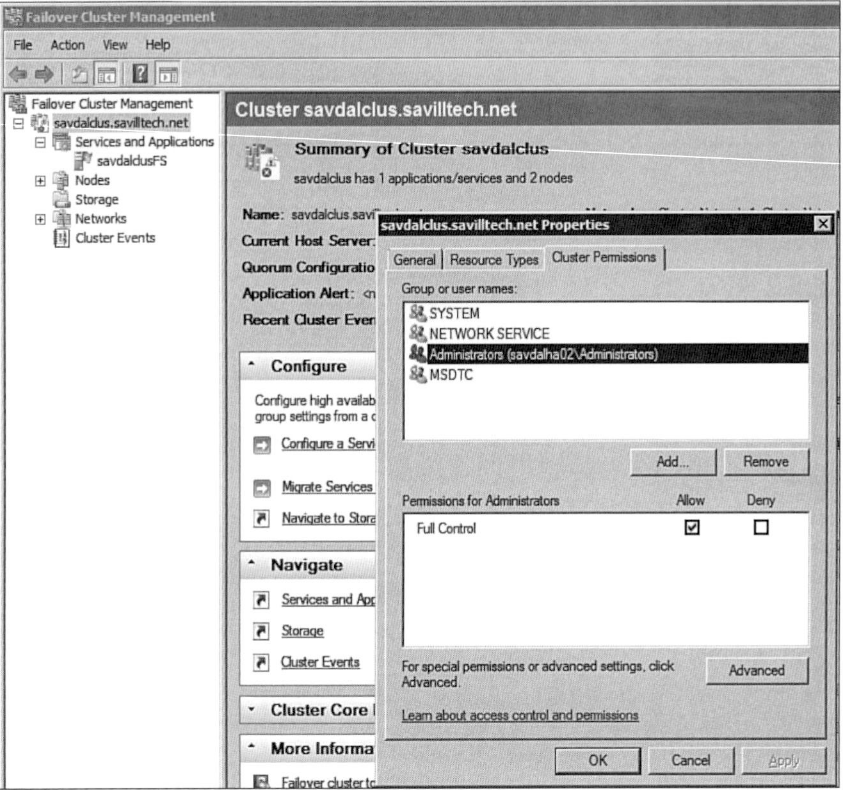

FIGURE 18-44 Permissions for the cluster management.

Command-Line Management

Nearly all the cluster properties can be configured via the `CLUSTER.EXE` command-line utility. There is not a separate PowerShell `cmdlet` for clustering, although there is a cluster WMI interface that can be accessed via PowerShell. Failover clustering does not support PowerShell, however, so for now steer clear of PowerShell with failover clustering.

You can get a lot of information about a cluster using the `CLUSTER.EXE` command. For example, to see all the internal properties, use the `/prop` switch:

```
C:\>cluster . /prop
Listing properties for 'savdalclus':

T  Cluster              Name                           Value
-- -------------------- ------------------------------ ----------------
M  savdalclus           AdminExtensions
D  savdalclus           DefaultNetworkRole             2 (0x2)
S  savdalclus           Description
B  savdalclus           Security Descriptor            01 00 14 80 ...
(212 bytes)
M  savdalclus           Groups\AdminExtensions
M  savdalclus           Networks\AdminExtensions
M  savdalclus           NetworkInterfaces\AdminExtensions
M  savdalclus           Nodes\AdminExtensions
M  savdalclus           Resources\AdminExtensions
M  savdalclus           ResourceTypes\AdminExtensions
D  savdalclus           QuorumArbitrationTimeMax       20 (0x14)
D  savdalclus           QuorumArbitrationTimeMin       7 (0x7)
D  savdalclus           DisableGroupPreferredOwnerRandomization 0 (0x0)
D  savdalclus           ClusSvcHangTimeout             60 (0x3c)
D  savdalclus           ClusSvcRegroupStageTimeout     7 (0x7)
D  savdalclus           ClusSvcRegroupOpeningTimeout   5 (0x5)
D  savdalclus           ClusSvcRegroupPruningTimeout   5 (0x5)
D  savdalclus           ClusSvcRegroupTickInMilliseconds 300 (0x12c)
D  savdalclus           HangRecoveryAction             3 (0x3)
D  savdalclus           SameSubnetDelay                1000 (0x3e8)
D  savdalclus           CrossSubnetDelay               1000 (0x3e8)
D  savdalclus           SameSubnetThreshold            5 (0x5)
D  savdalclus           PlumbAllCrossSubnetRoutes      0 (0x0)
D  savdalclus           CrossSubnetThreshold           5 (0x5)
D  savdalclus           BackupInProgress               0 (0x0)
D  savdalclus           RequestReplyTimeout            60 (0x3c)
D  savdalclus           WitnessRestartInterval         15 (0xf)
D  savdalclus           SecurityLevel                  1 (0x1)
D  savdalclus           ClusterLogLevel                3 (0x3)
D  savdalclus           ClusterLogSize                 100 (0x64)
D  savdalclus           WitnessDatabaseWriteTimeout    300 (0x12c)
```

To get status information about the groups in the cluster, use the `group/status` switches. For example, to see all cluster groups in the savdalclus cluster, use the following code. If you wanted only the status of one group, add the name of the group after the `group` keyword (for example, `cluster savdalclus.savilltech.net group savdalclusfs /status`):

```
C:\>cluster savdalclus.savilltech.net group /status
Listing status for all available resource groups:

Group                Node            Status
-------------------- --------------- ------
Available Storage    savdalha02      Offline
Cluster Group        savdalha01      Online
savdalclusFS         savdalha02      Online
```

To move a group to another node, add the `/move` switch and optionally a node to move it to. For example:

```
C:\>cluster savdalclus.savilltech.net group savdalclusfs
➥/move:savdalha01

Moving resource group 'savdalclusfs'...

Group                Node            Status
-------------------- --------------- ------
savdalclusfs         savdalha01      Online
```

Use the same format command to bring a clustered service or application online or offline by replacing the `/move` switch with /on or /off. The author recommends that you look at `cluster /?` if you are interested in running your cluster from a command prompt or automate actions via a script. With the new wizard interfaces, however, clustering is one area where the GUI is king. Limit the command line to basic moving of groups rather than the actual creation.

Upgrading from Windows 2003 Cluster to Windows 2008 Cluster

As mentioned earlier in the section, "Architecture of a Cluster," failover cluster in 2008 is totally rewritten. There is no compatibility between tools or nodes, so the familiar approach of a rolling upgrade (where one node in the cluster is upgraded while resources are failed over to another node; then resources fail back to the now-upgraded node and the other node is upgraded) is not possible because you cannot have 2003 and 2008 nodes in the same cluster. The old rolling upgrade approach is shown in Figure 18-45.

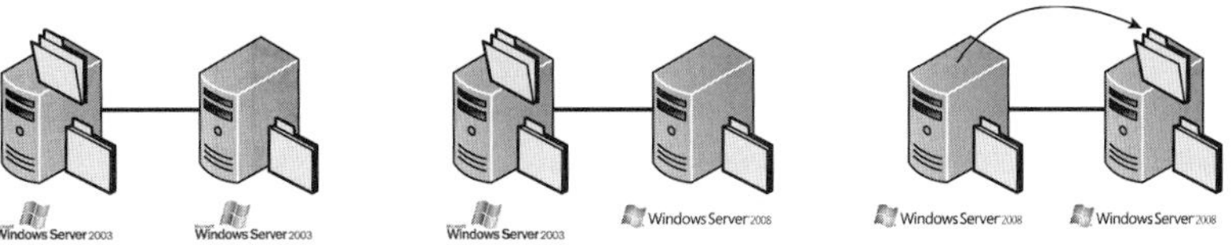

FIGURE 18-45 The rolling upgrade approach, which is not possible.

So what can you do? A powerful cluster-migration tool is included in Windows Server 2008 that helps move a cluster configuration and resources from one cluster to another, which is available via the Migrate Services and Applications link from the More Actions menu for a cluster in the 2008 Failover Cluster Management utility. When executed, the utility asks for a source 2003 cluster by IP address or name, displays a list of the resource groups available on the cluster, and migrates the resource groups into Windows Server 2008 services and applications. The migration utility does not copy actual file share content over; this needs to be done manually, and some additional manual steps are required if you migrate DHCP or WINS or any generic application, script, or service. As an example, for DHCP, you must install the server role, and for WINS, the server feature.

Therefore, there are two approaches possible because you can migrate settings from one cluster to another. You can perform an in-place migration involving only two servers. In this scenario, start with a two-node server cluster that is running Windows Server 2003, remove a server from the cluster, and install Windows Server 2008 on that server. Next, use that server to create a one-node failover cluster, and migrate the settings from the old server cluster node to that failover cluster. Finally, on the old server cluster node, install Windows Server 2008 and the failover cluster feature, add the server to the failover cluster, run validation tests to confirm that the overall configuration works, and then bring the migrated resources online, as shown in Figure 18-46. Although this might look like a rolling upgrade, remember that you are migrating resources and have two one-node clusters, so high availability is lost until you get both nodes upgraded to Windows Server 2008.

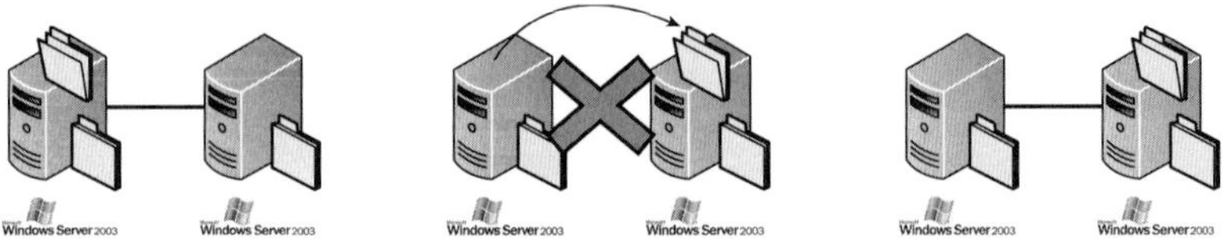

FIGURE 18-46 An in-place upgrade creating a new one-node interim cluster.

Alternatively, if you have new hardware, create a new cluster on the new hardware. After the new 2008 failover cluster is running, migrate the settings from the 2003 cluster and then retire the existing 2003, as shown in Figure 18-47.

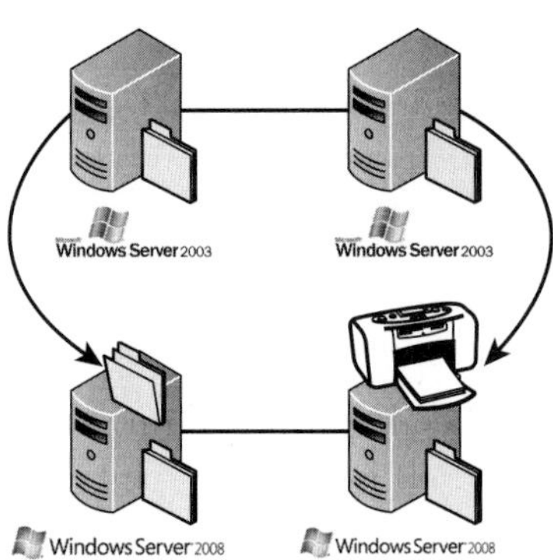

FIGURE 18-47 Performing a migration to a new cluster.

Microsoft has a helpful guide on this process: *Step-by-Step Guide for Migrating Settings from a Cluster Running Windows Server 2003 to a Cluster Running Windows Server 2008* is available at http://technet2.microsoft.com/windowsserver2008/en/library/6820ae3f-1ecc-43fd-8a76-fe8c2125cfe61033.mspx?mfr=true.

Summary

The big emphasis with 2008 clustering is embracing new technologies such as iSCSI, but most of the focus is on bringing clustering to the masses and making it easy. The new clustering interfaces are far more intuitive than with previous versions, and built-in inclusion of validation tools for failover clustering makes it much easier to ensure you have a supported configuration.

The wizards that create clusters are now automatic. Your quorum decisions are made for you based on the best option for the available hardware; as an administrator, you can concentrate on the applications and services you want to make highly available instead of the underlying cluster architecture.

With 2008, you see a lot more clusters, especially with features such as file share witnesses removing the need for shared storage, which enable multisite clusters. Many more applications are jumping onboard and using this new functionality.

Most of the changes in clustering revolved around failover clustering, because it needed the most work. However, do not overlook NLB and the critical areas in which it is the right high-availability solution.

CHAPTER 19

Virtualization and Resource Management

Virtualization is a buzzword in the Windows Server 2008 community, especially with the inclusion of a new virtualization platform: Hyper-V. However, there are numerous types of virtualization technologies and some alternatives.

The term "virtualization" brings to mind operating system (OS) virtualization facilitated by software, such as Virtual PC and Virtual Server. These types of software enable you to create virtual machines (VMs) on a computer running virtualization software. These solutions allow the VMs to have their own allocated memory, CPU access, network adapter mapping, and disk storage in the form of virtual hard disks (VHDs). The disks enable installation of complete OSs into virtual environments. This enables you to have a computer running Windows Vista and then, in VMs, run Windows XP, Windows 98, and Windows Server 2008, all on a single physical computer. This is great for testing and running applications that have compatibility issues. It's also helpful for separating applications that can't exist in the same OS instance as another application, and for general consolidation to reduce the overall number of physical servers (in many instances, servers are underutilized).

Many key virtualization technologies exist and, although this chapter focuses on Hyper-V, let's quickly look at the broader picture.

Virtualization 360 Picture

Microsoft has a Virtualization 360 initiative that breaks down virtualization into six key areas, from the desktop to the data center. It aims to break the bonds that exist without virtualization technologies.

Today, applications are installed locally on computers, OSs are installed on hardware and bound to it, networks are bound to specific locations, and storage is typically found on a hard drive. Virtualization removes these ties and allows these areas to be available as needed across the enterprise. The following are ways to isolate aspects of resources and infrastructure:

- **Virtual applications**. Running an application on a computer without installing the application.
- **Virtual presentation**. Separating the presentation of a process from the actual processing, which is essentially terminal services. Terminal services has the I/O on one computer and the work done on a different server. Refer to Chapter 9, "Terminal Services," for additional information.
- **Virtual operating system**. Running multiple instances of a component inside one OS without conflict, such as multiple IIS servers running with different configurations.
- **Virtual machine**. Removing a single OS on a single physical server.
- **Virtual storage**. Allowing data to follow users wherever they are and for data to be highly available.
- **Virtual network**. Allowing resources to be available anywhere—not just where you are physically connected—and enabling technologies such as VPN and terminal services over HTTP.

After these aspects are virtualized, you have a dynamic environment that enables resources and services to be allocated as needed. If you are getting Web requests, a new Web server instance is automatically created; if a user needs to run a new application, he runs it without worrying about conflicting with other applications or the installation time.

Virtual Applications

Getting a new application can be cumbersome. After installing the application, there might be compatibility issues with existing applications. The deployment and management of applications is advanced with today's infrastructure components. There is a group policy for the deployment of applications and updates, and other application deployment solutions—such as System Center Configuration Manager (SCCM). When you install an application, components are registered on the machine (including executables and dynamic link libraries), other files are copied to the file system, and information is written to the Registry. When you uninstall or upgrade an application, information is left behind; over time, the machine becomes polluted with leftover files, Registry information, and registered components, which might cause compatibility issues in the future.

Consider the startup time and resources available on a computer. Normally, when you install an application onto a computer, components are added that load when the computer starts. The Registry is bloated by the use of critical kernel memory, even if you don't use the application often.

Each application could run in a separate virtual OS, but with multiple OSs to maintain, that would be a maintenance nightmare. Terminal services could be another option because it enables remote execution of applications with the screen sent to the remote user's computer. This remote computing introduces single points of failure with the terminal server application, which wastes the resources on the user's computer because the workload is performed on the remote resources of the terminal server. Furthermore, if the user is offline, he has no way to run the applications hosted on the terminal server.

Considering these limitations, application virtualization is necessary. It virtualizes the application and its dependencies, but it's not the OS itself. This enables the application to run locally on the computer, but does not change the client OS.

SoftGrid Architecture

Application virtualization avoids issues like terminal service single points of failure, no offline access, and local computer resource "waste." Like a normal application execution, it runs on the user's PC, but in a sandbox, known as the SoftGrid SystemGuard environment. This prevents installation to the local OS. This virtualized environment contains all the elements that an application would attempt to contact, such as files, Registry information, COM objects, and environment information. Installation is not required on the hosting OS (the OS running the virtualization technology). The virtualized environment communicates with the hosting OS to avoid duplication in the virtualized space (see Figure 19-1). These components are layers over the actual host OS components. Figure 19-1 demonstrates how the application communicates with what appears to be normal OS facilities within its SystemGuard environment with full read and write access. The SystemGuard then communicates with the "real" OS with strict controls.

Configuration can only be read but never modified, whereas profile and documents data can be changed in the OS. This allows data to be saved and environmental preferences for an application to be maintained between sessions.

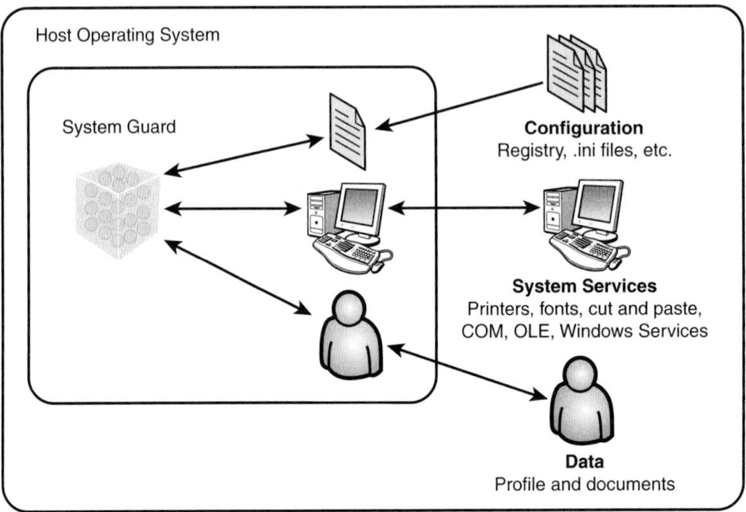

FIGURE 19-1 How a virtualized application communicates via the SystemGuard environment.

The virtual environment consists of several virtual elements for the OS areas used by applications. (For example, the Virtual Registry works as an overlay to the actual OS Registry.) If the application tries to read from the Registry and it's not in the Virtual Registry overlay, the read request is passed to the OS; however, any write request is always made into Virtual Registry overlay. The same process works for the Virtual File System. With dynamic link libraries, for example, this overlay ensures DLLs used by an application are always read from the SystemGuard environment first to avoid conflicts with local versions. If a file is not found, the read is passed to the underlying file system that the virtual file system layer has overlaid.

Additionally, there are virtualized components in the SystemGuard environment, as follows:

- Virtual Services components allow the service to function in the SystemGuard unknown to any other application running on the OS.
- Virtual COM environments allow the name spaces associated with these objects to be exposed to virtualized application. Although they

would normally conflict at the name level, COM/DCOM and the services that rely on them can work seamlessly.

- Virtual .INI files
- Virtual Process Environment
- Virtual Fonts

Figure 19-2 displays an application attempting to access the file system; the application has full access to the SystemGuard virtual file system, but only read access to the underlying OS file systems. As shown in Figure 19-2, the application's files are available in the virtualized application's file system layer; however, dependencies of the application, such as common controls, are accessed via the underlying OS.

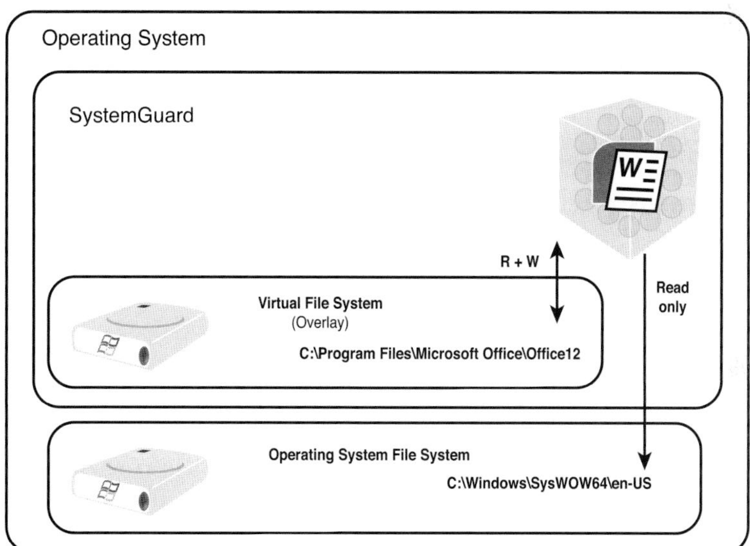

FIGURE 19-2 The file system layer from the SystemGuard in action.

This sounds great, but how does SoftGrid work, and how are these applications available on-demand? If run locally on the PC, SoftGrid still needs the information available to create the layers just discussed. Many components make up the SoftGrid solution:

- **System Center Virtual Application Server**. Streams the SoftGrid-enabled applications to the clients, and checks whether a client is authorized for the application. Clients query the virtual application server to find out what applications are available; they can then place shortcuts in the client environment to allow users to initiate execution.

- **SoftGrid Data Store**. Used to store information about the SoftGrid environment.
- **SoftGrid Management Web Service**. The interface between the management console and the data store. Uses .NET Framework 1.1 or above and needs IIS 5.0 or above with ASP.NET extensions enabled.
- **SoftGrid Client**. A locally installed service running on the user's machine; communicates with the virtual application server to receive the streamed application and caches it for use, even when the client is not connected to the network. The client also contains the SystemGuard environment for run-time virtualized application execution.
- **SoftGrid Sequencer**. A wizard-based tool that creates the streamable application from the original application media.

Creating a Virtualized Application

The SoftGrid Sequencer is the first step in virtualized applications; users of software like WinInstall are relatively familiar with it. Sequencing an application for virtualization consists of three phases:

1. Enter information about the application at the package configuration stage. This is just an information-gathering stage.
2. Perform installation of the application, where the SoftGrid Sequencing wizard monitors the OS for installation changes (including file system changes, component registration, Registry changes, and so on).
   This installation must be performed on a clean OS. No other applications can have ever been installed, even if they have been uninstalled (because files can be left behind). Remember, the process works by comparing differences on the computer before and after the application was installed. If you install an application on a computer that already has components installed, the wizard will not see the added components, and thus won't add them to the virtualized application package. When the virtualized application is run on another computer, the application stream is missing required information in the virtualized package and fails to run. Additionally, because you are virtualizing an application that runs

in overlay layers, the best practice is to create a new partition on the sequencing machine (for example, Q:). During the application installation, install it to the Q: drive via the advanced install option. This Q: drive does not need to exist on the clients. A virtual Q: drive is created by the SoftGrid environment for execution; it ensures no clashes with a computer's local file system. This is not mandatory—it's just a good practice.

3. Launch the application on the sequencing computer. This is important because a virtualized application is on-demand, so when the user runs a virtualized application for the first time, all the data needed has to be streamed from a SoftGrid server.

   Consider a full Word 2007 installation; this might be 100MB total size or more with all the various components, such as WordArt. If you execute Word 2007, you need only about 50MB to launch, so run each application during the sequencing process. This enables SoftGrid to see which installed pieces are needed to quickly launch the application. SoftGrid prioritizes the data to stream to the client based on what is first used (known as Feature Block 1 [FB1] of the stream) when the application starts. This prevents waiting for the entire stream to be sent before the application can begin. The rest of the application is then sent on-demand in 32KB chunks by default. If you are streaming applications to mobile users, stream all the data to them locally. This helps avoid the possibility of a user trying to run a piece of previously unused functionality with no way to pull down the required information.

You now have a complete sequenced application. The administrator loads this sequenced application onto the SoftGrid server; he specifies which users and groups can use the application, where shortcuts for the application will be placed (for example, the desktop or the Start menu), and which file types are associated with the virtualized application.

Using a Virtualized Application

The rest of your virtualized application experience is straightforward. The SoftGrid client, running on desktop computers and terminal services, communicates with the SoftGrid server at client logon or a preconfigured periodic interval. The client checks which virtualized applications are available for the logged-on user and downloads a small file describing the virtualized application. This file shows where to stream the application from and which icon file to use to display shortcuts on the system; the icon files are also downloaded. This information is saved in XML format in an OSD file, whereas the actual stream is stored in an SFT extension file.

When a user executes a shortcut, the FB1 stream is downloaded from the System Center Virtual Application server and the application launches. As other features are run, additional blocks are pulled down as needed. The stream is cached locally in the C:\Documents and Settings\All Users\Documents\SoftGrid Client folder; this means applications are not streamed down multiple times if different users use the same client. However, the same access checks are performed, so a user not authorized for an application cannot run it. Figure 19-3 displays the process of running an application. In step 1, the user runs the shortcut on his desktop. This tells the SoftGrid client to read the OSD file to determine where to pull down the stream. In step 2, the FB1 is downloaded. In step 3, the application launches. Notice the FB1 is cached locally on the computer. If the user tries to run functionality that's not part of FB1 (such as Word Art), the data needed for Word Art is pulled down from FB2 and again cached, as shown in step 4.

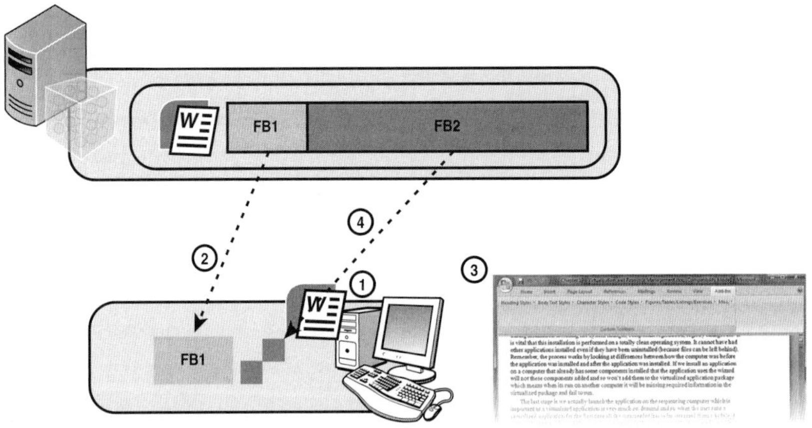

FIGURE 19-3 The application virtualization process.

The application virtualization process enables virtualized applications to start quickly. First, less information is being pulled down to the computer to initially launch the application than for a full installation. However, that's the difference between downloading 40MB over the network and writing to disk instead of 100MB. (On today's networks, this is not a big difference.) The key difference occurs when you install an application; the elapsed time is used up with registering components and performing system configuration, not with file system activity. With a virtualized application, because of the overlays, the application is already "installed"—the necessary information is written to the Registry and file system overlays, so applications can start quickly. The only requirement is to pull down the stream, which is effectively the installed application. After you've pulled down the FB1 stream (say 40MB), which takes a few seconds, the application opens! Figure 19-4 shows what a user sees the first time an application is launched. That's the power of the virtualized application. Normally, a user might have many unused applications installed just in case they are needed. With virtualized applications, the application icon is available and can be fired up in seconds if needed (depending on bandwidth). For computers without good connectivity, the virtualized applications should be prestaged in the computer's cache.

Figure 19-4 A virtualized application loading for the first time.

Virtualized Application Considerations

What does this sandbox add to the environment in terms of overhead? Well, not much. From a storage perspective, you use disk space to cache the application. At worst, this would be only slightly more than if the application was locally installed; this is more likely less, however, because you download FB1. FB1's percentage size of the total varies, but it is commonly about 25%, plus extra space for the virtualized Registry, COM, fonts, and services, which all live in the single stream cache. Therefore, if the entire content of FB1 and 2 were cached locally, it might use up slightly more disk space than a normal, locally installed application. Considering that Registry information still lives on disk, just in different places, it's a non-issue. Figure 19-5 shows the feature block information for Microsoft Word. Out of a total package size of 76MB, only 27MB has been downloaded and cached on the client to run the application.

In terms of the processor, which is logically where you might expect a hit, the application uses less than 1% more CPU than an unvirtualized application. Most of the extra work is done when the application initializes and not while it's running.

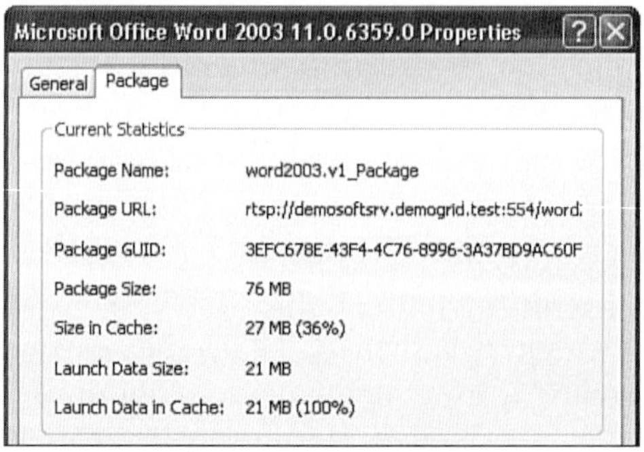

FIGURE 19-5 Example information for a virtualized application.

Memory use lessens when running a virtualized application. Installed applications have components load at system startup and configuration information stored in memory. Memory overhead can be broken into paged pool and nonpaged pool. Paged pool memory is where most applications operate; the content can be paged to disk as needed, and the amount used is the same for the virtualized application as if it was just installed locally. The only additional memory used is 20MB for the SoftGrid client. For nonpage pool memory (also known as kernel memory, which is used for important OS information that cannot be paged to disk), you use fewer resources. Normally, configuration data, which includes the Registry and other data, are pulled into kernel during computer start-up, taking up space—this means longer boot times for information in the hkey_local_machine and hkey_classes Registry areas or longer logons for hkey_current_user areas of the Registry.

Typically, as applications are installed, the Registry fattens up and takes up more space and nonpage pool memory. This is not the case for SoftGrid applications because nothing is written to the local machine Registry. Information needed by the application is loaded at run time. Imagine having 40 applications installed but running only 10 of them. With locally installed applications, this would significantly bloat the Registry, using up kernel memory. With the applications virtualized, nothing is written to the Registry; there is no bloat and information is loaded into memory as needed, so this means a 75% nonpaged pool memory save. Network bandwidth is also saved because SoftGrid pulls over only what is needed on-demand, instead of a full installation with many unused components. When using SoftGrid with terminal servers, the "therapeutic reboot" (a regular reboot to clear out memory) is not needed. This is due to the efficient garbage collection performed when an application closes, and its highly contained execution footprint.

Patching virtualized applications is easy to roll out. To patch an application, the patch is applied to the virtualized application in the sequencing environment and the delta is calculated between the pre- and post-patched application. This delta is sent to clients via the virtual application servers.

Additional components allow an MSI file to be created that contains information about a virtualized application for offline usage, which can be used with machines running the SoftGrid client in offline mode. This removes the requirement for SoftGrid client machines to check with the SoftGrid server for applications they should have access to. This allows SCCM and other distribution platforms to be used for the distribution of virtualized applications. A separate SoftGrid client is also available that is designed for terminal server-type environments, including Citrix.

The software and hardware requirements of the SoftGrid Virtual Application Server are reasonable. A data store is required for information about the application usage, licensing, server configuration, and so on. This data store can be hosted in SQL Server 2000 or 2005, and even Microsoft SQL Server Desktop Engine (MSDE) 2000, but the use of MSDE should only be for testing environments. This does not need to be on the same server as the application server; however, it should be on the same local fast network. A directory service is also required for the SoftGrid suite to function—for example, Active Directory (2000 or 2003) or even an NT 4.0 domain is sufficient, although it would be surprising if you used application virtualization, yet still used an NT 4.0 domain. During installation, an account must be specified with read access to the directory service. Two global groups are also needed to identify SoftGrid administrators and users who might use the SoftGrid services. (You can add the "domain users" group to this if all users in the domain need access.)

So, why is this so great? Each virtualized application runs in its own protected environment, and one virtualized application cannot see components from another virtualized application. This means compatibility and conflict problems between applications disappear because the applications cannot see each other. This is both a boon and a curse. Virtualized applications can't see each other, but a virtualized application can see applications installed locally on the host computer. This means one virtualized application cannot access APIs or facilities from another virtualized application, which is a problem if you have an application whose facilities need to be used by other applications. A good example is Microsoft Office, whose capabilities are used by many other applications. If Office was virtualized, the Enterprise Resource Planning (ERP) system would not be able to use it. The solution would be to sequence Office and the ERP system together, or more likely, install Office locally on the computer and virtualize the ERP system. In SoftGrid 4.5, a new feature, Dynamic Suite Composition (DSC), is introduced. This feature allows limited linking between two virtualized applications, known as *contexting*, which allows the two virtualized applications to see each other by running them in a single virtual environment. This is achieved by specifying one of the applications as the dependent package of the other, so Office would be the dependent application for the ERP system. In future versions, more complex contexting will be possible, allowing more than two applications to have a join.

NOTE I have a number of clients running virtualized application environments, and the whole process has been smooth. There are situations where virtualizing an application is not the best option, because there are some limitations (for example, you can't virtualize a driver), so some components still need to be manually installed. But it's a great solution to the problems of compatibility issues and deployment times. Without the compatibility problems, you spend far less time testing an application for deployment suitability; you don't have to do many rounds of regression and compatibility testing for coexistence if applications A, B, and C are installed. In the future, you will be seeing a lot more of application virtualization—it's available now as part of Microsoft's Desktop Optimization Pack.

Application virtualization is a key part of the Microsoft strategy. With SCCM R2, you can now package and deploy virtualized applications the same way you can deploy an MSI file. This is facilitated via a new XML manifest, which is created by the SoftGrid 4.5 sequencer. This sequencer can be imported into SCCM R2, which tells SCCM everything it needs to know to advertise a virtualized application.

Virtualized applications are considered first-class citizens. In addition to deploying virtualized applications, the SCCM 2007 R2 can also inventory virtualized applications via the SoftGrid 4.5 Windows Management Instrumentation (WMI) interface, so you get full virtualized application asset inventory.

Going forward, Microsoft is looking at virtualizing server services in the same manner as desktop applications. Instead of having services tied to an OS installation, which requires complex processes when making updates, the service and the OS are completely separate. To update the OS, apply the change in development, copy the tested OS into production, and then apply the virtualized service onto the new OS instance. When you add new model capabilities that say how a service should be used and executed, you get a plug-and-play server environment. This is where the OS, services, and configuration are picked and placed together as needed. This cuts down on the number of server OS images you need to manage.

Virtual Machines and Hyper-V

The first time I saw virtualization of an OS, I was at Tech Ed many years ago. The presenter was demoing Windows Server with multiple windows on a single PC, and he was running the VMWare product. I investigated and quickly got myself a copy of VMWare Workstation, which transformed how I did my testing. Prior to virtualization, I had six computers to test the various server components running together. With virtualization, they could all run on one powerful computer.

How is this possible? Let's take a high-level look at the basic virtualization of an OS. VM technology allows a portion of the CPU and a machine's memory to be dedicated to a process that emulates a physical machine environment. This environment is complete with its own virtual BIOS, graphics, and network adapter. This is called a virtual machine (VM). In addition, virtual hard disk (VHD) files are linked to VMs, which are actual files on the host computer's file system. These files contain a complete file system of their own, with a hierarchy of folders and files, much like a ZIP or CAB file. When you combine the allocated memory and CPU resources, along with virtual BIOS, network, CD drives, and links to VHDs, you have a complete computer environment. You can then start this virtual environment and do anything you can with a normal physical computer, such as install OSs (which can then run applications) and communicate over a network. You can basically do anything an OS on a physical computer can do. Figure 19-6 displays an example of a virtual server: A server is running Windows Server 2008, which has two VMs defined. Each machine has an amount of memory allocated, CPU resources, and a hard disk linked to a VHD file on the local file system. The VHD enables Windows NT 4 to be installed on one VM and Windows Server 2003 to be installed on the other.

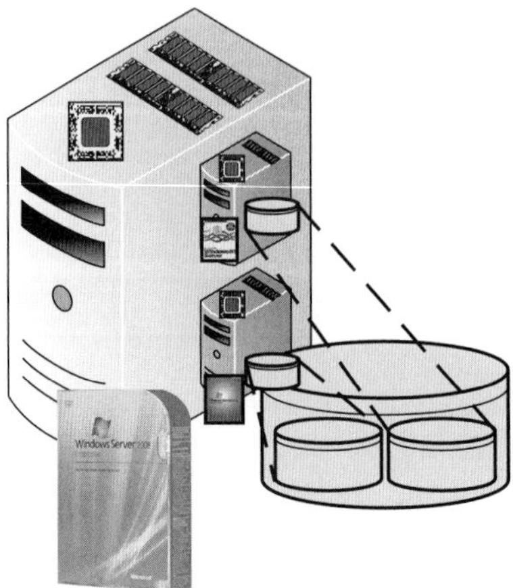

FIGURE 19-6 Example of a virtual server.

The only limitations are the capabilities of the virtual components seen by the VM, such as limited graphical hardware and possible performance limitations of the VHD files. However, some solutions allow VMs to link to actual physical hard drives, removing that performance complication (or you can use iSCSI storage). There are also limitations in various implementations of VM solutions that don't allow access to USB devices and other types of hardware, such as fiber cards.

Virtualization Technologies

Numerous technologies exist to facilitate the virtualization process. You are creating an entire computer environment inside a process that allows multiple OSs to run on one set of hardware. As such, the virtualization technology has to share out access to the CPU, network adapters, and other hardware access; at the same time, it's trying to minimize overhead to reduce the performance of the virtual environments.

Hosted Virtual Machine Manager (VMM)

As previously mentioned, several technologies are used for virtualization. Let's start with solutions like Virtual PC and Virtual Server, which are known as Hybrid or Hosted Virtual Machine Managers (VMMs); the VMM and the host OS both run in kernel mode, so they have equal pull on the CPU resources. The guest OSs run on top of the VMM, as shown in Figure 19-7. The VMM still runs within the host OS; however, it is shown side by side because it exists in kernel mode, as stated with the host

OS. The process for a VMM, such as Virtual PC, uses a great deal of kernel time; however, it still has to ask the host OS to get the cycles because the host OS controls the processor. The VMM can give the guest OS cycles as needed, so the performance is less than if the guest OS was running directly on its own hardware.

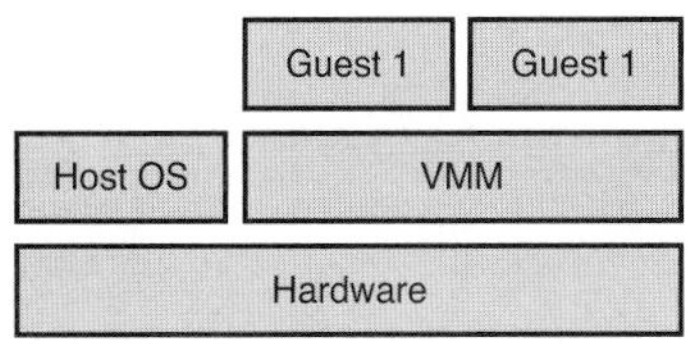

FIGURE 19-7 A hybrid or hosted VMM model.

Hypervisor Virtualization

The new type of virtualization technology is known as Type 1 VMM or Hypervisor Virtualization; the VMM sits directly on the hardware as a thin layer responsible for isolating separate environments, known as *partitions*, and for executing OSs. It also divides up memory, CPU cycles, and other hardware resources between the partitions running on top of the hypervisor. This division, which would include the "main" OS (such as Windows Server 2008), is tricky because an installed OS expects to have direct access to the processor in ring 0 of the kernel processor. To support a layer underneath the OS, the processor has to support the ring negative 1 (-1), which is provided only on specific 64-bit processors that support virtualization assist, namely AMD-V or Intel-VT. Additionally, Hardware Data Execution Protection (DEP) must be enabled via the BIOS (Intel XD bit or AMD NX bit, depending on processor). The hypervisor can then run in the ring -1 on the processor underneath the normal ring 0. Here the kernel of OSs installed in partitions on the hypervisor access ring 0 also, and other rings of the processor are used as normal—the device drivers run in ring 1 and applications run in ring 3 in normal user mode. This is important in hypervisor: VMs operate the same as a normal OS installed on hardware with direct access to ring 0, giving performance equivalent to running on the physical hardware (see Figure 19-8).

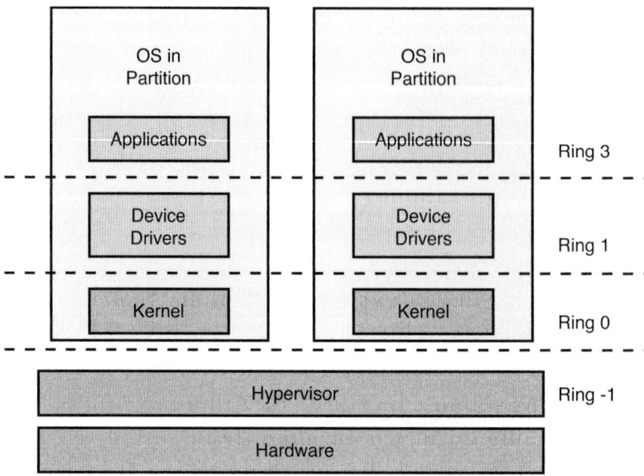

FIGURE 19-8 A view of CPU cycles and the OS and hypervisor components.

Two types of hypervisors exist: monolithic and microkernelized (see Figure 19-9). Hyper-V, which is used by the Windows Server 2008 virtualization, is a microkernelized hypervisor; VMware's ESX server uses a monolithic hypervisor. Discussion regarding which is the best is beyond the scope of this chapter, but let's look at why there are differences.

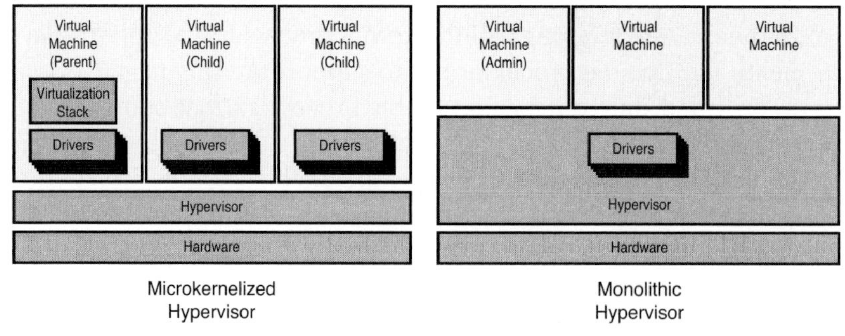

FIGURE 19-9 Hypervisor types.

With a monolithic hypervisor, the drivers responsible for communication with the hardware sit in the actual hypervisor. The hypervisor is a fairly complex kernel; it's basically a mini-OS. The VMs access the hardware via specialized device drivers, which perform well because the VMs can go directly to all hardware via these drivers. But, there are issues, of course. The first issue is that these shared drivers are specifically written for the hypervisor; this limits the hardware that is supported by a monolithic hypervisor, and virtualization solutions that use a monolithic hypervisor typically have a small hardware compatibility list. This shared driver base leads to the main concerns: security and stability. Because there's a shared driver for the VMs, if a malware driver was placed in the hypervisor, all the partitions would be vulnerable to attack and snooping. In addition, if a driver is updated in the hypervisor that has an issue, it causes problems for all the VMs.

Because of these problems, and particularly the limitations of hardware support, Windows Server 2008 uses the microkernelized hypervisor approach. This approach enables the drivers to exist in the actual VMs, which means the existing drivers for hardware can be used and the range of hardware that runs Windows Server can be supported. This also allows the hypervisor to remain closed to any third-party code, as nothing is ever added into the hypervisor.

The hypervisor governs the allocation of CPU cycles and RAM. It doesn't govern other types of devices, such as disk and Ethernet, because this would require the hypervisor to understand how these types of devices function. With Hyper-V, the first OS installed (Windows Server 2008) acts as a parent partition, which owns the non-CPU and memory resources; it performs direct communication with these other resources on behalf of itself and the other child VMs on the server. The other reason child partitions cannot directly access other hardware types is related to a Microsoft security guarantee, which states that child partitions cannot see, manage, or take over other child partitions or access any hardware directly. Isolation is a key aspect to the Windows hypervisor implementation; strict controls are in place that prohibit sharing of virtual devices between child partitions or shared memory, and neither a child nor parent partition can write data into the hypervisor.

Purpose of a Parent Partition

The parent partition hosts a virtualization stack that includes management components running in normal user mode, known as the Virtual Machine Manager (VMM), which contains the Virtual Machine Service (VM Service). This VM Service manages the Virtual Machine Worker Processes—one for each child partition running—which controls the state of the child partition, stopping, starting, and so on. You need the parent partition, along with the hypervisor, to do anything useful, such as creating child partitions. Although you can install the hypervisor on its own, it won't do much without a Windows Server 2008 parent partition.

Components also run in kernel mode, such as the Virtual Machine Bus (VMBus). This hosts a number of virtual service providers (VSP) to physical hardware, which correspond to a number of virtual service consumers (VSC) running in the child partitions; for example, you have a VSP and VSC for network, a pair for storage, and so on. When a child partition wants to access hardware resources that are not CPU or memory, its VSC makes a request to the VSP hosted in the VMBus on the parent partition; this performs the actual communication to the physical hardware, as shown in Figure 19-10. The VMBus is not shared between all the child partitions; there is one connection between each child and the parent, so no communication or data can be seen by other child partitions running on the same virtual server. This VMBus does bring in a performance hit because child partitions wanting to access hardware now have to communicate via the VSC to a VSP. This is done via the VMBus hosted on the parent partition, which communicates to the hardware. However, this path has been made as tight as possible by Microsoft. The benefit of a smaller, more secure, and more stable hypervisor is worth the small performance hit, especially when you consider no special device drivers are needed; this is vital considering the breadth of hardware available for Windows Server.

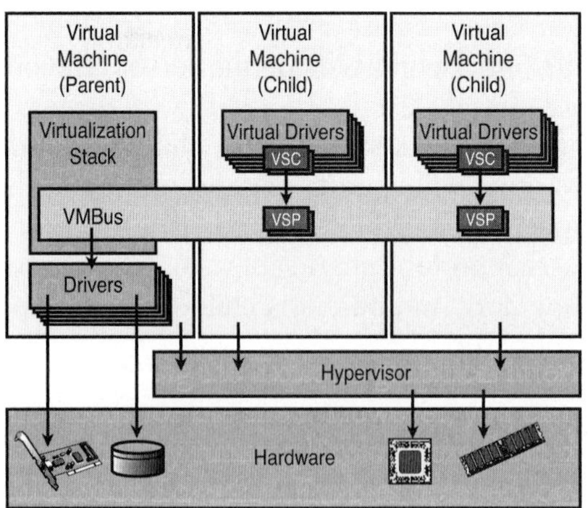

FIGURE 19-10 The VMBus implementation model.

If you consider what happens for nonenlightened child partitions that don't understand the VMBus, you have a far greater performance hit. For nonenlightened child partition requests, such as a network operation, the request goes from user mode in the child partition, to kernel mode in the child, to kernel in the parent (which hosts the emulated device the child partition sees). Finally, this ends up going to VM Worker Process in user mode on parent, which then makes the actual hardware request. This is a slow operation requiring context switching thousands of times. The VMBus avoids this because it runs in kernel and allows near direct hardware communication via the VSC and VSD. These are synthetic drivers, so machines see a virtual network device.

The parent partition hosts all the VM support components that are not part of the hypervisor; if the parent partition reboots or is unavailable, none of the child partitions are available either.

The virtualization stack also exposes a management interface, which is used not only by the built-in management tool but is publicly documented via an application programming interface (API). This allows other management solutions to manage the virtualization, such as the System Center Virtual Machine Manager (SCVMM), which is discussed later. A full WMI interface is also available for the management of the virtualization components.

Hyper-V

With all that theory out of the way, let's look at the actual implementation of Windows Server 2008 server virtualization. For those who followed the progress of Windows Server 2008, the virtualization story has not been an easy one—the Windows Server Virtualization (WSV) component (formally known as Viridian) was pulled from the standard release cycle of the OS, and instead promised to be available as a free download within 180 days of the Windows Server 2008 RTM as the Hyper-V role. A beta of Hyper-V was included as part of the 2008 RTM media. The final version of Hyper-V was released on June 26, 2008. It is available from Microsoft as update KB 950050.

Hyper-V runs only on 64-bit platforms, and the processor must support virtualization assist (for AMD, this is AMD-V, and for Intel, it is Intel-VT). The good news is that many new processors support these features, including most desktop and laptop computers. In addition, hardware data execute protection must be supported and enabled via the BIOS known as NX for AMD processors and XD for Intel.

Although the host OS must be 64-bit, the guest OSs can be 32-bit or 64-bit. Also, each VM can be configured with multiple-processors (up to four cores), in addition to up to 64GB of memory. Multiprocessing is only supported with Windows Server 2008 (32- and 64-bit) and Windows Vista SP1 (32- and 64-bit) child partitions. For Windows Server 2003, 32-bit, only two-way SMP is supported. For Windows Server 2003, 64-bit two cores are supported. Other platforms, such as Windows 2000 SP24 and SUSE Linux Enterprise Server 10, support only a single core, which is just down to time to test for Microsoft. There are no known issues, and support for other OSs with multiple processors will be added over time.

From an availability standpoint, clustering of Hyper-V servers is supported with the new VM cluster resource, which also allows a Quick Migration capability to move VMs between physical servers, plus the ability to migrate physical hosts into a virtual environment to aid in server consolidation. A VM VSS provider is also provided to allow VM snapshots to be taken.

Management is primarily via the MMC 3.0-based snap-in; however, you also have scriptable interfaces in addition to WMI. With the release of the Remote Server Administration Tools (RSAT) for Windows Vista SP1, you can install the Hyper-V MMC snap-in on a Vista box, which is available to download from Microsoft. To enable management from Vista, ensure that the Hyper-V and Hyper-V Management Clients firewall group exceptions are enabled, which are on by default. In addition, on the Vista machine, you need to enable a DCOM exception in the firewall (port 135), which is used for Hyper-V to send information back to the Hyper-V snap-in. The addition of the firewall rule on a Vista client fixed the "Cannot connect to RPC" errors. Here is the command to fix the problem:

```
netsh firewall add portopening protocol=tcp port=135
name=DCOM_TCP135
```

A cool feature of Hyper-V is pass-through disk access, which changes the performance of disk operations. (This has been a limiting factor in the use of virtualization.) Typically in virtualization, hard disks are provided via VHD files on the host OS's file system, which are serviced via a virtual storage stack. Pass-through disk access allows an entire physical disk to be presented to a child partition as a virtual drive; this allows all disk access to pass directly from the child partition's storage stack to the physical disk, bypassing the virtual storage stack and giving improved performance.

The OSs supported in the child partitions are broken down into two types: enlightened and nonenlightened. Child partitions communicate to the hypervisor by documented calls known as *hypercalls*. A partition OS can find out if it's running on a hypervisor (and even its version) via a hypercall if the OS is hypervisor-aware (also known as an enlightened guest OS). Operating systems such as Windows Server 2008 and Windows Vista (with Hyper-V RC0 integration components) are fully enlightened, whereas Windows Server 2003 is only partially enlightened—it understands only driver virtualization and not the hypervisor at a kernel level. An enlightened child partition understands it has a number of VSCs used to access storage, network, video, and input type hardware; VSC then communicates with the VSP in the parent partition via the VMBus, which performs the actual direct physical hardware communication. These VSC-VSP pairs are common in the Windows world, and hardware manufacturers will provide them in the future for additional hardware support.

NOTE Microsoft partnered with XenSource to create a series of VSCs for Linux, which enables Linux to run as an enlightened guest OS within a child partition and with full performance, like Windows Vista. This partnership also included the ability for Windows Server 2008 to run as an enlightened OS on the XenSource virtualization platform.

If an OS does not know it is running on a hypervisor, it is nonenlightened and does not have the capability to use the normal VSC-VSP pairs. Instead, it needs to see the normal emulated devices through an emulation layer that is commonplace with solutions, such as Virtual Server and Virtual PC. This results in a lower-performing guest OS because of this emulated hardware platform; the guest OS attempts normal hardware I/O, which is then trapped by the hypervisor and passed to the parent partition for handling. It is through this emulation that OSs that are not enlightened will be supported and be able to run under Hyper-V, although this performance is far less than with the VSC-VSP model.

The best way to look around Hyper-V is to get it installed and get some VMs fired up.

Installing Hyper-V

The installation of Hyper-V is done in the standard manner via Server Manager; however, because it is not part of the RTM Windows Server 2008 media, first download and install the Hyper-V final release update. In this book, I install the beta version of Hyper-V that is included as part of the RTM 2008. However, even as I write this, the second release candidate, RC1, is now available, which you should download and apply to your Windows Server 2008 boxes. A 64-bit update is available, which contains the updated Hyper-V and integration services, as well as a 32-bit update, which updates the integration services on 32-bit Windows Server 2008 child partitions. Use the final version of Hyper-V (or if it's not out, the latest RC). Microsoft made changes between the beta that ships with the RTM of 2008 and the final version that required recreating all the VM configurations. The earlier RCs were feature-complete and only bug fixes are made; this means changes to the VM configuration format did not happen.

Before installing Hyper-V, let's discuss where to install it. Ideally, Hyper-V is installed on Windows Server Core—Server Core uses fewer resources, has a smaller attack surface, has a lower management overhead, and requires less patching than a full install, which also means fewer changes of required reboots. In most cases, install Hyper-V under Core; a standalone server, Microsoft Hyper-V Server, is available for $28 (U.S.). This does not come with any Windows Server licenses to run as guest OSs; if you want to virtualize OSs you already have licenses for, such as Windows Server 2003 systems, this is a good option. Licensing is covered in more detail later.

To install via Server Manager, enable the Hyper-V role, and you are asked which Ethernet cards will be available for use by the VMs (see Figure 19-11). (However, additional configuration can be performed via the Hyper-V Manager mmc snap-in.)

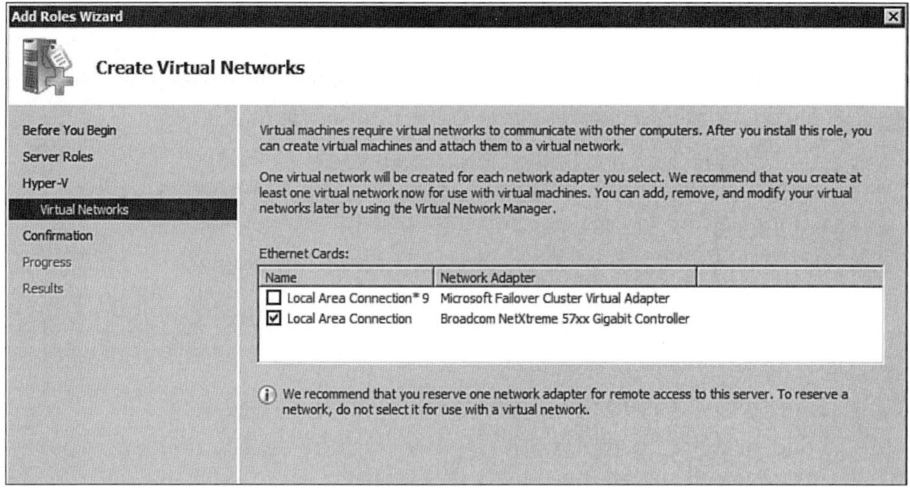

FIGURE 19-11 Selecting the network adapters for use by Hyper-V.

To install via the command line, add the role using `ocsetup`, as shown in the following code. Note that the first command is not mandatory, but it sets the boot configuration database to automatically enable the hypervisor if available, instead of having to install the Hyper-V role and reboot. This then asks for another reboot after it enables the hypervisor configuration:

```
C:\ >bcdedit /set hypervisorlaunchtype auto
The operation completed successfully.

C:\ >start /w ocsetup Microsoft-Hyper-V
```

After the configuration is complete, reboot the server.

Network Management

If you installed Hyper-V via Server Manager and selected a virtual network, a change was automatically made to your network configuration on the selected Ethernet adapters. If you examine your network devices, the selected Ethernet device has been unbound from all services except for the Microsoft Virtual Network Switch Protocol (see Figure 19-12). A new network connection has been created (in this case, Local Area Connection 3). The new network connection is configured for DHCP initially, so some configuration is required if you are using this network adapter for other purposes, such as remote management. However, the best practice is to dedicate the network adapter(s) to Hyper-V. This configuration might include specifying a static IP address; however, do not modify the network connection that is bound for the Microsoft Virtual Network Switch Protocol; modify only the new network connection that was created.

You should have a dedicated network interface card (NIC) for the VMs (or perhaps more than one, depending on load) and a separate dedicated NIC for the management of the actual Hyper-V server. You might also want additional NICs for connectivity to iSCSI-based storage if you are using iSCSI.

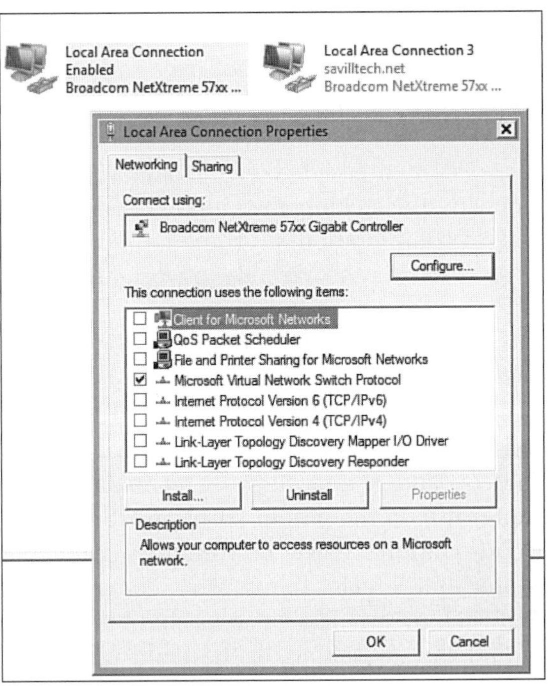

FIGURE 19-12 The network configuration after an adapter is specified for use by Hyper-V.

Virtual Machines with Hyper-V

After the server has rebooted, access the Hyper-V Manager via the Roles section in Server Manager or via the standalone MMC snap-in, for which a shortcut is available in the Administrative Tools folder.

The Hyper-V Manager snap-in can connect to multiple servers concurrently. This is vital if you're using Server Core because no graphical management tools can be run locally. Therefore, you need to run the Hyper-V Manager on a remote full Windows Server 2008 or Windows Vista installation and connect to the Hyper-V Server Core installation to manage. There is minimal configuration to perform on the actual Hyper-V platform. It consists of configuring the main server settings and the virtual network configuration.

If you connect to a Hyper-V server and run the Hyper-V Server Settings action, you can configure the default location for storing VHDs and machines (see Figure 19-13). The Virtual Machine configuration consists of an XML file that contains the configuration for the VM, BIOS configuration, virtual network adapter bindings, disk bindings, memory, and CPU allocation. Additionally, if a VM has its state saved or snapshots performed, these are saved in the VMs folder. You can also configure where Windows key combination keystrokes are sent, either locally or to the remote, in addition to the release key. This is the key combination used when a VM has focus that does not have the integration services running and thus locks the mouse into the virtual. The release key combination gives the mouse control back to the local session. Also available are options to unsave any credentials that might have been saved for connection to VMs, along with unchecking any Don't Ask Me This Again check boxes.

The server configuration has three types of available virtual networks, which are accessed via the Virtual Network Manager action:

- An **external network** is bound to a physical network adapter in the server; if this is the first time the adapter has been bound to a virtual network, there will be a disruption to the network connectivity. The adapter is bound to the Virtual Machine Network Switch Protocol, and a new network connection is created for network adapter use on the parent partition OS.
- An **internal network connection** is not bound to an Ethernet adapter but creates a network connection using the Microsoft VMSwitch driver. This enables communication between the parent OS and the guest OSs in the child partitions only. It's limited in scope to the single physical machine. Configure an IP address

scheme for the internal network that does not conflict with that used on the external networks.

- A **private network** creates no network connection on the host OS and is for use only by the VMs.

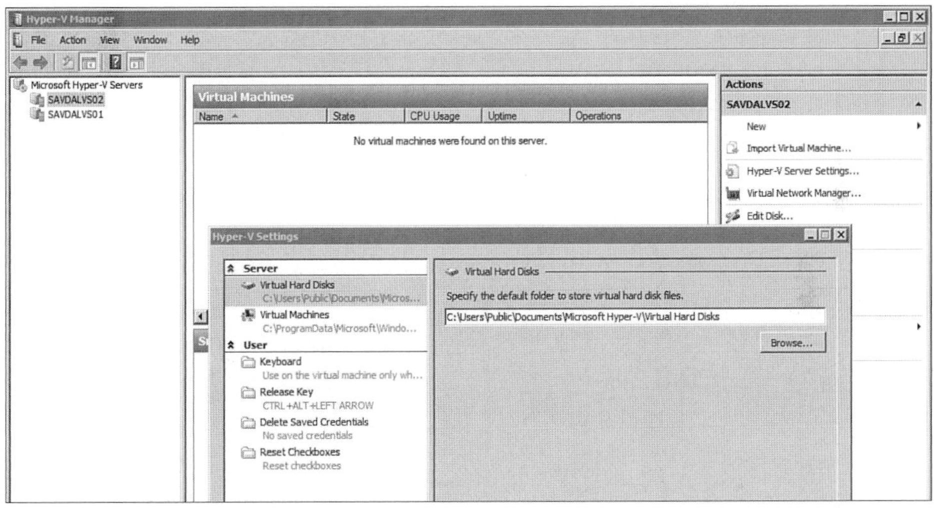

FIGURE 19-13 The server settings configuration.

Both internal and external virtual networks can also have a virtual LAN (VLAN) identification applied to them (see Figure 19-14). The VLAN is used only by the parent partition as the VLAN identified for communication over the virtual network.

You can also modify existing virtual networks or remove them via the Remove button. If you remove an external virtual network, the additional network connection created is removed. The original network connection is unbound from the VM network switch protocol and rebound to the original services, such as IPv4, IPv6, client for Microsoft networks, and so on. The original configuration of the network connection will be restored; if a static IP address had been configured previously, it will be enabled once again. The VMs see no difference in any of these networks; the only difference will be the connectivity available via them.

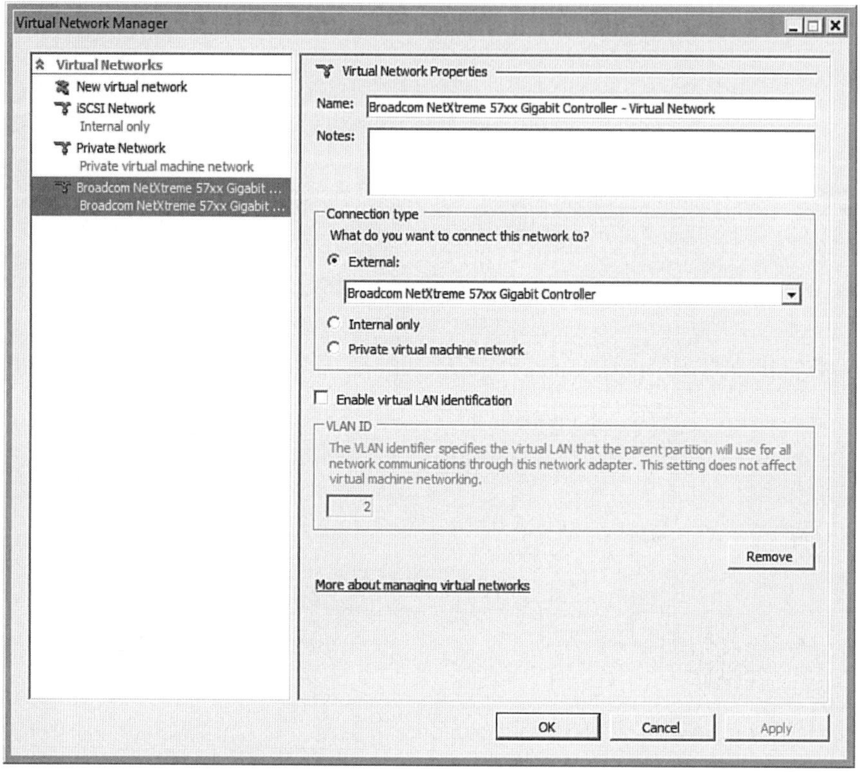

FIGURE 19-14 Details for a virtual network.

Creating a Virtual Machine

After the server and virtual networks are configured, you can create a VM, which is a wizard-driven process—a New action that creates hard disks, floppy disks, and VMs. Choose the latter option, which lets you create a new VM and new hard disks as needed, avoiding the need to create the VHDs in advance. There is also an Import Virtual Machine to import an existing VM that was previously configured. You can import only VMs configured under Hyper-V and not Virtual Server 2005 R2 or Virtual PC, which use a different format.

The first page of the wizard allows you to click Finish. This creates a new VM with default values. Alternatively, you can click Next to specify specific values; you'll be doing this in the walkthrough.

The Specify Name and Location stage of the wizard allows a name to be specified for the new VM. A good practice is to name the VM the same as the hostname given to the OS instance installed within the VM. Another option is to specify a different folder under which to store the new VM. By default, the new VM is created at the root of the virtual folder configured at a server level. If you enable Store the Virtual Machine in a Different Location, a new child folder is created (see Figure 19-15). This child folder is named the same as the VM. (This is recommended. It is not desirable to have one flat structure with all the VHDs in a folder, and then the VMs' XML configurations in the "Virtual Machines" subfolder named the GUID.)

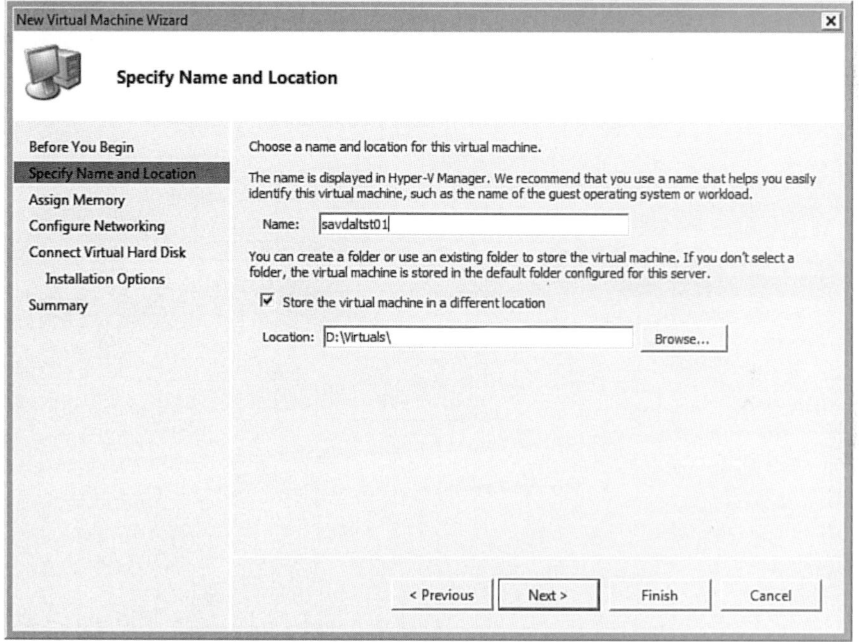

FIGURE 19-15 Configuring VM name and location.

The next stage enables the amount of memory to be allocated to the new VM. By default, 512MB is allocated; however, you can change this up to the amount of physical memory in the server or the 64GB VM limit, whichever is smaller.

The next stage defines which of the defined virtual networks on the server the default network adapter for the VM is connected to. By default, it is not connected to any virtual network; you can connect it to a defined network that can be changed at any time via the VM configuration; you can even add additional network adapters after creation. Each VM can have up to 12 network adapters, which are broken down into eight synthetic adapters (that use the VMBus) and four legacy network adapters. However, you should avoid legacy adapters if possible due to the performance impact associated with legacy.

The Connect Virtual Hard Disk stage allows a new VHD to be created with a configurable maximum size (default is 127GB). You can also use an existing hard disk or attach a hard disk after the VM is created via its properties (see Figure 19-16).

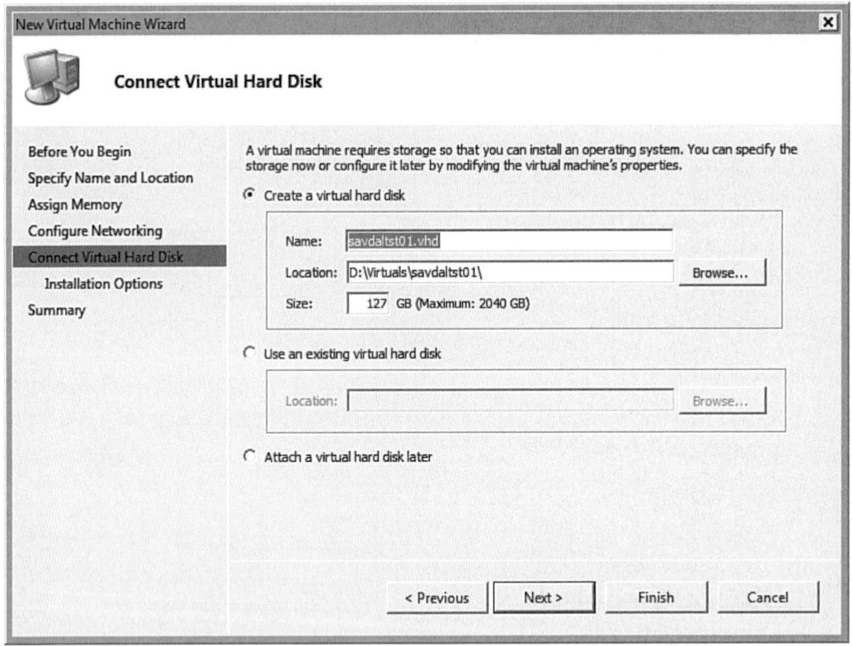

FIGURE 19-16 Hard disk options.

If a VHD was created or an existing disk used, an installation options stage is offered. This provides options to install an OS later, install an OS from a bootable CD/DVD, install an OS from a bootable floppy drive, or install an OS from the network. If you select the DVD/CD/floppy installation option, specify either a physical drive that contains the CD/DVD, or an image of a CD/DVD or floppy that contains the OS. These options connect a CD/DVD or floppy to the VM, so it's loaded on first boot. Plus, it updates the BIOS boot order so the media selected—that is, CD, floppy, or network—is first in the boot order list. Additionally, if you select to install over the network, a legacy network adapter is configured on the VM instead of a normal network adapter. This requires integration components and cannot enable install over the network.

The VM is now created. In the file system, there is a folder with the name of the VM. The folder contains the VHDs for the VM and a child folder named Virtual Machines that contains the XML configuration.

Configuring a Virtual Machine

After a VM is created or imported, you can perform additional customization or tweaking, which is done via the Settings action. Some settings can be changed while the VM is running; however, normally you should only make changes while the VM is stopped.

Figure 19-17 shows the basic settings. The default option is Add Hardware, which allows you to add additional SCSI controllers, network adapters, or legacy network adapters. A network adapter only works with the integration components installed on the OS; a legacy network adapter runs using hardware emulation, is available without integration components, and is required if you want to install the OS over the network. Adding these types of hardware enables you to create VMs that can connect to multiple networks, both external and internal, in addition to having SCSI connections.

NOTE One of the key changes with Hyper-V is the BIOS available to the VMs. Previously with Virtual PC and Virtual Server, a legacy AMIBIOS performed configuration of boot order; you had to configure via the VM by pressing the DEL key as the VM starts. Hyper-V has a much improved BIOS, which can be configured via the Hyper-V Manager. Configuration options available include the boot order for devices such as CD first, floppy first, legacy network adapter, and the default Num Lock state.

The Memory option enables the amount of RAM to be configured for the VM, whereas the Processor enables the number of logical processors that are visible to the VM (see Figure 19-18). (This number can range from 1 to the number of cores available in the server, up to a maximum number of 4.) In addition to the number of processors, you can specify some resource constraints and reservations for the processor. You can configure an amount of processor to be reserved for a VM; this is 0 by default, which means amounts of CPU are not set aside for a VM. However, a percentage can be configured, such as 20%, and this percentage is then represented as a portion of the overall processor resources. For example, if a VM has one logical processor, and the actual physical server has two cores, then a reservation of 20% of one processor is 10% of the overall system processor resource. In addition to reserving an amount of processor, you can also specify a maximum amount of resource a VM can use. Again, this percentage is expressed as a portion of the complete resources of the system, based on the number of logical processors exposed to the VM. The ability to limit processor functionality is also available for VMs that run the Windows NT 4.0 OS; this cannot handle certain features of the new processors and causes a Blue Screen of Death (BSOD) for the NT 4.0 child partition.

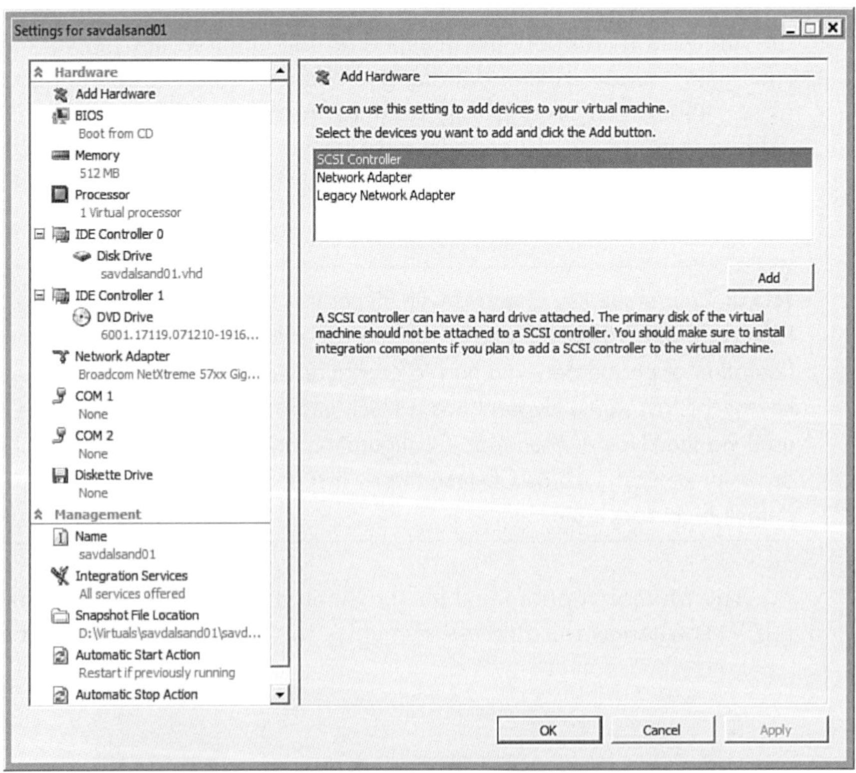

Figure 19-17 VM settings.

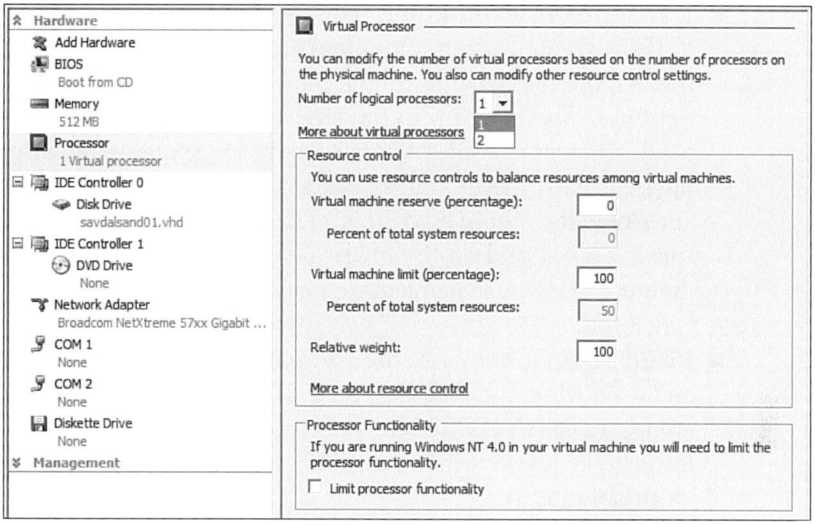

FIGURE 19-18 Processor configuration for a VM.

The next portion allows configuration of the ISD and SCSI controllers on the system, which can have disk drives and DVD drives attached. If a controller is selected, you have the option to add a new disk for IDE and SCSI or DVD drives for IDE controllers. You can also select a controller to be removed via the Remove Controller button.

For a SCSI controller, disks can use SCSI ID 0 through 255, and IDs already used on the SCSI controller are shown as being in use. For a SCSI controller, you can link a VHD or specify a physical disk on the system to be used in pass-through mode. Pass-through mode is also available for IDE controllers.

Pass-through disk access for VMs means a VM accesses an entire disk directly. When compared to a fixed-length VHD, pass-through disk access performance is pretty much the same. However, sometimes you might want a VM to not use a VHD but instead access a raw disk. You have to map an entire disk, not just a partition, and the disk to be passed through must not be mounted on the Hyper-V server. You can boot a VM from a pass-through disk. You can't boot from a disk connected to a virtual SCSI bus in Hyper-V; because there is no performance difference between virtual IDE and virtual SCSI, however, this is not a major issue.

When you create a new disk through the New, Hard Disk action or via the settings of a VM, there are three different types of VHD:

- **Dynamically expanding**. This is the most popular format. The VHD is created using a minimal amount of disk space. As the disk is used, the file expands on the file system to accommodate the data written to the disk (up to the size for the VHD). This option is the most efficient use of disk space because space is not used on the physical hard drives unless needed. However, there is a performance penalty. When a write is performed, the file has to grow and space is identified on the physical drive. This might result in a fragmented VHD. A dynamically expanding disk does not shrink if data is deleted.
- **Fixed size**. In this case, the size specified for the VHD is allocated and used when the disk is created. If a 127GB fixed-size VHD is created, a 127GB VHD file thus is created on the Hyper-V server. This leads to a less-fragmented VHD and faster performance during write operations.
- **Differencing**. This is linked to a parent VHD and stores the changes only from the parent hard disk.

After the type of VHD is selected, specify the name and location of the VHD along with a maximum size. Perform a VSS snapshot of a local disk to populate the VHD with the physical disk's content on the system (see Figure 19-19).

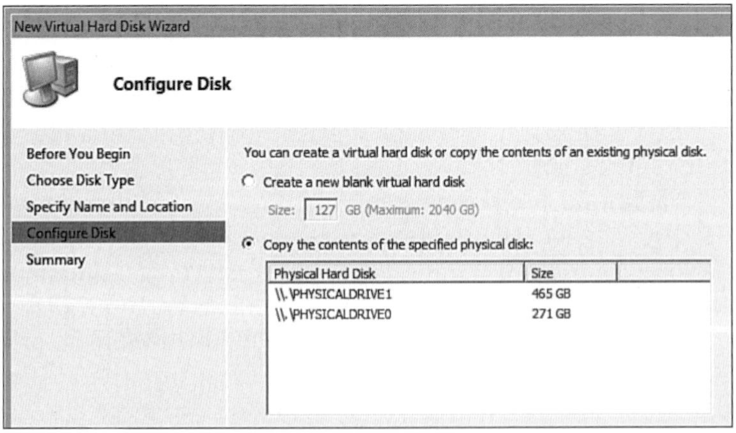

FIGURE 19-19 Configuring a new VHD to populate the content of a physical drive.

To get details for an existing VHD linked to an interface, click the Inspect button. This shows the current and maximum size. An Edit option is also available for disks. For the selected disk, you have the option to compact the disk (which removes blank space from a VHD file and shrinks its physical size on the server hard disk), convert a dynamic VHD to a fixed-size hard disk, or expand the size of a VHD to a larger size. These options are also available via the virtual server using the Edit Disk and Inspect Disk actions.

VHD FORMAT Let's look quickly at VHDs, which have the VHD extension. The VHD format is used outside of virtualization. Windows Backup in Windows Vista and Windows Server 2008 performs volume shadow copies of drives to a VHD file, which can be mounted inside a VM.

The VHD format has been fully documented as part of the Open Specification Promise, which is described at http://www.microsoft.com/presspass/press/2006/Oct06/10-17OSPVHDPR.mspx. As discussed previously, a VHD file is a cabinet-type structure that contains entire virtual file systems, which have folders, master boot records, files, and so on. The specification of the VHD can be found at http://www.microsoft.com/technet/virtualserver/downloads/vhdspec.mspx.

You can view the content of a VHD file by mounting the VHD file; this is possible via the `vhdmount.exe` command, which is provided as part of Virtual Server 2005 R2. If you don't want to install Virtual Server 2005 R2, download Virtual Server for the correct architecture (32- vs. 64-bit) and run the installation file. Select a custom installation and install only the VHD Mount feature (see Figure 19-20). I hope VHD Mount will be available with Hyper-V or as a separate download; I suspect it will.

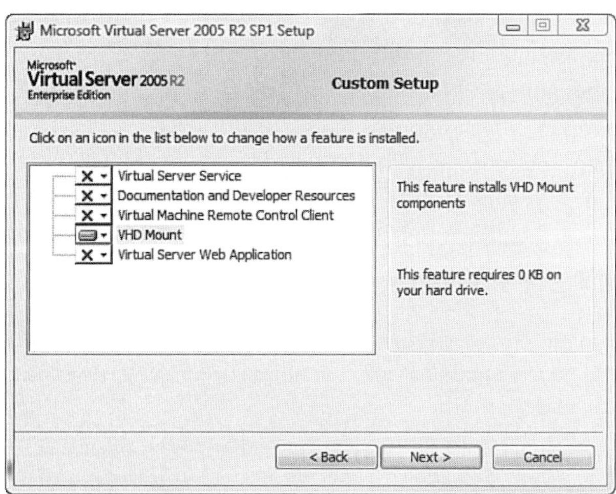

FIGURE 19-20 Installing the VHD Mount utility.

After installing it, the vhdmount.exe is found in the c:\program files\ microsoft virtual server\vhdmount folder. This folder also has a number of support files that are needed for its operation, although you can copy it to other machines to enable VHD mounting.

When a VHD file is mounted, an undo disk is automatically created. This enables any changes made to the VHD while mounted not to be committed if desired. However, you can use the /f switch not to create an undo disk, which means changes made cannot be undone.

To mount, use the /m switch and specify the VHD file to mount with an optional drive letter. If you don't pass a drive letter, one is automatically assigned, as shown in the mount:

```
C:\Program Files\Microsoft Virtual Server\Vhdmount>vhdmount
➥/m "d:\virtuals\xpvistadualboot\XPVistaDualBoot Hard
➥Disk2.vhd" y
```

The specified VHD is being plugged in using the default Undo Disk option. Use /c to commit or /d to discard the changes to the mounted disk.

The VHD is successfully plugged in as a virtual disk device, and the volumes on the disk have been successfully mounted.

```
C:\Program Files\Microsoft Virtual Server\Vhdmount>vhdmount
➥/q "d:\virtuals\xpvistadualboot\XPVistaDualBoot Hard
➥Disk2.vhd"
 PhysicalDrive7
➥d:\virtuals\xpvistadualboot\XPVistaDualBoot Hard Disk2.Vhd
```

The /q performs a query and shows which physical drive the virtual disk has been mounted as. In this case, mount passing drive letter Y so you can access the mounted VHD via Y. You can change this via the Disk Management MMC snap-in, which exposes the mounted VHD.

When you're done with the VHD file, dismount with the /u switch and either the /c switch to commit changes or /d to discard the changes. The ability to discard is available only if you did not disable the undo disk via the /f switch. An example dismount with discard of changes is shown here:

```
C:\Program Files\Microsoft Virtual Server\Vhdmount>vhdmount
➥/u /d "d:\virtuals\xpvistadualboot\XPVistaDualBoot Hard
➥Disk2.vhd"

Virtual disk device(s) successfully unplugged.
```

For DVD and floppy drives, the option to link the device to a physical device or an image file is available—for example, map to an ISO file, which is an industry standard image format for the contents of a CD/DVD.

The next major section is the network adapters: If the adapter is a legacy adapter that uses emulated hardware of a VSC network adapter, which requires the integration services. For each network adapter, the virtual network it is connected to can be configured. In addition, you can control the allocation of the virtual network adapter's MAC address; whether it is dynamically assigned by Hyper-V or if it is manually assigned, the static MAC address is configured. The VLAN ID can also be configured if connected to an external or internal virtual network.

The COM ports can be configured to connect to a named pipe, which can be local or remote, and a floppy drive image can be configured for the floppy drive, which is a VFD format file. There are numerous applications to help create virtual floppy disk images; I have used Magic ISO Maker, which creates floppy and CD/DVD images through an easy to use interface.

After the hardware aspects of a VM are configured, the next section is management. This section allows configuration of the VM name, along with a large description area, which can be used to make notes about the VM.

The Integration Services section allows you to select which services will be made available to the VM:

- Operating system shutdown allows the OS to be shut down gracefully from the Hyper-V management console via a Shut Down action. This is done instead of having to connect to the VM, logon, and select Shut Down from within the guest OS, or worse, Turn Off the VM from the Hyper-V Manager, which just turns off the power.
- Time synchronization keeps the VM clock synced with that of the parent OS.
- Data Exchange allows capabilities such as Cut and Paste between child OSs and the parent OS. With this enabled, you can copy data from a VM and paste into another VM or into the parent OS.
- Heartbeat keeps track of the state of the VM and its availability.
- Backup (volume snapshot) allows the consistent backup capability of a server and its virtuals without having to run commands on the actual VM.

Ideally, all these services should be enabled. However, they are not available until the integration services are installed.

The next configuration for management is the snapshot file location. By default, it's a child folder under the folder for the VM named the same as the VM. The snapshot file stores the snapshots taken of a VM, which are point-in-time views of a VM.

Finally, select the action to take when the physical Hyper-V server starts and stops. For the server start configuration, you can configure it to do nothing, automatically start the VM if it was running when the server was shut down, or always start the VM. You can also specify an optional delay in the start. This helps alleviate any contention between starting VMs. A great deal of CPU and disk use occurs when an OS loads. If you try to start five VMs at the same start, there will be significant contention. Using the delay shown in Figure 19-21 allows you to stagger the starting of VMs.

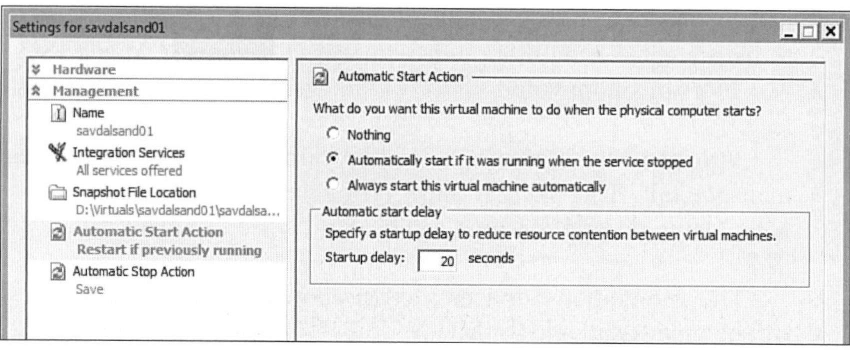

FIGURE 19-21 Start action for a VM.

For the stop action, save the VM state and turn off the VM. If the integration services are installed on the guest OS, shut down the guest OS.

Virtual Machines in Action

Let's start the VM via the Start action, which is available if the VM is currently shut down. Upon starting, the VM boots just like a normal service. It runs through its built-in BIOS and then boots according to the boot order configured for the VM. This could involve booting from a DVD, floppy, network, or the hard disk (if an OS has already been configured on the hard disk).

Although a small thumbprint of the current VM display is shown in the Hyper-V Manager, you can use the Connect action to get a full interface into the VM (see Figure 19-22). This enables you to interact with the VM. Until integration services are installed, the focus of the mouse and keyboard are locked into the VM. To release them, you need to run the release key combination: Ctrl+Shift+Left Arrow by default. (You can change this combination using the VM settings.)

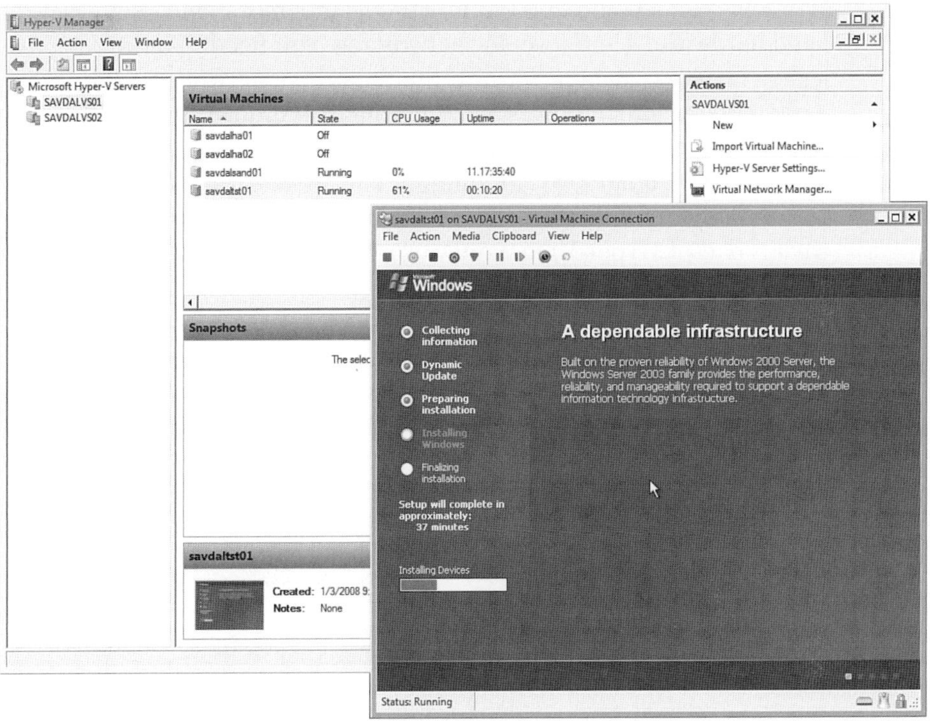

FIGURE 19-22 Accessing the VM during OS installation.

Figure 19-22 shows the Windows Server 2003 OS being installed. However, because you are working with VHDs instead of physical hard drives for each new VM, there are a number of options for installing the OS to your new VM. You can use traditional approaches, such as installation via media, or over the network using services such as Windows Deployment Services. Alternatively, you can perform an install of the OS on a reference VM and then run SYSPREP on the installation. Optionally, you can place a SYSPREP answer file on the system, so many of the configuration options are automatically configured the next time it boots. This SYSPREPd system is then captured and saved as a template OS. The template OS can be copied for a new VM that, when booted, runs through the minisetup wizard and is ready to use. Management solutions, such as SCVMM, help automate this type of template usage and facilitate fast, new VM creations.

After the VM OS installation is complete, you might have additional actions for the integration services, which are supported on various OSs, such as Windows Server 2003 SP2 and Windows Vista. Older OSs, such as Windows NT 4.0 and 2000, run without integration and use legacy, emulated hardware. Therefore, for networking, you need to ensure you have a legacy network adapter because the nonlegacy network adapter does not work without integration services installed. Windows Server 2008 has the integration components as part of the OS, so no further actions are required. For other OSs, the integration services can be installed via the Insert Integration Services Setup Disk action. This maps the vmguest.iso (that is part of Hyper-V) to the VM via the DVD, which autoruns the installations of the services. After the services are installed, the full integration of Hyper-V is available, and the VSC drivers are included; this stops the OS using the emulated hardware, which dramatically increases the performance. Figure 19-23 displays the Device Manager view of a system using the emulated hardware, and then the same machine after the integration services are installed, which enables the VSCs. For Linux, install integration services to enlighten the Linux OS.

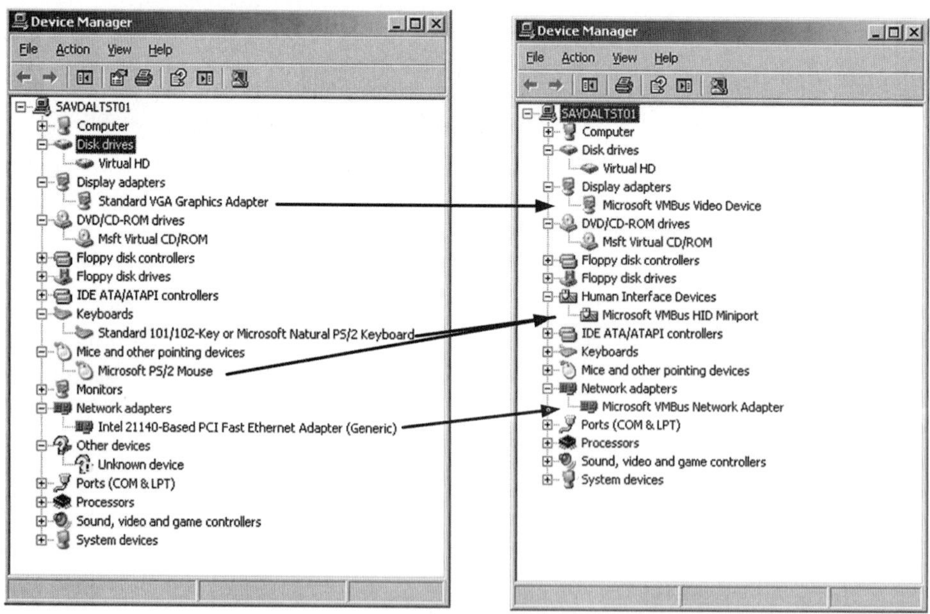

FIGURE 19-23 The device manager of a machine before and after the integration services are installed.

After a VM is running, you have various options. As the actions show for a VM, you can do more than just Turn Off (which performs a power down of the VM) or Shut Down (which attempts a clean shutdown of the guest OS), as shown in Figure 19-24.

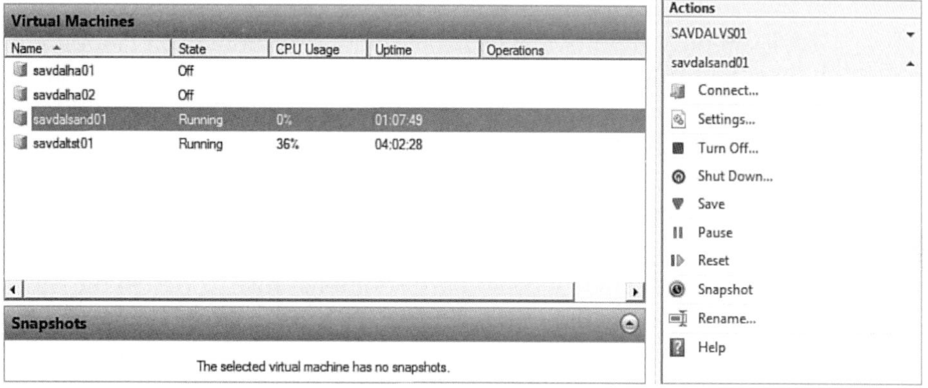

FIGURE 19-24 Control options for a VM.

The Save action takes the memory content for the VM and saves into a BIN and VSV file, which is effectively the VM's exact state. Because the memory is now saved to a file and the VM disk is not going to be changed, this is a frozen VM. This memory dump can then be read from file and placed back into memory via the Start action, which resumes the VM to its exact state at the time its state was saved.

You can also pause a VM. This temporarily freezes all activity on the virtual until the VM is resumed; this is in addition to performing a Reset, which is like a reset on a normal computer.

Licensing

The virtualization rights with Windows Server 2008 have not changed from Windows Server 2003, except for standard server. Windows Server 2008 has the following editions:

- **Standard Edition**. One physical instance and one virtual guest instance running at the same time. This is a new right in Windows Server 2008.

- **Enterprise Edition**. One physical instance and four virtual guest instances running at the same time.
- **Datacenter Edition**. One physical instance and an unlimited number of virtual guest instances running at the same time. Datacenter is a great option if you require many VMs to run on a single server.

Even on Windows Server 2008 Standard Edition, you can purchase a license and run Windows Server 2008 core or full installation and have a licensed virtual running on the server without additional purchasing. This new 1 + 1 licensing for standard makes the new Microsoft Hyper-V Server purchase attractive if you want a virtualization server running guest OSs that are not Windows Server. Standard 2008 now has one virtual license and has a full server capability on the server (not just restricted to the Hyper-V). The Hyper-V could have additional roles added in the future or repurposed, although as a best practice, the Hyper-V should run no roles other than the hypervisor. If you want the 2008 for virtualization only, buy Standard 2008 and install in its core mode with only the Windows Server Virtualization role, which is essentially what Hyper-V server is.

Snapshots

Normally, backups of virtual environments can be cumbersome. To get a good backup, take the backup inside the VM environment, or shut down the virtual environment and then back up the VHD files that the VM uses.

With Hyper-V, a snapshot can be performed on the host; this also snapshots the guest partitions and communicates through the applications in the guest partitions to ensure that a consistent snapshot is taken, with all necessary data flushed to disk. This is transparent to the guest OS and avoids the problems associated with just taking a snapshot of an in-use virtual disk file. Many backup solutions today perform snapshots of in-use data, which means data might not be flushed to disk. You are backing up a snapshot of an in-use disk, which is the same state as if the server crashed; this is known as a *crash consistent backup* because transactions might only be half committed.

Multiple snapshots of a VM can be taken. After a snapshot is taken, it is shown in the Snapshots section of the Hyper-V Manager. Snapshots can be applied to VMs to restore the VM back to its state at the time of the snapshot, as shown in Figure 19-25. If a snapshot is no longer needed, it can be deleted via the Delete Snapshot action. If you take multiple snapshots of a VM, you can rename the snapshots with a meaningful name. (For example, you could rename the snapshot so it reflects the actions taken, such as "Pre SP2 update snapshot.") Snapshots are also great for testing; if you want to try something that might break an environment, take a snapshot first and then break away. You can easily roll back to the snapshot state with a click of a button.

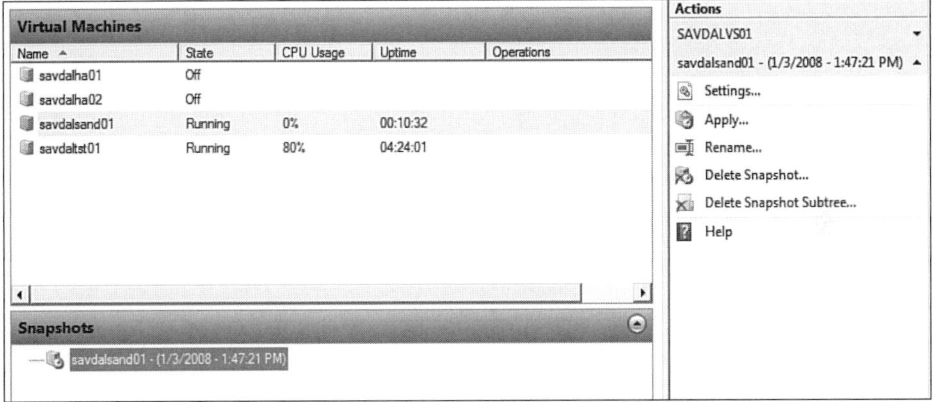

FIGURE 19-25 Snapshot management via the Hyper-V Manager.

Command-Line Management

At the time of writing, there are no command-line–specific tools to manage Hyper-V. A WMI interface is provided, however, which you can use from VBScript and PowerShell to perform any Hyper-V action that is possible via the graphical interface.

There are a number of scripts on http://www.ntfaq.com to manage Hyper-V from the command line; these include listing the state of VMs on a server, changing the state of a VM, and changing the states of all VMs on a server that are currently in a certain state. The latter script is useful if you want to quickly suspend all running virtuals, perform an action (such as a backup), and then restore them.

Here is a script that lists the state of virtuals. This gives you an idea of hooking into WMI and the power available.

```
' listhypervvirts.vbs John Savill
strComputer = "."
strState = "NA"
```

```
Set objWMIService = GetObject("winmgmts:" _
& "{impersonationLevel=impersonate}!\\" _
& strComputer & "\root\Virtualization")

Set colVMs = objWMIService.ExecQuery _
("Select * from Msvm_ComputerSystem")

For Each objVM in colVMs

Select Case objVM.EnabledState
Case 0
strState = "Unknown (0)"
Case 2
strState = "Enabled (2)"
Case 3
strState = "Disabled (3)"
Case 32768
strState = "Paused (32768)"
Case 32769
strState = "Suspended (32769)"
Case 32770
strState = "Starting (32770)"
Case 32771
strState = "Snapshotting (32771)"
Case 32772
strState = "Migrating (32772)"
Case 32773
strState = "Saving (32774)"
Case 32774
strState = "Stopping (32774)"
Case 32775
strState = "Deleted (32775)"
Case 32776
strState = "Pausing (32776)"
End Select

Wscript.Echo "Install VM: " _
& objVM.ElementName & " - " & strState

Next
```

This can be seen in action next. Notice that the first instance is the actual physical parent partition; this hammers home the point that the parent partition is also a VM.

```
D:\Temp>cscript listhypervvirts.vbs
Microsoft (R) Windows Script Host Version 5.7
Copyright (C) Microsoft Corporation. All rights reserved.

Install VM: SAVDALVS01 - Enabled (2)
Install VM: SAVDALCORE01 - Disabled (3)
Install VM: savdalsql01 - Enabled (2)
Install VM: savdaldc01 - Enabled (2)
Install VM: Vista Client - Suspended (32769)
```

If you want to list VMs that were running, you can change the select statement (for example, use "Select * from Msvm_ComputerSystem where EnabledState=2").

Microsoft's true command-line management solution is SCVMM. This has full management capabilities via the PowerShell cmdlets that are provided, which provide over 170 command-line functions.

Physical-to-Virtual Migration

Physical-to-Virtual Migration is part of the SCVMM. It is capable of taking a snapshot of a physical machine and making that snapshot a VM without having to shut down the physical server known as online P2V; you also can shut down the physical server and take the snapshot known as offline P2V. There are not P2V capabilities in Hyper-V in any automated sense; however, it would be possible to take a complete backup of a server, create a new VM in hyper-V with a similar hardware configuration, and then use the VHD generated from the backup. Some tweaking is required for this capability.

Quick and Live Migration

From a high-availability perspective, Hyper-V has quick migration to allow a failover cluster to be used. It also enables VMs to be quickly moved from one server to another. Quick migration is useful in a planned downtime situation. It typically takes a few seconds to move a VM from one server to another, but this depends on the amount of VM memory and the connectivity to the shared disk storing the VM. (For example, a VM with 2GB of memory connected to a disk via 1GB iSCSI might take 16 seconds to move, whereas it would take 8 seconds if it's connected via 2GB fiber, or 4 seconds if it's connected via 4GB fiber.)

For quick migration, each node must be running the Hyper-V role with the failover clustering feature configured using shared storage for the VMs (for example, a SAN over fiber or iSCSI). Each node must also have the same virtual networks defined; you can have up to 16 nodes in a Hyper-V cluster. This configuration is shown in Figure 19-26.

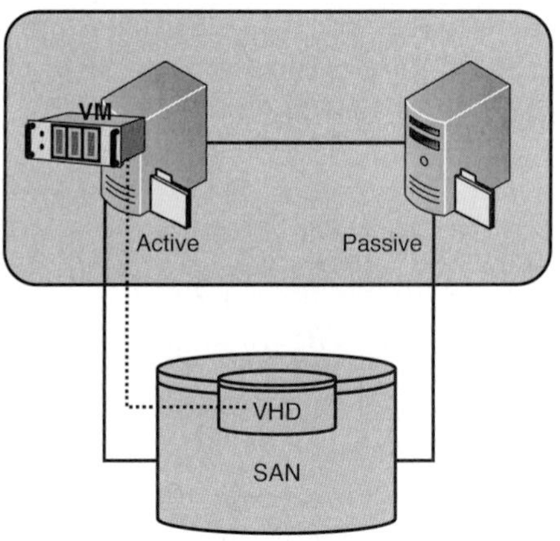

FIGURE 19-26 A cluster with Hyper-V and the VM configuration and data stored on shared storage.

After the failover cluster is defined, add a new Virtual Machine application via the High Availability wizard (see Figure 19-27).

A list of VMs configured on the nodes in the cluster is displayed, as shown in Figure 19-28. You should select the VMs you want to make highly available. Select only VMs that are stored on the shared storage, such as the SAN, or you receive an error that the VM cannot be managed by the cluster. The VM must also be stopped to be able to make it highly available. After the VM is cluster enabled, it can be managed via the Failover Cluster Management mmc snap-in and can be moved between nodes in the cluster as per a normal cluster service or application, as shown in Figure 19-29. Ensure that the disk drive that contains the VMs is part of the VM service or the failover will not function correctly; without the disk failing over the other node, there is no access to the VHDs or saved state.

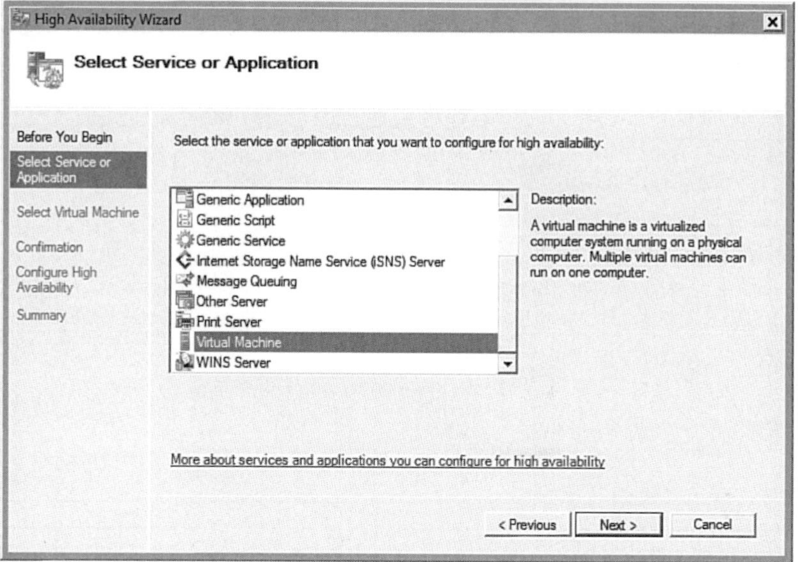

FIGURE 19-27 Adding a VM cluster service.

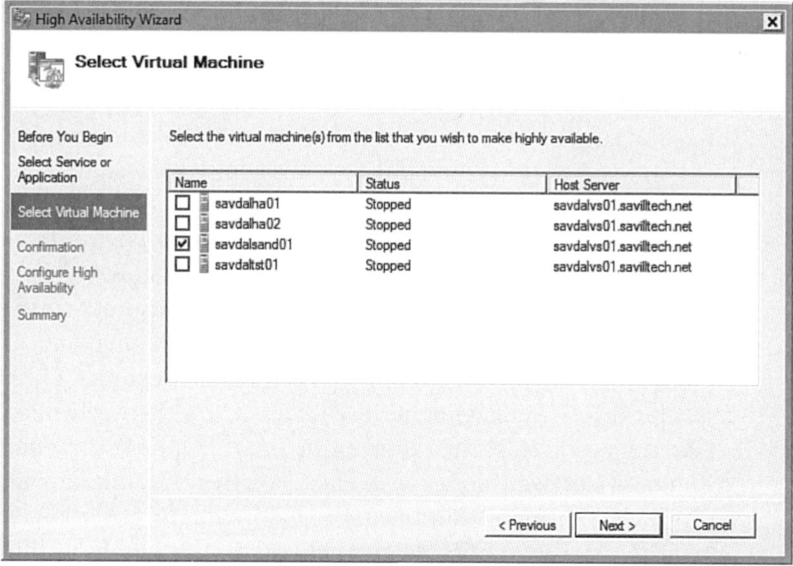

FIGURE 19-28 Selecting VMs to make highly available.

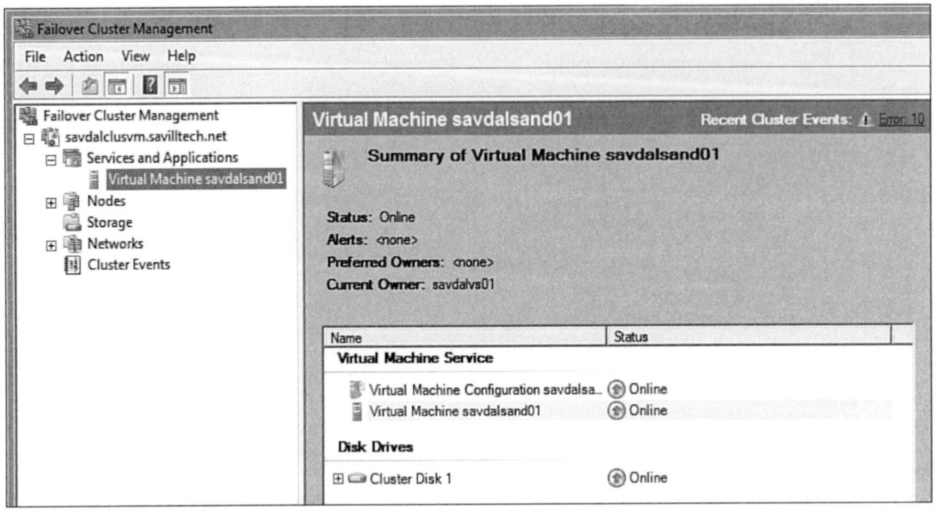

FIGURE 19-29 A cluster-enabled VM.

The actual process of a VM quick migration is not complex. It performs a save state, as you can do as part of normal VM management, and then the state is saved to the shared storage. The storage connectivity is then switched to the other cluster node so the node can access the storage containing the VM. The new active node reads the VM information and restores the saved state, which launches the VM. This is a fast process, but there is still server downtime during the saving of the state, migrating the resources for the cluster service, and then restoring the state. The actual guest VMs do not know they are running in a cluster environment; there is no clustering configuration performed on the actual guest OSs.

Keep in mind that if you bring up a VM on a different server, the VM has to be reactivated (refer to Chapter 3, "Installing and Upgrading Windows Server 2008," in the "Activation Option" section). The solution is to use a local Key Management Server (KMS) for your activations.

Live migration exists in a future version of Hyper-V; this enables a VM to be moved between nodes in a cluster with no visible downtime—not even a packet dropped during a PING operation. This is achieved by pumping the VM memory over the network to the server hosting the VM, and then switching over running the VM once the memory pump has completed. There is a short pause, which is necessary because some memory might have changed from the time of the memory pump and the actual cutover. This delta memory change is a tiny percentage and would be a subsecond service interruption, with nothing noticeable. Many clients say live migration is an absolute must (VMWare has this with their QMotion capability); however, when you start to probe, they don't actually need it. Most companies want it for planned VM move operations, such as removing all VMs from a virtual server so the virtual server can be patched/rebooted. This is typically done at 2 a.m., so can you accept a 15-second outage of those VMs? Most clients do not see this as a problem. That's not to say the live migration won't be great—it's just not the stumbling block many companies originally perceive it to be.

In future versions, you will see the capability to HotAdd on a running VM additional memory, processor, storage, and networking.

Advanced Management

One of the key ideas with Windows Server 2008 is that servers are role based (for example, that's your domain controller, that's your DHCP server, that's your SQL server). As you move into a virtualized world, assigning roles gets trickier: "Those are my 10 virtual servers and somewhere among all of them is my DC, DHCP, and SQL server" will become commonplace. Therefore, management of virtualization is the key to keeping track of the environment and keeping it efficient.

Managing both virtual and physical OSs the same way with one solution is the goal; this is where the System Center products are going, especially with the SCVMM. The SCVMM provides the following features:

- Centralized VM deployment and management via an intuitive administrator console, which breaks down the virtualization environment into groups of hosts, views of VMs, a central library, and a live thumbnail of the virtuals.
- Intelligent placement of VMs, which allows the administrator to request a new VM; SCVMM automatically decides on which server to place the VM based on current utilization. This assessment is constantly updated, and VMs might be moved at off-hours to rebalance utilization.
- Fast and reliable Physical to Virtual (P2V) and Virtual to Virtual (V2V) conversion.
- Comprehensive service-level enterprise monitoring with Microsoft Operations Manager.
- Rapid provisioning of new and VMs with templates and profiles.
- Centralized library of infrastructure components.

- Extend existing storage infrastructure, including local and network-based storage.
- Allow for delegated management of VMs via a Web-based provisioning portal.
- Monitor physical and VMs from one console.
- Fully scriptable using Windows PowerShell.

More information on SCVMM can be found at http://www.microsoft.com/systemcenter/scvmm/default.mspx. This page has trial versions for download and videos describing the product. SCVMM version 1 only works with Virtual Server 2005 R2; however, v2 supports Hyper-V virtualization platform and VMWare, which ships with the release of Hyper-V. The new SCVMM allows Virtual to Virtual migrations from VMWare to Hyper-V (but strangely, not the other way around).

Virtualization is fantastic, but don't forget you still have the same management responsibilities—you need to patch, monitor, back up, and do everything you normally do with a physical server. As you are building out your new virtual infrastructure, get a good management infrastructure in place, such as System Center. If you buy all the components, this is a lot cheaper than you might think; it will free up time from firefighting to getting an IT environment that facilitates the business, instead of limiting it.

The System Center family is a major selling point for Microsoft. With System Center, a management platform manages physical and VMs similarly, and also manages the environment from the hardware through to the actual services and applications. This is unique; it will be appealing to many clients to have a single management platform, as opposed to one for virtuals and one for everything else.

Hyper-V on Your Laptop

This is not as strange as you might think. Consider that Vista SP1 and Windows Server 2008 share the same kernel and many of the same capabilities (although there are obviously differences). Many people are choosing to run Windows Server 2008 on their desktops and laptops instead of a client OS like Vista. One of the major reasons for this is so Hyper-V can be run as their virtual server instead of software like Virtual PC. Licensing aside, there are some things you need to consider, because Hyper-V is designed for servers. Assuming you have all the Windows 2008 drivers for your laptop and can run all your software, it might work fine. However, consider the following before installing Hyper-V on your laptop/desktop:

- No support for wireless networking with Hyper-V.
- Cannot sleep or hibernate a system with Hyper-V installed.
- With a docking station, have to turn on and off to dock/undock; there is no hot remove.
- No hot swapping media bays.
- Use multiple spindles (one for system and one for VMs).

That being said, I plan to install Windows Server 2008 and Hyper-V on my laptop; just make sure your processor supports the virtualization requirements. I have a complete guide to configuring 2008 as a desktop OS at www.savilltech.com/docs/win2008desktopos.htm.

Windows System Resource Manager (WSRM)

Most of this chapter has been about virtualizing operating-system instances so multiple instances of OS can run on a single physical server. This keeps each OS instance separated from other virtualized OSs, with resource control via the Hyper-V product. Thanks to virtualization and partitioning, you can allow a specific amount of memory, CPU, and disk resource to be allocated to each virtual instance. However, every one of these OS instances requires management, patching, backing up, and potentially licensing. This is where you need the Windows System Resource Manager (WSRM).

If you have multiple services and applications that could coexist on a single OS instance, you might not do this because of a few concerns. There could be possible conflicts over resource allocation. In addition, one service might use up all the resources on a server, depriving the others and therefore impacting the other service's performance. For these reasons, there is another option beyond virtualization.

Introduced as part of Windows Server 2003 Enterprise edition, WSRM allows processes to be allocated portions of CPU and memory, with different amounts of resource allocation permitted at different times of the week. This allows a batch process to be given a large amount of CPU during nonbusiness hours (such as at night), but limited CPU usage during working hours (to not interfere with processes running during the day). These limits occur only in times of resource contention, so a process limited to 10% CPU can use more if no other system processes want the CPU. This type of limit is known as a *soft cap*.

WSRM is not a feature to manage clusters or groups of servers; each server is managed as a separate entity, although it is possible to export out configuration from one server and import into other servers. WSRM is not used to start or schedule applications, nor can it manage resource usage of OS processes; only non-OS processes can be managed with WSRM.

WSRM also has the ability to generate reports. These reports can show how many resource-specific processes users have used, which can be helpful (especially around proving service-level agreements).

If you are familiar with WSRM under Windows 2003, the actual configuration and functionality of WSRM is unchanged; the only change is that, under Windows 2003, WSRM was installed from a separate CD and was a separate installation step. With Windows Server 2008, WSRM is now a built-in feature that is installed via the Add Features wizard. When installed, the Windows Internal Database feature is also installed, which stores resource policies and resource usage for tracking purposes. (No configuration is performed during the install.)

After WSRM is installed, a shortcut is added to the Administrative Tools folder for the WSRM MMC snap-in; upon initialization, select this to connect to the local computer or a remote server.

Resource Allocation Policies

WSRM is focused around resource allocation policies, which consist of either a number of processes or users to which the resource allocation policy applies. You can also use generic resource allocation polices, which are provided out of the box (see Figure 19-30). The policies can be used to configure resource usage so it's spread equally between the processes, users, or sessions on the system (or even spread over IISAppPool instances on a IIS Web server). These resource allocation policies can then be configured to manage the resources on the system using the Set as Managing Policy option. If you just want to collect data on process usage based on the policy, use the Set as Profiling Policy action.

To create your own policy, first create a new process-matching policy to detail the applications or users/groups that the resource allocation policy will apply to. Select Process Matching Criteria in the console tree and select the New Process Matching Criteria action. A name is given to the criteria. Click the Add button to add a new rule for the matching criteria. This can consist of selecting running processes, services, an application, or IIS App Pool (see Figure 19-31), or users or groups can be selected. If an application is selected, a file Explorer dialog is opened, allowing executable or COM files to be selected; however, if Running Process is selected, a process list is displayed that allows processes to be chosen from those currently running. This is the same for registered services: a list of services is displayed that can be selected for inclusion in the policy. Each processing-matching criteria instance can be assigned portions of resources to be restricted to. Therefore, do not place multiple processes in a single-matching criteria instance that requires separate resource allocations. An existing process-matching criterion can be modified after it's created by viewing its properties.

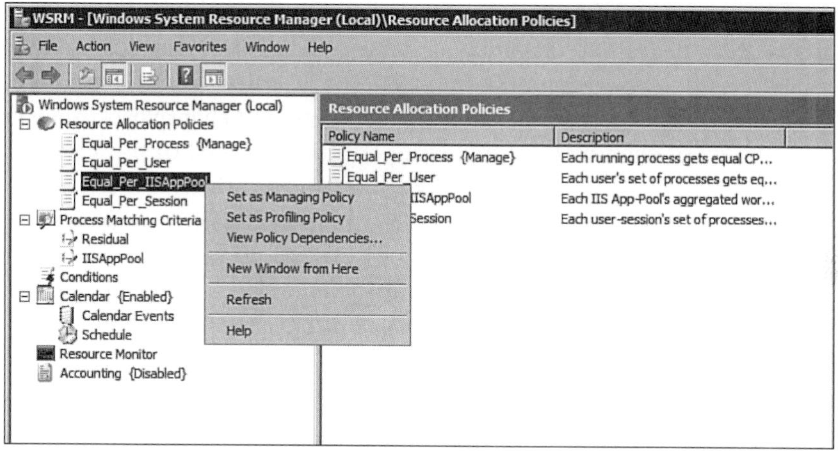

FIGURE 19-30 The WSRM main interface.

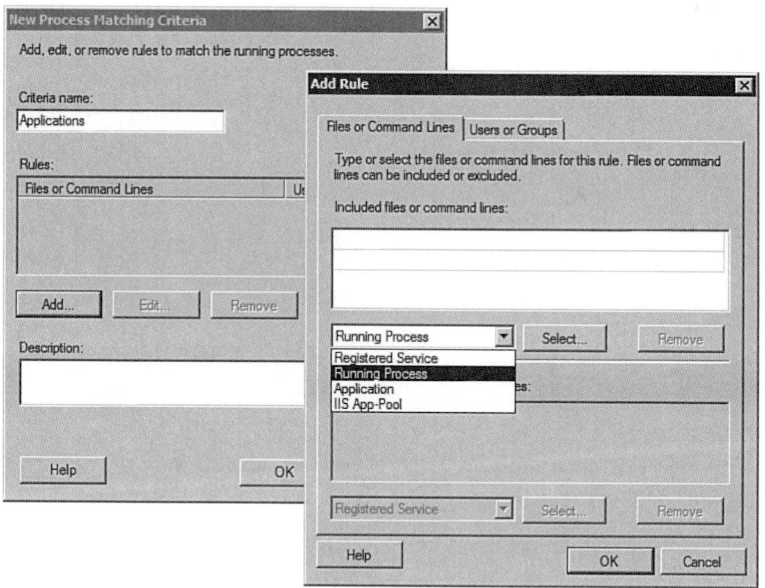

FIGURE 19-31 Adding a new process-matching criterion.

The next stage to create your own policy is to create a resource allocation policy via the New Resource Allocation Policy action when the Resource Allocation Polices console tree item is selected. A name must be given to the policy, and then process-matching criteria are added to the policy. Click the Add button to open the Add or Edit Resource Allocation dialog, as shown in Figure 19-32. The General tab allows a portion of the CPU to be allocated to the current process. The create resource allocation process keeps track of the amount of CPU currently allocated to processes and displays the amount of remaining CPU that can be allocated. The priority of each process-matching criteria is shown in the Priority column when viewing the resource allocation policy in the main WSRM manager; the lower the priority number, the higher the priority (priority 1 is the highest priority resource allocation). Any CPU not allocated to a process-matching criterion is left to the residual bucket, which is effectively available to any other non-OS processes on the system.

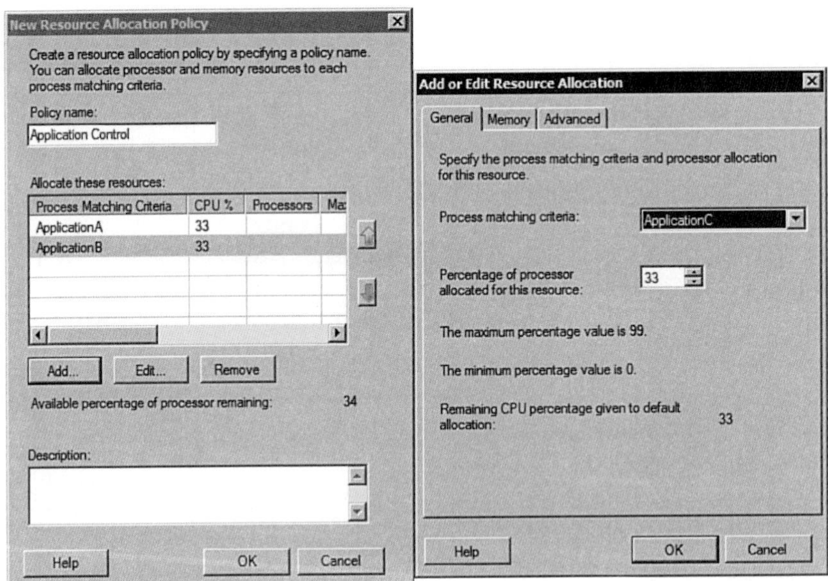

FIGURE 19-32 Adding process matches to a resource allocation policy.

The Memory tab allows configuration around maximum values for working set memory and committed memory. Remember that *working set memory* is the amount of data residing in memory, whereas *committed memory* is the amount of virtual memory for a process. The Advanced tab allows processes to be linked to a specific processor. A suballocation of processor resources can also be configured if multiple processes exist within a single process-matching criterion to spread processor in different ways up to the resource configured for the process group. General suballocations can be specified (such as spread evenly over the processes, sessions, or users), or a specific policy can be created (see Figure 19-33).

After the resource allocation policy is created, enable it via Set as Managing Policy action. This enforces resource use for the processes on the system that are included in the policy.

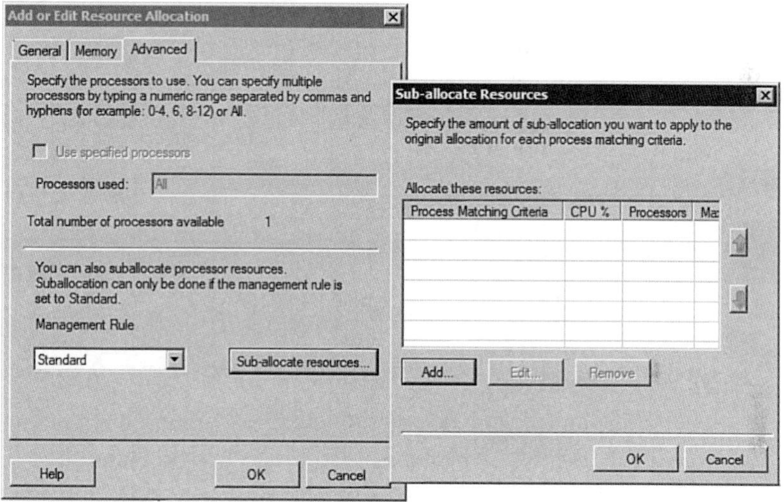

FIGURE 19-33 A granular suballocation of resources.

If you want to examine how processes on the system are being managed by an applied resource allocation policy, right-click the currently managing policy and select the View Process Matching. This shows all processes on the system and which process-matching criterion has been linked with the process (see Figure 19-34). Notice the OS processes are excluded because WSRM cannot control them.

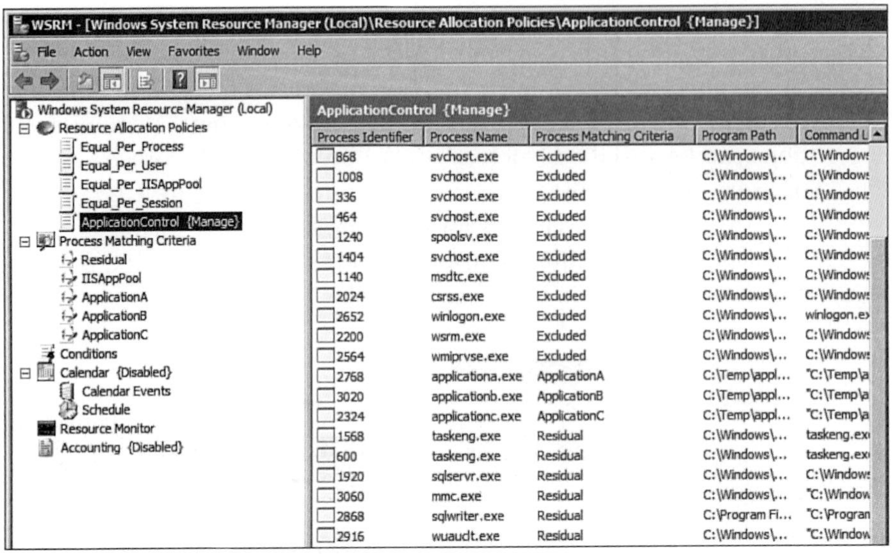

FIGURE 19-34 Viewing how processes are being matched for a resource allocation policy.

Scheduling Resource Allocation Policies Application

Setting a resource allocation policy as the manage policy works if an administrator is always available to set which policy should be enforced. However, if you want a more flexible schedule with different resource policies applied at different times of the day, manually setting the resource allocation policy is not an option. Instead, use the part of WSRM called the Calendar control.

You can create one-time or recurring events for the calendar. However, before we get to assigning events, let's look at schedules first. They are templates of resource allocation policy application over a 24-hour period that can then be used for one-time or recurring calendar events.

Access the Schedule console tree item, which can be found under Calendar, and select the New Schedule action. The dialog shown in Figure 19-35 appears. Give a name and description for the schedule—such as weekday, weekend, or month-end—and double-click hours to set which resource allocation policy should apply. After configuration is complete, click OK to save the new schedule template.

Schedules are not mandatory, but they help if you want to apply complex combinations of resource allocation policies multiple times. You can now create calendar events that are available via the Calendar Events console tree item to apply one-time or recurring events.

Use the New One Time Event action to create a single instance resource allocation, which allows either a resource access policy or schedule to be applied for a defined start and end date. If you select a schedule to be applied, you can't select start and end hours; it has to be allocated in 24-hour chunks, which matches the duration of a schedule.

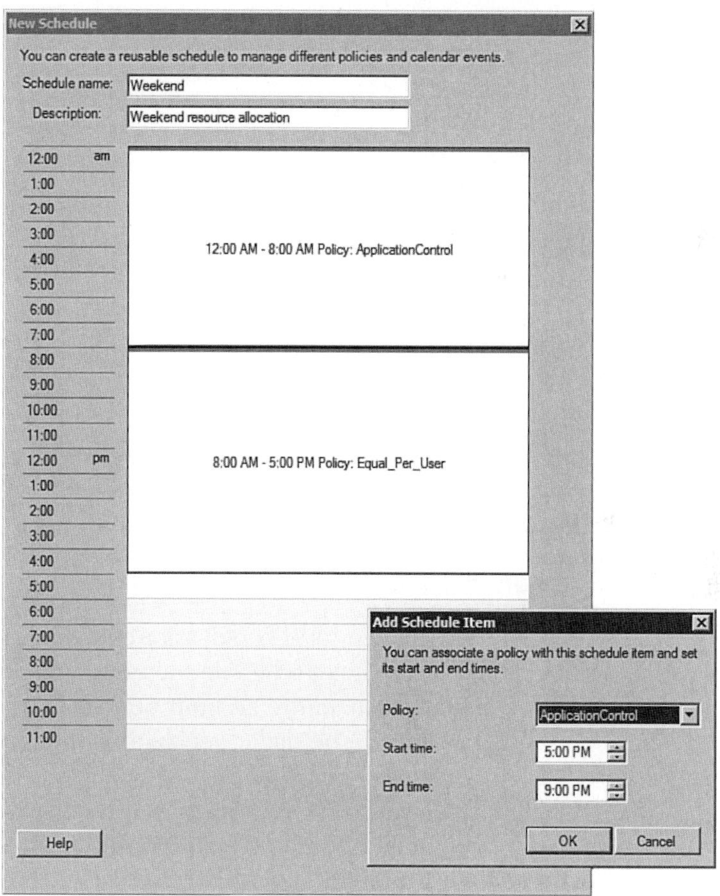

FIGURE 19-35 Creating a new 24-hour schedule.

The New Recurring Event action gives far more granular configuration, as shown in Figure 19-36. After a name and description is given for the new event, you must select if a resource allocation policy will be applied for the calendar event or if a predefined schedule will be used. This is where schedules come in handy, because you can apply only one resource allocation policy at a time with this dialog; however, a schedule can have multiple resource allocation policies applied over a 24-hour period.

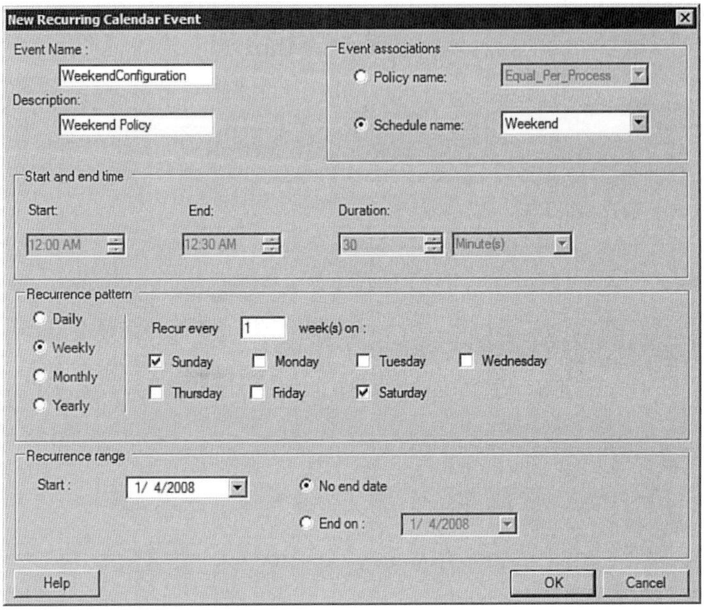

FIGURE 19-36 Creating a recurring event.

If a resource allocation policy is selected, a start and end time/duration must be configured. If you select a schedule, no hours can be configured because a schedule applies to an entire 24-hour period.

The recurrence pattern can be daily, weekly, monthly, or annually. If daily recurrence is selected, select after the gap in days between the event occurring; if this is set to weekly, select the days of the week on which to run the event, and an optional week interval. If monthly is selected, the day of the month on which the event should be run can be selected; and if annual, the day of the year to run is selected. The monthly and annual recurrence patterns are useful for setting policies that might be needed to apply for monthly or annual processing, so a policy can be configured for those times that gives more resource allocation to the batch processes.

The start date specifies when the calendar event starts its recurrence, and an optional end date can be configured.

After calendar events are created, they can be seen in the Details pane. For an actual calendar type view, select the Calendar node in the console tree. This shows a calendar with a day, week, or month timeline with the calendar events that apply.

NOTE If you enable a specific resource allocation policy, the calendar is disabled until you manually reenable the calendar via the Enable calendar action.

Conditions

It is possible for WSRM to switch to a different resource allocation policy when one of six preconfigured events occurs. These events are configurable via the Conditions console tree item and the Add/Edit Conditional Policies action. The conditions available are listed here, and each type can be used for specific resource allocation policy application:

- Hot addition of a processor or processors
- Hot addition of memory (RAM)
- A cluster service node comes online
- A cluster service node goes offline
- A cluster service resource group comes online
- A cluster service resource group goes offline

Accounting

The final component of WSRM is the Accounting module. This module is disabled by default due to the resources used to capture the data, both in terms of overhead and disk space in the internal database. The database used for the accounting information can be changed via the Set DB Server action.

To enable Accounting, run the Enable action; after activating, the Filter View action allows configuration of which information is displayed and over what time period. You can archive captured data or delete through the Archive or Delete information action, as shown in Figure 19-37. You also can select the computers for which data should be targeted, which can be archived or deleted via the relevant options.

After accounting data is captured, it can be viewed in the Details pane, which shows details of all processes on the system, along with detail on memory and CPU usage.

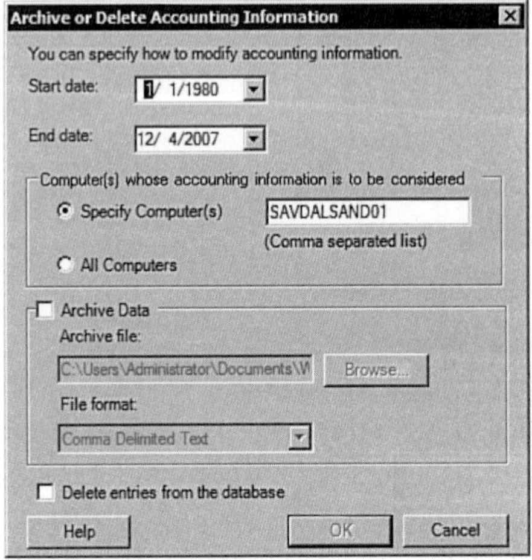

Figure 19-37 Configuring to delete or archive accounting information.

To modify the frequency of data collection, modify the server configuration, as discussed in the next section.

Server Configuration

Server configuration can be exported via the Export WSRM Information action, which is available when the root of the console tree is selected. The export creates a series of XML files containing information about policies and process-selection criteria, in addition to the calendar configuration. This information can then be read into other WSRM servers or used to restore WSRM configuration in the event of a WSRM configuration corruption. To reset WSRM configuration back to the default WSRM configuration, run the Reset WSRM Information action.

Additional configuration is available via the Properties action which opens up the server details. The Management tab allows the state of WSRM to be set. This also configures the state of calendaring, if profiling management is enabled, as well as the current resource allocation policy and the default calendar configuration (see Figure 19-38).

The Exclusion list shows the processes that are not controlled by WSRM. The user-defined processes can be modified if required; however, the system-defined list of processes cannot. It is best practice to not modify the user-defined list because they are key processes that are best not resource constrained. Ideally, no aspect of the OS should be resource constrained via WSRM.

The Notification tab allows email notifications to be sent to the configured email alias. This happens via the configured SMTP server for the event logs enabled in the event log message list.

The Accounting tab allows the frequency of accounting information to be captured, which can be changed from the default of 10 minutes. It is recommended not to set this value below two minutes because of the overhead it incurs on the system.

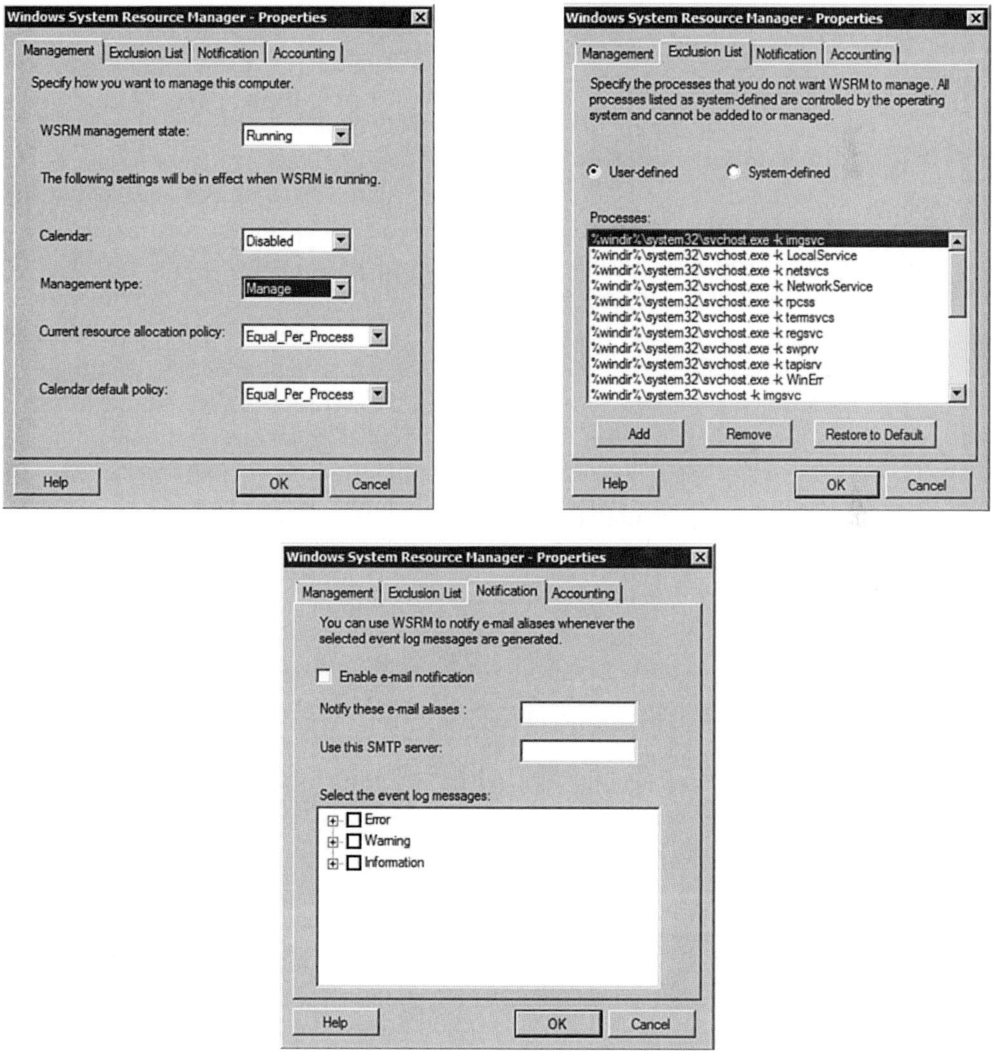

FIGURE 19-38 WSRM server properties.

If you need to disable WSRM, run the Stops WSRM management action.

Advantages of Virtualization and Consolidation

Virtualization and consolidation are the way to go. With today's more powerful hardware and new capabilities for virtualizing services and better controlling resource allocation, the days of one physical server per role are history. In five years, I doubt there will be any servers offering services that run directly on hardware. The flexibility provided by a VM—and the better use of hardware—make running on dedicated hardware a hard sell.

Consolidation via virtualization or resource management reduces costs in hardware and costs in power usage, and also reduces physical space, which leads to other cost savings. If you use resource management via WSRM, you also reduce the number of OS instances; this further cuts down not only on licensing costs but on the number of OSs that need managing, patching, and backing up. This leads to even further cost savings. And by consolidating, you have more resources available to processes because consolidated services typically run on more powerful hardware.

Now is a great time to look at virtualizing servers and consolidating. However, you should always ensure the services you virtualize are supported in a virtual environment by the vendor, or you might have supportability issues.

Summary

Virtualization is the future. Today, only 6% of servers are virtualized, leaving a huge amount to do. I would be surprised if, in five years, that number was not 50%. If you consider that 90% of servers run at less than 10% utilization, along with the money spent on new hardware, not virtualizing is insane. A common stumbling block has been application support when running under a virtual, but you can expect more and more services to be supported the same way under a virtual as on physical hardware. You can finally be rid of "best efforts" from vendors.

In some cases, you have different options for the level of virtualization. For example, Virtual Desktop Infrastructure (VDI) is when a virtual server (or many virtual servers) run VMs, which then run a client OS, such as XP or Vista. Users connect to one of these VMs, giving them their own VM environment in which they perform all their duties. Because the OSs are running on virtual servers, they can easily be destroyed and recreated; this prevents the need to "fix" problem environments, because it's faster to just recreate. On the user desktop side, the user would run a thin client, or perhaps legacy hardware running Windows fundamentals, as the remote desktop client or even a Linux shell.

Why is VDI even needed? We already have terminal services, which allow users to remote connect to their own session. The fundamental difference between VDI and a session on a terminal server is isolation. With a terminal server session, you are running processes and software on a shared OS; with VDI, you are the only session on that OS, so you have greater isolation. Ultimately, the right solution depends on your environment. Terminal services is very efficient, because you have to patch only the terminal servers. With VDI, you have to patch every VM, which is a lot, but VDI does have better isolation. The best solution might be a combination of both, depending on specific client needs.

Many people raise concerns over the performance and stability of Hyper-V—after all, it's new. There are few comparisons of performance between Hyper-V and the leading alternatives. This is mostly due to the fact that Hyper-V's competition have strict verbiage in the end-user agreements regarding what can be published (in terms of performance) without their permission. Unofficially, however, I've seen Hyper-V beating the competition in 90% of tests, so you don't need to worry about performance; more on this will be seen at release time. In terms of stability, many Microsoft clients have been using Hyper-V since beta with no problems. Microsoft itself runs MSDN exclusively on Hyper-V since release candidate 0.

Everything discussed in this chapter regarding server virtualization or consolidation via WSRM is favorable in terms of being "green." In 2008 and beyond, this is a big deal—we are running fewer servers, taking up less rack space, and better utilizing the resources we have. This is great for the environment, but also gives us more bang for the buck.

In the future, we will see everything virtualized: OSs, applications, and services. I hope this chapter has given you a solid understanding of how the technologies work.

CHAPTER 20

Troubleshooting Windows Server 2008 and Vista Environments

Problems in an environment will always occur—whether it's a server not starting correctly, a server not performing as expected, or other general errors that need to be diagnosed and resolved. Fortunately, many troubleshooting tools are available. Each chapter looks at troubleshooting each technology being discussed. This chapter deals with more generic troubleshooting tools that apply to the entire system.

Before we go any further, let's cover some basics regarding the units that an operating system (OS) uses for execution and general functionality. The following are discussed repeatedly in this chapter:

- A *process* is a container that executes an instance of a program. Each process has a unique process ID to identify the process. The process will run an executable program, which defines code to execute and data to be used. A process also comprises a private virtual address space. This space is the memory that the process uses, which is mapped to physical and virtual memory by the OS. This private virtual address space enables each process to have its own memory space without seeing the actual physical memory. Thus, it protects the memory content of one process being seen by another process, which is important from both a security and integrity perspective.

  An *access token* is linked to a process. This token defines the user, security groups, and privileges for the process. Each process also has a list of handles that hook into resources that a process uses (such as a file) and hook into internal OS objects (such as a semaphore). Finally, each process has at least one thread that executes.

- A *thread* schedules execution of instructions by the OS. A process can have more than one thread that share the processes resources, such as the private virtual address space. When a program uses multiple threads, it is considered multi-threaded, and this is one way a program can avoid becoming unresponsive while performing activity. A process can have one thread handling the user interface elements and another thread performing computations; even if the process is busy working, it is still responsive because it has a thread dedicated to the interface communication. Threads are also key to exploiting a multi-CPU (or even a multi-core single CPU) machine. A single-threaded application can execute only on one core at a time, whereas a multi-threaded app can execute each thread on a separate core or CPU.
- A *job* allows a group of processes to be managed as a single unit. This is necessary when a task requires multiple processes to function.
- A *handle* accesses objects. When an object, such as a file or database, is created or opened, a handle is returned that is used for access. User processes always use handles to access objects. Processes keep track of handles, so handles can be useful to see what objects a process is using.

That's enough high-level theory. Let's troubleshoot.

Boot Mode Options

In the next section, we look at Recovery Environment (RE), which might be the solution in the event of a problem. However, before you try to repair an environment, you have other options. The OS Loader for Windows Server 2008 has an advanced boot menu. The boot menu gives numerous boot options that can be useful to a troublesome system. These options are essentially unchanged from earlier versions of the OS, so if you are familiar with 2003, the 2008 advanced options should be familiar. And, in many cases, it will help you resolve a problem before you need to use RE, which requires a more "hands-on" approach that might make your situation worse.

To access the boot menu, first hit F8 at the Windows Boot Manager screen when you select the OS to boot. If you have only one OS configured, the boot menu might not display for any amount of time (because there is no choice to make). After the BIOS stage has completed the system startup, press F8 when the screen goes black. Keep pressing every second until the menu appears, as shown in Figure 20-1. If the Windows logo screen is displayed, you missed it and need to restart the computer. (If this happens, try pressing F8 more often and earlier after your computer restarts.)

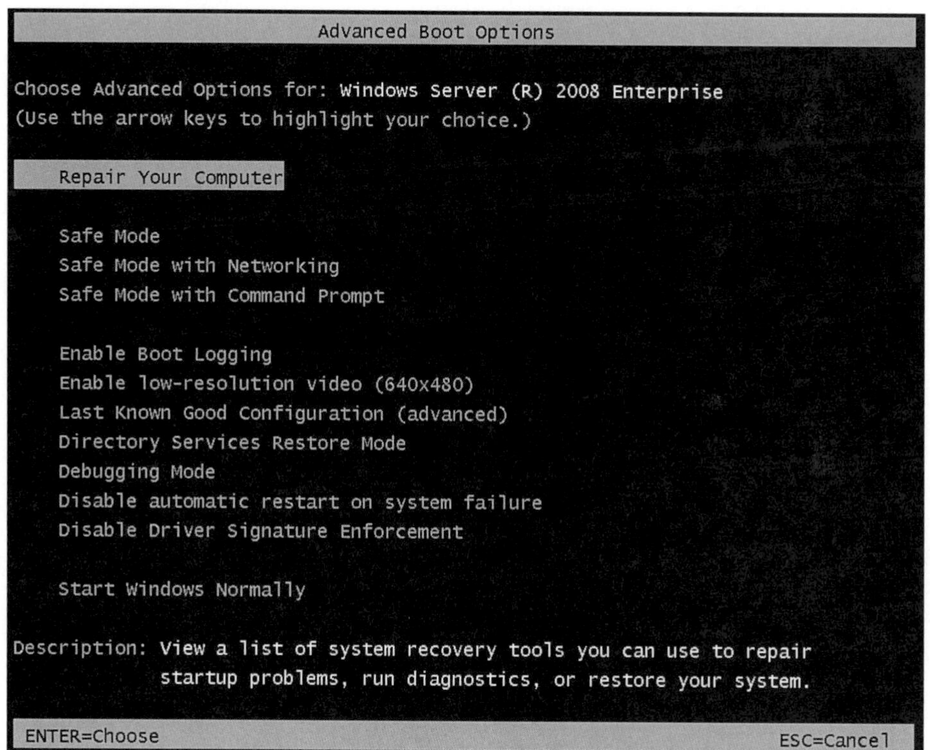

FIGURE 20-1 The advanced boot options for a Windows Server 2008 installation.

Notice the Repair Your Computer option. This option will be available only if you have installed the Windows RE locally to the server and configured it as the recovery platform for the OS via the bcdedit utility (covered later in this chapter).

The rest of the options are standard, as follows:

- **Safe Mode**. Starts the OS with only a minimal set of drivers and services that are core to the OS. The safe mode options are useful when a system can't boot normally due to some "extra" drivers or components that should not load as part of the core safe mode start-up. As the computer boots, the list of drivers being loaded appears. You know you are in safe mode because the words "Safe Mode" appear in each corner of the screen; a generic VGA driver is used, so a lower resolution is used. If safe mode works with no errors, the core settings and basic device drivers are working fine, and the problem is something extra on the system. Try starting additional programs on the server to see if you can force the problem.

  If you know the device that has been added or updated, safe mode is a good place to launch Device Manager and either disable/uninstall the device. If you updated the driver, roll back to the previous version of the driver.

  The only drivers that are loaded in safe mode are internal and external CD, DVD, floppy, and hard disk drives, as well as keyboards, mice, and VGA display cards. The only Windows services that load are the event log, plug and play, RPC, cryptographic services, and WMI (in addition to the core OS components).
- **Safe Mode with Networking**. Similar to safe mode, but this mode loads drivers and services needed to enable networking support. Safe mode with networking also loads network adapter drivers and starts the DHCP, DNC, firewall, network connections, and TCP/IP-NetBIOS helper services.
- **Safe Mode with Command Prompt**. Similar to safe mode, but instead of starting the Explorer graphical interface, only a command prompt loads for the shell. However, you can return to the normal Explorer shell by running Explorer.exe from the command prompt.
- **Enable Boot Logging**. Enables detailed logging of the loading of drivers during the boot process. This logging is written to the ntbtlog.txt file in the Windows folder; it is useful for advanced system debugging. If a boot log file already exists, the content of the new boot will be appended to the end of the file. The boot log will show drivers that attempted to load and failed. This indicates a problem; disable the device or uninstall/update the driver to remedy it.

- **Enable low-resolution video (640×480)**. Starts the OS normally but uses a base 640×480 graphical resolution mode. This is useful if you set a graphical resolution higher than can be viewed.
- **Last Known Good Configuration**. Each time a server starts up and a user logs on successfully, the Registry content related to the system configuration of services and drivers (that is, HKEY_LOCAL_MACHINE\System\CurrentControlSet) is backed up to a safe location; this is a known good configuration. If you made a change to the system that renders the system unbootable, try booting to the last known good configuration. This might help if the problem is related to some new driver trying to load at boot time or other configuration change. You can view the last known good control set by viewing the `HKEY_LOCAL_MACHINE\SYSTEM\Select\LastKnownGood` value.
- **Directory Services Restore Mode**. Restores data to the Active Directory. (See Chapters 10 through 13 for more information on the Active Directory.)
- **Debugging Mode**. This starts the system in a special mode used for debugging by troubleshooting experts and developers.
- **Disable automatic restart on system failure**. Normally, if Windows crashes, it automatically restarts. If it keeps crashing on every start attempt, it just loops, so this option will break that loop.
- **Disable Driver Signature Enforcement**. This will allow drivers that are not properly signed to load. This option is useful if the system will not start or function due to a reliance on a driver that cannot start. Be careful, however, because signed drivers protect the integrity of the system, so always use signed drivers.
- **Start Windows Normally**. Performs a normal Windows start.

If your system will not start and you just installed some new driver or application, try booting to the last known good configuration. If this does not work, try booting into safe mode. If this works, it probably means some extra driver is causing problems, so try disabling recent additions. If safe mode does not work, it's time for the RE.

Windows Recovery Environment

Let's start from the beginning. You have a server that will not boot correctly; or, the server is compromised in such a way that you don't want to boot into the environment for fear of removing evidence, or you need to access from outside the installed OS. Windows Server 2008 media contains a Recovery Environment (RE). This feature is essentially Windows PE that calls the recenv.exe image at startup. (This image is designed to help discover a problem environment.)

Accessing Windows RE

Windows RE is part of the Windows Server 2008 media. To access boot from the 2008 DVD, press a key when prompted to boot from the DVD. The Install Windows standard dialog appears and asks for the language, time and currency format, and keyboard layout. Enter these options as in a normal installation. Click Next.

The next dialog, as shown in Figure 20-2, prompts you to install Windows Server 2008. However, at the bottom of the dialog is a link that says Repair your computer. Select this link.

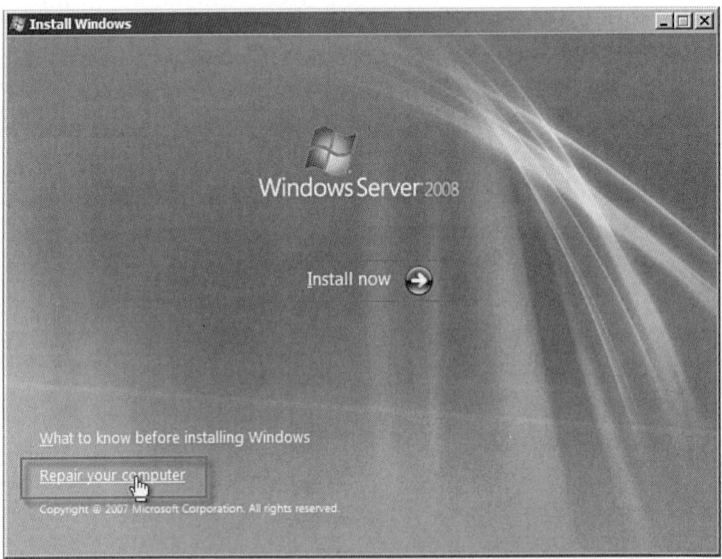

FIGURE 20-2 Selecting the repair computer option.

The computer is scanned, and all instances of Windows are displayed. The scan is performed only on storage devices that have drivers included with the Windows PE environment. If you added additional storage drivers during installation, these drivers need to be installed by clicking the Load Drivers button; after the proper drivers are loaded, this allows access to all storage on the system, and the list of Windows instances will be refreshed. Select the Windows instance you want to repair and click Next, as displayed in Figure 20-3.

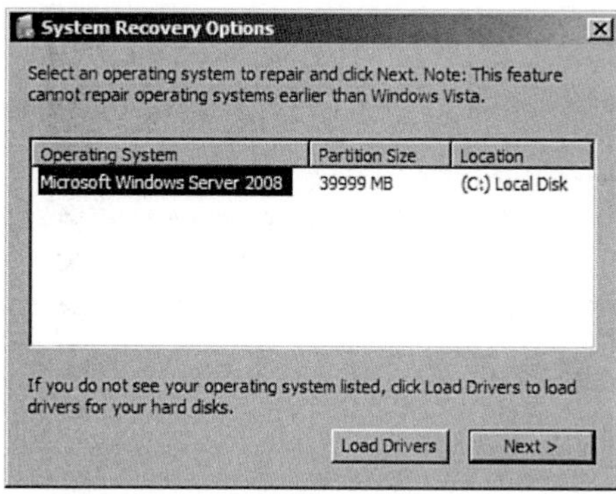

FIGURE 20-3 Selecting the installed instance to repair.

A check is also performed regarding the integrity of the system startup configuration. If any problems are found or Windows installations found that are not within the BCD start, a warning is given, along with an option to repair and restart (see Figure 20-4). Click the View details button to get detailed information on the actual problem found and the solution that will be applied.

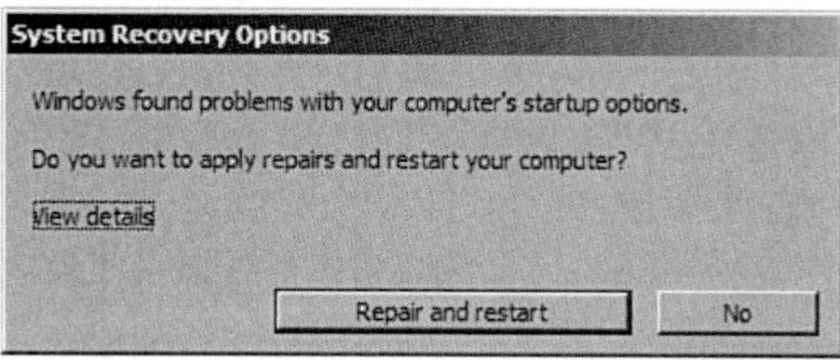

FIGURE 20-4 Automatic startup environment checking and resolution.

After selecting the instance of Windows, the list of recovery options is displayed (see Figure 20-5). The Windows Complete PC Restore option is covered in Chapter 17, "Managing and Maintaining Windows Server 2008," and it allows a backup of Windows to be restored in the event of a total corruption of the system.

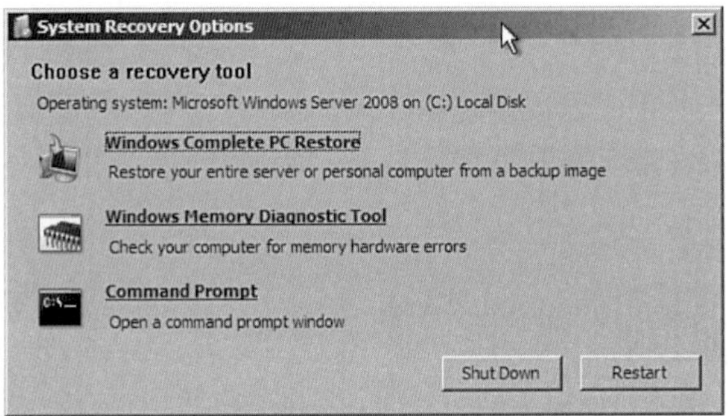

FIGURE 20-5 Selecting the recovery options.

The Windows Memory Diagnostic Tool runs at boot time. If you select the memory diagnostic tool, you are prompted to reboot the computer or run the test at the next scheduled reboot. When the memory tests start, press F1 to modify the number and type of tests that are run, and then press F10 to start the tests. Once complete, a summary of the results is shown and problems are highlighted. If you want to access the Windows Memory Diagnostic Tool on a computer without 2008 installed, boot from the media and keep pressing a key while the initial startup is being performed. This brings up the Windows boot manager menu.

The main item of interest is the Command Prompt option, which is the real Windows RE power. But, before the Command Prompt is discussed, let's look at removing the need to boot from the media.

Installing Locally on a Server

It might not be convenient to find the 2008 media and then boot from it in a problem situation; sometimes a server does not have a DVD drive available. It is possible to create a WIM image containing only the Windows RE environment. This image can then be used to deploy locally onto a server or distribute over the network through Windows Deployment Services to enable a problem server to boot over the network into the RE.

The first stage is to extract the Windows PE boot environment from the boot.wim on the Windows Server 2008 media. Install the latest Windows Automated Installation Kit (WAIK), which is available from Microsoft. Create two empty folders to store the new Windows RE environment and mount for modification purposes:

```
C:\>mkdir d:\temp\winre_image
C:\>mkdir d:\temp\winre_mount
```

Now extract the second image from the boot.wim, which is used by the RE into a new Windows RE-only WIM file:

```
C:\>imagex /export /boot v:\sources\boot.wim 2
➥d:\temp\winre_image\winre.wim "Windows RE"

ImageX Tool for Windows
Copyright (C) Microsoft Corp. All rights reserved.

Exporting: [v:\sources\boot.wim, 2] ->
           [d:\temp\winre_image\winre.wim]

Progress: 100%
Successfully exported image #2.
```

After the Windows RE environment is extracted to its own WIM file, mount the image and edit the PE startup information to automatically start the RE, recenv.exe. Mount the winre.wim, created using the imagex utility in writeable mode via the /mountrw switch, to the winre_mount folder that was created. You need the WIM filter installed to mount a WIM file. Right-click the wimfltr.inf file in the tools\<architecture> folder of the AIK and select Install from the context menu. After installing, restart the command prompt window and mount the WIM file:

```
C:\Program Files\Windows AIK\Tools\amd64>imagex /mountrw
➥d:\temp\winre_image\winre.wim 1 d:\temp\winre_mount

ImageX Tool for Windows
Copyright (C) Microsoft Corp. All rights reserved.

Mounting (RW): [d:\temp\winre_image\winre.wim, 1] ->
```

```
                [d:\temp\winre_mount]
Successfully mounted image (RW).
```

After the WIM is mounted, its content is visible via the folder that was selected via the `mount` command. Navigate to the windows\system32 folder of the mount and create a file called winpeshl.ini. Open it in Notepad and paste in the following content:

```
[LaunchApp]
AppPath=x:\sources\recovery\recenv.exe
```

If you need additional storage drivers to view all drives on the system, copy the additional storage drivers to the mount area and add a line to the winpeshl.ini pointing to the driver folder, for example:

```
peimg.exe /inf=<path> d:\temp\winre_mount\Windows
```

After the changes are made and drivers copied to the RE, unmount the WIM and save the changes:

```
C:\Program Files\Windows AIK\Tools\amd64>imagex /unmount
➥/commit d:\temp\winre_mount
ImageX Tool for Windows
Copyright (C) Microsoft Corp. All rights reserved.

Unmounting: [d:\temp\winre_mount]...
Successfully unmounted image.
```

The WIM image is now ready for deployment via WDS and for insertion into a normal Windows Server installation.

Ideally, the Windows RE is installed to its own partition and now the boot partition because, if the boot volume was having boot problems, having the RE on the same volume would not help. However, if you don't have other partitions that can be used, install the RE onto the Server 2008 partition.

To apply the RE WIM to a partition, use the `imagex /apply` command to specify the image file, the image within the file, and the target partition. For example:

```
C:\>imagex /apply winre.wim 1 e:
```

```
ImageX Tool for Windows
Copyright (C) Microsoft Corp. All rights reserved.

Progress: 100%
Successfully applied image.
```

Now add this to the bootmgr as a bootable option. In this example, the Windows RE partition is extracted to the E: drive. So, all partition information is for E:. If you installed to D:, replace the E drive with D. The installation creates a new entry of type OSLOADER, which gives a GUID for the new entry. Use that new GUID to set attributes for the entry before finally adding the new item to the end of the boot menu order:

```
C:\>bcdedit /create /d "Windows RE 2008" /application OSLOADER
The entry {57f9d851-b1b2-11dc-9cfd-e2c6c11635e9} was
successfully created.
C:\>bcdedit -set {57f9d851-b1b2-11dc-9cfd-e2c6c11635e9}
➥winpe yes
The operation completed successfully.
C:\>bcdedit -set {57f9d851-b1b2-11dc-9cfd-e2c6c11635e9}
➥osdevice partition=e:
The operation completed successfully.
C:\>bcdedit -set {57f9d851-b1b2-11dc-9cfd-e2c6c11635e9} device
➥partition=e:
The operation completed successfully.
C:\>bcdedit -set {57f9d851-b1b2-11dc-9cfd-e2c6c11635e9} path
➥\windows\system32\winload.exe
The operation completed successfully.
C:\>bcdedit -set {57f9d851-b1b2-11dc-9cfd-e2c6c11635e9}
➥systemroot \windows
The operation completed successfully.
C:\>bcdedit -set {57f9d851-b1b2-11dc-9cfd-e2c6c11635e9}
➥detecthal yes
The operation completed successfully.
C:\>bcdedit -displayorder {57f9d851-b1b2-11dc-9cfd-
➥e2c6c11635e9} -addlast
The operation completed successfully.
C:\>bcdedit

Windows Boot Manager
```

```
--------------------
identifier              {bootmgr}
device                   partition=C:
path                     \bootmgr
description              Windows Boot Manager
default                  {current}
displayorder             {current}
                         {57f9d851-b1b2-11dc-9cfd-e2c6c11635e9}
timeout                  30

Windows Boot Loader
-------------------
identifier              {current}
device                   partition=C:
path                     \Windows\system32\winload.exe
description              Windows Server (R) 2008 Enterprise
osdevice                 partition=C:
systemroot               \Windows
resumeobject             {43c836c6-b1a2-11dc-bfd9-806e6f6e6963}

Windows Boot Loader
-------------------
identifier              {57f9d851-b1b2-11dc-9cfd-e2c6c11635e9}
device                   partition=E:
path                     \windows\system32\winload.exe
description              Windows RE 2008
osdevice                 partition=E:
systemroot               \windows
detecthal                Yes
winpe                    Yes
```

The boot menu will now have an option for Windows RE, as shown in Figure 20-6.

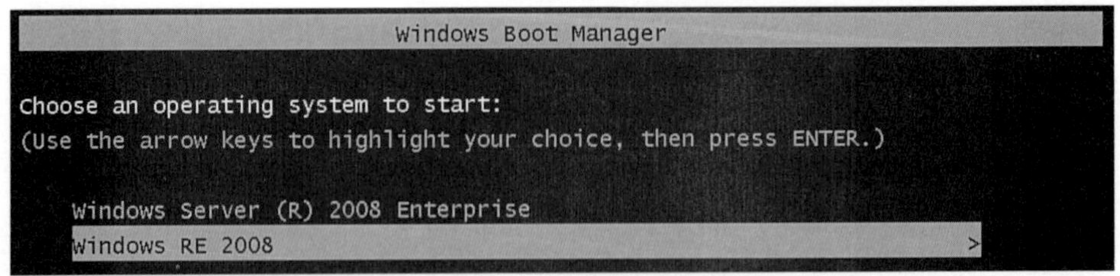

FIGURE 20-6 Selecting the Windows RE 2008 startup option.

If you do have to update a single partition, perform the following procedure to inject the recovery option as an advanced option for the main OS via the WIM file. To add an entry for a WIM file, create a RAM disk option in the BCD and add configuration for the WIM file, as shown in the following steps:

1. Copy the winre.wim you created and the boot.sdi file, which is found in the Tools\PETools\<architecture>\boot folder of the WAIK, to the root of the partition. Make sure you choose the correct architecture for the server where RE is being installed to. The next commands create a RAM Disk options object that points to the file used to generate the RAM disk, boot.sdi:

```
C:\>bcdedit /create {ramdiskoptions} /d "Ramdisk
➥options"
The entry {ramdiskoptions} was successfully created.
C:\>bcdedit /set {ramdiskoptions} ramdisksdidevice
➥partition=C:
The operation completed successfully.
C:\>bcdedit /set {ramdiskoptions} ramdisksdipath
➥\boot.sdi
The operation completed successfully.
```

2. Use the RAM disk object to add an entry using the RAM disk and a WIM file. Note that the partition must be placed in square brackets. These are the same commands as those used when adding an entry for a basic Windows PE environment, except that the device and osdevice paths are ramdisk entries that require us to pass the name of the WIM file and the ramdiskoptions object. Everything else is as if a normal partition entry were being added:

```
C:\>bcdedit /create /d "Windows RE WIM Load"
➥/application OSLOADER
The entry {57f9d854-b1b2-11dc-9cfd-e2c6c11635e9} was
successfully created.
C:\>bcdedit /set {57f9d854-b1b2-11dc-9cfd-e2c6c11635e9}
➥device ramdisk=[c:]\winre.wim,{ramdiskoptions}
The operation completed successfully.
C:\>bcdedit /set {57f9d854-b1b2-11dc-9cfd-e2c6c11635e9}
➥path \windows\system32\winload.exe
The operation completed successfully.
C:\>bcdedit /set {57f9d854-b1b2-11dc-9cfd-e2c6c11635e9}
➥osdevice ramdisk=[c:]\winre.wim,{ramdiskoptions}
```

```
The operation completed successfully.
C:\>bcdedit /set {57f9d854-b1b2-11dc-9cfd-e2c6c11635e9}
➥systemroot \windows
The operation completed successfully.
C:\>bcdedit /set {57f9d854-b1b2-11dc-9cfd-e2c6c11635e9}
➥winpe yes
The operation completed successfully.
C:\>bcdedit /set {57f9d854-b1b2-11dc-9cfd-e2c6c11635e9}
➥detecthal yes
The operation completed successfully.
```

3. Now add this to the BCD menu. However, you might not want to do this yet, as there is a second way to access the recovery console, but here is the standard command:

```
C:\>bcdedit /displayorder {57f9d854-b1b2-11dc-9cfd-
➥e2c6c11635e9} /addlast
The operation completed successfully.
```

A new boot option will now be available to boot from the WIM file. If selected, an OS must be selected to repair. (For example, if you're booting from media, you need the local administrator password for the installation entered to effectively authorize environmental changes.)

Enabling the Advanced "Boot Repair Your Computer" Option

You can optionally configure the RE environment to be added as a Repair Your Computer option for the Advanced menu of an OS. This means you would not add as a separate boot loader menu item (which is the last step). This can be enabled for either a WIM-based RE environment or an RE environment installed to a partition.

The first step to setting up the Boot Repair Your Computer option is to set the RE entry as the recovery OS by setting custom attribute 46000010 to Yes. The GUID here is the GUID of the RE environment:

```
C:\>bcdedit /set {57f9d854-b1b2-11dc-9cfd-e2c6c11635e9}
➥custom:46000010 yes
The operation completed successfully.
```

Now, set the Windows OS for which you want to have a Repair Your Computer option to use the recovery OS. The first GUID is the GUID of the Windows Server 2008 OS; the second GUID shown is the GUID of the RE entry:

```
C:\>bcdedit /set {57f9d850-b1b2-11dc-9cfd-e2c6c11635e9}
➥recoverysequence {57f9d854-b1b2-11dc-9cfd-e2c6c11635e9}
The operation completed successfully.
C:\>bcdedit /set {57f9d850-b1b2-11dc-9cfd-e2c6c11635e9}
➥recoveryenabled yes
The operation completed successfully.
```

A new RE boot entry will be written to the BCD and is accessed by opening the advanced boot options menu (F8) and selecting the Repair Your Computer option, as shown in Figure 20-7.

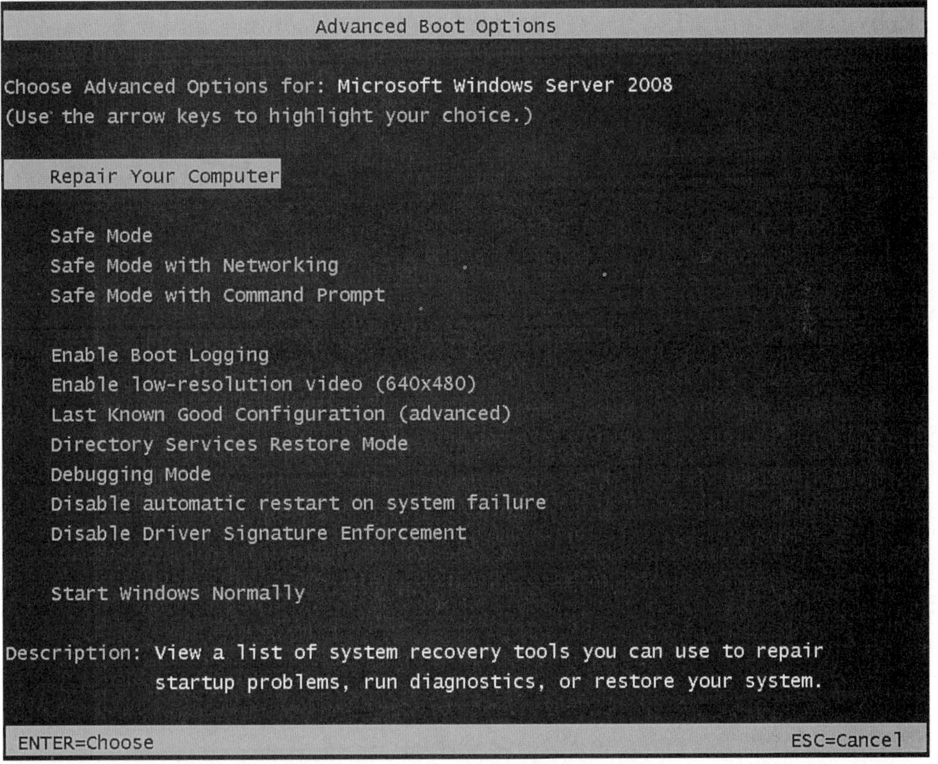

FIGURE 20-7 Selecting the repair option from a locally installed RE.

The advantage of this approach is that you are not prompted to enter an administrator password or select the OS to repair.

Using Windows RE Command Prompt

After selecting the command prompt from the RE main dialog, a command prompt will open in the X:\sources folder. This folder is the PE environment from the media or WIM file loaded into RAM running as the local system account. You can do almost anything to the accessible areas.

Windows RE is essentially the Windows PE environment, which is itself a subset of the Windows Server 2008 OS. Many of the normal command-line commands will work in PE and, therefore, RE (such as `copy`, `cd`, `del`, and `dir`). This is in addition to more powerful commands, such as the `net` suite of commands (like `net start` and `net stop`), and the `ipconfig`, `ping`, `tracert`, and `pathping` commands for network troubleshooting (even though, by default, the network is not running). Concentrate on the commands that are special to RE or applicable to the RE environment. You can also run other commands inside the RE that are available; however, because Windows PE is a subset of Windows Server 2008, there are limitations:

- No support for the .NET Framework.
- No Windows On Windows (WOW) support. 16-bit applications will not run on a 32-bit Windows PE, and 32-bit applications will not run on a 64-bit Windows PE.
- Windows PE automatically restarts after 24 hours to avoid being used as a normal OS.
- The following APIs are not part of PE, so any application that uses them will fail: access control, NetShow Theater Administration, OpenGL, power options, printing and print spooler, still image, tape backup, terminal services, user profile, Windows station and desktop, Windows multimedia, and the Windows shell.

Let's first look at a computer not starting. Aside from physical hardware problems (of which memory can be tested using the memory diagnostics), the actual OS load is performed via several stages and information sources.

The BIOS of the computer loads the Master Boot Record (MBR) from the boot disk. The MBR gives instruction on the loading boot sector from the system disk; this loads the Windows Boot Manager (bootmgr), which loads the BCD. The BCD resides in the \boot\bcd folder on the system volume (or \EFI\Microsoft\Boot for EFI installations stored on the EFI system partition). The BCD holds information about the OSs installed on the computer; when starting an OS, winload.exe is called. This in turn calls and starts the main Windows kernel and core services (for example ntoskrnl.exe), and then the rest of Windows starts (for example, winlogon.exe, and so on).

All these sources can be corrupted or erased. With the RE, you can recover each of them. A new command is available in Windows RE—the `bootrec` command. `Bootrec` is a single command that replaces the MBR boot sector and rebuilds the BCD database in the event of corruption.

These commands replace the information needed for the OS to start without wiping partition information, so don't fear that they might erase information. Delete the BCD database and run the `/scanos` command, which searches for any OSs that are not currently contained in the BCD database. This is why the old database needs to be removed before running it.

```
C:\>bootrec /fixmgr
The operation completed successfully.
C:\>bootrec /fixboot
The operation completed successfully.
C:\>del \boot\bcd
C:\>bootrec /scanos
Scanning all disks for Windows installations.
Please wait, since this may take a while…
Successfully scanned Windows installations.
Total identifier Windows installations: 1
[1] C:\Windows
The operating completed successfully.
```

If you run the bcdedit tool, which manages the BCD content, you see it is not available; it has been deleted. If you then run `/rebuildbcd`, you are given the option to add any missing OSs. Once entered, if you rerun the bcdedit, you see a boot manager and a boot loader for Windows Server 2008, as shown in Figure 20-8. This can be useful if OSs are not showing in your boot menu or if the boot database is corrupt. Boot into the RE, rename the existing database (instead of deleting it), and create a new one with the `bootrec` command. Follow these steps:

```
C:
cd boot
attrib bcd -s -r -h
ren bcd bcd.old
bootrec /rebuildbcd
```

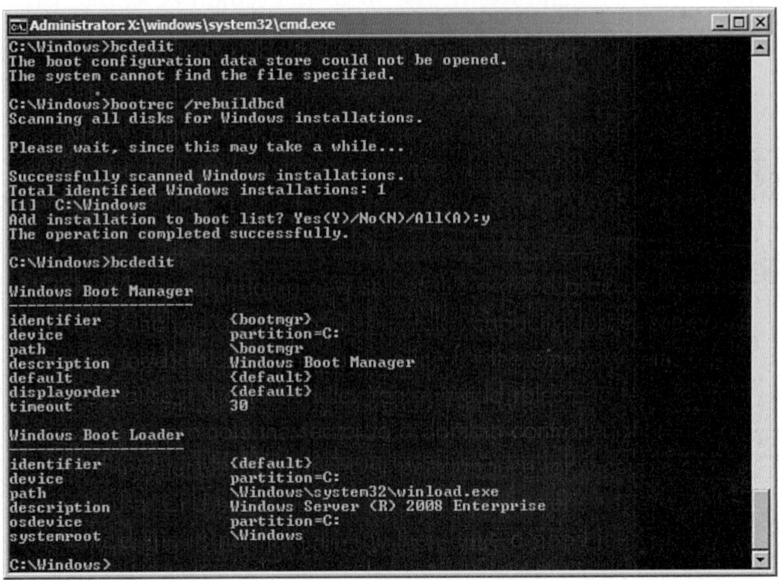

FIGURE 20-8 Automatic fixing of the BCD content.

Windows Vista had an option to automatically perform a check of the start-up environment in the RE menu. This is still present in the 2008 RE: You just have to start it from the command line. Execute `X:\sources\recovery\startrep.exe`. This performs a check on all the start-up elements of the environment, including the boot sector, master boot record, the boot manager, and the BCD store. If problems are found, they are fixed, and a report is given of the actions taken.

Managing Services and Drivers

Another big requirement from outside the OS is to manage a problem service or driver that might currently be stopping the OS from loading. For example, it is common to want to stop a driver or service from starting that is causing a system to not boot.

The Windows Server 2003 Recovery Console had some neat commands to enumerate and control services—`listsvc`, `enable`, and `disable`—that were removed with the Windows Server 2008 RE. To work around the loss of these useful commands, you need to directly modify the Registry and the start value of the services and drivers.

There are two ways of doing this. The `REG.EXE` command is supplied in PE, which means you have command-line access to query, copy, modify, delete, and manipulate the Registry in many ways. However, the better option for most users is to fire up the Registry editor (regedit.exe), browse the Registry, and edit in a more intuitive fashion.

When the Registry editor starts, don't make any changes. You are not editing the Registry of the Windows Server 2008 environment—you are editing the Registry of the Windows PE. And Windows PE is probably not the target you desire for the actions to be taken. In this scenario, you modify the state of services, so you need to load the System Registry hive.

Select HKEY_LOCAL_MACHINE in the tree hierarchy and select Load Hive from the file menu. Navigate to the c:\windows\system32\config folder (assuming Windows Server 2008 is installed in the c:\windows folder) and select the System file (it has no extension). You are prompted for a name under which to mount the hive (for example, 2008SystemHive). Click OK. As shown in Figure 20-9, the hive will be loaded along with all the sub-keys.

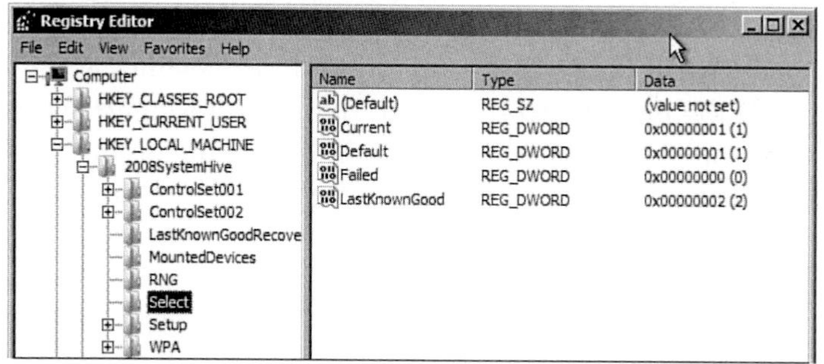

Figure 20-9 Viewing the system hive of an installed OS.

If you want to control services or drivers (device and file system), you are interested in the ControlSetnnn\Services key of the hive. However, there will always be at least two control sets on an installation: the control set that is being used and the last known good set. To know which control set to modify, select the Select key. This key will have a Default value whose data is the control set that is used. (For example, 1 means you need to edit ControlSet001, and your service keys will be under ControlSet001\Services.)

Chapter 17 looked at the various values available for services, but let's get a quick refresher. Each key represents a service or driver. The main values are DisplayName, which is the friendly name of the service/driver; ImagePath, which determines if a service will be an executable and if a driver will be an .SYS file; and Start, which controls if the service/driver will start. Possible values are 0, 1, and 2 (if it will start automatically), 3 (manually started), or 4 (disabled).

The most likely course of action is to stop a problem service or driver from starting; in this case, search the Registry for the Registry key. After you have the Registry key, change the Start value to 4. This stops the service or driver from starting. Then unload the Registry hive via the File–Unload Hive menu option and save changes.

Disk and File Access

Another useful capability of the Windows RE is that all partitions and data are available (encrypted files would not be visible). This means that you can replace normally locked files in the event that a system is unavailable and data needs to be captured prior to a server being wiped. You can then move it to an alternate location.

The file system access can also include replacing key files, such as Registry hives, if corrupt. A useful tip is taking the versions from the RegBack child folder of %windir%\system32\config, which contains versions of the files that were good as of the last system startup.

If you need to modify the disk partitions, the diskpart tool is available. Chapter 5, "File System and Print Management Features," discusses this tool, but basically, you can do anything with diskpart—clean away existing partitions, create new partitions, and shrink and grow existing partitions.

The `format` and `chkdsk` commands are available. In the event of a problem disk, run the `chkdsk /f <drive>:` command to perform a full scan of the disk sectors and recover information from bad clusters where possible.

Boot Configuration Editor (BCDEdit)

You saw the BCDEdit when you added a Windows RE entry to the BCD database via a series of commands. An easier way to manage your boot environment is to use MSCONFIG. MSCONFIG is covered later; however, you can't add new entries with MSCONFIG, but you can remove existing ones.

Windows Vista and Windows 2008 remove the legacy boot.ini file. Previously, legacy boot.ini controlled the initial selection of an OS at boot up along with the basic OS boot options. As previously mentioned, the BCD replaced it. This new format gives far more flexibility to boot configurations; however, it does mean slightly more complicated management in the form of the bcdedit.exe tool. But, this tool has a great deal of documentation, and adding a new OS is not that bad when you install Vista or 2008. In fact, it automatically updates the BCD, and the online help is great. For an example of adding an OS, refer to the section, "Windows Recovery Environment," where all the commands needed are discussed.

If you have pre-Windows Vista/2008 OSs dual-booted with your installation, there will be a legacy entry visible via a bcdedit /enum. The bcdedit /enum uses NTLDR to use and process the legacy boot.ini format, and its entries to boot into older OSs, as the following code shows. Normally, you will have one Windows boot manager entry, one or more boot loader application entries for each Vista or 2008 OS, and optionally, the legacy entry (if you have pre-Vista/2008 OSs installed):

```
Windows Legacy OS Loader
------------------------
identifier              {ntldr}
device                   partition=C:
path                     \ntldr
description              Earlier Version of Windows
```

BCDEDIT is used to rename entries in the BCD store by using the `/set` option for the entry's GUID and the description parameter. If you are renaming an entry that is the current or default entry instead of the GUID, you can pass the current identifier (such as {default} or {current}), and view via the `bcdedit /enum` command, as shown in the following code. If you want the actual GUID identifier, use the `/v` switch in addition to `/enum`. Additionally, to list boot managers, add `bootmgr` after the `enum` switch (for example, `bcdedit /enum bootmgr`). Likewise, to list only OS loaders, add `osloader` after the `/enum` switch—for example, `bcdedit /enum osloader`. Here is the output without any parameters passed of the `/enum` switch:

```
C:\>bcdedit /enum

Windows Boot Manager
--------------------
identifier              {bootmgr}
device                   partition=C:
description              Windows Boot Manager

Windows Boot Loader
-------------------
identifier              {default}
device                   partition=E:
path                     \Windows\system32\winload.exe
description              Microsoft Windows Server 2008
nx                       OptOut
hypervisorlaunchtype     Auto

Windows Boot Loader
-------------------
identifier              {current}
device                   partition=C:
path                     \Windows\system32\winload.exe
description              Windows Vista (TM) Ultimate
```

To change the Vista entry, use the following code, which passes the identifier ({current}) and the new description:

```
C:\>bcdedit /set {current} description "Windows Vista
➥Ultimate"
The operation completed successfully.
```

If you intend to change the BCD, export out the configuration to ensure it's available. If you need to export, use the `/export` command, and pass the file to export to:

```
C:\>bcdedit /export c:\bcd_backup
The operation completed successfully.
```

In the event of a problem, the BCD can be restored using the `/import` command.

To change the length of time the boot menu is displayed, use the `/timeout` setting. Specify a timeout value in seconds, such as `bcdedit /timeout 15`. To change the default boot loader, use the `/default` switch with the GUID of the new default entry. (Remember, to see the GUIDs, use the `/v` switch with bcdedit.)

```
C:\>bcdedit /default {a950120c-7f42-11dc-8830-eb567d4717dc}
The operation completed successfully.
```

NOTE All the other settings, such as setting Physical Address Extension (PAE) and removing some available memory to an OS, are possible via value settings, such as via the PAE and REMOVEMEMORY options. See http://msdn2.microsoft.com/en-us/library/aa906211.aspx for a list of advanced value settings. Chapter 17 uses BCDEdit to set DEP compatibility.

Reliability and Performance Monitoring

The Task Manager was covered in Chapter 2, "Windows Server 2008 Fundamentals: Navigating and Getting Started." Task Manager has a Performance tab, which is a great way to get quick insight into the overall CPU usage of the system (both overall and at a per-core level). The amount of physical memory in use can be viewed with the amount of kernel memory usage shown. There's also a summary of the number of handles, threads, and processes running on the system. The amount of time the server has been running since last boot is displayed, plus the amount of page file that is currently in use, as shown in Figure 20-10. When you have a performance issue on a server, run Task Manager to quickly identify if it's something simple (like CPU or memory maxed out). If it is the CPU or memory, jump to the Processes tab, sort by CPU or memory, and see the process that is using the most to help determine the problem. Also use the Networking tab to get an overall view of the networking usage on a system.

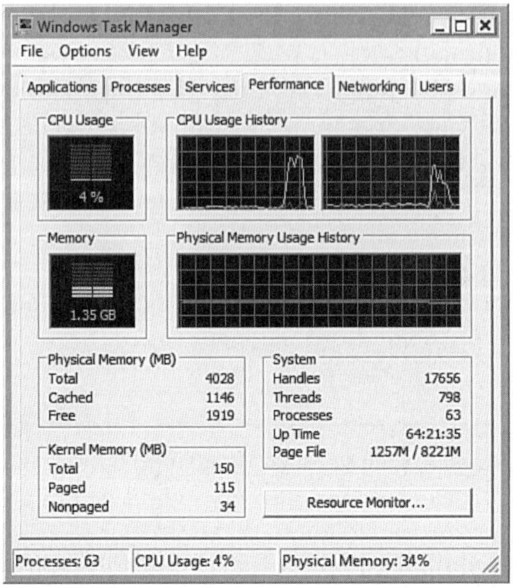

FIGURE 20-10 Quick information about a system's performance.

Many times, however, you need more information to troubleshoot a system or just to *benchmark a system* (see the following note for more details).

NOTE When you install a new server, it's a good practice to run some key performance analysis on the box in an "idle" capacity, just to see how it performs under no load. This becomes a baseline for the empty system, but that's not that useful because it should be idle. You can add roles and features to the system. For example, promote the server to a domain controller; then run a performance test on the system to monitor server performance for a couple of hours to see the memory use, CPU use, disk use, page file characteristics, and network utilization when it's doing its normal job. You then have a good idea of how the server should perform. Keep this normal-activity chart as a baseline for the server. Later in the server's lifecycle, if the server is having problems, run performance tests and then compare them to the baseline performance of the server to see any difference. You have a benchmark of performance to compare the server against. This makes it easier to see any differences between its memory, CPU, disk, and network use now and the use under normal conditions. Many people export the performance monitor counters to facilitate simple comparisons at regular intervals.

The tool used to capture a computer's performance statistics is the Performance Monitor, which is part of the larger Reliability and Performance component of Server Manager. The Reliability and Performance feature gives a performance and health view of the server. Access it via the Diagnostics console tree item in Server Manager, as shown in Figure 20-11, or by running perfmon.exe.

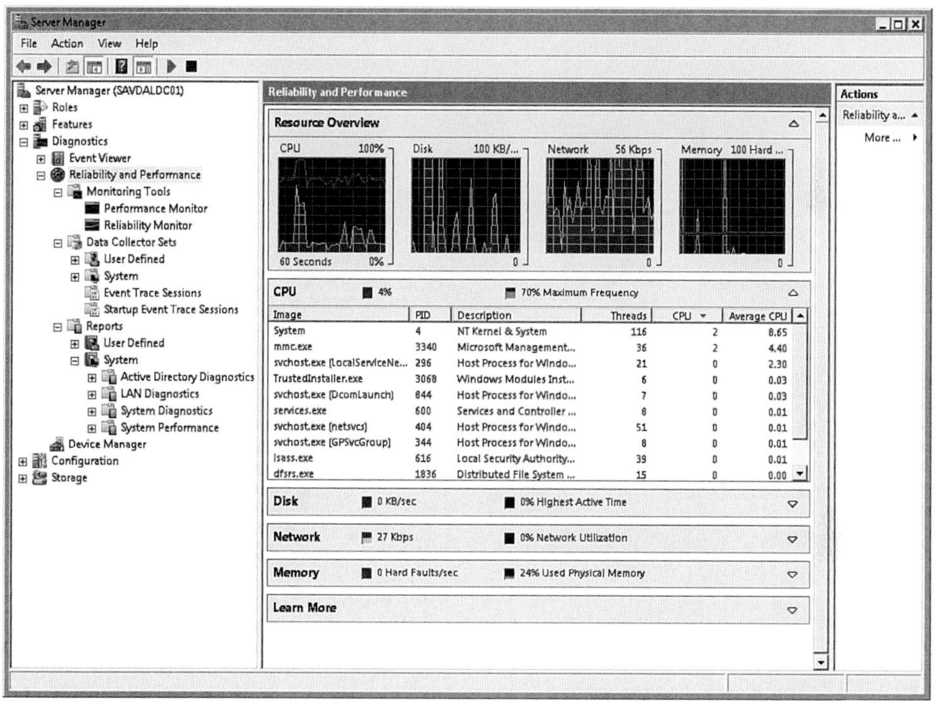

FIGURE 20-11 The Reliability and Performance interface.

The Reliability and Performance interface home page is known as the Resource View screen. It shows real-time information on the CPU, disk, network, and memory usage, as shown in the figure. To access the resource view screen in its own window, run perfmon.exe /res.

Each of the four resource elements can be selected to display detailed usage information for the resources, showing which processes are using what amount of the resource. Each column can be selected to sort the display.

The CPU usage shows the total current percentage usage in green; the blue line shows the CPU maximum frequency percentage, which is the current maximum frequency of the processor. Why is it not always 100%? To save power, a big driver for Windows Server 2008. If you access the Power Options control panel applet, you see several power plans: balanced, power saver, and high performance. Access the advanced power options via the Change Advanced Power Settings link by selecting Change Plan Settings. As shown in Figure 20-12, you can select the minimum and maximum processor state.

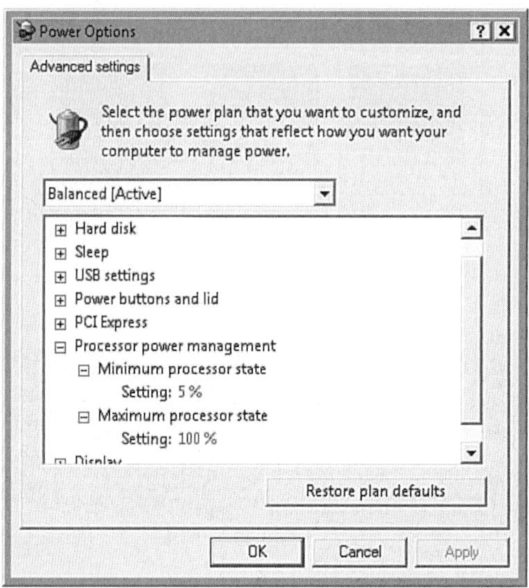

FIGURE 20-12 The processor advanced options.

Unless you are in the high-performance power option mode, the blue line tracks around 70% higher than the in-use CPU. This gives spare CPU resources in case more processor is required. However, if there is a large spike, there might be a slight lag while the maximum frequency is increased enough to cater for the resource need. In high-performance mode, the maximum frequency is always at 100%, ensuring there will never be a lag in the processor power needed.

The CPU detail display shows the image (executable) list of currently running processes, the process ID, the description of the process, the number of threads the process is using, the current CPU usage (% of the total CPU capability), and the average CPU usage of the process.

The disk resource overview shows the total number of KB/sec of the disk use (with the scale shown at the top-right—for example, 100 KB/sec). The blue line shows the highest active time percentage. The detail information is broken down by file handle for disk and shows the image name of the process and process ID, the file being accessed, and the amount of read and write activity in bytes per minute, along with the IO priority and response time in milliseconds for the disk activity (see Figure 20-13).

Disk | 16 KB/sec | 0% Highest Active Time

Image	PID	File	Read (B/...	Write (B...	IO Pr...	Respo...
ntfrs.exe	1340	C:\Windows\Debug\NtFrs_0005.log	0	8,192	Nor...	9
ntfrs.exe	1340	C:\$LogFile (NTFS Volume Log)	0	49,152	Nor...	13
svchost.exe (LocalService...	296	C:\Windows\ServiceProfiles\LocalService\Ap...	0	512	Nor...	9
System	4	C:\System Volume Information\DFSR\Config...	0	40	Nor...	0
System	4	C:\Windows\System32\config	0	4,004	Nor...	9
System	4	C:\Windows\System32\config\SOFTWARE	0	13,312	Nor...	10

FIGURE 20-13 The detailed disk output.

The network overview shows the total amount of network traffic by the green line (with the scale shown at the top-right—for example, 56 kbps). The blue line shows the percentage of available bandwidth used. The detailed view for the network shows the image and process ID that is communicating with a remote host, along with the send and receive in bytes per minute and the total (see Figure 20-14).

Network | 21 Kbps | 0% Network Utilization

Image	PID	Address	Send (B/min)	Receive (B/min)	Total (B/...
svchost.exe (NetworkService)	1128	savdalvst01	185,917	5,404	191,322
System	4	savdaldc01	9,374	13,486	22,860
lsass.exe	616	savdaldc01	5,913	6,448	12,361
svchost.exe (GPSvcGroup)	344	savdaldc01	4,942	6,703	11,645
lsass.exe	616	savdaldc01	6,703	4,942	11,645
dfssvc.exe	2200	savdaldc01	2,785	2,154	4,939
svchost.exe (rpcss)	912	savdaldc01	560	656	1,216
svchost.exe (NetworkService)	1128	savdaldc01	122	296	418
dns.exe	1872	savdaldc01	296	122	418

FIGURE 20-14 The detailed network output.

The Memory overview shows the number of hard page faults per second via the green line (with the scale for the line shown at the top-right—for example, 100 hard faults). The blue line shows the percentage of physical memory in use. Remember that a hard fault occurs when a page of memory is addressed that has been swapped out to the page file. This causes a performance hit because the page has to be moved back into physical memory before it can be used.

The detailed memory view breaks down the memory use into the process image and the ID, along with the number of hard faults per minute for the application. If high, this would indicate a cause for the process to run slowly. The *commit size* is the amount of virtual memory committed to the process (for example, page file allocation). This does not mean the process has that amount of memory paged out to page file, just that it has that amount reserved for it in the page file. The *working set size* is the amount of kilobytes residing in memory for the use of the application, the *shareable memory size* is memory other applications can use out of the working set; the private area is not shared out of the working set, as shown in Figure 20-15.

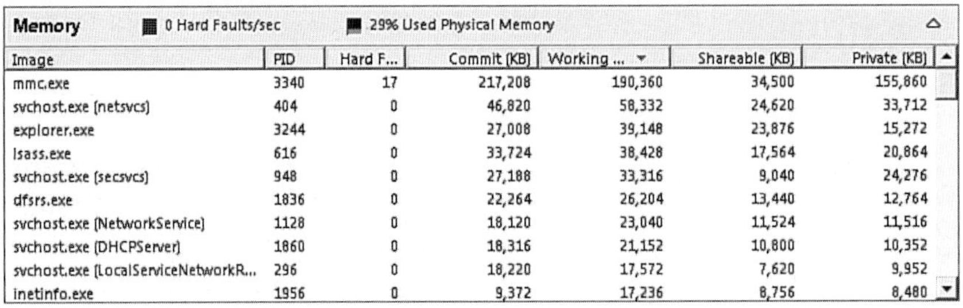

Memory | 0 Hard Faults/sec | 29% Used Physical Memory

Image	PID	Hard F...	Commit (KB)	Working ...	Shareable (KB)	Private (KB)
mmc.exe	3340	17	217,208	190,360	34,500	155,860
svchost.exe (netsvcs)	404	0	46,820	58,332	24,620	33,712
explorer.exe	3244	0	27,008	39,148	23,876	15,272
lsass.exe	616	0	33,724	38,428	17,564	20,864
svchost.exe (secsvcs)	948	0	27,188	33,316	9,040	24,276
dfsrs.exe	1836	0	22,264	26,204	13,440	12,764
svchost.exe (NetworkService)	1128	0	18,120	23,040	11,524	11,516
svchost.exe (DHCPServer)	1860	0	18,316	21,152	10,800	10,352
svchost.exe (LocalServiceNetworkR...	296	0	18,220	17,572	7,620	9,952
inetinfo.exe	1956	0	9,372	17,236	8,756	8,480

FIGURE 20-15 The detailed memory use view.

Performance Monitor

Performance Monitor has not changed much since its first incarnations in early Windows Server versions. Counters have been added; these are specific system attributes—to monitor total CPU usage, and to configure how often it should read the value of the counter (for example, every second) to make up a performance monitoring session.

The output of performance monitoring can appear as a live display or be saved to a log file or database that can be viewed at a later time. There are two main security groups related to performance monitoring:

- **Performance Log Users**. Members of this group can manage performance counters, logs, and alerts on a computer—both locally and from remote clients—without being a member of the Administrators group.

- **Performance Monitor Users**. Members of this group can monitor performance counters on a computer—locally and from remote clients—without being a member of the Administrators group or the Performance Log Users groups.

Adding Counters and Configuring Monitoring

When you first select Performance Monitor, you have an empty chart with 100 seconds of time at the bottom of the graph on the x axis and 0 to 100 on the y axis. Configure how the information will be collected and displayed; then, indicate what type of information to collect.

To configure the properties, click the Properties icon or select Properties from the context menu of Performance Monitor node in the console tree. Here, you can access several tabs:

- **General tab.** Allows element configuration to display, such as the legend (which lists the counters being displayed in the data display), the value bar (which allows a counter to be selected and shows the detail of the value), and the toolbar, as shown in Figure 20-16.

  The Report and Histogram Data section allows the configuration of what data is displayed, such as the minimum, average, maximum, and current values. Finally, the sampling can be configured to be taken automatically via the Sample Automatically check box. Select how often the automatic sampling is taken (by default, it is every second) and the amount of time to display on the graph (100 seconds by default). If you intend to sample over a long time—for example, because you were outputting to a log file—set a sample to be taken every 60 seconds; otherwise, the log would be huge. Also change the duration based around the sampling.
- **Source tab.** Allows configuration of where data to be displayed in performance monitor comes from (by default, it is current activity); however, it can also be a log file or a database, and once a source is selected, the time range to display is selected.

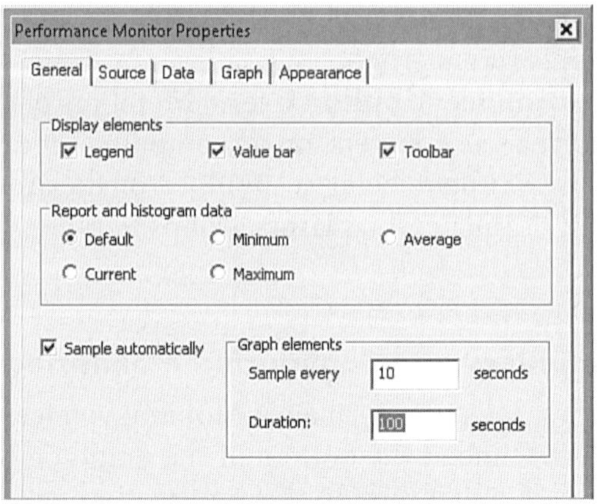

FIGURE 20-16 The General tab for Performance Monitor.

- **Data tab.** Allows monitored counters to be added and removed. Also, the display attributes for the counter can be configured, such as the color and the line width and style, as shown in Figure 20-17.

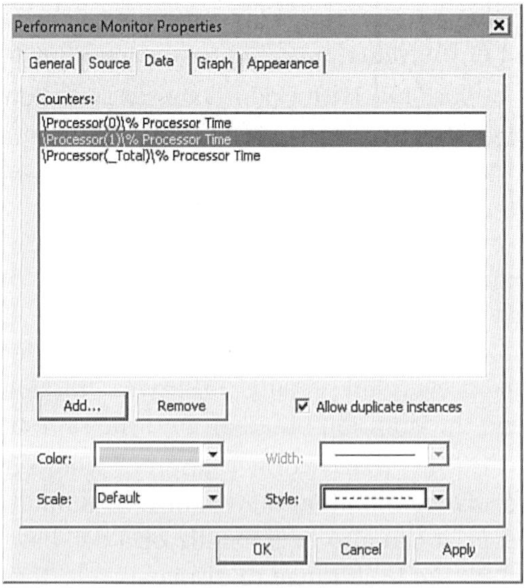

FIGURE 20-17 Setting properties for a Performance Monitor counter display.

- **Graph tab.** Allows the type of view to be chosen. This can be a line graph, histogram bar, or a text-based report. If the graph is a line, select if the display should wrap around on-screen or scroll off. Text descriptions for the Performance Monitor and the vertical access can be configured in addition to setting which elements are displayed, such as a grid for the vertical and horizontal and if numbers for the vertical axis scale and horizontal time axis should be displayed. Finally, the minimum and maximum for the vertical scale can be configured.

- **Appearance tab.** Allows a background for the display to be selected for each of the areas of Performance Monitor, plus setting a color for the text display and grid. Select the font for the display in addition to borders and separators for the group display.

Counters can be added and removed via the main Performance Monitor screen—not just via the Data tab. To add a counter by using the Performance Monitor, click the Add button or select Add Counters from the display context menu. The Add Counters dialog appears, as shown in Figure 20-18.

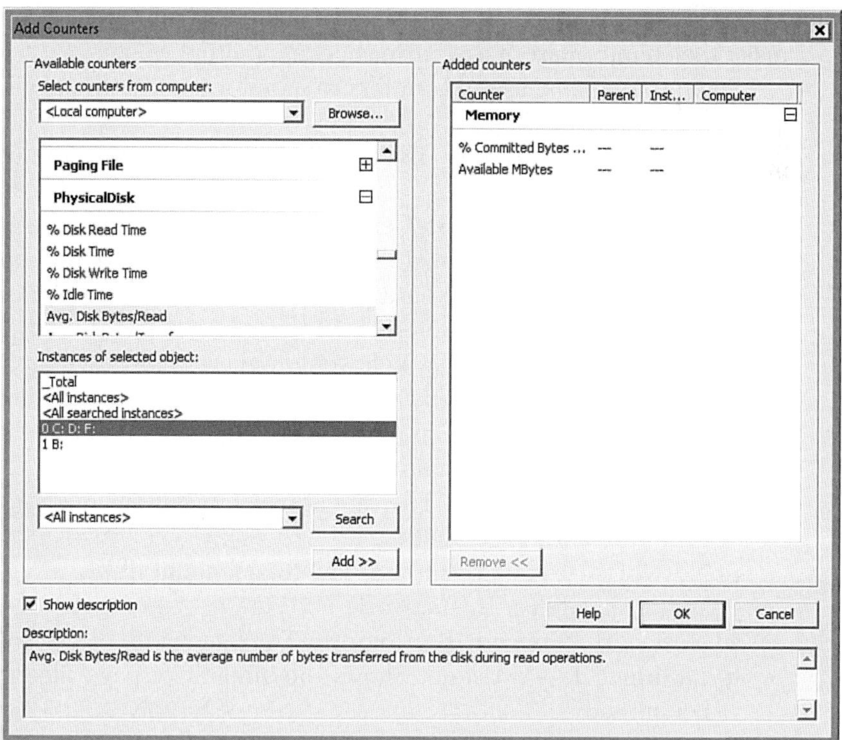

FIGURE 20-18 Adding counters to Performance Monitor.

Select which computer to add counters from. This allows for a mix of both local and remote counters within a single performance monitoring session. If you want to add counters from a remote machine, you need to be a member of the Performance Log Users and Event Log Readers group on a remote computer. The remote machine must have the Performance Logs and Alerts firewall exception enabled.

The available counters are grouped into various categories, such as Memory, PhysicalDisk (which are actual physical hard drives), LogicalDisk (which are volumes created on a physical disk), Processor, and many other groups. Some categories vary based on the roles and features installed on the server. For example, if DFS-R is installed, there are DFS Replication categories of counters. Select a section and then, within the section, select a counter to add. Some counters might have many instances on a single server; for example, if you select a physical disk counter, a list of all the physical disks is displayed in the instances section, in addition to an option to add counters for all instances and the total counters for all instances. If you have a large number of instances—say you were looking at processes—use the search capability to enter part of the instance name and search.

After the counter and the related instance is selected, click Add to make the counter part of the performance monitor.

Some of the most useful counters to monitor are as follows:

- **Memory—Available Bytes**. Shows the amount of available memory.
- **Memory—Page Faults/sec**. Shows how many times a page of memory is accessed that has been paged out to the page file (includes both soft and hard page faults).
- **Memory—Pages Input/sec**. The number of pages read per second from the page file, which would indicate hard page faults.
- **Memory—Pages Reads/sec**. The number of read operations performed to the page file to resolve hard page faults. This is the number of read operations and not the number of pages.
- **Memory—Pages/sec**. The rate at which pages are read or written to resolve hard page faults.
- **Network—Bytes Total/Sec**. The total amount of bytes being sent and received over the network.
- **Network—Current Bandwidth**. The bandwidth of the link.
- **Paging File—%Usage**. Shows the amount of page file currently being used.

- **PhysicalDisk—% Disk Time**. Shows the percentage of time the disk was busy servicing read or write requests.
- **PhysicalDisk—Current Disk Queue Length**. The number of outstanding requests for the disk. Ideally, this number should be two or less for any sustained amount of time; however, if you have multiple spindles, add 1 to this number for each spindle.
- **Processor—Interrupts per second**. Number of times in a second the processor is interrupted to handle hardware interrupts.
- **Processor—% Processor Time**. Shows how busy the processor is.
- **System—Processor Queue Length**. The number of threads in the processor queue waiting to be processed. This is a single queue for the system; if you have multiple cores, the acceptable value should be multiplied by the number of cores. For example, 10 or less per core is an acceptable number; if you have four cores in a server, the processor queue length should be 40 or less.

You now have a busy-looking graph, as shown in Figure 20-19. It is a good time to try the other views. If you click the view drop down, you see a histogram view, which is just a bar for each value, or the report view, which displays the current values. If you want to view a particular counter and are having trouble making out which line it is, select the counter in the legend and press Ctrl and H. This will highlight the counters data in the graph. If you right-click the display, you can save the content of the display as an HTML page (Save Settings). This embeds dynamic content in the page, allowing you to select counters when the page is displayed in Internet Explorer to see actual average, minimum, and maximum values, or save as a GIF file via the Save Image context menu option.

Saving a Configured Set of Counters

Creating a performance monitoring session is great, but we just added a bunch of counters. You don't want to have to reselect them every time you want to monitor the same set of attributes, but there is no option to save your actual configuration to reload at a later time—the save settings just creates an HTML file of the data!

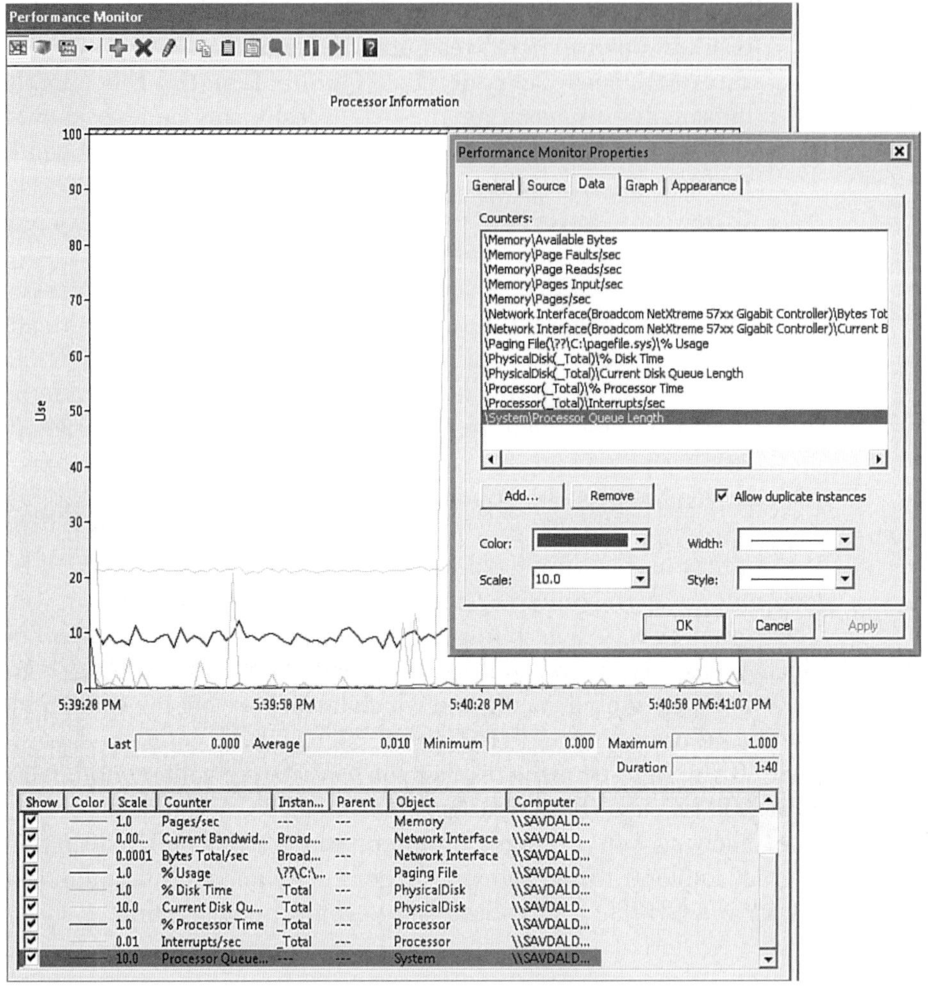

FIGURE 20-19 The most popular performance counters to view.

Don't panic. Right-click the Performance Monitor console tree item, select New–Data Collector Set. It's discussed more in a later section, but Data Collector Set is the new feature in 2008 for creating sets of predefined counters in addition to other sources of information or data collectors. (Data collector is the term for the sources of data available.)

The first stage in the Create New Data Collector Set wizard is to name the new set. (For example, in this case, it's called Key System Performance Counters.) Click Next.

The next stage allows you to configure where the data from the collector will be saved when not running in an interactive mode. By default, data is written to a subfolder of the PerfLogs folder that is created on the root of the system drive; however, change this path as needed. At this point, click Finish or Next to enable a specific user to be configured, under which to run the data set, or just accept the default of System. Click Finish. You now have a new data collector set under the Data Collector Sets area under User Defined.

Data Collector Sets and Reports

Although performance monitoring of counters gives great information on the system's performance counters at the time it's running, to get a full story, there might be other information that is needed, such as Registry key values and traces of other information (like various event logs). Windows Server 2008 introduces the concept of data collector sets that perform this combination of information gathering. In addition, the data collector set is used as the way to save a group of counters, as discussed in the last section.

The OS comes with several data collector sets designed to help health check and diagnose the core system. A clean Windows Server 2008 installation comes with three system defined data collection sets, as follows:

- **LAN Diagnostics.** Collects key LAN service-related information; this includes wired debugging logs, Registry values, and performance counter information.
- **System Diagnostics.** Captures a lot of system information via WMI calls, traces of the NT kernel, and performance counters.
- **System Performance.** Captures a huge number of counters about the system (all counters for key system attributes).

Some roles add additional data collector sets. For example, Active Directory Domain Services adds an Active Directory Diagnostic data collector set.

These data collector sets are not just performance counters. There is Windows Management Instrumentation (WMI) information, traces of system components, debug logs, event logs, and Registry information. You have a lot of input sources for the data collector sets. Select one of the system data collector sets, as shown in Figure 20-20. One of the data collectors configured is selected. This happens to be a configuration type collector, which is a series of WMI calls. The idea here is to be able to capture every aspect of data that would be needed to get the total view of a system and not rely only on performance counters.

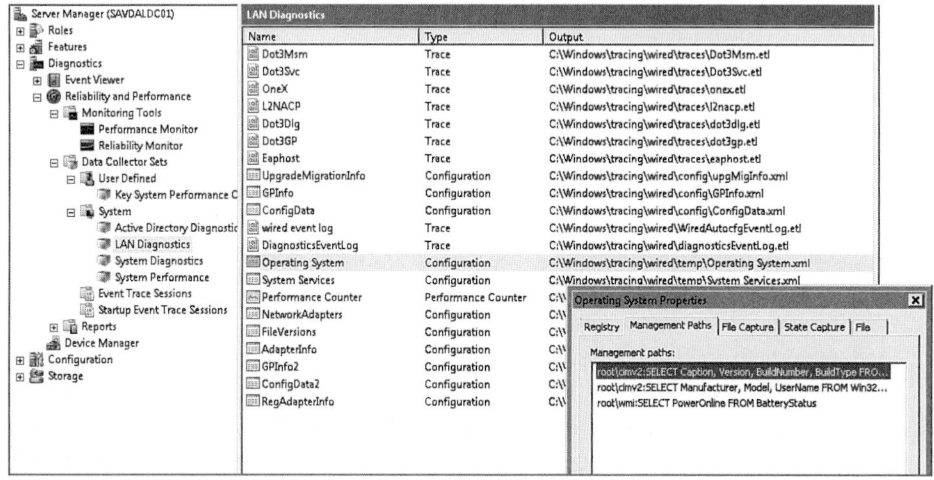

Figure 20-20 A view of the information captured by the LAN Diagnostics data collector set.

At this point, look around the built-in data collector sets. They have great examples of the various data collectors that are available around the general configuration of a data collector set. Let's look at the key configuration items.

Data Collector Set Properties

Right-click the data set collector and select Properties to access the key configuration options for the data collector set:

- **General tab.** Allows a description of the data collector set to be documented, which is a good idea to describe what the data collector set is used for and an overview of its information sources. Several keywords can also be defined for the collector set, and the user used to run the data collector set under can be changed from the default of System.

- **Directory tab.** Allows the specification of where to write the information that is gathered by the data collector set. Configure a root folder for the data; because the data collector might be run multiple times to ensure all instances of the data set execution are kept, specify a subdirectory name, which is again a static name. Even more useful, specify a subdirectory name format, which can include several special codes that relate to the date, time, and serial number in addition to just normal text, as shown in Figure 20-21. An example output of the generated folder name is displayed at the bottom of the dialog. To use text that is not a special sequence, prefix it with the backslash escape character (\).

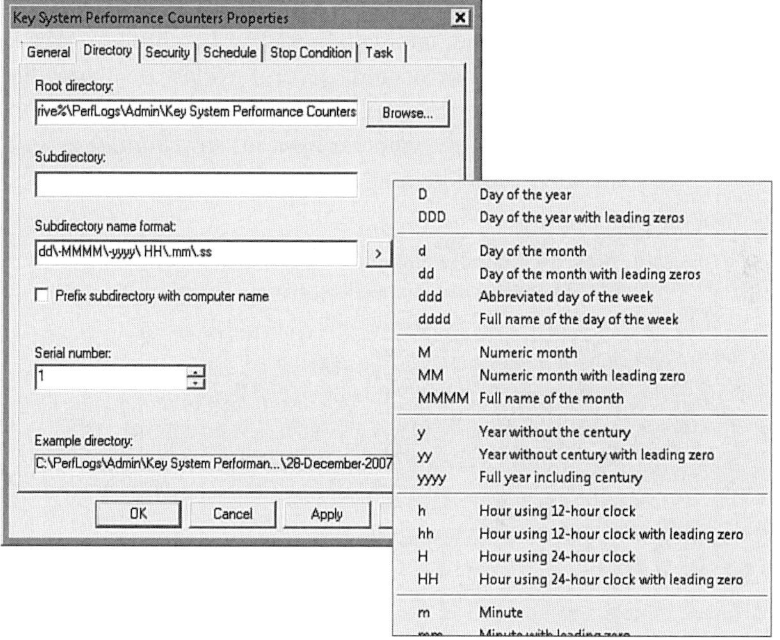

Figure 20-21 Configuring a unique subfolder name for storage of files related to a data collector set.

- **Security tab.** Allows delegation to groups and users around the usage of the data collector set—both those who can execute the set and those who can view generated data.
- **Schedule tab**. Enables the automatic execution of the data collector set on a predefined schedule and allows a start date with an optional expiration date. A time to run the set can be configured, in addition to which days of the week to perform the execution. Multiple schedules can be created, allowing any combination of executions possible.
- **Stop Condition tab.** Depending on the data being collected, you need to be able to specify when to stop collecting the data. The Stop Condition tab, shown in Figure 20-22, allows you to configure when to stop the data collector. Configure the collector to stop after a certain amount of time or when a specific limit is reached, which can be a time or when the data collection files reach a certain size. Alternatively, if the data collectors can be configured to stop after a certain action is performed, several cycles, or a specific time, you can configure the data collectors to stop after they complete collecting. Alternatively, you can have no stop condition, and you need to manually stop collecting.

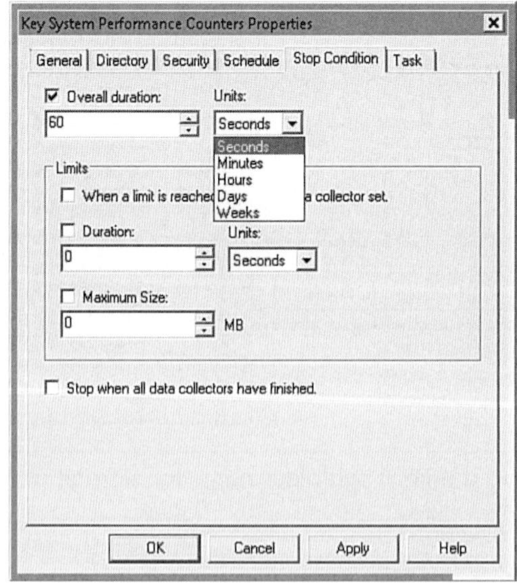

FIGURE 20-22 Configuring when the data collector should stop.

- **Task.** Allows a WMI task to be executed upon completion, which can be passed several arguments, including three special codes that can list the current log files, the running state, and a user text value.

A lot of information can be generated from the data collectors in a set. Manage this generated data via the Data Manager for a set, which is accessed via the Data Manager context menu option of a data collector set; this comprises settings related to how to handle the data, such as keeping a minimum amount of free space, specifying a maximum number of folders, and what to do regarding deleting the oldest or largest data (see Figure 20-23). The Apply Policy Before the Data Collector Set Starts check box configures the actions to occur before the next log file is created by the data collector set. Also specify a maximum total size for the folder structure associated with the set that, if reached, triggers the resource policy. Finally, configure and enable a report name and event file name via the Enable Data Management and Report Generation option. The Actions tab allows actions around older data, such as copying to a CAB file and deleting data when the data reaches a certain age or size.

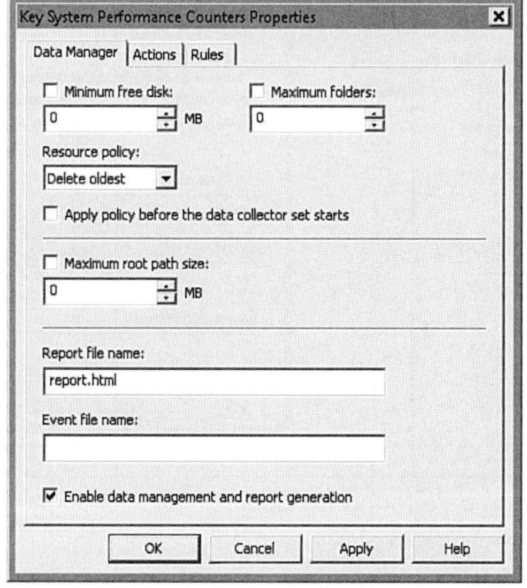

FIGURE 20-23 Data Manager options.

Adding and Configuring Data Collectors

The data set properties have been defined. Now add some actual data collectors to the set. If you created the data collector set from counters defined in Performance Monitor, you already have a data collector of type Performance Counter. Right-click it and examine its properties.

The actual properties available vary based on the type of data collector. Figure 20-24 shows a performance counter type; the Performance Counters tab shows all the counters that are being monitored. It also shows buttons to allow counters to be added or removed. To monitor every counter for a category, use the wildcard symbol (for example, Memory*). To add the wildcard, just select the category, and click Add without selecting a specific counter.

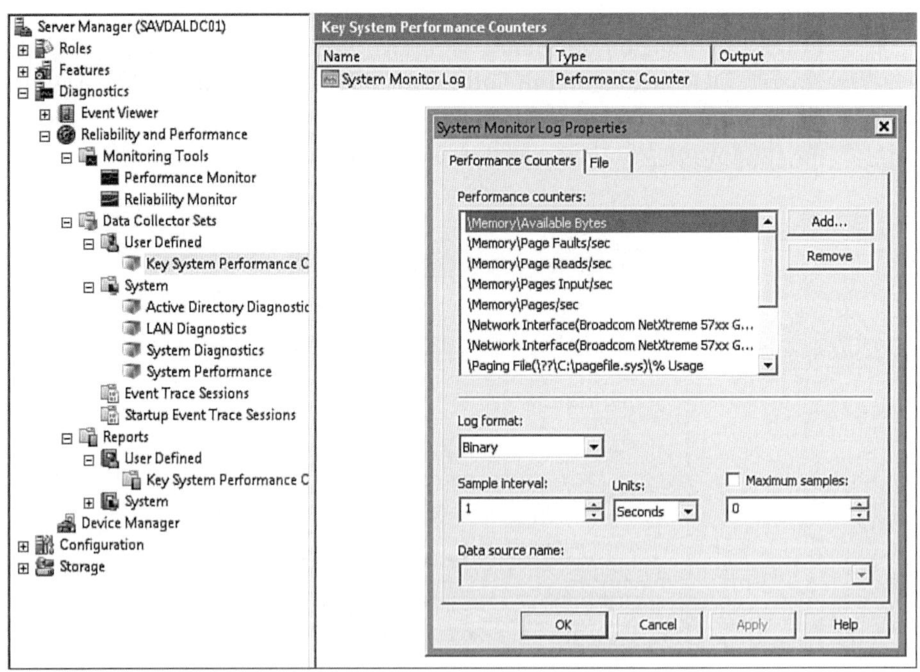

FIGURE 20-24 Properties of a Performance Counter data collector.

For a Performance Counter, select the log file format, because you will be writing to a file, in addition to how often to sample the data with an option to stop at a certain number of samples. For example, if you sample once a second and set the number of samples to 60, it stops after a minute. If the data collector set is configured with a stop condition of when all the data collectors have completed, it's important to set a maximum number of samples or the set can never finish. If, by contrast, you have configured the data collector set with a data size or time limit, you don't have to specify a maximum number of samples, but you could do it if you only needed a small amount of information about a specific data collector.

The File tab allows configuration of the name of the log file, which can be a static name; in addition, you can, like the data collector set subfolder, use a set of special characters that are expanded on to specify date and time. If you are already using a subfolder that is date and time specific for the data collector set, it's not as vital to use a unique name for the files written to by the data collector; the output will be to a unique folder each execution. Also configure the log mode for the file—that is, append data if the file already exists, overwrite existing data, or if you have a maximum file size, specify circular logging where the oldest data is overwritten as needed.

To add a new data collector to a set, right-click the set, select New from the context menu, and select Data Collector. You cannot modify the data collector sets that are part of the System—only user-defined sets.

The first page of the Create New Data Collector wizard is to give a name for the data collector and its type, which can be performance counter data, event trace data, configuration data, or performance counter alert (see Figure 20-25). The performance counter data collector is what you have seen already. It allows performance counters to be captured at a specified interval.

The Event trace data collector allows information to be captured about the system in addition to activities on the system. This is facilitated through several Event Trace Sessions listed in the Startup Event Trace Sessions child item of the Data Collector Sets console tree item, which lists all the trace sessions available and if they are enabled. If a trace session is not enabled that you want to use, right-click the item and select Start As Event Trace Session from the context menu. All the available trace sessions are found under Event Trace Sessions, including traces related to the Event Log, WMI, Spooler, and NTFS.

The Configuration data collector allows information to be read from the Registry and recorded; the performance counter alert allows information to be gathered when performance counters reach defined values that occur while the data collector set is running. It is also possible to add data from management paths, such as WMI.

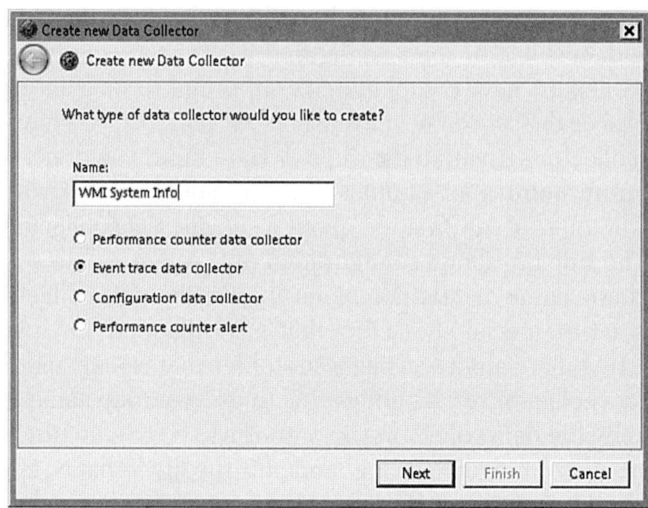

Figure 20-25 Selecting the type for a new data collector.

In this case, say that you want to capture some WMI information. Use the Configuration data collector. After the type of collector is selected, click Next to enter the details. You are prompted for Registry keys to monitor. Don't enter any keys and click Next. Then check the box to "Open properties for this data collector," and click Finish. The properties will open. Select the Management Paths tab, which enables you to add WMI paths. Click the Add button and enter the WMI query for the information you want to capture. For example, if you want to capture all the OS information, use the WMI command `root\cimv2:SELECT * FROM Win32_OperatingSystem`, as shown in Figure 20-26. Notice you can also capture file information and state information. The File tab allows configuration of where to save the information captured, which will be saved as an XML file.

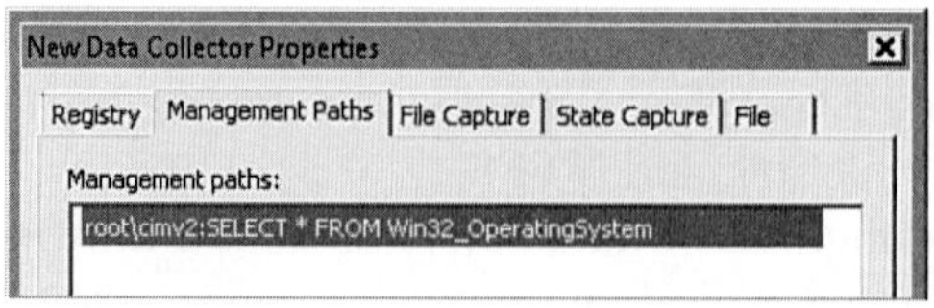

Figure 20-26 Specifying a WMI query.

Backing Up Data Collector Sets and Restoring

Once you have put in all this effort configuring a data set, it would be terrible to lose it or have to recreate it on every computer on which you want the same information. Save a data collector set as a template, which can then be imported into other machines or used as the basis for other data collector sets. Right-click on the data collector set and select "Save Template" from the context menu, which will prompt for an XML file to save the configuration of the data collector set to.

Then copy the XML file to another machine or make it available on a network location and import it by right-clicking on the User Defined–Data Collector Sets item and selecting New–Data Collector Set; this launches the Create New Data Collector Set wizard. However, unlike when you last created the data set, you now have an option to create from a template and click Next after entering a name for the data collector set.

The list of standard templates that are part of the OS are displayed (Basic, System Diagnostics, and System Performance); however, click Browse to select the XML file that was exported. At this point, click Finish or select Next to specify an alternate location to save the collected data to, in addition to specifying different credentials under which to run the data collector set.

Using a Data Collector Set

After a data collector set is created to use the collector, right-click on the set and select Start. This runs the data collectors in the set according to the configuration. While the data collectors are running, a play icon is placed over the set icon. If the data collector set has a defined time limit, it will stop on its own, or manually stop by selecting Stop from the displayed context menu.

After the data collector set has completed execution, its data is available in multiple forms. The raw data for the data collectors in the set is stored in the C:\PerfLogs\Admin\<data collector set>\<sub folder if specified> and will contain numerous files, such as a blg extension file containing the performance monitoring data, and XML files containing other types of data such as the WMI output. If you configured the data manager to produce a report, three additional files containing a summary of the data collector set execution are saved in HTML, XML, and XSL format.

Aside from going into the folder of the data collector set, the Reports console item has a similar hierarchy as the data collector set. Each data collector set has an entry and a summary of executions under the node, as shown in Figure 20-27. This gives you access to some of the data gathered.

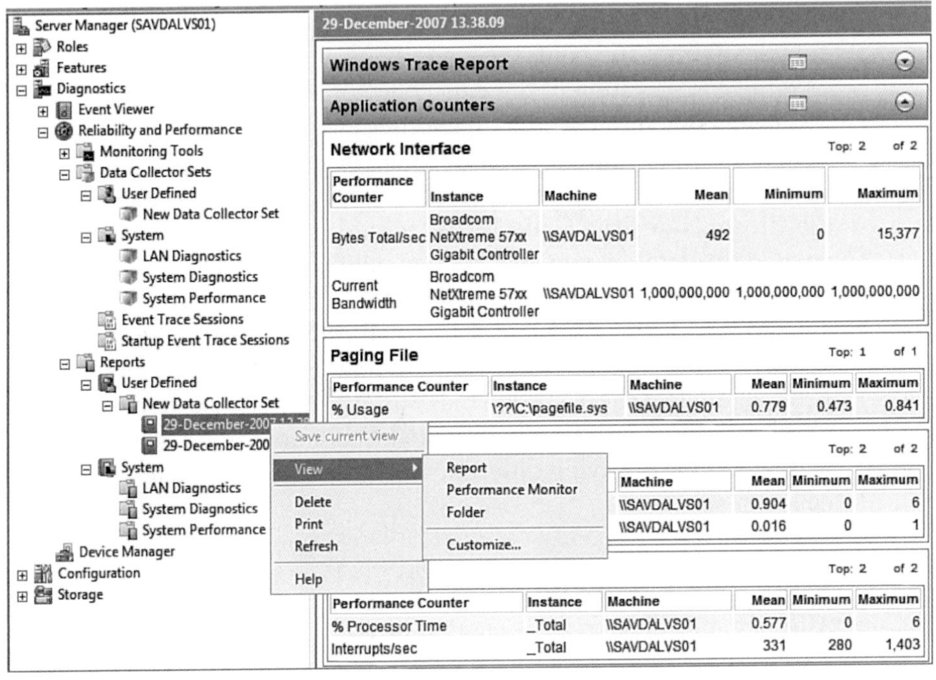

FIGURE 20-27 The cleaned-up output from a data collector set.

If the data manager is configured to create a report, the report will be displayed by default. This report gives information about trace and performance counter; however, no information from configuration data collectors is displayed. Access the XML files in the data collector set output folder to see these results.

Right-click the data collector set execution instance item to view Performance Monitor information. This information appears graphically by loading the performance counter log information into a Performance Monitor instance, as shown in Figure 20-28. Also select the Folder item to open the folder for the execution instance to get quick access to all the data collector information.

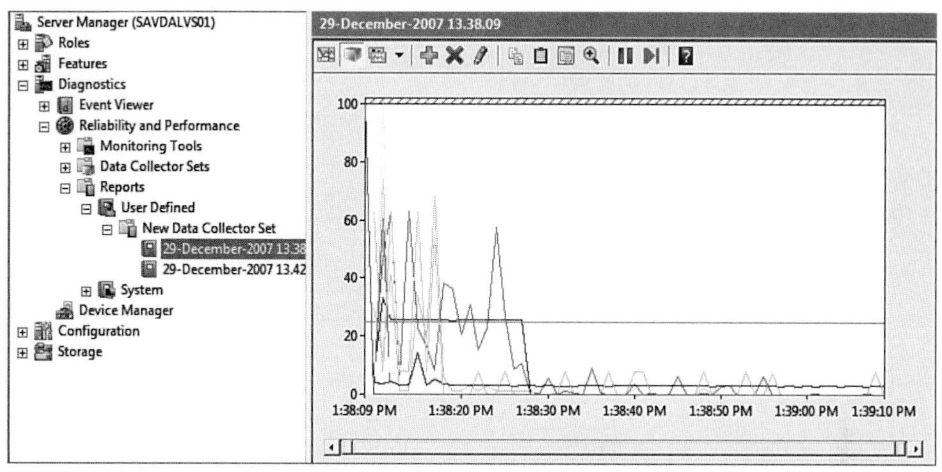

FIGURE 20-28 The Performance Monitor view of counter information from the data collector set execution.

Comparing Multiple Log Files

Although the Performance Monitor information from a data collector set is viewable via the Reports node, also load directly into the Performance Monitor by right-clicking the Performance Monitor, selecting Properties, and by the Source tab, change the data source from Current Activity to Log Files. Then, add the log files from which you want to display data. If you select a log file as the data source, the only counters you can add to the monitor are those whose data is captured in the log file.

If you start Performance Monitor in its standalone mode (perfmon /sys), you have the ability to open multiple log files concurrently and then overlay them to make it easier to compare performance. For this process to be useful, the same counters should be captured in both log files. Start two instances of Performance Monitor in stand-alone mode. In one instance, load one of the log files and add the counters. In the second instance, load the other log file. Then make one of the performance monitor instances semitransparent so it can be placed over the other performance monitor instance. To do this from the Compare menu, select either 40% or 70% transparency, as shown in Figure 20-29. After the transparency is selected, select Snap to Compare from the Compare menu to overlay the transparent performance monitor instance over the other, making it easy to compare values.

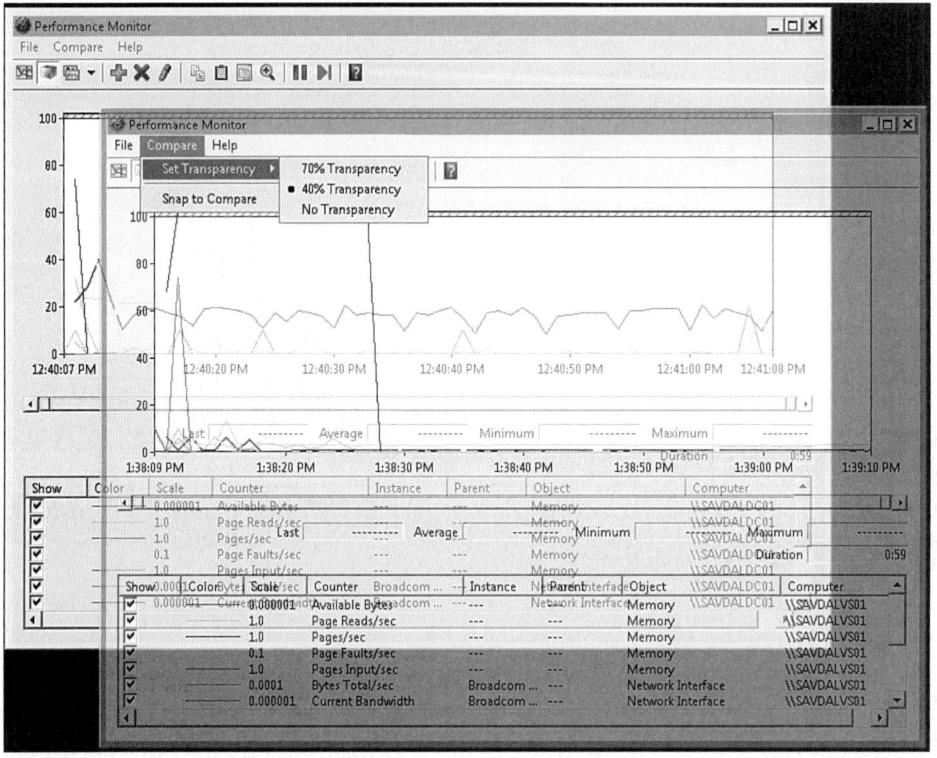

FIGURE 20-29 Comparing multiple log files.

Reliability Monitor

The Reliability Monitor is new to Windows Vista and Windows Server 2008. It indicates the stability of the system based on application, hardware, windows, and other failures, in addition to software installs and uninstalls.

As shown in Figure 20-30, for each day, the Reliability Monitor displays if there are any information, warning, or failures in each of the categories. Select the entries to get the actual driver, component, or application that the information refers to.

The Reliability Monitor gives you an idea on the quality of server's reliability. A large number of crashes or errors indicates a troublesome server that will have a lower stability index than a server that does not experience many problems. If you see more problems occurring and failures, follow the instructions that are displayed to remedy the problem.

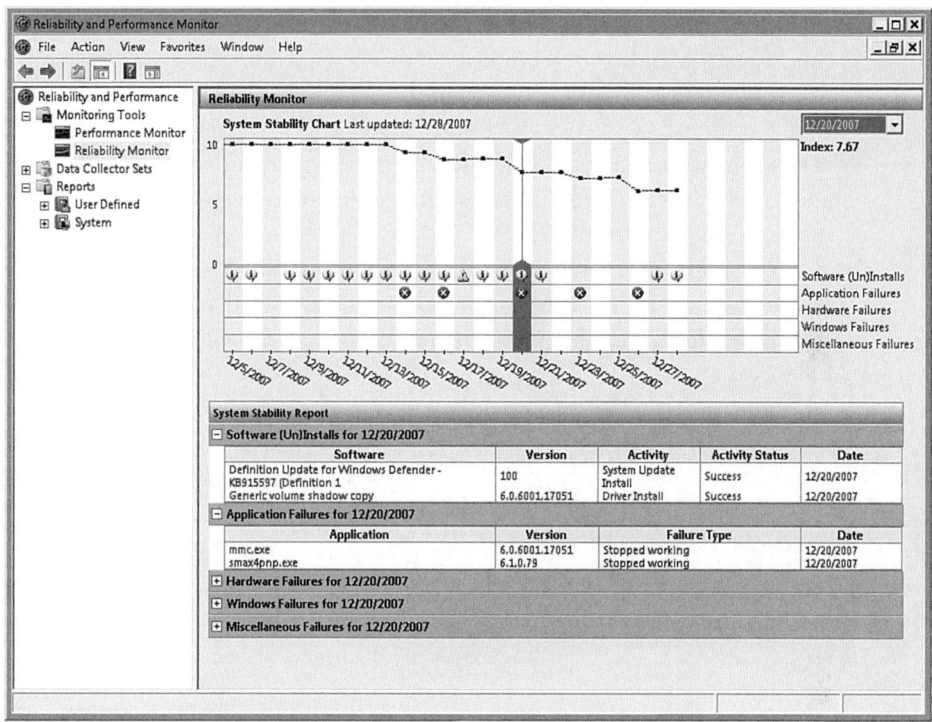

FIGURE 20-30 The Reliability Monitor.

Other Utilities

You use some tools again and again when troubleshooting performance and need information beyond what's shown in Task Manager. In 2007, Microsoft purchased Winternals.com, and made some fantastic utilities freely available that centered around core aspects of the Windows environment. Most of these utilities are still available for free (http://technet.microsoft.com/en-us/sysinternals/default.aspx). The next sections concentrate on two of the tools that relate to monitoring, Process Monitor and Process Explorer, but it is recommended that you view the site.

Process Monitor

Process Monitor allows the monitoring of all file system, Registry, thread, and DLL activity in real time. The site has several separate utilities that monitor just the Registry (regmon) or the file system (filemon); however, the Process Monitor does it all.

By default, Process Monitor monitors all processes running on the system except for the Process Monitor itself and the System process. A filter can be used to restrict actual information displayed; for example, you can add a filter so the process name has to match the program you want to monitor (see Figure 20-31).

If a program is having troubles, or you just want to see what resources it is using, use Process Monitor. This displays what is accessed and what was performed, and also shows if the resource access attempt succeeded or failed.

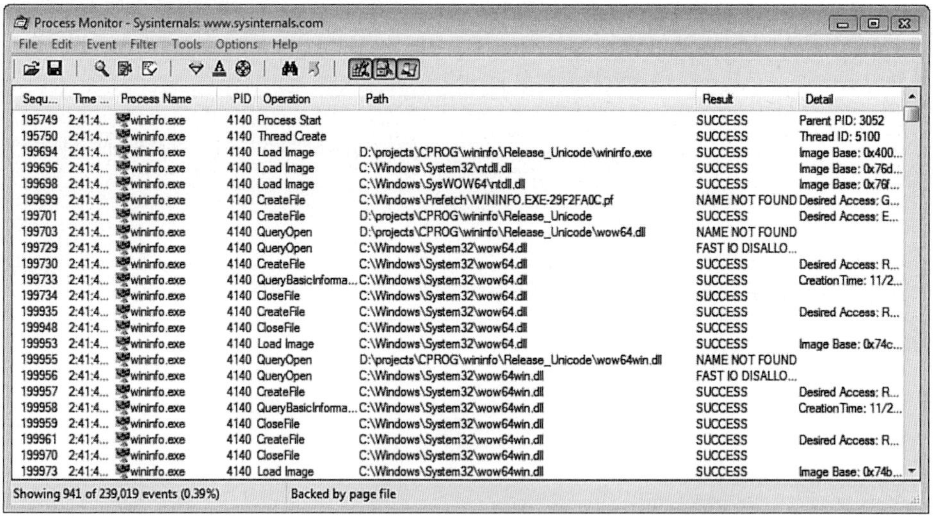

FIGURE 20-31 Process Monitor in action.

Process Explorer

Process Explorer is centered around the actual processes and allows you to view what files, Registry keys, and other handles a process is using in addition to components that it uses, such as DLLs.

As shown in Figure 20-32, select a process and all the handles and resources in use are displayed in the lower pane, which needs to be enabled via the View menu. In addition, as handles are opened and closed, they are highlighted by color to show activity. Also change processor affinity for a process and its priority via the Process Explorer, so in addition to viewing information about a process, you have some control.

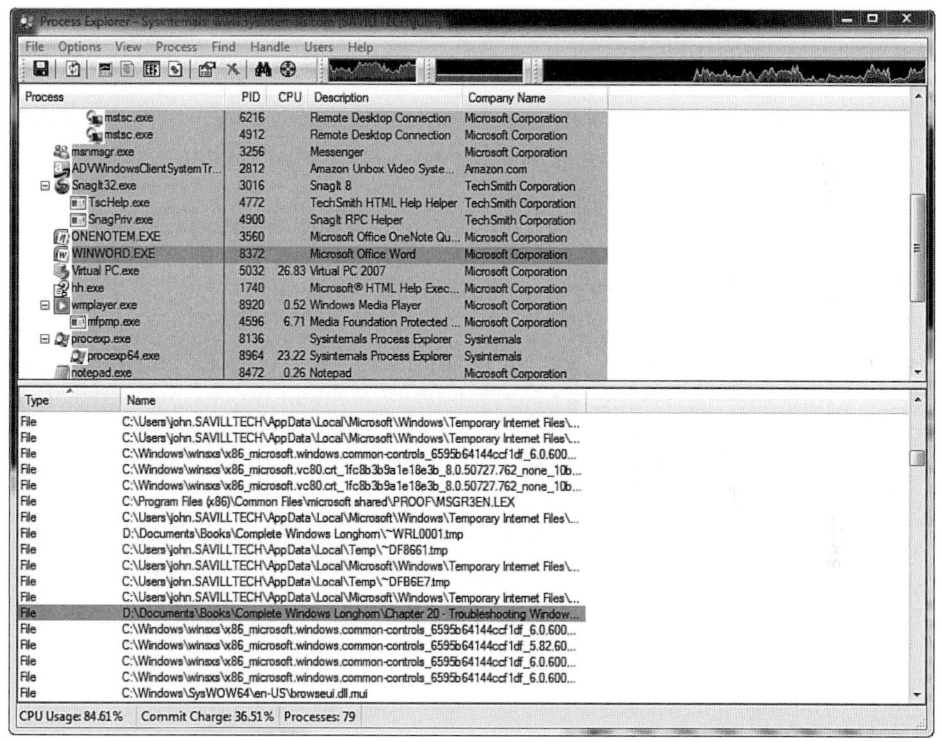

FIGURE 20-32 Process Explorer in action.

Event Viewer

The Event Viewer is the interface into a wealth of information contained in the Windows and Application/Services logs. Access the Event Viewer via the Diagnostics console tree item. Any action or problem is written into a log and, with Windows Server 2008, there are a lot of logs available. Here are three of the logs:

- **Application log**. Where applications and non-core services write information
- **Security log**. Where security information related to the system is written
- **System log**. Where logs about the system and its components write information

These logs are familiar to Windows users because they have been around since year one. All can be found under the Windows Logs node. In Windows Logs node, you also find Forwarded Events (which contains logs from other systems) and the Setup log (which contains information about role and feature configuration).

New to Windows Server 2008 is an Applications and Services group of logs. This is the solution to a crowded Application log, which is where almost everything is used to write its information, and to the solution of components, writing detailed information about processing or problems to text-based files. As shown in Figure 20-33, there are new logs for key service features, and additional logs are added as particular roles are added to the server, along with some non-OS services.

Figure 20-33 shows many other components listed under Microsoft, with these components having other logs. These include Admin, for information that administrators can act on; Analytic, which contains information on how a program is operating; Debug, for troubleshooting information; and Operational, for analyzing a component. By default, the Analytic and Debug logs are not displayed and must be enabled via the View–Show Analytic and Debug Logs action.

There are various types of event log entry. You often see Information- and Verbose-level logs, which are normal and are providing information. There are Warning-level logs, which might be an indication of a problem on the system or perhaps a misconfiguration. There are also Error-level logs, which are an actual problem that might be impacting the system's functionality, and Critical-level logs, which are failures that could not be automatically recovered from. The Security log has different types of logs, which contain Audit Success and Audit Failure type logs.

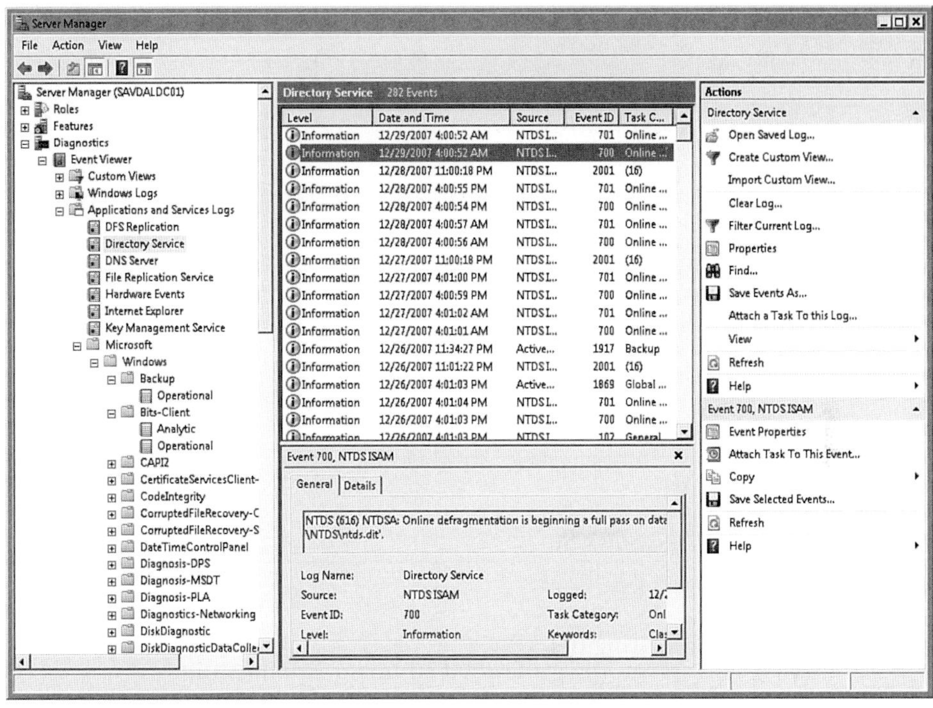

FIGURE 20-33 The Applications and Services log area.

Each event log has a source that generated the event log, and an ID that is unique for the type of the event log, which can be used to quickly search event logs for certain types of log. As shown in Figure 20-34, other information is captured, such as the date and time of the log, any keywords, and the computer. A link is also provided that redirects to a page on the Web that might contain additional information about the event log. The Details tab allows access to the raw event log information.

With Windows Server 2008, the best way to use the event logs is via the Server Manager views of roles. This is because each role's main page displays the event logs that are related to the role in one location, which are pulled from multiple event logs. These role-specific views are also available via Event Viewer in the Custom Views area, which is also used to create your own views.

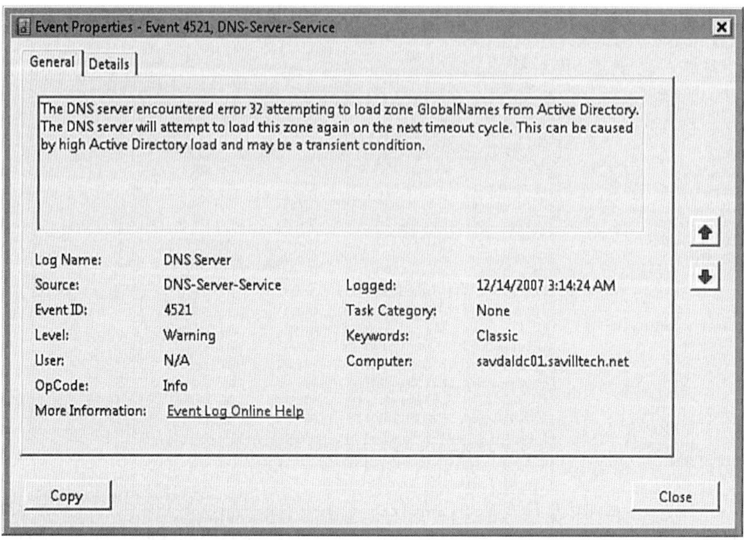

FIGURE 20-34 Example event log.

To view event logs, you need to be an Administrator or a member of the Event Log Readers group. To open the event viewer with a remote computer as the focus, start via the `eventvwr /r:<remote computer>` command.

Configuring Event Logs

Event logs require management as a lot of information is captured in the event logs, which might mean large event logs and using up large amounts of disk space. This is less of an issue today than in the past because we have such large disks. However, you still don't want to waste space and slow down the performance of your machine when you view event logs and have to trawl through 300 years of information.

In Windows Server 2008, the event logs are XML based, so it's easier to extract event log information into other applications and services that might act as consumers of event logs. When you view an event log, you have the option to see a human-friendly version of the event log and the raw XML via the Details tab.

Right-click a log (for example, Application, Security or an application/service log) and select Properties (or select Properties from the Action menu) to see details about the log. This detail includes the path to the file that contains the logs, which by default is %SystemRoot%\System32\Winevt\Logs\, and a file with an .evtx extension is specified.

The current size of the log is displayed, and a maximum log file size is specified, along with an action to perform when that maximum size is achieved. This can overwrite logs as needed, starting with the oldest logs, archiving the log when full, or not doing anything and relying on manual clearing of logs. There are implications here. Overwriting events as needed sounds like the best option; however, you are in danger of losing information. Imagine a server being compromised and your security log is configured to overwrite the oldest logs as needed. You might lose information that is needed to track what's happening. On the flip side, configuring the log to not overwrite events will cause the system to hang if the critical logs fill—such as system and security—and cannot be overwritten; the system has nowhere to write events to, so using this option is dangerous. Archiving the log is a good option for logs where information should not be lost, as events are archived as needed.

Manually archive a log by right-clicking on a log and selecting Save Events As, which prompts for a filename and folder to save to. The format to save the logs can be as an event XML file (evtx), an XML file, a tab-delimited text file, and a comma-separated text file. The format to save in depends on how you want to use the archived logs. To read the logs back into the Event Viewer, save in the evtx format. Open a saved log via the Open Saved Log action, which allows the evtx file to be selected; the log is opened in the Saved Logs area of the Event Viewer. Clear the contents of a log via the Clear Log action.

The ability to schedule a task is based around the occurrence of specific event logs. This was covered in Chapter 17, but the action in the Event Viewer is another easy interface to accomplish, triggering an action when certain events occur. A good example is if a certain warning occurred about running out of disk space, trigger an action to clean up the disk or notify the administrator.

Event Filtering

There are a huge number of potential logs on a system, so the ability to view only certain logs is vital. There are two ways of doing this. Create a custom view of the event log information, as previously covered. (Server Manager does this to show information related to the selected role.)

Alternatively, apply a filter to the currently selected event log, which is essentially the same thing as a view, except a view can display information from multiple event logs.

The process to create a custom view involves specifying which sources of event logs you want to include and the specific types of log you want to see. Custom views are stored under the Custom Views section of the Event Viewer; initiate the creation of a custom view from any event log via the Create Custom View action. This automatically sets the currently selected log as the source for the custom view. Or just create directly in the Custom Views section.

Figure 20-35 shows several configurable options. The first option is the Logged option which enables you to display logs only in the last 12 hours, 24 hours, 7 days, 30 days, or some other custom range. This option is used by the server role's screen to display only the last 24 hours of logs. It helps get a quick view of recent events because only events in the last 24 hours are displayed; if you see an error, you know it happened recently.

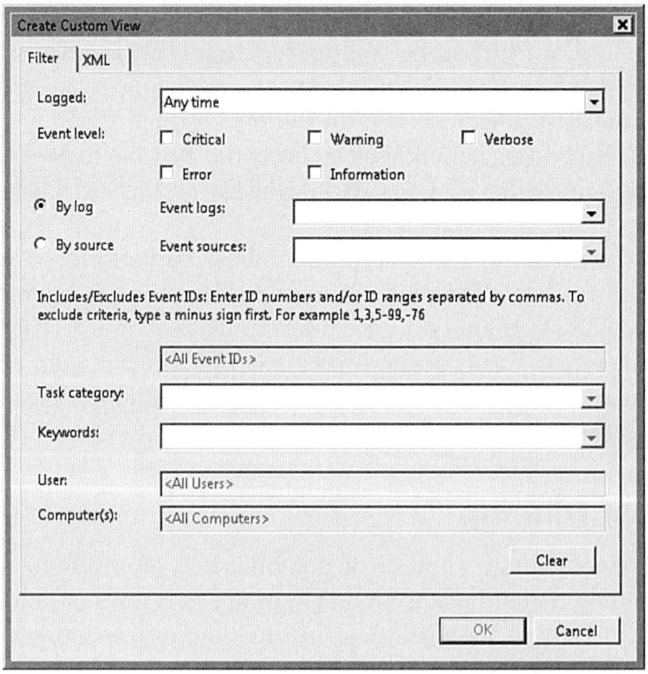

FIGURE 20-35 Creating a custom view.

The next item allows the selection of the event levels to display; for example, you might only want to see Critical, Error, and Warning logs, so you would select these options.

Next, select which events you want to see by which event log you will read from—for example, Security, System, Backup Operational log via the "By log" option, which allows the desired logs to be selected (see Figure 20-36). This can also be done by the source that generates the event log, which gives a list of all components on the system that generate event logs (for example, Winlogon, Task Scheduler), as shown in Figure 20-37. Choose only either event log or event source; you can't use a combination. However, both types are check boxes for their component logs/sources, allowing events to come from multiple logs/sources in a single view.

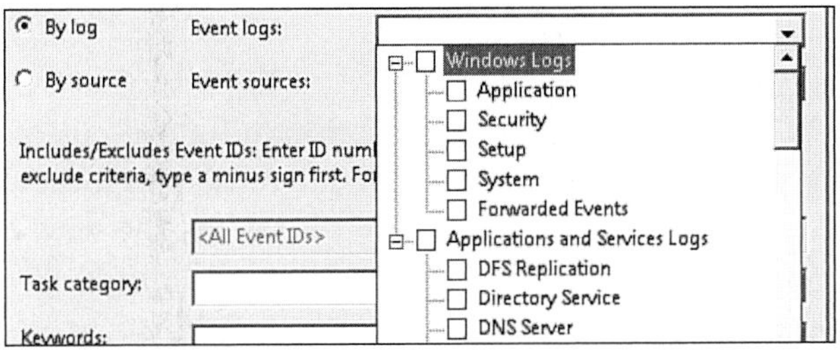

FIGURE 20-36 Selecting which logs to view in the custom view.

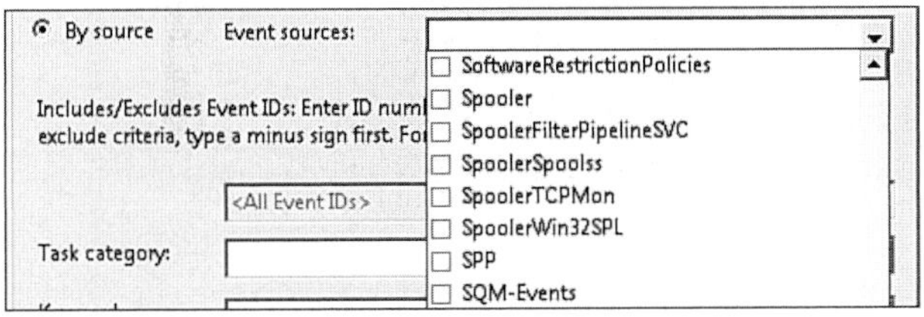

FIGURE 20-37 Selecting which sources to view in the custom view.

After selecting the source/log for the events, enter more granular view criteria, such as only viewing particular event IDs that you want to look for. Enter multiple event IDs separated via a comma or a range using the `<start event ID>-<end event ID>` format (for example, 5200–5205). If you don't want to view a certain event log, add a minus sign in front of it (such as –5204).

Also enter task categories and keywords from the drop-down list (if appropriate) for the source or logs selected. Display logs only for certain users and computers and separate multiple values by a comma.

The XML tab shows the actual XML that is used to construct the query. You directly enter XML via the Edit Query Manually button. Here is an example XML for a query that displays Critical, Error, and Warning event levels from the System log that happened in the last seven days:

```
<QueryList>
  <Query Id="0" Path="System">
    <Select Path="System">*[System[(Level=1  or Level=2 or
Level=3) and TimeCreated[timediff(@SystemTime) &lt;=
604800000]]]</Select>
  </Query>
</QueryList>
```

Finally, select a name and description for the custom filter and where to store it under Custom Views. Create folders to form a hierarchy of your views, as shown in Figure 20-38. After saving, the view is now available in the custom views and shows the applicable events.

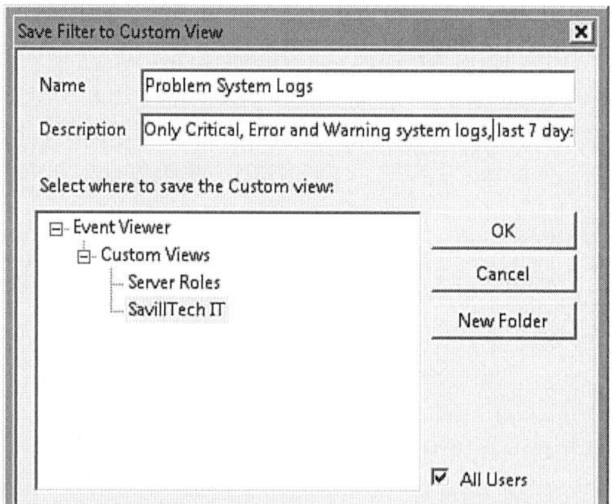

FIGURE 20-38 Saving the new custom view.

Custom views can be exported by the Export Custom View action. This saves the view to an XML file, which can be imported into other computers via the Import Custom View action. If you want another custom view on the same computer based on an existing custom view, select the Copy Custom View action, which enables a new name and location to be specified, and then customize the Filter via the Edit action for the view.

A custom view is great for a long-term, frequent need. The other option is when you are looking at an event log or custom view and want to view only some of the logs, filter down what you see. This is accomplished via the Filter action, which will be Filter Current Log or Filter Current View, depending on what entity currently has focus.

The Filter dialog is exactly the same as creating a custom view; select a logged time for the logs to display, the event levels, event ID, task, keyword, user, and computer. Everything is the same except you cannot select a log or source; you are filtering the events in the selected container, which is an event log or view. If you want to remove the filter, select the Clear Filter action or modify the filter by selecting the Filter action once more. If you create a filter that you want to be able to use again, run the Save Filter to Custom View option, which creates a custom view based on the filter that is currently being used. Also save all the logs that match the filter to a file via the Save Filtered Log File As—you have a lot of power with the filters.

A filter is great if you have a clear idea of what you are looking for—that is, you know that you want to see warnings or want to see event ID 7036; however, there might be times where you want to search a log for a text string. Maybe you want to see if there are any messages regarding a certain package or component; in this case, select an event log or view and select the Find action. This allows a text string to be entered, which is searched for in the entire event log and the match found.

Event Subscriptions

It is possible to subscribe to event logs from remote computers via an event subscription; however, configuration is required. On the remote computer, the Windows Remote Management (WinRM) service must be enabled along with the required firewall exception, which can be quickly configured via the `winrm quickconfig` command:

```
C:\>winrm quickconfig
WinRM is not set up to allow remote access to this machine for
management.
```

```
The following changes must be made:

Create a WinRM listener on HTTP://* to accept WS-Man requests
to any IP on this machine.
Enable the WinRM firewall exception.

Make these changes [y/n]? y

WinRM has been updated for remote management.

Created a WinRM listener on HTTP://* to accept WS-Man requests
to any IP on this machine.
WinRM firewall exception enabled.
```

The Windows Event Collector service must also be configured. Again, there is a quick configuration option. Run this command on the computer that collects the event logs:

```
C:\>wecutil qc
The service startup mode will be changed to Delay-Start. Would
you like to proceed ( Y- yes or N- no)?y
Windows Event Collector service was configured successfully.
```

Finally, add the computer account of the collecting server to the local Administrators group of the servers from which data is being collected. Remember to change the object type to computer when adding a computer account via the Local users and computers MMC snap-in.

Now subscribe to a remote event log. Select the Subscriptions console tree item and select the Create Subscription action. The properties for the new subscription opens, as shown in Figure 20-39. This allows a name and description for the subscription to be entered, in addition to selecting the computer whose events are subscribed to via the Select Computers button. It is also possible to initiate the feed of event logs from the source computer; however, this is a more complicated but a better option if you subscribe to many machines (it's covered in the 2008 help file). After you select the computer, click the Test button in the Select Computer dialog to ensure communication is possible.

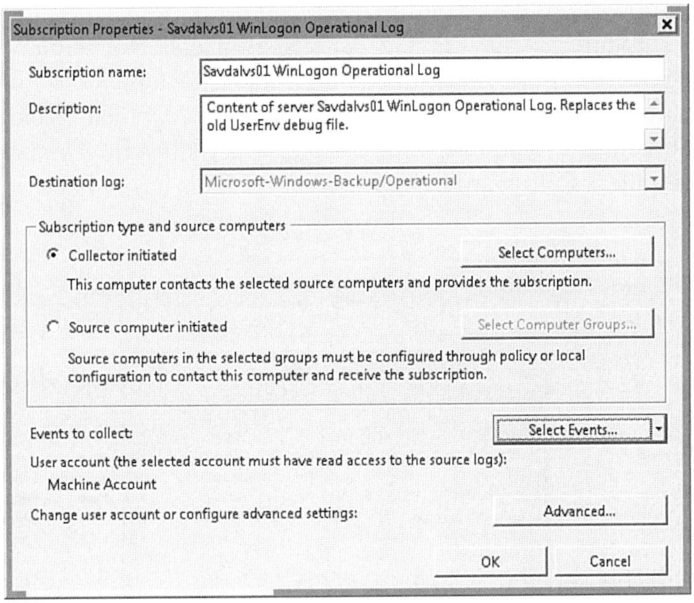

Figure 20-39 Adding a new subscription.

Finally, the events to subscribe to must be selected via the Select Events button, which uses the same Query Filter dialog box discussed in the last section. Select the event logs and types of events to subscribe to and click OK. The Advanced button allows configuration of the account used to read the event logs and the event delivery option. Because you are pulling the logs, the default pulls logs every 15 minutes in batches of five; you can change the number of batched items via the `winrm` command. There must be no space in the `winrm/config` component of the command:

```
Winrm set winrm/config @{MaxBatchItems="10"}
Winrm get winrm/config
```

Also select a Minimize Latency option. It receives logs every 30 seconds, but this makes far more chatter on the network. If the collection of logs is not urgent, select Minimize Bandwidth, which receives logs every six hours.

The subscription shows in the Subscriptions area, and events from other systems will be written into the Forwarded Events area under

Windows Logs based on the event delivery optimization that was selected (see Figure 20-40). This is known as a collector-initiated subscription because you perform all the configuration from the collector machine and detail the types of events you collect and from which machines. A source-initiated subscription is also possible, which is useful if you configure many computers to forward events to a server. This has a slightly different set of steps.

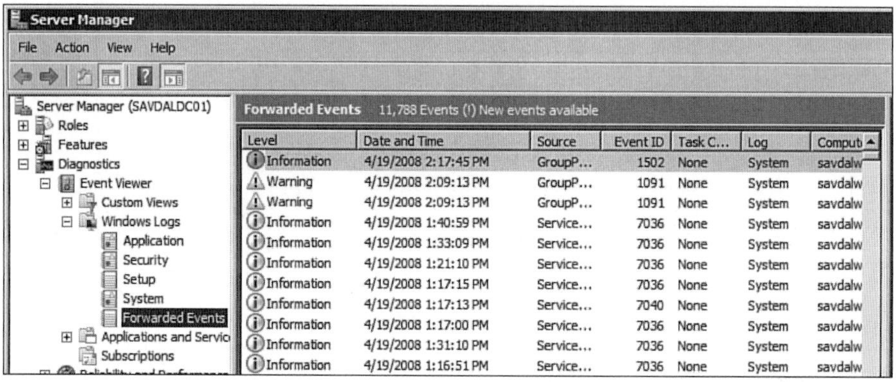

FIGURE 20-40 Viewing events gathered via a subscription. In hindsight, I should have picked a computer I was not currently installing Visual Studio 2008 on as the source machine.

On the source computer, run the winrm quickconfig because you use WS-Management; this time, however, also enable on the collector computer for WS-Management using the same winrm quickconfig, and then once again perform a quick configuration of the Windows event collector using the wecutil qc. So far, this is no different; you just configured WS-Management service on the collector in addition to the sources.

On each of the source computers, configure them with a subscription manager that they will use for their configuration, which can be set using local policy or via group policy, which can be applied to multiple servers. The setting is found under Computer Configuration—Administrative Templates—Windows Components—Event Forwarding. Double-click "Configure the server address, refresh interval, and issuer certificate authority of a target Subscription Manager." Enable the policy setting and click the Show button, which opens up a dialog to configure the subscription managers, as shown in Figure 20-41. Click the Add button and enter the URL of the subscription manager. HTTP is used in this example because the certificates are not configured for encrypted communication. You can have multiple subscription managers for one client. Click OK to all dialogs and then refresh the policy on the clients gpupdate /force.

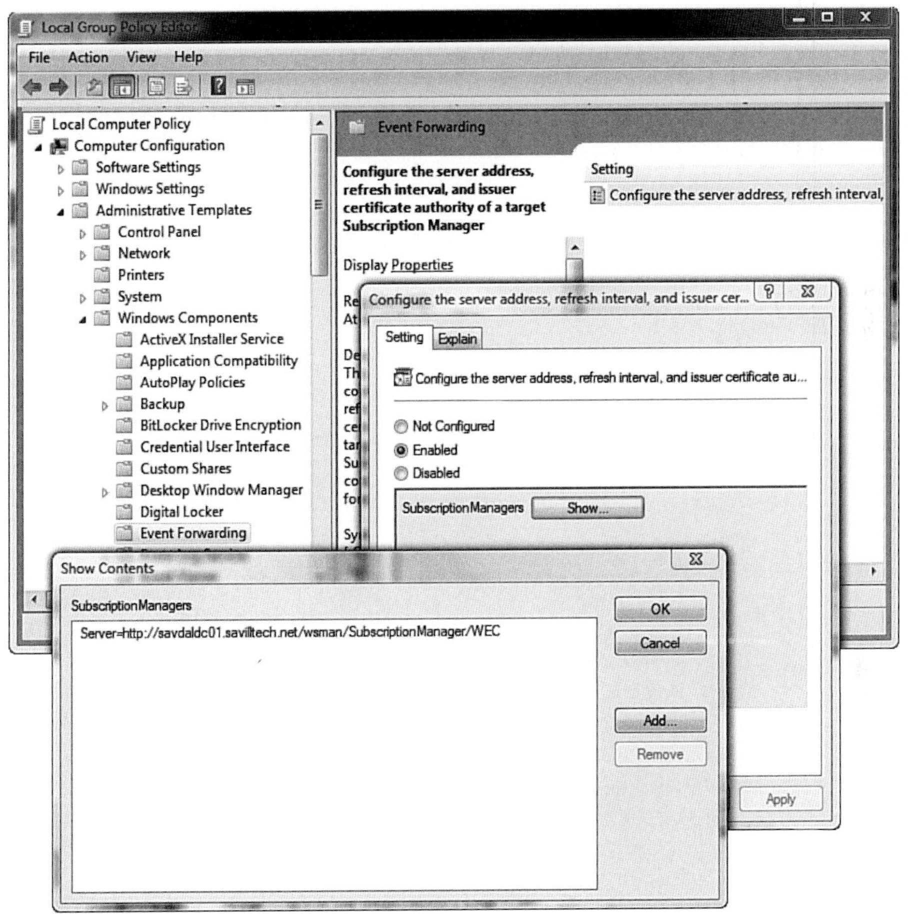

Figure 20-41 Configuring a subscription manager.

The final action is to import a subscription configuration in the collector machine, which will then be read in by the source computers at a refresh interval. If the subscription applies to them, the source computers send the events described in the subscription. A source computer can be part of multiple subscriptions to multiple machines.

The format of a subscription file is shown next. It applies to all source domain computers (that have the policy applied with the server as its subscription manager) and sends all system event logs. Modify the Select line (<Select>*</Select>) to gather only the logs you are interested in, plus change the Query Path to another event log. Note that <ReadExistingEvents> is set to true; this means you get all the current logs. Set this to false if you want only new ones!

```
<Subscription xmlns="http://schemas.microsoft.com/2006/03/
windows/events/subscription">
    <SubscriptionId>SourceInitiated</SubscriptionId>
    <SubscriptionType>SourceInitiated</SubscriptionType>
    <Description>Source Initiated Subscription Sample</
Description>
    <Enabled>true</Enabled>
    <Uri>http://schemas.microsoft.com/wbem/wsman/1/windows/
EventLog</Uri>

    <!-- Use Normal (default), Custom, MinLatency, MinBandwidth
-->
    <ConfigurationMode>Custom</ConfigurationMode>

    <Delivery Mode="Push">
        <Batching>
            <MaxItems>1</MaxItems>
            <MaxLatencyTime>1000</MaxLatencyTime>
        </Batching>
        <PushSettings>
            <Heartbeat Interval="60000"/>
        </PushSettings>
    </Delivery>

    <Expires>2018-01-01T00:00:00.000Z</Expires>

    <Query>
        <![CDATA[
            <QueryList>
                <Query Path="System">
                    <Select>*</Select>
                </Query>
```

```
            </QueryList>
        ]]>
    </Query>

    <ReadExistingEvents>true</ReadExistingEvents>
    <TransportName>http</TransportName>
    <ContentFormat>RenderedText</ContentFormat>
    <Locale Language="en-US"/>
    <LogFile>ForwardedEvents</LogFile>
    <AllowedSourceNonDomainComputers></AllowedSourceNonDomain-
Computers>

<AllowedSourceDomainComputers>O:NSG:NSD:(A;;GA;;;DC)(A;;GA;;;NS
)</AllowedSourceDomainComputers>
</Subscription>
```

Finally, import the subscription into your machine:

```
Wecutil cs <configuration file>.xml
```

Check if the subscription has been added using the `es` switch, as shown next. There are two event subscriptions. The first is the one that was collector initiated; the second is source imitated (a better name probably could have been chosen here):

```
C:\temp>wecutil es
savdaldc02 System Event Log
SourceInitiated
```

Get details of a subscription using the `gs` switch and get the current status using the `gr` switch. Use the ID of the subscription, so if you have spaces in the name, put the subscription ID in double quotes:

```
C:\temp>wecutil gs "savdaldc02 system event log"
Subscription Id: savdaldc02 system event log
SubscriptionType: CollectorInitiated
Description:
Enabled: true
Uri: http://schemas.microsoft.com/wbem/wsman/1/windows/
EventLog
ConfigurationMode: Normal
```

```
DeliveryMode: Pull
DeliveryMaxLatencyTime: 900000
HeartbeatInterval: 900000
Query: <QueryList><Query Id="0"><Select Path="System">*
[System[(Level=1  or Level=2 or Level=3 or Level=4 or Level=0
or Level=5)]]</Select></Query></QueryList>
ReadExistingEvents: false
TransportName: HTTP
TransportPort: 80
ContentFormat: RenderedText
Locale: en-US
LogFile: ForwardedEvents
PublisherName: microsoft-windows-eventcollector
CredentialsType: Default

EventSource[0]:
        Address: SAVDALDC02.savilltech.net
        Enabled: true

C:\temp>wecutil gr "savdaldc02 system event log"

Subscription: savdaldc02 system event log
        RunTimeStatus: Active
        LastError: 0
        EventSources:
                SAVDALDC02.savilltech.net
                        RunTimeStatus: Active
                        LastError: 0

C:\temp>wecutil gr SourceInitiated

Subscription: SourceInitiated
        RunTimeStatus: Active
        LastError: 0
        EventSources:
                savdalwks01.savilltech.net
                        RunTimeStatus: Active
                        LastError: 0
                        LastHeartbeatTime: 2008-04-
19T14:23:26.299
```

Hopefully, you can see when to use each option. To get events just from a few computers, you can use collector initiated. To get subscriptions to many machines, then source initiated is easier; configure the subscription detail once, and then any machine that has the collector server defined as a subscription manager sees the subscription and sends events. Use group policy to deploy the subscription setting to many machines.

To delete a subscription, use the `ds` switch (for example, `wecutil ds SourceInitiated`). Remember that you have to wait for machines to see the subscription before logs start flowing, so don't panic if logs don't appear instantly.

Command-Line Access

As with most of the components in Windows Server 2008, manage event logs from the command line. This includes configuration of the size of event logs, the actions to take when that size is hit, and viewing the content of event logs.

Some items can be configured only via the graphical interface, such as creating views and filtering; however, because these are graphical in nature, this limitation is not significant.

The command-line interface for the Event Viewer is wevutil.exe. Let's look at a number of options. To clear an event log and first back up its content, use the `CL` command with the name of the log to clear and the `/bu` switch with the name of the file to back up the logs to. The following command clears the application log and backs up to the d:\temp\application.evtx file. To archive without clearing the log, use the `EPL` command, specifying the log and filename to export to:

```
wevtutil cl application /bu:d:\temp\application.evtx
```

To configure a log's maximum size, use the `SL` command with the `/ms` switch, specifying the maximum size of the log in bytes (for example, `wevtutil sl <log name> /ms:<size in bytes>`). To set the retention policy, use a combination of the `/r` switch for retention and the `/ab` switch for automatic backup. To match the options in the GUI, set the switches as follows:

- Overwrite events as needed: `/r:false /ab:false`
- Archive the log when full; do not overwrite events: `/r:true /ab:true`
- Do not overwrite events (clear logs manually): `/r:true /ab:false`

Use these commands against a remote computer by adding the `/r` switch with the name of the remote computer—for example, `/r:<remote computer name>`—plus an optional username and password switches (`/u` and `/p`).

Query the event log via `wevtutil`, as well as via the `QE` command with the name of the log, and pass the number of events to return via the `/c` switch. Because you most likely want to see the newest events, enable the reverse direction via `/rd:true` with the output in text format (`/f:text`). In this case, query the system log and view the top two events:

```
C:\>wevtutil qe system /rd:true /c:2 /f:text
Event[0]:
  Log Name: System
  Source: Service Control Manager
  Date: 2007-12-30T17:28:17.000
  Event ID: 7036
  Task: N/A
  Level: Information
  Opcode: N/A
  Keyword: Classic
  User: N/A
  User Name: N/A
  Computer: savdaldc01.savilltech.net
  Description:
The Windows Modules Installer service entered the running
state.

Event[1]:
  Log Name: System
  Source: Service Control Manager
  Date: 2007-12-30T17:27:44.000
  Event ID: 7036
  Task: N/A
  Level: Information
```

```
  Opcode: N/A
  Keyword: Classic
  User: N/A
  User Name: N/A
  Computer: savdaldc01.savilltech.net
  Description:
The Windows Modules Installer service entered the stopped
state.
```

To view specific event logs, pass a query via the `/q` switch. Also search for specific event IDs (for example, to search for system OS information, which is event ID 6009 generated when a server boots). Use the same format command. Again, you see the most recent first via the `/rd:true` switch:

```
C:\>wevtutil qe system /q:*[System[(EventID=6009)]] /rd:true
➥/f:text /c:1
Event[0]:
  Log Name: System
  Source: EventLog
  Date: 2007-12-26T15:45:57.000
  Event ID: 6009
  Task: N/A
  Level: Information
  Opcode: N/A
  Keyword: Classic
  User: N/A
  User Name: N/A
  Computer: savdaldc01.savilltech.net
  Description:
Microsoft (R) Windows (R) 6.00. 6001 Service Pack 1, v.667
Multiprocessor Free.
```

Look at the XML used for a custom view to get help in viewing the format of query commands. For example, your custom view had the following search criterion to view the last seven days of critical, error, and warning logs:

```
*[System[(Level=1  or Level=2 or Level=3) and
TimeCreated[timediff(@SystemTime) &lt;= 604800000]]]
```

Apply that to your search and see the most recent one. Because you have spaces in the filter, place the query in double quotes, as follows:

```
C:\>wevtutil qe system /q:"*[System[(Level=1  or Level=2 or
➥Level=3) and TimeCreated[timediff(@SystemTime) <=
➥604800000]]]" /rd:true /f:text /c:1
Event[0]:
  Log Name: System
  Source: Microsoft-Windows-Kerberos-Key-Distribution-Center
  Date: 2007-12-30T09:45:49.000
  Event ID: 29
  Task: N/A
  Level: Warning
  Opcode: N/A
  Keyword: Classic
  User: N/A
  User Name: N/A
  Computer: savdaldc01.savilltech.net
  Description:
The Key Distribution Center (KDC) cannot find a suitable cer-
tificate to use for smart card logons, or the KDC certificate
could not be verified. Smart card logon may not function cor-
rectly if this problem is not resolved. To correct this prob-
lem, either verify the existing KDC certificate using
certutil.exe or enroll or a new KDC certificate.
```

MSConfig

The msconfig.exe utility can be used for detailed system configuration. The General tab of MSConfig allows configuration of the type of startup used at next boot. By default, this is Normal; however, a diagnostic startup can be selected. Diagnostic startup is essentially Safe Mode startup; there is also a selective startup option, which is Safe Mode plus selected services and startup programs that can be user selected.

The Boot tab, shown in Figure 20-42, allows options for the next boot to be selected. In addition, if the "Make all boot settings permanent" is selected, these options become the new defaults for the selected OS. The advanced options allow configuration of the number of processors that can be seen by the OS, in addition to a maximum amount of memory. You can also set generic options, such as the timeout for the display of the boot menu and setting the default OS.

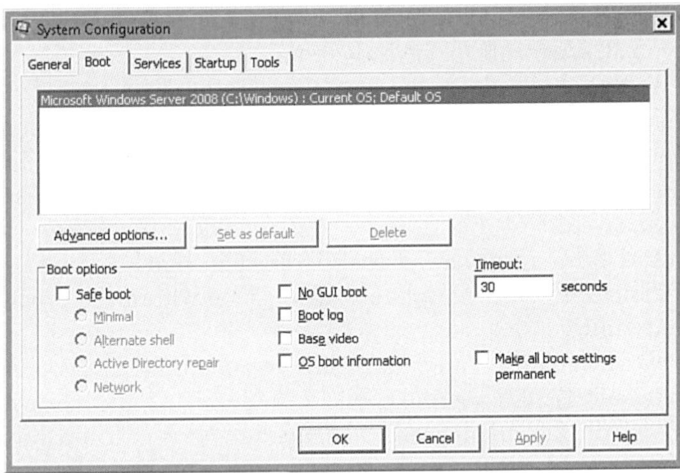

FIGURE 20-42 The boot options via MSConfig.

The Services tab allows control of which services will start at boot time, whereas the Startup tab allows configuration of the applications that launch at boot time and the location of the execution is shown (for example, the Registry RUN locations).

The Tools tab lists the most popular configuration tools available, with a description of what the tool does. Select the tool and click Launch to start.

Windows Error Reporting

When a crash occurs under Windows Server 2008 (and Vista), the error handling is performed via the Windows Error Reporting (WER) service. This is implemented via Wersvc.dll; this service calls the WER Fault Reporting executable, Werfault.exe, to display the actual crash dialog. Dr Watson is still alive in the form of the dwwin.exe executable; however, it is not used in the normal WER process. The advantage of moving the error handling out of the crashing process is if the crash was severe enough, it might not be possible to gather the data needed. The Dr Watson process used to be a child process of the crashing application, as opposed to a separate entity, which means Dr Watson would not run to help troubleshoot. The data gathered can then be sent to Microsoft, and a solution might be available, which is communicated back to the server or is logged at Microsoft for investigation.

You might prefer to not have your crash information from your servers and all your clients being sent directly to Microsoft; thus, you might implement WER services locally, which is a server that is housed in an organization. The data gathered by WER is sent to this server instead of Microsoft. Administrators of the in-house WER services server can then selectively forward error information to Microsoft in batches, and also get a good understanding of the problems being seen within the organization by the clients and servers.

WER services is not a major implementation task; you install the WER server, and then use group policies to configure the error-reporting components on the organization's clients and servers to forward to the WER server instead of Microsoft. To get access to WER, see the following web site: http://msdn2.microsoft.com/en-us/isv/bb190483.aspx.

NOTE If you are interested in the actual data Microsoft collects, read their privacy statement, which is available at http://oca.microsoft.com/en/dcp20.asp.

System Center

Microsoft previously had separate solutions for the management of the environment in the form of Systems Management Server (SMS) 2003 and monitoring in the form of Microsoft Operations Manager (MOM) 2005. In 2007, however, these products, along with new solutions, were combined under the System Center family umbrella.

System Center provides the solutions for the complete management of the IT infrastructure from a planning, deployment, management, monitoring, and optimization perspective. To achieve this, System Center comprises the following products. Each can be purchased and licensed separately—think of System Center as a new branding.

System Center Operations Manager

System Center Operations Manager (SCOM) is the latest version of the rebranded MOM product line—essentially MOM v3. SCOM provides detailed insight into the overall health of your IT infrastructure by monitoring key elements of the infrastructure; for example, performance counters and event logs.

SCOM has sets of knowledge known as Management Packs. Each understands a particular facet of the IT infrastructure. For example, there is an Active Directory Management Pack, DNS Management Pack, and Exchange 2007 Management Pack. These packs have specific product knowledge that help the SCOM agent, which runs on the server and knows what attributes on the server to look for. With some products such as SQL Server, the Management Pack might use synthetic transactions, which are transactions used by the Management Pack just to ensure connectivity and functionality of the target service. Microsoft provides Management Packs for nearly all their products, and additional Management Packs can be purchased for other non-Microsoft solutions, such as Unix platforms, Cisco switches, and so on. SCOM also supports industry standard SNMP communications for more basic monitoring of non-Microsoft services.

With this product expertise, SCOM has the ability to monitor services rather than specific products. For example, SCOM understands that messaging requires the Exchange server to be functioning, but also DNS services, Active Directory, and overall connectivity; thus, all of these components are combined to give an overall health state that messaging is performed. General views can be created showing basic traffic light health status of components, which can then be drilled into to get detail on the components making up a service.

In the event of a problem, SCOM has powerful notification options to alert operators that remedial actions are necessary; the real power of SCOM is its preventive nature and the ability to detect problems or non-best practice configurations before they impact service delivery. Although this alerting piece has always required a lot of expert tuning, the amount of effort has been reduced with SCOM 2007, thanks to self-tuning capabilities that automatically learn a normal threshold of activity and only alert for items outside of the "norm."

System Center Configuration Manager

System Center Configuration Manager (SCCM) is the newest version of the rebranded SMS product line, so SMSv4 includes all the functionality of SMS 2003 plus the additional feature packs and more. Where SCOM monitors, SCCM helps manage. SCCM attacks key areas of both desktop and server management, as follows:

- **OS Deployment**. SCCM has native support for the imaging format used for Windows Vista and Windows Server 2008, along with tools to help capture and create images of older OSs. Powerful task sequencing allows configuration of disk partitions, deployment of the OS, and then applications installed and patched. SCCM also has offline capabilities that allow an entire OS deployment process to be written to media, such as a DVD, which can then be sent to remote systems. This media contains not just the OS but any applicable applications and configuration. SCCM also has an online driver library allowing OS images to be standard for the organization and hardware-specific drivers downloaded during the OS installation from a central driver store.
- **Patching**. SCCM contains updated patching components, which use Windows Software Update Servers to ascertain available fixes for Microsoft products, and then package and deploy to the clients and servers in the enterprise. Support for deployment over Internet protocols is now included, meaning mobile clients no longer have to VPN into the office to obtain patches and applications. Maintenance windows can be defined for collections of computers to patches (and applications) and are only advertised at predefined maintenance times; this is useful for servers.
- **Application Deployment**. Microsoft Installer (MSI) packaged applications are easily deployed with SCCM, as well as non-MSI packages.
- **Inventory**. In addition to pushing information, the SCCM agent captures information from the machines from both a hardware and software perspective. This information is highly detailed, enabling reporting on machines of a certain processor specification, free disk space, and who has software installed.

- **Metering**. One step further than inventory is metering that, for selected applications, identifies how often and for what duration applications are run.
- **Reporting**. Built on SQL Report services, all information known to SCCM can be reported on—for example, a detailed report of OS deployment status, patches deployed in the environment, machines that are compatible with Windows Vista, and so on.
- **Desired Configuration**. This allows Configuration Items (CI) to be defined for computers, which describe how elements of the environment should be configured. If the configuration of a computer drifts away from the CI, this will be detected and can be corrected. This is considered to be an important feature because research shows a lot of system downtime is caused by misconfiguration.
- **Mobile Devices**. Full hardware, software, and file inventory for mobile devices, in addition to deploying software. Password and security policies can also be set.

System Center Data Protection Manager

The concepts of data recovery and data backup traditionally are handled by separate solutions. Data Protection Manager (DPM) builds on the Volume Shadow Copy functionality present in Windows Server 2003 that allows a share to periodically take snapshots of its content; this enables users to access previous point-in-time views of the share content and restore data as needed without involving administrators, and moves the snapshot cache to a centralized storage location managed by the DPM server.

The data protected by DPM is backed up to disk and then can also be copied from the disk backup to tape storage, which removes the need for the main server to be down for long periods as its data is backed up. Because the data is on disk, restoration time is fast.

To use the disk space efficiently, the DPM does not take copies of the entire data set of its protected content, but rather just the byte-level changes that are made between the last time a snapshot was taken. This byte-level change control not only saves disk space, but also saves network bandwidth by only replicating what has changed; this is vital if using DPM to back up remote servers in slower connected areas.

DPM contains special modules for Exchange, SQL Server, and SharePoint, enabling recoverability at granular levels—for example, with

SQL Server, a specific database can be restored to the original server or even another server for testing purposes.

System Center Virtual Machine Manager

With greater emphasis being placed on virtualizing environments, Microsoft has created a solution to help in the provisioning and management of virtual environments. The Virtual Machine Manager (VMM) not only helps to quickly provision new virtual environments, but also has Physical to Virtual (P2V) technologies, which helps take a physical server and migrate it into a virtual environment. This is useful for datacenter consolidations to fewer servers.

The VMM also performs constant performance checking on the virtual host environments and uses performance data and data provisioned from SCOM to choose the best location for a virtual environment.

Virtual template environments are fully supported, along with a library of "building blocks" that are used to populate virtual environments. Support for using a SAN as the storage of the virtual environments in addition to PowerShell scripting abilities make SCVMM appealing when dealing with virtual environments.

System Center Service Desk

Service Desk is designed to act as the interface point where users and administrators can interact around IT issues, along with visibility to senior management about the overall state of the IT infrastructure from a "ticket" perspective. Built on Microsoft Office SharePoint Server 2007 and Microsoft Office Forms Server 2007, the Service Desk is tightly integrated into the organization's information center.

Service Desk enables users to log tickets with the IT team, perform follow-on checking of ticket status, and even search on previous tickets for existing solutions. Workflow can be built on Service Desk to facilitate automated escalation and notification of IT issues. The other System Center offerings integrate into Service Desk; for example, system center operations manager can raise issues in Service Desk for problems.

System Center Capacity Planner

The number of servers needed to provide the IT infrastructure and their use is often a complex exercise. The Capacity Planner allows the modeling of the organization in terms of physical locations, connectivity between locations, and number of clients and servers; the Capacity Planner also can estimate the hardware needed to service the environment. Currently, the Capacity Planner supports Exchange 2007 and System Center Operations Manager 2007 and will detail the server environment required. In addition, simulations can be run that will test how the planned infrastructure would perform in terms of processor, memory, network, and disk utilization.

Capacity Planner is useful for simulating change scenarios. For example, 150 new users will be working at a new branch; how will that affect our Exchange 2007 environment? The Capacity Planner can simulate the use of the additional users and see how existing hardware would react and if additional servers should be added.

System Center Essentials

A scaled-down System Center solutions exists, which can support up to 30 servers and between 50 and 500 client computers. System Center Essentials (SCE) concentrates on the monitoring capabilities of SCOM; this includes a lot of the functionality of SCOM and the addition of update management, plus application and patch deployment and a special inventory engine that collects around 60 data points of the serviced machines. SCE has a single interface to manage all the elements of its functionality, which is intuitive and guides the administrator through the full configuration to get up and running quickly.

Over 50 reports are included in SCE, giving information about the environment and its health. Although SCE provides most of the SCOM functionality, the rest of its capabilities are SCE specific and are not based on System Center Configuration Manager, but instead are built on the Windows Server Update Services 3.0 engine. For smaller environments, SCE is a good introduction to System Center.

Summary

Windows Server 2008 has some great core improvements around its stability, so hopefully you won't need to troubleshoot. However, there are great capabilities that can be utilized.

For systems that can't start, there are powerful recovery tools in the form of the Windows RE that is so useful it's a great idea to install locally on each server. For systems that are not behaving, there are great monitoring and troubleshooting capabilities—for example, the Reliability and Performance Monitor deals with many aspects of troubleshooting in one place. Remember that the event log is your friend; when you have a problem with a service like the Active Directory or IIS, use Server Manager's role page as the first port of call, which shows event logs specific to a certain role and the state of services. The event logs are also a key source of troubleshooting information; in this chapter, you saw how to filter the logs to only see information you need and how to subscribe to event logs on other systems.

The System Center line should also be seriously reviewed by companies. When you consider that many problems are caused by misconfigurations and not detecting problem signs early enough, then System Center becomes a no-brainer.

CHAPTER 21

GROUP POLICY

One of the advantages for organizations with Windows 2000 and the AD was the introduction of Group Policy, which finally offered a comprehensive and reliable method of performing configuration in a persistent manner on servers and computers within an organization. Prior to the Group Policy feature, system policies were limited in their abilities and application.

System policies were managed with the System Policy Editor. By default, it had policy options for the default user and default computer, with the capability to add additional policies for specific users, groups, or computers. These policies were basic at best; they worked by manipulating Registry key values on the client through values set in template files with the adm extension type. It was possible to create custom adm files that set Registry keys on the client to achieve functionality beyond those in the included adm files stored in the Winnt\inf folder. An example policy is shown in Figure 21-1.

The policy file was saved with a .pol extension; in order to be read by NT-based clients, the file name was ntconfig.pol. The file was placed in the netlogon folder, which, under NT 4.0, usually pointed to the C:\Winnt\system32\Repl\Import\Scripts folder. (Place the file in the export folder, which then replicated it to the Import folder of all the other domain controllers.)

This Registry-based approach had a downside—it set Registry keys and then left them. If you removed a policy, the settings the policy had made were not removed from the client. This leaving of policy configuration on the client was known as *tattooing the system*, because its changes were permanent unless a definitive action was taken to remove them (via a manual cleanup, script, or other policy).

Interestingly enough, these policy template files (adm) remained unchanged in format from their first introduction with Windows NT all the way through to Windows XP/2003. Vista and Windows Server 2008 did finally include a change to the format, but this is discussed later in the chapter.

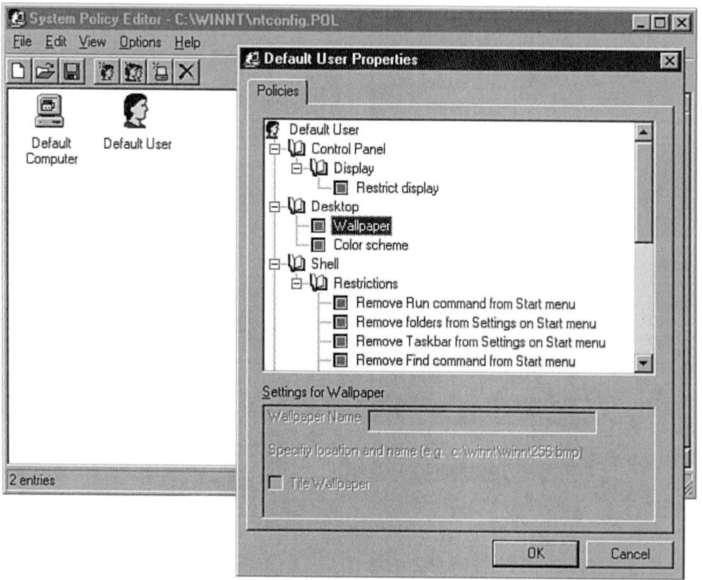

FIGURE 21-1 The old-style system policies of pre-Windows 2000 versions of the Windows operating system (OS) were basic at best.

Group Policy Structure

The Active Directory (AD) in Windows 2000 introduced a huge amount of change to nearly every aspect of the Windows infrastructure, including how policy is managed and applied. The old system policies with the tattoo-type Registry settings were gone (mostly) in favor of a new, far richer policy implementation: Group Policy.

Because the Group Policy implementation was written from the ground up and was being released as part of the new Windows 2000 brand (which included a desktop version, Windows 2000 Professional), a new component was included to enable the processing of the new Group Policy structure. Older, pre-Windows 2000 clients still require the ntconfig.pol file in the netlogon share created by the System Policy Editor. However, systems from Windows 2000 on prefer to process a Group Policy.

Group Policy Features

Unlike system policies with the single capability to write Registry keys, Group Policy can do a *lot* more, including the following:

- Deploy applications on a per-user or per-machine basis with granularity. These deployed applications can be self-healing if deployed using Microsoft Installer Format (MSI files). However, older style, non-MSI applications can also be deployed with a bit of ZAP (which is discussed later).
- Logon/logoff/machine startup/machine shutdown scripts. Notice this is not just computer startup and user logon. You can now run scripts at logoff and shutdown, which has long been a feature missing from the Windows capabilities.
- Ability to redirect folders such as My Documents to network-based locations.
- Configuration of local machine policies, including audit and security settings, in addition to rights on the machine.
- Configuration of certificate, IP Security (IPsec) policies, and so on.
- Environment and Internet Explorer configuration, such as setting the Internet Explorer home page to the corporate Web page.
- Capability to set the membership of local groups; for example, setting who the members of the local Administrators group are on machines to which the Group Policy is applied and ensuring other people are *not* members.
- Software restrictions that can prohibit certain applications from running; no more annoying office applications sidetracking the sales team from Solitaire.

Group Policy enables the management of your Windows-based infrastructure centrally via the AD. This is not just your desktop computers but also the servers, including your domain controllers.

Group Policy Objects (GPOs)

The main component in Group Policy is a Group Policy Object (GPO), which is a defined set of policies that describes a particular set of configurations. For example, a GPO might be created that is responsible for locking down the desktop (such as disabling the Run dialog and setting the Internet Explorer start page). For now just think of a GPO as a collection of defined settings from all those possible within Group Policy (which is a lot). On its own, however, a GPO does nothing; it's just a collection of settings that exist within the AD.

A Group Policy is broken down into two major sections: user and computer settings. Within those major sections, each has three child groupings of policy elements:

- **Software Settings**. Used for the deployment of software.
- **Windows Settings**. Used for configuration of scripts, policies, restriction of group membership, and software deployment.
- **Administrative Templates**. The adm(x)-based settings, which chiefly rely on settings made to the Registry of the target machines.

Figure 21-2 shows an example of a GPO. For now, understand that, in addition to the software settings, the settings are broken down into those that affect computers and those that affect users.

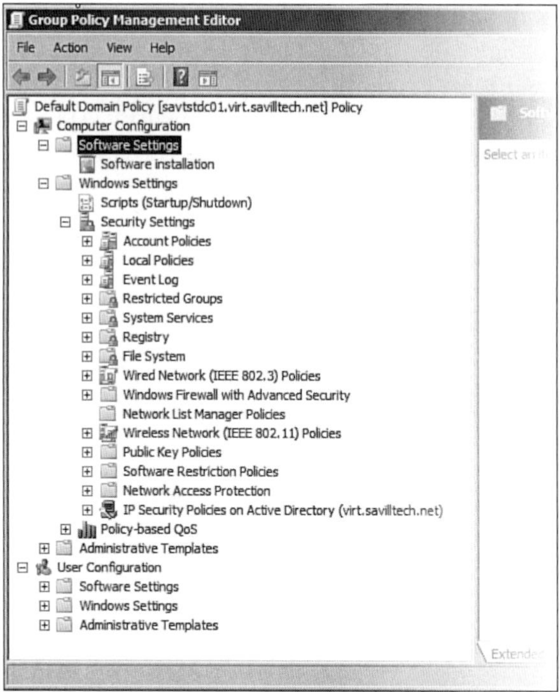

FIGURE 21-2 This gives an idea of the scope of options available in Group Policy; however, once you open it up and start selecting the actual settings, it gets more granular.

Using Group Policy Objects

For a GPO to be useful, it has to be linked to a specific container of user/computer objects; this is the first big change from system policies. With system policies, the ntconfig.pol sat in the netlogon folder of the domain controllers and was read by everyone, with some limited control of applications via user/group/computer specific settings. But that was ugly. GPOs can be linked at three levels (and another, but more on that in a second): an Active Directory Site, a domain, and an organizational unit (see Figure 21-3). The "and" in the last sentence is important. GPOs are stored within a domain but can be linked to any site, domain, or OU in the forest, although cross-domain GPO linkage is discouraged due to the time lag incurred in crossing domains. One GPO can be linked to many different containers in the same way one container—such as an OU—can have many different GPOs linked to it.

The linking of a GPO to one or more containers defines its scope of management—in other words, the users and/or computers that the GPO has an effect on. GPOs contain settings that affect the computer and user objects within the AD. You can apply a GPO to a site, domain, or OU, not just to security groups. An object in the AD can only exist in one place. However, an object in the AD does not receive the Group Policy settings contained in objects that link only to the object's parent container. In fact, the object (computer or user) cumulatively receives all policies applied at the site, domain, and OU that it resides in; because OUs can be nested, many levels of GPOs might be applied to the computer/user object.

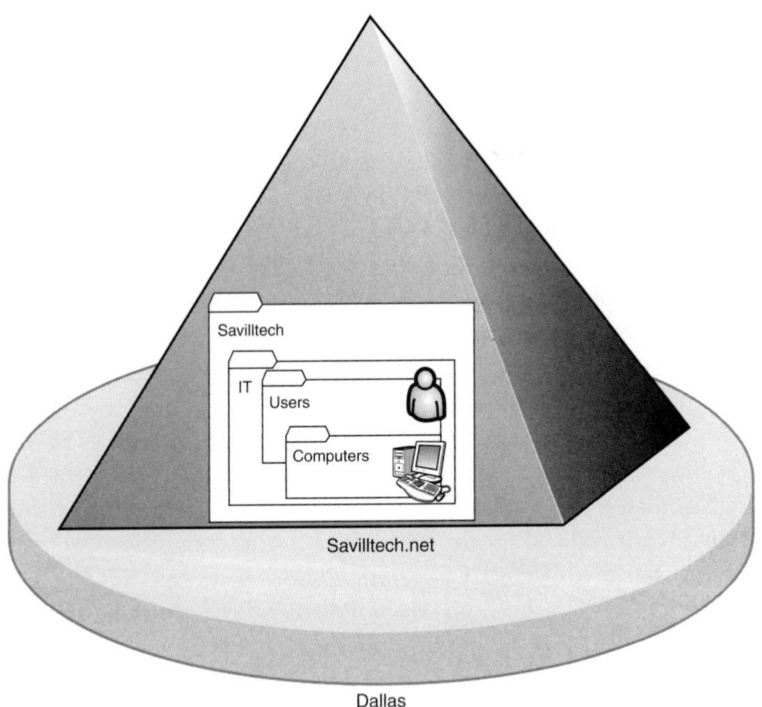

Figure 21-3 Typical organizational layout of a site, domain, and organizational units.

In this case, the computer and user reside in separate organizational units, which is common. So, how is Group Policy applied out of the three levels of site, domain, and organizational unit? Actually, it's in that order; the "furthest" policy is applied first (for example, the site). This allows more specific policies—that is, the domain- and OU-level policies—to overwrite settings that have been set at higher levels until the last policies applied are those applied on the actual parent container of the object itself. Let's take this example and assume there is one GPO linked at each level: the Dallas site, the savilltech.net domain, and at each of the Savilltech, IT, Users, and Computers organizational units. The policies are applied in the following order:

1. The site-linked GPOs—for example, the GPOs linked to Dallas (although in general, you don't want to link GPOs to sites because of the potential cross-domain linkage issues; sites form a forest-wide object and are not domain specific).
2. Next, the domain-linked GPOs would be applied for savilltech.net.
3. The GPOs linked at the Savilltech OU would be applied.
4. The GPOs linked at the IT OU would be applied.
5. Finally, GPOs linked at Users would be applied for the user, and the GPOs linked at Computers would be applied for the computer.

GPOs are cumulative; in our example, the user and computer would get the sum of all GPOs linked at all the levels: site, domain, and the multiple nested OUs. So, why the order at all? You could have conflicts in policy settings, or different GPOs might set the same setting with different values. If there is a conflict, the GPO closest to the user/computer object (that is, applied latest) would take precedence and be the setting the user/computer would receive. This is useful if you want to set a configuration at the domain level—for example, restricting access to the Run dialog, but then you want to enable it for the IT team. Create a GPO blocking the Run dialog and apply it at the domain level, and then create a GPO that enables the Run dialog and link to the OU that contains the IT team.

In fact, each container can have multiple GPOs linked to it. How are they prioritized? They are prioritized in the dialog used to manage Group Policy, which in Windows Server 2008 will always be the Group Policy Management Console (GPMC). This is because, unlike previous versions where GPMC was a separate download, GPMC is now part of the operating system (OS). When you select a possible Group Policy target (for example, a domain), a list of all the linked GPOs is displayed, as shown in Figure 21-4.

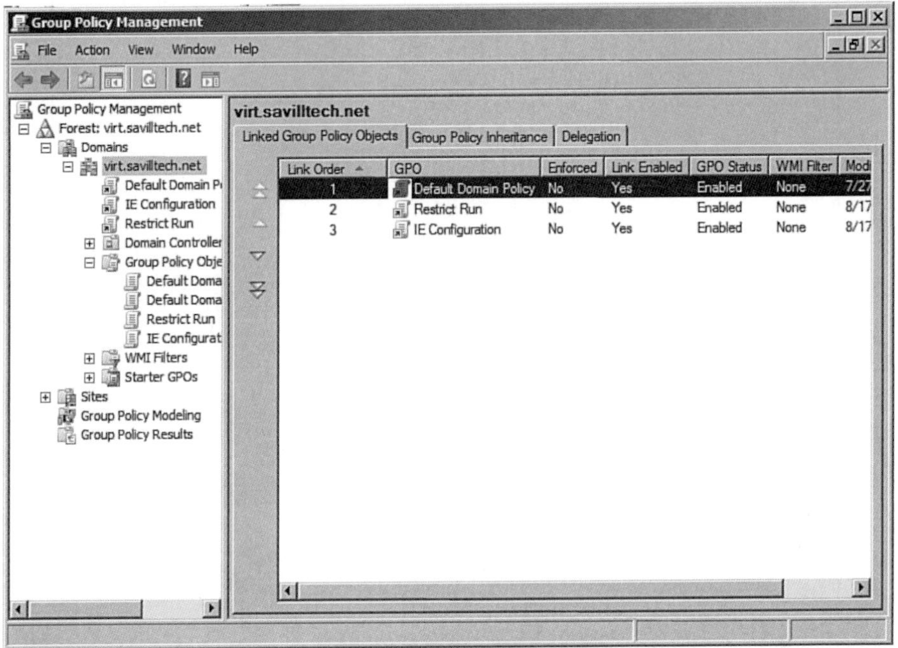

FIGURE 21-4 In this case, the domain has three GPOs linked.

Notice each GPO that is linked has a link order that can be modified by clicking the down and up arrows to the left. The higher the link order, the higher its precedence, meaning the GPO with link order 1 overwrites any setting defined in a GPO at link order 2, 3, 4, and so on. The link order 2 GPO overwrites settings in the link order 3 GPO, and so on. The GPOs are applied in reverse order, too; in this case, the IE Configuration GPO would be applied first, then the Restrict Run GPO would be applied, and finally the Default Domain Policy would be applied. This means the Default Domain Policy GPO could overwrite any setting that it had a conflict with in GPO Restrict Run and IE Configuration. To make this clear, let's create two GPOs: one sets Microsoft's Live.com as the home page, and the other sets Google.com as the home page. Figures 21-5 and 21-6 show whichever policy has the highest link order wins the conflict and is set as the home page.

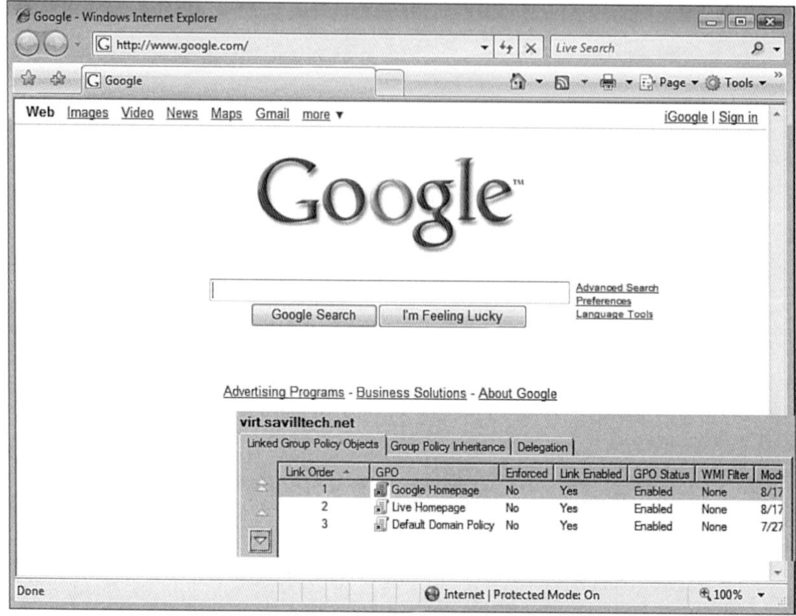

FIGURE 21-5 When the Google home page policy is above the Live home page policy, then Google is the user's home page.

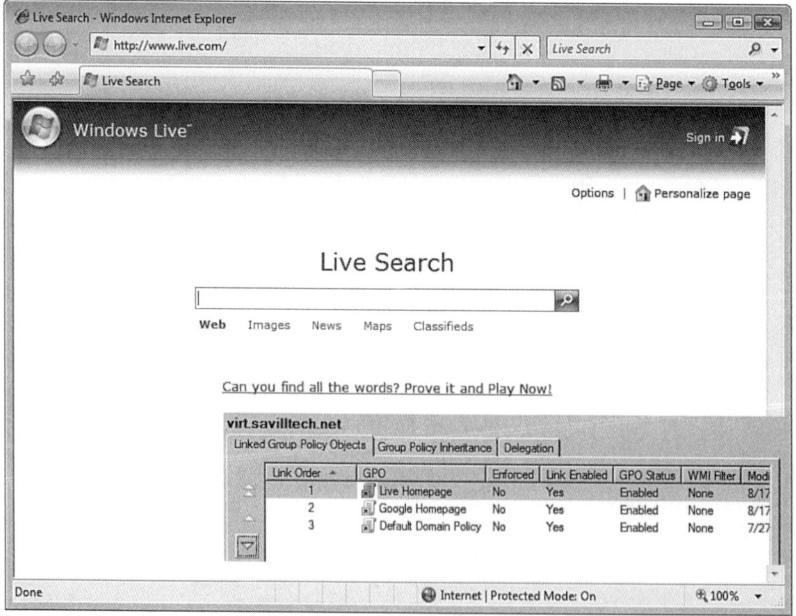

FIGURE 21-6 With the Live GPO, a link order position higher than the Google one ensures the user's home page is set to Live; this increases your chances of staying on good terms with Microsoft, which is encouraged for all.

There is a fourth level of Group Policy. Each computer has a local GPO. However, this is more typically locally managed on the computer and is overwritten by any domain-based policies. Prior to Windows Vista, only one local Group Policy existed. However, with Vista, multiple local GPOs can exist for administrators, non-administrators, and specific users, which is useful in non-domain environments. These settings are applied first, which means ANY setting applied via the Active Directory Group Policy overrides a local setting. The way to remember the order of application of policy is LSDOU:

Local -> Site -> Domain -> Organizational Unit

In a non-domain environment, the local policy is the only policy you can use; Group Policy is not available in non-domain environments. You do not have to link policies at each level, and in fact, it would not even be a best practice. It is not desirable to link GPOs at site levels; try to minimize the various layers that GPOs are linked to because this can adversely affect startup/logon times, as each GPO has to be processed.

Local Policy

Let's look at the local policy because you can do this from any Vista client (or even XP/2000; however, you can't see the multiple local policy options) without the need for a domain. First, create a Microsoft Management Console (MMC) interface for viewing the policy:

1. Start the MMC (Start, Run, mmc.exe).
2. Select Add/Remove Snap-in from the File menu.
3. Select the Group Policy Object Editor from the list of available snap-ins, and click the Add button, as shown in Figure 21-7.
4. You are prompted for the GPO to edit. Leave the default of Local Computer and click Finish.
5. Click OK to the Add or Remove Snap-ins dialog.

You now have a console that has the local computer policy loaded. In reality, you could have just run gpedit.msc, but it's good to see the complete process of building the custom console, which you want when defining multiple local GPOs. If you navigate the structure in the navigation pane, the local policy is structured in the same way as an AD-based GPO (with the Computer and User Configuration main sections), and then within each of those sections, the Software Settings, Windows Settings, and Administrative Templates sub-sections. Not all features are available in the local computer policy. For example, under Software Settings, there are no actions possible; you can't deploy software with a local computer policy.

There would not be much point. For example, expand User Configuration, Administrative Templates, Control Panel in the main details pane, and notice an option to Force Classic Control Panel view. Enable this, and the next time you start the Control Panel, you get the old Windows 2000 style view. Also, as you navigate around the Group Policy settings, notice the help that is shown, giving good details of what each policy does if you have the extended view option selected. Otherwise, the same help is available via the Explain tab when you double-click an actual setting. Notice that settings have an "At least Microsoft Windows 2000 or XP or Vista" and so on. This shows which client OS is needed to apply a policy setting. If a policy setting is read by an older OS, the setting is ignored. You don't need to create multiple GPOs for each client OS; one size fits all.

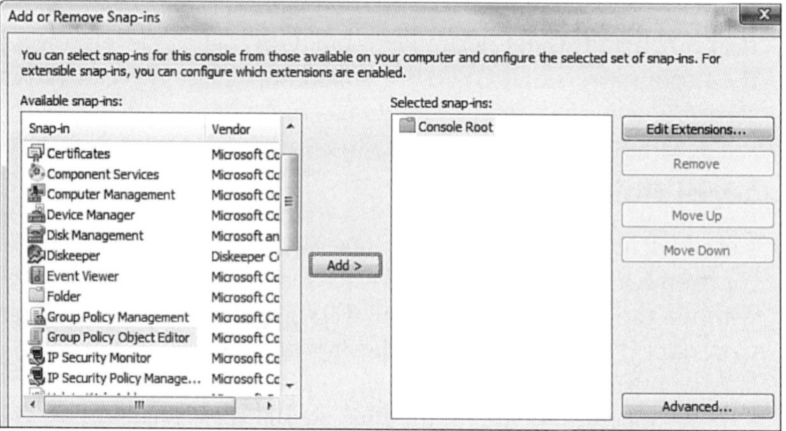

FIGURE 21-7 Vista enjoys the enhanced Add/Remove snap-in dialog that is part of MMC 3 and was first introduced as part of Windows 2003 R2.

How does Windows Vista and above support multiple local computer policies? Let's walk through the procedure. Remember, this is designed for use on stand-alone machines. For domain-joined machines, AD-based Group Policy makes more sense. You can create local GPOs only for the general user types of administrators or those that are not administrators, because a specific user cannot be both—and additionally, user-specific local GPOs. You can't create a local user-specific policy for a domain user. You create them only for local accounts; again, this should be considered only for machines that are not part of a domain.

When you define multiple local GPOs, an order of application is once again used, in case there are conflicts between the multiple local GPOs. The order of application works in the same manner as AD GPOs and is as follows:

1. The local computer GPO that contains both user and computer settings.
2. The Administrator or Non-Administrator local GPOs depending on the type of user.
3. User-specific local GPOs.

This means that any setting defined in the general local computer policy can be overridden by the more specific Admin or Non-Admin local GPO; those Admin or Non-Admin GPOs can be overridden by the user-specific GPO. The "closest" GPO always wins in the case of a conflict.

You created a custom console that has the local default GPO loaded; let's add to it now:

1. Select Add/Remove Snap-in from the File menu of the custom console.
2. Select the Group Policy Object Editor from the list of available snap-ins, and click the Add button, as you did previously when you created the console.
3. You are prompted for the GPO to edit. This time, click Browse and select the Users tab.
4. A list of the users that exist on the system is shown, in addition to an Administrators and Non-Administrators group. Select the user or group you want to set a policy for and click OK. Then click Finish, as shown in Figure 21-8. Repeat these steps to add and create multiple different local policies.

The snap-in created shows all the selected policies. Save this console to avoid having to re-add each user/admin Group Policy in the future. Notice that all the policies, except for the default local computer policy, have only a User Configuration element (see Figure 21-9).

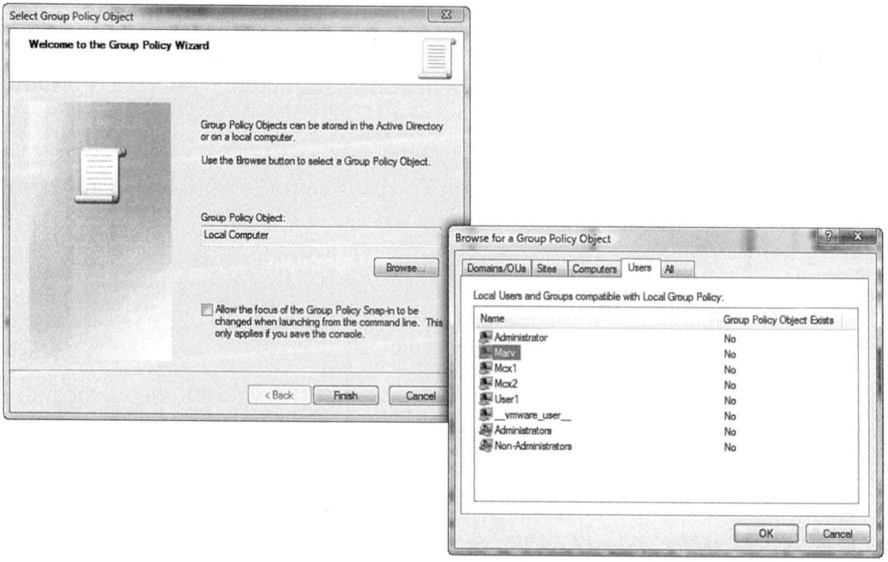

FIGURE 21-8 List of all the local users (including two Mcx accounts for the XBOX 360 media streaming support), along with the Administrators and Non-Administrators groups.

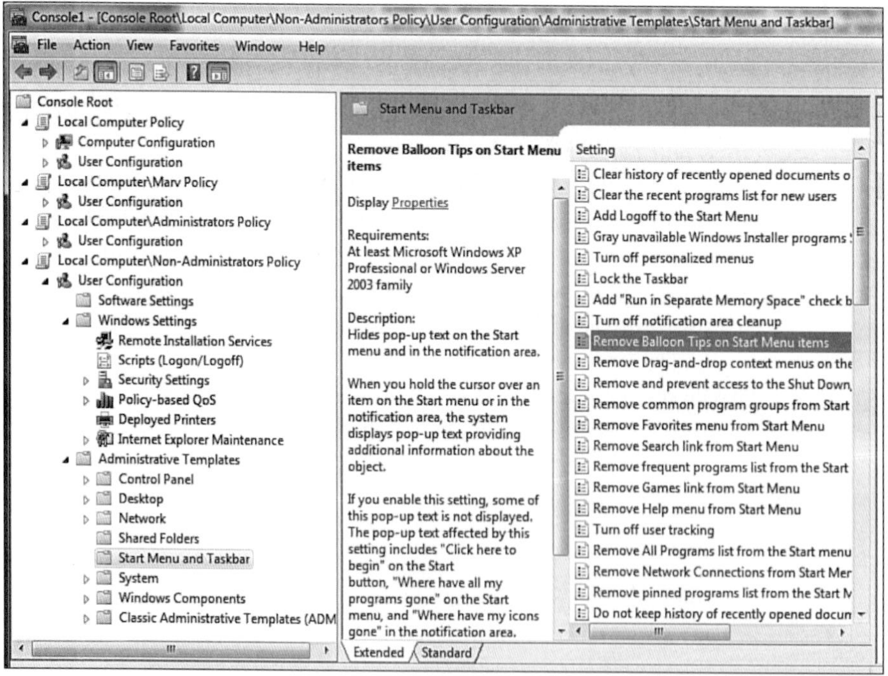

FIGURE 21-9 A Group Policy Object Editor with the local computer, both Administrator and Non-Administrator policies, and a user-specific policy for Marv.

Remember, if the system is part of a domain, the domain-based GPOs can override any setting that has been set locally. You should not be using local GPOs in a domain environment.

In a domain environment, you can disable the processing of local policies via a domain GPO. Enable the Turn off Local Group Policy Objects processing policy, which is found under the Computer Configuration, Administrative Templates, System, Group Policy area. It is available as part of the Windows Vista/2008 templates. This can also be achieved by creating a DWORD value named DisableGPO with data 1 in the Registry key HKEY_LOCAL_MACHINE\SOFTWARE\Policies\Microsoft\Windows\System.

Group Policy Application

AD GPOs can do wonders for computer management. But at what point do GPOs get applied to the computer and user? Is it the same as NT 4.0 policies that were applied at logon time? Yes, and then some.

Group Policy has multiple types of processing. The most basic is the initial processing that occurs at the computer startup, where computer portions of GPOs are applied. You can tell when the computer-based policy has completed when you see the Ctrl+Alt+Del screen appear, allowing logon. The other instance of initial processing is when a user logs on, and the user portions of the GPOs are applied. Typically, when the desktop is shown, the user GPO processing has completed. However, this does vary based on the client OS. Windows 2000 processes Group Policy synchronously which means that Group Policy is applied in order, and then the desktop or Ctrl+Alt+Del is displayed. However, Windows XP and above allows asynchronous Group Policy application; this means the logon dialog or user's desktop is displayed potentially before the Group Policy application has completed or while the Group Policy application is being done. This asynchronous application of Group Policy can sometimes cause issues resulting in multiple computer reboots or logons before all GPOs are correctly applied; however, the GPUPDATE tool often helps with this.

In reality, asynchronous and synchronous Group Policy application is available on all the Windows versions; only the default behavior is different. To force Windows XP and above to process Group Policy synchronously, enable the Always Wait for the Network at Computer Startup and Logon policy under the Computer Configuration, Administrative Templates, System, Logon area of the GPO (see Figure 21-10).

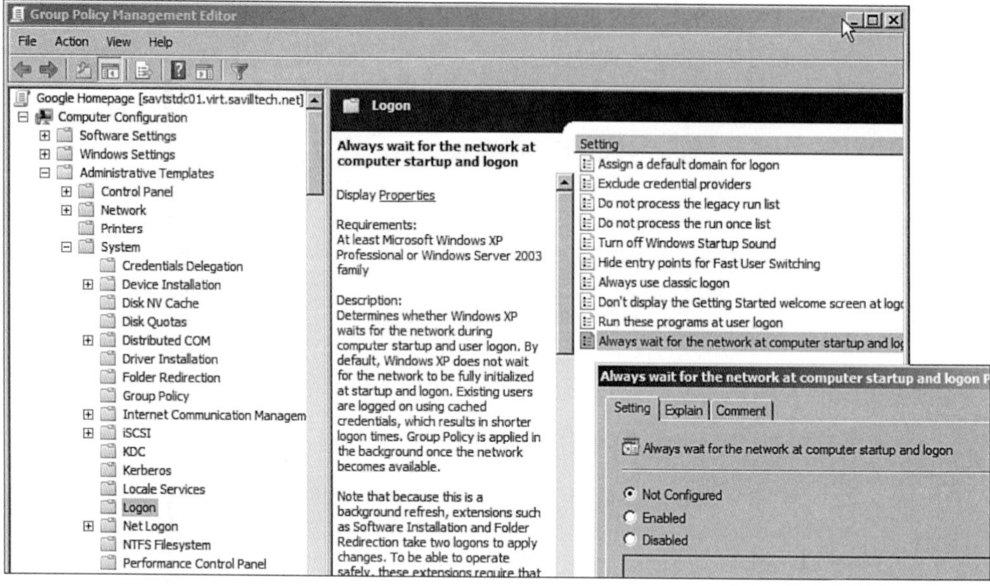

FIGURE 21-10 This setting might seem "legacy," but it can be useful to guarantee the application of folder redirection and software installation-type activities, which can be done only before activity/logon, that might not work with asynchronous Group Policy application.

This is the initial Group Policy application. In addition to the application at startup and logon, Group Policy is periodically refreshed by default every 90 minutes, plus a random offset of up to an additional 30 minutes. The additional time is designed to prevent all computers from refreshing Group Policy at the same time. Imagine that you have an office of 500 machines, where at 9 a.m. everyone comes in and turns on their computers. If 90 minutes later, they all refreshed Group Policy simultaneously, that would place considerable stress on the domain controllers and network to have everyone refreshing policy at the same time. With the random offset, this refresh is distributed more evenly.

The refresh policy can be modified via the Group Policy for both computers and users. To modify the users refresh policy, edit the Group Policy refresh interval for users setting under the Users Configuration, Administrative Templates, System, Group Policy area of the GPO. As shown in Figure 21-11, the default refresh interval of 90 minutes can be modified along with the random interval that is added. Care should be taken, however, not to modify these values without consideration, as reducing the intervals too much would generate excessive load on the domain controllers and network.

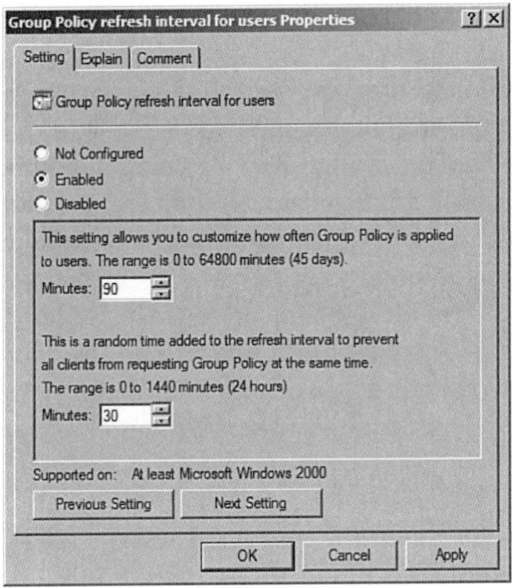

FIGURE 21-11 When enabled, the refresh interval policy can be changed from the defaults of 90 and 30 minutes.

Refresh of the computer portions of Group Policy can also be changed from the default of 90 minutes via the Group Policy Refresh Interval for Computers policy found under Computer Configuration, Administrative Templates, System, Group Policy. Under the same Group Policy area of the GPO, there is a Group Policy Refresh Interval for Domain Controllers setting. Why? Group Policy refresh for domain controllers behaves differently from normal members of a domain. By default, they refresh every five minutes with no random time addition (it's not normally needed because you have far fewer domain controllers than normal servers). It's far more important for domain controllers to have the latest Group Policy.

This refreshing is performed asynchronously and is useful when you make changes to a GPO. You don't have to wait for a user to log out or computer to restart until the updated policies take effect. For example, if you update a GPO to update the Internet Explorer home page, the user does not need to log off. The next time the Group Policy refreshes, the update to the settings takes effect. By default, on a non-domain controller, that would at most be 2 hours (90 minutes, plus a maximum of 30 minutes for the randomized offset). This background refreshing can be disabled (although it is not recommended), by enabling the Turn off Background Refresh of Group Policy in the Computer Configuration, Administrative Templates, System, Group Policy portion of your GPO. To force a setting to take effect faster, manually refresh policy on the computer via the `gpupdate` command.

Some settings don't get updated as part of background processing; specifically, software deployment and folder redirection are not updated. If these were changed during a live session, it could have a negative effect on your session. Imagine your documents folder being redirected to another location while working. That would be inconvenient. Or imagine the application you are running gets uninstalled. That might be even more inconvenient!

Group Policy has optimization during the refreshes that ensures only changed settings are applied to the computer. However, Security settings are treated differently because of their importance. By default, every 16 hours, security settings are reapplied regardless of any changes, with a 30-minute additional randomization factor (as usual). You can see these security applications by viewing the Application event log and looking for Event ID 1704 from the SceCli source, as shown in Figure 21-12.

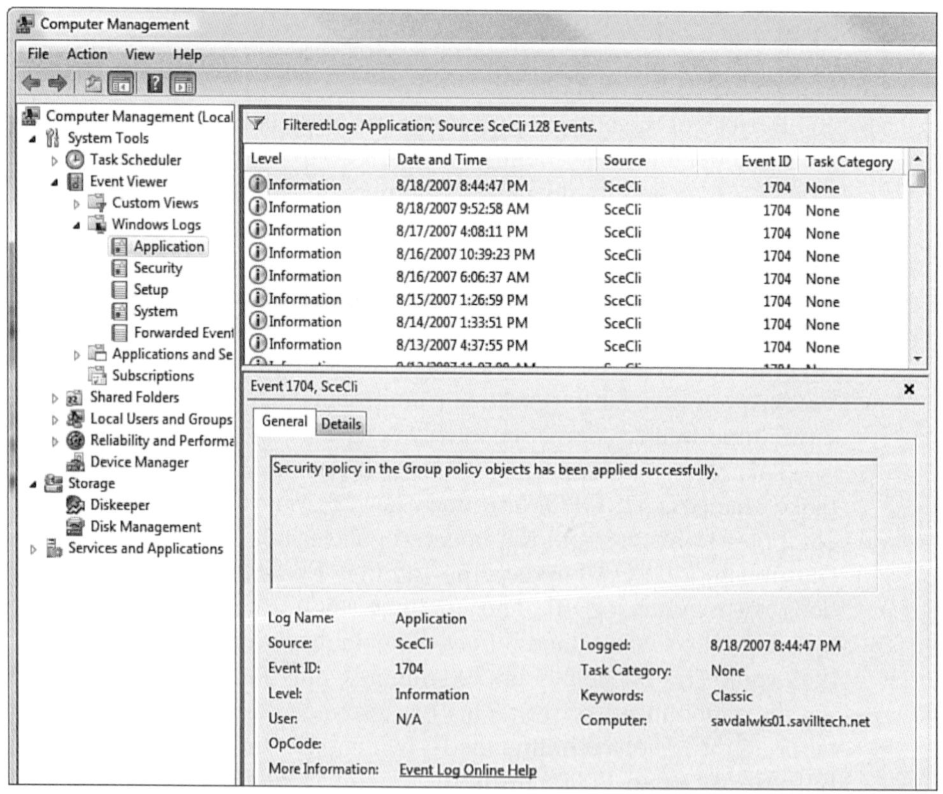

FIGURE 21-12 The dates between security applications are around 16 hours; however, this machine is not always running, so the times are not exact.

To modify the value of the security refresh from the default 960 minutes, edit the Registry value MaxNoGPOListChangesInterval under key HKEY_LOCAL_MACHINE\SOFTWARE\Microsoft\Windows NT\CurrentVersion\Winlogon\GPExtensions\{827D319E-6EAC-11D2-A4EA-00C04F79F83A} and set it to the number of minutes (see Figure 21-13). This is not simple or possible via a GPO, which gives some indication that you're not supposed to play with this value!

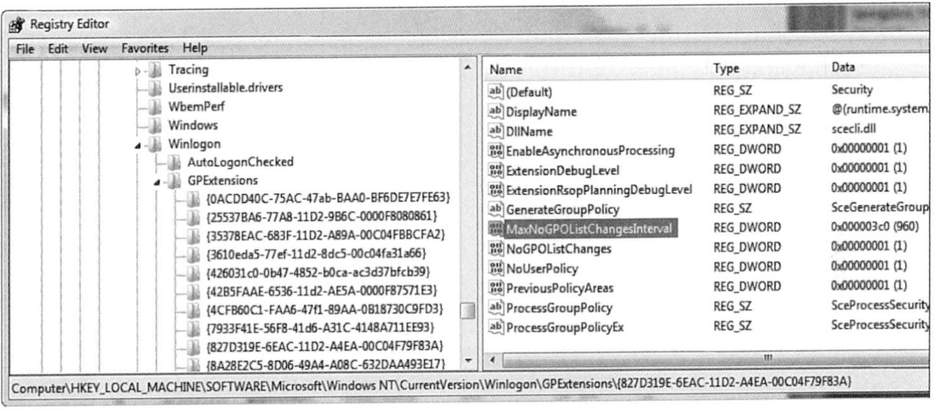

Figure 21-13 The obvious way to change the security application interval; however, you should not change it.

Forcing a Refresh

Although you can force a refresh by rebooting the computer or logging off and on, this is inconvenient. There might be times, especially during testing, when you don't want to wait the potential two hours for background refreshing to take effect. Refresh Group Policy manually using the GPupdate command-line utility locally on the computer whose policies need refreshing. For those Windows 2000 clients, GPupdate does not exist; instead, use the `secedit` command with the `/refreshpolicy` parameter and either `user_policy` or `machine_policy`—for example, `secedit /refreshpolicy user_policy`.

If you run GPupdate with no parameters, an update of the user and computer policy settings that have changed is performed, as shown here:

```
C:\Users\john>gpupdate
Updating Policy...
```

```
User Policy update has completed successfully.
Computer Policy update has completed successfully.
```

Remember that GPupdate applies an update of the settings that have changed. As mentioned previously, Group Policy utilizes optimization during a refresh and only applies settings that have been modified since the last application. There might be times you want to force the reapplication of all policies, and this is accomplished by adding `/force` to the `gpupdate` command.

Each of the User and Computer policies are applied separately; it is possible to update only the User or Computer parts of the Group Policy via the `/target` parameter and specify user or computer. For example, to update only the user portion of Group Policy, use the command `gpupdate /target:user`.

Other more advanced parameters are available with GPupdate. For example, by default, GPupdate waits 10 minutes for the policy to complete before returning control of the command session. You can change this timeout via the `/Wait` parameter, and the details can be found in the help (`gpupdate /?`). As mentioned previously, there are certain settings that can take effect only at computer startup (software installation) and user logon (software installation and folder redirection). If GPupdate encounters software installation or folder redirection, it is not able to process unless you add the `/logoff` or `/boot` switches; this performs a logoff or reboot, respectively, if GPupdate finds Group Policy changes that can take effect only from a computer's startup or logon. The final setting is the `/Sync` parameter, which when set forces the next initial Group Policy application to be done synchronously. In other words, it does not show the logon dialog until computer Group Policy processing is complete, and it does not show the desktop until user Group Policy processing is complete.

Slow Link Detection

One final point to consider about Group Policy application is the speed of the link through which the client is connected to receive policies. You obviously don't want clients trying to perform large software deployments when connected via a slow link. For example, if you are on a week's cruise in the Caribbean and connect via the ship's 32kbps connection to check email, you would be rather upset if Office 2007 started to download and install.

Group Policy, therefore, understands slow links; when a slow link is detected, certain policies are not applied. By default, pre-Windows Vista clients attempted to ping a domain controller four times; if the average ping time was greater than that defined for a slow link, then only certain Registry-based, EFS Recovery, IPSec, and security policies were applied.

By default, a slow link is considered 500Kbps or slower. However, you can change this via the Group Policy slow link detection policy under Computer Configuration, Administrative Templates, System, Group Policy. To disable slow link detection, set it to 0. However, this is not advisable because this causes *any* link to be considered fast, and the system processes all the elements of applicable GPOs.

This ping-based process has changed in Windows Vista and Windows Server 2008. Basing the network speed on ping tests had significant problems if ICMP was turned off at routers (ICMP is used for PING), or if a link was high bandwidth but had high latency (for example, with satellite connections). Pinging also had issues in VPN situations or if a computer was put into hibernate or standby. Also, if a computer was moved to a new network and the computer resumed the network link, speed tests were not re-performed.

Windows Vista has improved network awareness via Network Location Awareness (NLA) version 2.0, which no longer uses ICMP, so no more PING. The NLA informs the Group Policy modules when sufficient network connectivity is available to allow processing of Group Policy instead of the old time-out that had to occur via the PING scenario. When NLA tells Group Policy a domain controller is now able to be contacted, Group Policy application is performed, even if the connectivity is via a VPN. This is useful for disconnected computers who only connect via VPN; now, as soon as the VPN connection is made, the Group Policy client is notified and initiates a background refresh. This notification from the NLA improves Group Policy all around. If a network adapter is disabled or disconnected, Group Policy reduces its wait time because it knows the network is not available, which decreases startup times.

A final word: If you intend to use Network Quarantine (see Chapter 8, "Remote Access and Securing and Optimizing the Network," for more detail), there is additional configuration required. This is discussed when you configure Network Access Protection.

Group Policy Management Console (GPMC)

Now you understand where you can apply Group Policy and how it gets applied. How do you manage it? Two main tools are used: one tool to manage and apply Group Policy (and a lot more) and a second tool, which we've already seen, to edit the content of GPOs: the Group Policy Object Editor.

For the management of Group Policy, use the GPMC; this is available for Windows 2003 and Windows XP clients, but can manage Group Policy in Windows 2000-, Windows 2003-, and Windows 2008-based domains. It won't run on a Windows 2000 machine. GPMC can be downloaded from http://www.microsoft.com/downloads/; just search for Group Policy Management Console. Although GPMC was always provided as an add-on for the OS, it was a necessity. The basic functionality for managing and applying Group Policy without it was a tab of the properties of objects within Active Directory Users and Computers and the Sites and Services MMC snap-in, which was ugly at best (see Figure 21-14). Options and settings for GPOs were scattered over multiple Property, Options, and check boxes; it was hard to see exactly what a policy did and get a good view of what a GPO was doing in your organization. If you are using Windows 2003/2000 and are not using GPMC, go download it now!

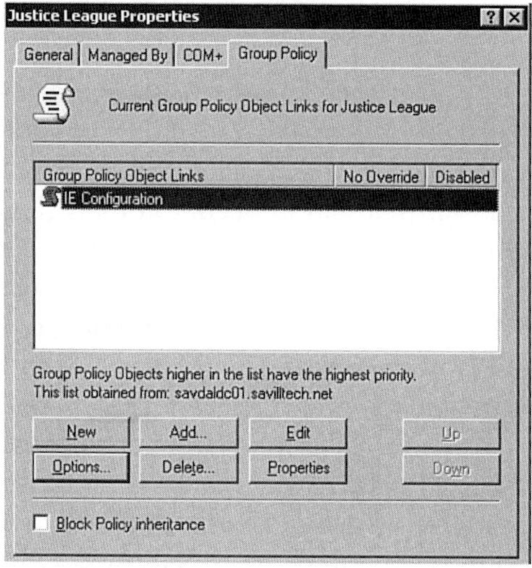

FIGURE 21-14 Hopefully you never have to use this. This shows the GPOs that are linked to a container.

Windows Vista originally shipped with the GPMC; this was great in that you could now manage Group Policy from Vista clients. However, Microsoft pulled the GPMC from Vista with SP1, effectively uninstalling GPMC during the service pack installation. Why? When GPMC was not part of the OS, many people complained that GPMC was so essential to managing Group Policy, it should be part of the OS. Instead of being an out-of-band release, Microsoft added GPMC into Windows Vista, making it available to any user of Vista. This turned out to be an issue; now every user could see Group Policies for the domain and could even back them up, taking to a friend/hacker who could then easily get an idea of the security at a company. In addition, making GPMC part of the OS meant that GPMC could be updated only as part of an OS update, which can take a considerable amount of time. Microsoft therefore decided it was better to remove GPMC from Windows Vista and make it out-of-band again, initially as part of the Remote Server Administration Tools (RSAT). Windows Server 2008 also ships with the GPMC.

In Windows Server 2008, the GPMC is accessible via a shortcut in the Administrative Tools Start menu group or with Windows Vista (pre SP1)—just run gpmc.msc. Once started, the Group Policy information is loaded from the computer's local forest, as shown in Figure 21-15.

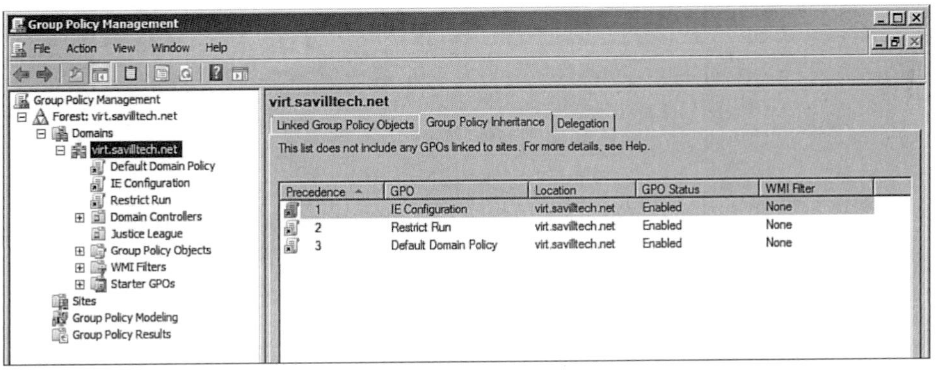

FIGURE 21-15 The GPMC gives an intuitive view of the state of Group Policy for your local forest.

Right-click on the root of the navigation pane, Group Policy Management to add additional forests that are trusted by the local forest to manage their Group Policy.

In a standard domain without any custom configuration, there are always two GPOs: the Default Domain Policy and the Default Domain Controllers Policy. If you select a container (such as a domain or organizational unit) in the details pane, Group Policy information is shown for that container. For example, if you select a domain in the details pane, you get three tabs: Linked Group Policy Objects, which are directly linked to the selected container; Group Policy Inheritance, which shows all GPOs that would apply to the container; and the Delegation tab, which enables delegation of control of Group Policy to selected users. Notice also that as child objects of the selected container, the GPOs that are linked to it are shown as in Figure 21-16. The GPOs are not stored in the containers; all GPOs are stored in the domain. The child nodes give an easy way to see which GPOs are linked at the various levels.

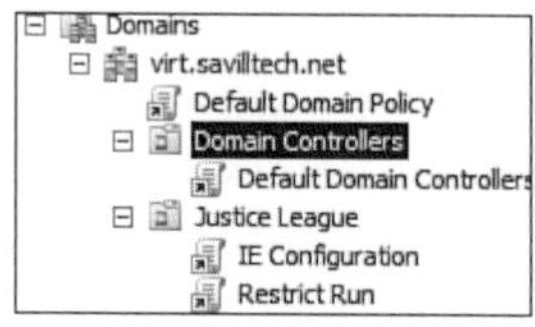

FIGURE 21-16 GPOs linked to containers are shown as child nodes in the navigation pane.

Three other nodes appear under the list of OUs for the domain, as follows:

- **Group Policy Objects**. Lists all the GPOs that are contained within the domain.
- **WMI Filters**. Enables the creation of Windows Management Instrumentation (WMI) Filter objects used to control application of GPOs, based on highly configurable computer settings accessed via WMI.
- **Starter GPOs**. Enables the storage of a collection of settings from multiple Administrative Templates to form the basis for GPOs created without having to define settings.

Creating a New Group Policy Object

Let's create a GPO that does something. Right-click on the Group Policy Objects node of the domain in the navigation pane and select New from the displayed context menu. You also can create a GPO and link it to a site, domain, or OU by right-clicking on the container in question and selecting Create a GPO in This Domain, and Link It Here… (see Figure 21-17).

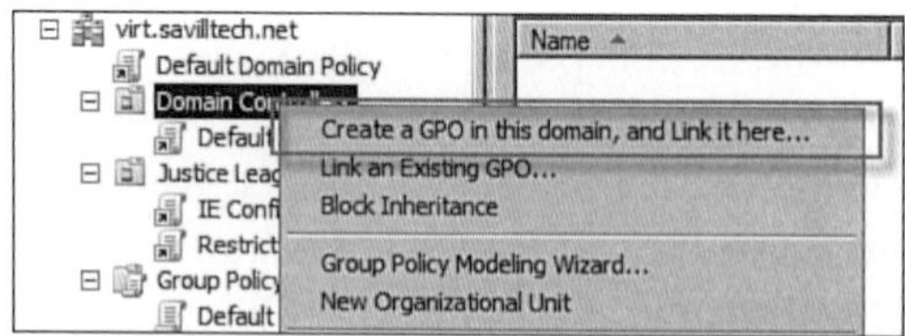

FIGURE 21-17 Create a GPO and link it at the same time to save the step of linking later.

Here's the "longer" way. Create the GPO first and then link it, as follows:

1. In the GPMC, right-click Group Policy Objects in the navigation pane within the domain in which you want to create a new GPO. Select New from the displayed context menu.
2. Enter a name for the new GPOs. If you use them, you can select a Source Starter GPO, which would autofill some of the settings, and click OK (see Figure 21-18).

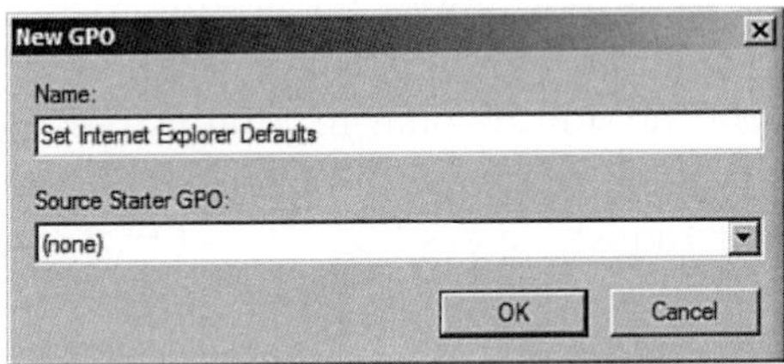

FIGURE 21-18 The GPO name must be unique within the domain.

After the GPO is created, create some settings in it. Right-click on the new GPO and select Edit from the context menu. This launches the Group Policy Management Editor with the selected GPO open (which, at this point, has no settings). You can now modify the GPO with settings. As you use Group Policy, you learn where the settings are. Because they are broken into areas of functionality, anything related to Registry keys generally lives under the Administrative Templates section, which is then broken down into areas like Control Panel, Network, and so on. If a setting is machine-wide, it is under Computer Configuration. If it's user specific, it is under User Configuration. However, there are still a LOT of settings. Fortunately, help is at hand. Microsoft has an Excel spreadsheet at http://www.microsoft.com/downloads/details.aspx?familyid=2043b94e-66cd-4b91-9e0f-68363245c495&displaylang=en that lists the various policy settings. This makes it easier to search for a setting you want to apply. The cool thing about the spreadsheet is it not only lists the policy item and where to find it; it also gives the Help/Explain text and, where applicable, the Registry key that is updated by the Registry policy (see Figure 12-19). When you configure settings in Windows Server 2008, you have the ability to add a comment for each setting made within a GPO. This helps you track the reason behind the setting and gives context to the setting's use within the organization. Enter this comment via the Comment tab that is available for most Group Policy settings.

D15 | Windows Components\Internet Explorer\Internet Control Panel\Security Page\Intranet Zone

	C	D	E	F	
1	Computer/User Node	Policy Path	Registry Settings	Supported on	Help/Explain Text
1073	User	Windows Components\Task Scheduler	HKCU\Software\Policies\Microsoft\Windows\Task Scheduler5.0!Prc	Microsoft Windows Server 2003, Windows XP, and Windo	Prevents users from
1074	Computer	Windows Components\Task Scheduler	HKLM\Software\Policies\Microsoft\Windows\Task Scheduler5.0!Prc	Microsoft Windows Server 2003, Windows XP, and Windo	Prevents users from
1075	User	Control Panel\Regional and Language Options	HKCU\Software\Policies\Microsoft\Control Panel\International!Hid	At least Windows Vista	This policy removes t
1076	User	Control Panel\Display	HKCU\Software\Microsoft\Windows\CurrentVersion\Policies\Syste	At least Microsoft Windows 2000	Removes the Screen
1077	User	Windows Components\Windows Media Player\User In	HKCU\Software\Policies\Microsoft\WindowsMediaPlayer!HideSecu	Windows Media Player 9 Series and later.	Hides the Security ta
1078	User	Control Panel\Display	HKCU\Software\Microsoft\Windows\CurrentVersion\Policies\Syste	At least Microsoft Windows 2000	Removes the Setting
1079	User	Control Panel	HKCU\Software\Microsoft\Windows\CurrentVersion\Policies\Explc	At least Microsoft Windows 2000	Hides specified Cont
1080	User	Control Panel\Add or Remove Programs	HKCU\Software\Microsoft\Windows\CurrentVersion\Policies\Unin	Microsoft Windows Server 2003, Windows XP, and Windo	Removes the "Add a
1081	User	Control Panel\Add or Remove Programs	HKCU\Software\Microsoft\Windows\CurrentVersion\Policies\Unin	Microsoft Windows Server 2003, Windows XP, and Windo	Removes the "Add pr
1082	User	Control Panel\Add or Remove Programs	HKCU\Software\Microsoft\Windows\CurrentVersion\Policies\Unin	Microsoft Windows Server 2003, Windows XP, and Windo	Prevents users from

Figure 21-19 An example of the information found in the spreadsheet.

While on the subject of Registry keys, this was obviously a bad thing with Windows NT 4 system policies. Registry changes were made that were permanent. If a policy was removed, the setting was not undone—the Registry was tattooed, which means the setting was left in the Registry. Is this still the case? No, at least not for the built-in administrative templates, which update special Registry areas reserved for policies. However, custom admx files can still affect other Registry areas that are not true Group Policies and are not undone if the policy is removed. These are known as preferences because they still tattoo. Most of these settings are under the HKEY_LOCAL_MACHINE/Software/Policies and HKEY_CURRENT_USER/Software/Policies, which are the preferred locations. However, some settings are also written to the HKEY_LOCAL_MACHINE\SOFTWARE\Microsoft\Windows\CurrentVersion\policies and HKEY_ CURRENT_USER\SOFTWARE\Microsoft\Windows\CurrentVersion\policies locations.

One great feature in the Group Policy Editor in Windows Server 2008 is its ability to search and filter. You can select Filter Options from the context menu of an Administrative Template. This opens a dialog that shows settings based on if they are managed, configured, and commented; it also includes keyword filters to search for a string in the policy setting title, explanation text, and even the comment. You can also enable requirement filters, so settings have to meet certain criteria. This is a great feature not just for finding settings but also limiting what you view. When you combine the filter with the All Settings node in Administrative Templates, it's a great way to quickly view what you care about in one place.

Let's assume you want to edit your Internet Explorer settings for users. After selecting Edit for your GPO, expand the User Configuration, expand Policies (preferences are covered in the "Group Policy Preferences" section), expand Windows Settings, and finally expand Internet Explorer Maintenance. Figure 21-20 shows that Internet Explorer maintenance is broken up into areas including the browser user interface (which enables customized graphics and titles), connection information such as proxy configuration and connection options, URLs, Security (which enables sites to be preconfigured into certain security zones), and Authenticode settings and Programs (which enable configuration of things such as the default application for Web page editing).

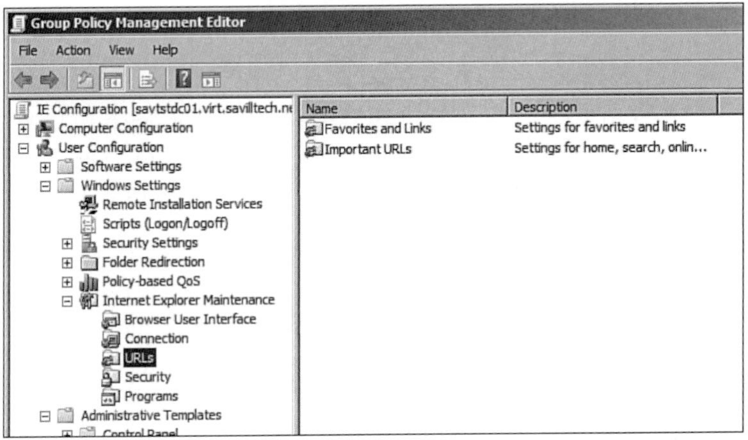

FIGURE 21-20 Internet Explorer confirmation is outside the Administrative Template section, with its configuration controlled by a specific Internet Explorer settings client-side extension (iedkcs32.dll).

For your purposes, you want to change the URL settings, so perform the following:

1. Select URLs under Internet Explorer Maintenance. There are two options in the details pane: Favorites and Links and Important URLs.
2. Double-click Favorites and Links, which opens the dialog to control the Favorites menu, as shown in Figure 21-21.

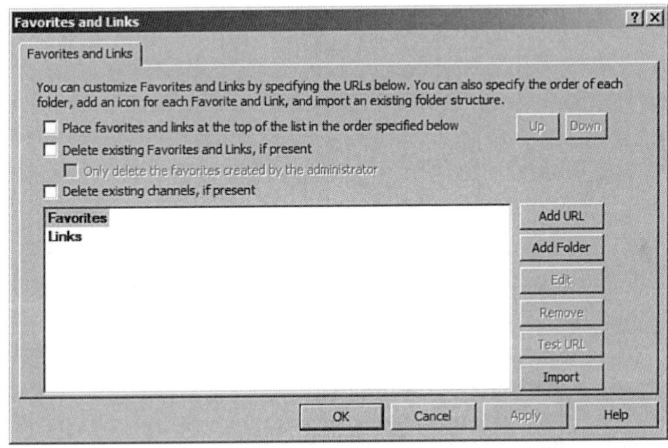

FIGURE 21-21 The default Favorites and Links screen provides only Favorites and Links as menu options.

3. To make the links specified in the Group Policy display at the top of the Favorites, select Place Favorites and Links at the Top of the List in the Order Specified Below. The Delete Existing Favorites and Links, if Present option removes all existing links (see Figure 21-22). However, if you also check the Only Delete the Favorites Created by the Administrator option, it only removes shortcuts created by previous policies.
4. Click the Add URL and Add Folder buttons to create an identical URL structure on all computers that have the GPO applied. For URLs you want users to see in Internet Explorer, place them in the Favorites section. For URLs to be shown as part of the Links toolbar, add them to the Links section. Once complete, click OK.

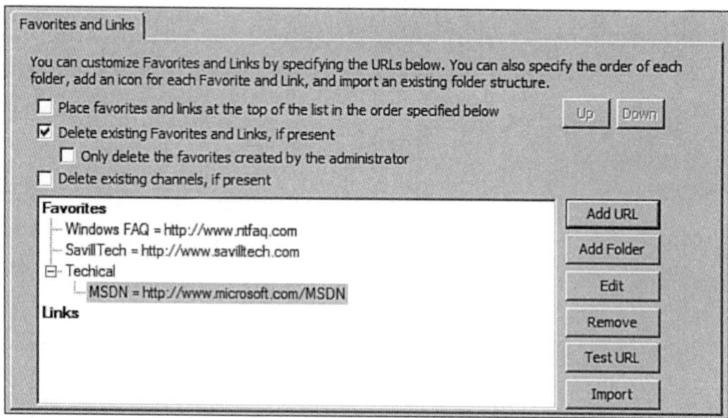

FIGURE 21-22 With this policy, any existing links would be removed on the client and replaced with those shown.

5. Now you can change the default home page (in addition to the search and help URLs). Double-click Important URLs and change the Home Page URL, as shown in Figure 21-23. Click OK and then close the Group Policy Editor.

The GPO is now created, but does absolutely nothing. Now link it to a possible target for a GPO, which is a site, domain, or organizational unit. Right-click a domain or organizational unit and select Link an Existing GPO from the context menu. A list of all the GPOs in the local domain is displayed. Alternate domains in the forest can be selected. However, this is not advisable due to the performance implications of such linkages. Select the GPO to link, and click OK, as shown in Figure 21-24.

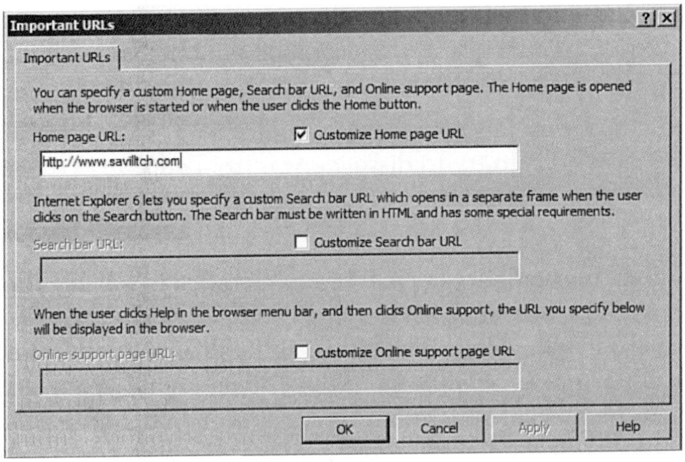

FIGURE 21-23 Check the box for the URL you want to change—for example, the Customize Home Page URL.

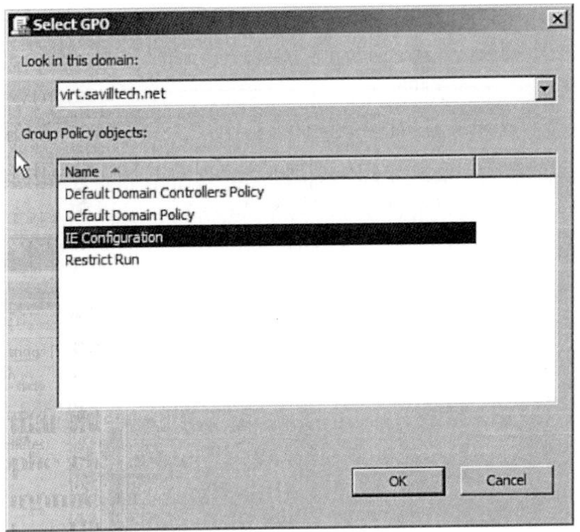

FIGURE 21-24 This domain only has two custom GPOs (in addition to the two standard ones).

Any users who are in the selected domain or OU (or a child) get the new policy at the Group Policy refresh. Of course, you can expedite this by running the `gpupdate` command on the client; once applied, the users favorites should contain those selected. URLs added by Group Policy are not removed from the client if removed from the policy. To enable URLs to be removed from the client, enable the policy to delete existing Favorites and Links created by Administrator, as described in step 3 previously.

Viewing Sites

Applying GPOs to a domain or organizational unit was covered earlier. But what about sites? Sites are displayed outside of a domain but as part of the forest configuration. However, when the site's branch is selected, there are no sites. This is to try to dissuade you from applying GPOs at a site level. To see sites, right-click on Sites and select Show Sites from the context menu, as shown in Figure 21-25. This is not a best practice, and the use of GPO linking at sites should have specific reasons.

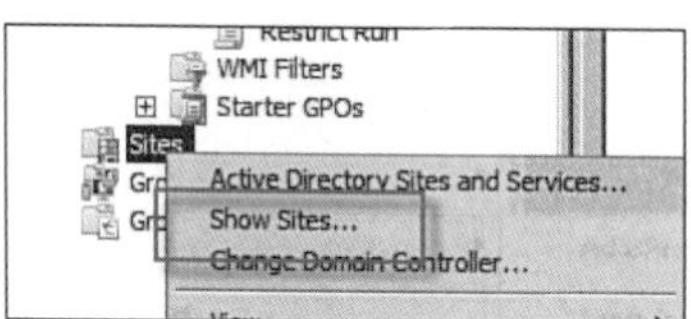

FIGURE 21-25 View the sites, but do not touch unless there are specific reasons (which would normally be network related, IPSec, and so on).

Why Not Link Cross Domain?

Why not link to a site? Linking at a site, which is a forest-wide concept, could mean the GPO is applied to users/computers who belong to different domains. That is the real problem: cross-domain GPO linking.

Cross-domain linking has three issues. The first is performance. When a user/computer has to apply a GPO in another domain, communication is required between domain controllers in the various domains, which in turn requires passing of credentials between domain controllers. In addition to performance, the management of GPOs cross domains is more complex with administrators in other domains having limited visibility into the contents of GPOs. This all folds into the third issue: troubleshooting. If you can't easily see GPO content, it is hard to troubleshoot problems.

Avoid linking cross domains. It's better to export and import the GPO into the other domains so it's executed locally.

Before going any further, let's look briefly at some of the useful Group Policy features in terms of policy and settings.

Software Deployment

Although more sophisticated solutions exist for software deployment, such as System Center Configuration Manager and even System Center

Essentials, Group Policy is still a great way to deploy software in the absence of a better solution. Group Policy has two types of software deployment:

- **Assigned**. When software is assigned, if the assignment is to a user, the software is installed when the user logs on to the computer; upon first execution, the software installation is finalized. If software is assigned to a computer, then the software is installed when the computer starts, and it is available to any users of the computer. Once again, the first time the software is used, the installation is considered finalized. The time to finalize an installation should be minimal (seconds) but depends on the application.
- **Published**. When software is published to a user, the software is displayed in the Add or Remove Programs control panel applet for manually triggered installation. You cannot publish software to a computer.

Notice that for assigned software, either the user must log on or the computer must be restarted. Software installations are not performed as part of a Group Policy refresh. They are only performed at startup/logon as part of foreground Group Policy processing.

One big advantage of using Group Policy to deploy software is the installation of the software is executed in a privileged context, which means the logged-on user does not need to be an Administrator or highly privileged/power user.

Distribution Point on the Network

The first requirement to deploy software is a distribution point on the network, where the installation files for the software can exist and be accessed from the clients; this is a share on a server, or for a more distributed organization, part of a distributed file system namespace. It is recommended to create a sub-folder for each product with a meaningful name (for example, Office2003SP1), which allows the folder structure to also be used outside of GPO deployments.

Microsoft Software Installer

This brings us to the second requirement. Software should be in the format of Microsoft Software Installer, preferably an MSI file for full Group Policy deployment support. Although you can deploy other types of installation media, the preferred and fully supported option is an MSI file.

The method to assign software is the same for both computer and user; it affects whether you select the User Configuration or Computer Configuration area of the GPO:

1. Open the GPO you want to use to deploy the software (ensuring the software installation files are already on a network location).
2. Expand Policies, Software Settings and right-click on Software installation; select New, Package from the displayed context menu (see Figure 21-26).

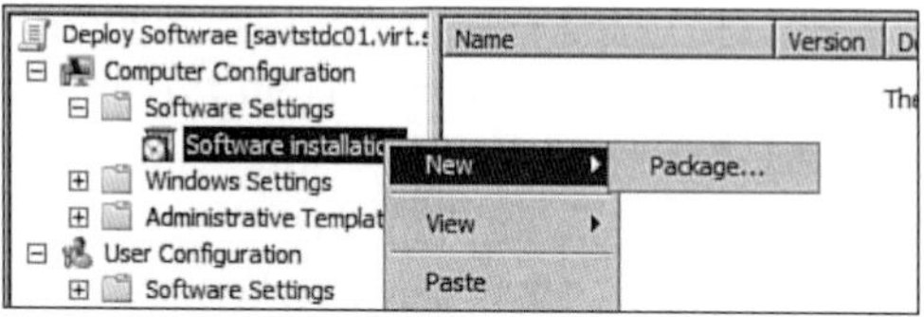

FIGURE 21-26 Select New, Package from the context menu.

3. In the Open dialog, enter the network path where the software resides (for example, \\savtstdc01\software) and select the MSI file you want to deploy. In this case, just deploy the administrative tools (see Figure 21-27). Click Open.

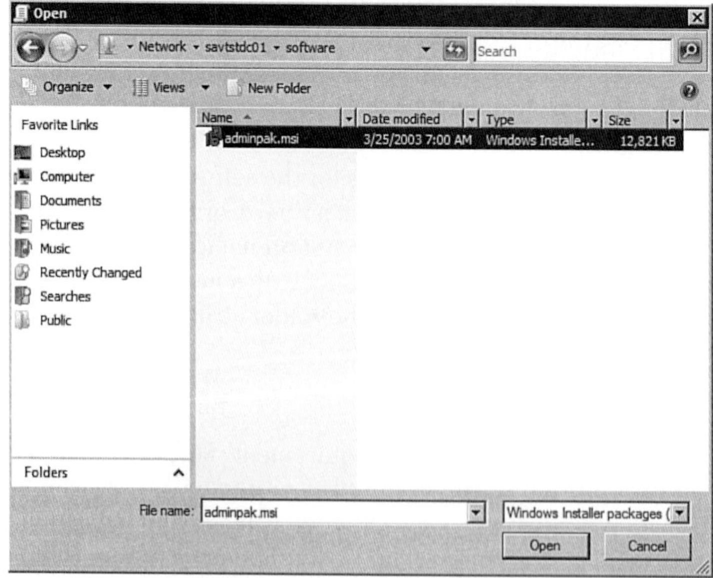

FIGURE 21-27 Enter the network path where the software resides.

4. A list of deployment options is displayed (see Figure 21-28). If you are pushing software for a computer, the option to publish is grayed out and you can only select Assigned. The Advanced option is beyond the scope of this chapter, but it enables the deployment properties to be modified, configuration of application categories, designation of the package as an upgrade to an existing package, and controlling the install based on security group. However, you can set most of these after initial configuration by changing the properties of the software.

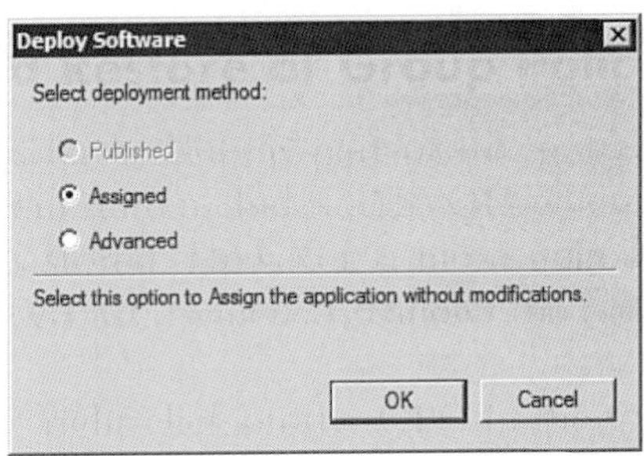

FIGURE 21-28 Choosing the deployment method for the application.

5. The new software is displayed in the Software installation window and installed on the computers for users who have the GPO applied on next startup/logon.

Right-click a Software installation entry and a dialog appears, enabling advanced configuration options, such as categories, upgrades, security, and so on, to be configured. One useful area in particular is under the Deployment tab. You can choose to uninstall the software if the GPO is no longer assigned to the user/computer, as shown in Figure 21-29. By default, this is not the case, and software stays installed. Software is removed only at computer startup/logon and not during a user session, when the user could be using the software.

The process to publish an application is identical, except the option of Published is selected in step 4. If you publish a lot of software applications, you might want to define categories to make it easy for users. Right-click on Software installation to show the options for software deployment. For example, you can set applications for certain file types under the File Extensions tab, so you can set Winzip application for ZIP file extensions. The Categories tab is used to add categories for the domain, which can then be selected for a published application to be displayed within via the software applications Categories tab. Figure 21-30 shows an application that has been published via Group Policy.

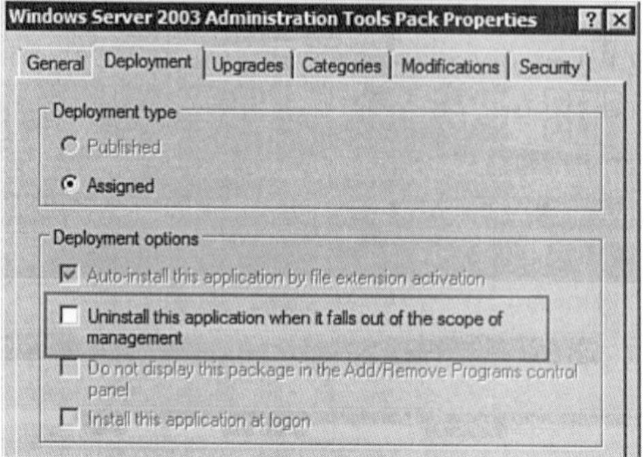

FIGURE 21-29 Uninstall This Application When It Falls Out of the Scope of Management can be a useful option to uninstall software, if the user/computer falls out of the scope of the GPO installing the software.

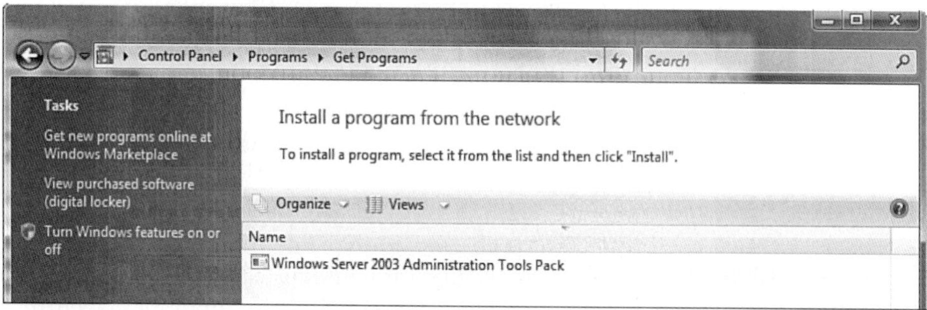

FIGURE 21-30 A published application shows as soon as Group Policy refreshes and does not require the foreground Group Policy to be listed because it's a manually triggered installation.

To remove software, right-click the entry under Software installation and select Remove from the All Tasks menu. When you remove an application, you are given the option to immediately remove the software from users and computers, or allow the software to stay installed but prevent new deployments of the application.

ZAP

Software deployment with MSI files is great, and most new applications come with MSI files to install software (except for Office 2007, which was a bit of a disaster). However, there is a way to deploy non-MSI–based software installations: Create a ZAP file. *ZAP files* are just text files that provide instructions for deploying older applications. However, there are some restrictions:

- ZAP-deployed applications cannot be assigned to users or computers; they can only be published, which means they are available only through user-based deployment.
- Applications do not automatically repair themselves because MSI is what gives an application self-healing capabilities.
- Applications do not install with elevated privileges, which means users require the privilege to install software.

(Given these restrictions, if you have more complex, non-MSI–based applications to install, you might be better off looking at SCCM/SMS.)

The ZAP file consists of two sections: the [Application] and [Ext] sections.

The application section ([Application]) contains the name of the setup command, a version to display, a friendly name, and a URL. The file extension section ([Ext]) lists extensions that should be associated with the new application. Note the full path to the application must be used for the `SetupCommand`; if any spaces exist in the path, enclose the entire path in double quotes:

```
 [Application]
FriendlyName = Project 64 1.6
SetupCommand = \\savtstdc01\software\setup_project64_1.6.exe
DisplayVersion =1.6
Publisher = Project 64
URL = http://www.pj64-emu.com/

[Ext]
z64=
```

The ZAP file is published the same way as a normal application. However, when the dialog is displayed, to select the installation file to install, change the type from MSI to ZAW (Zero Administration for Windows) Down-Level Application Packages (*.zap) and then select the required ZAP file (see Figure 21-31). Because ZAP files can only be published, and publishing is possible only for User Configuration, the option to select a ZAP is displayed only for User Configuration software installations—NOT Computer Configuration software installations. After a ZAP file is selected, the type of software deployment can only be Published; Assigned is grayed out.

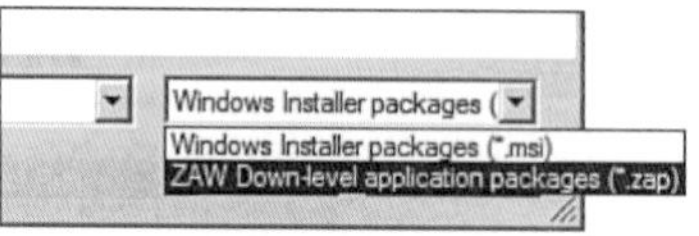

FIGURE 21-31 The ZAW Down-Level Application Packages option allows the section of a ZAP file for software installation.

The ZAP-based deployment displays in the same network-based software installation location for the Add or Remove Programs control panel applet.

Software Restrictions

In addition to helping deploy software, Group Policy can also be used to stop other software from being executed. Software Restriction policies are available for both User and Computer configurations and are found under Windows Settings, Security Settings, Software Restrictions. If you deploy software restrictions by computer, it stops anyone on the computer from running the restricted software; setting the restrictions by user configuration stops only specific users. Like software installation, software restrictions take effect only at foreground Group Policy processing, therefore requiring a computer restart/user logon, depending on where the policy is set.

There are sophisticated options for using software restrictions based on whether the software is from the Internet; if so, other options include the security zone site it downloaded from; certificate rules requiring digitally signed code to execute; hash rules, which are unique values based on the content of a file (this means you can block a file, and even if a user renames it, he still won't be able to run it); and the most simple approach, which is simply blocking or allowing a path. Because there is limited space, a path rule is covered here. However, a word of caution: Don't be too quick to restrict software. If, for example, you blocked everything under Program Files and then added exceptions, you might quickly render your OS unusable, so always test these on a limited audience first!

1. Right-click Software Restrictions and select New Software Restriction Policies (see Figure 21-32).

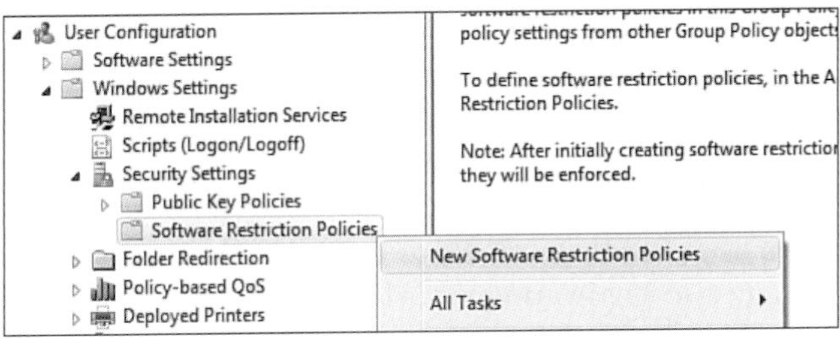

FIGURE 21-32 Select New Software Restriction Policies.

2. Two nodes display under Software Restriction Policies: Security Levels and Additional Rules. Select Security Levels.
3. Under Security Levels, three levels are displayed: Disallowed is for blocked software; Basic User is software that can run but runs without administrator credentials; and Unrestricted is software that can run with the access rights of the user. Right-click on any option but Unrestricted and the option to Set as default is shown, which forces the policy to that mode (Unrestricted is already the default). At this point, you have a choice: If you leave unrestricted as the default, you can then add entries to Disallowed to block certain applications/source. Alternatively, you can set Disallowed as the default and then add exceptions to Basic User/Unrestricted that can run, but this is a lot more work. However, it is necessary for a locked-down environment. For now, assume you leave Unrestricted as the default and want to block Lego Star Wars. Figure 21-33 shows the capability to set one of the levels as the default.

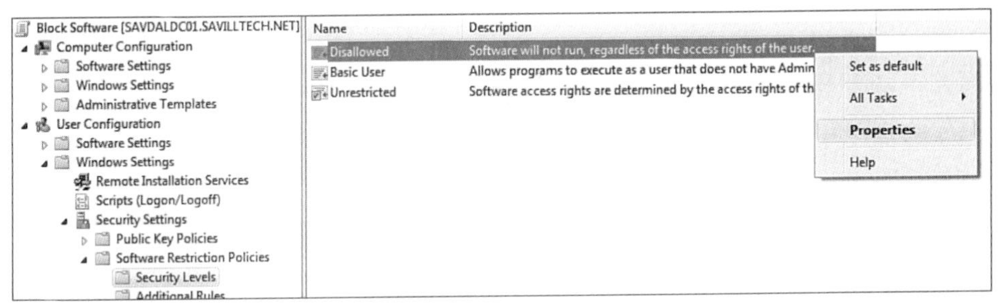

FIGURE 21-33 Think carefully before setting Disallowed as the default.

4. To set an exception, select Additional Rules.
5. Right-click on Additional Rules, and the various types of rule are shown (hash, certificate, Network Zone, and Path). Select New Path Rule.
6. Enter the path or file name, and enter a description. Browse if the path is locally available and click OK, as shown in Figure 21-34. You can use environment variables as part of path rules. For example, instead of using C:\Program Files, you can use %ProgramFiles% and %ProgramFiles(x86)% (for 64-bit platforms). You can also use a wildcard (*) as part of the path.

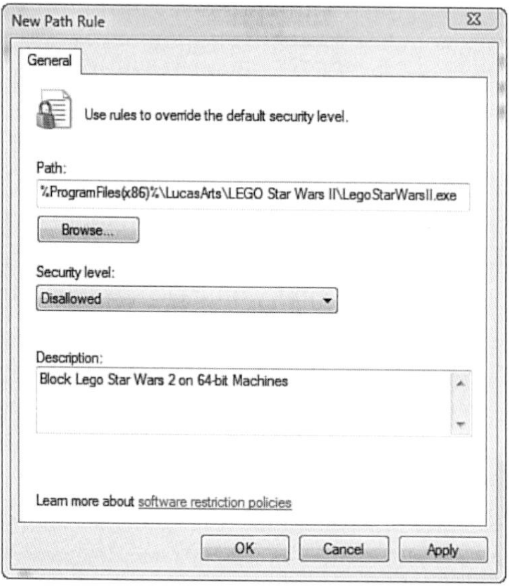

FIGURE 21-34 Boo to blocking Lego Star Wars 2.

Now when you try to start the Lego Star Wars 2 executable, you get an error informing you it is blocked by Group Policy, as shown in Figure 21-35.

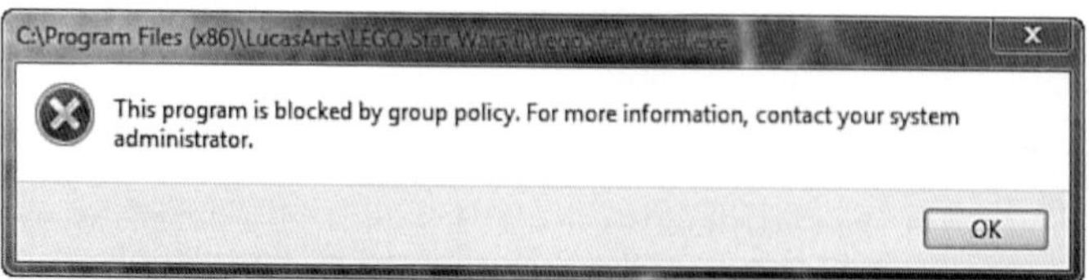

FIGURE 21-35 Well, it could be worse; it could have blocked Halo 2.

Restricting Group Memberships

One common issue is users getting added to the local Administrators group or wanting better control over group memberships. Group Policy can be used to configure the membership of local groups. Because only computers have groups, the configuration is available only as part of the Computer Configuration under Windows Settings, Security Settings, Restricted Groups. To use it, right-click on Restricted Groups and select Add Group from the displayed context menu. You are prompted for the group name (for example, Administrators). Click OK. You can now specify who should be a member of the group, as shown in Figure 21-36.

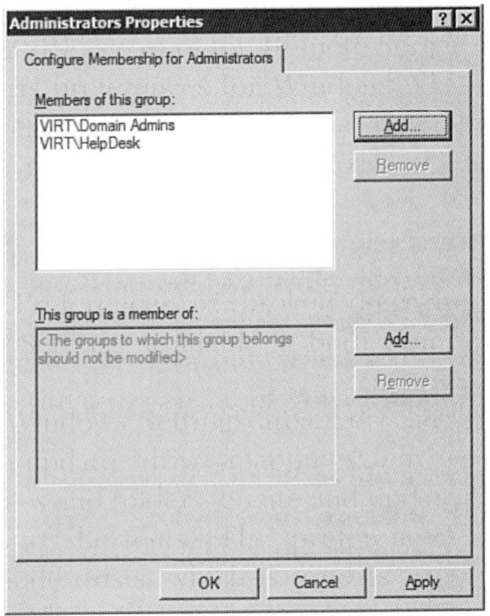

FIGURE 21-36 Here, the domain administrators and the helpdesk group are members of the local Administrators group.

When the Group Policy is refreshed, the members of the group named are replaced with those defined in the policy. If additional people were currently members of the group, they are removed when the restricted Group Policy is processed.

Updating File System and Registry Permissions

Under Computer Configuration, Windows Settings, Security Settings are areas for Registry and File System. Their use is intuitive, and they work the same as the other restrictions. For the file system, right-click and add a new folder or file; you can then set permissions on it. Those computers receiving the policy set the file system settings described in the Group Policy.

Modifying GPO Application Behavior

You now know how to create GPOs and link them to OUs, domains, and even sites if you need to; you also understand child objects. Even those in child containers get Group Policy applied to their parent containers; in the case of a conflict, the policy settings applied closest to the user/computer win, as shown in Figure 21-37. If there is a conflict between a computer setting and a user setting, under normal conditions the user settings are applied after the computer settings, so the user settings would take precedence. In this example, at each of the three layers for the user (the domain, the parent OU, and the child OU), there is an OU defining the default home page. As can be seen in the example, the user has the home page that is set on her OU.

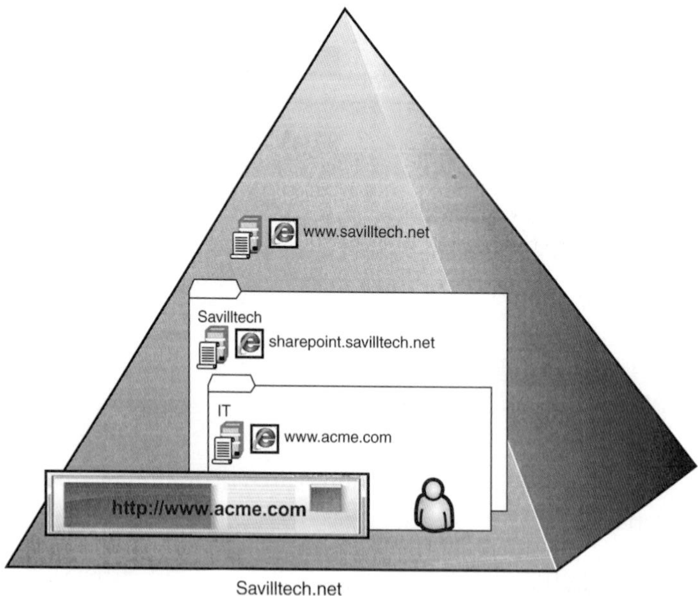

FIGURE 21-37 The normal flow of Group Policy, with the user receiving the default home page set in the GPO closest to them.

Well, this is not always the case. There are many times that the capability to control and manage Group Policy for organizational units is delegated to local support areas, which enables exactly the preceding scenario.

At the domain level, the domain administrators want a certain setting for the company—but then different people, who have control just at the level of organizational units, decide they want different settings that override those set at the domain. In many cases, this might be fine, and you stay away from the politics involved in such decisions. However, there might be times when a setting *must* be a certain value for legal or other compliance reasons, or is just what the company management wants. At the same time, you might not want to revoke the permissions for local support groups to manage their own Group Policies. You want to be able to set certain policies as definitive and that cannot be overwritten even by policies set on OUs closer to the user/computer. Thankfully, such functionality does exist. Notice on Linked Group Policy Objects that there is a column called Enforced, as shown in Figure 21-38.

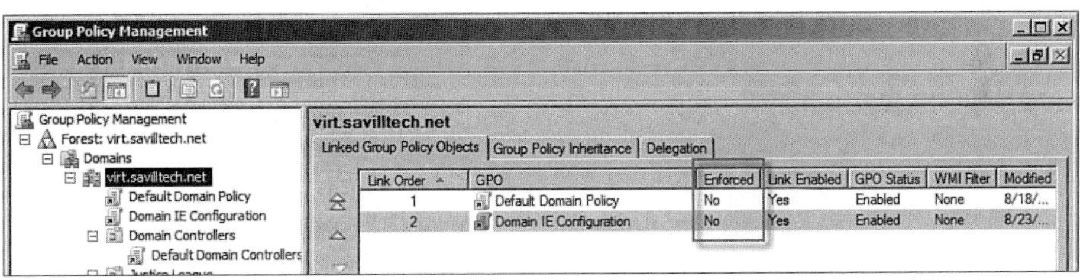

FIGURE 21-38 The GPMC gives great information about linked GPOs; that is one of the reasons it's such a welcome addition.

When you *enforce* a GPO link (also known as setting it as No Override), the settings contained in the linked GPO cannot be overwritten by settings applied by GPOs, which are applied subsequently (for example, child OUs). This affects only settings that conflict; all other settings from subsequently applied GPOs are combined as usual. To set a GPO link as enforced, right-click the link, and select Enforced from the context menu (see Figure 21-39). Click OK at the confirmation dialog.

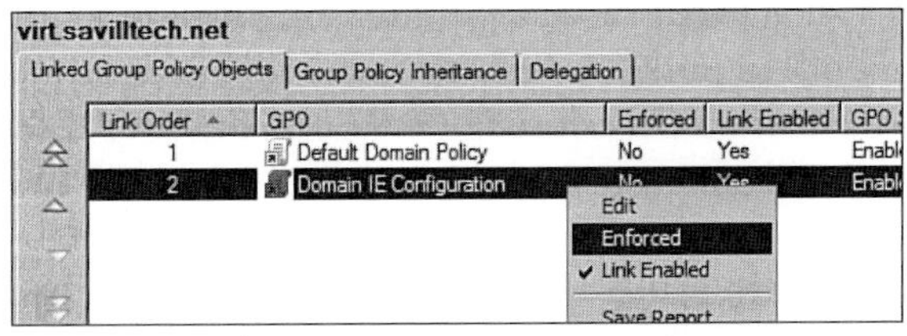

FIGURE 21-39 Enforcing makes this link of the GPO unchangeable once set, but ONLY this particular link. It's a setting on the link, NOT the actual GPO; if the GPO is used in other places, only this link instance is set as enforced.

When a link is enforced, the Enforced column is changed to Yes, and you see a padlock on the link icon. In the previous example, if you set the main SavillTech OU's link to its GPO with the IE configuration set to enforced, the client gets the home page configured in the GPO for the SavillTech OU; this is instead of that set in the user's local OU, as shown in Figure 21-40.

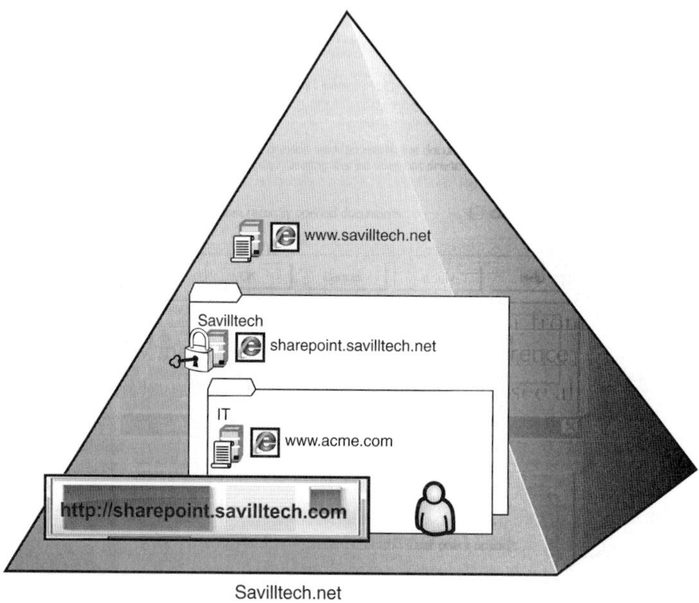

FIGURE 21-40 With the Savilltech OU Internet Explorer policy link set to enforced, the user gets a home page of sharepoint.savilltech.com instead of that set on its local OU.

What if multiple GPOs are set as enforced? It works in reverse of the normal rules. The FIRST GPO link set as enforced takes precedence, so the highest-enforced GPO link has precedence if policy settings conflict on multiple GPOs linked as enforced. Remember, only settings that conflict between policies are affected, not the entire GPO. Multiple levels of enforcement are possible and are quite common. However, in the interest of simplicity, try to not overuse enforcement.

There might be times when you do not want an organizational unit to receive any policies that were applied at higher levels, effectively blocking the normal inheritance of Group Policy. This might be desirable to a business unit that is self managed, has its own organizational unit, and wants no policies set from the domain. There is a facility to enable this blocking known as *Block Inheritance*. Unlike the No Override, which is GPO link-specific, the Block Inheritance is set at a container level—for example, the domain or organizational unit. When enabled by right-clicking on a domain or OU and selecting Block Inheritance, no GPOs linked at higher levels are applied. As shown in Figure 21-41, if IT enabled Block Inheritance on their OU, then no Group Policies set at site, domain, or the SavillTech OU would be read, and only those GPOs linked at IT explicitly would be processed.

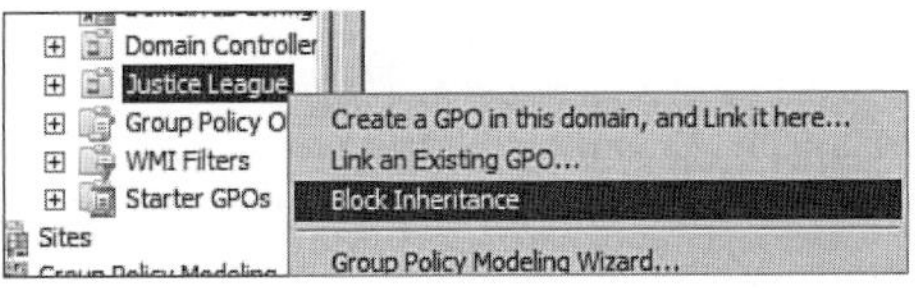

FIGURE 21-41 Just one click blocks the inheritance of other policies set from above.

What if you set a policy at the domain level that is enforced, and a child OU sets Block Inheritance? An Enforcement of a higher GPO link overrides a child's Block Inheritance. This is important, as it enables organizational administrators to ensure important policies are not blocked by lower-level administrators. This is shown in Figure 21-42 for the Justice League OU that has block inheritance enabled, which can be seen because the Default Domain GPO is not applied but the enforced Domain IE Configuration is still in effect.

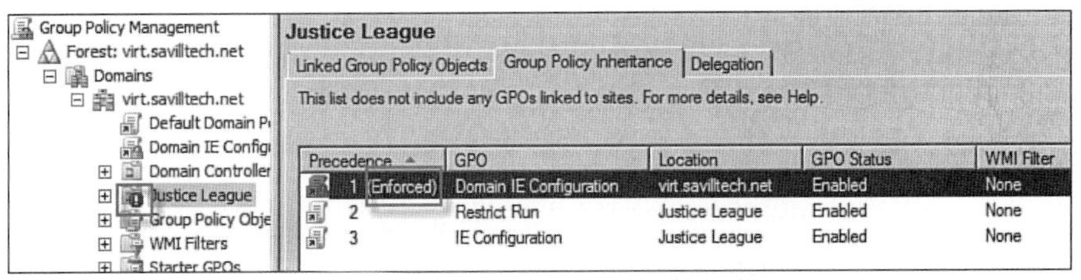

FIGURE 21-42 The exclamation mark over the OU shows that Block Inheritance is enabled, but it still has a policy that was set at the domain level.

Again, Enforcement and Block Inheritance should be used sparingly for ease of troubleshooting and maintenance.

While on the subject of performance, here's a good practice to get into. If you have a GPO for which you are using only the Computer Configuration portion or the User Configuration portion, disable the other part to save the Group Policy engine, checking half the GPO that has no settings. To enable/disable the User/Computer portions of a GPO, change the setting on the original GPO and not on a link, so this affects any linkage of the GPO you update.

Within the GPO branch of the domain that contains the GPO, right-click on the GPO and select the Edit context menu option. This opens up four options for the GPO, as shown in Figure 21-43.

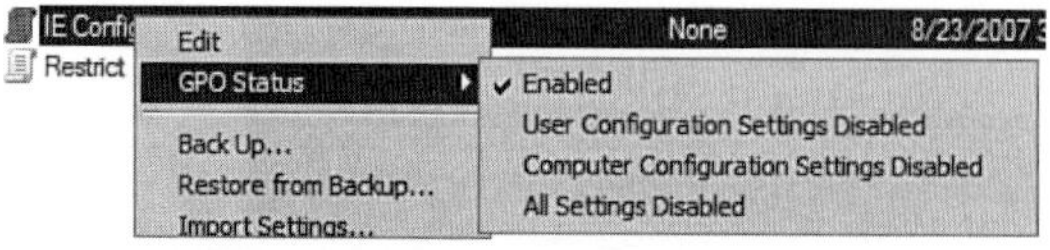

FIGURE 21-43 This context menu gives easy access to controlling the application of a GPO, no matter where it is linked.

The first option of Enabled controls whether the GPO takes effect when linked and whether both the User and Computer configurations are applied when linked. The second option of User Configuration Settings Disabled means only the Computer Configuration Settings are applied where the GPO is linked. Computer Configuration Settings Disabled means only user configuration is applied. All Settings Disabled means none of the GPO settings are applied, which disables the GPO, preventing it from having any functionality. Only one option is selected at any time.

If I had a GPO that had only User Configuration, as in my Internet Explorer configuration GPO, I would select the option Computer Configuration Settings Disabled. The status of a GPO is shown in the GPO Status column for linked GPOs and shows the same text as that shown on the GPO Status Edit menu (see Figure 21-44).

Linked Group Policy Objects | Group Policy Inheritance | Delegation

GPO	Enforced	Link Enabled	GPO Status
Restrict Run	No	Yes	Enabled
IE Configuration	No	Yes	Computer configuration settings disabled

FIGURE 21-44 The GPO Status column helps you to easily see which part of a GPO takes effect.

One final, useful function on a GPO link comes into play in this scenario. There are times you don't want to remove the link, but you also don't want it to be applied. Because a GPO might be used in multiple locations, you don't want to modify the GPO directly and set its status to All Settings Disabled; this would affect all other uses of the GPO. Instead, a link can be disabled by right-clicking the link and unselecting the Link Enabled context menu option. This sets its Link Enabled state to No, and its icon appears grayed out (see Figure 21-45).

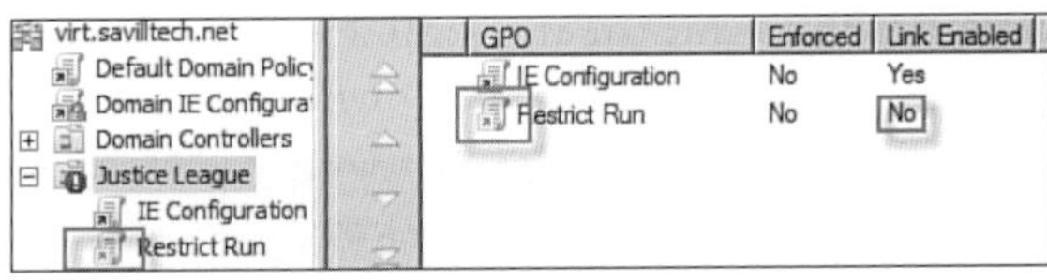

FIGURE 21-45 Link-disabled GPOs don't allow their policies to be applied while avoiding the need to re-link the GPO at a later time.

Loopback Processing

Normally, Group Policy application depends on where the computer object exists and where the user object exists. However, you might have special computers to which you want certain user GPOs to be applied, regardless of where the user object resides. For example, a kiosk machine would fit these criteria. No matter who logs on to the kiosk, you probably want strict user policies that can be configured on the OU containing the computer. This means the User Configuration is applied as if the user object was located in the computer's container, regardless of where the user object existed.

How do you accomplish creating the capability for the user policies applied to be based on where the computer resides? The answer is *loopback processing*. When enabled, loopback processing makes the user policies that are applied ascertained by the location of the computer account the user is logging on to, instead of where the actual user account resides.

To enable loopback processing, navigate to the Computer Configuration, Administrative Templates, System, Group Policy area of a GPO that is linked to the location of the computer object. Double-click the User Group Policy loopback processing mode and set it to Enabled, as shown in Figure 21-46. Once enabled, select the mode of the loopback processing. The options are Merge or Replace, as follows:

- **Merge Mode**. With Merge mode, the full list of User Configuration policies from GPOs, which would normally be applied to the user based on the user's location, are gathered and evaluated. Then the full list of User Configuration policies from GPOs based on the computer's location are gathered and added to the list of policies;

the user gets both sets of User Configuration. Because the computer location GPOs are applied last, they take precedence over the normal user policies. This means any more specific restrictions for User Configuration would be applied regardless of the user's normal configuration.

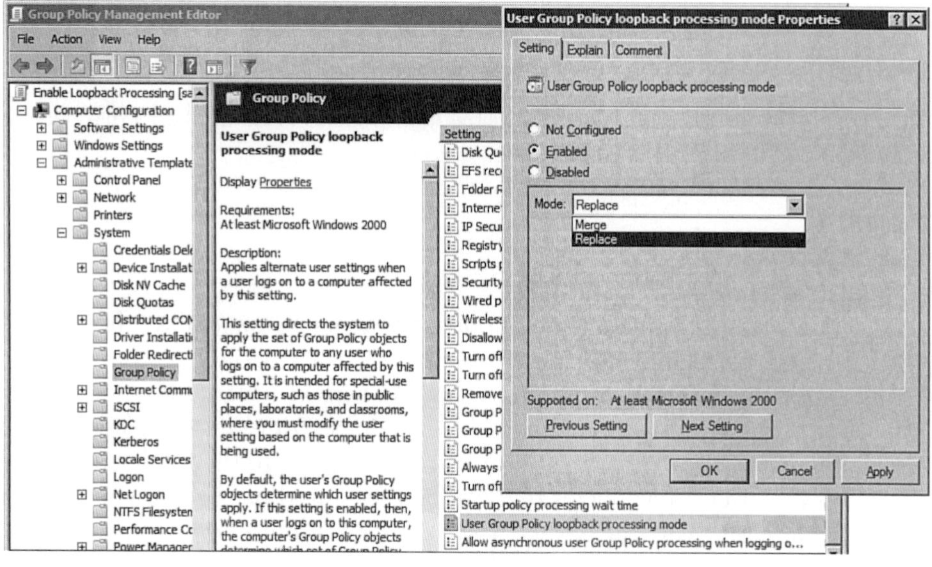

FIGURE 21-46 With loopback enabled, the user gets a policy based on the computer's location.

- **Replace Mode**. With Replace mode, only the User Configuration policies from GPOs based on the computer's location are gathered and applied, with none of the user's own location policies being applied.

This application of policy is shown in Figure 21-47, with an example of how the user configuration is applied in the three scenarios of normal processing, loopback replace mode processing, and loopback merge mode processing.

As Figure 21-47 demonstrates, in normal processing, the user receives the policy based on the user's location. With loopback replace processing mode, the user receives only the policy that is based on the computer that he is logged on to. Finally, with the loopback merge processing mode, the user first receives the policy based on his location, and then the policy based on the computer's location is applied. This means it can overwrite any settings that were set in the computer policy.

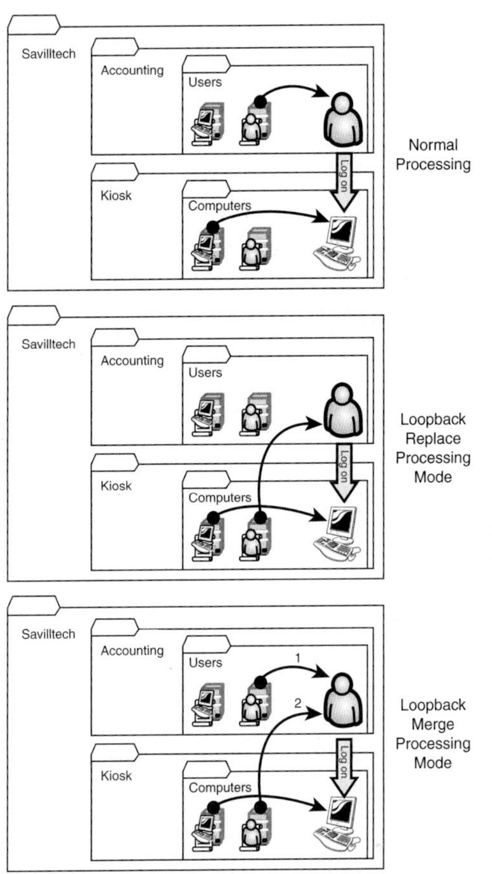

FIGURE 21-47 Group Policy processing modes.

Filtering Application of a Group Policy Object

The capability to apply GPOs to a site, domain, organizational unit, and even the local computer policy is great and granular. However, a user or computer object can exist only in one location; although OUs can be nested, there might be times when it's impractical to create a highly complex OU configuration just for a specific GPO application. For example, apply a GPO for any user who has a certain accreditation. However, you don't want to have to create a new sub OU anywhere the user exists just to link one policy, or because you want to apply a GPO only to computers that have certain hardware.

There are two pieces of functionality that enable this more-granular GPO application, but first a warning. These should be used sparingly—

they make troubleshooting more complex, and GPO application more resource intensive.

The first bit of functionality is the capability to modify the Access Control List (ACL) on a GPO. For users to have a GPO applied, they must have read and apply permissions on the GPO. By default, the Authenticated Users group has permission to apply Group Policy. This includes any user or computer in the domain. However, this group can be removed and other groups given those rights, as follows. Once again, these permissions are applied to the GPO, not the GPO link, so any changes affect any application of the GPO:

1. Select the GPO in the GPMC. This selection can be done via a link of the GPO or directly on the GPO under the GPOs container.
2. Select the GPO via a link, and a dialog is displayed with the following text: "You have selected a link to a GPO. Except for changes to link properties, changes you make here are global to the GPO, and impacts all other locations where this GPO is linked." Assuming you read, understand, and remember this warning, you can check the Do Not Show This Message Again option.
3. The Details pane shows information about the GPO. The Details tab is useful for showing the version numbers for the GPO. This is helpful for troubleshooting, along with the unique ID of the GPO. Notice that you can also set the GPO status (see Figure 21-48).

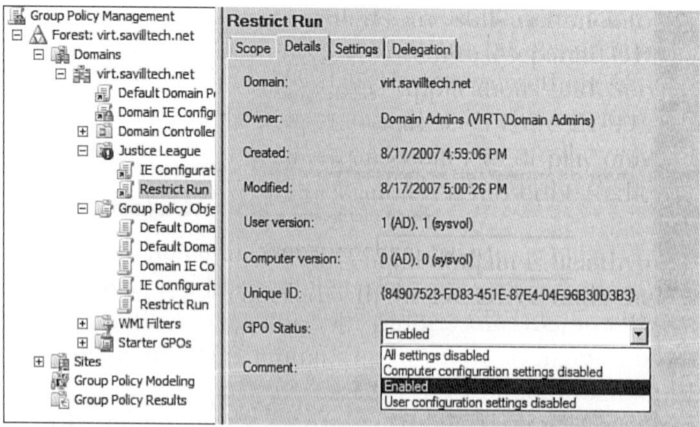

FIGURE 21-48 This information is useful when it comes time to troubleshoot GPO problems.

4. The Scope tab contains information related to the GPO (see Figure 21-49). A drop-down shows all the domains in the forest along with site information and, for the selected container, a list of locations where the GPO is linked. Also note the WMI Filtering displayed at the bottom. The Security Filtering section is used to limit who applies a GPO.
5. Select Authenticated Users and select Remove; as with Authenticated Users, include anyone in the domain who has permission to apply the GPO.
6. Click the Add button to get access to the normal dialog for the addition of objects, which by default are users and groups. However, click the Object Types button to also enable the capability to search for computers. Enter the objects to be given access (users, computers, and/or groups) and click OK. Click Advanced to search for matches or browse the objects in the domain or location specified.

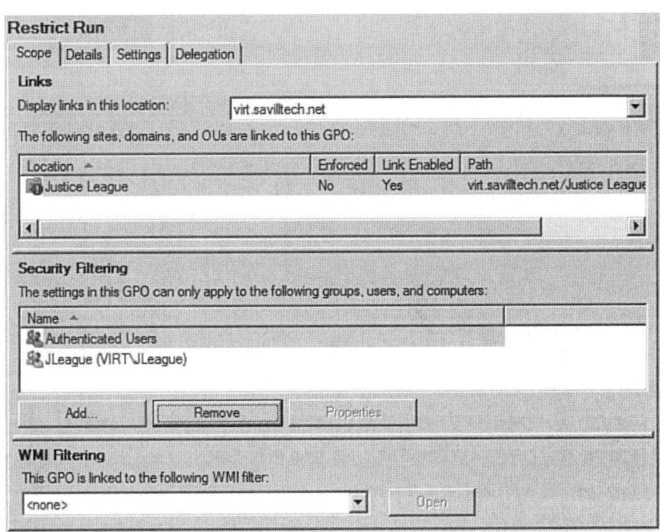

FIGURE 21-49 The Scope tab gives access to all the highly granular GPO application options.

Also note the Properties button that is available for groups; this button allows direct access to the properties of a group, giving easy access to add/remove members or view information.

You can test this. Initially, the JLeague group is empty. I have a user called John in the Justice League organizational unit to whom the Restrict

Run GPO is linked. This is important; the objects have to be within the container that has the policy linked. That seems obvious, but at first, I forgot John was in the default Users container and could not figure out why it was not working. Thankfully, my advanced Group Policy troubleshooting skills saved me (ahem).

So, user John in the Justice League OU updated the Group Policy by running gpupdate, but after running the policy, the `Run` command could still be accessed. This is correct because the application of the GPO is limited to users in the JLeague group. I then added John to the JLeague group, waited for replication to ensure the group membership update had been applied to all domain controllers in the domain, and then ran gpupdate again. User John now received the welcome news, as shown in Figure 21-50.

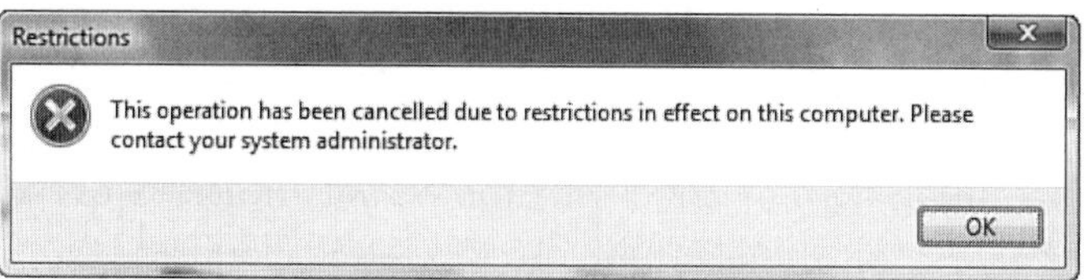

Figure 21-50 Users do not just get an error; they are informed that the action they attempted is not possible because of restrictions.

Security filtering is great for restricting GPO application based on permissions via a group. What about more dynamic restrictions? For example, what about something like deploying software or setting policies based on the specification of a machine deploying an application on a machine that has more than 10GB free disk space?

Most information about a machine can be accessed via WMI; you can access this in many ways, but it enables you to create a structured query as with SQL and return results. For our purposes, you want to query the root\CIMv2 namespace of WMI, which includes the Win32 classes that contain all your computer information. It's possible you are not sure of what you want to query. Fortunately, Microsoft has help for you in the form of the WMI Tools, which can be downloaded at http://www.microsoft.com/downloads/details.aspx?familyid=6430F853-1120-48DB-8CC5-F2ABDC3ED314&displaylang=en. (The link might change, so in that case, search for "Microsoft WMI Tools.") Once installed, a number of tools are made available that run within Internet Explorer as ActiveX components. The CIM Studio enables full access to the WMI space (see

Figure 21-51). However, more useful might be WMI Object Browser, which enables access to WMI, along with information about the values for the WMI attributes for the local machine.

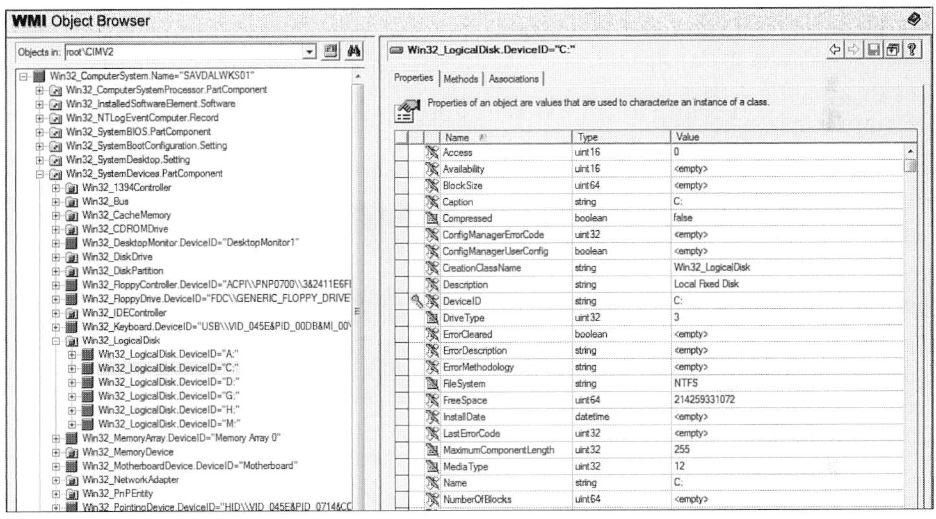

FIGURE 21-51 The WMI Tools application has a number of components. The WMI CIM Studio makes it easy to browse the objects and attributes available via WMI.

Take time to navigate around the tools to get a good idea of the information available. The example screenshot displays the C: drive; there is information around the file system type, the amount of free space, quota state, and much more. For now, create a WMI filter that applies only to computers that have more than 10GB of free space on the C: drive, so let's look at the FreeSpace and Caption attributes. The basic query would be as follows:

```
Select * from Win32_LogicalDisk where FreeSpace>10737418240 and
Caption = "C:"
```

What do you do with the WMI Query Language (WQL) statement? For your domain, you had a WMI Filters node in the navigation pane; now it's time to use it:

1. Select the WMI Filters navigation node item.
2. Right-click in the detail window and select New from the displayed context menu (see Figure 21-52).

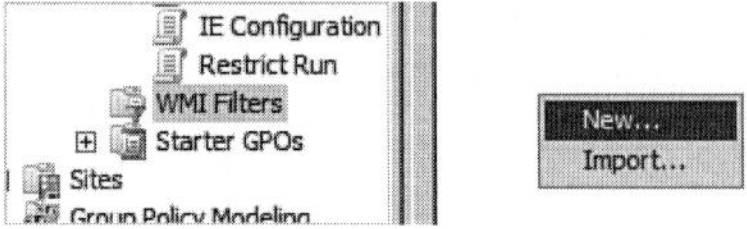

FIGURE 21-52 Creating a new WMI filter.

3. A name for the WMI filter should be given, along with a description (see Figure 21-53).

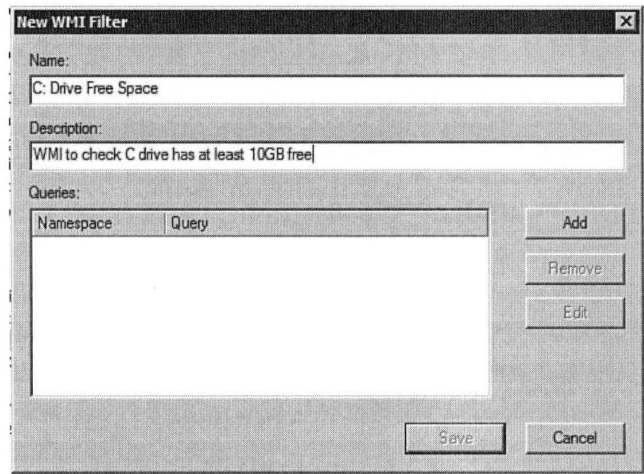

FIGURE 21-53 A descriptive name helps manage the GPO filters, especially as you add more to the environment.

4. Click the Add button to add a WMI Query to the filter.
5. The Browse button enables the namespace to be selected. However, the default root\CIMv2 is used in nearly all situations.
6. Enter the query in the Query area, as shown in Figure 21-54, and click OK.
7. The query is displayed in the main filter dialog. Click Save to complete the filter creation. When Save is selected, a syntax check is performed on the WMI query; if any errors are found, an alert is displayed.

After the filter is created, you can now link it to a GPO. Once again, a WMI filter is linked to the GPO directly. You cannot use a WMI filter on a specific link of a GPO. The WMI filter affects any instance of the GPO being linked to a container.

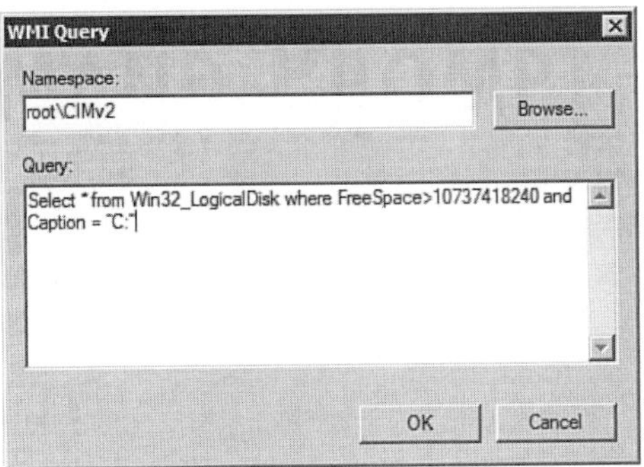

FIGURE 21-54 This query checks for at least 10GB of free space on the C: drive.

To apply the filter to a GPO, the same screen that was used to modify the Security Filtering is used. The bottom area, which is WMI Filtering, has a drop-down of all the defined WMI Filters in the domain (see Figure 21-55).

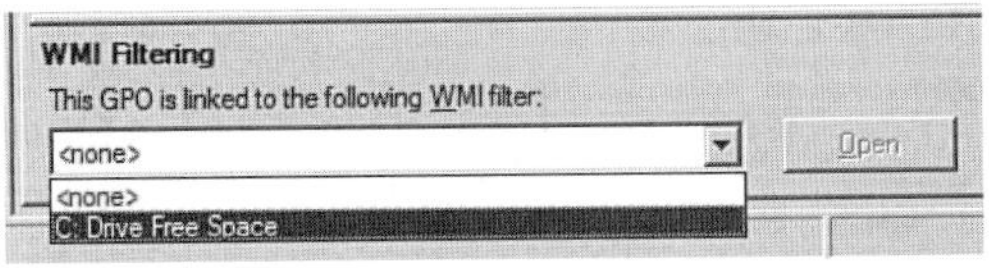

FIGURE 21-55 Applying WMI Filtering is a simple process.

After the WMI filter is applied, policies are applied only if the return value from the WMI query is true. This applies to both user and computer policies. If, for example, you enable a WMI filter for 10GB of free space and apply it to a GPO that performs user configuration, that user configuration takes effect only if the WMI filter returns true. It is not an issue that the settings are not computer-based.

WMI filters can become quite large and complex, and you might want to use the same filter in multiple domains. To support this, it is easy to export and import WMI filters. To export a WMI filter, right-click on the WMI filter, select Export from the context menu, and select a name for the export and a folder to write to (see Figure 21-56).

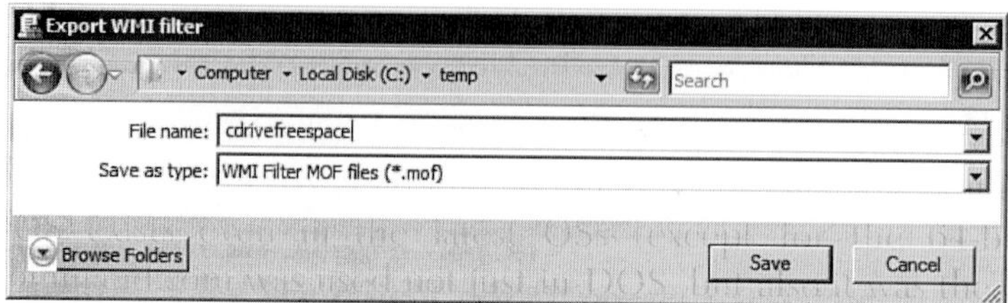

FIGURE 21-56 An easy way to export the WMI filter.

The export is a text file containing the content and description of the WMI filter, as shown in the following listing:

```
instance of MSFT_SomFilter
{
      Author = "administrator@VIRT.SAVILLTECH.NET";
      ChangeDate = "20070830005321.840000-000";
      CreationDate = "20070829213917.866000-000";
      Description = "WMI to check C drive has at least 10GB
free";
      Domain = "virt.savilltech.net";
      ID = "{8C417C0A-E988-47A0-9185-C1FAB0FC1B2C}";
      Name = "C: Drive Free Space";
      Rules = {
instance of MSFT_Rule
{
      Query = "Select * from Win32_LogicalDisk where
FreeSpace>10737418240 and Caption = \"C:\"";
      QueryLanguage = "WQL";
      TargetNameSpace = "root\\CIMv2";
}};
};
```

To import a filter, right-click WMI Filters, select Import, and then select the exported file. Security and WMI Filtering should be used with caution because they impact performance and complicate troubleshooting of the environment. However, they are useful components and help to complete the picture of fine granularity of GPO application.

Starter GPOs

Starter GPOs are stored in a special folder under the SYSVOL structure of the domain name StarterGPOs. The first time you select the Starter GPOs node of the navigation window, you are prompted to create the Starter GPOs folder by pressing the button (see Figure 21-57). Press the button to create the StartGPOs folder in the %sysvol%\<domain> folder.

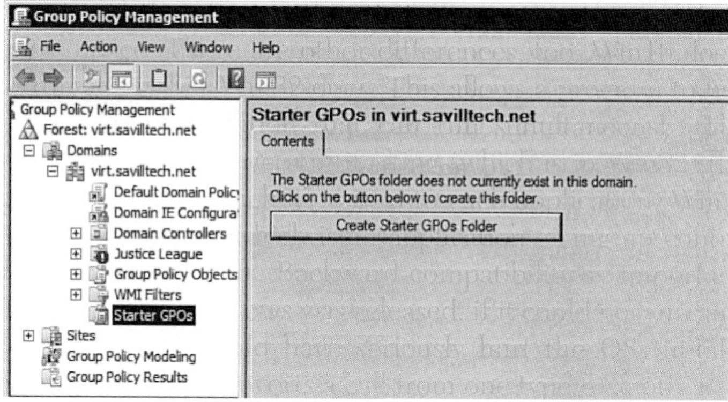

FIGURE 21-57 The GPMC that is part of Windows Server 2008 gives easy access to managing the Starter GPOs.

After the StarterGPOs folder is created, the details pane of the MMC is used for the creation and management of the Starter GPOs. The first item of business is to create a Starter GPO by right-clicking and selecting New from the context menu. Enter a name for the Starter GPO and a comment, as shown in Figure 21-58. Then click OK.

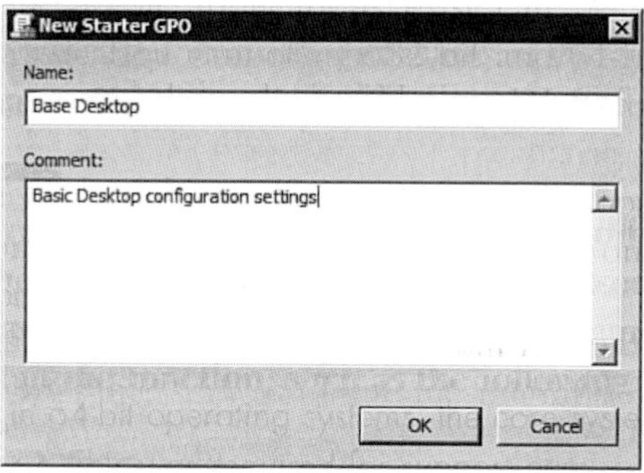

FIGURE 21-58 Name and comment for a new Starter GPO.

Once created, right-click on the Start GPO and select Edit, which opens the Starter GPO in a special "Starter" version of the GPO Editor. Notice immediately that only the administrative templates sections of the

GPOs are available for configuration. You cannot set non-administrative template values in a starter GPO (for example, Software and Windows Settings). Now set the base set of administrative template values you want to have in this foundation as you would with a normal GPO, and once complete, close the starter GPO Editor.

When you create a new GPO, you have the option to select from the created Starter GPOs (see Figure 21-59). Alternatively, you can right-click on the Starter GPO and select New GPO From Starter GPO to create a GPO based on the Starter GPO content.

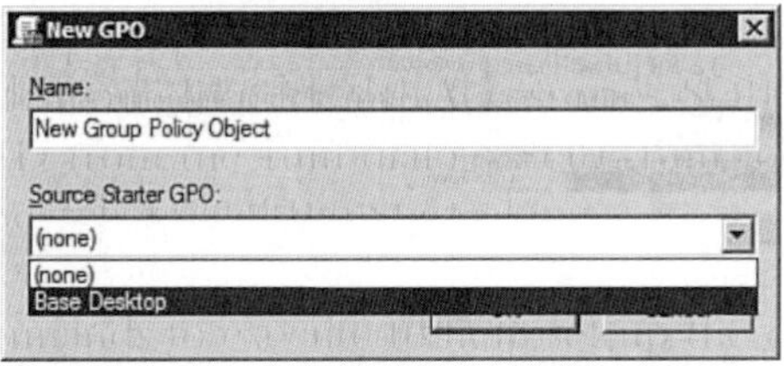

FIGURE 21-59 The new GPO has administrative settings, as defined in the Starter GPO.

What is the point of this functionality? The whole point of Group Policy is it's inheritable, so why would you want multiple GPOs based on the same set of settings? It would be better to set the common settings on the domain, and then any additional or conflicting settings could be set at an OU level. So, why bother with this at all? This option is meant for ISVs, IT professionals, or just the general community. It makes it easy to share GPO settings and configuration. Instead of describing a list of settings, you can pass around a cabinet file containing one or more Starter GPOs that have the entire configuration in it already.

Although the Starter GPOs can be backed up to a folder structure, this doesn't work well when it comes to sharing. Notice on the bottom of the details area of the Starter GPOs, you have a button to save a Starter GPO as a cabinet file (see Figure 21-60). By default, the name of the cabinet file is the name of the Starter GPO, and the location of the save can be selected by browsing the folders and selecting, as shown in Figure 21-61.

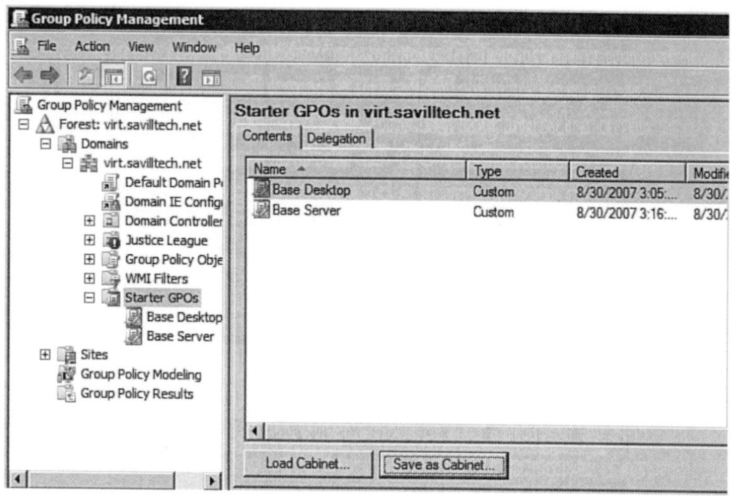

FIGURE 21-60 The Save as Cabinet button gives an easy way to export a Starter GPO to a file that can be shared and used by others.

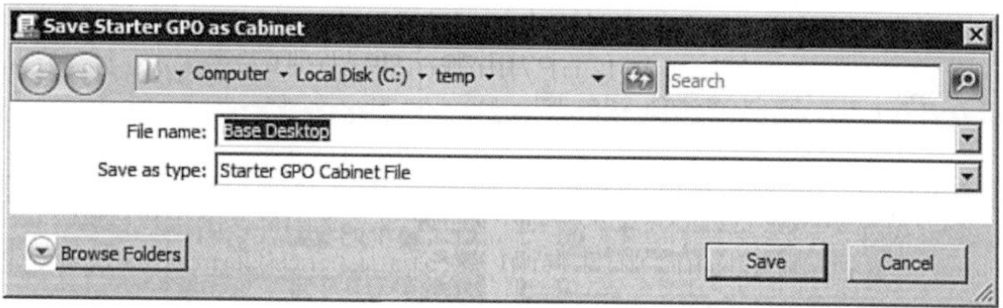

FIGURE 21-61 Ready for passing on to all your friends.

Once exported, you find a new cabinet file created. View it, to see that it contains a report of the GPO content, a template describing the GPO in XML format (a tmplx file), and the policy settings themselves. Conversely, to load in a Starter GPO from a CAB file, click the Load Cabinet button and then browse to the CAB file itself via the Browse for CAB button. Information is read from the contained template XML file and displayed; then the Starter GPO can be read into the domain by clicking OK (see Figure 21-62).

Hopefully, this gives you a good idea of why you would use Starter GPOs. More than likely, you will be on the receiving end of a CAB containing a Starter GPO—maybe from a software maker who needs certain settings, or from a security company who provides their locked-down desktop in the Starter GPO CAB format.

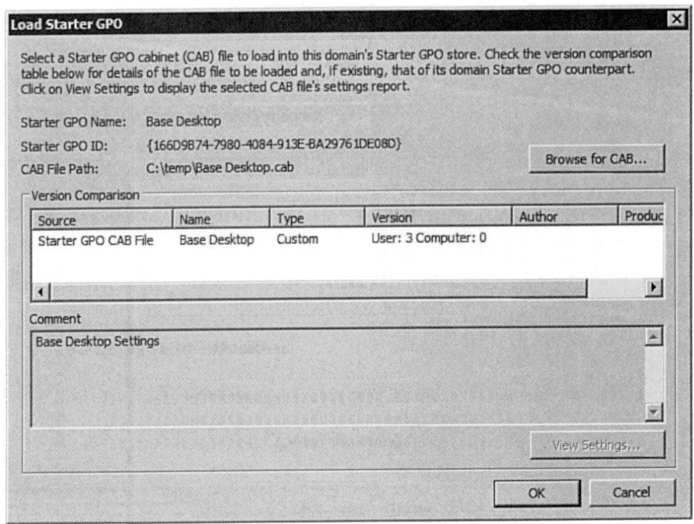

FIGURE 21-62 The CAB format makes for easy distribution of Starter GPOs.

Reporting on Group Policy Objects

If you are reading this book in order, then you know that the previous section discussed how the cabinet file contained a template file describing the starter GPO, the policy settings, and a report of the GPO. One of the great features that the GPMC introduced was the capability to create a report of the settings defined within a GPO. Previously, it was hard to see what and where settings were configured.

You can see this quickly; select a GPO and select the Settings tab, which is the report of the GPO contained within the EMC. Notice that it's dynamic HTML, which means you can elect to show and hide the various components of the GPO (see Figure 21-63). Also, notice the hierarchy of where the settings are located is still shown via nesting. The example shows that the Internet Explorer URLs are found under User Configuration, Windows Settings, Internet Explorer Maintenance by looking at the embedded folders.

Export this report out to a file by right-clicking on the GPO and selecting Save Report from its context menu. You are prompted for a location and the name of the HTML file to save the report as. Then double-click the created HTML file. However, notice that, by default, the show and hide options are not available; you have a warning at the top of the page that some content has been blocked; click for options, as shown in Figure 21-64. Select the Allow Blocked Content menu option and click Yes at the security warning confirmation; the hide and show options are displayed. This makes it easier to see the components of interest and mirror the view of the settings shown within the GPMC. It also provides some extra information concerning the details, links, security, and WMI Filtering and delegation that are normally shown in other tabs of the GPO.

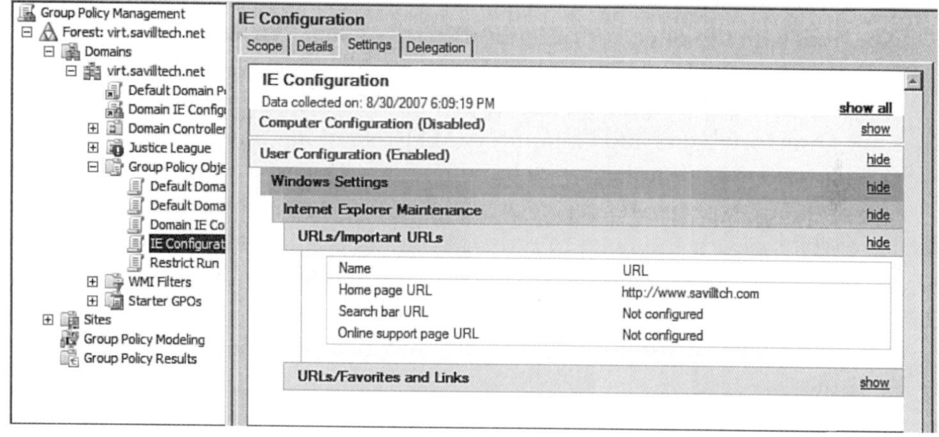

FIGURE 21-63 The Settings tab of the GPO provides easy viewing of the settings.

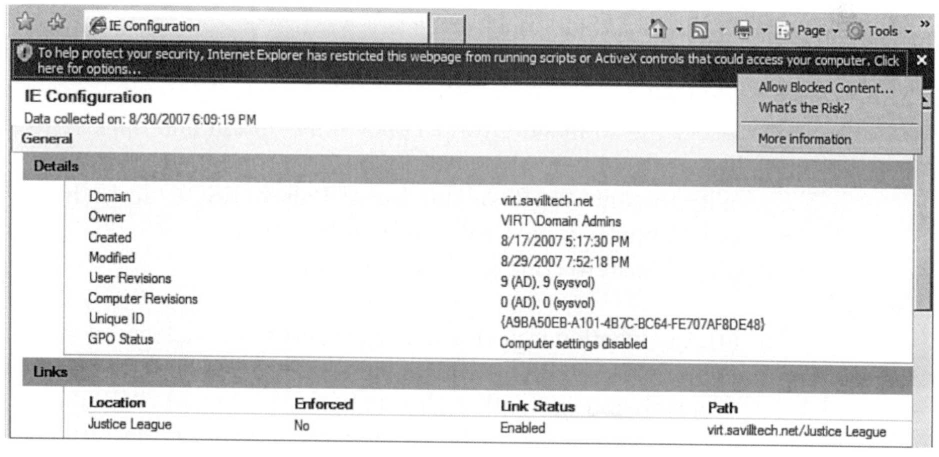

FIGURE 21-64 Note the standard warning for any page containing script or ActiveX controls.

Delegation

One of the great features of the AD and its new organizational unit objects is the capability to granularly delegate permissions to nonenterprise administrator permissions. This granularity of permissions also applies to Group Policy. In fact, Group Policy is one of the major design considerations for AD organizational units. Often in organizations, organizational units are designed for the purposes of applying Group Policy (and also for delegation).

General delegation for applying GPOs is controlled via the Active Directory Users and Computers MMC snap-in—for example, to give user John permission to use some resource (although this is poor procedure). When you delegate, create a group and delegate permission to the group, which avoids the need to redo delegation if someone else needs the same permissions or, even worse, if someone already has them and they need to be revoked. If a group is used for the delegation, users can easily be added and removed from the group that was delegated permissions. Let's do it properly:

1. Within the AD Users and Computers MMC snap-in, right-click on the domain or OU to which you want to delegate Group Policy permissions and select Delegate Control.
2. At the introduction wizard, click Next.
3. For the Users or Groups, click Add, select the Group Policy administrator group you have created, and click Next.
4. Select the Manage Group Policy links option and click Next (see Figure 21-65). Notice also the option to grant the user the capability to generate Resultant Set of Policy (RSOP) in both logging and planning modes, but more on that later.
5. Click Finish to complete the delegation.

After this delegation is performed, the users in the delegated group are now able to control GPO application for the OU/domain they were delegated permission on. Although GPOs can be linked and inheritance controlled, new GPOs cannot be created nor existing GPOs edited (see Figure 21-66).

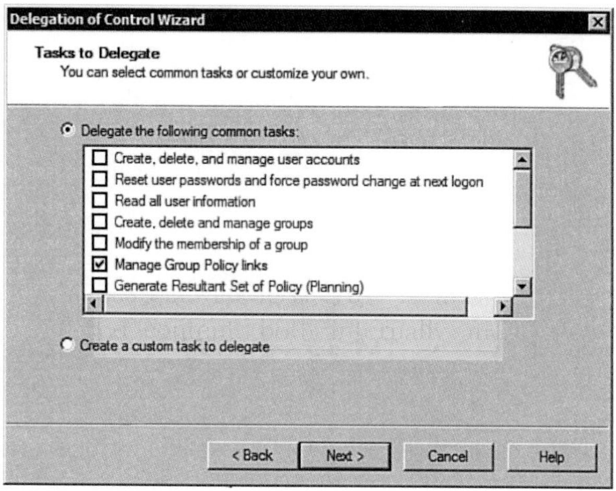

FIGURE 21-65 Notice other options of delegation are possible.

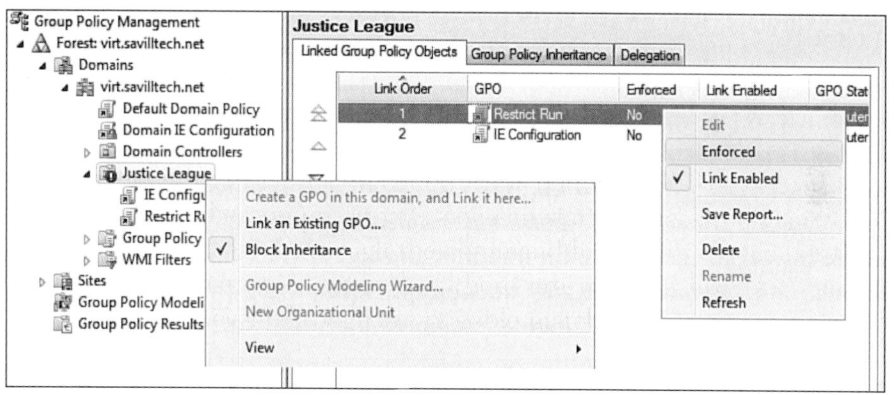

FIGURE 21-66 Once delegated, the manage Group Policy links capability; the delegated user can now link existing GPOs and unlink GPOs, but the option to create and edit are grayed out and unavailable.

The GPMC makes it easy to grant this delegation of linking GPOs by selecting the container (domain, site, or OU) in the GPMC. On the Delegation tab, select the Link GPOs permission and add the required user or group, as shown in Figure 21-67.

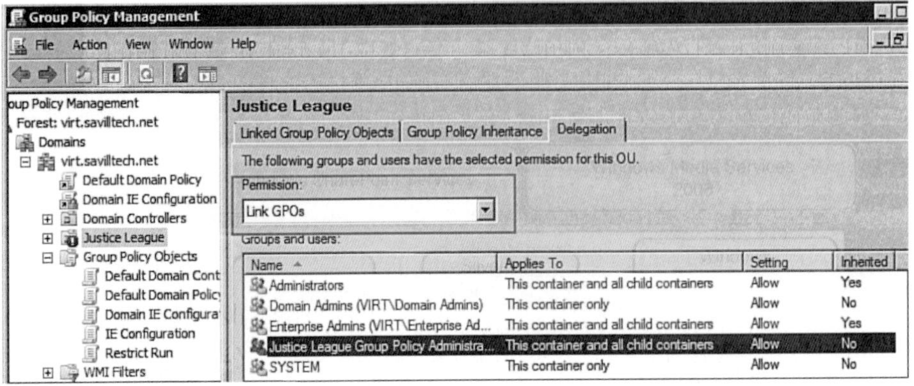

Figure 21-67 The GPMC makes delegating GPO permissions far easier than via AD Users and Computers.

To enable a user to edit a GPO, delegate permissions on the GPO directly. Remember, GPOs exist in the domain; a separate version is not created in each OU, for example. Giving a user or group the capability to edit a GPO means their changes apply anywhere the GPO is linked. Be careful in giving users the permission to edit a GPO. This might be a good time to create separate versions of a GPO (right-click a GPO and select Copy to easily create multiple versions) and give users the capability to edit only the version that has been designated for linkage to their OU (for example).

To delegate permissions to edit a GPO, perform the following steps:

1. Select the GPO on which you want to delegate Edit permissions under the GPOs, and select the Delegation tab in the details pane of the MMC (see Figure 21-68).

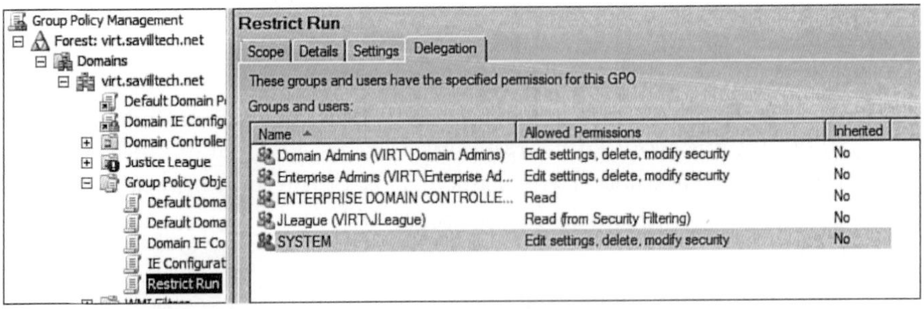

Figure 21-68 Delegation options.

Under Delegation, you see all the permissions that apply to a GPO. You used Security Filtering to set who could apply policy. Authenticated Users is not shown for this GPO, but JLeague does have Read permission; select Advanced view to see that the Apply Group Policy permission is also granted.

2. Add the group/user to which you want to delegate Edit permissions by clicking the Add button.
3. After entering the name of the user or group, you are prompted to select the permissions. The default is the Read permission. However, you can also select Edit settings or Edit settings, delete, and modify security permissions, as shown in Figure 21-69. Click OK. If you create a number of GPOs for each OU for the local administrators to configure, you want to prevent the administrators from being able to delete them; thus, don't give them too many permissions.

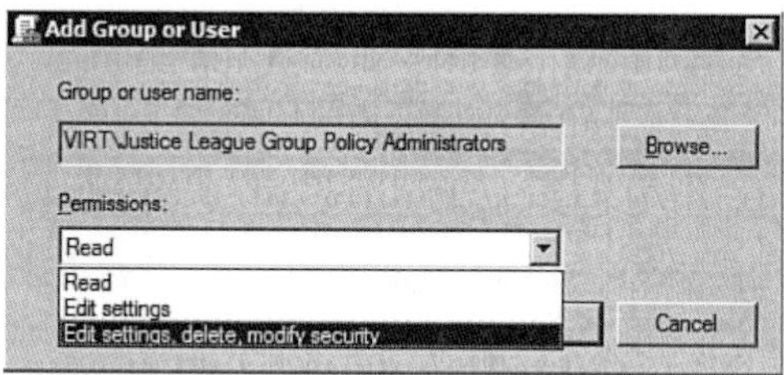

FIGURE 21-69 The permissions you want to give depend on the flexibility you want to give the users/administrators.

Now the delegated people have the Edit context menu option enabled within the GPMC.

Creating new GPOs is trickier. Remember, GPOs are created in the domain and not the OU, so you need to grant the users or group the capability to create Group Policy containers (objects) in the root of the domain. This means you need to be careful to whom you delegate this kind of permission. Most likely, you will not give out this permission; instead, create the GPOs as empty objects and delegate the users/groups the capability to edit the GPO you created for them. By default, only Domain and Enterprise Administrators, Group Policy Creator Owners, and SYSTEM can create new GPOs. The Group Policy Creator Owners group is probably the best option, because it allows members of this group to create new GPOs. However, they can only edit or delete GPOs that they have created. The Group Policy Creator Owners group also has no permission to link

GPOs to a container such as a domain or OU; that permission still must be given manually. To add a user or group, open the Group Policy Creator Owners group, which is found in the Users container of the domain, and add as required (see Figure 21-70).

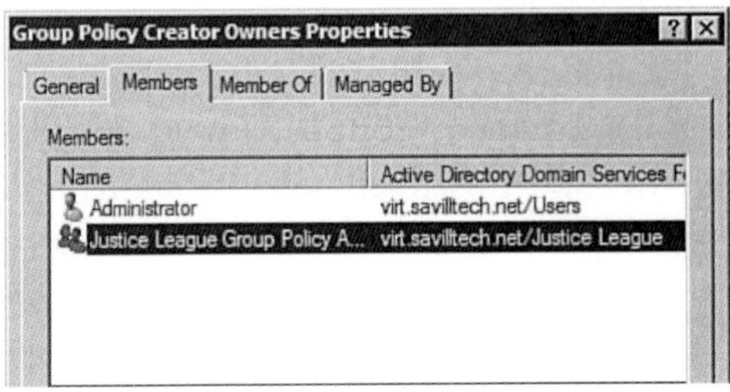

FIGURE 21-70 This group is an easy and supported way to give non-administrators the capability to create GPOs.

You can manually grant users or groups the capability to create groupPolicyContainers. However, there is another option. Select the Group Policy Objects container for the domain in the GPMC and select the Delegation tab in the details pane to see a list of all the users and groups that have rights to create GPOs in the domain. The Group Policy Creator Owners group is shown in Figure 21-71. To add other users and groups, click the Add button and enter the user/group name.

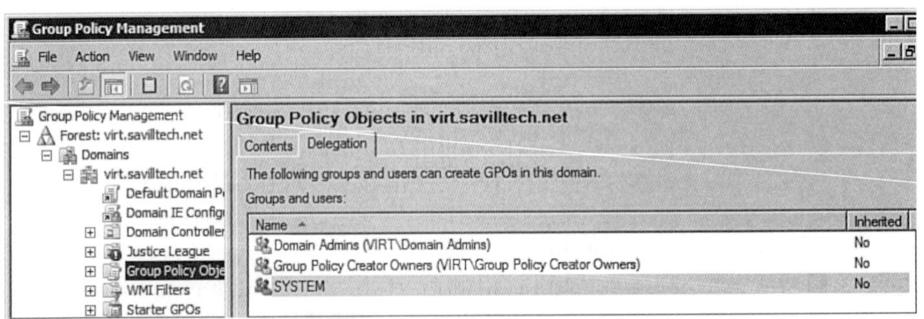

FIGURE 21-71 The GPMC makes both the management and delegation of Group Policy intuitive.

It's not surprising that the delegation of permissions to create WMI Filters and Starter GPOs is performed the same way. Select the Delegation tab when selecting the WMI Filters of the Starter GPO's container.

Group Policy Results

This chapter has discussed creating, linking, and seeing values of GPOs and delegating who can do what with a GPO. The next big item is being able to see the resultant set of policies a user or computer receives, based on all the GPOs that might be linked to a site, domain, and OU. At the bottom of the GPMC navigation window is a Group Policy Results option that is used to perform this RSOP calculation. The easiest way to understand it is to use it:

1. Right-click Group Policy Results and select Group Policy Results Wizard from the context menu (see Figure 21-72).

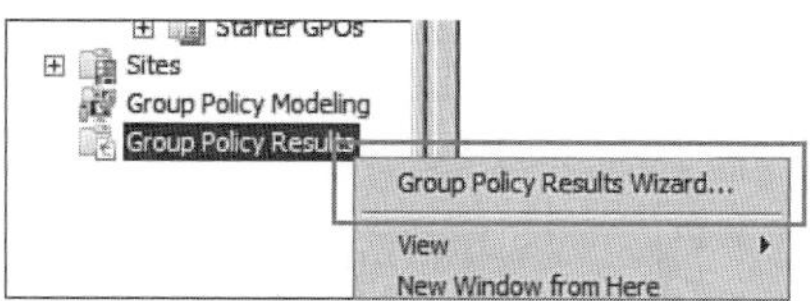

FIGURE 21-72 The Group Policy Results Wizard can be found on the Group Policy Results context menu.

2. The Welcome to Group Policy Results Wizard launches. Click Next at the dialog.
3. The first screen requiring configuration asks you to select the computer that the resultant policy should be focused on. Group Policy is based on the user and the computer account, with the computer account existing in a location in the AD both in the OU and sites. Computers have physical attributes, such as disk space and processor, which might affect WMI-Filtered policies. The dialog enables you to specify the local computer (which works if you are running GPMC on the machine you want to test), or select Another Computer and browse to the computer you want to RSOP against (see Figure 21-73). Another option is to check the Do Not Display Policy Settings for the Selected Computer in the Results, which ignores all computer-based settings and returns results concerning the User Configuration.

   In this case, select a workstation in the domain and click Next.
4. The next screen displays a list of the users of the machine and those domain users that have locally logged on to the target machine (see Figure 21-74). As with the previous screen, you can also select the option to ignore User Configuration settings and instead display the Computer Configuration settings. In this case,

you want to see the settings for the VIRT domain user John. Click Next.

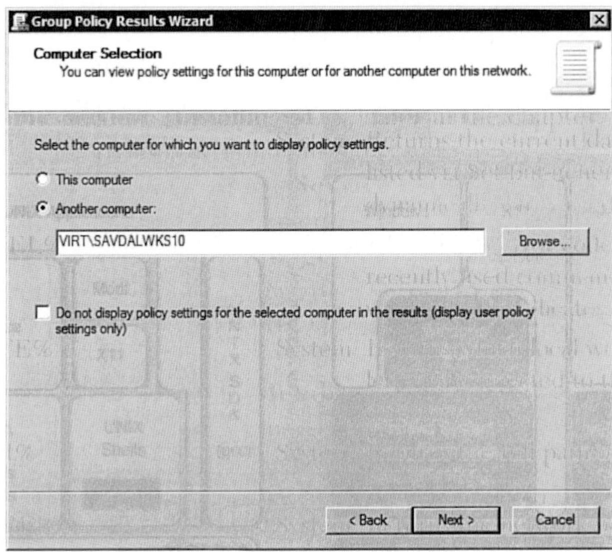

FIGURE 21-73 The Computer Selection page of the Group Policy Results Wizard.

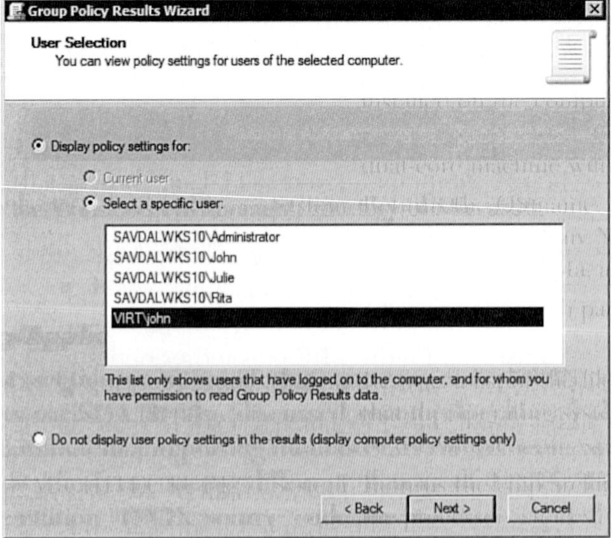

FIGURE 21-74 The User Selection page of the Group Policy Results Wizard.

5. A confirmation of the settings displayed is shown, confirming the computer and user names and the settings to display. Click Next, which starts the analysis.
6. After the analysis is complete, click Finish to display the output. It shows up in the format of a report under the Group Policy Results node (see Figure 21-75).

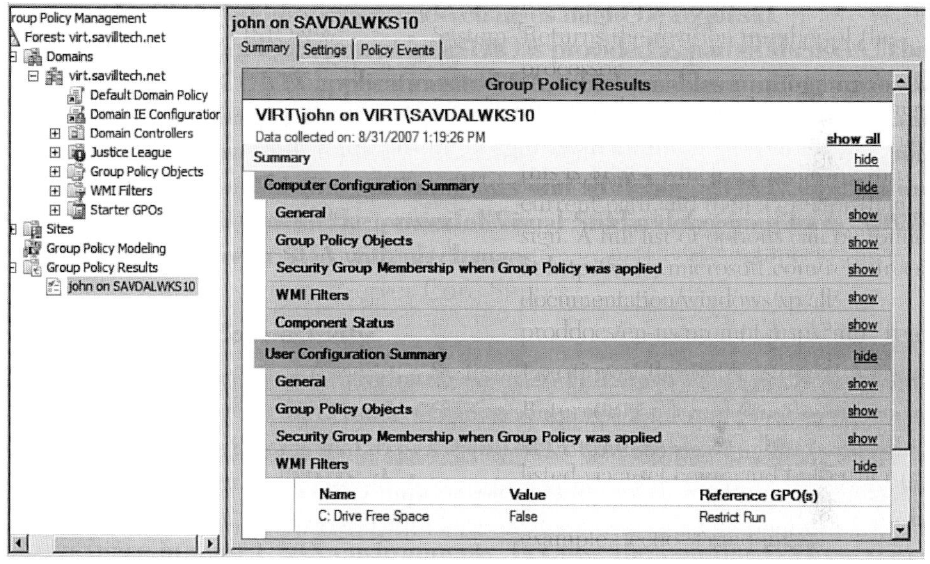

FIGURE 21-75 The Group Policy Results report breaks down the information about GPO for the user and computer.

Select the report to see three tabs, as shown in Figure 21-76. The Summary tab, as shown, is an HTML report with information about the GPOs that were applied, the Security memberships that were used for the application of GPO, and any WMI filters that were applied and their return status. This can be seen in the example. Notice the free drive space returned false, which means the Restrict Run GPO is not applied. This restriction of execution can be seen if you select the GPOs section of the report and select Denied GPOs. As shown in Figure 21-76, three policies were not applied for various reasons: the local policy was empty; the default domain policy was blocked because the Justice League OU blocks inheritance; and Restrict Run failed as the WMI filter did not pass.

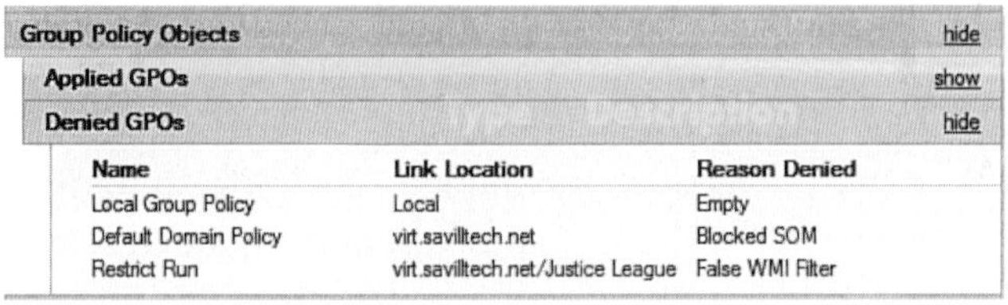

Group Policy Objects			hide
Applied GPOs			show
Denied GPOs			hide
Name	Link Location	Reason Denied	
Local Group Policy	Local	Empty	
Default Domain Policy	virt.savilltech.net	Blocked SOM	
Restrict Run	virt.savilltech.net/Justice League	False WMI Filter	

FIGURE 21-76 The Summary information is useful, and seeing the denied GPOs helps with troubleshooting GPO problems.

The Settings tab is the same for selecting a normal GPO, except it shows the combined settings of all the applicable GPOs for the user/computer object and for each policy of the GPO that set the setting.

Finally, the Policy Events tab scans the computer selected for all events that relate to Group Policy, which helps with troubleshooting in the event Group Policy is not applying correctly.

If settings or Group Policy change, which might affect the user or computer, right-click on the results and select Rerun Query from the displayed context menu. This uses the values already entered, but it re-evaluates the GPOs, security, WMI, and so on. Right-click the result and save it to a file for viewing offline or mailing to other involved parties. This feature, over many others, is key to troubleshooting GPO applications, especially those denied and the results of security and WMI.

There is another option on the actual client. You have already seen GPUPDATE force an update of the Group Policy for a user and computer. Another command-line tool, GPRESULT, is used to obtain the same information. If the command is run without any parameters, the RSOP for the logged-on user on the local computer is calculated and displayed, as shown in the following output:

```
C:\Users\john.VIRT>gpresult

Microsoft (R) Windows (R) Operating System Group Policy Result
tool v2.0
Copyright (C) Microsoft Corp. 1981-2001

Created On 8/31/2007 at 1:42:30 PM
```

```
RSOP data for VIRT\john on SAVDALWKS10 : Logging Mode
-----------------------------------------------------

OS Configuration:           Member Workstation
OS Version:                  6.0.6000
Site Name:                   N/A
Roaming Profile:            N/A
Local Profile:              C:\Users\john.VIRT
Connected over a slow link?: No


USER SETTINGS
--------------
    CN=John Savill,OU=Justice
League,DC=virt,DC=savilltech,DC=net
    Last time Group Policy was applied: 8/31/2007 at 12:30:37
PM
    Group Policy was applied from:      savtstdc01.virt.
savilltech.net
    Group Policy slow link threshold:   500 kbps
    Domain Name:                        VIRT
    Domain Type:                        Windows 2000

    Applied Group Policy Objects
    -----------------------------
        Domain IE Configuration
        IE Configuration

    The following GPOs were not applied because they were
filtered out
    -----------------------------------------------------------
        Restrict Run
            Filtering:  Denied (WMI Filter)
            WMI Filter: C: Drive Free Space

        Local Group Policy
            Filtering:  Not Applied (Empty)
```

By default, GPRESULT does not display the actual settings. However, by adding the `/V` switch, the actual settings are displayed. If you add `/Z`, a super-verbose mode is used that displays all the settings that attempted to be applied, even those that were overwritten by a higher-precedence GPO.

To generate RSOP for other users and computers via GPRESULT, use the `/s` switch to name the system and `/u` switch for the user. For example, the following command generates RSOP for domain user John on machine savdalwks10, which is the same detail used in the GPMC results wizard. If you want user or computer settings, add the `/scope` switch passing either `COMPUTER` or `USER`, depending on the settings you want to see:

```
gpresult /s savdalwks10 /user virt\john /v
```

NOTE Those using older versions of the OS probably remember the RSOP Wizard MMC snap-in (which is still included in Windows Server 2008); when executed, this could run in a Logging or Planning mode. The information you ran with GPRESULT and GPMC is equivalent to the RSOP Wizard MMC snap-in Logging mode. Ideally, use GPMC, as the RSOP MMC snap-in is deprecated.

Group Policy Modeling

There are many different ways to view the resultant set of policies configured for users and machines. What if you want to see what would happen if you did X without doing it? Group Policy Modeling has the capability to show the RSOP based on various design decisions that don't have to be implemented. Group Policy Modeling enables you to ask "what if" questions for any combination of policies for users/computers, scenarios where the user is in this OU instead of his normal OU, and so on:

1. Right-click Group Policy Modeling and select the Group Policy Modeling Wizard.
2. Click Next at the introduction screen.
3. Modeling must be run against a domain controller running Windows 2003 or above. The Domain Controller Selection dialog page enables the selection of a specific DC or any domain controller running Windows 2003 (see Figure 21-77).
4. The next screen, shown in Figure 21-78, enables the selection of a specific user or computer; alternatively, a container where the user or computer would exist can be selected as shown (because GPOs are applied at the site, domain, or OU level, you don't need an actual computer or user; just say where it would exist). Click Next after settings are selected.

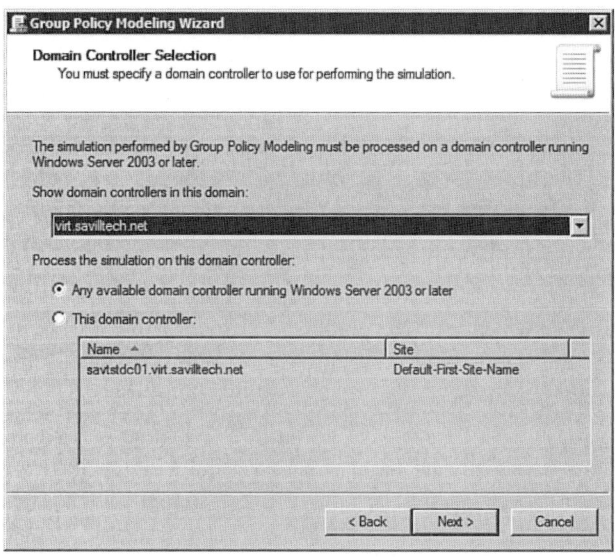

FIGURE 21-77 Modeling can be done against any domain controller running Windows 2003 or above.

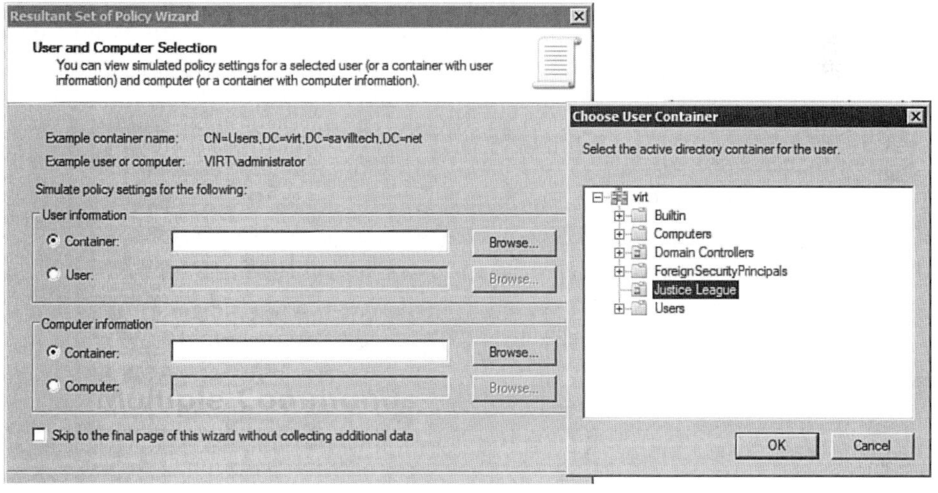

FIGURE 21-78 Select a user, computer, or container.

5. The next screen enables selection of other GPOs, affecting factors such as a slow link, if loopback processing is enabled, and in which site the computer is located (see Figure 21-79). Select the options you want and click Next.

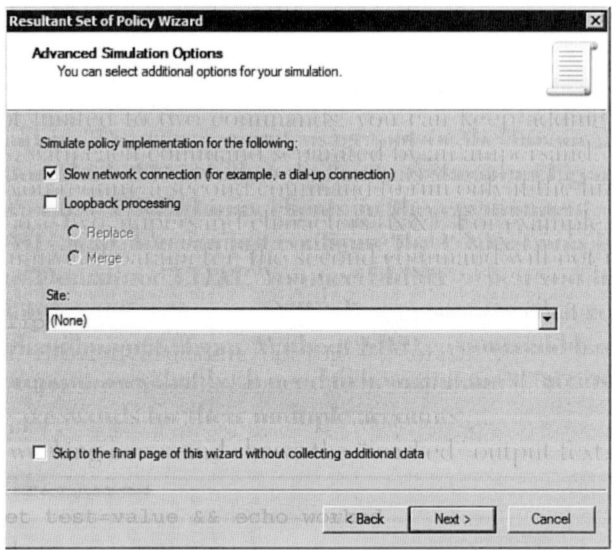

FIGURE 21-79 Set simulation options.

6. The next screen enables configuration of the groups the "user" would belong to. By default, the only security groups selected are Authenticated Users and Everyone. However, any group in the enterprise can be selected, which is pertinent if security filtering is used to restrict application of certain GPOs. Click Next after any additional groups for the modeling have been selected.
7. The next screen enables the same selection of groups, except for the computer object; once selected, click Next.
8. The WMI Filters for Users page, shown in Figure 21-80, enables selection of WMI filters that would be deemed as passed (GPOs restricted by the WMI filter would be applied). By default, it is assumed that all linked filters were passed. However, you can select Only These Filters, and click List Filters; this checks all GPOs that match the user/computer, or the selected containers that were chosen in the first screen, and individually selects only the ones you want to pass. Click Next after this is complete.
9. The next screen enables selection of WMI filters for computers in the same way as the previous screen did for users. Click Next.
10. The final screen displays a confirmation of all the options selected for the modeling (see Figure 21-81). Look it over and click Next.

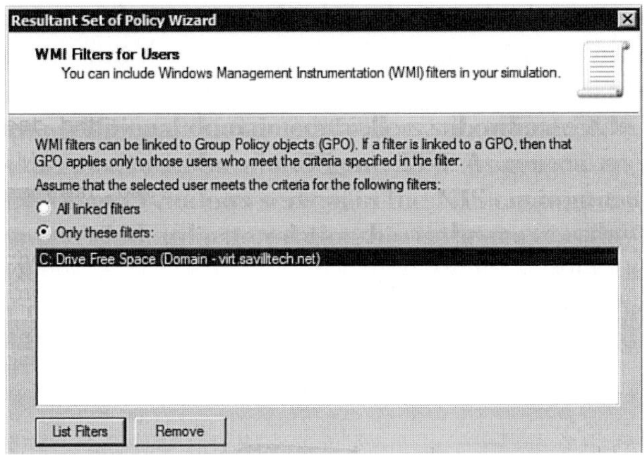

FIGURE 21-80 The WMI Filters for Users screen.

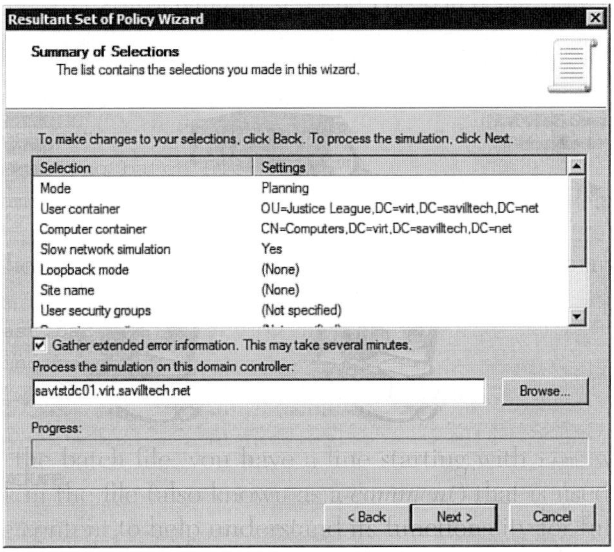

FIGURE 21-81 The Summary page.

11. After the modeling is complete, click Finish at the confirmation dialog. The output is displayed as a child item of the Group Policy Modeling in the same way as the Group Policy Results.

This modeling capability is a huge boon for Group Policy administrators and helps you develop an understanding of what happens if you reorganize your environment, moving users and computers. You can also re-run the saved model and modify settings as required; this helps you to avoid having to re-enter all information each time you run a model of a simulated environment.

Custom ADMX Files

Administrative templates are a large part of Group Policy and contain settings for most configurations. However, there might be custom settings you want to define via Group Policy that are Registry values. It's therefore possible to create custom template files that update Registry values on the client computers.

These custom administrative templates, however, are not true policies; they update Registry values outside the normal "policy" areas. If you remove the application of the Group Policy using a custom administrative template, the Registry values that were set by the template are not removed; the Registry keeps the values. It has been tattooed by the policy, in the same way as system policies worked with NT 4.0. These custom updates are known as *preferences*.

Previously, Group Policy administrative templates were .adm files that were stored in the SYSVOL folder. However, in a multi-language environment, problems were experienced because only one version could be stored. Ideally, different versions of the template file would be available for different languages. In Vista and Windows Server 2008, the administrative template files are stored in two parts: the main admx file with the settings, which is language neutral, and a language-specific adml file containing language-specific settings. Interoperability is maintained with pre-Windows Vista versions of the Windows OS and support for adm files is maintained. However, new settings contained in admx files are available only via Windows Vista/2008 tools; going forward, manage Group Policy from a Windows Vista/2008 machine.

The new admx files can be found in the C:\Windows\PolicyDefinitions folder. By default, there is a language-specific en-US file containing the English U.S.-specific version, assuming you are running the English U.S. version of the OS. Although custom adm files are supported in the new tools that were manually created, if any modifications were made to the standard adm files (for example, system.adm files that are replaced by new admx files), those customizations are lost. This is a good reason to never modify the built-in administrative templates.

Going forward, to create a custom administrative template, create both an admx file with settings that is language independent and a language-specific adml file. The full syntax for creating these files is beyond a section in a chapter of a book; Microsoft has good online help, available at http://technet2.microsoft.com/windowsserver2008/en/library/1db6fd85-d682-4d7d-9223-6b8dfafddc1c1033.mspx, which talks you through the complete admx syntax, structure, and best practices for its use. Let's create a basic customized file setting two possible Registry values. In this example, you want to control the creation of the default administrative shares on workstations and servers, which is managed by the values AutoShareWks and AutoShareServer under the `HKEY_LOCAL_MACHINE\SYSTEM\CurrentControlSet\Services\lanmanserver\parameters` key. An admx file that uses the WindowsComponents category is part of the `Microsoft.Policies.Windows` namespace as a parent for a custom category. Because this is a HKEY_LOCAL_MACHINE Registry key, this is a MACHINE policy setting. There is a lot to this file, but take note of the main Category and Policies sections, which are the bulk of our customized work. The following is saved as customshare.admx:

```
<?xml version="1.0" encoding="utf-8"?>
<policyDefinitions xmlns:xsd="http://www.w3.org/2001/XMLSchema"
xmlns:xsi="http://www.w3.org/2001/XMLSchema-instance"
revision="1.0" schemaVersion="1.0"
xmlns="http://www.microsoft.com/GroupPolicy/PolicyDefinitions">
  <policyNamespaces>
    <target prefix="CustomSharePolicy"
namespace="Microsoft.Policies.CustomSharePolicy"/>
    <using prefix="windows" namespace="Microsoft.Policies.
Windows" />
  </policyNamespaces>
  <resources minRequiredRevision="1.0" />
  <categories>
    <category name="CustomShares" displayName="$(string.
CustomShare)" explainText="$(string.CustomShareHelp_Help)">
      <parentCategory ref="windows:WindowsComponents" />
    </category>
  </categories>
  <policies>
      <policy name="ConfigureShareWks" class="Machine"
      displayName="$(string.ConfigureAdminShareWksPolicy)"
      explainText="$(string.ConfigureAdminShareWksPolicy_Help)"

key="SYSTEM\CurrentControlSet\Services\lanmanserver\parameters"
      valueName="AutoShareWks">
      <parentCategory ref="CustomShares" />
      <supportedOn ref="windows:SUPPORTED_Win2k" />
      <enabledValue>
            <decimal value="1" />
```

```
        </enabledValue>
        <disabledValue>
              <decimal value="0" />
        </disabledValue>
        </policy>
        <policy name="ConfigureShareSrv" class="Machine"
        displayName="$(string.ConfigureAdminShareSrvPolicy)"
        explainText="$(string.ConfigureAdminShareSrvPolicy_Help)"

key="SYSTEM\CurrentControlSet\Services\lanmanserver\parameters"
        valueName="AutoShareServer">
        <parentCategory ref="CustomShares" />
        <supportedOn ref="windows:SUPPORTED_Win2k" />
        <enabledValue>
             <decimal value="1" />
        </enabledValue>
        <disabledValue>
             <decimal value="0" />
        </disabledValue>
        </policy>
  </policies>
</policyDefinitions>
```

In the previous file, a number of `$(string.xxxx)` values are referenced. These are the language-specific variables that are read from your adml file, which is shown here and would be saved as customshare.adml:

```
<?xml version="1.0" encoding="utf-8"?>
<!--  (c) 2006 Microsoft Corporation  -->
<policyDefinitionResources
xmlns:xsd="http://www.w3.org/2001/XMLSchema"
xmlns:xsi="http://www.w3.org/2001/XMLSchema-instance"
revision="1.0" schemaVersion="1.0"
xmlns="http://schemas.microsoft.com/GroupPolicy/2006/07/
PolicyDefinitions">
  <displayName>CustomShare</displayName>
  <description>English CustomShare ADML</description>
  <resources>
    <stringTable>
      <string id="CustomShare">Custom Shares</string>
      <string id="CustomShareHelp_Help">Manage Custom
Shares</string>
      <string id="ConfigureAdminShareWksPolicy">Workstation
Specific Setting</string>
```

```
      <string id="ConfigureAdminShareWksPolicy_Help">Enable for
creation of admin shares on workstations</string>
      <string id="ConfigureAdminShareSrvPolicy">Server Specific
Setting</string>
      <string id="ConfigureAdminShareSrvPolicy_Help">Enable for
creation of admin shares on servers</string>

    </stringTable>
  </resources>
</policyDefinitionResources>
```

After you have your customized admx and adml files, copy the admx file to your %windir%\policydefinitions folder and the adml file to the %windir%\policydefinitions\<language—for example, en-US>. Once copied to the folder, unlike the old adm files that had to be added to the administrative templates, the content of the admx file is automatically read in and available in your policies. In fact, the first time you start the Group Policy Editor, you'll get errors if you made any mistakes in the admx/adml files.

In the example, Windows Components is selected as the parent category, so your new settings should be available under Computer Configuration, Policies, Administrative Templates, Windows Components, Custom Shares, and as shown in Figure 21-82, *failure*!

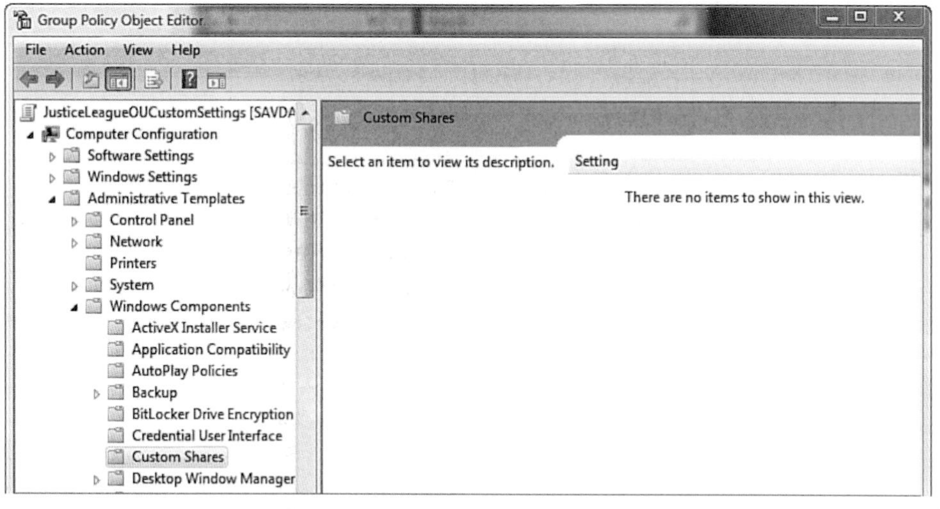

FIGURE 21-82 Your two settings are not showing. What gives?

Actually, you haven't failed. The GPMC is just being a little bit snobbish about what it's willing to display. By default, the GPMC displays only true policies; because your admx is updating Registry keys outside the safe policy areas, the policy won't display. To enable the viewing of preferences (custom policies updating Registry keys), perform the following:

1. Right-click Administrative Templates and select Filtering from the displayed View menu (see Figure 21-83).

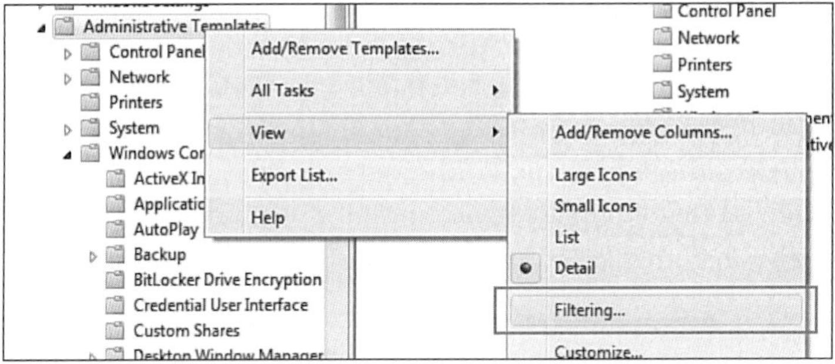

FIGURE 21-83 Choose Administrative Templates and select Filtering from the context menu by choosing View, Filtering.

2. Uncheck the Only Show Policy Settings That Can Be Fully Managed setting. Click OK (see Figure 21-84).

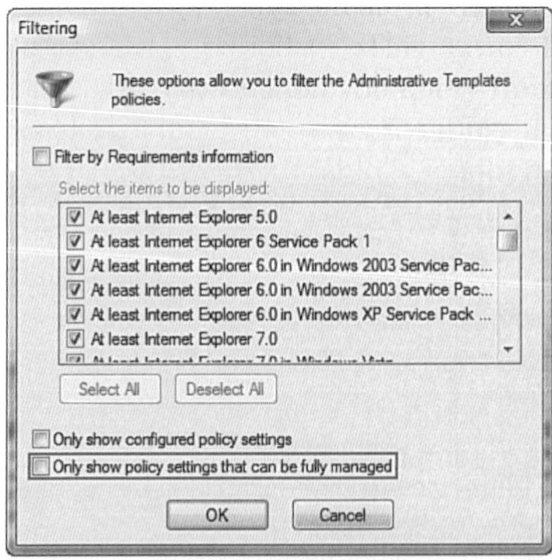

FIGURE 21-84 Make sure Only Show Policy Settings That Can Be Fully Managed is unchecked.

3. Now check the Group Policy Object to make the settings available with a slightly different icon; this icon shows that they are less well-thought of and indicates a warning that this is considered a preference (see Figure 21-85).

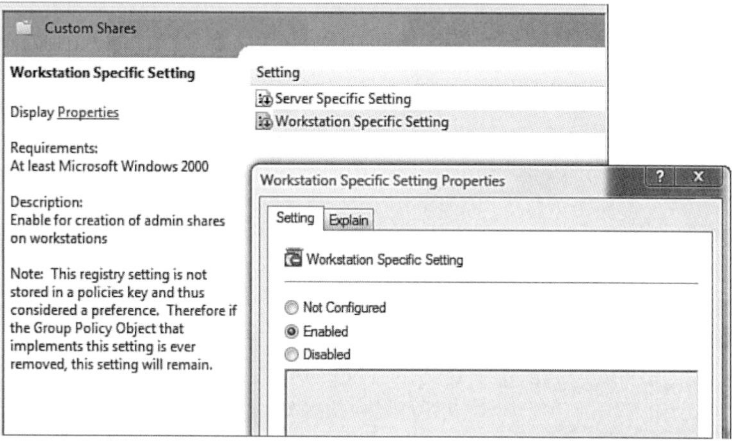

FIGURE 21-85 With the Only Show Policy Settings That Can Be Fully Managed filter turned off, you can see your custom admx content.

Central Store

In the past, adm files were stored as part of every GPO on SYSVOL. It took around 4MB of storage space for every GPO. In addition, problems arose because a user editing a GPO on one machine might have had different local adm files that gave different options. To solve the problems regarding wasted space of administrative templates being copied multiple times, and different local versions of administrative templates with Windows Server 2008, you can create the central store. This is simply a folder replicated between all domain controllers. After the central store is created, all 2008-aware Group Policy Editor clients ignore their local PolicyDefinitions folder and only use the templates in the central store.

There is no automated way to create the central store, but the process is easy. In the following steps, it is assumed your computer is a member of the domain you are copying the policies to, using the userdnsdomain environment variable. If the machine is not in the domain, replace the use of `%userdnsdomain%` with the actual DNS domain name:

1. Log on to a domain controller.
2. Create the root folder for the central store. It should be `%systemroot%\sysvol\<domain>\policies\PolicyDefinitions` on your domain controller:

   ```
   C:\Windows\SYSVOL\sysvol\virt.savilltech.net\Policies>
   ➥mkdir PolicyDefinitions
   ```

3. Create a subfolder under PolicyDefinitions for the language as defined in http://msdn.microsoft.com/library/default.asp?url=/library/en-us/indexsrv/html/ixuwebqy_7gfn.asp—for example, en-US, for U.S. English.
4. Copy the admx files from a Vista or Windows Server 2008 machine to the domain controller from a command prompt on the Vista box:

   ```
   xcopy %systemroot%\PolicyDefinitions\*
   %logonserver%\sysvol\%userdnsdomain%\policies\
   PolicyDefinitions\
   ```

5. Copy the language files for the Group Policy templates:

   ```
   xcopy %systemroot%\PolicyDefinitions\en-US\*
   %logonserver%\sysvol\%userdnsdomain%\policies\
   PolicyDefinitions\en-US\
   ```

Once created, when editing of a Group Policy occurs, the policy file source is the central store. This avoids the replication hit that would occur with multiple GPOs and a change to an administrative template (although the new DFSR replication counters some of that). If you create custom administrative templates, copy them to the central store instead of the local machine PolicyDefinitions folder.

If you have legacy adm files, Microsoft provides the ADMX Migrator at http://www.microsoft.com/downloads/details.aspx?FamilyId=0F1EEC3D-10C4-4B5F-9625-97C2F731090C&displaylang=en. It enables custom adm files to be converted to an admx file. In addition to just converting, an admx editor is provided, which makes creating customized admx files much easier.

Once installed, to convert an adm file, access the ADMX Migrator Command Window shortcut and run the `faAdmcConv` command. For example, to convert the adm file blocksharecreate.adm to an admx file, use the following command (where `d:\temp` is the location to save the generated admx file to and `/x` says to save an admx file):

```
C:\Program Files\FullArmor\ADMX Migrator>faadmxconv
➥d:\temp\adminshare.adm d:\temp /x
ADMX Migrator Application converts ADM file into ADMX format
file(s).
Copyright (c) 2006 FullArmor Corporation. All rights reserved.

ADMX Template generated successfully
```

An admx file and an adml file are saved to the destination folder, ready for Vista and Server 2008 usage.

Backup and Restore of Group Policy

Group Policy is backed up as part of the system state of a domain controller; the system state includes SYSVOL, where the file-based portion of Group Policy is stored. However, a more granular backup and restore is possible via the GPMC, which also allows the policies to be backed up and restored.

To back up, right-click on the GPO in the Group Policy Objects container and select Backup from the displayed context menu. However, you can also select multiple GPOs simultaneously, and they are all backed up. In addition, you can right-click on the Group Policy Objects container directly and select Back Up All from its context menu. The only information required is a backup location, a description, and selecting Back Up, as shown in Figure 21-86.

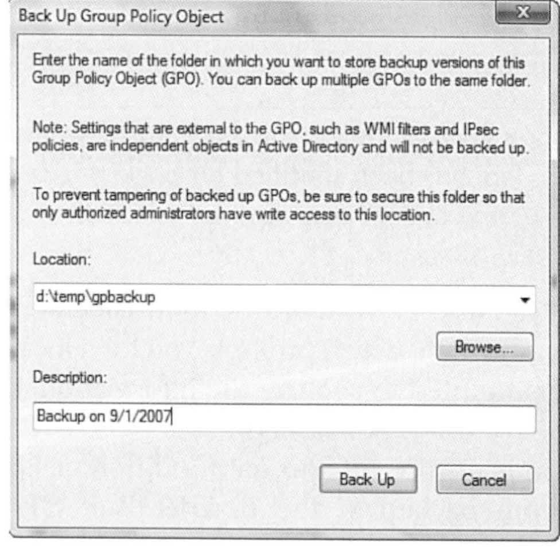

FIGURE 21-86 Backing up GPOs with the GPMC is easy.

Right-click Group Policy Objects and notice a context menu item Manage Backups. The Manage Backups option enables a location to be specified that shows all backed-up GPOs in that location, along with the time of the backup and the description (if one was given during the actual backup). From the Manage Backup screen, a GPO can be selected and restored if needed (perhaps due to a settings change or corruption), as shown in Figure 21-87.

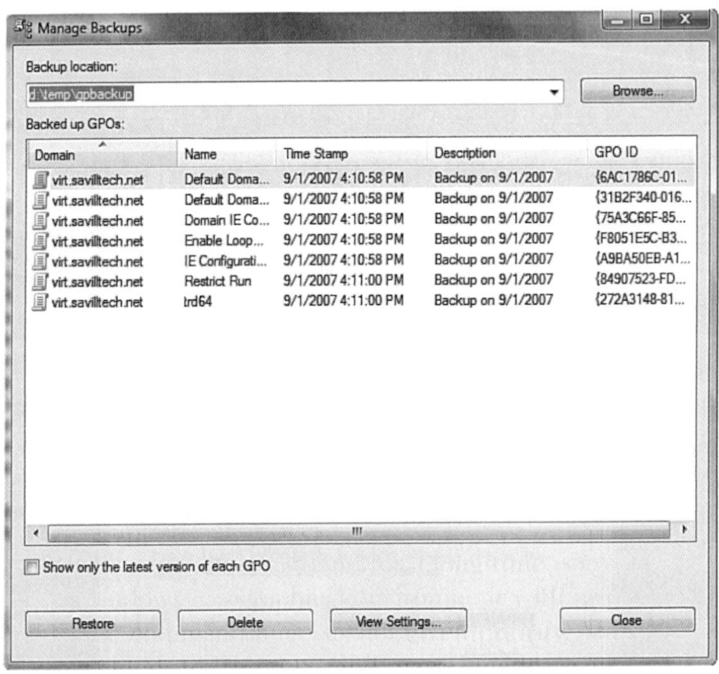

FIGURE 21-87 The Manage Backups option gives a great view into the backup state of your GPOs. Any location that has been specified for backup is available in the backup location drop-down menu, and custom paths can be selected.

A GPO can also be restored by right-clicking the GPO and selecting Restore from Backup, which prompts you for a location of the GPO's backup. You are prompted to confirm the information on the backed-up GPO, and then the restore is performed.

You cannot restore a GPO onto a different GPO—for example, you can't take your backup of the Restrict Run GPO and restore the IE Configuration GPO to it. When you try to restore it, you will not find a matching backup that can be restored. However, you can perform an Import as follows:

1. Right-click on the GPO from which you want to bring in the settings from another GPO's backup, and select Import Settings from the context menu.
2. The welcome dialog is displayed, which notifies you that only the settings are imported; other items like links, delegations, security, and WMI Filtering are not restored. Click Next.
3. A dialog is displayed, prompting you to back up the GPO you are importing into, because all its settings are lost by clicking the Backup button. You can perform a backup now, or just click Next to continue.
4. You are prompted for the location of the backup (see Figure 21-88). This is the folder where you have copied the backup of the GPO you are importing; you need to select the correct location. Click Next.

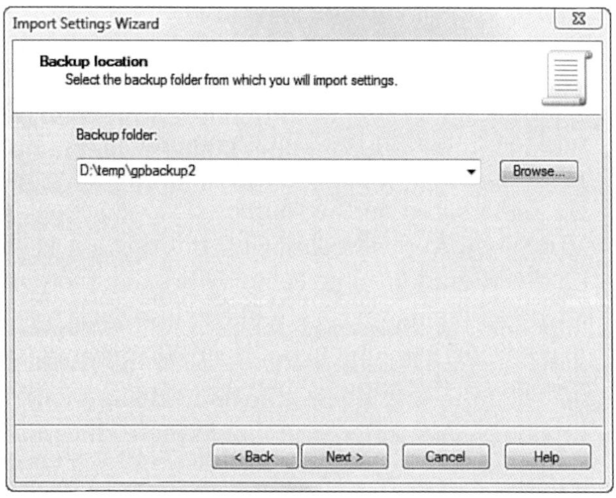

Figure 21-88 Set the location of the backup folder.

5. A list of the backed-up GPOs in the location specified is displayed (see Figure 21-89). You can select any of the GPOs listed and click the View Settings button to see an HTML report of the policies that are included in the GPO. After you have selected a GPO to import, click the Next button.

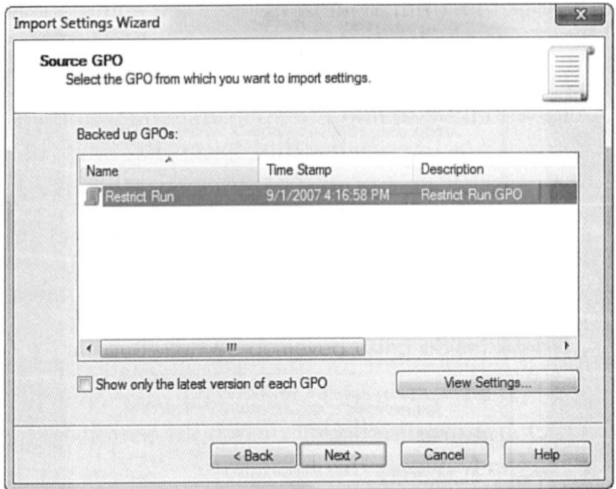

FIGURE 21-89 List of the backed-up GPOs is displayed.

6. A scan is performed on the GPO for any special security principals on UNCs used in the GPO being imported. If any were found, a migration table would be used to specify the value used on the target GPO based on the source GPO values—for example, convert VIRT\john to savilltech\savillj. Information in the GPMC help is on the Migration Table Editor. Normally, the scan comes back negative and no mappings are needed, so click Next.
7. A confirmation screen is displayed as to the actions to be performed for the import. Click Finish.

After the import is complete, a notification is shown of any aspects of the GPO that were lost in the import (see Figure 21-90). In the example, the WMI filter that was attached is no longer available. Remember, you can right-click on WMI filters and export the filter to a MOF file. You can then import it to the target domain, so everything is transportable.

Importing GPOs is not limited to within a domain or even a forest. You can back up a GPO and restore it to a domain in a totally separate organization. However, if this is a requirement, you might want to look again at Starter GPOs, which might be more applicable to this type of portability need.

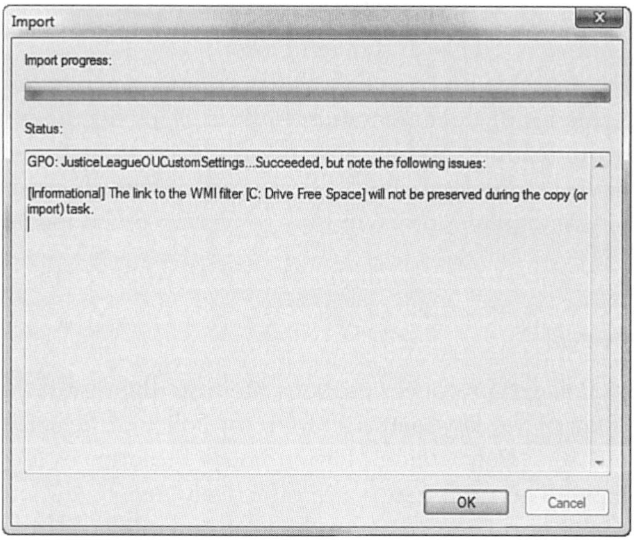

Figure 21-90 Importing GPOs is a simple process.

Group Policy Preferences

Group Policy Preferences was a last-minute addition to Windows Server 2008. It was so last minute that I'm writing this during the editing phase of this book, because Group Policy Preferences were not added until Release Candidate 1 of Windows Server 2008. You might wonder why a feature was added so late in the release cycle without the normal beta testing cycles, so let's look at where Group Policy Preferences originated.

Origin

Microsoft purchased a company named Desktop Standard in October 2006. This company had a number of core tools around Group Policy. Three of the Desk Standard tools—PolicyMaker Standard Edition, PolicyMaker Share Manager, and Registry Extension—have been merged into the Windows OS to make up the new Group Policy Preferences capability.

One other main tool was acquired: GPOVault. It is part of the Microsoft Desktop Optimization Pack that is available to Software Assurance customers and is now known as Advanced Group Policy

Management (AGPM). It helps in the management, delegation, and version control of GPOs, and much more.

Because this functionality was previously a separate product, it has a huge amount of documentation built in. This documentation is detailed and worth reading. And because this preferences feature already existed as a complete, functional, and tested product with documentation, it could safely be integrated into Windows Server 2008 and made part of a release candidate.

Features

Group Policy Preferences are separate from the rest of the GPO functionality. One of the key features of Group Policy is the settings are enforced on the Group Policy client. Group Policy Preferences are not enforced on the client. The preferences are effectively many additional settings available via Group Policy that can be used to better control the desktop; the changes made by Group Policy Preferences can be overridden by the user if he prefers. Although a normal GP policy removes the option to change the setting from the client interface—for example, graying out a setting and preventing the user from enabling it—a GP preference does not prevent the user from modifying the setting.

Although Group Policies write to specific Registry locations that the OS examines, Group Policy Preferences don't have special Registry areas and can write anywhere. The best way to think of preferences is as custom administrative templates that write to anywhere in the Registry but are not true policies. In this case, Microsoft supplies lots of these settings baked into the OS; thanks to new Client-Side Extensions (CSEs), you can do far more than functionality that is tied to a Registry change.

You can make GP Preferences emulate policies slightly by configuring the preference to apply each time the policy is refreshed. This means that although the user can change the setting, it would get reverted back to the preference value each time the Group Policy was refreshed. Obviously, this would quickly irritate the user. This is not a true policy because the user can change the setting, but it does help enforce a certain configuration. Normally, GP Preferences would not be configured to apply at every GP refresh; instead, apply preferences only when a change was made.

Another big difference between GP Preferences and custom administrative templates is that GP Preferences do not always tattoo the client computer. If you remove a GP Preference from the GPO, the change that preference executed also would be removed from the client, assuming the preference supported being undone. If the preference falls out of scope to a target, its settings are removed from the client; if the preference overwrote an existing value, however, the old value is not put back. Instead, the value is deleted and the application/OS component default setting is used where no configuration is present.

In addition to many new settings, preferences are highly targetable. With a normal GPO, you can link it to a site, domain, or OU, with some granularity available via WMI filters or security modifications. With preferences, you can target specific settings within a preference to particular users. For example, if you have five printers defined in a preference, you could target each printer to a different user.

To manage Group Policy Preferences, you need an updated version of the GPMC, which is part of Windows Server 2008, and is available for Windows Vista SP1 as part of the Remote Server Administration Tools. No GPMC supports preferences for Windows XP or Windows Server 2003. The Preferences portion of the GPMC is rich in terms of usability and is a real boon for Group Policy administrators.

New Settings

Group Policy Preferences are broken down into Windows Settings and Control Panel Settings, available at both Computer and User levels (see Figure 21-91).

With the Windows Settings area, you can set items such as network share creation/update, drive mappings, environment variable management, create files and folders, create and update INI files, set Registry values, and create shortcuts. The preferences are also extensible. An Applications node exists, which is used to configure settings for specific applications that have had a preference plug-in installed.

The Control Panel Settings area allows configuration of many of the key control panel applet options such as Data Sources, Devices, Folder Options, Internet Settings, network options allowing VPN and DUN connection management, creating/modifying local users and groups, power options, printers, regional options, scheduled tasks, service management, and start menu items. Not all control panel applet settings are available at both user and computer levels, which you see as you explore the preferences.

Some settings are available as both policies and preferences. This gives you the option of enforcing the setting via a policy or making it an initial configuration via a preference. If you configure an item in both policy and preference, the policy takes precedence no matter where the settings are made. For example, if a policy is used for a setting that is linked at domain level, and a preference is used to set the same setting at OU level, the policy value still takes effect, even though the preference was linked at a closer level to the object.

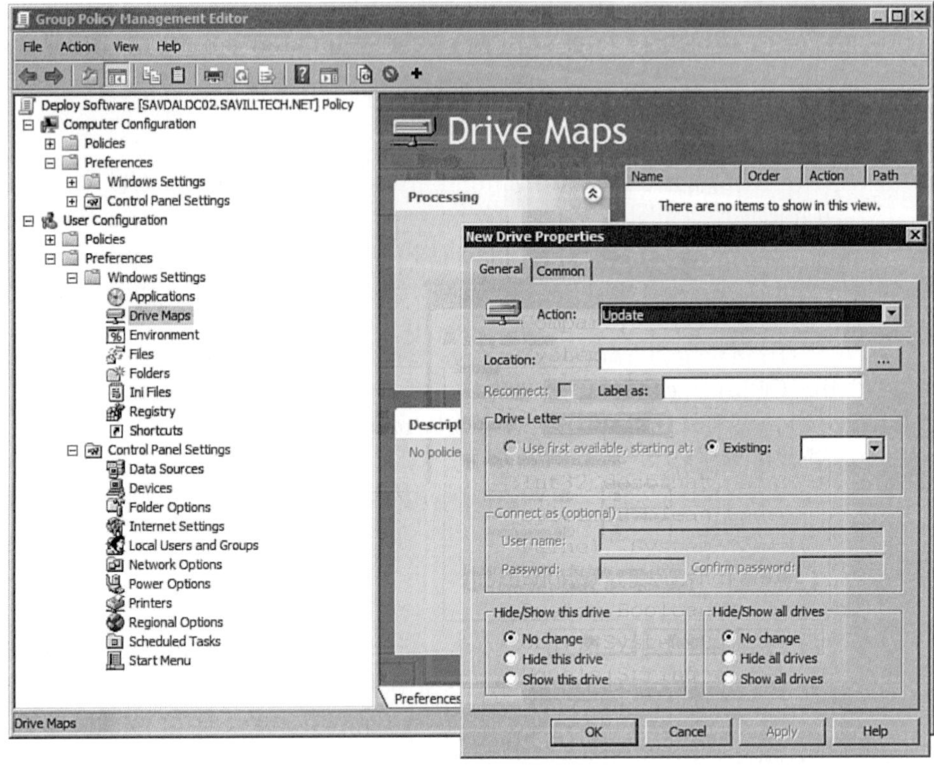

Figure 21-91 There are a number of Preference options under Windows Settings and Control Panel Settings. Here, you add a new mapped drive via a preference.

One great piece of functionality is you can take a Group Policy preference and drag it to the desktop or anywhere else to create an XML version of the preference. You can then drag this into another preference, where the setting is automatically created.

Configuring a Preference

The Preferences interface is graphically rich. In most instances, the configured options look the same as if you were configuring the setting locally on a client computer—especially the Control Panel options.

In this instance, let's create a new Start Menu configuration via the User Configuration—Preferences—Control Panel Settings—Start Menu option; select New—Start Menu (Windows Vista), as shown in Figure 21-92. Because some settings are implemented differently in the various options, specify which target OS the setting is for.

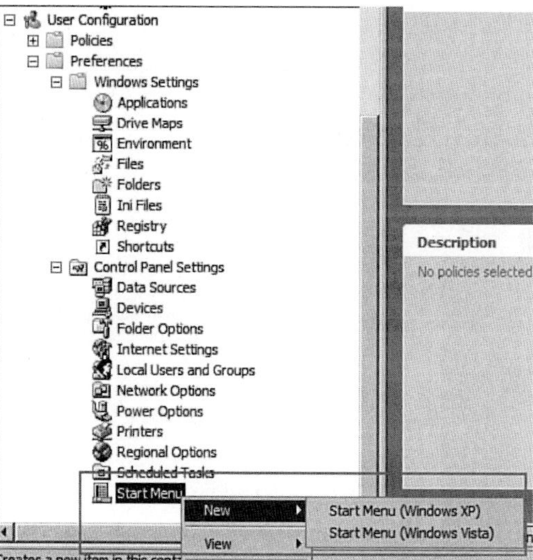

Figure 21-92 Start Menu options vary based on XP or Vista.

Select a new preference item, and the dialog for that setting is displayed and consists of a number of tabs, depending on the preference you are configuring (see Figure 21-93). If an item is underlined in green, it means it can be set via the preference; if the item is red dashed, it cannot be set. The Common tab is shown in Figure 21-94. F5 enables all the settings in a preference item, F6 enables the currently selected setting in a preference item, F7 disables the currently selected setting in a preference item, and F8 disables all the settings in a preference item. The Common tab has settings that are available to all preferences that pertain to the preferences application.

Stop Processing Items in This Extension if an Error Occurs

Normally, if a preference item experiences a problem, the other preference items in the same extensions within the GPO are implemented and are not affected. If the Stop Processing Items in This Extension if an Error Occurs option is enabled, any preference item in the same extension is not processed. Preference items are applied bottom to top, so only settings that occur before the problem item are not processed; items already processed are not undone.

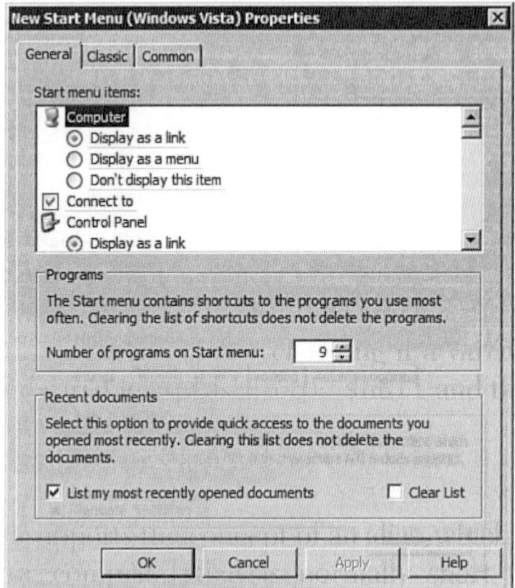

Figure 21-93 These show the type of interfaces for a preference.

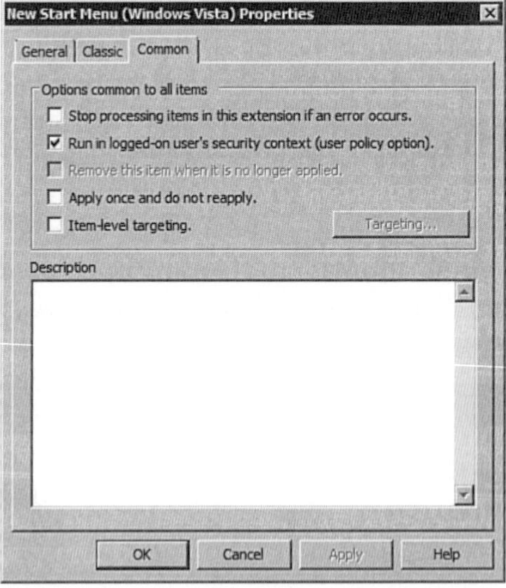

Figure 21-94 The Common tab that is available for all preference items.

Run in Logged-on User's Security Context (User Policy Option)

Normally, Group Policy is applied via the SYSTEM security context; however, if you enable this setting, the particular preference item is applied using the logged-on user's security context. This is useful if the item pertains to something specific to the user's environment that the system context might not have access to. Some preference items enable this setting automatically.

Remove This Item When It Is No Longer Applied

By default, if a GPO that contains preferences is no longer in scope for a user or computer, the preferences defined are not removed unlike a policy. If you enable the Remove This Item When It Is No Longer Applied option, the setting is removed if the preference extension detects the setting is no longer in scope for the target. This is not available for all settings that cannot undo the changes made.

Apply Once and Do Not Reapply

Normally, preferences are applied every time Group Policy is refreshed. To apply the preference item only once, enable this setting.

Item-Level Targeting

This is one of the huge features of Preferences. With normal Group Policy, you can use certain filters such as WMI and security permissions to control application of GPOs; preferences, however, have item-level targeting to allow configuration for whether an item applies to specific users or groups, in addition to a large number of other conditional checks. In fact, there are 29 different types of targeting available, such as if a battery is present in the computer, CPU speed, amount of RAM, domain, time range, and many more.

Item-level targeting can use these different targets in combinations via Boolean logic operators such as And, Or, and Not. For example, you can apply a preference item if the machine has more than 2GB of RAM and more than 10GB of free disk space and is not running Windows Vista. This information about the machine uses native Windows APIs and not WMI, which means the checks are faster to execute than they would be if using WMI.

Figure 21-95 shows the main item-level targeting interface, which is displaying all the target options available that can be used as part of the targeting. Access the Targeting Editor by enabling item-level targeting and then clicking the Targeting button.

After you add target items, set the values required for the target item and join multiple target criteria together through the And and Or operators. In addition, you can state if the setting you are configuring needs to be a value or NOT be a value, as shown in Figure 21-96.

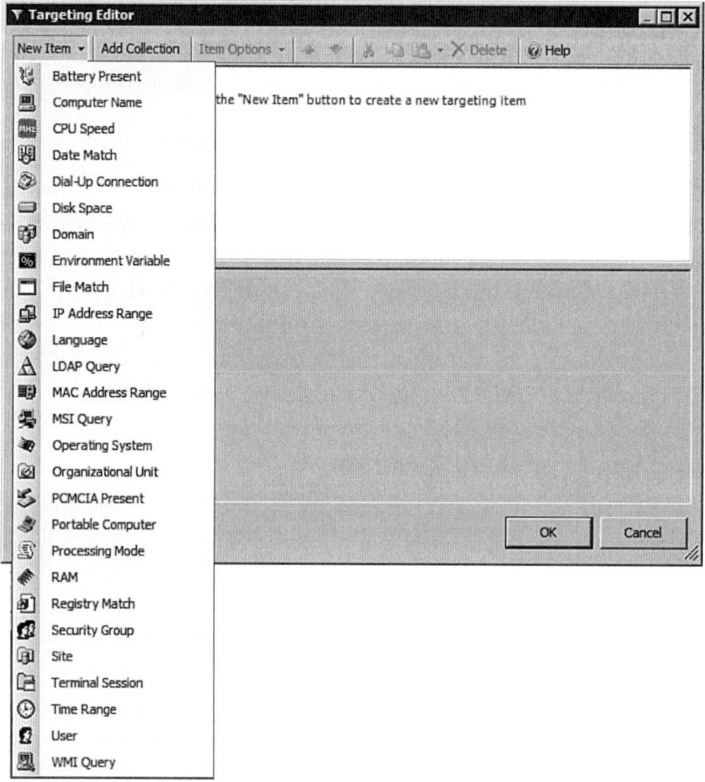

FIGURE 21-95 Notice all the target items available.

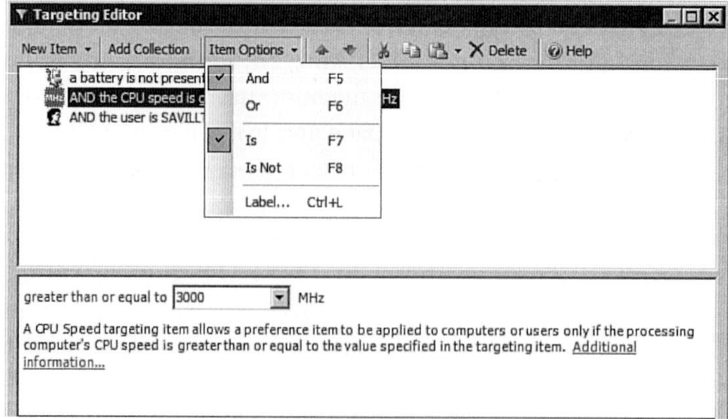

FIGURE 21-96 You can add multiple target criteria, and each criterion has various settings, such as speed for CPU. You can combine multiple criteria through And/Or combinations.

You can even group a number of items into a collection, which allows you to create more complex combinations of expressions. This is done by adding a collection to the target expression and then adding target items under the collection that should be evaluated together. In Figure 21-97, we've grouped the check that you are running Vista SP1 and that the computer name does not have "lab" as part of the NetBIOS name into a single expression.

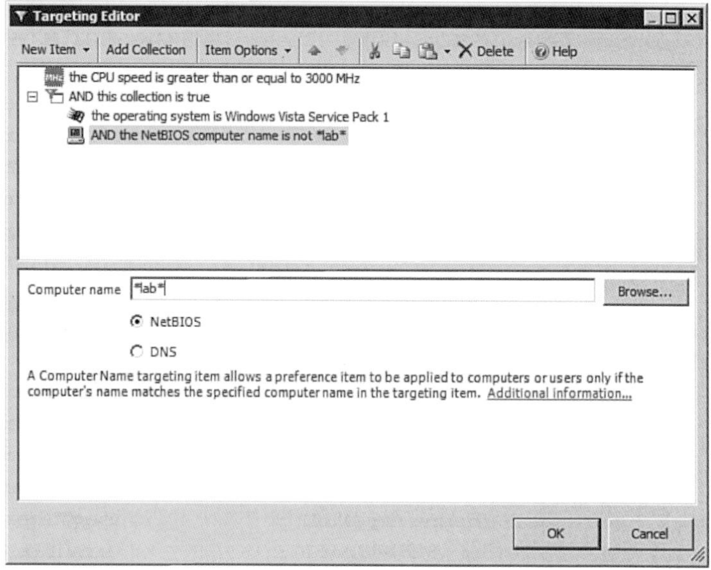

FIGURE 21-97 Combining multiple target items into a single logical collection item.

Client Support

Although Windows Server 2008 has the CSEs needed to process Group Policy Preferences, the other Microsoft OSs do not. Group Policy Preference CSEs are being made available for Windows Vista, Windows XP SP2, and Windows Server 2003 SP1. The XmlLite update is also required for XP and 2003, which is available at http://support.microsoft.com/kb/914783/en-us. These CSEs are available from Microsoft. Search for "Group Policy Preferences client-side extensions download" at Microsoft.com. Separate CSEs are available for the 32- and 64-bit versions of each supported OS. There is no support for any version of Windows 2000.

The Group Policy Preference CSE is update KB943729; it is supplied as a Microsoft Update (MSU) file for Windows Vista and as an executable file for Windows XP and Windows Server 2003. You can deploy the update CSE as you would a normal update to Windows; however, because you have no MSI deployment wrapper, it's not easy to deploy using Group Policy. By the time this book hits the shelves, hopefully Microsoft will have provided an MSI wrapper to detect the client OS and install the right CSE, along with any other prerequisites. If that's not the case, however, Jakob Heidelberg created a script to do just this at http://heidelbergit.blogspot.com/2008/03/how-to-install-gpp-cses-using-startup.html.

Reporting

GP Preferences are displayed as part of normal settings reports, as well as when you view Group Policy results. However, item-level targeting is not shown in reports and is always assumed to be true. An example report view is shown in Figure 21-98.

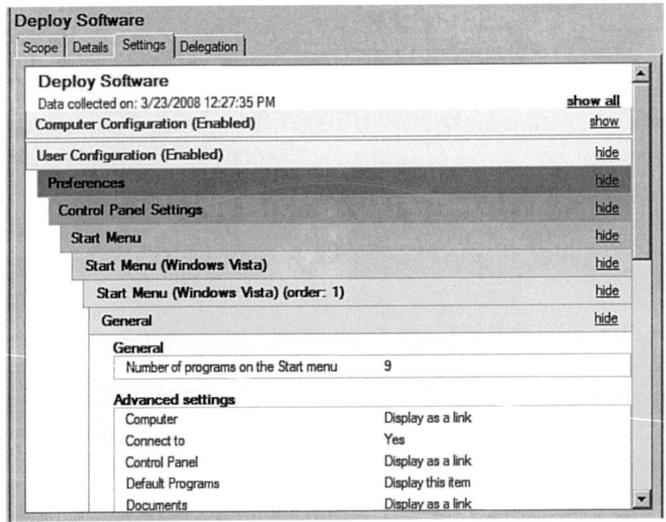

FIGURE 21-98 Viewing preferences settings through GPMC.

Because with preference items, multiple values can be applied, the Group Policy results display only the last value applied.

Troubleshooting

Two of the best tools for troubleshooting are the gpresult and GPMC logging tools. They can be used to determine which GPOs are being applied to a client, and if they are not applying, they show why. They can reveal things like whether the GPO is being blocked by WMI or security filtering. In reality, 99% of Group Policy problems are basic instances of the policies being applied in the wrong place, such as in the wrong OU. But let's look beyond the basic reasons for Group Policy not doing what you wanted.

The use of RSOP helps you more easily identify any issues caused by the linkage of GPOs, any no overrides, block inheritance, and link order/status. The output of the RSOP easily helps you see the order of GPO application. If you have a Group Policy that's not behaving as expected, check the server that facilitated the user logon by checking the logonserver environment variable; then connect to that domain controller via GPMC and inspect the content:

```
C:\Users\john>echo %logonserver%
\\SAVDALDC01
```

GPOs exist within the AD, but where are they stored? GPOs are stored in two parts. The first part is in the SYSVOL folder on all domain controllers (C:\Windows\SYSVOL\sysvol), which is the Group Policy Template portion that contains all the actual settings, information, scripts, and so on. The second part is in the AD itself in the form of a Group Policy Container, which stores versioning, status, and WMI Filtering information, along with components that have actual settings in the GPO. This is important to remember, as SYSVOL and the AD are replicated separately. It's possible that if there are network problems or replication issues, one part of the GPO might not have replicated, which causes problems with application of the GPO. Although the GPO is stored in two locations, all the management tools treat them as one, and it should never be necessary to manually manipulate only one part of a GPO. For example, when a permission change is made, the GPMC updates both the SYSVOL portion of the GPO and that stored in the AD.

The replication used for SYSVOL now uses DFSR (which is covered in Chapter 15, "Distributed File System"), which is a delta-based replication technology; only the changed parts of a file are replicated, not the entire file. This means replication is far less likely to be a problem, but what if replication is not working correctly—for example, the SYSVOL and AD portions are not in sync? A great way to check this replication state is with the GPOTOOL, which has a number of purposes, including the following:

- Checks the consistency of GPOs between the SYSVOL- and AD-based portions of GPOs
- Checks GPO replication
- Searches GPOs
- Targets specific domain controllers (DCs) to enable testing of specific DC Group Policy status
- Displays GPO information
- Checks cross-domain GPOs

GPOTOOL, along with other GPO tools such as GPMONITOR, are part of the support tools and are described in huge detail in the Microsoft help files (search for Group Policy tools).

Previously, most logging information related to Group Policy was found in userenv.log. However, the content was often cryptic and hard to use. With Windows Vista, the Group Policy now has its own service and has a new logging engine that uses the new Vista/2008 Crimson event-logging technology. The Crimson technology creates its own XML-based Group Policy log with logs separated into Administrative and Operational events.

Although administrative alerts are still written into the application event log, operational events are written to a separate GP Operational log, which is found in Event Viewer, Applications and Services, Microsoft, Windows, Group Policy, Operational (see Figure 21-99). This provides a lot of functionality; you can create a filter to display only certain types of Group Policy logs, save queries, and even subscribe to the operational logs on other machines.

In nearly all cases, if your general domain is healthy in terms of replication (which can be checked with the DCDIAG and other AD replication tools), then your Group Policy technically behaves; any problems are probably caused by linking and filtering of GPOs.

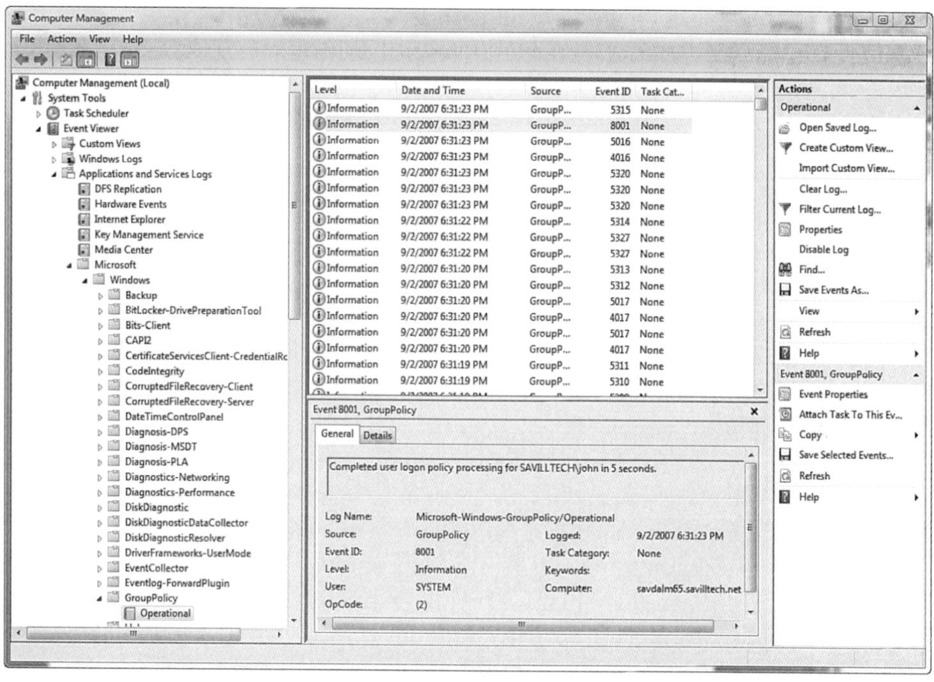

FIGURE 21-99 This Operational log makes it easy to see Group Policy-related events.

Microsoft Templates

With all the facilities of Group Policy, a number of logical usage scenarios, depending on the type of clients and purpose of a machine, arise and can consist of a huge number of settings. Fortunately, Microsoft provides templates for the most common types of Group Policy usage; although you can implement all the settings yourself, it is recommended to use the Microsoft templates supplied at http://www.microsoft.com/downloads/details.aspx?familyid=354b9f45-8aa6-4775-9208-c681a7043292&displaylang=en as a foundation for your settings.

Here are the main templates that are supplied and their use:

- **Lightly Managed**. In this scenario, you are dealing with power users and developers who have a good understanding of the OS environment and who need flexibility to perform their day-to-day functions. In this case, Group Policy is most likely used to deploy core applications, such as Office, anti-virus applications, and perhaps patch update settings. The "free-seating" approach applies for the lightly managed configuration, where users can sit at any computer that is lightly managed and have access to the application and resources that are needed.

- **Mobile**. This is directed at mobile and laptop users, so a great deal of emphasis is given to computers that are in a disconnected state from the network and who synchronize infrequently. The main configuration item here is ensuring data is available at all times, which requires configuration of offline copies of folders and the data therein.
- **Multiuser**. Multiple users use one computer, such as in a lab or library, which allows users to have limited customizations (like background picture or color scheme) but no major configuration changes. No cache is maintained on the computer, so at logoff, all data about the logon session is removed. This means all user data and configuration is stored on a server.
- **AppStation**. This is a highly restricted environment that runs only a few applications with minimal customization possible and with no access to applications like Internet Explorer, Office, and so on. When the computer boots, only access to the specified applications is allowed, with some optional access to a desktop (but this can be restricted).
- **TaskStation**. This scenario has access to only one application (the only application available when the computer starts), with no Start menu or desktop. This is used in call centers and sales centers, and it limits the users to the specific application. The application becomes the shell of the environment.
- **Kiosk**. This scenario is designed for a public location, such as in a demonstration booth or in an airport. The desktop runs in an automated logon at startup, which at shutdown removes all configuration data. This is a highly secure configuration with everything locked down except for the specified applications.

Summary

This chapter has shown the power of Group Policy; it is a vital tool in your infrastructure management. Trying to manage a Windows-based infrastructure without using Group Policy severely handicaps your capabilities. Take the time now to understand the capabilities of Group Policy and put policies in place to enforce your organization's standards. Companies have tried to run an infrastructure without Group Policy; they create their own version of Group Policy through a nightmare combination of logon scripts, Registry files, and other custom pieces of code (which eventually becomes unusable), with client logon times taking tens of minutes as hundreds of individual scripts and checks are performed.

Partner Group Policy with a good OS, patch, and application deployment technology (such as System Center Configuration Manager), and you have a server and desktop environment that requires little handholding.

CHAPTER 22

THE COMMAND PROMPT AND POWERSHELL

You might have heard the term "Monad" frequently talked about in the past few years. Monad is the codename for the first major revision to the command-line world in the history of Windows. Monad was supposed to be big, and it is—you know it by its final name: PowerShell! However, before the newest command-line environment is discussed, let's look at what you can do with the simple command prompt, which is still powerful.

Even though Windows is thought of as a graphical operating system—especially with Vista, its new, prettier interface—the command-line aspect should not be ignored. Nearly every task you perform via the graphical interface can be performed in at least one way via the command-line or scripting interface. In fact, this was a big driver for Windows 2003: All management should be possible via the command line; that makes it easier to automate via scripts or remotely. (These commands are talked about throughout this book; actual commands are not covered specifically in this chapter.) Although point and click is nice, the command line is also handy to do something faster and with less ambiguity. For example, if you want to check your IP address, a quick ipconfig shows that your basic IP information or ipconfig /all gives full IP stack information, including DNS configuration. To check a computer's name, run `hostname`:

```
C:\Users\john.SAVILLTECH>hostname
savdalwks01
```

Let's go to the root of the command prompt.

Command.com

The earliest version of the command line in the Microsoft world was MS-DOS, which was based around command.com. Although antiquated, MS-DOS exists even in the latest OSs (except for the 64-bit versions). Command.com was used not just in DOS, but also it was the default shell for Windows 95, 98, and Me. The first program to run at boot time was responsible for parsing and executing the autoexec.bat and config.sys content. Command.com (a 16-bit environment) was replaced as the shell for Windows NT, and a new 32-bit command line interface (and, subsequently, a 64-bit version) was provided for Windows NT (known as CMD.EXE, which the next section discusses). However, command.com was and is still supplied for 16-bit application backward-compatibility. When run, it executes in NTVDM (NT Virtual DOS Machine), which is the name of the process if you look at a command.com instance.

To start command.com from the Run windows, press Start key+R and type **command.com**. The title of the Window will be as follows:

```
Microsoft(R) Windows DOS
(C)Copyright Microsoft Corp 1990-2001.

C:\USERS\JOHN~1.SAV>
```

Notice its title is Windows DOS, and instead of showing the full path of the user, it shows only its 8.3 representation, because the 16-bit DOS window does not understand long filenames. You are essentially in a legacy DOS environment. One difference from the old-style command.com is that autoexec.bat and config.sys have been replaced with autoexec.nt and config.nt. These files are stored in the %systemroot%\system32 folder instead of the root of the system partition. Any commands or environmental configuration you want applied to the command.com environment should be placed into these .nt files. This NTVDM runs any MS-DOS or Win 16 executable (a 16-bit program). If you try to execute a 32-bit program from command.com, it passes it up to the 32-bit command shell for handling and subsequent execution.

Thunking and WOW

Why is command.com not available in the 64-bit versions of Windows 2003, XP, Vista, and Windows Server 2008 Server? Let's review the versions of Windows Server 2008 that are available: 64-bit and 32-bit (previously, there was 32-bit and 16-bit, which are different memory addressing schemes). Let's look at 16-bit and 32-bit first. Win16 used a segmented memory model (which means a memory address is based on a memory segment and the offset within that segment), whereas Win32 uses a flat memory space. There are other differences, too: Win16 does not support multithreading, but Win32 does. This allows a program to be run as separate threads of execution that can run simultaneously. These separate threads tie to symmetric multitasking (which is in Win32) that uses slices of processor time, which are given to each application. Win16 uses cooperative multitasking, which is an application giving up control before the next program can run. Backward-compatibility is important. When the 32-bit version of Windows was released, if it could not run any older 16-bit applications, this would have seriously hurt the OSs uptake. A process known as *thunking* converts a call from one type to another—for example, converting the 16-bit memory address to a 32-bit memory address (and vice versa) to allow the application to run. A large part of this functionality is implemented using the wow32.dll.

A similar problem exists for running 32-bit code on a 64-bit operating system, and once again, a conversation layer is implemented: Windows On Windows (WOW) is responsible for all the conversions needed, including processor, memory, and handling 32-bit application access to the Registry and file system. For example, an application running via WOW is redirected via folder redirection from %systemroot%\system32 to the %systemroot%\sysWOW64 folder, which is where legacy executables and libraries where 32-bit applications exist can be found. This is needed because an application cannot mix 32-bit and 64-bit DLLs, so any 32-bit application has to use the redirected legacy DLLs found in the sysWOW64 folder.

You can't run 32-bit applications on a 16-bit operating system, nor 64-bit applications on a 32-bit operating system. It's only backward support—forward support is some time away!

NOTE Even in 64-bit operating systems, the core system library folder is still named system32. This was required for support purposes. Remember that although 32-bit applications can run on 64-bit Windows, 32-bit drivers will not work; all drivers must be 64 bit.

So, why is the 16-bit command.com not available on 64-bit windows? Two levels of emulation are not possible within Windows, and you need that for 16 bit to 32 bit and 32 bit to 64 bit.

CMD.EXE

CMD.EXE was introduced with Windows NT, not as the core kernel of the operating system, but as a command-line interface into the operating system. Although the image and process is cmd.exe, it is often referred to as the command prompt or command shell. A shortcut to the command prompt can be found under the Accessories Start Menu group. You can also run CMD from the Run dialog (Start–Run) or just type **command** in the Instant Search area of the Start menu.

When a command prompt starts, it checks the following Registry locations for commands to execute to help set up the command prompt environment:

- HKEY_CURRENT_USER\Software\Microsoft\Command Processor\AutoRun
- HKEY_LOCAL_MACHINE\SOFTWARE\Microsoft\Command Processor\AutoRun

By default, these AutoRun values do not exist, and no special commands are executed. Also by default, command prompts open at the user's profile area (%UserProfile%):

```
Microsoft Windows [Version 6.0.6000]
Copyright (c) 2006 Microsoft Corporation.  All rights reserved.

C:\Users\john.SAVILLTECH>
```

If you run `cmd /?`, you can find a list of switches. Some of the useful switches are the following:

- **/c <command>**. Used to start a command window, run the command, and then close the command session.

- **/k <command>**. Same as `/c` except the window remains open. For example, `cmd /k ipconfig` starts a command window, runs IP config, and then leaves the command prompt open.
- **/d**. Stops execution of the values in the autorun areas of the Registry.

CMD.EXE Properties

The default command prompt window is 80 characters by 25 lines with a buffer of 300 lines of text, which allows you to scroll the information displayed to view information that has scrolled off the screen. (However, if required, press Ctrl+S to suspend screen output and then press again to resume screen updates.) This screen and number of lines remembered can be changed by right-clicking the command prompt window title and selecting Properties. This opens most of your configurable items.

As can be seen in the Options tab, shown in Figure 22-1, the cursor size can be changed from the default of little more than the underscore character. For commands, the buffer size value and number can be changed, along with the capability to store or discard duplicate commands via the Discard Old Duplicates option. The Edit options also are useful. By default, Insert mode should be left checked; however, if you uncheck this, the command prompt uses an old style overstrike mode (which most people are not used to anymore). QuickEdit mode allows the mouse to easily cut and paste information by simply selecting text on the screen by clicking the left mouse button, and then holding down while dragging over the text to be selected. You then release the left mouse button and press Enter; the selected text is now stored in the Windows Clipboard. To paste quickly back into the command prompt, right-click anywhere in the command prompt window. Normally, you have to right-click on the Command Prompt title bar and select Mark from the Edit menu of the displayed context menu, select the area, and press Enter. It is recommended to enable the QuickEdit mode.

If you perform a lot of command prompt work, change the size of the font used by the command prompt (see Figure 22-2). If you use the Lucida Console font instead of selecting a size for each character, like a raster font, select the font size as if in Word or any other true-type font application.

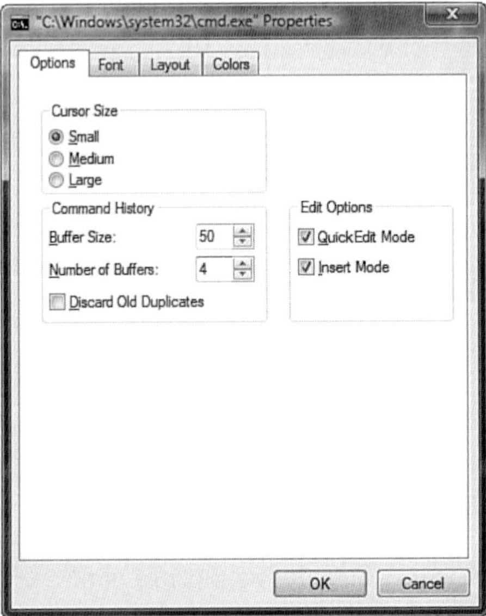

Figure 22-1 The Options tab gives access to basic items, such as the cursor size, but also the more useful buffer size and Edit options.

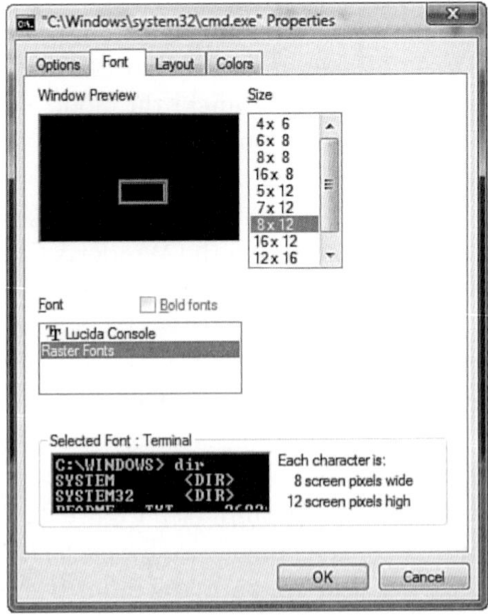

Figure 22-2 The Font tab allows the size of the command window text to be selected.

If you have information scrolling off the screen, go to the Layout tab to fix this problem (see Figure 22-3). Window Size is the actual visible, onscreen displayable area of the command window, which is by default 80 characters by 25, but it can be changed to any custom size—obviously, the bigger the size, the more screen real estate used. Screen Buffer Size is where you configure the history of output to be stored from the standard 300 up to a possible 9,999 lines, which is a lot of directory listings.

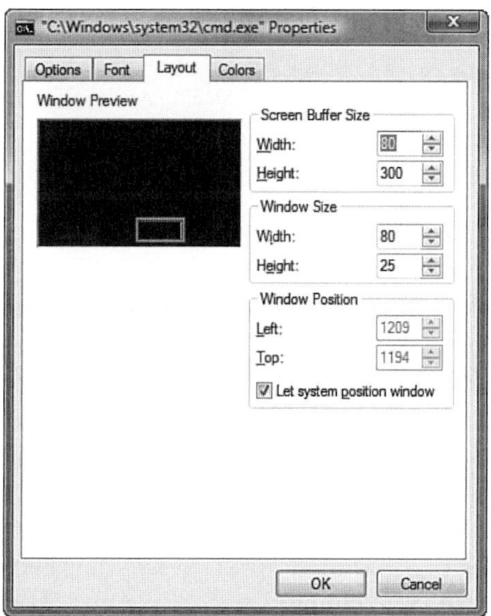

Figure 22-3 The Layout tab allows the configuration of how the command prompt is displayed onscreen and how much output it remembers.

The final tab is the Colors tab (see Figure 22-4) that enables you to change the color-display configuration. A nice combination is dark blue for the background with white for the text (which, as a nod to its artistic quality, is the same scheme Microsoft uses as the default for PowerShell) .

All these options configured are stored in the Registry under key HKEY_CURRENT_USER\Console, and a value exists for each item. (For example, the command history buffer size is set in value HistoryBufferSize.)

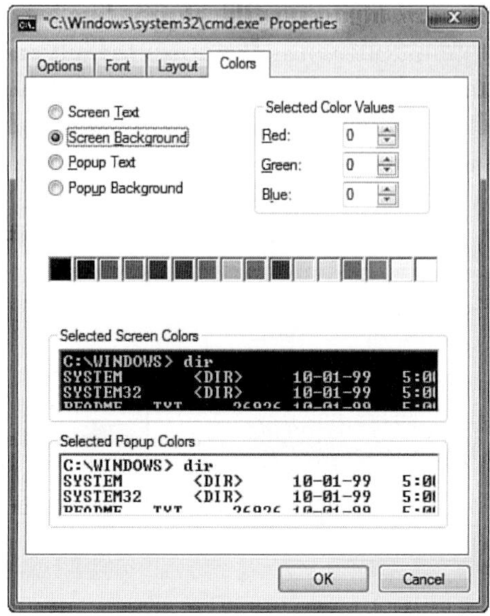

FIGURE 22-4 Interesting color combinations are possible via the Colors tab.

DOSKEY

One drawback of a command prompt is typing the actual commands, especially if you are performing repetitive commands and have to retype the same sequence of commands. (Although if that is the case, scripting might be the answer.) In the days of DOS, the solution was introduced with MS-DOS 5.0 in the form of DOSKEY, which allows easy access to the history of commands entered. (The number of commands remembered is configured via the command prompt buffer size for the command history, 50 by default.) This functionality is now a core part of the OS; the commands history is normally accessed by pressing the up and down arrows, with up moving back toward the older commands and down moving forward toward the newest entered command.

Type **`doskey /history`** to see a full list of the commands available. The function keys also provide a useful service when browsing command history. If you press F7 from within a command prompt window, a pop-up appears that displays the command history (see Figure 22-5). Scroll up and down, and select a command by pressing Enter.

Administrator: C:\Windows\system32\cmd.exe
/INSERT Specifies that new text you type is inserted in old text.
/OVERSTRIKE Specifies that new text overwrites old text.
/EXENAME=exename Specifies the executable.
/MACROFILE=filename Specifies a file of macros to install.
macroname Specifies a name for a macro you create.
text Specifies commands you want to record.
UP and DOWN ARROWS
command history; AL
history; F9 selects
F7 displays
ommand
definitions.
The following are s
$T Command sepa
$1-$9 Batch parame
$* Symbol repla
ons:
o.
ms.
command line.
D:\temp>doskey /his
dir
d:
cd temp
dir/ah
doskey /?
doskey /history
D:\temp>
0: dir
1: d:
2: cd temp
3: dir/ah
4: doskey /?
5: doskey /history

FIGURE 22-5 The pop-up gives an easy view of the command history.

Additionally, if you remember the number of a command in the history, press F9, enter the command's number, and press Enter. (For example, in Figure 22-5, if you press F9, a pop-up asking for the command number is displayed; if you type **3** and press Enter, the text "dir/ah" is entered into the prompt, ready for execution.) For both F7 and F9, pressing the Esc key closes the pop-up. Finally, you can start typing a command and then press F8 to search through the command history for commands that start with the characters entered; if there are multiple matches, continue to press F8 to cycle through the possible matches.

Commands

So what can you do inside a command prompt? So far, you can change its color and browse through a history of commands. Two types of commands are available in a command prompt: internal and external.

Internal Commands

Internal commands are part of the cmd.exe environment (for example, commands such as `cd`, which is used to change directory; `del`, which deletes a file; and `dir`, which lists the content of a folder). These commands don't have a separate executable and are just part of the command environment. Logic and control commands are also available as internal commands, such as `for`, `if`, `goto`, and `exit`, which are useful when writing scripts. For example, using `if`, you can easily perform a function based on a piece of logic; in this case, if a file exists, you output to screen Hello World:

```
IF EXIST helloworld.txt (echo Hello World) ELSE (echo Goodbye
Cruel World)
```

As this shows, if the file `helloworld.txt` is found, a pleasant message is displayed; if not, a rather dramatic response appears. The brackets denote which items relate to the conditional item by grouping. Programmers are familiar with this structure.

Here's another neat feature. When navigating the file system or even passing a filename or folder to a script or program in the command line, if you press the Tab key, it auto-completes the filename or folder based on characters you have typed so far. With each Tab strike, it cycles through any matches. So, if you're at the root of the Windows folder, type the following:

```
C:\Windows>cd s
```

NOTE To change the default completion character from Tab to something else, modify Registry value HKEY_CURRENT_USER\Software\Microsoft\Command Processor\CompletionChar to the ASCII value for the character you want to use. (See http://www.asciitable.com/ for a full list.)

Press the Tab key to scroll through all folders starting with s (for example, cd SchCache, then cd schemas, then cd security, and so on). This saves you a lot of typing when working with files and folders from the command line. Alternatively, you can turn on a separate file and directory completion by starting the cmd session with `/F:ON` switch, which enables Ctrl-F to complete files and Ctrl-D to complete directories. In addition, when using the `cd` command, if you want to move up a directory level, use .. as the directory name—for example, `cd ..` would move from d:\temp\folder to d:\temp. To move to the root of a disk, use the forward slash (\)—for example, `cd \`. To change the drive, type the name of the drive with a colon and nothing else—for example, **c:** to change to the C drive.

In addition to these internal commands, extensions were added with Windows 2000 and are enabled by default. (HKEY_LOCAL_MACHINE\SOFTWARE\Microsoft\Command Processor\EnableExtensions set to 1 means enabled; 0 is disabled.) These extensions modify the behavior of certain commands and enable additional functionality, which is explained further in the cmd help (`cmd /?`).

External Commands

External commands are programs with their own executables (normally residing in the %systemroot%\system32 folder) that are written to be used from the command line and return output in console format that provide useful functionality often beyond those internal commands. For example, you have the internal `copy` command. However, you also have the external `xcopy` command, which can do everything that `copy` can do—copying files with some configuration around overwriting behavior and user interaction—plus an additional 20 parameters (which are options passed when a command is run). This creates the capability to copy only the files that match certain criteria (attributes, date, and so on) to determine how subdirectories are handled and how security access can be copied with restartable network copy options, and more. To see what a command can do (both internal and external), run the command with the `/?` switch. This displays its help; for example, `xcopy /?` will list all the switches and what they do.

External commands are executed from the cmd.exe process (meaning cmd.exe is the parent of the executed command) and are normally contained in the %systemroot%\system32 folder; however, they can be placed anywhere. The advantage to location in the %systemroot%\system32 folder is that folder is part of the default search path, which avoids you having to type the full path to the location of the file. (For example, you don't have to type c:\windows\system32\xcopy.) This is not done by searching the entire file system every time, or using search features that are part of the Vista/Windows Server 2008 operating system. Instead, this is accomplished by simply searching the file system, but only a small part of it.

Finding Commands in the Command Prompt

The entire OS has a path environment variable that applies to all users and processes on the system, which is normally accessed via the Environment Variables button of the Advanced tab of the System control panel applet.

When applications install, many of them update this path variable to include their installation folders; this enables Windows to find applicable resources, both from the normal windows shell and the command environment. In addition to this systemwide path variable, there is also a user-specific path variable that is only valid for the currently logged-in user. When a new process starts, it adds the user path to the end of the system path to make a single path where the system will look for programs. From the command prompt, type **echo %path%** to see your full path:

```
C:\Users\john.SAVILLTECH>echo %path%
C:\Program Files\Windows Resource Kits\Tools\;C:\Windows\sys-
tem32;C:\Windows;C:\Windows\System32\Wbem;C:\Program
Files\Microsoft SQL Server\90\Tools\binn\;C:\Program Files\Win-
dows Imaging\;C:\Program Files\QuickTime\QTSystem\;C:\Program
Files\Diskeeper Corporation\Diskeeper\;C:\Program Files\IDM
Computer Solutions\UltraEdit-32;C:\Windows\System32\WindowsPow-
erShell\v1.0\;d:\temp
```

In this example, viewing the path, you see SQL Server 9.0 installed, the Windows imaging add-on, QuickTime, Diskeeper, UltraEdit, and PowerShell, in addition to the default C:\windows and C:\windows\system32 entries (among others). Also d:\temp is at the end, which was the path variable for the user and is, therefore, added to the end.

When you run an external command, this path is searched, so as soon as a match is found, the search is stopped. Because the user path variable is appended to the system, path variable files stored in system locations will always take preference. In the case of this path variable, the start of the search order is as follows:

1. C:\Program Files\Windows Resource Kits\Tools\
2. C:\Windows\system32
3. C:\Windows

The exception is the application's current folder, which is always checked before resorting to looking at the path entries. If you run a command and want to know where it is being called from, use the `where` command with the name of the program:

```
C:\>where whoami
C:\Windows\System32\whoami.exe
```

You use the `whoami` command for more than just programs; it also works on DLLs and any other file type, which is useful if you are seeing strange behavior and want to understand which file a program might be using via the searchpath.

Variables

Variables were covered at a high level early in the book, limited mainly to `%systemroot%`, which is the root of the Windows installation, usually C:\windows. There are many other environment variables, and other options. Environment variables are variables that the command environment and overall OS sets and utilizes. Other variables can be created for use by your scripts or programs but their scope is limited to that particular command instance and are known as local variables.

The internal `set` command is useful for viewing and setting variables. For example, if `set` is run without any arguments, it lists out all variables (both environmental and local). Table 22-1 lists some of the most common variables and their type.

Table 22-1 Operating System Environment Variables

Variable	Type	Description
%ALLUSERSPROFILE%	Local	Returns the location of the All Users Profile.
%APPDATA%	Local	Returns the location where applications store data by default.
%CD%	Local	Returns the current directory string.
%ALLUSERSPROFILE%	System	Path of where to store program data for all users; by default, C:\ProgramData.
%CMDCMDLINE%	Local	Returns the exact command line used to start the current Cmd.exe session. This is not listed via Set but returned when used.
%CMDEXTVERSION%	System	Returns the version number of the current Command Processor Extensions. This is not listed via Set but returned when used.

(continues)

Table 22-1 Operating System Environment Variables *(continued)*

Variable	Type	Description
%COMPUTERNAME%	System	Returns the name of the computer.
%COMSPEC%	System	Returns the exact path to the command shell executable.
%DATE%	System	Returns the current date. This is not listed via Set but generated dynamically when used.
%ERRORLEVEL%	System	Returns the error code of the most recently used command. A nonzero value usually indicates an error.
%HOMEDRIVE%	System	Returns which local workstation drive letter is connected to the user's home directory.
%HOMEPATH%	System	Returns the full path of the user's home directory.
%HOMESHARE%	System	Returns the network path to the user's shared home directory if set.
%LOGONSEVER%	Local	Returns the name of the domain controller that validated the current logon session—for example, \\SAVDALDC01.
%NUMBER_OF_PROCESSORS%	System	Specifies the number of cores installed on the computer. This is not physical processors—for example, a dual-core machine will list as 2.
%OS%	System	Returns the OS name. This will be Windows_NT on any NT-based OS, including 2003, Vista, and 2007.
%PATH%	System	Specifies the search path for executable files.
%PATHEXT%	System	Returns a list of the file extensions that the operating system considers to be executable.
%PROCESSOR_ARCHITECTURE%	System	Returns the chip architecture of the processor—for example, AMD64, x86.

Table 22-1 Operating System Environment Variables

Variable	Type	Description
%PROCESSOR_IDENTIFIER%	System	Returns a description of the processor.
%PROCESSOR_LEVEL%	System	Returns the model number of the processor installed on the computer.
%PROCESSOR_REVISION%	System	Returns the revision number of the processor.
%PROMPT%	Local	Returns the command prompt settings for the current interpreter. By default, this is PG, which is displaying the current path and then a greater-than sign. A full list of options can be found at http://www.microsoft.com/resources/documentation/windows/xp/all/proddocs/en-us/prompt.mspx?mfr=true.
%PUBLIC%	System	Location of the Public storage area.
%RANDOM%	System	Returns a random decimal number between 0 and 32767. This is not listed via a set command but rather is created dynamically when used—for example, "echo %random%".
%SESSIONNAME%	System	Returns a string indicating the name of the session. Console sessions will show as Console; other remote sessions would show as the name—for example, RDP-Tcp#2.
%SYSTEMDRIVE%	System	Returns the drive containing the Windows root—for example, C:.
%SYSTEMROOT%	System	Returns the location of the Windows root directory—for example, C:\Windows.
%TEMP% and %TMP%	System and User	Returns the default temporary directories that are used by applications available to users who are currently logged on.
%TIME%	System	Displays current time. This is not listed via Set but generated dynamically when used.

(continues)

Table 22-1 Operating System Environment Variables *(continued)*

Variable	Type	Description
%USERDOMAIN%	Local	Returns the name of the domain that contains the user's account—for example, SAVILLTECH.NET.
%USERNAME%	Local	Returns the name of the user who is currently logged on—for example, john.
%USERPROFILE%	Local	Returns the location of the profile for the current user.
%WINDIR%	System	Returns the location of the operating (same as SystemRoot).

The `set` command can only change local variables and not system variables. For example, you can create a new variable using the format `set <variable name>=<value>` (for example, `set johnval=local`); however, this variable would only be available in your current command prompt instance or script and is not persistent in any way. (Persistent in this case means it is a permanent change beyond a single session.) To change system and user environment variables in a persistent fashion, use the external command, `setx` (x at the end for eXternal). `setx` is powerful; it can set variables based on values in the Registry and contents of a file, and can modify remote machines. Its default mode is to set variables in the user environment, but using the `/M` switch sets systemwide. The basic usage is simply to pass the name of the variable to set its value; for example:

```
C:\>setx currentchapter 22
SUCCESS: Specified value was saved.
```

If you looked at the Environment Variables dialog (which is available via the Advanced tab of the System Control Panel applet), this variable is now created and its value set (see Figure 22-6). `setx` without the `/M` switch creates the environment variable in the user space and, therefore, is stored under the HKEY_CURRENT_USER\Environment Registry key. Conversely, system variables are stored in Registry key HKEY_LOCAL_MACHINE\SYSTEM\CurrentControlSet\Control\Session Manager\Environment.

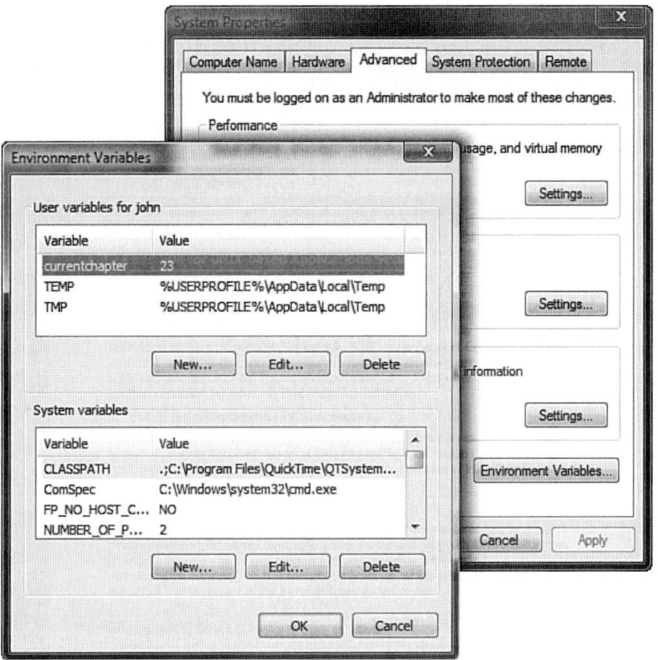

FIGURE 22-6 The user variable created via `setx` without the `/m` switch.

To use `setx` to change the path system variable, you can use the `/M` switch but remember to include the original `%path%` in the value, or the existing path locations will be lost, which will cause the system problems:

```
C:\>setx /m path "%path%;d:\temp"
SUCCESS: Specified value was saved.
```

If you placed `d:\temp` at the start of the path, `d:\temp` would be searched before the rest of the path areas, so consider the order of your path. The more paths you put before the default Windows areas, the longer the rest of the OS searches will take because it now has to look in your custom locations before finding its core files.

Redirecting Input and Output

There are many instances where the output from a command line would be more useful in a file, which is easily achieved using the greater-than (>)

sign. The sign tells the command to output to the filename given after the sign. For example, to send the output of `ipconfig` to a file `ipconfig.txt`, add `> ipconfig.txt` to the end:

```
C:\>ipconfig > ipconfig.txt
```

Now instead of seeing anything onscreen, the output was redirected to the file. If a file named `ipconfig.txt` already exists, its content would be replaced. If you want to append the output to an existing file, use `>>` instead of `>`. This is useful if you want to repeat a command periodically for logging purposes as an example.

The exception to this redirection of output is errors; by default, errors will still be displayed to screen. However, using `2>` allows the redirection of error output to a separate file. If you want errors redirected to the same file as normal output, use `2>&1`, for example:

```
C:\>ipconfig > ipconfig.txt 2>&1
```

These numbers refer to the various handles—for example, the `STDOUT` handle, which in a normal command prompt window is numerical handle 1, the `STDERR` handle is numeric handle 2, and the `STDIN` is numeric handle 0. `STDOUT` is where normal output is directed, `STDERR` is where error output is directed, and `STDIN` is where input is expected.

Likewise, you can use the less-than (<) symbol to allow a command to read its input from a file. For example, if you had a list of names, you could use the `sort` command to place them in order:

```
C:\>type names.txt
Hector
Achilles
Paris
C:\>sort < names.txt
Achilles
Hector
Paris
```

To make this even more useful, you could then output to another file:

```
C:\>sort < names.txt > sortednames.txt
```

Finally, if you don't want to use files, you can "pipe" output from one command to another using the | character and send the output of one command to another, for example:

```
Command 1 | command 2
```

This code sends the output from `command 1` as the input to `command 2`. For example, if you want to perform a directory listing of a directory and return only the files that have a certain text string in their name, use the following command:

```
C:\Windows>dir *.* | find "log"
11/17/2006  06:02 PM            19,133 comsetup.log
02/07/2007  04:05 PM           323,041 DirectX.log
11/17/2006  05:53 PM             4,231 DtcInstall.log
12/23/2006  06:39 AM               738 KB926139.log
03/14/2007  07:54 AM            57,198 PFRO.log
03/14/2007  04:22 PM           165,507 setupact.log
11/17/2006  06:01 PM               491 setuperr.log
11/17/2006  05:35 PM             1,313 TSSysprep.log
11/17/2006  05:00 PM         1,116,147 WindowsUpdate (1).log
03/15/2007  07:46 PM         1,823,540 WindowsUpdate.log
03/09/2007  10:06 AM               510 windows_r2setup.log
09/30/2006  08:25 AM               861 wsftperr.log
```

One common use of the pipe capability is adding `| more` to the end of a command, which sends the output to the `more` command. The `more` command displays a screen of output and then waits for the Enter key to be pressed to display an additional line of text. This is useful for commands that don't have the capability to slowly display information. One final tip is `| clip`, which takes the output and sends it to the Clipboard.

Multiple Commands

It is possible to chain commands together with varying levels of complexity. The simplest method is to use a single ampersand symbol (&), which simply runs multiple commands consecutively:

```
command1 & command2
```

Command1 runs first and then command2 runs, regardless of the success of command1. For example, running `netstat & echo %time%` would list the active connections and then write out the current time. You are not limited to two commands; you can keep adding additional commands, with each command separated by an ampersand.

If you require a second command to run only if the first command succeeds, use two ampersand characters (&&). For example, if you run `clip` with an invalid parameter, the second command will not run:

```
C:\>clip /error && echo worked
ERROR: Invalid argument/option - '/error'.
Type "CLIP /?" for usage.
```

A working command shows the "worked" output text:

```
C:\>set test=value && echo worked
worked
```

Taking the first example, you can use a double `||` to run a command only if the previous command fails:

```
C:\>clip /error || echo not working
ERROR: Invalid argument/option - '/error'.
Type "CLIP /?" for usage.
not working
```

Chaining is fine; however, often you require more complex sequences of commands with more granular logic beyond just success or failure, and you want to run the sequences with ease. Files are used with batches of commands known as "batch files," which are simply text files with a .bat extension. (Although a `.cmd` extension also works and is treated the same as a batch file.)

The commands used before and mentioned in other chapters can all be used in a batch file. In its basic form, a batch file can consist of nothing more than a series of commands; for example, a batch file could contain the following:

```
rem test.bat
echo Starting batch file
hostname
```

If `test.bat` is executed, it runs as expected, except every line of the batch file is output to the screen, as shown here:

```
C:\>test.bat

C:\>rem test.bat

C:\>echo Starting batch file
Starting batch file

C:\>hostname
savdalwks01
```

Output of the actual commands can be suppressed by adding @ to the start of each line or adding `echo off` to the top of the batch file. In fact, normal convention is to add `@echo off` to the start of batch files to avoid the `echo off` displaying to screen. The batch file now becomes the following:

```
@echo off
rem test.bat
echo Starting batch file
hostname
```

When executed, you get the output from the commands:

```
C:\>test.bat
Starting batch file
savdalwks01
```

In the batch file, you have a line starting with `rem`, which is simply a remark in the file (also known as a *comment*) that is used to comment on the file content to help understand its functionality for future editing.

Although a batch file on its own might be useful, there will also be times that you will want to pass data to be used in its actions. For example, you might want to pass a computername, username, or any other value, or perhaps a combination of values. The passing of data to a batch file is made possible simply by adding the percent (%) sign to the number of the argument's position when passed to the batch file, with %0 being the actual name of the batch file. Let's say you run a batch file as follows:

```
Dosomething.bat john 32 vista
```

Within the script, %0 would equate to `dosomething.bat`, %1 would be john, %2 32, and %3 vista. For example, you could write a `mapdrive.bat` that accepts the UNC path as a parameter and maps the path to a drive letter:

```
@echo off
rem Map drive
rem mapdrive <unc path> <drive letter>

net use %2: %1
```

If you want to check for errors, you can examine the `errorlevel` environment variable, which contains the execution result of the last command run as the following:

- 0—Command completed with no error
- 1—A general error
- 2—An execution error
- -2—A mathematical error

This `errorlevel` can be checked using the general `%errorlevel%`, for example:

```
if %errorlevel% neq 0 echo A problem occurred
```

Alternatively, for `errorlevel,` the `if` command has a separate way of handling that allows a certain `errorlevel` to be checked for

```
if errorlevel 2 echo A problem occurred
```

Batch files are great for many things; however, when you start trying for more complex logic and interaction with the operating system and other interfaces, such as the Active Directory, batch file capabilities are limited. This is where Windows Scripting Host comes in.

Windows Scripting Host

Windows Scripting Host is not a language of its own. It's an environment into which scripts written in other languages can run (for example, VBScript and JScript). Available as an add-on for Windows 95 and

Windows NT 4.0, Windows Scripting Host later became a core part of the operating system with Windows 98/Windows 2000 and later operating systems. This allows Windows Scripting Host to be used as part of logon scripts to perform more powerful functions than those possible with batch files, which were the previous supported logon process environment.

In addition to the raw power of now being able to write scripts in a language that might be already well known (for example, VB and JScript), using the power of these languages provides easy access to other components. Commonly accessed features via languages include the Active Directory Scripting Interface (ADSI), which allows powerful manipulation of the Active Directory environment, and the Windows Management Interface (WMI), which allows access to information and to control all elements of an OS and, if supported by the manufacturer, the underlying hardware itself. Those are just two examples; many other types of service, such as databases, have scriptable interfaces. This is all possible because the languages are all object-oriented; the language itself just needs to interact with an object representing some entity. In the case of the Active Directory, for example, an object exposed to VBScript or JScript via ADSI could represent a computer or a user. This object exposed via ADSI will give the scripting language full access to the properties and functions supported without the scripting language having to understand the object itself.

Hello World

This section looks at VBScript (because we don't like anything starting with J; for those of you who know Java, JScript is also supported out-of-the-box). Let's look at the most basic VBScript possible:

```
WScript.Echo( "Hello World" )
```

If this line is saved as `helloworld.vbs` (the `vbs` extension indicates that the file is of type vbscript), you can execute from the command line, and Hello World appears—but not as expected. Instead of appearing in the command prompt window, a dialog box appears, as shown in Figure 22-7.

FIGURE 22-7 Your first VBScript program, and it's impressive, to say the least.

The reason the text appeared in a window is that the Windows Scripting Host has two script host environments:

- A command-line host environment, cscript
- A graphical host environment, wscript (the default)

You can force a script to run in a particular host by specifying the name of the host before the script name. For example, to force helloworld.vbs to run in the command host, use the following:

```
C:\>cscript helloworld.vbs
Microsoft (R) Windows Script Host Version 5.7
Copyright (C) Microsoft Corporation. All rights reserved.

Hello World
```

To run in the graphical host, use the following:

```
C:\>wscript helloworld.vbs
```

In many instances, the command host is more useful, particularly if there are multiple lines of output. In the graphical environment, each line of output will appear as a separate dialog box; this gets cumbersome and soon becomes painful for your clicking finger. To set the default host to be the command host run command, do the following:

```
C:\>cscript //H:cscript
Microsoft (R) Windows Script Host Version 5.7
Copyright (C) Microsoft Corporation. All rights reserved.

The default script host is now set to "cscript.exe".
```

To switch back to wscript as the default, and therefore, the graphical host run command, do the following:

```
C:\>wscript //H:wscript
```

VBScript Basics

An in-depth look at the VBScript language is beyond the scope of this book; however, let's look at some of its common tasks because, as an Administrator, you will find yourself challenged with a task where a script might be the right answer. First, like a batch file, you probably want to pass parameters to the script. Arguments are accessed via the array `Wscript.Arguments()`, where the number in the bracket is the element of the array. For example, `Wscript.Arguments(0)` is the first argument to the script; to check the total number of arguments, use the `.Count` function of an array, such as `Wscript.Arguments.Count`. This is useful at the start of a script that expects a certain number of arguments to make sure they were passed. For example:

```
' Check all arguments required have been passed
If Wscript.Arguments.Count < 1 Then
  Wscript.Echo "Arguments   required. For example:" & vbCrLf _
    & "cscript helloworld.vbs worldname"
  Wscript.Quit(0)
End If

Wscript.Echo "Hello " & Wscript.Arguments(0)
```

Notice that the first line is a comment. (A *comment* is anything after the apostrophe character ['].) A check is performed to ensure that the number of arguments is not less than one; if there are less than one, a message is displayed describing the correct syntax. Then the script exited via the `Wscript.Quit(0)` function. If a planet is passed, it will not run the quit and write to screen Hello with the passed planet. (In this example, the script is not smart enough to point out that Pluto is, in fact, not a proper planet, just a dwarf one.) For example:

```
D:\temp>helloworld.vbs pluto
Microsoft (R) Windows Script Host Version 5.7
```

```
Copyright (C) Microsoft Corporation. All rights reserved.

Hello Pluto
```

Calling WMI from VBScript

Some of the most common actions you perform with a script are to communicate with the Windows Management Instrumentation (WMI) to look at information on a local or remote computer. Let's start with a script to get the operating system information about a machine:

```
strComputer = "."
Set objWMIService =
GetObject("winmgmts:{impersonationLevel=impersonate}!\\" &
strComputer & "\root\cimv2")
Set colOperatingSystems = objWMIService.ExecQuery("Select *
from Win32_OperatingSystem")
For Each objOperatingSystem in colOperatingSystems
      WScript.Echo "Name - " & objOperatingSystem.Caption
        WScript.Echo "Architecture - " &
objOperatingSystem.OSArchitecture
      WScript.Echo "OS Build - " & objOperatingSystem.Version
      WScript.Echo "Windows Directory - " &
objOperatingSystem.WindowsDirectory
Next
```

Looking at this script, first create a variable named `strComputer`, which has a value of a period (.). This means the local machine WMI instance—that is, the information you query from WMI—will be gleaned from the local machine that is executing the script. Don't define `strComputer` in advance. A variable is required in some languages to be defined in advance, but not VBScript. You can create variables as needed in VBScript; however, good programming practice encourages you to define variables at the start of the program to help make the code more understandable and to remove the possibility of errors in the code.

Next, the `objWMIService` variable is created. It's set to point to an object that points to the WMI service and the `\root\cimv2` namespace. There are other namespaces, such as SECURITY, but this list will vary based on the OS and other software that might be installed.

The next line sets the `colOperatingSystems` variable to a query run against the WMI object that you linked to select all information from the `Win32_OperatingSystem WMI` class. Many different classes are listed at http://msdn2.microsoft.com/en-us/library/aa392727.aspx along with an overall description. By selecting a class, all the attributes and methods of the class are shown. Because you want information about the operating system, you need to select from the `Win32_Operating System` class. Notice that the format of the selection of information is like that of a SQL database; select * from `Win32_OperatingSystem`.

The next line sets up a loop to process through each returned record. (Although in this instance, you will only get one record returned because there is only one operating system instance on a single machine; other types of selection could return many records, such as hotfix information, software installed, and so on.) Within the `FOR` loop, each record can be accessed by the passed `objOperatingSystem` pointer.

Within the `FOR` loop, write to screen various attributes of the operating system's return record (for example, the Caption [which is the OS name], architecture [32- or 64-bit], and so on). To access a property of an object, type the name of the object, followed by a period, followed by the name of the property, so **`objOperatingSystem.Caption`** is pointing to the Caption attribute of object `objOperatingSystem`. If you run this script on a Vista machine, you see the following output:

```
D:\projects\VBScripts>cscript checkos.vbs
Microsoft (R) Windows Script Host Version 5.7
Copyright (C) Microsoft Corporation. All rights reserved.

Name - Microsoft® Windows Vista™ Ultimate
Architecture - 32-bit
OS Build - 6.0.6000
Windows Directory - C:\Windows
```

To experience the cumbersome clicking mentioned in the "Hello World" section, try running `wscript checkos.vbs` and enjoy clicking the four dialog boxes. With a few minor changes, you can make this script far more appealing; let's enable it to function on remote boxes and tidy the code to force all variables to be declared at the start of the program via the `Option Explicit` command:

```
Option Explicit

Dim strComputer, objWMIService, colOperatingSystems,
objOperatingSystem

If Wscript.Arguments.Count < 1 Then     ' If no machine name
passed
  strComputer = "."   'Point to local machine   ' Make machine
the local
else
  strComputer = Wscript.Arguments(0)
End If



Set objWMIService =
GetObject("winmgmts:{impersonationLevel=impersonate}!\\" &
strComputer & "\root\cimv2")

Set colOperatingSystems = objWMIService.ExecQuery("Select *
from Win32_OperatingSystem")

For Each objOperatingSystem in colOperatingSystems

      WScript.Echo "Name - " & objOperatingSystem.Caption
      WScript.Echo "Service Pack - " &
        objOperatingSystem.CSDVersion
      WScript.Echo "OS Build - " & objOperatingSystem.Version
      WScript.Echo "Windows Directory - " &
        objOperatingSystem.WindowsDirectory

Next
```

Now declare the variables you will use at the start of the code via the `DIM` command, and then check to see if an argument is passed. If passed, set as the `strComputer` value allowing remote execution; otherwise, set to a period that is the local machine. The architecture output to the service pack version was also changed because only Windows Vista and Windows Server 2008 support this attribute. (You can run this script on older remote machines.) As shown here, you can now execute the script locally by passing no parameters or remotely by passing the name of the machine:

```
D:\projects\VBScripts>checkos.vbs
Microsoft (R) Windows Script Host Version 5.7
Copyright (C) Microsoft Corporation. All rights reserved.

Name - Microsoft® Windows Vista™ Ultimate
Service Pack -
OS Build - 6.0.6000
Windows Directory - C:\Windows

D:\projects\VBScripts>checkos.vbs savdaldc01
Microsoft (R) Windows Script Host Version 5.7
Copyright (C) Microsoft Corporation. All rights reserved.

Name - Microsoft(R) Windows(R) Server 2003 Enterprise x64
  Edition
Service Pack - Service Pack 2
OS Build - 5.2.3790
Windows Directory - C:\WINDOWS

D:\projects\VBScripts>checkos.vbs longhorn1
Microsoft (R) Windows Script Host Version 5.7
Copyright (C) Microsoft Corporation. All rights reserved.

Name - Microsoft® Windows Server™ Code Name "Longhorn"
Service Pack -
OS Build - 6.0.6001
Windows Directory - C:\Windows
```

Obviously, problems will happen, and by default, the scripting host halts on errors; however, you can tell the script how to react via the following:

```
on error resume next
```

This will cause the script to carry on even if an error is encountered. If this is in place after running commands, you can check for errors using the following logic:

```
if err.number<>0 then
    wscript.echo err.number, err.description
    err.Clear
end if
```

Like a batch file, the `err.number` should be 0 if successful; otherwise, it signifies an error that can then be acted upon. For more information on scripting, visit the Microsoft scripting center at http://www.microsoft.com/technet/scriptcenter/learnit.mspx.

So, all this sounds great, right? Why do you need PowerShell? What is PowerShell exactly?

PowerShell

PowerShell has been around for a couple of years. Prior to its late 2006 release under the codename Monad, PowerShell was to re-envision how the command line is seen and used. The goal was simply to create the best Windows-based scripting environment with full access to all facets of the OS and supporting services.

Windows has been around for a long time, so why release PowerShell now? Windows is a graphical environment with most users relying on the GUI. The command line was not given priority. Many new features were being added to the OS and were made available via Application Programmer Interfaces (APIs) that, being binary in nature, don't work well from a command line and other management interfaces. Over time, however, more Windows Servers were introduced into environments and placed in data centers. This meant that the old-style management using the GUI did not scale to hundreds of servers; instead, a scriptable, command shell interface was required and delivered with PowerShell.

The actual PowerShell language is based on the POSIX standard shell defined in IEEE Specification 1003.2, but it's obviously modified to center around Windows structures (in particular, the .NET Framework). All other shells have to convert results to text for manipulation and display in the command shell, but PowerShell just processes the underlying objects of the OS, providing far more flexibility. Additionally, PowerShell does not care about whitespace (such as spaces and new lines) and is not case-sensitive.

Installing PowerShell

PowerShell is a feature of Windows Server 2008, is installed via the Add Features Wizard within Server Manager, and has no dependencies or prerequisites. PowerShell is also available for Windows XP, 2003, and Vista with all the major architectures supported (x86, x64, and IA64). You can download PowerShell from http://www.microsoft.com and search for "powershell download." After downloading, the installation is a simple install wizard procedure with the only prerequisite of having .NET Framework 2.0. You should also search Microsoft for the "Windows PowerShell Documentation Pack" that includes four documents:

- A Windows PowerShell Getting Started Guide
- A Windows PowerShell Primer, which has more in-depth information on PowerShell than the Getting Started Guide
- A PowerShell Quick Reference Guide that is a one-page foldable help sheet
- Release notes

After installing, PowerShell is accessible via the Windows PowerShell shortcut under the Windows PowerShell program folders. Although it looks like the normal command prompt, PowerShell is not running as part of the command prompt but as a separate environment (powershell.exe).

NOTE To customize PowerShell, right-click the Windows PowerShell window title and select properties and colors, edit modes, layout, and so on. This is the same as for a regular command prompt.

---

cmdlets

In the same way that the command prompt has internal commands, PowerShell has cmdlets (command-lets) that perform a single function.

Additional cmdlets can be installed into the environment, and they are already available from several third parties, including Quest and PowerGadgets. Microsoft also has several products that extend PowerShell as the new central management point for Windows; for example, Exchange 2007 relies heavily on PowerShell.

NOTE PowerShell can access all the external commands that were available in the command environment (such as `hostname`, `ipconfig`, and `net`); however, after you start to learn PowerShell, much of the functionality offered via these external commands can be achieved using object interaction.

One big plus of the PowerShell is consistency. With normal shells, the commands can vary in complexity; however, given the object-oriented nature of PowerShell, most cmdlets are fairly basic in their usage and are highly consistent. The power comes in using combinations of cmdlets. The cmdlet naming convention is for the first part to be a verb (for example, get-, format-, out-, or set-) that dictates what the cmdlet does (such as get information, format information, direct information, or set information). The next part is a noun, which specifies what is being acted on. Everything is based around this verb-noun pair; for example, `get-process w*` retrieves information about processes whose names start with the letter w, as shown here:

```
PS C:\Users\john.SAVILLTECH> get-process w*

Handles  NPM(K)    PM(K)      WS(K) VM(M)   CPU(s)     Id ProcessName
-------  ------    -----      ----- -----   ------     -- -----------
     62       3     1836       4592    60     0.19   1120 WinCinemaMgr
     97       4     1344       2920    32     0.25    504 wininit
    130       3     1976       3844    38     0.56    652 winlogon
    498      30    48964      86972   314   209.02   6108 WINWORD
    145       4     1636       3840    48     0.05   1732 wmdc
    871      34   214372     142876   376   836.75   4184 wmplayer
    447      18    15524      14104   125     1.47   3900 wmpnetwk
```

Although the output is in tabular format, this is not how the data is returned in the PowerShell. It's referenced in its.NET object format, but the default display format is a table. You can easily tell it to output in other formats, such as a list, by piping the output of the `get-process` to the `format-list` cmdlet:

```
PS C:\Users\john.SAVILLTECH> get-process w* | format-list


Id      : 1120
Handles : 62
CPU     : 0.1875
Name    : WinCinemaMgr

Id      : 504
Handles : 97
CPU     : 0.25
Name    : wininit
..
..
```

Probably the greatest cmdlet (and the best verb-noun combination) you will use is `get-help`. On its own, `get-help` gives you basic information, but it can show you the names of other cmdlets, so you can get detailed help on them. For example, `get-help format-*` will list all the cmdlets starting with `format-` to help you see the options available to you:

```
PS C:\Users\john.SAVILLTECH> get-help format-*

Name           Category  Synopsis
----           --------  --------
Format-List    Cmdlet    Formats the output as a list of prop...
Format-Custom  Cmdlet    Uses a customized view to format the...
Format-Table   Cmdlet    Formats the output as a table.
Format-Wide    Cmdlet    Formats objects as a wide table that...
```

To generate a list of all the available cmdlets, run the `get-command` cmdlet. This returns a high-level description of their syntax for usage. To see all the available members of a cmdlet, run the cmdlet and pipe to the `get-member` cmdlet. For example, to return all the available members of `get-process`, run the following:

```
get-process | get-member
```

In addition to getting detailed help about a cmdlet, use the `get-help` command with the name of the cmdlet followed by `-detailed` to get all available help. Add `-full` to just view a portion of the help. For example, add `-examples`, as follows:

```
Get-help format-list -examples
Get-help format-list -full
Get-help format list -detailed
```

If you look at the `get-` commands and then combine them with `get-help` to access more detailed information, you quickly see some powerful functionality. For example, to look at a certain Registry value in PowerShell, you can access it just like a file:

```
PS C:\Users\john.SAVILLTECH> $reg = get-itemproperty
➥"HKLM:\Software\Microsoft\Windows NT\CurrentVersion"
PS C:\Users\john.SAVILLTECH> write-host $reg.registeredowner
John Savill
```

This code creates a variable (`$reg`)—variables always start with the dollar character—which points to the properties of the HEY_LOCAL_MACHINE path given. The next line just outputs the attribute of the path (`registeredowner`). (This is accessed consistently with property access to an object; just place the attribute name after a period following the object name.) This command could also be written as a single, long line:

```
PS C:\Users\john.SAVILLTECH> write-host (get-itemproperty
➥"HKLM:\Software\Microsoft\Windows NT\CurrentVersion").
➥registeredowner
John Savill
```

Variables

In PowerShell, variables have no type and are not declared; they are simply created as needed in the PowerShell variable namespace (which you'll see in the "Aliases" section, later in the chapter). What you can do with a variable, however, is cast it. This only allows it to hold a certain type.

Casting is done by placing the data type in square brackets (for example, [int], [string], [datetime], [double], [wmi], and [adsi]), which only allows that type of data to be stored. (Where possible, it converts that data so it can be stored.) Any data type can be cast by using the full .NET Framework class name. Here is an example of this casting:

```
PS C:\> [int] $varnum = 2
PS C:\> $varnum
2
PS C:\> $varnum = "005"
PS C:\> $varnum
5
PS C:\> $varnum = "ten"
Cannot convert value "ten" to type "System.Int32". Error:
"Input string was not in a correct format."
At line:1 char:8
+ $varnum  <<<< = "ten"
```

You originally create the variable `varnum` as an integer with a value of 2, which outputs fine. Then set to a string value of "005," which PowerShell converts to the integer 5 (because the preceding zeros mean nothing for a number). You receive an error only when you try to save a string into the variable. (Maybe the next version of PowerShell will handle conversion of numeric text names!)

Depending on the type of data stored in a variable, the various members for that data type's .NET class are available. For example, if you store a string in a variable, you could use the `ToUpper()` method:

```
PS C:\> $strVar = "This is a MiXture"
PS C:\> $strVar.ToUpper()
THIS IS A MIXTURE
```

When you type the period (.) after the variable name, you can press Tab to cycle through all the methods that are available. Alternatively, you can pass the variable to the get-member cmdlet to list them:

```
PS C:\> $strVar | get-member


   TypeName: System.String

Name              MemberType           Definition
----              ----------           ----------
Clone             Method               System.Object Clone()
CompareTo         Method               System.Int32 CompareTo(Object
                                       value), System.Int32
                                       CompareTo(String strB)
Contains          Method               System.Boolean Contains(String
                                       value)
CopyTo            Method               System.Void CopyTo(Int32
                                       sourceIndex, Char[] destination,
                                       Int32 destinationIn...
EndsWith          Method               System.Boolean EndsWith(String
                                       value), System.Boolean
                                       EndsWith(String value, ...
Equals            Method               System.Boolean Equals(Object
                                       obj), System.Boolean
                                       Equals(String value), Syste...
GetEnumerator     Method               System.CharEnumerator
                                       GetEnumerator()
GetHashCode       Method               System.Int32 GetHashCode()
GetType           Method               System.Type GetType()
GetTypeCode       Method               System.TypeCode GetTypeCode()
get_Chars         Method               System.Char get_Chars(Int32
                                       index)
get_Length        Method               System.Int32 get_Length()
..
```

You can always check the type of a variable by running the `.GetType()` method on the variable, for example:

```
PS C:\> $var=7
PS C:\> $var.GetType()

IsPublic IsSerial Name                                     BaseType
-------- -------- ----                                     --------
True     True     Int32                                    System.Value-
                                                           Type
```

```
PS C:\> $var="String now"
PS C:\> $var.GetType()

IsPublic IsSerial Name                                     BaseType
-------- -------- ----                                     --------
True     True     String                                   System.Object
```

It is possible to create variables with spaces in the name. Just create and use the variable with its name surrounded by braces. However, this does not lead to easy code, so it's not highly recommended:

```
PS C:\> ${johns variable} = "WHY?"
PS C:\> ${johns variable}
WHY?
```

You can put any characters you want in braces to make up your variable name, but it is advisable to stay away from using a colon (:). If PowerShell sees a colon in a variable name, it treats the variable as a path and stores it as such:

```
PS C:\> ${d:\temp\varnum} = "Colossus"
PS C:\> dir d:\temp\varnum


    Directory: Microsoft.PowerShell.Core\FileSystem::D:\temp


Mode                LastWriteTime     Length Name
----                -------------     ------ ----
-a---          3/20/2007   1:49 PM        10 varnum


PS C:\> get-content d:\temp\varnum
Colossus
```

The scope of a variable can also be configured:

- **Global**. Available to all child scopes.
- **Local (default)**. Variables are only available in the specific PowerShell instance.
- **Script**. Only visible within the script and are removed when the script closes.

To see full information about scope, run `get-help about_scope` within the PowerShell. To create a variable in another scope or reference from another scope, add the scope name before the variable (such as `$<scope>:<variable>`). For example, to create/access a global variable named room, use `$global:room`. Cmdlets exist to remove, clear, set, and get the value and create new variables.

There are a few reserved constant variables, such as `$null` (which means no value), `$true`, and `$false`. You can set your own values as constants by adding `-constant` after the name of the variable at creation time. `$null` can be useful for checking if a variable exists—for example, testing if the variable equals `(-eq) $null` and then acting accordingly.

Aliases

PowerShell supports the concept of an alias, which is just another name for a cmdlet or command that is normally short. Many are included in PowerShell by default to ease the transition from the command prompt. (For example, an alias exists for the `get-ChildItem` cmdlet in the form of `dir`, which many are already used to.) To see all aliases, run `get-alias` with no parameters and use the `set` verb to create a new one (for example, `set-alias <alias> <cmdlet>`). Looking at the alias for familiar commands, such as `cd`, helps in understanding the underlying PowerShell cmdlets and their uses.

You cannot, however, create an alias to a cmdlet or command that also has parameters; this is known as a *function*, and it can be created in the following format:

```
Function <function name> {<command and arguments>}
```

For example:

```
PS C:\Users\john.SAVILLTECH> function getsysroot {write-output
➥$env:systemroot}
PS C:\Users\john.SAVILLTECH> getsysroot
C:\Windows
```

To list all the functions on the system, use the cmdlet `Get-ChildItem` with the function:* parameter, such as `Get-ChildItem function:*`, which lists all the child items in the function: data store. If you run this, you notice a number of functions already existing, particularly for the various drive letters to enable easy access to changing drives. This helps the adjustment from the normal cmd environment, where to change drives. Type the drive letter followed by a colon. You see a function for every letter, as follows:

```
Function        D:                              Set-
Location D:
```

Let's go back a step. Earlier in this chapter, you wrote out the registered owner of the operating system by navigating to a child item under HKLM:, which represents the Registry hive HKEY_LOCAL_MACHINE. This was used in the same way as navigating the file system. Is this true? In the preceding paragraph, all the functions were listed by the content of the function data store.

To see a list of the data stores available to the PowerShell, use the `get-psdrive cmdlet` with no parameters, as shown here:

```
PS C:\Users\john.SAVILLTECH> get-psdrive

Name         Provider       Root                       CurrentLocation
----         --------       ----                       ---------------
A            FileSystem     A:\
Alias        Alias
C            FileSystem     C:\                        Users\john.SAVILLTECH
cert         Certificate   \
D            FileSystem     D:\
Env          Environment
Function     Function
HKCU         Registry       HKEY_CURRENT_USER
HKLM         Registry       HKEY_LOCAL_MACHINE
Variable     Variable
```

In this list, you see the familiar drive letters you would expect, but also data stores for Alias, cert (certificate store), env (environment), function, HKCU (HKEY_CURRENT_USER Registry hive), HKLM (HKEY_LOCAL_MACHINE Registry hive), and variable. All of these can be navigated to using the `Set-Location` cmdlet (or the `cd` alias, if you're not ready for PowerShell native cmdlets yet). Let's move to HKLM and then list it out and move around:

```
PS C:\Users\john.SAVILLTECH> cd hklm:
PS HKLM:\> dir
```

```
   Hive: Microsoft.PowerShell.Core\Registry::HKEY_LOCAL_MACHINE

SKC  VC Name                           Property
---  -- ----                           --------
  2   0 BCD00000000                    {}
  4   4 COMPONENTS                     {StoreFormatVersion,
StoreArchitecture, PublisherPolicyChangeTime, PoqexecFai...
  4   0 HARDWARE                       {}
  1   0 SAM                            {}
    Get-ChildItem : Requested registry access is not allowed.
    At line:1 char:3
    + dir <<<<
 51   1 SOFTWARE                       {(default)}
  9   0 SYSTEM                         {}


PS HKLM:\> cd 'HKLM:\SOFTWARE\Microsoft\Windows NT\
CurrentVersion'
PS HKLM:\SOFTWARE\Microsoft\Windows NT\CurrentVersion> dir


   Hive:
Microsoft.PowerShell.Core\Registry::HKEY_LOCAL_MACHINE\SOFT-
WARE\Microsoft\Windows NT\CurrentVersion

SKC  VC Name                           Property
---  -- ----                           --------
  1   0 Accessibility                  {}
  1   2 AeDebug                        {UserDebuggerHotKey,
                                       Debugger}
  0  10 APITracing                     {LogFileDirectory,
InstalledManifests, LogApiNamesOnly, LogApisRecursively...}
  2   1 AppCompatFlags                 {ApphelpUIExe}
  0 174 Compatibility                  {_3DPC, _BNOTES,
                                       _LNOTES, ACAD...}
  0   1 Compatibility32                {winword}
  3   0 Console                        {}
```

You received a permissions error when listing the root of HKLM. This was the SECURITY key to which you don't have access; however, you can navigate through the rest of the Registry and list out child keys using the standard `dir` command alias. The SKC column is the Subkey count of the key, and the VC is the value count. As you move around the Registry, you can press Tab for completion. With PowerShell, you can perform wildcard completion. (For example, if you wanted "Windows NT," you could type **wi*nt** and press Tab, and it would expand accordingly.) You can even use TAB expansion on cmdlet names, which can help if you are unsure of the name of the cmdlet.

To look at the properties of the current Registry key, use the `get-itemproperty` cmdlet with `*` as the name:

```
PS HKLM:\SOFTWARE\Microsoft\Windows NT> get-itemproperty *

PSPath                    :
Microsoft.PowerShell.Core\Registry::HKEY_LOCAL_MACHINE\
SOFTWARE\Microsoft\Windows NT\CurrentVersion
PSParentPath              :
Microsoft.PowerShell.Core\Registry::HKEY_LOCAL_MACHINE\
SOFTWARE\Microsoft\Windows NT
PSChildName               : CurrentVersion
PSDrive                   : HKLM
PSProvider                : Microsoft.PowerShell.Core\Registry
CurrentVersion            : 6.0
CurrentBuildNumber        : 6000
CurrentBuild              : 6000
SoftwareType              : System
CurrentType               : Multiprocessor Free
InstallDate               : 1163804828
SystemRoot                : C:\Windows
ProductName               : Windows Vista (TM) Ultimate
```

Likewise, you can do far more than just view the data. This is not read-only information—you can also set values and move data (as if it were files), but obviously care should be taken. Deleting files or moving files can be inconvenient, but mostly you won't corrupt the system (unless you are playing in the systemroot area). However, changing Registry keys can have a damaging impact. Let's say you want to change the registered user; you use the `set-itemproperty` cmdlet:

```
set-itemproperty -path . -name RegisteredOwner -value
'Achilles'
```

Notice that you passed a path of `.`, which is the current location, the name of the property to change, and its new value.

You've already seen the normal file systems, the Registry, and the function data store. Let's look only at the `env` store, which is the environment store. If you change store to `env:` and then execute `dir` (or `get-childitem`), you see all the environment variables:

```
PS D:\> cd env:
PS Env:\> get-childitem | Sort-Object -property name

Name                           Value
----                           -----
ALLUSERSPROFILE                C:\ProgramData
APPDATA                        C:\Users\john.SAVILLTECH\
                               AppData\Roaming
CLASSPATH                      .;C:\Program
Files\QuickTime\QTSystem\QTJava.zip
CommonProgramFiles             C:\Program Files\Common Files
COMPUTERNAME                   SAVDALWKS01
ComSpec                        C:\Windows\system32\cmd.exe
currentchapter                 22
FP_NO_HOST_CHECK               NO
..
..
```

Although this does provide a way to inspect environment variables, there is another method. It is possible to just use `$env:<name of environment variable>`. This is because you are outputting a variable that is stored in the environment (`env`) namespace. For example, to view the `systemroot` variable, use `$env:systemroot`:

```
PS D:\> Write-Host $env:systemroot
C:\Windows
```

PowerShell fully supports creating new drives. For example, suppose you often use an area on a disk such as `d:\documents`. You could create a drive to point to this location:

```
PS C:\Users\john> new-psdrive -name DataDr -psprovider
➥FileSystem -root "d:\documents"
```

```
Name       Provider     Root               CurrentLocation
----       --------     ----               ---------------
DataDr     FileSystem   D:\documents
```

Looking at the command, specify the name of the `psdrive`, the target folder (`-root`), and the type of provider to use (in this case, FileSystem). However, others are available both as a default in the PowerShell, which are typically .NET assemblies to expose data (such as Registry and certificate store) or via third-party solution partners. To get a list of all available providers, use the `get-psprovider` cmdlet. To remove a drive, "remove" the verb with the `psdrive` noun, followed by the `-name` parameter with the name of the drive to be removed:

```
PS C:\Users\john> remove-psdrive -name datadr
```

As you saw in the VBScript examples, access to WMI was fairly simple. However, with PowerShell, that access is even simpler by connecting to a WMI object and querying its content. Here is an example:

```
PS C:\Users\john> $os = get-wmiobject win32_OperatingSystem
PS C:\Users\john> Write-Host $os.Caption
Microsoftr Windows VistaT Ultimate
```

The first command simply creates a variable, `$os`, that points to the `win32_OperatingSystem` WMI object (which was attached via the `get-wmiobject` cmdlet). The next line outputs the `Caption` attribute of the attached object.

You can also view all the items available as part of the `win32_OperatingSystem` WMI object by formatting the properties of the object created:

```
PS C:\Users\john> $os | format-list -property *

Status                                          : OK
Name                                            : Microsoftr Windows
VistaT Ultimate |C:\Windows|\Device\Harddisk0\Partition1
FreePhysicalMemory                              : 1976940
FreeSpaceInPagingFiles                          : 3469992
FreeVirtualMemory                               : 5446920
__GENUS                                         : 2
```

```
__CLASS                                    : Win32_
OperatingSystem
__SUPERCLASS                               : CIM_
OperatingSystem
__DYNASTY                                  : CIM_
ManagedSystemElement
__RELPATH                                  : Win32_
OperatingSystem=@
__PROPERTY_COUNT                           : 65
__DERIVATION                               : {CIM_
OperatingSystem, CIM_LogicalElement, CIM_ManagedSystemElement}
__SERVER                                   : SAVDALM65
__NAMESPACE                                : root\cimv2
__PATH                                     :
\\SAVDALM65\root\cimv2:Win32_OperatingSystem=@
BootDevice                                 : \Device\
HarddiskVolume1
BuildNumber                                : 6000
BuildType                                  : Multiprocessor Free
Caption                                    : Microsoftr Windows
VistaT Ultimate
..
..
```

Performing Actions with PowerShell

So far, you've just been viewing items, because when learning, it's the safest thing to do—it's hard to destroy something by just looking at it. However, more often than not, you want to do something; for example, list all running processes via the `get-process` cmdlet or simply list processes that contain a certain string, such as `win`, using the following:

```
PS C:\Users\john.SAVILLTECH> get-process *win*

Handles  NPM(K)    PM(K)      WS(K) VM(M)   CPU(s)     Id ProcessName
-------  ------    -----      ----- -----   ------     -- -----------
     62       3     1828       4456    56     0.08   1328 WinCinemaMgr
     98       4     1340       2980    32     0.66    500 wininit
    126       3     1948       3900    33     1.02    552 winlogon
    385      19    32548      70864   263    22.00   3144 WINWORD
```

You can then send the output of these matching processes to the `stop-process` cmdlet to stop those processes. But are you sure? As you start performing actions that are more "suspect," it would be great if you could run the command and just see what it would do without doing it; hence, `-whatif`. Adding `-whatif` to the end of a command runs the command and shows you what it would do without doing it, for example:

```
PS C:\Users\john.SAVILLTECH> get-process *win* | stop-process -
➥whatif
What if: Performing operation "Stop-Process" on Target
"WinCinemaMgr (1328)".
What if: Performing operation "Stop-Process" on Target
"wininit (500)".
What if: Performing operation "Stop-Process" on Target
"winlogon (552)".
What if: Performing operation "Stop-Process" on Target
"WINWORD (3144)".
```

You probably don't want to stop `wininit` or `winlogon`, so you're lucky you ran `-whatif`! In addition to `-whatif`, there is another option, `-confirm`. Before doing any modification operation, `-confirm` will prompt the user, as shown:

```
PS C:\Users\john.SAVILLTECH> get-process *win* | stop-process -
➥confirm

Confirm
Are you sure you want to perform this action?
Performing operation "Stop-Process" on Target "WinCinemaMgr
(1328)".
[Y] Yes  [A] Yes to All  [N] No  [L] No to All  [S] Suspend
[?] Help (default is "Y"): y

Confirm
Are you sure you want to perform this action?
Performing operation "Stop-Process" on Target "wininit (500)".
[Y] Yes  [A] Yes to All  [N] No  [L] No to All  [S] Suspend
[?] Help (default is "Y"): n
```

While in PowerShell, use the following code to easily kill Media Player:

```
PS C:\Users\john.SAVILLTECH> get-process *wmplay* | stop-
➥process -confirm

Confirm
Are you sure you want to perform this action?
Performing operation "Stop-Process" on Target "wmplayer
(4660)".
[Y] Yes  [A] Yes to All  [N] No  [L] No to All  [S] Suspend
[?] Help (default is "Y"): y
```

You can apply `-whatif` to many items. For example, you can list all services that are stopped and then send to the `start-service` cmdlet:

```
get-service | where-object { $_.status -eq "Stopped"} | start-
service -whatif
```

In this sequence, you list all services with `get-service` and then select only objects whose status attribute equals `Stopped`. These stopped services are then sent to the `start-service` cmdlet (with `-whatif` because you don't want to start all these services). The `$_` has special meaning: It's a placeholder for the current pipeline object; in this case, pipe the services to the next block of commands so the `$_` is the current service pipelined, and then look at its status attribute.

Scripts

How do you create a script with PowerShell? Unlike WSH, which is a host for other language interpreters, PowerShell has its own native format. It has a `ps1` extension, which is nothing more than PowerShell commands stored in a file. Let's start with the most basic, "`Hello World`". Save the following as `helloworld.ps1`:

```
write-host "Hello World"
```

To run this command, add ./ to the front of the script name, because by default PowerShell does not execute commands out of the current folder. You give it a path (which is the current location). You can also use the `Invoke-Expression` cmdlet or the ampersand (&) symbol to execute a script, but let's just type the name of the script:

```
PS C:\Users\john.SAVILLTECH> ./helloworld.ps1
File C:\Users\john.SAVILLTECH\helloworld.ps1 cannot be loaded
because the execution of scripts is disabled on this system.
Please see "get-help about_signing" for more details.
At line:1 char:16
+ ./helloworld.ps1 <<<<
```

You have a shell that can't run scripts? This is the default state of PowerShell for security purposes. No scripts can be run; however, this can be changed by using the `Set-ExecutionPolicy` cmdlet to control which scripts can be executed. Various levels are available, as follows:

- **Restricted**. Does not load configuration files or run scripts. "Restricted" is the default setting and means you can't run scripts.
- **AllSigned**. Requires that all scripts and configuration files be signed by a trusted publisher, including scripts that you write on the local computer. This is cumbersome.
- **RemoteSigned**. Requires that all scripts and configuration files downloaded from the Internet be signed by a trusted publisher. This only works for files that are correctly labeled in the Zone Identifier Stream by the tool that downloads the script—for example, Internet Explorer or Outlook.
- **Unrestricted**. Loads all configuration files and runs all scripts. If you run an unsigned script that was downloaded from the Internet, you are prompted for permission before it runs.

Set the policy to RemoteSigned, which allows you to run locally created scripts but protects remote scripts from running, which could potentially be malicious in nature:

```
PS C:\Users\john.SAVILLTECH> set-executionpolicy remotesigned
```

The execution policy setting is stored in Registry string value ExecutionPolicy under key HKEY_LOCAL_MACHINE\SOFTWARE\Microsoft\PowerShell\1\ShellIds\Microsoft.PowerShell. The data is the policy setting (for example, "RemoteSigned"). Now you can run your script!

```
PS C:\Users\john.SAVILLTECH> ./helloworld.ps1
Hello World
```

If you want to comment scripts, use the pound sign (#). Use # at the start of the line; if you use it in the middle of a line, put a space in front of it. Also, if the # is in quotes, it has no effect. This can be seen in the three output commands shown next. Notice that only the middle version does not display the content after the pound sign because in the middle example, the word `world` is now considered a comment.

```
PS C:\Users\john.SAVILLTECH> Write-Host hello#world
hello#world
PS C:\Users\john.SAVILLTECH> Write-Host hello #world
hello
PS C:\Users\john.SAVILLTECH> Write-Host "hello #world"
Hello #world
```

Let's recreate the VBScript that outputs basic information about the operating system installation:

```
$os = get-wmiobject win32_OperatingSystem
Write-Host "Name - " $os.Caption
Write-Host "Service Pack - " $os.CSDVersion
Write-Host "OS Build - " $os.Version
Write-Host "Windows Directory - " $os.WindowsDirectory
```

This code is less than the same code written using VBScript earlier in the chapter, and is simpler to read. To execute, run it as follows:

```
PS C:\users\john> ./checkos.ps1
Name -  Microsoftr Windows VistaT Ultimate
Service Pack -
OS Build -  6.0.6000
Windows Directory -  C:\Windows
```

In the previous script, you were able to optionally pass a computer name and browse that computer. Arguments to a script are made available in the `$args` array, so the following code can be saved as `hello.ps1`:

```
write-host "Hello " $args
```

It can run as follows:

```
PS D:\Temp> .\hello john
Hello  john
PS D:\Temp> .\hello john bob
Hello  john bob
PS D:\Temp> .\hello john bob dutch hank billy bob
Hello  john bob dutch hank billy bob
```

Notice that it does not just write out the first name; it writes out all of them because `$args` is an array. If you ran a `$args.count` in your last example, it would have a value of 6 since you passed six names. You could access individual elements using standard array notation, which is the array element in square brackets starting from 0—for example, the first argument would be `$args[0]`, the second `$args[1]`, and so on. There is, however, a more formal method: The `param` statement can be used as the first line of a script to give names to variables. Any undefined variables are placed in `$args`, for example:

```
param($name)
write-host "Hello" $name
write-host $args
```

When run, the code now gives you this:

```
PS D:\Temp> .\hello john bob dutch hank billy bob
Hello john
bob dutch hank billy bob
```

Notice that the first argument was stored in `$name`, and the rest were placed in `$args` as usual. You can cast parameters as well. For example, the PowerShell script can be configured to expect a string by placing the cast in front of the variable—for example, `param([string] $name)`. Additional parameters are set by just placing the brackets:

```
param($name, [string] $name2)
```

Now you can pass a computer name optionally to your script and use if passed:

```
param([string] $computername)

if ($computername.Length -eq 0)
      {$os = get-wmiobject win32_OperatingSystem}
else
      {$os = get-wmiobject -computer $computername
win32_OperatingSystem}

Write-Host "Name - " $os.Caption
Write-Host "Service Pack - " $os.CSDVersion
Write-Host "OS Build - " $os.Version
Write-Host "Windows Directory - " $os.WindowsDirectory
```

You can do one better! You can eliminate the logic check for whether computername is set; this works by setting computername to a period (.), which means local computer if no value is passed:

```
param([string] $computername=".")

$os = get-wmiobject -computer $computername
win32_OperatingSystem

Write-Host "Checking computer - " $computername
Write-Host "Name - " $os.Caption
Write-Host "Service Pack - " $os.CSDVersion
Write-Host "OS Build - " $os.Version
Write-Host "Windows Directory - " $os.WindowsDirectory
```

If an argument is passed, then computername is set to the passed value; however, if no argument is passed, then it's set to the value set in the param statement. This can be seen in the following executions. Notice that a line was added in the code to show the computername, so you can see this default value being used:

```
PS D:\projects\PowerShell> .\checkos.ps1 savdaldc01
Checking computer -  savdaldc01
Name -  Microsoft(R) Windows(R) Server 2003 Enterprise x64
  Edition
```

```
Service Pack -  Service Pack 2
OS Build -  5.2.3790
Windows Directory -  C:\WINDOWS
PS D:\projects\PowerShell> .\checkos.ps1 longhorn1
Checking computer -  longhorn1
Name -  Microsoftr Windows ServerT Code Name "Longhorn"
Service Pack -
OS Build -  6.0.6001
Windows Directory -  C:\Windows
PS D:\projects\PowerShell> .\checkos.ps1
Checking computer -  .
Name -  Microsoftr Windows VistaT Ultimate
Service Pack -
OS Build -  6.0.6000
Windows Directory -  C:\Windows
```

When a script is complete, call `exit` at the end with an optional number, which is considered the error level of the script execution. (By default, this is 0, meaning success or, at least, no errors.)

POWERSHELL AND THE RUN DIALOG

If you try to run a PowerShell script from a RUN box—for example, powershell.exe d:\projects\powershell\checkos.ps1—it appears not to work. Actually, it did, but PowerShell immediately closes. Instead, run the `-noexit` parameter (for example, `powershell -noexit d:\projects\powershell\checkos.ps1`).

Script Functions

Functions were discussed earlier, and they're no different in PowerShell scripts. Use the `function` keyword with the associated code, and the function appears inside curly braces. Optionally, parameters can come after the name of the function, such as the following:

```
Function <name of function> (<parameter list>) {<statement
  list>}
```

For example:

```
PS D:\ > Function addnumbers ($num1, $num2) {$num1 + $num2}
PS D:\ > addnumbers 1 2
3
```

This equally works without the parameter component:

```
PS D:\ > Function addnumbers {$args[0] + $args[1]}
PS D:\ > addnumbers 1 2
```

Functions must be defined in the script before they are used. So normally, functions are placed at the beginning of the script file:

```
# Function to add numbers together
function addnumbers {$args[0] + $args[1]}

# Here we will pass just numbers 4 and 5
$result = addnumbers 4 5
write-host $result

# Here we pass the first number passed to the script and 5
$result = addnumbers $args[0] 5
write-host $result

# Here we pass both numbers that were passed to script
$result = addnumbers $args[0] $args[1]
write-host $result
```

Run this script passing the numbers 10 and 20 as arguments:

```
PS D:\projects\PowerShell> .\addtogether.ps1 10 20
9
15
30
```

Notice here that the use of the `args` is perhaps not what was expected. Within the function, the `$args` variable represents the values passed to the function, whereas in the rest of the script, the `$args` variable represents the values passed to the script when executed. This is why you see different values when you pass combinations to the function from within the script. In the first call, you pass 4 and 5, so you get a response of 9. Next, you pass the first number passed to the actual script (10) and the number 5, so you get the answer of 15. Finally, you pass to the function the two arguments actually given to the script, which gives you the desired answer of 10 + 20, which is 30. PowerShell has awesome computational power!

Error Handling

There will be times when the environment might cause issues. You need to be ready to handle problems. By default, these errors normally appear on the screen; however, this might not be useful in a script, and it does not allow you to automatically perform other actions in certain error situations. Like everything in PowerShell, an error is not just a string giving the name of an error message, but a full `ErrorRecord` object. Let's take a common problem of looking at a file/folder that does not exist. (You'll use `Get-ChildItem`, but you can still use the dir alias to save typing; you need to get used to the underlying cmdlet verb-noun format.)

```
PS D:\> Get-ChildItem nothere
Get-ChildItem : Cannot find path 'D:\nothere' because it does
not exist.
At line:1 char:14
+ Get-ChildItem  <<<< nothere
```

In fact, you can capture the response to your commands to a variable and ensure errors are also sent there using the same error redirection format as a batch file (2>&1):

```
PS D:\> $err = Get-ChildItem nothere 2>&1
```

You can't use `$error` because it's reserved. It contains all the error objects known to the PowerShell session (which is a useful tool) stored in an array, with the latest error stored in the lowest array entry, such as 0. You can output the entire array or look at individual entries. As new errors are added to the start of the array, the older errors "shift down" in effect. (For example, `$error[1]` becomes `$error[2]`, and so on.) This `$error` is useful in the event you don't do the advance "capture" of errors by redirecting the error stream. The exact number of errors kept is defined by the `$MaximumErrorCount` variable, which is 256 by default:

```
PS D:\> $error[0].Exception
Cannot find path 'D:\nothere' because it does not exist.
```

Back to your custom `$err` variable, you can now inspect the `$err` object by looking at its members. After they are known, you can inspect the content of the properties as required. For example:

```
PS D:\> $err | Get-Member


   TypeName: System.Management.Automation.ErrorRecord

Name                     MemberType Definition
----                     ---------- ----------
Equals                   Method     System.Boolean
Equals(Object obj)
GetHashCode              Method     System.Int32 GetHashCode()
GetObjectData            Method     System.Void
GetObjectData(SerializationInfo info, StreamingContext context)
GetType                  Method     System.Type GetType()
get_CategoryInfo         Method     System.Management.
                                    Automation.
                                    ErrorCategoryInfo get_
                                    CategoryInfo()
get_ErrorDetails         Method     System.Management.
                                    Automation.ErrorDetails
                                    get_ErrorDetails()
get_Exception            Method     System.Exception
get_Exception()
get_FullyQualifiedErrorId Method    System.String get_
                                    FullyQualifiedErrorId()
get_InvocationInfo       Method     System.Management.
                                    Automation.InvocationInfo
                                    get_InvocationInfo()
get_TargetObject         Method     System.Object get_
                                    TargetObject()
set_ErrorDetails         Method     System.Void set_
                                    ErrorDetails(ErrorDetails
                                    value)
ToString                 Method     System.String ToString()
```

```
CategoryInfo              Property   System.Management.
                                     Automation.
                                     ErrorCategoryInfo
                                     CategoryInfo {get;}
ErrorDetails              Property   System.Management.
                                     Automation.ErrorDetails
                                     ErrorDetails {get;set;}
Exception                 Property   System.Exception Exception
                                     {get;}
FullyQualifiedErrorId    Property    System.String
                                     FullyQualifiedErrorId
                                     {get;}
InvocationInfo            Property   System.Management.
                                     Automation.InvocationInfo
                                     InvocationInfo {get;}
TargetObject              Property   System.Object TargetObject
                                     {get;}
```

```
PS D:\> $err.Exception
Cannot find path 'D:\nothere' because it does not exist.
PS D:\> $err.targetobject
D:\nothere
```

This assignment works great, except you have to rely on redirecting the error stream so the errors are no longer displayed. Another option is available via the `-ErrorVariable` parameter, which allows a variable to be passed for the storage of errors related only to a particular command:

```
PS D:\> Get-ChildItem nothereeither -ErrorVariable err
Get-ChildItem : Cannot find path 'D:\nothereeither' because it
does not exist.
At line:1 char:14
+ Get-ChildItem  <<<< nothereeither -ErrorVariable err
PS D:\> $err.count
1
PS D:\> $err[0].targetobject
D:\nothereeither
PS D:\> $err[0].exception
Cannot find path 'D:\nothereeither' because it does not exist.
```

Notice that the error was still displayed onscreen; however, it was also stored in the err variable. You did not use $ in front of the variable name because the `ErrorValue` parameter works by storing the data directly into the variable. These are sophisticated error-collection techniques, but just as in other languages and scripts, all you might want to do is see if an error occurred. To view the last error code, view the content of `$LASTEXITCODE`. To see if there was an error in the last command, view the content of `$?`. This contains a Boolean TRUE/FALSE simply showing if the last command ran without error; a value of TRUE means no error occurred.

```
PS D:\> get-childitem temp

    Directory: Microsoft.PowerShell.Core\FileSystem::D:\temp
..
..

PS D:\> write-host $?
True
PS D:\> get-childitem notfound
Get-ChildItem : Cannot find path 'D:\notfound' because it does
not exist.
At line:1 char:14
+ get-childitem  <<<< notfound
PS D:\> write-host $?
False
```

Error-Handling Methods

Methods also exist to set what to do when an error occurs for an entire session via the setting of the `$ErrorActionPreference` variable (Continue, which is the default to output error and move on; SilentlyContinue, which outputs nothing to screen but still writes to `$error` and sets `$?`; and Continues and Stop, which aborts an error). You can also set this on a command-by-command basis using the `-ea` parameter, for example:

```
PS D:\> get-childitem notfound -ea silentlycontinue
PS D:\> write-host $?
False
PS D:\> get-childitem notfound
Get-ChildItem : Cannot find path 'D:\notfound' because it does
not exist.
At line:1 char:14
+ get-childitem  <<<< notfound
```

In the example, when the command listing the invalid object was set to `silentlycontinue`, no message was written, but `$?` was still set to error. If you run the same command with no `-ea` parameter, the error appears. PowerShell also exhibits sophisticated error handling by using the `trap` and `throw` statements in addition to the `Set-PSDebug` cmdlet to enable debugging by stepping through your code; however, this is beyond the scope of this chapter.

Summary

Huge amounts of information are available, both at Microsoft and on the Web, about command-line usage, including batch files, VBScript, and PowerShell. This book looks at using the environments as they relate to the various components of the OS. With PowerShell's great built-in help, logical verb-noun syntax, and consistent usage, you will be amazed with what is possible after a little practice, thanks to the piping of one cmdlet output to another and then to another, as needed.

Why would you ever need to use a command line or script with Windows, especially with the advanced remote management facilities available? Consider installations of Windows Server 2008 such as Core, which has a limited graphical interface, as well as the WS-Management capabilities of Windows, which are command-line driven. The only way to perform sequences of actions in an unattended fashion, such as in a scheduled process, is via a script; because of this, the powerful command-line and scripting capabilities of Windows Server 2008 are a blessing.

CHAPTER 23

Connecting Windows Server 2008 to Other Environments

Although a Microsoft-only infrastructure might sound appealing, Windows is often integrated with other platforms, such as UNIX, Linux, or NetWare. This integration can be ongoing, where Windows and the other platforms coexist indefinitely, or might involve migrating from these platforms, which is often the case with NetWare.

The actual level of integration depends on the services needed to share. For example, the integration can be as basic as file sharing but can extend all the way to synchronizing directory services; facilities exist to cover all these integration challenges.

In years past, integration was a huge challenge. Before you even got to services, just communicating was a challenge: NetWare used IPX/SPX, DEC had Decnet/OSI, and so on. Common protocols didn't exist; protocol gateways were needed to enable different platforms to talk. Today, that's no longer an issue. Every platform uses TCP/IP, so you no longer have to worry about the protocol levels of communication. Instead, you can concentrate on the services shared between platforms.

This chapter covers the services that are part of Windows Server 2008 and some that are available for download from Microsoft. (These services are particularly useful around migrations from NetWare.) There are many other solutions for synchronizing different direct services, such as Microsoft Identity Lifecycle Manager (ILM). ILM is not covered in this chapter, but you should look at ILM because it has great capabilities beyond the tools covered here.

UNIX/Linux is the focus of the Microsoft interoperability story because it frequently coexists with Windows—there are services currently that run on UNIX, whereas NetWare is on its way out. NetWare is being replaced with Microsoft technologies, so typically the reason Windows touches a NetWare environment is to pillage its resources and services.

This chapter is divided into UNIX and NetWare interoperability. Although it's hands-on for some of the technologies, unlike most of the other chapters, this chapter is more high level and discusses the solutions available without walking through every one.

Macintosh is not covered in this chapter. Windows 2008 no longer has services for Macintosh because IP is used on new Macintosh computers, and Macintosh clients support SMB for file access in a secure fashion in addition to authenticating against an Active Directory (AD) domain. A good place for information on Macintosh and Windows integration is www.macwindows.com. Macintosh also has some good AD integration information at http://www.apple.com/itpro/articles/adintegration/ and in the whitepaper at http://images.apple.com/itpro/pdf/AD_Best_Practices_2.0.pdf.

UNIX Integration

Numerous services today run only on UNIX or require UNIX interaction. Although Microsoft is pushing service migrations to the Microsoft platform, it puts a lot of effort into UNIX integration services. UNIX integration services fall into one of two groups: the capability for UNIX and Microsoft platforms to communicate and share information, and the capability to run UNIX applications and functions directly on the Microsoft platform.

NOTE Before looking at the services in Windows Server 2008 that support UNIX and the Windows-UNIX interoperability story, check out Microsoft's web site at UNIX: http://www.microsoft.com/windowsserver/compare/compare-windows-to-unix.mspx. This site is based around how the Microsoft platform can be used in place of UNIX and mainframe-based systems. It's an interesting read and has some valid, although biased, points.

Subsystem for UNIX-Based Applications

The Subsystem for UNIX-based Applications (SUA) is not a brand-new component of Windows Server 2008; instead, it is the evolution of a technology that has been available in Windows since version 3.51 as the Interix solution.

The SUA provides a number of features, which include UNIX shell environments for running UNIX commands and scripts. This makes it possible to have a UNIX operating environment within Windows. In addition to just shell and command support, the actual UNIX environment is supported, which is beyond the normal level of support that Windows provides.

The SUA provides a complete compilation environment. This means you can build UNIX code on your Windows installation with SUA installed and then execute UNIX code—all on your Windows Server 2008 installation. In addition to this UNIX environment, the SUA also enables you to run UNIX applications directly on the Microsoft platform. With Windows Server 2008, this includes the ability to communicate with Oracle databases via the Oracle Call Interface (OCI). The OCI is a major feature because Oracle is the database of choice in many UNIX environments.

Why is SUA needed? Why not just move to Microsoft Windows platform native applications? In reality, that is often not possible. There might be applications that are only available for UNIX, or there are no resources available to migrate applications to Windows-based calls and functionality. Therefore, you need to be able to run UNIX code and interoperate with UNIX in the Microsoft world.

Here is the good news: Not only does the environment resemble a POSIX-compliant UNIX on your Windows servers, but also because SUA runs directly on the Windows kernel, the UNIX functionality is provided without any emulation taking place. This is great from a performance perspective, and it provides true UNIX functionality that adheres to standards that would not be possible if emulation was used. The SUA runs next to the native Windows subsystems, such as the Win32 subsystem. This is a complete UNIX environment running natively on the Windows kernel. Figure 23-1 displays this concept, which Microsoft uses to show the SUA in the Windows stack.

SUA is supported on both 32-bit and 64-bit versions of Windows. This new model also enables something called *mixed mode*, which removes the labeling of a UNIX application as running under SUA at all. Instead, no distinction is made, and the UNIX application executes as a native Windows application. When a UNIX call is made, it is intercepted and routed through the SUA and then handled by the SUA subsystem. This means that a UNIX application can now make calls to Windows DLLs, which helps migrate applications to Windows; however, mixed mode has limited support for Windows Server 2008. It is designed to address UNIX applications connecting to Oracle and SQL. This functionality will be expanded in the future. Mixed mode is not the default and, under normal circumstances, UNIX applications will run under the SUA. Sample code is provided as part of the download from Microsoft to explain how to make an application using mixed mode. This download is discussed in more detail in the section, "Installing SUA," later in the chapter.

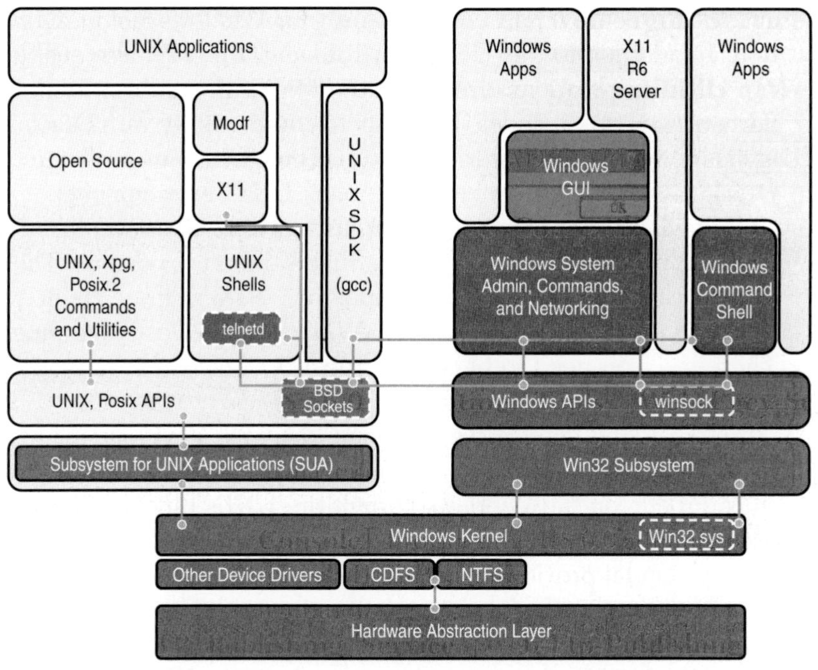

FIGURE 23-1 SUA in the Windows environment, courtesy of Microsoft.

Porting Applications

The last section mentioned that you can run UNIX applications on Windows via SUA. It also discussed recompiling the applications in the SUA environment and porting them over. If you've been exposed to UNIX, you know there are many different flavors of UNIX. For each UNIX implementation, UNIX source code has to be compiled for the target UNIX environment, and that is the same for SUA. Think of SUA as a flavor of UNIX, and the recompiling of source code to enable it to run on

UNIX is the same exercise you would perform to move a UNIX application from one version of UNIX to another. The important point is that this is just a recompilation. You're not changing the actual source code with different syntax or API calls; you are simply recompiling unchanged source code to run on SUA.

There are some caveats, however. Some UNIX implementations have implementation-specific libraries and calls that might not be available under SUA. In those cases, code changes might be required.

A software development kit (SDK) is provided as part of the SUA. This kit helps port UNIX applications to SUA, which enables running any code written for UNIX to run on the SUA. The SDK is supported from any developer product; however, there is tight integration with Microsoft Visual Studio. This integration allows you to debug a UNIX application running in SUA with the powerful Visual Studio debugging tools. UNIX scripts run under SUA with no changes.

Database Connectivity

One new feature with Windows Server 2003 R2 and Windows Server 2008 is the support for the Oracle Call Interface (OCI). An application can use OCI to talk to Oracle databases. With SUA now supporting OCI, an application written for UNIX that communicates with an Oracle database via OCI can now run in SUA. This is huge because Oracle is the database of choice in most UNIX environments. Because the point in UNIX services is to allow the Windows environment to be used for UNIX interoperability, running code that talks to Oracle is a huge leap in enabling Windows to run UNIX applications, which previously could not be ported to Windows because of the lack of database support.

SUA also supports Open Database Connectivity (ODBC). ODBC connects to Microsoft SQL Server, so it's now possible to have a UNIX application running on SUA that can communicate via OCI to Oracle and ODBC to SQL Server.

Installing SUA

In Windows Server 2008, you can install SUA via the Add Features Wizard. SUA is also available on Windows Vista, if you want to experiment, and is installed via the Turn Windows Features On or Off link in the Programs and Features Control Panel applet (see Figure 23-2).

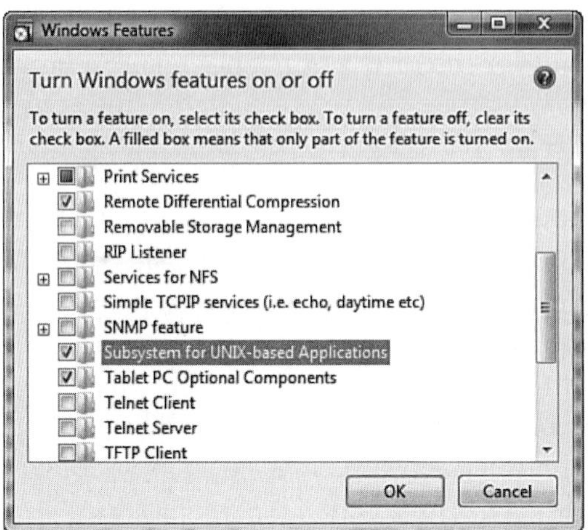

FIGURE 23-2 Install SUA on Vista.

After SUA is installed, a new startup group is added, called Subsystem for UNIX-Based Applications. This startup group contains a help file and a link to the Microsoft web site. The web site is where you download the Utilities and SDK for SUA. You need to do this to get exposure to the various shells provided as part of SUA, the SDKs, and Visual Studio add-ins.

The SUA download is around 250MB. Separate versions are available for the 32- and 64-bit platforms, so make sure you download the correct version. When you install, various options are available as part of the Utilities and SDK installation, as follows:

- **Base Utilities**. Core utility component that is installed by default. It includes the utilities from the Berkeley Software Distribution (BSD) UNIX implementation, which are the most commonly used utilities, including the C shell and Korn shell.
- **SVR-5 Utilities**. Utilities based on the SVR-5 UNIX implementation. This includes the SVR-5 Korn shell.
- **Base SDK**. Installed by default. Installs the headers, libraries, and utilities used to build UNIX and X-Windows applications on SUA.
- **GNU Utilities**. GNU is a free set of utilities that run on UNIX. This includes compression utilities (gzip, gunzip), difference utilities, and processing languages, such as BC.
- **GNU SDK**. GNU development components, such as gcc, g++, and dynamic shared libraries.

- **Perl**. Installation of Perl that runs in the SUA environment.
- **Visual Studio Debugger Add-in**. The add-in for Visual Studio to enable debugging of SUA-based applications.

After the components are selected, you must modify certain security settings, as shown in Figure 23-3.

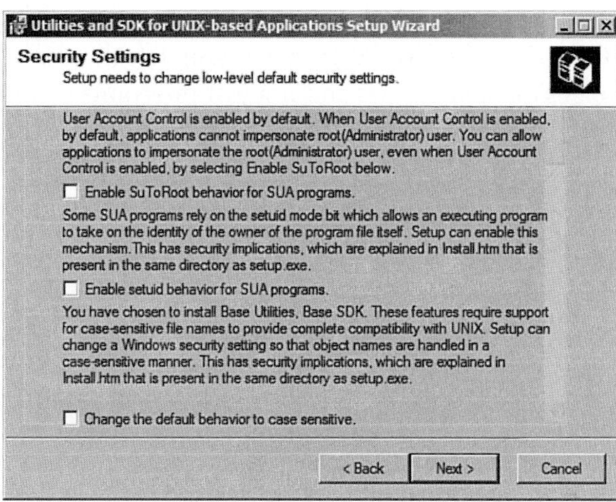

FIGURE 23-3 Advanced security options.

The security settings enable the SUA environment to work with some of the new Windows Server 2008 features, such as User Access Control, by enabling the superuser (SU) to impersonate the Administrator account.

The Enable Setuid Behavior for SUA Programs option relates to functionality that is defined as part of the POSIX standard, which enables a process executing a file to take the User or Group ID (UID or GID) defined on the file being executed. If the UID/GID is a higher privilege than the user, the process running the program gains those high privileges. This is the setuid functionality's purpose: It allows a nonprivileged user to execute a program that can run with higher privileges. This has security implications if used incorrectly because, depending on the file settings, normal users could run administrator functions. Thus, this option is disabled by default. To set it after installation, change the Registry value EnableSetuidBinaries under the HKEY_LOCAL_MACHINE\SOFTWARE\Microsoft\SUA key to 1 to enable setuid or 0 to disable. You must restart Windows for this change to take effect.

The next setting is related to case sensitivity. Windows preserves the case of a file but is not case sensitive. For example, you can run notepad.exe, NOTEPAD.EXE, and nOtEpAd.ExE. Windows does not care about the casing. In a single folder, you cannot have a file of the same name, so you could not have both notepad.exe and NOTEPAD.EXE.

UNIX, however, is case sensitive, so notepad.exe and NOTEPAD.EXE are two different files that can both be stored in the same folder. By selecting Change the Default Behavior to Case Sensitive, the Windows behavior can be changed to be case sensitive and match the default UNIX behavior. This changes all of Windows and not just programs running in SUA. (There is a security implication with this setting. Suppose your system is compromised, and some malware places itself on your computer and names itself NOTEPAD.EXE, which now sits next to the built-in notepad.exe. If you run notepad.exe, you might run the Trojan NOTEPAD.EXE instead of the correct Windows notepad executable.)

The casing option can be changed at any time by setting the `obcaseinsensitive` value under HKEY_LOCAL_MACHINE\SYSTEM\CurrentControlSet\Control\Session Manager\kernel to 0 to enable case sensitivity, or 1 to disable case sensitivity and restore Windows to its normal mode. After changing the Registry value, you must restart Windows. The installation then executes. When complete, new links are available in the SUA Start menu. You then have a link to the C shell and the Korn shell.

Configuring the SUA Shell

You can execute the shortcuts for any of the installed shells. Doing so opens a command prompt that emulates the shell and gives a UNIX-like environment.

The Korn shell, which is a POSIX 2.0-compliant shell found in the /bin folder, is file `ksh`. The C shell is found in the /bin folder, and it is file `csh`. The C shell is an implementation of the Tenex C shell (`tcsh`). The Korn shell is the default shell on most UNIX environments. It combines the best features from the Bourne shell and the C shell; however, there are differences between Korn and the C Shell, particularly around script execution. You will likely pick a specific shell to work from and develop under, and, in some cases, you might pick one shell to work on interactively.

You can launch either the Korn or C shell from Start, SUA. Alternatively, use the `ksh` and `csh` commands. You have the option of adding the `-l` switch to perform the shell's logon process.

NOTE UNIX commands and using the shell are not discussed here—that is beyond the scope of this chapter. If you need to use SUA, you likely already know UNIX. Instead, this chapter talks about some issues you might experience when running UNIX environments on Windows.

One important difference is how new lines are handled between Windows and UNIX. With Windows, when you press Return, two characters are added in a text file under Windows: a carriage return and a line feed (CRLF). Under UNIX, only a line feed character is used; this would cause problems if you attempted to run a script that you edited in notepad.exe under a SUA shell because there would be an unexpected carriage return. If you viewed a Windows text file from within SUA, you would see a Ctrl+M (^M) character at the end of each line. This character is the extra carriage return. Don't worry—you don't need to edit every file to remove the ^M from every line. SUA provides a utility (called flip) to toggle between CRLF and LF. To convert a file to Windows format (CRLF), use the `-m` switch. To convert to UNIX style (LF), use the `-u` switch. For example:

```
% chdir /dev/fs/C/temp
% ls
2linefile.txt
% flip -m 2linefile.txt
% view 2linefile.txt
[WOULD see ^M at end of each line]
% flip -u 2linefile.txt
% view 2linefile.txt
[WOULD NOT see ^M at end of each line]
```

You can now run UNIX scripts. As mentioned earlier, after you recompile UNIX source code, it executes under the SUA subsystem. The main step is to update the make file to use the correct SUA folders. (For example, the BINDIR should be /dev/fs/C/Windows/SUA/bin.) After you update all the settings, make the file via the `make` command. `make` calls the compiler and linker to create the SUA-compatible UNIX executable.

Identity Management for UNIX

Identity Management for UNIX (IdMU) allows integration between UNIX directories and the AD. Many Linux/UNIX implementations already support Windows Domain account usage out of the box or, at a minimum, LDAP (for which AD is fully compliant, as shown in Figure 23-4). If you just have a few UNIX/Linux clients in the environment, you might not need IdMU at all. You can just configure the UNIX/Linux boxes to use the Windows Domain or LDAP. You need IdMU when you have an existing Network Information Service (NIS) directory service that you need to integrate with and migrate from. Without IdMU, you would have two separate account repositories that both need to be maintained. So, users would have multiple passwords for their multiple accounts.

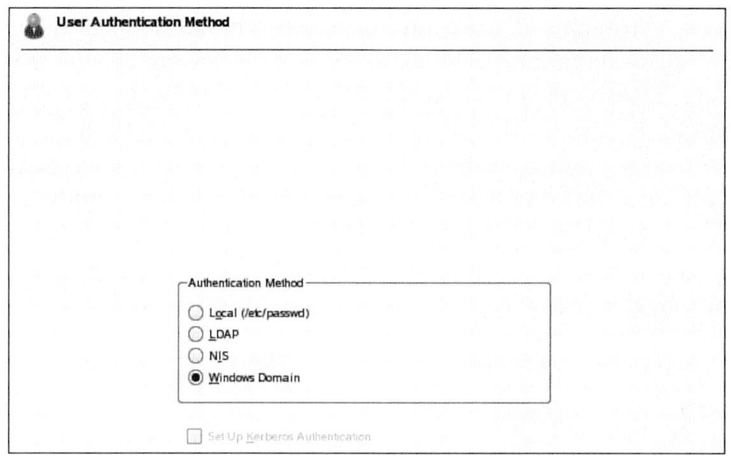

FIGURE 23-4 Many UNIX/Linux implementations support Windows domains out of the box.

Here's one great change with Windows Server 2008: The 2008 schema supports IdMU without any schema changes. Everything needed for IdMU is built into the default 2008 schema. This makes integration and testing easier and helps if you want to use Windows Server 2008 as an LDAP authentication server for UNIX clients.

With the Windows Server 2008 Service for NIS, a Windows Server 2008 domain controller can act as the Master server in a UNIX NIS environment. Actual UNIX servers can act as NIS subordinates to the Windows DC, and UNIX clients can authenticate to the UNIX NIS subordinates or the DC NIS Master; the Windows NIS service then fully integrates with the UNIX environment. It is also possible to install the service for NIS on other Windows Server 2008 domain controllers. You can make those additional domain controllers subordinate NIS servers, which provides the structure shown in Figure 23-5. As you can see, there's a mixture of UNIX and Windows servers in the NIS environment.

This master/subordinate relationship is the same as the Windows NT 4 PDC/BDC relationship, where the master NIS server is the only server that can make changes to the security database. The changes are then replicated to the subordinate NIS servers, which can then authenticate clients.

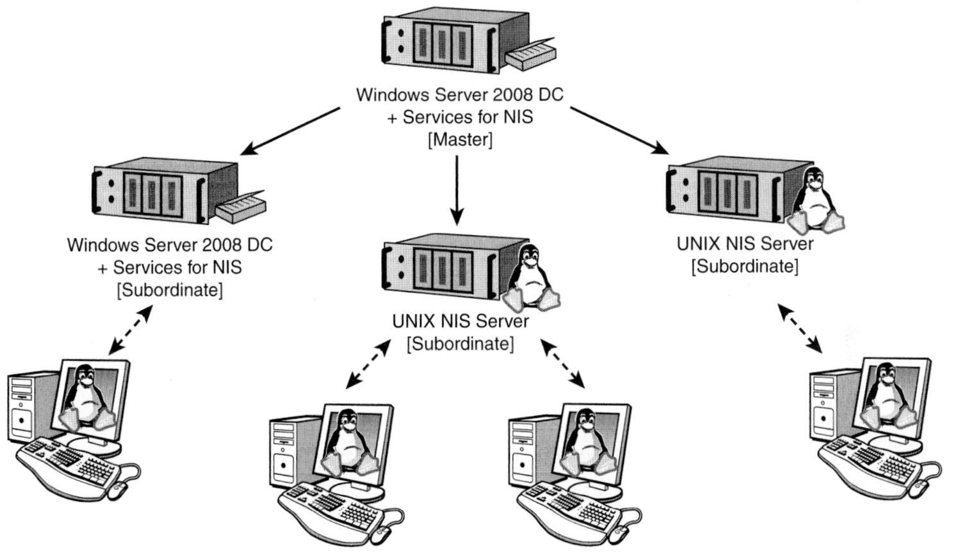

FIGURE 23-5 NIS structure.

Synchronization of multiple account sources means you must map UNIX users to AD users. This is achieved via AD mapping. With AD mapping, UNIX account information is stored within the AD. This is possible because the AD schema is RFC 2307 compliant. A set of attribute types and object classes are proposed, along with specific guidelines for interpreting them.

NOTE RFC 2307 is a standard that describes an experimental mechanism for mapping entities related to TCP/IP and the UNIX system into X.500 (X500) entries, so that they might be resolved with the Lightweight Directory Access Protocol (RFC 2251).

The intention of the RFC is to assist the deployment of LDAP as an organizational name service. No proposed solutions are intended as standards for the Internet. Rather, it is hoped that a general consensus will emerge as to the appropriate solution to such problems, leading eventually to the adoption of standards. The proposed mechanism has already been implemented with some success.

After Services for NIS are installed and configured, NIS clients can use Windows 2008 domain controllers for authentication or UNIX subordinates. Now the Windows 2008 DC is the NIS master, and UNIX accounts can be administered using the same tools as the AD accounts—for example, using the AD Users and Computers MMC snap-in.

Installation and Configuration

The IdMU components are role services that are part of the AD role. Therefore, they are installed via the Add Role Services Wizard, as shown in Figure 23-6. After the IdMU role services are installed, you must restart the server.

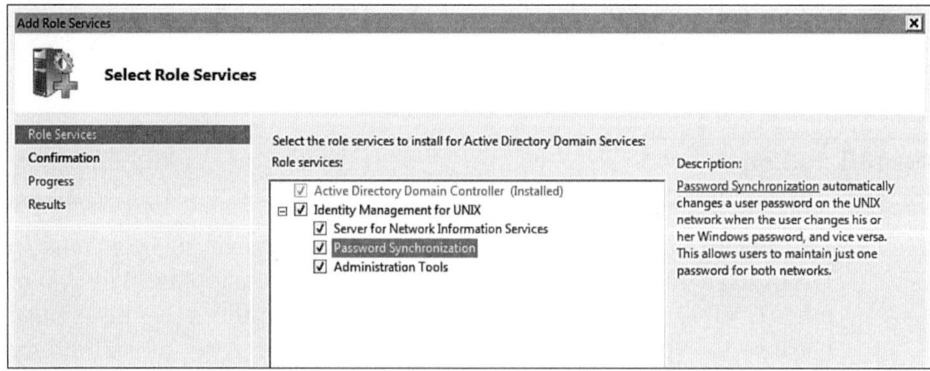

FIGURE 23-6 Installing the IdMU role services.

As soon as the domain controller reboots, the local domain for the DC is automatically exposed as a new NIS domain that UNIX/Linux computers can use. Computers view it as a UNIX NIS server, and the NIS status can be seen via the Microsoft Identity Management for UNIX snap-in, as shown in Figure 23-7. You can now add additional subordinate NIS servers running Windows Server or UNIX. UNIX clients see the NIS domain as the name of the AD DNS name (for example, savilltech.net).

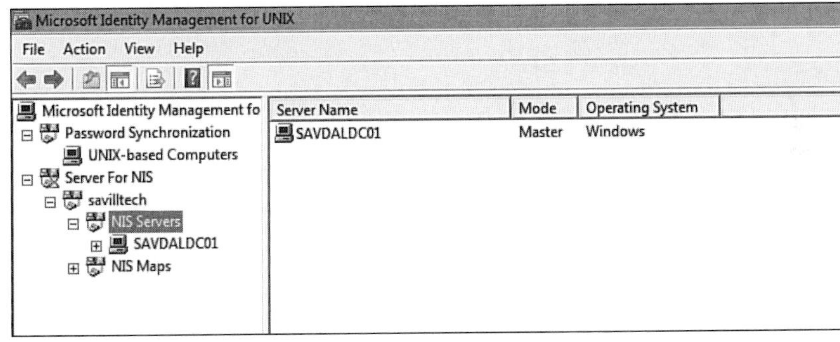

FIGURE 23-7 A Windows domain now available as a NIS domain.

After you install the Administration Tools on a domain controller, the AD Users and Computers MMC snap-in is enhanced with new UNIX-specific attributes to facilitate a UNIX client logging on via the UNIX Attributes tab, as shown in Figure 23-8. The main setting is the NIS domain. After it is configured, you can configure items such as the UID, login shell, home directory, and the primary group name (GID) for the user. The group has to be an AD group that also has its UNIX attributes configured with an NIS domain and GID. All groups that have UNIX attributes configured will be listed in the Primary Group drop-down dialog. These attributes previously required the AD schema to be updated but are a core part of Windows Server 2008.

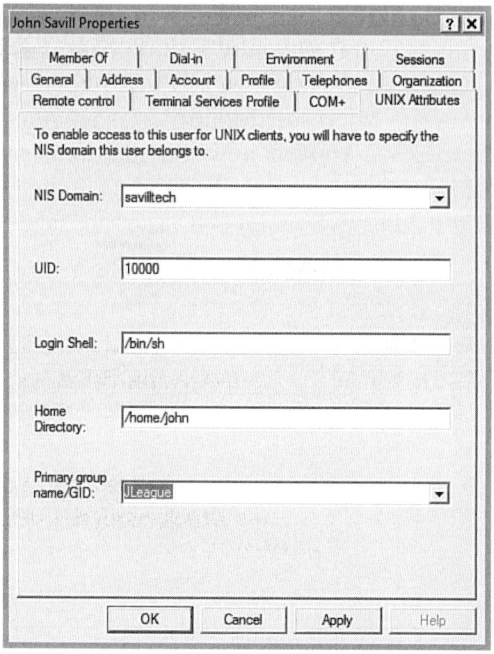

FIGURE 23-8 Configuring UNIX attributes for a user.

Adding Additional UNIX NIS Domains/Servers

To add a server as a replica of an existing UNIX NIS domain, select Server for NIS; then run the Start NIS Data Migration Wizard action and follow the prompts. Although you can also use the nis2ad.exe command-line utility, we'll do a walkthrough of the NS Data Migration Wizard. Before running the wizard, map files from the UNIX server that hosts the NIS domain (stored in the /etc folder). This also applies to a stand-alone UNIX/Linux server. The wizard does not distinguish, so if you have a normal UNIX server from which you want to migrate users, pull the files from that server.

By default, files are in UNIX format. This means that new lines have a line feed; if you view them in Windows, the files appear as one long run-on line. If you run the `flip -m <file>` on a copy of the file in one of the SUA shells, it adds the carriage return and makes the file easier to read. However, do *not* flip the original file because the NIS Data Migration Wizard expects the file to be in UNIX format.

An example section of a UNIX password file is shown here:

```
Bruce:x:501:501:Bruce Wayne:/home/Bruce:/bin/bash
Clark:x:502:502:Clark Kent:/home/Clark:/bin/bash
```

Notice that you have the user name, ID, full name, home folder, and the shell. To import objects, such as users, do the following:

1. Click Next on the NIS Data Migration Wizard's welcome screen.
2. Enter the name of the UNIX-based NIS source domain and then click Next.
3. You are prompted for administrator credentials on the local AD domain or, if logged on as an administrator, you can select to use your current information.
4. The next screen lets you select which maps are migrated. For example, select passwd for users, as shown in Figure 23-9, and hosts for computers. Click Next. Each map contains a different type of object or resource information.

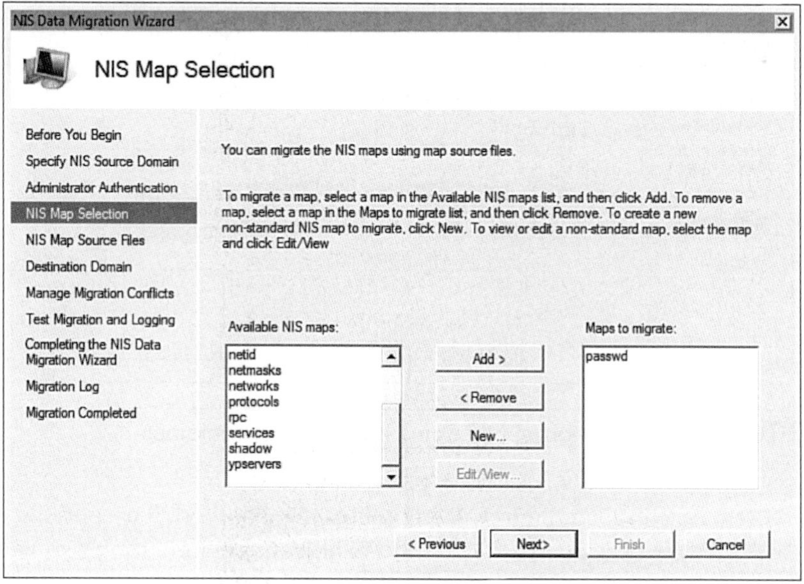

FIGURE 23-9 Specifying the maps to use.

5. The next screen prompts for the folder that contains the NIS map source files. This folder should contain the files from UNIX for the maps that are taking place. For example, if migrating passwd, I copy the passwd file from the /etc folder on the UNIX server and place it in the folder specified.
6. The Destination Domain must be selected, which, by default, is the existing domain. Alternatively, a new NIS domain can be created on the DC, plus a container to store the migrated objects in (such as an OU, as shown in Figure 23-10). If you specify a container, it must be the fully distinguished name. For example, an OU UNIXMigration in domain savilltech.net would be OU=UNIXMigration,dc=savilltech,dc=net.

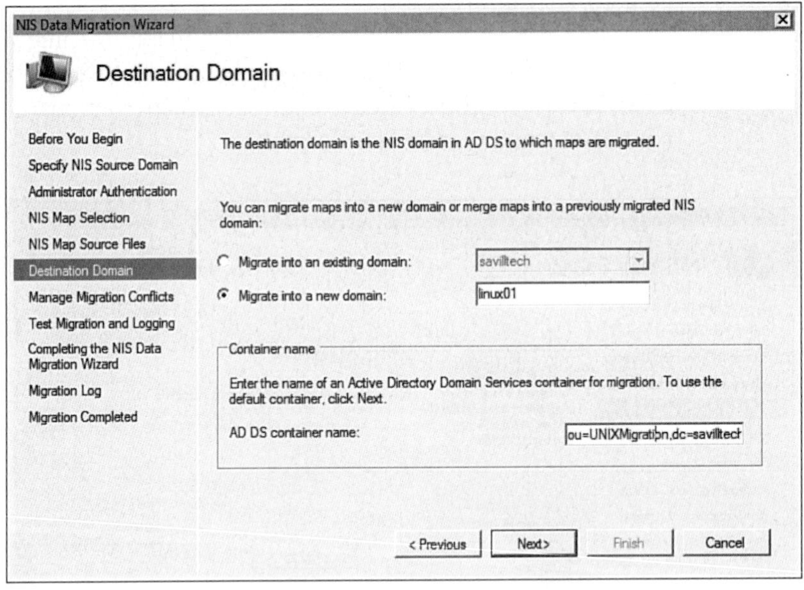

FIGURE 23-10 Specifying the target NIS domain and object container.

7. Next, configure how conflicts are handled. The options can be to overwrite existing Windows objects, rename the existing object, or preserve the existing object. Conflicts are written to the C:\Windows\IDMU\log\conflicts.log file by default.

8. Perform a test of the migration via the Do Not Migrate (Log Only) option, or you can migrate the objects via the Migrate and Log option. The log is written to C:\Windows\IDMU\log\nis2ad.log by default.
9. A confirmation of the settings appears. Click Next to perform the migration.
10. At the end of the migration, a dialog appears. It links to the two log files that list conflicts and the overall progress. Here is an example entry in the nis2ad.log for a successfully created object. Notice that the object name and AD container are shown:

```
SUCCESS
Adding the object in Active Directory Domain Services.
Object = 'Clark'
Object class = 'User'
container =
'CN=users,CN=linux01,ou=UNIXMigration,dc=savilltech,dc=
net'.
```

You now have migrated objects in your AD, as shown in Figure 23-11. If you look at your container, it might appear empty because, if you migrated the objects into a new NIS domain in AD, a container (named the NIS domain) is created in the target container specified. By default, the NIS domain is not displayed. Select the View menu within AD Users and Computers and enable the Advanced Features option. This action shows your new container. This new NIS domain is now available in user and group objects for the NIS domain.

After you have migrated NIS to AD, configure the UNIX NIS servers and clients to use AD. This configuration is documented in the online IdMU help file in "Server for NIS Administration," as shown in Figure 23-12.

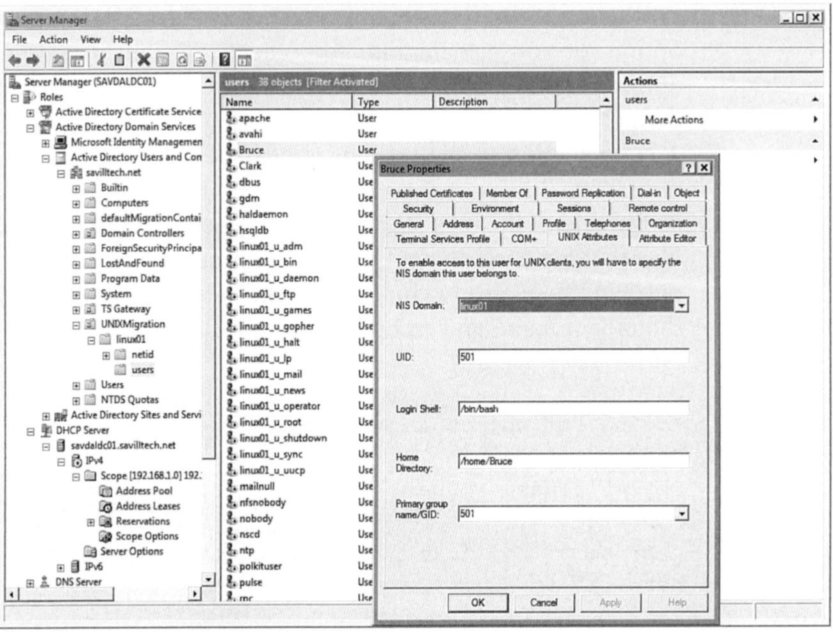

FIGURE 23-11 Migrated UNIX environment.

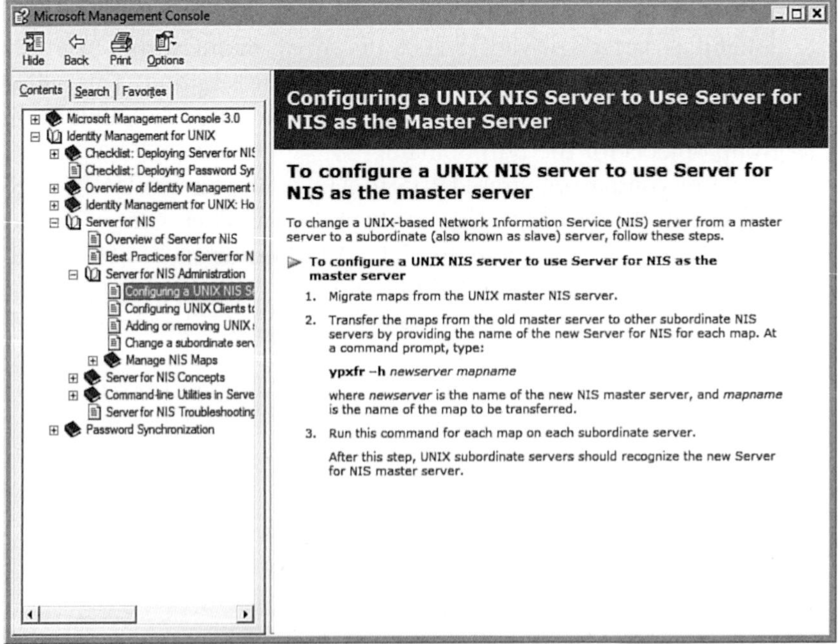

FIGURE 23-12 NIS online help.

Password Synchronization

Consider an environment consisting of a mixture of UNIX and Windows servers. Each server maintains its own security databases, which means users have one account for UNIX access and one account for Windows access. Multiple accounts mean multiple passwords. This type of heterogeneous environment is an issue from a password management perspective, but with password synchronization, you can enable synchronization between UNIX NIS domain account passwords and the users' accounts in the Windows Server 2008 AD. This synchronization is bidirectional; it requires you to install the password synchronization component on all domain controllers in the domain.

Password synchronization is granular, and individual user accounts can be excluded or included. The process works by having a component installed on both the UNIX and Windows Server side.

If a password is changed on the UNIX side, the UNIX password module calls a Pluggable Authentication Module (PAM). PAM intercepts the password change request, encrypts the password with strong encryption (Triple DES), and then sends the password to the AD domain controller running IdMU. This controller decrypts the encrypted password and applies the updated password to the AD account. In fact, you can also use password synchronization to synchronize to local user accounts on a normal Windows server and not a domain controller.

As part of the password synchronization component, PAMs are available for HP-UX 11i, Sun Solaris 7 and 8, IBM AIX 5L 5.2, and Red Hat Linux 8 and 9. Use them to perform synchronization to AD. The source code also is available, so if you are running a different version of UNIX or Linux, you can compile the PAM onto any version.

If a password is changed on the Windows side, the Password Synchronization Service intercepts the password change, encrypts the password using strong encryption, and transmits the encrypted password to the Single Sign on Daemon (SSOD) running in the background on the UNIX side. SSOD then decrypts the password and applies it to the UNIX user database. Once again, SSOD is supplied for the four major UNIX/Linux versions, plus the source code is installed. This allows the SSOD to run on any UNIX/Linux implementation. SSOD can be downloaded from Microsoft.com as ssod.tar.gz for Windows Server 2008. (Search Microsoft.com for ssod.tar.gz.) These password synchronization components are seen in action in Figure 23-13.

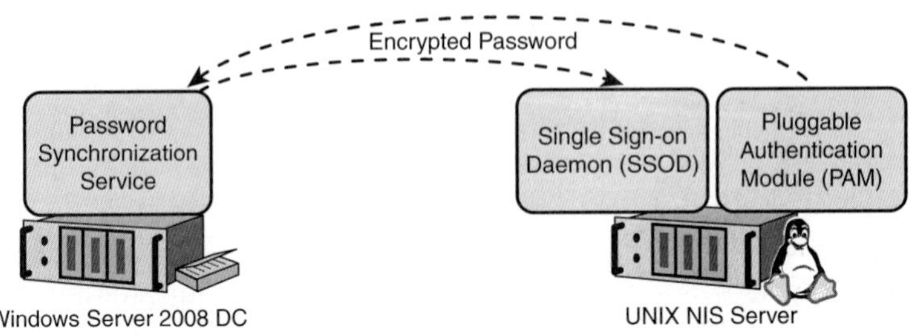

FIGURE 23-13 The password synchronization components.

Password encryption is performed via a shared key known to the Windows and UNIX servers partnered in the password synchronization. This key can be different for each set of password synchronization relationships and can be set with the Add Computer action, as shown in Figure 23-14.

Add Computer

General

Computer name : linux-vm01

Direction of password synchronization

☑ Synchronize password changes to this computer

☑ Synchronize password changes from this computer

Encryption and decryption

If you change the encryption key, or generate a new key, you must also configure UNIX-based computers to use the new key.

Key: 9lhDe_24Q6fKLj#fP08k

Generate

Port configuration

Password Synchronization monitors this port for password changes.

Port number: 6677

OK Cancel Apply

FIGURE 23-14 Adding a new UNIX computer for password synchronization.

Always click the Generate key to create a new key. (You don't want to use the ABCDZ#efgh$12345 value because everyone knows this key.) Make a note of the newly generated key because you need to enter this into the UNIX-side component to enable a common encryption/decryption capability.

Now configure the UNIX side. Take the ssod.tar.gz file, expand it, and then, depending on your UNIX platform, you have two options. The first is to take UNIX-specific precompiled versions, place them in the UNIX /usr/bin folder, and rename the binary files to remove the UNIX version from the files extension. If your UNIX version is not one of those supplied, use the second option—you need to compile the source file to create the password synchronization UNIX-side components.

The next step is to update the ssod.cfg, which has to be copied to the /etc folder. Then, in the ssod.cfg file, update a number of properties, as follows:

- Rename the extension to be .conf instead of .cfg, so it is recognized as a configuration file.
- Within the file, give the details of the system that password synchronization will be performed with—for example, the PORT_NUMBER plus the SYNC_HOSTS value, which specifies the host to synchronize passwords with. You also have to enter the encryption key as part of the entry in the format SYNC_HOSTS=(<host or IP address of DC>,<port>,<encryption key>).
- Update the password encryption key to match that on the Windows side (ENCRYPT_KEY).
- Configure the users that will have the password synchronized via the SYNC_USERS value, which is ALL by default.

When a password is changed on the UNIX side, the password is sent to the Windows DC specified and, likewise, a change made on the Windows side is sent to the UNIX server.

The Properties dialog for the Password Synchronization component has two tabs. These tabs allow general control of password flow configuration, such as Windows to UNIX and UNIX to Windows, as shown in Figures 23-15 and 23-16, along with the default port number used for monitoring and a general encryption key, which you won't use. The Configuration tab allows retry settings and logging options. Finally, there's the option to automatically enable password synchronization for any accounts migrated from NIS to AD. You can view similar properties for each of the specific UNIX server connections.

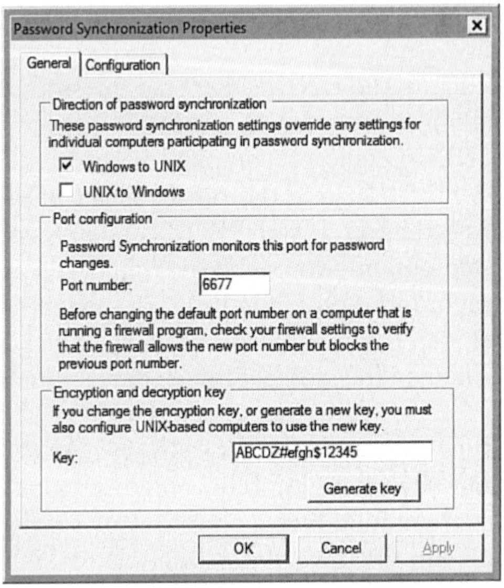

FIGURE 23-15 The General properties for password synchronization.

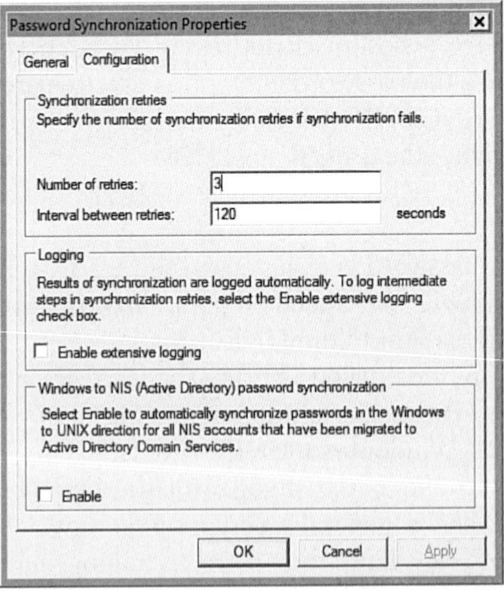

FIGURE 23-16 The Configuration properties for password synchronization.

Microsoft Services for Network File System

The last component this section discusses is related to file sharing between UNIX/Linux and Microsoft systems. UNIX shares files through the Network File System (NFS). To enable Microsoft clients to view files on a UNIX box, install the NFS client. To allow UNIX clients (and any other client that supports NFS, such as Macintosh) to see files on a Windows Server, install the NFS Server.

Many recent UNIX and Linux implementations now understand the Windows environment, as shown in Figure 23-17. They can directly connect to a Windows share, but some implementations cannot.

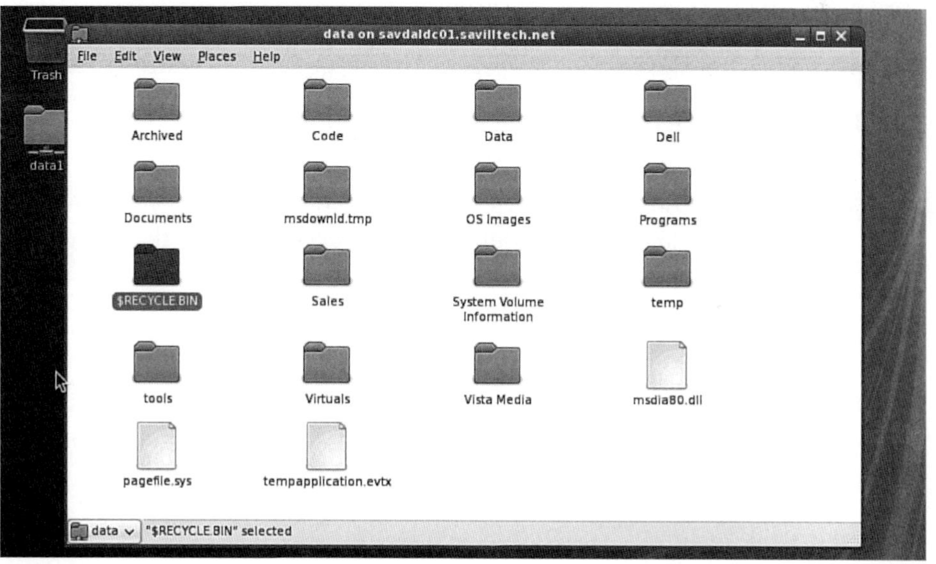

FIGURE 23-17 A Linux box connecting to a Windows share using SMB.

Windows Vista contains only the Client for NFS, plus administrative tools. Windows Server 2008 has the complete Services for NFS role service; this includes the NFS Server in addition to the NFS client and is added via the File Services role, as shown in Figure 23-18.

After Services for NFS are installed, a new link is available in the Administrative Tools folder (Services for NFS) that enables the configuration of both the client and server portion of NFS.

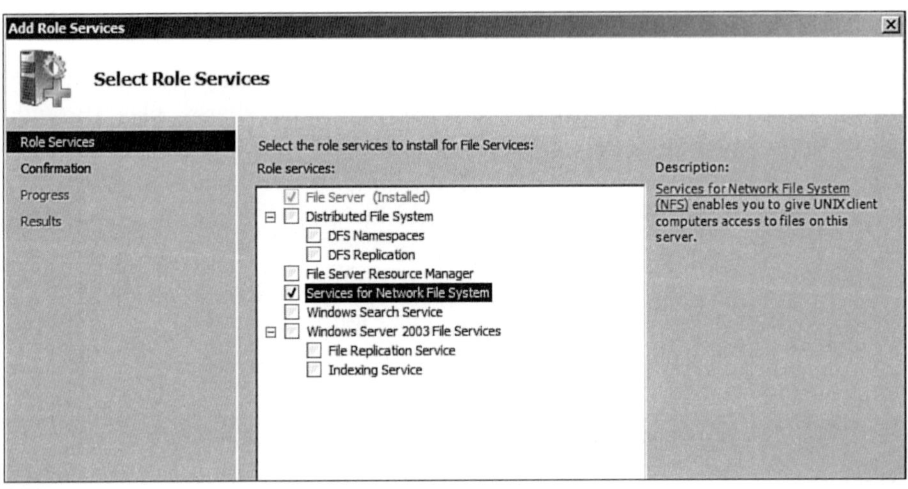

FIGURE 23-18 Installing the NFS Services.

Before you can use either function, configure mapping between the UNIX users and the AD users to enable access to files that have security configured on them. In Windows Server 2008, this is done via AD mapping.

NFS Configuration

There is not much to configure for NFS. Assuming you have mapped data within the AD by importing a NIS, just access the properties of the Server for NIS via the Services for Network File System MMC snap-in.

The first (and only required) action is to tell Service for NFS how to perform the UNIX mapping. To do this, right-click the Service for NFS console tree item (not Server for NFS) and select Properties. In the displayed box, check AD Domain Name and enter the AD name, which has UNIX mapping information, as shown in Figure 23-19. You can also configure this from the command line via the `nfsadmin mapping config adlookup=yes addomain=savilltech.net` command.

The next stage is to configure the folders that are shared with NFS. This is performed through Explorer or the command line. Right-click the folder in Explorer and select Properties. Then select the NFS Sharing tab. Click the Manage NFS Sharing button; enable the share option and set the NFS share options, as shown in Figure 23-20. Specific permissions can be set via the Permissions. Hosts and host groups are created and managed via the nfsadmin server creategroup <group> and nfsadmin server addmembers <group> <host> commands. The default settings for permissions are also set, which is Read Only by default with no root access; to enable root access, check the Allow Root Access box. If you allow anonymous authentication, enable the anonymous user to be included in the Everyone group, which is achieved by enabling a group policy setting—Computer Configuration—Windows Settings—Security Settings—Local Policies—Security Settings—Netware Access: Let Everyone Permission Apply to Anonymous Users. For domain controllers, you need to set this on the default domain controllers policy, but for any other server, it can be set via group policy or in the local computer policy. This does have other security implications by enabling anonymous to be included in Everyone, so consider this carefully.

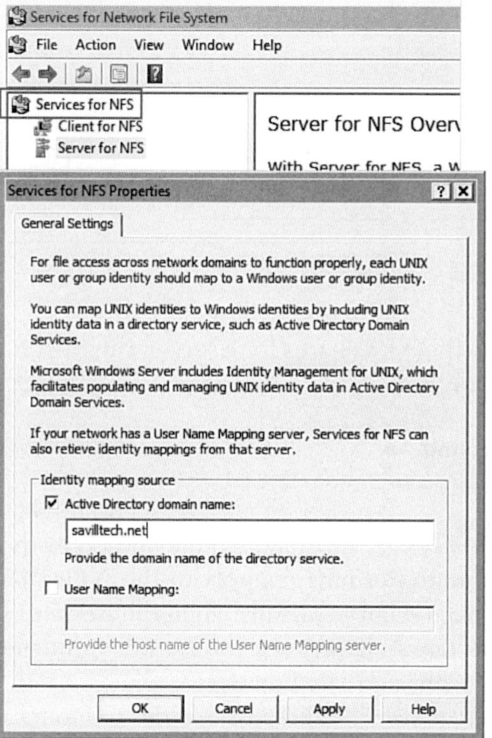

FIGURE 23-19 Configuring how the NFS mapping of credentials are performed.

To configure from the command line, use the nfsshare command (for example, nfsshare <nfs share name>=<drive>:\<path>).

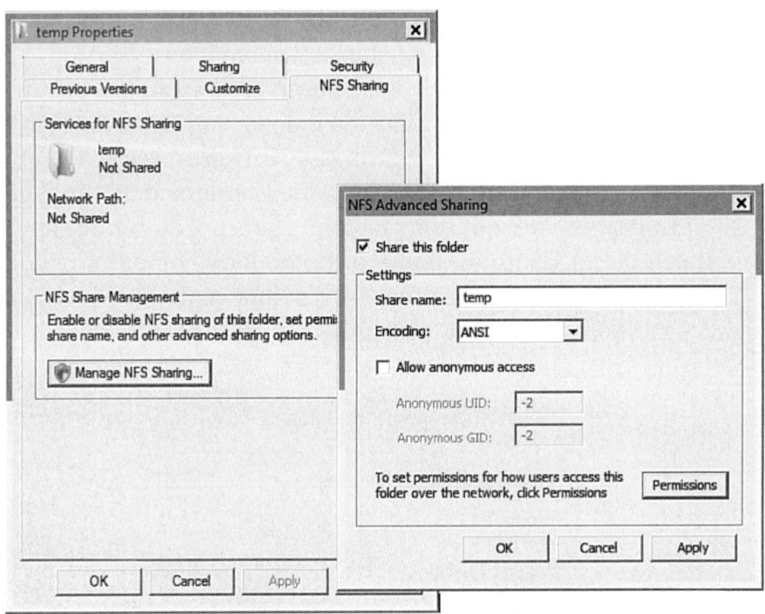

FIGURE 23-20 Configuring NFS sharing.

To view the NFS shares for a server, run the showmount -e command on the server, as follows:

```
C:\>showmount -e
Exports list on SAVDALDC01:
/DataTemp                                  All Machines
```

NFS clients can now connect to the NFS share. The firewall exceptions are enabled automatically when the Services for NFS are installed.

For Windows clients, use the mount command (for example, mount <server>\<share> *). For UNIX, clients use the NFS format, which is <server>:/<share>, and pass a folder to mount to. You can also use the UNIX format from the Windows mount command, for example:

```
mount savdaldc01.savilltech.net:/temp /mnt/tmpmount
```

To unmount an NFS mount, use the umount command. You can run the showmount command remotely from an NFS client to query what NFS shares are available by passing a server/IP address after the -e. Then, from the Linux client, mount and view the data, as shown in Figure 23-21.

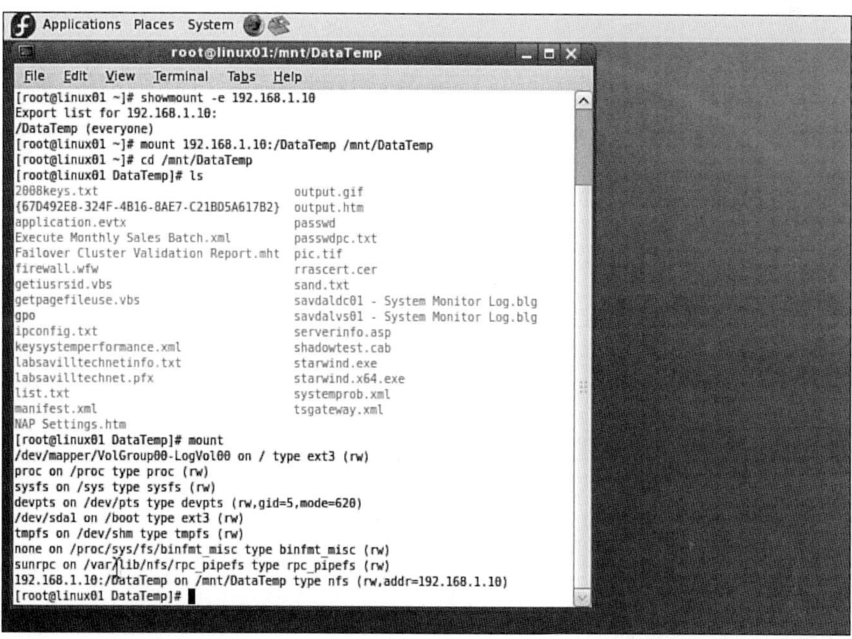

FIGURE 23-21 Connecting to the NFS Server from a Linux client.

You can tune aspects of NFS sharing via the Server for NFS properties. This allows a number of NFS version support configurations, including filename handling (see Figure 23-22), file locking handling, and the amount of logging to perform.

If you enable the logging of mount/unmount, you can see these type of requests. For example, the following is a mount request and a good way to troubleshoot:

```
Log Name:      Microsoft-Windows-Server For NFS/Operational
Source:        Microsoft-Windows-Server For NFS
Date:          2/1/2008 4:43:54 PM
Event ID:      1
Task Category: None
Level:         Information
```

```
Keywords:
User:          SYSTEM
Computer:      savdaldc01.savilltech.net
Description:
Mount operation succeeded.

Address:192.168.1.64
Share:D:\temp
```

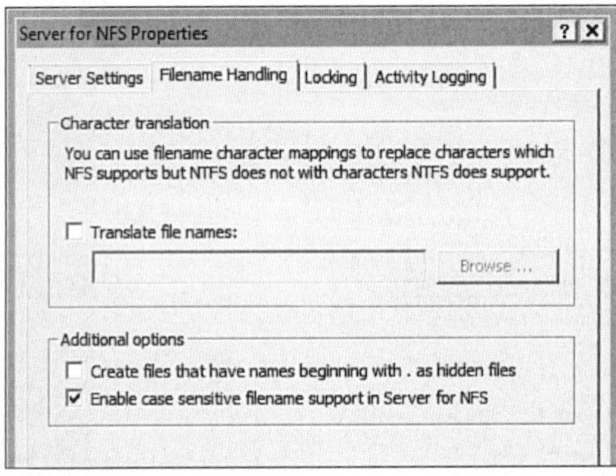

Figure 23-22 Converting filenames with NFS.

Windows as an LDAP Authentication Server

Although Windows Server 2008 can act as an NIS server, many UNIX vendors are moving away from NIS and using LDAP authentication. Windows Server 2008 AD, running in at least Windows Server 2003 mode with the Windows Server 2008 schema applied, supports LDAP authentication for UNIX clients out of the box.

The only action you have is to install the IdMU tools on at least one domain controller. This allows access to the UNIX attributes tab, where you can configure the NIS domain, User ID (UID), logon shell, home folder, and primary group.

At this stage, UNIX/Linux clients could be configured to use the LDAP service from AD. For security reasons, you might want to configure certificate services. This enables encrypting the LDAP bind requests from the clients with SSL. The certificate can be from an Internet trusted certificate authority (CA), or you can install Active Directory Certificate

Services (ADCS) in your environment and issue the domain controllers a certificate from that authority. Doing this requires importing the CA root certificate from the enterprise CA into all the UNIX clients, so they trust the certificates from the domain controllers.

Another item you might want to configure is a normal user account with a nonexpiring password. UNIX clients can use this password as a proxy account when they want to connect to the directory service and browse for information without authenticating. After you create this proxy account in AD, it is configured into the UNIX-side LDAP configuration.

NOTE The actual process to configure a UNIX client to use LDAP varies. Consult the individual UNIX/Linux documentation.

NetWare Integration and Migration

Microsoft has a similar set of solutions for NetWare as it does for UNIX. However, the Services for NetWare (SFN) solution provides a slimmer solutions set that is not part of Windows Server 2008. SFN is focused on introducing Windows into a NetWare environment and then migrating the NetWare resources—such as users, groups, and data—to a Windows platform.

NOTE This section is based on the solution set for Windows Server 2003, which can be found at http://www.microsoft.com/windowsserver2003/sfn/default.mspx. The solution is covered, but you will need a Windows 2003 domain controller. Windows Server 2008 does not support the "Client service for NetWare," which is a requirement for the Services for NetWare. In a pure Windows Server 2008 domain, use the Novell DirXML (Identity Access Manager) solution to synchronize user objects from eDirectory to AD. If you need to migrate file/folder resources, look at third-party solutions, such as those from Quest Software.

The Microsoft NWLink protocol is not supported in Windows Vista or Windows Server 2008. Although it is possible to take the files from a 32-bit Windows XP installation and copy to a 32-bit Windows Vista and get some

NWLink communication, it's not supported. Plus, it has configuration issues. Novell's own client for Windows Vista no longer supports the IPX/SPX protocol.

Services for NetWare 5.03, which is the most recent version of SFU, includes two components:

- **Directory Synchronization Services**. Enables synchronization and migration with Novell Directory Services (NDS), eDirectory, and Bindery network services
- **File Migration Utility**. Migrates file-based resources from the NetWare environment to a Windows server while preserving security settings on the files

To use SFN, install the Novell Client for Windows: http://www.novell.com/products/clients/. Both 32-bit and 64-bit versions are available. During the installation of MDSS, the schema of the AD forest is updated automatically. You need to reboot your server.

NOTE Another component is File and Print Services for NetWare (FPNW). This feature allows NetWare clients to view file and print resources hosted on a Microsoft Windows server. However, this chapter does not cover FPNW in detail.

The Client Services for NetWare, which was part of the operating system that allowed connectivity to file and printer resources on NetWare, has been removed, as has the Gateway Services for NetWare. NetWare is no longer the dominant player it was when Windows NT first entered the market, and if Microsoft clients need to communicate with NetWare file and print resources, the Novell client can be downloaded. Microsoft is focusing on moving these NetWare resources over to Microsoft.

Synchronization Within Microsoft Directory Synchronization Services

The Microsoft Directory Synchronization Services (MSDSS) is responsible for synchronizing AD with either NDS or eDirectory in a uni- or bidirectional fashion, NetWare 3.x bindery services in a unidirectional fashion, and AD to bindery-only mode.

Two types of synchronization are available with MSDSS, as follows:

- **Forward**. Replicates data from AD to Novell
- **Reverse**. Pulls data from Novell to AD

The direction of synchronization depends on how the organization functions, and the directory might vary over time. When you first install MSDSS, you might have replication running in reverse mode. As Windows becomes more widely used, bidirectional synchronization will be needed. After the focus shifts to AD and changes are made only on AD, the synchronization can be forward with only changes made in AD pushed to the Novell directory.

Forward Synchronization

Ideally, run forward synchronization only because it's far more efficient than reverse synchronization. Forward synchronization queries the AD for any changes since the last forward synchronization. Any change to an object is pushed and updated on the Novell side. Only the attribute changes; the entire object is not sent to Novell directories. If a new object is created in AD, the entire object and its attributes are sent to Novell. This works great because MSDSS is running on the Windows side, so it has full information about the AD and what has changed. Reverse synchronization does not have such a luxury.

Reverse Synchronization

Reverse synchronization, available for NDS and eDirectory only, is a far more data-intensive process. This is because the Novell directories do not provide a mechanism to query for changes to objects. Instead, the reverse synchronization has to look at every object on the Novell directory side and compare it to the AD object. If the Novell object is new, it is created in AD. If an attribute has changed, that attribute is updated on the AD side. This is a lot of data that requires much resource use, so typically reverse synchronization is performed less frequently than forward synchronization; however, this also means that changes on the Novell side take longer to update on the AD side.

Differences Between Forward and Reverse Synchronization

One difference between forward and reverse synchronization is shown in Figure 23-23. Forward replication sends over only the new object or the modified attributes, and the process to discover the new/modified objects/attributes is a simple, low-resource query to AD. With reverse replication, MSDSS has to ask Novell for every object, which includes the new objects and modified attributes; then on the MSDSS server it performs a comparison of the current AD content with the information brought over from Novell. Imagine that you have 50,000 objects instead of four. That's a big difference in network utilization for sending only changes compared to the entire directory content. In reality, it's not this bad; algorithms are used to improve the comparisons and attempt to minimize data sent. However, there is still a big difference between forward and reverse synchronization.

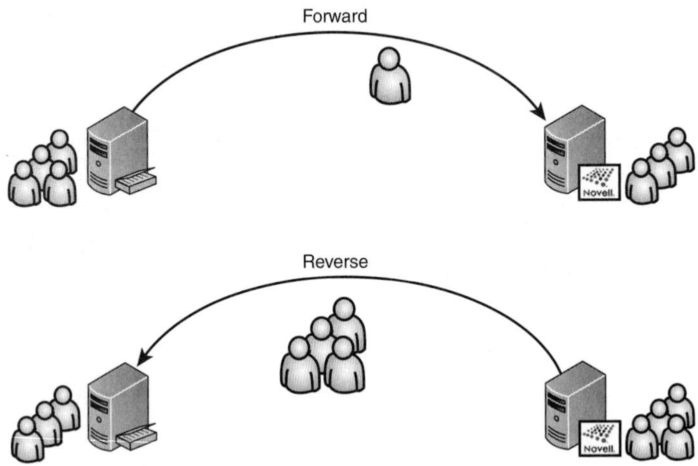

FIGURE 23-23 MSDSS forward and reverse replication.

Although Figure 23-23 shows user objects, the same process is performed for group and organization unit (OU) information. This replication is not constant. Instead, it runs on a schedule, which by default is every 15 minutes for forward synchronization and once an hour from midnight to 06:00 for reverse synchronization. However, you can modify this behavior to meet your organization's needs. In addition, manual synchronizations can be performed for urgent changes, such as a disabled user. It is also possible to configure the replication to replicate only certain areas of the directory service or only certain types of objects.

Additionally, reverse replication can be used in a migration mode to perform a one-time population of AD from Novell objects and then not synchronize again. This is one of the most common uses of MSDSS for NetWare to AD migrations. It populates AD with the NDS objects, assuming you are doing a big-bang migration with no changes to NetWare after the object migration is performed. Therefore, no future synchronization is required.

To enable this synchronization between directory services, schema changes are required on the AD to support object replication or migration; a schema change is also required on the NDS side if bidirectional replication will be used, and these changes are walked through in the Services for Network documentation. As previously mentioned, the schema change is made automatically on the Windows side during the installation process.

The MSDSS snap-in creates these synchronization relationships. The process of establishing the relationships is as follows. Because you are performing a migration, you are not prompted to set an object mapping scheme.

1. Select the New Session context menu item to start the New Session Wizard.
2. Select the type of Novell directory source and the synchronization directions to be used, in this case the migrate option from NDS to AD, which performs a one-time pull of objects from NetWare to AD.
3. Select the AD domain controller to be used for the synchronization, and the root container where migration will take place, as shown in Figure 23-24.
4. The next screen prompts for the root container on the Novell side (for example, NDS://NDSTREE/O=NDSOrg) and a Novell Administrator account. You can browse the NDS tree to view the correct container. For the account, you might need to enter the full administrator name instead of just admin, depending on the organization the account exists in.
5. If you are performing synchronization from NDS, you are prompted for how the initial reverse synchronization password are handled, which by default is to use random values, and you are informed an event log will be written showing the location of the log file (see Figure 23-25). By default, this log is written to the C:\Windows\system32\Directory Synchronization\Sessions Logs folder with a name like session1.pwd.

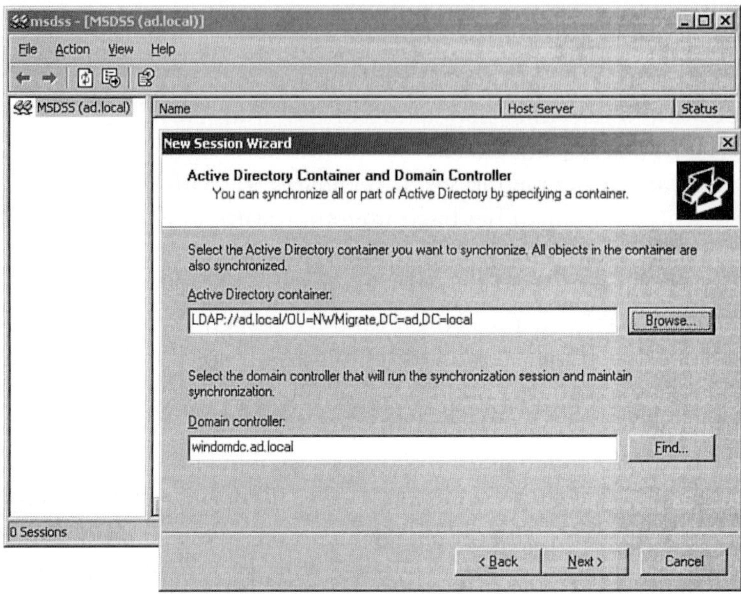

FIGURE 23-24 Selecting the AD side for the replication.

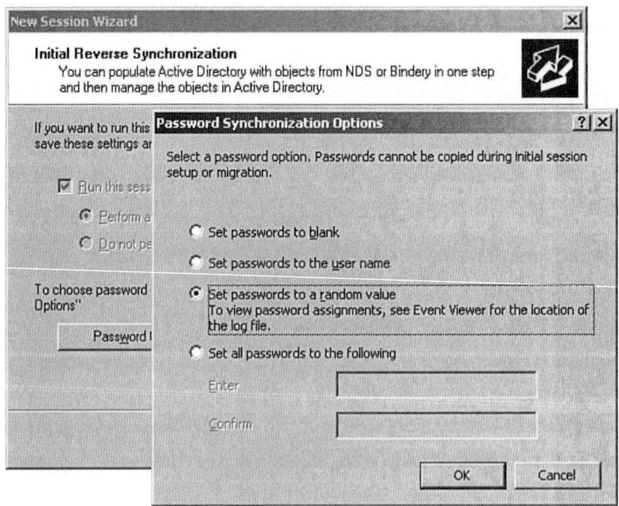

FIGURE 23-25 The default password policy option.

6. A summary appears. Click Finish to perform an initial migration, as shown in Figure 23-26.

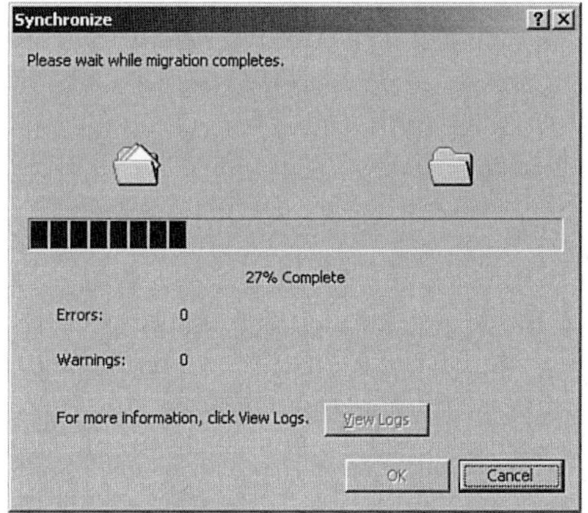

Figure 23-26 The migration process.

After the migration is complete, click the View Logs button to see the MSDSS Log. The log shows warnings, such as duplicate accounts. A summary log is written to confirm the number of objects moved, as shown here:

```
Event Type:  None
Event Source:      MSDSS
Event Category:    None
Event ID:  59
Date:         2/1/2008
Time:         12:16:55 PM
User:         N/A
Computer:     WINDOMDC
Description:
Session (1): {21AD8B68-2A42-459e-BD29-F082F47E71B2}

The reverse synchronization session has terminated success-
fully.
12 objects were read,
12 objects were mapped.

Among the objects mapped,
12 objects were written.
0 objects failed.
0 objects were added to the Failed Object List.
```

```
From the Failed Object List,
0 objects were successfully written,
0 objects expired.
For more information, see Help and Support Center at
http://go.microsoft.com/fwlink/events.asp.
```

A migration log is also written to the C:\WINDOWS\system32\Directory Synchronization\Session Logs folder with an incremental number text filename. For example, 1.txt that has the object mappings between NDS and AD can be used for the file-migration utility. This is important. Here is a sample of the file generated:

```
Session 1: {21AD8B68-2A42-459e-BD29-F082F47E71B2}
Started: 02-01-2008 12:16
NDS Tree: NDSTREE
AD Server: windomdc.ad.local
O=NDSOrg/CN=NFAUUser
User
CN=NFAUUser,OU=NWMigrate,DC=ad,DC=local
user
O=NDSOrg/CN=NFAUWorld
Group
CN=NFAUWorld,OU=NWMigrate,DC=ad,DC=local
group
```

Many entries are removed, but the structure is four lines for each user, group, OU, or organization:

- **Line 1**. The Novell object distinguished name—for example, O=NDSOrg/CN=NFAUUser for user NFAUUser in organization NDSOrg.
- **Line 2**. The type of Novell object—for example, User.
- **Line 3**. The AD fully distinguished name for the replicated object—for example, CN=NFAUUser,OU=NWMigrate,DC=ad,DC=local for user NFAUUser in organizational unit NWMigrate in domain ad.local.
- **Line 4**. The object type for the AD created object—for example, a user or group. Because this log is used for file migrations and in Windows only, users and groups can be used for Access Control Entities, and any Organization or Organizational Unit object in Novell is converted to a Group in AD.

Understanding this structure is useful because you might want to edit it. Let's say you already have AD installed, and all users have AD accounts. You also have NetWare NDS. Users have a separate account on NDS, and you want to finally retire NDS and migrate all the data on NetWare over to a Windows server. In this case, you might not want to synchronize the NDS user accounts with your AD accounts, but you do want to maintain file permissions. You could migrate all the NDS objects into an OU within the AD to get the migration log with the NetWare user/group and its mapping of the created user/group. At this point, delete the NetWare migration OU you created, edit the migration log file, and replace the distinguished name of the AD object from the object created during the migration to the user's real AD account. For example, suppose you had the following for user John in the log file:

```
O=NDSOrg/CN=John
User
CN=John,OU=NWMigrate,DC=savilltech,DC=net
user
```

John's real AD account is CN=John,OU=Users,OU=America,DC=savilltech,DC=net, so update the migration log file to read as follows:

```
O=NDSOrg/CN=John
User
CN=John Savill,OU=Users,OU=America,DC=savilltech,DC=net
user
```

Now when this migration log is used by the file migration utility, any permissions for user John in NetWare are given to the normal account for John.

Passwords

Extracting user passwords from Novell is not possible because of the encryption used, a good thing for Novell directory services but a problem for synchronization. Any password changes have to be made on the AD side, which can then be replicated to Novell; however, sometimes a password is set on the Novell side. For example, the first time you synchronize with Novell, you might import 40,000 users, all of whom have passwords, or a new user is created on the Novell side during normal operation. What happens?

Any user object imported from Novell that has a new password created in AD has User Must Change Password at Next Logon set for their account. When the user changes the password, this new password is then synchronized with Novell via forward replication. There is an exception, however: If the password is changed on the Novell side, but the user account in AD already has a password configured, the Novell password is ignored, and the user now has different passwords on the AD and Novell side. For this reason, when you have both AD and Novell, allow users to change passwords only on the AD side. Configure the Novell side to not allow password changes, and make sure the Novell side does not have minimum and maximum password ages defined.

There are a number of password schemes available for user objects replicated from Novell, as follows:

- **Set passwords to a blank**. On first logon, the user does not need to enter any password.
- **Set passwords to the name of the user**. Sets the password to the username of the account, and this is the default scheme.
- **Set passwords to a random value**. Creates a random password for each user that is written to the synchronization log file, which can then be used to mail users about their temporary AD user account password. This log is found in C:\Windows\system32\Directory Synchronization\Sessions Logs by default with a .pwd extension.
- **Set all passwords to the following value**. Use a static value for the password of all migrated user accounts.

During the creation of the MSDSS replication, if you select the random value, the .pwd file has a list of usernames and their passwords. For example:

```
Session 1: {21AD8B68-2A42-459e-BD29-F082F47E71B2}
Started: 02-01-2008 12:16
nfauuser    ndQ%9Y5$Ir
admin       sx)VyH5X%4
```

You could write something to process the generated file that would parse this generated file and perhaps email users with their new AD password.

File Migration Utility

After the accounts and groups are migrated or at least synchronized with the AD, the next major task for a migration is to migrate the data from the NetWare servers over to the Windows Servers. A raw data copy would not be a problem; however, on the NetWare side, there will likely be access controls placed on files and folders allowing users and groups specific permissions. These permissions need to be maintained in most environments, which requires a utility that will not only move the data file but also inspect the access permissions on the NetWare side. For each user or group permission, find the corresponding AD user or group; after the file is migrated to Windows, set the same permissions that were present before but using the AD user and/or group.

This mapping of NetWare users to AD users is not done automatically by the File Migration Utility; instead, you need to have performed at minimum a one-time migration of NDS or bindery user and group directory objects to AD. During the initial configuration of object migration from NDS to Windows, select the option to migrate files; this generates a log file that maps objects from NDS to AD and is used by the file migration utility to distinguish which AD account to give permissions on the migrated file (see Figure 23-27). There are separate mappings created for users mappings, group mappings, and NDS OU and organizations to AD group mappings. The reason NDS OUs and organizations map to groups in AD and not AD OUs is because with Windows Server, an OU cannot be granted access to resources.

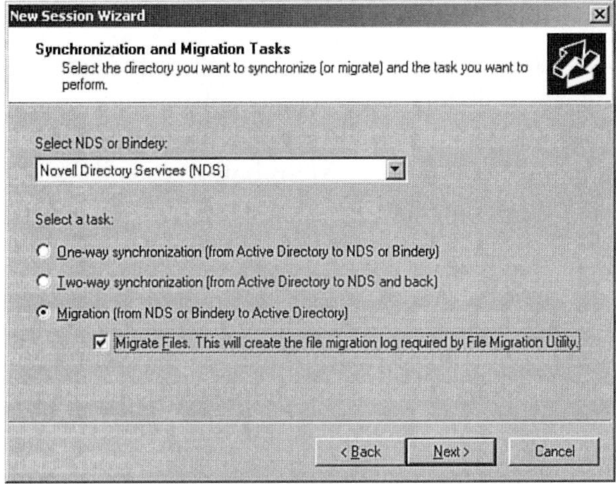

FIGURE 23-27 Requesting the creation of the log for file migration purposes.

When you first run the File Migration Utility, the utility checks the environment and connects to both AD and the NDS environment, as shown in Figure 23-28.

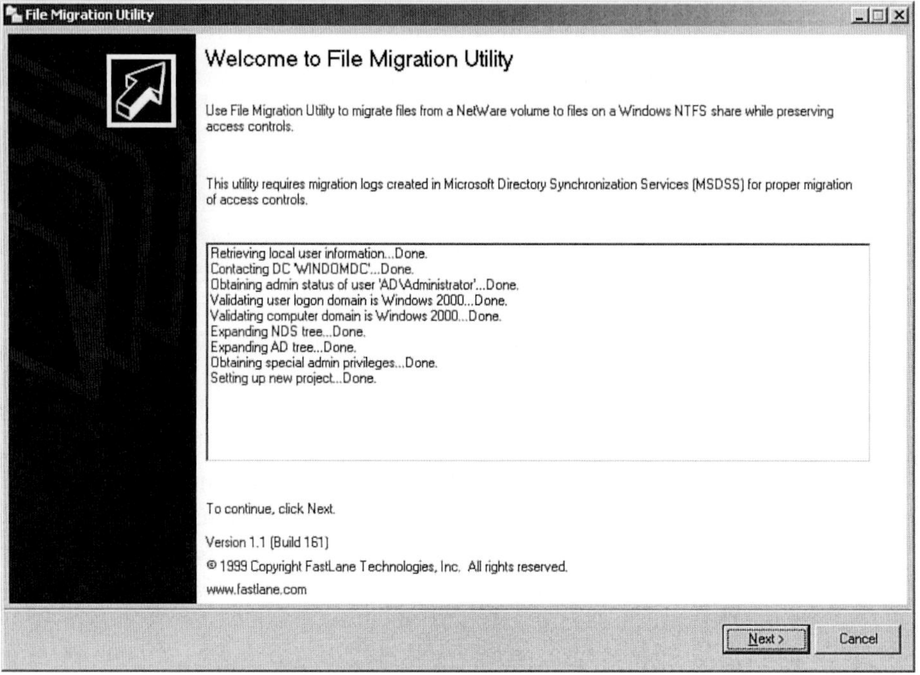

FIGURE 23-28 The initial File Migration Utility screen.

When you press Next, the first step is displayed, which is the mapping of Novell accounts to AD accounts. This is where you specify the migration log file and then click the Load Data button. I recommend checking the Validate Active Directory Maps before you click the Load Data button; this checks the AD objects specified in the log file, which is especially important if you have edited the log file to map NDS objects to AD objects other than those originally created during the migration stage (see Figure 23-29).

After the data is loaded, you can view the mappings via the View Maps button, and the Access Rights enables you to configure if the NetWare Modify right equates to Read right on Windows or Read & Write.

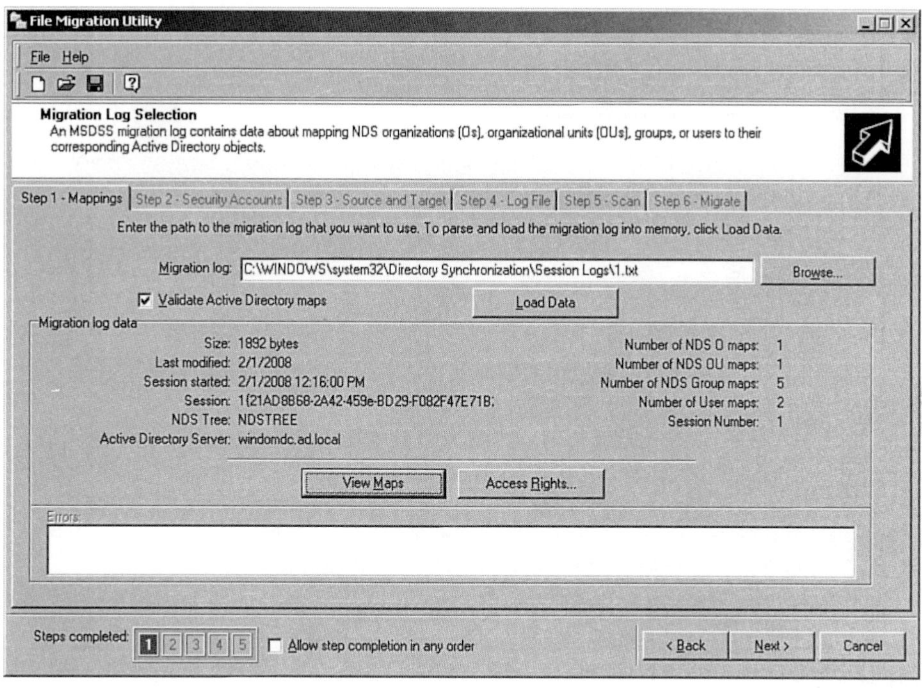

FIGURE 23-29 The first stage of the file migration is to map Novell objects to AD objects.

The next stage displays the AD account that is used and buttons to display the current NetWare connections. Then, log on, as shown in Figure 23-30, if you are not currently connected to NetWare. If you click NetWare Connections and it's blank, you have not connected to NetWare. Therefore, you need to log on to NetWare first via the Log On to Novell button.

Next, select the folders to migrate from the Novell side and the folder it maps to on the Windows side. Select the source and target folders, as shown in Figure 23-31. Click the Map button to create a map between them. You can add multiple maps to facilitate file migration from multiple folder hierarchies and servers in one file-migration utility execution.

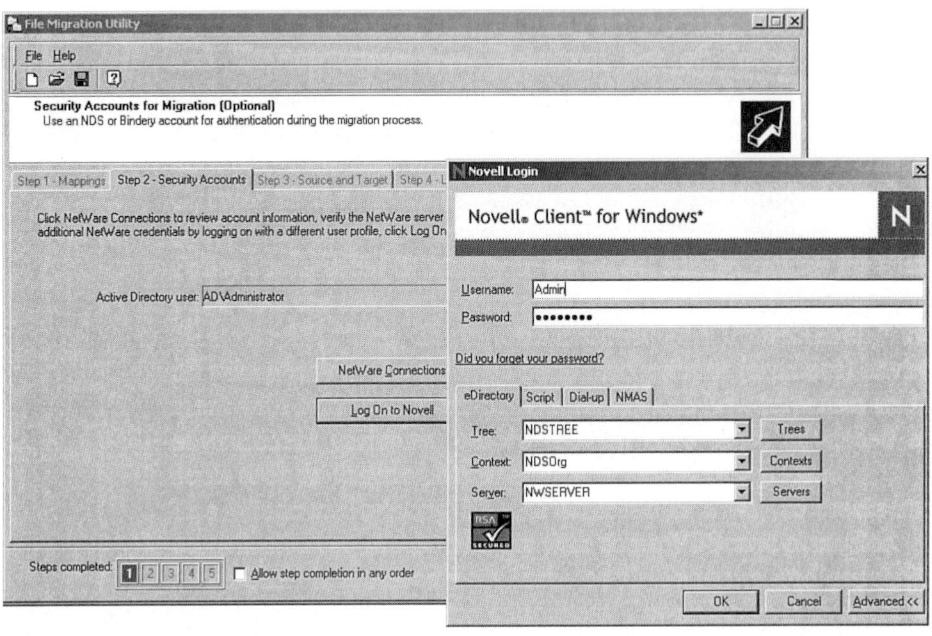

FIGURE 23-30 Logging onto NetWare.

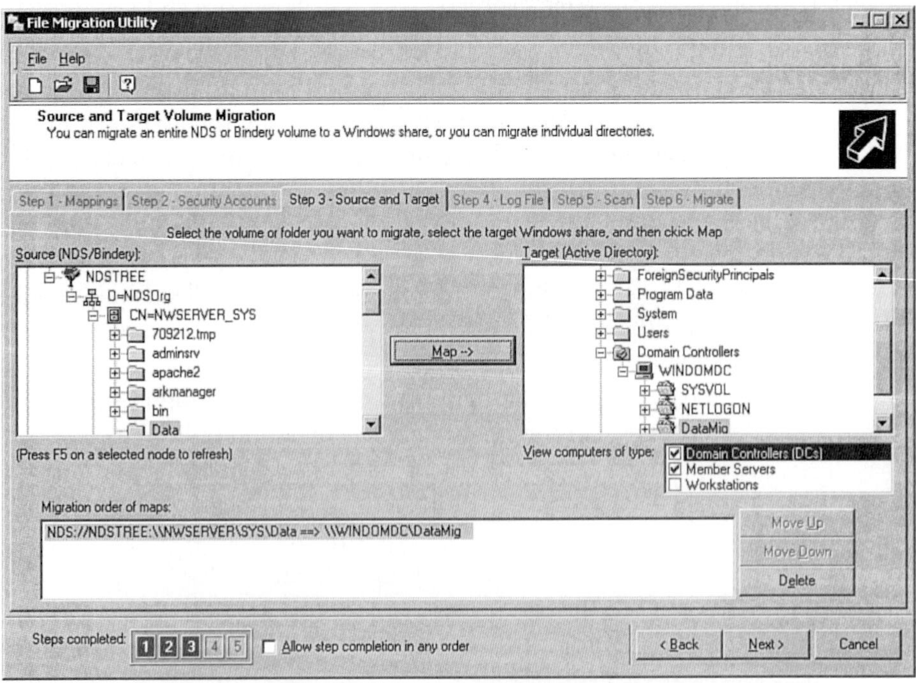

FIGURE 23-31 Creating a map between the Novell source and Windows target.

Now, select Log File Creation, which is disabled by default due to the huge amount of information generated. However, you can specify to compress the file via NTFS compression (if created on an NTFS partition) and a maximum log file size, along with the log level of detail.

This step performs a scan of the files and the target environment to ensure there is enough space, and a summary of data appears, as shown in Figure 23-32. As you can see, I have only two test files in my environment and, with my limited NetWare skills, that was a challenge!

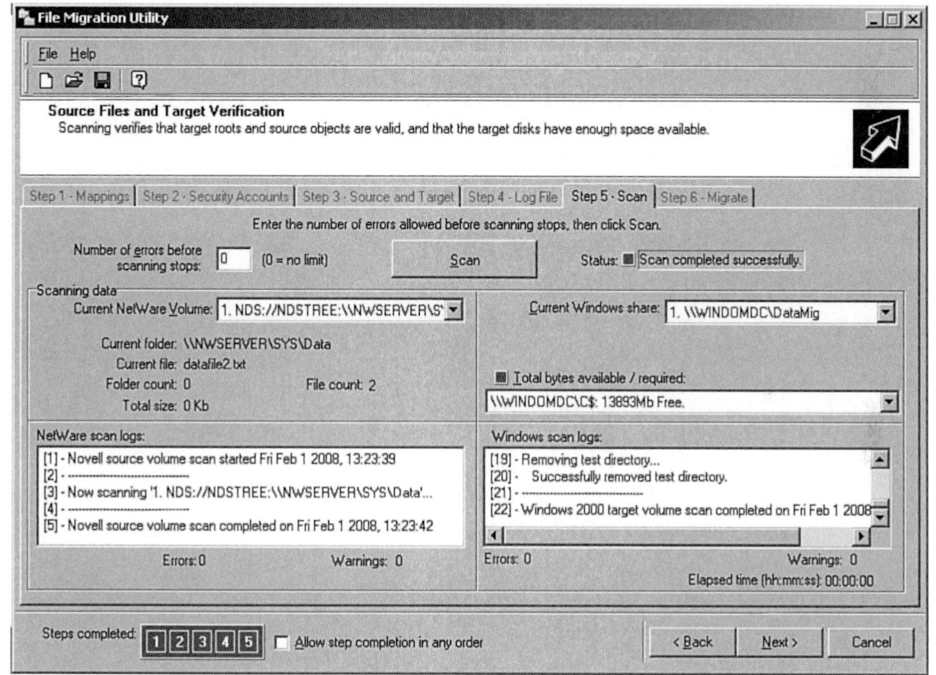

Figure 23-32 The detail of files to be migrated.

The final stage has a Migrate button. This performs the data migration, and depending on the amount of data, this might take some time. Strangely, with two text files, it completed quickly, as shown in Figure 23-33. When you click Next, a success message appears, and you can close the utility. You are also prompted to save the settings to a migration file to enable easy future file migrations using similar configurations.

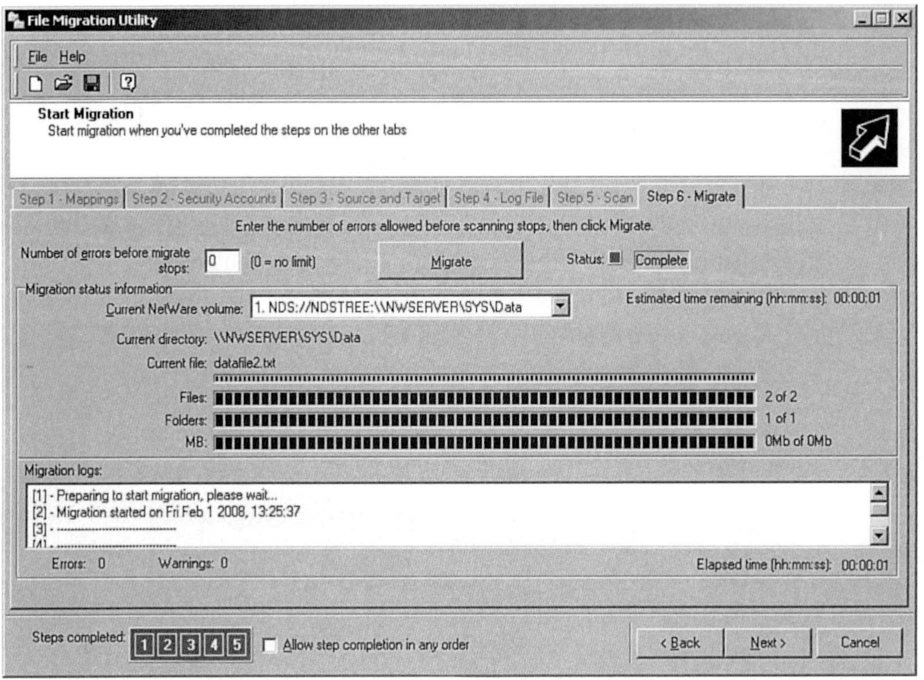

FIGURE 23-33 A large-scale file migration completed.

You can then inspect the migrated files and see that the permissions shown match those on NetWare, based on the user and group mappings defined in the migration log file specified.

Summary

Windows Server 2008 has a great interoperability connection with UNIX; with its capability to run many UNIX applications and now to connect to Oracle, there is a compelling story for standardizing more systems onto Windows and consolidating servers.

The Server for NIS components allow Windows to act as a server for NIS domains, enabling older UNIX clients to use a centralized authentication scheme, whereas new UNIX clients can likely take advantage of LDAP authentication or even AD domains directly.

The Services for NetWare are simple to use. They perform well and help the migration from NetWare to Windows. In large environments, however, the services do start to suffer in terms of usability; thus, for larger migrations, consider third-party tools, such as Quest Software's NDS Migrator, which Microsoft recommends.

Although we live in a world where not every server is running Microsoft Windows, we have a great set of tools to minimize the overhead of heterogeneous environments.

CHAPTER 24

Internet Information Services

Internet Information Services (IIS) is a rich platform for delivering Internet-enabled content, both internally and externally. IIS acts as a dependency for many other roles and features within Windows Server 2008 in that it provides Web and Web protocol-enabled services. It is also an area of constant evolution on the server and, to a lesser extent, the client.

IIS is a powerful platform for applications and services that do not have to be Microsoft based. Although IIS 7.0 (the version included in Windows Server 2008) is highly integrated with .NET, other types of language are supported, such as Personal Home Page (PHP), which is fully supported on IIS 7.0. IIS is a huge topic as both a Web server and an application/services platform. This chapter only skims the surface of some of IIS's major features and highlights changes from previous versions. The areas discussed include an overview of the main IIS components and core management actions, such as creating a new site, plus the new Uniform Resource Locator (URL) authorization features. The chapter covers local, remote, and command-line management of IIS, in addition to the core aspects of protecting an IIS instance.

NOTE IIS is such a huge topic that it warrants its own book. Touching on any part in detail is not possible within a single chapter. www.iis.net is recommended for great media presentations on IIS features and product walkthroughs.

IIS 7.0 Architecture

IIS 7.0 forms a central piece of the Windows Server 2008 Web platform. It is comprised of Windows Server 2008, and also .NET Framework 3.x,

ASP.NET, Windows SharePoint Services, and Windows Media Services 2008. This central role is shown in Microsoft's Web platform stack (see Figure 24-1).

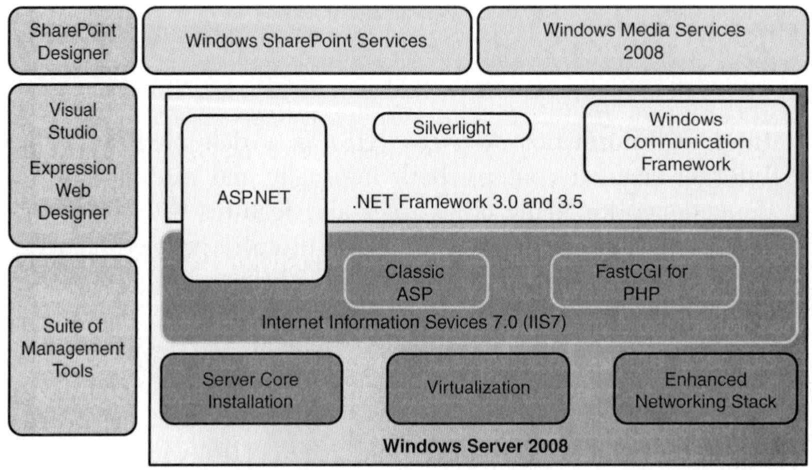

FIGURE 24-1 Windows Server 2008-based Web platform.

IIS 7.0 has undergone a large number of changes in its latest version. One of the biggest is its new modular structure. This change was based on customer feedback from those wanting a more granular level of control over the pieces of IIS that were installed on their services to ease management and possible attack vulnerabilities. The other great aspect of this modular approach is that IIS is also expanded with new modules from both Microsoft and third parties. This gives great extensibility with the capability to replace certain modules. If you don't like the way a component works, you can even write your own.

Features

All IIS 7.0's features are contained in modules, which enables you to have precise control over the available features, and even which types of security are installed and made available. Here are the various features, grouped by their primary role:

- **Common HTTP Features [Web-Common-Http]**. Supports basic Hypertext Transfer Protocol (HTTP) functionality for Web

Services, including the delivery of basic file formats and some server properties, such as custom error messages and redirections.

- **Static Content [Web-Static-Content]**. Allows publication of static content such as HTML (Hypertext Markup Language) pages and images.
- **Default Document [Web-Default-Doc]**. Allows configuration of the list of default documents that are checked for and their order when a user selects a folder instead of a specific file. For example, common default documents include default.htm and index.htm—users don't need to worry about file names and can just browse at folder levels.
- **Directory Browsing [Web-Dir-Browsing]**. When enabled, directory browsing allows a user to view the entire content of a selected folder via the URL. This is often not recommended, however, as it might expose more information than is desirable.
- **HTTP Errors [Web-Http-Errors]**. Allows the creation of customizable error pages for end user display when an error condition is found.
- **HTTP Redirection [Web-Http-Redirect]**. Allows a user to be redirected to another page, which is useful to automatically handle changing URLs.

- **Application Development [Web-App-Dev]**. Provides the infrastructure to support hosting and development of Web-based applications, such as dynamic Active Server Pages (ASP) pages.
  - **ASP.NET [Web-ASP-NET]**. Provides support for server-side managed code via ASP.NET and allows ASP.NET pages to be rendered and executed for display to the end user.
  - **.NET Extensibility [Web-NET-Ext]**. Allows the .web server's NET functionality to be extended.
  - **ASP [Web-ASP]**. Enables support for classic ASP used to generate dynamic Web pages that can interact with many other stores of information and can execute VBScript and Jscript on the Web server.
  - **CGI [Web-CGI]**. Supports Common Gateway Interface (CGI)-based scripting, which is largely not used today due to performance overhead. However, CGI is supported in multiple languages and might be required in some environments.
  - **ISAPI Extensions [Web-ISAPI-Ext]**. Internet Server Application Programming Interface (ISAPI) extensions allow additional components to be run from within IIS to perform

tasks. ISAPI extensions are applications that have full access to all the capabilities of IIS; for example, ASP.NET is processed via an ISAPI extension, aspnet_isapi.dll.

- **ISAPI Filters [Web-ISAPI-Filter]**. ISAPI Filters can be used to check requests to the Web server and if a match made per the filter criteria actions can be performed, such as pre-processing of the request before being actioned by IIS. A good example might be to handle compression.
- **Server Side Includes [Web-Includes]**. Allows the dynamic generation of HTML pages based on a script and typically is used to insert one file into another file.

- **Health and Diagnostics [Web-Health]**. Provides the capabilities to manage, monitor, and troubleshoot the entire Web server environment.
  - **HTTP Logging [Web-Http-Logging]**. Allows the logging of configured events to the relevant logging module.
  - **Logging Tools [Web-Log-Libraries]**. Tools to manage the logging on Web server.
  - **Request Monitor [Web-Request-Monitor]**. Used mainly to troubleshoot a problem site by monitoring an IIS worker process and viewing the HTTP requests that the IIS worker process is currently executing when it's having problems.
  - **Tracing [Web-Http-Tracing]**. Allows the tracking of problem scenarios by buffering information related to a request to disk if certain error conditions are met.
  - **Custom Logging [Web-Custom-Logging]**. Allows logging of IIS information into any format defined by your own custom logging module, which is registered as a COM component.
  - **ODBC Logging [Web-ODBC-Logging]**. Allows IIS logging to an ODBC-connected database.
- **Security [Web-Security]**. Provides control of Web server security features, such as denying anonymous requests and setting the authentication scheme.
  - **Basic Authentication [Web-Basic-Auth]**. Credentials are sent over the network using basic encryption that is easily hacked but supported by many browsers. Never use this on an Internet-facing Web browser—it should be used only as a last resort internally. If you do have to use Basic, consider encrypting pages with SSL, which will then also encrypt the basic authentication requests. Users are prompted via a dialog to enter their username and password.

- **Windows Authentication [Web-Windows-Auth]**. Allows domain-based credentials to be used to authenticate a web site. Realistically, this can be used only on an internal network. It allows pass-through authentication when accessing a site, assuming the web site is within the "local intranet" security zone.
- **Digest Authentication [Web-Digest-Auth]**. Uses a hash of the user's password, which is sent to a domain controller for authentication. This is more secure than basic authentication.
- **Client Certificate Mapping Authentication [Web-Client-Auth]**. Uses a digital ID from a trusted source (in this case, Active Directory) for authentication by one-to-one mapping. A certificate authority (CA) is required in the domain to give the users certificates for their accounts.
- **IIS Client Certificate Mapping Authentication [Web-Cert-Auth]**. Uses a digital ID from a trusted source (which, in this case, is IIS) for one-to-one or many-to-one mapping.
- **URL Authorization [Web-Url-Auth]**. Allows rules to be defined to restrict access to Web content based on users, groups, or HTTP header content. This enables you to stop users' access to a page who are not members of particular groups.
- **Request Filtering [Web-Filtering]**. Allows the filtering of requests that match a defined criteria. This is useful to minimize the effect of certain types of attacks that have specific characteristics.
- **IP and Domain Restrictions [Web-IP-Security]**. Allows restriction based on a client's originating IP address or domain.

- **Performance [Web-Performance]**. Provides components to increase performance via output caching technologies and compression.
  - **Static Content Compression [Web-Stat-Compression]**. Allows compression of static HTML content using less bandwidth.
  - **Dynamic Content Compression [Web-Dyn-Compression]**. Allows compressions of dynamic content, which will save bandwidth. Because dynamic content will vary for each request, the compression is performed for each response, which will use CPU resources to perform the compression. A decision must be made if the saving of bandwidth is worth the expense of processor resources.

- **Management Tools [Web-Mgmt-Tools]**. The tools to manage the IIS infrastructure with SMTP and FTP management (via the IIS 6.0 version of the management tools).
  - **IIS Management Console [Web-Mgmt-Console]**. The main tool to manage IIS 7.0 components.
  - **IIS Management Scripts and Tools [Web-Scripting-Tools]**. Command-line tools and scripts for management of IIS via the command line and scripts.
  - **Management Service [Web-Mgmt-Service]**. Allows remote management of IIS.
  - **IIS 6.0 Management Compatibility [Web-Mgmt-Compat]**. Allows the use of IIS 6.0 scripts that use Admin Base Object (ABO) and ADSI APIs to manage IIS 7.0 Web servers.
    - **IIS 6.0 Metabase Compatibility [Web-Metabase]**. Allows the use of applications and scripts designed for IIS 6.0 to communicate with the IIS 7.0 metabase.
    - **IIS 6.0 WMI Compatibility [Web-WMI]**. Provides IIS 6.0 WMI compatibility.
    - **IIS 6.0 Scripting Tools [Web-Lgcy-Scripting]**. Provides the tools that were used for IIS 6.0 scripting management.
    - **IIS 6.0 Management Console [Web-Lgcy-Mgmt-Console]**. Provides the IIS 6.0 administrative console for remote IIS management and local FTP and SMTP configuration.
- **FTP Publishing Service [Web-Ftp-Publishing]**. Components that provide an FTP service. An enhanced FTP service is available from http://www.iis.net that is superior in functionality and manageability and integrates with the IIS 7.0 management interface.
  - **FTP Server [Web-Ftp-Server]**. Role service to enable the service listening on port 21 for the upload and download of files via the FTP protocol.
  - **FTP Management Console [Web-Ftp-Mgmt-Console]**. Snap-in for IIS manager 6.0 to manage the FTP server.

In addition, the Windows Process Activation Service (WAS) feature is key to IIS. This feature is comprised of four components, as follows:

- **Windows Process Activation Service [WAS]**. Decouples certain IIS features from the HTTP protocol. By using WAS, any application that hosts Windows Communication Foundation (WCF) services can take advantage of IIS.

- **Process Model [WAS-Process-Model]**. Hosts Web and WCF services.
- **.NET Environment [WAS-NET-Environment]**. Supports managed code activation in the process model.
- **Configuration APIs [WAS-Config-APIs]**. Allows configuration of the Windows Process Activation Model programmatically via this API.

IIS has many components; however, a number of them are installed by default when you install the Web Server (IIS) role. Some of these role services (components) are not available under Windows Vista, and some are not available under a core installation of Windows Server 2008. This is because of the core's inability to run managed code, which is discussed later in the section, "Server Core Support."

IIS Processing

How are all the IIS modules used? How are custom modules implemented? When a request is sent to the Web server, the request is sent through a series of events to which code can be configured to trigger when the events occur. This is known as the *request processing pipeline*. Under IIS 6.0, the request processing pipeline was monolithic, with no real control for an administrator or developer to define what happens in the pipeline other than turning the feature on or off (for example, compression or windows authentication). To add functionality to IIS 6.0, this had to be written as a DLL and plugged in via an ISAPI filter or extension—that was the only way. ISAPI is an old technology, and ISAPI components are called late in the pipeline, which limits the access to some of the features.

IIS 7.0's features are all modularized. Features presented in installed modules are triggered by events in the pipeline as they occur. New modules can be written in .NET or native code, such as C++, which can plug directly into the pipeline—not via ISAPI. There are separate modules in action in the IIS worker process, which loads the various providers and components (see Figure 24-2).

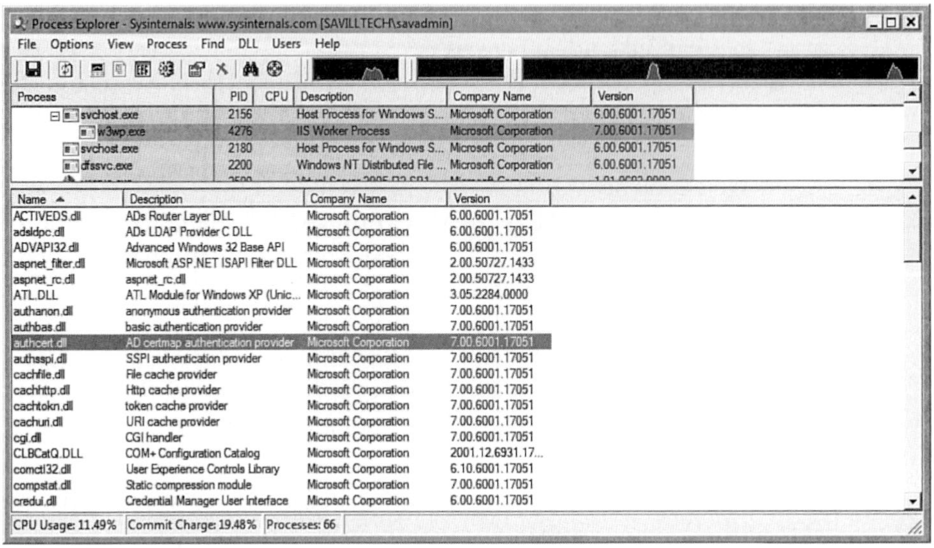

FIGURE 24-2 The DLLs loaded for the IIS worker process.

For ASP.NET in IIS 7.0, you have two modes, as follows:

- **ASP.NET integrated mode (default)**. With this mode, ASP.NET acts as a wrapper over the IIS pipeline. ASP.NET modules run at any point in the pipeline, and they can interact at all stages and for all components. Therefore, instead of being able to run only at the ISAPI hook stage, ASP.NET can run at key stages, such as initial request processing for header processing. This allows developers to write new features for IIS 7.0 using managed code that can plug in anywhere in the pipeline. This integration with ASP.NET gives IIS 7.0 its great extensibility.
- **Classic ASP.NET mode**. The classic ASP.NET approach is available with ASP.NET functionality provided as an ISAPI extension, which will mainly be used for compatibility purposes.

NOTE Microsoft's community portal, http://www.iis.net, has great information and module extensions, such as new FTP server components, FrontPage extensions, and FastCGI engines. Updates are done via MSI installation files that expand the IIS functionality and integrate fully, as shown in Figure 24-3. FTP is a great example of a module that is available via iis.net and replaces the FTP modules supplied as part of Windows Server 2008. The updated FTP from iis.net is the version that should have shipped with 2008 and removes the need to use the IIS 6.0 manager interface, which is required for the 2008 in-box FTP solution.

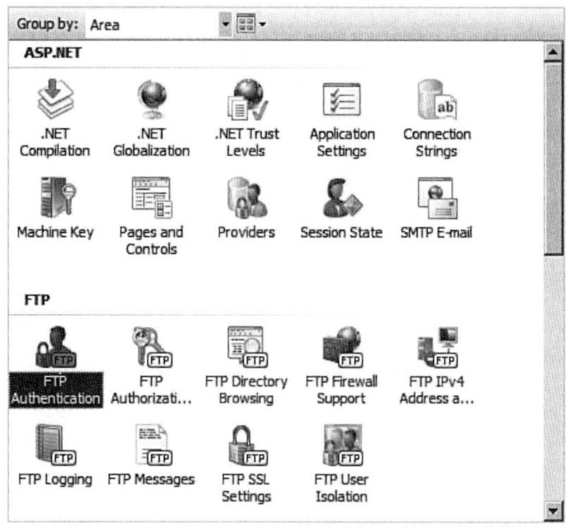

FIGURE 24-3 Totally integrated experience with downloaded modules for IIS 7.0.

IIS Configuration

In many larger enterprises or even organizations that have a strong reliance on their Web presence, multiple Web servers might be used. These are seen as a single unit using load-balancing technologies, known as a *Web farm*. Because each server is still a separate instance, it is vital that the configuration of each server maintains a consistent configuration. IIS 7.0 has improved in terms of shared configuration scenarios, as follows:

- Replication of configuration and having the same configuration on multiple servers
- Synchronization of configuration between multiple servers
- Portability of sites and applications between servers
- Staged deployment to enable a controlled staging of changes with rollback capabilities to meet change control requirements

To meet these goals, the metabase is no longer needed in IIS 7.0. (It's available as an optional component only.) Instead, a new ApplicationHost.config file contains all the configuration of the sites, application pools, and the services at a global level.

ApplicationHost.config does not even have to physically exist on a single server. This is what facilitates one aspect of the shared configuration. It is possible to place this configuration file on a share on the network and then, via the redirection.config file on each server, redirect IIS to look at the specified location. You can also configure the redirection via the Shared Configuration management feature in the IIS manager.

Typically, a shared configuration text-based file would be problematic from a change and locking perspective. However, granular locking of the configuration is possible to enable configuration distribution. This text-based file configuration approach and granular locking is designed to enable XCopy deployment of the Web server configuration between servers. This means that the ApplicationHost.config file is machine independent and contains no machine-specific information, which required some changes in how anonymous access is handled; previously, an IUSR_<machine name> account was created on the IIS server, used the password that was stored in the metabase, and would be machine specific. With IIS 7.0, the IUSR account is built-in, so password storage isn't required. In addition, a pre-configured SID (S-1-5-17) is used to give full portability of configuration and security settings. The account is now named IUSR, so it obviously has no machine component in its name. The account cannot be used for logon, and because it's built into the system, it's not even a local account.

Another change in IIS 7.0 is that the IIS_WPG local group is no longer used. This group used to contain all application pool identities. Instead in IIS 7.0, there is a built-in IIS_IUSR group to which pool identities are automatically added.

A Web.config exists with the content, such as a Web application, and it can be stored locally on a server or on a UNC path. Just like the ApplicationHost.config, Web.config is server agnostic. It can be copied between servers to enable the portability and distribution of a web site or an application's configuration.

Both the Web.config and ApplicationHost.config are XML-based files that enable viewing and editing with XML editors/readers and through XML APIs. They're also easy to back up and restore because they're text files. These two files give various management options by controlling who is delegating permissions to write to the files and which content. For example, store all configuration data in the applicationHost.config file for a centralized management approach. This can be replicated between servers or stored in a single location, or you can delegate write permissions to particular Web.config files for certain sites and applications. This gives the site owners some control over parts of the Web server environment. The delegation is at a property level, so a site owner can be given permission to change a value specific to a certain configuration, such as enabling or disabling basic authentication, but nothing else locally or remotely. This would be useful for allowing a web site developer some configuration control over a specific site without giving full administrator permissions.

This combination of configuration files can lead to a hierarchy of information related to IIS 7.0 and .NET configuration. The .NET Framework configuration is stored in a global machine.config file, a global ASP.NET configuration is stored in a global Web.config file, the IIS 7.0 global configuration is stored in ApplicationHost.config, and a web site-specific Web.config file stores Web-specific information about both .NET and delegated IIS 7.0 settings (see Figure 24-4). The site and contained applications effectively receive the sum of all the different configuration locations.

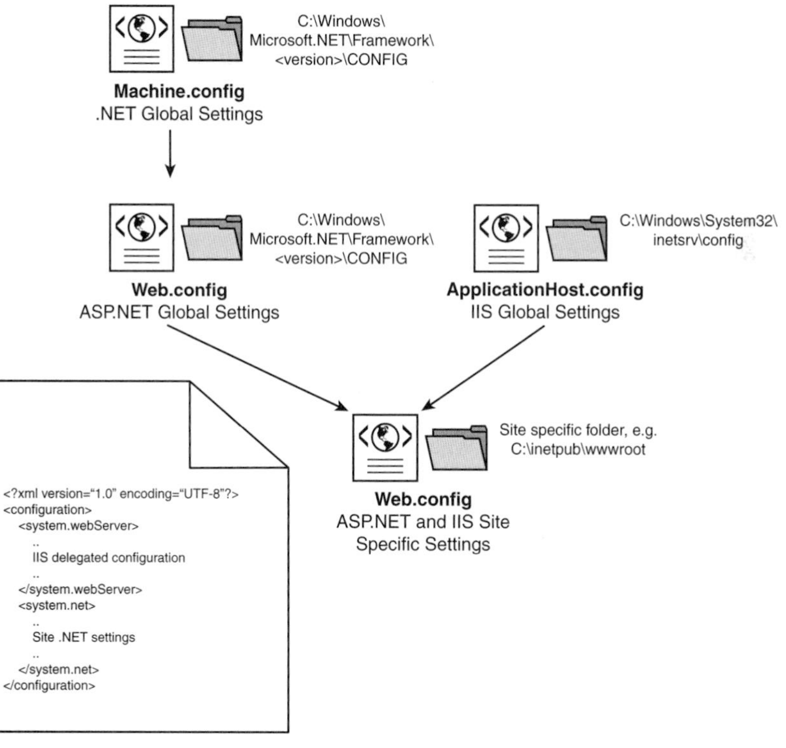

FIGURE 24-4 Configuration flow.

From an administrative perspective, IIS 7.0 has a brand-new interface for the management of both IIS and ASP.NET. The interface is now focused around the features of IIS, which are modules installed on the system. If custom modules are written and loaded on an IIS server, a management extension is included. The custom module will also display in the IIS management interface, as shown in Figure 24-5. One neat point is that the IIS Manager is firewall friendly and communicates over HTTP/HTTPS, so no special ports are needed. Notice how integrated the ASP.NET configuration is with the rest of IIS management, which was a request from customers.

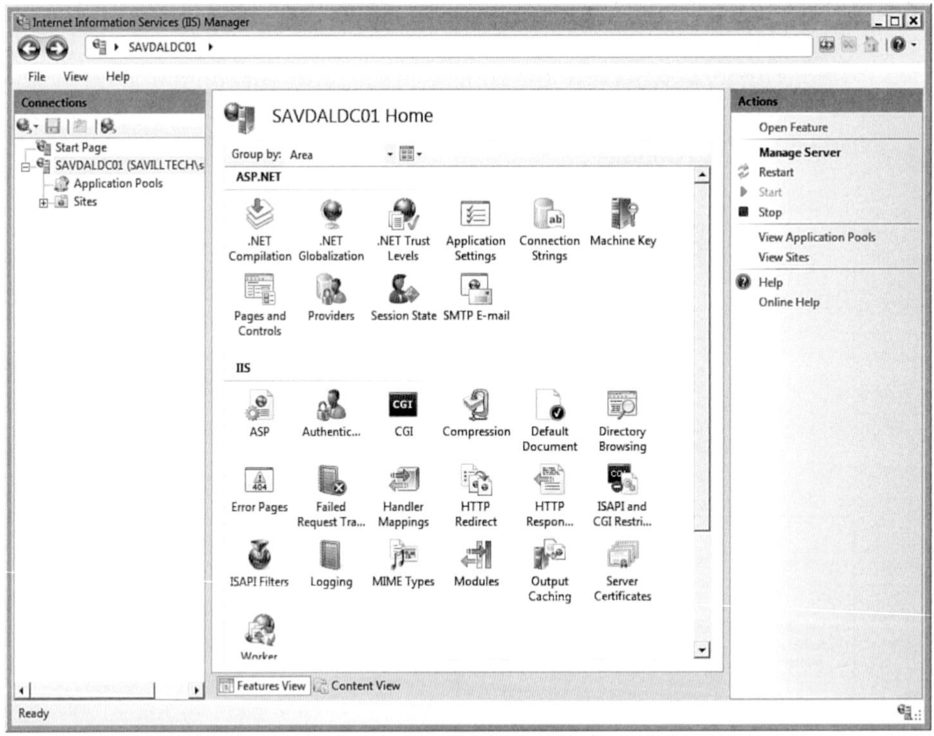

FIGURE 24-5 The main IIS Manager interface.

As a web site administrator or developer, the new error reporting for server content is a major improvement. It gives detail on the actual error and where in the page source the problem originated, facilitating debugging. For security purposes, however, detailed error pages by default are returned only if the request comes from the local server. Detailed error pages give information about your server, which would be potentially dangerous if that information was made public. Therefore, any nonlocal host client will receive a custom error page that shows the error code and description. Figures 24-6 and 24-7 show the difference for the same error viewed remotely and locally.

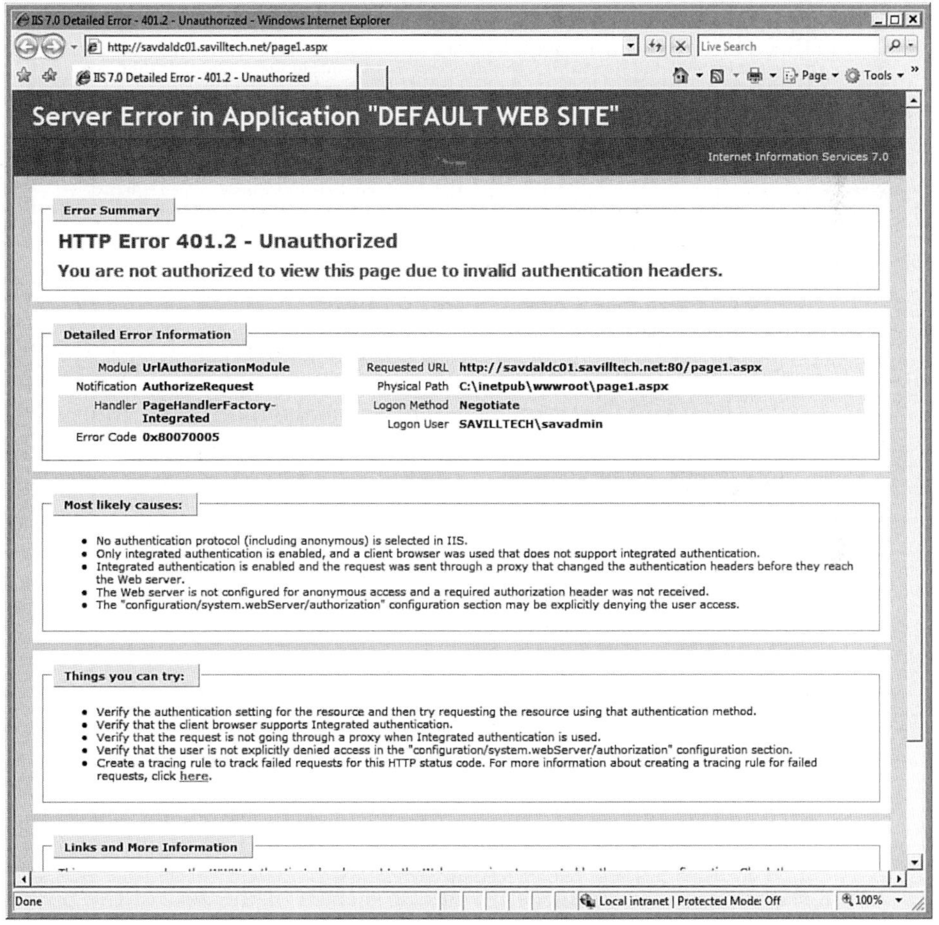

FIGURE 24-6 The detailed error message shown on the local server.

Staying with diagnostics, a list of all current requests for the IIS worker process can be viewed. The request information shows the URL being accessed for the request, the type of request (for example, if it's a GET), and how long the request has been running. In the Diagnostics section, there is a lot more functionality.

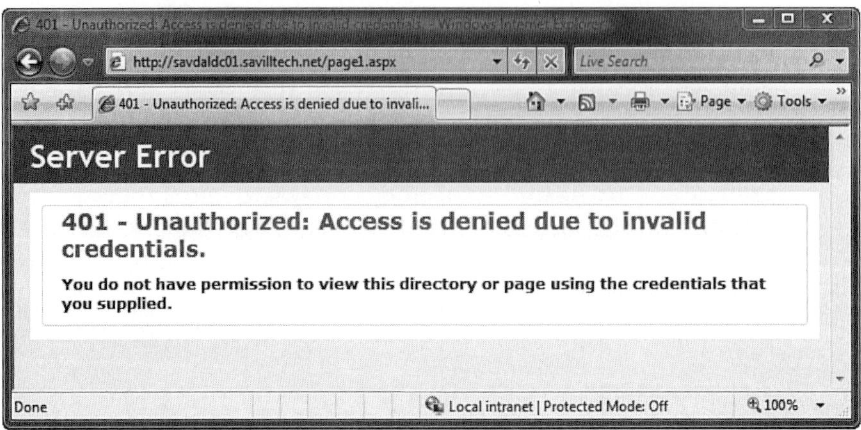

FIGURE 24-7 The error message shown on a remote client.

From a performance perspective, IIS 7.0 has had architectural changes with the SSL and Windows authentication now taking place in kernel-mode, which gives performance improvements up to 150% from the user-mode authentication processing. IIS 7.0 also has improved compression for both static and dynamic content, in addition to improved output-caching capabilities at multiple levels, including URL, query string, and total request header, with an API that allows configuration to place responses into the output cache.

The final major change within IIS 7.0 is security. Microsoft had a good start in this area. IIS 6.0 was released four years ago, and since then, there has not been a single critical IIS hotfix. 54% of the Fortune 1000 companies use IIS for their Web server needs, including, Microsoft. So what changed? The major change is the modular approach (discussed previously); you only install the modules you intend to use. This minimizes your attack surface by not having features and potential vulnerabilities for technology you are not using. Plus, you have the ability to now run on a core installation, which reduces the attack surface of the rest of the operating system.

With IIS 7.0, the application pool isolation is enabled by default. This protects any shared memory areas from possible modification. Previously, a new application/site would be placed in the default appPool that required you to create a new appPool and then move the application. This is no longer necessary. It is also possible to have multiple application pools for a single site; however, this is not the default and would require manual configuration.

Finally, new request filtering and URL authorization features are included. These features enable an administrator to have more control over access to sites based on group membership requirements that are defined as part of the Web.config file and remove requests that match defined criteria, such as denial of service (DOS) attacks.

IIS 7.0 is a major step forward with great modularity. Now, how do you get your hands on it?

Installation

Many roles in Windows Server 2008 have a number of role services; IIS has 30 separate role services, which is a testament to its highly modular architecture and is the most services of any role by far. The command-line version of server manager, called servermanagercmd.exe, had its `-allsubfeatures` added just to support IIS and enables all the features of IIS to be installed at once.

The command-line tool is useful to list all the roles within IIS. Here is an excerpt of the Web server roles. You have control over the installation of parts of the Web server role.

```
[X] Web Server (IIS)  [Web-Server]
    [X] Web Server  [Web-WebServer]
        [X] Common HTTP Features  [Web-Common-Http]
            [X] Static Content  [Web-Static-Content]
            [X] Default Document  [Web-Default-Doc]
            [X] Directory Browsing  [Web-Dir-Browsing]
            [X] HTTP Errors  [Web-Http-Errors]
            [X] HTTP Redirection  [Web-Http-Redirect]
        [X] Application Development  [Web-App-Dev]
            [X] ASP.NET  [Web-Asp-Net]
            [X] .NET Extensibility  [Web-Net-Ext]
            [X] ASP  [Web-ASP]
            [X] CGI  [Web-CGI]
            [X] ISAPI Extensions  [Web-ISAPI-Ext]
            [X] ISAPI Filters  [Web-ISAPI-Filter]
            [ ] Server Side Includes  [Web-Includes]
        [X] Health and Diagnostics  [Web-Health]
            [X] HTTP Logging  [Web-Http-Logging]
            [X] Logging Tools  [Web-Log-Libraries]
            [X] Request Monitor  [Web-Request-Monitor]
```

```
            [X] Tracing   [Web-Http-Tracing]
            [ ] Custom Logging   [Web-Custom-Logging]
            [ ] ODBC Logging   [Web-ODBC-Logging]
        [X] Security   [Web-Security]
            [X] Basic Authentication   [Web-Basic-Auth]
            [X] Windows Authentication   [Web-Windows-Auth]
            [ ] Digest Authentication   [Web-Digest-Auth]
            [X] Client Certificate Mapping Authentication   [Web-
Client-Auth]
            [ ] IIS Client Certificate Mapping Authentication
[Web-Cert-Auth]
            [ ] URL Authorization   [Web-Url-Auth]
            [X] Request Filtering   [Web-Filtering]
            [ ] IP and Domain Restrictions   [Web-IP-Security]
        [X] Performance   [Web-Performance]
            [X] Static Content Compression   [Web-Stat-
Compression]
            [ ] Dynamic Content Compression   [Web-Dyn-
Compression]
    [X] Management Tools   [Web-Mgmt-Tools]
        [X] IIS Management Console   [Web-Mgmt-Console]
        [ ] IIS Management Scripts and Tools   [Web-Scripting-
Tools]
        [ ] Management Service   [Web-Mgmt-Service]
        [X] IIS 6 Management Compatibility   [Web-Mgmt-Compat]
            [X] IIS 6 Metabase Compatibility   [Web-Metabase]
            [ ] IIS 6 WMI Compatibility   [Web-WMI]
            [ ] IIS 6 Scripting Tools   [Web-Lgcy-Scripting]
            [ ] IIS 6 Management Console   [Web-Lgcy-Mgmt-
Console]
    [ ] FTP Publishing Service   [Web-Ftp-Publishing]
        [ ] FTP Server   [Web-Ftp-Server]
        [ ] FTP Management Console   [Web-Ftp-Mgmt-Console]
```

When you install the Web Services (IIS), the WAS, and its Process Model and Configuration APIs, subcomponents are required because IIS is dependent on these due to the separation of the IIS process from HTTP. This dependency is shown in Figure 24-8 and is enabled by clicking the Add Required Features button. No more configuration is required.

Adding and removing IIS features is the same as other Windows Server 2008 role services and features. With IIS 7.0, you do have an alternative to Server Manager to install Role Services.

Add Roles Wizard

Add features required for Web Server (IIS)?

You cannot install Web Server (IIS) unless the required features are also installed.

Features:
Windows Process Activation Service
Process Model
Configuration APIs

Description:
Windows Process Activation Service generalizes the IIS process model, removing the dependency on HTTP. All the features...

Add Required Features | Cancel

Why are these features required?

FIGURE 24-8 The dependency dialog for Web Server (IIS).

It is also possible to manage the installed modules via the Modules IIS management feature. This feature displays the modules installed, and they can be grouped by module type, as shown in Figure 24-9. This grouping confirms the modules that won't work under Core because managed code is not available; therefore, any module type of Managed is not core compatible. Select a module and use the Remove action. This unloads the module from IIS but unlike Server Manager, it does not uninstall the binaries related to the module.

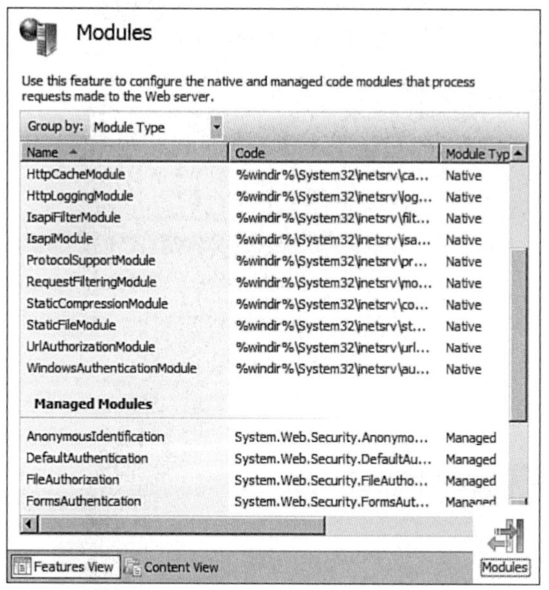

FIGURE 24-9 IIS Module information broken down by type.

After IIS is installed, manage your IIS installation and make it do something useful.

IIS Management

The IIS Manager has undergone extensive surgery. It can be accessed via its role area within Server Manager, via its shortcut in Administrative Tools, or by running Inetmgr directly.

The IIS Manager's main start page is based around commonly used activities, as shown in Figure 24-10. The start page is grouped by recent connections, allowing connections to the localhost, a specific server, a site, or to an application, in addition to links of various online resources. Also displayed are IIS News items, which are disabled by default. However, they do give useful information about new modules for IIS and other resources.

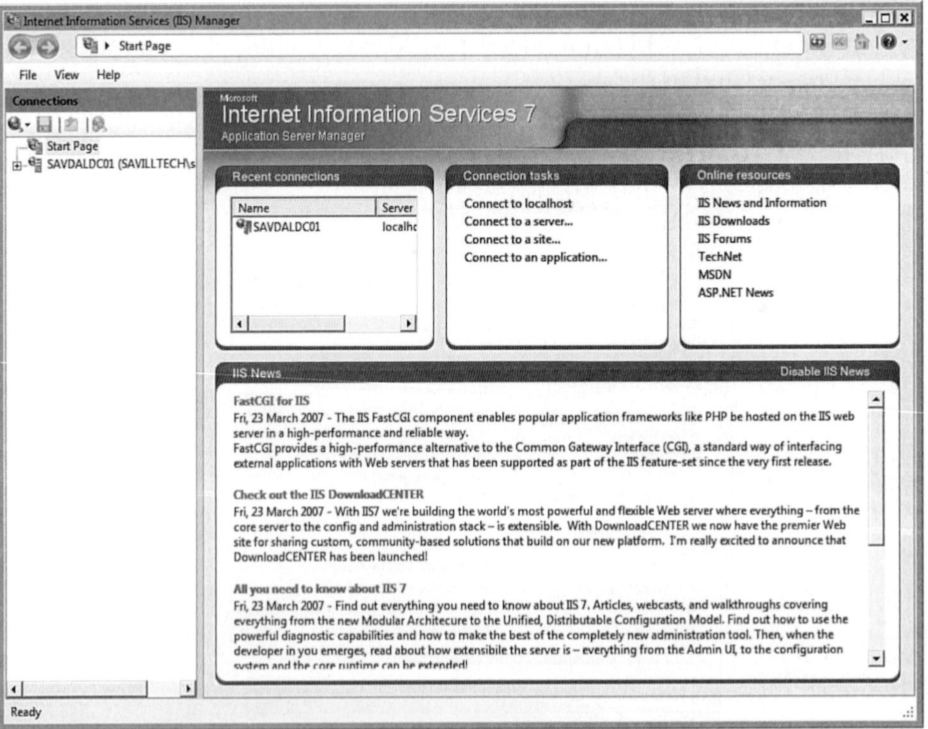

FIGURE 24-10 The main IIS Manager start page.

After a connection is made to an IIS server, you see a familiar tree view showing Application Pools, Sites, and the site content in the console tree. In the main window, the features of IIS are displayed with context-sensitive actions shown in the actions pane, depending on the currently focused object (see Figure 24-11). Figure 24-11 shows the server level, so any changes here will be made to the global configuration files. The management is focused around modules of functionality, giving access to configuring authentication, document selection, and so on. Remember that you only see the modules that are installed on the server. For example, the FTP Server is not downloaded from IIS.net, so it's not shown. The default view is the Features View. If you select the Content View for an IIS server, you will see containers for the application pools and for the sites. However, if Content View is selected for a specific site, the files that comprise the site would be displayed with any applications used in the site.

FIGURE 24-11 The main management interface for an IIS server's global configuration.

To manage the application pools, select the Application Pools console tree item. This will display all the configured application pools, which can have their settings modified individually. Alternatively, configure the default properties for application pools via the Set Application Pool Defaults action, as shown in Figure 24-12.

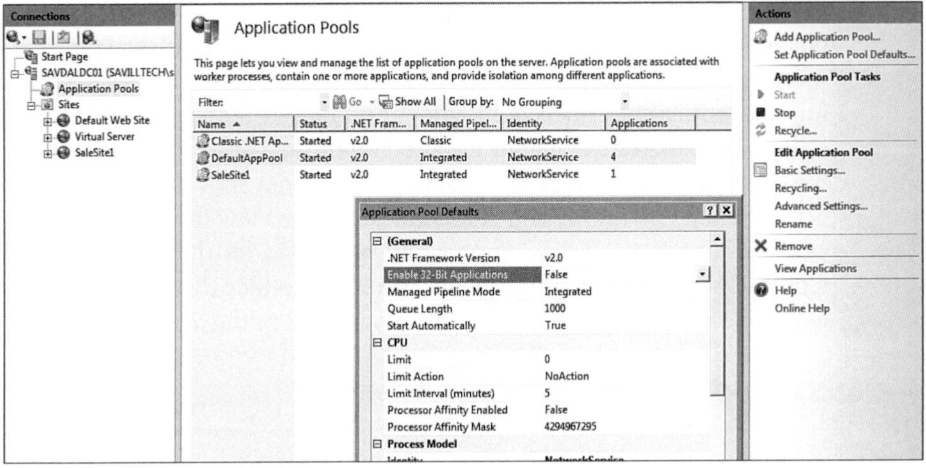

FIGURE 24-12 Configuring application pool defaults.

Adding a New Web Site

Creating a new site is a simple exercise: Select the Sites console tree item and run the Add Web Site action. This opens the Add Web Site dialog, as shown in Figure 24-13. Give the site a friendly name, which you use to reference and remotely connect. As the name of the site is typed, the application pool name matches the site name; this shows how, in IIS 7.0, the default behavior is one application pool per site. Modify this via the Select button, which will list the existing application pools.

A physical path must be selected. This is where static content for the site is contained in addition to files that generate dynamic content, such as ASP and ASPX files; in addition, site-specific content is stored in this folder.

By default, connection to the web site will use pass-through authentication, which means the credentials used will be those of the application pool. Elect to always use a specific user via the Connect As button, which will require selecting an account.

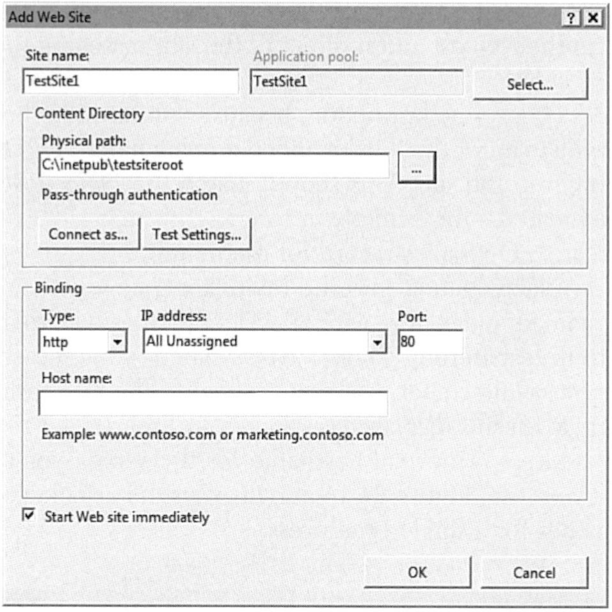

FIGURE 24-13 Specifying details for the new site.

The next section is the binding, which specifies whether the HTTP or HTTPS protocol is used for connectivity (you can modify this later). This section also addresses whether a specific IP address is used for the new site or if all unassigned IP addresses on the server should be used, and which port should be used for the protocol. Normally, port 80 is used for HTTP and port 443 for HTTPS. However, if you are hosting multiple sites on one IP address, a problem arises: Which site should a user be sent to if he enters http://192.168.1.10? Multiple sites are bound to the same IP address, and they are all using port 80. The end-user experience would not be consistent, so hosting multiple sites on one IP address is not allowed. To bind multiple sites to one address, you have multiple options.

- Create multiple IP addresses on the same server and then bind each site to a unique IP address so they can all use port 80/443. You would then create multiple DNS host records, with one name pointing to each IP address so users would use a different host name, and therefore URL, for each of the sites.
- Use a port other than 80 and 443 for all but one of the sites. Then users must add this port number to the URL—for example, http://www.savilltech.net:8080 could be used for a second site if it was configured to use port 8080 instead of 80.

- Specify a hostname for the site. IIS can use this hostname to inspect in the request and redirect to the site matching the hostname.

Let's choose the last option, because you have the hostname field that allows you to enter the fully qualified domain name (FQDN) that users will pass to get to the site. This should match the DNS host record/alias that will be created—for example, reference this new site as test.savilltech.net and create a DNS alias record for that name.

Now place content into the folder for a new site. For example, place a file named index.htm with a welcome message to the site into the c:\inetpub\testsiteroot folder. Now, when you access the site using http://test.savilltech.net, you are directed to the new test site, and you see your HTML skills displayed, as shown in Figure 24-14. Whether you use the IP address or normal hostname for the server, you're directed to the default web site. Figure 24-14 also displays the nslookup showing the multiple names for a single IP address.

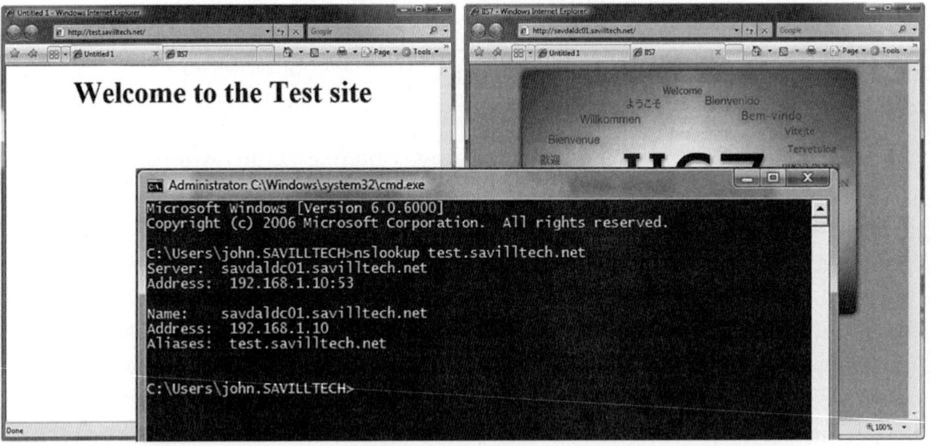

FIGURE 24-14 Two sites on one IP address, both bound to HTTP (port 80).

Create actual folders under the file system for your web site. For example, create an IT folder under c:\inetpub\testsiteroot and place content there, which is then accessible via the URL http://test.savilltech.net/IT/page1.aspx. Alternatively, add virtual directories via the Add Virtual Directory context menu item for a site. This allows an alias to be specified; this alias is the child folder name that the content appears to exist under, but the physical path of the folder can exist elsewhere on the server or network (see Figure 24-15). This enables a web site to have content distributed outside of a single folder structure, and even reference material on other servers. If you select a folder on a remote server, ensure that IIS has the proper credentials to connect to the remote data, or IIS will be denied access.

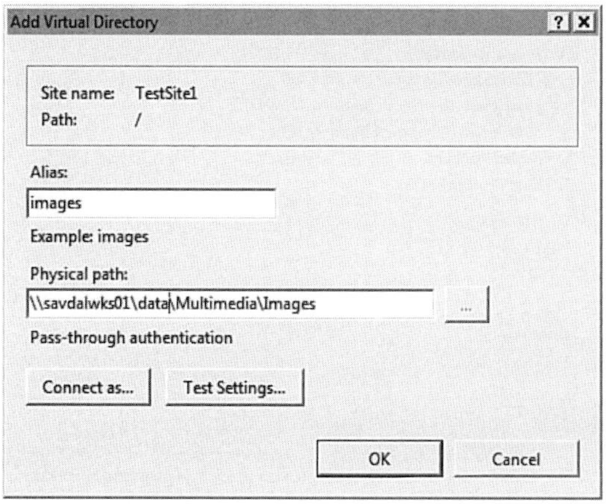

FIGURE 24-15 Adding a virtual directory.

You now have a site that can be configured via the functions within the IIS Manager, and enhanced configurations, such as SSL enablement, can be performed.

To configure elements of a site that are not exposed via a function such as connection limits, use the Advanced Settings action for the site, as shown in Figure 24-16. Here, you can view the site ID, its path, and its default start status.

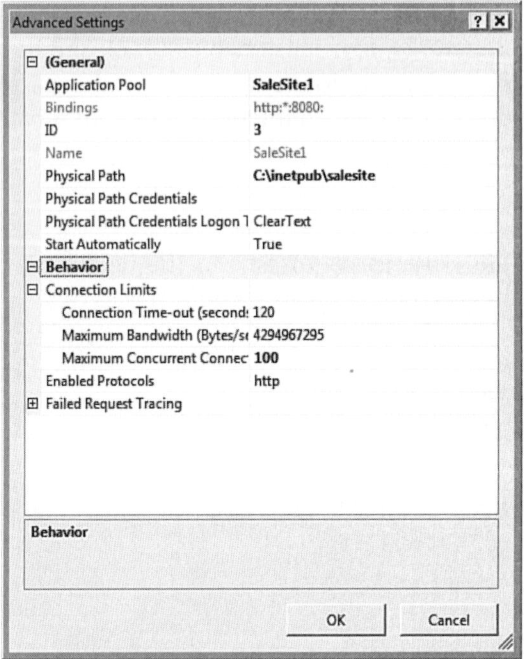

FIGURE 24-16 Configuring advanced settings of a site.

Configuring URL Authorization for a Web Site

A new IIS 7.0 feature, URL Authorization, exposes a number of elements of the IIS configuration, such as authorization features. By default, your IIS installation will have a default web site. For this test, make sure you have installed the ASP.NET role service in addition to the Windows Authentication and URL Authorization role services. When you connect to an IIS web site, it connects anonymously by default and uses the built-in IUSR account for any permission checking. Confirm this by creating a small ASP.NET page:

```
<%@Language="C#"%>
<%
    string currentUser = Request.ServerVariables["LOGON_USER"];
    if (currentUser == "")
        currentUser = "anonymous";
%>

<html>
```

```
<head>
<title>Welcome <%Response.Write(currentUser);%></title>
</head>
<body>
<p>Hello user <%Response.Write(currentUser);%></p>
</body>
</html>
```

Save this code as page1.aspx in the default web site's default folder (c:\inetpub\wwwroot); however, confirm that this path is correct by viewing the advanced settings of the site, which has a Physical Path attribute to confirm its root folder. Then connect using the FQDN of your server (such as savdaldc01.savilltech.net) and pass the name of the page1.aspx filename, as shown in Figure 24-17. You connect as an anonymous user.

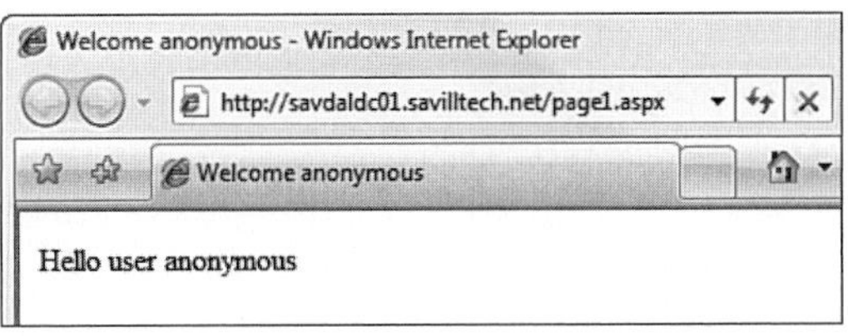

Figure 24-17 Anonymous access.

If you want to use your domain account, disable anonymous access and enable Windows Authentication. You could do this at a global or site level. In this case, turn it off at the site level, so select the Default Web Site and select the Authentication feature, which allows you to disable Anonymous Authentication and enable Windows Authentication (see Figure 24-18).

Authentication

Group by: No Grouping

Name	Status	Response Type
Anonymous Authentication	Disabled	
ASP.NET Impersonation	Disabled	
Basic Authentication	Disabled	HTTP 401 Challenge
Forms Authentication	Disabled	HTTP 302 Login/Redirect
Windows Authentication	Disabled	HTTP 401 Challenge

Actions: Enable; Help; Online Help

Figure 24-18 Configuring the authentication methods available for a site.

If you connect again, the name of the account you are logged on with should be shown. However, you receive a 401–Unauthorized access page—you don't want your Web browser sending your windows credentials to any site just because it asks for them. Instead, you have to tell your Web browser which sites should be allowed to receive this information. By default, only sites in your Local intranet zone are sent your credentials.

1. In Internet Explorer, go into the Tools–Internet Options menu.
2. On the Security tab, select Local intranet, and click the Sites button.
3. Click the Advanced button and then add the URL of the site that should be included in the zone, as shown in Figure 24-19.

If you click the Custom Settings button on the Security tab and scroll down, you see a User Authentication section that shows Automatic Logon Only in Intranet Zone by default.

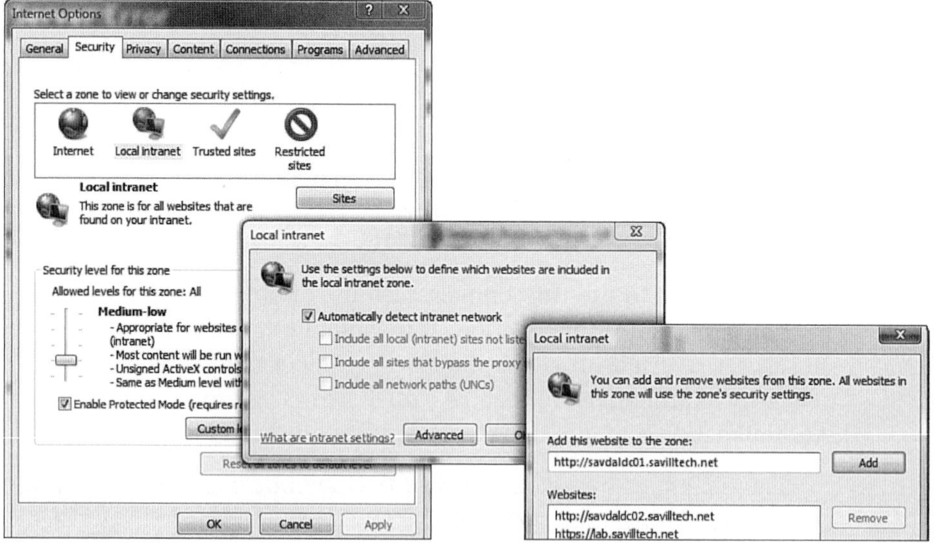

FIGURE 24-19 Configuring a local intranet site.

If you connect again, your Windows domain account shows Hello User SAVILLTECH\john. Now modify the authorization rules. Ensure that the site and folder where the content you want to restrict access to is contained, and click the Authorization Rules icon. By default, this icon displays a single rule for All Users with the mode set to Allow. Ideally, you would not set this on the root of a site, but you would have a child folder that you wanted to lock down, and it is possible to configure at any level.

Remove this default Allow rule and add enable rules for specific users, groups, and verbs, or leave the allow rule and then add specific deny rules (see Figure 24-20). There are generic options for all users, all anonymous users, and then specific roles, groups, users, and verbs.

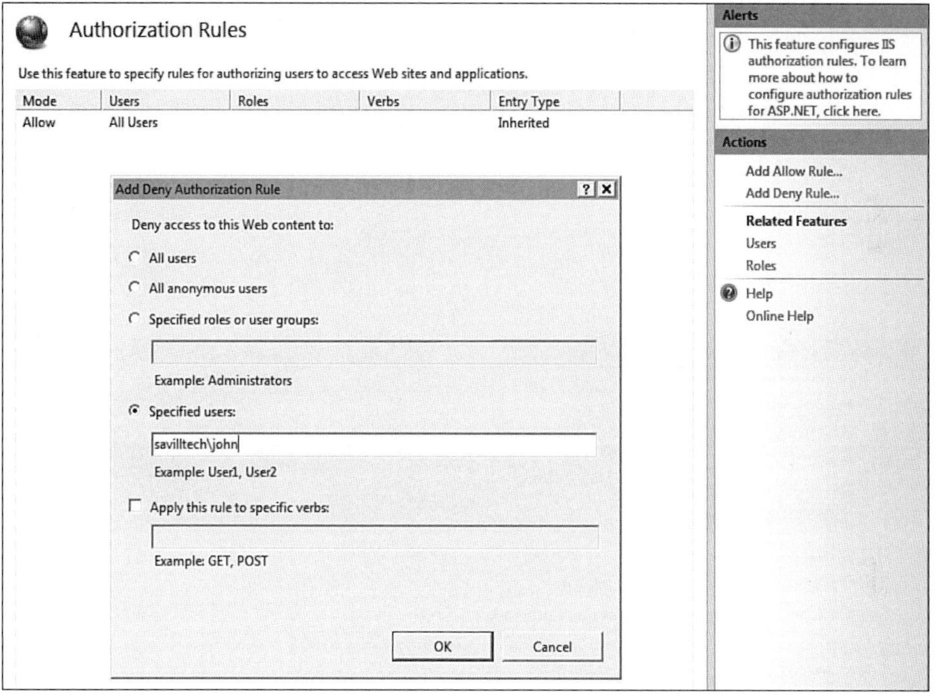

FIGURE 24-20 Adding an explicit deny rule for domain user John.

The change is immediate. If you try to connect as user john, you will be prompted for credentials because john has no access. If you can't provide alternate credentials, you will get a 401.2 unauthorized response that says you have no access. However, this is a great example of the detail of errors you get with IIS 7.0, as shown in Figure 24-21. In the error page, you are given a list of the most likely causes. The final cause is accurate—the user is explicitly denied access. If you open the Web.config file in the folder where the URL authorization was configured, you will see the denial, as shown next. This same configuration is possible on a specific page level, in which case, the site's Web.config would have a section for the page in the same format as shown but part of a `<location path="<page.name>">` section:

```
<?xml version="1.0" encoding="UTF-8"?>
<configuration>
    <system.webServer>
        ..
        <security>
            <authorization>
                <add accessType="Deny" users="savilltech\john"
/>
            </authorization>
        </security>
    </system.webServer>
    <system.net>
        ..
    </system.net>
</configuration>
```

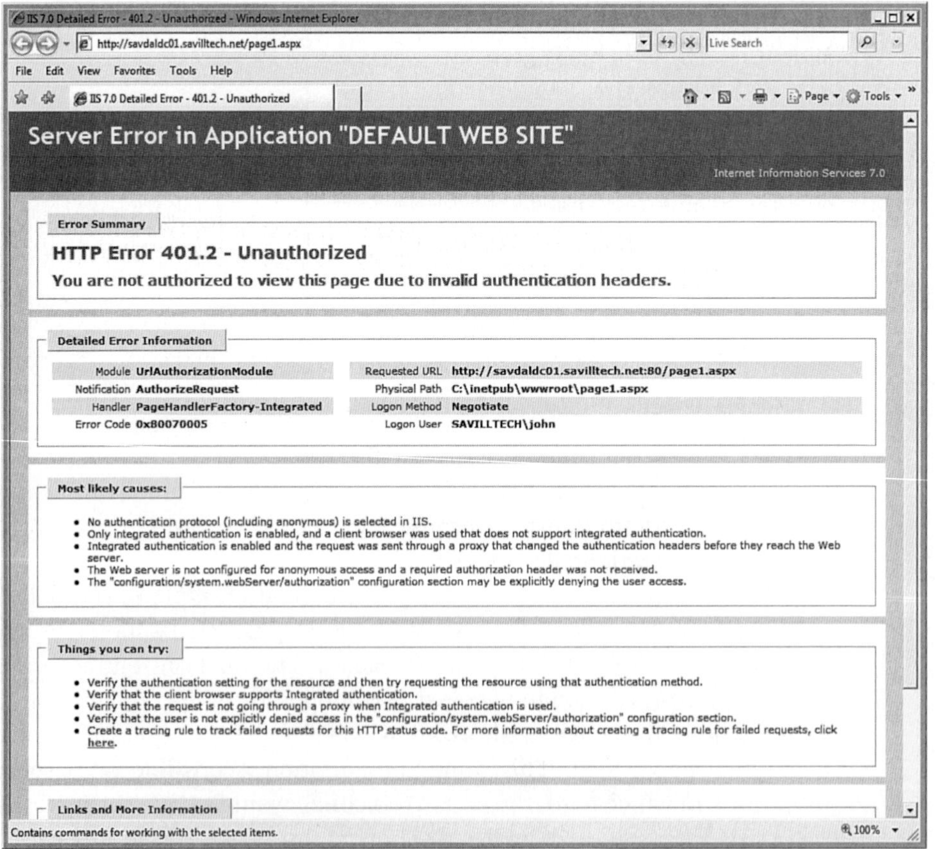

FIGURE 24-21 Error page in IIS 7.0.

Remote Management of IIS

A major goal of IIS 7.0 was better management. As mentioned, IIS can be fully managed remotely; however, this is not default. Before any remote management can be attempted, you must first enable the management service, which therefore must be installed.

After installation, configure at the server level. Select the server in the IIS manager and, in the Management section of features, execute the Management Service icon. This management view will look the same as Figure 24-22 with the remote connections not enabled. Check the Enable Remote Connections box and select whether only Windows credentials can be used or IIS Manager credentials can be used. (These are credentials used only by IIS and managed via the IIS Manager Users function that is part of Management.) Also, select the specific certificate and port to use. Finally, click Apply in the actions and then click the Start action to begin the management service (WMSVC). A firewall exception is automatically enabled for port 8172 that the management traffic uses. If you change this port, manually modify the firewall exception.

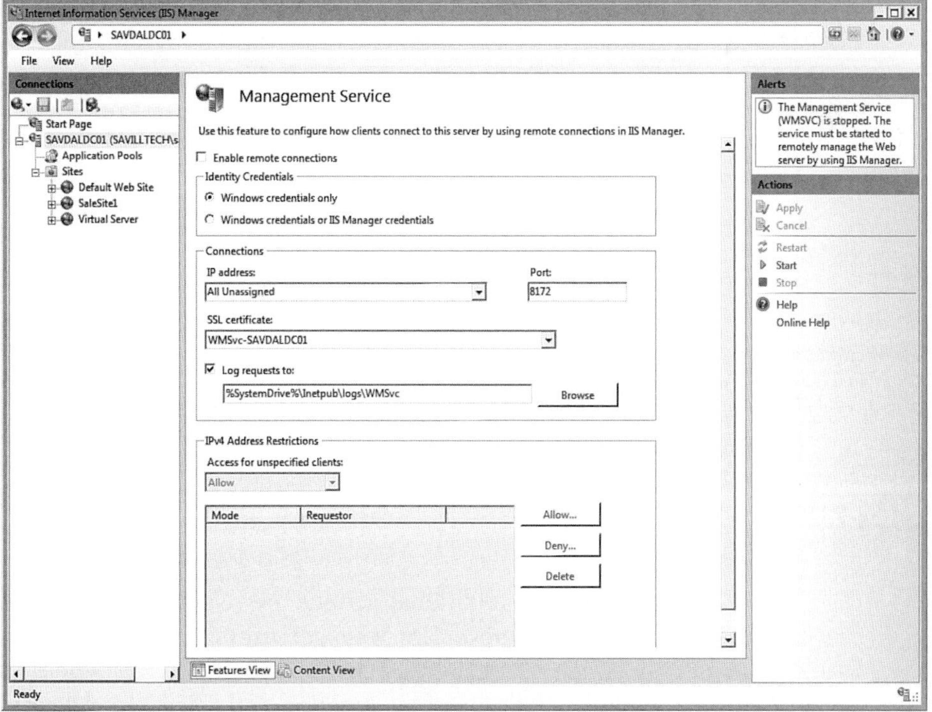

FIGURE 24-22 Enabling remote management.

Confirm the service is listening via netstat:

```
C:\>netstat -a | findstr 8172
  TCP    0.0.0.0:8172          savdaldc01:0          LISTENING
  TCP    [::]:8172             savdaldc01:0          LISTENING
```

Feature Delegation

Feature Delegation is available at a server level and has a number of steps. Enable IIS remote management and create IIS Manager Users via the IIS Manager Users function of the server or a Windows account. For this example, you'll create an IIS Manager account. The IIS Manager accounts would mainly be used if you have users who manage some functions of the site but are not members of the domain, so Windows accounts cannot be used. Click the Add User action. Enter a name and password for the new IIS Manager user, as shown in Figure 24-23.

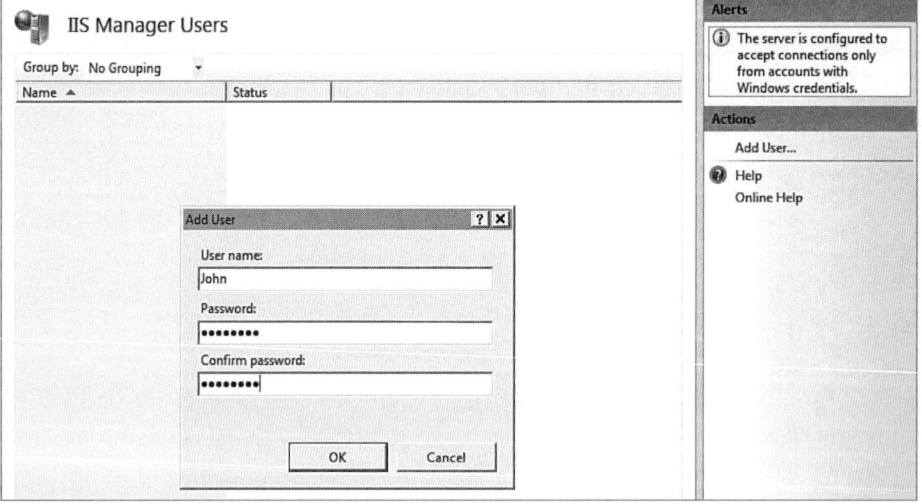

FIGURE 24-23 Creating an IIS Manager.

After users are added, additional actions are available to reset passwords, and disable and remove IIS Manager users. The next step is to allow the users to connect to a site via IIS Manager. To do this, select a site and run the IIS Manager Permissions function and select the Allow User action, which will ask for either a Windows account or an IIS Manager account. This account will now be able to connect to the site. Without this step, any attempt to connect would result in an authorization error. If you are an administrator on the server, you do not need to be given per-site access and will be able to connect.

The next task is to set delegation, and the server has default delegation states for lower levels of IIS Manager connection—for example, a site or application. The Feature Delegation function shows which features are delegated at lower levels by default, as shown in Figure 24-24. Change the default delegation state by selecting the feature and selecting the new delegation, such as Read/Write.

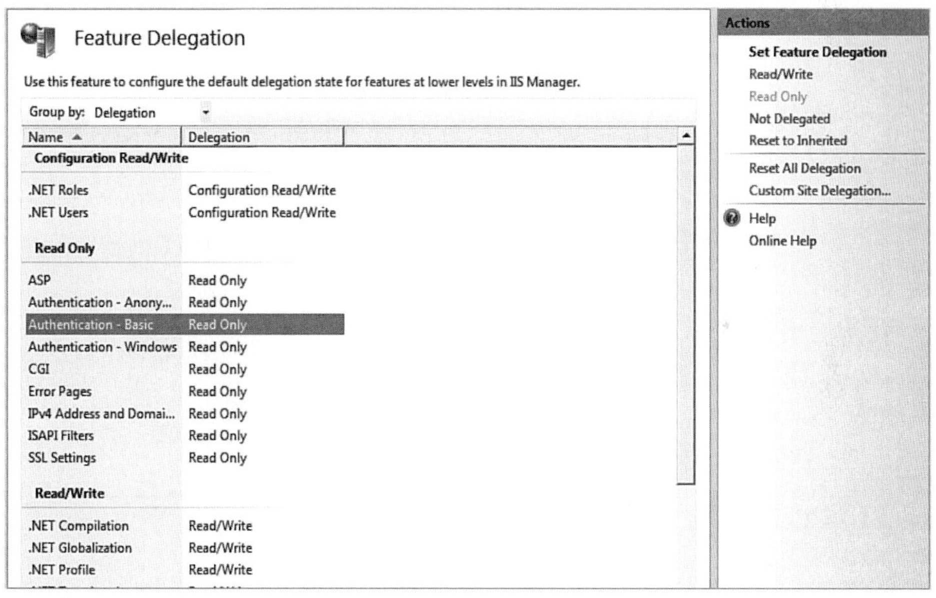

FIGURE 24-24 Configuring functions that are available for delegation at site and application levels.

You can also have custom delegations for specific sites by selecting the Custom Site Delegation action within the Feature Delegation function, which exposes settings for each site on the server. Notice that you don't delegate at a user level. You are making specific users IIS Managers for a site. After you make them site managers, they can perform functions that have been delegated as actionable by a site admin.

The final action is to connect. On the main IIS page, select the "Connect to a site" task and enter the server name hosting the web site and the name of the site to connect to, as shown in Figure 24-25. You will then be prompted for credentials, which can be IIS Manager user credentials or Windows user credentials. Finally, you will be asked for a connection name. By default, the connection name is just the site name; however, you might want to add the name of the server to the end to make it unique.

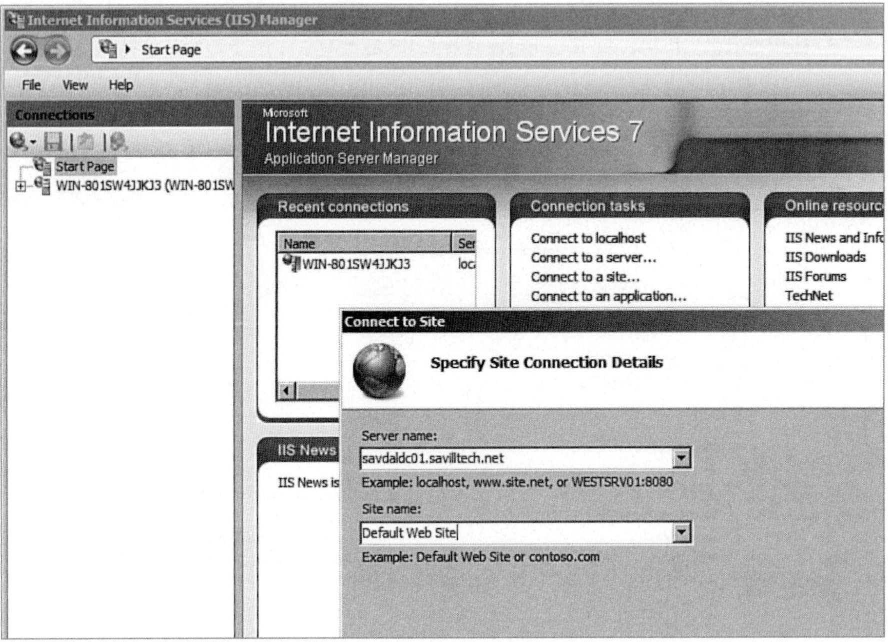

FIGURE 24-25 Connecting to a remote server and site.

Once connected, the functions of IIS Manager can be accessed with permissions based on delegation. If a feature is not delegated, it is not visible; if it's delegated as read-only, you view the settings, but they are not modifiable.

NOTE IIS 7.0 Manager is available on www.iis.net to enable remote management of IIS 7.0 from Windows Vista SP1, XP, and 2003 clients. There is no requirement for the IIS 7.0 component to be installed on the client remotely managing, which means that you can manage and connect from most modern clients.

Command Line

Appcmd gives full access to the management of IIS. It's found in the %windir%\system32\inetsrv folder. If you intend to use the command often, add the folder to the path of your system to avoid having to always execute it from the inetsrv folder.

Although appcmd is not part of the PowerShell, its structure is similar. The help for appcmd gives a great overview of its structure, as shown in Figure 24-26.

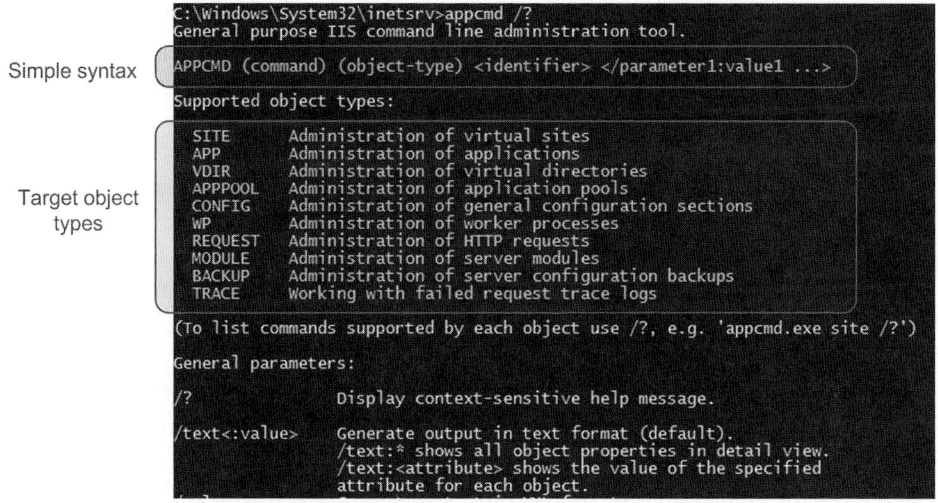

FIGURE 24-26 Overview of appcmd syntax.

Let's look at a few simple commands using appcmd. The easiest way to start is by viewing information. If you want to see all sites, use the `list` command with the site object type, as follows:

```
C:\Windows\System32\inetsrv>appcmd list site
SITE "Default Web Site"
(id:1,bindings:http/*:80:,https/*:443:,state:Started)
SITE "Virtual Server"
(id:2,bindings:http/:1024:,state:Started)
SITE "SaleSite1" (id:3,bindings:http/*:8080:,state:Started)
```

Making modifications is also possible using the `SET` command. Here, set the number of maximum connections for a site to 120:

```
C:\Windows\System32\inetsrv>appcmd set site "SaleSite1"
➥/limits.maxConnections:100
SITE object "SaleSite1" changed
```

To see all possible configurations for a site, run `appcmd set site "<site>" /?"`. This will list all available properties. Also, stop and start sites using the `appcmd stop site "<site>"` command and `appcmd start site "<site>"` command, respectively. If you need to recycle an application pool, use the `appcmd recycle apppool "<appPool name>"` command.

You also still have iisreset.exe, which should be the last line of IIS restart used, because it shuts down all aspects of IIS, including the Web Server services, the WAS, and administration services. A number of switches are available, including the `/restart` switch to stop and then start all the mentioned services. There are also switches to view the status of the services, and `/noforce` is used to not forcefully terminate a process that is attempting a graceful stop. To see a full list of switches, use the `iisreset /?` command.

There is currently no PowerShell provider specific for IIS 7.0, however, a new WMI provider is available (in addition to maintaining support for the old WMI provider): winmgmts:root\WebAdministration. Like the rest of the management, this WMI provider is used for both IIS and ASP.NET management. For example, to create a new site, use the following:

```
Set oService = GetObject("winmgmts:root\WebAdministration")

' Create site
oService.Get("Site").Create _
   "SaleSite", array(oBinding), "C:\inetpub\saleroot"
```

NOTE From a .NET perspective, a fully remotable API exists, called Microsoft.Web.Administration, that allows full configuration and runtime information gathering. Microsoft has a lot of documentation on its web site. This .NET API is fully accessible via PowerShell, so although there are no PowerShell-specific cmdlets, there is still functionality that PowerShell can easily hook into.

Appcmd is powerful, and this section only touched the surface of what it can do. Take some time to look at the online help, and you'll find that appcmd can do everything from configuration to showing information about individual handles and requests for a worker process within a web site. Take a look at http://learn.iis.net/page.aspx/114/getting-started-with-appcmdexe/ to get started.

Certificates and Encryption

Although Web communication is by default over port 80 and unencrypted HTTP, for secure communication, using HTTP over Secure Socket Layer (SSL), called HTTPS (port 443), is preferred. However, encryption requires certificates that have a private and public key component.

Create and load certificates at a server level via the Server Certificates function, and there are various options for what source of certificate to use.

The easiest type of certificate is a self-signed certificate that, as the name implies, is a certificate generated by the IIS server itself and then self signed. Remember that a certificate should be signed by a party trusted by the client to prove it is valid. Clients typically don't trust certificates that are self signed, so the self-signed certificate is useful only in testing purposes; this will likely require exporting the certificate and importing onto each client's trusted root certification authorities folder.

The next level of certificate is one issued by an internal certificate authority (CA), such as the Active Directory Certificate Services, known as a domain certificate. Typically computers within a domain will trust certificates issued by a domain CA, so this type of certificate is useful if a service only needs encryption internally, such as an internal Web portal.

For both self-signed and domain certificates, if a client does not trust the issuer of the certificate, he will receive a warning that the certificate is not trusted, but SSL encryption will still be used.

The best level of certificate (which you should use for any Internet-facing web site) is a certificate issued by an Internet-trusted CA, such as Verisign, which all common operating systems trust.

If you activate the Server Certificates function, a list of certificates will appear. If you installed the Management service, a self-signed certificate exists for that service's encryption. In the actions pane, a list of actions can be selected around certificate management.

If you have a certificate that was previously exported to a file, import it via the Import action. To create a self-signed certificate for SSL testing, run the Create Self-Signed Certificate action. The only information needed is a name for the certificate, as shown in Figure 24-27.

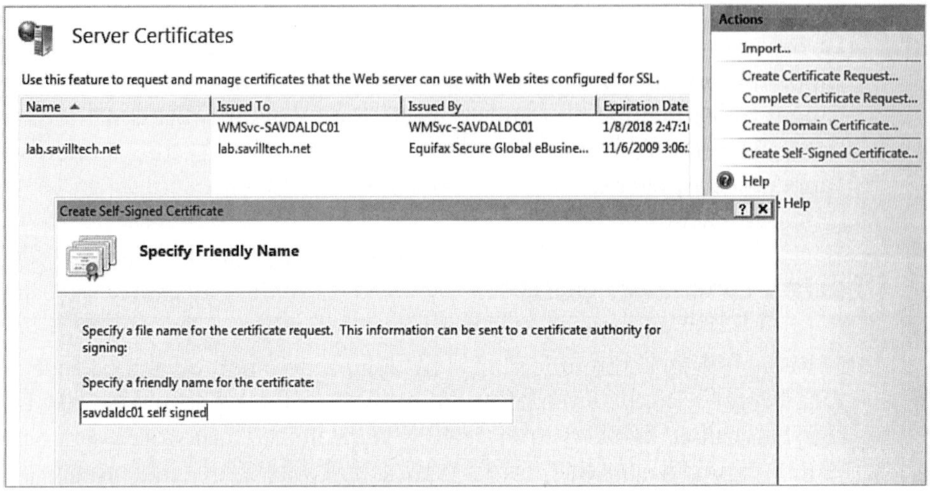

FIGURE 24-27 Creating a self-signed certificate.

If you have a domain CA, run the Create Domain Certificate action, this will prompt for information about the certificate, such as its common name, organization, and location, followed by the local CA that will respond to the request.

Receiving a certificate from a third party is more complex. Run the Create Certificate Request action to fill in the necessary information, which will create a request file that you submit to the online CA using any process they support (normally a web site). You then receive a response that contains the certificate, which requires you to run the Complete Certificate Request action to get the certificate loaded.

In Figure 24-27, Equifax issued the certificate. There are two main types of certificates from third parties related to SSL: one for a specific name (for example, www.savilltech.net), or a wildcard certificate. The wildcard certificate is more expensive, but covers any name under the requested domain; thus, with one certificate, you could cover www.savilltech.net, lab.savilltech.net, unclebob.savilltech.net, and so on.

The reason all certificates are not wildcard, or *, certificates, is due to both the cost and the fact that some SSL features simply don't support wildcards. However, this lack of support is now a minor problem because wildcard certificates are now more common. When you request a certificate, make sure that the common name on the request matches the final name that will be used to access the web site, because a certificate is tied to a single name. If you request a certificate with a common name of savdaldc01.savilltech.net and then try to use the certificate with clients using www.savilltech.net, they will receive an error that the name on the certificate does not match that of the site being accessed.

After you have a certificate on the server that you want to use for encryption, there is still a configuration to perform. The first action is to tell a web site to bind to the SSL port, which will also enable you to select a certificate. Select a web site (for example, default web site) and run the Bindings action.

The Site Bindings dialog will open and, as shown in Figure 24-28, the type of protocol binding should be selected. In this case, you are adding an HTTPS binding, which will default to port 443, and then select a certificate to use for the encryption. After a certificate is selected, select the View button to see the detail of the certificate.

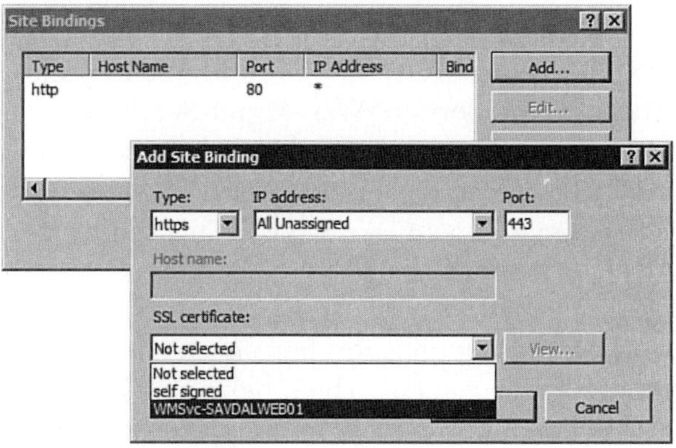

FIGURE 24-28 Specifying a site binding.

You could now use https to navigate to the site with the new binding enabled; however, from any client, you will receive a warning that there is a problem with the server's security certificate because the certificate is not issued by a trusted authority. Click the Continue to this web site link because you are just testing. Continue SSL configuration via the SSL Settings function of a site to make SSL required for connectivity, and to a further level require 128-bit SSL encryption.

Server Core Support

Initially, Web Server was not going to be a supported role under Windows Server Core because of its integration with .NET and the fact that the .NET Framework and managed code is not supported under Server Core. This changed, but certain roles of IIS are not supported under Server Core because of their reliance on .NET and managed code.

Server Core imposes two limiting factors: You can't support managed code, and you don't have many of the components needed to render graphical interfaces. Therefore, the following are unavailable under a Server Core installation:

- ASP.NET [Web-ASP-NET]
- .NET Extensibility [Web-NET-Ext]
- IIS Management Console [Web-Mgmt-Console]
- Management Service [Web-Mgmt-Service]
- IIS 6.0 Management Console [Web-Lgcy-Mgmt-Console]
- FTP Management Console [Web-Ftp-Mgmt-Console]
- .NET Environment [WAS-NET-Environment]
- Configuration APIs [WAS-Config-APIs]

Obviously, the big omission here is no support for ASP.NET and no local graphical management. The other capabilities of IIS are still included, such as classic ASP and PHP support, but if you require ASP.NET, install a full server installation and not core. The decision to use core will depend on the features offered by the full versus core version of IIS and the management overhead advantages in running core. The management process must be considered for Server Core because you cannot run the IIS management interface, but thankfully, you have `appcmd` (covered earlier in this chapter).

IIS and Windows Vista

IIS is provided in both the server and desktop versions of the operating system, and IIS 7.0 is also included as part of Windows Vista. The features available under Windows Vista depend on the version of Vista that is installed.

The features available in the versions of Vista differ between the high-end and business editions (Ultimate, Enterprise, and Business). The Home Premium edition with the Vista Home Basic and Starter editions have no real hosting capabilities. The main differences relate to the security features—because the Home edition cannot be part of a domain, any infrastructure requiring types of authentication such as windows, digest, and client certificate mapping (AD and IIS) are unavailable. In addition, Vista Home cannot support an FTP server. Windows Vista Ultimate, Enterprise, and Business can support 10 concurrent connections, whereas the other Vista versions can only support three. Vista isn't intended as a Web server platform; it can be used to test IIS functionality in a development environment or in a limited home usage scenario, but you need one of the server-line products for serious Web-hosting capabilities.

Windows Web Server 2008

An entire SKU is dedicated to running the Web Server role, with enhanced hardware support in the 2008 version supporting up to four processors and 32GB of RAM on the 64-bit edition. Windows Web Server 2008 also supports Windows SharePoint Services, Windows Media Services 2008, and SQL Server to allow for local Web applications.

Because Web Services is a role in Windows Server 2008, it is not surprising that Windows Web Server 2008 is a minimal server install, containing only the Web Services (IIS) role, as shown in Figure 24-29. As with the rest of the Windows Server 2008 family, a Server Core installation option is available to give the Web Server a minimal footprint and ease management and lower its attach surface.

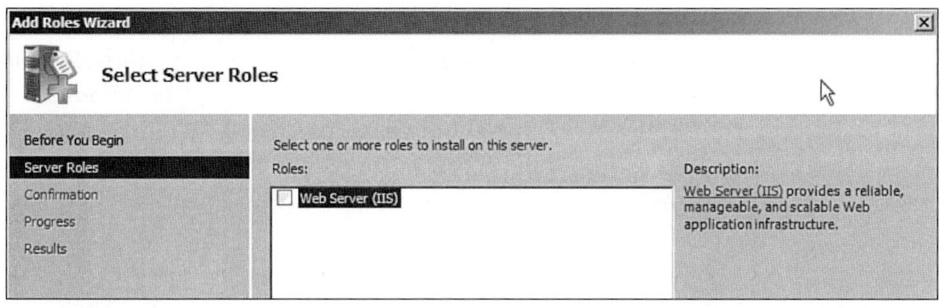

Figure 24-29 <sarcasm>The huge number of roles available for Windows Web Server 2008.</sarcasm>

Many of the normal Windows Server 2008 features are available in Windows Web Server 2008, giving full access to technologies such as Network Load Balancing, SMTP Services, Windows Internal Database, Windows Server Backup, and Windows System Resource Manager.

WINDOWS MEDIA SERVICES 2008 Windows Media Services is available as a download from iis.net. It provides a platform for streaming live or on-demand audio and video content over the Internet or intranet. In addition, a new Cache Proxy plug-in enables edge servers in the network to be Cache Proxy servers. This enables them to cache the content for on-demand streaming and split the stream for live streaming events. This reduces network traffic and results in significant bandwidth savings and improved network and source server performance.

Summary

IIS 7.0 is a major improvement for IIS, with its support for Server Core, modular architecture, and complete integration with ASP.NET.

Windows Server 2008 has a powerful management capability from both a graphical and command-line interface; although there aren't yet PowerShell cmdlets for IIS 7.0, the appcmd.exe interface provides huge insight into the workings of IIS and enables you to do almost anything.

This chapter discussed the modules in IIS and some of their major features. Some of the vital points you will encounter with IIS were covered, such as certificates and delegation. In most cases, however, IIS will be configured automatically for you by the roles and features that require IIS. If you are interested in raw IIS for hosting, hopefully the general concepts are now clear, and the IIS Manager's intuitive interface will help you get things started. For high-availability web site options, you should review Chapter 18, "Highly Available Windows Server 2008." Keep a close eye on www.iis.net because new modules and information for IIS are constantly posted to improve what is already a strong Web platform.

HOW TO QUICK REFERENCE

A

B

C

D

E

F

G

H

I-L

M

N

O

P-Q

R

S

T

U

V

W-Z

INDEX

B

C

E

F

G

H

I

N

T

X - Y - Z

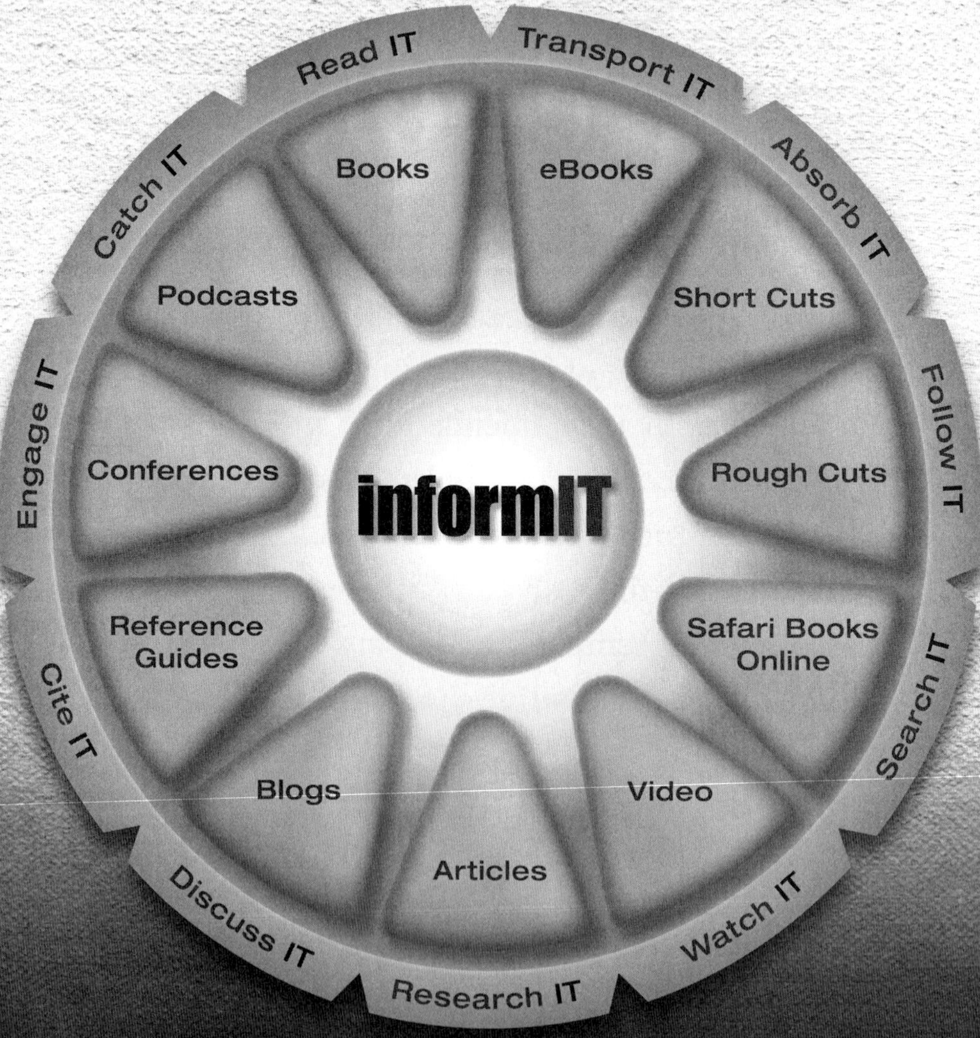